Y0-CML-597

FUNK & WAGNALLS
NEW ENCYCLOPEDIA

fw

VOLUME 14
ISRAEL to
LACCADIVE, MINICOY, AND
AMINDIVI ISLANDS

FUNK & WAGNALLS NEW ENCYCLO-PEDIA

JOSEPH LAFFAN MORSE, Sc.B., LL.B., L.H.D., LL.D.
Editor in Chief, Funk & Wagnalls Encyclopedias, 1946–69
WILLIAM H. HENDELSON, Editorial Director,
and successor Editor in Chief

Funk & Wagnalls, Inc., New York

Funk & Wagnalls
New Encyclopedia
Copyright © 1972, 1973
By Funk & Wagnalls, Inc.

Library of Congress Catalog
Card Number 72–170933

Copyright Under the Articles of the Copyright Convention of the Pan-American Republics and the United States

PRINTED IN THE UNITED STATES OF AMERICA
ALL RIGHTS RESERVED

jgc

FUNK & WAGNALLS
NEW ENCYCLOPEDIA

LIST OF ABBREVIATIONS USED IN THE TEXT*

abbr.	abbreviated	fr.	from	ONF.	Old Norman French
AC; a-c	alternating current	Fr.	French	O.T.	Old Testament
A.D.	*anno Domini* (Medieval Lat., in the year of the Lord)	ft.	foot	oz.	ounce
		g	gram	P.M.	*post meridiem* (Lat., after noon)
		Gael.	Gaelic		
		gal.	gallon	Pol.	Polish
alt.	altitude	Ger.	German	pop.	population
A.M.	*ante meridiem* (Lat., before noon)	Gr.	Greek	Port.	Portuguese
		Heb.	Hebrew	prelim.	preliminary
AM	amplitude modulation	Hind.	Hindustani	pron.	pronounced
amu	atomic mass unit	h.p.	horsepower	q.v.	*quod vide* (Lat., which see)**
anc.	ancient	hr.	hour		
Ar.	Arabic	Hung.	Hungarian	r.	reigned
AS.	Anglo-Saxon	Hz	hertz or cycles per second	R.	River
A.S.S.R.	Autonomous Soviet Socialist Republic			rev.	revised, revision
		I.	Island	R.R.	railroad
at.no.	atomic number	i.e.	*id est* (Lat., that is)	Rum.	Rumanian
at.wt.	atomic weight	in.	inch	Russ.	Russian
b.	born	Ind.	Indian	Ry.	railway
bbl	barrel	Ir.	Irish	S.	south; southern
B.C.	before Christ	It.	Italian	sec.	second
bd.ft.	board feet	K.	Kelvin	S.F.S.R.	Soviet Federated Socialist Republic
bev	billion electron volts	kg	kilogram		
		km	kilometer	Skr.	Sanskrit
b.p.	boiling point	kw	kilowatt	Sp.	Spanish
B.T.U.	British Thermal Unit	kw hour	kilowatt hour	sp.gr.	specific gravity
		lat.	latitude	sq.	square
bu.	bushel	Lat.	Latin	sq.mi.	square mile
Bulg.	Bulgarian	lb.	pound	S.S.R.	Soviet Socialist Republic
C.	centigrade	long.	longitude		
cent.	century	m	meter	St.; Ste.	Saint
Chin.	Chinese	M.	Middle	Sum.	Sumerian
cm	centimeter	mev	million electron volts	Sw.	Swedish
Co.	County			temp.	temperature
colloq.	colloquial	mg	milligram	trans.	translation
cu.	cubic	mi.	mile	Turk.	Turkish
Czech.	Czechoslovakian	min.	minute	U.A.R.	United Arab Republic
d.	died	M.L.	Medieval Latin		
Dan.	Danish	mm	millimeter	U.K.	United Kingdom
DC; d-c	direct current	mod.	modern	U.N.	United Nations
Du.	Dutch	m.p.	melting point	U.S.	United States
E.	east; eastern	m.p.h.	miles per hour	U.S.A.	United States of America
ed.	edition; editor	Mt(s).	Mount, Mountain		
Egypt.	Egyptian	N.	north; northern	U.S.S.R.	Union of Soviet Socialist Republics
Eng.	English	Norw.	Norwegian		
est.	estimated	N.T.	New Testament	var.	variant
ev	electron volt	OE.	Old English	vol.	volume
F.	Fahrenheit	OF.	Old French	vs.	versus or against
fl.	flourished	OHG.	Old High German	W.	west; western
FM	frequency modulation	ON.	Old Norse	yd.	yard

* For a more extensive listing of abbreviations, widely used by authoritative sources in many fields, see ABBREVIATION. Charts of pertinent abbreviations also accompany the articles BIBLE, CANON OF THE; DEGREE, ACADEMIC; ELEMENTS, CHEMICAL; MATHEMATICAL SYMBOLS; WEIGHTS AND MEASURES. Accent marks and special letters are explained in the article DIACRITIC MARK.

** The abbreviation (q.v.) stands for the Latin words "quod vide", meaning "which see": The placement of this abbreviation after a word—or a name or term—indicates that the word itself is the title of a separate article in the encyclopedia. By looking up the article on this word, or the entries on each word in a series that is followed by the plural form (qq.v.) of the abbreviation, the reader will find specific information about the words used as well as additional data about the main topic of the article he is reading.

FUNK & WAGNALLS NEW ENCYCLOPEDIA

ISRAEL, republic in the Middle East, established in 1948 and occupying much of the territory of ancient Palestine (q.v.). Located on the E. shore of the Mediterranean Sea, Israel is bounded on the N. by Lebanon, on the N.E. by Syria, on the E. by Jordan, and on the S.W. by the Arab Republic of Egypt. Its southernmost tip extends to the Gulf of 'Aqaba. The northernmost point lies at about lat. 32°45′ N.; the southernmost is approximately lat. 29°30′ N. On the W. Israel extends to about long. 34°30′ E. and on the E. to approximately long. 35°30′ E. According to the armistice agreement that followed the war of 1948–49 between Israel and neighboring countries, Israel covers 7978 sq.mi. (see *History*, below).

THE LAND

Israel has an extreme length of 262 mi., a width that varies from 10 mi. to about 70 mi., and can be divided into five distinct topographical areas: the highlands of Galilee; the Plain of Jezreel (*see* JEZREEL, PLAIN OF); the Judean and Samarian hills; the coastal plains; and the Negev (q.v.).

The hills of Galilee dominate the N. section of Israel, extending eastward about 25 mi. from a narrow coastal plain across to Lake Tiberias (Sea of Galilee). To the S. of the highlands of Galilee lies the Plain of Jezreel, about 36 mi. long and 15 mi. wide, running across Israel from the vicinity of Haifa on the Mediterranean coast to the Jordan River (q.v.). Formerly a malarial swampland, the valley has been drained and is now a densely populated and productive agricultural region.

Extending about 120 mi. along the Mediterranean, the coastal plains range from a width of a few hundred yards, particularly in the N., to a maximum of 20 mi. They consist of the Plain of Zevulun, extending about 10 miles N. of Haifa along the Bay of Acre; the Plain of Sharon, extending S. from the vicinity of Haifa to Tel Aviv-Jaffa; and the Plain of Judea, from Tel Aviv-Jaffa to Gaza (q.v.). The coastal plains contain most of Israel's large cities, industry, and commerce. The Judean Hills, and N. of them the Samarian Hills, form a barrier running N. and S. throughout most of Israel.

The Negev is a desert region to the S. The desert extends N. from the Gulf of 'Aqaba to a line from the S. end of the Dead Sea (q.v.) to the Mediterranean, passing just S. of Beersheba.

The chief river of Israel is the Jordan. It descends from Mount Hermon (q.v.) on the Lebanon-Syrian border to Lake Tiberias, 665 ft. below sea level, and ultimately into the Dead Sea, about 1292 ft. below sea level.

The coastline of Israel has few indentations. The only natural harbor on the Mediterranean is Haifa, on the Bay of Acre. A new port, Ashdod, has been created in the S.

Climate. The climate is generally subtropical, with rainfall limited to the winter months. Conditions vary however. Rainfall is poorly distributed, varying from about 40 in. annually in Galilee to about 20 in. around Tel Aviv-Jaffa, and about 1 in. at the S. port of Elath.

Natural Resources. Known in Biblical times as a land of milk and honey, Palestine has more recently been regarded as barren and infertile. Israel has both mineral and agricultural resources, however. Geological surveys have indicated that minerals in the Negev include copper, iron phosphates, manganese, granite, marble, mica, feldspar, gypsum, glass, flint-clay, and ball clay. Commercially exploitable deposits of oil and natural gas have also been discovered. Vast quantities of bromine and potash are available in the waters of the Dead Sea, and some peat and iron ore are to be found in Galilee.

The soil of Israel is generally poor, but along the coastal plain are rich alluvial soils, and the lands reclaimed from the swamps of the Plain of Jezreel are also extremely fertile.

ISRAEL

ISRAEL

INDEX TO MAP OF ISRAEL

Districts

Central	B 3
Haifa	C 2
Jerusalem	B 4
Northern	C 2
Southern	B,D 5
Tel Aviv	B 3

Cities and Towns

Acre	C 2
Afiqim	D 2
'Afula	C 2
Ahuzzam	B 4
Akko (Acre)	C 2
Arad	C 5
'Arrabe	C 2
Ashdod	B 4
Ashdot Ya'aqov	D 2
Ashqelon	A 4
Atlit	B 2
Avihayil	B 3
Bat Shelomo	B 2
Bat Yam	B 3
Be'er Tuveya	B 4
Be'eri	A 5
Beersheba	D 4
Bene Beraq	B 3
Bet Dagan	B 4
Bet Hagaddi	B 5
Bet Qama	B 5
Bet She'an	D 3
Bet Shemesh	B 4
Binyamina	B 2
Carmiel	C 2
Dafna	D 1
Dalyat al-Karmel	B 2
Dan	D 1
Dimona	D 4
Dor	B 2
'Ein Harod	C 2
El 'Auja	D 5
Elath (Elat)	D 5
Elyakim	C 2
Elyashiv	B 3
Even Yehuda	B 3
Gal'on	B 4
Gan Yavne	B 4
Gat	B 4
Gedera	B 4
Gesher	D 2
Gesher Haziv	C 1
Gevar'am	B 4
Gilat	B 5
Ginnosar	D 2
Giv'at Brenner	B 4
Giv'at Hayyim	B 3
Giv'atayim	B 3
Gosh Halav (Jish)	C 1
Habonim	B 2
Hadera	B 3
Haifa	B 2
Hazerim	B 5
Helez	B 4
Herzeliyya	B 3
Hod Hasharon	B 3
Hodiyya	B 4
Holon	B 3
Iksal	C 2
Jerusalem (cap.)	C 4
Jish	C 1
Kafar Kanna	C 2
Kafar Yasif	C 2
Karkur	C 3
Kefar Atta	C 2
Kefar Blum	D 1
Kefar Gil'adi	D 1
Kefar Ruppin	D 3
Kefar Sava	B 3
Kefar Vitkin	B 3
Kefar Yona	B 3
Kefar Zekhariya	B 4
Kinneret	D 2
Lod (Lydda)	B 4
Lydda	B 4
Magen	A 5
Mash' Abbe Sade	B 6
Mavqi'im	B 4
Megiddo	C 2
Me'ona	C 1
Metula	D 1
Migdal	C 2
Mikhmoret	B 3
Mishmar Hanegev	B 5
Mivtahim	A 5
Mizpe Ramon	D 5
Moza Illit	C 4
Mughar	C 2
Muqeible	C 2
Nahariyya	C 1
Nazareth	C 2
Negba	B 4
Nes Ziyyona	B 4
Nesher	C 2
Netanya	B 3
Nevatim	B 5
Newe Yam	B 2
Nir Am	B 4
Nir Yitzhaq	A 5
Nizzanim	B 4
Oron	C 6
Pardes Hanna	B 2
Peduyim	B 5
Petah Tiqwa	B 3
Qadima	B 3
Qedma	B 4
Qiryat Bialik	C 2
Qiryat Gat	B 4
Qiryat Haayin	B 2
Qiryat Motzkin	C 2
Qiryat Shemona	C 1
Qiryat Tiv'on	C 2
Qiryat Yam	C 2
Ra'anana	B 3
Ramat Gan	B 3
Ramat Hasharon	B 3
Rame	C 2
Ramla	B 4
Rehovot	B 4
Re'im	A 5
Revadim	B 4
Revivim	D 5
Rishon Le Ziyyon	B 4
Rosh Pinna	D 2
Ruhama	B 4
Sa'ad	B 5
Safad (Zefat)	C 2
Sakhnin	C 2
Sedot Yam	B 3
Shave Ziyyon	B 2
Shefar'am	C 2
Shefayim	B 3
Shoval	B 5
Tayibe	C 3
Tel Aviv-Jaffa	B 3
Tiberias	C 2
Tirat Hakarmel	B 2
Tirat Zevi	D 3
Tur'an	C 2
Umm el Fahm	B 5
Urim	B 5
Uzza	B 4
Yad Mordekhai	A 1
Yagur	C 2
Yavne	B 4
Yavne'el	C 2
Yehud	B 3
Yeroham	B 6
Yesodot	C 2
Yesud Hama'ala	D 1
Yirka	C 2
Yoqne'am	C 2
Zavdi'el	B 4
Ze'elim	A 5
Zefat	C 2
Zikhron Ya'aqov	B 2
Zippori	C 2

Other Features

'Araba, Wadi (dry river)	D 5
Beer Ef'e (well)	C 5
Beer Sheva', Wadi (dry river)	B 5
Besor, Wadi (dry river)	B 5
Carmel (cape)	B 2
Carmel (mt.)	C 2
Dead (sea)	C 4
'Ein Gedi (well)	C 5
'Ein Netafim (well)	D 5
Galilee (region)	C 2
Galilee, Sea of (sea)	D 2
Gerar, Wadi (dry river)	B 5
Hadera (river)	B 3
Haifa (bay)	C 2
Hatira (mt.)	B 6
Hemar, Wadi (dry river)	C 5
Jordan (river)	D 3
Judaea (region)	B 5
Lakhish, Wadi (dry river)	B 4
Meiron (mt.)	C 1
Negev (region)	D 5
Paran, Wadi (dry river)	D 5
Qarn (river)	C 1
Qishon, Wadi (dry river)	C 2
Ramon (mt.)	D 5
Rubin, Wadi (dry river)	B 4
Tabor (mt.)	C 2
Tiberias (Galilee) (sea)	D 2
Tseelim, Wadi (dry river)	C 5
Tsin, Wadi (dry river)	D 5
Yarmuk (river)	D 2
Yarqon, Wadi (dry river)	B 3

Gaza Strip

Cities and Towns

'Abasan	A 5
Bani Suheila	A 5
Beit Hanun	A 4
Deir el Balah	A 5
Gaza	A 5
Jabaliya	A 4
Khan Yunis	A 5
Rafah	A 5

Plants and Animals. The plant life of Israel is different in three distinct regions: the Mediterranean coast, the Asian steppe, and the desert regions of the Arabian Peninsula. The country has about 2500 species of plants, most of them xerophytic, that is, able to survive prolonged dry spells. Economically valuable products include citrus fruits, bananas, cotton, tobacco, grapes, dates, figs, olives, plums, and almonds. Dwarf oak and various other deciduous and coniferous trees have increased in number in recent years. Reforested areas cover 3 percent of the land.

The wildlife of Israel includes about 100 species of mammals and about 400 species of birds. Chief among the beasts of prey are the otter, wolf, mongoose, jackal, and hyena. Gazelles, porcupines, and hedgehogs are plentiful, and the wild boar is hunted. Locusts, though not native to the area, invade it periodically.

Water. The water supply of Israel is extremely limited and unevenly distributed. The exploitation and allocation of water resources are the responsibility of Mekorot, the national water-supply authority, the responsibilities of which include the preservation of flood waters, purification of sewage, location and utilization of all natural deposits of sweet water, desalinization of brackish and saline water, and the completion of a huge conduit to carry water from the Jordan R. to the Negev. The first part of this conduit was finished in 1964. Electric power was produced by fuel oil in the early 1970's (see *Manufacturing*, below).

THE PEOPLE

The population of Israel is predominantly urban and, although 85 percent Jewish, contains a remarkable racial, cultural, and ethnic diversity. Approximately 41 percent of the Jews in Israel in

Haifa, the chief seaport of Israel, lies on the south shore of the Bay of Acre. Israel Office of Information

the early 1970's were Israeli-born, but their immediate forebears came from more than 100 different countries and spoke, among them, about eighty-five different languages or major dialects. The two major groupings are European or Western ("Ashkenazi") Jews, who make up about 31 percent of the Jewish population, and Asian and North African ("Sephardic") Jews, who make up about 28 percent.

Population. The population of Israel (census 1961) was 2,183,332; the United Nations estimated (1971) 3,013,000. The overall population density is about 367 per sq.mi. (U.N. est. 1970). The non-Jewish population totaled more than 438,000, of whom about 326,000 were Muslims, 76,000 Christians, and 36,000 Druzes and others. Nearly 80 percent of the Jewish population is urban. Of the Israeli Arabs, on the other hand, 75 percent are rural.

Political Divisions. Israel is divided into six administrative districts: the Northern District, Haifa, Central District, Tel Aviv, Jerusalem, and the Southern District. Each is administered by a commissioner appointed by the minister of the interior. In practice, the influence of the central government is evident directly in every part of the country. Local government is carried out through 27 municipal councils, 116 local councils, and 47 regional councils.

Principal Cities. The largest city in Israel, Tel Aviv–Jaffa (pop. est. 1971, 382,900), is also the leading industrial center. The capital is Jerusalem (pop. est. 1971, 283,100, including inhabitants of the Old City). Haifa had a population of about 214,500 in 1971.

Religion. The affairs of the three major religions, Judaism, Islam, and Christianity (qq.v.), are administered by the ministry of religious affairs, through councils established by the various religions. Jewish holy days and the Sabbath are, by law, observed throughout the country, and only kosher food is served in the army, in hospitals, and in other official institutions.

Languages. Hebrew and Arabic are the official languages. The most widely spoken language is Hebrew, but Arabic is also used in schools, in law courts, in legal documents, and in the legislature.

Education. The educational tradition of Israel reaches back to Biblical times, although the country did not become a modern independent state until 1948. During the ancient period schools on all levels were organized, and through the centuries elementary and secondary education and, to a large extent, higher learning continued in Palestine under the vari-

Above: In striking architectural contrast in Jerusalem are the white-domed Shrine of the Book, which houses the Dead Sea Scrolls, and the building of the Knesset, the Israeli legislative body. Right: The historic Wailing Wall, in the Old City of Jerusalem. The central barrier separates men from women. UPI

In a giant vat at a Dead Sea phosphate plant, workers break up and remove dried potash. UPI

ous ruling factions, whether Roman, Arab, Turkish, or British.

The Compulsory Education Law of 1949 provides for free and compulsory elementary education for all children five to fourteen years of age. Reform continued with the State Education Law of 1953, which established a national system of public secondary schools. Higher education is governed by a law enacted in 1958, which set up a council to control universities and other higher educational institutions, such as the Hebrew University of Jerusalem, the Technion (Israel Institute of Technology) in Haifa, Bar-Ilan University in Ramat Gan, Tel Aviv University, and the Weizmann Institute of Science in Rehovot. Students in secondary schools receive aid from state and local authorities in amounts up to 100 percent of costs, depending upon parents' incomes.

In addition to the secular system of elementary, secondary, and higher education, a parallel system of Jewish religious schools exists, culminating in postgraduate schools of independent study and research. Mission schools conducted by various Christian groups are also widely attended. An educational problem peculiar to Israel is that of assisting immigrants of many linguistic and ethnic backgrounds to adjust to Israeli society.

ELEMENTARY AND SECONDARY SCHOOLS. In the early 1970's preprimary and primary schools numbered about 4850 with approximately 560,000 pupils. Secondary schools totaled more than 230, with an aggregate enrollment of about 62,300 students.

SPECIALIZED SCHOOLS. Vocational, teacher-training, and other specialized schools totaled about 690, with an enrollment of more than 94,000.

Culture. Israeli culture reflects the diverse background of the people. The most successful writers draw their inspiration from Jewish tradition. Such writers include the novelist Shmuel Yosef Agnon, winner of the 1966 Nobel Prize in literature, and the philosopher Martin Buber (qq.v.). The impetus to create an indigenous Israeli literature is strong, but the cultural diversity of their countrymen is a problem for Israeli writers and artists. The foremost orchestra of the nation, the Israel Philharmonic attracts each year a number of world-famous conductors and soloists. A vigorous tradition of folk song, in which the influence of Oriental Jewish music is strongly felt, thrives in Israel, as does the dance. The Habimah (q.v.) is notable among theatrical organizations.

LIBRARIES AND MUSEUMS. Israel has more than 130 museums, the two most prominent being the Tel Aviv Museum and the Israel Museum in Jerusalem, which houses a large collection of Jewish folk art, a collection of modern sculpture, and Biblical and archeological artifacts, including a notable collection of Dead Sea Scrolls (q.v.). Of the more than 500 public libraries in the country, the most important is the Jewish National Library on the campus of the Hebrew University of Jerusalem, with more than 1,500,000 volumes.

ARCHEOLOGY. Archeology is a national pastime. The numerous ancient sites date from pre-Biblical, Biblical, and post-Biblical periods, and new finds are frequent. Restorations that may be visited include King Solomon's stables at Megiddo, the town of Caesarea, and the Herodian palace at Masada.

THE ECONOMY

The Israeli economy is beset by a chronic balance of payments deficit and a shortage of the raw materials necessary to a modern industrial economy. High expenditures are devoted to arms and to the task of absorbing large numbers of immigrants. In a recent year the national budget showed revenues at $1,434,000,000 and expenditures at $2,328,000,000.

Agriculture. Israeli agriculture meets some three fourths of the national food needs, and certain items, chiefly citrus fruits and eggs, are exported. Annual agricultural production in the early 1970's included about 1,000,000 tons of citrus fruits, 142,000 tons of potatoes, 37,000 tons of cotton, 21,000 tons of groundnuts, 18,000 tons of barley, 527,000 tons of milk, and about 1,393,000,000 eggs.

Irrigation pipe is moved with specially designed wheels on a farm in the Negev. Modern irrigation methods are bringing new life to the region, which is developing industrial as well as agricultural settlements. UPI

The success of Israeli agriculture has been made possible by reliance on scientific research and advanced technology, particularly in land reclamation and irrigation programs.

Israeli farming settlements are organized into three principal types. In the collective settlement *(kibbutz),* people live in communal dwellings and share equally in the work and its profits. In the cooperative settlement *(moshav),* individual farms are worked separately but the produce is pooled and marketed by the settlement. In the small-holders' settlement *(moshava),* individual farms are worked as private enterprises. The first two types of settlement are established on land owned by one of the various colonizing organizations, principally the Jewish National Fund, and leased to the settlers.

Forest and Fishing Industries. A major portion of the land reclamation and conservation program is afforestation, or the establishment of forest cover, mainly in the hilly areas. An additional 150,000 acres of Israeli land are covered by natural forest and forest reserves. In the early 1970's Israeli fishermen were netting approximately 28,000 tons of fish annually. About one third of this quantity consisted of freshwater fish raised mainly in artificial fish ponds.

Mining. The chief assets of the mining industry are the huge quantities of potash, bromine, and other salt deposits of the Dead Sea; potash production in the early 1970's amounted to

A shepherd drives his flock to pasture from a kibbutz (background), a type of communal or cooperative farm community that is common in Israel.

Israel Office of Information

Women of the Israeli army march in Jerusalem in a parade marking an anniversary of the founding of Israel.
UPI

about 570,000 tons annually. Copper production of about 10,400 tons meets domestic requirements. Annual petroleum production exceeds 6,000,000 tons, and output of natural gas is about 161,000,000 cu.yd. Extensive quarrying of marble and granite meets domestic construction needs.

Manufacturing. Factories are mainly concentrated in Haifa and Tel Aviv–Jaffa, although an important industrial complex is developing around the new port of Ashdod. The principal industrial products are construction materials, tires, metal products, pharmaceuticals, soap, cosmetics, and textiles. Wines and olive oil are also produced, and the diamond-cutting industry flourishes. Israeli industry is increasing its production in the fields of petrochemicals, weapons, and electronics. Private and industrial consumption of electricity in the early 1970's amounted to about 7,640,000,000 kw hours.

Currency and Banking. Israel has a flourishing banking industry. The official bank, the Bank of Israel, issues currency and is the sole bank of the government. The unit of currency is the Israeli pound, consisting of 100 agorot (4.20 Israeli pounds equal U.S.$1; 1973).

Commerce and Trade. Principal imports are machinery, grain and flour, motor vehicles, iron and steel products, fuel, and weapons. Principal exports are polished diamonds, citrus fruits and by-products, metal products, textiles and clothing, and chemicals.

Transportation. The artificial harbor at Ashdod is now the chief Israeli port, having surpassed Haifa in 1966. A third port is Elath, on the Gulf of 'Aqaba. Elath is the only Israeli outlet to the Red Sea, Israeli ships being denied access to the Suez Canal (q.v.). In the early 1970's the Israeli merchant fleet included nearly 115 vessels with a capacity of approximately 698,000 gross tons. Railroads are state-owned and totaled about 600 mi. Paved roads totaled some 2500 mi. Most passenger and freight transportation within Israel is by truck and automobile. In addition to its own airline, El Al, Israel is served by several other international airlines. Internal service is also supplied by Arkia Airline. The principal airport is at Lod, outside Tel Aviv–Jaffa.

Communications. Radio and television services are provided exclusively by Kol Israel (the Voice of Israel), which transmits on some twenty-two different wavelengths in both principal languages, Hebrew and Arabic.

All postal, telegraph, and telephone services are operated by the ministry of posts. In the early 1970's Israel had some 500 post offices, about 660,000 radios, 345,000 television receivers, and more than 584,000 telephones.

Israel has 23 daily newspapers. Approximately 400 other periodicals are published either weekly, biweekly, or monthly.

Labor. The total number of persons employed in the late 1960's was more than 875,000, of whom 250,000 were women. The most distinctive feature of Israeli labor is the Histadrut, the General Federation of Labor. Its membership comprises about 60 percent of the working pop-

ISRAEL

ulation. The Histadrut not only functions as a labor union but is also one of the largest employers in the country, with a variety of commercial and industrial enterprises.

GOVERNMENT

Israel is a parliamentary democracy with supreme authority vested in the legislature. The nation has no written constitution.

Central Government. The head of state, the president, is elected by the legislature for a five-year term. The executive body is a cabinet of about fifteen ministers headed by a prime minister. It remains in office as long as it retains the confidence of the legislature.

HEALTH AND WELFARE. The overall administrative and coordinating authority is the ministry of health, with fifteen offices and thirty-four hospitals throughout the country. Medical insurance funds are largely private or cooperative, the largest, covering two of every three Israelis, being run by the Histadrut, the Israeli labor federation. Government insurance, pensions, maternity benefits, and aid to dependent children covered about 900,000 people in the late 1960's.

Legislature. The Israeli legislature, or Knesset, is a unicameral body of 120 members elected for four years on the basis of proportional representation. Suffrage is granted to all citizens eighteen years of age and over.

Political Parties. Political parties in Israel include ten Jewish parties and two parties representing Muslims, Christians, and Druzes. Because no party has ever won a majority of seats in the Knesset, coalition governments have been the rule. The governing coalition, formed in 1967, is based upon the Mapai (the largest Labor party), Ahdut Ha'avoda (a Zionist party), Rafi (the Israel Labor List), the Gahal, the National Religious Party, and the Mapam (United Workers' Party). The first three merged in 1968 to form the Israel Labor Party; the Mapam joined in 1969.

Judiciary. Israel has two court systems, one civil, one religious. The civil court consists of a supreme court, the chief administrative and highest appellate court of the land. Beneath it are the district courts, which hear major civil and criminal cases and appeals from lower courts, and magistrates and municipal courts, which have limited jurisdiction. Religious courts have control of marriage, divorce, alimony, and confirmation of wills. They may also rule on other matters of personal status if all the parties involved consent.

Defense. In the early 1970's Israel maintained a standing army of 61,500 men and an additional 200,000 men as reserve forces. All men between eighteen and twenty-six years of age must serve for 36 months and those between twenty-seven and twenty-nine for 2 years. Unmarried women between eighteen and twenty-six must serve for 20 months. Men up to forty-nine and childless women up to age thirty-four are liable for service in the reserves. An air force of about 9000 men equipped with some 350 first-line jet planes (mostly of French or U.S. manufacture) and a small navy augment the highly mobile land forces.

HISTORY

Zionism (q.v.), the movement for an independent Jewish state in Palestine, had its roots in the beginning of organized Jewish settlement during the 19th century. The first modern Jewish agricultural colony, Petah Tiqwa, was founded

Members of a kibbutz, in traditional dress, perform a peasant dance. UPI

ISRAEL

about 1870, and a number of others followed soon thereafter. In the last decade of the century, Theodor Herzl (q.v.), an Austrian writer, organized a world Zionist movement, and made it an effective political force. The movement rapidly gained adherents during the first decade of the 20th century, as anti-Semitism and pogroms (qq.v.) in Eastern Europe stimulated Jewish nationalism and caused growing numbers of Jews to see in Zionism a solution to their problem. Meanwhile, the earliest settlements in Palestine, attacked occasionally by marauding Arabs, organized a loose defensive group known as Hashomer (Heb., "Watchmen"). This group was the antecedent of the Israeli army, and it came into being in response to the Jews' first confrontation with Arab opposition, one of the two major obstacles to the achievement of their own state. The other important obstacle, opposition from the Ottoman Empire (q.v.), was eliminated after British troops, supported by specially recruited Jewish forces, ousted the Ottoman Turks from Palestine during World War I, in 1918. The year before, Arthur James Balfour (q.v.), then British foreign secretary, had stated that Britain pledged itself to support the establishment of a Jewish "National Home" in Palestine; see BALFOUR DECLARATION.

The Mandate. This pledge was incorporated into the League of Nations (q.v.) mandate for Palestine in 1922, under which Britain was instructed to "facilitate" Jewish immigration and settlement upon the land. Its intention was supported by Faisal I, King of Iraq (see under FAISAL), in an exchange of letters with Dr. Chaim Weizmann (q.v.), the Zionist leader who later became the first president of Israel. The postwar influx of Jewish immigrants was met by two setbacks, however. First, the mandatory government divided Palestine into two parts. The area east of the Jordan R. was designated a separate entity called Transjordan, and Jews were forbidden to enter or settle there; see JORDAN, HASHEMITE KINGDOM OF: History. Secondly, Palestinian Arabs began to organize political opposition to Zionism.

With the advent of the National Socialist regime in Germany, in 1933, Jews faced with persecution left Europe in increasing numbers, and the Jewish population of Palestine began to swell; see NATIONAL SOCIALISM. In 1936, fierce Arab rioting broke out in protest against further Jewish immigration, and deaths occurred daily for the next three years. In response to this rioting, two Jewish armed forces were organized. In 1936, the Hashomer was replaced by an underground army, the Haganah ("Defense"), which enlisted large numbers of able-bodied Jewish men and women. The Haganah operated on a principle of "self-restraint", and dedicated itself solely to defending Jewish lives and property. In 1937, the smaller Irgun Zvai Leumi ("National Military Organization") was founded. Following the political leadership of Vladimir Jabotinsky (1880–1940), then head of the militant New Zionist Organization, the Irgun sought out and conducted retaliatory attacks against Arabs, on the theory that Arab rioting was encouraged by the British and could not be halted merely by defensive tactics.

In 1939, on grounds of being obliged to find some means of restoring order in Palestine, the British government issued a white paper. This document asserted that a Jewish national home had already been established in Palestine, with the existence there of a large and flourishing community. By thus implying that the term "national home" did not mean a state, but simply a functioning community, the British claimed that this part of the mandatory obligation already had been satisfactorily discharged. Then, on the ground that Britain was obliged to respect the wishes of the "local inhabitants", the white paper assured the Arabs of a continuing majority in Palestine by restricting further Jewish immigration to 75,000, to be apportioned over the ensuing five years. It also strictly limited Jewish purchase of Palestinian land. The result was a virtual cessation of Arab violence, and the beginning of anti-British violence by Jews, conducted by the Irgun.

After the outbreak of World War II the Haganah and the Irgun joined Great Britain in the war effort and about 30,000 Palestinian Jews enlisted in the British Middle Eastern forces. The Irgun was split in 1940, however, by a small faction, the Fighters for the Freedom of Israel, or "Stern Group". Its leader, Abraham Stern (1907–42), killed by British police who claimed that he attempted to escape after being apprehended by them, believed that the immigration of Jews from Europe, which had been all but halted by the British authorities, was of primary importance. His group attempted to force a change of policy through a campaign of assassination directed at British officials. After Germany's collapse, when the fate of Jews under National Socialism was more fully known, Palestinian Jews pressed for admission of the concentration-camp survivors into Palestine. When the election of a Labour government in Britain, in August, 1945, failed to produce a change in immigration policy, anti-British fighting flared again. The Stern Group and the larger and stronger

ISRAEL

Irgun claimed that the British administration, by violating the immigration and land settlement provisions of the mandate, had become an unlawful occupying power.

A two-year crisis of continuously mounting intensity began. While Arabs, impressed by Jewish strength, looked on passively, the British government and the Jewish groups maneuvered for position. Under David Ben-Gurion (q.v.), the Jewish Agency, the official Zionist and semi-governmental organization of Jewish Palestine, denounced what it called the terrorism of the Irgun and the Stern Group. But the Agency's position was strengthened by their activities, which it told the British it could not prevent unless concessions were granted. Meanwhile, Jews and their sympathizers in America, aroused by the reports of fighting and of captured immigration ships, contributed increasing amounts of money for support of the Jewish cause and put pressure on the government of the United States to urge a change in British policy. The British refused to increase the immigration quota, and began to intern captured would-be immigrants on the island of Cyprus. Early in 1947, the imminent execution of a captured Irgun leader brought the tension to fever pitch. In March the British army imposed martial law on Tel Aviv (now Tel Aviv-Jaffa) and the Jewish sections of Jerusalem. Then, despite an Irgun warning of retaliation if its members were executed, four Irgunists were hanged. When the Irgun retaliated by hanging two British soldiers, the incident produced a clamor in Britain for a change in policy.

The mandate government, having succeeded only in strengthening and uniting its opposition, feared that greater repressive measures might bring about an outright alliance between the moderate Jewish forces and the more militant underground groups. On the other hand, to allow Jewish immigration would antagonize the nations of the Arab League (q.v.). Accordingly, the British government decided to submit the Palestine problem to the United Nations (q.v.).

Fighting in Palestine ceased when a special meeting of the U.N. General Assembly resulted in the appointment of an eleven-nation investigation commission, the U.N. Special Committee on Palestine (U.N.S.C.O.P.). The U.N.S.C.O.P. proceeded to Palestine in the summer of 1947, and, on Aug. 31, submitted a majority report recommending the partition of the country into separate Arab and Jewish states, and the creation of an international zone including Jerusalem and its environs. Both States were to have democratic governments, and were to cooperate with each other economically. A detailed plan of partition procedure was passed by the General Assembly on Nov. 29. Representatives of the Arab nations left the meeting after the vote, declaring their refusal to accept the plan.

Fighting broke out in Palestine immediately after the vote of the General Assembly. Bands of Arabs attacked Jewish farms and settlements, and Jews retaliated. The five-nation commission (Bolivia, Czechoslovakia, Denmark, Panama, and the Philippines) that had been appointed to supervise the partition not only lacked military forces to control the violence, but was prevented by the British from entering Palestine until the following spring. As the communal fighting increased, the British failed, on Feb. 1, to evacuate a port for Jewish use in bringing refugees and supplies, as specified in the U.N. timetable. Meanwhile, Palestinian Arabs were being reinforced by detachments of irregulars, trained and armed in the surrounding Arab countries. During the early months of 1948 the British abandoned more and more of the administration of the country, which was taken up haphazardly by local Jewish and Arab authorities, and announced that they would depart completely on May 15. In February the Palestine commission requested an international military force to quell the fighting and implement partition, but neither the U.S. nor the Soviet Union, the dominant powers in the U.N., approved of this proposal.

Independence and War. On May 13, the Arab League declared that the forces of its member nations would enter Palestine immediately after the British departure to "administer" it until an Arab state could be established throughout the country. On May 14, the British high commissioner and the last of the British troops sailed from Haifa harbor. That night, the State of Israel was proclaimed by Jewish leaders, and a provisional government was established. Almost simultaneously, the regular armies of Syria, Lebanon, Egypt, Iraq, and Transjordan crossed the Palestine frontier and attacked Jewish settlements. The State of Israel began its official existence at midnight. Eleven minutes later, it was accorded *de facto* (in fact) recognition by the U.S., and two days later, it was recognized *de jure* (in law) by the U.S.S.R. The Israeli provisional government was headed by David Ben-Gurion, prime minister and defense minister, and Moshe Shertok, who changed his name to Moshe Scharett (1894–1965), foreign minister. On May 16 Dr. Chaim Weizmann was elected president of the council of the provisional government.

ISRAEL

The Israelis were at first hard pressed. Lacking sufficient arms, they initially suffered heavy casualties. At that time the Israeli army, formed from the Haganah, did not yet embrace the Irgun and the Stern Group. These kept most of their effectives in Jerusalem, in an attempt to assure its inclusion in the new state. At this high point of the Arab advance, Lebanese troops, and Lebanon-supported irregulars, occupied western Galilee while Syrian army units attacked Israeli settlements in eastern Galilee. Iraqi troops occupied the strategic Tulkarm-Jenin-Nablus "triangle" in the northern Judean Hills. Transjordan forces, British armed and led, constituting the strongest Arab army, attacked Jerusalem and destroyed Israeli settlements south of Bethlehem. Egyptian troops moved up the Mediterranean shore, taking Gaza, and struck inland to occupy Beersheba and Hebron.

The U.N. proposed a truce and appointed Count Folke Bernadotte (1895–1948), head of the Swedish Red Cross, as U.N. mediator. The Arabs at first rejected the truce proposal, but, when their attack bogged down, they accepted it. A four-week truce went into effect on June 11, 1948, and during this period, the Israelis managed to strengthen their forces. When the cease-fire ended on July 9, they launched offensives in the northern and central sectors, capturing western Galilee, thus gaining all of northern Palestine, and capturing Lydda, important for its airport and its location near the strategic Tel Aviv-Jerusalem highway. Under the circumstances, the Arabs readily agreed to another truce, which went into effect on July 17.

On Sept. 17, while trying to bring about a permanent armistice, Bernadotte was killed by Israeli partisans in Jerusalem. Three days later, the Israeli government ordered the disbanding of nongovernmental military forces. The Irgun, most of whose members had already been transferred to the Israeli army, and the Stern Group complied with the order (and subsequently transformed themselves into militant, hard-line political parties). The Bernadotte plan for conciliation, which the count had completed shortly before his death, was presented to the U.N. by Dr. Ralph Bunche (q.v.), Bernadotte's American assistant, who became acting mediator. Recognizing Israel as an established fact, the plan called for its admission to the U.N. and a final arrangement of boundaries, awarding western Galilee to Israel and the Negev region to the Arabs, and placing Jerusalem under U.N. administration. Jews and Arabs both objected: the Arabs continued to oppose the existence of any Jewish state, and Israel maintained that surrender of the Negev would reduce the state by two thirds of its territory. The plan failed to receive U.N. approval and was abandoned.

Charging Egyptian truce violations, in October, 1948, Israel launched an attack which cleared most of the Negev desert region. The fighting was stopped and the new front stabilized through the mediation of Dr. Bunche. After Israeli-Egyptian armistice talks had continued for some weeks without apparent success, Israel again attacked, with one of its detachments striking more than 40 mi. into the Sinai Peninsula (q.v.), in Egypt, before withdrawing to the Negev. This fighting between Israel and Egypt was also halted by the intervention of Dr. Bunche, and an agreement was signed on Feb. 24, 1949. Under its terms, Israel retained the entire Negev except for a small coastal strip that included Gaza, which remained in Egyptian hands.

From Armistice to Suez Crisis. On March 11, 1949, Transjordan signed an agreement with Israel, under which the New City of Jerusalem remained in Israeli possession, and the Old City remained under Arab control. The agreement also provided for the withdrawal of Transjordan forces along some portions of the front in order to adjust the border with Israel. Lebanon signed an armistice on March 23, and, with the withdrawal of Iraqi troops from all of Palestine, and an Israeli-Syrian armistice in process of negotiation, fighting ceased on all fronts.

Meanwhile, on Jan. 25, the new republic had held its first elections. More than 350,000 persons voted. Ben-Gurion became prime minister of the new government, with the support of the religious bloc and some of the smaller parties. On Feb. 17, Chaim Weizmann was elected president of Israel by the Knesset.

Despite a $100,000,000 loan granted by the Export-Import Bank of the United States (q.v.) and large-scale financial assistance from Jewish communities in the U.S. and elsewhere, the new state faced great economic difficulties. Drained of resources by the fighting, Israel had the additional problem of sheltering and absorbing the hundreds of thousands of new immigrants who, often penniless, poured into the country. Accordingly, a drastic austerity program was inaugurated, modeled after the one in Britain.

Israel became a member of the U.N. in May, 1949. In December of that year the General Assembly affirmed its previous (1947) decision to internationalize Jerusalem and environs. Both Israel and Jordan (the name Transjordan had been changed in 1949) vigorously opposed the

Two Near Eastern emigrés selling their produce in an Israeli market. UPI

Assembly action. The Israeli foreign minister notified the General Assembly that his country intended to keep the New City. Jerusalem was made capital of Israel on Jan. 23, 1950.

More than 583,000 immigrants reached Israel between 1949 and 1951. About 50 percent of them were impoverished refugees from underdeveloped Middle Eastern countries. The cost of transporting, housing, and rehabilitating the immigrants severely taxed the Israeli economy.

In February, 1951, the Knesset authorized the sale of a $500,000,000 bond issue in the U.S. Ben-Gurion resigned (Feb. 14) because of disagreements within the government coalition on economic policies and on religious education in the immigrant camps. The prime minister agreed to head a caretaker government pending the outcome of elections scheduled for July 30. In the elections the conservative General Zionist Party gained thirteen seats and became the second-largest party in the Knesset. The Mapai lost one seat, but remained the largest party. After weeks of negotiation, the Mapai and the religious parties formed (Oct. 7) a new coalition government with Ben-Gurion again as prime minister.

In February, 1952, the U.S. government granted Israel $50,000,000 for the relief and resettlement of refugees. In June Israel arranged to receive aid under the U.S. Point Four Program (q.v.). West Germany agreed in September to ship to Israel over the next twelve years capital goods worth about $715,000,000, as reparations for the destruction of Jewish life and property under the Hitler regime.

President Chaim Weizmann died on Nov. 9, 1952. The veteran Mapai leader Itzhak Ben-Zvi (1883–1963) was installed as the second president of Israel on Dec. 10. Later that month the cabinet resigned, and Ben-Gurion formed a new government composed of Mapai and General Zionist members.

During 1953 Syria and Jordan registered strong protests against Israeli construction of a canal for a hydroelectric project on the Jordan R. The two countries lodged (Sept. 22) a complaint with the U.N. Security Council that the project would deprive them of water for irrigation. When Israel failed to halt work on the canal pending U.N. investigation, the U.S. government announced (Oct. 20) that financial assistance to Israel would be suspended. Israel halted construction on Oct. 28 and U.S. economic aid was resumed.

In December, 1953, Prime Minister Ben-Gurion resigned for reasons of health. He was succeeded by Foreign Minister Moshe Sharett, who favored reliance on diplomacy rather than force in dealing with the Arabs. While Sharett improved Israeli relations with the Soviet Union, India, Burma, and other nations, relations with the Arab states continued to deteriorate. He resigned in June, 1955.

Beginning in September, 1955, Israel was subjected to raids by groups of fedayeen, Arab volunteers who penetrated deeply into Israeli territory from bases in Egypt, inflicting heavy damage and casualties and terrorizing the population. Egypt arranged to exchange its cotton for Soviet and Czechoslovak military equipment, including jet aircraft. Striving to keep pace with the Egyptian arms buildup, Israel managed to purchase supplies of weapons from France, Canada, and other countries. Israel directed urgent appeals for arms to the U.S., but the U.S. government, unwilling to encourage an arms race in the Middle East, turned down the appeals.

The U.N. Secretary-General, Dag Hammarskjöld (q.v.), visited Israel and the neighboring

ISRAEL

Arab states in April, 1956, and attempted to win cease-fire pledges from both sides. Although such pledges were given, violence soon erupted along the Jordanian and Egyptian borders of Israel. Labor Minister Golda Meir (q.v.), who favored a tough policy toward the Arabs, succeeded Sharett as foreign minister in June. Hammarskjöld toured the Middle East again in July and renewed his efforts to secure peace.

On July 26 the Egyptian government nationalized the Suez Canal (q.v.) and denied Israel its use. Israel, together with the U.S., Great Britain, France, and other nations, condemned the act, demanded the restoration of international control of the canal, and insisted on the right of all nations to use it without interference. Subsequent negotiations, in London, Cairo, and New York, failed to settle the dispute.

Suez Canal Crisis, 1956. On Oct. 29 Israeli troops invaded the Sinai Peninsula with the declared objective of wiping out fedayeen bases in that area. The U.S. moved on Oct. 30 to censure Israel in the U.N. Security Council, but Great Britain and France vetoed the move. The same day the British and French governments, with the professed intention of protecting the Suez Canal, issued a joint ultimatum demanding cessation of hostilities and withdrawal of both Israeli and Egyptian forces from the canal area. The two powers threatened military intervention should either side fail to comply. Israel accepted the ultimatum, but Egypt rejected it, whereupon British and French aircraft attacked Egyptian airfields and military installations.

By Nov. 2 the Israeli army had driven to within 10 mi. of the Suez Canal, gaining control of the Gaza strip and almost all of the Sinai Peninsula. Israeli officials claimed the capture of many thousands of Egyptian soldiers and of large amounts of matériel. The U.N. General Assembly called for a cease-fire on Nov. 2, but the fighting continued.

On Nov. 4 the Israeli army completed its conquest of the Sinai Peninsula and suspended military operations. Its commander announced that only 165 Israeli soldiers had been killed during the week of fighting. British and French forces invaded the Suez Canal area on Nov. 5. The next day Great Britain, France, and Israel, yielding to American pressure and to Soviet threats to "crush the aggressors . . . through the use of force", accepted the U.N. cease-fire order. The invaders undertook to evacuate Egyptian territory as soon as a specially constituted U.N. police force could take their place. The first U.N. police contingents arrived in Egypt on Nov. 15. Israel began a gradual withdrawal of its forces a few days later. The withdrawal was followed by a temporary cessation of border incidents.

Relations between Israel and Egypt (which united with Syria to form the United Arab Republic, or U.A.R., on Feb. 1, 1958, and then, after Syria subsequently withdrew from the merger, retained the new name until 1971) continued strained and hostile. On several occasions the Egyptians confiscated Israeli cargo in foreign-flag vessels going through the Suez Canal. Mediation by U.N. Secretary-General Hammarskjöld was unsuccessful, and the situation remained unchanged throughout 1960.

Domestic Affairs in the Early 1960's. On May 23, 1960, Prime Minister Ben-Gurion announced the capture of Adolf Eichmann (1906–62), a former National Socialist Party official accused of having taken a leading part in the extermination of 6,000,000 Jews during World War II. Captured in Argentina by Israeli secret agents, Eichmann was brought to Israel to stand trial. Despite Argentine protests over violation of sovereignty, the Israeli government refused to return the captive. He was tried, found guilty, and executed.

On Jan. 31, 1961, Ben-Gurion resigned as prime minister after months of bitter controversy over the exoneration by a cabinet committee of Pinhas Lavon (1904–   ), former defense minister allegedly responsible for a grave security mishap in 1954. The Mapai party rallied behind Ben-Gurion by removing Lavon from his position as head of Histadrut, the powerful labor federation of Israel, but the resulting political upheaval made formation of a new coalition government impossible. On March 28 the Knesset was dissolved. In the elections of Aug. 15 the Mapai party lost strength but retained its plurality in the Knesset. Ben-Gurion, dissatisfied with the failure to win a majority, at first refused the president's invitation to form a cabinet. On Nov. 2, however, the Knesset voted its confidence in a new Ben-Gurion cabinet consisting mostly of Mapai and religious party ministers.

Israeli President Itzhak Ben-Zvi died on April 23, 1963, and on May 21 Schneor Zalman Shazar (1889–   ), formerly head of the Jewish Agency Department of Education and Culture for the Diaspora, was chosen as his successor. A second major government change was the resignation on June 16 of Prime Minister Ben-Gurion. His successor, former Minister of Finance Levi Eshkol (1895–1969), who was appointed on June 19, was committed to following the same policies.

On May 5, 1964, Israel announced that the first stage of its project to divert Jordan R. waters to irrigate the Negev was completed and

After their conference in June, 1973, Prime Minister Golda Meir of Israel shakes hands with Chancellor Willy Brandt of West Germany outside her Jerusalem office.
Starphot–Pictorial Parade

that Jordan waters were already flowing through the pipeline from Lake Tiberias to the desert region. The Arab states, at a summit meeting (Sept. 5–11), agreed jointly to build three dams that would divert Jordan waters before they reached Israel. In a party dispute over Ben-Gurion's demands to reopen the Lavon controversy, Prime Minister Eshkol and his cabinet resigned on Dec. 14. They returned to office on Dec. 22 following a Knesset vote of confidence. Israel and West Germany formally established diplomatic relations on May 13, 1965. The move, a controversial one in Israel, was defended as necessary for Israel's security.

Throughout 1965 and 1966 incidents continued along the Jordanian and Syrian frontiers, steadily increasing in intensity. In April, 1967, Syria complained of an Israeli troop buildup along its borders.

No evidence was found by U.N. inspectors, but in May Syria and the U.A.R. began massing troops along their borders with Israel. President Gamal Abdel Nasser (q.v.) of the U.A.R. then demanded the withdrawal of the U.N. peacekeeping force from the Gaza Strip and from Sharm el Sheikh at the entrance to the Gulf of 'Aqaba. These forces were replaced by U.A.R. troops and by forces of the Palestine Liberation Army, made up of fedayeen and other Arab irregulars. President Nasser then announced a blockade of the Straits of Tiran, the only access of Israel from the Gulf of 'Aqaba to the Red Sea. An emergency session of the U.N. Security Council was called to discuss the crisis. Meanwhile, as both sides approached full mobilization of their armed forces, Prime Minister Eshkol formed a new coalition government.

The Six-Day War. War broke out on June 5, 1967. In a series of lightning predawn raids, Israeli planes destroyed about 400 Arab planes, mostly on the ground, demolishing the Syrian, Jordanian, and U.A.R. air forces. At the same time Israeli troops and armor advanced into the Sinai Peninsula to meet advancing U.A.R. forces. Fighting also broke out around Jerusalem and on the Syrian border. Before the U.N. cease-fire took effect on June 10, the Israelis had taken the Gaza Strip and the Sinai Peninsula from the U.A.R. and Palestine Liberation Army forces, the Old City of Jerusalem and the West Bank of the Jordan R. from Jordan, and the Golan Heights overlooking Galilee from Syria. Thousands of prisoners and vast amounts of matériel were also taken. Israel lost about 700 men. The war cost Israel an estimated $750,000,000.

An Uneasy Peace. Although militarily the victor, Israel was unable to consolidate the victory. Arab intransigence in the U.N., combined with new Soviet military support, forced a stalemate. The Soviet Union and other Eastern European nations broke diplomatic relations with Israel (June 10). After annexing the Old City of Jerusalem, Israel placed the other captured areas under military control. From 1967 into the early 1970's sporadic fighting took place along the Suez Canal and along Israel's borders. Palestinian guerrilla forces made terrorist raids into Israel, and Israeli commandos retaliated with raids on guerrilla strongholds. Air skirmishes with Egypt, Syria, and Lebanon were frequent.

In July, 1970, the U.S. proposed a ninety-day cease-fire, which was accepted by Premier Golda Meir (q.v.), who had succeeded Levi Eshkol in March, 1969. The cease-fire expired in 1971, but open warfare was not renewed. In addition to the efforts of the U.N. mediator, Gun-

ISRAEL

nar V. Jarring (1907–) of Sweden, mediation attempts were made by a U.S. official and by a committee of four African chiefs of state.

Palestinian terrorist attacks in 1972 included two raids on Lod Airport, near Tel-Aviv, in May, which caused numerous fatalities. At the Olympic Games (q.v.), held in Munich, West Germany, in September, a Palestinian commando raid on the Israeli compound resulted in the deaths of nine Israeli athletes, five commandos, and one German police officer. The guerrillas also initiated a campaign of mailing letter bombs to prominent Israelis and prominent persons in other countries. Israeli reprisals against Lebanon and Syria caused hundreds of civilian and military casualties.

On April 10, 1973, Ephraim Katchalski (1917–), candidate of the ruling Labor Party, was elected president of Israel; he thereupon changed his name to Ephraim Katzir, in conformity with government policy requiring state officials to have Hebrew names.

The War of 1973. On Oct. 6, Yom Kippur, the Jewish Day of Atonement, major war again erupted as Egyptian troops attacked along the Suez Canal and Syrian forces on the Golan Heights. The Arabs, at first, made significant gains, in contrast to the sweeping Israeli victory in the 1967 war. Late in October the Soviet Union and the U.S. introduced a resolution in the U.N. calling for a cease-fire and the beginning of negotiations. The combatants accepted the proposal, but violations were numerous. Thereafter the U.N. voted to send a 7000-man emergency force to police the cease-fire, and tentative steps were taken toward direct Arab-Israeli negotiations.

Parliamentary elections scheduled for Oct. 30 were postponed until Dec. 31, and the war and the negotiations to follow were expected to be significant factors in the campaign and voting.

ISRAEL, Hebrew patriarch; see JACOB.

ISRAEL, KINGDOM OF, political unit in the Middle East. It originated with the Hebrew conquest of Canaan (q.v.) after the exodus from Egypt, about the 13th century B.C.; see HEBREWS; JEWS. The kingdom itself came into existence under King Saul (q.v.) in the 11th century B.C. When the country was divided after the death of King Solomon (q.v.), in 922 B.C., Israel was the name retained by the northern kingdom. Judah (q.v.), the southern kingdom, continued to exist until the 6th century and the Babylonian Captivity (q.v.). The inhabitants of Israel, however, had been effectively dispersed in the last third of the 8th century B.C. (see SAMARIA). See also PALESTINE: History.

ISSACHAR, in the Old Testament (Gen. 30:18), ninth son of the Hebrew patriarch Jacob (q.v.) and traditional founder of the tribe of Israel that bore his name. According to the Jewish historian Flavius Josephus (q.v.), the land of Issachar "extended in length from Carmel to the Jordan, in breadth to Mount Tabor". The territory was among the most fertile lands belonging to the kingdom of Israel (q.v.) during Biblical times.

ISSUS, town of ancient Asia Minor, located near the site of present-day Iskenderun (Alexandretta), Turkey. It was a seaport, built on a narrow strip of coast between high mountains and the Gulf of Issus (now Alexandretta). Issus is celebrated as the site of three battles. In the first occurred the defeat of Darius III, King of Persia (see under DARIUS) by Alexander III (q.v.), King of Macedonia, known as the Great, in 333 B.C. In a second battle, in 194 A.D., Lucius Septimius Severus (q.v.) defeated a rival claimant to the Roman throne. Heraclius (q.v.), Byzantine Emperor, in the third battle at Issus, in 622 A.D., was victorious against the Persians during a war to regain territory formerly lost to the Persians.

İSTANBUL, formerly CONSTANTINOPLE, largest city of Turkey, and capital of İstanbul Province. The name was officially changed to İstanbul in 1930; see TURKEY: History. The province and the city are situated on both sides of the Bosporus (q.v.), the strait that separates Europe from Asia. İstanbul Province is bounded on the N. by the Black Sea, on the E. by Kocáeli Province, on the S. and S.W. by the Sea of Marmara, and on the W. by Tekirdağ Province. Located in a large agricultural region, İstanbul Province produces cotton, fruit, olive oil, silk, and tobacco. The city is the chief seaport and commercial and financial center of Turkey. A large share of the trade of Turkey passes through the Golden Horn, a narrow inlet of the Bosporus that forms an excellent natural harbor. Industries in İstanbul include shipbuilding, liqueur distilling, and the manufacture of cement, cigarettes, foodstuffs, glass, leather products, and pottery. The city is an important rail center with several international lines terminating on the European side and a railroad beginning on the Asian side.

In 324 the Roman emperor Constantine I (q.v.) selected the ancient city of Byzantium (q.v.) as the site of his new capital, which he later named Constantinople. Like Rome, Constantinople was built on seven hills and at one time was surrounded by walls. The walls erected by Emperor Theodosius II (401–50) in 413 are today largely in ruins. The oldest of the many old sections of the city is Stambul, W. and S. of the Golden Horn, built on the site of Byzantium.

The Dolma Bagtcheh, on the shores of the Bosporus in İstanbul.
American Export Lines

Phanar, the Greek quarter, lies within Stambul. Across the Golden Horn and N.E. of Stambul is the commercial quarter of Galata, which is connected to Stambul by two floating bridges. Residential areas include Beyoğlu (Pera) and Üsküdar on the Asian side of the Bosporus. Üsküdar, also called Scutari, was the site of a hospital where the British nurse Florence Nightingale (q.v.) served during the Crimean War (q.v.).

Among the many imposing structures of historic significance in the city is the Hagia Sophia (see SAINT SOPHIA), a 6th-century church converted to a mosque in the 15th century. Many buildings dating from the Ottoman Empire, including the mosques of Bajazet II (see under BAJAZET) and Suleiman I (q.v.) reflect the stylistic Byzantine influences of the Hagia Sophia, but are uniquely Turkish in that they have tall, slim minarets on the exteriors and extensive surface ornamentation on the interiors (see ISLAMIC ART AND ARCHITECTURE). The Seraglio, which comprises buildings grouped around three courts, includes the former palace of the sultans. In the 19th century the royal residence was moved to the Dolma Bagtcheh, on the Bosporus; the president of Turkey uses it occasionally.

The oldest institution of higher learning in the city is İstanbul University, founded in 1453. The city also has a business academy, technical university, and the American Colleges in İstanbul, comprising three separate schools: Robert College, Robert Academy, and the American College for Girls. İstanbul is the headquarters of the Ecumenical Patriarch of the Eastern Orthodox Church and the archdiocese of the Patriarch of the Armenians in Turkey; the city has nearly 200 Christian churches.

History. İstanbul is historically important as the capital first of the Byzantine Empire and later of the Ottoman Empire (q.v.). In its influence on the development of Roman law, Greek philosophy and art, and Christian theology, and on church history, Byzantine-ruled İstanbul rivalled the cultural contributions of Athens, Jerusalem, Rome, and Paris.

İstanbul is famous as one of the most often besieged cities in the world. Prior to the Turkish conquest its assailants included the Arabs from 673 to 678, and from 717 to 718; the Bulgarians in 813 and 913; and the armies of the Fourth Crusade (see CRUSADES), which twice succeeded in taking the city, in 1203 and 1204. After Constantinople fell to the Turks in 1453, the city became the capital of the Ottoman, or Turkish, Empire; it was the capital of present-day Turkey until 1923, when the newly founded Turkish Republic declared Ankara (then Angora) the capital. From 1918 until 1923 Great Britain, France, and Italy occupied the city. Pop. (greater city; 1970 prelim.) 2,247,630.

ISTHMIAN GAMES, one of the four national festivals of ancient Greece (see GAMES, ANCIENT), so called because the celebrations took place on the Isthmus of Corinth. The games were held

ISTRIA

in honor of Poseidon (q.v.), god of the sea; according to tradition, they had been founded either by him or by the legendary Attic hero Theseus (q.v.). Available records indicate that the first Isthmian Games were held in 582 B.C.; thereafter they were held biannually in the spring. Athletic, equestrian, and musical competitions were featured. The victors were originally awarded wreaths of parsley or wild celery; later, the wreaths were of fir or pine needles. The games are believed to have continued until about the 4th century A.D., when the acceptance of Christianity as the religion of the Roman Empire, which then included Greece, brought an end to the practice of many pagan customs.

ISTRIA, or ISTRIAN PENINSULA, mountainous peninsula of Yugoslavia, in the Croatian and Slovenian republics, projecting into the Adriatic Sea, between the gulfs of Trieste and Kvarner, and bounded on the N. by the Karst Plateau. The area is heavily forested and chiefly agricultural, with cereals, fruit, and olives the main crops. Fishing, lumbering, and the manufacture of wine are the principal industries. Ancient Istria was the home of Illyrian tribes (*see* ILLYRIA). It was conquered by the Romans in 177 B.C., and was under nominal Byzantine rule until 752 A.D., after which it was dominated by a series of overlords. In 1347, the northeastern part passed to the Hapsburg (q.v.) family and, in 1420, the southwestern region to Venice. In the 18th century, it became a crownland of Austria and following World War I was awarded to Italy. After World War II, the Free Territory of Trieste was partitioned from the northern region of Istria, and the remainder of the peninsula was ceded to Yugoslavia. Area, about 1500 sq.mi.

ITALIAN ART AND ARCHITECTURE, term that in its broadest sense includes a number of styles in art and architecture that appeared in Italy after Roman times. The Early Christian, Byzantine, Romanesque, Gothic, and Rennaissance periods succeeded one another in the period from the 5th to the 15th century. Only the Renaissance period, however, had a uniquely Italian character, inasmuch as the others were international in scope or had their greatest development in other countries. Men of the Renaissance found models for painting, sculpture, architecture, and writing in classical vestiges that were being unearthed at the time. Italy of the Renaissance was the cultural capital of the entire Western world, and took the lead in all the arts from the 15th to the 17th century. In the Renaissance for the first time after the Roman Empire the names of artists became generally known and the creative work of painting and building was no longer cloaked in the group anonymity common to the work of medieval guilds and bands of artisans. Artists and architects became famous as individuals and sought to develop their personal styles; the pattern they established has continued in use in the present day.

Further information on individual architects, painters, and sculptors (and in some cases on their families) whose life data are not given below will be found in separate articles.

ARCHITECTURE

Renaissance architecture is divided into three periods: (1) Early Renaissance, from about 1420 to 1500; (2) High Renaissance, from about 1500 to 1580; and (3) baroque, from 1580 to 1780. In general, Renaissance architecture differs from Gothic, the preceding style, in emphasizing horizontal rather than vertical lines, round rather than pointed arches, and the carrying of roof structures on continuous walls rather than on isolated thrust-absorbing members.

Early Renaissance. Architectural experiments of this period took the form of decorative use of classical motifs taken from Roman coins, candelabra, and busts, applied in terra-cotta to facades of buildings that remained Gothic in mass and plan. The finely chiseled and highly detailed ornamentation is close in feeling to contemporary goldsmith work. The best examples occur in the north in Lombardy, for instance, on the facade of the Certosa at Pavia. This style was carried by the Lombards to Venice, where it gave rise to the most richly decorative of all the local Renaissance schools of building, through the free use of multicolored marble incrustations and surface carving. More important to the full revival of classic types of building mass and plan was the work at Florence of Filippo Brunelleschi, the greatest designer of the Early Renaissance. In the Pazzi Chapel (1425) and the two great basilican churches of Santo Spirito and San Lorenzo he used Roman moldings and details to emphasize the structural lines of the buildings. The Medici-Riccardi Palace, built by Michelozzo for the Medici family during this first period of the Renaissance, also shows Roman inspiration in scale and minor details, although it is fundamentally a contemporary Florentine palace type. Leon Battista Alberti (1404-72) was the first to attempt strictly classical exterior design in both religious and secular architecture by an integrated use of superposed orders, pilasters, entablatures, and Roman arches. Florentine architects of later date, such as Bernardo Rosselino (1427-79) and Francesco di Giorgio (1439-1502), carried the new style to

The Farnese Palace is one of the most magnificent early Rennaisance palaces of Rome.
Italian Government Travel Office

Pienza, Siena, and Cortona; others such as Benedetto da Maiano (1442–97), Luciano da Laurana (1420–79), and Giuliano da Sangallo (1445–1516), brought it to Naples, Urbino, and Rome. Laurana's ducal palace at Urbino was regarded by contemporaries as the ideal princely residence.

High Renaissance. Bramante, a native of Lombardy, outgrew the goldsmith and decorator limitations of most of his compatriots and predecessors. He was a master builder, and the first to synthesize structure, space, and detail in the classic manner. Severe and grandiose, given to plain surfaces and colossal details, the new style was embodied in the small, domed structure called the Tempietto, or temple, of San Pietro in Montorio in Rome, and in the designs for Saint Peter's Basilica (q.v.). The center of the new movement had shifted from Florence to Rome, where ancient ruins could be seen everywhere and where powerful popes gave the impetus to ambitious building projects, both religious and secular. The study of the Roman architect Vitruvius and the measuring and drawing of Roman ruins became a standard part of every architect's training. After Bramante, the younger architects Raphael, Baldassare Peruzzi, and Antonio da Sangallo (1455–1534) took the lead, and their formal, symmetrical use of tiers of Roman orders and pedimented windows may be seen in the Farnesina, Massimi, and Farnese palaces. Michelangelo, a giant figure in architecture as well as in painting and sculpture, ushered in a new phase of personal adaptation of classic elements. Earlier lessons learned from Vitruvius and Roman ruins had been thoroughly assimilated, and now a freer play of personal stylistic elements became dominant. The dome, either single or grouped, and the tunnel and cross vaults, often coffered, continued the orthodox forms of roofing, but internal piers became heavier, columns frequently took the place of pilasters on the exterior, and the single, colossal order, replacing tiers of superposed orders, reigned supreme. Saint Peter's, remodeled by Michelangelo, became the archetype for Renaissance churches. His Capitoline group of buildings in Rome established the free use of balustrades and sculptured figures as architectural adjuncts to the facade itself. Certain elements of the Capitoline groups as well as details of the interior of the Laurentian Library in Florence foreshadow baroque architectural freedom. The more sedate work of Giacomo da Vignola (1527–73) set the style for villa architecture centering in Rome. He built the Villa Caprarola and the Villa de Papa Giulio.

The continuing domination of classic formulas is seen both in the writings and work, especially at Vicenza, of Andrea Palladio. This phase is known as Palladian for the scientific-theoretical style which was exemplified also by Vignola, Sebastiano Serlio (1475–1554), and Vincenzo Scamozzi (1552–1616), all of whom published books on architecture in addition to practicing

ITALIAN ART AND ARCHITECTURE

Air view of Saint Peter's. The photograph also shows the colonnade, designed in the baroque style by Giovanni Lorenzo Bernini. Italian Government Travel Office

as architects. Palladio's sober, carefully studied interrelation of classic elements was first embodied in the arcade around the basilica at Vicenza, which was followed by examples such as the Chieregati and Barbarano palaces, and the Teatro Olimpico. He also built in Venice the churches of Santa Maria Maggiore and the Redentore.

Baroque. Opposed to Palladian severity, the baroque style was characterized by defiance of tradition, broken lines and curves, unexpected theatrical perspectives, and unusual placement of figures and objects. Associated with the Counter-Reformation demand for lavish and appealing effects in the churches, aimed at holding and attracting worshipers, the style made use of richly colored marbles and decorative cupids, scrollwork, and animated figures, and often imitated drapery in metal and stone. Domenico Fontana, Carlo Maderna (1556–1629), Giovanni Lorenzo Bernini, and Francesco Borromini (1599–1667) were its greatest representatives. One of the most grandiose works of the style is Bernini's colonnade and approach to St. Peter's.

Following the baroque period, Italian styles no longer dominated the European scene. In the 18th century, France set the architectural styles, and French rococo and the later archeological neoclassic were imitated all over Europe, including Italy. The huge palace grounds of Caserta, near Naples, reminiscent of Versailles, is one of the few ambitious architectural projects carried out in Italy after the Renaissance and before recent times. Italian 19th-century building showed the eclectic stylistic trends common to the Western world. The 20th century brought the collective efforts sponsored by the fascist government under Benito Mussolini. Many modern ferroconcrete and glass railroad stations, factories, public buildings, and housing projects were constructed with state backing. Notable examples are the modern piazza at Brescia, the railroad station at Florence, and the new town of Sabaudia in the Pontine Marshes.

SCULPTURE

The 13th-century sculptor Nicola Pisano employed both medieval and classical forms in his work. His son Giovanni Pisano was the dominant influence on Italian sculpture of the 14th century because his large, expressive forms gave new life to the Gothic formula. A greater realism and renewed interest in classic forms took place in the 15th century; the nude human figure as a subject for grand concepts made its reappearance in sculpture. Lorenzo Ghiberti produced a pair of bronze doors for the baptistery of the church of San Giovanni in Florence, a delicate masterpiece of relief sculpture which became known as the "Gates of Paradise" and influenced all similar projects after that time. Jacopo della Quercia combined in his relief of "Adam and Eve", at Bologna, the robust quality of the

ITALIAN ART AND ARCHITECTURE

Rome, executed by assistants of Bernini after the master's design, displays the lavishly ornamental character of the baroque.

PAINTING

From the 13th century through the 16th the development of Italian art centered in Siena, Florence, and Venice. Siena was the most isolated center, and the character of Sienese art remained close to the Romanesque-Byzantine tradition. To this tradition the Sienese school added a touch of naturalism and delicate sentiment in order to illustrate Biblical tales more clearly. Duccio di Buoninsegna, the greatest master of the Sienese school, introduced a more rhythmic and complex style of composition into painting. He also added a gracious characterization to the figures in his paintings of early Christian legends. Among other notable painters of Siena were the brothers Ambrogio Lorenzetti

"Saint John the Baptist" by Donatello.
National Gallery of Art, Kress Collection

antique with the dramatic spirit of the Renaissance. Donatello, the outstanding sculptor of the 15th century, acquired a complete knowledge of human anatomy, and gave humanness of expression to his grand classic forms. His work represented a vigorous pageant of life as contrasted to a medieval religious symbolism. His dramatic figure "Lo Zuconne" carved for the Campanile, Florence, is the embodiment of the Early Renaissance spirit. Antonio Pollaiuolo and Andrea del Verrocchio were representative of the scientific realism in Florentine sculpture of the late 15th century. Verrocchio's equestrian state of "Colleoni" in Venice utilized a forceful realism and a monumental scaling to achieve a new power.

The dominant personality in High Renaissance sculpture was Michelangelo. His work represented a vigor, drama, and exaltation unique within the realm of Western sculpture. The climax of his style was reached in the tombs in the Medici Chapel, for which he designed both the architecture and sculpture; in the nude figures "Night" and "Day" he used the human form as universal symbols. Benvenuto Cellini utilized the Michelangelesque forms for decorative purposes; his rendering of graceful detail and his remarkable work as a goldsmith made him extraordinarily popular. The baroque style, with its insistence on exaggerated emotional effects and sharply illustrative technique, was summed up in the work of Giovanni Lorenzo Bernini. "The Fountain of the Four Rivers" at

"David with the head of Goliath" by Andrea Verrocchio.

ITALIAN ART AND ARCHITECTURE

and Pietro Lorenzetti, Simone Martini, and Stefano di Giovanni (1392–1450), known as "Sassetta". They added refinement of color and subtlety of composition to the native tradition. Elements of pathos, narration, and rich decoration were revealed by a rare purity of style within the framework of small panels and altarpieces.

Beginnings of the Renaissance. Giotto, one of the supreme artists of medieval Italy, transformed the role of painting into one of grandeur, naturalism, and depth of human feeling by his series of murals at Padua and Assisi. The monumental scale of his designs established Florence as the fountainhead of European art, and the bold innovations in his work paved the way for the work of the Renaissance. At the beginning of the 15th century Masaccio introduced a new ease and freedom of gesture in the figures of murals. Aerial perspective, that is, the effect of atmosphere suffusing distant objects, and the constructing of figures by strong areas of light and shade were Masaccio's special contributions. His mural "The Tribute Money" in the Branacci Chapel, Florence, exemplified his art at its peak. Andrea del Castagno combined an austerity with a sculptural solidity that foreshadowed the grand art of Michelangelo. Castagno's "Last Supper" welded a vigorous realism to bold, complex space composition. Other 15th-century masters were Paolo Uccelo, Andrea Mantegna, and Piero della Francesca. Francesca, in his set of frescoes at Arezzo, representing the "Story of the True Cross", revealed a world of arrested action and a mood of withdrawal from the ordinary aspects of life in his classically articulated designs and monumental figure groupings. In his works, the union of the physical and the spiritual was lifted to the level of sublime detachment. In contrast to Piero della Francesca, Domenico di Tommaso Ghirlandajo and Benozzo Gozzoli were popular illustrators of the Bible in terms of everyday life; their work was full of picturesque sentiment and tapestrylike detail. The gentle and spiritual art of Giovanni da Fiesole, known as Fra Angelico, was suffused with a lyrical religious sentiment and stood apart from the main currents of the time, being more closely related to the early Sienese masters. His devout life as a Dominican monk was undoubtedly a chief factor in lending his art its rare grace and fervor.

The exploration of the external world, based upon the rational interpretation of experience as opposed to medieval mysticism, was the fundamental principle of the Early Renaissance. The mastery of the physical world in terms of realistic images was a long and involved process. Uccello experimented with new principles of perspective (lines converging into space) in his famous battle pictures, such as "Battle of San Romano", now in the Uffizi Gallery, Florence. Piero della Francesca had written books on scientific perspective. Antonio Pollaiuolo made exhaustive studies of the nude in contorted postures and contributed to the study of anatomy during this period. Luca Signorelli, through analysis of the structure of the skeleton and dissection of cadavers, acquired a remarkable skill in rendering physical movement. In his mural "Torments of the Damned" (Cathedral, Orvieto), the writhing of men in agony is vividly portrayed. Sandro Botticelli illustrated myths from antiquity in elaborately decorative paintings, full of nostalgic charm and sensuousness. He added to Italian art one of the most intricately graceful uses of line ever created by a Western artist. Moreover, his art represented the beginning of a secular art that eventually superseded religious painting in the course of the 16th century. "The Birth of Venus" (Uffizi) is Botticelli's supreme painting in this field.

The Great Age. Leonardo da Vinci, in the 15th and the beginning of the 16th century, summed up for the Renaissance both the passion for scientific inquiry and the spirit of humanism in art. He examined thoroughly formalistic problems of space, anatomical and psychological aspects of character, and chiaroscuro (q.v.) effects to lend mystery and drama to his work. His mural "The Last Supper" (in the monastery of Santa Maria delle Grazia, Milan) and the "Mona Lisa" (Louvre, Paris) are his most famous works. He exerted a great influence on the work of 16th-century painters, particularly that of Raphael and Michelangelo. Michelangelo, one of the giant figures of the 16th century, was a sculptor, architect, painter, and poet. He created a grand concept of the human form, more expressive and monumental than it had ever been before. His decorations for the ceiling of the Sistine Chapel (q.v.) in the Vatican recorded the epic of mankind from the Creation to the Last Judgment. Michelangelo's figures create a sense of superhuman conflict with the universe. Raphael combined some of the lyric qualities of Leonardo da Vinci with the dramatic power of Michelangelo, adding a gracious harmony and sentiment of his own. He painted many fine portraits and popular versions of the Madonna, and created one of the finest series of frescoes of his period, including "The School of Athens" in the Vatican at Rome. In representing groups of scholars and philosophers surrounded by

Italian Art. Plate 1. Above: "The Deposition" by Giotto, a 13th-century precursor of the Renaissance. The fresco is one of a series on the life of Christ in the Annunziata dell' Arena chapel, Padua. Right: Detail of "The Last Judgment", showing Saint Peter and other saints, by Fra Angelico, whose art reflected the piety of his life as a Dominican monk.

Italian Art. Plate 2. Four masters of the Renaissance. Top, left: "The Virgin with the Rose", one of many versions of the Madonna by Raphael. Top, right: Detail from "The Madonna with Saints" by Giovanni Bellini, founder of the great age of painting in Venice. Above: "The Mona Lisa", one of the most celebrated portraits in the world, by Leonardo da Vinci. Left: "La Bella", portrait of Eleanora Gonzaga by Titian.

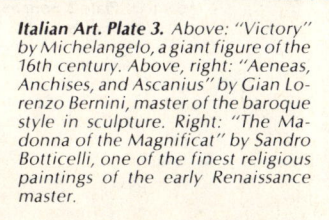

Italian Art. Plate 3. *Above: "Victory" by Michelangelo, a giant figure of the 16th century. Above, right: "Aeneas, Anchises, and Ascanius" by Gian Lorenzo Bernini, master of the baroque style in sculpture. Right: "The Madonna of the Magnificat" by Sandro Botticelli, one of the finest religious paintings of the early Renaissance master.*

Italian Art. Plate 4. Above: "Pietà" by Il Tintoretto, Venetian master of the High Renaissance. Below, left: "Martyrdom of Saint Peter" by Michelangelo da Caravaggio, leader of a 17th-century realistic movement. Below, right: "Bacchus and Ariadne", ceiling detail of the grand hall of the Palazzo Labia in Venice, by Giovanni Battista Tiepolo, who dominated 18th-century Italian painting.

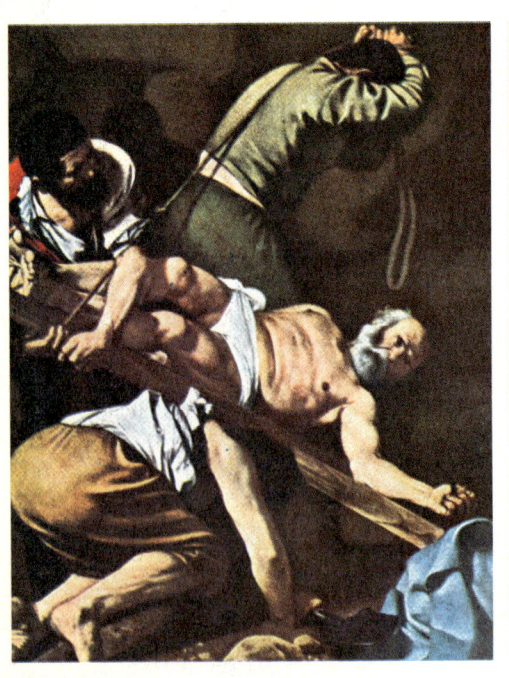

ITALIAN ART AND ARCHITECTURE

"The Birth of Venus" by Botticelli. Alinari

spacious architectural vaults, he summed up, pictorially, the homage of Renaissance man to ancient Greece.

Venetian painting represented both a more luxurious and a more worldly attitude toward life than did either the Sienese or Florentine schools. The founder of the great age of painting in Venice, during the 15th century, was Giovanni Bellini, whose work covered all phases of religious humanism, and in several late paintings created the beginning of secular and Romantic art. His favorite subject was the Madonna and Child, many versions of which express a human warmth, grace, and serenity unequaled in Italian painting. Among his late works is a splendid bacchanale, "The Feast of the Gods" (National Gallery, Washington, D.C.), which combines a paganism with a lofty classical spirit. This picture represented the dawn of Romanticism in Renaissance art, and its mood and spirit was both sustained and deepened in the work of Bellini's pupil Il Giorgione. The Romantic motifs of this painter, such as the "Sleeping Venus" (Dresden) and the "Pastoral Symphony" (Louvre, Paris), together with his use of sensual forms, richness of color, and an Arcadian landscape world, broke through the boundaries of religious painting and created a poetical sphere in art which proclaimed the glory of the physical life. With Titian, pupil of Bellini and Giorgione, art flowered into a full-bodied, vigorously sensual experience, a frank expression of the dominance of man's individuality. Portraiture assumed a major role in the history of painting, representing the glory and beauty of Venetian society as exemplified by wealthy princes, merchants, and their families. Titian recorded the fullest splendor of the High Renaissance. The herculean compositions of Il Tintoretto and the sumptuous festival scenes of Paolo Veronese were rooted in the tradition of Titian and complete the history of Renaissance painting.

After the Renaissance. In the 17th century Italian painting became both academic and eclectic. The painters attempted to create a lofty style by a cold imitation of the great previous masters. Lodovico Carracci and Annibale Carracci of Bologna were the leading exponents of the new manner. Their elaborate works are characterized by bombast and theatricality. A realistic movement was led by Michelangelo da Caravaggio, who painted scenes of everyday life with striking light effects and careful representation of nature. His work was immensely popular and exerted a wide influence on painters. With Caravaggio, a new, more obviously illustrative current entered the mainstreams of art.

ITALIAN GREYHOUND

The 18th century was dominated by Giovanni Battista Tiepolo, whose large fresco decorations emulated the work of Veronese, but were more light and airy in tone. His style was both highly skillful and theatrical in character. In Venice, too, a group of painters developed a school of architectural and landscape art, depicting canal scenes surrounded by buildings and bridges. It was an intimate, localized school of painting, and its best-known masters were Antonio Canaletto, his pupil Bernardo Bellotto (1720–80), and Francesco Guardi. Pietro Longhi (1702–62) painted the everyday life, manners, and frivolities of well-to-do Venetians. Giambattista Piranesi (1717–78) made great contributions as engraver and architect. His fantastic prints of prisons and grand architectural interiors were daring in conception. Antonio Canova was the leader of the Classic Revival in Italy, spurred by a renewed interest in Greek sculpture of the highly graceful Hellenic period.

Although Italy still remained an art center during the 19th century, the mainstream of art was developed in Spain and France. In modern times, Italy's chief contributions to painting were the movement of futurism (q.v.) initiated by Gino Severini (1883–1966), Umberto Boccioni (1882–1916), and Giacomo Balla (1871–1958); and a metaphysical, surrealist school of painting founded by Giorgio di Chirico and Carlo Carra (1881–1966). See also BAROQUE; BYZANTINE ART; FLORENTINE PAINTING AND SCULPTURE; FRESCO; RENAISSANCE; SIENESE SCHOOL; VENETIAN SCHOOL OF PAINTING.

ITALIAN GREYHOUND, miniature type of English greyhound (q.v.) that is more slender in all proportions. It belongs to the toy dog class. The Italian greyhound is believed to have originated in Asia Minor over 2000 years ago by the interbreeding of small specimens of the full-sized greyhound. From Asia Minor the breed spread into southern Europe and then into England, where it became a favorite of queens and ladies of the nobility. The Italian greyhound was introduced into the United States in the late 19th century. The dog has a long and narrow head; large, bright eyes; soft and delicate ears; a deep, narrow chest; a back that curves and droops at the hind quarters; and a rather long tail that is held low. The dog is of various colors, including white, fawn, red, blue, and black, but is usually gold or silver fawn in color. It weighs about 8 lb.

ITALIAN LANGUAGE, term used generically to denote those modern types of Latin speech spoken in the Italian peninsula, in Sicily, Corsica, and northern Sardinia, along the northeastern shore of the Adriatic Sea, and on the southern watershed of the Alps as a whole. Considered as a single language with numerous dialects, Italian is one of the group of Neo-Latin or Romance languages (q.v.) that are the direct offspring of the Latin tongue as spoken by the Romans and imposed by them upon the nations under their dominion. The chief subdivisions of the Romance group are French, Spanish, Portuguese, Provençal, Rumanian, and Italian, although certain Italian dialects are so peculiar that they are classified as a separate branch of Romance or in another language system altogether. Of all the Romance languages, Italian retains the closest resemblance to Latin. The struggle between the written but dead language and the various forms of the living speech, most of which were derived from Vulgar Latin (see LATIN), was nowhere so intense or so protracted as in Italy.

During the long period of evolution many dialects sprang up. In the north and northwest the Gallo-Italian dialects predominate; they are Piedmontese, Lombard, Ligurian, and Emilian or Bolognese, all of which display a close affinity to French in their pronunciation and truncated terminations. The Venetian dialect is spoken in the Italian Tirol and parts of what used to be Dalmatia and Istria, in addition to the Venetian area itself. South of these districts the centro-southern Italian dialects are found; these are Tuscan, Corsican, north Sardinian, Roman (with which are included the closely related dialects of Umbria and The Marches), Campanian (with which are included Abruzzese and Apulian), Sicilian, and Calabrian. South and central Sardinian dialects are so distinct from this entire group of dialects that they constitute a separate branch of the Romance languages, while an Italian dialect of the eastern Alps, Friulian, which is spoken in northeastern Venetia, is considered by most philologists to be a member of the Rheto-Romansch languages.

The multiplicity of these dialects, and their individual claims upon their native speakers as a pure Italian speech, presented a peculiar difficulty in the evolution of an accepted form of Italian which would reflect the cultural unity of the entire peninsula. Even the earliest popular Italian documents, produced in the 10th century, are dialectal in language, and during the following three centuries Italian writers wrote in their native dialects, producing a number of competing regional schools of literature. During the 14th century the Tuscan dialect began to predominate, because of the central position of Tuscany in Italy, and because of the aggressive commerce of its most important city, Florence. Moreover, of all the Italian dialects, Tuscan departs least in morphology and phonology from classic Latin, and it therefore harmonizes best with the Italian traditions of Latin culture. Finally Florentine culture produced the three literary artists who best summarized Italian thought and feeling of the late Middle Ages and early Renaissance: Dante Alighieri, Francesco Petrarch, and Giovanni Boccaccio (qq.v.); see ITALIAN LITERATURE.

Grammarians during the 15th and the 16th centuries attempted to confer upon the pronunciation, syntax, and vocabulary of 14th-century Tuscan the status of a central and classic Italian speech. Eventually this classicism, which might have made Italian another dead language, was widened to include the organic changes inevitable in a living tongue. In the dictionaries and publications of the Accademia della Crusca, founded in 1583, which have been accepted by Italians as authoritative in Italian linguistic matters, compromises between classic purism and living Tuscan usage have been successfully effected.

In modern Italian the Latin qualities of the Florentine dialect are preserved, but the vocabulary of Latin has been made to meet the changing conditions of Italian life. The simplicity of the phonetic changes from Latin, along with a nearly perfectly phonetic orthography, makes the acquisition of Italian easy for a person who knows Latin or any of its modern Romance forms.　　　　　　　　　　　　　　　M.P.

ITALIAN LITERATURE, literature written in the Italian language (q.v.) in the period from about the 13th century to the present. Prior to the 13th century the literary language of Italy was Latin, which served for the writing of chronicles, historical poems, heroic legends, lives of the saints, religious poems, and didactic and scientific works. In addition to those who wrote in Latin, a number of the early Italian poets wrote in French or in Provençal, and borrowed most of their verse forms and literary themes from foreign sources; see PROVENÇAL LANGUAGE AND LITERATURE. Among the most important verse forms are the Provençal *canzone, sirventese, tenzone, tornata,* and *stanza.* The literary themes include the deeds of ancient heroes, of Arthurian knights, and of Holy Roman Emperor Charlemagne (q.v.) and his paladins. The *geste,* or tales, of Charlemagne first appeared in a Franco-Venetian vernacular and were later Italianized in Tuscany. Besides attaining lasting popularity in Italy, the tales furnished themes of chivalry (q.v.) for subsequent Italian poets.

ITALIAN LITERATURE

13th Century. The earliest poetry written in Italian was that of the so-called Sicilian school connected with the German Hohenstaufen court of the Italian-speaking Holy Roman Emperor Frederick II (q.v.) and his son Manfred (1232?–66). They chose to administer their far-flung empire mainly from Sicily, which, partly under the impact of Arab civilization, had become one of the chief cultural centers of 13th-century Europe. The poetry of the Sicilian school, although written in Italian, had otherwise no native quality. It was largely a court type of love poetry, almost slavishly and often clumsily imitative of the current Provençal models. The most remarkable poets of the school were Giacomo Pugliese (fl. about 1230–50) and Rinaldo d'Aquino (fl. 1240–50).

After the fall of the Hohenstaufen dynasty in 1254, the center of Italian poetry shifted to two cities, Arezzo, known for the work of Guittone d'Arezzo (d. 1294), and Bologna, distinguished by the innovations of Guido Guinicelli (about 1240–76). Guittone d'Arezzo and his followers produced little poetry of distinction. Guinicelli was the creator of the *dolce stil nuovo* ("sweet new style"). In this style the poet did not exalt the worldly, fashionable type of love cultivated in the courts of princes, as in Provençal and Sicilian love poetry. He wrote instead of a Platonic love relationship in which the loveliness of the adored woman spiritualized the lover, lifting his soul to a comprehension of divine beauty; see PLATO. The greatest of Italian poets, Dante Alighieri, who had a high regard for Guinicelli, wrote his first book, *La Vita Nuova* (1292; Eng. trans., *The New Life,* 1861) in the new style. In prose narrative interspersed with lyrics, Dante describes his idealized love for his beloved, Beatrice; see BEATRICE PORTINARI. Dante and the other poets of the *dolce stil nuovo,* notably Guido Cavalcanti, and Cino da Pistoia (1270–1337), made it one of the great schools of Italian poetry.

Meanwhile another native and original type of poetry had appeared, a devotional poetry inspired by Saint Francis of Assisi, whose *Canto dell' Amore,* translated sometimes as "Canticle of Creatures", sings of love for all of God's creation rather than for any single human being. The same feeling was expressed in a collection of legends in verse, *Fioretti* ("Little Flowers"), based on the life of the saint. Other Franciscan poets followed in the 13th century, among them a poet of Dantesque imagination, Jacopone da Todi (1230–1306). He contributed splendid polemical verses to the religious controversies about the Franciscan friars, but more enduring

35

Dante Alighieri
Bettmann Archive

are his beautiful hymns, among them the famous "Our Lady of the Passion" and "Stabat Mater".

14th Century. The 14th century has been called the golden century of Italian literature because, besides Dante, such masters, as Petrarch and Giovanni Boccaccio are identified with it.

Dante is one of the great figures of world literature. He is remarkable for the loftiness of his thought, the vividness and fluency of his verse, and the boldness of his imagination. He was one of the founders of Italian literature through his use of the vernacular for some of his greatest works. About 1302 he wrote in Latin *De Vulgari Eloquentia* (Eng. trans., *On the Vernacular Speech,* 1529), in which he analyzed the qualities of Italian as a literary language and advocated its use.

Dante mastered the knowledge of his time and stands out as the greatest interpreter of the ideals of medieval Europe. His *Il Convivio* ("The Banquet"), written during the first years of the 14th century, is an almost encyclopedic summary of European culture. To his scholarship Dante added experience drawn from a varied and active civic life. He served as a magistrate of Florence and took part in the political controversies of this time. His political convictions, for which he suffered exile, were expressed plainly in his Latin treatise on government, *De Monarchia* (about 1313; Eng. trans., *On Monarchy,* 1904), which projected enlightened imperial rule as the ideal system in which multiple conflicting states would be absorbed in one, church and state would be separated, and justice would be founded on Roman law.

Dante's greatest work is his epic poem *La Divina Commedia (The Divine Comedy),* probably begun about 1307, and written in the vernacular for the sake of a full and direct communication of its thought. It is a dramatization of medieval philosophy and theology partly in terms of the controversies and personalities of 13th- and 14th-century Italy. In some respects it is a literary guided tour through the three worlds of medieval theology: hell, purgatory, and paradise. Dante's guides are Beatrice, the object of his chaste adoration, and the Roman poet Vergil (q.v.); see DIVINE COMEDY, THE.

With Petrarch a new feeling enters Western culture. Unlike Dante or other medieval thinkers such as the Italian scholastic philosopher Saint Thomas Aquinas and the French philoso-

ITALIAN LITERATURE

Petrarch

pher Peter Abelard (q.v.). Petrarch is not concerned so much with using the material of the ancient classical writers as with acting in the classical spirit. A great Latinist, he helped to restore classical Latin as a literary and scholarly language and to discredit the use of medieval Latin, which had served as an international medium of communication. After this period Latin lost currency as a spoken tongue and became useful only to writers and scholars. See LATIN.

Petrarch is often referred to as the "modern man" because of his interest in individuality; his *Vita Solitaria* (1480; Eng. trans., *Solitary Life*, 1924) and his *De Remediis utriusque Fortunae* (1468; Eng. trans., *Physicke against Fortune*, 1579) are considered the first essays to express this new attitude. He has been called also the first Italian nationalist, as contrasted with Dante, who was a universalist and for whom Italy was a part to be fitted into an imperial whole. To Petrarch, Italy was the heir and successor of ancient Rome, the civilizing mission of which he glorified in his Latin epic *Africa* (critical edition, 1926), dealing with the Punic Wars (q.v.) between Rome and Carthage. He believed that the various states of Italy should be united to resume the mission of ancient Rome in the Christian world.

Impressive as were Petrarch's contributions to classical scholarship, his greatness rests on his Italian lyrics. His *Canzoniere* (1470; Eng. trans., 1777), a collection of love poems addressed to Laura, probably the Frenchwoman Laure de Noves (1308?–48), the counterpart of Dante's Beatrice, departs from the idealized approach of the *dolce stil nuovo*. It introduced an intensity and inwardness of feeling and perception heretofore unknown in European poetry.

Boccaccio, like Petrarch, was conscious of belonging to a new age. He was strongly influenced by Petrarch and the two men became close friends. Boccaccio had a strong narrative bent, as evidenced by his prose romances *Filocolo*, written between 1331 and 1338; *Ameto* (1339?); and *L'Amorosa Fiammetta* (about 1341).

Boccaccio's greatest work is his *Decamerone* (1353; Eng. trans., *Decameron*, 1702), a masterpiece in which he draws directly from life instead of from literary models. It is a collection of a hundred short stories presumed to have been told during a period of ten days by seven gentlemen and three ladies of Florence living in a remote country villa in which they had taken refuge from an epidemic of the plague; see DECAMERON, THE.

Unlike Petrarch, Boccaccio valued Dante very highly; his last work was a biography and a series of lectures on the work of the great poet. Boccaccio's writings gained an international public and were drawn upon for plots and characters by writers in other countries. For example, his epic poem *La Teseide* (1341) was used by the English poet Geoffrey Chaucer (q.v.) as the basis for his "Knight's Tale" and by the English poet John Dryden (q.v.) in his poem "Palamon and Arcite".

Giovanni Boccaccio — Bettmann Archive

37

ITALIAN LITERATURE

Dante, Petrarch, and Boccaccio were the first Italian writers to make literary use of the Tuscan dialect spoken in Florence, Siena, and other towns of north-central Italy, and they won for it general acceptance as the language of culture. Modern Italian is based upon the Tuscan dialect.

Among other notable writers of the 14th century are Saint Catherine of Siena, whose works are esteemed for their literary as well as for their devotional value, the historians Dino Compagni (1260–1324) and Giovanni Villani, and the orator Domenico Cavalca (d. 1322).

The Renaissance. The Renaissance (q.v.) in Italy was a period of expanding economic, political, and cultural activity. The towns and cities emerged from feudal conditions to become centers of commerce and industry. Some cities, like Venice and Genoa, won control of Mediterranean empires. A constant struggle of military and political interests took place among the towns and cities, the leaders of which aimed at broadening their power by conquest and by establishing spheres of influence. The period was marked by a rebirth of culture based upon the discovery of ancient manuscripts and the reevaluation of classical literature and philosophy, which spread eventually throughout Europe.

The great figures of Early Renaissance literature were scholars concerned with philological research into and the translation of the Greek and Latin classics. They were known as humanists because of their interest in human rather than transcendental ideals, as opposed to the scholars and thinkers of the Middle Ages; see HUMANISM. Many humanists turned for inspiration to the works of the Greek philosopher Plato in preference to those of his pupil Aristotle (q.v.), who was the dominant influence in medieval scholarship.

15th Century. In the Renaissance appeared many examples of the so-called universal man, who achieved greatness in more than one field. Among the most famous figures of this type were the architect, painter, organist, and writer Leon Battista Alberti; the painter, sculptor, architect, engineer, and scientist Leonardo da Vinci; and the sculptor, painter, architect, and poet Michelangelo. This universality of mind and talent was true also of the princes who ruled the Italian towns, the most brilliant of whom was Lorenzo the Magnificent, a member of the Medici family (see under MEDICI) that ruled Florence. Lorenzo was a brilliant statesman and administrator, a patron of the arts, a poet, and a critic of distinction.

Angelo Poliziano, called Politian, is generally considered the outstanding poet of the period. His verse play *Orfeo* (1480?; Eng. trans., 1880) ranks as the first important work in the Italian drama, and his collections of lyrics are of a high order. Politian is famous also for his scholarly editions of Greek texts and for his translations from Greek into Latin of the works of the classical writers.

In this period the Carolingian *geste* and the pastoral continued to provide literary themes. Among the outstanding works in the first of these genres were the *Morgante Maggiore* ("The Greater Morgante", 1483) of Luigi Pulci (1432–84) and the *Orlando Innamorato* ("Roland in Love", 1487) of Matteo Maria Boiardo. The finest work in the pastoral genre was *Arcadia* (1504), by Jacopo Sannazaro, which attained continental recognition. In their preoccupation with worldly rather than religious values Renaissance writers departed widely from the Christian concepts of the Middle Ages. The popes themselves patronized atheist and so-called pagan authors. Some of these writers, above all the humanist Lorenzo Valla (1406–57), whose bold exposure of dubious papal documents almost cost him his life, mentioned Christian authors only to find fault with them. The sermons and polemical writings of the reformer Girolamo Savonarola, who attempted to reverse this trend, provide graphic descriptions of revived pagan tastes and practices. He instituted a theocratic republic in Florence but it lasted less than three years. He was abandoned by the people and suffered martyrdom for his defiance of Pope Alexander VI (see under ALEXANDER), who was famous for his patronage of pagan culture.

16th Century. The 16th century brought the Renaissance to its fulfillment. Italian, long eclipsed by the humanists' preoccupation with Greek and Latin, rose to a new and conscious dignity as a medium of serious literary expression. Pietro Bembo, who exercised tremendous influence in the first half of the century, contributed greatly to this development. In his treatises, especially *Le Prose della Volgar Lingua* ("Prose in the Vernacular", 1525), he established Boccaccio's writings as the model for prose. His *Rime* (1530), imitative of Petrarch's verse, marked the effective beginning of the movement known as Petrarchism. Other writers of this period who made much more creative use of the heritage of humanism were the statesman and political philosopher Niccolò Machiavelli and the poet Ludovico Ariosto.

Both from his experiences as an official and diplomat and from his historical studies, Machiavelli arrived at the realistic conception of statecraft with which his name has since been linked. It is elaborated in *Il Principe* (1532; Eng. trans., *The Prince*, 1640), an analysis of the basis and exercise of political power which formed part of a larger work, his commentary on *The Annals of the Roman People* by the Roman historian Livy (q.v.). The premise of *The Prince* is that "the preservation of the state is the supreme law" transcending all other obligations. Machiavelli's ideal prince anticipated the socalled benevolent despots of later periods who consolidated state power and deployed it in international affairs. In his thinking he departed from medieval theocratic concepts and presaged modern scientific political economy. Some historians conjecture that had his views been realized Italy might have been united under a strong ruler and spared the subsequent French and Spanish invasions. Other works by Machiavelli include a treatise on the art of war, a history of Florence, the biography *Vita di Castruccio Castracane* ("Life of Castruccio Castracani", 1520), poems, and a number of plays. His most famous play, *La Mandragola* (1524; Eng. trans., *The Mandrake*, 1957; performed in New York City, 1958), is a bitter, pessimistic analysis of human instincts. In it he applies to social and religious life the principle of analysis that he applies in *The Prince* to political life.

The historian and statesman Francesco Guicciardini, Machiavelli's friend, is best known for his *L'Historia d'Italia* (1561; Eng. trans., *The History of Italy*, 1753), a work outstanding for its objectivity and its astute discussion of personalities and events. His *Ricordi Politici e Civili* (Eng. trans., *Political and Civil Memoirs*, 1857) is based upon his thorough experience as a political participant in the affairs of Florence.

The genius of Ariosto, the supreme poet of the century, found its best expression in the epic poem *Orlando Furioso* ("The Mad Roland", 1516), a work of originality and power in continuation of Boiardo's *Orlando Innamorato*. The events related in the poem concern the struggle of Charlemagne and his paladins against the Saracens (q.v.). Against this unifying background, the epic weaves together adventure, romance, magic, heroism, villainy, pathos, sensuality, and contemporary reality into a sophisticated, ever-varying narrative enlivened by humor and gentle irony. The poem achieves the universal appeal of a masterpiece because Ariosto's extraordinary imagination is based upon a profound understanding of human nature and psychology. His comedies are of lesser value, although they influenced later developments in both Italian and French literature.

Two popular treatises on manners belong to this period of cosmopolitan refinement and worldly accomplishment. *Il Cortegiano* (1528; Eng. trans., *The Courtier*, 1561), by the diplomat Baldassare Castiglione, is a discussion of etiquette, social problems, and the advantages of intellectual pursuits. It served as a handbook for the training of gentlemen on the Continent and in England. *Galateo* (1558; Eng. trans., 1576), by the prelate Giovanni della Casa (1503–56), discusses the practices of etiquette from the point of view of a broad understanding of human nature.

A violent reaction against this cult of fancy, beauty, and refinement is found in the mock epic *Baldus* (1517) by Teofilo Folengo (1496–1544). Written in the macaronic style, a comical burlesque of scholarly Latin, it is an extremely and often vulgarly funny parody of the world of chivalry and belles-lettres, and satirizes many aspects of contemporary life. The French writer François Rabelais (q.v.) found inspiration and material in *Baldus*. Another rebel, of much greater contemporary prestige, was Pietro Aretino, a talented playwright and pamphleteer whose pen was for hire. His *Ragionamenti* ("Reasonings", 1532–34) and the six volumes of his letters (1537–57) best represent his scurrilous and harsh wit.

The great artists of the period made several notable contributions to literature. The sonnets of Michelangelo are impassioned expressions of inner feeling and religious conviction. Da Vinci's treatises on art and science contain principles of analysis that have profoundly influenced modern thinkers. The remarkable autobiography of the sculptor Benvenuto Cellini ranks among the greatest personal documents in all literature. The various biographies of famous painters, sculptors, and architects written by the painter and architect Giorgio Vasari constitute a pioneer source book of modern art criticism.

The short narrative tale is best represented in the 16th century by the *Novelle* (4 vol., 1554–73) of Matteo Bandello. These tales, modeled on those of Boccaccio, formed the basis of many European literary works, including probably Shakespeare's play *Romeo and Juliet*.

The second half of the 16th century was dominated by the Counter-Reformation (*see* REFORMATION), which began with the Council of Trent in 1545. In the resultant wave of piety and submission to authority the frank enjoyment and exploration of life cultivated by the humanists and their successors was replaced by a superficial regard for morality and public welfare. The

ITALIAN LITERATURE

exuberant freedom of expression and form characteristic of Ariosto was frowned upon, while such freedom of thought and utterance as Machiavelli's became downright dangerous. In literature this change was intensified by a new classicism, which relied upon the authority of Aristotle's rediscovered *Poetics* and spread later throughout all Europe. In 1548 the *Poetics* was published in the original with a Latin translation and commentary by Francesco Robortelli (1516–67). Many other versions as well as treatises on the *Poetics* followed, the most important of which were the *Poetics* (1561) of Julius Caesar Scaliger (1484–1558), and the commentary (1570) by Ludovico Castelvetro (1505–71), in

Torquato Tasso — Bettmann Archive

which the dramatic unities of time and place were first set forth.

Despite the prevailing climate of repression, one great lyric and imaginative poet, Torquato Tasso, produced a masterpiece, *Gerusalemme Liberata* (1575; Eng. trans., *Jerusalem Delivered*, 1884). This beautiful epic treatment of the First Crusade (see CRUSADES) is much shorter and simpler and more unified and serious than the *Orlando Furioso*. It aroused so much pedantic criticism, however, that the author later rewrote it, producing a work of inferior quality. Another great mind and bolder spirit, the philosopher Giordano Bruno, wrote dialogues attacking pedantry and authoritarianism and daring to uphold views forbidden by the church. He was burned at the stake as a heretic in Rome in 1600.

17th Century. Italy in the 17th century was exhausted by unending wars, particularly the invasions of the rival Spanish and French kings who made the country their battleground. The once free-spirited Italian communities offered little resistance to tyranny. World trade was shifting from the Mediterranean Sea to the Atlantic Ocean, and the cosmopolitan Italian ports and industrial cities began to stagnate into provincial communities.

The predominant style of the century, not only in literature but in the fine arts and music, was baroque (q.v.), that is, characterized by exuberant and often gloomy emotion. Poetry and the drama became extravagant in imagination, rhetorical in expression, and richly metaphorical in imagery.

Typical of the century in this respect is the poetry of Giambattista Marini, whose *Adone* ("Adonis", 1623) is a masterpiece of literary virtuosity. A remarkable study of the universality of love, it masks sense under sentiment and discovers amorous tendencies in all nature.

Much of the writing of the period is morbid in spirit. Representative of this genre are the tragedies of Federigo della Valle (1565–1629), whose *La Reina di Scotia* ("The Queen of Scotland", 1628) centers around the trials of Mary, Queen of Scots (q.v.). A dissatisfaction with life, especially with the social order of his time, is expressed in the work of the poet, scientist, and philosopher Tommaso Campanella, whose speculations about ways of improving society cost him imprisonment and exile. His most important work is *Civitas Solis* ("City of the Sun", 1623), which he wrote in prison. It is a utopian vision of an egalitarian state maintained by careful regulation.

18th Century. Toward the end of the 17th century a movement arose in opposition to the affectations and unrestraint of the baroque style. The principle exponents of this tendency belonged to Arcadia, a society founded in Rome in 1690. In conformity with the simplicity traditionally associated with the term "Arcadian", this group advocated a conscious naïveté of expression. The Arcadian writers borrowed from classical sources, chiefly from the Greek pastoral poets.

The outstanding Arcadian figure was the poet and dramatist Metastasio. Much of Italy was under Austrian rule during this period, and Metastasio became the court poet in Vienna, capital of the Austrian emperors. He succeeded Apostolo Zeno (1668–1750), author of dramas and opera librettos, and a pioneer literary critic who was the co-founder (1710) of the first jour-

40

nal of criticism *Giornale dei Letterati d'Italia* ("Journal of Italian Literature"). Metastasio's plays, such as *Artaxerxes* and *Semiramide*, which became widely popular during his lifetime, are remarkable for the melodic fluency of their lines. Several were used as librettos for operas; *see* OPERA.

The influence of Arcadia is discernible in the comedies of Carlo Goldoni, one of the great playwrights in Italian literature. His best comedies include *La Locandiera* (1752; Eng. trans., *The Mistress of the Inn*, 1912), *Il Ventaglio* ("The Fan", 1763), and *Le Baruffe Chiozzotte* (1760; Eng. trans., *Squabbles at Chioggia*, 1914). Goldoni's genius is at its best in rendering situations simply and forcefully and in depicting the milieu from which his characters derive their distinctive qualities.

According to some critics, Goldoni developed his style of writing in reaction to the famed *commedia dell'arte* (q.v.), or guild comedy, which flourished during the 16th to 18th centuries. The guild comedy was based on routine comic situations, the plot outlines of which were composed by wandering companies of actors. The characters were fixed types called *maschere* ("masks"), such as Pantaloon, Harlequin, and Columbine; the actors improvised the dialogues for different performances. The most effective use of the guild-comedy style was made by the dramatist Count Carlo Gozzi (1720–1806), who was opposed to Goldoni's type of dramatic writing. Gozzi dramatized a number of popular fairy tales, establishing a new form known as the "fairy" play. Two of his plays later served as the basis for the operas *The Love of Three Oranges*, by the Russian composer Sergei Prokofiev and *Turnadot*, by the Italian composer Giacomo Puccini (qq.v.).

In its scientific and ethical aspects, Italian literature was influenced during the 18th century by the ideas of the French scientist and philosopher René Descartes (q.v.) and by the writers of the French Enlightenment; *see* ENLIGHTENMENT, AGE OF. The principal organ of Italian intellectual life, which was centered in Milan, was the periodical *Il Caffè* ("The Coffeehouse", 1764–66). The most influential thinker of the Enlightenment in Italy was the jurist Cesare Bonesana Beccaria, who advocated humane treatment of prisoners and abolition of capital punishment. An unfortunate result of the general French influence was the infusion of French words and expressions into Italian at a time when the language already was overladen with Grecisms and Latinisms revived by the Arcadians. An important counterinfluence was that of English literature and ideas, which were popularized in Italy by the work of Giuseppe Baretti, a resident of England for many years. His periodical *Frusta Letteraria* ("Literary Scourge", 1763–65) communicated English cultural values through translations and informative articles.

Among those writers who reacted most vigorously and effectively against excessive foreign influences, especially those from France, and strove to arouse a sense of national pride and unity against foreign domination, were the poets Giuseppe Parini (1729–99) and Conte Vittorio Alfieri. Parini is best known for his social satire in the mock-heroic poem *Il Giorno* ("The Day"), published in several parts between 1763 and 1801. He attacks by ridicule and irony the uselessness, frivolity, and immorality of the aristocracy, and praises in contrast the sober frugality of the working classes. Although he strove to free his work from undue foreign influences, the spirit of social indignation characteristic of *Il Giorno* is very much the same as that found in many French writings which led to the French Revolution (q.v.). In contrast, however, Parini displayed greater moderation and respected the classical traditions and the church.

Alfieri, whose autobiography describes one of the stormiest and most romantic figures in literature, turned from a youthful life of aristocratic self-indulgence, as empty as that satirized by Parini, to a mature life of vigorous and prolific activity as a man of letters. Freedom was his ob-

Conte Vittorio Alfieri   Italian Cultural Institute

ITALIAN LITERATURE

session and tyranny his favorite target, both in his treatises and minor lyrics and in his famous tragedies. Except for *Agamennone* ("Agamemnon", 1777), *Saul* (1783; Eng. trans., 1835), and *Mirra* ("Myrrh", 1787), his best-known plays such as *Filippo* ("Philip the Second", 1781), have a strong political emphasis, which earned them great popularity in the struggle for national liberation marking the following century.

Other important 18th-century writers are the literary critic, historian, and archeologist Ludovico Muratori and the philosopher Giovanni Battista Vico, whose influence was revived by the work of his 20th-century disciple Benedetto Croce. In his *Principii d'una Scienza Nuova* ("Principles of a New Science", 1725), Vico attacked the concept of body and mind as separate entities, which was stressed by Descartes, propounded a cyclical view of history, and anticipated the romantics' interest in the past.

THE 19TH CENTURY

The extraordinary influence on Italy of the French Revolution and of the French emperor Napoleon I (q.v.) is directly evident in the works, which belong mainly to the 19th century, of Vincenzo Monti (1754–1828), Ugo Foscolo (1778–1827), and Carlo Porta (1775–1821). Monti's writings mirror the instability of his convictions. He began as a foe of the French Revolution, as shown in his poem *La Bassvilliana* (1793), about the assassination of the French envoy Hugo Bassville (1753–93), and later favored the French cause, extolling Napoleon in a series of poems. Monti is best known for his translation of the Greek epic poem the *Iliad* (q.v.).

Ugo Foscolo was a more stable personality than Monti. He served as a soldier and teacher in Italy during the French occupation, and upon the return of the Austrians, he went to England, where he died. Foscolo's fâme was established by an epistolary romance, *Le Ultime Lettere di Jacopo Ortis* (1798; Eng. trans., *The Last Letters of Jacopo Ortis*, 1818), patterned on *The Sorrows of Werther* by the German poet and novelist Johann Wolfgang von Goethe (q.v.). Foscolo's novel is a fusion of romantic love and ardent patriotism. Later his patriotism yielded to a resigned contemplation of the past glories of his divided country, the fairest provinces of which remained under foreign rule. In this mood his masterpiece *I Sepolcri* (1807; Eng. trans., *The Sepulchers,* 1860) was written. In his later poems he turns from his passion for Italy to celebrate the ancient world.

The poet Carlo Porta, who wrote in a Milanese dialect, was concerned in his work with describing the miserable life of the Italian common people during the Napoleonic period. He condemns the role of the clergy and nobility, but without excessive bitterness. The poems in which these thoughts are most effectively presented are "Bongee", "Appointment of the Chaplain", and "Prayer", included in the volume *Poesie in Dialetto Milanese* ("Poetry in the Milanese Dialect", 1821).

Conte Giacomo Leopardi stands out as one of the greatest lyric poets in Italian literature. In the loneliness of his secluded home, he made himself a classical scholar, and then, schooled by his translations of Greek and Latin poetry, emerged as a poet of deep feeling. His first compositions were patriotic, such as "To Italy" and "On the Monument of Dante". Later a pessimistic strain pervaded his work. His poems were published singly or in partial collections. The first complete edition, *I Canti* ("Songs"), appeared in 1831. His pessimism was expressed also in his prose writings, notably *Operette Morali* (1827; Eng. trans., *Essays and Dialogues,* 1882), *Zibaldone* ("Miscellany", 7 vol., 1898–1900), and his masterly letters. He did not look kindly upon romanticism, yet his introspection, his desolation, and his nostalgia for the unattainable link him with the romantics. On the other hand, the aristocratic purity and elevation of his literary style, his use of classic forms, and his rationalism link him with the classicists.

Nationalist Literature. Liberation and unification had been a hope of Italian writers since the 13th century. At that time nationalism had been manifested, among other ways, by the development of an Italian literary language. The hope of liberation was stimulated further by the French Revolution, which released a fervent nationalism throughout Europe. From the beginning of the 19th century until 1870, when the evacuation of French troops from Rome removed the last trace of foreign domination, the prevailing influence in Italian literature and in almost every phase of Italian life was nationalism, in its particular Italian form called the risorgimento. See ITALY: *History: Risorgimento.*

Outstanding among the political writers of the risorgimento was the patriot Giuseppe Mazzini, whose political activities cost him imprisonment and exile. He ranks with the statesman Conte Camillo Benso di Cavour and the patriot Giuseppe Garibaldi (qq.v.) among the fathers of Italian liberty. Mazzini's impassioned yet polished political writings continue to be read with interest.

Nationalism gave rise to two other strains in 19th-century Italian literature. One was a new regional feeling that manifested itself in a realistic presentation of regional life, often in the dialect of the region. The other rose out of the conflict over the temporal power of the papacy. A major obstacle to the unification of Italy had been the Papal States (q.v.), which the foreign powers, notably France, had supported in their own national interests. On this issue Italian nationalism came into conflict with religion, and the conflict was resolved variously by different writers. The more nationalist or revolutionary writers expressed antagonism to the church; other writers withdrew to what they considered the more serene values of the pre-Christian classical civilization; still others made of their writing a reaffirmation of Christian faith.

Foremost among the last-named group of writers is Alessandro Manzoni, the author of the famous 19th-century masterpiece of Italian romantic fiction *I Promessi Sposi* (1825–27; Eng. trans., *The Betrothed*, 1834). It is basically the story of two humble lovers struggling against oppression and a hostile fate in 17th-century Italy, then under Spanish domination. Safeguarded by historical accuracy, Manzoni was able thus to ridicule and attack foreign oppression of any kind in any period, and to his fellow patriots the parallel with the contemporary domination by Austria was clear. The universal message of the work, however, which together with its masterly style has gained it world renown, is the need for man to trust to Divine Providence rather than to human plans for the eventual triumph of good over evil. His *Inni Sacri* ("Sacred Hymns", 1810) revealed Manzoni's preoccupation with religious thought, and his later work is imbued with a strong pietistic spirit. Manzoni acquired European fame with an ode written on the occasion of Napoleon's death and translated into German by Goethe. Manzoni's two plays, *Il Conte di Carmagnola* (1820; Eng. trans., *Count of Carmagnola*, 1868), about a Renaissance *condoittiere*, or commander of mercenaries, and *Adelchi* (1822; Eng. trans., 1868), about the heir of the last king of the Lombards, anticipate the religious and patriotic themes of *The Betrothed*.

Manzoni's clear and effective prose has none of the classical embellishments found in the works of Foscolo and Monti. His search for a mystic order in history, his preoccupation with the Middle Ages, and his sense of the imperfection and incompleteness of mortal life link him with the romantics. In his opposition to classicism he criticizes the classical theory of the dramatic unities. In his *Lettera sul Romanticismo* ("Letter on Romanticism", 1823) he declares that romanticism repudiates mythology and ignores the rules of the rhetoricians, who demand imitation, not creative study, of the classics. According to Manzoni, history should take the place of mythology; truth should be the aim of the writer.

Alessandro Manzoni — Bettmann Archive

Manzoni was also deeply concerned with the Italian language. In the course of the centuries the basically Tuscan Italian vocabulary had been enriched by contributions from other regional vernaculars. This development, in Manzoni's opinion, had resulted in a swollen and confusing repetitive vocabulary, and he advocated a return to the Florentine vernacular as spoken by the cultivated classes.

Toward the middle of the 19th century the influence of Manzoni and romanticism in general provoked a reaction accompanied by a classicism more aggressive than that of Monti. The reaction culminated in the work of the poet Giosuè Carducci, who extolled Italian hope and Roman glory. His work was an assertion of classic reason as opposed to romantic mysticism and Catholic piety. Among his outstanding writings are *Levia Gravia* (1861–77; Eng. trans. in *Political and Satiric Verse of Giosuè Carducci*, 1942), *Rime Nuove* (1861–87; Eng. trans. in *Poems by Giosuè Carducci*, 1907), *Odi Barbare* (1877; Eng. trans., 1939), and *Rime e Ritmi* (1897–98; Eng. trans., *Lyrics and Rhythms*, 1942). Carducci was awarded the Nobel Prize in 1906.

ITALIAN LITERATURE

Verist Literature. A reaction against classicism and romanticism as unrealistic marks the second half of the 19th century. It is a revolt against a literature obsessed by the past and its own past achievements, and with its roots in books rather than in life. Shunning conscious lyricism and rhetoric, this reaction advocated everyday speech and a simple style. The poets exalted reality as the truth and named the movement *verismo,* which connotes the "real" and the "true".

The verist trend imparted a new significance to the regional dialect poetry which characterizes this period as well as the beginning of the 20th century. Earlier poets had written in dialect, notably Giovanni Batista Basile, who wrote *Lo Cunto de li Cunti* (1634; Eng. trans., *The Tale of Tales,* 1932) in Neapolitan; and Porta, who wrote in Milanese. The 19th-century dialect poets included a master of even greater significance, Gioacchino Belli (1791–1863). Belli wrote more than two thousand brilliantly descriptive sonnets in Roman dialect depicting the Roman populace grumbling humorously at social conditions and at the mismanagements of the pontifical administration. Among other dialect poets are the Neapolitan Salvatore di Giacomo (1860–1934) and the Pisan Renato Fucini (1843–1921).

The verist movement affected drama and fiction as well as lyric poetry. The one great novelist of this movement is Giovanni Verga, a leader of the Sicilian realists. His major works include the novels *I Malavoglia* (1881; Eng. trans., *The House by the Medlar Tree,* 1890), and *Mastrodon Gesualdo* (1889; Eng. trans., *Master Don Gesualdo,* 1923). Two of his collections of short stories have been translated as *Little Novels of Italy* and *Cavalleria Rusticana and Other Tales. Cavalleria Rusticana* was made into an opera by the Italian composer Pietro Mascagni. Verga's fiction presents realistic pictures of the humble and often miserable lives of the Sicilian peasantry.

Opposed to and yet influenced by the verist trend was the poet Giovanni Pascoli (1855–1912). His lyrics have an idyllic note and in their evocations of rustic life come close in spirit to the *Georgics* of Vergil. His classicism contained no anti-Catholicism; on the contrary, he hailed Dante for his Christian spirituality. Pascoli's style is marked by loose metrics and avoidance of rhetoric. His work prepared the way for Italian free verse. Another antagonist of realism was the poet and novelist Antonio Fogazzaro. Although a sincere Catholic, he campaigned for the acceptance of Darwinism (*see under* DARWIN), and in *Il Santo* (1905; Eng. trans., *The Saint,* 1908) he espoused a form of religious modernism which brought him condemnation by Catholic authorities. His novels, dealing with the problems raised by the advances in science and by social revolution, seek a way out of the moral crisis resulting from these advances. Fogazzaro's novels include *Malombra* (1881; Eng. trans., *The Woman,* 1907), *Daniele Cortis* (1885; Eng. trans., 1887), and *Piccolo Mondo Antico* (1896; Eng. trans., *The Patriot,* 1906). The latter, also translated as *Little World of the Past* (1962), is generally considered his best work.

Several other Italian writers are not associated directly with the literary trends of the period. The traveler and author Edmondo De Amicis (1846–1908) is noted for his novels and travel books. His best-known work of fiction is *Cuore* ("Heart", 1886), written in the form of a journal kept by an Italian schoolboy. Carlo Lorenzini (1826–90), using the pen name Carlo Collodi, wrote the famous children's story *Le Avventure di Pinocchio* (1883; Eng. trans., *The Adventures of Pinocchio,* 1892).

Francesco De Sanctis (1818–83) is the foremost critic of the period and the founder of modern Italian literary criticism. Such works as *Saggi Critici* ("Critical Essays", 1881), *La Letteratura Italian nel Secolo XIX* ("Italian Literature in the 19th Century", 1897), and especially *Storia della Letteratura Italiana* (1871; Eng. trans., *History of Italian Literature,* 1931) apply sociological and psychological perceptions to literary evaluations with great judgment and skill.

THE 20TH CENTURY

The 19-century Italian writer whose influence carried over most strongly into the 20th century was Gabriele D'Annunzio. He broke through the limitations of romanticism, realism, and classicism in his aspiration to be the modern example of the Renaissance universal man. His writings include poetry, fiction, drama, and opera librettos. D'Annunzio claimed recognition also as a soldier and political leader and as a philosopher influenced at different times by the German philosophers Arthur Schopenhauer and Friedrich Nietzsche (qq.v.). Some of D'Annunzio's best writings are the collection of poetry *Laudi* ("Hymns of Praise", 3 vol., 1903–12), the novel *Il Trionfo della Morte* (1894; Eng. trans., *The Triumph of Death,* 1896), and the play *La Figlia di Iorio* (1904; Eng. trans., *The Daughter of Jorio,* 1907), as well as political works and patriotic addresses.

Another important transitional figure was Ettore Schmitz (1861–1928), who wrote under the pen name Italo Svevo. Svevo's work was neglected completely until it was evaluated by the

French journalist and novelist Valéry Larbaud (1881–1957) and the Irish writer James Joyce (q.v.), and brought to the attention of Italian critics. Svevo's strength lies in his realistic portrayal of psychological motivations. His fame rests upon the novels *Una Vita* (1893; Eng. trans., *A Life,* 1963), *Senilità* (1898; Eng. trans., *As a Man Grows Older,* 1932), and *La Coscienza di Zeno* (1923; Eng. trans., *The Confessions of Zeno,* 1930).

Several other writers of various tendencies belong to both the end of the 19th century and the beginning of the 20th century. The philosopher Giovanni Gentile (1875–1944) is the author of many valuable works, notably *Origini e Dottrina del Fascismo* ("Origins and Doctrine of Fascism", 1929) and *La Filosofia dell' Arte* ("The Philosophy of Art", 1931). The historian and author Guglielmo Ferrero was outstanding as a sociological historian and an opponent of fascism (q.v.). His principal work is *Grandezza e Decadenza di Roma* (1902–07; Eng. trans., *The Greatness and Decline of Rome,* 1907–09). The dramatist Sem Benelli became famous as the author of *La Cena delle Beffe* (1909; Eng. trans., *The Jester's Supper,* 1924–25; produced in New York as *The Jest,* 1919) and *L'Amore dei Tre Re* (1910; Eng. trans., *The Love of Three Kings,* 1923). Grazia Deledda was known for regional novels about the Sardinian peasantry, such as *La Madre* (1920; Eng. trans., *The Mother,* 1923). She received the Nobel Prize in 1926. The writer Matilda Serao (1856–1927) was a notable psychological novelist. Among her works are *Il Paese di Cuccagna* (1891; Eng. trans., *The Land of Cockayne,* 1901) and *La Ballerina* (2 vol., 1899; Eng. trans., *The Ballet Dancer,* 1901).

Partly through the influence of foreign literary trends, various movements developed at the beginning of the 20th century in opposition to rhetoric and lyricism in poetry. The most effective and extremist of these movements, which advocated a simplification of syntax and metrics, was futurism (q.v.). The founder of futurism, the poet Emilio Filippo Tommaso Marinetti (1876–1944), used language stripped to essentials. Insisting that 20th-century literature should express the characteristic dynamism of industry, he advocated a type of writing that would emulate the speed and tension of machines. He also became a leading proponent of Italian intervention in World War I and later of fascism.

A unique figure of the first three decades of the century was the novelist, short-story writer, and playwright Luigi Pirandello, who was awarded the Nobel Prize in 1934. He introduced into his plays original dramatic devices that tended to bring actors and the audience into closer relation. Many of his plays are dramatizations of earlier stories, and most of them treat philosophical problems, such as relativism and multiple personality, with subtle psychological insight illuminated by graceful wit. The most famous of his plays include *Sei Personaggi in Cerca d'Autore* (1918; Eng. trans., *Six Characters in Search of an Author,* 1922; produced in New York City in 1922), *Enrico IV* (Henry IV", 1922), and *Come Tu Mi Vuoi* (1930; Eng. trans., *As You Desire Me,* 1931). His novels include *Il Fu Mattia Pascal* (1904; Eng. trans., *The Late Mattia Pascal,* 1923) and *I Vecchi e i Giovani* (1913; Eng. trans., *The Old and the Young,* 1928).

The most important thinker in 20th-century Italy was the philosopher, statesman, literary critic and historian Benedetto Croce, whose influence became worldwide. His bimonthly periodical *Critica* (1930–44) and his literary and philosophical works developed the ideas of the 18th-century philosopher Giovanni Battista Vico and stressed the importance of intuition in art and of freedom in the development of civilization. His position of idealism (q.v.) was in strong opposition to the positivistic thinking then current in Italy; see POSITIVISM. Croce believed that the intellectual should participate in public life and was himself openly opposed to fascism. His major philosphical work, *Filosofia come Scienza dello Spirito* (1902–17; Eng. trans., *Philosophy of the Spirit,* 1909–21), consists of four volumes

Gabriele D'Annunzio   Italian Cultural Institute

dealing respectively with aesthetics, logic, practical thinking, and history. His autobiography, published in 1918, is the record of a rich and varied life.

Besides *Critica,* two other periodicals acted as the forum of different groups of Italian writers. *Voce* (1908–16), directed by the writer Giuseppe Prezzolini (1882–   ), helped to modernize Italian culture and introduce into Italy significant French, British, and American ideas. Outstanding among Prezzolini's collaborators were the painter and writer Ardengo Soffici (1879–1964) and the philosopher and writer Giovanni Papini (1881–1956). The other important periodical, *Ronda* (1919–23), was reactionary in tendency and classical in inspiration. From its circle came the writers Antonio Baldini (1889–1962) and Riccardo Bacchelli (1891–   ).

The emergence of Fascism in Italy under the leadership of the dictator Benito Mussolini (q.v.) endangered the vitality of Italian literature. Fascism failed to create a type of literature congenial to the government in power. The outstanding authors of the time reacted variously to the stifling intellectual conditions and to the contempt for human freedom contained in the fascist political philosophy. Many were outspoken in their opposition, among them the writer and scholar Giuseppe Antonio Borgese (1882–1952). He realistically appraised the political situation in *Goliath, The March of Fascism* (1937), which was written in English, but which was not translated into Italian until ten years later. The novelist Ignazio Silone, who went into exile, became more famous abroad than in Italy for his searching political novels, notably *Fontamara* (1933; Eng. trans., 1934) and *Pane e Vino* (1937; first published in English, *Bread and Wine,* 1936). Croce was forced into retirement under fascism; the journalist and diplomat Curzio Suckert (1898–1957), who wrote under the pen name Malaparte, served the government in an official capacity but ended by repudiating Mussolini. His most powerful work, *Kaputt* (1944; Eng. trans., 1946), pictures the moral and cultural degeneration of Europe under fascism.

Literature after World War II. After World War II a number of Italian writers came into international prominence, among them the poets Giuseppe Ungaretti (1888–1970), Eugenio Montale (1896–   ), and Salvatore Quasimodo. Ungaretti, who ranks with Montale among the foremost European poets of the 20th century, published his first book of verse, *Il Porto Sepolto* ("The Buried Harbor"), in 1916, marking the beginning of a period of great revival in Italian poetry. His works, the most important of which are *Allegria di Naufragi* ("Gaiety of the Outcasts", 1919), *Sentimento del Tempo* ("Feeling of Time", 1933), *Il Dolore* ("The Pain", 1947), and *La Terra Promessa* ("The Promised Land", 1954), have been collected under the title *Vita di un Uomo* (Eng. trans., *Life of a Man,* 1958). His poetry is characterized by a sparing use of words and by his power to create illuminating images of unusual lyric intensity. Montale's major poems are found in three books: *Ossi di Seppia* ("Cuttlefish Bones", 1925), *Le Occasioni* ("The Occasions", 1939), and *La Bufera e Altro* ("The Whirlwind and More", 1956), some of which, accompanied by English translations, were published in book form in England (*Poems,* 1964) and in the United States (*Selected Poems,* 1966). His verse, often highly compressed and hermetic, contains a harsh and intellectual criticism of life and is at times deeply pessimistic in tone. Quasimodo's collections of poems, including *Ed è Subito Sera* ("And Suddenly It Is Evening", 1942), *Giorno Dopo Giorno* ("Day After Day", 1947), *La Vita non è Sogno* ("Life Is Not a Dream", 1949), and *Il Falso e Vero Verde* ("The False and True Green", 1953), reveal a passionate lyrical awareness of tragedy in modern life. Quasimodo was awarded the Nobel Prize for literature in 1959. *The Selected Writings of Salvatore Quasimodo* (1960) and *To Give and to Have and Other Poems* (1969) are his two major collections published in English.

A few years after the war a new type of realism appeared in the Italian cinema, which enjoyed a period of unique creativity, and simultaneously critics began to speak of an Italian literary neorealism. Among the outstanding figures were Carlo Levi (1902–   ), who exposed the plight of the tenant farmers of southern Italy in his best-seller *Cristo si è Fermato a Eboli* (1946; Eng. trans., *Christ Stopped at Eboli,* 1947); the novelists Elio Vittorini (1908–66), author of *Conversazione in Sicilia* (1941; Eng. trans., *In Sicily,* 1949); Vasco Pratolini (1913–   ), who wrote *Cronache di Poveri Amanti* (1947; Eng. trans., *A Tale of Poor Lovers,* 1949); the novelist and film scenarist Mario Soldati (1906–   ), noted for his *Lettere da Capri* (1954; Eng. trans., *Affair in Capri; The Capri Letters,* 1957); the poet, critic, and novelist Cesare Pavese (1908–50), whose works include *Tra Donne Sole* (1949; Eng. trans., *Among Women Only,* 1959), *Il Diavolo sulle Colline* (1949; Eng. trans., *The Devil in the Hills,* 1959), *La Luna e i Falò* (1950; Eng. trans., *The Moon and the Bonfires,* 1953); and the novelist Vitaliano Brancati (1907–54), a keen critic of contemporary Sicilian society as shown in *Il Bell' Antonio* (1949; Eng. trans., *Antonio the*

Alberto Moravia — Italian Cultural Institute

Great Lover, 1952). A novel that enjoyed international acclaim, *Il Gattopardo* (1958; Eng. trans., *The Leopard*, 1960), by Giuseppe Tomasi di Lampedusa (1896–1957), is set against the background of Sicilian life.

Besides Pirandello, the best-known modern Italian writer, especially in the U.S., is the novelist and short-story writer Alberto Moravia, a prolific author notable for his fictional studies of contemporary human situations. He writes in a spare, realistic prose style about the moral dilemmas of men and women trapped in social and emotional circumstances. His most popular work is *La Ciociara* (1957; Eng. trans., *Two Women*, 1958), a novel about a mother and her daughter in war-torn Italy. The story was made into a successful motion picture.

Among the more notable recent novelists are Italo Calvino (1923–   ), who wrote *Il Barone Rampante* (1957; Eng. trans., *The Baron in the Trees*, 1959) and *Le Cosmicomiche* (1965; Eng. trans. *Cosmicomics*, 1968); Carlo Emilio Gadda (1893–   ), author of *Quer Pasticciaccio Brutto de Via Merulana* (1957; Eng. trans., *That Awful Mess on Via Merulana*, 1965) and *La Cognizione del Dolore* (1963; Eng. trans., *Acquainted with Grief*, 1969); Elsa Morante (1918–   ), who wrote *L' Isola di Arturo* (1957; Eng. trans., *Arturo's Island*, 1959); Giose Rimanelli (1926–   ), author of *Tiro al Piccione* (1953; Eng. trans., *The Day of the Lion*, 1954); and Lalla Romano (1909–   ), who wrote *Le Parole Tra Noi Leggere* ("The Words Between Us Are Light", 1969).

See also DRAMA: *National Drama: Italy;* and separate articles on artists and writers whose dates are not given above.   A.T.M. & L.R.

ITALIAN MUSIC, music created by the Italian people from the beginnings of the Christian Era to the present.

Chant and Polyphony. Italian music is one of the oldest in the Western world and has played a crucial role in music development. The first major Italian contribution to Western music was the development during the first thousand years of the Christian Era of two repertories of Christian chant (q.v.): Ambrosian chant, which developed at Milan, and Gregorian chant, which developed at Rome and eventually became the official liturgical chant of the Roman Catholic Church. At first, chant melodies were transmitted orally from one place and generation to another. As the repertories became larger, however, and as the church sought greater uniformity in chant melodies, musical notation became necessary. Italians played a crucial role in inventing a satisfactory notation. References to written music date from the 6th century, and samples of it date from the 9th century. The Italian Benedictine monk, Guido d'Arezzo (q.v.) established the use of the staff, which has remained a basic feature of musical notation.

The most important musical development in Europe from the 11th to the 14th centuries, the rise of polyphony (q.v.), took place in France; see FRENCH MUSIC; MUSIC: *The Gothic Period.* During the 14th century the rigorous techniques of French polyphony were adapted to the Italian taste for graceful melody by one of the great Italian masters of composition, the blind organist Francesco Landini (1325–97).

Renaissance Music. In the Renaissance (q.v.) European music was dominated by musicians from the Netherlands. At the end of this period Italy again produced a master composer, Giovanni Pierluigi da Palestrina (q.v.). Palestrina's music, with its smooth flowing vocal lines and euphonious sonorities, was considered the ideal manifestation of the religious spirit, not only in its own time but for many succeeding generations. Italian composers of the late 16th century were noted for the colorful ways they depicted contrasting emotions and visual images in music, especially in the madrigals composed by Luca Marenzio (1553–59) and Carlo Gesualdo (1560?–1613). Another Italian contribution during the 16th century was the development of music printing. The Venetian printer Ottaviano Petrucci (1466–1539) produced the first printed editions of polyphonic music beginning in 1501.

As the baroque era (1600–1750) approached, Italy became an increasingly active musical na-

ITALIAN MUSIC

tion. This was the era when instrumental music was first cultivated as an independent genre, and the Italian love of colorful and sensuous sound seems to have made the country an ideal place for the development of musical styles that would exploit the special features of various instruments. The types of instrumental music that evolved included the canzona, concerto, fantasia, sonata, and toccata (qq.v.). Instrumental music was further aided by the development of string instruments (see VIOLIN) in Cremona by the Amati and Guarnieri families and by Antonio Stradivari (qq.v.). Simultaneously, Italian violinist-composers were expanding the range of violin technique in large quantities of music. These composers included Arcangelo Corelli, Giuseppe Tartini, and Antonio Vivaldi (qq.v.). The modern piano (q.v.) was largely the invention of a harpsichord maker in Padua, Bartolommeo di Francesco Cristofori (1655–1731).

Italians and other composers working in Italy in the late 16th and early 17th century developed a polychoral style of music using two or more ensembles of voices and instruments situated in different parts of a large space such as a cathedral. The multiple choir lofts at Saint Mark's Church (q.v.) in Venice made this building an especially attractive setting for such music, which was written in Venice by the organist Andrea Gabrieli (1520?–86), his nephew Giovanni Gabrieli (1557–1612), and many others.

Opera (q.v.) was an Italian invention that developed in Florence at the beginning of the 17th century and reached its first peak in the works of Claudio Monteverdi (q.v.). The Italian tradition of beautiful and agile singing, called *bel canto* (It., "beautiful singing") developed later in the century and created an enormous demand for Italian singers throughout Europe. In France an Italian composer, Jean-Baptiste Lully (q.v.), founded a distinctively French style of opera; see FRENCH MUSIC: *The Baroque Era*. The work of the late 17th century composer Alessandro Scarlatti (q.v.) was influential in the development of German music.

During the second quarter of the 18th century, the symphony (q.v.) appeared, first in Italy and then in the rest of Europe. From this point on, Italy began to lose its musical hegemony, except in opera, which retained the Italian style until the 19th century. The operatic composers Vincenzo Bellini, Gaetano Donizetti, and Gioacchino Antonio Rossini (qq.v.) carried the Italian *bel canto* tradition into the first half of the 19th century. Thereafter Giuseppe Verdi (q.v.) dominated Italian opera, sharing an influence over worldwide trends with the German composer Richard Wagner (q.v.). The most notable of the later Italian operatic composers were Ruggiero Leoncavallo, Pietro Mascagni, and Giacomo Puccini (qq.v.).

Italian music of the 20th century has in general followed the lead of other nations. The influence of French impressionism (q.v.) affected the musical style of Ottorino Respighi (q.v.). The neoclassical movement, largely French inspired, was embraced by the conductor, pianist, and composer Alfredo Casella (1883–1947). The aesthetic tenets of neoclassicism were formulated most forcefully by another Italian, the pianist and composer Ferruccio Benvenuto Busoni (q.v.). The innovations of the Austro-American composer Arnold Schoenberg (q.v.) have influenced the music of the Florentine Luigi Dallapiccola (1904–   ). With the rise of radical avant-garde tendencies in the late 1950's and 1960's, Italy has again begun to produce innovative composers. The works of Luigi Nono (1924–   ), Luciano Berio (1925–   ), and others are representative of the newest trends.   J.V.

ITALIAN SOMALILAND. See SOMALIA.

ITALIC, style of type in which the letters are designed with an upslope to the right. The style was first used by the Italian printer Aldus Manutius (see under MANUTIUS) in his edition of Vergil's works published in 1501. Italic type gradually came to be used for a number of special purposes in works otherwise printed in roman letters; today it is often used for prefaces, introductions, notes, and indexes outside of the main body of a book, and for quotations, footnotes, and word emphasis inside the body of a book. See TYPE.

These letters are in italic type.

ITALIC LANGUAGES, important subfamily of the Indo-European languages (q.v.), formerly spoken chiefly in ancient Italy and today, chiefly in Italy, France, Spain, Portugal, Belgium, Switzerland, and Rumania. The entire subfamily is usually divided into two branches: Osco-Umbrian, a group of dead languages formerly spoken in ancient Italy and containing two members, Oscan and Umbrian; and Latinian, or Latin-Faliscan, the major branch, that contains Latin (q.v.) and the entire group of languages usually called in whole or part the Romance languages (q.v.), which represent the survival of the Latin language (q.v.) in territories once part of the Roman Empire.

The predominance of Latin from classical Roman until modern times was in large measure the result of more or less deliberate political pressure. In prehistoric Italy, however, and even well into classical times, other Italic and non-Italic tongues claimed numbers of speakers who at times amounted to an actual majority of the population of the Italian peninsula. For example, Etruscan (see ETRURIA), a nonIndo-European language, was at one time the dominant language of western Italy north of the Tiber R. In southern Italy and on the island of Sicily, ancient Greek (see GREEK LANGUAGE) was spoken in numerous Greek colonies and maintained a close relationship with the Italic languages. Other languages of ancient Italy concerning whose affiliations there is still doubt were Messapian, spoken in the so-called heel of boot-shaped Italy; Sicel, spoken in Sicily and Calabria; and Venetic, Liguric, and Rhaetic, used in the north. Gaulish, a Celtic language, was spoken in the northwestern part of Italy. In Carthaginian colonies in western Sicily and in Sardinia, Punic, a Semitic tongue, was spoken prior to the First Punic War (see PUNIC WARS).

Of the Italic tongues themselves, Umbrian and Oscan were second in importance only to Latin, and became the repositories of fairly extensive literatures; they were suppressed before the beginning of the Christian era through the political influence of Rome; see ROME, HISTORY OF. Oscan was the language of Samnitic tribes (see SAMNITES), and was spoken in most of the southern half of Italy except for the southernmost peninsulas. Umbrian, spoken in central Italy, is of importance chiefly because of its literature, which is of far greater extent than that of any other ancient Italic language except Latin and Oscan. Most of the texts in ancient Umbrian are contained in the so-called Iguvine Tablets, found in Gubbio, Italy. Oscan texts have been traced to a number of southern Italian localities, notably Pompeii and Capua (qq.v.).   M.P.

ITALY (It. *Italia*), republic of S. Europe, bounded on the N. by Switzerland and Austria; on the E. by Yugoslavia, the Adriatic Sea, and the Ionian Sea; on the S. by the Strait of Messina, which separates it from Sicily; and on the W. by the Tyrrhenian Sea, the Ligurian Sea, and France. It comprises, in addition to the Italian mainland, the Mediterranean islands of Elba, Sardinia, and Sicily (qq.v.), and many lesser islands. The country lies between about lat. 36°39′ N. and lat. 47°5′ N. and long. 6°33′ E. and long. 18°31′ E. The area of Italy, including the islands and Vatican City (q.v.), an independent papal state within Rome, is about 116,230 sq.mi.

THE LAND

More than one half of Italy consists of the Italian peninsula, a long projection of the continental mainland. Shaped much like a boot, the Italian peninsula extends generally southeastward into the Mediterranean Sea. From N.W. to S.E., the country is nearly 710 mi. long; with the addition of the southern peninsular extremity, which extends N. and S., it is about 846 mi. long. The maximum width of the mainland portion of Italy is about 250 mi. from E. to W., the maximum width of the peninsula is 150 mi. On the northern frontiers are the Alps (q.v.), which extend in a wide arc from Ventimiglia on the W. to Gorizia on the E. Between the Alps and the Apennines (q.v.), which form the backbone of the Italian peninsula, spreads the broad plain of Lombardy, comprising the valley of the Po River (q.v.). The northern Apennines project from the Maritime Alps along the Gulf of Genoa to the sources of the Tiber R. Monte Cimone (7096 ft.) is the highest summit of the Northern Apennines. The Central Apennines, beginning at the sources of the Tiber, consist of several chains. In the E. portion of this rugged mountain district is Monte Corno (9560 ft.), the highest Apennine peak. The Southern Apennines stretch southeasterly from the valley of the Sangro R. to the coast of the Gulf of Taranto, where they assume a more southerly direction. Maximum elevations of the Apennine ranges of the Calabrian peninsula, as the southern extremity of the Italian peninsula is known, are Botte Donato (6329 ft.) and Montalto (6422 ft.). The Apennines form the watershed of the Italian peninsula. The main uplifts are bordered, particularly on the W., by less elevated districts, known collectively as the sub-Apennine region.

Only about one third of the total land surface of Italy is made up of plains, of which the greatest single tract is the plain of Lombardy. The coast of Italy along the N. Adriatic Sea is low and sandy, bordered by shallow waters, and, except at Venice, not readily accessible to oceangoing vessels. From a point near Rimini southward, the E. coast of the peninsula is fringed by spurs of the Apennines. Along the middle of the W. coast, however, are three stretches of low and marshy land, the Campagna di Roma, the Pontine Marshes (qq.v.), and the Maremma.

The W. coast is broken up by bays, gulfs, and other indentations, which provide a number of natural anchorages. In the N.W. is the Gulf of Genoa, the harbor of the important commercial city of Genoa. Naples, another leading west-coast port, is situated on the beautiful Bay of Naples, dominated by the volcano Vesuvius (q.v.). A little farther S. is the Gulf of Salerno, at the head of which stands the port of Salerno. The S.E. end of the peninsula is deeply indented

ITALY

by the Gulf of Taranto, which divides the so-called heel of Italy (ancient Calabria) from the toe (modern Calabria). The Apennine range continues beneath the narrow Strait of Messina and traverses the island of Sicily, where the volcano Etna (q.v.), 11,053 ft. high, is located. Another active volcano rises on Stromboli, one of the Lipari Islands (q.v.), N. of the Strait of Messina.

Rivers and Lakes. Italy has many rivers, of which the Po and the Adige (q.v.) are the most important. The Po, 418 mi. long, is navigable from Turin to its outlet on the Adriatic Sea and with its tributaries affords about 600 mi. of inland waterways. The Adige, about 220 mi. long, enters Italy from the Austrian province of Tirol, flows E., and, like the Po, empties into the Adriatic. The beds of these rivers are slowly being elevated by alluvial deposits from the mountains.

The rivers of the Italian peninsula are shallow, often dry during the summer season, and consequently of little importance for navigation or industry. The chief peninsular rivers are the Arno and the Tiber (qq.v.). From its sources in the Apennines, the Arno flows W. 150 mi. through a well-cultivated valley and the cities of Florence and Pisa. The Tiber rises not far from the sources of the Arno and runs through the city of Rome. Both the northern and peninsular regions of Italy have numerous lakes. The principal lakes of northern Italy, in the order of size, are Garda, Maggiore, Como, and Lugano (qq.v.); the peninsular lakes, which are considerably smaller, include Trasimeno (q.v.), Bolsena, and Bracciano.

Climate. The climate of Italy is highly diversified, with extremes ranging from frigid, in the higher elevations of the Alps and Apennines, to semitropical along the coast of the Ligurian Sea and the W. coast of the lower peninsula. The average annual temperature, however, ranges from 52° to 66° F.; it is about 55° F. in the Po valley, 64° F. in Sicily, and 58° F. in the coastal lowlands. Climatic conditions on the peninsula are characterized by regional variations, resulting chiefly from the configurations of the Apennines, and are influenced by tempering winds from the adjacent seas. In the lowland regions and lower slopes of the Apennines bordering the W. coast from northern Tuscany to the vicinity of Rome, winters are mild and sunny, and extreme summer temperatures are modified by cooling Mediterranean breezes. Temperatures in the same latitudes on the E. of the peninsula are much lower, chiefly because of the prevailing N.E. winds. Aong the upper E. slopes of the Apennines climatic conditions are particularly bleak. The climate of the peninsular lowlands below the latitude of Rome closely resembles that of southern Spain. In contrast to the semitropical conditions prevalent in southern Italy and along the Gulf of Genoa, the climate of the Lombardy plain is continental. Warm summers and severe winters, with temperatures as low as 5° F., prevail in this region, which is shielded from sea breezes by the Apennines. Heaviest precipitation occurs in Italy during the fall and winter months, when westerly winds prevail. The lowest mean annual rainfall, 18 in., occurs in the Apulian province of Foggia in the south; the highest, 60 in., occurs in the Venetian province of Udine in the N.E.

Natural Resources. Italy is poor in natural resources, the land being unsuitable for agriculture due to mountainous terrain or unfavorable climate. Italy, moreover, is seriously deficient in such basic natural resources as oil, coal, and iron ore. The most important mineral resources are natural gas and sulphur. Other mineral deposits are lead, manganese, zinc, and bauxite. Italy is rich in various types of building stone, notably marble. The coastal waters of Italy teem with fish, of which the sardine, tunny, and anchovy have the greatest commercial importance. Freshwater fish include eels and trout.

Plants and Animals. The flora of the central and S. lowlands of Italy is typically Mediterranean. Among the characteristic vegetation of these regions are such trees as the olive, orange, lemon, palm, and citron. Other common types, especially in the extreme S., are fig, date, pomegranate, and almond trees, and sugarcane and cotton. The vegetation of the Apennines closely resembles that of central Europe. Dense growths of chestnut and oak trees occupy the lower slopes, and at higher elevations are extensive stands of pine and fir.

Italy has fewer varieties of animals than are found generally in other comparable areas of Europe. The marmot, chamois, and ibex are found exclusively in the Alps. The bear, numerous in ancient times, is now virtually extinct, but the wolf and wild boar still flourish in the mountain regions. Another fairly common quadruped is the fox. Among the predatory species of bird are the eagle, hawk, vulture, buzzard, falcon, and kite, confined for the most part to the mountains. The quail, woodcock, partridge, and various migratory species abound in many parts of Italy. Reptiles comprise several species of lizards and snakes, including three species of the poisonous viper family. Scorpions and tarantulas are also found.

Waterpower. The most important natural resource is waterpower, which contributes more

ITALY

INDEX TO MAP OF ITALY

Regions

Abruzzi	D3
Aosta	A2
Apulia	F4
Basilicata	F5
Calabria	E4
Campania	G4
Emilia-Romagna	D1
Friuli-Venezia Giulia	D4
Latium	B2
Liguria	B2
Lombardy	D3
Marche	E4
Molise	A2
Piedmont	F4
Puglia (Apulia)	B4
Sardinia	E6
Sicily	C1
Trentino-Alto Adige	C3
Tuscany	D3
Umbria	C2
Venetia	

Provinces

Agrigento	D6
Alessandria	B2
Ancona	D3
Aosta	A2
Arezzo	C3
Ascoli Piceno	D3
Asti	B2
Avellino	F4
Bari	D1
Belluno	E4
Benevento	B2
Bergamo	C1
Bologna	G4
Bolzano	D6
Brescia	B5
Brindisi	D6
Cagliari	E4
Caltanissetta	E4
Campobasso	F5
Caserta	E3
Catania	F5
Catanzaro	D5
Chieti	F5
Como	A2
Cosenza	D1
Cremona	E6
Cuneo	C3
Enna	E4
Ferrara	D2
Florence	
Foggia	
Forlì	

Frosinone	D4
Genoa	B2
Gorizia	C3
Grosseto	B3
Imperia	B2
L'Aquila	G4
La Spezia	D1
Latina	D1
Lecce	C3
Leghorn	B2
Lucca	C4
Macerata	Q2
Mantua	F4
Massa-Carrara	E5
Matera	B2
Messina	F7
Milan	B3
Modena	E2
Naples	D6
Novara	B4
Nuoro	B2
Padua	F4
Palermo	D3
Parma	D5
Pavia	C2
Perugia	D3
Pesaro e Urbino	E3
Pescara	A2
Piacenza	D6
Pisa	C3
Pistoia	D2
Pordenone	E4
Potenza	F4
Ragusa	E6
Ravenna	F1
Reggio di Calabria	E4
Reggio nell'Emilia	C3
Rieti	D3
Rome	F6
Rovigo	C4
Salerno	B4
Sassari	B2
Savona	G4
Siena	D6
Sondrio	B1
Syracuse	E4
Taranto	F4
Teramo	F3
Terni	D3
Trapani	D5
Trento	F5
Treviso	D2
Trieste	A2
Turin	E6
Udine	D1
Varese	C3
Venice	B2
Vercelli	D2

Verona	C2
Vicenza	C2
Viterbo	C3

Cities and Towns

Acireale	E6
Acqui Terme	B2
Acri	F5
Adrano	E6
Adria	D2
Agira	E6
Agrigento	D6
Agropoli	E4
Alassio	A2
Alba	B2
Albano Laziale	F7
Albenga	B3
Albino	C4
Alcamo	B2
Alessandria	B4
Alghero	B2
Altamura	F4
Amalfi	D3
Ancona	D5
Andria	C2
Anzio	D3
Aosta	E3
Aprilia	A2
Aragona	D6
Ariano Irpino	C3
Arezzo	D2
Ascoli Piceno	E4
Assisi	D3
Asti	B2
Augusta	E6
Avellino	E4
Aversa	D3
Avezzano	C3
Avola	D5
Bagheria	B4
Barcellona Pozzo di Gotto	E5
Bari	F4
Barletta	D1
Bassano del Grappa	C2
Belluno	F6
Benevento	F3
Bergamo	B6
Biancavilla	B2
Biella	F4
Bisceglie	C1
Bitonto	D2
Bologna	A2
Bolzano	D1
Bordighera	B2
Borgomanero	B2
Bosa	B4

Bra	A2
Bracciano	C3
Brescia	C1
Bressanone	G4
Brindisi	B2
Bronte	E6
Busto Arsizio	B5
Cagliari	E6
Caltagirone	D6
Caltanissetta	C3
Camaiore	D6
Campobasso	E4
Canicatti	E6
Canosa di Puglia	B2
Cantù	A2
Capua	B2
Caravaggio	B5
Carbonia	B5
Carini	B5
Carloforte	E4
Carmagnola	A2
Carpi	C2
Carrara	B2
Casale Monferrato	C3
Cascina-Navacchio	F5
Caserta	E4
Cassino	D2
Castelfranco Veneto	D5
Castellammare del Golfo	
Castellammare di Stabia	E4
Castelvetrano	F5
Castrovillari	E4
Catania	D3
Catanzaro	F7
Cava de' Tirreni	E6
Cecina	C3
Ceglie Messapico	F4
Celano	D3
Cerignola	D2
Cernobbio	B2
Cesena	D2
Cesenatico	B2
Chiari	D1
Chiavari	B4
Chieti	E3
Chioggia	B2
Chivasso	F4
Ciampino	A2
Città di Castello	D3
Cittanova	F5
Cividale del Friuli	D1
Civitavecchia	B2
Colle di Val d'Elsa	B4

Comacchio	D2
Comiso	E6
Como	D2
Conegliano	F4
Conversano	F7
Corato	F7
Cori	F5
Corigliano Calabro	F5
Corleone	C6
Correggio	D3
Cortina d'Ampezzo	D1
Cosenza	F5
Cremona	B2
Crema	B2
Crotone	F5
Cuneo	A2
La Maddalena	B4
Lanciano	E3
L'Aquila	D3
La Spezia	B2
Latina	D4
Lavello	E4
Lecce	E6
Lecco	C2
Legnago	C3
Legnano	D3
Lendinara	D3
Lentini	F4
Leonforte	D6
Licata	C1
Lido di Ostia	D2
Lido di Venezia	F4
Livorno (Leghorn)	C3
Lodi	B2
Lucca	E4
Lucera	D2
Lugo	D2
Macerata	D3
Macomer	B4
Maglie	G4
Manduria	E6
Manfredonia	E4
Mantua	D3
Marino	F4
Marsala	D6
Martina Franca	C2
Massa	A2
Massa Marittima	F4
Massafra	D4
Matera	E3
Mazara del Vallo	G4
Mazzarino	D6
Melfi	B2
Menfi	E4
Merano	E6
Mesagne	G4
Messina	C1
Mestre	E5
Milan	F7
Desenzano del Garda	C2
Domodossola	B4
Dorgali	B5
Eboli	C2
Empoli	C2
Enna	C2
Este	C2
Fabriano	D3
Faenza	D2
Fano	D3
Fasano	F5
Favara	E4
Feltre	D2
Fermo	D6
Ferrandina	C1
Ferrara	F4
Fidenza	B2
Finale Emilia	D6
Finale Ligure	C2
Firenze (Florence)	F7
Fiumicino	E6
Florence	D3
Floridia	C3
Foggia	E4
Foligno	E5
Fondi	D3
Forlì	D4
Formia	D2
Fossano	A2
Francavilla Fontana	F4
Frascati	F6
Frosinone	D4
Gaeta	B2
Galatina	E3
Galatone	G4
Gallarate	B2
Gallipoli	A2
Gela	F7
Gemona	D3
Genoa (Genova)	F5
Genzano di Roma	C3
Giarre	E6

Continued on page 54

ITALY

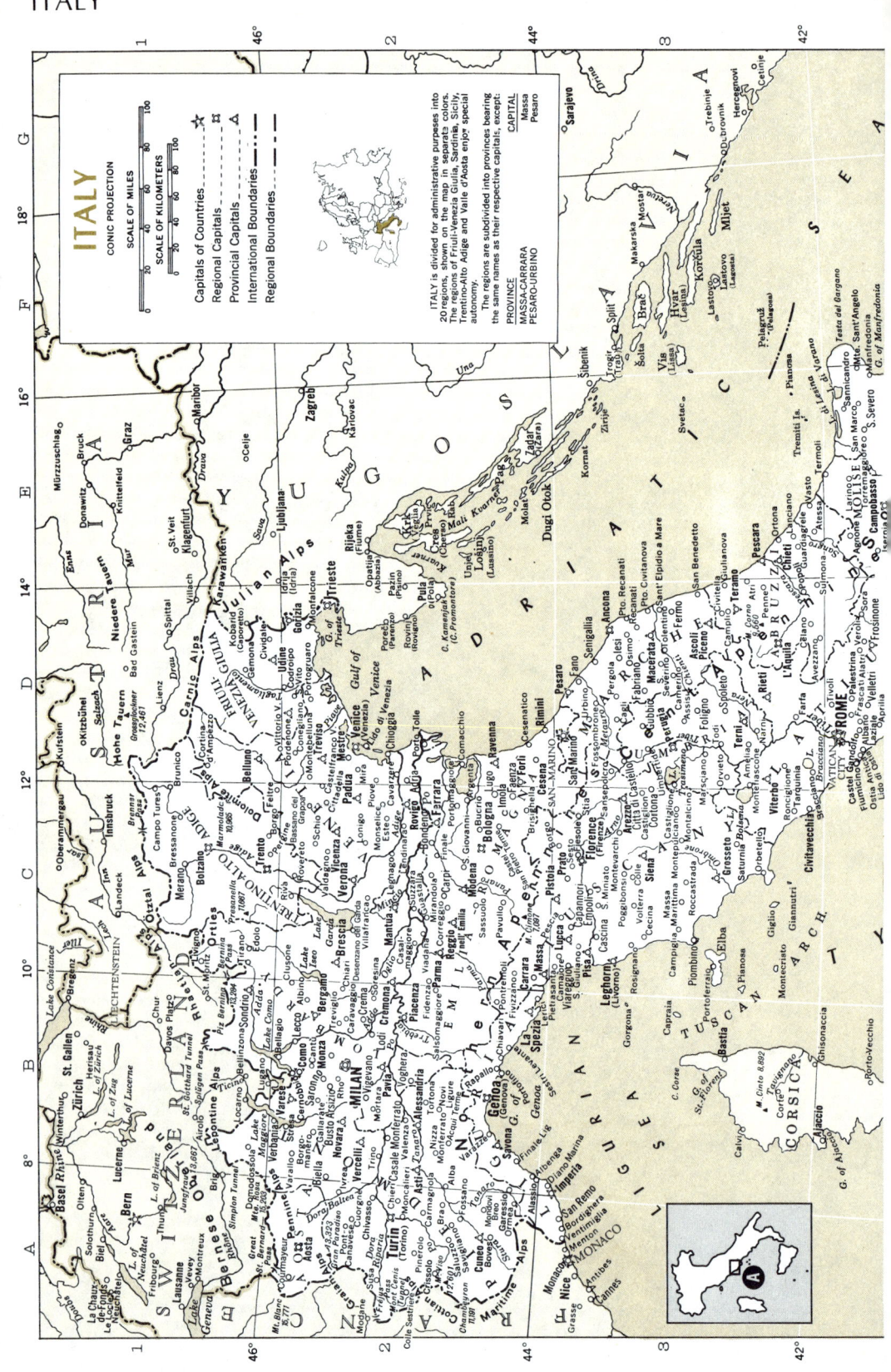

ITALY

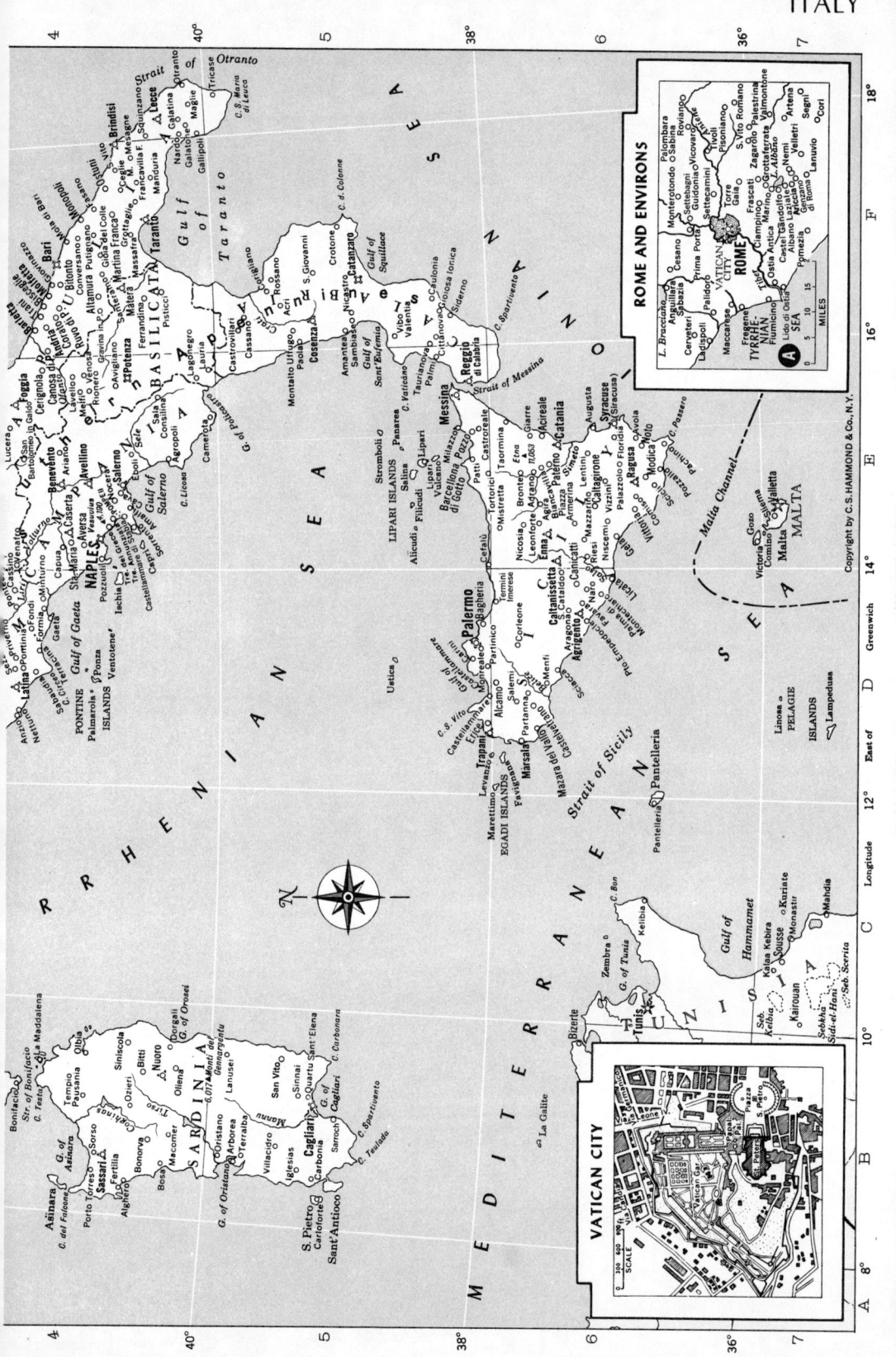

ROME AND ENVIRONS

VATICAN CITY

ITALY

Index to Map of Italy — Continued from page 51

Milazzo	E 5
Mirandola	C 2
Mira Taglio	B 3
Mistretta	D 6
Modena	C 2
Modica	E 6
Mola di Bari	F 4
Molfetta	F 4
Moncalieri	A 2
Mondovì Breo	A 3
Monfalcone	D 2
Monopoli	F 4
Monreale	C 5
Monselice	C 2
Monterotondo	D 3
Monte Sant'Angelo	F 4
Montevarchi	C 3
Monza	B 2
Mortara	B 2
Naples	E 4
Nardò	F 4
Naro	D 6
Nettuno	D 4
Nicastro	F 5
Nicosia	E 6
Niscemi	E 6
Noto	E 6
Novara	B 2
Nocera Inferiore	E 4
Novi Ligure	B 2
Nuoro	B 4
Olbia	B 4
Oliena	C 3
Orbetello	C 3
Oristano	B 5
Ortona	E 3
Orvieto	D 3
Osimo	D 3
Ostuni	F 4
Ozieri	B 4
Pachino	E 6
Padua	C 2
Palazzolo Acreide	E 6
Palermo	D 5
Palestrina	F 7
Palma di Montechiaro	D 6
Palmi	E 5
Paola	F 5
Parma	C 2
Partanna	D 6
Partinico	D 5
Paterno	E 6
Patti	E 5
Pavia	B 2
Perugia	D 3
Pesaro	D 3
Pescara	E 3
Pescia	C 3
Piacenza	B 2
Piazza Armerina	E 6
Pietrasanta	C 3
Pinerolo	A 2
Piombino	C 3
Pisa	C 3
Pisticci	F 4
Pistoia	C 3
Poggibonsi	C 3
Popoli	E 3
Pordenone	D 2
Porto Civitanova	D 3
Porto Empedocle	D 6
Portoferraio	C 3
Portofino	B 2
Portogruaro	D 2
Porto Torres	B 4
Potenza	F 4
Pozzallo	E 6
Pozzuoli	E 4
Prato	C 3
Prima Porta	D 4
Priverno	D 4
Putignano	F 4
Quartu Sant'Elena	B 5
Ragusa	E 6
Rapallo	B 2
Ravenna	D 2
Recanati	D 3
Reggio di Calabria	E 5
Reggio nell'Emilia	C 2
Rho	B 2
Rieti	D 3
Rimini	D 3
Rionero in Vulture	E 4
Riva	C 2
Rome (cap.)	D 4
Rossano	F 5
Rovereto	C 2
Rovigo	C 2
Ruvo di Puglia	F 4
Sala Consilina	F 4
Salemi	D 6
Salerno	E 4
Salsomaggiore Terme	B 2
Saluzzo	A 2
Sambiase	F 5
San Bartolomeo in Galdo	E 4
San Benedetto del Tronto	E 3
San Cataldo	D 6
San Giovanni in Fiore	F 5
San Giovanni in Persiceto	C 2
San Marco in Lamis	E 4
Sannicandro Garganico	E 4
San Remo	A 3
Sansepolcro	D 3
San Severo	E 4
Santa Maria Capua Vetere	E 4
Santeramo in Colle	F 4
San Vito dei Normanni	F 4
Saronno	B 2
Sassari	B 4
Sassuolo	E 3
Savigliano	A 2
Savona	B 2
Sciacca	D 6
Scicli	E 6
Segni	D 3
Senigallia	C 3
Sesto Fiorentino	B 2
Sestri Levante	B 2
Sezze	D 4
Siderno	C 3
Siena	C 3
Siracusa (Syracuse)	E 6
Sondrio	B 1
Sora	D 4
Soresina	C 2
Sorrento	E 4
Sorso	B 4
Spoleto	D 3
Squinzano	G 4
Sulmona	D 3
Suzzara	C 2
Syracuse	E 6
Taranto	F 4
Tarquinia	C 3
Taurianova	E 5
Tempio Pausania	B 4
Teramo	D 3
Termini Imerese	D 6
Termoli	E 3
Terni	D 3
Terracina	D 4
Terralba	B 5
Tivoli	D 3
Tolentino	D 3
Torino (Turin)	A 2
Torre Annunziata	E 4
Torre del Greco	E 4
Torremaggiore	E 4
Tortona	B 2
Trani	F 4
Trapani	D 5
Trento	C 2
Treviglio	B 2
Tricase	G 5
Trieste	E 2
Trino	A 2
Turin	A 2
Udine	D 1
Urbino	C 3
Valdagno	C 2
Valenza	B 2
Varazze	B 2
Varese	B 2
Vasto	E 3
Velletri	D 4
Venice (Venezia)	D 2
Venosa	E 4
Ventimiglia	A 3
Verbania	B 2
Vercelli	B 2
Verona	C 2
Viareggio	C 3
Vibo Valentia	F 5
Vicenza	C 2
Vigevano	B 2
Villacidro	B 5
Villafranca	C 2
Viterbo	D 3
Vittoria	E 6
Vittorio Veneto	D 2
Vizzini	E 6
Voghera	B 2
Volterra	C 3

Other Features

Adda (river)	B 2
Adige (river)	C 2
Adriatic (sea)	E 3
Albano (lake)	F 7
Alicudi (isl.)	C 5
Apennines (range)	D 3
Arno (river)	C 3
Asinara (isl.)	A 4
Bernina (mt.)	B 1
Blanc (mt.)	A 2
Bolsena (lake)	D 3
Bonifacio (strait)	B 4
Bracciano (lake)	D 3
Brenner (pass)	C 1
Cagliari (gulf)	B 5
Capraia (isl.)	B 3
Capri (isl.)	E 4
Carbonara (cape)	D 5
Carnic Alps (range)	D 1
Cimone (mt.)	C 2
Circeo (cape)	D 4
Colonne (cape)	G 5
Como (lake)	B 1
Corno (mt.)	D 3
Cottian Alps (range)	A 2
Crati (river)	F 5
Dolomite Alps (range)	C 1
Dora Baltea (river)	A 2
Dora Riparia (river)	A 2
Egadi (isls.)	C 6
Elba (isl.)	C 3
Etna (volcano)	E 6
Favignana (isl.)	C 6
Filicudi (isl.)	E 5
Frejus (pass)	A 2
Gaeta (gulf)	D 4
Garda (lake)	C 2
Gennargentu (mts.)	B 5
Genoa (gulf)	B 2
Giannutri (isl.)	C 3
Giglio (isl.)	C 3
Gorgona (isl.)	B 3
Graian Alps (range)	A 2
Gran Paradiso (mt.)	A 2
Great Saint Bernard (pass)	A 2
Ionian (sea)	F 6
Ischia (isl.)	D 4
Iseo (lake)	C 2
Julian Alps (range)	D 1
Lampedusa (isl.)	D 7
Lepontine Alps (range)	B 1
Levanzo (isl.)	B 5
Licosa (cape)	E 4
Ligurian (sea)	B 3
Linosa (isl.)	D 7
Lipari (isls.)	E 5
Maggiore (lake)	B 1
Malta (channel)	E 6
Mannu (river)	B 5
Marettimo (isl.)	C 6
Maritime Alps (range)	A 2
Marmolada (mt.)	C 1
Mediterranean (sea)	C 6
Messina (strait)	E 6
Metauro (river)	D 3
Mincio (river)	C 2
Mont Cenis (tunnel)	A 2
Montecristo (isl.)	C 3
Ogliastro (river)	C 3
Ombrone (river)	C 3
Orosei (gulf)	B 4
Ortles (range)	C 1
Otranto (strait)	G 4
Ötztal Alps (range)	C 1
Panarea (isl.)	E 5
Panaro (river)	C 2
Pantelleria (isl.)	C 7
Passero (cape)	E 6
Pelagie (isls.)	D 7
Pennine Alps (range)	A 2
Pescara (river)	D 3
Pianosa (isl.)	C 3
Piave (river)	D 2
Po (river)	D 2
Policastro (gulf)	E 5
Pompeii (ruins)	E 4
Pontine (isls.)	D 4
Ponza (isl.)	D 4
Presanella (mt.)	C 1
Rosa (mt.)	A 1
Salerno (gulf)	E 4
Salina (isl.)	E 5
Salso (river)	D 6
Sangro (river)	E 4
San Pietro (isl.)	B 5
Santa Maria di Leuca (cape)	G 5
Sant'Antioco (isl.)	B 5
Sant'Eufemia (gulf)	F 5
San Vito (cape)	D 5
Sardinia (island)	B 4
Sicily (island)	E 6
Sicily (strait)	E 6
Simeto (river)	E 6
Spartivento (cape)	F 6
Spartivento (cape)	B 7
Splügen (pass)	B 1
Squillace (gulf)	F 5
Stromboli (isl.)	E 5
Tagliamento (river)	D 2
Tanaro (river)	B 2
Taranto (gulf)	F 5
Testa (cape)	B 4
Testa del Gargano (cape)	F 4
Teulada (cape)	B 5
Tiber (river)	D 3
Tirso (river)	B 4
Trasimeno (lake)	C 3
Trebbia (river)	B 2
Tremiti (isls.)	E 3
Trieste (gulf)	D 2
Tuscan (arch.)	B 3
Tyrrhenian (sea)	C 4
Ustica (isl.)	D 5
Varano (lake)	E 3
Vaticano (cape)	E 5
Venice (gulf)	D 2
Ventotene (isl.)	D 4
Vesuvius (volcano)	E 4
Viso (mt.)	A 2
Volturno (river)	E 4
Vulcano (isl.)	E 5

SAN MARINO

San Marino	D 3

VATICAN CITY

Vatican City	B 6

than 35 percent of the total national output of electrical energy. In the early 1970's more than 41,000,000,000 kw hours of hydroelectric power were produced annually.

THE PEOPLE

The Italian population, which consists almost entirely of native-born persons, belongs to the ethnic grouping known as the Caucasian race (q.v.). The country is largely urban in the north and rural in the south. In recent years the population has generally migrated from rural to urban areas. The overwhelming majority of the people speak Italian, one of the Indo-European family of languages; see ITALIAN LANGUAGE.

Population. The population of Italy (census 1971) was 54,025,211. The United Nations estimated the overall population density at about 463 persons per sq.mi. in 1970.

Political Divisions. Administratively, Italy is divided into twenty regions, each of which is subdivided into provinces, with a provincial capital, and communes.

REGIONS OF ITALY

Region	Area (sq. mi.)	Population (1961)	Chief Town or City
Abruzzi	4170	1,206,266	Aquila
Aosta	1259	99,754	Aosta
Apulia	7470	3,409,687	Bari
Basilicata	3856	648,085	Potenza
Calabria	5823	2,045,215	Reggio di Calabria
Campania	5249	4,756,094	Naples
Emilia-Romagna	8543	3,646,507	Bologna
Friuli-Venezia Giulia	2948	1,205,222	Udine
Latium	6628	3,922,783	Rome
Liguria	2099	1,717,630	Genoa
Lombardy	9191	7,390,492	Milan
Marche	3743	1,347,234	Ancona
Molise	1785	358,052	Campobasso
Piedmont	9804	3,889,962	Turin
Sardinia	9301	1,413,289	Cagliari
Sicily	9926	4,711,783	Palermo
Trentino-Alto Adige	5256	785,491	Trento
Tuscany	8876	3,267,374	Florence
Umbria	3282	788,546	Perugia
Venetia	7095	3,833,837	Venice
Total	116,230	50,463,762	

A great degree of local autonomy, granted by the constitution of 1947, prevails in five of these regions—Sicily, Sardinia, Aosta, Trentino–Alto Adige, and Friuli–Venezia Giulia.

Principal Cities. Rome, capital and largest city (pop., 1971 est., 2,778,872), is also a cultural center and is the site of Vatican City, autonomous administrative center of the Roman Catholic Church. Other cities with populations of more than 300,000 in 1970 include Milan (about 1,707,576), the most important industrial and commercial city in Italy; Naples (1,277,438), the second-largest port in Italy; Turin (1,183,864), transportation junction and second-largest industrial city in Italy; Genoa (841,978), the leading port in Italy and a major trade and commercial center; Palermo (661,477), capital and chief seaport of Sicily; Bologna (493,070), a major transportation center and agricultural market; Florence (460,944), a cultural, commercial, transportation, and industrial center; Catania (414,619), a manufacturing and commercial city of Sicily; Venice (367,528), a leading seaport and a cultural and manufacturing center; and Bari (356,250), a major commercial city.

Religion. The official religion of Italy is Roman Catholicism, the faith of about 99 percent of the people. Roman Catholic religious instruction is part of the curriculum of all primary and secondary schools. The Italian constitution guarantees complete freedom of worship to the religious minorities, which are primarily Protestant, Greek Orthodox, and Jewish.

Education. The Italian impact on European education dates back to the ancient Roman educators and scholars, outstanding among whom were Marcus Tullius Cicero, Quintilian, and Lucius Annaeus Seneca (qq.v.). Later, during the Middle Ages, Italian universities became the model for those of other countries. During the Renaissance, Italy was the teacher of the liberal arts to virtually all of Europe, especially for Greek language and literature. The educational influence of Italy continued through the 17th century, when its universities and academies were continental centers of teaching and research in the sciences. After a decline during the 18th and 19th centuries, Italian education regained international notice in the 20th century as a result of the method of Maria Montessori (q.v.) for teaching young children.

The modern educational system of Italy dates from 1859, when a law was enacted providing for a complete school system that extended from the elementary through the university levels. Improvements were introduced in the 19th century. In 1923 the philosopher Giovanni Gentile (1875-1944), minister of public instruction under the dictator Benito Mussolini (q.v.), promoted complete governmental control of education, and the control was reinforced by the School Charter of 1939. With the collapse of fascism (q.v.) in 1944, however, Italy undertook to organize the school system along democratic lines. The constitution of 1947 and later laws raised the general educational level and encouraged experimentation, such as televised adult education (*telescuola*), which attracted international notice.

Traditionally, the goal of the Italian educational system has been a well-trained minority

ITALY

rather than a widely educated majority. Children aged three to five may attend kindergarten. Education is free and compulsory for all children aged six to fourteen. The compulsory term includes five years of elementary and three years of secondary education. The required part of secondary education is taken in an intermediate school of general studies. This period may be followed by study in a higher secondary school to gain specialized training or to prepare for university.

ELEMENTARY AND SECONDARY SCHOOLS. In the early 1970's about 60,000 elementary schools with some 270,000 teachers were giving instruction to about 6,400,000 pupils. About 2,100,000 students were enrolled in about 9000 junior secondary, or intermediate, schools.

SPECIALIZED SCHOOLS. Higher secondary studies leading to university entrance may be taken in classical, scientific, teacher-training, technical, or business schools. A postintermediate student may also enter an art institute or conservatory of music. Areas of specialized training include industry, navigation, and agriculture.

UNIVERSITIES AND COLLEGES. Much attention is given higher education in Italy. During the last quarter of the 19th century, the gain in Italian university graduates was about seven times the corresponding rate of increase of the Italian population. Matriculation for all forty-two Italian universities and higher institutes in the early 1970's averaged over 679,000 students annually. Six Italian universities were founded in the 13th century and five in the 14th century. The oldest is the University of Bologna, dating from 1200. Other notable institutions are those of Padua, Pisa, Siena, Perugia, and Rome.

Culture. From antiquity to modern times Italy has played a central role in world culture. Italians have contributed some of the world's most admired sculpture, architecture, painting, literature, and music, particularly opera. Although the

The narrow stone-paved streets are thoroughfares for people and livestock in villages such as this one in Cosenza Province.
United Nations

"Trulli" houses, distinguished by conical stone roofs, are traditional in the southeastern region of Apulia.
United Nations

nation was politically unified about a century ago, the Italians do not consider themselves to be a "new" people, but see themselves instead as the direct descendants of the ancient Romans. Moreover, regional differences persist because of natural geographical boundaries and the disparate cultural heritage that has come down from the Greeks, Etruscans, Arabs, Normans, and Lombards. Regional particularism is evidenced in persistent local dialects, holidays, festivals, songs, and regional cuisine. Central to all Italian life is the tradition of the family as a guiding force and focus of loyalty.

See ARCHITECTURE: *History: Greece and Rome*; DRAMA: *Roman Drama: National Drama: Italy*; ITALIAN ART AND ARCHITECTURE; ITALIAN LITERATURE; ITALIAN MUSIC; MOTION PICTURES, HISTORY OF: *The 1960's*; ROMAN ARCHITECTURE; ROMANESQUE ART AND ARCHITECTURE.

LIBRARIES AND MUSEUMS. Italy is rich in important library collections. Among the largest and most valuable libraries are the national libraries in Florence, Palermo, and Rome. Smaller collections, rich in local manuscripts and incunabula (q.v.), are found in most Italian cities.

World-famous art collections are housed in numerous Italian cities. Among the most important art museums are the Uffizi Gallery and Medici Chapel in Florence, the National Museum in Naples, and, in Rome, the Villa Giulia Museum, the Galleria Borghese, and the National Museum of Rome. Vatican City has important art collections in its museums and chapels, the most famous of which is the Sistine Chapel (q.v.). An international biennial exhibition of visual arts sponsored by the *Biennale di Venezia* is world renowned.

ARCHEOLOGY. See ETRURIA; POMPEII; see also articles on Rome and other Italian cities.

THE ECONOMY

A largely agricultural country before World War II, by the late 1960's Italy had developed a thriving industrial plant in the N. which contributed heavily to a flourishing and balanced economy. Between 1955 and 1965 the gross national product expanded by nearly 10 percent annually, one of the highest rates of increase in the world. Italy has essentially a private-enterprise economy, although the government has a controlling interest in a number of large commercial and business enterprises, such as the oil industry through the Italian state petroleum company. Also, the state owns the transportation and telecommunication systems. Budget figures for 1971 showed about $19,700,000,000 in revenue with about $24,000,000,000 in expenditures.

Agriculture. About one third of the land area of Italy is devoted to agriculture, which engages about 25 percent of the employed population. Variations of climate, soil, and altitude favor the cultivation of all European crops. Italy leads the world in the production of grapes. In the early 1970's annual wine production was nearly 1,500,000,000 gal., about 23 percent of world production. See WINE: *Foreign Wines: Italian Wines*. The output of olive oil, about 350,000 tons annually, usually ranks first or second in

ITALY

the world. In the early 1970's the chief field crops, with approximate annual production figures in tons, included wheat (9,600,000), potatoes (3,700,000), oats (486,000), sugar beets (9,000,000), corn (4,700,000), and rice (819,000). Other field crops are barley, rye, tomatoes, beans, tobacco, and hemp. Orchard crops, prominent in the Italian economy, include olives, apples, oranges, figs, dates, pomegranates, and nuts. Dairy farming is a major Italian industry. About fifty kinds of cheese are produced, the most notable being Gorgonzola, pecorino, and Parmesan. The livestock population in the early 1970's numbered about 9,600,000 cattle, 917,000 sheep and goats, 9,200,000 hogs, 485,000 horses and mules, and 295,000 donkeys.

Forest and Fishing Industries. The forestry industry is limited in Italy. Neither forestry nor fishing production meets domestic demand.

Mining. Mining comprises only 1 percent of the gross national product; however, production of available minerals is sizable. In the early 1970's annual production of economic significance included, in tons, petroleum (1,400,000); pyrites (1,500,000); lignite (1,400,000); marble (1,000,000); iron ores (755,000); sulfur (355,000); coal and similar fuels (2,235,000); zinc (244,000); and bauxite (224,000).

Manufacturing. Since World War II Italian industry has expanded rapidly, and production more than doubled between 1955 and 1965. In the early 1970's the annual production of the textile industry, the largest and most important Italian industry, included cotton yarn (about 194,000 tons); rayon and acetate (83,000); and wool yarn (59,700). Annual production of the chemical industry, which is also important to the national economy, included sulfuric acid (about 5,300,000 tons), superphosphate (1,400,000), and ammonia (1,600,000). Among other major Italian industries are the manufacture of automobiles, rubber, heavy machinery, electrical ware, and foodstuffs, particularly macaroni; shipbuilding, the processing of hemp and tobacco, and sugar refining are also important.

Currency and Banking. The unit of currency is the lira, consisting of 100 centesimi (586.51 liras equal U.S.$1; 1972). The Bank of Italy is the only bank of issue and exercises control over credit. It is a public institution and has branches in each provincial capital. Italy has 6 chartered banks, 3 banks of national interest, 188 incorporated banks, 6 cooperative banks, and 787 agricultural banks.

Commerce and Trade. Increased trade between Italy and the other countries of the European Economic Community (q.v.) characterized the late 1960's. The dependence of Italy upon the importation of coal, petroleum, and other essential raw materials creates an unfavorable balance of trade. This imbalance is partially offset by the expenditures of tourists, remittances from Italian nationals in foreign lands, and shipping revenues. In the early 1970's exports were valued at more than $13,200,000,000 and imports at about $14,940,000,000 annually. Remittances from Italians in other countries totaled about $440,000,000 annually in the same period. Exports include vegetables and fruits, automobiles, heavy machinery, and clothing; imports consist mainly of crude oil, coal, wool, cotton, foodstuffs, machinery, and chemicals.

The bulk of Italian export trade is with the countries of the European Economic Community (q.v.), and with the United States, Canada, and Great Britain. In order of importance, the leading sources of Italian imports are West Germany, France, the U.S., Great Britain, and the Netherlands.

Transportation. In the early 1970's the gross tonnage of the Italian merchant marine totaled about 7,600,000. Italy had about 12,600 mi. of railroad lines. About 80 percent of these lines, which included more than 5100 mi. under electrification, were owned and operated by the state. Highways totaled about 177,000 mi., including about 26,500 mi. of state roads. The longest automobile tunnel in the world, the Mont Blanc Tunnel linking Italy and France, was opened in 1965. Several airlines provide Italy with both domestic and international service.

Communications. Some 70 daily newspapers are published in Italy, with a combined daily circulation of about 2,570,000. In the early 1970's some 11,700,000 radios and 10,300,000 television sets were in use; telephones numbered about 10,300,000.

Labor. Of the total labor force of about 19,500,000 in the early 1970's over 8,000,000 belonged to four major trade union federations: the Communist-dominated Confederazione Generale Italiana del Lavoro, or C.G.I.L. (over 3,500,000 members); the Catholic-oriented Confederazione Italiana Sindacati Lavoratori, or C.I.S.L. (about 2,500,000); the Unione Italiano del Lavoro, or U.I.L. (500,000); and Confederazione Italiana Sindacati Nazionali dei Lavoratori, or C.I.S.N.A.L. (76,000). The C.G.I.L. is controlled by the Communist Party and the C.I.S.L. is closely connected to the Christian Democratic Party. Labor-union contracts set wages and salaries in every major field.

GOVERNMENT

Italy has been a democratic republic since June

Industry and agriculture in Italy. Above, left: Modern machinery and materials, largely manufactured in Italy, are used in the construction of an apartment building in the capital. Above, right: Dock workers in the port city of Genoa prepare bales of fabric for hoisting aboard ship and export to nations of the European Common Market. Right: Farm workers in southern Italy take their midday meal in the open fields. United Nations

ITALY

2, 1946, when the monarchy was abolished by popular referendum. By the terms of the constitution that was made effective in January, 1948, the reestablishment of the Fascist Party (see FASCISM) is prohibited; direct male heirs of the House of Savoy (see SAVOY, HOUSE OF) are ineligible to vote or hold any public office and are, in fact, banished from Italian soil; and official recognition is no longer accorded to titles of nobility, although titles in existence prior to Oct. 28, 1922, may be used as part of the bearer's name.

Central Government. The president of the republic is elected for a seven-year term in a joint session of parliament augmented by three delegates from each of the twenty regional councils except the Aosta, which sends one. The president, who must be at least fifty years old, is ordinarily elected by a two-thirds majority. The president has the right to dissolve the Senate and Chamber of Deputies at any time except during the last six months of his tenure. The president, the prime minister chosen by the president, and the cabinet chosen by the prime minister comprise the executive branch.

HEALTH AND WELFARE. National health insurance in the mid-1960's aided some 28,000,000 Italians annually at a cost of about $1,250,000. Italy, however, has a shortage of medical personnel and of hospitals, particularly in rural areas. Social-welfare insurance, funded largely by employers, is extended to the infirm and the aged, as well as to persons pensioned by the state, to small farmers, unemployed agricultural workers, and apprentices.

Legislature. The Italian parliament consists of a Senate and Chamber of Deputies elected by popular suffrage for terms of six and five years respectively. The Senate had 322 members in 1970 elected on a regional basis as well as a number of life members; the latter comprise past presidents and their honorary nominees (each president is entitled to make five such Senate appointments). The Chamber of Deputies consisted of 630 members; each member of the Chamber is required to be at least twenty-five years of age.

Political Parties. Italy has eight major political parties and a number of minor ones. The Partito Democrazia Cristiana (Christian Democratic Party) has been the core of all postwar governments. It represents a wide range of views, which sometimes results in internal dissension. The Partito Communista Italiano (Communist Party of Italy), one of the largest Communist parties in Western Europe, has advocated most of the policies of the Soviet Union in foreign affairs and reform of the state in domestic affairs.

The Italian Unified Socialist Party was formed from the merger in November, 1966, of the Italian Socialist Party and the Italian Social Democratic Party. The reunified party is a member of the Socialist International, and its ideological position is close to that of other European Social Democratic parties. The Liberal Party of Italy, founded in 1848, is anticlerical, right of center, and strongly supports the North Atlantic Treaty Organization (q.v.). The Italian Social Movement, on the extreme right, is imbued with the traditions of fascism and the memory of Mussolini. The Italian Proletarian Socialist Party was formed when it broke away from the Socialist Party in 1964. The Italian Democratic Party of Monarchical Unity is a rightist group formed in 1959 by the unification of two monarchist parties. The Republican Party of Italy is a small, left-center party with a tradition going back to the 19th-century struggle to unite Italy.

Local Government. The Italian state is highly centralized. The chief executive of each of the ninety-two provinces, the prefect, is appointed by, and answerable to, the central government. An elected council and a provincial executive committee administer each province. The constitution provides for twenty autonomous regions with limited governing powers. Five special regions were to have their own parliaments and governments, coordinated with the national government. By the late 1960's these five, Sardinia, Sicily, Trentino-Alto Adige, Aosta (formerly Valle d'Aosta), and Friuli-Venezia Giulia, had been established. Elections in 1970 established legislatures and governments for the fifteen ordinary autonomous regions. Every part of Italy forms a portion of a commune, the basic unit of local government, which may range in size from a small village to a large city like Naples. Each commune is governed by a communal council elected for a four-year term by universal suffrage. A mayor and a group of aldermen, elected by the council, administer the commune.

Judiciary. Italy has a Court of Cassation, which is the highest court of appeal in all cases except those concerning the constitution. A constitutional court, analogous in function to the Supreme Court of the United States (q.v.), is composed of fifteen judges, five of whom are appointed by the president of the republic, five by the Senate and Chamber of Deputies jointly, and five by the supreme law courts. The administration of justice is divided among 23 appeal court districts, subdivided into 159 tribunal districts, and these into 899 *mandamenti* (local courts).

Defense. The armed forces of Italy have been greatly expanded since the country joined the North Atlantic Treaty Organization in 1947. In the early 1970's the Italian permanent armed forces totaled about 425,500 men. Compulsory military service extends for fifteen months in the army and air force and twenty-four months in the navy.

HISTORY

For the history of Italy to the 5th century A.D., see ROME, HISTORY OF. For additional data on the development of modern Italy see ETRURIA; FLORENCE; GENOA; LOMBARDY; MILAN; NAPLES; PAPAL STATES; SAVOY; SICILY; TUSCANY; VENICE.

The Early Middle Ages. In 476 the last independent Roman emperor of the West, Romulus Augustulus (q.v.), was dethroned by the invading Germanic chieftain Odoacer (434?–493), who thereupon succeeded to the throne. In 488 Theodoric (q.v.), King of the Ostrogoths (see GOTHS), invaded Italy, and, after defeating and slaying Odoacer, became the sole ruler in Italy. Theodoric ruled until his death in 526. At that time Justinian I (q.v.), Emperor of the Eastern Roman Empire (see BYZANTINE EMPIRE), dispatched his two great generals Belisarius (q.v.) and Narses (478?–573?) to expel the Germanic invaders from Italy. A fierce war ensued, ending in 552 with the death of Teias, the last of the Gothic kings. The Byzantine rule was of short duration, however, for in 568 Italy was invaded by the Lombards (q.v.), another Germanic tribe. Alboin (q.v.), King of the Lombards, made Pavia the capital of his realm, and from that city launched a series of campaigns which presently deprived the Byzantine power in Italy of everything except the southern portion of the province and the exarchate of Ravenna in the north.

After the death of Alboin in 572, the Lombards for a time had no king. Separate bands thereupon united under regional leaders known as *duces*. The Lombards, like the Goths before them, espoused the heretical creed called Arianism (see ARIUS), with the result that they were in perpetual religious conflict with the native Italians, who overwhelmingly supported orthodox Christianity. This conflict was intensified as the temporal power of the popes increased. At length, Agiluf, a new Lombard king, was converted to orthodox Christianity, and for some time comparative harmony prevailed. To consolidate their political power, however, the Lombards began to encroach on papal territory, even threatening Rome, the center of church authority. In 754 Pope Stephen II (see under STEPHEN) summoned help from the Franks (q.v.), who had accepted the spiritual authority of the Church a century earlier. Under the vigorous leadership of Pepin the Short (see under PEPIN) and his son Charlemagne (q.v.), the Franks conquered the Lombards, deposing the last Lombard king in 774. On Christmas Day, 800, Charlemagne was crowned Emperor of the West by Pope Leo III (see under LEO).

When, in the 9th century, the Saracens (q.v.) subdued Sicily and threatened Rome, Pope Leo IV called to his aid Louis II, King of France (see under LOUIS), Charlemagne's great-grandson, who checked the progress of the invaders. The Muslims overran southern Italy after the death of Louis, and compelled the popes to pay tribute. For many years thereafter, the history of Italy is the record of the rise and fall of successive petty kings. Chief among these rulers were Guy of Spoleto (d. 894), Berengar I, Marquis of Friuli (d. 924), and Hugh of Provence (d. 947). The period of anarchy ended in 962, when the Germanic leader, Otto I (see under OTTO), after obtaining possession of northern Italy and the Lombard crown, was crowned emperor by Pope John XII (see under JOHN). This event marked the establishment of both the Holy Roman Empire (q.v.) and the German nation; see GERMANY: *History*.

The Papacy versus the Holy Roman Empire. Until the close of the Middle Ages the Holy Roman emperors claimed and, in varying degrees, exercised sovereignty over Italy, but for practical purposes imperial authority became completely nominal by the beginning of the 14th century. Meanwhile, the south of Italy had remained under Byzantine and Lombard sway. In the 11th century, however, the Normans (see NORSEMEN) broke the Byzantine power and expelled the Lombards. The Normans united their territorial conquests in Italy, in 1127, with Sicily, which they had wrested from the Saracens. These developments coincided with a resurgence of papal power, long secondary to that of the emperors. Imperial and papal friction reached a peak in the great investiture struggle. By the famous Concordat of Worms, negotiated in 1122, the emperor surrendered to the college of cardinals the right to elect the pope. Simultaneous with the increasing influence of the papacy, strong opposition to the continued rule of the Holy Roman emperors appeared in the form of the rising Italian city-states. In Italy the feudal system had never attained the high degree of development which was characteristic of France and Germany; see FEUDALISM. The relative weakness of Italian feudalism was due in great part to the survival of Roman traditions and to the large number of cities in Italy, for feudalism was a

ITALY

A view of the prosperous and powerful city of Venice in 1338 (from an illustrated manuscript). Bettmann Archive

rural rather than an urban phenomenon. The northern cities in particular defied the power of Frederick I (q.v.), Holy Roman Emperor, called Frederick Barbarossa, who fought fierce but inconclusive wars with them. At length the Lombard League (q.v.), an alliance of Italian cities, was formed in 1167; Frederick was vanquished at Legnano in 1176, and in 1183, with the signing of the Peace of Constance, the cities of northern Italy secured virtual autonomy. A final and unsuccessful attempt to crush both the papacy and its allies was made by Frederick II (q.v.), the last great ruler of the royal house of Hohenstaufen (q.v.). Italy itself was divided by the struggles between imperial partisans and their opponents. These factions were known respectively as Guelphs and Ghibellines (q.v.), names which continued to be the designations of fiercely contending parties long after the Holy Roman emperors had lost their hold upon the country.

Meanwhile, in 1266 southern Italy and Sicily came under the domination of the French house of Anjou. In 1282, however, Sicily threw off the French yoke and placed itself under the power of Aragón; see SICILIAN VESPERS.

The Rise of the City-States. Through commerce, some of the northern Italian cities had meanwhile grown wealthy and had established oligarchical governments which were tending to become democratic. The prosperous merchants of these cities, having secured their independence from the authority of the Holy Roman emperors, soon began to contest the authority of their powerful nobles. Gradually these nobles were divested of their power and compelled to abandon their extensive land holdings. Venice, by its participation in the Fourth Crusade (see CRUSADES), had secured extensive possessions in the Byzantine East. Pisa, Genoa, Milan, and Florence had likewise become powerful. A bitter struggle for ascendancy soon developed between Genoa and Venice. The conflict ended with a Venetian victory toward the close of the 14th century.

In every city of northern and central Italy the population had long been divided into Guelphs and Ghibellines. The former party was substantially progressive in character, the latter conservative. Civil strife was almost incessant, and the triumph of one party frequently resulted in the banishment of members of the other. On occasion, the banished party sought to regain power with the aid of other cities, so that city often warred against city, producing throughout the late Middle Ages a shifting succession of alliances, conquests, and temporary truces. This turbulence was highly disadvantageous to commerce and industry, the chief interests of the northern cities. In consequence, the office of *podestà,* or chief magistrate, was established to mediate the differences of the contending parties. It proved ineffective, however, and the *podestà* came in time to be primarily a judicial officer. His place as head of the city was taken by "a captain of the people", representing the dominant party. As military accomplishment was a requisite in this position, it was usually held by a noble. The people, longing for peace, acquiesced in the establishment of centralized authority. Thus, almost every city came to have its despot, or absolute ruler; the office in many cases became hereditary in some noble families, such as the Scala at Verona, the Este at Ferrara (q.v.), the Malatesta at Rimini, and the Visconti and later the Sforza (q.v.) at Milan. Under the rule of the despots wealth increased, life became more luxurious, and literature and the arts flourished. Gradually the smaller cities passed under the influence of the larger ones.

Period of Prosperity. By the middle of the 15th century Italy had achieved great prosperity and comparative tranquility. The country stood in the forefront of European nations culturally, having pioneered the great revival of learning and the arts; *see* RENAISSANCE. Preeminent in this revival was Tuscany, which had produced the great religious poet Dante Alighieri and the painter and sculptor Giotto (qq.v.). Near the end of the 15th century Italy became the object of a succession of aggressive wars, waged by France, Spain, and Austria, which culminated in the ascendancy of the Spanish and Austrian Hapsburgs; *see* HAPSBURG. In 1494 Charles VIII, King of France (*see under* CHARLES) undertook to conquer the Kingdom of Naples, then under the rule of the house of Aragón. Charles was induced to conduct this campaign by the Milanese regent Ludovico Sforza, and by the citizens

An estate of the Medici at Caffagiolo, near Florence, as depicted at the end of the 15th century. Bettmann Archive

ITALY

of Florence, who were restive under the tyranny of the Medici (q.v.) family. He invaded Italy, occupied Naples, and concluded a treaty with Florence, by the terms of which the Medici were expelled and the pope was brought to submission. In consequence, however, of a league formed against him by Spain, the pope, Maximilian I (q.v.), Holy Roman Emperor, and the Italian cities of Venice and Milan, Charles was forced to retire from Naples and fight his way out of Italy. This French invasion, although it produced no great political results, was highly important as one of the means by which Italian culture was disseminated throughout Europe.

Period of Decline. In 1499 Louis XII (q.v.), the successor of Charles VIII, subjugated Milan,

The Grand Canal, principal waterway of Venice, which divides the city into two nearly equal sections. Below: The Palazzo Vecchio, built in the 14th century as the seat of government of Florence. The bell in the 308-ft. tower was once used to sound alarms.

Ruins of the Colosseum in Rome. The amphitheater, built in the year 80, is believed to have seated some 50,000 persons.

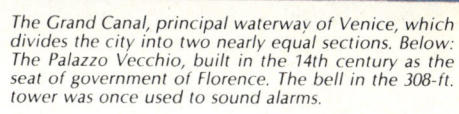

Italy. Plate 1.

Italy. Plate 2. *Above: View of the central range of the Apennines, in Macerata Province. The mountain chain forms the backbone of the Italian peninsula. Right: The picturesque mountainside town of Amalfi, on the Gulf of Salerno, a popular tourist resort.*

ITALY

which changed hands several times among the French and the Germans until 1535, when Charles V (q.v.), Holy Roman Emperor, incorporated it into his Spanish realm. In 1501 Ferdinand V (q.v.), King of Castile, reunited the Two Sicilies under one crown. The rivalry between Charles V and Francis I (q.v.), King of France, led to another French invasion of Italy. With the Florentines, Genoese, and Venetians as allies, the French were at first successful, but were finally defeated. In the Peace of Cambrai of 1529 Francis renounced all claims to territory in Italy. He later renewed the conflict with Charles V, but his domination over Italy could not be broken. On the extinction of the Sforza dynasty, in 1535, Charles V took possession of Milan, which became part of the Spanish realm. Naples remained for more than 200 years in the possession of the Spanish Hapsburgs. Of all the free cities of Italy only four survived, and of these four Genoa and the Republic of Venice alone remain noteworthy. Venice, in its last notable achievement as an independent city, conquered the Peloponnesus in 1684, but lost it in 1715. Thereafter, and until as late as the 19th century, Italy was at the mercy of foreign powers, and partitioned as suited their policy.

The Napoleonic Period. The Napoleonic Wars (q.v.) began in 1796 when Napoléon Bonaparte, later Napoleon I (q.v.), Emperor of France, invaded Italy. His victories over the imperial armies led, in 1797, to the Treaty of Campoformio by which the Cisalpine Republic (q.v) and the Ligurian Republic (see LIGURIA) were established, with their respective capitals at Milan and Genoa; see CAMPOFORMIO, TREATY OF. Venice and the bulk of its territory were given to Austria. Napoleon was crowned King of Italy at Milan in 1805. The following year he took possession of the Kingdom of Naples, which was given first to his brother Joseph Bonaparte (see under BONAPARTE), and after the latter acceded to the Spanish throne, to the French general Joachim Murat (q.v.). In 1810 Rome became part of the French Empire.

Napoleon's hold on Italy began to weaken following his defeat at Leipzig in 1813. The Austrians invaded northern Italy, and a British force occupied Genoa. The Congress of Vienna led to a restoration, with only slight modifications, of the situation prevailing in Italy before the Napoleonic Wars; see VIENNA, CONGRESS OF.

Risorgimento. The period succeeding the Napoleonic rule and extending to the final unification of Italy in 1870 was characterized by a growing movement for national unity and independence, which has been termed the *risorgimento*. Despite the suppressive measures of their despotic rulers, the Italian people maintained a network of secret societies, notably the Carbonari (q.v.), which agitated ceaselessly for the establishment of constitutional government. Risings in Naples and Piedmont were ruthlessly suppressed.

Napoléon Bonaparte negotiating the terms of the Treaty of Campoformio. Bettmann Archive

ITALY

The French Revolution of 1830, which drove the Bourbons (see BOURBON) from the throne of France, had strong repercussions in Italy. In 1831 insurrections took place in the Papal States (q.v.). A congress of representatives from the insurgent Papal States (except Rome and a few cities in the March of Ancona) met in Bologna and adopted a constitution establishing a republican form of government. Austria quickly intervened, suppressed the revolutionary movement in the papal dominions, and placed Bologna under stringent military surveillance.

Following the death of Charles Felix, King of Sardinia (1756–1831), the Sardinian crown passed to Charles Albert, Prince of Savoy and Piedmont (1798–1849). At this time the Italian patriot and scholar Giuseppe Mazzini (q.v.) issued an exhortation to the new king, who was known to hold more liberal views than others of his house, to become the leader and liberator of Italy. The king ignored the appeal, but nevertheless, as the movement toward Italian unification gathered impetus, more and more of its supporters looked to the Sardinian monarchy for the realization of their objective. It seemed to them clear that Austria, unrelenting in its reactionary policy, would have to be driven from the Italian peninsula by a power strong enough to assume the leadership in Italy. Mazzini himself abandoned reliance on royal leadership of the cause and founded the secret political society known as Young Italy to support the principles of the Carbonari.

The movement toward a national uprising was quickened by Pope Pius IX (see under PIUS), the first pope to be elected without the influence of Austria since the establishment of the Austrian hegemony over Italy. Immediately after his election, in 1846, he entered upon an extensive program of reforms in the Papal States. An amnesty was proclaimed for political offenders, political exiles were permitted to return, freedom of the press was introduced, the highest government offices were opened to laymen, and a council of notables was established to initiate new reforms. The pope's example was followed by a number of Italian princes. Broad reforms were introduced in Lucca, Tuscany, and, notably, in Piedmont, where a great advance was made toward constitutional government. Instead of allaying the revolutionary movement, however, these reforms served only to intensify it. In January, 1848, the people of Palermo rose and drove out the forces of Ferdinand II (q.v.), King of the Two Sicilies, who thereupon granted his Italian subjects a constitution and summoned a separate parliament for Sicily. At the same time Leopold II Grand Duke of Tuscany (1797–1870), issued a constitution for his duchy, and Pope Pius IX consented to a constitution for the Papal States (March, 1848), albeit unwillingly, because he had begun to regard the course of events with apprehension.

The outbreak of the Revolution of 1848 in Vienna, which drove the statesman Prince Klemens von Metternich (q.v.) from power, served as the signal for an uprising in Milan on March 18. The Austrian troops were driven from the city after a battle with the populace. On March 22 the Austrians were expelled from Venice, and on the following day a Venetian republic was proclaimed. The autocratic rulers of Parma and Modena were likewise forced to flee. In Piedmont sentiment ran high for a war to drive the Austrians completely from Italian soil. Charles Albert, after considerable hesitation, finally mobilized his army and marched to the assistance of Lombardy, which he entered on March 25, acclaimed as the liberator of Italy.

Italian nationalist hopes were checked when, in July, the Piedmontese were overwhelmingly defeated by the Austrians, who reentered Milan a few days later. An armistice concluded on Aug. 9 stipulated that Charles Albert was to evacuate Lombardy, Venetia, and the duchies of Parma and Modena. In spite of these reverses, the Sardinian king considered it his duty not to retire without attempting again to free the Lombards from Austrian domination. Accordingly, in March, 1849, the armistice was suspended. Charles Albert met the Austrians in battle at Novara, was badly defeated, and on March 28 abdicated the Sardinian throne in favor of his son, Victor Emmanuel II (see under VICTOR EMMANUEL).

GIUSEPPE GARIBALDI. Meanwhile, Pope Pius IX, who perceived that the revolutionary movement had exceeded his expectations in both scope and intensity, indicated his intention to rescind the benefits he had conferred upon the Papal States. Before he could act, an insurrection led by Mazzini drove him from Rome. The temporal power of the pontiff was abolished and Rome was proclaimed a republic. In April a French army was dispatched to suppress the Roman republic. Despite gallant Italian resistance led by the patriot Giuseppe Garibaldi (q.v.), the French occupied Rome in July, and papal authority was reestablished.

Victor Emmanuel II remained true to the cause of Italian independence. He adhered faithfully to the liberal constitution promulgated by his father, retained the tricolor flag, symbolic of free Italy, perpetuated freedom of

King Victor Emmanuel II of Sardinia and Giuseppe Garibaldi, both leaders of the 19th-century movement to liberate and unite the Italian peninsula, meeting at Teano, in southern Italy. Bettmann Archive

the press, and encouraged political refugees from the Italian mainland to make Sardinia their asylum. In 1852 Conte Camillo Benso di Cavour (q.v.) became the Sardinian prime minister. He led Sardinia into the Crimean War (q.v.) on the side of Great Britain and France and urged at the subsequent peace conference in 1856 the immediate consideration of Italy as a problem of international concern. In 1858 Cavour arranged an agreement with Napoleon III (q.v.), Emperor of France, providing for a joint declaration of war against Austria. The Franco-Italian coalition won the battles of Magenta and Solferino in 1859, but on the eve of complete victory Napoleon, through the influence of the Empress Eugénie (q.v.) and the clerical party in France, deserted the Italians and concluded the preliminary Treaty of Villafranca, in July, 1859, with the Austrians. In November, France, Austria, and Sardinia signed the Treaty of Zürich, by the terms of which Austria ceded all of Lombardy to France, which then transferred it to Sardinia. In a plebiscite held in March, 1860, the people of Romagna and the duchies of Parma and Modena voted for union with Sardinia. As the price of French assistance in the war against Austria, Napoleon exacted from Sardinia the regions of Savoy and Nice, which became part of France.

Palermo rose, in April, 1860, against Francis II, King of the Two Sicilies (*see under* FRANCIS). In May, Garibaldi headed an expedition from Genoa against Sicily. Sicily was taken after nearly three months of fighting, and then Garibaldi crossed to the Italian mainland in a move against Naples. Meeting with negligible resistance, he entered Naples on Sept. 7. Francis II fled after vainly attempting to save his throne by the grant of a constitution and the promise of sweeping reforms. The Sardinian government, while openly in sympathy with the Garibaldi mission, had carefully abstained from affording any pretext for the intervention of the European powers. This diplomatic neutrality was threatened, however, when Garibaldi, not content with the conquest of the Two Sicilies, prepared to invade the Papal States. Meanwhile, the Sicilies, Umbria, and the Marches voted in a plebiscite for union with Sardinia.

Kingdom of Italy. In February, 1861, the first Italian parliament was convened in Turin by Victor Emmanuel II, on whom the title King of Italy was formally conferred. The death of Cavour in June was a grave loss to the new Italian government. Soon thereafter Garibaldi went to Sicily to organize an expedition against Rome. In fear of French intervention, Victor Emmanuel issued a proclamation denouncing the action of Garibaldi as rebellious. Undeterred, the Sicilians enthusiastically rallied to the cause of Roman liberation. In 1862, the royal government dispatched a Sardinian force against Garibaldi's volunteers, who had landed in Calabria. The insurgents were met by the troops of Victor Emmanuel and compelled, after a brief en-

ITALY

gagement, to surrender. In 1866 Italy became the ally of Prussia in the Seven Weeks' War (q.v.) against Austria, by which the Italian kingdom acquired the territory of Venice. The following year Garibaldi headed a new expedition against the remaining parts of the Papal States, but was defeated by a French force at Mentana. At length, in 1870 French reverses in the Franco-German War (q.v.) forced Napoleon III to withdraw his troops from the last remnants of the papal dominions, known as Patrimony, and on Sept. 20, Italian forces triumphantly entered Rome. In October the Roman people declared overwhelmingly for union with the Italian kingdom. Rome became the capital of a united Italy on July 2, 1871.

In January, 1878, Victor Emmanuel died, and his eldest son, Humbert I (q.v.), succeeded to the Italian throne. Mounting labor disturbances, for the most part in the industrial cities of northern Italy, culminated on July 29, 1900, in the assassination of Humbert by an Italian anarchist. Humbert's son ascended the throne as Victor Emmanuel III. Meanwhile, prompted by the example of France and Great Britain, Italy launched its colonial empire. Early in 1885 an Italian expedition occupied a portion of eastern Africa, and five years later Italian African possessions were consolidated into the colony of Eritrea (q.v.). Encouraged by this success, the Italian premier Francesco Crispi (q.v.) laid ambitious plans for a vast colonial empire in Africa. In February, 1890, an Italian protectorate was established over the Somali coast south of British Somaliland; see SOMALIA: History. After unsuccessful attempts by two private companies to administer the territory, the Italian government assumed complete control in 1905. In September, 1911, following Turkey's rejection of an Italian ultimatum, Italian troops occupied and blockaded the Libyan coast; see LIBYA, UNITED KINGDOM OF: History. By the Treaty of Lausanne, which concluded in October, 1912, the ensuing Italo-Turkish war, Italy's possession of the Libyan coast was confirmed.

WORLD WAR I. Although Italy had been formally allied with both Germany and Austria-Hungary since 1882, the Italian government declared its neutrality on the outbreak of World War I in August, 1914. In the spring of 1915, however, after signing the secret Treaty of London with the Allied powers, Italy declared war on Austria and Turkey; war was not declared against Germany until more than a year later. The Italian role in World War I commenced with the occupation of the seaport town of Vlonë in southwest Albania. Italy then dispatched a large force into the Trentino region, in the southern Tirol. In 1916 the Austrians launched a series of attacks northeast of Trent and along the eastern bank of the Adige R., capturing the towns of Asiago and Asiero. Most of the lost territory was later regained by the Italian commander in chief Conte Luigi Cadorna (q.v.). Cadorna then mounted an offensive along the Isonzo R. in Venezia Giulia, capturing Gorizia on Aug. 9. The Italian armies made little progress thereafter. On Oct. 24, 1917, a combined Austrian and German force attacked, winning a speedy victory at Caporetto in Venezia Giulia. The Italian commander in chief withdrew from Gorizia and the Karst plateau, and by Oct. 20, Austria threatened the Italian line from the Julian Alps to the Adriatic Sea. General Armando Díaz (q.v.) replaced Cadorna as Italian commander in chief, and Allied divisions were dispatched to the Italian front. The Austrians began a general offensive along the Piave R. on June 15, 1918, and crossed to the opposite side, but were there repulsed. In July the Italians drove the Austrians from the Piave delta. American aviators serving with the Italian army were presently joined by the 332nd United States Infantry Regiment. The third Battle of the Piave opened on Oct. 24, leading rapidly to the collapse of Austrian resistance and the suspension of hostilities on Nov. 4. Italian casualties during World War I totaled 462,000. Following the general armistice concluded between the Allies and the Central Powers (q.v.) on Nov. 11, 1918, Italy and Yugoslavia signed the Treaty of Rapallo. A provision of this treaty established Fiume as a free state, connected with Italy by a territorial corridor along the Adriatic Sea. In August, 1920, Italy signed with Turkey the subsequently discredited Treaty of Sèvres, which granted the Italian government substantial concessions in Anatolia; see SÈVRES, TREATY OF. Italy became one of the charter members of the League of Nations (q.v.) in January of the same year.

THE RISE OF FASCISM. During most of 1920, 1921, and 1922 Italy was torn by bitter political strife. Armed bands, with a strongly nationalistic program, and known as Fascisti (see FASCISM) clashed repeatedly with the Communists (see COMMUNISM) in Rome, Bologna, Genoa, Trieste, Alessandria, and Parma. On Oct. 24, 1922, Benito Mussolini, leader of the fascist movement, demanded that the Italian government be turned over to the Fascist Party, threatening to seize power by force if his demands were refused. Three days later, as the black-shirted Fascisti mobilized for a march on Rome, the Italian premier Luigi Facta (1861–1930) resigned. Mussolini

ITALY

was summoned to the capital by King Victor Emmanuel III and given a free hand in the formation of a new government. In the ensuing years, the history of Italy was, to a large extent, identified with the career of Mussolini. Many reforms were instituted and the administration was strongly centralized. Following clashes with Greece and Yugoslavia, the Italian government negotiated a treaty with the latter country by which Fiume was ceded to Italy.

ITALY

The Fascist Dictatorship. Public indignation aroused by the murder of the Socialist deputy Giacomo Matteotti (1884-1924), allegedly by a fascist mob, and the widespread charges that the crime had been perpetrated with the complicity of the fascist government, provided Mussolini with a convenient pretext for suspending constitutional guarantees, ostensibly in the interests of law and order. The premier proceeded to consolidate his dictatorial power by forbidding the Italian parliament to initiate legislation; by making himself responsible to the king alone; by ordering parliament to authorize him to issue decrees having the force of law; by establishing absolute censorship of the press; by abolishing secret societies; and, in 1926, by suppressing all opposition parties. By the terms of an industrial law of 1926, thirteen syndicates or associations were recognized as having legal status. These syndicates were grouped into corporations, which included the employers and workers of the various industries. The same law prohibited strikes and lockouts.

In 1928 further measures were taken to transform the nation into a thoroughly fascist state. Supreme power was lodged in the Fascist Grand Council comprising the top leadership of the party, with the prime minister as chairman. The Grand Council was to select the list of candidates for the Chamber of Deputies and to be consulted on all important business of the government, especially the choice of an heir to the throne and successor to Mussolini. By another law of 1928 the exclusive right to nominate candidates for deputy was given to the national federations of employer and employee syndicates. In 1934 another step was taken in the reorganization of the economic life of Italy with the formation of twenty-two corporations, or guilds, representing workers and employers in all phases of the economy. Each corporation included Fascist Party members on its governing council and had Mussolini as its president. These councils were organized into a National Council of Corporations. Mussolini scored one of the greatest diplomatic triumphs of his career when, in 1929, he concluded the Lateran Treaty (q.v.) of reconciliation between the Italian state and the Holy See. This concordat settled the sixty-year-old controversy concerning the temporal power of the pope by the creation, at Rome, of Vatican City, a state in which the Holy See is the sole authority.

During the world economic depression, which began in 1929, the Fascist government increasingly intervened to prevent the collapse of normally sound industries. The construction of new factories or the expansion of old ones without governmental consent was prohibited. Near the end of 1933, Mussolini announced that the Italian Chamber of Deputies would be called upon to legislate itself out of existence and to transfer its functions to the National Council of Corporations. This step was finally taken in 1939. The Chamber of Deputies was replaced by a Chamber of Fasci and Corporations, composed of some 800 appointive members of the National Council of Corporations. In their respective industries the corporations were entrusted with regulating prices and wages, planning economic policies, and discharging other economic functions.

On the international scene, the appointment of Adolf Hitler (q.v.) as chancellor of Germany was greeted with enthusiasm by the controlled Italian press. Hitler in turn expressed sympathy and friendship for Italian Fascism. Meanwhile, Italy participated in the general disarmament conference of 1933, which, after months of discussion, came to nothing when on Oct. 14 Germany withdrew.

A temporary improvement in Franco-Italian relations resulted from German attempts to force the incorporation of Austria into the Third Reich of Germany in 1934. Mussolini rushed 75,000 Italian troops to the Italo-Austrian frontier, announcing that he would intervene if Germany took overt action. Italy drew even closer to her allies of World War I when, in April, 1935, the Italian government, with the governments of France and Great Britain, formed the *Stresa Front*, a bloc organized in protest against Germany's repeated violations of the Treaty of Versailles; *see* VERSAILLES, TREATY OF.

THE ETHIOPIAN CAMPAIGN. The event that upset European alignments and brought the fascist and National Socialist dictatorships into close accord was the invasion by Italy of Ethiopia on Oct. 3, 1935; *see* ETHIOPIA: *History*. Ethiopia, generally regarded as within the Italian sphere of influence, was bound to the fascist state by many commercial and diplomatic pacts. Italy, however, intent on acquiring an outlet for its excess population and gaining vital natural resources, sought every opportunity to integrate Ethiopia into the Italian colonial empire. The Italo-Ethiopian war was preceded by a Franco-Italian accord concluded in January, 1935, in which Italy agreed to support French opposition to German rearmament in exchange for French territorial concessions in French colonial Africa and a share in the ownership and management of the Djibouti-Addis Ababa railroad. In addition to the foregoing provisions, the agreement between the two countries contained a secret clause which subsequently gave rise to conflicting interpretations in Rome and Paris. Mussolini contended that Pierre Laval (q.v.), the French foreign minister, had given him a free hand to carry out his conquest of Ethiopia. Laval formally denied having made such a promise, although his reluctance in supporting the League of Nations in its efforts to stop Italy seemed to belie his words. Great Britain, regarding Italian aggressive expansion as a menace to British interests in Africa, vigorously opposed Mussolini's plan of outright seizure of Ethiopia.

The Italian invasion of Ethiopia began on Oct. 3, and four days later the Council of the League of Nations declared Italy guilty of violating its obligations under the League Covenant, and the decision was made to impose economic sanctions against the aggressor. The failure of the League of Nations to enforce these sanctions, particularly its refusal to impose an embargo on oil shipments to the fascist state, contributed largely to an Italian victory. On May 9, 1936, Mussolini formally annexed Ethiopia and proclaimed King Victor Emmanuel III emperor.

The fascist dictator's successful defiance of the League of Nations, and especially of Great Britain and France, gained for him and his party further popular favor within Italy. On June 1, an Italian decree incorporated Ethiopia with Eritrea and Italian Somaliland into a single colony, Italian East Africa. In October, after Germany had recognized the Italian conquest of Ethiopia in July, 1936, Hitler and Mussolini concluded an agreement providing for joint action in support of their common goals.

THE SPANISH CIVIL WAR. With the outbreak of Spanish Civil War new stresses upon the Italian economy resulted from the active espousal by Mussolini of the fascist insurgent cause of General Francisco Franco (q.v.); see SPAIN: *History*. Mussolini pursued this policy hoping to secure an economic and strategic foothold in the western Mediterranean and also of checkmating France and the Soviet Union, who had rendered some assistance to the Spanish loyalist, or prorepublican, forces. Italian troops played an important role at the battles of Malaga and Santander, the Italian air force participated in a number of Spanish engagements, and Italian submarines allegedly sank many neutral ships bound for loyalist ports with oil, food, and other supplies to the republican armies. On the Guadalajara front, however, Italian forces were routed by the Spanish loyalists in March, 1937. An official report placed Italian casualties at about 4000 killed and 15,000 wounded.

PARTNERS IN EXPANSION. By 1937, cooperation between Italy and Germany had begun to produce results. Although Italian influence in the Danubian and Balkan regions was progressively supplanted by that of Germany, Mussolini was compensated by German support of his expansionist policy in the Mediterranean area. Following Mussolini's visit to Germany in September, Italy announced its adherence to the Anti-Comintern Pact between Germany and Japan, and soon thereafter withdrew from the League of Nations. The first major result of Italian policy toward Germany was Mussolini's refusal to aid Austria, diplomatically or militarily, when that republic was absorbed by Germany in March, 1938. Meanwhile, the increasing influence of the racist doctrine of the Hitler regime upon fascist Italy found expression in a series of measures designed to curb the economic, political, and cultural activities of Italian Jews. These measures were presently supplemented by additional racist legislation, including a law that excluded all Jews from the civil and military administrations of the state and the Fascist Party. During the negotiations which led to the conclusion in September, 1938, of the Munich Pact (q.v.) and to the subsequent dismemberment of Czechoslovakia, Mussolini gave firm support to the demands put forth by Hitler. The two dictators signed a military assistance pact in May, 1939. This move followed the German seizure of Bohemia and Moravia, and the Italian annexation of Albania.

World War II (1939–45). At the outbreak of World War II in September, 1939, the Italian government took the position that it was under no obligation to aid Germany militarily because Hitler had rebuffed an Italian proposal for the arbitration of German-Polish differences. The Fascist government then removed a number of strongly pro-German ministers and high-ranking military officials from office. At the same time Italy attempted to regain its former trade connections with the Balkan countries, thus entering into some competition with Germany. German successes during the first year of the war led Mussolini to reverse his policy of nonbelligerence. In June, 1940, when France lay prostrate in defeat and Great Britain alone faced the powerful German armies, Italy entered the war and granted France an armistice.

In August, 1940, Italian forces in East Africa scored an important victory with the conquest of British Somaliland, and the following month fascist armies in Libya and Italian East Africa began a gigantic pincers movement designed to overwhelm the British defenses in Egypt. On

ITALY

Oct. 28, 1940, fascist forces in Albania invaded Greece, apparently to divert British naval and military forces from Egypt and to secure Italian air and sea bases on the Greek peninsula. The inadequately prepared invasion was completely frustrated by the Greeks, who drove the Italians from Greece and Albania. This debacle, followed by British naval and military victories in the Mediterranean area and in Egypt, rocked the Fascist regime in Italy to its foundations. Italian prestige was shattered throughout the world, and two decades of fascist diplomacy in the Balkans, the Middle East, and Africa were undone. To stave off total military collapse, Mussolini had to ask Hitler for aid. Thereafter, Italian policy in all fields fell increasingly under German control. Sweeping changes in the Fascist military hierarchy were instituted by Mussolini in an effort to restore morale and retrieve his government's damaged prestige. These replacements, following a succession of military reverses, only undermined confidence in both Mussolini and his regime. Rising political discontent among the Italian masses was spurred by a steady decline of living standards and by a general increase of economic difficulties caused, among other factors, by the Allied blockade and a poor wheat crop.

In 1941 Italy suffered successive military and naval disasters and growing economic privation. By November the Italian colonial empire in East Africa was completely liquidated. Anti-fascist sentiment spread among all sections of the Italian population, including the professional army officers, who held Mussolini and his associates responsible for Italy's military setbacks. The successful end of the Balkan campaign, as a result of German intervention, somewhat offset the fascist reverses, however. Italy acquired portions of the Dalmatian coast, almost all the islands off the Dalmatian Peninsula, the Kossovo-Mitoyan province of eastern Yugoslavia, six of the Cyclades Islands in the Aegean Sea, the island of Corfu, and a small district on the Greek mainland, adjoining the Albanian frontier. By arrangement with Germany, almost all of Greece, including Athens, was occupied by Italian troops. Many Italians soon realized that their territorial gains in the Balkans were largely illusory, because the Germans actually controlled these areas. Also, Italy was forced to pay an increasingly high price for Hitler's military assistance. Italian stocks of foodstuffs, raw materials, and other commodities began to run low, due in large part to heavy shipment to the Third Reich in return for German coal and oil. Italy declared war on the Soviet Union on June 22, 1941, on the day of the German invasion, and five weeks later the first Italian division was sent to the Soviet front. As difficulties developed in

Benito Mussolini, Adolf Hitler, and aides leave a conference in Munich, Germany, in September, 1938: (left to right) Hermann Göring, Mussolini, Hitler, Conte Galeazzo Ciano. Behind and slightly to the left of Hitler is Rudolf Hess.
Wide World

the German offensive against the Soviet Union, Hitler became more pressing in his demands upon Mussolini for further aid.

U.S. ENTRY INTO THE WAR. At the same time relations between the U.S. and Italy were rapidly approaching a showdown. In March the U.S. government had seized twenty-eight Italian merchant ships in American ports and arrested officers and seamen who sabotaged the machinery of the vessels on orders from the Italian naval attaché in Washington, D.C. The immediate recall of the attaché was demanded, whereupon Italy forced the recall of the U.S. military attaché in Rome. When Italian assets in the U.S. were impounded in June, the fascist government promptly took similar measures against American assets in Italy. Later in the same month all consular offices were ordered closed in both countries. The process of alienation was climaxed on Dec. 11, four days after Japan's surprise air attack upon Pearl Harbor, Hawaii, when Mussolini announced Italy's declaration of war against the U.S.

The military and political outlook for fascist Italy in 1942 was gloomy. In northern Africa, temporary Italo-German gains were liquidated by a vigorous British offensive which lifted the Axis siege of Tobruk in Libya and recaptured Benghazi; see AXIS POWERS. Axis forces, including several Italian divisions, suffered serious reverses in the Soviet Union. About 500,000 Italian troops occupying conquered Albania, Yugoslavia, and Greece suffered heavy losses from organized guerrilla bands; see GUERRILLAS. At home the Italian people endured a bitter winter with very short rations of food and fuel. Manufactured goods were scarce and of poor quality. War industries were handicapped by acute shortages of materials and manpower. Increasing German control of all phases of Italian life, corruption and inefficiency among fascist officials, and evasion of the rationing laws by the wealthy and influential contributed to the demoralization and unrest of the Italian people. In October the British Royal Air Force launched a series of bombing raids on the industrial cities of northern Italy, damaging a considerable portion of Italian war industry and causing heavy civilian casualties. Simultaneously, advancing British and American forces in northern Africa established bomber bases in Algeria and Cyrenaica from which the cities and military installations of southern Italy were attacked. Politically, the prestige of Mussolini and his regime continued to decline.

In February, 1943, Mussolini dismissed twelve of the most important members of his government and announced that he was assuming full responsibility for the management of political affairs and the conduct of military operations. With the collapse of Axis forces in Tunisia in May, Mussolini hastily strengthened the fascist militia and ordered the establishment of a council of defense to prepare for an expected Allied invasion of the Italian mainland. All efforts to reinvigorate the Fascist Party, bolster military defenses, and raise national morale were nullified, however, by the inexorable Allied air offensive.

INVASION OF ITALY. Following the capitulation of the strategic Italian island of Pantelleria in the Mediterranean, an emergency meeting of the fascist directorate was convoked at which Mussolini's disastrous conduct of the war was bluntly assailed. Then, on July 10, Allied forces invaded Sicily. Six days later, U.S. President Franklin Delano Roosevelt and British Prime Minister Sir Winston Churchill (qq.v.) addressed a joint radio message to the people of Italy urging their surrender to avoid greater devastation and warning that their continued toleration of the German-controlled fascist regime would have disastrous consequences. This admonition, although underscored by heavy Allied air raids on Naples, was scornfully rejected by the fascists in a radio broadcast to the Italian nation. The next day Allied planes dropped leaflets over Rome advising of a possible raid on military installations in the vicinity of the Italian capital but assuring that the utmost care would be taken to avoid destruction of residential buildings and cultural monuments. About 500 Allied bombers, mostly American, then devastatingly attacked the San Lorenzo and Littorio railroad freight yards, war factories, and the Ciampino airfield.

The bombing of Rome precipitated a large-scale exodus of the Roman population and brought the political crisis in Italy to a climax. During the raid on Rome Mussolini was at Verona conferring with Hitler on measures to meet the next phase of the Allied invasion of Italy. The Italian dictator acceded to a German plan for a gradual withdrawal from Sicily and from south and central Italy to a defense line extending through the southern limits of Tuscany. Rome was to be abandoned, the evacuated regions to be stripped of all food stores and rolling stock in order to force the invading Allies to feed and sustain the population. Upon Mussolini's return to Rome he was confronted with a demand for the convening of the Fascist Grand Council to consider the Italian military crisis. After a stormy debate the session concluded

ITALY

with a no-confidence vote of nineteen to five against Mussolini. It was thereupon decided to submit the German defense plan to the king. Victor Emmanuel flatly rejected the plan. He then ordered, on July 25, the resignation of Mussolini and his government and summoned Marshal Pietro Badoglio (q.v.) to form a new ministry. The ousted dictator and a number of his chief aides were arrested. The Badoglio cabinet decreed the dissolution of the Fascist Party, the Fascist Grand Council, and the special fascist tribunals for the defense of the state. The liquidation of all other fascist organizations and institutions followed.

ARMISTICE. The fall of Mussolini precipitated clamorous peace demonstrations throughout Italy. At the same time popular demands were made for the end of martial law, the restoration of constitutional government, and the punishment of fascist leaders. Meanwhile the Allies continued their advance in Sicily. Churchill offered Italy the choice of breaking off its alliance with Germany or suffering destruction; General Dwight David Eisenhower (q.v.), Allied commander in chief, promised the Italian people an honorable peace and a beneficent occupation if they ended their aid to the German war effort. The Badoglio government made two unsuccessful secret peace overtures to British officials early in August. Then, in mid-August, a fully authorized representative of Premier Badoglio arrived in Lisbon, Portugal, with an offer to join the Allies against Germany when the Allied invasion of the Italian mainland began. At the direction of President Roosevelt and Prime Minister Churchill, General Eisenhower dispatched American and British staff officers to negotiate with the Italian representative on the basis of Italy's unconditional surrender. The armistice was signed on Sept. 3, the same day the British Eighth Army began the invasion of southern Italy. The Italian capitulation was kept secret at General Eisenhower's insistence, and did not become effective until the Allied commander in chief personally broadcast the announcement five days later. The armistice was then confirmed by Premier Badoglio over the Rome radio.

The announcement of the armistice set off a furious race between the Allies and the Germans for possession of the territories, bases, arms and supplies, communications, and other war facilities formerly under Italian control. A large Anglo-American amphibious force landed on the beaches of Salerno just south of Naples, hoping to drive inland and trap the German units facing the British Eighth Army farther south. British forces began a drive up the eastern coast of the peninsula in coordination with other British units advancing from Calabria up the western coast. The Germans were prepared for the emergency and acted swiftly. They attacked and held the invasion force at Salerno until German units in southern Italy could retire. They also seized the cities and strategic centers of northern and central Italy, disarmed all Italian troops except those under pro-Nazi commanders, and rounded up thousands of suspected enemies among Italian officials and civilians. On Sept. 10 the Germans occupied Rome, from which King Victor Emmanuel III and Premier Badoglio had fled two days previously to Allied-held territory in the south of Italy. Complete German domination was also rapidly extended over Greece, Yugoslavia, and the Italian Aegean islands. The Allies were more successful in the race for control of the still powerful Italian fleet. In response to a message broadcast by Sir Andrew Browne Cunningham (q.v.), Allied naval commander in the Mediterranean, virtually all seaworthy Italian warships left their bases at La Spezia and other Italian-held ports to surrender to the Allies in accordance with the armistice terms.

Politically the Germans sought to retain the support of pro-fascist and anti-Allied Italians by announcing in September that a so-called Fascist National Government had been established in Italy in opposition to the Badoglio government, and was functioning in the name of Mussolini. The former Italian dictator had been rescued from prison by a surprise raid of German parachute troops, thus balking Badoglio's promise to deliver the deposed dictator to the Allies.

WAR ON GERMANY. In line with pledges made to the Allies and to the Italian people, Premier Badoglio declared war on Germany on Oct. 13 and undertook to reorganize his government on a broader and more democratic basis. During the latter part of October he sought to induce leaders of various anti-German political groups to enter his cabinet. He conferred with Count Carlo Sforza (q.v.), former Italian foreign minister, who had just returned to Italy after a voluntary exile of almost fifteen years, and with leaders of six political parties, disbanded by Mussolini, which had united to form a National Liberation Front. These liberal elements served notice that they would consent to form a representative government only if Victor Emmanuel abdicated. The king refused to comply with this condition, and Badoglio declined any part in the move to oust him. As a temporary solution, the premier in the following month organized a so-called technical government of nonparty experts to carry on administrative functions. Allied policy had been based upon the subordination of political questions until the Germans were expelled from all of Italy and until the whole Italian people could determine their form of government by democratic process, but the violence of the controversy between opponents and supporters of the king made the implementation of such a policy increasingly difficult. In November the Committee of National Liberation voted nonconfidence in the Badoglio government, and called upon Victor Emmanuel to abdicate. On Feb. 11, 1944, the Allied Advisory Council for Italy turned over control of Sardinia, Sicily, Salerno, Potenza, and Bari to the Italian royal government. Badoglio thereupon asked that Italy be received as an ally with full diplomatic relations. He also indicated that his administration would be broadened democratically after the liberation of Rome but that the king would not abdicate.

In April the king announced his decision to withdraw from public affairs and to appoint his son Humbert, later Humbert II, King of Italy (1904–), as lieutenant general of Italy, the appointment to become effective upon the entry of Allied troops into Rome. These developments cleared the way for a government representing the National Committee of Liberation. The advance toward national unity and democracy was followed by the liberation of Rome by Allied armies on June 4. Victor Emmanuel then transferred all royal authority to Humbert as lieutenant general of the realm (regent). The party leaders of the Committee of National Liberation unanimously refused to serve under Badoglio. On June 9 the premiership was given to the statesman and ex-Socialist Ivanoe Bonomi (1873–1951), who formed a coalition government. Count Sforza received one of the ministries without portfolio.

Because the new government was under Allied jurisdiction and control, its plans for broad domestic reforms and for vigorous participation in the war effort were largely nullified. American and British officials, fearful of internal developments that might impede the Allied war effort, vetoed or deferred all proposals for social and economic change. Allied authorities also looked with disfavor upon the Italian anti-fascist volunteers and resistance fighters, most of whom were extreme radicals. The new cabinet largely agreed on basic political issues. Middle-class liberals and proletarian radicals were united in the belief that the armistice terms should be modified and that Italy should be allowed to reshape itself into a self-governing democracy. Communists and Socialists, elsewhere bitter adversaries, unanimously advocated economic reform. Even Communists and Catholics found areas of agreement; a small group of enthusiastic fusionists even called themselves Catholic Communists.

WINTER OF 1944–45. The winter of 1944–45 was a period of intense suffering in Italy, particularly in the ravaged areas left in the wake of the retreating Germans. Throughout the central provinces were burned villages, idle or flooded fields, and ruined factories, railroads, power plants, and bridges. Two million acres of arable land were uncultivated. Prices of necessities rose prohibitively in an inflation aggravated by the Allied issue of invasion currency. As a result of the widespread misery among the Italian people, the Action and Socialist parties sharply criticized Premier Bonomi's leadership.

On Feb. 25, 1945, the Allied Control Council transferred to the Italian government most of its authority in the liberated regions of Italy (except military zones near the fighting front), thereby enabling the Italian cabinet to conduct foreign relations, make diplomatic appointments, and enact legislation without the ratification of the Control Council. Industrial stagnations, mass unemployment, and skyrocketing inflation continued to frustrate the government in its efforts to rehabilitate the national economy.

DEATH OF MUSSOLINI. The final Allied offensive in Italy began in April, 1945, and by the end of the month the German armies on Italian soil had been completely smashed; Italy north of the Apennines was liberated from the domination of Mussolini's regime. Mussolini, his mistress, and a number of his high-ranking colleagues were captured by Italian partisans at a small town near Lake Como. The entire group was summarily tried and, on April 28, executed. Italian partisans inflicted brutal vengeance on Mussolini's followers throughout northern Italy after the German surrender, which became effective on May 2. More than 1000 fascists were shot in Milan alone.

In accordance with a previous pledge to dissolve his government after the liberation of northern Italy, Premier Bonomi resigned on June 12. A coalition government, representing the entire Committee of National Liberation, was formed on June 21. The new government, which was headed by Ferruccio Parri (1890–), a prominent anti-fascist and leader of the Action Party, inherited, in addition to all of the economic problems of its predecessor, mounting

ITALY

popular demands for a Constituent Assembly and a referendum on the future of the monarchy. Without a peace settlement of such matters as frontier, reparations, and the status of the Italian colonies, the Parri government was little more than a stopgap regime, unable to grapple effectively with the economic, political, and social problems confronting Italy. The Italian people grew restive, particularly after repeated failures of the so-called Big Four (France, Great Britain, the U.S., and the U.S.S.R.) Council of Foreign Ministers to agree on a draft of the Italian peace terms. In October spokesmen for Italian monarchism and leaders of the Liberal Party accused Premier Parri of violating the truce on the question of the monarchy. Warning Italy to beware of resurgent fascism and of possible civil war, Parri resigned in November. The ensuing crisis was accompanied by riotous demonstrations in southern Italy against the high cost of living. After unsuccessful attempts by Vittorio Orlando (q.v.), a conservative, and Francesco Nitti (1868–1953), a leader of the Liberal Party, to form a government, the Committee of National Liberation offered the premiership to Alcide de Gasperi (q.v.), a Christian Democrat and the foreign secretary of the Parri cabinet. In one of his initial moves, de Gasperi, who took office on Dec. 9, proclaimed April 30, 1946, the date for election of a Constituent Assembly.

The year 1946 was a period of unparalleled hardship for most of the Italian people. Although the privations provoked occasional riotous demonstrations, the general mood of the populace was apathetic during the campaign preceding the national referendum and elections, which were postponed until June. The prevalence of opposition to the monarchy was indicated when, on April 27, the convention of the Christian Democratic Party, composed largely of liberal Roman Catholics, voted three to one in favor of a republic. King Victor Emmanuel III abdicated on May 9 and his son ascended the throne as Humbert II.

Republic of Italy. In 1946 nearly 25,000,000 voters, approximately 89 percent of the eligible electorate, which included women for the first time in Italian history, voted in the general elections of June 2 and 3. Of the voters, 54.3 percent voted for a republic. On June 10, 1946, when the popular mandate was officially proclaimed, Italy became a de facto republic. The cabinet then transferred all royal powers to the premier. On June 13 King Humbert abdicated and left the country.

In the vote for the Constituent Assembly the Christian Democrats won a plurality of 207 seats and emerged as the first party in Italy. The Socialist and Communist parties won 115 and 104 seats respectively and four minor parties shared the remaining 117 seats. The Liberal, Labor Democratic, and Action parties, components of the erstwhile Committee of National Liberation, practically disappeared from Italian politics. On June 28 Enrico de Nicola (1877–1959), a member of the Liberal Party and a compromise candidate of the Marxist and Christian Democratic parties, was elected provisional president of the republic by the Constituent Assembly. De Gasperi, who remained as premier, reorganized the cabinet as a coalition of the three leading parties and the Republican Party.

PARTY DIFFERENCES. In the deliberations preceding approval of the new republican government by the Constituent Assembly, irreconcilable disagreements between the Communists and Christian Democrats became evident. The Communists charged that papal influence played an important role in the formulation of Christian Democratic policy and the Christian Democrats accused the Communist Party of being an instrument of Soviet policy. The Communists were accused also of fomenting industrial strife, then becoming serious in Italy. The friction between the two camps was intensified by persistent semi-famine and the generally chaotic Italian economy. In October the radical wing of the Christian Democratic Party joined the leftist parties in attacking De Gasperi's policies. As the prestige of the De Gasperi government declined, the Socialist and Communist parties drew together with the stated objective of taking power. Municipal elections in November, 1946, indicated a decline in Christian Democratic support and gains for the Communist, Socialist, and rightist parties.

PARIS PEACE CONFERENCE. The despairing mood of the Italians had been aggravated meanwhile by preliminary decisions of the Big Four council of foreign ministers as revealed at the Paris Peace Conference, which opened in July, 1946. These decisions contemplated the internationalization of Trieste (q.v.), see TRIESTE, FREE TERRITORY OF; the cession of most of the remainder of Venezia Giulia (now Friuli-Venezia Giulia) and several Adriatic islands to Yugoslavia; the cession of the Dodecanese Islands and certain small border areas to France; and the award of $100,000,000 in reparations to the U.S.S.R. The proposed treaty provided also for additional reparations to other nations victimized by Fascism, for severe restrictions on the Italian armed forces, and for British administration over Italian East Africa pending a Big Four agreement on final disposition of the colonies. Despite official and popular Italian protests, the treaty was signed by the Allied powers at Paris on Feb. 10, 1947, and was ratified subsequently by the Italian Constituent Assembly, with Communist and Socialist delegates abstaining; it came into effect on Sept. 15. Allied occupation forces withdrew from Italy shortly thereafter.

Although the Italian people generally opposed the peace treaty, many were mollified and encouraged by the attitude of the U.S. government, which had helped to frustrate Soviet demands for harsher terms and had also concretely demonstrated its friendly intentions toward Italy. On a mission to Washington, D.C., in early 1947 De Gasperi had obtained $50,000,000 in payment for purchases by U.S. forces in Italy, a credit of $100,000,000 from the Export-Import Bank of the United States (q.v.), immediate shipments of basic foodstuffs, and pledges of additional aid.

BREAKUP OF COALITION GOVERNMENT. While De Gasperi was abroad the Italian Socialist Party, reflecting a trend then occurring in Europe, split into two groups on the issue of collaboration with the Communists. Pietro Nenni (1891–   ), foreign minister in De Gasperi's cabinet and a leader of the pro-Communist faction of the Socialist Party, resigned on Jan. 15. The entire cabinet then withdrew and De Gasperi formed another coalition ministry, including both the Communists and Socialists, on Feb. 2. Relations between the leftists and moderates deteriorated steadily thereafter. In the mounting diplomatic struggle, popularly termed the "cold war", between the Western democracies and the Soviet bloc, Italian political parties and factions chose sides according to their ideological orientation. During this period the extreme right, composed mainly of former adherents of Mussolini and monarchists, became increasingly bold. On May 1 an armed band of anti-Communists attacked a Communist-led parade at Greci, Sicily, killing eight persons. The massacre, together with disagreements in the Constituent Assembly on such government policies as increased taxation and dismissals of civil employees, precipitated a cabinet crisis from May 13 to 31, when De Gasperi formed a ministry of Christian Democrats and nonparty specialists and excluded Communists and Socialists. The new regime immediately began a purge of leftists from important public positions.

Bitter political strife followed the breakup of the coalition government. By means of mass demonstrations, general strikes, and other tactics the leftists tried to dislodge the De Gasperi government. They denounced the U.S. and De Gasperi's approval of the European Recovery Program (q.v.). Reflecting hostility to the Italian government, on Oct. 1 the Soviet delegate to the Security Council vetoed Italy's application for United Nations membership. In the same month the Italian Communist Party became a founding member of the Communist Information Bureau (Cominform), established to combat American influence in Europe and to extend Communism.

ELECTIONS OF 1948. Meanwhile the Constituent Assembly had drafted a constitution for Italy. Approved on Dec. 22, 1947, by a vote of 453 to 62, the document became effective on Jan. 1, 1948. National elections for the new Italian parliament were postponed until April, 1948. The ensuing campaign was one of the most bitter and dramatic in Italian history. Coinciding with a general intensification of the cold war internationally, the contest repeatedly brought Italy to the verge of civil war. Displays of force became a central feature in the strategy of both camps. The Communist-led coalition, operating through the General Confederation of Labor, frequently used strikes as a political weapon. As part of its program of reprisals against the left, the government confiscated arms and ammunition from Communist partisans and conducted intimidatory military demonstrations in various urban areas. On March 10, Pope Pius XII sanctioned anti-Communist activity by the Italian clergy. Less than a week later Premier De Gasperi accused the U.S.S.R. and the Cominform of directing the Communist bid for power in Italy. Reflecting American concern over possible developments in Italy, Secretary of State George Catlett Marshall (q.v.), warned, on March 19, that no aid would be extended that nation under the European Recovery Program (E.R.P.) in the event of a Communist victory; E.R.P. relief shipments to Italy were authorized on April 9, however.

In the elections on April 18 and 19 the Christian Democratic Party, which received more than 12,750,000 votes, won overwhelmingly. This total, nearly 49 percent of all ballots cast, gave the Christian Democrats 307 seats in the Chamber of Deputies and 151 seats in the Senate. The Popular Front, the coalition of Communists and left-wing Socialists, polled slightly more than 8,000,000 votes and won 182 seats in the Chamber of Deputies. Senators elected by the Popular Front numbered 31. The right-wing Socialists elected 33 deputies, and the remaining 52 seats were distributed among minor parties.

ITALY

CONTINUED COMMUNIST OPPOSITION. The decisive mandate of the Italian people in the general elections markedly reduced political tension in Italy. Because of the relative strength displayed at the polls by the Communists, however, reconciliation of the differences which had divided the nation into two camps appeared unlikely. On May 11, Luigi Einaudi (q.v.), the candidate of the Christian Democrats and right-wing Socialists, was elected president of the republic. De Gasperi, who was reappointed premier on the following day, announced his cabinet on May 23, which differed little from its predecessor.

Supplies and credits made available under the E.R.P. had meanwhile begun to flow into Italy, creating favorable conditions for reconstruction of the national economy. Adhering to their policy of irreconcilable struggle against the E.R.P., the Italian Communists promoted, beginning about the middle of June, a widespread strike for higher wages. The movement culminated, on July 2, in a general twelve-hour walkout. Within two weeks Italy was plunged into another grave crisis as the result of the attempted assassination, on July 14, of Palmiro Togliatti (1893–1964), head of the Communist Party. The General Confederation of Labor, charging the De Gasperi government with political responsibility for the crime, immediately called a nationwide general strike to force the premier to resign. During the next two days riotous demonstrations occurred in practically every city of Italy. By mobilizing more than 300,000 troops and police, the government succeeded in ending the strike on July 16.

FOREIGN PROBLEMS AND TREATIES. In 1949, the Italian Popular Front confined its struggle against the Christian Democratic regime chiefly to the chambers of parliament. The principal object of Communist attacks during this period was the proposed North Atlantic Treaty Organization (q.v.), a defensive alliance of the U.S., Canada, and ten Western European nations. Nevertheless, with the unanimous approval of his cabinet and a large majority of the Chamber of Deputies, De Gasperi signed the North Atlantic Treaty at Washington, D.C., on April 4, 1949.

The Big Four meanwhile had failed to agree on the disposition of Italian prewar colonies in Africa, and the matter had been referred to the General Assembly (q.v.) of the United Nations (q.v.). During its third session, from April 5–May 18, the General Assembly considered an Anglo-Italian plan of disposition, but the plan failed to receive the required support of a two-thirds majority. The Assembly then voted to table the question until its fourth session, scheduled to open in September. A plan developed by the Political and Social Committee of the General Assembly was adopted (48 to 1) on Nov. 21, with Ethiopia casting the negative ballot and nine members abstaining. Among salient features of the plan were provisions for granting independence to Italian Somaliland after ten years as a U.N. trust territory under Italian administration; for granting independence to Libya by Jan. 1, 1952; and for disposition of Eritrea on the basis of a report to be prepared by a special commission of the U.N.

In foreign affairs, Italy continued to collaborate with the Western democracies after its ratification of the North Atlantic Treaty. The government, in its first contribution to the North Atlantic defense system against possible Soviet aggression, announced in July, 1950, that the Italian army would be built up to 250,000 men, the limit imposed by the World-War-II peace treaty. Further expansion of the military establishment was announced in December. As a result of Italian efforts to secure revision of the treaty, the U.S., Great Britain, France, and eight other Western countries waived in December, 1951, the clauses limiting Italian rearmament.

In June, 1952, the Italian parliament ratified the treaty (popularly known as the Schuman Plan) establishing the European Coal and Steel Community (q.v.).

FALL OF THE DE GASPERI GOVERNMENT. The prewar fascists, previously barred by a constitutional provision from voting and holding public office, regained these rights on Jan. 1, 1953, upon expiration of the five-year limitation on punitive action against them. In an attempt to improve the effectiveness of the executive branch of the government, the Christian Democrats and their allies secured passage, on March 29, of an electoral-reform bill ensuring the party in power of a working majority in parliament. The bill provided that the party or coalition of parties polling 50 percent or more of the popular vote will receive 65 percent of the seats in the Chamber of Deputies.

Parliamentary elections on June 7 to 8, with the closest results in Italian history, reflected the trend established in the local elections of 1951–52. The Christian Democrats, emerging again as the strongest single party, polled 40 percent of the votes. The Communists were second (22.6 percent) and the parties of the right, which registered the biggest gains (12.7 percent as compared with 4.2 percent in 1948), were third. Following the elections De Gasperi was succeeded by the Christian Democratic leader Gieuseppe Pella (1902–   ), former minister of the treasury,

ITALY

Representatives of the governments of Belgium, France, West Germany, Italy, Luxemburg, and The Netherlands at the signing in Rome of the treaty that established the European Economic Community, on March 25, 1957.

who won the neutrality of the Socialists and the support of the Monarchists. But intraparty differences brought about the collapse of several governments in the next two years, including those of former Minister of the Interior Mario Scelba (1902–) and of Antonio Segni (1891–), also a Christian Democrat, who had held portfolios of agriculture and education.

Late in 1953 the question of the future status of the Free Territory of Trieste brought Italy and Yugoslavia to the verge of war, but tensions abated after the U.S., Great Britain, and France agreed to work out a formula acceptable to both sides. On Oct. 5, 1954, Italy, Yugoslavia, Great Britain, and the U.S. signed a Memorandum of Understanding on the Trieste problem. The settlement allocated a zone that included the city of Triesto to Italy; Yugoslavia received the rest of the Trieste region.

In 1955 a left-wing Christian Democrat, Giovanni Gronchi (q.v.), who had been speaker of the Chamber of Deputies, was elected president of the republic on April 29. Italy became a member of the United Nations on Dec. 14.

CHRISTIAN DEMOCRAT ASCENDENCY. The repudiation of the former Soviet dictator Joseph Stalin (q.v.) at the 20th Congress of the Soviet Communist Party in February demoralized Italian Stalinists and plunged the powerful Italian Communist Party into confusion. The revelations about Stalin's crimes disillusioned Italian left-wing Socialists, perennially staunch admirers of the Soviet system, and weakened their alliance with the Communists. After the Hungarian uprising in October against Soviet domination many Communists turned in their membership cards and the number of Communist sympathizers dwindled. The decline of the Communist Party strengthened pro-democratic forces in Italy.

In July, 1957, the Chamber of Deputies ratified the treaties for the proposed European Economic Community and the European Atomic Energy Community (Euratom); in October senatorial ratification was obtained. In March, 1958, Gronchi dissolved the Senate and Chamber of Deputies and ordered elections for the third parliament of the Italian Republic. In the elections, which were held on May 25–26, the center coalition obtained majorities in both houses of parliament.

A new coalition government composed of

ITALY

Christian Democrats and right-wing Socialists and led by Amintore Fanfani (1908–) was sworn in on July 2. He was succeeded in January, 1959, by Antonio Segni, whose cabinet consisted entirely of Christian Democrats. Widespread criticism and debate over Gronchi's visit to the Soviet Union in February, 1960, led to the fall of the government later that month. In July Fanfani returned to office and, with the voting support of three centrist parties, succeeded in obtaining approval of a cabinet composed entirely of Christian Democratic ministers. An agreement concluded on Oct. 11 provided that the U.S.S.R. would supply Italy with 12,000,000 tons of oil over four years in exchange for finished steel, pipeline equipment, and synthetic rubber.

The 1960's and '70's. The first Italian rocket was launched on Jan. 12, 1961, in Sardinia. During March the government announced plans to assist underdeveloped nations so far as this did not hinder efforts to assist the depressed economy of southern Italy. Premier Fanfani and Foreign Minister Segni paid an official visit to the Soviet Union in August. Nikita S. Khrushchev (q.v.), the chairman of the Supreme Soviet, warned that in the event of a nuclear war Italy would be destroyed utterly. With the dispute over the South Tirol (see TIROL) still unsettling relations between Italy and Austria, the U.N. General Assembly on Nov. 28 unanimously adopted a resolution calling on the two countries to resume negotiations.

On May 6 the parliament elected Antonio Segni, a Christian Democrat, to the presidency. Local elections in 1962 demonstrated strong popular support for the progovernment parties, and the Communists lost strength for the first time in many years.

Subsequently dissension arose among the parties supporting the government. It had its base in Communist criticism of Fanfani's policies, including charges that the premier had failed to push domestic economic reforms and the removal of NATO missile bases from Italy. Although the parties agreed in January, 1963, to continue their support of his government, it was weakened by the results of parliamentary elections on April 28–29. The popular vote for Christian Democrats (38.3 percent) declined while the Communist vote (25.3 percent) increased. Fanfani resigned on May 16 but remained head of a caretaker government until Giovanni Leone (1908–), President of the Chamber of Deputies, formed on June 21 a minority government of all Christian Democrats as a temporary expedient. On Oct. 29 the moderate elements of the left-wing Italian Socialist Party, led by Pietro Nenni, agreed to enter a center-left government for the first time since 1947. A four-party coalition cabinet was then organized by Christian Democrat Aldo Moro (1916–), who assumed the premiership of Italy on Dec. 5.

During 1964 the conservative and left-wing elements in the government persistently and fundamentally disagreed. The situation was rendered more serious by signs that the six-year economic boom would be ending because the factions were unable to agree on a policy to counter the threatened downturn. The political climate was unsettled also by the loss of two influential leaders: Palmiro Togliatti, head of the Italian Communist Party for twenty years, died on Aug. 21; President Segni, crippled by a stroke on Aug. 7, resigned on Dec. 6. On Dec. 28 Giuseppe Saragat (1898–), the head of the Social Democratic Party, was elected president. On March 4, 1965, the four parties in the coalition government agreed to set aside their political differences in order to take unified action against the economic slump.

FLOODS OF 1966. Throughout 1965 and 1966 the government headed by Aldo Moro maintained the confidence of the coalition parties. In early November, 1966, floods swept through central and northern Italy, causing extensive damage. Florence was severely battered and major art works and historical archives were destroyed or damaged. The government voted $75,200,000 in flood relief and began reconstruction, aided by foreign contributions.

GROWING POLITICAL AND ECONOMIC UNREST. An uneasy center-left coalition government, in 1967, dealt with a succession of challenges, such as the longest parliamentary filibuster in postwar Italian history over the proposal by Moro to establish fourteen new autonomous regions with their own assemblies. The bill finally became law in 1968.

In the late spring of 1968 the country was disturbed by a number of clashes between police and students in Rome and other cities. The students, who were demanding reforms in the educational system, had seized several university buildings. They were joined by industrial workers demanding increased economic benefits.

In parliamentary elections on May 20, the Unified Socialist Party lost a number of seats and withdrew from the ruling coalition, precipitating the fall of the Moro government on June 5. An interim minority government was formed on June 25, which remained in office until December. Mariano Rumor (1915–), secretary-general of the Christian Democratic Party, then succeeded in forming a new coalition with the Socialists and Republicans. In July, 1970, Rumor's government fell and was succeeded the following month by one formed by the Christian Democratic leader and treasury minister Emilio Colombo (1920–).

In the early 1970's Italy was beset by severe economic, social, and political problems. Symbolic of the political difficulties was the election on Dec. 25, 1971, of Giovanni Leone as president; the election took place after sixteen days and a record twenty-three ballots.

Under pressure of differences within his coalition, Colombo resigned in January, 1972. After collapse within a week of a minority government formed by Giulio Andreotti (1919–), a Christian Democrat, general elections were held on May 7–8. The Christian Democrats won a clear popular mandate, and Andreotti formed a centrist coalition government. The economy maintained a steady growth rate, but the benefits were unequally shared, with the south and Sicily continuing to lag behind the more industrialized north. Unemployment reached serious proportions in some southern districts, prices rose, and a wave of strikes brought the economy nearly to a standstill. After the fall of succeeding center-to-left coalition governments, the former premier Mariano Rumor formed still another center-left government, including Socialist members, on July 9, 1973. He promised "shock therapy" against inflation and promptly imposed a price freeze.

In August and September several Italian cities were struck with a cholera epidemic.

ITASCA, LAKE, small lake in Minnesota, situated in a State park of the same name about 25 miles s.w. of Bemidji in the n.w. section of the State. The lake is sometimes referred to as the source of the Mississippi R., but geologists assert that many other lakes of the surrounding morainic region contribute to the headwaters of the Mississippi. Area, 2 sq.mi.

ITCH, or PRURITUS, uneasy sensation of the skin which causes the desire to scratch the parts affected. It may or may not be accompanied by an observable inflammation of the skin such as in poison ivy; see ALLERGY; IVY POISONING. The basic cause is stimulation of the sensory nerve endings in the skin and persistent itch may be a symptom of an otherwise unnoticed systemic disease such as diabetes (see DIABETES MELLITUS). Treatment should be both palliative for the itch and specific, if possible, for the cause.

Itch is the name sometimes applied to scabies, which is a skin infestation caused by small parasites called itch mites, which burrow into and irritate the skin. The commonest of these is the female of *Sarcoptes scabiei,* a round, pearly-white arachnid, about $\frac{1}{60}$ in. long, with pointed mouth parts; see PARASITE. This mite burrows into sensitive folds of the skin, such as those found in the armpit and between the digits; it occasionally infects the smooth skin of the face. Treatment of this condition, which can be transmitted from person to person, consists of avoiding scratching, careful cleansing of the infested parts, and application of sulfur ointment. Itch is also caused by the chigger (q.v.).

ITHACA, city in New York State, and county seat of Tompkins Co., at the s. end of Cayuga Lake, 55 miles s.w. of Syracuse. Ithaca is notable as the site of Cornell University (q.v.) and Ithaca College, and as a popular summer resort area near the Finger Lakes (q.v.). The city is a trade center for local agricultural products. The chief industries include the manufacture of business machines, machine tools, clothing, and cement.

Lying in a hilly region overlooking Cayuga Lake, Ithaca and the surrounding area are famous for their scenic beauty. Three streams traverse the city, flowing through deep gorges, and the rapids and waterfalls are one of its distinctive features. The municipal park system contains bird and wild-fowl sanctuaries and varied recreational facilities. Three State parks, Buttermilk Falls, Robert H. Treman, and Taughannock Falls, are situated within 10 mi. of the city. Ithaca was founded about 1788. It became the county seat in 1818, was incorporated as a village in 1821, and chartered as a city in 1888. Pop. (1960) 28,799; (1970) 26,226.

ITO, Marquis Hirobumi (1841–1909), Japanese statesman, born near Shimonoseki, and educated in Japan and Great Britain. Ito served as prime minister four times between 1885 and 1901; see JAPAN: *History.* During his career he made several visits to the United States and Europe, and subsequently was instrumental in introducing Western political ideas and economic reforms into Japan. With the Japanese statesman Kimmochi Saionji (1849–1940), he drafted a constitution for Japan, patterned on European models, which was in effect from 1890 to 1945. Following the Sino-Japanese War (*see* CHINA: *History*), Ito negotiated in 1895 the Treaty of Shimonoseki, which ended the war and made Korea (q.v.) independent. He negotiated an Anglo-Japanese alliance with Great Britain, which was signed in 1902. After conducting negotiations that eventually led to the establishment of a Japanese protectorate over Korea, Ito served as resident-general of Korea from 1905 until his assassination at Harbin, Manchuria.

ITURBI, José (1895–), Spanish pianist and conductor, born in Valencia, and educated in Valencia and Paris. From 1919 to 1923 he taught piano at the Geneva Conservatory. He made his American debut in 1928 with the Philadelphia Orchestra and subsequently gave concerts throughout the world, often appearing in duo-piano recitals with his sister Amparo Iturbi (1899–1969). In 1933 Iturbi conducted fifteen concerts in Mexico City and thereafter was guest conductor of several major orchestras. From 1936 to 1944 he was conductor of the Rochester Philharmonic Orchestra, and in 1956 he became musical director of the Valencia Symphony Orchestra. He also appeared as a concert pianist in several motion pictures.

ITURBIDE, Agustín de (1783–1824), Mexican revolutionary leader and self-proclaimed emperor (1822), born in Valladolid de Michoacán (now Morelia). Iturbide began his career as an officer in the Spanish Royalist army in New Spain (now Mexico) at the time of the Mexican war of independence; see MEXICO: *History*. In 1820 he commanded the Royalist troops assigned to quell an uprising led by the Mexican revolutionist Vicente Guerrero (1783?1831). Instead of fighting Guerrero, however, Iturbide joined him in a conspiracy against Spanish authority. Together, in February, 1821, they issued the so-called Plan of Iguala, which included provisions for Mexican independence under a monarchical form of government. Iturbide and Guerrero gained broad popular support and subsequently imposed successive defeats on the Royalists near Mexico City. The last Spanish viceroy, Juan O'Donojú (1755?–1821), resigned and in August, 1821, signed the Treaty of Córdoba, by which Mexico became independent. Within a month Iturbide became provisional head of the government.

Iturbide proclaimed himself emperor as Agustín I in 1822. His reign became wasteful and despotic, however, and he was forced to abdicate ten months later by Antonio López de Santa Anna (q.v.). Iturbide went into exile in Italy, but returned to Mexico in 1824; he was then arrested, condemned as a traitor by the Mexican congress, and executed.

ITYS. See PHILOMELA.

ITZÁ, tribe of Mayan Indians who lived in what is now known as the Yucatán peninsula in Central America; see YUCATÁN. Archeologists believe that the Itzá were originally members of the Chontal language group who lived in the Veracruz and Tabasco States of present-day Mexico. The Itzá migrated north about 900 A.D. to the city of Chichén-Itzá (q.v.), in the modern State of Yucatán, Mexico. Sometime in the 11th century, after Chichén-Itzá had been invaded by the Toltec, a group of Indians from central Mexico, the city became the most important center of Mayan culture. Civil war erupted among the Mayan city-states, however, and the Itzá abandoned Chichén-Itzá. They established Tayasal, near Lake Petén Itzá (now Flores, Guatemala) as their new capital. The Itzá were the last Mayan tribe to surrender to the Spanish, who conquered Tayasal in 1697. See also MAYA; MEXICO: *History*.

IVAN, name of three grand princes or dukes and three rulers of Russia, of whom the following are important in the history of Russia; see also RUSSIA: *The Rise of Muscovy*.

Ivan I Danilovich, called IVAN KALITA ("the moneybag") (d. 1341), Grand Prince or Duke of Moscow (1328–41). As a vassal of the Tatars (q.v.) he collected taxes for the Tatar khan and thus earned his epithet; see also GOLDEN HORDE. Ivan moved his court from the city of Vladimir to Moscow and persuaded the metropolitan of Kiev, one of the leading ecclesiastics of the Russian Orthodox Church, to transfer his see to Moscow. During his reign Ivan also extended the boundaries of his principality.

Ivan III Vasilievich, called IVAN THE GREAT (1440–1505), Grand Duke of Moscow (1462–1505), the son of Basil II (1415–1462), whom he

Ivan III Vasilievich, called Ivan the Great.

succeeded. Ivan strengthened the hegemony of Moscow over other Russian principalities (*see* Moscow: *History*), and he described himself as "Sovereign of all Russia". In 1470 he launched a war against the republic of Novgorod, which he conquered and annexed in 1478, thereby acquiring all of northern Russia from Lapland to the Ural Mts. In 1480, by refusing to make the customary payment of tribute to the Tatar khan, Ivan ended the subservience of the Muscovite rulers to the Tatars. Subsequently, he further increased his domain by conquest, by purchases of territory, and by exacting allegiance from weaker princes. Ivan invaded Lithuania in 1492 and again in 1500, and forced Alexander (r. 1501–06), the ruler of that country, to cede a score of Lithuanian towns to him in 1503; *see* Lithuania: *History*. Ivan also succeeded, through his marriage in 1472 to Zoë Sophia, niece of the last Byzantine emperor Constantine XI Palaeologus (*see* Palaeologus), in establishing himself as the protector of the Orthodox Church (q.v.). Soon after his marriage Ivan added the two-headed eagle of the Byzantine escutcheon to his own coat-of-arms and, modeling his regime on that of the autocratic Byzantine rulers, drastically curtailed the powers and privileges of the Russian aristocracy. Ivan also issued the first Russian code of court procedure.

Ivan IV Vasilievich, called IVAN THE TERRIBLE (1530–84), Grand Duke of Moscow (1533–47) and Czar of Russia (1547–84). He was the grandson of Ivan III, succeeding his father, Basil III (1479–1533), at the age of three. He was the first Russian ruler to assume the title of czar. The first thirteen years of Ivan's reign comprise one of the greatest periods of internal reform, external expansion, and centralization of state power in the history of Russia. In 1550 Ivan convoked the *Zemski Sobor,* the first national representative assembly ever summoned by a Russian ruler. In the same year he initiated a comprehensive revision and modernization of the Russian law code. Ivan conquered and annexed the Tatar khanates of Kazan and Astrakhan' in 1552 and 1556, respectively, bringing the Volga R. within the borders of Russia and ending the influence of the Tatars over Russian territory. The reign of Ivan after 1560 is remarkable more for repeated displays of erratic behavior and wanton brutality by the czar than for his statesmanship. He surrounded himself with a select group of noblemen, whom he allowed to exercise despotic power over his entire domain. In 1570 he ravaged the town of Novgorod and ordered the slaying of thousands of its inhabitants, because they had been reported, on dubious authority, to be conspiring against him. Ten years later Ivan brought personal tragedy upon himself, when, in a fit of anger, he struck and killed his eldest and favorite son. The sole achievement of Ivan's later years was the acquisition of Siberia in 1581, after that vast territory had been brought under Russian control by Ermak Timofeev (d. 1584), the Cossack leader; *see* Cossacks. Shortly before his death, Ivan, overcome with feelings of guilt and remorse, entered a religious order of hermits.

IVANOVO, formerly IVANOVO-VOZNESENSK, city of the Soviet Union, in the Russian S.F.S.R., and capital of Ivanovo Oblast, about 150 miles N.E. of Moscow. The city is an important center for the production of textiles, especially cotton. Other principal industries include the manufacturing of chemicals and machinery. Ivanovo dates from the 14th century; it became a commercial center in the 17th century. The city was incorporated with Voznesensk in 1871 and renamed Ivanovo in 1932. Pop. (1970) 419,000.

IVES, Charles Edward (1874–1954), American composer, born in Danbury, Conn. He received his early musical education from his father and later studied music at Yale University, from which he graduated in 1898. After he served for several years as church organist in and around New York City, he ceased being a professional musician and founded an insurance business. Musical composition, thereafter, was his avocation. He composed primarily for his own pleasure, and most of his works remained unperformed until many years after their composition.

Ives's music contains much Americana; it includes familiar American tunes. Although Ives wrote in traditional genres, such as the symphony and sonata (qq.v.), he incorporated radical innovations in harmony which were many years in advance of American and European composers. Some of his ideas went beyond the mere extension of the traditional musical language. These ideas included the use of blocks of sound as the primary structural element in a composition rather than melodic and harmonic relationships. He also allowed performers to alter significantly parts of a composition. His technical innovations, as well as the freedom of his imagination, have inspired younger composers of the mid-20th century in all parts of the Western world. Ives's compositions include five symphonies, four violin sonatas, two piano sonatas, more than one hundred songs, choral music, short pieces for piano and organ, and chamber music.

IVES, Frederick Eugene (1856–1937), American inventor and scientist, born in Litchfield, Conn.

IVORY

With little formal education, in his late teens Ives became director of the photographic laboratory at Cornell University. He was a pioneer in the development of photomechanical processes (q.v.) and color photography. His inventions include the first halftone photoengraving process (q.v.); the first trichromatic halftone photogravure method, which anticipated modern rotogravure; and the short-tube, single-objective binocular microscope. He is the author of *The Autobiography of an Amateur Inventor* (1928).

IVORY, opaque, creamy-white, hard, fine-grained, modified dentine that composes the upper incisor teeth (tusks) of elephants. Ivory is composed of curved layers of dentine, alternating in shade, which intersect one another; the resulting lozenge-shaped structure is highly elastic and finely grained. The layers of an elephant's tusk are deposited from the pulp, so that the innermost layer is the newest. The base of the tusk, which is imbedded in the skull, is filled with pulp at the widest part. The pulp cavity becomes progressively narrower toward the tip of the tusk, ending as a minute, threadlike channel.

Most commercial elephant ivory is obtained from the tusks of the African elephant, *Loxodonta africana;* see ELEPHANT. Elephants formerly roamed over all of Africa south of the northern desert region, but the encroachment of civilization has driven them into the interior. The primary sources of ivory are eastern and central Africa, especially Mozambique, Tanzania, and Uganda. Most of the ivory of the western half of Africa is hard, whereas that from the eastern half is soft. Hard ivory is relatively glassier in texture, more difficult to cut, and more susceptible to cracking than soft ivory. The largest ivory tusks are 9 ft. long and weigh about 225 lb. The value of ivory depends on the size and condition of the tusks. Standard commercial grades are based primarily on weight. The usual four grades are: (1) tusks weighing 60 lb. or more, (2) tusks weighing 40 to 60 lb., (3) tusks weighing 20 to 40 lb., and (4) tusks weighing less than 20 lb. Less than one quarter of commercial ivory is obtained from freshly killed elephants; the remainder is obtained from collections made by natives from the carcasses of elephants that died natural deaths. The principal ivory markets are the ports of Antwerp, London, and Liverpool.

Fossil ivory, called odontolite, is a blue variety found in small quantities in the frozen soils of northern Siberia. The ivory was produced by the extinct mammoths of the Pleistocene geological epoch; its blue color results from saturation by metallic salts.

Tusks of several other animals, such as hippopotamuses, narwhals, sperm whales, and walruses, are commonly called ivory and have similar physical properties. As genuine ivory has become rarer and more expensive, numerous plastic substitutes for ivory have been developed; see PLASTICS. Several ivorylike vegetable parts are also used as imitation ivory; the ivory palm (q.v.), for example, produces large, white, hard seeds, called ivory nuts, the endosperm of which is commonly known as vegetable ivory.

Carved ivory has been used for decorative purposes since the time of the ancient Egyptians; see IVORY CARVING. Small pieces of ivory are used for high-quality furniture inlays, chessmen, and small jewelry. Larger pieces of ivory have been sometimes used in the manufacture of billiard balls, piano keys, and toilet articles.

IVORY CARVING, art of carving ivory for ornamental or useful purposes, practiced from prehistoric to modern times. The ivory most frequently used is obtained from elephant tusks, but other types of ivory or substitute material include the tusks, teeth, horns, and bones of other animals, as well as vegetable ivory and synthetic ivories. See IVORY; IVORY PALM.

Ancient Carvings. The earliest ivory carvings known were made in the Old Stone Age which ended about 8000 B.C. Aurignacian man produced great numbers of ivory, bone, and horn carvings, with nude female figures being the most common subject. Representations of animals, especially reindeer, occur most often in the subsequent Magdalenian Period. See ARCHEOLOGY: *Old Stone Age or Paleolithic Period.*

In Egypt the art of ivory and bone carving was developed in predynastic times. Large numbers of carved figures of men and women and also carved combs, hairpins, and handles have been found in tombs dating from predynastic and early dynastic periods. Objects found in Egyptian tombs of later date include carved ivory weapon hilts and furniture and caskets inlaid with ivory carvings. Mesopotamian ivories frequently show strong Egyptian influence. They include a series of tablets carved with figures in low relief, made at the ancient Assyrian capital Nineveh (q.v.).

The Minoans (see MINOAN CULTURE), and later the ancient Greeks, were noted for their ivory carvings. The Greeks were famous especially in the 5th century B.C. for their chryselephantine statues, often of heroic size, in which the flesh was represented in carved ivory and the hair and garments in sculptured gold. Among the Romans, particularly in late imperial times, carved ivories were much in demand. A popular

IVORY CARVING

Three examples of Chinese ivory carving of the Ch'ien Lung period, in the mid-18th century.
Parke-Bernet Galleries

type was the consular diptych, a two-leaved tablet decorated with portraits and scenes commemorating the inauguration of a consul (q.v.).

Medieval Work. Ivory carving flourished under the Byzantine Empire, particularly in the 5th and 6th centuries, and from the 10th to the 13th century. Christian figures, symbols, and scenes were the subjects most commonly depicted on ivory book covers, icons, boxes, shrines, crosiers, crucifixes, door panels, and thrones. Most Byzantine carvings, however, were in the form of a triptych.

In Europe during the reigns of Charlemagne (q.v.), Holy Roman Emperor, and his successors in the 9th and 10th centuries elaborately carved ivory book covers and altarpieces were produced. Gothic ivories from the 13th to the 15th century primarily included objects of ecclesiastical use as in preceding periods, but objects which were secular in character were also carved by Gothic craftsmen. One of the most popular devotional subjects was the Virgin and Child, executed in the round or in relief.

Post-Renaissance Craftsmanship. During the 15th and 16th centuries, ivory carving was not popular but in the baroque and rococo periods (qq.v.) it again came into vogue, especially in Germany and the Netherlands. The German craftsmen were known for richly ornamented ivories; the Flemish craftsmen produced statuettes and other sculpture-inspired ivory carvings. France again became an important ivory-carving center, in the 17th and 18th centuries. The chief cities of the industry were the Dieppe

87

IVORY COAST, REPUBLIC OF THE

and Paris, where large numbers of crucifixes and other religious objects were produced. During the 18th century, however, the demand for ivories diminished, and did not increase substantially until the end of the 19th century. Ivory carvings then became popular once more, and are still in demand today.

Arabic, Eastern, and American Indian Work. Arabic Muslims have long used ivory in creating patterned inlay work on furniture and woodwork. In the Far East the best-known ivories are those of India and Japan, and particularly of China. The Indians carved figures of their gods, and ornate caskets. The Japanese netsukes, small carved ornaments used as part of a costume or placed on view in the home, are often made of ivory. The Chinese have traditionally esteemed ivory, and Chinese artists were encouraged to work in this medium. The art still flourishes today and objects created include statuettes, chessmen, fans, screens, toilet articles, chopsticks, and models of buildings and boats. The Chinese are world-famous for their ivory curiosities, particularly the concentric ivory balls carved one inside the other by Cantonese craftsmen. In Eskimo, African, and North American Indian cultures, carving in ivory, horn, and bone has been practiced from the earliest times to the present day.

IVORY COAST, REPUBLIC OF THE, nation in w. Africa, bounded on the N. by Mali and Upper Volta, on the E. by Ghana, on the S. by the Gulf of Guinea (340-mi. coastline), and on the w. by Liberia and Guinea. It is situated between about lat. 5° N. and lat. 10° N. and long. 2° 30′ W. and long. 7° 30′ W. The country has an area of about 124,504 sq.mi.

THE LAND

The coast is fringed by a number of large lagoons, most of which are inaccessible to shipping because of off-shore shoals. Bordering the coast a zone of dense forests extends about 165 mi. inland in the E. and W., and about 60 mi. in the center. Beyond this, in the N. and center, lies an extensive savanna. The W. region is undulating, with mountain chains in the Odienné and Man regions. Some of the summits are over 5000 ft. The principal rivers are the Cavally, Sassandra, Bandama, Nzi, and Comoé, none of which is navigable because of rapids and low water in the dry season.

Climate. The Ivory Coast lies within the Torrid Zone; the weather is generally hot and humid, and the rainfall is quite heavy. Temperatures range from 76° F. to 83° F. in the lagoons and from 57° F. to 103° F. in the forest area. Average annual rainfall varies from 79 to 128 in. in the la-

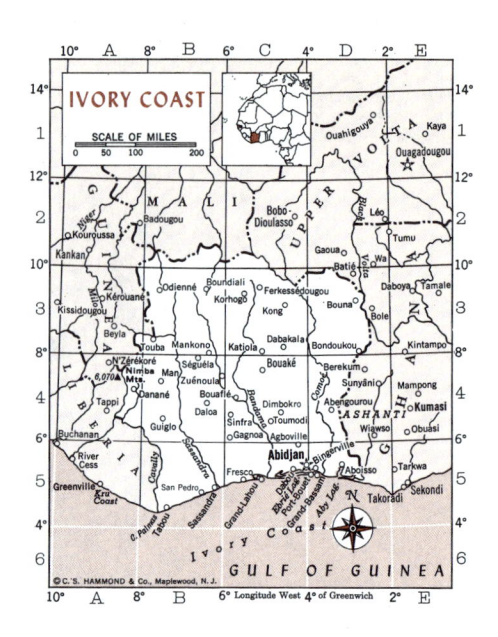

INDEX TO MAP OF IVORY COAST

Cities and Towns

Abengourou	D 4
Abidjan (cap.)	C 5
Aboisso	D 5
Agboville	C 5
Bingerville	D 5
Bondoukou	D 3
Bouaflé	B 4
Bouaké	C 4
Bouna	D 3
Boundiali	B 3
Dabakala	C 3
Dabou	C 5
Daloa	B 4
Danané	B 4
Dimbokro	C 4
Ferkessédougou	C 3
Fresco	C 5
Gagnoa	C 4
Grand-Bassam	C 5
Grand-Lahou	C 5
Guiglo	B 4
Katiola	C 3
Kong	C 3
Korhogo	C 3
Man	B 4
Mankono	B 3
Odienné	B 3
Port-Bouet	C 5
San Pedro	B 5
Sassandra	B 5
Séguéla	B 4
Sinfra	C 4
Tabou	B 5
Touba	B 3
Toumodi	C 4
Zuénoula	B 4

Physical Features

Aby (lagoon)	D 5
Bandama (river)	C 4
Cavally (river)	B 5
Comoé (river)	D 4
Ebrié (lagoon)	C 5
Guinea (gulf)	D 6
Ivory Coast (region)	C 6
Nimba (mts.)	A 4
Sassandra (river)	B 5

goons and from 39 to 98 in. in the forests. The S. has two rainy seasons, from March to July and from September to November. In the N. the rainy season is from March to July.

Natural Resources. The principal resources of the Ivory Coast are its rich soil, which favors agriculture, and the forests, which contain dense stands of commercially valuable hardwoods. Mineral deposits include diamonds and manganese ore. Two hydroelectric plants on the Bia R. have an annual capacity of nearly 300,000 kw. A major power station scheduled for construction on the Bandama R. is expected to have a potential of about 500,000,000 kw hours.

Plants and Animals. The central band of the Ivory Coast is covered by forest with over 225

Garden produce is displayed for sale in a new outdoor market, built on the traditional plan, in Abidjan, capital of the Ivory Coast. UPI

species of trees, among which are obeche, mahogany, and iroko. Animals include the jackal, hyena, panther, elephant, chimpanzee, crocodile, and various lizards and venomous snakes.

THE PEOPLE
Ethnically the population is very diverse, comprising more than sixty tribes. The principal ethnic groups are the Ashanti (q.v.), Agni-Baule, Kru, Mandingo, and Senufo. The people are primarily agricultural workers.

Population, Religion, and Language. The population of the Ivory Coast (census 1958) was 3,100,000; the United Nations estimated (1971) 4,420,000. The overall population density is about 34 per sq.mi. (U.N. est. 1970).

In religion, about 12 percent are Christian, chiefly Roman Catholic, 23 percent are Muslim; and 65 percent practice animism (q.v.). French is the official national language.

Political Divisions and Principal Cities. The country is divided into six departments, each administered by a centrally appointed prefect and an elected council. The main cities are Abidjan, the capital, with a population of about 650,000, and Bouaké (pop. 100,000), an important administrative and commercial center. Gagnoa, a marketing center, has 45,000 inhabitants.

Education. In the late 1960's about 465,000 pupils were attending primary schools and about 60,000, secondary schools. The University of Abidjan, opened in 1963, has an attendance of about 3700. A substantial number of Ivory Coast students were studying abroad at the same time. The literacy rate is about 20 percent.

Culture. The modernized sector of the population has been greatly influenced by French culture, although the indigenous culture of the country is well known for its artistic creations, especially masks. The French language is almost universally used in literature to the exclusion of African languages.

THE ECONOMY
The economy of the Ivory Coast is primarily agricultural, with some 90 percent of the total

IVORY COAST, REPUBLIC OF THE

labor force employed in farming. Recent annual budget figures show in revenue and expenditures about $170,000,000.

Agriculture. The main cash crops are coffee, cocoa, bananas, and pineapples. Other crops which are mainly used for local consumption include rice, corn, millet, and yams. The government is actively encouraging the development of palm-oil and rubber plantations.

Forest and Fishing Industries. The production of timber is growing rapidly, and with it the number of sawmills, plywood factories, and furniture plants. The most important export timbers are mahogany, iroko, sipo, obeche, and makore. About 12,200,000 cu.yd. were produced annually in the early 1970's. Fishing is conducted along the coast; the annual catch is about 62,600 tons.

Mining and Manufacturing. Mining has not been greatly developed to date. The principal products are diamonds (about 326,000 carats annually in the early 1970's) and manganese ore (about 10,400 tons). Industrial enterprises include food processing plants, lumber and textile mills, oil refineries, automobile and bicycle assembly plants, and factories producing shoes, steel containers, and aluminum sheets.

Currency, Banking, and Trade. Ivory Coast is a member of the seven-nation West African Monetary Union. The currency is the C.F.A. franc, issued by the Central Bank for the States of West Africa (200 C.F.A. francs equal U.S.$1; 1973).

In the early 1970's annual imports totaled about $415,000,000 and exports about $475,000,000. France is the chief trading partner of the Ivory Coast in both imports and exports; other important trading countries are the United States and Great Britain. Trade with all members of the European Economic Community, with which Ivory Coast is associated, is significant. Coffee, wood, and cocoa are the major exports.

Transportation and Communications. In the late 1960's the port of Abidjan handled over 4,000,000 tons of merchandise. A new port exists at San Pedro, which is linked to Mali (q.v.) by rail. A railroad links Abidjan to Bobo-Dioulasso and Ouagadougou in Upper Volta. Of about 20,000 mi. of roads, 540 are paved.

The government operates two radio broadcasting stations and a television station.

Labor. Most of the labor force of approximately 1,900,000 are engaged in agriculture, hunting, and fishing. About 100,000 workers belong to 190 unions grouped in the General Workers Union of Ivory Coast.

GOVERNMENT

According to the constitution of 1960 executive authority is vested in an elected president assisted by a cabinet of his selection. Both the president and the eighty-five members of the legislative assembly are elected for five-year terms by universal adult suffrage. All deputies are members of the Ivory Coast Democratic Party. The judicial system includes a supreme court that comprises constitutional, judicial, administrative, and auditing chambers. A high court of justice is empowered to try government officials, including the president, for high crimes. Other courts include appellate, state security, and first-instance courts.

HISTORY

Very little is known of the early history of the region now constituting the Ivory Coast. Ancestors of most of the present population seem to have moved into the area in recent times, mostly from the northeast and east. The Kru tribe, however, came from the west across the Cavally R. Portuguese explorers reached the coast in the 15th century and began trading in slaves and ivory. Strong tribal kingdoms flourished in the northeastern and eastern parts of the country. Europeans did not penetrate inland until the 1830's, when the French signed treaties with coastal rulers. As part of the French expansion of their holdings in western Africa, Ivory Coast was made a colony in 1893. French penetration was bitterly resisted, and frequent revolts occurred. In 1904 the Ivory Coast became a constituent territory of the Federation of French West Africa. Faced with dissidence, the French resorted increasingly to direct rule, undermining the powers of traditional rulers.

In 1919 the northern part of the colony was detached to form part of the new colony of Upper Volta, which was dissolved in 1932, only to be reconstituted in 1948. In 1944 Félix Houphouët-Boigny (1905–), a Baoulé chief, farmer, and doctor, founded a union of African farmers. From this organization emerged the interterritorial African Democratic Rally and its constituent section, the Democratic Party of the Ivory Coast, both led by Houphouët-Boigny, who was elected to the French National Assembly in 1946. The party was actively opposed by the French administration; the resultant tension flared into open violence in 1949. In 1950 Houphouët-Boigny reversed his policy and began active cooperation with the French. On Dec. 4, 1958, the Ivory Coast was proclaimed a republic within the French Community. After national elections in 1959 Houphouët-Boigny became premier and was elected president in November, 1960, following the achievement of full independence on Aug. 7 of that year. He was reelected in 1965 and 1970. The country became a member of the United Nations and of the African-Malagasy-Mauritius Common Organization (OCAM). In the early 1970's the Ivory Coast was one of the most stable of the new African nations.

In December, 1971, Houphouet-Boigny achieved a reconciliation of his country with that of President Léopold Sédar Senghor (q.v.) of Senegal, an event viewed as of major significance for French-speaking Africa.

IVORY PALM, common name of a low-growing tree, *Phytelephas macrocarpa,* belonging to the Palm (q.v.) family, native to N. South America. The short, prostrate stem of the ivory palm produces a large tuft of lightgreen, pinnately compound leaves, which grow from 30 to 40 ft. high and resemble immense ostrich plumes. The small imperfect flowers are borne on crowded spadices arising from the center of the leaf cluster. The fruit clusters, large as the head of a man, consist of six or more four-celled fruits, and contain numerous seeds, each the size of an egg from a hen. These seeds are called corozo nuts or tagua nuts or ivory nuts, and contain a hard, white endosperm. The endosperm, commonly called vegetable ivory, was used extensively as a substitute for ivory in the manufacture of buttons and small trinkets but has been largely supplanted by plastics. Another member of the palm family, *Metroxylon amicarum,* native to Polynesia, produces seeds which are a minor source of vegetable ivory.

IVY, common name applied to woody vines of the genus *Hedera,* belonging to the Ginseng family. The genus is native to temperate regions of the Old World. Ivy plants produce two kinds of leaves during the climbing phase. The leaves have three to five distinct lobes, but during the flowering stage they usually have three indistinct lobes or may even be lobeless. The flowers, which are borne in terminal umbels, have a five-parted calyx, five-parted corolla, five stamens, and a single pistil. The fruit is a smooth berry that contains a poisonous glucoside. The plant is supported by adventitious rootlets that become attached to trees or bare walls.

The English ivy, *H. helix,* is commonly cultivated in Europe and North America in gardens where it is trained to cover masonry walls of buildings. It has small leaves that are usually dark green. The African ivy or Algerian ivy, *H. canariensis,* native to the coast and islands of N.W. Africa, produces large, pale green, lobed leaves. The Asian ivy, *H. colchica,* bears dark green leaves that are usually faintly lobed or entirely lobeless. Easily cultivable from cuttings, ivy protects the walls on which it is grown from the corrosive effects of weathering. Ivy has no destructive effect on stone or brick walls except when rootlets are established in fissures, which they expand.

Several plants of the Vine family are commonly called ivy. The American ivy or Virginia creeper, *Parthenocissus quinquefolia,* and the Boston ivy or Japanese ivy, *P. tricuspidata,* are shrubby climbers that cling to tendrils. American ivy has long-petioled leaves composed of five leaflets; Boston ivy has three-lobed leaves. Both species of *Parthenocissus* grow readily from cuttings.

Ground ivy (q.v.) is a small, creeping member of the Mint (q.v.) family. German ivy, *Senecio mikanioides,* is a small creeping herb, native to South Africa, which belongs to the Composite (q.v.) family. *Rhus toxicodendron,* commonly known as poison ivy (q.v.), is a member of the Cashew family.

IVY POISONING, inflammation of the skin caused by contact with the sap of poison ivy,

American ivy or Virginia creeper, Parthenocissus quinquefolia
John H. Gerard —
National Audubon Society

poison oak, or poison sumac plants, all members of the *Rhus* genus of plants; *see* SUMAC. Ivy dermatitis is a true allergic hypersensitivity reaction and repeated exposure to its sap causes a distinct inflammatory response; *see* ALLERGY. Although only about half of white persons under sixty are highly sensitive, almost anyone will produce a reaction with repeated exposures. Older persons and those with darker skin pigment are less sensitive. Sensitization and skin inflammation can occur only when the skin makes direct contact with the sap of the plant, which is released only when some part of it is bruised or crushed. The contact dermatitis which it causes can result from direct contact with the plant or the sap can be carried in smoke from burning plants, by clothes, or by animals. Temporary (seasonal) reduction of sensitivity can be achieved by established desensitization procedures prior to exposure. Prevention of poison ivy after contact with the sap can be achieved sometimes by washing with ordinary kitchen or laundry soaps, which are strongly alkaline, a few minutes after contact.

The skin in typical cases of ivy poisoning becomes red, swollen, and covered with many water blisters, associated with severe burning, tingling, or itching. The inflammation may be spread from an affected area of the body to other parts by dispersal of the watery, irritating contents of the blisters. The inflammation usually lasts one to four weeks. Chemicals such as potassium permanganate, boric acid solution, calamine lotion, or cold saline compresses are used to allay the discomfort caused by itching. Present-day treatment of severe cases may include hormone therapy, such as the administration of ACTH or cortisone (qq.v.) or the external application of hydrocortisone ointment.

See PLANTS, POISONOUS; POISON IVY, POISON OAK, AND POISON SUMAC.

IWO, city of Nigeria, in Western State, about 25 miles N.E. of Ibadan. Iwo is a road hub within 5 mi. of a railroad station. Local industries include cacao and palm processing, cotton weaving, and indigo dyeing. Pop. (1971 est.) 191,684.

IWO JIMA, island in the Pacific Ocean, largest of the Volcano Islands (q.v.), about 710 miles s. of Tokyo, Japan. About 5½ mi. long and 2½ mi. wide, the island is mountainous and volcanic in origin. Mount Suribachi (546 ft.), an extinct volcano, is the highest elevation. Principal industries include sulfur mines and a sugar refinery. The Volcano Islands were annexed by Japan in 1887. During World War II, the island of Iwo Jima, the site of a Japanese air base, was captured in 1945 by the United States Marine Corps in one of the bitterest battles of the war; *see* IWO JIMA, BATTLE OF. In accordance with the peace treaty signed between the Allies and Japan in 1951, the Volcano Islands were placed under the provisional administration of the United States Navy. They were returned to Japan in 1968, but Iwo Jima has a U.S. air base.

IWO JIMA, BATTLE OF, one of the most costly battles of the Pacific campaign of World War II (q.v.), fought in February and March, 1945, on the island of Iwo Jima (q.v.). More than 4000 men of the United States Marine Corps (q.v.) lost their lives in capturing the island from the Japanese; Japanese losses were estimated at about 20,000. The conquest of the island provided American air units with the first base inside the Japanese inner-defense system from which to attack the heart of industrial Japan with medium bombers escorted by fighters.

Before the actual invasion on Feb. 19, the island was subjected to air and sea bombardment for three months. In spite of the preinvasion assault, some Japanese were still firmly entrenched in underground fortifications in the soft volcanic soil. The marines secured the island after a month of the most severe fighting in their history. Mount Suribachi, the highest point on the island and an important defense position, was captured on Feb. 23. The campaign was officially declared ended on March 16.

I.W.W. *See* INDUSTRIAL WORKERS OF THE WORLD.

IXELLES, industrial suburb of Belgium, in Brabant Province, adjoining Brussels on the S.E. Industrial products include chemicals, metal and wood products, and textiles. The city has a communal museum. A 17th-century monastery houses a military cartographic institute and a school of decorative arts. In Flemish the suburb is called Elsene. Pop. (1971) 85,805.

IXION, in Greek mythology, the first man to murder one of his kinsmen. He murdered his father-in-law to avoid presenting the promised bridal gifts, but was purified by the god Zeus (q.v.), who brought him to Mount Olympus. There Ixion sought to seduce Hera (q.v.), the wife of Zeus. Zeus formed a cloud in his wife's image which deceived Ixion and made him the father of the monstrous Centaurs (q.v.). As punishment, Ixion was fastened to a fiery wheel that revolved forever in the underworld.

IXTACCIHUATL. *See* IZTACCIHUATL.

IXTLILXOCHITL, Fernando de Alva Cortés (1568?–1648), Mexican historian, and lineal descendant of the Mexican chief Ixtlilxochitl II (1500?–50). He was commissioned by the Spanish viceroy of Mexico to write histories of the ancient Mexican inhabitants.

The ruins of the Temple of Hadrian, built in the 2nd century, near İzmir, Turkey.

IZHEVSK, city of the Soviet Union, in the Russian S.F.S.R., and administrative center of the Udmurt A.S.S.R., on the Izh R., about 600 miles N.E. of Moscow. Izhevsk, a major steel-milling center, is in an industrial region. The city also manufactures machinery and small arms. Izhevsk was founded in 1760. Pop. (1970) 422,409.

İZMIR, formerly SMYRNA, city and seaport in Turkey, and capital of İzmir Province, at the head of the Gulf of İzmir, about 210 miles s.w. of İstanbul. İzmir, the third largest city in Turkey, is one of the chief seaports of the nation and is served by several railroads. İzmir also is a commercial and industrial center; dyes, soaps, and textiles are manufactured and foods and tobacco are processed. The chief exports include carpets, foodstuffs, and minerals.

Founded in the 11th century B.C. by the Aeolians, a Greek people, the city was seized by the Ionians (see IONIA) before 688 B.C. Later in the 7th century B.C., Smyrna was devastated by the Lydians, a people of Asia Minor (see LYDIA). Antigonus I, King of Macedonia (see under ANTIGONUS), restored the city in the 4th century B.C., and subsequently it was fortified and improved by Lysimachus (about 361–281 B.C.), a general in the service of Alexander III (q.v.), King of Macedonia, known as Alexander the Great. Smyrna was conquered later by the Romans and subsequently became an early center of Christianity, referred to as one of the "seven churches of Asia" (Rev. 1:11). During the 4th century A.D. the city was made a part of the Byzantine Empire (q.v.), and from the 11th to the 15th century was alternately ruled by the Byzantines and the Turks. In 1402 Smyrna was ravaged by the Mongols under Tamerlane (q.v.), and after 1424 belonged to the Ottoman Turks. The Greeks claimed Smyrna after World War I, and by the terms of the Treaty of Sèvres, drawn up in 1920, the administration of the city and its Ionian hinterland was assigned to Greece for five years; see SÈVRES, TREATY OF. The Greek occupation was contested by the Turks, who seized Smyrna in 1922. By the provisions of the Treaty of Lausanne in 1923, the city was awarded to Turkey. Pop. (1970) 520,686.

İZMIT, city in Turkey, and capital of Kocaeli Province, at the head of the Gulf of İzmit, 55 miles S.E. of Istanbul. It is an important naval base and the trade center of a tobacco-growing region. Industries include the manufacture of tobacco and paper products, chemicals, cement, and beer. İzmit is an ancient city, but few antiquities remain. After the destruction of the Megaran colony of Astacus, the city of Nicomedia was founded here in 264 B.C. as capital of Bithynia. Hannibal (q.v.), the Carthaginian leader, died here in 183 B.C. Later the residence of the Roman emperors Diocletian and Constantine, the city was captured by the Seljuk Turks in the 11th century and by the Ottoman Turks in 1338. Pop. (1970) 123,016.

IZTACCIHUATL, or IXTACCIHUATL (Aztec, "white woman"), dormant volcanic mountain of Mexico, about 35 miles S.E. of Mexico City and 10 miles N. of Popocatépetl (q.v.). It has three summits, the central one being the tallest (17,343 ft. above sea level). Its summits are constantly covered with snow, and from Mexico City the mountain resembles a reclining figure. Iztaccihuatl, therefore, is popularly referred to as "the sleeping woman".

Jj

J, tenth letter and seventh consonant in the English alphabet. It is the latest addition to English script and has been inserted in the alphabet after I, from which it was developed, just as V and W follow U, the letter from which they arose. In form, J was originally merely a variation of I; J appeared first in Roman times, when it was used sometimes to indicate the long *i* vowel sound, but often was used interchangeably with I. The Romans pronounced *i* as a vowel in some words, such as *iter,* and as a semivowel in others, for example, *iuvenis,* spelled presently *juvenis.* The only difference in spelling, however, was the occasional use of double i for the *y* sound, for example, in *maiior,* spelled presently *major.* In the Middle Ages the elongated form (J) was used as an ornamental device, most often initially and in numeral series; many Old French manuscripts indicate the numeral 4 by the letter sequence iiij. The use of J as an initial led ultimately to its specialized use to indicate both the old semivowel sound *y,* found in German, and the new palatal consonant sounds (ʒ) and (dʒ), found in French, Spanish, and English. Not until the middle of the 17th century did this usage become universal in English books; in the King James Bible of 1611, for example, the words Jesus and judge are invariably Iesus and iudge. Long after the invention of printing, j thus became more than a mere calligraphic variation of i (which in Latin could be either vowel or semivowel), and j became restricted to a consonantal function at any position in a word.

In English, j has the composite sound of d + zh, as in journal. In French, on the other hand, the zh sound alone is given the letter, as in *jour;* German has retained the original *y* sound of the Latin i consonant, as in *jahr;* and Spanish has introduced a new sound resembling a guttural *ch,* as in *Jerez.* In Middle English, before the differentiation of i and j, the combination gi was sometimes used to represent the *dzh* sounds, as in *Giew* for Jew, and in modern times the soft g is used for the same sound, as in general.

As an abbreviation, the capital J is used for Joule's equivalent, or the mechanical equivalent of heat (q.v.), in physics; for a variety of titles such as Judge and Justice; and in Old Testament criticism for any Jehovistic document included in one of the books of the Hexateuch (q.v.), the oldest being designated as J¹, and the more recent as J², J³, J⁴, until the end of the series. As a symbol the capital or lowercase J is used to indicate the tenth in a class, order, group, or series, and occasionally to indicate 10 as a number or numeral. J was used in medieval Roman numerals for the number 1 and was interchangeable with I; this use survives in medical prescriptions, in which a lowercase final j is used as a variant for i in numbers such as iij (3) or vij (7). The lowercase *j* is also used in electrical engineering as the mathematical symbol for the imaginary quantity $\sqrt{-1}$; see IMAGINARY NUMBER. M.P.

JABBAR, Kareem Abdul, original name (FERDINAND) LEW(IS) ALCINDOR (JR.), (1947–), American athlete, born in New York City. Educated at the University of California at Los Angeles, he led the university basketball team to three National Collegiate Athletic Association championships, 1967–69. In 1970 Alcindor, a center with the Bucks of Milwaukee, Wis., was unanimously named outstanding rookie of the National Basketball Association. The 7-ft.-2-in. player averaged 28.8 points and 14.5 rebounds per game in his first professional season.

JABIR. See GEBER.

JABORANDI. See PILOCARPINE.

JACAMAR, common name for any of fifteen species of small, robin-sized tropical American birds in the family Galbulidae of the woodpecker order Piciformes. The term refers especially to those in the genus *Galbula.* The bird has a long, sharp bill and long tail; it is usually greenish-gold above and reddish below and has a white throat patch. It nests in holes on or near the ground; the female lays three or four glossy white eggs each year. The jacamar subsists chiefly on insects which it catches in flight.

JACANA, common name of any of seven species of tropical birds in the family Jacanidae of the order Charadriiformes. It has extremely broad feet, long, thin toes tipped with sharp claws, and a short tail, and is similar in appearance to the rail (q.v.). The bird has a leaf-shaped plate covering the forehead, and a long sharp spur at the bend of each wing. It is 6½ to 11 in. long. The jacana frequents marshes and quiet streams, making its way over the surface of the water in search of insects, small shellfish, small frogs, and seeds by walking on pieces of floating vegetation. The bird usually nests on such vegetation anchored near a shore; the female lays about four tan eggs.

The Mexican jacana, *Jacana spinosa,* is the only one of these birds sometimes found in the southern United States. It ranges generally from Mexico to Central America, and is also found in Cuba and Haiti. This bird, which is 8½ in. long, is chiefly chestnut, with black head and neck and green wing feathers.

JACARANDA, tropical American trees belonging to the genus *Jacaranda* in the Bignonia family. They have opposite, twice-pinnate leaves and irregular, panicled blue flowers, each having a five-parted calyx, five-lobed corolla, five stamens (one of which is sterile), and a two-celled ovary. The fruit is a dry capsule containing many flat, winged seeds.

Brazilian rosewood (*see* ROSEWOOD), *Dalbergia nigra,* a tree in the Legume family, is called jacaranda locally. Jacaranda wood is heavy, hard, and brown, with a faint roselike aroma, and is used extensively in cabinetmaking.

JACINTH. *See* ZIRCON.

JACKAL, common name of three species of Old World wild dogs. The Asian jackal, *Canis aureus,* is common from southeastern Europe to India and also throughout Africa. The black-backed jackal, *C. mesomelas,* and the side-striped jackal, *C. adustus,* inhabit eastern and southern Africa. The animal is about the size of a fox, standing no more than 15 in. high at the shoulder. The narrow head and pointed muzzle are foxlike, but its other physical characteristics are similar to those of wolves. The Asian jackal is grizzled tawny buff in color; the tip of the bushy tail is dark. This animal feeds on carrion, wounded animals, small poultry, and occasionally fruit; it hunts at night, sometimes in small groups, more frequently in pairs, and habitually utters its cry, called the *pheal,* when hunting.

Jackals inhabit plains, deserts, and prairies, living twelve to fifteen years. During the day the jackal lives in holes in the ground. Jackals commonly interbreed with domestic dogs, and may be tamed with little difficulty.

JACKASS, common name for male ass (q.v.).

JACKDAW, *or* DAW, common name for a European crow, *Corvus monedula* of the family Corvidae. The jackdaw is smaller than the common crow (q.v.), attaining a maximum length of about 13 in. It is black, with a whitish-gray neck and purplish wings and tail. It feeds on insects, worms, and snails. The jackdaw builds its nest in hollow trees and in buildings; the female lays about five bluish-white eggs that are usually speckled with brown. The bird is easily tamed and a remarkable mimic.

JACK-IN-THE-PULPIT, *or* INDIAN TURNIP, common names of a perennial herb, *Arisaema triphyllum,* belonging to the Arum (q.v.) family, Araceae. The plant is native to moist woodlands of temperate North America. It commonly has two leaves, each divided into three pointed leaflets. In late spring a fleshy spike of flowers is surrounded by a large, convoluted, green or purple spathe, sometimes flecked with white dots, which arises from the base of the spike and forms a pulpit-like canopy over it. Small male flowers are borne at the upper end of the spike and large female flowers at the lower end.

Jack-in-the-pulpit, Arisaema triphyllum

JACK RABBIT

Cross-pollination is assured in most plants by the abortion of the male flowers of some stalks and the female flowers of others. Pollination between plants is usually effected by fungus gnats. The fruit, ripening in late summer, consists of a cluster of small, brilliantly scarlet berries. The underground portion of the plant is a turnip-shaped, wrinkled, starchy corm (bulb), which contains poisonous microscopic needles of calcium oxalate. At one time the Iroquois Indians used the corm as food, after boiling it to remove the poisonous characteristics.

JACK RABBIT. See Rabbits and Hares.

JACKSON, city in Michigan, and county seat of Jackson Co., on the Grand R., about 70 miles w. of Detroit. It maintains a municipal airport, and is served by several railroads. The city is a commercial and industrial center, and the trading center for the surrounding agricultural area, which contains many lakes. The principal industries in Jackson are the manufacture of fabricated metal products, nonelectric machinery, rubber tires, and transportation equipment. In the city is Jackson Junior College and nearby is the State Prison of Southern Michigan, one of the largest walled prisons in the world. Points of interest include illuminated cascades in a city park donated by one of Jackson's leading industrialists. Jackson was first settled in 1829, and was incorporated as a village in 1843. On July 6, 1854, the Republican Party (q.v.) was founded in Jackson. Jackson was chartered as a city in 1857. Pop. (1960) 50,720; (1970) 45,484.

JACKSON, city and capital of Mississippi, and a county seat of Hinds Co., on the Pearl R., about 40 miles E. of Vicksburg. The chief products of the surrounding region are cattle, cotton, and oil. The city, the largest in the State, is an important industrial, rail, and shipping center and is served by several air lines, motortruck lines, and railroads. Industry is highly diversified and includes cotton-seed processing, meat packing, and the manufacture of aircraft parts, burlap bags, cement, clothing, cork tile, corrugated boxes, cotton products, feeds, fertilizer, fluorescent lamps, foodstuffs, furniture, glass bottles and containers, household cleansers, kitchenware, machinery, mattresses, oil products, power mowers, store fixtures, and tile.

Among the many imposing public buildings are the new State Capitol, completed in 1903 and similar in design to the national capitol; the old State Capitol, occupied in 1839, and now the State Historical Museum; the governor's mansion, completed in 1842; and city hall, erected in 1854.

The foremost educational and cultural institutions are Belhaven College, founded in 1883; Jackson State College, founded in 1877; Millsaps College, founded in 1892; the State library; and a municipal art gallery. The city is also the site of the State fairgrounds.

History. The first settlement on the site of the city was a trading post known as Le Fleur's Bluff. In 1821 it was selected as the site of the State capital and named in honor of Andrew Jackson (q.v.), and incorporated in 1833. In 1861 the old State capitol was the site of the Secession Convention, which severed Mississippi from the Union. The city suffered heavily during the Civil War, notably on July 17, 1863, when it was occupied and partially burned by Federal troops led by General William Tecumseh Sherman (q.v.); see Civil War, The American. During the first half of the 20th century the city grew rapidly in population and economic importance. Pop. (1960) 144,422; (1970) 153,968.

JACKSON, city in Tennessee, and county seat of Madison Co., on the South Fork of the Forked Deer R., 75 miles N.E. of Memphis. The city is situated within an agricultural area in which cotton and fruit are grown, and livestock is raised. Jackson is an industrial city and the trading center and shipping point for the surrounding region. Industrial establishments in Jackson include factories manufacturing aluminum products, building materials, ceramic tiles, clothes, cotton bagging, foodstuffs, hardware, lumber products, and store fixtures. The city is the site of Lambuth College, founded in 1843; Lane College, founded in 1882; and Union University, founded in 1825. On the outskirts of Jackson is the West Tennessee Agricultural Experiment Station, of the University of Tennessee. Jackson was first settled in 1819, incorporated as a town in 1823, and chartered as a city in 1845. Pop. (1960) 34,376; (1970) 39,996.

JACKSON, Andrew (1767–1845), seventh President of the United States, born in Waxhaw settlement (in what is now South Carolina), the son of Irish immigrants. After the death of his parents and two brothers, he studied law in Salisbury, N.C., and was admitted to the bar in 1787. Appointed prosecutor for the western district of North Carolina (now Tennessee), he moved to Nashville, where he later established a plantation known as the Hermitage. In 1791 he married Mrs. Rachel Donelson Robards (1767–1828), a divorcee. A subsequent dispute over the finality of her divorce resulted in gossip that was bitterly resented by Jackson.

In 1797 he helped to frame the Tennessee constitution and served briefly as the first representative of that State in the U.S. House of

Andrew Jackson, a portrait by the 19th-century American artist Asher Brown Durand. New York Historical Society

Representatives and later in the Senate. After resigning from the Senate he served on the Tennessee supreme court from 1798 to 1804. During the War of 1812 (q.v.), he led the Tennessee militia against a rebellion of the Creek Indians in 1814. Commissioned major-general in the United States Army, he decisively defeated the British at New Orleans in 1815; see NEW ORLEANS, BATTLE OF. After the war, he waged a campaign against the Seminole Indians, pursuing them into Spanish Florida and evoking a protest from the Spanish government. He was appointed governor of the Territory of Florida in 1819; see FLORIDA: *History*.

Known as "Old Hickory", Jackson became increasingly popular with the American people, and in 1822 he was nominated for President by the Tennessee legislature. The election of 1824 brought him a popular vote larger than that of his opponent, but because no candidate received an electoral majority, the election was decided by the House of Representatives which chose John Quincy Adams (q.v.) as the sixth President; see ELECTORAL COLLEGE. Jackson then began a vigorous campaign against Adams, and was elected President in 1828. His defeat of the Whig (q.v.) candidate Henry Clay (q.v.) in the election of 1832 was an important factor in the development of the Democratic Party (q.v.).

Jacksonian Democracy. Jackson's administration, crucial in the growth of popular democracy, was marked by the extension of the electoral franchise and by the emergence of the convention system for the nomination of Presidential candidates; see CONVENTION; ELECTIONS.

The power of the Presidency also increased under Jackson, who made extensive use of the veto and of political patronage; see SPOILS SYSTEM. His personal advisers, assembled in the so-called kitchen cabinet (q.v.), assisted the President in decisions on national policy and economic reform.

One of the most important of these questions involved the issue of nullification (q.v.), by which an individual State might attempt to reject Federal authority. Jackson's opposition to this principle in a tariff dispute with South Carolina led to the resignation of Vice-President John Caldwell Calhoun (q.v.), an advocate of States' rights (q.v.).

The issue of Federal authority was also involved in a controversy over the Bank of the United States; see BANK AND BANKING: *United States Banking System*. Jackson, expressing widespread popular resentment and his own opposition to excessive governmental control, vetoed a bill that would have rechartered the institution. He then persuaded his secretary of the treasury, Roger Brooke Taney (q.v.), to withdraw government deposits from the bank and to place all newly collected tax money in certain State banks, called "pet banks". When the State banks, encouraged by the new policy, began to support land speculators by issuing paper currency, Jackson announced that government land could be purchased only with gold or silver. His restrictions were often blamed for the financial panic of 1837.

In other matters of national policy, Jackson advocated the movement of the Indian tribes to tracts west of the Mississippi R., and negotiated commercial agreements with France and Great Britain. Seeking to avoid war with Mexico, he moved cautiously in debates on the annexation of Texas; see TEXAS: *History*.

Near the end of his second term, Jackson was confronted by numerous opponents, many of whom united to form the Whig Party (q.v.). In the election of 1836, however, he successfully supported the candidacy of his close associate Martin Van Buren (q.v.). "Old Hickory" subsequently retired to the Hermitage, well-remembered for his military and political achievements. N.W.P.

JACKSON, Charles Thomas (1805–80), American geologist, chemist, and physician, born in Plymouth, Mass. He received his medical degree from the medical school of Harvard University and studied both medicine and geology in Paris. Jackson undertook an investigation of cholera (q.v.) in Vienna, Austria, during the epidemic of 1831. He returned to Boston the following year

JACKSON, HELEN HUNT

to practice medicine. In 1836 he abandoned medicine to establish a laboratory for instruction in analytical chemistry and to pursue work in the field of mineralogy. He became State geologist of Maine in 1837, and later of Rhode Island and New Hampshire. Appointed by Congress as United States geologist in 1847, he studied and reported on the mineral wealth of public lands in the Lake Superior region.

During his career Jackson became involved in two noted scientific controversies: He claimed credit for suggesting to the American inventor Samuel Finley Breese Morse (q.v.) the idea of the telegraph (q.v.); he also disputed the discovery of surgical anesthesia (q.v.) with the American dentist William Thomas Green Morton and the American surgeon Crawford Williamson Long (qq.v.). In 1852 the French Academy of Sciences ruled that both Jackson and Morton should be credited with the discovery, but today Long and Morton are given credit.

JACKSON, Helen Hunt (1830–85), American novelist and poet, born HELEN MARIA FISKE in Amherst, Mass. After her marriage to a banker in 1875, she lived for some time in the West, where she became intensely interested in the American Indians and worked actively to better conditions among them. Her *Century of Dishonor* (1881) was a sharp, documented criticism of the United States government for the treatment of the Indians. In 1882 she was appointed a special commissioner to investigate conditions among the Indians of the California missions, the setting of her novel *Ramona* (1884).

JACKSON, Robert Houghwout (1892–1954), American jurist, born in Spring Creek, Pa., and educated at Albany Law School, Albany, N.Y. After practicing law for some years in Jamestown, N.Y., he became general counsel for the United States Bureau of Internal Revenue in 1934. He was assistant attorney general of the U.S. from 1936 to 1938, and distinguished himself by his able conduct of a number of prosecutions of major American corporations charged with violating the antitrust laws. In 1938 and 1939 he served as solicitor general of the U.S. and from 1940 to 1941 as U.S. attorney general. In 1941 President Franklin Delano Roosevelt (q.v.) appointed him an associate justice of the United States Supreme Court. In 1945 Jackson was granted a leave of absence from the Court to serve as chief U.S. prosecutor in the trials of the major German war criminals, held in Nuremberg, West Germany; see WAR-CRIMES TRIALS: *Nuremberg Trials*. His writings include *The Case Against the Nazi War Criminals* (1946), and *The Nürnberg Case* (1947).

JACKSON, Thomas Jonathan, known also as STONEWALL JACKSON (1824–63), American soldier, born in Clarksburg, Va. (now in W.Va.), and educated at the United States Military Academy at West Point. Following his graduation from West Point in 1846 he participated in the Mexican War (q.v.) until 1848. In 1851 he became an instructor at Virginia Military Institute (V.M.I.) and the next year he resigned from the army. On the outbreak of the American Civil

Stonewall Jackson

War in 1861, he left V.M.I. to enter the Confederate army. He was commissioned a colonel, and within several months he was given the rank of brigadier general. Jackson earned his nickname at the first Battle of Bull Run (see BULL RUN, BATTLE OF), where his troops stood against the Union forces "like a stone wall", according to a colleague, General Bernard Bee (1824–61). While commanding his troops, the so-called Stonewall Brigade, during a campaign in the Shenandoah Valley in the spring of 1862, Jackson executed a remarkable tactical maneuver against three Union armies then menacing Richmond. After driving back the army of General Nathaniel Prentiss Banks (1816–94), which was advancing from the north, Jackson turned and defeated the armies threatening to attack his rear ranks from the east and west.

Jackson subsequently took part, with General Robert E. Lee, in the defeat of General George B. McClellan (qq.v.) in the Seven Days' Battle (q.v.) at Richmond. In August, 1862, Jackson defeated the army of General John Pope (1822–92), thus assuring a Confederate victory at the second Battle of Bull Run. Jackson then crossed the Potomac into Maryland with Lee, who ordered him to capture Harpers Ferry (q.v.). His task accomplished in September, 1862, Jackson rushed north to Antietam Creek to aid Lee who was under attack by an overwhelming Union force; see ANTIETAM, BATTLE OF. Jackson commanded the right wing of the victorious Confederate army at Fredericksburg in December, 1862; see FREDERICKSBURG, BATTLE OF. During the Rappahannock campaign in Virginia the following spring, by launching a surprise attack on the rear columns of the Union army, Jackson prevented the threatened encirclement of the Confederate forces by the troops of General Joseph Hooker (q.v.). On May 2, 1863, while leading his forces at Chancellorsville (see CHANCELLORSVILLE, BATTLE OF), Jackson was accidentally shot and fatally wounded by his own men.

Jackson is considered by military authorities to have been an outstanding leader, a skilled tactician, and one of the ablest Confederate commanders. See also CIVIL WAR, THE AMERICAN.

JACKSON HOLE. See GRAND TETON NATIONAL PARK; NATIONAL PARK SERVICE.

JACKSONVILLE, city of Arkansas, in Pulaski Co., about 14 miles N.E. of Little Rock. Manufactures include furniture, chemicals, electric equipment, and metal products. Pop. (1960) 14,488; (1970) 19,832.

JACKSONVILLE, largest city and a port of entry in Florida, coextensive with Duval Co., on the Saint Johns R. 25 miles w. of its mouth at the Atlantic Ocean, about 325 miles N.E. of Miami, and about 135 miles s. of Savannah, Ga. It is served by railroad and steamship; major airlines operate out of the municipal airport. The city is now linked to the Eastern seaboard by the Inland Waterway. Situated in a predominantly rural area, Jacksonville is the chief commercial, industrial, financial, cultural, and medical center of northeastern Florida and southeastern Georgia. It is also one of the principal distribution, insurance, and convention centers of the Southeastern United States, and it has three large United States Navy bases, to which 27,000 military personnel are assigned. In 1968 the city of Jacksonville was consolidated with Duval County under a new charter providing for a mayor-council form of government. The consolidation added more than 300,000 people to the city, and its area was expanded from 39 sq.mi. to 827 sq.mi., making it the largest city in land area of the U.S. Jacksonville is a summer and winter vacation resort, with excellent recreational facilities. The city maintains a park system of some 700 acres.

Commerce and Industry. The important port of Jacksonville has extensive shipping and storage facilities. The principal exports, both foreign and domestic, are naval stores, lumber, canned goods, citrus fruits, and iron and steel products; the leading imports are coffee, oil, and chemicals. Industrial establishments in the city include shipbuilding yards, chemical plants, lumber and planing mills, pulp and paper mills, canneries, automobile-assembly plants, and factories manufacturing cigars, glass, and fertilizers.

History. The first settlement in the vicinity of Jacksonville was made by a colony of French Huguenots (q.v.) under René Goulaine de Laudonnière (fl. 1562–82), in 1564. Fort Caroline, which they built on a bluff above the river, was destroyed by a force from the Spanish settlement at Saint Augustine in 1565. After the English had established supremacy in Florida, permanent settlement of the site was made in 1816, and in 1822 a town was laid out and named in honor of Andrew Jackson (q.v.), the first territorial governor of Florida. The town was incorporated in 1832. Jacksonville was occupied by Federal troops during the Civil War in order to control the operations of blockade runners on the St. Johns R.

Population. The population of Jacksonville increased between 1910 and 1950 from 57,699 to 204,517. In 1960 the population was 201,030. As a result of the consolidation of the city and Duval County, the population in 1968 exceeded 500,000. In 1970 it was 528,865.

JACKSONVILLE, city in Illinois, and county seat of Morgan Co., about 70 miles s.w. of Decatur. The leading products of the surrounding agricultural area are corn, livestock, oats, poultry, and wheat. In Jacksonville the principal industries are dairy processing, meat packing, metal fabricating, and the manufacture of brick and tile, caps, and concrete. It is the site of Illinois College, founded in 1829; MacMurray College, established in 1846 as the Illinois Conference Female Academy; several schools for the handicapped; and a State hospital for the insane. Prominent persons who made their home in Jacksonville at one time include the American political leaders Stephen Arnold Douglas and William Jennings Bryan (qq.v.). Jacksonville was founded and made the county seat in 1825. Pop. (1960) 21,690; (1970) 20,553.

JACKSONVILLE, city in North Carolina, county seat of Onslow Co., on the New R., about 100 miles s.e. of Raleigh. Jacksonville, pri-

JACOB

marily a resort city, has some manufacturing. Nearby is the United States Marine Corps base, Camp Lejeune. Pop. (1960) 13,491; (1970) 16,021.

JACOB, or ISRAEL, in the Old Testament, one of the Hebrew patriarchs, son of Isaac (q.v.) and Rebekah, and grandson of Abraham (q.v.). After depriving his brother Esau (q.v.) of their father's blessing and of his birthright by trickery, Jacob

An illustration of the Old Testament story of the encounter between Jacob and an angel of God.

fled to the house of his uncle, Laban, where he worked for many years, and married Laban's daughters, Leah and Rachel. His wives and their handmaidens, Zilpah and Bilhah, bore him twelve sons, who became the patriarchs of the twelve tribes of Israel. Leah bore Issachar, Judah, Levi, Reuben, Simeon, and Zebulun; Rachel bore Joseph and Benjamin; Zilpah bore Gad and Asher; and Bilhah bore Dan and Naphtali.

The story of Jacob is told in Gen. 25–35. Outstanding events in Jacob's life were the vision (of "Jacob's ladder") and blessing received at Bethel (Gen. 28:10–22) and the bestowal of the name Israel upon him by a divine adversary after they had struggled (Gen. 32:24–32). As the figure of Esau is taken to represent the nation of Edom (Gen. 36:8), so the figure of Jacob, or Israel, personifies the nation of Israel. Thus the prophet Hosea (q.v.) saw Jacob's experiences as typifying those of his people (Hos. 12) around 1700 B.C. *See* JEWS: *The Hebrews in Canaan.*

JACOB, François (1920–), French geneticist, born in Nancy, and educated at the University of Paris. For his service from 1940 until 1945 in the Free French underground forces of World War II he was awarded the *croix de guerre*. In 1950 he joined the Pasteur Institute in Paris. In 1964 the chair of professor of cellular genetics was created for him at the Collège de France, Paris. Jacob shared the 1965 Nobel Prize in medicine and physiology with his colleagues, the French scientists André Lwoff and Jacques Monod (qq.v.) for their work at the Pasteur Institute on the nature of the gene, that structure within the living cell that determines hereditary characteristics and controls production of enzymes and other proteins. Their work led to the discovery of a type of gene that regulates the activity of other genes. *See* HEREDITY.

JACOBI, Karl Gustav Jakob (1804–51), German mathematician, born in Potsdam, and educated at the University of Berlin. He became professor of mathematics at the University of Königsberg in 1827 and held this chair until 1842. Jacobi was one of the founders of the theory of elliptic functions (*see* ELLIPSE; FUNCTION). He made valuable contributions to the theory of numbers and to the study of determinants, one of which, the functional determinant, bears his name (*see* DETERMINANT; NUMBERS, THEORY OF); and he did research on differential equations (*see* CALCULUS: *Differential Calculus*). Several monographs on his findings were published during his career.

JACOBINS, name given to the members of a radical French political club that played a controlling part in the French Revolution (q.v.). It was founded in 1789 as the Society of Friends of the Constitution; the name "Jacobins" derives from the meeting place of the club, a former Jacobin monastery in Paris. The Revolutionary leaders Comte de Mirabeau and Maximilien Robespierre (qq.v.) were early members of the club, and Robespierre subsequently became its principal figure. Although comprising only 3000 members in Paris, the club had national scope through its control of 1200 related societies located throughout France. Its great political power resulted from the close organization of these affiliated groups and from the skillful hold on public opinion exercised by its leaders.

At its outset the club was in favor of a constitutional monarchy, but after the attempted escape from France of Louis XVI (q.v.), King of France, in 1791, the Jacobins, like most of the French people, turned against any form of royal rule. Simultaneously with the formation of the National Convention, the French ruling body from 1792 to 1795, the club reached the zenith of its power; it developed into so powerful a political party that no important action was undertaken by the convention until the matter had first been discussed in the meetings of the Jacobins. Extremist elements of the group took control during this period, and they plunged the country into the Reign of Terror, a state policy of suppressing all opposition by violence. The Jacobins insisted on the death of the king, destroyed the moderate Girondists (q.v.), and incited the working class against the middle class. The club lost much of its power with the downfall of its leader Robespierre, and was finally banned by the convention on Nov. 11, 1794.

JACOBITES, in English history, the name, derived from that of James II (q.v.), King of England, given to the adherents of the House of Stuart after the Glorious Revolution of 1688, when James was dethroned and exiled. After apparently accepting the change of dynasty, the Jacobites engaged for some years in minor, futile plots. Then in 1715 a group of Jacobite nobles led an uprising in Scotland and in the English Border country in favor of the son of the king's son, James Francis Edward Stuart (q.v.), who was known as the Old Pretender. After an indecisive battle with the government forces at Sheriffmuir, the Jacobite forces surrendered at Preston, and Stuart returned to exile in France. Seven noblemen were sentenced to death for their part in the revolt, but only James Radcliffe, Earl of Derwentwater (1689–1716) and William Gordon, Viscount Kenmure (d. 1716), were executed.

The high point of the Jacobite movement was the second Jacobite rebellion, known as "The Forty-Five". In July, 1745, the king's grandson, Charles Edward Louis Philip Stuart (q.v.), called Bonnie Prince Charlie, and also known as the Young Pretender, landed in Scotland and in September entered Edinburgh with 2000 men. Jacobite forces subsequently won three battles in Scotland and invaded England as far as Derby. Jacobite sentiment was strong only in the Scottish Highlands, however; their forces retreated, and were completely defeated at the Battle of Culloden. The revolt collapsed, and Bonnie Prince Charlie fled to France. Again, a number of nobles were executed for taking part in the rebellion. Nearly a thousand others were condemned to death, but had their sentences commuted. With the crushing of "The Forty-Five", the political significance of the Jacobite movement ended; it survived only in local sentiment and as a theme in romantic literature. *See* STUART. *See also* ENGLAND: *History: James II.*

JACOBS, William Wymark (1863–1943), British writer, born in London, England, and educated at the University of London. About 1885 he began writing short humorous stories about sea life and dock workers. His first collection of these tales, *Many Cargoes* (1896), established his literary reputation. In addition, he wrote several plays and novelettes. Jacobs is best known for his horror tale *The Monkey's Paw* (1902), a story, dramatized many times, about the supernatural effects a monkey's paw has on its owners.

JACOB'S-LADDER, or GREEK VALERIAN, common name for perennial herbs of the genus *Polemonium,* belonging to the Phlox family. Such plants have pinnate leaves which look like primitive ladders. The blue, pale-blue, or white, bell-shaped flowers, borne in corymbs, have a five-lobed calyx, five-lobed corolla, five stamens, and a solitary pistil. The fruit is a three-celled loculicidal capsule. The American Jacob's-ladder, *P. reptans,* has blue flowers, and grows in wooded areas of E. United States. Another blue-flowered species, *P. vanbruntiae,* is native to swampy areas of the U.S. Both are occasionally cultivated in gardens.

JACOPO DELLA QUERCIA. *See* QUERCIA, JACOPO DELLA.

JACQUARD, Joseph Marie. *See* LOOM: *Power Looms.*

JACQUERIE (from *Jacques Bonhomme*), in French history, uprising of peasants in 1358, during the Hundred Years' War (q.v.), and name derisively applied by the French nobility to the peasantry. Taking advantage of the revolutionary crisis precipitated by the English victory over France at Poitiers, the peasantry sought revenge upon their oppressors, particularly the nobility. The uprising, initiated by a minor clash between some peasants and soldiers late in May near Beauvais, swiftly spread to various parts of N.E. France. Supported by the burghers in some areas, the peasants sacked and burned numerous castles and killed a number of nobles. Royalist forces under Charles II, King of Navarre (*see under* CHARLES), then captain general of Paris, decisively defeated an army of peasants on June 10 near Meaux, killing about 7000 and crushing the uprising. Reprisals were inflicted on the peasantry in the ensuing period; according to some accounts about 20,000 were murdered in the course of two weeks.

JACQUES-CARTIER, city of Canada, in Québec Province, on the Saint Lawrence R., adjoining Longueuil on the N., and opposite Montréal, 4 miles E. of the city center. It is part of the Montréal metropolitan area, and industries include ironworking and the manufacture of metal and foundry products. The Louis Braille Insitute of the Blind is located here. The city,

Long-tailed jaeger, Stercorarius longicaudus
Charles J. Ott —
National Audubon Society

first known as Ville-Jacques-Cartier, is also called Cité de Jacques-Cartier. Pop. (1966) 51,734.

JADE, compact, opaque, gem stone, ranging in color from dark green to almost white. The term is applied to specimens cut from the minerals jadeite and nephrite.

Jadeite, the less common and more highly prized of the two minerals, is a silicate of sodium and aluminum, $NaAl(SiO_3)_2$, usually containing some iron, calcium, and magnesium. It belongs to the group of minerals called pyroxenes (q.v.). Jadeite crystallizes in the monoclinic system (*see* CRYSTAL: *Crystallography*), but rarely occurs in distinct crystals and is usually found in fibrous, compact, massive aggregates. It has a hardness ranging from 6½ to 7 and a sp.gr. ranging from 3.3 to 3.5; it is extremely tough and difficult to break. The luster on fresh fracture is dull and waxlike, but polished jadeite has a vitreous luster. Jadeite is found chiefly in eastern Asia in Burma, as well as in sections of Tibet and southern China.

Nephrite, a member of the amphibole group of minerals, is a silicate of calcium and magnesium, with a small amount of iron generally replacing part of the magnesium. It is a tough, compact variety of the mineral tremolite (q.v.) with hardness 6 to 6.5 and sp.gr. 2.96 to 3.1. Polished nephrite has an oily luster. It is found in Alaska, Mexico, New Zealand, Siberia, and Turkestan.

Jade was used in prehistoric times for weapons, utensils, and ornaments. A variety of jade called axstone is used by the natives of the South Sea islands for making hatchets. Jade has always been prized by the Chinese and Japanese as the most precious of all stones, and the most beautiful specimens of carved jade in the form of ornamental pieces, such as vases, bowls, tablets, and statues, many of which are now museum pieces, were made in China. Jade is a highly valued gem stone used in rings, necklaces, earrings, and other articles of jewelry. See GEM.

JADOTVILLE. See LIKASI.

JAEGER, or BOATSWAIN, common name for any large sea bird in the genus *Stercorarius* of the family Stercorariidae, which also contains the skua (q.v.). Jaegers are powerful fliers, and look somewhat like large gulls. They average 16 to 23 in. in length, depending upon the species. The birds are usually grayish brown or blackish above and white or light gray below. They have slightly hooked beaks, long, narrow wings, two long tail feathers, and webbed toes with long, sharp talons. Jaegers are noted for attacking slower and weaker sea birds such as terns and gulls in midair, forcing them to give up whatever food they have in their beaks or even forcing them to disgorge what they have swallowed. Jaegers feed on fish, on small rodents, and on the eggs and young of other birds. They nest in arctic regions on cliffs or plains; the female lays two or three spotted, dull-colored eggs in an unlined depression in the ground.

Three species of jaeger winter in North America, where they are commonly known as "sea hawks", "robber gulls", and "teasers" because of their thieving habits. The pomarine jaeger, *Stercorarius pomarinus,* is common in the winter off the coast of New England; the parasitic jaeger, *S. parasiticus,* is found along both coasts of the United States in winter; and the long-tailed jaeger, *S. longicaudus,* winters off the Atlantic coast of the U.S. The latter species breeds in the north in both the Old and New worlds.

JAÉN, city in Spain, and capital of Jaén Province, about 180 miles s. of Madrid. Jaén is the agricultural and trade center for the province. Industrial establishments in the city include chemical works, tanneries, distilleries, and textile factories. After the Moorish invasion of Spain during the 8th century, the city, then known as Jayyan, was developed as a trade center. Remains of the Moorish fortifications and citadel still stand. Jaén is the seat of a Roman Catholic bishopric. Of particular interest is the Renaissance-style cathedral, begun in 1532 and completed in the 18th century. Pop. (1970) 74,522.

JAFFA (anc. *Joppa*), historic city and seaport of Palestine, since 1949 part of of Tel Aviv–Jaffa (q.v.), a city of Israel, on the Mediterranean Sea, just S. of the mouth of the Hayarqon R., 35 miles N.W. of Jerusalem.

Jaffa is mentioned in the Old Testament as a seaport and border possession of the tribe of Dan (q.v.). In antiquity it was besieged on different occasions by the Egyptians, Persians, and Greeks. During the Jewish War of 68 A.D., it was destroyed by the Roman emperor Vespasian (q.v.). Christ's disciple Peter (q.v.) spent some time in Jaffa, and there restored the Christian woman Tabitha to life. Jaffa was captured by the Crusaders in 1126 and again in 1191, and in each case it was reconquered by the Muslims; see CRUSADES. Confronted with the threat of another Crusade in 1345, the Muslims destroyed the town. About the beginning of the 18th century it was reestablished as a seaport. British troops captured the city in 1917, during World War I, and from 1923 until 1948 it was part of the British-mandated territory of Palestine. By the terms of the United Nations partition plan of 1947, Jaffa was allocated to the Arabs, becoming a coastal outpost in Jewish territory. The city was attacked by Jewish forces in April, 1948, during the war between the Arab League (q.v.) and the Jews of Palestine, and all but about 15,000 of the Arab population fled, and in 1949 the city was incorporated into the newly established State of Israel (q.v.).

JAFFNA, city and seaport in Ceylon, and capital of Northern Province, on a peninsula, about 200 miles N. of Colombo. The city is the trading center for the surrounding region in which coconuts, rice, and tobacco are grown. As early as 204 B.C. Jaffna was inhabited by the Tamils, a Dravidian (q.v.) people. The city was occupied by the Portuguese and Dutch, successively, in the 17th and 18th centuries. The British seized the region in 1795. Pop. (1971 prelim.) 108,000.

JAGUAR, large feline mammal, *Panthera onca*, that is the most powerful of the American cats; see FELIDAE. A mature jaguar is about 6 ft. long, and stands 2 ft. high at the shoulder. It is found from southern Texas through South America, and is especially abundant in the dense forests of Central America and Brazil. In color, the jaguar is yellowish-tan, spotted with black; its head and body are massive, and its legs are short and thick. The animal is an adept climber and an excellent swimmer, feeding on arboreal, terrestrial, and aquatic animals. It rarely attacks man. The jaguar is extensively hunted in South America by professional hunters hired by ranchers to prevent depredations on cattle.

Jaguar, Panthera onca
Karl Weidmann—National Audubon Society

JAHN

JAHN, Friedrich Ludwig (1778–1852), Prussian patriot and teacher of gymnastics, known as *Turnvater* ("father of gymnastics"), born in Lanz, and educated at universities in Halle, Göttingen, and Greifswald. During the occupation of Prussia by the French in the Napoleonic Wars (q.v.), he determined to help bring about the emancipation of his country. Believing that the practice of gymnastics would result in a moral as well as physical regeneration of his countrymen, he established, in 1811, an open-air athletic field in Berlin. The courses in mass gymnastics he conducted there later formed the basis for the exercises of the German athletic clubs known as the *Turnvereine; see* GYMNASTICS. After serving for two years in the army, he was appointed (1815) state teacher of gymnastics, and organized the *Burschenschaften,* student patriotic fraternities, which became famous for their advocacy of the unification of Germany. As a result of his views, Jahn was imprisoned by the Prussian government from 1819 to 1825. During the Revolution of 1848 he was prominent in the German national parliament, which met at Frankfurt.

JAHVE, or JAHWE. See JEHOVAH.

JAI ALAI, or (Sp.) CESTA PUNTA, ball game of the Basques of northern Spain and the adjacent French Basque area in which opposing individuals or teams alternately bounce a small, hard ball against one, two, or three walls and catch it upon its return. Jai alai is a type of handball. The objective of the game is to amass a given number of points by forcing the opponent to miss the ball or to hit it out of bounds. The ball is caught and propelled with a glovelike, scoop-shaped wicker basket, the cesta, which is strapped to the player's wrist. Jai alai matches are usually played in a large auditorium known as a frontón; the court on which the game is played is called a cancha. The cancha is rectangular in shape, with walls about 40 ft. high. Although the court can vary in dimension, the shorter sides of the rectangle, the front and back walls, are usually about 55 ft. wide. They are connected along the left side of the court by a wall that ranges in length from 160 to 200 ft. Along the right or fourth side of the rectangle is a wire screen behind which the spectators sit.

The jai alai ball, or pelota, is made of a core of strands of hard rubber wound under tension, covered with an inner layer of linen thread and two outer layers of goat skin. About 2 in. in diameter, the pelota is approximately three-quarters the size of a baseball and much harder. During fast rallies the ball travels at speeds exceeding 150 m.p.h. Cestas, which are custom-made to player specification, vary somewhat in size and are usually about 2 ft. long.

The number of points required to win a jai alai game varies according to local custom and the number of participants. Singles matches are usually played to thirty points and doubles matches to forty points. Two types of jai alai matches are played, partidos and quinielas. The former are matches between two individuals or two teams of two players each, similar to a singles or doubles match in tennis. A quiniela is a bet in which the bettor chooses two men or teams to finish first and second in any order.

A game of jai alai commences when in one continuous motion the server bounces the pelota on the surface of the court, catches it in his cesta, and hurls it against the front wall. The ball must fall between short and long lines painted usually in red across the court, or the server loses the point, which goes to the opponent or opposing team. If the ball lands on the floor or against the side or back wall in foul territory, the server loses the point and the right to serve reverts to the other team. If the ball lands in fair territory and bounces twice before the receiver can return it to the front wall, the server gains a point and continues to serve. A contestant may hit the ball either before it reaches the playing surface or after it has bounced once. Balls must also be caught and returned in one nearly continuous motion. If the ball is juggled in the cesta the player loses the point. If the receiver returns the ball successfully, a rally ensues in which both teams hit the ball alternately until one or another loses the point by missing the ball, by allowing it to bounce twice, or by driving it out of bounds. During such rallies the ball remains in play if, after rebounding from the front wall, it strikes fair territory on the side or back wall before bouncing on the floor. The returned ball must always strike the front wall. Probably the most difficult maneuver in a jai alai game is that in which a player catches the ball as it comes off the back wall and returns it in a single motion to the side or front wall.

Cesta punta, as the game is called in Spain, is one of a number of Spanish ball games of Basque origin. Most professional jai alai players are Basques from northern Spain, although a few have appeared from Cuba, Mexico and the Philippines. Other forms of Basque ball, or *pelota vasca,* are *pelota mano* (handball), *pelota pala* (played by women with 2-ft. long rackets similar to large ping-pong paddles), and several forms in which the ball is batted from a heavy, stiff cesta. In one form no cancha is employed, but two teams, each having a large number of players, play on a large field. In Spain *pelota vasca* matches often took place as part of a feast day or holiday celebration. (Jai alai in the Basque language means "holy day", "holiday" or in a corrupted translation "merry festival".) When *cesta punta* was imported into Cuba about 1900, the name jai alai was applied to the game itself. This is the name by which most of the world outside of Spain knows the game.

Introduced into Latin America during the last decade of the 19th century, the game became a national pastime in many countries of that region. It spread to the U.S. in the early 20th century but is thus far played only in Florida, which has frontons in Miami, Daytona Beach, Tampa, Dania, and Miami Beach. It is also played professionally in Italy and the Philippines.

JAIL. *See* PRISON.

JAINISM, religion of India concentrated for the most part in the north, in parts of Bombay, and in the State of Mysore as well as in the larger cities of the Indian peninsula. The Jains totaled only 1,500,000 in the 1960's, but they exert an influence in the predominantly Hindu community far out of proportion to their numbers; they are mainly traders, and their wealth and authority have made their comparatively small sect one of the most important of living Indian religions.

Origins. Jainism is somewhat similar to Buddhism (q.v.), of which it was an important rival in India. It was founded by Vardhamana Jñātiputra or Nātaputta Mahāvīra (599–527 B.C.) called *Jina* ("spiritual conqueror"), a contemporary of Buddha (q.v.). Like the Buddhists, the Jains deny the divine origin and authority of the Vedas (*see* VEDA) and revere certain saints, preachers of Jainist doctrine from the remote past, whom they call *tīrthaṅkaras* ("prophets or founders of the path"). These saints are liberated souls who were once in bondage but became free, perfect, and blissful through their own efforts; they are saviors from the ocean of phenomenal existence and bondage to the cycle of rebirths. Mahāvīra is believed to have been the twenty-fourth *tīrthaṅkara*. Like adherents to their parent sect, Brahmanism (q.v.), the Jains admit in practice the institution of caste (q.v.), perform a group of sixteen essential rites, called *saṁskāras*, prescribed for the first three *varṇa* (caste) of Hindus, and recognize some of the minor deities of the Hindu pantheon; nevertheless, their religion, like Buddhism, is essentially atheistic. Fundamental to Jainism is the doctrine of two eternal, coexisting, independent categories known as *Jīva* (animate, living soul: the enjoyer) and *Ajīva* (inanimate, nonliving object: the enjoyed). Jains believe, moreover, that the actions of mind, speech, and body produce subtle *karma* (infra-atomic particles of matter), which becomes the cause of bondage, and that one must eschew violence to avoid giving hurt to life. The cause of the embodiment of the soul is thought to be karmic matter; one can attain salvation *(mokṣa)* only by freeing the soul of *karma* through the practice of the three "jewels" of right faith, right knowledge, and right conduct. In Jainist belief, however, women can never reach salvation.

Differences in Doctrine. These principles are common to all but differences occur in the religious obligations of the religious and lay orders, which are known respectively as the *Yatis* (monks of Śvetāmbara and Digambara sects) and the *Śrāvakas*. The *Yatis* must observe five great vows *(pañca-mahāvrata)*: refusal to inflict injury *(ahiṁsā)*, truthfulness *(satya)*, refusal to steal *(asteya)*, sexual restraint *(brahmacarya)*, and refusal to accept unnecessary gifts *(aparigraha)*. In keeping with the doctrine of nonviolence, they carry the Jainist reverence for animal life to its most extreme lengths; the *Yati* of the *Śvetāmbara* sect, for example, wears a cloth over his mouth to prevent insects from flying into it and carries a brush to sweep the place on which he is about to sit, to remove any living creature from danger. The observation of the nonviolent practices of the *Yatis* was a major influence on the philosophy of the Indian nationalist leader Mohandas Karamchand Gandhi (q.v.). The secular *Śrāvaka*, in addition to his observance of religious and moral duties, must engage in the adoration of the saints and of his more pious brethren, the *Yatis*.

The two main sects of Jainism, the *Digambara* (space-clad, or naked) and the *Śvetāmbara* (white-clad, wearers of white cloth), have produced a vast body of secular and religious literature in the Prakrit and Sanskrit languages; *see* SANSKRIT LITERATURE. The art of the Jains, consisting primarily of cave temples elaborately decorated in carved stones, and illustrated manuscripts, usually follows Buddhist models but has a richness and fertility that mark it as one of the peaks of Indian art; *see* INDIAN ART AND ARCHITECTURE. Some sects, particularly the *Ḍhuṇḍiā* and the *Luṇkā*, which reject the worship of images, were responsible for the destruction of many works of art in the 12th century, and Muslim raids were responsible for the looting of many temples in northern India. In the 18th century another important sect of Jainism was founded; it exhibited Islamic inspiration in its iconoclasm and rejection of temple worship. Complex ritu-

JAIPUR

als were abandoned in favor of austere places of worship called *sthānakas,* from which the sect is called *Sthānakavāsī*. R.W.W. & R.V.J.

JAIPUR, city in the Republic of India, and capital of Rajasthan State, about 150 miles w. of Agra. The city is within an agricultural and mining region, and is an important transportation junction and commercial center for the area. In Jaipur are to be found a large banking business, railroad workshops, and plants producing jewelry and textiles. The city follows a grid plan, with rectangular blocks created by broad intersecting avenues and streets. It is surrounded by a fortified wall, 20 ft. thick. Among places of interest are an astronomical observatory, the vast palace of the maharajas, and the University of Rajasthan, founded in 1947. Several institutions of higher learning, including a free college and a school of art, are located in the city. Jaipur was founded in 1728 and was the capital of the former Jaipur State, until the State was made a part of Rajasthan in 1949.

Pop. (1971) 613,144.

JAKARTA. *See* Djakarta.

JALAPA ENRÍQUEZ, city in Mexico, and capital of Veracruz State, on the slopes of the Sierra Madre Oriental, about 160 miles n.e. of Mexico City. The city is the agricultural center for the surrounding area in which coffee, fruit, sugar, and tobacco are grown. Because of its cool and healthful climate Jalapa Enríquez is a popular summer resort. The chief industries include the manufacture of cigarettes and cotton textiles. The city has a Franciscan convent thought to have been founded around 1555, and a museum containing an excellent archeological collection. Jalapa Enríquez was made a city in 1830 and the bishopric of the State in 1864. Pop. (1970) 127,000.

JAMAICA, independent member of the Commonwealth of Nations, third-largest island of the Greater Antilles of the West Indies, situated about 95 miles s. of Cuba. The island lies between lat. 17°43′ N. and lat. 18°32′ N. and long. 76°11′ W. and long. 78°21′ W. Jamaica has a maximum length, from e. to w., of about 145 mi.; the maximum width is about 50 mi. The total area of the island is 4411 sq.mi.

THE LAND

The terrain is extremely mountainous, except for several tracts of lowlands in the s. coastal area. The principal uplift, situated in the e. section of the island, is the Blue Mts. range, of which Blue Mt. Peak (7402 ft.) is the highest summit in the West Indies. A series of lesser mountains, with numerous transverse spurs, extends generally w. to the extremity of the island, surmounting an extensive plateau. The coastline, about 500 mi. long, is irregular, particularly in the s. Jamaica has a number of excellent natural harbors, including those at Kingston (q.v.), Saint Ann's Bay, Montego Bay, and Port Maria.

Thermal springs occur in various areas. No other volcanic phenomena are apparent, but the island is subject to severe earthquakes. Many small unnavigable rivers traverse the island.

Snorkeling is a popular sport in the waters off Jamaica.
British West Indian Airways

JAMAICA

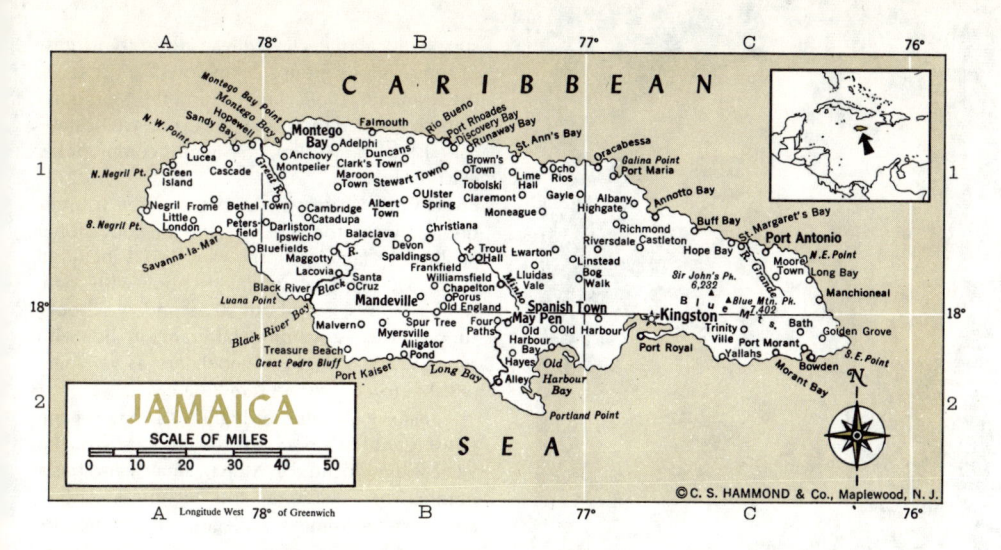

INDEX TO MAP OF JAMAICA

Cities and Towns

Adelphia	B1
Albany	C1
Albert Town	B1
Alley	B2
Alligator Pond	B2
Anchovy	B1
Annotto Bay	C1
Balaclava	B1
Bath	C2
Bethel Town	B1
Black River	B1
Bluefields	A1
Bog Walk	B1
Bowden	C2
Brown's Town	B1
Buff Bay	C1
Cambridge	B1
Cascade	A1
Castleton	C1
Catadupa	B1
Chapelton	B1
Christiana	B1
Claremont	B1
Clark's Town	B1
Darliston	B1
Devon	B1
Discovery Bay	B1
Duncans	B1
Ewarton	B1
Falmouth	B1
Four Paths	B2
Frankfield	B1
Frome	A1
Gayle	B1
Golden Grove	C2
Green Island	A1
Hayes	B2
Highgate	C1
Hope Bay	C1
Hopewell	A1
Ipswich	B1
Kingston (cap.)	C2
Lacovia	B1
Lime Hall	B1
Linstead	B1
Little London	A1
Lluidas Vale	B1
Long Bay	C1
Lucea	A1
Maggotty	B1
Malvern	B2
Manchioneal	C1
Mandeville	B1
Maroon Town	B1
May Pen	B2
Moneague	B1
Montego Bay	B1
Montpelier	B1
Moore Town	C1
Morant Bay	C2
Myersville	B2
Negril	A1
Ocho Rios	B1
Old England	B1
Old Harbour	B2
Old Harbour Bay	B2
Oracabessa	C1
Petersfield	A1
Port Antonio	C1
Port Kaiser	B2
Port Maria	C1
Port Morant	C2
Port Rhoades	B1
Port Royal	C2
Porus	B1
Richmond	C1
Rio Bueno	B1
Riversdale	C1
Runaway Bay	B1
Saint Ann's Bay	B1
Saint Margaret's Bay	C1
Sandy Bay	A1
Santa Cruz	B1
Savanna-la-Mar	A1
Spaldings	B1
Spanish Town	C2
Spur Tree	B2
Stewart Town	B1
Tobolski	B1
Treasure Beach	B2
Trinityville	C2
Trout Hall	B1
Ulster Spring	B1
Williamsfield	B1
Yallahs	C2

Physical Features

Black (river)	B2
Black River (bay)	B2
Blue (mts.)	C1
Blue Mountain (peak)	C1
Galina (point)	C1
Grande (river)	C1
Great (river)	B1
Great Pedro (bluff)	B2
Long (bay)	B2
Minho (river)	B1
Montego (bay)	A1
Montego Bay (point)	A1
North East (point)	C1
North Negril (point)	A1
North West (point)	A1
Old Harbour (bay)	B2
Portland (point)	B2
Sir John's (peak)	C1
South East (point)	C2
South Negril (point)	A1

Climate. Tropical climatic conditions prevail in the coastal lowlands. The mean annual temperature in this region is almost 80° F., but oceanic winds frequently moderate the extremes of heat and humidity. Mean annual temperatures in the plateau and mountain areas range from about 73° F. at elevations below 3000 ft. to about 60° F. at the 5000-ft. level. Annual precipitation, averaging slightly more than 66 in., is characterized by wide regional variations. Over 200 in. of rain are deposited annually in the N.E. section; in the vicinity of Kingston the average is about 32.5 in. The months of maximum precipitation are May, June, October, and November. The region is at times rent by violent hurricanes.

Natural Resources. Because of the rich soil Jamaica is primarily agricultural. Mineral deposits, such as gypsum, lead, and salt are found. The bauxite deposits, in the central section of the island, are the richest in the world.

Plants and Animals. Luxuriant and remarkably diversified vegetation characterize the flora. More than 2000 species of flowering plants have been classified. Among indigenous trees are cedar, mahoe, mahogany, logwood, rosewood, ebony, palmetto palm, coco palm, and pimento (allspice). Such valuable trees and plants as the mango, breadfruit, banana, and plantain also flourish on the island and are widely cultivated.

The Jamaican fauna, as that of the West Indies generally, includes highly diversified bird life.

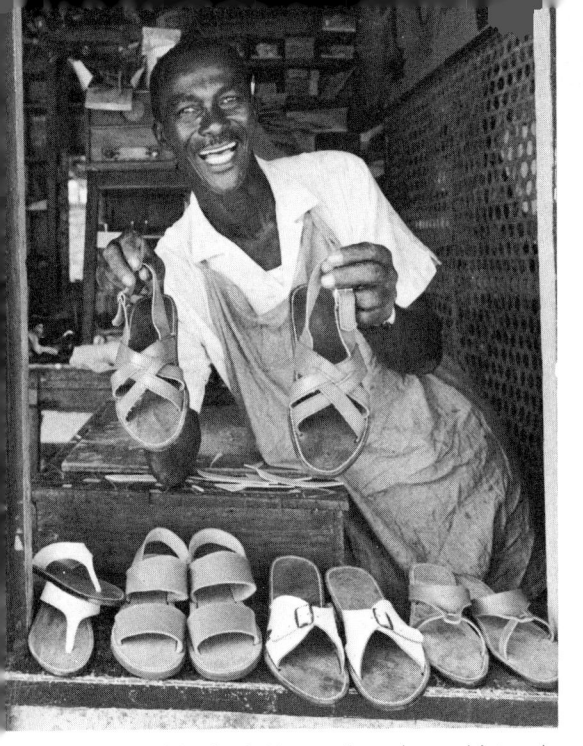

A sandal maker in Montego Bay makes sandals to order while the customer waits.   Jamaica Tourist Board

Varieties are said to number over forty. Parrots, hummingbirds, cuckoos, and green todies are especially abundant. No large indigenous quadrupeds or venomous reptiles exist.

THE PEOPLE

Nearly 90 percent of the population of Jamaica consists of Negroes, most of whom are descendants of African slaves. Persons of mixed Negroid-Caucasoid ancestry comprise most of the remainder; other minorities include East Indians, Europeans, and Chinese. About two-thirds of the population is rural.

Population. The population of Jamaica (census 1970) was 1,865,400. The United Nations estimated the overall population density at about 445 persons per sq.mi. in 1970. A rapid increase in population (estimated at 3 percent annually) has resulted in serious unemployment and overcrowding.

Political Divisions and Principal Cities. The island is divided into fourteen parishes. Eleven of the parishes are administered by popularly elected councils; the remaining parishes are administered by elected commissions.

Kingston (pop., 1970 est., 117,400), the capital of Jamaica, is a commercial seaport and the largest city in the country. Other important communities are Spanish Town (15,000), Savanna-la-Mar (10,000), and Port Antonio (8000).

Language and Religion. English is the official language, although many of the Jamaicans speak a local dialect. Anglicans form the largest of the religious groups. Numerous Baptist sects, the Roman Catholic Church, and the Methodist Church are also represented. Several well-established Jewish, Muslim, and Hindu communities exist.

Education. Primary education is free to children between the ages of 6 and 15. Educational facilities in Jamaica in the early 1970's included about 800 public elementary schools with some 400,000 pupils, and about 90 secondary schools, supported by governmental grants-in-aid, with some 42,000 students. Schools are as yet inaccessible to children in remote areas.

A major institution of higher learning for the entire Caribbean region is the University of the West Indies, located at Mona. Jamaica also has a number of vocational and technical schools and teacher-training colleges, and more are being built.

Culture. The position of Jamaica as a dependency of Great Britain for more than 300 years is reflected in the language and some of the customs practiced by the predominantly Negro population. Many images and drawings that were executed by the Arawak Indians, the aboriginal inhabitants of Jamaica, have been discovered in caves on the island.

Contemporary cultural life in Jamaica combines African influences, particularly in music and religion, with Western traditions imported by the British governing class.

THE ECONOMY

The economy of Jamaica is primarily agricultural, but recent gains in mining, manufacturing, and tourism are leading to a more diversified economy. Recent annual budget figures showed revenues of about $294,200,000 and expenditures of about $343,700,000. In the early 1970's about 1,637,000,000 kw hours of electricity were produced.

Agriculture. Some 40 percent of the total labor force is engaged in agricultural production. The chief crop is sugarcane; from the annual average harvest in the early 1970's, more than 394,000 metric tons of refined sugar were produced. Other leading agricultural products are bananas, citrus fruits, tobacco, cacao, coffee, coconuts, corn, hay, peppers, ginger, mangoes, potatoes, and arrowroot. Jamaica grows nearly the entire world supply of allspice.

In the early 1970's the livestock population included some 270,000 cattle, 270,000 goats, and 190,000 pigs.

Mining and Manufacturing. The bauxite and alumina (enriched bauxite ore) industries are a mainstay of the Jamaican economy and account

JAMAICA

for more than 45 percent of the total exports. In the late 1960's alumina production was nearly 870,000 tons, and bauxite production amounted to more than 12,500,000 tons. In the late 1960's the largest alumina plant outside of the United States was built at Saint Elizabeth.

Manufacturing is becoming an increasingly important factor in the island economy; in the late 1960's some 180 industries had been established. The government has granted concessions, such as duty-free importation and tax-relief programs, to further industrialization. Along with established food and beverage industries, new plants manufacturing such products as printed fabrics, transistor radios, nylon stockings, and fertilizers have been set up. A new steel mill, using local scrap iron and capable of producing 50,000 to 70,000 tons per year, was erected in 1966.

Banking, Commerce, and Trade. The unit of currency is the dollar, consisting of 100 cents (1 dollar equals U.S.$1.11; 1973). In 1969 Jamaica converted from the metric to the decimal system. The Bank of Jamaica is the central bank and bank of issue. Several commercial banks are also in operation.

Foreign trade is primarily with the U.S., Great Britain, and Canada. In the early 1970's, chief exports were minerals, sugar, rum, molasses, and bananas, and all exports were valued at $566,000,000 annually. Flour, textiles, motor vehicles, tobacco, machinery, and petroleum products were the major imports; the value of all imports amounted to about $363,000,000 annually.

Tourism is vital to the economy and provides a considerable portion of foreign-exchange earnings. In the late 1960's some 407,000 persons visited the island annually; spendings were estimated at about $102,000,000 per year for this period.

Transportation and Communications. Jamaica has 225 mi. of railroads. First-class highways, totaling 2682 mi., are maintained by the ministry of communications and works. Secondary roads, suitable for light automobile traffic, and totaling 6898 mi., are maintained by the local governments. Numerous international airlines and Air Jamaica serve the island, and internal flights are provided by a local airline.

The island operates two radio stations and one television station. About 1350 mi. of telegraph lines, 20,850 mi. of telephone lines, and some 300 post offices are maintained.

Labor. In the late 1960's the labor force numbered some 650,000. The main trade unions in-

Sugar, important to the economy of Jamaica in its own right and as an ingredient of rum, awaits processing at the Caymanas refinery, near Kingston.
Jamaica Information Service

JAMAICA

cluded the National Workers' Union of Jamaica (N.W.U.), and the Bustamante Industrial Trade Union (B.I.T.U.). The N.W.U., the largest, had 150,000 members; the B.I.T.U. had over 100,000 members. Each union was closely identified with one of the two main political parties: the N.W.U. with the People's National Party, and the B.I.T.U. with the Jamaica Labour Party.

GOVERNMENT

The Jamaican constitution, promulgated in 1962, established a parliamentary system of government patterned after that of Great Britain. The prime minister is the head of the government. The British crown is represented by a governor-general.

Central Government. Executive power is vested in a cabinet. The cabinet consists of at least eleven ministers, and is headed by the prime minister. The governor-general appoints the ministers and the prime minister.

Jamaica has a two-party political system. The ruling party in 1972 was the People's National Party (P.N.P.); the Jamaica Labour Party (J.L.P.) formed the opposition.

Legislature. Legislative authority is vested in the bicameral parliament. The fifty-three members of the House of Representatives are popularly elected to terms of five years. The twenty-one members of the Senate are appointed by the governor-general, thirteen in accordance with suggestions by the prime minister, and the remaining eight on the advice of the leader of the minority party.

Judiciary. The legal and judicial system is based on English common law and practice. The judicature comprises the supreme court, a court of appeals, resident magistrates' courts, petty sessional courts, and other courts.

HISTORY

Members of the Arawak tribe, an important group of the Arawakan (q.v.) linguistic stock of American Indians, were the aboriginal inhabitants of Jamaica (Arawakan *Xaymaca,* "Isle of Springs"). The Italian-born navigator Christopher Columbus (q.v.) discovered the island on his second voyage, and it became a Spanish colony in 1509. Saint Jago de la Vega (now Spanish Town), the first settlement and, for the ensuing 350 years, the capital, was founded about 1523. Colonization proceeded slowly under Spanish rule. Enslaved by the Spanish, the Arawak quickly died out as a result of harsh treatment and diseases. African slaves were imported to overcome the resultant labor shortage.

Jamaica was captured by an English naval force under Sir William Penn (1621–70) in 1655. The island was formally transferred to England in 1670 under the provisions of the Treaty of Madrid. During the final decades of the 17th century, growing numbers of English emigrants arrived; the sugar, cacao, and other agricultural and forest industries were rapidly expanded; and the consequent demand for plantation labor led to large-scale importation of Negro slaves. Jamaica soon became one of the principal slave-trading centers in the world. In 1692 Port Royal, the chief Jamaican slave market, was destroyed by an earthquake. Kingston was established on a nearby site in the same year. Parliamentary legislation provided for the abolition of slavery after Aug. 1, 1838. The act made available $30,000,000 as compensation to the owners of the nearly 310,000 liberated slaves.

Large numbers of the freedmen abandoned the plantations following emancipation and took possession of unoccupied lands in the interior, gravely disrupting the economy. Labor shortages, bankrupt plantations, and declining trade resulted in a protracted economic crisis. Oppressive taxation, discriminatory acts by the courts, and land-exclusion measures ultimately caused widespread unrest among the Negroes. In October, 1865, an insurrection occurred at Port Morant. Imposing martial law, the government speedily quelled the uprising and inflicted brutal reprisals on Negroes. Jamaica was reduced to the status of a crown colony, thus losing the large amount of self-government it had enjoyed since the late 17th century. Representative government was partially restored in 1884.

Jamaica was one of the British colonies that on Jan. 3, 1958, was united in the Federation of the West Indies; see WEST INDIES, THE. Disagreement over the role Jamaica would play led to the breakup of the federation, and on Aug. 6, 1962, the island gained independence. The Jamaica Labour Party won the elections of April, 1962, and its leader, Sir William Alexander Bustamante (1884–   ), became prime minister. In 1967 he retired and was succeeded by Hugh Lawson Shearer (1923–   ). In 1968 Jamaica was a founding member of the Caribbean Free Trade Area (CARIFTA). In elections on Feb. 29, 1972, Shearer's party was upset by the People's National Party. Michael Norman Manley (1923–   ), head of the party and president of the Caribbean Bauxite and Mine Workers Federation, became prime minister and promised a regime of economic development.

JAMAICA PEPPER. See PIMENTO.

JAMES, longest river in Virginia, formed at Iron Gate, Alleghany Co., by the union of the Jackson and Cowpasture rivers. It flows generally S.E. to Lynchburg, then N.E. to Scottsville, in central

JAMES (Aragón)

Virginia, where it turns S.E., passing Richmond. Below Richmond the river generally widens to Hampton Roads (q.v.), the estuary through which it flows to empty into Chesapeake Bay (q.v.). The James R. is navigable to Richmond, about 120 mi. from its mouth, for vessels up to 150 tons. The total length of the river is about 340 mi. The falls at Richmond furnish abundant waterpower for the industries of the city. Tributaries of the James include the Appomattox and the Rivanna rivers. Jamestown (q.v.), the first permanent English settlement in America, was founded on the banks of the James R. in 1607.

JAMES, book of the New Testament (see BIBLE), in the King James Version, THE GENERAL EPISTLE OF JAMES. It is one of seven New Testament Epistles that are known collectively as the General Epistles because they are each addressed to the entire Church rather than to a specific group. Ecclesiastical tradition has ascribed the Epistle to the Apostle James, called "the Less" (see under JAMES). Today, however, most Bible scholars suggest that the traditional claim is supported neither by ancient nor by recent evidence. They believe rather that the author was a Greek Christian who had a fine command of the Greek language, who apparently knew or had read some of the letters of Saint Paul and Saint Peter (qq.v.), and who thus probably wrote after the close of the 1st century A.D.

James is a miscellaneous collection of moral instructions and exhortations, similar in style, for example, to the book of Ecclesiasticus (q.v.) and other Jewish Apocryphal wisdom literature (see BIBLE: *The Apocrypha*). The main themes developed in the Epistle are concerned with the application of Christianity to everyday living. Men should seek and prefer patience, "wisdom that is from above" (3:17), humility, and "the prayer of faith" (5:15); for great riches, a boasting tongue, and "envying and strife" (3:14) always corrupt. Men with an unwavering faith may endure the severest temptations. But faith by itself is no safeguard in everyday life, for "faith, if it hath not works, is dead, being alone" (2:17); men must also show their faith by good deeds.

Although the Epistle of James was recognized as canonical as early as the 2nd century A.D. (see BIBLE, CANON OF THE), not all persons then, or later, accepted it without reservation. The German religious reformer Martin Luther (q.v.), to mention one notable dissenter, objected strongly to the book. He felt that parts of it contradicted the teachings of St. Paul, and he called it an "epistle of straw". In recent years, however, James has been more favorably received.

JAMES, name of three saints, figures in the Christian Church of the 1st century.

Saint James, known as the "brother" of Jesus Christ (Mark 6:3, Gal. 1:19). According to the New Testament, he was a leader of the early Church, in Jerusalem (Acts 12:17, 15:13). James was put to death by the Sanhedrin (q.v.), the Jewish high council, about 63 A.D. Tradition sometimes identifies him with Saint James the Less (see below), but modern scholars consider this identification unlikely, as they do his authorship of the book of James (q.v.).

Saint James the Great, an Apostle (q.v.), the son of Zebedee and Salome and brother of Saint John the Evangelist (q.v.). Jesus called the two brothers *Boanerges* (Gr., "sons of thunder") because of their zeal (Mark 3:17). With Saint Peter (q.v.) and Saint John, James was one of the three privileged disciples who witnessed the Transfiguration of Jesus and His agony in the garden of Gethsemane (q.v.). Beheaded by Herod Agrippa I (see under HEROD), ruler in Judea, about 44 A.D., James was the first of the twelve discples to be martyred (Acts 12:1–2). He is especially venerated in Spain because of an unsubtantiated tradition that he preached there shortly before his death. His feast day is July 25.

Saint James the Less, an Apostle and the son of Alpheus (Mark 3:18). Virtually nothing is known of him other than that he was one of the twelve disciples of Jesus Christ. His feast day is combined with that of Saint Philip (q.v.) on May 3.

JAMES, name of two kings of Aragón.

James I, called EL CONQUISTADOR (1208–76), King (1213–76), son of King Pedro II (1174–1213), born in Montpellier, France. He succeeded his father as king of Aragón in 1213. Sixteen years later James began his conquest of the Balearic Islands (q.v.), gaining full control in 1235. After a three-year campaign he then captured the Moorish city and kingdom of Valencia (q.v.). He promulgated a new legal code in 1247 and brought an end to the conflicting territorial claims of Aragón and France by concluding with Louis IX (q.v.), King of France, the Treaty of Corbeil in 1258. He spent the remaining years of his life attempting to drive the Moors from the Spanish peninsula. Before his death he divided his kingdom among his two sons, a division which ultimately led to conflict.

James II, called JAMES THE JUST (1260?–1327), King (1291–1327), second son of King Pedro III (1238–85), and grandson of James I. James II succeeded his father as king of Sicily in 1285, and in 1291, upon the death of his elder brother King Alfonso III (see under ALFONSO), James relin-

111

JAMES (England)

quished Sicily to become king of Aragón. In return for Sicily Pope Nicholas IV (see under NICHOLAS), made James king of Sardinia and Corsica. To bring about peace with the Anjou (q.v.) rulers, James married a daughter of Charles II, King of Naples, (see under CHARLES). About 1300 James founded the University of Lérida.

JAMES I (1566–1625), King of England (1603–25), and, as James VI, King of Scotland (1567–1625). He was born in Edinburgh Castle, Scotland, the only son of Mary, Queen of Scots and Henry Stewart, Lord Darnley (qq.v.). On the abdication of his mother in 1567, James was proclaimed king of Scotland. A succession of regents ruled the kingdom until 1576, when James became nominal ruler. The boy king was little more than a puppet in the hands of political intriguers until 1581. In that year, with the aid of his favorites James Stewart, Earl of Arran, (d. 1596), and Esmé Stuart, Duke of Lennox (1542?–83), James assumed actual rule of Scotland. Scotland was at that time divided domestically by religious conflict between the Protestants and Roman Catholics, and in foreign affairs by those favoring an alliance with France and those supporting England. In 1582 James was kidnaped by a group of Protestant nobles headed by William Ruthven, Earl of Gowrie (1541?–84), and was held virtual prisoner until he escaped the following year.

In 1586 by the Treaty of Berwick, James formed an alliance with his cousin Elizabeth I (q.v.), Queen of England, and the following year, after the death of his mother, he succeeded in reducing the power of the great Roman Catholic nobles. His marriage to Anne of Denmark (1574–1619) in 1589 brought him for a time into close relationship with the Protestants. After the Gowrie Conspiracy of 1600, James repressed the Protestants as strongly as he had the Catholics. He replaced the feudal power of the nobility with a strong central government, and, maintaining the divine right (q.v.) of kings, he enforced the superiority of the state over the church. See SCOTLAND: *History*.

In 1603 Queen Elizabeth died childless, and James succeeded her as James I, the first Stuart (q.v.) king of England. In England his policy, based on divine right, led to prolonged conflict with Parliament. He alienated the Nonconformists (q.v.) in 1604 by convoking the Hampton Court Conference, at which he authorized a new translation of the Bible, generally called the King James Version; see BIBLE, ENGLISH TRANSLATIONS OF THE. His undue severity toward Roman Catholics gave rise to the abortive Gunpowder Plot (q.v.) in 1605. James tried unsuccessfully to

James II of England, a portrait by the contemporary English artist Sir Godfrey Kneller. British Information Services

advance the cause of religious peace in Europe, giving his daughter Elizabeth (q.v.) in marriage to the elector of the palatinate, Frederick V (1596–1632), the leader of the German Protestants. He also sought to end the conflict by attempting to arrange a marriage between his son, later King Charles I (q.v.), and the Infanta of Spain, then the principal Catholic power. His efforts were unsuccessful, and due to the failure of his planning, England was drawn into the Thirty Years' War (q.v.). He was succeeded as king of England and Scotland by Charles I. See ENGLAND: *History*.

JAMES II (1633–1701), King of England, Scotland, and Ireland (1685–88), born in London, England, the second surviving son of King Charles I and Henrietta Maria (qq.v.). He was created duke of York and Albany in 1634. After the execution of his father he was taken to the Continent, and in 1657 he entered the Spanish service in the war against England. At the Restoration (q.v.) of the monarchy in 1660, his brother became king as Charles II (q.v.) and James was made lord high admiral of England. In the same year he married Anne Hyde (1637–71), daughter of Edward Hyde (q.v.), Earl of Clarendon. In 1672 James made a public profession of his conver-

JAMES (Scotland)

sion to the Roman Catholic faith. In 1673 the English Parliament passed the first of the Test Acts (q.v.) disqualifying Catholics from holding office, and James resigned as lord high admiral. Shortly after, he married the Catholic Mary Beatrice of Modena (1658–1718). In 1679 the House of Commons unsuccessfully attempted to bar James from the throne.

On the death of Charles in 1685, James became king. In the same year he crushed a revolt in Scotland led by James Scott, Duke of Monmouth (q.v.) and Archibald Campbell, Earl of Argyll (see under CAMPBELL). James alienated many supporters by his severe reprisals, especially by a series of repressive trials, the Bloody Assizes (q.v.). James attempted to win the support of the Dissenters (q.v.) and the Roman Catholics in 1687 by ending religious restrictions, but instead increased the religious tensions. The birth of his son (see STUART, JAMES FRANCIS EDWARD), on June 10, 1688, seemed to insure a Roman Catholic succession. The opposition leaders soon thereafter invited James' son-in-law, William of Orange, later William III (q.v.), to take the English throne, thus touching off the Glorious Revolution. William landed in England in November, 1688, and marched on London. He was hailed as a deliverer, and James, deserted by his troops, fled to France, where he was aided by King Louis XIV (q.v.). In 1690, aided by a small body of French troops, James landed in Ireland in an attempt to regain his throne. He was defeated in battle at the Boyne (q.v.), and returned to France, where he remained in Saint-Germain-en-Laye until his death. See ENGLAND: *History: James II.*

JAMES I (1394–1437), King of Scotland (1406–37), only surviving son of King Robert III (q.v.), born in Dunfermline. In 1406, shortly before the death of his father, James was sent to France for safety from rebellious Scottish nobles. The ship was seized by the English, and James was kept a prisoner until 1423. The following year, having inherited the Scottish throne in 1406, James returned to Scotland and was crowned. He married Jane Beaufort (d. 1445), niece of the English king Richard II, and granddaughter of John of Gaunt (qq.v.). By 1429 James forced the Scottish nobles to submit to royal authority. He introduced representative government and for the first time caused parliamentary acts to be published in the language of the common people. He drew closer the bond of alliance with France and gave his eldest daughter Margaret (1425?–45) in marriage to the Dauphin, later King Louis XI (q.v.). James, however, had antagonized the Scottish nobles by forfeiting their estates and was assassinated in 1437. He was succeeded by his son James II (q.v.).

JAMES II (1430–60), King of Scotland (1437–60), son of King James I (q.v.), born in Edinburgh. He was crowned shortly after the murder of his father in 1437. A regency led by the Douglas (q.v.) family ruled until 1449, when James began to govern by himself. His efforts to promote social welfare were greatly obstructed by the nobles, and especially by William, 8th Earl of Douglas (1425?–52), who was involved in treason and who was stabbed to death by the king. James crushed a revolt of the Douglas family in 1452 and seized their estates. He then became entangled in the contest between the houses of York and Lancaster; see ROSES, WARS OF THE. In 1460 at the head of an army, he was killed during the siege of Roxburgh Castle in Scotland. He was succeeded as king by his son James III (q.v.).

JAMES III (1451–88), King of Scotland (1460–88), son of King James II (q.v.), born in Stirling. He was crowned king in 1460 after the death of his father. A regency ruled until 1469 when he began his personal rule. Through his marriage to Margaret of Denmark (1457?–86) in the same year, James gained control of the Orkney and Shetland islands. James was unpopular with the Scottish nobles who were led by his brother Alexander Stewart, Duke of Albany (1454?–85). The nobles seized the king, and kept him prisoner in the castle at Edinburgh. Under the duke of Albany, the English forces took Berwick and advanced to Edinburgh. In 1487, James made peace with the English, thereby further alienating his turbulent nobles, who rose in rebellion and induced James' son, later James IV (q.v.), to become their nominal head. In the ensuing rebellion at Sauchieburn between the nobles and the Royalists, James was thrown from his horse and murdered by a noble disguised as a priest. He was succeeded by James IV.

JAMES IV (1473–1513), King of Scotland (1488–1513), son of King James III (q.v.). Within a few months after becoming king he ended a revolt of the Scottish nobles. He expanded the navy and encouraged commerce. His romantic disposition induced him to support Perkin Warbeck (1474–99), a claimant to the English throne, and to invade England in behalf of Warbeck. In 1497, however, a truce for seven years was concluded between Scotland and England. In August, 1503, James married Margaret Tudor (q.v.), the eldest daughter of Henry VII (q.v.), King of England. This marriage led eventually to the union of the crowns of England and Scotland. After 1509 when Henry VIII (q.v.) became king of England,

113

JAMES (Scotland)

relations between the two countries became strained. In 1513 James invaded England and was killed at Flodden (q.v.). He was succeeded by his son James V (q.v.).

JAMES V (1512–42), King of Scotland (1513–42), son of King James IV and Margaret Tudor (qq.v.), born in Linlithgow. He was seventeen months old when his father was killed. His mother acted as regent until her marriage in 1514 to Archibald, 6th Earl of Angus (see under Douglas). In that year John Stewart, Duke of Albany (1481–1536), became James' protector. In 1525, during the continued struggle for control of the country, James was taken prisoner by his stepfather. Three years later the king escaped and assumed control of Scotland. He instituted judicial reforms and took measures to protect the peasantry by whom he was much admired. His uncle, Henry VIII (q.v.), King of England, tried to induce James to repudiate the authority of the Catholic Church, but James refused and relations between the two countries became strained. War broke out in 1542, and in November the Scottish force was routed at Solway Moss. Within a month James died. He left one legitimate child, Mary, Queen of Scots (q.v.), who was six days old at his death.

JAMES, family of American men of letters and philosophers; best known were the following.

Henry James (1811–82), religious philosopher, lecturer, and writer, born in Albany, N.Y., and educated at Union College. Greatly influenced by the theological writings of the Swedish philosopher Emanuel Swedenborg (q.v.), he wrote a number of philosophical religious works, including *Christianity, the Logic of Creation* (1857).

William James (1842–1910), philosopher and psychologist, eldest son of the preceding, born in New York City, and educated at Harvard University and the Harvard Medical School. In 1869, after having interrupted his studies to go to South America on an exploring expedition up the Amazon R. and to Germany to study psychology and philosophy, he received an M.D. degree at Harvard Medical School; three years later he was appointed to its faculty. He taught anatomy and physiology until 1880; from 1880 to 1907 he taught psychology and philosophy. Interested in the physiological and biological bases of psychology, James established the first American laboratory for psychology at Harvard in 1876.

His monumental book *The Principles of Psychology* (1890) established him as one of the most influential thinkers of his day. The work advanced the principle of functionalism (q.v.) in psychology, thus removing psychology from its traditional place as a branch of philosophy and placing it among the laboratory sciences based on experimental method.

In the next decade James applied his empirical methods of inquiry to questions of religion and philosophy. He studied the problems of the existence of God, of the immortality of the soul, and of the possibility of life after death, and of free will (q.v.) as opposed to determinism (q.v.). His views on these subjects were expounded in the lectures and esssays published in such books as *The Will to Believe and Other Essays in Popular Philosophy* (1897), *Human Immortality* (1898), and *The Varieties of Religious Experience* (1902). The last-named work was especially welcome to religious leaders because it provided scientific psychological justification for their beliefs.

Later lectures published as *Pragmatism: A New Name for Old Ways of Thinking* (1907) summed up his epoch-making theory of the method known as pragmatism (q.v.), a term first used by the physicist and logician Charles Sanders Peirce (q.v.). James generalized the pragmatic method, developing it from a critique of the logical basis of the sciences into a basis for evaluation of all experience. He maintained that the value of ideas is found only in terms of their usefulness or actual consequences. He was vehemently opposed to absolute conceptions and lectured polemically against monism (q.v.), the system that maintains that reality is a unified whole.

In *Essays in Radical Empiricism* (1912), he denied that the world can be explained in terms of a mystic force or scheme that determines the interrelation of things and events. He held that the interrelations, whether they serve to hold things together or apart, are just as real as the things themselves.

By the end of his life, James had become world famous as a philosopher and a psychologist. In both fields he functioned more as an originator of new thought than as a founder of dogmatic schools. His pragmatic philosophy was continued and developed by the American philosopher John Dewey (q.v.) and others; later studies in physics by the American theoretical physicist Albert Einstein (q.v.) made the theories of interrelations advanced by James appear prophetic.

Henry James (1843–1916), novelist, younger brother of the preceding, born in New York City, educated in New York, London, Paris, and Geneva. In 1875 he settled permanently in England; in 1915 he became a British subject. While

JAMESON

Henry James

still in his early twenties he began to contribute short stories and articles to American periodicals. The American novelist William Dean Howells (q.v.) encouraged him and introduced his work to the magazine *The Atlantic Monthly*.

James' work is characterized by leisurely pacing and subtle delineation of character rather than by dramatic incidents or complicated plots. His major writings, highly sensitive examples of the objective psychological novel, describe the world of leisure and sophistication he had grown to know intimately in Europe; see NOVEL: *Psychological Novel*.

In his earlier novels James dealt with the impact of European culture on Americans traveling or living abroad. Examples of this phase, written between 1875 and 1881, are *Roderick Hudson* (1876), *The American* (1877), *Daisy Miller* (1879), *Washington Square* (1881), and *Portrait of a Lady* (1881). Next he explored the types and manners of the English scene, as in *The Tragic Muse* (1890), *The Spoils of Poynton* (1897), and *The Awkward Age* (1899). His last three great novels, *The Wings of the Dove* (1902), *The Ambassadors* (1903), and *The Golden Bowl* (1904), take up again the theme of contrast between American and European societies. In general his later works are more complex and psychologically analytical than the earlier ones, and their characters and settings seem to exist only in the minds of the other characters.

Two of the most famous works of Henry James are stories, "The Aspern Papers" (1888) and "The Turn of the Screw" (1898), both of which have been dramatized and adapted for motion pictures. His own writing for the stage, though unsuccessful, helped to form his style and observation of character.

James was a prolific writer, and one or more of his books was published every year until the end of his life. His reputation as a major force in English literature was not firmly established until the 1940's. Particularly responsible for the revival of interest in James was the American critic and editor Leon Edel (1907–   ).

JAMES, Jesse Woodson (1847–82), American outlaw, born in Clay County, Mo. In the period before the American Civil War, he joined the guerrilla forces of rebel William Clarke Quantrill (q.v.), who was then raiding the border towns of Missouri and Kansas. James continued making raids with Quantrill during the war and soon earned a reputation for reckless daring. In 1866, he organized his own band of brigands, which he led until his death. His exploits, both real and legendary, in bank and train robberies, won him worldwide notoriety. In 1882, tempted by a reward of $10,000 offered by Governor Thomas Theodore Crittenden (1832–1909) of Missouri for James' capture, dead or alive, one member of his own band killed him in his home in Saint Joseph, Mo. The events of James' life and death have been made popular in stories and ballads.

JAMES BAY, southern extension of Hudson Bay (q.v.) in Canada, extending about 300 mi. from N. to S. and averaging about 150 mi. in width. The longest rivers flowing into the bay include the Attawapiskat, Eastmain, and Fort George. Akimiski Island and a number of smaller islands are located in the bay. It is generally too shallow for navigation. James Bay was discovered by the English navigator Henry Hudson (q.v.) in 1610 but was named for another English navigator, Captain Thomas James (1593?–about 1635), who explored it in 1631.

JAMES EDWARD, Prince. See STUART, JAMES FRANCIS EDWARD.

JAMESON, John Franklin (1859–1937), American historian and educator, born in Somerville, Mass., and educated at Amherst College. In 1882 he received the first doctorate in history awarded by Johns Hopkins University and taught at the university until 1888. He was professor of history at Brown University from 1888 to 1901, and professor and head of the department of history at the University of Chicago

115

from 1901 to 1905. He also served as director of historical research at the Carnegie Institution of Washington (q.v.) from 1905 to 1928 and first director of manuscripts at the Library of Congress from 1928 to 1937. Jameson was deeply involved in historical scholarship. He was a founder and editor of the *American Historical Review,* the journal of the American Historical Association. He wrote many books on American history, but he is best known for his efforts in bringing about the publication of the monumental *Dictionary of American Biography* (20 vol., 1928–36).

JAMESON, Sir Leander Starr (1853–1917), British physician and statesman, born in Edinburgh, Scotland, and educated at the University of London. In 1878, because of ill health, he went to South Africa and practiced medicine in Kimberley. There he met the British administrator Cecil John Rhodes (q.v.). Jameson assisted Rhodes in negotiations with South African natives and induced the Matabele chief Lobengula (1833–94) to grant mineral concessions to Great Britain in what is now part of Rhodesia. In 1891 Jameson became administrator of the region and three years later ensured British control by putting down a revolt. Although unauthorized, he then attempted to assist the Uitlanders, the British residents of the Transvaal and the Orange Free State (qq.v.), who were planning an uprising in Johannesburg against the government of the Boers (q.v.). Jameson, on Dec. 29, 1895, led a force of about 500 men in a raid into the Transvaal. The raid was met with resistance and at Doornkop on Jan. 2, 1896, after thirty-six hours of fighting, Jameson surrendered. He was turned over to the British government for punishment and was sentenced to serve ten months in prison. He was released after eight months because of ill health.

The Jameson raid was one of the most important causes of the South African War (q.v.), in which Jameson fought against the Boers. He became a member of the Cape Colony (now the Province of the Cape of Good Hope) legislature in 1900 and served as prime minister from 1904 to 1908. He was created a baronet in 1911. See SOUTH AFRICA, REPUBLIC OF: *History.*

JAMESON RAID. See JAMESON, SIR LEANDER STARR.

JAMESTOWN, city of New York, in Chautauqua Co., at the S. end of Chautauqua Lake, 70 miles S.W. of Buffalo. Jamestown is served by several railroads, and maintains a municipal airport. The city is a manufacturing and wholesale shipping center noted for the production of metal and wood furniture. Educational institutions in the city include Jamestown Community College. Jamestown was founded about 1806, incorporated as a village in 1827, and chartered as a city in 1886. Pop. (1960) 41,818; (1970) 39,795.

JAMESTOWN, city in North Dakota, and county seat of Stutsman Co., on the James R., about 100 miles N.E. of Bismarck. The chief industries are construction, dairying, and food processing. Jamestown is the site of Jamestown College, founded in 1884. In the vicinity is Arrowwood National Wildlife Refuge, frequented by many forms of water fowl and other wildlife. Jamestown was settled in the early 1870's near the site of a United States Army post, and incorporated in 1892. Pop. (1960) 15,163; (1970) 15,385.

JAMESTOWN, former village of Virginia, in present-day James City Co., on an island in the James R., about 45 miles S.E. of Richmond. It is part of the 9430-acre Colonial National Historical Park; see NATIONAL PARK SERVICE.

The first permanent English settlement in America was founded here on May 14, 1607, by a small group led by Captain Christopher Newport (1565?–1617), an English mariner hired by the London Company (q.v.) to transport colonists. Many of the settlers died from famine and disease in the winter of 1609–10. The survivors would have deserted the village the following June, but were encouraged to stay by the arrival of a shipload of supplies and new settlers. In 1612 tobacco growing was started. The colony prospered, and was the capital of Virginia until 1699. In 1619 the first representative assembly in America was held in the village. In the same year, at Jamestown, the first Negro slaves were introduced into the original thirteen colonies. In 1676 the village was burned by the English colonial leader Nathaniel Bacon (1647–76); see BACON'S REBELLION. The seat of government was moved from Jamestown to the Middle Plantation (now Williamsburg) in 1699, and the village was deserted. An area on the island is separate from the national park and is owned by the Association for the Preservation of Virginia Antiquities. It contains several interesting remains, including a church tower dating from 1639, the foundations of the State houses, ancient tombstones, and statues of Pocahontas and John Smith (qq.v.). The Jamestown Archeological Laboratory contains relics unearthed by excavations carried on by the National Park Service. See also COLONIAL LIFE IN NORTH AMERICA.

JAMESTOWN WEED. See JIMSONWEED.

JAMI, pen name of NURUDDIN ABDURRAHMAN IBN AHMAD (1414–92), Persian poet, born

Early morning on the Jhelum River, near Srinagar, capital of Kashmir. Government of India Tourist Office

in Jam, in Khurasan Province. Foremost among his works is a collection of seven poems entitled *Haft Aurang* ("The Seven Thrones"), which includes the allegory *Salāmān u Absāl* (*Salaman and Absal*, 1856). His works are held in high esteem among the Persians. Jami is also known for his interest in the mystic philosophy Sufism (q.v.).

JAMMU, city of the Republic of India, in Jammu and Kashmir State, about 100 miles s. of Srinagar. The city is located in an agricultural area in which maize, rice, and wheat are the principal crops. In Jammu are several colleges affiliated with the University of Jammu and Kashmir, a large palace, and a fort. Jammu was conquered by the religious community of the Sikhs (q.v.) under their leader Ranjit Singh (1780–1839) in 1819. From 1846 until the partition of British India in 1947, British supremacy was recognized in Jammu. Pop. (1971) 338,219.

JAMMU AND KASHMIR, State of the Republic of India, more commonly known only as Kashmir, bounded on the N. by Afghanistan and China, on the E. by mainland China, on the S. by the Territory of Himachal Pradesh and the State of Punjab, and on the W. by West Pakistan Province of Pakistan. The Chinese boundary is not precisely defined. Pending a plebiscite most of Kashmir, which is claimed by both Pakistan and the Republic of India, is under the control of a pro-Indian republican government; the remainder is governed by a pro-Pakistani, so-called Free Kashmir, regime. See *History*, below. The capital and chief city of pro-Indian Kashmir is Srinagar. Other important towns in Indian Kashmir include Jammu and Leh. The capital of Pakistani Kashmir is Muzaffarabad. Area of Kashmir, 86,024 sq.mi.; pop. (1971) 4,615,176.

Kashmir is almost entirely mountainous, and is topographically divided into three regions: the valley of the Jhelum R., which includes the valley of Kashmir, in the central portion; the mountains around Jammu in the S.; and the great mountains of the Karakoram range in the N. The Karakorams, which are part of the Himalayas, include Mt. Godwin Austen (28,250 ft.), the second-highest mountain in the world. Nanga Parbat, another peak, towers 26,660 ft. above sea level. The Indus River (q.v.) flows through Kashmir, and the Jhelum R. rises in the N.E. portion of the State. Kashmir possesses a more equable climate than that of southern and central India, and the valley of Kashmir is a noted resort region.

The State, internationally famous for its hunting, is the habitat of numerous game animals, including the markhor and ibex (wild goat), stag, and bear. Most of the population is engaged in agriculture; the principal crops are rice, corn, wheat, and oilseeds. Among livestock raised are buffalo and other cattle, sheep, goats, and poultry. Silk weaving is the principal industry; the weaving of cashmere (q.v.) shawls has been almost supplanted by carpet weaving. An-

JAMMU AND KASHMIR

other important industry is the manufacture of small art objects and jewelry in wood, silver, and papier-mâché.

History. Kashmir is an ancient country, deriving its name, according to tradition, from the Khasi, a people who lived in the northern mountains several centuries before the Christian era. The country was originally a stronghold of Hinduism (q.v.). Buddhism (q.v.) was introduced about 245 B.C., and during the succeeding millennium the two religions profoundly influenced the development of Kashmir. Beginning in the mid-14th century, Muslim sultans controlled the area for the next two centuries. Akbar (q.v.), the Mogul emperor of Hindustan, conquered Kashmir between 1586 and 1592, and it became a part of the Mogul empire. In 1819, after a period of Afghan rule extending from 1756, Kashmir was conquered by Ranjit Singh (1780–1839), the Sikhist maharaja of the Punjab. In 1846 Gulab Singh, the ruler of Jammu, concluded a treaty with Great Britain, which by then dominated most of India, and was confirmed as ruler also of Kashmir.

Following the partition in August, 1947, of British India into Pakistan and the Republic of India, a large section of the predominantly Muslim population of Kashmir demanded accession to Pakistan, a Muslim state. The reigning maharaja, Sir Hari Singh (1895–1961), a Hindu, resisted the pro-Pakistani movement. The Pakistanis invaded the area and, encountering feeble resistance, swiftly occupied western and central portions and began to advance on Srinagar. With the fall of his capital imminent, Sir Hari acceded on Oct. 27, 1947, to the Indian Republic, which thereupon dispatched troops to Kashmir. In the ensuing severe conflict the invaders gradually yielded ground.

Meanwhile the insurgent Muslims had formed a pro-Pakistani, Free Kashmir government in the region under their control, eventually reduced to about one quarter of the area of the State. The remainder of Kashmir was ruled by a government nominally responsible to the maharaja of the State under the State Premier Sheikh Muhammad Abdullah (1905–), a pro-Indian Muslim.

On Jan. 1, 1948, the Indian government lodged a formal complaint with the United Nations against Pakistani intervention in Kashmir. The Security Council approved in April the formation of a commission to mediate the continuing war and create conditions for a free and impartial plebiscite on the future status of the state. Following negotiations with the commission the Indian and Pakistani governments, on Jan. 1, 1949, concluded a cease-fire agreement. Subsequent U.N. efforts to secure troop withdrawals and develop a plebiscitic plan mutually satisfactory to the contending sides were unsuccessful.

In April, 1952 Premier Abdullah, renouncing his support of accession to India, declared that Kashmir should become a sovereign state. His position found few adherents among other Kashmiri political leaders, and in August, 1953, he was replaced by pro-Indian Deputy Premier Bakshi Ghulan Muhammad (1895–). Later in August Pakistan and the Republic of India reached direct agreement on plans for a plebiscite in Kashmir. Preliminary negotiations by the two governments to implement the agreement ended on Dec. 26, 1953, in another deadlock, which persisted throughout 1954. Pakistan demanded in October of the latter year that the U.N. conduct a plebiscite in Kashmir, but the Indian government refused to cooperate.

In April, 1956, Indian Prime Minister Jawaharlal Nehru (q.v.) proposed that Kashmir be partitioned between India and Pakistan along the cease-fire line, with minor border adjustments. Pakistan refused to consider partition. In November the constituent assembly of pro-Indian Kashmir adopted a constitution, effective Jan. 26, 1957, which made the republic an integral part of the Indian Republic. On Jan. 16 Pakistan asked the U.N. security Council to dispatch U.N. troops to Kashmir and to order India to agree to a plebiscite at an early date. On Jan. 24, the U.N. Security Council approved another resolution calling for a plebiscite in Kashmir. The Kashmir question again was brought before the Security Council by Pakistan on April 27, 1962. The Indian delegate told the Council that the accession of Kashmir to India was irrevocable and therefore could not be the subject of a plebiscite. In early August, 1965, large-scale infiltration from Pakistan began. On Aug. 16 Indian troops crossed the Kashmir cease-fire line. On Sept. 23, both sides accepted a U.N. cease-fire resolution. Prime Minister Lal Bahadur Shastri (1904–66) of India and Muhammad Ayub Khan (1907–), then president of Pakistan, signed an agreement in Tashkent, U.S.S.R., on Jan. 10, 1966, which provided for the withdrawal of forces to the points held prior to Aug. 5, 1965, and for efforts on the part of both sides to search for a peaceful settlement. In the early 1970's negotiations had not as yet been finalized.

JAMNAGAR, city of the Republic of India, in Gujarat State, on the Kathiawar Peninsula, 45 miles N.W. of Rajkot and 165 miles S.W. of Ahmadabad. Poultry is raised and cotton, millet, potatoes, and oilseed are grown in the area. In the city, important industries include cotton and flour milling, oilseed processing, dyeing, tanning, and the manufacture of chemicals, textiles, tiles, salt, and soap. Brass and copperware, embroideries, baskets, and pottery are made by local craftsmen. Jamnagar is the site of colleges of arts and sciences and of medicine, affiliated with Gujarat University, and of the palace of a maharaja. Bedi, 4 miles N.W. on the Gulf of Kutch, is the port for the city. Founded in 1540 by Rajputs, Jamnagar was capital of Navanagar princely state until 1948. The city was also called Navanagar or Nawanagar. Pop. (1971) 214,853.

JAMSHEDPUR, city of the Republic of India, in Bihar State, on the Subarnarekha R., 140 miles N.W. of Calcutta. The city is an industrial center based on the Tata iron and steel plants, which were begun in 1907 and are now the largest in India. Other industrial plants produce chemicals, locomotive parts, agricultural equipment, machinery, tinplate, cable, and wire. The Jamshedpur Cooperative College, affiliated with Bihar University, is located in the city. A technical institute operated by the Tata Iron and Steel Company, and national metallurgical laboratories are also situated here. Pop. (1971) 340,564.

JANÁČEK, Leoš (1854–1928), Czech composer, born in Hukvaldy, and educated at the Community of the Austin Friars in Brünn, at the Organ School in Prague, and at the Leipzig Conservatory. In 1882 he became conductor of the Philharmonic Society of Brünn (now Brno), and in the same year founded the Brünn Organ School, where he taught until 1920, when the new Czechoslovakian state took over the school and he was appointed professor at the State Conservatory of Prague.

Public recognition was withheld from Janáček until very late in his life. His best-known opera, *Jenufa*, first produced in 1904, had no popular success until its performance in Prague in 1916, when the composer was 62. From this time onward, however, his reputation rose steadily. His numerous theater, choral, and chamber works derive most of their stylistic features from Moravian folk material.

JANESVILLE, city in Wisconsin, and county seat of Rock Co., on the Rock R., 12 miles N. of the Illinois boundary, and about 35 miles S.E. of Madison. It is the commercial and industrial center for the surrounding tobacco-growing area. Industrial establishments in the city include factories manufacturing automobiles, automobile bodies, foodstuffs, fountain pens, furniture and fixtures, glasses, and machinery. Janesville is the site of a museum housing old books from New England and Indian relics. Janesville was settled in 1835 and incorporated as a city in 1853. It became the county seat in 1859. Pop. (1960) 35,164; (1970) 46,426.

JANET, Pierre (1859–1947), French psychologist, born in Paris, and educated at the École Normale and the École de Médecine in Paris. From 1881 to 1898 he taught philosophy at the lycées of Chateauroux and Havre, at the Collège Rollin, and at the lycées Louis-le-Grand and Condorcet. His interest in neurology and psychology, which he studied under Jean Martin Charcot (q.v.), was already in evidence at this time, and from 1889 to 1898 he was director of the psychological laboratory of the Salpétrière in addition to his other duties. From 1898 to 1902 he lectured on psychology at the Sorbonne, and from 1897 taught psychology at the Collège de France, where he served as professor of psychology from 1902 until his death. Janet did important pioneer work on the scientific treatment of neuroses and hysteria (q.v.); his investigations of hypnosis (q.v.) as an aid to the understanding of the mind and the diagnosis of its disorders greatly influenced the early work of another pupil of Charcot, Sigmund Freud (q.v.). Among Janet's works are *Major Symptoms of Hysteria* (1920), *Neuroses* (1909), and *Principles of Psychotherapy* (1923).

JANINA. See IOANNINA.

JANIZARIES, or JANISSARIES, regular standing army of the Ottoman Turks, formed by Sultan Orkhan (1279–1359) in 1330; see TURKEY: *History*. Orkhan had previously organized a regular paid army, but the Turcomans from which the organization was recruited were unsatisfactory soldiers. Orkhan adopted a system of troop procurement under which the children of Christian subjects were taken from their parents and trained as *yeni cheri* (Turk., "new troops"). The Janizaries were led by an *aga*, who was held in reverential respect and who had the power of life or death over his soldiers. The Janizaries served as police during peacetime. In wartime they served on foot, and were noted for the wild impetuosity of their attacks. The bodyguard of the sultan was composed of selected Janizaries.

In the middle of the 15th century the Janizaries, who had been an orderly body of troops until that time, began the first of a long series of revolts. By the 17th century the organization had become completely corrupt, exacting tribute from each new sultan at his accession. In 1825 Sultan Mahmud II (q.v.) ordered his subjects to attack the mutinous Janizaries. De-

JAN MAYEN

serted by their aga and other officers, the soldiers were defeated, with a loss of 16,000 men. The organization was dissolved by proclamation in 1826, and all opposition was put down by bloodshed. Thousands of Janizaries were killed, and more than 20,000 were banished.

JAN MAYEN, island of Norway, in the Arctic Ocean, between Greenland and Norway, about 300 miles N.E. of Iceland. Jan Mayen is 39 mi. long and 9 mi. wide. The highest point is Beerenberg (7470 ft.), a dormant volcano. The island was discovered in 1607 by the English navigator Henry Hudson (q.v.), who named it Hudson's Tutches. The present name was derived from that of a Dutch sea captain, Jan Mayen, who had a whaling base on the island between 1611 and 1635. In 1929 the island was annexed by Norway. Whalers and seal hunters occasionally visit Jan Mayen, but the island is uninhabited except by the operators of a wireless and meteorological station, established in 1921 by the Norwegian government. During World War II a United States Navy weather station was maintained on the island.

JANSEN, Cornelis (Lat. *Cornelius Jansenius*) (1585–1638), Dutch Roman Catholic theologian, founder of Jansenism, born in Acquoi, near Leerdam, and educated at the universities of Utrecht, Louvain, and Paris. During his school days he came in contact with the disciples of the Flemish Roman Catholic theologian Michael Baius, who was also known as Michael de Bay

Cornelis Jansen   Bettmann Archive

(1513–89), and began a lifelong friendship with Jean Duvergier de Hauranne (1581–1643), who later became abbot of Saint Cyran and chaplain of the convent of Port Royal. In 1617 Jansen became head of the Dutch theological college of Saint Pulcheria, at Louvain, and in 1630 became professor of exegesis at the University of Louvain. He was made bishop of Ypres in 1636 and died of the plague just after completing his great work, the *Augustinus,* which was published two years after his death.

The main object of this work was to prove that the teachings of the 5th-century theologian Saint Augustine (q.v.) against the Pelagians (*see* PELAGIANISM) on grace, free will, and predestination (qq.v.) were directly opposed to the doctrines of contemporary schools, especially those of the Jesuits (q.v.). This work and the *Frequent Communion* (1643) of the French theologian and philosopher Antoine Arnauld (q.v.) contained the principal tenets of the Jansenist movement. They included denial of the orthodox Roman Catholic doctrine of freedom of the will; refusal to admit the existence of sufficient grace, maintaining that all interior grace is irresistible; and denial of the dogma that Christ died for all mankind, holding that He died only for those predestined to salvation. The principal promoters of the movement were Duvergier de Hauranne and Arnauld and, later, the French religious writer Pasquier Quesnel (1634–1719), who wrote *Moral Reflections on the New Testament* (1687–94), a work reproducing their teachings. Prominent among the defenders of the movement were the scholars and divines of the convent of Port Royal and the French scientist and philosopher Blaise Pascal (q.v.).

The *Augustinus* was prohibited by a decree of the Inquisition (q.v.) in 1641 and in the following year was condemned in general terms by Pope Urban VIII (*see under* URBAN). In 1705 Pope Clement XI (1649–1721) issued the bull *Vineam Domini* ("The Lord's Vineyard"), closing the convent of Port Royal, and in 1713, the bull *Unigenitus* ("Of One Race"), condemning 101 propositions in Quesnel's *Moral Reflections.* Many of the Jansenists appealed from the decision of the pope to a general council (q.v.), forming a party known as the Appellants; the remaining members of the movement, the Acceptants, agreed to the pope's decision. A firm policy on the part of the papacy and the French state brought the Appellants into disfavor; many submitted, and the recusants were subjected to severe penalties. Jansenism declined in France, but survived in Febronianism and Gallicanism. A large number of Appellants emigrated to the

Netherlands, where they formed a community with Utrecht as the center, eventually merging with the Old Catholics (q.v.) and joining with them and other minority religious groups in the Union of Utrecht (1889).

JANSENISM. See JANSEN, CORNELIS.

JANUARY, first month of the year in the Gregorian calendar, consisting of thirty-one days. The name of the month is derived from Janus (q.v.), the Roman god of gates and doors, and hence of openings and beginnings. January was the eleventh month of the year in the ancient Roman calendar; in the 2nd century B.C., however, it came to be regarded as the first month. On the first day of January the Romans offered sacrifices to Janus so that he would bless the new year. See CALENDAR; CALENDAR REFORM.

JANUS, in Roman mythology, the god of doors and gateways, and also of beginnings, which the Romans believed ensured good endings. His principal temple in the Forum (q.v.) had doors facing east and west for the beginning and ending of the day, and between them stood his statue with two faces, gazing in opposite directions. In every home the morning prayer was addressed to him, and in every domestic undertaking his assistance was sought. As the god of beginnings, he was publicly invoked on the first day of January (q.v.), the month that was named for him because it began the new year. He was invoked, too, at the beginning of wars, during which the doors of his temple in the Forum always stood open; when Rome was at peace, the doors were closed. Janus has no counterpart in Greek mythology.

JAPAN, in Japanese *Dai* ("great") *Nihon* or *Nippon* ("origin of the sun"), hence, Land of the Rising Sun, a constitutional monarchy off the E. coast of Asia, bounded on the N. by the Sea of Okhotsk, on the E. by the Pacific Ocean, on the S. by the Pacific Ocean and the East China Sea, and on the W. by the Sea of Japan. The Japanese islands are situated between lat. 28° N. and lat. 45°30′ N. and long. 128°30′ E. and long. 146° E. and extend in an irregular crescent from the island of Sakhalin (U.S.S.R.) to the island of Formosa, or Taiwan (Republic of China). Japan proper consists chiefly of four large islands: Hokkaido, the northernmost; Honshu, the largest, called the mainland; Shikoku; and Kyushu (qq.v.), the southernmost; the combined area of which is 142,672 sq.mi. In addition, Japan includes seven secondary islands and island groups: Awaji, Oki, Okinawa (qq.v.), Sado, Tsushima, Iki, and Izu Shichito, and more than 1000 lesser adjacent islands. The total area of Japan is 142,734 sq.mi.

The Kuril Islands (q.v.), N. of Hokkaido and formerly included in Japan proper as Chishima-retto, were occupied by the U.S.S.R. at the conclusion of World War II under an agreement concluded at the Yalta Conference (q.v.) in 1945. Until the unconditional surrender of Japan to the Allied powers on Sept. 2, 1945, the Japanese Empire controlled, in addition to present Japan and the Kuril Islands, an area of about 637,500 sq.mi., including Korea, Formosa, Manchuria, the leased territory of Kwantung, the Pescadores, Karafuto (southern half of Sakhalin), and the South Sea Mandated Territories, comprising the Marshall, Mariana (except Guam, a United States possession), and Caroline islands (qq.v.), which were made a Japanese mandate by the Treaty of Versailles in 1919, after World War I. For the disposition of these territories and others acquired by Japanese conquest during World War II, see *History*, below.

THE LAND

The islands of Japan are the projecting summits of a huge chain of mountains originally a part of the continent of Asia from which they were detached in the Cenozoic Period (q.v.). The long and narrow main island, Honshu, measures less than 200 mi. at its greatest breadth; no part of Japan is more than 100 mi. from the sea. The coastline of Japan is exceedingly long in proportion to the area of the islands, and totals with the many bays and indentations, about 15,500 mi. The greatest amount of indentation is on the Pacific coast, the result of the erosive action of the tides and severe coastal storms. The W. coast of Kyushu, on the East China Sea, is the most irregular portion of the Japanese coast. Few navigable inlets are found on the E. coast above Tokyo, but S. of Tokyo Bay are many of the best bays and harbors in Japan. Between Honshu, Shikoku, and Kyushu is the Inland Sea (q.v.), dotted with islands and connected with the Pacific Ocean and the Sea of Japan by three narrow straits through which oceanic storms rarely pass; see JAPAN, SEA OF. The W. coast of the islands of Japan, on the almost tideless Sea of Japan, is relatively straight, and measures less than 3000 mi.; the only conspicuous indentations in the coastline are Wakasa and Toyama bays in Honshu.

Topographically, Japan is a rugged land of high mountains and deep valleys, with many small plains. The alternating sequence of mountain and valley, and the rocky soil, account for the fact that only an estimated 15 to 18 percent of Japan is arable land.

Rivers and Lakes. Although Japan is abundantly watered, every valley having a stream, no

JAPAN

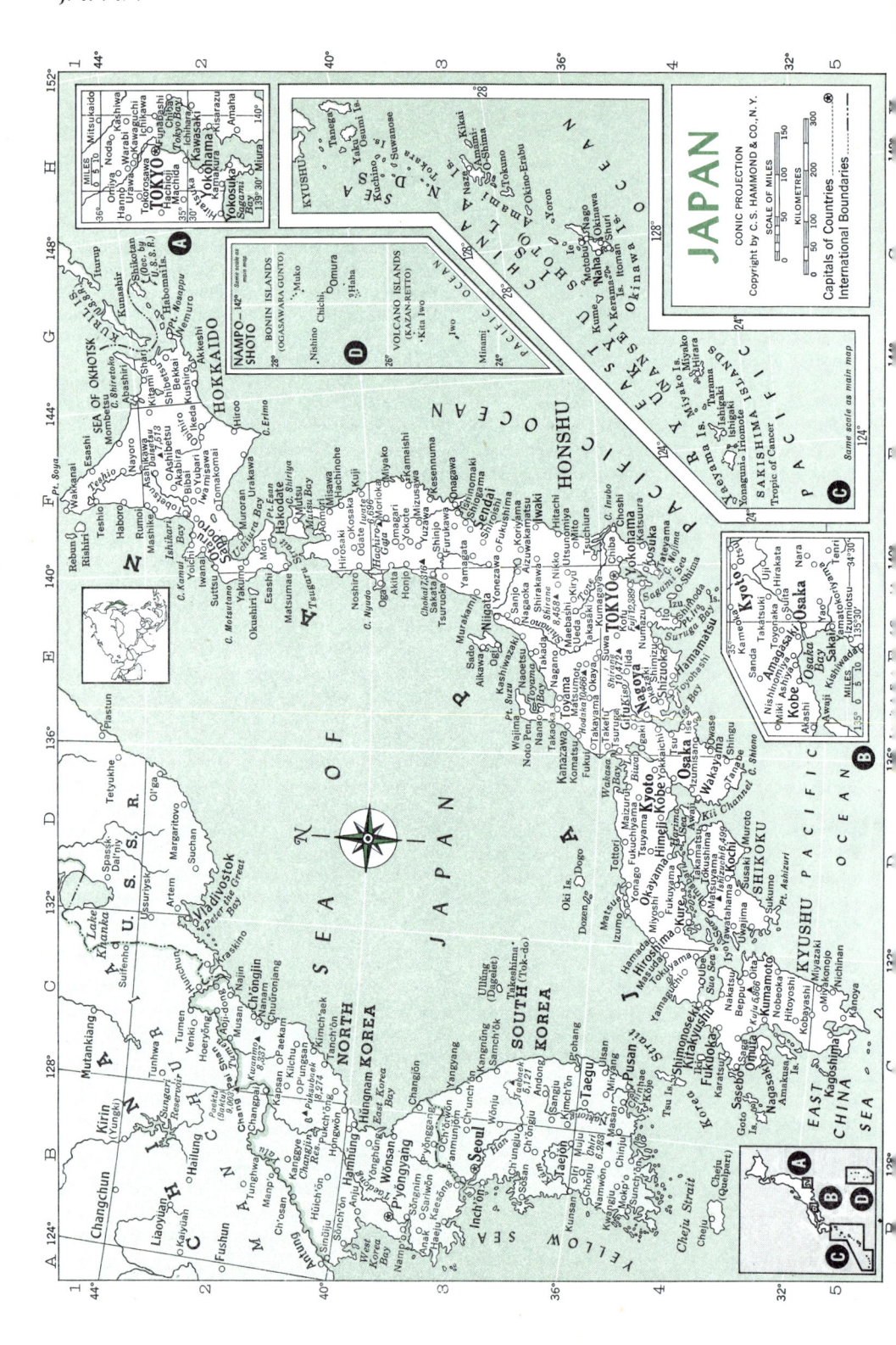

JAPAN

INDEX TO MAP OF JAPAN

Cities and Towns

Abashiri	G1
Aizuwakamatsu	F3
Akabira	E4
Akashi	E4
Akita	E3
Akkeshi	G2
Amagasaki	F2
Aomori	F2
Asahikawa	F2
Ashibetsu	G2
Ashiya	C4
Bekkai	G2
Beppu	C4
Bibai	F2
Chiba	F4, H2
Choshi	F4
Fukuchiyama	D3
Fukui	C4
Fukuoka	F3
Fukushima	D4
Funabashi	H2
Furukawa	F3
Gifu	E4
Haboro	F1
Hachinohe	F2
Hachioji	C4
Hakodate	E2
Hamada	C4
Hamamatsu	E4
Hanno	H2
Himeji	D4
Hirakata	E4
Hirara	G1
Hiratsuka	H2
Hirosaki	F2
Hiroshima	C4
Hitoyoshi	C5
Honjo	E3
Ichihara	H2
Ichikawa	H2
Iida	E4
Imabari	D4
Ise	E4
Ishigaki	F4
Ishinomaki	F3
Ito	E4
Itoman	G4
Iwaki	F3
Iwamisawa	F2
Izumiotsu	E5
Izumisano	D4
Izumo	D4
Kagoshima	C5
Kamaishi	F3
Kamakura	H2
Kameoka	E4
Kanazawa	E3
Kanoya	C5
Karatsu	H2
Kashiwa	H2
Kashiwazaki	E3
Katsuura	H2
Kawaguchi	H2
Kawasaki	H2
Kesennuma	F3
Kiryu	H2
Kisarazu	H2
Kishiwada	E5
Kitakyushu	C4
Kitami	G2
Kobayashi	C5
Kobe	D4, E4
Kochi	D4
Kofu	F3
Komatsu	D3
Koriyama	F3
Kuji	F2
Kumagaya	E3
Kumamoto	C4
Kure	D4
Kushiro	G2
Kyoto	D4, E4
Machida	H2
Maebashi	E3
Maizuru	D4
Masuda	C4
Matsue	D4
Matsumoto	E3
Matsuyama	D4
Miki	E4
Mito	F3
Mitsukaido	H1
Miyako	F3
Miyakonojo	C5
Miyazaki	C5
Miyoshi	D4
Mizusawa	F3
Morioka	F3
Motobu	G3
Murakami	E3
Muroran	E2
Muroto	D4
Mutsu	F2
Nagano	E3

Nagaoka	E3
Nagasaki	C4
Nago	G4
Nagoya	E4
Naha	G4
Nakatsu	C4
Nanao	E3
Naoetsu	E3
Nara	F1
Nayoro	G2
Nemuro	H2
Nichinan	C5
Niigata	E3
Nikko	E3
Nishinomiya	C4
Nobeoka	C4
Noda	H1
Noshiro	F2
Numazu	F2
Obihiro	G2
Odate	F2
Ogaki	E4
Oita	C4
Okaya	E3
Okayama	D4
Okazaki	E4
Omagari	F3
Omiya	H1
Omura	C4
Omuta	C4
Osaka	D4, E4
Otaru	F2
Otsu	E4
Owase	E4
Rumoi	F2
Saga	C4
Sakai	E4
Sakata	E3
Sanjo	E3
Sapporo	F2
Sasebo	C4
Sendai	F3
Shibetsu	G2
Shimizu	E4
Shimoda	E4
Shimonoseki	C4
Shingu	E4
Shinjo	F3
Shiogama	F3
Shirakawa	F3
Shiroishi	F3
Shizuoka	E4
Shuri	G4
Suita	E4
Susaki	D4
Suwa	E3
Takada	E3
Takamatsu	D4
Takaoka	E3
Takasaki	E3
Takatsuki	E4
Takayama	E3
Tanabe	D4
Tateyama	E5
Tenri	E4
Tokorosawa	H2
Tokushima	D4
Tokuyama	C4
Tokyo (cap.)	H2, F4
Tomakomai	F2
Tottori	D4
Toyama	E3
Toyohashi	E4
Toyonaka	E3
Tsu	D4
Tsuchiura	F3
Tsuruga	E4
Tsuruoka	E3
Tsuyama	D4
Ube	C4
Ueda	E3
Uji	E4
Urawa	F4
Utsunomiya	F3
Uwajima	D4
Wajima	E3
Wakayama	E4
Wakkanai	F1
Warabi	H2
Yamagata	F3
Yamaguchi	C4
Yamatokoriyama	E4
Yao	F3
Yawatahama	D4
Yoichi	F2
Yokkaichi	E4
Yokohama	C4
Yokosuka	H2
Yokote	F3
Yonago	D4
Yonezawa	F3
Yubari	F3
Yuzawa	E4

Physical Features

Amakusa (isls.)	C4
Amami (isls.)	H3
Ashizuri (point)	D4
Awaji (isls.)	D4, E5
Biwa (lake)	D4
Bonin (islands)	G2
Chichi (island)	G2
Chokai (mt.)	E3
Daisetsu (mt.)	D3
Dogo (isl.)	D3
Dozen (isls.)	D3
East China (sea)	C5, G3
Erabu (isl.)	H3
Erimo (cape)	F2
Esan (cape)	E2
Fuji (mt.)	F2
Goto (isls.)	E3
Habomai (isls.)	G2
Hachiro (lagoon)	F3
Haha (island)	G2
Harima (sea)	D4
Hokkaido (isl.)	G2
Honshu (isl.)	F3
Inubo (cape)	C4
Iriomote (isl.)	F4
Iro (point)	F4
Ise (bay)	E4
Ishigaki (isl.)	F4
Ishikari (bay)	F2
Ishizuchi (mt.)	D4
Iwate (island)	F3
Iwo (island)	H2
Iyo (sea)	C4
Japan (sea)	D3
Kamui (cape)	F2
Kazan-Retto (Volcano isls.)	G3
Kerama (isls.)	G4
Kii (channel)	D4
Kikai (isl.)	H3
Kita Iwo (island)	H3
Kuchino (isl.)	C5
Kuju (mt.)	C4
Kume (isl.)	G4
Kyushu (isl.)	D4, H2
Minami (island)	G3
Miyako (isl.)	G4
Miyako (isls.)	F4
Muko (island)	G2
Mutsu (bay)	F2
Nampo-Shoto (isls.)	G2
Nishino (island)	F4
Nojima (cape)	G2
Nosappu (cape)	E3
Noto (pen.)	E2
Nyudo (cape)	F1
Ogasawara-Gunto (Bonin) (isls.)	G2
Okhotsk (sea)	G1
Oki (isls.)	D3
Okinawa (isl.)	G4
Okinawa (isls.)	F2
Okushiri (isl.)	E4
Osaka (bay)	E4
O-Shima (isl.)	F1
Rebun (isl.)	F1
Rishiri (isl.)	F1
Sado (isl.)	E3
Sagami (bay)	H2
Sagami (sea)	E4
Sakishima (isls.)	F4
Shikoku (isl.)	D4
Shinano (riv.)	E3
Shiono (point)	E4
Shirane (mt.)	E4
Shiretoko (cape)	G1
Shiriya (cape)	F2
Soya (point)	F1
Soya (sea)	C4
Suo (sea)	C4
Suruga (bay)	H3
Suwanose (isl.)	C5
Suzu (point)	E3
Tanega (isl.)	H2
Terama (isl.)	D4
Teshio (riv.)	D3
Tokara (isl.)	H3
Tokuno (isl.)	H3
Tokyo (bay)	H2
Tsu (isls.)	E2
Tsugaru (strait)	E2
Volcano (islands)	G3
Wakasa (bay)	D4
Yaeyama (isls.)	F4
Yaku (isl.)	C4
Yonaguni (isl.)	F4
Yoron (isl.)	H3

123

Traditional Japanese architecture contrasts with modern buildings across the Imperial Moat in Tokyo.
Japan National Tourist Organization

long navigable rivers exist. The larger Japanese rivers vary in size from swollen freshets during the spring thaw or the summer rainy season to small streams during dry weather. Successions of rapids and shallows are so common that only boats with extremely shallow draft can navigate. The longest river in Japan is the Shinano, on Honshu, which is 229 mi. long; other large rivers on Honshu are the Tone, Kitakami, Tenryu, and Mogami. The important rivers of Hokkaido include the second-largest river of Japan, the Ishikari (227 mi. long), and the Teshio and Tokachi. The Yoshino is the longest river in Shikoku. The many Japanese lakes are noted for their scenic beauty. Some are located in the river valleys, but the majority are mountain lakes and many are summer resorts. The largest lake in Japan is Biwa (q.v.), on Honshu, which is 40 mi. long by 7 mi. wide.

Plains and Mountains. The Japanese plains lie chiefly along the lower courses of the principal rivers, on plateaus along the lowest slopes of mountain ranges, and on lowlands along the seacoast. The most extensive plains are in Hokkaido: along the Ishikari R. in the w. part of the island (480,000 acres), along the Tokachi R. in the s.e. (744,000 acres), and around the cities of Nemuro and Kushiro on the e. central shore (1,229,000 acres). Honshu has several large plains; that of Osaka contains the cities of Kobe, Kyoto, and Osaka, the plain of Kwanto is the site of Tokyo, and Nagoya lies in the plain of Nobi. The plain of Tsukushi is the most important level area in Kyushu.

The mountains of Japan are the most conspicuous feature of the topography. Mountain ranges extend across the islands from n. to s., the main chains sending off smaller ranges which branch out laterally or run parallel to the parent range, and frequently descend to the coast, where they form bays and harbors. In the n., the island of Hokkaido is marked by a volcanic range which descends from the Kurils and merges in the s.w. part of the island with a chain branching from Point Soya on the n.w. tip. These mountains branch into two lines near Uchiura Bay, on the s.w. coast, and reappear on the island of Honshu in two parallel ranges. The minor range, situated entirely in the n.e., separates the valley of the Kitakami R. from the Pacific Ocean. The main range continues toward the s.w. until it meets a mass of intersecting ridges which enclose the plateau of the Shinano R. and forms a belt of mountains, the highest in Japan, across the widest part of the island. The highest peak, 12,389 ft., is Fuji (q.v.), an extinct volcano near Yokohama, which, because of its

JAPAN

beauty, is one of the favorite themes of Japanese decorative art. One of the subsidiary chains in the central mountain mass is called the Japanese Alps because of the grandeur of the landscape; the highest elevation in the chain is Mt. Yariga (10,433 ft.). Farther s. is another chain of high peaks; Mt. Shirane (10,472 ft.), is the highest. The islands of Shikoku and Kyushu are dotted with mountain ranges, although none contains any peak higher than Ishizuchi (6499 ft.) on Shikoku. Volcanoes are common in the Japanese mountains; some 200 volcanoes are known, about 50 of which are still active.

Earthquakes. Thermal springs and volcanic areas emitting gases are exceedingly numerous.

Earthquakes are frequent in Japan. A survey made during a recent period showed that seismic disturbances, mostly of a minor nature, occurred more than three times a day. Geological research has shown that, possibly under the continuous impact of these disturbances, the w. coast of the Japanese islands is settling, while the Pacific coast is rising. The E. coast is frequently subject to earthquakes affecting large areas and usually accompanied by tidal waves; these shocks seem to begin at the bottom of the ocean near the N.E. coast of Honshu, where a gigantic crater is thought to exist more than 5 mi. below the surface. The most disastrous earthquake in Japanese history occurred in 1923 in Segami Bay, near Tokyo and Yokohama, in which more than 91,000 persons were killed; see EARTHQUAKE: *Devastating Earthquakes.*

Climate. The Japanese islands extend through approximately 17 degrees of latitude, and climatic conditions vary widely. Average mean temperatures range from about 41° F. in Nemuro (Hokkaido) to about 61° F. in Okinawa. Short summers and severe long winters characterize Hokkaido and the N. part of Honshu. The severity of the winters is caused in great part by the N.W. winds blowing from Siberia and the cold Okhotsk Current which flows s. into the Sea of Japan. To the s. and E. of this region the winters are considerably moderated by the influence of the warm Kuroshio Current (q.v.). In Shikoku, Kyushu, and s. Honshu the summers are hot and humid, almost subtropical, and the winters are mild with comparatively little snow. Japan lies in the path of the S.E. monsoons which add considerably to the oppressive humidity of the summers. Yearly precipitation ranges from about 40 in. on Hokkaido to 150 in. in the mountains of central Honshu. From June to October tropical cyclones, also called typhoons (*see* CYCLONE), occur and cause great damage, especially to shipping.

Natural Resources. The most important natural resources of Japan are primarily agricultural. Although arable land is limited, Japan has the highest per-acre crop yield in the world and the country is almost self-sufficient in food production. Japan's large waterpower potential has been extensively developed but mineral resources are limited. The country must import most of its mineral requirements.

Plants. The great variety and luxuriance of Japanese plant life is mainly caused by the heat and moisture of Japanese summers. More than 17,000 species of flowering and nonflowering plants are found and many are widely cultivated. The white and red plum and the cherry bloom early and are particularly admired. The Japanese hills are colorful with azaleas in April, and the tree peony, one of the most popular cultivated flowers, blossoms at the beginning of May. The lotus blooms in August, and in November the blooming of the chrysanthemum, the national flower of Japan, occasions one of the most celebrated of the numerous Japanese flower festivals. Other flowers include the pimpernel, bluebell, gladiolus, and many varieties of lily. Few wild flowers are found, the small area of arable land permitting little space for uncultivated vegetation in the plains.

The predominant variety of Japanese tree is the conifer; a common species is the sugi, or Japanese cedar, which sometimes attains a height of 150 ft. Other evergreens include the larch, spruce, and many varieties of fir. In Kyushu, Shikoku, and s. Honshu subtropical trees, such as the bamboo, camphor tree, and banyan are found, and the tea plant and wax tree are cultivated. In central and N. Honshu the trees are those of the Temperate Zone, such as the beech, willow, chestnut, and many conifers. Lacquer and mulberry trees are cultivated extensively, and the cypress, yew, box, holly, and myrtle are plentiful. In Hokkaido the vegetation is subarctic, and similar to that of s. Siberia. Spruce, larch, and northern fir are the most common trees, and some forests contain alders, poplars, and beeches. The most common Japanese fruits are peaches, pears, and oranges.

The Japanese practice a unique kind of landscape gardening. Japanese gardens attempt to reproduce in miniature a stylization of natural landscapes. The Japanese also cultivate dwarf trees, such as the cherry or plum, which, through skillful pruning, are kept as low as 12 in. The potted flora that are dwarfed by special methods of culture are called *bonsai.*

Animals. As compared with its luxuriant flora, Japan suffers a dearth of animal life. Yet Japa-

JAPAN

nese fauna includes at least 140 species of mammals, 450 species of birds, and a wide variety of reptiles, batrachians, and fish. The only primate mammal is the red-faced monkey, the Japanese macaque, found throughout Honshu. The thirty-two carnivora include the red bear, black bear, and brown bear. Foxes are found throughout Japan, as are badgers. Other fur-bearing animals include the marten, Japanese mink, otter, weasel, and several varieties of seal. Rodents are numerous and include squirrels, flying squirrels, hares, rabbits, rats, and mice, though the common house mouse is not found. Many varieties of bat exist; insectivores include the Japanese mole and shrewmouse. Of the two species of deer, the more common is the small Japanese deer which has a spotted white coat in summer and a brown coat in winter.

The sparrow, house swallow, and thrush are the commonest Japanese birds. Water birds comprise almost 25 percent of the known species, and include the crane, heron, swan, duck, cormorant, stork, and albatross. Songbirds are numerous, the bullfinch and two varieties of nightingale being the best known. Among other common birds are the robin, cuckoo, woodpecker, pheasant, and pigeon.

The coastal waters of Japan teem with fish, which are caught in enormous quantities for use as fresh food or for canning, and also for fertilizer. Various seaweeds are also eaten.

Waterpower. Japan is richly endowed with waterpower because of the abundant rainfall and favorable topography. In the early 1970's total electric power generation capacity, including thermal capacity, was some 76,480,000 kw. In this period Japan ranked fourth as world producer of hydroelectric power, surpassed by the U.S., the Soviet Union, and West Germany, and third in total electric power generated. The generating capacity of Japan is divided into one third waterpower and two thirds thermal power.

THE PEOPLE

The modern Japanese are essentially a Mongoloid race and are similar in appearance to the Chinese and Koreans; the Japanese, however, are slightly smaller in stature. Japan is an industrialized urban society, and more than two thirds of the population live in metropolitan areas. Japanese is the official language, but English is widely used in commerce.

Population. The population of Japan (census 1970 was 104,665,171. The overall population density in 1971 was 737 persons per sq.mi. Japan is the fifth most densely populated country in the world, among those nations with 5,000,000 or more inhabitants.

Political Divisions. Japan is divided into forty-seven chief administrative divisions, most of which are called *ken,* or prefectures. The prefectures listed include Okinawa, which was occupied by the U.S. after World War II and returned to Japan in 1972.

The island of Hokkaido constitutes a *do,* or special administrative division. The cities of Kyoto and Osaka each comprise an urban prefecture, or *fu,* and the city of Tokyo comprises a metropolis, or *to.*

Principal Cities. The capital and largest city of Japan is Tokyo, the financial and commercial center of the country, with a population (1970 census) of about 8,840,902. Other leading cities include Osaka (2,980,487), an important seaport and airline terminal; Yokohama (2,238,264), with excellent harbor facilities, a leading seaport and shipbuilding center; Nagoya (2,036,053), a manufacturing center noted for its lacquer ware, textiles, and pottery; Kyoto (1,419,165), famed for the manufacture of art goods, including silk brocades and textiles, and a center of heavy industry; and Kobe (1,288,937), a leading seaport and shipbuilding and transportation center.

POLITICAL DIVISIONS OF JAPAN

Prefecture	Area (sq. mi.)	Population[1]	Prefecture	Area (sq. mi.)	Population[1]	Prefecture	Area (sq. mi.)	Population[1]
Aichi	1961	5517	Kagawa	718	915	Saga	943	831
Akita	4502	1233	Kagoshima	3514	1708	Saitama	1468	4062
Aomori	3718	1428	Kanagawa	908	5695	Shiga	1564	908
Chiba	1960	3519	Kochi	2742	786	Shimane	2555	767
Ehime	2187	1420	Kumamoto	2871	1685	Shizuoka	2999	3138
Fukui	1551	747	Kyōto (*fu*)	178	2274	Tochigi	2485	1604
Fukuoka	1907	4025	Mie	2225	1556	Tokushima	1599	789
Fukushima	5320	1941	Miyagi	2808	1838	Tokyo (*to*)	828	11,477
Gifu	4051	1777	Miyazaki	2987	1046	Tottori	1347	568
Gumma	2446	1676	Nagano	5260	1966	Toyama	1643	1036
Hiroshima	3257	2478	Nagasaki	1573	1560	Wakayama	1893	1047
Hokkaido (*do*)	30,307	5188	Nara	1424	958	Yamagata	3600	1218
Hyogo	3213	4734	Niigata	4855	2356	Yamaguchi	2348	1513
Ibaraki	2351	2179	Oita	2445	1161	Yamanashi	1724	764
Ishikawa	1620	1011	Okayama	2720	1731			
Iwate	5881	1364	Okinawa	848	934			
			Osaka (*fu*)	700	7785			

[1] 1971 estimate in thousands.

JAPAN

About forty-five other cities have populations of 250,000 or more inhabitants.

Religion. The principal religious faiths of Japan are Shinto (q.v.), a cult based on ancestor and nature worship, with about 200 sects and denominations, and Buddhism (q.v.), with about 207 sects and denominations. Christianity, represented in Japan by the Protestant, Roman Catholic, and Greek Orthodox faiths, is practiced by only a small fraction of the population. Virtually all the Japanese, with the exception of the Christians, are regarded as being Shintoists, and the majority of the Shintoists are also Buddhists. In the latter half of the 19th century Shinto was made a state religion, stressing worship of the emperor as a divinity and the racial superiority of the Japanese; all Japanese, regardless of their religious affiliation, were forced to worship at Shinto shrines. In 1946 the Allied occupation authorities ordered Shinto disestablished and reduced it to the level of a sect. On Jan. 1, 1946, Emperor Hirohito (q.v.) renounced all claim to divinity. The constitution promulgated in 1947 reestablished absolute freedom of religion and ended state support of Shinto.

Education. The educational system of Japan is the most highly developed in Asia. The illiteracy rate, consequently, is less than 5 percent for the entire nation. English, as the chief language for foreign contacts, is a required course of study in secondary schools.

The early history of Japanese education was profoundly affected by the Chinese. From the Chinese, the Japanese acquired new crafts and, most important, a system of writing. The acquisition of writing cannot be precisely dated, but by about 400 A.D. Korean scribes were using Chinese ideographs for official records at the Japanese imperial courts. Education in ancient Japan, however, was more aristocratic than the Chinese system, with noble families maintaining their own private schooling facilities. During the medieval military-feudal period, Buddhist churches assumed much responsibility for education.

With the onset of the enlightened rule of Emperor Meiji (r. 1867–1912), Japan in 1868 underwent a radical transformation in education as well as in social and economic matters. A ministry of education was created in 1872, and in the same year a comprehensive educational code that included universal primary education was formulated. The government sent educational missions to Europe and America to learn new educational approaches; it also invited foreign educators to carry on educational programs and initiate changes in Japanese schools. In 1877, during this period of innovation, Tokyo Imperial University was founded. As a result of these reforms, Japan emerged as a modern nation with a full educational system in line with much of Occidental practice.

The defeat of Japan in World War II resulted in educational changes, many of which were recommended in 1946 by a U.S. educational mission; some of these changes were discontinued when Japan regained sovereign status as a nation in 1952. The teaching of nationalistic ideology was banned, greater emphasis was placed on social studies, and classroom procedures were redesigned to encourage self-expression.

Education in Japan is centralized under the ministry of education. Its school system operates under the Fundamental Law of Education of 1947 and subsequent legislation, and makes it possible for all students to compete for admission to institutions of higher education. One of the continuing problems facing Japanese educators is the teaching of the complex Japanese language, which utilizes several scripts.

ELEMENTARY AND SECONDARY SCHOOLS. Education is

Gymnastics is an important pursuit among athletes in Japan, where sports have become increasingly popular.
UPI

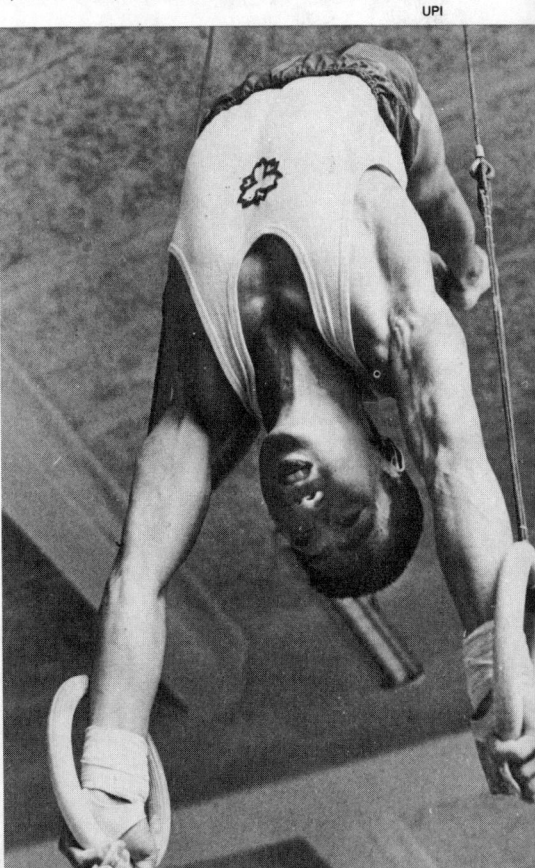

JAPAN

free and compulsory for 9 years, that is, 6 of elementary school and 3 of junior high school. Beyond the junior-high-school level, education is optional, and a small tuition fee is charged, even in public senior high schools and public institutions of higher learning. In the late 1960's Japan had about 26,000 primary schools annually attended by some 9,631,000 students, and about 11,000 secondary schools with about 5,000,000 students. Elementary school teachers numbered about 375,000. Approximately 9,100,000 students were enrolled in high schools, and teachers in high schools numbered about 479,000. About 400 special schools are attended by approximately 50,000 of the physically handicapped, blind, or deaf children in need of special education. Technical, commercial, and vocational schools are also maintained.

UNIVERSITIES AND COLLEGES. Japan has seven national (formerly called imperial) universities, located in Tokyo, Kyoto, Sendai, Fukuoka, Sapporo, Osaka, and Nagoya. The largest and oldest is the University of Tokyo (q.v.). In the late 1960's about 400 junior colleges were attended by about 200,000 students, and more than 440 colleges and universities had a total enrollment of more than 1,684,000. Nearly all of these institutions are coeducational.

Culture. The Japanese culture derives from the early contacts of the islands with the early civilizations of China and Korea. Classic influences of ancient China are found in Japanese literature, art, and music. Religion, especially Buddhism, has played an important role in the cultural life of Japan. Western influences, which began in earnest during the 19th century, exist side by side and often intermingle with the traditions and stylized forms of Japanese culture. *See* JAPANESE ART AND ARCHITECTURE; JAPANESE DRAMA; JAPANESE LANGUAGE; JAPANESE LITERATURE; JAPANESE MUSIC.

LIBRARIES AND MUSEUMS. Tokyo outranks all other Japanese cities in the number of its important libraries. Of the nearly one hundred leading libraries in the nation, more than forty are located in the capital city. Among the most important are the National Diet Library, an international book exchange and information center of Japan. It comprises many divisions, and the combined collection totals some 5,500,000 volumes. The Cabinet Library in Tokyo contains about 500,000 volumes. Among the important university collections in Tokyo are those at Tokyo University Library with more than

Residents of Naha, Okinawa, shop for tropical fruits at the stalls of peasant farmers. UPI

The art of wearing the traditional kimono is demonstrated to shoppers in a Tokyo department store. UPI

3,000,000 volumes, Meiji University Library with about 730,000 volumes, and Nihon University Library with nearly 710,000 volumes. Major collections are found in the libraries of the provinces, The Osaka Prefectural Library houses more than 650,000 volumes and Kobe City Library has more than 240,000 volumes. Important university libraries are located throughout the country.

The museums of Japan, with the exception of several modern galleries in the large cities, represent treasure halls and are usually found in temples and shrines. Among the most famous of these is the Myohin Temple in Kyoto. Tokyo contains nearly twenty important museums and art galleries. The largest art museum in Japan is the Tokyo National Museum. Major specialized collections in Tokyo are contained in the Calligraphy Museum, the National Museum of Western Art, the Meiji Shrine Treasure Museum, and the Japanese Folkcraft Art Museum. Important museum collections are found in virtually every major city.

ARCHEOLOGY. Discoveries in recent years indicate that the Japanese islands may have been inhabited as early as 6000 to 7000 years ago. The earliest major culture, however, dates from about the third millennium B.C. Known as the Jōmon culture, it is classified as mesolithic, meaning that the people made pottery, but did not yet practice agriculture. The Jōmon people lived in sunken-pit dwellings and survived by hunting and gathering roots, nuts, and shellfish. Their pottery, which was not made on a potter's wheel, shows great artistic skill and richness of design.

A new culture, called Yayoi, influenced by the continent, developed about the 3rd or 2nd century B.C. It was characterized by a more delicate, wheel-made pottery and by the practice of agriculture and the use of bronze and iron implements and weapons. The third major prehistoric culture superseded the Yayoi around the middle of the 3rd century A.D. It is called the Tomb culture from the large earthen, and later stone, burial mounds which are a characteristic feature. The largest of these are as much as 1500 ft. in length and 120 ft. high. The tombs and their contents reveal a highly aristocratic society led by a warrior class equipped with horses, armor, and well-wrought iron weapons. The Tomb culture lasted into the 7th century and merged into the fully historical Japanese civilization.

THE ECONOMY

In recent years the Japanese economy has expanded rapidly. The industrial base of Japan has shifted from light industries to heavy and chemical industries, the production of which accounts for some 55 percent of the total volume of exports. In the late 1960's, the annual gross national product of Japan was the second largest in the world after the United States (excluding the nations of the Soviet bloc). The 1971–72 budget estimate gave revenues and expenditures at approximately $36,100,000,000. In 1971 the per capita product of Japan was estimated at $1995.

Agriculture. The number of Japanese farm

JAPAN

households and the farm population have declined in recent years. The importance of agriculture, however, has not decreased. Almost half of the approximately 23,000 sq.mi. of arable land is devoted to rice production, which in the late 1960's represented about 45 percent of the total crop income. Rice remains the staple of the Japanese diet; however, alterations in the national diet and development of better-yielding strains of rice have brought about a significant overproduction. Wheat and barley are other important grain crops. In the early 1970's annual production of rice was about 14,000,000 tons, of wheat, 440,000 tons, and of barley, 503,000 tons. Other crops are potatoes, soybeans, cabbages, onions, and oranges and other fruits.

Livestock is of much less importance to Japanese agriculture. Because arable land is scarce and consequently valuable, relatively little acreage is used for livestock. The arable land is divided into small farms and almost 70 percent of the land consists of farms of 2 acres or less. Nearly 80 percent of the farmers also work part-time in industry. The land is tilled intensively; almost all farms have electricity and most use modern machinery. Japanese farmers frequently raise two or more crops yearly. Much of the land suffers from soil exhaustion. Heavy use of chemical fertilizers, improved strains, and advanced techniques, however, have made Japanese farms among the most productive in the world.

Forest and Fishing Industries. Nearly 70 percent of the total land area of Japan is woodland, 40 percent of which contains softwoods. More than half of the forest area is privately owned. Although Japan ranks high in world produc-

A busy fish market in a Japanese port.
Japan National Tourist Organization

A component of a steam turbine is assembled at a plant in Tokyo.
Japan National Tourist Organization

tion of round timber, the steadily increasing domestic demand for lumber requires the country to import about 30 percent of its needs.

Fish is a food staple for the Japanese and is second in importance only to rice. Consequently, fishing is one of the most important industries, both for the domestic and export markets. The industry may be divided into three principal categories: coastal, offshore, and deep-sea fishing. Coastal fishing, either by small boats, set nets, or breeding techniques, represents about 40 percent of the total value of production. Offshore fishing by medium-sized boats accounts for about 40 percent of the catch, but only about 25 percent of the total value. Deep-sea fishing by large vessels that operate in international fishing grounds represents about 20 percent of the catch. In the early 1970's the annual catch totaled almost 10,000,000 tons and included bonito, crab, pike, prawn, salmon, saury, sea bream, tuna, and yellowtail. The number of whales caught was about 15,500. In the same period Japan ranked first in the world in whaling, and second in total catch.

Mining. The mineral resources of Japan are varied but limited in quantity. Coal is the principal mineral, but it is primarily low-grade bituminous coal. Other minerals include copper, lead, zinc, manganese, limestone, pyrites, and quartzite, but quantities are insufficient to meet domestic demand.

Manufacturing. Japanese industry suffered extensive damage in World War II. Subsequently, the country began an industrial reconstruction which has brought about complete modernization of its industrial facilities. Primary emphasis was placed on the chemical and petrochemical industries and the heavy-machinery industry. By the mid-1950's industrial production had surpassed prewar levels. In the early 1970's Japan was the leading shipbuilding country in the world and among the leading world producers of electrical products, steel, and motor vehicles. Aluminum output during this period totaled about 893,000 tons annually; crude steel production totaled about 88,500,000 tons, and pig iron about 74,600,000 tons. The iron and steel industry accounted for approximately 9 percent of the total value added by manufacture and about 14 percent of total Japanese exports. The machine industry of Japan represents about 45 percent of the total exports of the country. Among the products of light industry are radio and television sets, cameras, optical goods, transistors, tape recorders, computers, and automation equipment.

In the early 1970's Japan was among the leading world producers of basic chemical raw ma-

131

JAPAN

terials. Japan remains one of the leading textile manufacturers in the world and in recent years has been among the three largest world producers of synthetic fiber. Silk and cotton production during this period, however, were declining in importance to the economy.

Before and during World War II much of the Japanese economy was controlled by about a dozen wealthy families, called the *Zaibatsu* ("wealth cliques") collectively. The greatest of these families were the Mitsui, Iwasaki (operating under the company name Mitsubishi), Sumitomo, and Yasuda; they controlled most of the coal, steam-engine, pulp, and aluminum industries. In 1945–46 family ownership of these immense trusts was dissolved by the occupation authorities. The business organizations remained intact, however, and have since acquired even greater economic power by expanding into shipping, banking, and other industries.

Currency and Banking. The Bank of Japan, established in 1882, is the central bank, acts as general fiscal agent for the government, and is the sole issuer of currency. About ninety private banks constitute the financial system. The yen is the basic unit of currency, consisting of 100 sen (about 265 yen equal U.S.$1; 1973). Twice in recent years, during international currency realignments in 1971 and 1973, the yen was revalued by a total of about 33 percent relative to the U.S. dollar (see DEVALUATION).

Commerce and Trade. Prior to World War II Japan was ranked as the fifth nation in world trade. In 1939 Japanese exports amounted to over $928,000,000 and imports totaled over $757,000,000. Most Japanese exports went to territories controlled by the empire, such as Manchuria and occupied China. Trade balance with other countries, such as the U.S. and Great Britain, was unfavorable; imports from the U.S., for example, exceeded exports to that country by more than $70,000,000. Allied occupation authorities permitted a resumption of foreign trade by private enterprises in 1946. By the early 1970's imports totaled about $19,000,000,000, about 20–25 percent of which were from the U.S., and exports totaled about $24,000,000,000, ranking Japan third as an export nation. Manufactured goods accounted for about 93 percent of total exports; imports of raw materials and foodstuffs accounted for about 75 percent of total imports.

Foreign trade is essential to the Japanese economy. The domestic market is unable to fully absorb the manufactured goods that are produced by Japanese industry. Furthermore, because Japan must import much of the raw material on which its industries depend, the country also must export a substantial proportion of its gross national product to effect a favorable balance of trade.

The foreign markets for Japanese goods shrank after World War II. Certain markets, such as Manchuria and Korea, were lost to Japan as a result of the breakup of the empire. Trade with China declined for political reasons after the establishment of the Communist regime, and trade with the U.S. declined because of the economic barriers set up to protect its own industries from low-priced Japanese competition. To offset the shrinkage of former export markets, Japan attempted with some success during the 1950's to expand its trade with other countries of the Far East. By the early 1970's concentration of Japanese trade with the U.S. (between 25 and 30 percent) created trade imbalances favoring Japan. Several trade agreements with quotas resulted, particularly limitations on Japanese textile exports to the U.S. The primary trading partner of Japan, however, remains the U.S., followed by Australia and Canada.

Transportation. The major railroads of Japan were nationalized in 1907. Total railroad trackage is about 17,300 mi., of which some 12,900 mi. are owned and operated by the government and about 3360 mi. are electrified. In 1965 the Japanese National Railways initiated service by the all-electric Tokaido line, a railroad that provides 125-m.p.h. service between main industrial centers on the eastern seaboard.

Japan has about 94,000 mi. of roads, 17,000 mi. of which are national. Motor vehicles in the early 1970's totaled about 19,670,000, including about 10,500,000 passenger cars and 9,100,000 commercial vehicles.

Japan ranks second in the world in the size of its merchant fleet, with more than 7000 vessels, aggregating a total of about 35,000,000 gross tons. Japan Air Lines, established in 1953, provides service from Tokyo to Europe, the U.S., the Middle East, and Southeast Asia. All-Nippon Airways, a domestic service, connects all major cities in Japan.

Communications. In the early 1970's more than 30,000,000 telephones, as well as about 60,000,000 radios and 23,000,000 television sets, were in use. Some 115 daily newspapers are published; their combined circulation is approximately 53,000,000. Japanese dailies have the highest combined circulation in the world after those of the U.S.

Labor. An enormous increase in the number and membership of trade unions took place in

JAPAN

Japan after World War II. In 1946 more than 12,000 trade unions represented a combined membership of about 3,700,000. In the late 1960's, the number of unions had increased to about 59,000 and the combined membership rose to about 11,000,000, or about 20 percent of the total employed persons. Two principal confederations exist, the General Council of Trade Unions of Japan, consisting mainly of large unions, and the Japanese Confederation of Labor, to which the smaller unions belong. Both confederations seek to better the wages and working conditions of their members.

GOVERNMENT

Japan is governed according to the provisions of the constitution of 1947. Under the terms of this document, which was formulated under the guidance of the Allied occupation authorities after World War II, the emperor is the symbol of the nation.

Central Government. Between 1889, when the first modern Japanese constitution was promulgated, and the end of World War II in 1945, the supreme executive power in Japan was officially designated as resident in the sacred and inviolable person of the emperor, called the *Dai Nippon Teikoku Tenno* ("Emperor of the Empire of Great Japan"). The throne is hereditary and descends only in the male line of the imperial family; in default of a direct male heir, an emperor may be chosen only from four princely families equal in rank to the imperial house. Emperor Hirohito, who succeeded to the throne in 1926, is said to be the 124th of his line.

Executive power is vested in a cabinet, which is headed by a prime minister. The prime minister, who is named by the national legislature (diet), chooses his cabinet, subject to the approval of the diet, from among its members. The prime minister and the cabinet are responsible to the diet.

Health and Welfare. In the early 1970's about 16 percent of the total budget was allocated for social welfare purposes. A medical insurance system has been in effect in Japan since 1927. Self-employed people and employees in the private and public sectors are included under the plan. In recent years about 60 percent of all medical expenses incurred was paid for by medical insurance.

Social welfare services have greatly expanded since World War II; legislation enacted or amended in the postwar years includes the Livelihood Security Law for Needy Persons, the Law

A tanker is painted before launching at a shipyard in Nagasaki.　　　　　　　　Japan National Tourist Organization

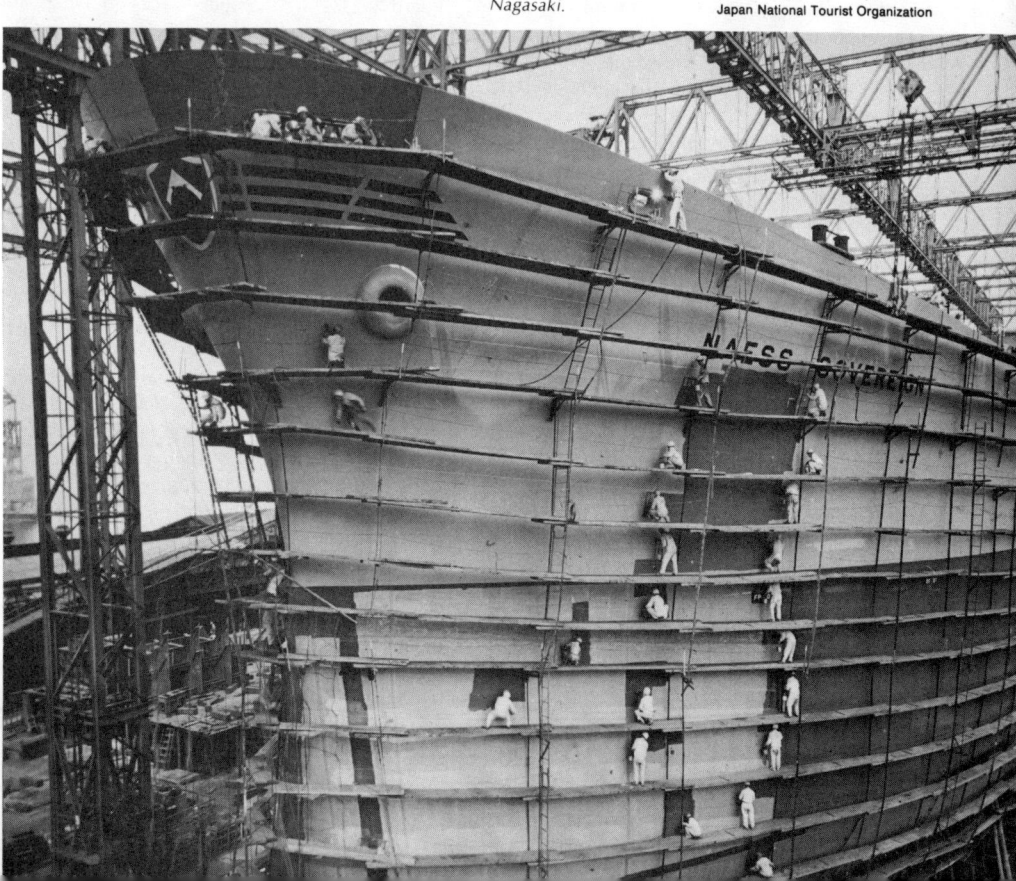

JAPAN

for the Welfare of Disabled Persons, the National Health Insurance Law, the Welfare Pension Insurance Law, Old Age Welfare Law, and the Maternal and Child Welfare Law. The entire population is covered by various insurance systems.

Legislature. The diet, the supreme organ of government power, is a bicameral body, elected by universal suffrage and consisting of the House of Representatives (lower house) and the House of Councillors (upper house). Lower-house members, totaling 486, are elected for a term not to exceed four years. Upper-house members, totaling 250, are elected for six-year terms; elections for one half the membership are held every three years. One hundred councillors are elected at large, and the remainder from the prefectural districts. Decisions by the House of Councillors may be vetoed by the lower house, which also retains control over legislation dealing with treaties and fiscal matters.

Before the Japanese defeat in World War II legislative power resided in a House of Peers (composed of hereditary peers, distinguished commoners nominated by the emperor, and a limited number of elective seats) and a House of Representatives elected by male citizens over twenty-five years of age. Cabinet ministers were responsible to and appointed by the emperor.

Political Parties. The three major political parties in Japan are the Liberal-Democratic Party, the Socialist Party, and the Democratic Socialist Party. The Liberal-Democratic Party, in power in the early 1970's, advocates free enterprise, the expansion of foreign trade, government aid to small businessmen, and close relations with the U.S. The Socialist Party advocates nationalization of major industries and expanded social welfare; it also favors a policy of neutralism in foreign affairs. The Democratic Socialist Party was formed in 1960 by a group that broke away from the Socialist Party; it follows so-called middle-of-the-road policies. The largest of the minor parties is Komeito, a Buddhist religious party. The Communist Party of Japan is also represented in the diet.

Local Government. Including Okinawa, which was returned to Japan by the U.S. in 1972, the country is divided into forty-seven prefectures, which contain municipalities. Each municipality has a legislature composed of popularly elected representatives. The municipalities have fairly broad powers; they control public education and may levy taxes.

Judiciary. The Japanese judicial system is entirely separate from and independent of the executive authority. Except for reasons of health, judges may be removed only by public impeachment. The highest court in the nation is the supreme court, established by the constitution and consisting of a chief justice appointed by the emperor upon the recommendation of the cabinet and fourteen associate justices appointed by the cabinet. Four types of lower courts are prescribed by the constitution: high courts, district courts, family courts, and summary courts. The supreme court is the tribunal of final appeal in all civil and criminal cases and has authority to decide on the constitutionality of any act of the legislature or executive. High courts hear appeals in civil and criminal cases from lower courts. District courts have both appellate and original jurisdiction. Family and summary courts are exclusively courts of first instance.

Defense. The National Police Reserve, created under the direction of the occupation authorities in 1950, formed the nucleus of the defense forces subsequently organized when the Japanese regained national sovereignty. In the early 1970's the Japanese Self-Defense Forces consisted of about 293,000 personnel. These comprised an army (169,000 active; 30,000 reserve), a navy (43,000), an air force (40,000), and a coast guard (11,000). All police forces in Japan are under the control of the central government.

HISTORY

Traditionally, Japan dates from 660 B.C. The earliest surviving records of Japanese history, aside from Chinese accounts, are contained in two semimythical chronicles, the *Kojiki* and the *Nihonshoki* (or *Nihong*), completed, respectively, in 712 and 720 A.D. These chronicles purport to deal with events from about the 7th century B.C. to the 7th century A.D. The chronicles and other collections of legends were the basis of the traditional accounts of the history of Japan. The *Nihonshoki* gave 660 B.C. as the year in which Jimmu, the first Emperor of Japan ascended the throne, thereby founding the Japanese Empire; in the 19th century A.D. the founding was precisely dated as Feb. 11 of that year.

Early Settlement. Archeological and historical research have shown that the Ainu (q.v.), a tribal people whose origins are unknown, were probably the earliest inhabitants of the Japanese archipelago. They may have populated all the Japanese islands in the 2nd and 1st millennia B.C. Invading peoples from nearby areas in Asia began expeditions of conquest to the islands. Gradually the Ainu were forced to the northern and eastern portions of Honshu by the invaders. According to the chronicles, Jimmu after having established his rule in Kyushu, led his forces northward, and extended his domains to Yamato, a province in central Honshu, which gave its name to the imperial house and eventually, to all of ancient Japan.

The Imperial Clan. The mikado, the Yamato chieftain, consolidated his power by making a primitive form of Shinto the general religion and, thus, a political instrument. In the early centuries of the Christian era the Yamato chieftains exerted indirect control over various autonomous tribal units known as uji. Each uji had its own clan gods and its own domain. Of the uji the most important were the Omi, claiming divine descent, and the Muraji, claiming descent from nobles of the pre-Yamato era. The rule of the imperial clan, regarded as the head clan, was more nominal than actual, though its principal deity, the sun-goddess, was worshiped nationally.

About 360 A.D. Empress Jingo, a legendary ruler who came to be considered a goddess, took over the government at the death of her husband, Emperor Chuai. The warrior empress is said to have fitted out an army and invaded and conquered a portion of Korea (q.v.). Korean culture, greatly influenced by adjacent China, had already advanced to a comparatively high level. During the next several centuries intercourse between Japan and Korea, including the movement of people, considerably stimulated the developing civilization of the islands. Chinese writing, literature, and philosophy became popular at the court of Yamato. About the beginning of the 5th century the Chinese script came into use at the Yamato court. About 430 the imperial court appointed its first historiographers, and more dependable records were kept. The most important event of the period was the importation of Buddhism. About 552 the king of Pakche, in southwestern Korea, sent Buddhist priests to Japan, together with religious images, Buddhist scriptures, and calendars and methods of keeping time. The Koreans drove out the Japanese invaders about 562, but the imported culture was already strongly rooted in the archipelago. By the early 7th century Buddhism had become the official religion of Japan.

In 604, the first Japanese constitution, comprising a simple set of maxims for good government, was drafted. It was strongly influenced by the centralized government of China. Originally twelve, and later eight, hierarchical ranks of court officials were established. A great council, the Dajokan, ruled the realm through local governors sent out from the capital. Nara in Yamato became the fixed capital in 710; in 794 Kyoto was made the imperial residence and, with few interruptions, remained the capital until 1868. By the 9th century the Yamato court had come to rule all of the main islands of Japan except Hokkaido.

Fujiwara Leadership (858–1160). During the 9th century the emperors began to withdraw from public life. Delegating the affairs of government to subordinates, they went into seclusion and, in time, came to be regarded as abstractions in the national life rather than its directors. The retirement of the emperors was accompanied by the rising power of the Fujiwara, the leading family of court nobles. In 858 the Fujiwara became virtual masters of Japan, maintaining their power for the next three centuries. In that year a Fujiwara prince, Yoshifusa (804–72), became regent for his grandson then less than one year old. The Fujiwara monopolized most of the court and administrative offices. In 884 Fujiwara Mototsune (836–91) became the first official civil dictator (kwampaku). The greatest of the Fujiwara leaders was Michinaga (966–1027), whose five daughters married successive emperors, and who was the leading figure at the court from 998 to 1027.

The period of Fujiwara supremacy was marked by a great flowering of Japanese culture, and by the growth of a civilization greatly influenced but not dominated by the Chinese civilization, which had been its fountainhead. The dictatorship of Michinaga is regarded as the classical age of Japanese literature (q.v.). The character of the government also changed under the Fujiwara ascendancy. The centralized administration, which became rife with corruption, weakened, and the country in time was divided up into large, hereditary estates, owned by the nobles, as tax-free emoluments for their official positions. Most peasants were only too willing to attach their lands to such estates in order to escape the heavy burden of taxes on the public lands, which had been meted out to them. Thus, great private estates became characteristic of land ownership throughout the empire.

In the provinces local groups of warriors banded together for protection, forming protofeudal groups of lords and vassals. The leaders of these groups were often members of the Taira and the Minamoto clans, both of which had been founded by imperial princes. The Taira warriors acquired their military renown and power in the southwest; the Minamoto, in the east. In the 12th century both great military clans started to extend their power to the court itself, dominated by the Fujiwara, and a struggle

JAPAN

Yoritomo, first Minamoto ruler of Japan. Bettmann Archive

for control of Japan ensued. In 1156 a civil war began between the forces of two rival emperors and, after a second war, in 1160, the Taira crushed the Minamoto and seized control of Japan from the Fujiwara. The Taira leader, Kiyomori (1118–81), was named prime minister in 1167 and, modeling his policies on those of the Fujiwara, married his daughter to an imperial prince, their infant son becoming emperor in 1180. In the same year the Minamoto leader, Yoritomo (1147–99), led an uprising in eastern Japan and the Taira were driven from the capital. The civil war endured five years, ending in 1185 with the naval battle of Dan no Ura, near present Shimonoseki on the Inland Sea. Yoritomo became the leader of Japan, ending the era of imperial administration and inaugurating a military dictatorship that ruled Japan for the next seven centuries.

Early Shoguns (12th–16th Centuries). Stressing the almost complete division between the civil military phases of government, Yoritomo established a separate military capital at Kamakura, on Tokyo Bay, in 1185. During the Kamakura period, which lasted from 1185 to 1333, Japanese art flourished; *see* JAPANESE ART AND ARCHITECTURE: *Painting and Sculpture.* Also from that time forward Japanese feudalism (q.v.) developed until it was stronger than the imperial administration had ever been. In 1192 Yoritomo was appointed to the office of *Seiitaishogun* ("barbarian-subduing great general"), usually shortened to *shogun,* the military commander in chief. Through his military network, Yoritomo was already the virtual ruler of Japan and his shogunate made him titular leader as well. The emperor and court were largely powerless before the shogun. Kamakura became the true court and government, while Kyoto remained a titular court, without power.

In 1219 the Hojo family, by means of a series of conspiracies and murders which eliminated Minamoto heirs and their supporters, became the military rulers of Japan. No Hojo ever became shogun; instead, the family prevailed on the emperor to appoint figurehead shoguns, sometimes small children, while a Hojo leader governed as the *shikken,* or regent, with the actual power. For more than 100 years the Hojo maintained their rule. In 1274 and again in 1281 the Mongols (q.v.), then in control of China and Korea, attempted to invade Japan, each time unsuccessfully. The invasions were a serious drain on Hojo resources and the Hojos were unable to reward their vassals for support during the invasions. An able emperor, Daigo II (1287-1339), led a rebellion that was climaxed in 1333 with the capture of Kamakura and the downfall of the Hojo. For the next two years Daigo tried to restore the imperial administration. One of his vassals, Ashikaga (1305-58), revolted and, driving Daigo from Kyoto, set up his own candidate for emperor in 1336. Daigo and his supporters fled to Yoshino, a region south of Nara in Honshu, and established a rival court. For the next fifty-six years civil war between Daigo and his successors and the emperors controlled by the Ashikaga, who became shoguns, ravaged Japan. At length, in 1392, an Ashikaga envoy persuaded the true emperor at Yoshino to abdicate and relinquish the sacred imperial regalia. With their nominees acknowledged as rightful emperors, the Ashikaga shoguns felt empowered to establish their own feudal control over all Japan. By this time, however, there had developed in all parts of Japan a class of hereditary, feudal lords, called daimyo. The Ashikaga shoguns were never able to exercise absolute control over the powerful daimyo. In general, the period of Ashikaga ascendancy was one of great refinement of manners, of great art and literary endeavor, and, notably, of the development of Buddhism as a political force. For some centuries Buddhist monasteries had been so wealthy and powerful that they were great forces in the country. Buddhist monks, clad in armor and bearing weapons, often turned the tide of medieval battles with their strong organizations and fortified monasteries. Local wars among feudal lords became common by the 16th century, which is still known in Japanese history as the "Epoch of a Warring Country".

Three great contemporary warlords finally established order in the strife-torn empire. Nobunaga (1534-82), a Taira general, broke the power of the monasteries between 1570 and 1580, destroying Buddhism as a political force. Toyotomi Hideyoshi (1536-98), a follower of Nobunaga, united all of Japan under his rule by 1590. Using his power to its greatest extent, the dictator marked out the boundaries of all feudal fiefs.

The Tokugawa Shogunate (1603-1867). In 1603 the successor to Hideyoshi, Iyeyasu (1542-1616), became the first of the Tokugawa (q.v.) shoguns who ruled Japan for the succeeding two-and-a-half centuries. Iyeyasu made Edo (later Tokyo) his capital. In a short time the city became the greatest in the empire, developing culturally and economically as well as politically. Iyeyasu brought the feudal organization that had been planned by Hideyoshi to fulfillment. The daimyos and administrators, as well as the emperor and his court, were put under the strict control of the shogunate. Social classes became rigidly stratified. The form of feudalism established by Iyeyasu and succeeding Tokugawa shoguns endured until the end of the feudal period in the late 19th century.

Another result of Tokugawa domination was the imposed isolation of Japan from the Western world. The first Europeans to visit Japan were Portuguese traders who had landed on an island near Kyushu about 1542. Saint Francis Xavier (q.v.), the Jesuit missionary, had brought Christianity to Japan in 1549. During the remainder of the century about 300,000 Japanese were converted to Roman Catholicism, despite disapproval and persecution by Hideyoshi. Portuguese, Spanish, and Dutch traders visited Japan more and more frequently. The shoguns became convinced that the introduction of Christianity (q.v.) was designed to serve as a preliminary to European conquest. In 1612 Christians became subject to official persecution and various massacres occurred. The Spanish were refused permission to land in Japan after 1624 and a series of edicts in the next decade forbade travel abroad, prohibiting even the building of large ships. The only Europeans permitted to remain in Japan were a small group of Dutch traders restricted to the artificial island of De-shima in the harbor of Nagasaki and continually subjected to indignities and limitations on their activities. During the succeeding two centuries the forms of Japanese feudalism remained static. Bushido (q.v.), the code of the feudal warriors, became the standard of conduct for the great lords and the lesser nobility, the professional warriors called samurai (q.v.). Japanese culture, closed to outside influence, grew inward and received intensive development resulting in extreme nationalism.

During the 18th century, however, new social and economic conditions in the islands began to indicate the inevitable collapse of rigid feudalism. A large, wealthy merchant class rose in great strength. At that time, too, peasant disturbances became more frequent because of the impoverishment of the landless peasantry.

The awakening consciousness of Japan to the outside world was formally evidenced in 1720 when the Tokugawa shogun Yoshimune (1677-

JAPAN

1751) repealed the proscription on European books and study. By the early 19th century visits from Europeans, mostly traders and explorers, became comparatively frequent, though the ban was still officially in force. The United States was particularly anxious to make a treaty of friendship and, if possible, one of commerce with Japan. One of the major factors on which this American policy was compounded was the circumstance of the wrecking of American whaling ships on the Japanese coast. In 1853 the American government sent a formal mission headed by Commodore Matthew Calbraith Perry (see under PERRY) with a squadron of ships, to the emperor of Japan. After almost a year of negotiations, Perry and representatives of the emperor signed a treaty on March 31, 1854, establishing trade relations between the U.S. and Japan. In 1860 a Japanese embassy was sent to the U.S., and two years later Japanese trade missions visited European capitals to negotiate formal agreements.

The opening of Japan was achieved more through the show of superior force by Western nations than by an actual desire for foreign relations on the part of Japanese leaders. The Japanese warlords, equipped with medieval weapons and trained in small-scale warfare, were dismayed by Western military equipment and dared not, at first, resist. Nevertheless, a militant antiforeign faction immediately developed and attacks on foreign traders became common occurrences in the 1860's. The leaders of the antiforeign movement were the great clans which had always resented Tokugawa rule from Edo. They rallied around the emperor at Kyoto and, with imperial support, initiated military and naval attacks on foreign ships in Japanese harbors. The antiforeign movement was short lived, ending in 1864, following a show of force by the Western powers, but it resulted in the decline of the shogunate and the restoration of imperial administration.

Restoration of Imperial Rule. In 1867 the last shogun, Hitotsubashi (1837–1902), resigned and the emperor, Mutsuhito, (1852–1912), regained the position of actual head of the government, with the support of the southwestern clans. Mutsuhito took the name of Meiji ("Enlightened Government") to designate his reign. Meiji became the posthumous title of Mutsuhito. The imperial capital was transferred to Edo, renamed Tokyo ("Eastern Capital"). In 1869 the lords of the great Choshu, Hizen, Satsuma, and Tosa clans surrendered their feudal fiefs to the emperor and, after a succession of such surrenders by other clans, an imperial decree in 1871 abolished all fiefs and created centrally administered prefectures in their stead.

Under the direction of such farsighted statesmen as Prince Tomomi Iwakura (1835–83) and Marquis Toshimichi Okubo (1830?–78) the Japanese remained untouched by the European imperialism that, at the time, was engulfing other Asian countries and, by concerted imitation of Western civilization in all its aspects, set out to make Japan itself a world power. French officers were engaged to remodel the army, British seamen reorganized the navy, and Dutch engineers supervised new construction in the islands. Japanese were sent abroad to analyze foreign governments and to select their best features for duplication in Japan. A new penal code was modeled on that of France, and a ministry of education was established in 1871 to develop a system of universal education based on that of the U.S. Universal military service was decreed in 1872 and four years later the samurai class of professional warriors was abolished by decree.

Changes in the Japanese political system were imposed from the top, and were not the result of political demands by the people. In 1881 the emperor promised formally to establish a national legislature and in 1884, preparing for an upper house, he created a peerage with five orders of nobility. A cabinet modeled on that of Germany was organized in 1885 with Marquis Hirobumi Ito (q.v.) as the first prime minister, and a privy council was created in 1888, both being responsible to the emperor. The new constitution, drafted by Marquis Ito after constitutional research in Europe and the U.S., was promulgated in 1889. A two-house diet was designed to have a house of peers of 363 members, and a 463-member lower house elected by citizens paying direct annual taxes of not less than fifteen yen. The emperor's powers were carefully safeguarded; he was permitted to issue decrees as laws, and only he could decide on war or the cessation of war. Moreover, the lower house could be dissolved and the upper prorogued by imperial decree. Rapid industrialization, under government direction, accompanied this concentrated political growth.

The empire also embarked upon an aggressive foreign policy. In 1879 Japan had taken over the Ryukyu Islands (q.v.), a Japanese protectorate since 1609, designating them the prefecture of Okinawa. The struggle for control of Korea became the next step in Japanese expansion. Conflict with China in Korea resulted in the Sino-Japanese War of 1894–95, in which the modernized Japanese forces completely and easily defeated the Chinese army and navy. By

138

the terms of the Treaty of Shimonoseki in April, 1895, China gave Japan Formosa, the Pescadores, and a large monetary indemnity. The treaty had originally awarded the Liaotung Peninsula (southern Manchuria) to Japan, in addition; but intervention by Russia, France, and Germany forced Japan to accept an additional indemnity instead.

The decisive Japanese triumph indicated to the world that a new, strong power was rising in the East. As a preliminary to negotiating full equality with the great powers, Japan, in 1890, had completely revised its criminal, civil, and commercial law codes on Western models. Thus, the empire was in a position to demand the revocation of extraterritoriality (q.v.) clauses from its treaties. By 1899 all the great powers had signed treaties abandoning extraterritoriality in Japan. In 1894 the U.S. and Great Britain were the first nations given the freedom of the entire empire for trade.

The 20th Century. In pursuing its interests in Korea, Japan inevitably came into conflict with Russia. Resentment against Russia was already high because that country had been the principal agent in depriving Japan of the Liaotung Peninsula after the Chinese war. The two countries signed a treaty pledging the independence of Korea in 1898, but allowing Japanese commercial interest to predominate. In 1900, following the Boxer Rebellion (q.v.) in China, Russia occupied Manchuria (q.v.) and, from bases there, began to penetrate northern Korea.

In 1904, after repeated attempts to negotiate the matter had failed, Japan broke off diplomatic relatons with Russia and attacked Russian-leased Port Arthur (now part of Lüta) in southern Manchuria, beginning the Russo-Japanese War (q.v.). Japan won its second modern war in less than eighteen months. The peace treaty, mediated by U.S. President Theodore Roosevelt (q.v.), was signed in Portsmouth, N.H., on Sept. 5, 1905. Japan was awarded the lease (to 1923, later extended to 1997) of the Liaotung Peninsula, including the Kwantung territory, and the southern half of Sakhalin (q.v.), thereafter known as Karafuto. Moreover, Russia acknowledged the paramount interest of Japan in Korea. Five years later in 1910 Korea was formally annexed to Japan and named Chosen.

Japanese-American relations had for some years been strained by difficulties over Japanese emigration to the U.S. Thousands of Japanese had settled in the States of California, Oregon, and Washington, and the American residents of these States demanded the exclusion of the Japanese by legislation similar to the Chinese Exclusion Acts of 1882, 1892, and 1902. This agitation was led by American labor unions, resenting the fact that Japanese laborers were willing to work for lower wages and longer hours than those called for by American labor policies. Formal protests against the treatment of Japanese in Pacific-coast States were delivered by the Japanese ambassador in Washington in 1906, and, after a series of negotiations, Japan and the U.S. concluded a so-called gentleman's agreement in 1908. By this extralegal agreement, confirmed in 1911, Japan consented to withhold passports from laborers, and the U.S. Department of State promised to disapprove anti-Japanese legislation. The problem, however, was never fully resolved and was a contributing factor to anti-American feeling in Japan, which increased in the following three decades.

WORLD WAR I. In August, 1914, following the outbreak of World War I, Japan sent an ultimatum to Germany, demanding the evacuation of the German-leased territory of Kiaochow in northeastern China. When Germany refused to comply, Japan entered the war on the side of the Allies. Japanese troops occupied the German-held Marshall, Caroline, and Mariana islands in the Pacific Ocean. In 1915 the empire submitted the Twenty-One Demands to China, calling for industrial, railroad, and mining privileges, and a promise that China would not lease or give any coastal territory to a nation other than Japan. These demands, which were quickly granted, were the first statement of the Japanese policy of domination over China and the Far East. A year later, in 1916, China ceded commercial rights in Inner Mongolia and southern Manchuria to Japan.

As a result of the World War I peace settlement, Japan received the Pacific islands, which it had occupied as mandates from the League of Nations (q.v.), the empire having become a charter member of that organization. The territory of Kiaochow was also awarded to Japan, but the empire restored Kiaochow to China in 1922 as a result of an agreement, the Shantung Treaty, made during the Washington Conference (q.v.) in 1922. This conference also resulted in the replacement of the Anglo-Japanese Alliance by the Four-Power Treaty, by which Japan, France, Great Britain, and the U.S. pledged themselves to respect one another's territories in the Pacific Ocean and to consult if their territorial rights were threatened. The Nine-Power Treaty (Belgium, Great Britain, the Netherlands, Portugal, Japan, France, Italy, China, and the U.S.) bound the signatories to re-

JAPAN

spect the territorial integrity and sovereignty of China. An additional treaty between Great Britain, the U.S., Japan, France, and Italy dealt with naval disarmament on a 5-5-3-1.7-1.7 ratio, respectively, the Japanese navy being limited to 315,000 tons of capital ships; see DISARMAMENT.

With the adoption of the Shantung and Nine-Power treaties, Japan demonstrated a conciliatory attitude toward China. Nevertheless Japanese commercial interests in China were still regarded as paramount over Chinese interests. Russo-Japanese relations, which had become strained after the Russian Revolution in 1917 and the subsequent invasion of Siberia and northern Sakhalin by the Japanese in 1918, became more amicable after Japan recognized the Soviet regime in 1925. This less aggressive attitude on the part of Japan was due partially to a surge of political liberalism stimulated by the victory of the democratic nations in World War I. Beginning with 1919 the government was assailed with increasing demands for universal suffrage, an issue that occasioned rioting in the cities. To placate these demands the government, in 1919, passed a reform act doubling the electorate (to 3,000,000); but the universal suffrage issue became more intense until it was granted by a 1925 bill, increasing the electorate to 14,000,000. Reflecting the rising interest in popular government, the political trend during the 1920–30 decade was toward party cabinets and away from oligarchic rule by the so-called elder statesmen, the nobility, and military leaders. This movement lasted only until about 1932, when totalitarianism became the trend of Japanese government.

Hirohito, adopting *Showa* ("Enlightened Peace") as the official designation for his reign, succeeded as emperor in 1926. One year later General Baron Gi-ichi Tanaka (q.v.) became prime minister, and declared the resumption of an aggressive policy toward China. The impelling factor in this change of policy lay in the expansion in Japanese industry, which began with the declaration of World War I in 1914 and was then continuing at a great pace, requiring new markets for the increased output.

OCCUPATION OF MANCHURIA. In the late 1920's Japan, in effect, gained domination of the administrative and economic affairs of Manchuria. The Chinese, however, increasingly resented Japanese interference in what was, technically, part of China. On Sept. 18, 1931, the Japanese army in Kwantung, claiming that an explosion on the Japanese-owned South Manchuria Railroad had been caused by Chinese saboteurs, seized the arsenals of Mukden and of several neighboring cities. Chinese troops were forced to withdraw from the area. Entirely without official saction by the Japanese government, the Kwantung army extended its operations into all of Manchuria and, in about five months, was in possession of the entire region. Manchuria was then reestablished as an independent state, Manchukuo, controlled by Japan through a puppet ruler, Henry P'u-i (see HSÜAN T'UNG).

All pretense of party government in Japan was abandoned as a result of the occupation of Manchuria. Viscount Makoto Saito (1858–1936) formed a so-called national cabinet composed, chiefly, of men who belonged to no party. The international repercussions of the Manchurian incident resulted in an inquiry by a League of Nations commission, acting by authority of the Kellogg-Briand Pact (q.v.). When, in 1933, the League Assembly requested that Japan cease hostilities in China, Japan instead announced its withdrawal from the League, to take effect in 1935. To consolidate its gains in China, Japan landed troops in Shanghai to quell an effective Chinese boycott of Japanese goods. In the north the Japanese Manchurian army occupied and annexed the province of Jehol, and threatened to occupy the cities of Peiping and Tientsin. Unable to resist the superior Japanese forces, China, in May, 1933, recognized the Japanese conquest by signing a truce.

The independent action of the army evidenced the power of the military leaders in Japanese politics. In 1936 the empire signed an anti-Communist agreement with Germany and, one year later, a similar pact with Italy. The establishment of almost complete military rule, with the cooperation of the Zaibatzu, or family trusts (see MONOPOLY AND COMPETITION: *History: Historic Cartels*), made aggression and expansion the avowed policy of the empire.

WAR WITH CHINA. On July 7, 1937, a Chinese patrol clashed with Japanese troops on the Marco Polo Bridge near Peiping (present-day Peking). Using the incident as a pretext to begin hostilities, the Japanese army in Manchuria moved troops into the area, precipitating another Sino-Japanese War, never actually declared. A Japanese force quickly overran northern China. By the end of 1937 the Japanese navy had completed a blockade of almost the entire Chinese coast. The army advanced into eastern and southern China throughout 1937 and 1938, capturing, successively, Shanghai, Soochow, Nanking, Tsingtao, Canton, and Hankow, and forcing the Chinese army into the west. A Japanese force occupied the island of Hainan (q.v.). Protests by foreign governments concerning property owned by their nationals and mistreatment, by Japanese troops, of foreigners resident in China, were, in effect, ignored by the empire. By the end of 1938 the war reached a virtual stalemate. The Japanese army was checked by the mountains of central China, behind which the Chinese waged guerrilla warfare against the invaders.

Japan, meanwhile, was subjected to controlled war economy. In 1937 a cabinet headed by Prince Fumimaro Konoye (q.v.) relegated the entire conduct of the war, without government interference, to military and naval leaders.

The beginning of World War II in Europe, in September, 1939, gave Japan new opportunity for aggression in Southeast Asia. These aggressive acts were prefaced by a series of diplomatic arrangements. In September, 1940, the empire concluded a tripartite alliance with Germany and Italy, the so-called Rome-Berlin Axis, pledging mutual and total aid for a period of ten years. Japan considered, however, that a 1939 neutrality pact between Germany and the Soviet Union had released the empire from any obligation incurred by the 1936 anti-Communist alliance. In September, 1941, therefore, Japan signed a neutrality pact with the Soviet Union, thus protecting the northern border of Manchuria. A year before, with the consent of the German-sponsored Vichy government of France, Japanese forces occupied French Indochina; see INDOCHINA. At the same time Japan tried to obtain economic and political footholds in the Netherlands East Indies; see INDONESIA, REPUBLIC OF.

These acts, in Indochina and the East Indies, contributed to increasing hostility between Japan and the U.S. The protection of American property in eastern Asia had been a source of friction since the Japanese invasion of China in 1937. Continued protests from Joseph Clark Grew (1880–1965), then U.S. ambassador to Japan, were fruitless. In October, 1941, General Hideki Tojo (q.v.), who was militantly anti-American, became the Japanese premier and minister of war. Negotiations continued in Washington throughout November, even after the decision for war had been made in Tokyo. ATTACK ON PEARL HARBOR. On Dec. 7, 1941, without warning and while negotiations between America and Japanese diplomats were still in progress, Japanese carrier-based airplanes attacked Pearl Harbor (q.v.), the main American naval base in the Pacific. Simultaneous attacks were launched by the Japanese army, navy, and air force against the Philippines, Guam, Wake Island, Midway Island, Hong Kong, British Malaya, and Thailand. On Dec. 8 the U.S. Congress declared war on Japan, as did all the Allied powers except the U.S.S.R. See WORLD WAR II.

For about a year following the successful surprise attacks, Japan maintained the offensive in Southeast Asia and the islands of the South Pacific. The empire designated eastern Asia and its environs as the "Greater East Asia Co-Prosperity Sphere" and made effective propaganda of the slogan "Asia for the Asians". Moreover, nationalistic elements in many of the countries of eastern Asia gave tacit and, in some cases, active support to the Japanese, because they saw an apparent way to free themselves from Western imperialism. In December, 1941, Japan invaded Thailand, forcing the government to conclude a treaty of alliance. Japanese troops occupied Burma, British Malaya, Borneo, Hong Kong, and the Netherlands East Indies. By May, 1942, the Philippines were in Japanese hands. Striking toward Australia and New Zealand, Japanese forces landed in New Guinea, New Britain, and the Solomon Islands. A Japanese task force invaded the North American continent, occupying Attu, Agattu, and Kiska in the Aleutian Islands off the Alaskan coast. Ultimately, however, the war became a naval struggle for control of the vast expanses of the Pacific Ocean.

The tide of battle began to change in 1942, when an Allied naval and air force defeated a Japanese invasion fleet in the Battle of the Coral Sea (see CORAL SEA, BATTLE OF THE) between New Guinea and the Solomon Islands. A month later a larger Japanese fleet was defeated in the Battle of Midway (see MIDWAY ISLANDS). Using combined operations of military, naval, and air units under command of the American general Douglas MacArthur (q.v.), Allied forces fought northward from island to island in the South Pacific, invading and driving out the Japanese. In July, 1944, after the fall of Saipan, a major Japanese base in the Mariana Islands, the Japanese leaders realized that Japan had lost the war. Tojo was forced to resign, weakening the hold of the military oligarchy. In November, 1944, the U.S. began a series of major air raids over Japan by B-29 Superfortress bombers based on Saipan. In early 1945 an air base even closer to Japan (750 mi.) was acquired with the conquest, after the fierce Battle of Iwo Jima; see IWO JIMA, BATTLE OF. During the same period Allied forces under the British admiral Louis Mountbatten (q.v.), 1st Earl Mountbatten of Burma, defeated the Japanese armies in Southeast Asia. In the next four months, from May through August, bombing attacks devastated Japanese communications, industry, and what was left of the navy. These at-

JAPAN

tacks were climaxed on Aug. 6 by the dropping of the first atomic bomb (see NUCLEAR WEAPONS) on the city of Hiroshima. Two days later, on Aug. 8, the Soviet Union declared war on Japan, and on Aug. 9 a second atomic bomb was dropped on Nagasaki. Soviet forces invaded Manchuria, Korea, and Karafuto. The Allied powers had agreed during the Potsdam Conference (q.v.) that only unconditional surrender would be acceptable from the Japanese government. On Aug. 14 Japan accepted the Allied terms, signing the formal surrender aboard the American battleship U.S.S. *Missouri* in Tokyo Bay on Sept. 2.

The U.S. army was designated, by the Allied powers, as the army of occupation in the Japanese home islands. Japan was stripped of its empire. Inner Mongolia, Manchuria, Formosa, and Hainan were returned to China. The U.S.S.R. was awarded the Kuril Islands and Karafuto, and the control of Outer Mongolia; Port Arthur and the South Manchurian Railway were placed under the joint control of the U.S.S.R. and China. All the former Japanese mandated islands in the South Pacific were occupied by the U.S. under a United Nations trusteeship; see UNITED NATIONS, THE.

On Aug. 11, 1945, following the Japanese offer of unconditional surrender, Douglas MacArthur was appointed Supreme Commander for the Allied Powers (SCAP) occupying Japan. Representatives of China, the U.S.S.R, and Great Britain were named to an Allied Council for Japan, sitting in Tokyo, to assist MacArthur. Broad questions of occupation policy became the province of the Far Eastern Commission, sitting in Washington, D.C., representing the U.S., Great Britain, the U.S.S.R., Australia, Canada, China, France, India, the Netherlands, New Zealand, and the Philippines. A number of Japanese war leaders were tried for war crimes by an eleven-nation tribunal, which opened May 3, 1946, and closed Nov. 12, 1948; see WAR-CRIMES TRIALS: *Tokyo and Other Trials*.

AMERICAN OCCUPATION. The American occupation of the Japanese islands was in no way resisted. The objectives of the occupation policy were declared to be, basically, the democratization of the Japanese government and the reestablishment of a peacetime industrial economy sufficient for the Japanese population. MacArthur was directed to exercise his authority through the emperor and existing government machinery as far as possible. Among other Allied objectives were the dissolution of the great industrial and banking trusts, the assets of which were seized in 1946 and later liquidated through SCAP. A program of land reform, designed to give the tenant farmers an opportunity to purchase the land they worked, was in operation by 1947, and an education program along democratic lines was organized. Women were given the franchise in the first postwar Japanese general election in April, 1946, and thirty-eight women were elected to the Japanese diet. Subsequently the diet completed the draft of a new constitution; the latter became effective in May, 1947.

The rehabilitation of the Japanese economy was more difficult than the reorganization of the government. The scarcity of food had to be offset by imports from the Allied powers, and from the U.S. in particular. Severe bombings during the war had almost nullified Japanese industrial capacity. By the beginning of 1949 aid to Japan was costing the U.S. more than $1,000,000 a day.

Beginning in May work stoppages took place in various Japanese industries, notably coal mining. The government accused the Communist Party, which had polled 3,000,000 votes in a recent national election, of instigating the strike movement for political purposes, and SCAP concurred in this view. Subsequently the government launched a large-scale investigation of Communist activities. MacArthur's labor policies were sharply criticized in June, 1949, by the Soviet member of the Allied Control Council. In his reply, MacArthur accused the U.S.S.R. of fomenting disorder in Japan through the Communist Party and of "callous indifference" in repatriating Japanese prisoners of war. For the next year Communism and repatriation were dominant issues in national politics. The Soviet Union announced in April, 1950, that, excluding about 10,000 war criminals, all prisoners (94,973) had been returned to Japan, but according to Japanese records over 300,000 prisoners were still in Soviet custody.

Allied negotiations during 1950 relative to a Japanese peace treaty were marked by basic differences between the U.S. and the Soviet Union on several issues, especially whether Communist China should participate in the drafting of the document. On May 18 the American statesman John Foster Dulles (see under DULLES), adviser to the U.S. secretary of state, was named to prepare the terms of the treaty. More than a year of consultations and negotiations with and among the Allied powers, Japan, and the Far Eastern nations that had fought against Japan culminated, on July 12, 1951, in the publication of the draft treaty. The U.S.S.R., which had been consulted also, maintained that the document

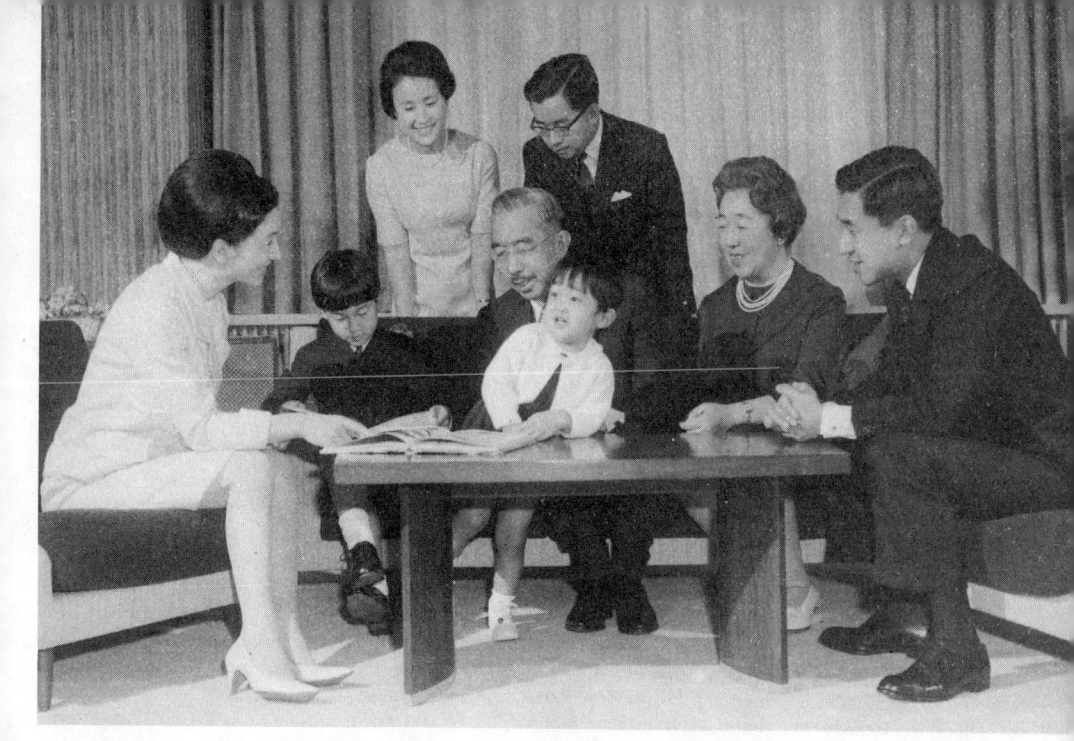

The Japanese royal family poses for a portrait in 1967: (seated, left to right) Crown Princess Michiko, Prince Naruhito, Prince Fumihito, Emperor Hirohito, Empress Nagako, Crown Prince Akihito; (standing) Princess Hanako, Prince Masahito. UPI

was conducive to the resurgence of Japanese militarism. The U.S. government invited fifty-five countries to attend the peace conference. Nationalist China and Communist China were not invited.

The peace conference opened in San Francisco, Calif., on Sept. 4. Of the nations invited, India, Burma, and Yugoslavia refused to attend. During the conference discussion was limited to the previously prepared treaty text, a procedure that nullified Soviet attempts to reopen negotiations on its various provisions. Forty-nine countries, including Japan, signed the treaty on Sept. 8; the U.S.S.R., Czechoslovakia, and Poland refused to do so.

THE PEACE TREATY, 1951. By the terms of the treaty Japan renounced all claims to Korea, Formosa, the Kurils, Sakhalin, and former mandated islands and relinquished any special rights and interests in China and Korea; the right of Japan to defend itself and enter into collective-security arrangements was recognized; Japan accepted in principle the validity of reparations claims, to be paid in goods and services in view of the country's insufficient financial resources.

Also on Sept. 8, the U.S. and Japan signed a bilateral agreement providing for the maintenance of U.S. military bases and armed forces in and around Japan to protect the disarmed country from aggression or from large-scale internal disturbances.

Meanwhile, MacArthur had been relieved of his post as SCAP on April 11. Lieutenant General Matthew Bunker Ridgway (1895–), then commander of the U.N. forces in Korea, succeeded him. On June 30 the U.S. had terminated economic aid to Japan, but the detrimental effect of this action on the Japanese economy was largely offset by American military procurement orders for the Korean War (q.v.). The country's chief economic problem stemmed mainly from the wartime loss of overseas markets, especially the Chinese mainland. Recognizing the importance of the Chinese market, on Oct. 1, 1951 the U.S. granted Japan the right to carry on limited trade with mainland China.

On April 28, 1952, the Japanese peace treaty became effective and full sovereignty was restored to Japan. By the terms of the Japanese-American treaty of 1951 U.S. troops remained in Japan as security forces. The Japanese government concluded treaties of peace or renewed diplomatic relations during 1952 with Taiwan, Burma, India, and Yugoslavia.

The question of rearmament was widely debated throughout 1952. The government was reluctant to commit itself in favor of rebuilding the country's defenses, mainly because of economic difficulties and legal obstacles (in the Japanese constitution of 1947 war is renounced "forever").

After heated debate the diet approved, on

JAPAN

July 21 a bill to suppress subversive activities of organized groups, including the Communists. The Communist Party itself was not outlawed, however. In general elections on Oct. 1, the first since the end of the occupation, Yoshida was again named premier.

On March 14, 1953, Premier Yoshida, after losing a vote of confidence on proposals for increased centralization of the school system and the police force, scheduled new elections. The electorate went to the polls in April and again returned the Liberals to power. Yoshida was renamed premier on May 19.

During 1953 the U.S. government, seeking further to safeguard the country against possible Communist aggression, actively encouraged Japan to rearm. On Aug. 6 the two countries signed a military-aid treaty that contained provision for the manufacture of Japanese arms according to American specifications. In a joint statement on Sept. 27 Premier Yoshida and Mamoru Shigemitsu (1887–1957), Progressive Party leader, officially recommended that Japan rearm for self-defense. Negotiations with the U.S. government led to the signing on March 8, 1954, of a mutual-defense pact by the two nations.

Premier Yoshida's policy of close collaboration with the U.S. was subjected to strong criticism by dissidents within the Liberal Party during the second half of 1954. On Nov. 24 the insurgent Liberals formed the Japan Democratic Party. Premier Yoshida, who was removed as head of the Liberal Party a few days later, resigned the premiership on Dec. 7 after failing to muster a majority in the diet. On Dec. 9, by virtue of Socialist Party support, the Democratic Party leader Ichiro Hatoyama (1883–1959) was elected premier. He promised, in exchange for Socialist support, to dissolve the diet in January, 1955, and hold national elections.

The Democratic Party failed to win a majority in the diet in the election held on Feb. 27, 1955, but by virtue of Liberal support Hatoyama was returned, on March 18, to the premiership. The Democratic and Liberal parties merged on Nov. 22, giving the government an absolute majority in the diet.

On Oct. 19 the Soviet Union and Japan agreed to end the technical state of war that had existed between the two countries since August, 1945. The agreement provided for the reestablishment of normal diplomatic relations, for the repatriation of Japanese prisoners of war still remaining in the U.S.S.R., for the effectuation of fishing treaties negotiated earlier in the year, for Soviet support of Japanese entry into the U.N., and for the return to Japan of certain small islands off its northern coasts upon the conclusion of a formal Soviet-Japanese peace treaty. On Dec. 18 the U.N. General Assembly voted unanimously to admit Japan to the U.N. Tanzan Ishibashi (1884–1973), the minister of international trade and industry, succeeded Hatoyama as premier on Dec. 20. While maintaining close relations with the U.S., Ishibashi sought to expand trade with the U.S.S.R., and mainland China as a means of reducing unemployment.

In February, 1957, Premier Ishibashi resigned from his post because of poor health. The diet elected his former foreign minister Nobusuke Kishi (1896–   ) to succeed him. In the same month agreements were signed ending the state of war with Czechoslovakia and Poland. In July the Soviet Union, despite Japanese objection that the action violated international law, banned all foreign ships from Peter the Great Bay, near Vladivostok, thus limiting Japanese fishing waters. Japan agreed in November to pay $230,000,000 to Indonesia as World War II reparations. In addition, the Indonesian trade debt of $177,000,000 to Japan was canceled.

Japan became a nonpermanent member of the U.N. Security Council in January, 1958. In March a private Japanese trade delegation concluded a trade agreement with China. The agreement subsequently was approved by the Japanese government despite the fact that Taiwan canceled its existing contracts with Japan in reprisal. The trade agreement did not go into operation, however, because China demanded, in effect and without success, diplomatic recognition from Japan. The House of Representatives was dissolved by Premier Kishi in April and elections were held the following month.

On Oct. 9, the Socialist Party ordered a strike of its members in both chambers of the diet to protest a government bill providing for an increased power for the police. By the beginning of November, about 4,000,000 workers were also on a protest strike; subsequently Premier Kishi agreed to withdraw the bill. Elections in June, 1959, for half the seats in the House of Councillors proved a victory for the Liberal-Democratic Party. Shortly afterward the government was completely reorganized.

In November, 1959, more than 500 people were injured when violent anti-U.S. riots broke out in Tokyo during a discussion in the diet of a new security pact with the U.S. The treaty was signed in Washington, D.C., in January, 1960, and at the same time it was announced that President Dwight David Eisenhower (q.v.) would visit Japan in June. By mid-June, how-

Japan. Plate 1. *Right:* A shrine of the Heian period (8th to 12th centuries) in Kyoto. *Below:* An ancient Shinto shrine on one of the many smaller islands of Japan. *Bottom:* The harbor of Yokohama, a major seaport and shipbuilding center on Honshu island.

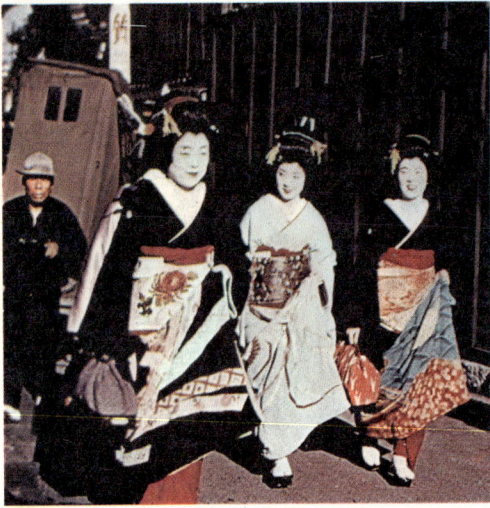

Japan. Plate 2. *Above, left: The Star Festival is celebrated at the city of Sendai. Left: Colorfully attired geisha, members of a class of professional singing and dancing girls. Above: A court dance is performed at the historic Itsukushima shrine, on the islet of the same name. Below: Scene from a nō drama, a stylized form of theatrical performance dating from the 14th century.*

Pictures, Plates 1 and 2 Japan National Tourist Office

JAPAN

ever, anti-U.S. feelings in Japan had grown to the extent that the visit was canceled because of fears for President Eisenhower's safety.

Premier Kishi resigned on July 15 and was succeeded by Hayato Ikeda (1899–1965), the new president of the Liberal-Democratic Party. In elections to the House of Representatives in October, the Liberal-Democrats won a major victory, and Ikeda formed a new cabinet in December.

It was announced on Jan. 8, 1962, that Japan agreed to provide $250,000,000 toward a $6,000,000,000 emergency fund for currency stabilization to be administered by the International Monetary Fund (q.v.). Japan was making a strong effort to improve its trade deficit, much of which was incurred by heavy imports of machinery and raw materials to support the country's rapid industrial growth. During the year Japanese-Soviet trade was increased by one third over that of 1961, and a five-year expanded-trade agreement with China was negotiated.

In 1963 the governing Liberal-Democrats sought to amend a constitutional provision banning maintenance of military forces and other war potential in Japan. The amendment, necessary to legalize further increases in the Japanese armed forces, needed approval of a two-thirds majority in the House of Representatives. Lacking such a majority, Premier Ikeda dissolved the diet and scheduled elections for Nov. 21. Contrary to his hopes, his party's majority was reduced by 13 seats by the vote and leftist parties gained a few more seats.

The Japanese economy continued to lead the world in its growth rate for 1964. In its drive to expand trade the Japanese government made an agreement with China that each would establish unofficial trade liaison offices in the other's capital city. The usual five-year limit on Soviet credit was exceeded when Japan arranged the sale of a fertilizer plant to the Soviet Union with payment extended over eight years. Premier Ikeda, who had been reelected president of the Liberal-Democrats on July 10, was incapacitated by illness in September and resigned as premier on Oct. 25. He was succeeded on Nov. 9 by former Minister of State Eisaku Sato (1901–   ), also a Liberal-Democrat. The 18th Olympic Games were held in Tokyo from Oct. 10 to 24. Japan had prepared for the event by investing $2,000,000,000 in city improvements, including new highways, subways, and buildings.

In March, 1965, the South Korean foreign minister became the first Korean to have an audience with the Japanese emperor since World War II. During his visit the Japanese and South Korean governments reached far-ranging agreement on mutual relations.

In the late 1960's Japan experienced widespread and sometimes violent demonstrations by radical students protesting Japanese support of U.S. foreign policy. The government took a firm line, and relations between Japan and the U.S. were further strengthened when Okinawa was returned to Japan in 1972.

As the 1970's began, the rapid growth of the Japanese economy continued. Japan in the 1960's surpassed every nation of Western Eu-

Eisaku Sato, prime minister from 1964 to 1972, a student of calligraphy, relaxes at home writing Chinese characters with a writing brush.
Japan National Tourist Organization

JAPAN CURRENT

rope in terms of gross national product and ranked next to the U.S. as a world industrial power. The Japan World Exposition, staged at Osaka in 1970, demonstrated the nation's restored position in world affairs; see EXHIBITIONS AND EXPOSITIONS: *Famous 20th-Century Expositions: Expo '70.* In 1971 Japan was the third-largest exporter of the world, next to the U.S. and West Germany, and the fifth-largest importer.

Nevertheless, differences arose between Japan and its trading partners, caused by wide export-import gaps in Japan's favor. In September, 1972, Kakuei Tanaka (1918–), who had succeeded Premier Sato in July, met in Hawaii with President Richard M. Nixon (q.v.) and agreed on measures to alleviate the American trade imbalance. Japan also increased its aid to developing countries. In February, 1973, when the U.S. devalued the dollar, the yen was allowed to float.

In September, 1972, Tanaka visited the People's Republic of China and agreed on immediate resumption of diplomatic relations. Japan also severed its ties with Taiwan. Negotiations were begun on a peace treaty with the Soviet Union.

In 1973 the government announced a strong plan to stem inflation, involving a tightening of credit and expansion of imports.

JAPAN CURRENT. See KUROSHIO CURRENT.

JAPANESE ART AND ARCHITECTURE, works of art produced in Japan from the 6th century A.D. to the present. Pottery and sculpture produced prior to the 6th century give evidence of two distinctly different cultures, each of which contributed to the historic Japanese character as it came to be expressed in later art. One culture, known as the Jōmon, or "Sword" (about 9000 B.C.–about 300 B.C.), produced carefully decorated pottery and simple houses. Primitive clay statuettes, *dogu,* characterized this culture. The other major cultural period, the Yayoi (about 200 B.C.–about 200 A.D.), sometimes referred to as the "Chrysanthemum", was marked by greater refinement of design and technique and came to maturity in the Kōfun (Tomb Mound) period (about 300–about 700 A.D.). The *haniwa,* mostly hollow, cylindrical human and animal figures of reddish clay, typified Yayoi culture. The Japanese were at first strongly and repeatedly influenced by the arts of Korea and China, but they rapidly assimilated the lessons learned from the Chinese and developed their own forms and techniques. In painting, architecture, and the other arts, the Japanese have almost always preferred working in such light materials as wood, paper, and silk to obtain the efflorescent, spacious, and naturalistic effects for which they are known. Although they often used stone and bronze, most of their production has been in nondurable materials; nevertheless, a great number of early works have been preserved through diligent care.

The Shinto shrine architecture that developed in the Kōfun period is distinguished by remarkably precise carpentry and the simplicity of form characteristic of Yayoi culture. These features persist to the present day in the periodic rebuilding of shrines, such as Ise and Izumo. Such structures are markedly different from the Buddhist temple buildings, which are based on architectural principles that originated in Korea and Japan. See BUDDHISM; SHINTO.

The Japanese garden, so completely integrated with the house, constitutes perhaps the greatest single contribution of the Japanese to the whole history of world art. Created throughout the centuries and maintained in a state of perfect preservation today, the garden masterpieces of Katsura, Ryoanji, and Tenryuji represent a unique element of Japanese art. Many miniature or "pocket-handkerchief" gardens display the perfection of the Japanese garden on a smaller scale.

Architecture. Since the 6th century, the basic structure in Japanese architecture has been a skeletal framework of timbers carrying a peaked roof or series of roofs. As in related Chinese and Korean architecture, the principal building material is wood; stone, a secondary material, is often used for foundations, stairways, and terraces. The most distinctive external feature is the roof, gabled or hipped, with a concave curved sweep and wide eaves. The latter are turned up at the corners, but at a less pronounced angle than in China. See CHINESE ART. The bracketed framework that supports the roof is mortised or halved into round or square posts spaced at regular intervals. The walls, usually on the south and east sides of a building, are replaced, in the skeletal post-and-lintel type of architecture, by sliding translucent paper screens called *shōji*. These in turn are protected from the weather by widely overhanging eaves and wooden panels called *amadō.* The interiors are partitioned with sliding paper screens (rendered opaque by double layers with space between) called *fusuma,* which are often enriched with paintings on the paper composing them.

Although the main tradition of Japanese architecture begins with the adoption of Buddhism as the state religion in the 6th century, a few vestiges of pre-Buddhist indigenous architecture survive. One example, the Imperial Ise

Right: The Imperial Ise Shrine, still used by the royal family, is a relic of pre-Buddhist architecture of Japan. Below: The 12th-century Nijō Palace in Kyōto is a popular attraction for Japanese school children and foreign visitors.

Japan National Tourist Organization

Japan Air Lines

A horse in terracotta, from the Kōfun period.
Cleveland Museum of Art

Shrine, a complex of plain white wood structures thatched in bark, built before the 4th century, exists today because it has been rebuilt in exact replica every twenty years since it was first erected. Buddhism, imported by Korean monks from Pakche, a kingdom in southern Korea, brought with it the modified building styles of the Chinese Six Dynasties (221–589) and, later, of the T'ang (q.v.) dynasty. Extant examples of Chinese style modified and carried to Japan by Koreans include the early 7th-century pagoda and "Golden" temple hall at Hōryūji near Nara, which are believed to be the oldest preserved wooden buildings in the world, and other Buddhist monasteries, much rebuilt, in Nara and its environs. More purely Japanese modification of the Chinese style is seen in the Yakushiji temple (7th cent.) near Nara. Much of the subsequent history of Japanese architecture may be traced in terms of successively waxing and waning influences from China, and also in the special demands of various religious sects. A large number of Buddhist temples, Shinto shrines, and palaces have survived. Castles have survived from the Momoyama period (1568–1615) and the early years of the ensuing Edo period (1615–1868).

The style of the present-day typical dwelling house began to take form in the Fujiwara and Kamakura periods (794–1333) with the development of a new domestic and palace architecture. The Muromachi period (1393–1568) produced the *tokonoma*, a recess for the display of paintings and ornaments; the *chaseki*, a space for the performance of tea ceremonies; and the *tatami*, floor mats measuring 3 by 6 ft. Not until the Tokugawa period (1600–1868) was the evolution of the common house completed. Today the standard dwelling consists of one or two stories; the rooms are divided by fixed or sliding panels covered with paper made from mulberry bark. Each room is planned to fit a given number of floor mats, and the chief room contains the *tokonoma*, as well as, more often than not, subsidiary rooms, especially for guests. Rooms are not assigned special functions, and by removal of the sliding panels two or more rooms can be converted into one. At night wooden shutters close off the exterior. Recently the furnishing of one room in Western style has become fashionable in urban areas, but it is still used infrequently, and then usually only for the reception of Occidental guests; the Japanese family man usually prefers to live on the traditional *tatami*-covered floor, dangling his legs into a *kotatsu* (pit under a low-legged table), or sitting cross-legged or on his ankles directly on the *tatami*, or on the flat cushion called the *zabuton*. The Japanese still, as a general rule, converse, eat, and sleep on the mats covering the floors from wall to wall throughout the house.

The common dwelling house has had a direct influence on modern Western architecture. Although Western architects use steel and concrete more often than wood and tile, they recently emulated the characteristics of Japanese residential architecture: the integration of structure and garden, and the general tendency toward low-lying horizontal proportions, spaciousness, and cleanness of line. Reciprocally, the Japanese since the late 19th century have extensively followed Western styles in the design of nonresidential buildings. Modern reinforced concrete and glass are common building materials for Japanese factories, department stores, and public buildings.

Painting and Sculpture. Cultivated (as opposed to primitive) Japanese painting and sculpture began at the end of the 6th century with the introduction of Buddhism from Korea during the reign of the Empress Suiko (r. 592–628), after whom the period is named. The Suiko bronze Buddhas were like the 5th- and 6th-century Korean Buddhas. One of the major works of the Suiko period is a large wood carving of Miroku, the "Messiah of Buddhism", in contemplation, in the temple of the Chūgūji, a nunnery serving as a sub-temple of the Hōryūji. In the 7th century, attempts were made to discard the clumsier features of the primitive models and achieve more graceful and delicate effects. Many statuettes of bodhisattvas (aspirants to Buddhahood) date from this period, depicting the Buddhist conception of a being who has advanced so far in wisdom and insight, and in the renunciation of fleshly ties, as to be on the point of entrance into Nirvana (q.v.) and salvation.

In 708 copper was discovered in Japan in large quantities, making possible the casting of bronze images of large size, including the largest ever cast, a colossal image of Roshana Buddha dating from 753 and housed in the Daibutsuden of the Tōdaiji temple at Nara; only fragments survive today, incorporated in the present inferior Edo-period restoration. The style of this bronze work was a synthesis of the new Buddhist ideals coming from India through the classic-minded T'ang dynasty of China and the gentle quality of the 7th-century Japanese statuettes. New delicacy of feeling and remarkable finish combine with great dignity and grace, in the classic grand manner, to mark this work. A supreme example of the new group of large bronze deities is the Black Bronze Trinity at the Yakushiji (about 720).

The long Fujiwara or Heian period (794–1185) is divided on the basis of changing styles in art, and especially in sculpture, into three distinct subperiods: the Jōgan period (794–897), the Middle Fujiwara period (897–1086), and the Late Fujiwara period (1086–1185). At the end of the 8th century, Buddhist art underwent great changes in Japan. Mystical Buddhist art was introduced into Japan from China, where the T'ang period flourished in the 8th century. The priest and saint Kukai (774–835), posthumously named Kōbō Daishi, visited China in 804–06 and brought hundreds of paintings and sculptures back to Japan. The architecture and sculpture of the pagoda and Golden Hall of the Murōji, supposedly executed by Kōbō Daishi in a single night, constitute a major example of Jōgan art.

In the 9th and 10th centuries a new style of architecture, painting, and sculpture developed, combining late-T'ang classic elements with sensuous Pala-Sena Indian influences to form a unique Jōgan-period style in Japan; see INDIAN ART AND ARCHITECTURE. Painting was often regarded as a branch of calligraphy (artistic handwriting), and many fine calligraphic works were produced during this period by Buddhist monks. The priest Eshin (941–1017) probably painted a triptych depicting the savior Amida welcoming the soul of a dying man. Far more important than this work is the masterpiece of architecture, garden design, sculpture, and mural painting, all finished in 1053 as the Hō-ō-dō (Phoenix Hall) at the Uji, representing Middle Fujiwara art at its best.

Miroku Bosatsu, the bodhisattva in contemplation, a wooden statue of the Suiko period, in the Chūgūji Nunnery, Nara.

The painter Toba Sōjō (1053–1140) marked the beginning of secular art in Japan as opposed to the previous religious forms in sculpture and painting. He used black and white instead of color in his painting, and developed a new flexible line of great motion. A noteworthy example attributed to him is the first in a series of four hand-scroll paintings (*emakimono*) preserved in the Kōzanji, near Kyōto, and called "Animals at Play".

In the late Fujiwara period, Japanese art developed a unique individuality, depicting crowded scenes of street pageantry, fairs and temple courts, dramatic groupings, and scenes of violent action. The important hand-scroll

JAPANESE ART AND ARCHITECTURE

masterpieces of this period include the three Ban Dainagon hand scrolls, attributed to Tokiwa Mitsunaga, and the three Shigisan Engi hand scrolls, by an unknown master. Exuberant genre pictures became typical; see GENRE PAINTING.

During the feudal age of the Kamakura period (1185–1333), Japan developed her dominant art, national in form and content. The so-called Nara Renaissance produced the powerfully realistic sculptures in the "joined-blocks", or *yosegi*, technique of wood carving, the overwhelmingly powerful architecture of the Great South Gate of Tōdai-Ji at Nara, the culminating development of hand-scroll paintings, in the "Burning of the Sanjō Palace" (mid-13th cent.), and the series of twelve scrolls by En-i in 1299 illustrating the life of his late fellow priest, Ippen Shōnin. An innovator in painting, Fujiwara Takanobu (1142–1205), made popular the representation of everyday types of Japanese countenance, and infused a new realism into all subjects. He also painted many fine portraits, which typify the vigorous realism of the new era. Fujiwara Nobuzane (about 1177–about 1265), the son of Takanobu, used sweeping and powerful line work for his greatest painting, which was a panoramic account, in nine wide scrolls, of the life of Sugawara Michizane (d. 903), a scholar of Chinese literature who became ambassador to China in 894. Kamakura art is as purely Japanese as any ever created; it represents a peak achievement of the Japanese genius.

The art of the Nambokuchō (1333–93) and the Muromachi (1393–1568) periods marked a new wave of importation of works of Chinese art, especially the ink paintings of the Southern Sung dynasty (1127–1279) inspired by Ch'an Buddhism, the Chinese forerunner of the Zen (q.v.) of Japan. Many Muromachi painters assimilated this Chinese art and created their own distinctively Japanese version of it. Between 1378 and 1428 the great bulk of original black-and-white paintings from the Sung dynasty was imported from China. Japanese art responded to the new Chinese stimulus with a large force of fine painters educated at well-established schools. Shūbun, who flourished in the first half of the 15th century, followed the tradition of imitating Chinese landscapes. Sesshu (q.v.), who also worked during this period, was one of the greatest of all Japanese painters. His works included religious, historical, symbolic, and biographical subjects; he painted scenes of palaces, temples, farms, and mountain valleys, all in black and white. He was a supreme landscape artist, with a vigorous line full of short, dramatic accents continuously interwoven.

During the 16th century the Kanō school was developed. The leading figure of this school was Kanō Motonobu (1476–1559), who managed to fuse Chinese black-and-white painting with newly decorative painting under Japanese influences. About 1510 the first fabrication of decorated porcelains in the fashion of the Ming dynasty (1368–1644) was introduced from China into Japan. Kanō Eitoku (1543–90), with his use of rich, glazed color in painting, was an exponent of the most brilliant school of secular art Asia ever produced. This school was characterized by a sumptuously decorative mural painting, especially created for the new castles of the Momoyama period (1568–1615).

The two main streams of art in the Tokugawa period (1615–1868) were the aristocratic and the plebeian. Representative of the aristocratic art was the 17th-century Kanō Tanyū (1602–74), a court painter who created a great eclectic school, making transcripts of old masterpieces, both Chinese and Japanese. He also made many studies of nature, severe and dignified in style. Koetsu (1557?–1637) was a great lacquerer and adapter of nature designs to fine pottery. The Sōtatsu-Korin school, founded by Tawaraya Sōtatsu (fl. early 17th cent.) and advanced most decisively by Ogata Korin (1658–1716), produced the foremost painters of decoratively treated tree, flower, and other landscape forms. Representative of plebeian realistic art was the painter Maruyama Ōkyo (1733–95). His subjects, originally influenced by imported Dutch paintings and drawings and the Occidental practice of working directly from nature and the posed model, were taken chiefly from the scenery and animal life of his native Kyoto. He also designed patterns for silk weavers and bronze casters, embroiderers, fine lacquerers and potters in Kyoto, which had been the center of fine-art manufacturers since the days of Fujiwara. Ōkyo became famous not only for his paintings of waterfalls, cranes, turtles, mountains, and the like, all based on direct observation, but also for his fanciful representations of dragons, ascending and descending, and of tigers (which he had probably never seen). His most celebrated work, however, is a pair of folding screens, "Pine Trees in Snow", in the Mitsui Collection in Tokyo. He founded a flourishing school, the Maruyama-Shijō school, which had many offshoots; the last distinguished master of this school was Takeuchi Seihō (1864–1942).

The ukiyoye school (17th–19th cent.) of Japanese painting was foremost among those that portrayed Japanese city life, above all that of pleasure-seekers in the gay quarters of Edo (the

Japanese Art. Plate 1. Masters of the ukiyoye school of art. Above: "The Wave" by Katsushika Hokusai, one of a series of woodblock prints depicting Mt. Fuji. Left: "The Bridge over Nishigawa" by Ando Hiroshige, among the greatest of Japanese landscape artists.

Japanese Art. Plate 2. Above: Procession of warriors, detail of a 17th-century painted scroll. Right: "Young Girl in the Rain" by the 18th-century ukiyoye artist Suzuki Harunobu. Below: Portrait of the Kabuki actor Yooso by the 18th-century painter Toshusai Sharaku.

former name of Tokyo) and of Kyoto. One popular subject for ukiyoye folding screens was called "Rakuehu-Rakugai" ("Views Inside and Outside Kyoto"). Another was the "Namban" ("Western Barbarians") folding screens, depicting Dutch and Portuguese visitors to Japan as seen, often comically, through Japanese eyes. The most flourishing branch of ukiyoye was wood-block printmaking, first developed perhaps by Hishikawa Moronobu (1618–1703). The outlines of his prints were stamped from a wood block and the color applied afterward with a brush. His pupil Torii Kiyonobu (1664–1729) began to apply both outline and color from blocks. Suzuki Harunobu (1725–70) increased the number of blocks to complete the design with background and atmosphere. He is generally considered the founder of the polychrome wood-block print known as "Nishiki-e" ("Brocade Picture"). Katsukawa Shunsho (1726–92) portrayed a large variety of actors in character. Torii Kiyonaga (1752–1815) and Utamaro Kitagawa (1753–1806) are noted for portraits of beautiful plebeian women. The most popular and versatile of Japanese print masters, Hokusai (q.v.), produced many landscape masterpieces and witty figure sketches. Immensely prolific, he was the dominant figure of the ukiyoye school. Ando Hiroshige (q.v.), the second best-known print master of the school, excelled in rendering scenes of sleet, snow, rain, and other atmospheric effects, most notably in his famous series, "Fifty-three Views Along the Takaido". These were produced to sell to travelers stopping overnight at inns on the chief road between Edo and Kyoto. They are remarkable for their rich variety of compositional effects. The work of both Hokusai and Hiroshige had a considerable influence on Western art dating from about 1860. See IMPRESSIONISM.

After the accession (1867) of Emperor Meiji (1852–1912), who westernized many Japanese institutions, numerous Japanese artists looked to the Occident for inspiration. Shibata Zeshin (1807–91) was one of the few important artists who continued to adhere to traditionalist painting. Within a little more than a decade, however, Japanese interest in native artistic traditions was revived, largely through the efforts of the American Orientalist Ernest Francisco Fenollosa (1853–1908). During the 1880's and 1890's noteworthy paintings were produced by several artists whose work was essentially Japanese, although somewhat influenced by contemporary movements in European art. These artists included Kawabata Gyokushō (1842–1913), Hashimoto Gahō (1835–1908), and Kanō Hōgai (1828–88). Among early 20th-century Japan's most noteworthy traditional artists were Takeuchi Seihō (1864–1942) and Yokoyama Taikan (1868–1958). After World War II, Japanese painters turned almost exclusively to the medium of oil, and developed in it the whole succession of styles occurring in contemporary Occidental art. As in the Nara period (646–794), when the Japanese showed such remarkable powers of assimilation of classic T'ang Chinese art as to create in their own right comparable masterpieces, contemporary Japanese sculptors and painters have produced works comparable to those produced elsewhere, while carrying on a vital Japanese tradition. One of the most striking instances of such a synthesis is to be found in the works of Sōkyū Ueda (1900–) and other members of a group called Keisei-kai, who use the traditional brush strokes of Japanese calligraphy to create abstract expressionist compositions; see EXPRESSIONISM.

JAPANESE BEETLE, *Popillia japonica,* insect pest in the Scarab family. The Japanese beetle was introduced accidentally into New Jersey from Japan in 1916, and is now widespread over the eastern United States. The adult has a broad, thick body about ½ in. long, and is iridescent green, with tan wing covers. It attacks the foliage of a wide variety of plants and also eats their fruit, causing widespread destruction. The Japanese beetle is most common in July and August, at which time the female lays its eggs 5 to 6 in. below the surface of the ground. The white grubs feed on the roots of grasses until fall, when they descend a foot or more underground

Japanese beetle, Popillia japonica   U.S. Dept. of Agriculture

JAPANESE CHIN

and hibernate, to emerge in midspring and pupate in June after attaining a length of slightly less than 1 in. DDT (q.v.) sprays are useful in controlling the adult; the soil may be grub-proofed with chlordane, DDT, aldrin, or deildrin. Parasitic wasps, largely responsible for the control of the insect in Japan, were imported into the U.S. in the 1920's; they reduce the beetle population by preying upon the grubs. The grubs are also subject to certain diseases, caused by bacteria, fungi, nematodes, and viruses. Most important for biological control are milky disease, caused by *Bacillus popilliae* and *B. lentimorbus,* and a virus infection, called blue disease. See ENTOMOLOGY, ECONOMIC.

JAPANESE CHIN or **JAPANESE SPANIEL,** toy dog that reputedly originated in China many centuries ago and was later introduced into Japan, where it was the pet of royalty and the nobility, and developed its present characteristics. Several specimens were presented to the American commodore Matthew Calbraith Perry (*see under* PERRY) as a sign of esteem when he was negotiating (1853) a trade treaty with Japan. The dog was imported into the United States in large numbers at the beginning of the 20th century.

The Japanese chin has a broad skull that is round in front; a flat face; prominent, dark, and lustrous eyes, set wide apart; small v-shaped ears also set wide apart; a short nose; and a silky coat. The tail is covered with a profusion of long hair; from its base the tail curves naturally to one side and rises upward over the back to fall on the opposite side. The dog is either black and white or red and white in color; it weighs about 7 lb. The Japanese chin is intelligent, clean, loyal, and affectionate.

Japanese Chin

JAPANESE DRAMA, drama written and performed in Japan from about the 7th century A.D. to the present time. Throughout this period Japanese drama evolved a wide variety of genres characterized generally by the fusion of dramatic, musical, and dance elements. The music and dance, and the subjects, settings, costumes, and acting styles were rigidly stylized and, until recent times, offered relatively few realistic or naturalistic qualities. Some genres utilize almost exclusively a fixed repertoire of plays, often many centuries old.

The earliest known type of Japanese theatrical entertainment is *gigaku,* which was introduced into Japan in 612 A.D. from southern China; it is thought to have been ultimately of Indian or possibly even of Greek origin. *Gigaku* dances, performed with masks, seem to have been humorous in nature. In the 8th century *gigaku* fell into disfavor because its frivolous character displeased the Japanese rulers of the period. It was supplanted largely by *bugaku,* an entertainment introduced into Japan from China. *Bugaku* dances portrayed simple situations such as the return of a general from war. The performers wore impressive robes, and their dances, introduced from China and central and southeastern Asia, had exotic splendor. The Japanese rulers, intent on imitating Chinese court etiquette, favored *bugaku,* both because of its solemnity and because of its similarity to Chinese court entertainments, and it quickly acquired a ritual character. *Bugaku* may now be seen only at ceremonies.

A type of acrobatic entertainment known as *sangaku,* transmitted similarly to Japan from the Asian continent and popular in the 8th century, was also influential in the history of the Japanese drama. Typical acts, according to surviving accounts, included tightrope walking, juggling, and sword swallowing. A combination of these secular entertainments and the sacred dances and songs associated with the Shinto (q.v.) religion gradually evolved into more complex and sustained forms of drama.

Surviving documents from the 11th century describe comic playlets, and one play still performed, the ritual dance *Okina,* may date from this period. Plays were also performed at shrine festivals in support of prayers for harvests or to depict the history of the shrine. The actors and musicians were organized into troupes.

Nō Drama. By the 14th century the theater had evolved one of its foremost artistic achievements, *nō* drama. These plays included solemn dances intended to suggest the deepest emotions of the principal character and were written in the poetic language of the Japanese classics. A program also often included *kyōgen,* or farces written in colloquial language.

Nō was brought to the level of great art by the genius of two dramatists, Kanami Kiyotsugu (1333–84) and his son Zeami Motokiyo (1363–1443). *Nō* was patronized by the Ashikaga shogunate after the shogun Yoshimitsu (r. 1368–94) saw the boy Zeami perform in 1374. Zeami developed *nō* into refined aristocratic drama, but it tended to lose its creative vitality and become ritualistic after his death. Many *nō* plays performed at present are by Zeami, and his books of criticism are considered the final authority in discussions of the subject. For a short period after the Meiji Restoration (1868) *nō* was threatened with extinction because of its long connections with the discredited shogunate; *see* JAPAN: *History.* It survived the threat, however, and thereafter enjoyed popularity.

The entire program of *nō* drama traditionally consists of five *nō* plays and four *kyōgen* farces performed alternately, a *nō* play beginning and ending the program. *Kyōgen* farces feature representational acting, and the actors wear neither masks nor makeup. *Nō* plays avoid representational accuracy in favor of a symbolic treatment of subjects concerning the worlds of the living and the dead. The principal types of *nō* plays are those dealing with deities, the ghosts of warriors, women with tragic destinies, mad persons, and devils or festive spirits. The actors, who often wear masks, are richly and elaborately costumed.

The *nō* drama is performed in a theater with a roofed stage. The audience is seated on two or, less commonly, three, sides of the stage. The actors reach the stage by a passageway, called the "bridge", which is marked by three pine trees. The only backdrop is a large painted pine. The scenery consists entirely of impressionistic props suggesting the outlines of a building, a boat, or any other object of importance to the play. Only male actors perform in *nō* dramas. When they play the roles of women or of men whose age is markedly different from their own, they wear masks, many of which are exceptionally beautiful. The *nō* drama also includes a chorus that sits at one side of the stage and recites for the actors when they dance, but that has no identity in the drama. Full programs are seldom presented any longer, but *kyōgen* continues to be an indispensable part of the entire performance, for it presents the humorous aspects of life with which *nō* is never concerned.

Puppet and *Kabuki* Theater. At the end of the 15th century two new popular forms appeared;

A Kabuki actor, dressed for the role of an ancient Japanese warrior. Bill Doll & Co.

they were the puppet theater, *jōruri,* and a form known as *kabuki.* The puppet theater combines three elements, the puppets, the chanters who sing and declaim for the puppets, and the players of the samisen, a three-stringed instrument, who provide the accompaniment. The greatest Japanese dramatist, Chikamatsu Monzaemon (1653–1725), wrote chiefly for the puppet theater, the artistic level of which is perhaps higher in Japan than anywhere else in the world.

The puppet theater, after attaining its greatest popularity in the 18th century, lost in public favor to the *kabuki,* the most popular dramatic genre until the 20th century. *Kabuki* tends to be spectacle rather than drama. Original *kabuki* texts, as opposed to those adapted from the puppet theater, are of lesser importance than the remarkable acting, the music and dance, and the brilliantly colored settings. *Kabuki* plays are performed in large theaters, with a *hanamichi,* or raised platform, extending from the back of the theater to the stage.

In addition to the traditional drama a modern theatrical repertory consisting of original Japanese plays in a modern idiom and of translations of European plays has been active in Japan since the beginning of the 20th century. Some 20th-century playwrights have attempted to compromise between traditional Japanese forms and essentially Western idioms, either by introducing modern psychology into their treatment of the ancient tales, or by making *kabuki*-style

JAPANESE LANGUAGE

plays out of such European classics as *Macbeth*. Highly successful modern presentations of traditional themes are offered in *Five Modern Nō Plays* (1956) by Yukio Mishima (1925–70). Other plays, notably *Twilight Crane* (1949) by the playwright Junji Kinoshita (1914–), are derived from old folk tales. Many contemporary Japanese playwrights deal with such themes as conflict in modern Japanese society and problems of social injustice; others prefer to work out Japanese equivalents of modern symbolic drama or of the American musical comedy.

See also JAPANESE LITERATURE; JAPANESE MUSIC.

D.K.

JAPANESE LANGUAGE, agglutinative language spoken by the more than 100,000,000 inhabitants of Japan and by a few hundred thousand Japanese immigrants living in Hawaii and on the North and South American mainland, especially in Brazil. Because of its structural similarity to Korean, Manchu, Mongolian, and Turkish, Japanese is considered to belong with them to the Altaic family of languages. Several scholars doubt this theory, however, because of the lack of vocabulary links. Luchuan, the language of the Ryukyu Islands, is so similar to Japanese that it is considered a dialect variant of it.

Compared with the Indo-European languages (q.v.), Japanese is vague and imprecise. The Japanese seem to prefer a certain kind of imprecision to precision, and they deliberately phrase their sentences vaguely. This is especially true in regard to visual impressions. For instance, the Japanese word *aoi* may mean either blue, green, or pale. On the other hand, the language is minutely precise in regard to auditory or tactile impressions. It contains a vast number of onomatopoeic expressions, and different words for minute differences of sound or tactile sensation. It contains, for example, different words for the clatter of hoofs and the clatter of wooden-soled shoes and many words for the different sounds of rain and of rain falling on different places.

Originally the vocabulary of Japanese was extremely limited. Beginning in the 3rd century A.D., however, a large number of Chinese words were incorporated into the language. The number of words in present-day Japanese that were originally Chinese is much greater than the number of native Japanese words. Japanese words of Chinese origin are somewhat comparable in function to English words derived from Greek and Latin. During the periods when the Japanese adopted them, these words were pronounced in Japanese approximately as they were in Chinese, but subsequently their pronunciation was modified considerably. Japanese has borrowed many words from European languages during the last hundred years, mostly from English. This process has been greatly accelerated in the post-World War II period.

The Japanese language has a simple phonology consisting of only five vowels, which are Romanized as *a, i, u, e,* and *o,* and are pronounced somewhat as in Italian; and of nineteen consonants, Romanized as *k, s, sh, t, ch, ts, n, h, f, m, y, r, w, g, z, j, d, b,* and *p*. The consonants are pronounced rather like the corresponding English consonants, but *r* is produced by flapping the tip of the tongue far forward in the mouth. In the body of a word, *g* is often nasalized, in a manner somewhat comparable to the *ng* in the English word "sing". This feature is most prominent in the educated speech of Tokyo. The *f* is also different from the English *f* in that it is produced with the lips not touching each other, and in some speakers it is almost indistinguishable from an *h*. Japanese vowels and consonants may be either short or long. Certain syllables are emphasized in Japanese by differences of pitch or tone, but the language possesses no true stress accent.

The order of words in a Japanese sentence is usually that of subject, object, and verb; modifiers normally precede the words they modify. The Japanese verb denotes neither number nor person, and has no tense as this term is understood in relation to the Indo-European languages. Despite the lack of a true future tense in Japanese, the verb carefully indicates whether or not an action is completed. Japanese has three conjugations of verbs, each with five basic forms: the negative, the continuative, the conclusive, the conditional, and the imperative. Four important irregular verbs also occur in Japanese, including the copula. Japanese nouns have neither gender nor number. Although no articles or prepositions exist in Japanese, the nouns are governed by postpositions (a relatively small group of words corresponding in use to Indo-European case endings and prepositions) that directly follow them. An example is the word *no* ("of") in the phrase *mizu no oto,* which means "sound of water", but translated word for word reads "water of sound". Many pronouns exist in Japanese, but are rarely used. Adjectives in Japanese, like the verbs, are highly inflected, and function to a great extent like verbs, in that they contain the copula, and by difference of inflection indicate a present state, a completed state, or a continuing or connective state. For instance, *shiroi* means "is white", *shirokatta* means "was white" (a completed state), and *shirokute* means "is white and";

JAPANESE LITERATURE

Probably the linguisitic feature that more than any other distinguishes Japanese from other languages is the large number of polite, honorific, and humilific words, and of word forms such as prefixes and suffixes. Only Korean and Javanese contain a comparable number of words indicating status. Although many dialectal variants occur within the Japanese language, the educated speech of Tokyo has been accepted as standard.

The ancient Japanese had no writing system of their own. They first learned to write about fifteen hundred years ago when the Chinese and the Koreans taught them the Chinese method of writing by characters or ideograms; see CHINESE LANGUAGE. Because each Chinese character represents one particular word, it was difficult to use characters for the highly inflected words of the Japanese language. For a long period the Japanese followed the Chinese method, but by the 8th century A.D. they were using Chinese characters as phonetic symbols, each representing one syllable. In the 9th century these Chinese characters were abbreviated to create the two native *kana* syllabaries, so called because the Japanese word *kana* denotes a symbol that represents a syllable. In these syllabaries, known as *katakana* and *hiragana*, each syllable is represented by a symbol derived from a more complex Chinese character. In *katakana* one part of a Chinese character was adopted as the phonetic symbol, and in *hiragana* the whole character was written in a cursive manner. For example, the character 宇 gave rise to the *katakana* ウ and the *hiragana* う. At first *kana* alone was used to write Japanese, but gradually a system evolved wherein characters were used wherever possible, and *kana*, usually *hiragana*, was used to represent postpositions and inflections. *Katakana* was used later primarily to write imported Western words and in telegrams, and occasionally in official documents. The use of Chinese characters led to the introduction of a great number of Chinese words into the Japanese vocabulary. Shortly after World War II the number of Chinese characters in common use was reduced to 1850, thereby simplifying the written language considerably.

The study of Japanese increased greatly in the United States during World War II because of the requirements of the military establishment. The spoken language received its most careful analysis at Yale University and primers for the study of the written language were produced at Harvard University. Since about 1960 much attention has been given to the teaching of Japanese as a foreign language, and the number of American schools, colleges, and universities offering Japanese language courses continues to increase. V.H.V.

JAPANESE LITERATURE, literature written by Japanese in the Japanese language as well as in the Chinese language (qq.v.). The present article is concerned primarily with works in the Japanese language.

Japanese literature developed primarily in the forms of fiction, poetry, the essay, and the drama; see JAPANESE DRAMA. This development is divided usually into five periods, the Yamato, Heian, Kamakura-Muromachi, Edo, and modern periods; the first four are so called from the site of the main administrative center of Japan during each period. See JAPAN: *History*.

Yamato Period (archaic times to late 8th cent. A.D.). Although no written literature existed before the 8th century, a large number of ballads, ritual prayers, myths, and legends were composed in the previous centuries. These compositions subsequently were recorded and are included in the *Kojiki* ("Record of Ancient Matters", 712), written largely in Japanese with Chinese characters, and the *Nihonshoki* ("History Book of Ancient Japan", 720), written almost exclusively in Chinese. The earliest extant histories of Japan, these works explain the origin of the Japanese race, the formation of the Japanese state, and the essence of the national polity. Although both works contain much the same mythical and historical material, the *Kojiki* is clearly intended for exclusive use by the Japanese, whereas the *Nihonshoki*, showing the influence of Chinese thought, is broader in scope. From the early ballads included in these collections developed a lyric poetry that was collected in the first great Japanese anthology, the *Man'yōshū* ("Anthology of a Myriad Leaves"), compiled by Ōtomo no Yakamochi after 759. In this anthology a primitive syllabary is used, known as *man'yōgana*, in which Chinese characters serve as phonetic symbols of syllables rather than of words. The two most important poetic forms in the anthology are the *chōka* (long poem), consisting of alternate lines of five and seven syllables, followed by a final line of seven syllables to which is appended one or more *hanka* (envoy); and the *tanka* (short poem), consisting of thirty-one syllables, written in five lines according to a pattern of five, seven, five, seven, and seven syllables. The *tanka* (q.v.) became the preeminent Japanese verse form, maintaining its vitality until the modern period, whereas the *chōka* soon waned in popularity. The foremost poet of the *Man'yōshū* is Kakinomoto no Hitomaro (fl. late 7th cent.), who han-

JAPANESE LITERATURE

dled freely all forms of verse. The prevailing mood of the anthology is characterized by the term *makoto* (truth or sincerity), which to the Japanese implies the full involvement of the whole person.

Heian Period (late-8th to late-12th cent.). In the late-8th century the seat of government was shifted to Heian (present-day Kyōto), and a new type of literature emerged among the aristocratic court society. The creation of the Japanese syllabaries in this century aided the growth of fiction as well as of poetry. The *Kokinshū* ("Anthology of Ancient and Modern Poems", 905) reflects clearly the change in mood from that of personal sincerity, which characterized the previous period, to one of *mono no aware*, or empathy with the essence of things, a bond linking nature and man. The chief compiler, Ki no Tsurayuki (d. 946), who provided the basis for Japanese poetics in his preface, was himself a poet of note, and his poems are included in the anthology. Most of the poems, however, are taken from earlier periods. Ki no Tsurayuki is noted also as the author of the *Tosa Nikki* ("Tosa Diary"), the first example of an important genre, the literary diary.

The literature of the early-10th century was either in the form of fairy tales such as the *Taketori Monogatari* ("The Tales of the Bamboo-Hewer") or of poem-tales such as the *Ise Monogatari* ("The Tales of Ise"). The greatest works of Heian literature appeared in the late-10th and early-11th centuries, notably *Genji Monogatari* ("The Tales of Genji") by Baroness Murasaki Shikibu (fl. 11th cent.) and Sei Shōnagon's *Makura no Sōshi* ("The Pillow-Book"). *Genji Monogatari*, a detailed panoramic picture of Heiam court life, may be considered the first important novel (q.v.) in world literature. It includes also many *tanka* written by the characters in various situations. The novel traces in fifty-four long chapters the life and loves of Prince Genji and Kaoru, his presumed son. It becomes increasingly profound toward the end, an indication probably that the author had perfected her mastery of the craft of fiction. *Makura no Sōshi*, the earlier of the two works, is a witty, often brilliant, collection of sketches revealing the more wordly aspect of the same court society.

Kamakura-Muromachi Period (late-12th through 16th cent.). The collapse of the manorial system in Japan culminated in the defeat of the Taira clan by the Minamoto clan, who established the government in Kamakura in 1192. From the end of the 12th until the early-17th century Japan was in almost constant warfare and turmoil. The dominant figures in Japanese society were the warrior, who engaged in a life of action, and the Buddhist priest, who devoted his life primarily to contemplation; *see* BUDDHISM. The first imperial anthology, the *Shinkokinshū* (New Collection of Ancient and Modern Poems", 1205) compiled by Fujiwara Teika (1162–1241), reflects the change in mood to one of gloom and solitude. Japanese scholars use the term *yūgen* (mystery), which has definite religious overtones, to characterize the entire literature of this period. One of the major poets of this anthology is, significantly, a religious figure, the priest Saigyō (1118–90). The defeat of the Taira by the Minamoto clan became the subject of the most famous prose piece of the period, the *Heike Monogatari* ("The Tales of the Taira Clan"). Kamo no Chōmei's *Hōjōki* ("Account of My Hut", 1212) contrasts the vanity of the world with the virtues of Buddhist contemplation. Abutsu Ni's *Izayoi Nikki* ("Diary of the Waning Moon", 1277) is a literary diary consisting of prose and poetry, the latter sections being of greater importance. *Tsurezuregusa* ("Essays in Idleness", 1340) by Yoshida Kenkō (1283–1350) is reminiscent of *Makura no Sōshi* but more melancholy in mood, reflecting undoubtedly regret at the disturbances of the times. The major type of fiction was the *otogizōshi,* the generic name for collections of popular short stories intended exclusively for entertainment, the authors of which are unknown.

The foremost poetic development in the period after the early-14th century was the creation of the *renga,* or linked verse, a form circumscribed by many regulations, wherein three or more poets cooperate in composing one long poem, consisting of alternate verses, one containing lines of seven, five, and seven syllables and the other two lines of seven syllables each. The three greatest masters of this form, Sōgi (1421–1502), Shōhaku (1443–1527), and Sōchō (1448–1532), together composed the famous *Minase Sangin* ("Three Poets at Minase") in 1488.

Edo Period (17th cent. to 1868). With the establishment of peace in 1603 under the Tokugawa clan, which had its seat of government in Edo, pesent-day Tokyo, commerce flourished and towns developed, producing a merchant class that soon created its own literature, a bawdy, wordly fiction radically different in character from the literature of the preceding period. The first important figure of the period is Ihara Saikaku (1642–93), whose *Kōshoku Ichidai Otoko* ("The Man Who Spent His Life at Love-Making", 1682) is a brilliant work of fiction full of humor and wit, presenting a panoramic view of the sensual life of mercantile society.

His *Nihon Eitaigura* ("Eternal Storehouse of Japan", 1688), a collection of anecdotes, is a kind of guide to commercial success. Many imitators of Saikaku wrote during the 18th century, but none equaled his achievements. The early-19th century brought into prominence three important, if somewhat limited, writers of fiction. Jippensha Ikku (d. 1831) is the author of *Dōchū Hizakurige* ("On Foot Along the Tōkaidō"), a delightful picaresque work relating the misadventures of two scamps; Shikitei Samba (1775–1822) wrote *Ukiyoburo* ("The Up-to-date Bath-House", 1809), a light, almost trivial novel relating the gossip of various classes of people in the city of Edo as they pass in and out of the public bath; and Takizawa Bakin (1767–1848) wrote *Nansō Satōmi Hakkenden* ("The Eight Retainers of Satōmi", 9 vol., 1814–41), a long work infused with Confucian morality and containing a large admixture of legend and fantasy; see Confucianism.

The poetic form *haiku* (q.v.), perfected in this period, is possibly the greatest Japanese aesthetic achievement; it can be described as the distilled essence of poetry and reflects the influence of Zen (q.v.), a form of Buddhism that prevailed in Japan at this time. Three poets are preeminent for their use of *haiku*. The first is the Zen Buddhist lay-priest Matsuo Bashō (1644–94), who took excursions to remote regions, composing as the mood struck him, so that his poetry is set within travelogues, the prose sections of which are also significant. He is revered as the greatest of Japanese poets for his sensitivity and profundity. The second is Yosa Buson (1716–81), whose *haiku* express his experience as a painter. The third is Kobayashi Issa (1763–1828), a poet of humble origin who drew his material from the village life he knew so well. Comic poetry, in a variety of forms, also flourished during this period.

Modern Period (1868 to the present). Throughout this period Japanese writers were influenced by other literatures, primarily those of the West, and refashioned many foreign literary concepts and techniques in fiction and poetry. The humorist Kanagaki Robun (1829–94) is a transitional figure who attempted vainly to adapt himself to the new age but basically adhered to the comic style of the Edo period. Translations from Western literature, at first primarily from works of British authors, gave impetus to the political novel, an interesting if not highly literary genre that prevailed throughout the 1880's. *Kajin no Kigū* ("Chance Meeting with Two Beauties") by Tōkai Sanshi (1852–1922) is an extravagant and unintentionally humorous work tracing the travels and fortunes of a young Japanese politician. The critical work *Shōsetsu Shinzui* ("The Essence of the Novel", 1885) by Tsubouchi Shōyō (1859–1935) argues for a prose art grounded in realism, on the Western model. The next step forward in modernization is *Ukigumo* ("The Floating Cloud", 1887) by Futabatei Shimei (1864–1909), the first serious novel in the colloquial language.

Yasunari Kawabata, winner of the Nobel Prize in literature in 1968.
Consulate General of Japan

The *Ken'yūsha* ("The Society of the Friends of the Inkstone"), a student literary society founded by Ozaki Kōyō (1867–1903), became important in Japanese literary life after 1890. The society influenced the creation of a new literature that maintained traditional aesthetic values while incorporating Western techniques. A young woman writer, Higuchi Ichiyo (1872–96), deftly traces the psychology of children and young lovers through a number of short stories. Her *Takekurabe* ("Comparing Heights", 1896) is generally considered to be her masterpiece.

French naturalism early attracted young Japanese authors, who soon developed a naturalism (q.v.) of their own with less social content and far greater subjectivity. In this naturalistic style, the leading figure is Shimazaki Tōson (1872–1943), whose *Hakai* ("The Breaking of the Commandment", 1906), describing the confession of an outcast youth, firmly established the movement. Two exceedingly important figures, Mori

JAPANESE LITERATURE

Ōgai (1862–1922) and Natsume Sōseki (1867–1916), stood aloof from this dominating tendency. Mori Ōgai drew his inspiration primarily from German literature. He was active in writing poetry, the drama, the novel, and historical biography. Perhaps his best work of fiction is *Gan* ("The Wild Goose", 1911–13), which examines with remarkable acuity the feelings of a girl who is forced to be the mistress of a usurer. Natsume Sōseki was a scholar of English literature before he turned to imaginative writing. His monumental achievement in the psychological novel makes him unquestionably the greatest writer Japan has produced in modern times. In his works written between 1905 and his death he created a fictional world that constitutes a ruthless indictment of modern man's egoism. His incomplete last work, *Meian* ("Light and Darkness"), is perhaps the only modern Japanese novel that in scope and depth resembles the achievement of the Russian masters.

In the period from 1910 to 1930 a new school of aristocratic writers, the *Shirakabaha* (White Birch School), produced a number of idealistic, humanitarian works. During the same period Akutagawa Ryūnosuke (1892–1927), a disciple of Sōseki, created a highly structured, polished short-story form that, in English translation, has found admirers throughout the world.

The militarist domination of Japanese life in the 1930's largely stifled literature, although a few writers retreated into an uncontroversial aestheticism. Yasunari Kawabata (q.v.), the recipient of the 1968 Nobel Prize for literature, and Tanizaki Jun'ichiro (1886–1965) are foremost among the authors who emerged from World War II to continue perfecting their craft. Their work is known to readers of English through the excellent translations by the American writer and translator Edward Seidensticker (1921–   ) of Kawabata's *Snow Country* (1956) and Tanizaki's *Some Prefer Nettles* (1955) and *The Makioka Sisters* (1957). Another of Japan's most highly regarded postwar writers, Yukio Mishima (1925–70), wrote a number of novels, plays, and short stories dealing with his despair over the Westernization of his country and his desire for a return to the nobler Japan of earlier times. His best works are generally thought to be *The Temple of the Golden Pavillion* (1956) and the first two volumes of his tetralogy, *The Sea of Fertility* (1969–71). Although poetry has been less important than fiction in the modern period, the name of Masaoka Shiki (1867–1902) deserves mention as the creator of modern forms of the *tanka* and *haiku*. Since the end of the 19th century a vigorous movement for the writing of poetry in the Western style has arisen, and several prominent poets have emerged in this genre.

In the period after World War II various aspects of Japanese literature have received a careful and sympathetic appraisal by several American scholars, foremost among whom has been Donald Keene (1922–   ). Through their work of criticism and translation, Japanese literature is coming into consideration as a vital part of world literature.

JAPANESE MUSIC, traditional music of Japan. This music is performed by small ensembles of instruments and/or voices. Compositions often follow a three-part pattern called *jo-ha-kyū*, which consists of an introduction, a scattering effect in the central section, and a rushing effect near the end of the piece. This pattern has permeated much of Japanese music and applies to individual musical phrases as well as to entire compositions.

Music for Worship. The music of the ancient Japanese religion known as Shinto (q.v.) is called *kagura* ("god music"). It is used on formal occasions at shrines or imperial functions and at Shinto folk festivals. The songs and dances are meant to praise the gods and to entertain them. Music at seasonal festivals is performed on drums, rattles, and flutes. Dancers at these festivals perform inside and outside the shrines; their performances are interspersed with chants to the gods.

Music at a Buddhist temple in Japan is chanted in one of three languages: Indic, Chinese, or Japanese. The music is marked by highly ornamental singing and free rhythm; bells and chimes are sounded intermittently. The *Bon-odori* dances of the *o-bon* festival are mainly restrained in motion; they are accompanied by singers, and sometimes by flute, drum, and samisen, a three-stringed lute.

Court Music. The ancient court music of Japan (called *gagaku*) has its origins as far back as the 8th century; it is derived mainly from China and Korea; see CHINESE MUSIC. *Gagaku* orchestras may consist of as many as seventeen musicians playing woodwinds, plucked string and percussion instruments. The winds include a flute, usually of the type known as *ryūteki*; a short double-reed pipe called *hichiriki*; and a *shō*, a mouth organ consisting of seventeen bamboo pipes inserted in a bowl-shaped wind chest with a mouth hole. The flute and the double-reed pipe play the melody while the mouth organ provides a cluster of background tones. Phrases of music are marked off by the sounds of a small horizontal two-headed drum (*kakko*),

Young girls wear the traditional kimono for lessons in playing the koto (a type of zither) and the three-stringed samisen. UPI

a large hanging drum (*taiko*), and a small gong (*shokō*), as well as by short melodies and arpeggios played on a four-stringed lute (*biwa*) and a thirteen-stringed zither (*koto*). *Gagaku* music utilizes six modes, or scales, of Chinese origin, all derived from two basic scales, *ryo* and *ritsu*. The meters in *gagaku* music are basically duple.

RYO

RITSU

Dramatic music. Theatrical music during the early Middle Ages was influenced by earlier Buddhist music (see BUDDHISM) and consisted of lute accmpaniments to narrations called *heikebiwa* and of music for Nō dramas; see JAPANESE DRAMA. The lute accompaniments consist of set melodic and rhythmic patterns often representing specific emotions or situations. The Nō music contains parts for voices as well as for instruments. The actors or a chrous sing while instrumentalists accompany them on the shoulder drum (*ko tsuzumi*) and hip drum (*o tsuzumi*). The entire instrumental ensemble (called *hayashi*) also includes a flute (*nōkan*), which signals formal divisions within the drama, adds color to lyric moments, and accompanies dances, for which a stick drum, or *taiko*, is also used. Nō music makes use of set melodic and rhythmic patterns within prescribed forms, but it is played in flexible tempi. Variations in tempo are signaled by the drummers.

The most popular form of traditional Japanese theater is Kabuki, which is said to have begun in 1596 and was well established by the mid-17th century. Kabuki music makes use of instrumentalists and singers, most of whom sit at the back of the stage; others remain off stage to provide sound effects and special incidental music. The main form of dance music in Kabuki is *nagauta*, performed by the Nō instrumental group and the samisen. The most famous form of music used in puppet plays is called *gidayū*.

Chamber Music. After 1500 music for the solo instruments, the samisen and the koto became popular. Originally the music for both instruments consisted of suites of short, unrelated songs, *kumiuta*. Koto music, however, developed some forms that were wholly instrumental and others that were partly instrumental and partly vocal. An example of the wholly instrumental form is *danmono*, which consists of a theme and variations. An example of the combined instrumental and vocal form is the *jiuta*, in which vocal and instrumental interludes appear alternately. One to three kotos are used in the instrumental interludes, often supplemented by a samisen and a *shakuhachi*, an end-blown flute. Samisen music is of two types: *utaimono*, lyric pieces for home entertainment; and theatrical music for Kabuki drama and puppet plays. The koto is usually tuned in one of two scales, the *in* and *yō*.

JAPAN, MARTYRS OF

The Modern Period. When Mutsuhito (1852–1912) became emperor of Japan in 1867, Western influences began to be accepted in Japanese life and art, and composers developed new forms based on Western models. Japan now has many excellent orchestras and opera companies, and the music taught in public schools is primarily Western. Nevertheless, ancient traditional music remains popular.

Folk Music. Japanese folk music, which is of ancient origin, exists primarily in the form of religious festival music, work songs, and dance accompaniments. Folk entertainments, such as masked dances, folk theatricals, and community dancing, all include musical parts or accompaniments. The non-Japanese tribes of Northern Japan, the Ainu (q.v.), have a separate musical tradition similar to that of the American Indians (q.v.).
 — T.C.G.

JAPAN, MARTYRS OF, twenty-six Christians who were crucified on Feb. 5, 1597, in Nagasaki, Japan. Six Franciscans, among them Saint Paul Miki, a prominent Japanese preacher; three Jesuits; and seventeen laymen composed the group of martyrs. Of the possibly thousands of Japanese Roman Catholics martyred, these twenty-six are the only ones to have been canonized; they were canonized in 1862 by Pope Pius IX (*see under* PIUS). In 1962 a shrine was built in their honor on the hill where their martyrdom took place. Their feast day is Feb. 6.

JAPANNING. See LACQUER WORK.

JAPAN, SEA OF, arm of the Pacific Ocean, lying between Japan on the E. and the Asian mainland on the W. It is connected to the Sea of Okhotsk, on the N., by La Pérouse Strait and Tatar Strait; to the Pacific Ocean, on the E. and S.E., by Tsugaru Strait and Bungo Strait, respectively; and to the East China Sea, on the S., by Korea Strait and Tsushima Strait. Area, 391,100 sq.mi.; maximum depth, 12,280 ft.

JAPHETH, son of the Biblical patriarch Noah (q.v.) and survivor of the Deluge (q.v.). *See also* JAPHETIDES.

JAPHETIDES, *or* JAPHETIC PEOPLES, in ethnology, loose designation for the Caucasian peoples of Europe and certain parts of Asia, supposed to be descended from Japheth, a son of the Old Testament patriarch Noah (q.v.).

JAPURÁ, tributary of the Amazon R., rising in the Andes Mts. of Colombia, where it is called the Caquetá. The Japurá flows in a S.E. direction into Brazil where it shifts to an E. course, joining with the Amazon R. through a system of channels. It is about 1500 mi. long.

JAQUES-DALCROZE, Émile (1865–1950), Swiss composer and teacher, born in Vienna, Austria, and educated in Paris and at the Geneva Conservatory. He became a professor of harmony at the Conservatory in 1892, and developed a system of musical training designed to "create by the help of rhythm a rapid and regular current of communication between brain and body, and to make feeling for rhythm a physical experience." In 1915 he founded the Institut Jaques-Dalcroze in Geneva for the teaching and further development of this system, which became known as "Dalcroze Eurythmics", and has since taught in schools and colleges all over the world. Jaques-Dalcroze was also an active composer; his works include several operas, two violin concertos, three string quartets, piano pieces, and many songs. His literary works include *Méthode Jaques-Dalcroze* (1907–14) and *Rhythm, Music and Education* (1921).

JARGON, vocabulary used by a special group or occupational class and only partly comprehensible to outsiders. The special vocabularies of such fields as medicine, law, banking and fiance, science and technology, education, military affairs, the entertainment world, and sports all fall under the heading of jargon. Jargon, which accordingly constitutes well over half of all the words listed in a comprehensive dictionary, is highly legitimate in many callings, saving time and labor to those who know what it means. Falling under the general heading of jargon are such expressions as *perorbital hematoma* (black eye, to the layman), in medicine; sums held in *escrow* and *rediscount rate,* in finance; *coaxial cable,* in communications; and *unacceptable damage,* in insurance. In order to have a jargon the occupational group need only be engaged in the same activity or field of knowledge. For example, soldiers use such terms as *grunt* (enlisted man), loggers use *cat* (tractor), railroad men use *pig* (locomotive), and popular musicians use *licorice stick* (clarinet).

On the borderline between jargon and slang are extensive areas of the English language as used by young people. The vocabulary of the young changes rapidly and extensively. Such terms as *shafts* or *gams* (legs), *prehistorics* (parents), and to *bump gums* (to chat) may be short-lived; more enduring may be *chicken* (yellow) and *soul food* (food usually associated with the Southern United States).

Cant is the variety of jargon specifically used in the underworld, ranging from *skylarker* (suspicious character) and *breeze* (jailbreak) to expressions that have penetrated the general language such as *mugging* (either photgraphing for police purposes or an attack from behind), *ice* (diamonds), and *payola* (pay, graft, or blackmail).

Jargon has a long and traceable history. Among samples of 16th-century criminal cant are *hooker* (pickpocket), *jarkman* (forger), and *prigger* (horse thief). The special language variously described as Cockney or Australian is characterized by rhymes such as *bees and honey* (money) and *gay and frisky* (whiskey). See also DIALECT; SLANG. M.P.

JARRAH, common name of two trees belonging to the genus *Eucalyptus* (q.v.) of the family Myrtaceae; see MYRTLE.

JASHER, BOOK OF, one of the lost books of the Hebrews. Most scholars adopt the conjecture of the Syriac and Arabic translators that the Book of Jasher was a collection of national ballads. The book is mentioned twice in the Old Testament, once in the book of Joshua (Josh. 10:13), where Joshua's commanding of the sun and moon to stand still is said to have been reported therein, and again in 2 Samuel (2 Sam. 1: 18), where David's lament is given. Some held it to be a composition of the age of Solomon, and the work of the prophets Nathan (fl. 10th cent. B.C.) and Gad (*see under* GAD). In the 12th to the 14th centuries no less than three works professing to be the lost Book of Jasher were produced, and in 1751 another forgery was traced to a London printer.

JASMINE, or JESSAMINE, common names applied to plants of the genera *Jasminum*, true jasmine, and *Gelsemium*, false jasmine, which belong to closely related families of the Gentian order. The true jasmines, which belong to the Olive family, are a genus of shrubs and climbing plants, including 200 or more species, most of which are native to tropical regions of the Old World. The salver-shaped jasmine flower has a five or eight-cleft calyx, five- or eight-lobed corolla, two stamens, and a solitary pistil. The fruit is a two-lobed berry. The common white jasmine, *J. officinale*, is native to s. Asia, and naturalized in s. Europe. It is a tall climbing plant, usually 6 to 10 ft. high, bearing pinnate leaves and fragrant white flowers. Spanish jasmine, *J. grandiflorum*, is a bushy shrub, native to Indonesia, which bears white flowers flecked with pink. Arabian jasmine, *J. sambac*, is a white-flowered climbing plant, native to India, which grows about 5 ft. high. Flowers of all three species contain an essential oil, called oil of jasmine, which is used in making perfumes. White, Spanish, and Arabian jasmine, as well as several other forms of the genus, are cultivated in tropical and warm temperate regions of the world.

The false jasmine genus, which belongs to the Logania family, contains two Asian and one North American species. The latter is the yellow or Carolina jasmine, *G. sempervirens,* the State flower of South Carolina. Yellow jasmine has fragrant yellow flowers with a five-parted calyx, five-lobed, funnel-shaped corolla, five stamens with arrowhead-shaped anthers, and a solitary pistil. The fruit is a two-celled, septicidal capsule. The roots contain a crystalline alkaloid called gelsemine, $C_{20}H_{22}N_2O_2$, formerly used as an antispasmodic and diaphoretic.

JASON, in Greek mythology, son of Aeson, a king in Greece, whose throne had been taken away from him by his nephew, Pelias (q.v.). Jason, the rightful heir to the throne, had been sent away as a child for his own protection. When Jason grew to manhood, however, he courageously returned to Greece to regain his kingdom. Pelias pretended to be willing to relinquish the crown, but said that the young man must first undertake the quest of the Golden Fleece (q.v.), which was the rightful property of their family. Although Pelias believed that Jason could not come back alive from the quest, the young man scoffed at the dangers ahead. Jason assembled a crew of heroic young men from all parts of Greece to sail with him on the ship *Argo*. After a voyage of many almost incredible perils, the Argonauts reached Colchis (qq.v.), the country in which the Golden Fleece was held by King Aeetes. Aeetes agreed to give up the Golden Fleece if Jason would yoke two fire-breathing bulls with bronze feet, and sow the teeth of the dragon that Cadmus (q.v.), the founder of Thebes (q.v.), had long before slain. From the teeth would spring up a crop of armed men who would turn against Jason.

Jason successfully accomplished this task with the aid of Medea (q.v.), the king's daughter. Unknown to Jason, the goddess Hera (q.v.) had intervened in his behalf by making Medea fall in love with him. Medea gave Jason a charm to sprinkle on his weapons that would make him invincible for the day of his ordeal and helped him steal the fleece that night by charming a sleepless dragon that guarded it. In return for her help, Jason promised to love Medea always and to marry her as soon as they were safely back in Greece. Carrying the fleece and accompanied by Medea, Jason and his crew managed to escape from Aeetes.

JASPER

Upon reaching Greece, the crew of heroes disbanded, and Jason with Medea took the Golden Fleece to Pelias. In Jason's absence Pelias had forced Jason's father to kill himself, and his mother had died of grief. To avenge their deaths, Jason called upon Medea to help him punish Pelias. Medea tricked Pelias' daughters into killing their father and then she and Jason went to Corinth, where two sons were born to them. Instead of feeling grateful to Medea for all she had done, Jason treacherously married the daughter of the king of Corinth. In her grief and despair, Medea employed more sorcery to kill the young bride. Next, fearing that her young sons might be left alone for strangers to mistreat, she killed them. When the furious Jason determined to kill her, she escaped in a chariot drawn by dragons.

JASPER, opaque, cryptocrystalline variety of quartz (q.v.). The mineral takes a high polish and is used as a gem stone. It is usually stained by impurities and occurs in various colors, such as red, green, yellow, and blue. When the colors are arranged in bands, the mineral is called riband jasper; a variety containing alternating bands of red and green is known as Siberian jasper. Mottled yellow or brown varieties of jasper are called Egyptian jasper. Agate jasper is intermediate in structure between true jasper and chalcedony (q.v.). Inclusions of red jasper occur in heliotrope (see BLOODSTONE).

The jasper mentioned in the Bible as one of the stones in the breastplate of the high priest (Ex. 28:20) and as the foundation of the wall of the New Jerusalem (Rev. 21:18) is believed to have been a dark-green, opalescent stone. The jasper of the ancients was a partially translucent stone, probably containing some chalcedony and a variety of the latter known as chrysoprase. Many medicinal values were attributed to jasper, and as late as the beginning of the 17th century it was believed that this stone, if worn about the neck, had powers to strengthen the stomach.

JASPER NATIONAL PARK. See ALBERTA: *The Land: Parks and Other Places of Interest.*

JASPERS, Karl (1883–1969), German philosopher, born in Oldenburg, and educated in law and medicine at the universities of Heidelberg, Munich, Berlin, and Göttingen. He served at Heidelberg both as psychiatrist and professor of philosophy at the university hospital and medical school from 1909 until 1937 when he was dismissed by the National Socialist government. After the war, Jaspers was reinstated at Heidelberg, and in 1948, was appointed professor of philosophy at the University of Basel, Switzerland. Jaspers, a leading existentialist philosopher, held that man had the responsibility of examining each of his actions in relation to his life as a whole. Among his works are the three-volume *Philosophie* (1932; Eng. trans., *Philosophy,* 1969), *Vom Ursprung und Ziel der Geschichte*

Karl Jaspers.   Swiss National Tourist Office

(1949; Eng. trans., *On the Origin and Goal of History,* 1953); *Vernunft und Existenz* (1935; Eng. trans., *Reason and Existence,* 1955); *Die Atombombe und die Zukunft des Menschen* (1958; Eng. trans., *The Future of Mankind,* 1961); *Die Schuldfrage* (1946; Eng. trans., *The Question of German Guilt,* 1961); and *Der Philosophische Glaube* (1948; Eng. trans., *The Perennial Scope of Philosophy,* 1949). See EXISTENTIALISM.

JASSY. See IAŞI.

JATS, Indo-Aryan people, living mainly in the States of Punjab, Rajasthan, and Uttar Pradesh in northwestern India. Jats are tall, with light brown skin, and dark eyes and hair. They may be Hindus, Muslims, or Sikhs. Their principal occupation is farming.

JAUNDICE, *or* ICTERUS, yellowing of the skin, conjunctivae, and mucous membranes caused by excessive amounts of bile (q.v.) pigments in blood and tissues. Small amounts of these pigments, normally present in blood as a result of the breakdown of hemoglobin (q.v.) in red blood cells, are filtered through the liver (q.v.) and excreted in feces; see GALL BLADDER. Excessive amounts produce jaundice of three types.

Hemolytic jaundice, caused by the abnormal breakdown of red blood cells and hemoglobin, results in increased production of bile pigment exceeding the liver's filtering capacity. Breakdown occurs in abnormal red cells and those damaged by infection, toxins, and antibodies created by mismatched blood transfusions; see BLOOD: *Blood Tranfusion*. A newborn infant may be jaundiced for a short time due to a self-correcting condition or by a prenatal mismatch between the Rh factor (q.v.) in his blood and that of his mother. Treatment involves aiding the patient with blood transfusions while the causative toxins, bacteria, or antibodies are neutralized or eliminated. A baby can be prenatally desensitized against his mother's negative Rh blood factor or can have an exchange blood transfusion after birth.

Hepatocellular jaundice occurs when liver cells are damaged by viruses (see HEPATITIS, VIRAL), toxins, or excess alcohol and lose the ability to filter pigment which accumulates in the blood. Treatment involves rest, to minimize the load on the liver, proper diet, and control of the responsible damaging agents.

Obstructive jaundice follows physical obstruction of the ducts that transport pigment filtered by the liver to the small intestine. This may be caused by gall stones, tumors, scar tissue, or inflammation, forcing pigment to regurgitate through the liver into the blood. Treatment generally involves surgical removal of the obstruction.
D.S.T.

JAUREGG, Julius Wagner von. See WAGNER VON JAUREGG, JULIUS.

JAVA, one of the islands of the Malay Archipelago (q.v.), bounded on the N. by the Java Sea, on the E. by Bali Strait, on the S. by the Indian Ocean, and on the W. by Sunda Strait, and forming part of the Republic of Indonesia. Java, together with Madura (q.v.), was formerly an administrative division of the Netherlands Indies (q.v.).

Java extends in a generally E. and W. direction for a distance of about 650 mi. The maximum width of the island, which lies about midway between the fifth and tenth parallels of south latitude, is about 127 mi. Djakarta (q.v.), is the largest city of Java and capital of the republic. Other important cities are Djokjakarta, Bandung, Semarang, Surabaja, Tjirebon (qq.v.), Pekalongan, Sukabumi, Malang, and Surakarta. The area of Java is 48,842 sq.mi. The island is the most densely populated region of the world, with a population (1969 est.) of 74,000,000.

The Land. Java is traversed from E. to W. by a volcanic mountain chain. This longitudinal uplift has approximately 110 volcanic centers, including about 35 active craters. Semeru (12,060 ft.), situated in the E. portion of the island, is the highest volcano and one of the most active. Elevations in W. Java are generally lower, rarely exceeding 5700 ft. Besides Semeru, the most active volcanoes of Java include Bromo, Kawah Idjen, and Tangkubanperahu. Java has

Outsized sails drive boats on one of the large canals that connect Djakarta with the sea. Standard Oil Co. (N.J.)

Women at work raising rice, the principal food crop of Java, in paddies near Bandung.

Standard Oil Co. (N.J.)

been the scene of a number of disastrous volcanic eruptions, notably that of Mt. Ringgit in 1686, when about 10,000 lives were lost, and that of Papandayan in 1772, when about 3000 persons were killed. A low coastal plain, with a maximum width of about 40 mi. adjoins the central mountain chain on the N. The southern part of the island is occupied by a series of limestone ridges, which form a precipitous coastal escarpment. With few exceptions, the rivers of Java are swift, narrow, and shallow. The Lasolo R., about 335 mi. in length, is the largest stream. The best natural harbors of Java are on the N. coast of the island.

Climate. Temperatures as high as 99° F. occur at midday in the coastal and lowland regions of Java, and the relative humidity often exceeds 80 percent. During the rainy season, from November to April, ocean breezes and frequent thunderstorms exercise a cooling influence. At elevations above 2000 ft. temperate climatic conditions prevail, and temperatures as low as 27° F. occur at extreme elevations. The mean annual precipitation is about 80 in. Wide regional variations occur, however, with extremes ranging from an annual maximum of about 166 in. at Bogor to an annual minimum of about 35 in. at Assembagus.

Plants and Animals. The vegetation of Java is luxuriant, particularly along the lower slopes of the central mountain chain and on the coastal plain. In addition to a broad variety of plants, numerous species of trees, including palms, bamboo, acacia, rubber, and teak, abound in this zone, which is confined largely to the area below 1700 ft. The teak forests, one of the most valuable natural resources of Java, are extensive. Among the trees common to the higher slopes of the central uplift are the magnolia, rasamala, oak, elm, laurel, maple, and chestnut. Stands of timber occupy approximately 7,627,000 acres, or about 23 percent of the total surface of the island. Java also has a numerous and diversified fauna. Noteworthy quadrupeds are the one-horned rhinoceros, tiger, leopard, banteng (wild ox), wild pig, lemur, and several species of ape. The island is the habitat of more than 400 species of birds, including the red jungle fowl *(Gallus gallus)*, the green peacock, two species of parrot, the swift *(Collocalia)*, 10 species of pigeon, 2 species of cuckoo, and 11 species of heron. Among the reptilian fauna are the great python (*Python reticulatus*), cobra, a species of adder, and the crocodile. Specimens of the last-named animal sometimes attain 30 ft. in length. The coastal and inland waters teem with fish, including many edible varieties. Crabs, crayfish, and lobsters are numerous.

The People. The population of Java is composed largely of Malayan peoples (q.v.) who speak various dialects of the Malay language (see MALAY LANGUAGE AND LITERATURE); a majority of the population belongs to the Sundanese, the Javanese, and the Madurese dialect-speaking groups. The Sudanese inhabit the extreme w. portion of the island, the Javanese inhabit the central part, and the Madurese inhabit the E. part. An overwhelming majority of the population is Muslim.

History. The earliest Javanese civilization of record was Hindu, probably introduced about the 1st century A.D. Archeological evidence of Hindu culture dates from about the middle of the 8th century. Little is known of Javanese political developments prior to the 13th century, but after 1293 records exist of several Hindu and Buddhist kingdoms, including that of Majapahit, which endured until 1520, when the Muslims came to power. Subsequently Islam became the religious faith of the Javanese people. Portuguese traders visited the island early in the 16th century. Toward the close of that century, Dutch traders broke the Portuguese commercial monopoly in Java. The Dutch swiftly enlarged their sphere of influence and by 1755 controlled a large portion of the islands; see EAST INDIA COMPANY: *Dutch East India Company*. In 1811, during the Napoleonic Wars (q.v.) in Europe, a French expeditionary force expelled the Dutch. The French were driven out later that year by the British, who remained in Java until 1816, when the island was returned to Dutch sovereignty. Between 1825 and 1830 Dutch authority in Java was unsuccessfully challenged by a Javanese rebellion. Thereafter, the island remained under the rule of the Netherlands until the Japanese occupation, begun in March, 1942, during World War II. For later developments, see INDONESIA, REPUBLIC OF.

JAVA MAN. See MAN, ANCIENT: *Pithecanthropines*.

JAVITS, Jacob K(oppel) (1904–), American politician, born in New York City. He was awarded an LL.B. degree from New York University Law School in 1926 and began the practice of law the following year. In partnership with

The residents of Djakarta travel about the city inexpensively on betjaks, *or bicycle taxis.* UPI

JAY

his brother, Benjamin Abraham Javits (1894–1973), Jacob soon became a well-known trial lawyer. A long-time member of the Republican Party, he made his entrance into politics in 1946. In the first of what was to become an unbroken series of successful political campaigns, Javits was elected to the United States House of Representatives from the 21st Congressional District of the State of New York. After serving four successive terms in the House, Javits was elected in 1954 to a four-year term as New York State Attorney General. He vacated the attorney generalship after two years, when he was elected to the United States Senate. He was reelected to the Senate in 1962 and 1968.

JAY, common name for a group of birds in the subfamily Garrulinae of the Crow family, found in temperate and warm regions throughout the world. Most jays are smaller and more brightly colored than crows; many of them have crests. Jays eat large insects, seeds, nuts, small amphibians, invertebrates, and sometimes the eggs and young of other birds.

The common European jay is *Garrulus glandarius,* about 14 in. long. It is chiefly brownish-pink in color, with a black and white crest. The blue jay, or common American jay, *Cyanocitta cristata,* found throughout the eastern United States from the Great Plains to the Atlantic coast, is 11½ to 12 in. long, and has a large crest. It is grayish blue above and pale gray below. Its tail is bright blue; its wings are bright blue banded with black and spotted with white. An irregular circle of black rings its neck and lower throat. The gray jay or Canada jay (also called whiskey jack, moosebird, or camp robber), *Perisoreus canadensis,* is a crestless jay of northern North America, found as far south as northeastern New York. This bird, which is known for stealing food from hunters' camps, is about 12 in. long; it is dirty gray in general body color, with a white forehead. Other crestless jays include the scrub jay, *Aphelocoma coerulescens,* and the piñon jay, *Gymnorhinus cyanocephala,* of the western U.S.

JAY, John (1745–1829), American statesman and jurist, first chief justice of the Supreme Court of the United States (q.v.), born in New York City, and educated at King's College (now Columbia University). He was admitted to the bar in 1768. He represented the point of view of the American merchants in protesting British restrictions on the commercial activities of the colonies, and was elected to the Continental Congress (q.v.) in 1774 and again in 1775. He drafted the first constitution of New York State, and was appointed chief justice of the State in 1777. In the following year he was again elected to the Continental Congress and was chosen its president. In Paris in 1782 he was one of the commissioners who negotiated the Treaty of Paris with Great Britain, ending the American Revolution (q.v.); *see* PARIS, TREATY OF.

From 1784 to 1789 Jay served as secretary for foreign affairs. The ineffectiveness of the Articles of Confederation (q.v.) led him to become a proponent of a strong national government. In collaboration with the American statesmen Alexander Hamilton and James Madison (qq.v.), Jay wrote the notable series of articles known as *The Federalist* (q.v.), which successfully urged ratification of the Constitution of the United States (q.v.). In 1789 President George Washington (q.v.) appointed Jay chief justice of the U.S. In 1794, when war with Great Britain threatened over unsettled controversies arising in part from the Treaty of Paris, Jay was appointed by Washington to negotiate a settlement. Jay went to Great Britain and concluded the agreement known as Jay's Treaty (q.v.).

On his return to the U.S. Jay discovered that during his absence he had been elected governor of New York State. He resigned from the Court, and served as governor from 1795 to 1801. Jay spent the rest of his life in retirement.

JAYHAWKER, popular name for a resident of the State of Kansas. Derived from the name of a mythical large-beaked bird, the jayhawk, the term has been applied to various bands of Kansas guerrillas and raiders, including abolitionists

Blue jay, Cyanocitta cristata
Alvin E. Staffan – National Audubon Society

JAY'S TREATY

John Jay is burned in effigy by a crowd critical of the treaty Jay negotiated with Great Britain in 1794 (after a contemporary woodcut).
Granger Collection

and Union troops during the American Civil War and outlaws and rustlers following the war. See CIVIL WAR, THE AMERICAN; KANSAS: *History.*

JAY'S TREATY, treaty negotiated in 1794 by the American statesman and jurist John Jay (q.v.) and the British foreign secretary Baron William Wyndham Grenville (*see under* GRENVILLE), resolving the outstanding differences between the United States and Great Britain.

The differences that the treaty was intended to settle arose chiefly from violations of the Treaty of Paris (*see* PARIS, TREATY OF), which terminated the American Revolution (q.v.). Jay's Treaty provided for evacuation by the British of posts on the northwestern border of the U.S. and for the appointment of arbitration commissions to define boundaries of the U.S. It also provided for a commission to determine compensation by Great Britain for the illegal seizure of American ships and for the payment by Americans of prewar debts owed to British merchants. By the terms of the treaty severe restrictions were placed on American trade with the British West Indies, and the British were allowed to trade with the U.S. on a most-favored-nation basis.

Jay's Treaty aroused great public indignation in America. Jay was burned in effigy and the American statesman Alexander Hamilton (q.v.) was stoned while speaking in favor of the treaty; even President George Washington (q.v.) was criticized. After heated debate, the treaty was ratified by the United States Senate on June 24, 1795. Despite initial unpopularity, the treaty came to be recognized as the best that the U.S. could have obtained in the circumstances. In time Jay's Treaty was credited with averting war between America and Great Britain.

JAZYGES, ancient tribe of the group called Sarmatians (q.v.), originally occupying the shores of the Black Sea.

JAZZ, designation for a type of music first developed by American Negroes in the late 19th century in New Orleans, La. Although the term has been applied to many types of 20th-century music, it properly refers only to a type of improvisatory music in which the combinations of basic elements are determined largely by an individual performer during the course of his performance, rather than by a composer, as in art music and much popular music; see MUSIC; MUSICAL. It differs from folk music (q.v.) in that it usually modifies musical traditions to express the temperament of an individual rather than preserving them as the relatively unified and unchanging expressions of a people. Because jazz has influenced so much modern music, however, it can usually be distinguished in its true form only by the relative freedom of the performer from the requirements of a written score and by his subtle and individual variations of a basic musical pulse.

ELEMENTS OF JAZZ

The typical musical form of jazz consists of variations on a basic theme. The theme may be provided by almost any type of music, including marches and hymns, or by such musical elements as harmonic progressions and even the consecutive notes of a musical scale. From the basic material the jazz performer produces a virtually infinite number of variations and developments, usually through improvisations in the course of a performance. Written scores are used merely as guides, and the variations make extensive use of the element of syncopation (q.v.), which gives jazz its quality of rhythmical freedom. The nature of the variations, however, and the particular qualities of the musical pulse depend largely on the taste and temperament of the performer, and result in the individuality of expression and the intense feeling of personal creative involvement that constitute the distinctive characteristics of jazz.

Improvisation. True improvisation uses a basic melody or theme as a starting point from which the player develops and extends his musical thoughts. This development may consist of chord changes, the interpolation of additional notes into the basic melodic structure, and the alternation of melodic variations among contrasting instrumental combinations. A key element in all improvisation is the degree to which the performer can impress his own sense of musical rhythm on the basic musical pattern. The style of a jazz performer depends, in addition, on the originality of his musical improvisations and on the manner in which he executes them.

Rhythm. Jazz rhythm is distinguished by a quality called swing (q.v.), the subtle conflict between a regular, ongoing beat and a player's personal rhythmic articulation of a phrase. The player swings, that is, he superimposes rhythmic accents alternatively with, and against, the basic beat, producing a pattern of complex rhythms. Styles of swing have changed over the years, primarily because jazz players have become increasingly adroit in their use of rhythms, but the principle remains the same. The player who swings the most is the one who exercises the greatest degree of personal subtlety in his articulation of individual rhythms against the basic beat.

Texture. Much of the characteristic sound of jazz results from a bending of the pitch (q.v.) of the third, fifth, and seventh degrees of the diatonic scale (see SCALE); this produces a sound sometimes described as wailing or moaning, as in the specialized form of jazz known as the blues (q.v.). The most important instruments in jazz are the clarinet, the saxophone, the trombone, and the trumpet, with important rhythmic accompaniments from drums and the string bass; the piano is used both as a percussive instrument, and, like the banjo or guitar, as a means of providing harmonic background. Although these harmonic and instrumental elements occur in other types of music, they have become particularly effective when used by those jazz musicians who have developed great skill in improvisation. Attempts to describe the sound of various types of jazz include use of such terms as "cool", "hot", and "smooth".

ORIGINS OF JAZZ

The history of jazz is marked by a movement toward an ever greater freedom in improvisation, accompanied by the development of increasingly complex rhythmic patterns. Jazz today is played throughout the world, by many skilled performers. The most significant part of the history of jazz, however, has occurred in the United States, and all of the musicians mentioned in this article are Americans.

African Influences. The origins of jazz can be traced to the musical traditions carried to North America by African Negro slaves in the 17th century; see NEGROES IN THE UNITED STATES. Similarities therefore exist between African music (q.v.) as we know it in this century and the earliest forms of jazz as recorded for the phonograph beginning in 1917. African music is formally organized around a repeated refrain; jazz uses an almost identical form, a series of variations on a basic musical idea. The call-and-response patterns of African music have their counterparts in the interacting solo and ensemble devices of jazz, and both types of music incorporate extensive collective improvisation in which each voice or instrument has a specific function.

The elements of African music were maintained through the various forms of music such as field hollers, rowing chants, lullabies, and especially the type of religious song known as the spiritual (q.v.). During the 18th and 19th centuries these basic musical forms were affected by contact with European music. As early as 1845 the American composer Louis Moreau Gottschalk (q.v.) used Negro themes, often with syncopation, in his concert works, suggesting new forms of instrumental treatment for this material. Many Negroes in New Orleans received extensive education in European music; frequent contact between these urban musicians and the rural workers, who used essentially African forms of musical expression, undoubtedly played an important role in the early artistic hybridization that led to jazz. For example, an attempt to combine the African five-note scale with the European eight-note scale may have produced the so-called blue notes, tones slightly higher or lower than those of the eight-note scale. Such notes, which also may have been derived from the techniques of West African singers, became very important elements in the characteristic sound texture of jazz.

Ragtime. Another early source of jazz was the music played on the "banjar", or banjo, first on the plantation and later in the minstrel show (q.v.). As adapted by musicians in New Orleans this music led to ragtime, a syncopated style of piano playing drawn also from the march music of the late 19th century and from European dance pieces. The best-known exponent of ragtime was the composer and pianist Scott Joplin (1868–1917), who used the ragtime style in operas and orchestral works. Ragtime was most important for the effect it had on such major piano soloists of the late 1920's and 1930's as Ferdinand Joseph La Menthe ("Jelly Roll") Morton (1885–1941), James Price Johnson (1891–1955), Thomas ("Fats") Waller (1904–43), and Arthur ("Art") Tatum (1910–56).

Brass-Band Music. In the late-19th and early-20th centuries Negro brass bands became prominent, especially in New Orleans, but also in Texas, Oklahoma, and throughout the Midwest. The bands played traditional themes, modified frequently by syncopation and acceleration, at picnics, weddings, street parades, and funerals. It was characteristic of these bands to play dirges on the way to funerals and then to syncopate and accelerate the same tunes into lively marches on the way back. This type of music was made popular by the American Negro composer, cornetist, and bandmaster William Christopher Handy (q.v.), who led and toured with a brass band composed of musicians mainly from Louisiana and Mississippi at the turn of the century.

EARLY JAZZ

The first major jazz musician was the trumpeter Charles ("Buddy") Bolden (1868–1931).

New Orleans Jazz. As the leader of a band that played for the public dances at Congo

Early figures in jazz. Left: Bix Beiderbecke, cornetist and pianist, developed a style that influenced many older musicians in the Chicago era. Center: Bessie Smith, one of the legendary blues singers. Right: Louis Armstrong, one of the first jazz virtuosos, was the teacher by example of many famous musicians.

Columbia Records   Columbia Records   RKO Pictures

JAZZ

Square in New Orleans, Bolden developed an early form of jazz in which volume was more important than finesse. Little individual improvisation took place. The trumpet generally played a vociferous melodic lead, the clarinet piped a simple harmony line, the trombone played rhythmic slides and pedal notes. Rhythmic accompaniment was provided by the wind tuba. Among later trumpeters influence by Bolden's style were William Geary ("Bunk") Johnson (1879–1949) and Freddie Keppard (1889–1933). The so-called Dixieland jazz consisted of the New Orleans style as played by white musicians. It was popularized later by the band leader Albert Edwin ("Eddie") Condon (1905–73).

In 1917 a group of white musicians known as the Original Dixieland Jazz Band made the first phonograph records of jazz music. A more important organization, the Creole Jazz Band, was led by Joseph ("King") Oliver (1885–1938), an influential stylist in the Bolden manner. Oliver's group, in 1923, was the first black band to produce a series of phonograph records. The most original member of the group was the trumpeter Louis ("Satchmo") Armstrong (q.v.), whose subsequent recording with his own groups, the Hot Five and the Hot Seven, established new standards for solo playing. Armstrong was the first musician to demonstrate that jazz improvisation could consist of something more than melodic ornamentation. He built new melodies with chord changes.

Another type of jazz that developed during the early 1920's is known as boogie-woogie. Played on the piano, it consists of a short and sharply accented bass pattern played over and over by the left hand while the right plays freely, using a variety of rhythms. Boogie-woogie was particularly popular in the late 1930's and 1940's. Leading boogie-woogie pianists included Meade Lux Lewis (1905–64), Albert Ammons (1907–49), Peter ("Pete") Johnson (1904–   ), and Clarence ("Pine Top") Smith (1904–29).

Chicago Jazz. Armstrong's innovations influenced many jazz musicians of the 1920's, especially in Chicago, where such groups as The New Orleans Rhythm Kings worked out their own versions of the New Orleans style. Among the best known of the Chicago jazz musicians were the trumpeter Leon Bismarck ("Bix") Beiderbecke (q.v.) and the singer Bessie Smith (1894–1937). Many of the latter's vocal improvisations were influential in the further development of instrumental jazz.

Big-Band Jazz. As a result of technical developments achieved during the 1920's, large groups of jazz musicians began to play together,

Benny Goodman (standing, center) plays the clarinet and directs his swing orchestra, while blues specialist Jimmy Rushing (1903–73) sings. Robert Parent

JAZZ

Duke Ellington, composer, arranger, pianist, and orchestra leader, examines an orchestral score during a recording session. Columbia Records

forming the so-called "big bands", which became especially popular during the 1930's. One major development was the substitution of string bass for the wind tuba; this smoothed the two-beat rhythm that had been used in New Orleans into a more flowing four beats to the bar. In addition, musicians learned how to use short melodic phrases, known as ensemble riffs, in call-and-response patterns. To facilitate this type of playing, orchestras were divided into instrumental sections, and opportunities were provided for musicians to play extended solo passages.

Such developments were achieved largely through the work of Edward Kennedy ("Duke") Ellington (q.v.) and James Fletcher ("Smack") Henderson (1898–1952). During the late 1920's, Ellington led a band at the Cotton Club in New York City. There he composed music that made his orchestra a cohesive ensemble, with solos written for the unique qualities of specific instrumentalists. Henderson's compositions, less complex than those of Ellington, helped to introduce written scores into jazz music. In his written arrangements for large groups he attempted to capture the quality of improvisation that characterized the music of smaller ensembles. Other bands were led by James Melvin ("Jimmie") Lunceford (1902–47), William ("Chick") Webb (1902–39), and Cabell ("Cab") Calloway (1907–).

Another style of big-band jazz was developed in the organization led by William ("Count") Basie (1904–) during the mid-1930's. The various instruments of this band exchanged ensemble riffs in a free and strongly rhythmical interplay, with occasional pauses to accommodate extended instrumental solos. The playing of tenor saxophonist Lester Willis ("Pres") Young (1909–59), in particular, was marked by a rhythmic freedom that was rarely apparent in the playing of soloists from the Ellington and Henderson bands. Among other groups that played in this style were the Clouds of Joy led by Andrew Dewey ("Andy") Kirk (1898–), the Blue Devils of Walter Sylvester Page (1900–57), and the band of Earl ("Fatha") Hines (q.v.). New instrumental effects were developed by the vibraphonists Lionel Hampton (1913–) and Kenneth ("Red") Norvo (1908–).

Jazz singing in the 1930's became increasingly flexible and stylized. Ivie Anderson (1904–49), Mildred Bailey (1907–51), Ella Fitzgerald (1918–), and Billie ("Lady Day") Holiday (1915–59), whose original name was Eleanor Gough McKay, were the leading singers. Louis Armstrong, already a major influence on instrumental playing, became equally influential as a singer.

The pioneering efforts of Armstrong, Ellington, Henderson, and others made jazz a dominant influence on American music during the

Trumpeter Miles Davis, a significant influence in modern jazz. UPI

175

JAZZ

Dave Brubeck, pianist and composer, an exponent of West Coast jazz. Columbia Records

1920's and 1930's. Such popular musicians as Paul Whiteman (q.v.) used some of the more obvious rhythmic and melodic devices of jazz, although with far less improvisational freedom and skill than was displayed in the music of the major jazz players. This so-called symphonic jazz influenced such American composers as George Gershwin and Jerome Kern (qq.v.) and was widely imitated in Europe. The music played by the bands of the clarinetist Benny Goodman (q.v.), the drummer Gene Krupa (1909–73), and the trumpeter Harry Hagg James (1916–) was closer to the authentic jazz tradition of improvisation and solo virtuosity. *See also* SWING.

MODERN JAZZ

During the 1940's the alto saxophonist Charles Christopher (Charlie "Bird") Parker (1920–55) developed a form of jazz variously called rebop, bebop, and bop. Like the music of Lester Young in the Basie band, Parker's innovations included intricate rhythmical patterns. Parker's style also resembled that of the tenor saxophonist Coleman ("Bean") Hawkins (1904–69) in his use of complex chord alterations and substitutions. Other notable jazz musicians of the 1940's included John Birks ("Dizzy") Gillespie (1917–), Thelonious Monk (1920–), Oscar Pettiford (1922–), Earl ("Bud") Powell (1924–), and Max Roach (1925–).

Another cycle of jazz began to develop in the late 1940's, when a modified, or "cool" version of bop appeared. Inspired by trumpeter Miles Davis (1926–) it was adopted and refined by players like tenor saxophonists John Haley ("Zoot") Sims (1925–) and Stanley ("Stan") Getz (1927–) and baritone saxophonist Gerald Joseph ("Gerry") Mulligan (1927–).

In the early 1950's, the pianist David ("Dave") Brubeck (1920–) and the alto saxophonist Paul Desmond (1924–) developed a form of bop known as West Coast jazz.

Parker's music continued to influence many jazz musicians of the 1950's, and a number of jazz movements were largely derivatives of the Parker style. Among them were soul jazz, played by Horace Silver (1928–), the brothers Julian Edwin ("Cannonball") Adderly (1928–) and Nathaniel ("Nat") Adderly (1931–), and Robert Henry ("Bobby") Timmons (1935–); hard bop, developed by Art Blakey (1919–) and the many young musicians who have played with him; the experimental jazz of pianist Leonard Joseph ("Lennie") Tristano (1919–) and alto saxophonist Lee Konitz (1927–); and the polished neo-bop of Clifford Brown (1930–56). As these players became accustomed to the complex harmonic and rhythmic patterns of modern jazz, they began to return to the simultaneous improvisation of several lines of melody by a whole group of musicians, which had characterized the earliest form of jazz.

Jazz Ballet. Music in jazz styles has been used for dance works, particularly in the U.S. The American choreographer Jerome Robbins (q.v.) has created many jazz dances, including those for two musicals by the American composer and conductor, Leonard Bernstein (q.v.), *On The Town* (1944) and *West Side Story* (1957). The finest jazz dance is considered to be Robbins' *N.Y. Export: Op. Jazz* (1958, revised 1969).

Contemporary Jazz. The two key figures in the jazz of the 1960's were the tenor saxophonist John William Coltrane (1926–67), and the alto saxophonist Ornette Coleman (1930–). As a player with the influential Miles Davis group, Coltrane improvised within set modes or scales, in contrast to a method of completely free improvisations developed by Coleman. By the early 1960's, Coltrane had exceeded the limits of modal improvisation and was moving toward a true melodic-rhythmic improvisational style, based on a rhythmic accompaniment from drummer Elvin Ray Jones (1927–).

In the 1960's, jazz no longer dominated American music as it had in the 1930's. Its popularity with large audiences was taken over by a new type of music based primarily on derivatives of Anglo-Saxon folk music and on a type of Negro

The Bobby Hutcherson–Harold Land Quintet performs at the annual Pori Jazz Festival in Helsinki, Finland.
UPI

music called rhythm and blues. Although this music uses some of the harmonic and melodic freedom of jazz, it has a rhythmical base so pronounced that opportunities for free improvisation are limited. Further, the dominance of such singers as Elvis Presley (1935–) and such vocal groups as the Beatles led to a lack of interest in instrumental soloists. Jazz continued to be played extensively, however, and such players as clarinetist-composer James Peter ("Jimmy") Giuffre (1921–), composer-bassist Charles Mingus (1922–), composer George Allan Russel (1923–), woodwind specialist Eric Allan Dolphy (1928–), tenor saxophonist Theodore Walter ("Sonny") Rollins (1929–), and pianist Cecil Percival Taylor (1933–) continued to develop new methods of improvisation. In addition, jazz musicians adopted several of the techniques of contemporary concert music, including atonality and the twelve-tone scale (see Music: *History: Contemporary Music*); and they became increasingly receptive to music of varied cultures, including that of the Indian composer Ravi Shankar (1920–).

See also Popular Music.

JEAN BAPTISTE DE LA SALLE, Saint (1651–1719), French cleric and educator, born in Reims. After entering the priesthood, he became a canon of the cathedral at Reims. He devoted his life to the teaching of poor children and attracted numerous assistants to his cause. He resigned his canonry and in 1684 founded for his assistants an order called the Christian Brothers, or, as it became known officially, Brothers of the Christian Schools (q.v.). The order was the first organized exclusively for the advancement of Christian education. In 1685 at Reims he also founded, for the training of his teachers, a school that is often considered the first normal school; see Teaching and Training of Teachers. He was canonized in 1900 and declared patron of teachers in 1950. His feast day is April 7.

JEANMAIRE, Renée Marcelle (1924–), French dancer and actress, born in Paris. After a period of study at the Paris Opera Ballet School, she became a dancer with several European companies. In 1948 she joined the ballet troupe of Roland Petit (q.v.), whom she later married. She first achieved fame for her performance in 1949 in the title role of the Petit ballet version of the opera *Carmen* by the French composer Georges Bizet (q.v.). The following year she danced in *La Croquese de Diamante* ("The Diamond Cruncher"). Her appearances in American motion pictures include *Hans Christian Anderson* (1952) and *Anything Goes* (1956). Her American stage appearances include *The Girl in the Pink Tights* (1954) and *Zizi* (1962). She was awarded the Chevalier des Arts et Lettres decoration.

177

JEANNE D'ARC

JEANNE D'ARC. See JOAN OF ARC, SAINT.

JEAN PAUL. See RICHTER, JEAN PAUL FRIEDRICH.

JEANS, Sir James Hopwood (1877–1946), British mathematician, physicist, and astronomer, born in London, England, and educated at the University of Cambridge. Jeans was professor of applied mathematics at Princeton University from 1910 to 1912, and research associate at the Mt. Wilson Observatory in 1923. He was secretary of the Royal Society of London for Improving Natural Knowledge from 1919 to 1929. He is best known for his successful application of mathematics to problems in physics and astronomy, for his work in cosmogony (q.v.), and for his research on the kinetics and radiation of gases (see KINETIC THEORY). Jeans was knighted in 1928, and awarded the Order of Merit in 1939. His works include *Radiation and the Quantum Theory* (1914), *Problems of Cosmogony and Stellar Dynamics* (1919), and *Eos, or the Wider Aspects of Cosmogony* (1928). He also wrote books for the layman, such as *The Universe Around Us* (1929), *The Stars in Their Courses* (1931), *Through Space and Time* (1934), *Science and Music* (1937), and *The Growth of Physical Science* (published posthumously in 1948).

JEDDA. See JIDDA.

JEEP, sturdy, all-purpose, small but high-powered open automobile, first mass-produced for the United States armed forces in 1940. Combining the ruggedness of a truck with the speed and mobility of a light car, the original jeep (called a "peep" during World War II) was about 11 ft. long and 5 ft. wide, carried six passengers, and could travel about 65 m.p.h. Essential features were a powerful engine, two- and four-wheeled drive, and deep-treaded tires. A standard jeep can haul a load of a half a ton or more and maneuvers well over mud or hilly terrain. Besides their military indispensability, jeeps are also sold commercially today, often with engines capable of speeds up to 90 m.p.h. or more. The popular name derives from the abbreviation of "general purpose" vehicle.

JEFFERS, (John) Robinson (1887–1962), American poet, born in Pittsburgh, Pa., and educated at Occidental College and at the medical school of the University of Southern California. His works are naturalistic and he depicts man at the mercy of the forces of the universe. Recurring themes in his poetry, variously symbolized, are the worthlessness of modern man, perversion, violence, and man's desire for self-destruction. His poetic works include *Tamar and Other Poems* (1924), *Dear Judas and Other Poems* (1929), *Descent to the Dead* (1931), *The Double Axe and Other Poems* (1948) and *Hungerfield and Other Poems* (1953). In 1947 his English adaptation of *Medea*, by the Greek dramatist Euripides (q.v.), was seen in New York City.

JEFFERSON, river in S.W. Montana, and one of the three rivers that unites to form the Missouri R. It rises in the Red Rock lakes, in Beaverhead County, and flows N.E. for about 200 mi. to the confluence of the Jefferson, Madison, and Gallatin rivers at Three Forks.

JEFFERSON, Joseph (1829–1905), American actor, member of a family of actors descended from the British actor Thomas Jefferson (1732–97), born in Philadelphia, and privately educated. He made his stage debut at the age of three and toured with his family for many years. He gained recognition in the company of the American actress Laura Keene (q.v.) in New York City. In 1865 Jefferson visited London and played for the first time the title role in *Rip Van Winkle,* by the Irish dramatist Dion Boucicault (q.v.). Thereafter his name was especially identified with this character and also with that of Bob Acres in *The Rivals,* by the British dramatist Richard Brinsley Sheridan (q.v.). Jefferson also attained distinction as a landscape painter and wrote an *Autobiography* (1890).

JEFFERSON, Thomas (1743–1826), third President of the United States, born in Shadwell, near Charlottesville, Va. His father was the Virginia magistrate and surveyor Peter Jefferson (1707–57), and his mother, Jane Welsh Jefferson (1720–76), belonged to one of the most prominent families in the colony. Jefferson was educated at the College of William and Mary and was admitted to the Virginia bar in 1767. In 1772 he married Martha Wayles Skelton (1748–1782), the daughter of a Virginia lawyer.

One of the most prominent members of a notable generation of Virginia statesmen, Jefferson served in the legislative assembly of that colony from 1769 to 1775. His literary skill quickly became evident, as did his libertarian political philosophy. In his *A Summary View of the Rights of British America,* a set of resolutions presented to the Virginia convention in 1774, he rejected the claim of the British Parliament to authority over the American colonies. Such views received their most eloquent expression in the Declaration of Independence (q.v.), which Jefferson drafted as a member of the Continental Congress (q.v.) in 1776. Returning to Virginia, he served in the legislature and, from 1779 to 1781, as governor during the American Revolution (q.v.). A proponent of religious liberty (q.v.), he brought about the passage of a bill establishing freedom of worship in the State. In a radical departure from established policy, he proposed a system of public education and a reform of the penal code; although he himself was a slaveowner, he proposed the emancipation of slaves. Elected again to the Continental Congress in 1783, he secured adoption of the system of decimal coinage and proposed a plan for the government of the Northwest Territory (q.v.). From 1785 to 1789 he served as minister to France, succeeding the aging American statesman Benjamin Franklin (q.v.).

Jeffersonian Democracy. The French Revolution (q.v.) strengthened Jefferson's belief in the rights of man. When he became secretary of state under President George Washington (q.v.), his concept of individualistic democracy and a simple agrarian society brought him into conflict with Alexander Hamilton (q.v.), the secretary of the treasury. Jefferson considered Hamilton's unprecedented proposal for a national bank unconstitutional, and criticized his colleague's advocacy of a strong central government. Their differences led to Jefferson's resignation from the cabinet in December, 1793, and to the emergence of two political factions: the Federalist Party (q.v.), supporting Hamilton's principles, and the Democratic-Republican Party (q.v.) led by Jefferson.

As the Presidential candidate of his faction, Jefferson was defeated by the Federalist John Adams (q.v.) in the election of 1796. Under the provisions of the Constitution that prevailed at that time, he became Vice-President, but took little part in the Adams administration; *see* CONSTITUTION OF THE UNITED STATES: *Article II*. He vigorously opposed the Alien and Sedition Acts (q.v.), which he regarded as an attack on individual liberties. In the election of 1800 Jefferson became President after receiving a tie in the electoral college (q.v.) with his fellow Democratic-Republican Aaron Burr (q.v.). The election was decided in the House of Representatives, largely through the influence of the Federalist Hamilton, whose distrust of Burr outweighed his opposition to Jefferson.

The first President to take office in Washington, D.C., Jefferson called for national unity, declaring that "We are all Republicans, we are all Federalists". His recommendations for frugality in government were hindered by the costs of the Tripolitan War, against the pirates of the Barbary Coast (q.v.), and by the Louisiana Purchase (q.v.). The latter, perhaps Jefferson's greatest achievement as President, marked the beginning of a period of national expansion, which was furthered by his support of the Lewis and Clark Expedition (q.v.) for the exploration of the newly acquired territory. Jefferson also

Thomas Jefferson

supported the expeditions conducted by the soldier Zebulon Montgomery Pike (q.v.) in his search for the source of the Mississippi R. and in his exploration of the Southwest.

Reelected in 1804, Jefferson worked to protect American neutrality during the Napoleonic Wars (q.v.) between France and Great Britain. He responded to the harassment of American shipping and the impressment of sailors by proposing such measures as the Embargo Act (q.v.), which proved largely ineffective. He remained committed to peaceful diplomacy, however, even after the British frigate *Leopard* fired on the U.S. warship *Chesapeake* (q.v.) in June, 1807. In 1808 Jefferson, declining a third term, supported his secretary of state James Madison (q.v.) as his successor. Jefferson died on July 4, 1826, the 50th anniversary of the Declaration of Independence, only a few hours before the death of his old colleague and rival, John Adams.

An American Intellectual. Jefferson was one of the most prominent American representatives of the period of intellectual activity known as the Enlightenment; *see* ENLIGHTENMENT, AGE OF. A profound thinker and a man of extraordinary intellectual energy, he proposed numerous reforms in the laws of his State and was a major advocate of education, notably in the University of Virginia (*see* VIRGINIA, UNIVERSITY OF), which he founded in 1819. His architectural designs, de-

JEFFERSON CITY

rived from the classical ideals of the 18th century, were realized in the buildings of the university, in the State Capitol at Richmond, and in "Monticello", his estate near Charlottesville, Va. Interested in science and art, he conducted the first American archeological activities and, as a skillful violinist, became one of the early important figures in American music (q.v.). His conception of the rights of the individual against the encroachments of government constitutes one of the most important theoretical principles in the American system of law; see CIVIL RIGHTS AND CIVIL LIBERTIES. N.W.P.

JEFFERSON CITY, city and capital of Missouri, and county seat of Cole Co., on the Missouri R. at the center of the State, about 115 miles s.w. of Saint Louis. It is a transportation center served by railroads and domestic airlines. In the city are printing and publishing plants, and factories manufacturing shoes and cosmetics. Jefferson City is the site of Lincoln University, founded in 1866 by members of two Negro Civil War regiments following their discharge from the Union army; it was made a State institution in 1879. The city is also the site of a national cemetery established in 1867. The marble State Capitol, completed in 1917, is built on a bluff overlooking the river. Other notable buildings are the Missouri State Museum, and the Supreme Court Building, housing one of the finest law libraries in the United States. The site of the present city was chosen in 1821 to be the capital of the State, and in 1822 the town was laid out. The first State House was built in 1826. Jefferson City became the county seat in 1828 and was chartered as a city in 1839. Pop. (1960) 28,228; (1970) 32,407.

JEFFERSON NATIONAL EXPANSION MEMORIAL NATIONAL HISTORIC SITE, United States memorial to President Thomas Jefferson's foresight in promoting the Louisiana Purchase (q.v.) and to America's westward expansion, in Saint Louis, Mo., historically the gateway to the West. The central feature of the memorial is the 630-ft.-high steel Gateway Arch, designed by the American architect Eero Saarinen (see under SAARINEN), and completed in 1965; it fronts the Mississippi R. on the site of the original village of St. Louis. The Museum of Westward Expansion is underground, below the arch. Also part of the site are the Old Courthouse, scene of the Dred Scot Case (q.v.), and the Old Cathedral, which is still in use. The site is administered by the National Park Service (q.v.).

JEFFERSONVILLE, city and river port in Indiana, and county seat of Clark Co., on the Ohio R., about 105 miles s.e. of Indianapolis, and about 2 miles E. of Louisville, Ky. Machinery, soap, cement, clothing, riverboats and foundry and wood products are manufactured in the city. It is the site of a regional campus of Indiana University, established in 1820. Pop. (1960) 19,522; (1970) 20,008.

JEFFREY, Francis, Lord Jeffrey (1773–1850), Scottish literary critic and jurist, born in Edinburgh, and educated at the universities of Glasgow and Oxford. In association with the British author Sydney Smith (q.v.) and others, he founded the *Edinburgh Review,* a literary periodical (*see* PERIODICALS), in 1802. Jeffrey was editor of the review until 1829, and became famous for his trenchant style and caustic treatment of the works of such poets as William Wordsworth, John Keats, and Percy Bysshe Shelley (qq.v.). He also was an able and eloquent barrister and in 1830 was appointed lord advocate. Four years later he was created a peer and was appointed judge of the Court of Session. He served in that capacity until his death.

JEFFREYS, George, 1st Baron Jeffreys of Wem (1648–89), English jurist, born in Denbighshire, Wales, and educated at the University of Cambridge and the Inner Temple, London. He was called to the bar in 1668. Jeffreys' brilliant eloquence soon won him a large private practice. He secured the favor of influential courtiers, and was employed in the confidential legal business of Charles II (q.v.), King of England. In 1677 he was knighted and appointed solicitor general to the Duke of York and Albany, later James II (q.v.) King of England. Jeffreys became chief justice of Chester in 1680, lord chief justice of England, and member of the privy council in 1683.

Jeffreys was an able and upright judge in civil cases, and had few superiors in the clarity with which he expressed his decisions. His conduct of criminal trials, however, was so brutal, even for his period, that he earned the sobriquet "the Hanging Judge". In 1683 he presided at the trials of the conspirators in the Rye House Plot (q.v.) to kill Charles II and the Duke of York. His conduct toward the accused was regarded as so unjust that he became infamous throughout England.

In 1685 James II made Jeffreys a baron. Later in the same year, Jeffreys conducted a series of trials of men charged with complicity in a rebellion against James II, led by James Scott, Duke of Monmouth (q.v.). Because he conducted these trials with ruthless disregard for legal procedure, they became known as the "bloody assizes" (q.v.). James II appointed him lord chancellor of England and keeper of the great seal. In the following years Jeffreys upheld the king in his most tryannical assertions of authority, and, when James II fled the country in December, 1688, during the Glorious Revolution (q.v.), Jeffreys also attempted to escape, disguised as a seaman. He was recognized and arrested, and imprisoned in the Tower of London (q.v.), where he died four months later.

JEFFRIES, James J. (1875–1953), American boxer, born in Carroll, Ohio. He entered the professional boxing ring in 1896. On June 9, 1899, he fought the British pugilist Robert Fitzsimmons (1862–1917), then heavyweight champion of the world, in New York City, and knocked him out in the eleventh round, winning the title. Jeffries successfully defended his crown on five occasions during the next five years. In each bout except the first, which resulted in a decision, he won by a knockout. He retired undefeated in 1905. Attempting a comeback in 1910, he met the American world champion Jack Johnson (q.v.) at Reno, Nev. Johnson knocked him out in the fifteenth round.

JEHOASH. See JOASH.

JEHOIAKIM (died about 598 B.C.), King of Judah (609–598 B.C.), son of Josiah (q.v.). Originally a vassal king under the control of the Egyptians, Jehoiakim submitted to the conqueror of Egypt, Nebuchadnezzar II (see under NEBUCHADNEZZAR), the Neo-Babylonian overlord of Palestine, in 605 B.C., after the Battle at Carchemish. Some three years later, he rebelled against Nebuchadnezzar and was subdued and possibly assassinated. He was succeeded by his son, Jehoiachin (615?–560? B.C.), who ruled for several months before being deposed and carried into captivity (2 Kings 23:34–24:6); see BABYLONIAN CAPTIVITY. See also ZEDEKIAH.

JEHOSHAPHAT (Heb., "Jehovah has judged), according to the Old Testament (1, 2 Kings, 2 Chron.) King of Judah (873–849 B.C.) succeeding his father, Asa (q.v.). Jehoshaphat allied himself with Israel against the Syrians and joined Ahab (q.v.), King of Israel, in a military expedition to Ramoth Gilead, which has been variously identified with such towns of present-day Jordan as 'Ajlun, Es Salt, and Jarash. He later renewed the alliance with Ahab's son and successor, Ahaziah, King of Judah (r. 850 B.C.), and joined Ahaziah's brother and successor, Jehoram, King of Israel (r. about 849–842 B.C.), in a war against the Moabites (q.v.). Jehoshaphat was succeeded by his oldest son, Jehoram, King of Judah (r. 849–842 B.C.), whose wife was Ahab's daughter, the notorious Athaliah, who was later to attain the throne of Judah by murder (r. about 842 B.C.).

JEHOSHAPHAT, VALLEY OF, traditional name of the northern extension of the Vale of Kidron, in Jordan, lying just outside the eastern wall of the Old City of Jerusalem (q.v.). According to Joel 3, containing the only scriptural citation, the Valley of Jehoshaphat is the place in which Jehovah will pass judgment against the enemies of His people.

JEHOVAH, name of the God of the Hebrew people as erroneously transliterated from the Masoretic Hebrew text; see GOD; MASORA. The word consists of the consonants JHVH or JHWH, with the vowels of a separate word, AdOnAI (Lord). What its original vowels were is a matter of speculation, for because of an interpretation of such texts as Exod. 20:7 and Lev. 24:11, the name came to be regarded as too sacred for expression; the scribes (see SCRIBE), in reading aloud, substituted "Lord" and therefore wrote the vowel markings for "Lord" into the consonantal framework JHVH as a reminder to future readers aloud. The translators of the Hebrew, not realizing what the scribes had done, read the word as it was written down, taking the scribal vowel markings as intrinsic to the name of their God rather than as a mere reminder not to speak it. From this came the rendition Jehovah. The evidence of the Greek Church fathers (see FATHERS OF THE CHURCH) shows the forms *Jabe* and *Jaô* to be traditional, as well as the shortened Hebrew forms of the words *Jah* (Ps. 68:4, for example) and *Jahu* (in proper names). It indicates that the name was originally spoken *Jahweh* or *Yahwe* (often spelled Yahweh in modern usage). Etymologically, it is a third person singular, imperfect, probably of the verb *hawah* (or *hajah*), signifying "to be". The older interpreters explain the verb in a metaphysical and abstract sense; the "I am" of Scripture is "He who is", the absolutely existent. S.L.

JEHOVAH'S WITNESSES, Christian sect, founded in 1872 in Pittsburgh, Pa., by the American clergyman Charles Taze Russell (1852–1916), and comprising congregations in more than ninety countries. Members of the sect originally were known by the popular name of Russellites. The legal governing body of Jehovah's Witnesses is the Watch Tower Bible and Tract Society of Pennsylvania, incorporated in 1884. European members belong to the affiliated International Bible Students Association, incorporated in London, England, in 1914. International headquarters are located in Brooklyn, N.Y.

Members of the sect believe in the second coming of Christ and regard themselves as practitioners of primitive Christianity and consider each Witness a minister. The sect stresses Bible study and absolute obedience of Biblical precepts. Its teachings are spread primarily by

JEHU

members who preach from door to door and distribute literature to passersby on street corners. Bible study classes frequently are conducted in private homes. The meeting places of Jehovah's Witnesses are known as Kingdom Halls.

Witnesses acknowledge allegiance solely to the Kingdom of Jesus Christ. They refuse consequently to salute any flag, vote, perform military service, or otherwise signify allegiance to any government. This policy has brought them into conflict with governmental authorities in many countries, including the United States.

Jehovah's Witnesses teach that Christ began His invisible reign as King in 1914. They believe that soon the forces of good, led by Christ, will defeat the forces of evil, led by Satan, at the battle of Armageddon (q.v.). Thereafter Christ will rule the earth for a thousand years. During this millennium (q.v.) the dead will rise again and all men will have a second opportunity to achieve salvation. At the end of the millennium Satan will return to earth, and he and those who support him finally will be destroyed. A perfected mankind will then enjoy eternal life on earth.

The sect maintains an extensive publishing program, issuing books and pamphlets in many languages. Its best-known periodical, *The Watchtower*, is printed in seventy-four languages. In the late 1960's the world membership of active adherents numbered about 1,160,000; in the U.S., where Jehovah's Witnesses are most numerous, active members totaled some 425,000 in the early 1970's.

JEHU (Heb., "He is Jehovah"), in the Old Testament (1, 2 Kings, 2 Chron.), King of Israel (r. 842–815 B.C.). Jehu was originally a soldier of Ahab (q.v.), King of Israel, and rose to the rank of general. Exhorted by Elisha (q.v.), the prophet, Jehu slew Jehoram, King of Israel (r. about 849–842 B.C.); Ahaziah, King of Judah (r. about 842 B.C.); and Jezebel (q.v.), Ahab's notorious wife. He was anointed king of Israel by the prophet Elijah (q.v.) and controlled the kingdom of Judah. Jehu paid tribute to the Assyrian king, Shalmaneser III (r. 859–825) and fought Hazael (d. about 801 B.C.), who was king of Damascus from about 843 B.C. Jehu was succeeded by his son Jehoahaz (d. 800? B.C.).

JEKYLL AND HYDE, names given to the two personalities of the title character in the psychological novel *The Strange Case of Dr. Jekyll and Mr. Hyde* (1886), by the Scottish writer Robert Louis Balfour Stevenson (q.v.).

JELLICOE, John Rushworth, 1st Earl Jellicoe (1859–1935), British naval officer, born in Southampton, England. He received an appointment as a naval cadet in 1872 and was commissioned a sublieutenant in 1880. After service (1882) in the war in Egypt he studied at the Royal Naval College. By 1897 he had attained the rank of captain. In 1900 he led one of the units of the international force sent against Peking during the Boxer Rebellion (q.v.).

Jellicoe advanced steadily in rank, becoming rear admiral in 1907, vice admiral in 1910, and second sea lord of the admiralty in 1912. At the beginning of World War I he was appointed acting admiral and commander in chief of the British Grand Fleet. In 1916 Jellicoe directed British naval forces at the Battle of Jutland (see JUTLAND, BATTLE OF), the most important naval conflict of the war. Although both Britain and Germany claimed the victory, the German fleet was blockaded for the duration of the war. Jellicoe supervised British antisubmarine operations after November, 1916, when he became first sea lord and chief of naval staff. Following the war he was promoted (1919) to the rank of admiral of the fleet and appointed (1920) governor general of New Zealand. He retired in 1924. Among honors conferred on Jellicoe for his war services were membership in the Order of Merit and elevation to the peerage as Viscount Jellicoe of Scapa. In 1925 he was created an earl.

JELLIFFE, Smith Ely (1866–1945), American neurologist and psychoanalyst, born in Brooklyn, N.Y., and educated at the Brooklyn Polytechnic Institute and Columbia University. He taught at the College of Pharmacy of Columbia University from 1897 to 1907, and from the latter year until 1912 was clinical professor of mental diseases at Fordham University. From 1911 until his death he was adjunct professor of diseases of the mind and nervous system at the New York Post-Graduate Hospital and Medical School.

Jelliffe was the author of about 400 papers and many books on varied scientific subjects, many of which dealt with the theory and practice of psychoanalysis (q.v.). He became one of the pioneer psychoanalysts in the United States as well as one of the most effective advocates among physicians and psychiatrists for psychoanalytic doctrine. In 1913, with the American psychiatrist William Alanson White (1870–1937), he founded the *Psychoanalytic Review*, of which he was coeditor until his death; he was also managing editor of the *Journal of Nervous and Mental Diseases* from 1902 until his death. His most important editorial work, also in collaboration with White, was the "Nervous and Mental Disease Monograph Series", founded in 1907, for which he wrote several volumes.

JELLYFISH or **MEDUSA,** common name for any of the marine species of free-swimming coelenterate animals constituting the class Scyphozoa. They are found in most temperate and cold waters of the world. The animals are transparent and disk-shaped or bell-shaped. Water constitutes almost 96 percent of their body weight, so that if left to dry in the sun they virtually disappear in a short time. In structure they resemble the hydromedusa state of the Hydrozoa (q.v.), differing chiefly in the absence of the velum. Some scyphozoans pass through a very minute polyp stage during which they are anchored at the ocean bottom. The chief order of jellyfish is Semaeostomeae, which contains the large red species, *Cyanea arctica,* common off the north Atlantic coast of the United States. This species attains a diameter of 7½ ft. and a tentacle length of 120 ft. Jellyfish are dried, flavored, and used as food in the Orient. *See* COELENTERATA.

JENA, city in East Germany, on the Saale R., about 25 miles E. of Erfurt. It was chartered in the 13th century and in 1423 passed from the control of Meissen to that of Saxony. Jena is the site of the University of Jena, founded by John Frederick, Elector of Saxony (1503–54), and chartered in 1558. Between 1758 and 1828 Johann Gottlieb Fichte, Georg Wilhelm Friedrich Hegel, Friedrich Wilhelm Joseph von Schelling, Johann Christoph Friedrich von Schiller, and August Wilhelm von Schlegel (qq.v.) taught at Jena. Johann Wolfgang von Goethe (q.v.) wrote *Hermann und Dorothea* in the ducal palace, later destroyed and replaced by university buildings. Also of interest is the Church of Saint Michael, dating from the 15th century. North of the city is the site of the Battle of Jena at which Napoleon I (q.v.), Emperor of France, defeated the Prussians in 1806 during the Napoleonic Wars (q.v.).

The celebrated Zeiss optical works are situated in Jena. Other industrial establishments are machine shops, printing shops, and plants manufacturing scientific instruments, glass, and chemicals. Pop. (1963 est.) 82,113.

JENA, UNIVERSITY OF, officially FRIEDRICH-SCHILLER-UNIVERSITÄT, institution of higher learning, located in Jena (q.v.), East Germany. The university is under the jurisdiction of the minister for higher education and is supported by the government. The university was founded as an academy in 1548 and given the status of a university in 1558. It consists of the faculties of philosophy, law, theology, medicine, mathematics and natural sciences, and agriculture. A Diplom, the approximate equivalent of an American baccalaureate degree, is awarded after a four- to five-year course of study. After an additional three years of study and the completion of a dissertation the doctorate is awarded. Further study and the completion of a second dissertation lead to a second doctorate (Habilitation), which qualifies the recipient to teach in a university. Habilitation represents the approximate equivalent of the American Ph.D. The library contains about 1,433,000 bound volumes and approximately 6600 manuscripts. In 1968–69 the student body numbered more than 4700 and the faculty, about 400.

JENGHIZ KHAN. *See* GENGHIS KHAN.

JENKINS' EAR, WAR OF, in British history, name given to the trade war begun in 1739 between Great Britain and Spain. The war developed from British attempts to circumvent the Peace of Utrecht (*see* UTRECHT, PEACE OF), which in 1714 terminated the War of the Spanish Succession; *see* SPANISH SUCCESSION, WAR OF THE. The commercial provisions of the treaty severely restricted British trade with Spanish colonies in America, and many British merchants consequently resorted to smuggling. In 1731 Robert Jenkins (fl. 1731–38), a British smuggler in command of the brig *Rebecca* was seized by the crew of a Spanish coast guard vessel who compelled him to surrender his cargo and then cut off one of his ears. The incident received little attention at the time, but subsequent outrages against British seamen engendered widespread anti-Spanish sentiment in Great Britain. The affair was hotly debated in Parliament in 1738, and in the following year, confronted by an implacable opposition, the British statesman Sir Robert Walpole (*see under* WALPOLE) was obliged to declare war against Spain.

Hostilities (1739–41) were confined to the New World. The struggle later became part of the War of the Austrian Succession; *see* SUCCESSION WARS: *War of the Austrian Succession.*

JENNER, Edward (1749–1823), British physician, born in Berkeley, Gloucestershire, England, and educated privately by several physicians, including the celebrated British surgeon John Hunter (q.v.). Jenner is best known for his discovery of the principles of vaccination (q.v.), considered the basis of the modern science of immunology; *see* IMMUNITY. Having observed that people infected with cowpox were immune to smallpox (qq.v.), a much more severe disease, Jenner in 1796 injected a young boy with cowpox; six weeks later attempts to produce smallpox in the boy were unsuccessful. In 1798 Jenner published his discovery in "An Inquiry into the Cause and Effects of the Variolae Vaccinae". Vaccination against smallpox met with great opposition among the medical profession, but enough important British physicians and surgeons were convinced by Jenner's arguments to establish the practice. Jenner received several parliamentary grants for his discovery.

JENNY, William Le Baron. See AMERICAN ARCHITECTURE: *Modern American Architecture: Technology and Tall Buildings (1830's–1950's).*

JENNINGS, Hugh Ambrose (1870–1928), American professional baseball player, born in Pittston, Pa. He began his professional baseball career in 1890 and subsequently played in the American Association, the National League, and the American League. He became famous as shortstop with the Baltimore Orioles of the National League and was a noted base runner. From 1907 to 1920 he was manager of the Detroit Tigers of the American League; during this period the team won three American League pennants. From 1920 to 1925 Jennings was a coach for the New York Giants of the National League. He was named to the Baseball Hall of Fame in 1945; *see* BASEBALL HALL OF FAME AND MUSEUM, NATIONAL.

JENSEN, Johannes Hans Daniel (1906–), German physicist, born in Hamburg, and educated at the University of Hamburg. After teaching (1937–41) at the University of Hamburg and (1941–49) at the Technical University at Hannover, Jensen joined the faculty of the University of Heidelberg. He shared half of the 1963 Nobel Prize in physics with the German-American physicist Maria Goeppert Mayer (q.v.); the other half was awarded to the German-American physicist Eugene P. Wigner (q.v.). Jensen was cited for his independent work on the structure of the atomic nucleus. He produced a model of the nucleus having protons and neutrons grouped in concentric shells.

JENSEN, Johannes Vilhelm (1873–1950), Danish writer, born in Farsø, Jutland, and educated at the University of Copenhagen. His writings are notable for their profound understanding and sympathetic portrayal of common people. He first gained recognition for *Himmerlandshistorier* ("Tales from the Himmerland", 3 vol., 1898–1910), a collection of folk tales of the people of Himmerland, his native province. Jensen was deeply interested in the theory of evolution, and is best known for a series of six novels published from 1909 to 1920, in which he expounded his view of the development of mankind from savagery to lofty intellectual aspiration. These novels were combined into two volumes under the title *Den Lange Rejse*, in 1938, after they had been translated into English under the title *The Long Journey* (3 vol., 1922– 24). Among his numerous other writings are a collection of lyric verse, *Digte* ("Poems", 1906); essays on evolution; and seven collections of a unique literary genre called *myter* ("myths"), which combine elements of both the essay and the prose tale. Jensen, who wrote over sixty volumes of poetry, plays and novels, was awarded the 1944 Nobel Prize in literature.

JENSON, Nicolas. See TYPE.

JEOPARDY, in criminal law, peril incurred by a defendant, charged with a crime, on trial before a court of competent jurisdiction. In past ages it was not uncommon for persons acquitted of criminal charges, by the verdict (q.v.) of a jury (q.v.), to be tried a second time on the original charge; persons so treated were generally so-called political criminals or opponents of rulers and governments, and were said to be placed in double jeopardy. To exclude the possibility of such persecution in the United States, the Fifth Amendment to the Constitution of the United States (q.v.) provides: "nor shall any person be subject for the same offense to be twice put in jeopardy". The courts have interpreted this provision to apply only to criminal cases, and have ruled that jeopardy begins only when an accused person is placed on trial, and ends upon acquittal (q.v.) or with his sentencing after conviction; *see* CRIMINAL PROCEDURE.

JEPHTHAH, according to the Old Testament (Judg. 11–12), eighth of the judges of Israel, considered one of the most important. Driven out of his native Gilead (a region of present-day Jordan) because he was of illegitimate birth, he became the leader of a band of freebooters and led successful wars against the Ammonites (q.v.) and Ephraimites (*see* EPHRAIM). A judge for six years, he is recalled in the New Testament (Heb. 11:32) as an example of a man of faith.

JERBA. See DJERBA.

JERBOA, common name for any of the Old World jumping rodents in the family Dipodidae, found particularly in the arid regions of Africa and central Asia. These animals have short front limbs and long hind limbs on which they leap about like tiny kangaroos. They are about 6 in. long from head to rump, and have hind legs about 4 in. long. Jerboas are sandy above and white below, often with the tip of the tail black. Some species have large, broad ears. The Egyptian jerboa, *Dipus sagitta*, is a well-known species which is often tamed and kept as a pet. The jerboa is related to the kangaroolike rodent of the western United States called the pocket rat. The animal may cover from two to six feet in a single jump. *See* KANGAROO RAT. *See also* KANGAROO; POCKET MOUSE.

JEREMIAH, book of the Old Testament (*see* BIBLE), in the King James Version, THE BOOK OF THE PROPHET JEREMIAH. It is entitled *The Prophecy of Jeremias* in some English versions of the Bible used by Roman Catholics. According to the traditional view, the entire book was composed by the Hebrew prophet Jeremiah or dictated by him to the scribe Baruch (qq.v.). Many modern Bible scholars, however, maintain that chapters 26–45 are a biography of the prophet written by Baruch; and some scholars further maintain that chapters 46–51 were added sometime after the middle of the 6th century B.C. by anonymous authors or editors. Quite possibly the book was worked on by editors for several hundred years after Jeremiah's death, for the present text almost certainly appears to have been compiled from other sources over a long period of time.

The book of Jeremiah falls into three distinct parts. The first portion (chapters 1–25) consists largely of prophecies against Judah (q.v.) and Jerusalem uttered by Jeremiah during the reigns of the Judean kings Josiah, Jehoiakim, Jehoiachin, and Zedekiah (qq.v.). The prophecies are mostly in the first person and may have been recorded, partly as prose and partly as poetry, by Baruch (36:4–6). Also included in this first portion are an account of Jeremiah's call (1:4–19), a number of innovative introspective laments (see, for example, 18:18–23), biographical details such as Jeremiah's Temple sermon (7:1–15), and his activities in support of King Josiah's religious reforms (11:1–17). The last two chapters recount two visions concerning the fall of Judah and the Babylonian Captivity (q.v.).

The second distinct part of Jeremiah (chapters 26–29, 32–45) is an account, almost entirely in prose, of Jeremiah's activities, trials, and persecutions from roughly 608 B.C. to his last days. Presumably (because the prophet appears throughout in the third person), these chapters are from Baruch's pen. The historical events are accurately reported, but the original order has been changed by later writers or editors; chapters 26 and 45, for instance, record events in the reign of King Jehoiakim, while much of the material in chapters 27–44 dates from the reign of King Zedekiah. Chapters 30 and 31, the so-called "Little Book of Comfort", predict the restoration of Israel (q.v.) and Judah, their reunification, and a new covenant (q.v.) "with the house of Israel and the house of Judah" (31:31).

The third distinct part of Jeremiah consists of a collection of pronouncements against foreign nations (chapters 46–51) and an historical appendix (chapter 52). The oracles appear as "The word of the Lord which came to Jeremiah the prophet against the Gentiles" (46:1); present-day scholars, however, are uncertain as to how much of this collection is actually from Jeremiah. Chapter 52 seems to have been drawn from 2 Kings 24:18–25:30 (*see* KINGS). It gives the number of Jews taken into captivity, an historically valuable statistic not recorded in 2 Kings.

A number of theological teachings contained in Jeremiah have significantly affected the development of postexilic Judaism (q.v.). Preeminent among these is the view that the God of Israel and Judah could be worshiped away from the sanctuaries at Shiloh (q.v.) and Jerusalem, a view that enabled the Jews of the Diaspora (q.v.) to preserve and perpetuate their religion. Another significant contribution is the emphasis given to the concept of individual responsibility (see especially 31:30), which ultimately was to find its fitting expression in a new covenant between the Lord and His chosen people (31:31–34).

JEREMIAH *or* JEREMIAS (fl. 7th cent. B.C.), in the Old Testament, one of the major prophets (*see* PROPHECY), principal figure of the book that bears his name. In Hebrew, the name means "whom Jehovah appoints".

Born in Anathoth near Jerusalem, he came into prominence during the reign of Jehoiakim, King of Judah (609–598 B.C.), when he denounced the idolatry of the Jews and proclaimed the forthcoming destruction of Jerusalem and the Temple; *see* TEMPLE: *Temple at Jerusalem*. After Jerusalem was destroyed (587 B.C.) by Nebuchadnezzar II (*see under* NEBUCHADNEZZAR), Jeremiah moved to Egypt, where he continued to prophesy, and where he probably died.

With his emphasis on individual union with God, Jeremiah is regarded as the most personal of the prophets and one of the most sensitive human beings in the Old Testament. His prophecies of the destruction of Jerusalem and his weeping over the doomed city have been likened to Christ's foretelling of the destruction of the Temple and His lament over Jerusalem (Matt. 23:37–24:2).

JEREMIAH, LETTER OF, book of the Old Testament Apocrypha (*see* BIBLE), in the King James Version, THE EPISTLE OF JEREMY. It is appended to the Apocryphal book of Baruch (q.v.) as chapter 6 in the King James Version, but in several ancient Greek and Syriac manuscripts and versions of the Bible it appears as a separate book. Some modern English translations of the Bible, for example, the Revised Standard Version, also print the letter separately (*see* BIBLE: *Manuscripts, Versions, Editions, and Translations*). It is included in the Roman Catholic canon of the Bible (see BIBLE, CANON OF THE) as one of the deuterocanonical books (q.v.).

The Letter of Jeremiah proclaims itself "A copy of an epistle, which Jeremy sent" (1:1) to the Judean exiles in Babylon (see BABYLONIAN CAPTIVITY). It is long (73 verses), repetitious, and much more like a sermon than a letter; it seems to have been appended to the book of Baruch merely because of its own claim and the historical relationship of the scribe Baruch to the Hebrew prophet Jeremiah (q.v.). The letter predicts a long captivity, warns against the danger of apostasy, and repeatedly exhorts the exiles to shun the worship of idols, for "they are known not to be gods: therefore fear them not" (1:16).

Modern scholars generally agree that the letter was not written by Baruch, since it dates from a later time. The actual date of composition is still undetermined, ranging from the end of the 4th century B.C. to about the end of the 2nd century B.C. The language of the original also remains conjectural. Some scholars maintain it was Greek, others that it was Hebrew, still others that it was Aramaic (see ARAM).

JEREZ DE LA FRONTERA, city of Spain, in Andalusia, near the Atlantic Ocean, 14 miles N.E. of Cádiz. Situated in a fertile agricultural region, it is a commercial center for fruit, vegetables, and grains, and also livestock, cork, and timber. Jerez is the sherry wine capital of the world; the word "sherry" is a corruption of Xerez, the former name of the city. Jerez also produces cognac, bottles, barrels, and cement. The picturesque city has narrow, winding streets and many wine cellars. Architectural monuments include a Moorish fortress, the 15th century church of Santiago, the Gothic church of San Miguel, and the ruins of San Francisco convent. Jerez was under Moorish control from 711 to 1264, when it was recovered by Alfonso X (q.v.), King of León and Castile. Pop. (1970) 149,867.

JERICHO (Ar. *Ariha*), village of Jordan, about 15 miles N.E. of Jerusalem, 5 mi. from the northern end of the Dead Sea, and about 800 ft. below sea level. The town is near the site of the ancient city of Jericho, the name of which is retained in the Arabic name of the modern city. Modern Jericho is a vacation resort, frequented by Arab residents of Jerusalem. Bananas, figs, and oranges are grown in the region.

Biblical Jericho. Archeologically important ruins in the vicinity include massive, winding double walls. Excavated early in the 20th century, these walls are generally identified as the fortifications of the original Jericho, a city of Canaan (q.v.). In the first Biblical reference to Jericho (Josh. 2), the Hebrew leader Joshua (q.v.) dispatched two spies to the Canaanite city from Shittim (in what is now Jordan), the place of encampment of the Israelites. Subsequently besieged by the Israelites, Jericho fell after its walls were leveled miraculously by seven trumpet-blowing priests (Josh. 6). All the inhabitants were massacred, according to the story in the book of Joshua, and the city was cursed by Joshua and destroyed. Historically, there probably was no massacre, and the Hebrews and Canaanites were able to live side by side in peace and even, later, to intermarry.

According to 1 Kings 16:34, Jericho was rebuilt about 500 years later, during the reign of the 9th-century Israelite king Ahab (q.v.), by the Bethelite Hiel. The city is mentioned in later books of the Old Testament, notably (2 Kings 25) as the scene of the defeat (586 B.C.) of Zedekiah (q.v.), the last king of Judah, by the Chaldeans (see BABYLONIA: *History*) under King Nebuchadnezzar II (see under NEBUCHADNEZZAR). During the reign (37–4 B.C.) of the Judean ruler Herod the Great (see under HEROD), Jericho was the winter capital of the kingdom; its fortifications were strengthened, and several palaces, an amphitheater, and other imposing structures were built. After Herod's death, which occurred in the city, it was destroyed by rebellious slaves. Later rebuilt on a nearby site, the city figured prominently in the life of Jesus Christ (q.v.). According to Matt. 20:30, for example, it was there that He restored sight to two blind men. Jesus passed through Jericho on His last journey to Jerusalem (Luke 19).

History. The ancient city was razed by the Romans under Caesar Vespasian (q.v.) during his campaign (66 A.D.) against the Jews. Its site was later occupied and settled by the Crusaders, who were expelled in turn by the Muslims. British forces captured the modern village in February, 1918, during World War I, and in 1920 Jericho became part of the British Mandate of Palestine. By the terms of the United Nations partition plan for Palestine (1947), Jericho was allocated to Arab control; following the Arab-Israeli War (1948–49), the village became part of Jordan. Since the 1967 outbreak of hostilities between Israel and the Arab countries, Jericho has been included in Israeli-occupied Jordan. Pop. (1962 est.) 11,649.

JEROBOAM (Heb., "may the people grow numerous"), name of two early kings of Israel.

Jeroboam I, according to the Old Testament (1, 2 Kings, 2 Chron.), the first king of the Kingdom of Israel (r. 922–901 B.C.), a member of the tribe of Ephraim (q.v.). Before gaining the throne he led an unsuccessful plot against the life of King Solomon (q.v.) of Israel and Judah and fled to Egypt, remaining there until Solomon's death. He returned to Palestine to lead a revolt against Solomon's son and successor, Rehoboam (q.v.), and succeeded in establishing himself as king of the ten northern tribes of Israel, with Shechem as his capital. He set up shrines at Dan (now in Israel) and Bethel (qq.v.) and fostered cults alien to Judaism. He was succeeded at his death by his son Nadab, who reigned for only a year.

Jeroboam II, King of Israel (r. 786–746 B.C.), son of Joash, King of Israel (*see under* JOASH). During his reign Jeroboam recovered the lost provinces of Ammon and Moab (q.v.) from Damascus (q.v.). His reign, recorded in 2 Kings 13–15, was outwardly successful and prosperous, but he was denounced by the prophets (*see* PROPHECY) Amos and Hosea (qq.v.) for contributing to the ultimate doom of Israel. Jeroboam, considered the last of the powerful kings of Israel, was succeeded at his death by his son Zechariah, who was assassinated within a year.

JEROME, Saint (Lat. *Eusebius Hieronymus*) (345?–420), Father and doctor of the Church, Biblical scholar, born in Stridon, on the border of Dalmatia and Pannonia (roughly, present-day Yugoslavia). In 379 he was ordained a priest. He then spent three years in Constantinople (now İstanbul, Turkey) with the Eastern Father, Gregory of Nazianzus (q.v.). In 382 he went to Rome, where he became secretary to Pope Damasus I (*see under* DAMASUS) and gained much influence. Many persons placed themselves under his spiritual direction, including a noble Roman widow named Paula (347–404) and her daughter, both of whom followed him to the Holy Land in 385. He fixed his residence at Bethlehem in 386, Paula (later Saint Paula) having founded there four convents, three for nuns and one for monks; the latter was governed by Jerome himself. Here Jerome pursued his literary labors, accomplishing his most important work, the translation of the Bible into the common, or vulgar (popular), tongue; *see* VULGATE. He engaged in controversy not only with the heretics Jovinian (fl. 4th cent.) and Vigilantius (fl. 4th–5th cent.) and the adherents of Pelagianism (q.v.), but also with the monk and theologian Tyrannius Rufinus (345?–410) and the great Latin Father Saint Augustine (q.v.). Because of his conflict with the Pelagians, he went into hiding

Saint Jerome, an oil painting by the 16th-century Flemish artist Quentin Massys.
Metropolitan Museum of Art

JEROME, OF PRAGUE

for about two years; he died soon after his return. His feast day is Sept. 30. *See* FATHERS OF THE CHURCH.

JEROME OF PRAGUE (1360?–1416), Bohemian religious reformer, born in Prague (now in Czechoslovakia). He studied for some time at the University of Oxford, in England, where he became converted to the unorthodox doctrines of the English theologian John Wycliffe (q.v.). On returning to Prague in 1407, he became an associate of the Bohemian religious reformer John Huss (q.v.) and joined him in preaching against the abuses of the hierarchy of the Church and the profligacy of the clergy. When Huss was denounced by the Council of Constance (*see* CONSTANCE, COUNCIL OF) and arrested, Jerome hastened to Constance to defend him, but, on learning that he, too, would be condemned for his preaching, he attempted to return to Prague. He was arrested in Bavaria, however, and was returned to Constance. At first he recanted his views, but later withdrew his recantation and was burned at the stake as a heretic. *See also* REFORMATION.

JEROME, Jerome Klapka (1859–1927), British humorist and playwright, born in Walsall, Staffordshire, England. In his early years he was employed as a clerk, a teacher, an actor, and a journalist. He first gained a reputation as a writer with the publication in 1889 of two witty, anecdotal books, *Idle Thoughts of an Idle Fellow* and *Three Men in a Boat*. A few years later he became coeditor of the periodical *Idler* (1892–97) and editor of the weekly *To-Day* (1893–97). His first success in the field of drama was *The Passing of the Third Floor Back* (1908), which has been revived several times. He also wrote the amusing book *Stageland: Curious Habits and Customs of Its Inhabitants* (1890).

JERSEY, largest and southernmost of the Channel Islands (q.v.), situated in the English Channel, about 15 miles W. of the coast of Manche Department, France, and about 17 miles S.E. of Guernsey (q.v.). Generally oblong, it is about 10 mi. long and from 4 to 6¼ mi. wide. Precipitous rocky headlands, with elevations up to 500 ft., a deeply indented coast, and an interior tableland broken by numerous valleys are the outstanding physical features. Climatic conditions are equable, the highest and lowest recorded temperatures being 89° F. and 31° F. respectively. Precipitation averages about 25 inches annually.

Saint Helier, a seaport on the S. coast, is the administrative center and largest town. Other towns include Saint Aubin, and Gorey.

The raising of Jersey cattle, a breed that originated on the island, the cultivation of potatoes, tomatoes, fruits, and flowers, fishing, and tourism are the principal occupations.

Among points of interest in Jersey are numerous prehistoric megalithic monuments (q.v.), an 11th-century church, and the ruins of two medieval castles. Cargo and passenger steamships operate on regular schedules between the island and Guernsey, Saint Malo, France, and points in England. The island is also linked to Great Britain and France by air-transport lines.

Area of island, 45 sq.mi.; pop. (1971) 69,329.

JERSEY CATTLE. *See* CATTLE.

JERSEY CITY, second-largest city in New Jersey, and county seat of Hudson Co., on a peninsula bounded on the E. by Upper New York Bay and the Hudson R. and on the W. by Newark Bay and the Hackensack R., and about 7 miles E. of the center of Newark. The city is opposite the S. end of Manhattan Island, with which it is connected by several tunnels. It is served by railroad, an interurban subway system, and by overseas and coastwise steamships. The extensive commerce carried on at its 11 mi. of waterfront is part of the shipping trade of the Port of New York.

Most of Jersey City lies in a low and swampy area, but an extension of the Palisades (q.v.) runs through the city from N. to S.; the residential section of the city is largely centered on this height. Among the interesting structures in Jersey City is a huge electric clock, measuring 50 ft. in diameter, on one of the Colgate-Palmolive-Peet factories along the Hudson river front. The minute hand of the clock weighs more than a ton and moves 31 in. a minute. The city is the site of Saint Peter's College (Roman Catholic; men), established in 1872, and Jersey City State College, a teachers college. The city is governed under the mayoral system.

Commerce and Industry. Jersey City is one of the leading manufacturing centers on the Atlantic Coast. Industrial establishments, several of which produce products with widely known trade names, include railroad shops, foundries, machine shops, and factories manufacturing soap, perfume, lead pencils, cans and containers, electrical machinery, patent medicines, packed meats, macaroni, cheese, chemicals, gypsum, paints, varnishes, steel, cigarettes, and antiseptics.

History. The region was first settled by the Dutch and was part of the patroonship of Pavonia, granted to Michael Pauw in 1630. The site of the present city was known as Powles Hook (Paulus Hoeck), and was first settled in 1633. A highway between New York and Philadelphia was built through the settlement in 1764, and in the same year a ferry to New York was established. During the American Revolution the British took the American fort at Powles Hook in 1776 and occupied it until 1779, when it was retaken by the Americans commanded by Major Henry ("Light-Horse Harry") Lee (*see under* LEE). In 1804 a town was laid out at Powles Hook by a private corporation, and in 1820 it was incorporated as the City of Jersey, a part of Bergen Township. It was reincorporated as a separate town in 1838, made the county seat in 1840, and chartered as a city in 1855. During the 1920's the mayor of Jersey City, Frank Hague (1876–1956), became political boss of the entire State. He held power until 1949, when accusations of widespread corruption caused his downfall.

Population. Between 1910 and 1950 the population of Jersey City increased from 267,779 to 299,017. In 1960 the population was 276,101; in 1970 it was 260,545.

JERUSALEM (Ar. *El Quds esh Sherif*; Heb. *Yerushalayim*; anc. *Hierosolyma*), partitioned city of the Palestine region of Asia, comprising New Jerusalem (the "New City"), which is the capital of Israel, and Old Jerusalem (the "Old City"), which is part of the Hashemite Kingdom of Jordan. Jerusalem is about 35 miles E. of the Mediterranean Sea, about 15 miles W. of the northern extremity of the Dead Sea, and some 35 miles S.E. of Tel Aviv-Jaffa. The Old City, divided into Armenian, Christian, Jewish, and Muslim sections, is enclosed by a wall with gates. The extant walls are remnants of those constructed in the 16th century by the Turks. The Christian section, in the N.W., contains the New Gate, shares the Jaffa Gate with the Armenian section on the S., and shares with the Muslim section on the N. the Damascus Gate. The Muslim section, in the northeastern portion of the Old City, contain Herod's Gate, Saint Stephen's Gate, and the Golden Gate, E. of which is located the Mount of Olives (*see* OLIVES, MOUNT OF) and the Garden of Gethsemane (q.v.). The Jewish section, occupying the southern portion, contains the Zion Gate, S. of which is Mt. Zion and King David's Tomb. To the W. and S.W. of the Old City is New Jerusalem, which has developed since the middle of the 19th century; it extends over the surrounding hills into garden suburbs and then desert, and its broad avenues, modern apartments, and office buildings are in contrast to the narrow, twisting streets and alleys, and meager dwellings of the Old City. The population of Jerusalem (1972) is 314,100 (Jews, 232,400; non-Jews, 81,700).

The Old City is sacred to Christians as the site of Jesus Christ's (q.v.) last days on earth; it is sacred to Jews as the historic symbol of the Jewish homeland and capital of the first Jewish kingdom; and it is sacred to Muslims as the site of the ascent into heaven of their prophet Muhammad (q.v.). The notable structures of the Old City are the Christian Church of the Holy Sepulcher, built over the 4th-century basilica, which in turn was erected over the traditional tomb of Christ; the Jewish Wailing Wall, the remnant of the great Temple built by Herod the Great (*see under* HEROD), King of Judea; the Muslim Dome of the Rock, better known as the Mosque of Omar, built upon the site where Muhammad is said to have ascended to heaven; and the Mosque of Al Aksa, one of Islam's most sacred shrines. The chief historical landmark of the New City is the Citadel, a 14th-century structure on the site of Herod's fortress. Other points of interest are the Palestine Archeological Museum, Hebrew University of Jerusalem, and the buildings of the Israeli Knesset (Parliament).

Holy City of the Jews. The site of Jerusalem was occupied during the Stone Age; these aborigines were driven out much later, in the period 5000–4000 B.C., by a people called in the Old Testament the Canaanites (q.v.), who had advanced into the Bronze Age; *see* PALESTINIAN ARCHEOLOGY. The invaders, a mixed people among whom the Jebusites were dominant, came under Egyptian rule in the 15th century B.C., during the conquests of King Thutmose III (*see under* THUTMOSE). Then, in about 1250 B.C., the Hebrews began their conquest of Canaan (*see* JEWS: *The Hebrews in Canaan*), initially under their leader Joshua (q.v.). So powerfully fortified was Jerusalem, however, that it did not fall until more than 200 years later, when David (q.v.) finally captured it some years after being anointed king of Israel (2 Sam. 5:6–9; 1 Chron. 11:4–7).

According to the Old Testament, David decided to make Jerusalem his residence and the capital of his country. The new king brought the Ark of Jehovah (*see* ARK OF THE COVENANT) to his capital from its obscurity at Kirjah-Jearim (a holy place of the time, W. of Jerusalem) and installed it in a new tabernacle (2 Sam. 6:1–17), built a royal palace and a number of other buildings, and strengthened the city's fortifications. David's son and successor Solomon (q.v.) continued the development of Jerusalem. He built a city wall and many buildings on a scale of magnificence previously unknown to Israel. Solomon's principal buildings were a Temple (*see* TEMPLE: *Temple at Jerusalem*) and a new royal palace, encircled by a wall. The palace, built on

In Jerusalem the building of the Young Men's Christian Association, with its domed tower, blends Western and Eastern architecture. UPI

successive terraces, consisted of a house, constructed of cedar beams and pillars brought from the forests of Lebanon, that was 50 cubits wide, 100 cubits long, and 30 cubits high (perhaps 75 ft. wide, 150 ft. long, and 45 ft. high); the throne hall; the palace proper, or royal apartments; and the prison (1 Kings 5–7, Neh. 3:25–27, Jer. 32:2). The courts and buildings of the Temple were constructed on a level above the palace. The main building of the Temple was considered of great beauty, but was comparatively small, being only 20 cubits wide and 60 cubits long (about 30 ft. wide and 90 ft. long), exclusive of the porch and the side chambers. The Temple was built of cedar and of stone (1 Kings 6:3–6) and was surrounded by a court that contained the altar of burnt offerings and a "molten sea" or bronze water tank (1 Kings 7:9–12, 23–47).

Jerusalem continued to expand after Solomon's reign until the ten northern tribes of Israel seceded from the rule of the house of David, after which the importance of the city, now the capital of but two tribes, Judah and Benjamin (qq.v.), diminished greatly. Jerusalem was wracked for the next two centuries by a succession of sieges, incursions, and unsuccessful military undertakings that were physically and financially costly. Not until the reigns of King Uzziah of Judah (r. 783–742 B.C.) and his son Jotham (r. 742–735 B.C.) did the city begin to regain its previous status (2 Chron. 26, 27). Between this period and the rise of the powerful Maccabee family (see MACCABEES), about six centuries later, the history of Jerusalem is that of the Jews (see JEWS: *The Kingdom* and *Subject Judea*); see also PALESTINE: *History*. Under the Maccabees, Jerusalem entered upon an era of unprecedented prosperity. It was the holy city of Judaism and the great pilgrim shrine of the Jewish world.

Roman Occupation. Conquest by the Romans under the general and statesman Pompey the Great (q.v.) in 63 B.C. resulted in no serious material disaster to the city. Its greatest prosperity was attained under Herod the Great. Besides a complete reconstruction of the Temple on a scale truly magnificent, involving the expenditure of vast sums of money, he undertook the building of the Xystus, an open place surrounded by a gallery; his own great palace, on the western side of the city; and a hippodrome, theater, and large reservoir. In addition to these works, minor improvements were made, including the general strengthening of the fortifications. Less than a century later, however, during a rebellion of Jews against Roman authority, Titus (q.v.), son of the Roman emperor Vespasian (q.v.), captured and razed the city in 70 A.D.;

only a few remnants of the western fortifications were left standing. With this calamity, the history of ancient Jerusalem came to a close.

The Roman emperor Hadrian (q.v.) visited the city, which was largely in ruins, about 130 A.D. and began its reconstruction. The desperate rebellion of the Jews, led by Bar Cocheba (q.v.), against the Romans between the years 132 and 135 caused the emperor to make the new city a pagan one and to prohibit all Jews from entering it. The new city was called Aelia Capitolina (q.v.). The wall with which Hadrian encircled it was, in general, on the line of the old wall, except on the s., where it left a large portion of the former city outside of the enclosure.

A Christian City. Little is known of the city from the time of Hadrian to that of Roman emperor Constantine I (q.v.), called the Great, when Christianity became the religion of the Empire. The population of Jerusalem was gradually supplemented by Christians, and pilgrims flocked to the city. The Church of the Holy Sepulcher was built at the order of Emperor Constantine. Other buildings of like character were subsequently built, and Jerusalem became a Christian city. Among the noteworthy buildings belonging to this period are the Church of Saint Stephen, N. of the city, built by the Byzantine empress Eudocia (d. about 460), who also rebuilt the ancient southern wall; and the great Church of Saint Mary on the temple hill, built by the Byzantine emperor Justinian I (q.v.).

The Christian city, after being captured by the Persians under King Khosrau II (see under KHOSRAU) in 614, but recovered by the Byzantine emperor Heraclius (q.v.) in 628, was taken in 637 by the Muslims under the caliph Omar I (q.v.). A shrine, the Dome of the Rock, was erected over the rock that was believed to be the altar place of Solomon's Temple. The Christians were treated leniently by their Muslim conquerors, but when the Egyptian Fatimid caliphs (see CALIPH) became the rulers of Jerusalem, in 969, the situation became more precarious. The Seljuk Turks (see SELJUKS) conquered the city in 1071, and their maltreatment of Christians and destruction of the Church of the Holy Sepulcher were causes of the Crusades (q.v.). In 1099 the Crusaders, under the French nobleman Godfrey of Bouillon (q.v.), gained possession of the city and slaughtered many of its inhabitants. Jerusalem became once more a Christian city and the capital of the so-called Latin Kingdom (see JERUSALEM, LATIN KINGDOM OF) until its capture in 1187 by the Muslim leader Saladin (q.v.).

The Recent History of Jerusalem. Concerned with the contemporary histories of Palestine and the state of Israel (q.v.), Jerusalem was the site of some of the most bitter fighting between the Jews and the Arabs in the conflict over partition of Palestine. The General Assembly of the United Nations, in its original partition plan of Nov. 29, 1947, proposed to establish Jerusalem and its environs as an international enclave, some 280 sq.mi. in area. The objective was to assure free access for all religious groups to the holy places of the city. In the spring of 1948, however, during the war over partition between the Jews and the Arab League (q.v.), the opposing armies of Israel and of Jordan seized Jerusalem, with Israel occupying the western portion of the city, containing the modern residential and business sections, and Jordan occupying the eastern portion, including the Old City. In addition, the Israeli forces held a corridor to Jerusalem extending from Tel Aviv-Jaffa on the coast. In the armistice signed on April 3, 1949, between Israel and Jordan, both sides recognized the other's holdings in Jerusalem. The Israeli government proposed the internationalization of the Old City, but Jordan conditioned consent to this proposal upon the rest of the city's being placed under international administration. In 1950 the New City was made the capital of Israel. During the Arab-Israeli war of June, 1967, Israeli forces captured the Old City, and, subsequently, the Israeli Knesset unilaterally decreed the reunification of the entire city of Jerusalem.

JERUSALEM ARTICHOKE. See ARTICHOKE, JERUSALEM.

JERUSALEM, LATIN KINGDOM OF, kingdom, centered in Jerusalem but also including other parts of Palestine and parts of ancient Syria, established by the Crusaders in 1099 and lasting until 1291, although in ever-changing form; see CRUSADES. When, on July 15, 1099, Jerusalem was taken, it became necessary for the Christian conquerors to establish some permanent rule for the Holy City and for such other conquests as Antioch (now Antâkya, Turkey) and Edessa (now Urfa, Turkey). They adopted the feudal system of government, the only system they knew well; see FEUDALISM. The French nobleman Godfrey of Bouillon (q.v.) was elected baron and defender of the Holy Sepulcher by the nobles and churchmen who controlled the First Crusade. Thereafter, the succession was not elective but hereditary. When Godfrey died in 1100 he was succeeded by his brother, Baldwin I (see under BALDWIN), who took the title of king and ruled until 1118. He in turn was succeeded by his cousin, Baldwin II, who was followed by his son-in-law, Fulk V the

JERVIS BAY

Young, Count of Anjou (1092–1143). Under Fulk the kingdom reached the highest point in its development, and most of Syria was in the hands of the Christians. In 1187 Saladin (q.v.), Sultan of Egypt and Syria, reconquered the city of Jerusalem, but the Latin Kingdom persisted. The Crusaders regained the city in 1228 under Frederick II (q.v.), Holy Roman Emperor, who was crowned king of Jerusalem the following year. The Muslims retook Jerusalem in 1244 in the first of a series of victories for Islam that finally, with the reconquest of Acre (now in Israel) in 1291, brought the Latin Kingdom to an end.

JERVIS BAY, harbor of Australia, inlet of the Pacific Ocean, on the E. coast of New South Wales, 90 miles S.W. of Sydney. The harbor, 3 mi. across at the mouth, widens to 6 mi., and is 10 mi. long. Summer resorts are on the W. and S. shores. In 1915, the harbor and 28 sq.mi. of the S. peninsula sheltering it were transferred by New South Wales to the federal government to serve as a port for Canberra. Port facilities, however, have not been extensively developed.

JESSAMINE. *See* JASMINE.

JESTBOOK, once popular literary genre, consisting of a collection of jokes and anecdotes, some satirizing contemporary institutions and others developed from folklore. Jestbooks were especially popular in Italy during the 15th century; the earliest examples were written in Latin and were known as *facetiae* ("jokes"). Notable among the early Italian collections was the *Liber Facetiarum* written by the Italian humanist scholar Giovanni Francesco Poggio Bracciolini; *see* POGGIO BRACCIOLINI. This work was a collection of satires, sometimes coarse, on the monks and secular orders of the Church of the period, and many of his jokes found their way into the anecdotal literature of Italy, France, Germany, and England.

Jestbooks began to flourish in England and other European countries in the 16th century, and continued to be popular for about 200 years. A notable early English jestbook was *A Hundred Merry Tales* (about 1526). Authorship of many of these collections was attributed by publishers to well-known persons in order to enhance the sales value of the jestbooks. A notable example in England was *Joe Miller's Jests,* or *The Wit's Vade Mecum* (1739), in which only three of the jokes had been coined by Joseph Miller (1684–1738), a contemporary popular comedian. At a later date, after jestbooks had ceased to have a popular vogue, jokes and anecdotes of the same type were included in novels of manners. The older English jests were collected and edited by the literary historian William Carew Hazlitt (1834–1913) under the title *Old English Jest Books* (3 vol., 1863–64).

JESUITS or **SOCIETY OF JESUS,** religious order (*see* ORDERS, RELIGIOUS) of men in the Roman Catholic Church, founded by Ignatius of Loyola (*see* LOYOLA, IGNATIUS OF, SAINT) in 1534 and confirmed by Pope Paul III (*see under* PAUL) in 1540. The motto of the order is *Ad Majorem Dei Goriam* (Lat., "To the greater glory of God"), and its object is the spread of the church by preaching and teaching or the fulfillment of whatever else is judged the most urgent need of the church at the time. Education has been its chief activity almost from the outset, and it has made notable contributions to scholarship in both theology and the secular disciplines.

Preparation for Membership. The preparation required of a candidate, especially for membership as a priest rather than as a brother (temporal coadjutor), is considerably longer than that required for the secular priesthood or for membership in other religious orders. After two years in seclusion and prayer as a so-called novice, the candidate takes simple vows of poverty, chastity, and obedience, and becomes a so-called scholastic. He then typically spends two years of study in review of classical subjects and three years studying philosophy, mathematics, and the physical sciences. Several years of teaching follow, succeeded by three years' study of theology, after which ordination to the priesthood takes place. Following a fourth year of theological study and a year of retirement and prayer, the candidate is awarded his final grade, becoming either a so-called coadjutor or a so-called professed. The coadjutors take final simple vows of poverty, chastity, and obedience, but the professed take these vows as solemn vows and add an additional solemn vow to go wherever the pope may send them; furthermore, the professed take five simple vows, among them the renunciation of ecclesiastical office beyond their order unless by directive of the order. The order is governed by a superior general, residing in Rome, who is elected for life by the general congregation of the order, consisting of representatives of the various provinces; there are now some sixty-five regional provinces in the world, each under its own father provincial.

History. The aim of Ignatius of Loyola in forming his band was to make a pilgrimage to the Holy Land to convert the Muslims; all access to the Holy Land was barred, however, by the outbreak of war with the Ottoman Turks, and the members of the order submitted to the pope a constitution which bound them to go as mis-

Saint Ignatius of Loyola, founder of the Society of Jesus, an early 17th-century painting by the Flemish artist Peter Paul Rubens. Bettmann Archive

sionaries to any place the pope might direct; *see* PALESTINE: *History*. After the constitution was approved, Loyola was elected the first superior general of the order.

The development of the order was rapid. Its members took leading parts in the Counter-Reformation (*see* REFORMATION: *Counter-Reformation*), establishing schools and colleges (principally offering a high-school education) throughout Europe. For 150 years they were the leaders in European education; by 1640 they had more than 500 colleges throughout Europe; by about a century later the number of colleges had increased to more than 650 and, in addition, the order had total or partial charge of two dozen universities. There were also more than 200 seminaries and houses of study for Jesuits. The education of Jesuits in the period of the Counter-Reformation was designed to strengthen Roman Catholicism against Protestant expansion. Among the laity the Jesuits were concerned chiefly with the education of the nobility and those of wealth, although they did conduct trade schools and, in mission countries, schools for the poor.

In the mission field (*see* MISSIONARY MOVEMENTS) the expansion of the order was equally great. Missions were established by Francis Xavier (q.v.) in India and Japan, and the order spread to the interior of China and the coast of Africa. Letters from the Jesuit missionaries in Canada, containing ethnological, historical, and scientific information, were published as the *Jesuit Relations* and form a unique and valuable source of information concerning the aboriginal tribes of that country. The most famous work of the Jesuit missionaries in the New World, however, was the establishment in the order's South American provinces of so-called reductions, or village communities of native Indians under the spiritual and temporal direction of the priests. The most resoundingly successful were the reductions of Paraguay. In that country for almost 200 years the Jesuits conducted a communal nation of Indians, founding thirty-two villages with a total population of about 160,000; they taught the Indians agriculture, mechanical arts, and commerce and trained a small army for defense of the settlements.

The history of the Jesuit order has been marked by a steadily increasing prejudice against it, especially in Roman Catholic countries. Their devotion to the papacy called forth opposition from nationalistic rulers and leaders, and their zeal for ecclesiastical reform antagonized the clergy. At one time or another the order has been expelled from every country in Europe, and in 1773 a coalition of powers under Bourbon (q.v.) influence induced Pope Clement XIV (see under CLEMENT) to issue a brief suppressing the order. Frederick II, King of Prussia, and Catherine II (qq.v.), Empress of Russia, both admirers of Jesuit education and scholarship, however, refused to give the brief the publication necessary to make it effective, and in those countries the order survived in local organizations until 1814, when Pope Pius VII (see under PIUS) reestablished the Jesuits on a worldwide basis. Political and religious opposition also revived; since the reestablishment of the order, it has been free from attack only in Denmark, Sweden, Great Britain, and the United States.

Membership. In the mid-1960's the order had about 36,000 members; about one fourth were in the U.S. The order maintained in this country twenty-eight colleges and universities and forty-nine secondary schools, as well as eighteen seismological stations and a number of radio broadcasting stations. The Jesuits here and elsewhere carry on an extensive program of periodical publication, and they are prolific authors of books and articles. W.N.C.

JESUITS' BARK. See CINCHONA.

JESUP, Morris Ketchum (1830–1908), American banker and philanthropist, born in Westport, Conn. He entered the banking business in New York City in 1852 and retired from it thirty-two years later. During his business career, he was an active member of the New York City Mission and Tract Society, of which he became president in 1881. He was a founder of the Young Men's Christian Association (q.v.) in the United States, and in 1872 he became president of the association. His financial contributions to further the advancement of science (about $2,000,000) were distributed principally through the American Museum of Natural History (q.v.), which he helped to found in 1869 and of which he was president from 1881 to 1907. He also made large contributions to the arctic expeditions led by Robert Edwin Peary (q.v.) and financed the Jesup North Pacific Expedition (1897–1903). Jesup was also a generous contributor to the National Association of Audubon Societies and to many other educational institutions. From 1889 to 1907 he served as president of the New York Chamber of Commerce.

JESUS, son of Sirach. See ECCLESIASTICUS.

JESUS CHRIST (between 8 and 4 B.C.–about 29 A.D.), the central figure of Christianity (q.v.), born in Bethlehem in Judea (see PALESTINE). The chronology of the Christian era is reckoned from a 6th-century dating of the year of His birth, which is now recognized as being from four to eight years in error. Jesus is believed by the great majority of Christians to be the incarnate Son of God, and to have been divinely conceived by Mary, the wife of Joseph, a carpenter of Nazareth; see JOSEPH, SAINT; MARY, SAINT. The name "Jesus" is derived from a Greek rendering of the Hebrew name Joshua, or in full *Yehoshuah* ("Jehovah is deliverance"). The title Christ (q.v.) is derived from the Greek *Christos*, a translation of the Hebrew *māshīakh* ("anointed one") or Messiah (q.v.). "Christ" was used by Jesus' early followers, who regarded Him as the promised deliverer of Israel (q.v.; see JEWS; JUDAISM), and later was made part of Jesus' proper name by the Church, which regards Him as the redeemer of all mankind.

The principal sources of information concerning His life are the Gospels (see GOSPEL), written in the latter half of the 1st century to facilitate the spread of Christianity throughout the ancient Western world. The Epistles of Saint Paul (q.v.) and the book of Acts (see ACTS OF THE APOSTLES), also contain information about Jesus. The scantiness of additional source material, and the theological nature of Biblical records, caused some 19th-century Bible scholars to doubt His historical existence. Others, differently interpreting the available sources, produced naturalistic, so-called biographies of Jesus. Today, however, scholars generally agree that His existence is authenticated, both by Christian writers and by a number of Roman and Jewish historians.

Birth and Early Life. Two of the Gospels, those of Saint Matthew and Saint Luke (qq.v.), provide

JESUS CHRIST

information about Jesus' birth and childhood; see MATTHEW, GOSPEL ACCORDING TO SAINT; LUKE, GOSPEL ACCORDING TO SAINT. They also provide genealogies tracing Jesus' descent through the Hebrew patriarch Abraham and the 10th-century King David (Matt. 1:1–17; Luke 3:23–38). Presumably, the genealogies are offered as proofs of Jesus' Messiahship. According to Matthew (1:18–25) and Luke (1:1–2:20), Jesus was miraculously conceived by his mother. Christ was born at Bethlehem, where Joseph and Mary had gone to comply with the Roman edict of enrollment for the census; see CHRISTMAS. Matthew alone (2:13–23) describes the flight into Egypt, when Joseph and Mary took the child out of reach of the Judean king Herod the Great (see under HEROD). See also EPIPHANY. Only Luke relates the compliance of Joseph and Mary with the Jewish law, which required circumcision (q.v.) and presentation of the firstborn son at the Temple in Jerusalem (2:21–24); Luke also describes their later journey (2:41–51) with the young Jesus to the Temple for the Passover or Pesach (q.v.) feast. Nothing is told in any of the Gospels concerning Jesus from the time He was twelve until the time He began His public ministry, about eighteen years later.

Beginning of His Public Ministry. All three Synoptic Gospels (the first three Gospels, so called because they present a similar overall view of the life of Christ) record Jesus' public ministry as beginning after the imprisonment of John the Baptist (q.v.), and as lasting for about one year. The Gospel of John (see JOHN, GOSPEL ACCORDING TO SAINT) describes it as beginning with the choosing of His first disciples (1:40–51), and as lasting for perhaps three years.

The account of the public ministry and immediately preceding events is generally the same in the Synoptic Gospels. Each describes the baptism of Jesus in the Jordan River by John the Baptist. Each reports that after the baptism Jesus retired to the neighboring wilderness for a forty-day period of fasting and meditation. All three Synoptists mention that in this period, which some Bible scholars view as a time of ritual preparation, the Devil, or Satan, tried to tempt Jesus. Matthew (4:3–9) and Luke (4:3–12) add descriptions of the temptations brought forth by the Devil.

After Jesus' baptism and retirement in the wilderness, He returned to Galilee, visited His home in Nazareth (Luke 4:16–30), where His fellow townsmen objected to Him, and then moved to Capernaum and began teaching there. About this time, according to the Synoptists, Jesus called His first disciples, "Simon who is called Peter and Andrew his brother" (Matt. 4:18), and "James the son of Zebedee and John his brother" (Matt. 4:21). Later, as His followers increased, Jesus selected a total of twelve disciples to work closely with Him; see APOSTLE.

Growth of Jesus' Following. Using Capernaum as a base, Jesus, accompanied by His twelve chosen disciples, traveled to neighboring towns and villages, proclaiming the advent of the Kingdom of God as had many of the Hebrew prophets before Him (see PROPHECY). When the wounded in body and spirit asked help from Him, He sought to heal them with the power of faith. He stressed the infinite love of God for the lowest and meanest of mankind, and promised pardon and eternal life in Heaven to the most hardened sinners, provided their repentance was sincere. The essence of these teachings is presented in Matt. 5:1–7:27, in the so-called Sermon on the Mount, containing the Beatitudes (5:3–12) and the Lord's Prayer (6:9–13). His emphasis on moral sincerity rather than strict adherence to Jewish ritual incurred the enmity of the Pharisees (q.v.), who feared that Jesus' teachings might lead to disregard for the authority of the Law, or Torah (q.v.). Other Jews feared that Jesus' activities and followers might prejudice the Roman authorities against any restoration of the monarchy.

Despite this growing opposition, His popularity with the populace, especially with social outcasts and the oppressed, increased. Eventually, the enthusiasm of His followers led them to make an attempt to "take him by force, to make him a king" (John 6:15). Jesus, however, frustrated this attempt, withdrawing with His disciples by ship over the Sea of Galilee (Lake Tiberias) to Capernaum (John 6:15–21). In Capernaum, He delivered a discourse in which He proclaimed Himself "the bread of life" (John 6:35). This discourse, emphasizing spiritual communion with God, bewildered many in His audience. They thought the discourse a "hard saying" (John 6:60), and thereupon they "went back, and walked no more with him" (John 6:66).

Thenceforth, Jesus divided His time into periods of traveling to cities in and outside the province of Galilee, and periods of instruction (of His disciples) and retirement in Bethany (Mark 11:11–12) and Ephraim (John 11:54), two villages near Jerusalem. The Synoptists generally agree that Jesus spent most of His time in Galilee, but John centers His public ministry in the province of Judea, reporting that Jesus made numerous visits to Jerusalem. His discourses and the miracles He performed at this time, particu-

JESUS CHRIST

larly the raising of Lazarus in Bethany (John 11:1–44), made many people believe "on him" (John 11:45). The most significant moment in Jesus' public ministry, however, was Simon Peter's realization at Caesarea Philippi that Jesus was the Christ (Matt. 16:16; Mark 8:29; Luke 9:20), although Jesus had not previously revealed this (according to the Synoptic Gospels) to Peter or the other disciples. This revelation, and the subsequent prediction by Jesus of His death and Resurrection (q.v.), the conditions of discipleship that He laid down, and His Transfiguration (at which time a voice from Heaven was heard proclaiming Jesus to be the Son of God, thus confirming the revelation) are the primary authority for the claims and historical work of the Christian Church. (Explicit authorization by Jesus is recorded in Matt. 16:17–19.)

The Last Days. On the approach of Passover, Jesus traveled toward Jerusalem for the last time. (John mentions numerous trips to Jerusalem and more than one Passover, whereas the Synoptists roughly divide the public ministry into a Galilean section and a Judean section and record one Passover, which came after Jesus left Galilee for Judea and Jerusalem.) On the Sunday before the Passover, Jesus entered Jerusalem, where He was met by crowds of people who acclaimed Him enthusiastically; see PALM SUNDAY. There (on Monday and Tuesday, according to the Synoptists), He drove from the Temple the traders and money changers who, by long-established custom, had been allowed to transact business in the outer court (Mark 11:15–19), and He disputed with the chief priests, the scribes, the Pharisees, and the Sadducees (q.v.), questions about His authority, tribute to Caesar (see AUGUSTUS), and the Resurrection. On Tuesday, Jesus also revealed to His disciples the signs that would usher in His Parousia or Second Coming; see SECOND ADVENT OF CHRIST.

On Wednesday, Christ was anointed in Bethany in preparation for His burial (Matt. 26:6–13; Mark 14:3–9). Meanwhile in Jerusalem, the priests and scribes, concerned that Jesus' activities would turn the Romans against them and the Jewish people (John 11:48) conspired with Judas Iscariot, one of His disciples, to arrest and kill Jesus by stealth, "for they feared the people" (Luke 22:2). John 11:47–53 places the conspiracy before Jesus' triumphal entry into Jerusalem. On Thursday, Jesus ate the Passover supper with His disciples, and during the meal referred to His imminent betrayal and death as a sacrifice for the sins of mankind; see MAUNDY THURSDAY. In blessing the unleavened bread and wine during the Passover services, He called the bread His body and the wine His "blood of the new testament, which is shed for many for the remission of sins" (Matt. 26:23), and bid the disciples partake of each. This ritual, the Lord's Supper (q.v.), has been repeated by Christians in worship services ever since, and has become the central sacrament (q.v.) in the Christian Church.

After the meal Jesus and His disciples went to the Mount of Olives, where, according to Matthew (26:30–32) and Mark (14:26–28), Jesus said that He would be "raised up" (from the dead). Knowing then that the hour of His death was near, Jesus retired to the Garden of Gethsemane, where, "being in an agony" (Luke 22:44), He meditated and prayed. A crowd sent by the chief priests and the elders of the Jews, and led by Judas Iscariot, arrested Him in Gethsemane.

Trial and Crucifixion. According to John (18: 13–24), Jesus was brought after His arrest to Annas, the father-in-law of the High Priest Caiaphas, for a preliminary examination. The Synoptists make no mention of this incident: they report only that Jesus was taken to a meeting of the supreme council of the Jews, the Sanhedrin (q.v.). At the council meeting, Caiaphas asked Jesus to declare whether He was "the Christ, the Son of God" (Matt. 26:63). Upon His affirmation (Mark 14:62), the council condemned Jesus to death for blasphemy. But only the Roman procurator was empowered to inflict capital punishment; and so, on Friday morning, Jesus was led before the procurator, Pontius Pilate, for sentencing. Before judging, Pilate asked Him if He was King of the Jews. Jesus replied, "Thou sayest it" (Mark 15:2). (In Matthew, Jesus remains silent, but He answers at length in John 18:33–38.) Thereafter, Pilate tried several expedients to save Jesus before ultimately leaving the decision to the people. When the populace insisted on His death, Pilate (Matt. 27:24) ordered Him executed. (The actual role of Pilate has been much debated by historians. The early Church tended to place the major blame on the Jews, and to deal less harshly with Pilate.)

Jesus was taken to Golgotha and nailed to a cross (q.v.), the Roman punishment for political offenders and criminals; see CRUCIFIXION. Two robbers were crucified also, one on each side of Him. And on the cross, above His head, "they put the charge against him, which read 'This is Jesus the King of the Jews'" (Matt. 27:37). Late in the day, His body was taken down, and, because of the approach of the Sabbath (q.v.), when burial was not permitted, was hastily laid in a nearby tomb by Joseph of Arimathea. (John 19:39–42 relates that Joseph was assisted by Nicodemus); see GOOD FRIDAY.

JESUS CHRIST

"The Deposition", an early 16th-century painting by the Flemish painter Gerard David.
Frick Collection

The Resurrection. Early on the following Sunday, "Mary Magdalene, and Mary the mother of James" (Mark 16:1), going to the tomb to anoint Jesus' body for burial, found the tomb empty. (Matt. 28:2 reports that an angel appeared after an earthquake and rolled back the stone.) Inside the tomb, "a young man" (Mark 16:5) clothed in white announced to them that Jesus had risen. (This news is announced by the angel in Matt. 28:5–6, and by two men "in shining garments" in Luke 24:4. According to John 21:11–18, Mary Magdalene saw two angels and then the risen Christ.) Later on the same day, according to Luke, John, and Mark (see MARK, SAINT; MARK, GOSPEL ACCORDING TO SAINT), Jesus appeared to the women and to other of the disciples in various places in and around Jerusalem. Most of the disciples did not doubt that they had again seen and heard the Master they had known and followed during the time of His ministry in Galilee and Judea. A few disciples, however, doubted it at first (Matt. 28:17); and Thomas, who had not been present at these first appearances, also doubted that Jesus had risen (John 20:24–29). As recorded in the New Testament, the Resurrection of Jesus became one of the most compelling doctrines of Christianity; for, according to this doctrine, by rising from the dead, Jesus gave man hope of a life after death in the Kingdom of Heaven. See also EASTER.

All the Gospels add that for a brief time after His Resurrection Jesus further instructed His disciples in matters pertaining to the Kingdom of God. He also commissioned them to "Go . . . and teach all nations, baptizing them in the name of the Father, and of the Son, and of the Holy Ghost" (Matt. 28:19); see BAPTISM; TRINITY Finally, according to Luke (24:50–51), at Bethany He was seen to ascend into the heavens by His disciples. Acts 1:2–12 reports that the Ascension (q.v.) occurred forty days after Jesus' Resurrection. The doctrines that Jesus expounded and

197

JET

those concerning Him were subsequently developed into the principal tenets of Christian theology.

Theology. The life and teachings of Jesus were often matters for dispute and varying interpretation in Christian history; see CHRISTIAN CHURCH, HISTORY OF THE. Early in the life of the Church, for example, it became necessary to regularize beliefs about Jesus and His role, to aid in conversion and to answer those Christians who adopted views unacceptable to Church leaders. For discussion of some of these questions, see such separate entries as CHRISTOLOGY; HERESY; INCARNATION; THEOLOGY. Traditions later coalesced around various events concerning the life of Christ; see, for example, CHURCH CALENDAR; FESTIVALS AND FEASTS. For the central teachings of present-day Christianity, see CHRISTIANITY. See also RELIGION: *The Religions*.

See separate articles on persons and places mentioned.

JET, hard, compact, deep-black variety of lignite (q.v.) or brown coal. It has a hardness ranging from 2 to 2.5 and a sp.gr. ranging from 1.15 to 1.3. It is easily cut and carved; it takes a high polish and is used in making ornaments and inexpensive jewelry. The most important center for production of jet and manufacture of jet articles is Whitby, Great Britain. Pennsylvania anthracite coal is often used in place of jet; other substitutes are black, cryptocrystalline varieties of quartz, black glass, and certain plastics.

JET PROPULSION, thrust imparting forward motion to an object as a reaction to the rearward expulsion of a high-velocity liquid or gaseous stream.

A simple example of jet propulsion is the motion of an inflated balloon when the air is suddenly discharged. While the opening is held closed, the air pressure within the balloon is equal in all directions; when the stem is released, the air expands and the internal pressure is less at the open end than at the opposite end, causing the balloon to dart forward. It is not the pressure of the escaping air pushing against the outside atmosphere but the difference between high and low pressures inside the balloon that propels it.

An actual jet engine does not operate quite as simply as a balloon, although the basic principle is the same. More important than pressure imbalance is the acceleration to high velocities of the jet leaving the engine. This is achieved by forces in the engine that enable the gas to flow backward forming the jet. From Newton's second law (see NEWTON'S LAWS OF MOTION), it can be seen that these forces are proportional to the rate at which the momentum of the gas is increased. For a jet engine, this is related to the rate of mass flow multiplied by the rearward-leaving jet velocity. From Newton's third law, which states that for every force there must be an equal and opposite reaction, the rearward force is balanced by a forward reaction, known as thrust. This thrusting action is similar to the recoil of a gun, which increases as both the mass of the projectile and its leaving velocity are increased. High-thrust engines, therefore, require both large rates of mass flow and high jet exit velocities, which can only be achieved by increasing internal engine pressures and by increasing the volume of the gas by combustion.

Jet-propulsion devices are used primarily in high-speed, high-altitude aircraft, in spacecraft, and in missiles; see AIRPLANE: *Propulsion;* ASTRONAUTICS; GUIDED MISSILES. The source of power is a high-energy fuel that is burned at intense pressures to produce the large gas volume needed for high jet exit velocities. The oxidizer required for the combustion may be the oxygen in the air that is drawn into the engine and compressed, or the oxidizer may be carried in the vehicle, so that the engine is independent of a surrounding atmosphere. Engines that depend on the atmosphere for oxygen include turbojets, turbofans, turboprops, ramjets, and pulse jets; see below. Nonatmospheric engines are usually called rocket engines; see below. See also ROCKET.

ATMOSPHERIC JET ENGINES

All atmospheric engines depend on the flow of a large mass of air that is first compressed, then burned with the addition of fuel, and finally expanded to low pressures through a nozzle in order to achieve a high jet exit velocity.

Turbojet Engines. The most widely used atmospheric engines are turbojets (see diagram, *a*). After air has been drawn into the engine through an inlet, the air pressure is increased by a compressor before it enters the combustion chamber (*see* AIR COMPRESSOR). The power required to drive the compressor is provided by a turbine, which is placed between the combustion chamber and the nozzle.

Practically all airborne jet engines utilize an axial-flow compressor, in which the air flows generally in the direction of the shaft axis through alternate rows of stationary and rotating blades, called stators and rotors respectively. The blades are arranged so that the air enters each row at a high velocity. As it flows through the blade passage the air is decelerated to a lower velocity, and the pressure is increased. Modern axial-flow compressors can increase the

JET PROPULSION

pressure twenty-four times in fifteen stages, with each set of stators and rotors making up a stage.

The compressed air then enters the combustion chamber, in which it is mixed with finely atomized fuel and then burned. For best performance, the combustion temperature should be the maximum obtainable from the complete combustion of the oxygen and the fuel. This temperature, however, would make the turbine too hot; turbine inlet temperatures, which currently limit turbojet performance, cannot exceed about 2000° F. because of the limitations of the materials. To reduce the temperature of the turbine inlet, only part of the compressed air is burned. This combustion is achieved by dividing the air as it enters the combustion chamber. Part of the air is mixed with the fuel and ignited; the remainder is added until the temperature is reduced to acceptable limits.

In the turbine, which acts in opposite fashion to the compressor, the gases are partially expanded through alternate stator and rotor passages. At the entry to each blade row, the velocity is low, allowing the gas to expand and speed up in the passage while it turns the rotor. The turbine must provide the power to drive the compressor, to which it is connected by a shaft through the center of the engine, and it also provides the power for the fuel pump, generator, and other accessories.

The gases, which are now at an intermediate pressure, are finally expanded through the rearward-facing nozzle to reach the desired high jet-exit velocity. The greatest thrust would be obtained if the nozzle expanded the gases to the pressure of the surrounding atmosphere. In practice, however, such nozzles would be too large and too heavy. Actual nozzles are made shorter in order to provide higher exit pressures and a somewhat reduced engine performance.

A turbojet engine cannot start directly from rest; the engine must first be induced to spin by an external starting motor. The fuel is then ignited by a heated plug. Once the engine is running, however, combustion is maintained without spark plugs.

The thrust delivered by a turbojet decreases as the surrounding air temperature increases, because the decreased density of the hot air reduces the mass flow through the engine. On hot days, takeoff thrust can be increased by injecting water at the compressor inlet and allowing the evaporating water to cool the air.

In military engines, bursts of speed or additional thrust for takeoff and climb can be provided by a second burner, or afterburner, in-

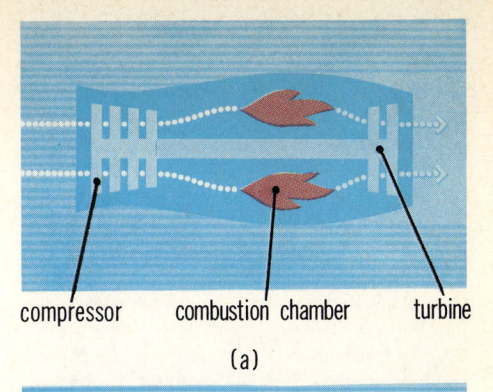

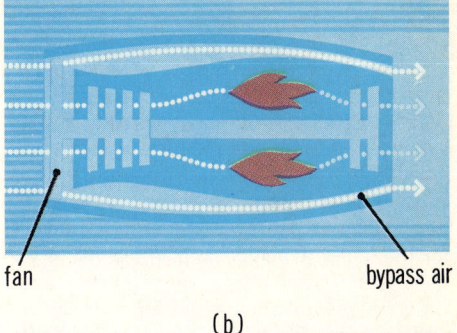

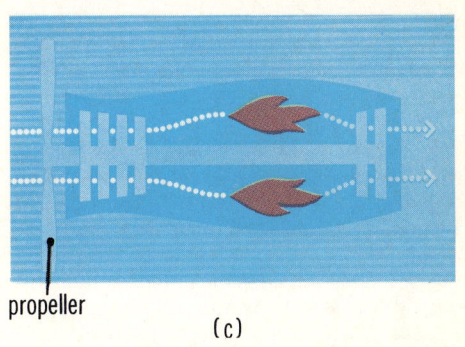

Schematic diagrams of three jet-propulsion engines: (a) turbojet engine; (b) turbofan, or bypass turbojet, engine; (c) turboprop engine. Pratt and Whitney Aircraft

stalled between the turbine and the nozzle. In the afterburner, more fuel is added to burn the oxygen in the air that is not used in the combustion chamber; this process increases both the air volume and the jet velocity. The low efficiency of an afterburner, however, restricts its use to situations requiring a great burst of speed.

Turbofans or Bypass Engines. The turbofan engine (see diagram, *b*, and Color Plate 1) is an improvement on the basic turbojet. Part of the incoming air is only partially compressed and then bypassed in an outer shell beyond the turbine. This air is then mixed with the hot tur-

JET PROPULSION

bine-exhaust gases before they reach the nozzle. A bypass engine has greater thrust for takeoff and climb, and increased efficiency; the bypass cools the engine and reduces noise level.

In some fan engines the bypass air is not remixed in the engine but exhausted directly. In this type of bypass engine, only about one sixth of the incoming air goes through the whole engine; the remaining five sixths is compressed only in the first compressor or fan stage and then exhausted. Different rotational speeds are required for the high- and low-pressure portions of the engine. This difference is achieved by having two separate turbine-compressor combinations running on two concentric shafts or twin spools. Two high-pressure turbine stages drive the eleven high-pressure compressor stages mounted on the outer shaft, and four turbine stages provide power for the fan and four low-pressure compressor stages on the inner shaft. The engine shown weighs 8470 lb. and can develop a takeoff thrust of about 45,000 lb. This is more than double the thrust available for the largest commercial planes prior to the Boeing 747.

Current research in turbojet and turbofan engines is largely directed to achieving more efficient operation of the compressors and turbines, to devising special turbine-blade cooling systems to permit higher turbine-inlet temperatures, and to reducing jet noise.

Turboprop Engines. In a turboprop engine (see diagram, c), a propeller mounted in front of the jet engine is driven either by a second, or free, turbine or by additional stages from the turbine that supplies power to the compressor. About 90 percent of the energy of the expanding gases is absorbed in the turbine portion that drives the propeller, leaving only about 10 percent to accelerate the exhaust jet. The exhaust jet, therefore, contributes only a small fraction to the overall propulsive thrust. Turboprops have certain advantages for small and medium-sized planes at speeds up to about 300 to 400 m.p.h. They cannot compete, however, with turbojets or fanjets for very large planes and for higher speeds.

Ramjets. The air rushing toward the inlet of an engine flying at high speeds is partially compressed by the so-called ram effect. If the air speed is high enough, this compression can be sufficient to operate an engine without either compressor or turbine. A ramjet has been called a flying stovepipe, because it is open at both ends and has only fuel nozzles in the middle. A straight stovepipe would not work, however; a ramjet must have a properly shaped inlet-diffusion section to produce low-velocity, high-pressure air at the combustion section, and it must also have a properly shaped exhaust nozzle. Ramjets can operate at speeds above 200 m.p.h., although they become practical for military applications only at very high, supersonic speeds. Because the ramjet depends on the compression of the inrushing air for its operation, a vehicle powered by a ramjet must first be accelerated by other means to a sufficiently high speed.

Pulse Jets. A pulse jet is similar to a ramjet, except that a series of spring-loaded shutter-type valves are located ahead of the combustion section. In a pulse jet, combustion is intermittent or pulsing rather than continuous. Air is admitted through the valves, and combustion is initiated, which increases the pressure, closing the valves to prevent backflow through the inlet. The hot gases are expelled through the rear nozzle producing thrust and lowering the pressure to the point that the valves may open and admit fresh air. Then the cycle is repeated. The most widely known pulse jet was the German V-1 missile, or buzz bomb, used near the end of World War II, which fired at a rate of about 40 cycles per second.

The pulsing effect can also be achieved in a valveless engine, or wave engine, in which the cycling depends on pressure waves traveling back and forth through a properly scaled engine. A pulse-jet engine delivers thrust at zero speed and can be started from rest, and the maximum possible flight speeds are below 600 m.p.h. Poor efficiency, severe vibrations, and high noise limit its use to low-cost, pilotless vehicles.

NONATMOSPHERIC OR ROCKET ENGINES

Nonatmospheric engines carry both fuel and oxidizer and are therefore not dependent on a surrounding atmosphere for a supply of oxygen. Rockets are generally classified by the type of fuel burned; solid-propellant rockets carry a solid mixture of fuel and oxidizer, similar to gunpowder, which burns completely after ignition. The burning generates a large volume of high-pressure gases in the engine chamber, and the gases are then converted to a high-velocity jet by expansion through a nozzle. The burning rate is controlled by shaping the charge of solid fuel so that combustion gases are released at a nearly uniform rate. Thrust control is limited, restricting the use of solid-propellant rockets in multistaged space vehicles to the first, or takeoff, stage.

In most liquid-fuel rockets, fuel and oxidizer, stored in separate tanks, are metered and in-

Jet Propulsion. Plate 1. The largest airplane ever designed for commercial service, the Boeing 747 jet airliner (above), is propelled by four wing-mounted Pratt & Whitney JT9D-3 turbofan engines (see the cutaway picture, below). The most powerful jet engine in commercial service, each JT9D-3 engine generates a thrust of 43,500 lb., enabling the giant airplane to cruise at a height of 35,000 ft. and speed of about 625 m.p.h. The aircraft carries an average payload of 374 passengers, their baggage, and 40,000 lb. of cargo a distance of over 5000 mi.

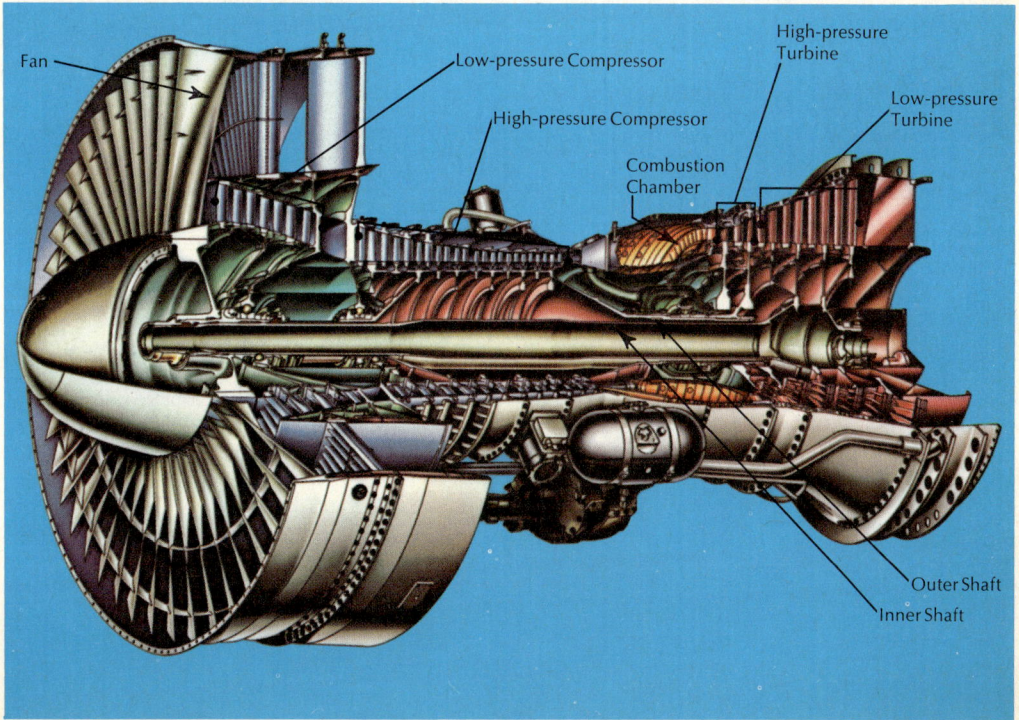

The Boeing Company

Pratt & Whitney Aircraft

Jet Propulsion. Plate 2.

Left: The F4-C Phantom interceptor and attack aircraft of the U.S. Air Force is powered by two General Electric J79-15 jet engines. The supersonic aircraft has a combat ceiling of 71,000 ft., can carry a payload of 16,000 lb., and is equipped to carry tactical nuclear weapons. Right: The British V/STOL (vertical/short takeoff and landing) Hawker Harrier is powered by a Rolls-Royce Bristol Pegasus Mark 101 engine which generates a 21,500-lb. thrust. The ground-support aircraft is capable of an in-flight speed of 737 m.p.h. and can operate at an altitude exceeding 50,000 ft.

Naval Photographic Center, Washington, D.C.

Lockheed-California Co.

Two commercial airplanes equipped with the most sophisticated jet-propulsion systems yet developed: the American Lockheed L-1011 TriStar (above) and the Anglo-French supersonic transport Concorde (below). The TriStar is equipped with two Rolls-Royce RB.211-22B high-bypass turbofan engines on the wings and one in the tail of the fuselage. Each engine develops a 42,000-lb. take-off thrust, enabling the TriStar to carry up to 345 passengers at a speed of about 620 m.p.h. on long or short-haul flights. The Concorde has four Rolls-Royce/SNECMA Olympus 593 turbojet engines, each developing up to 38,300-lb. thrust. Designed to carry 132 passengers at speeds of up to 1400 m.p.h., the Concorde has a cruising altitude of between 52,000 and 62,000 ft. and a range of over 4000 mi.

British Aircraft Corp.

JET PROPULSION

jected at high pressures into the engine chamber, in which they are atomized, mixed, and burned. Fuel metering and the ability to shut off and restart a liquid-propellant rocket make it ideal for the upper stages of space vehicles. A combination of liquid hydrogen and liquid oxygen is one of the most efficient fuel-oxidizer combinations; in spite of the difficulty and danger in handling them, they have been used successfully in the American space-flight program.

Future rocket engines for long-range space missions include nuclear rockets, plasma jet rockets, and ion engines.

HYDRAULIC JET PROPULSION

Jet-propulsion devices are not limited to using gases as the working fluid; liquids, such as water, may also be utilized. A simple example of a liquid jet device that operates on the reaction principle is the swirling lawn sprinkler.

Attempts to develop hydraulic jet propulsion for ships were made by British and Swedish engineers as early as the 1920's. In such a system, water is inducted at the forward end of the ship, passed through high-pressure pumps, and then exhausted at the stern through one or more nozzles that produce high-speed water jets. Both highly efficient pumps and high speeds are required to make hydraulic jets competitive with other means of ship propulsion. Although water-jet propulsion has not proven successful for large vessels, it is currently employed in some high-speed boats and pleasure craft.

HISTORY

Jet power as a form of propulsion has been known for hundreds of years, although its use for propelling vehicles that carry loads is comparatively recent. The earliest known reaction engine was an experimental, steam-operated device developed about the 3rd century B.C. by the Greek mathematician and scientist Hero of Alexandria (q.v.). Known as the aeolipile, Hero's device did no practical work, although it demonstrated that a jet of steam escaping to the rear drives its generator forward. The aeolipile consisted of a spherical chamber into which steam was fed through hollow supports. The steam was allowed to escape from two bent tubes on opposite sides of the sphere, and the reaction to the force of the escaping steam caused the sphere to rotate.

The development (1629) of the steam turbine is credited to the Italian engineer Giovanni Branca (1571–1645), who directed a steam jet against a turbine wheel, which in turn powered a stamp mill. The first recorded patent for a gas turbine was obtained in 1791 by the British inventor John Barber (1734–1801).

In 1910, seven years after the first flights by Orville and Wilbur Wright (see under WRIGHT), the French scientist Henri-Marie Coanda (1885–1972) designed and built a jet-propelled biplane, which took off and flew under its own power with Coanda as pilot. Coanda used an engine that he termed a reaction motor, but, discouraged by the lack of public acceptance of his aircraft, he abandoned his experiments.

During the next twenty years the gas turbine was developed further both in the United States and in Europe. One result of the experimental work of that period was the perfection in 1918 of a turbosupercharger driven by an exhaust gas turbine for conventional aircraft engines. In the early 1930's many patents covering gas turbines were awarded to a number of European engineers. The patent granted the British aeronautical engineer Frank Whittle (q.v.) in 1930 is generally conceded to have outlined the first practical form of the modern gas turbine. In 1935 Whittle applied his basic design to the development of the W-1 turbojet engine, which made its first flight in 1941.

Meanwhile the French aeronautical engineer René Leduc (1898–1967) had exhibited (1938) a model of the ramjet in Paris, and a jet airplane, which was powered by an axial-flow turbojet designed by the German engineer Hans Pabst von Ohain (1911–), made its first flight in 1939. In the following year, under the direction of the aeronautical engineer Secundo Campini (1904–), the Italians developed an airplane powered by a turboprop engine with a reciprocating-engine-driven compressor. The first American-built jet airplane, the Bell XP-59, was powered by the General Electric I-16 turbojet, adapted from Whittle's design in 1942. The first jet engine of exclusively American design was produced by Westinghouse Electric Corporation for the United States Navy in 1944.

From a principle first described in 1906, the pulse jet was developed by a German engineer Paul Schmidt, who received his first patent in 1931. The V-1, or buzz bomb, was first flown in 1942. Also in the mid-1940's occurred the first commercial airline flights using turboprop engines. In 1947 the Bell X-1 experimental airplane, powered by a four-chambered liquid-rocket engine and carried to the stratosphere in the belly of a bomber for launching, was the first pilot-operated craft to break through the sound barrier. Subsequently the Douglas Skyrocket experimental airplane, powered by a jet engine in addition to a liquid-rocket engine, broke the sound barrier at low altitude after taking off under its own power.

JET STREAM

The first commercial jet airplane, the British Comet, was flown in 1952, but this service was stopped after two serious accidents in 1954. In the U.S., the Boeing 707 jet was the first jet airplane to be tested commercially, in 1954. Commercial flights began in 1958.

The continuous development of jet propulsion for air power has resulted in such advances as piloted aircraft capable of attaining speeds several times greater than the speed of sound, and intercontinental ballistic missiles and man-made satellites launched by powerful rockets.

F.La.

JET STREAM. See METEOROLOGY: *History; Circulation of the Atmosphere.*

JEVONS, William Stanley (1835–82), British economist and mathematician, born in Liverpool, England, and educated at University College, University of London. He is known for the development of the theory of marginal utility (q.v.), which states that utility determines value. Jevons demonstrated the relationship between utility and value in mathematical terms. Among his writings are *The Coal Question* (1865), *Lessons in Logic* (1870), *The Theory of Political Economy* (1871), *Principles of Science* (1874), and *Principles of Economics* (posthumously published in 1905).

JEWEL CAVE NATIONAL MONUMENT, area of geological interest in s.w. South Dakota, about 14 miles w. of the town of Custer. It is administered by the National Park Service (q.v.).

JEWELRY, personal adornments worn since prehistoric times by men and women of all cultures, as ornaments, as badges of social or official rank, and as emblems of religious or superstitious belief. In its widest sense the term "jewelry" encompasses objects made of many kinds of organic and inorganic materials such as hair, feathers, leather, scales, bones, shells, wood, ceramics, metals, and minerals. More narrowly, and as used here, the term refers to mounted precious or semiprecious stones, and to objects made of valuable or attractive metals such as gold, silver, platinum, and copper. Jewelry has been worn on the head as crowns, diadems, tiaras, aigrettes, hairpins, hat ornaments, earrings, nose rings, ear plugs, and lip rings; on the neck as collars, necklaces, and pendants; on the breast as pectorals, brooches, clasps, and buttons; on the limbs as rings, bracelets, armlets, and anklets; and at the waist as belts and girdles, with pendants such as chatelaines, scent cases, and rosaries. Much present knowledge of jewelry is derived from the preservation of personal objects in tombs. Information about the jewelry of cultures that did not bury valuables with the dead comes from portraits in surviving painting and sculpture. See DIAMOND; ENAMEL; GEM; GEM CUTTING; GEM ENGRAVING.

Egyptian Work in Metal and Stone. In ancient times, the Egyptians, who were familiar with most of the processes of ornamenting metal that are still practiced today, produced skillfully chased, engraved, soldered, repoussé, and inlaid jewelry. They commonly worked in gold and silver, inlaying with semiprecious stones such as carnelian, jasper, amethyst, and lapis lazuli. Their jewelry included diadems, necklaces, pectorals, bracelets, and rings. Many Egyptians wore two bracelets on each arm, one on the wrist and one above the elbow. The most popular ornament by far was the signet ring, usually carved in the form of a scarab (q.v.) and engraved with the owner's emblem. Vast quantities of jewelry have been found in Egyptian tombs. The notable finds of XII-Dynasty (1991–1778 B.C.) jewelry at Dahshur and Lisht are exhibited at the Egyptian Museum in Cairo, Arab Republic of Egypt, and at the Metropolitan Museum of Art, New York City.

Babylonian, Assyrian, and Phoenician Jewelry. Jewelry found in Babylonian and Assyrian tombs of the 3rd and 2nd millennia B.C., particularly at Ur, includes headdresses, necklaces, earrings, and animal amulet figures in gold, silver, and semiprecious stones. The University Museum, Philadelphia, Pa., contains representative examples of this type of jewelry. See ASSYRIA; BABYLONIA.

The Phoenicians, as international traders from about 1000 to about 500 B.C., were active in carrying foreign jewelry from country to country. They also produced native work based largely on Egyptian and Assyrian forms. An example of their art is the sculptured bust known as the "Lady of Elché" (now in the Louvre, Paris), that bears an elaborate diadem and three necklaces carrying urn-shaped pendants. See PHOENICIA.

Greek and Roman Techniques of Decoration. The ancient pre-Greek jewelers, although working at opposite ends of the Aegean region, in Troy and Crete, executed earrings, bracelets, and necklaces of a common type that persisted from about 2500 to about 500 B.C., the beginning of the classical period. Typical work consisted of thin coils and chains of linked and plaited wire, and thin foil decorated in petals and rosettes. Stamping and enameling were common. Free use was also made of gold granulation, or the decorating of gold surfaces with microscopic grains of gold. Stone inlay was rare. Prevailing motifs were spirals and naturalistic pat-

JEWELRY

terns drawn from cuttlefish, starfish, and butterflies. Jewelry found at Mycenae and Crete, and now in the National Museum in Athens, includes a great number of small gold disks, perforated so that they could be attached to clothing, and gold diadems made of long oval plates covered with repoussé rosettes. See AEGEAN CIVILIZATION.

Archaic Greek jewelry and Etruscan and other Italian jewelry made in the period between 700 and 500 B.C. was almost entirely inspired by Egyptian and Assyrian examples imported by Phoenician merchants. The techniques remained fundamentally the same as in the preceding period; embossed or stamped plates were the basic element in the work; granulation continued and was developed in Etruria (q.v.) to an extraordinary degree of refinement.

In the Greek classical period, 5th and 4th centuries B.C., granulation disappeared, enamel reappeared, and filigree became important. The style was one of delicacy and refinement. Plaited gold necklaces bore flowers and tassels; hoop earrings with filigree disks and rosettes became popular. In the succeeding Hellenistic phase, pendant vases, winged victories, cupids, and doves became common motifs. At the same time an important innovation was the introduction of large colored stones, especially garnets, at the center of designs. This scheme was developed by the Romans, who multiplied the variety of stones and set them in rows bordered with pearls. In Rome the art of cameo (q.v.) cutting reached its peak of virtuosity, and cameos often of great size were produced in large numbers. Rings were extremely popular among the Romans, and at the height of the empire were often worn on all ten fingers. Exotic ornaments made of amber in which flies were embedded were also in great demand. Toward the end of the Roman Empire, from the 3rd century A.D. on, necklaces and bracelets were formed of gold coins set in elaborate mountings of arcaded pattern; classical figure work died out. Extensive collections of Greek and Roman jewelry are to be seen in all the large European museums, as well as in the Metropolitan Museum of Art, New York City. See GREEK ART.

Byzantine Use of Jewels, Gold, Bronze, and Enamel. Byzantine jewelry was often worn in lavish profusion. An example can be seen in the 6th-century mosaic portrait of Empress Theodora (q.v.) in the church of San Vitale at Ravenna: the dress is stiff with gold and set with jewels; pearls, rubies, and emeralds mounted in gold are worn at the neck and shoulders, and hang in festoons from the temples to the breast.

A usual type of Byzantine earring was of crescent shape in gold repoussé openwork with a central cross in a circle flanked by peacocks. The favorite breast pendant was the cross. Most finger rings bore Christian symbols, and the extant examples are more often made of gilded bronze than of gold. Enamel work, especially cloisonné enamel, was developed to a high point by the Byzantines and had a strong influence on European jewelry of succeeding periods. Fine collections of Byzantine jewelry can be seen at the British Museum, London, the Cleveland Museum of Art, Cleveland, Ohio, and the Metropolitan Museum of Art, New York City. See BYZANTINE ART.

The Work of European Jewelers from the 4th to the 11th Century. Throughout the Roman territories, even after the fall of the empire, common forms and techniques remained in general use. Gold filigree persisted, and the Roman fibula or safety-pin form was elaborated into complicated brooches. The most important development, adopted all over Europe from the 3rd to the 8th centuries, was the use of garnet slices set, like enamel, into metal cells. Outstanding examples were discovered in the 4th-century treasure unearthed at Petrossa, near Bucharest, Rumania. Another pervasive influence at the time came from Byzantine cloisonné enamel. Both the Roman and Byzantine traditions fused in the work of the barbarian jewelers, who also introduced native variations. Among the distinct local styles developed in the period from the 5th to the 11th centuries are the Ostrogothic, Visigothic, Frankish, Scandinavian, Anglo-Saxon, and Celtic. Remarkable examples of the work of this period include the 7th-century crown of Reccesvinthus, King of the Visigoths (in the Archeology Museum, Madrid) and the famous 9th-century Alfred Jewel (in the Ashmolean Museum, Oxford, England).

Jewelry as a Medieval Industrial Art. In the Middle Ages, beginning in the 11th century, jewelry became one of the industrial arts, first practiced in the monasteries and then in town workshops. The Roman fibula form had disappeared, but the brooch continued to be the typical ornament. It took the form of a ring with a pin held in place by the weight of the cloth through which it passed. Chased or enameled devotional pendants frequently mounted in an architectural frame were another characteristic adornment. By the 14th and 15th centuries jewelry became more and more an integral part of dress. It was attached to clothes and was used to decorate belts and hairnets. A famous example of medieval jewelry is the 12th-century Eagle

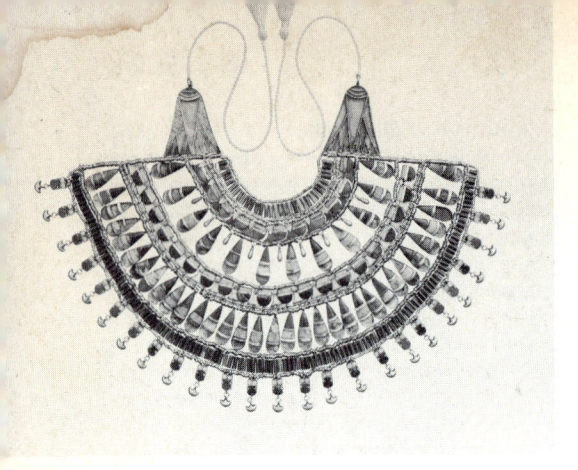

An Egyptian gold necklace of the XVIIIth Dynasty, 1567–1320 B.C.   Metropolitan Museum of Art

Brooch in the Mainz Museum, Mainz, Germany. Knowledge of medieval jewelry is also derived from a book on goldsmith work written (about 1100) by the monk Theophilus of Essen, and from paintings such as the 15th-century "Legend at Saint Eloi and Saint Godeberta" by Petrus Christus (q.v.), which shows the interior of a Flemish goldsmith's shop.

The Rich Designs of Renaissance Artists. In the latter half of the 15th century, during the Renaissance, jewelry together with the other arts, received tremendous stimulus. In Italy especially, the goldsmiths, no longer anonymous artists as they had been in the medieval guilds, became famous as free artists. Many sculptors, painters, and architects also executed jewlery; the most celebrated of these artists was Benvenuto Cellini (q.v.). The jewelry of the period is characterized by rich color in gems and enameling and by a type of design which is often architectural in character. Color was so much in demand that diamonds, prized highly in later times, were much less valued than emeralds or rubies. Costume and jewelry were closely linked, and often an entire garment was encrusted with jewels. Religious subjects, prevalent in medieval jewelry, diminished sharply in popularity, and classical or naturalistic themes increased. These changes were adopted in France, Germany, and the rest of Europe as the Renaissance spread from Italy. Outside of Italy, famous painters such as Holbein, Dürer, and Rubens (qq.v.) drew numerous designs for jewelers. Notable examples of Renaissance jewels include the 16th-century Phoenix Jewel in the British Museum, London. Another famous example of the Renaissance jeweler's art is the Cellini Cup (Metropolitan Museum of Art, New York City.

In the fad of a season in the 1960's, "body jewelry" includes earrings, necklaces, and multiple belts of glittering stones and twisted gold.   UPI

Modern Tastes and Themes. In subsequent styles such as the baroque, rococo, neoclassic, and neogothic, jewelry reflected the prevailing taste in other arts. For instance, in the Neoclassic period at the end of the 18th and the beginning of the 19th century, the wearing of ancient Greek and Roman jewelry, or facsimiles of originals excavated at Pompeii (q.v.), was fashionable. At the same time the characteristic jewel arrangement was the parure, or matching set of earrings, necklace, brooch, and ring.

In the 18th century in the United States, the manufacture of jewelry was one of the first artistic industries. Trinkets for the Indians and common articles such as snuffboxes were much in demand. Later, in the 19th century, in the U.S. and in Europe industrial development brought mass production of cheap jewelry of all types and styles; the techniques utilized included alloying, hammer-plating, and electroplating. Simultaneously, demand increased for the most costly gems and settings. The Second Empire in France set the style for opulent jewels rich in diamonds and pearls; see FRANCE: *History: The*

Second Empire. With emphasis on lavish display and the intrinsic value of precious stones, the workmanship of the metal settings was neglected and became inferior. At the beginning of the 20th century, the French designer René Lalique (1860–1945), among others, launched a revival of the goldsmith's art. Ignoring historic styles, he took his themes from plants, birds, and insect forms. Emphasizing design more than the costliness of material, he used enamel, ivory, glass, and horn as often as semiprecious stones and gems.

Modern jewelry is generally a part of dress, and changes with changing fashions. After World War I the vogue for short hair resulted in the disappearance of previously popular jeweled combs and hair ornaments. In the same period jeweled vanity cases, wrist watches, and cigarette cases came into style. The diamond has remained the most esteemed among precious gems, and although platinum is preferred as a setting, newly discovered metals such as iridium and palladium have also become popular. Today there is also demand for handicraft jewelry of hammered copper, and various metals worked in other ways. Plastics are often used for inexpensive jewelry. Arts-and-crafts shops produce a vast selection of abstract and naturalistic designs in rings, bracelets, earrings, necklaces, and brooches.

Oriental and Other Jewelry. In the Orient, techniques and styles of jewelry have been unbrokenly continued from remote antiquity to the present day. Indian goldsmiths, expert in the techniques also common in the West since ancient times, produce enameled, soldered, granulated, and filigreed work of great refinement. Some of the best work, especially silver filigree, is produced in Cuttack, Kashmir, and Bengal. Fine historic examples of Indian work shown at the Victoria and Albert Museum, London, include a crescent-shaped gold brooch with granulated gold balls and pendants. Other examples, especially from the south of India, bear in relief subjects from Hindu mythology. See INDIAN ART AND ARCHITECTURE.

In Persian jewelry the characteristic material is enameled gold; the main center for this work is Shiraz. The technique is often applied to the making of the charms and amulets common in Persia. It is also seen in an elaborate pair of earrings in the Victoria and Albert Museum, London, formed of two domelike tiers fringed with pearls and leaf pendants. See PERSIAN ART.

Silver is used in Chinese traditional jewelry more often than gold, and the silver is gilded to prevent tarnishing; silver and gold are frequently enameled in blue, a favorite color, and often decorated with kingfisher feathers; and jade is the most valued among precious stones. Under the Chinese Empire jeweled emblems such as the buttons on the hats of mandarins indicated rank, and extremely elaborate silver and gold filigree headdresses were worn by women of high position. Dragons, phoenixes, and many Buddhist symbols were used and continue to be used as decoration or charms on necklaces, rings, and bracelets. Outstanding examples of Chinese jewelry are exhibited at the Freer Gallery of Art, Washington, D.C. The gold and silver work of Nepal, Burma, and Thailand is related to Indian and Chinese work, and is also outstanding in craftsmanship. The Japanese have excelled in lacquer and ivory ornaments such as combs and buttons, and pendants worn at the waist. See CHINESE ART; JAPANESE ART AND ARCHITECTURE.

The jewelry of African, Pre-Columbian, and Oceanic cultures, often displayed in natural history museums such as the Museum of Natural History, New York City, or in art museums such as the Cleveland Museum of Art and the National Gallery, Washington, D.C., shows a great variety of materials and techniques; along with precious metals and stones, great use was made of skins, feathers, claws, and other such materials. W.M.M.

JEWETT, Sarah Orne (1849–1909), American writer, born in South Berwick, Maine, and educated at Berwick Academy. Her stories of New England life depicted the fading glamour of the provincial New England countryside. Her works won her a place as one of the most important writers of the local-color literary genre in the United States. Among Sarah Jewett's works are *Deephaven* (1877); *A Country Doctor* (1884); *The Life of Nancy* (1895); *The Country of the Pointed Firs* (1896), her most outstanding work; and *The Tory Lover* (1901).

JEWFISH, or SPOTTED GROUPER or GIANT SEA BASS, the largest grouper (q.v.) to be found along the coasts of the Americas. The jewfish, *Epinephelus itajara,* is known from Florida to Brazil; and the same species, or a similar species, is found in the waters off Bermuda, in the eastern Atlantic Ocean, and in the eastern Pacific Ocean. A good table fish, the jewfish is sought by commercial and sport fishermen. It is reported to reach a maximum weight of about 750 lb.

JEWISH ART AND ARCHITECTURE, art produced by the Jews as a nation until the time of their dispersal after the capture of Jerusalem in 70 A.D. by Titus (q.v.), or that produced later

A Torah crown in silver and gilt repoussé and cast work, of 18th-century Galicia, Poland. Much Jewish art work was designed for the protection and decoration of the Torah scrolls, which contain the written first law.
Frank J. Darmstaedter – Jewish Museum, N.Y.

women, were adopted in early Christian churches and have survived to the present time in buildings of the Eastern Church. Syrian synagogues of the 3rd and later centuries stood side by side with closely similar Christian churches. The well-known synagogue of Dura-Europos (about 250 A.D.) is decorated with mural paintings of Old Testament scenes executed in a style typical of the region and period. In 1962, a monumental synagogue, paved with precious mosaics, was discovered in Sardis (q.v.), ancient Lydia.

Since ancient times, Jewish art has formed part of the culture and period in which it was produced. Notable examples are the medieval synagogue in Prague, Czechoslovakia, the Renaissance synagogue in Venice, Italy, and the oldest synagogue in the United States at the Touro Synagogue National Historic Site in Newport, R.I. During the 19th century many synagogues all over the Western world were built in the neo-Byzantine manner in order to suggest the Middle Eastern origin of Judaism (q.v.). Contemporary synagogues, like most public buildings, are built in a great variety of styles, and occasionally the most advanced innovations in modern architecture are selected.

A number of Jewish illuminated manuscripts (q.v.) survive from medieval times, but there have been relatively few well-known Jewish painters. In Renaissance and later times, several painters of Jewish descent achieved fame, but their work is a part of their era and shows no distinguishing Jewish cultural elements. Modern artists such as the sculptor Jacques Lipchitz and the painter Marc Chagall (qq.v.) may be classed as Jewish artists because they emphasized their

by scattered groups of Jews continuing their ancient religious and cultural traditions. The term is also used loosely to describe painting, sculpture, and architecture done by Jews of all nationalities up to the present day.

Ancient Jewish architecture, pottery, and seals bore a resemblance to those of earlier Phoenician, Babylonian, and Assyrian cultures. Although no traces remain of Solomon's Temple (10th cent. B.C.), the most famous of Jewish monuments, the Wailing Wall in Jerusalem has come to be regarded as an original part of the wall surrounding Herod's Temple. During the 1st century B.C. under Herod the Great (q.v.), Palestine was largely rebuilt in the style of Roman buildings; the few remaining ancient synagogues in Galilee, the recently excavated city of Caesarea with its amphitheater, and the palace in Masada, belong to this time and the following century. Tombs from all parts of Palestine are similar to the late Hellenistic and Roman sepulchers throughout Syria. Many elements of synagogue construction, such as the sanctuary and the separate areas for men and

A modern menorah, a candelabrum used in a variety of worship services.
Percival Goodman

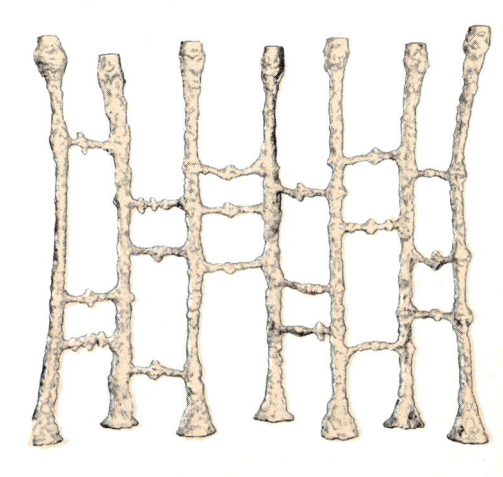

cultural tradition. The State of Israel has a modern art museum and the Shrine of the Book, containing Dead Sea Scrolls (q.v.), in Jerusalem. A number of Western-oriented painters live in Israel, and an independent style is slowly emerging. N.N.G.

JEWISH AUTONOMOUS OBLAST, commonly called BIROBIDZHAN, administrative division of the Soviet Union, in the Russian S.F.S.R., in eastern Siberia about 200 miles w. of the Tatar Strait. Part of the Khabarovsk Territory, the oblast is bordered on the N. by the Bureya Range and on the S. by the Amur R., which extends along the entire southern border, forming a boundary with China. The mountainous northern sector of the oblast is covered with a thick, coniferous forest, the basis for a prosperous timber industry. The region is rich in minerals. Resources include tin (from Khingansk) and iron ore (mined south of Izvestkovy), as well as graphite, marble and limestone. The Bira and Bidzhan rivers, tributaries of the Amur, flow S. through what was once a swampy plain. Through drainage, this extensive southern section has been coverted to fertile farmland. Agricultural products include wheat, oats, and soybeans; cattle and pigs are raised. All important urban centers of the oblast are located along the route of the Trans-Siberian Railroad which traverses the northern part of the oblast. The capital and largest city is Birobidzhan (q.v.) in which about one third of the population of the oblast resides. The second most important city is Obluch'ye, where tin ore is processed. In addition to mining and lumbering, the principal industries include the manufacture of shoes, textiles, clothing, building materials, and furniture.

In 1928 the area was set aside by the Soviet government as a resettlement district for the Jews of the U.S.S.R. The region was sparsely settled and economically undeveloped. Because Jews had no historical connection with the territory, it was understood that the purpose of the government in making this land allocation was to speed up settlement of the area as a defensive measure against possible aggression on the far eastern borders of the Soviet Union. In 1934 the area was designated an autonomous oblast. A limited number of Jews migrated to the area. Jewish population of the area has been estimated at less than 10 percent; most of the population is composed of Russian and Ukrainian settlers. Area 13,896 sq.mi.; pop. (1971 est.) 176,000.

JEWISH COMMUNITY CENTER, general name for what were formerly the Young Men's Hebrew Association and Young Women's Hebrew Association. Although the names Y.M.H.A. and Y.W.H.A. are still used by some centers, they are no longer separate.

In 1854 the first Y.M.H.A. was founded in Baltimore, and an auxiliary for women, the Y.W.H.A., appeared in New York in 1888. The forerunners of these organizations were informal Jewish literary associations which flourished in America during the mid-19th century, and which became the Young Men's Hebrew Literary Associations. About 70 similar organizations were founded during the next 30 years, but were not united into a national association until 1913, when the National Council of Young Men's Hebrew and Kindred Associations was formed. This, in turn, merged in 1921 with the National Jewish Welfare Board (q.v.), which had served the spiritual and welfare needs of Jews in the United States armed forces.

Jewish community centers in the United States are established locally, but linked through their national association, the National Jewish Welfare Board, and have a combined membership of 750,000, ranging in age from 3 to 90; there are 447 centers in 200 U.S. cities. The center is maintained by and for the residents of a given Jewish community, although in most cases membership is open to non-Jews as well. Activities may vary according to specific needs and interests, but generally include arts and crafts, dramatics, physical education, lectures and forums. Camps and outdoor recreation facilities are staffed by professional social workers and specialists in child education and adult Jewish education. The programs are basically aimed at strengthening Jewish family life, and providing shared experiences for all age groups; activities stress participation in community affairs and provide leadership training. Many cultural and exchange programs are engaged in with similar agencies in Israel, Europe, Latin America, Asia, and Africa.

JEWISH LANGUAGE. See HEBREW LANGUAGE; YIDDISH LANGUAGE.

JEWISH LITERATURE, literature written by Jews (q.v.), principally in Hebrew, and also in other languages, including Aramaic (see ARAM), Greek, Arabic, Spanish, and German. Hebrew was the principal literary language of the Jews until the 19th century, when European languages came into use for works of modern Jewish scholarship and Yiddish became a vehicle of literary expression. For the writings of Jewish authors in Yiddish, see YIDDISH LITERATURE.

The Scriptures. Jewish literature may be divided chronologically into twelve periods. An-

JEWISH LITERATURE

Maimonides, 12th-century Spanish Jew whose writings embraced science, law, and theology.
Zionist Archives and Library

cient Jewish literature consists mainly of the Old Testament (see BIBLE: *The Old Testament*), and the first three periods of Jewish literature were devoted to the writing of various portions of the Old Testament. In the first period, which extended from earliest times to about 950 B.C., were written many of the lyrics found in the Old Testament. To the second period (about 950–586 B.C.), belong most of the historical narratives concerning the kings of Israel and Judah (qq.v.), some of the psalms, and the oracles of certain of the prophets (see JEWS: *The Kingdom*). The third period (586–165 B.C.) was the time of composition of the books of the Bible known as the Writings, specifically, Ecclesiastes, Job, Proverbs, and a large part of Psalms (qq.v.). During this period, many apocryphal writings (see BIBLE: *The Apocrypha*) originated, and a major portion of the Old Testament was translated from Hebrew into Greek by Jewish scholars living in Egypt; see JEWS: *Subject Judea*.

In the fourth period (165 B.C.–135 A.D.), the Midrash (q.v.), which had been begun during the Babylonian Captivity (q.v.), was divided into two parts, the Halakah and the Haggada (qq.v.). Among other works of this period were a number of the apocalyptic writings (q.v.) of the Old Testament, including those pseudonymously ascribed to the prophet Daniel, the patriarch Enoch, the lawgiver and prophet Moses, and the priest and reformer Ezra (qq.v.); the Dead Sea Scrolls (q.v.), attributed to Jewish monastic communities of the Essene type (see ESSENES); and the writings of the philosopher Philo Judaeus (q.v.) and of the historian Flavius Josephus (q.v.). See also TARGUM.

The Talmud. The major accomplishment of the fifth period (135–475) was the Talmud (q.v.). During this period the version known as the Palestinian Talmud was completed, and the more important version known as the Babylonian Talmud took shape. In addition, the period was rich in stories, fables, and historical and ethical treatises. The sixth period (470–740) witnessed the completion of the Babylonian Talmud, the collection of some of the early versions of the Haggadoth (plural of Haggada), and the writing of marginal notes, called Masora (q.v.), to the Scriptures.

In the seventh period (740–1040), the earliest Hebrew prayer books were compiled (about 880) and the first dictionary of the Talmud was written (about 900). The era was also notable for *The Book of Precepts* (published about 770) by Anan ben David (fl. 8th cent.), the founder of the Jewish sect of the Karaites (q.v.). Another important writer of the ninth period was Saadia ben Joseph (892–942), who translated most of

Baruch Spinoza, 17th-century Dutch Jew whose pantheism influenced later philosophers.

JEWISH LITERATURE

the Old Testament into Arabic and composed the first system of Jewish religious philosophy, *Doctrines and Beliefs*. Rhymed Hebrew poetry was first written in the 8th century, and the forms and rules of modern Hebrew poetry originated in the 10th century. The great centers of Jewish scholarship in the early part of this period were northern Africa and Italy; in the latter part, Spain and Egypt.

European Writers. The eighth period (1040–1204) was dominated by Jewish scholars and writers in Europe. The Spanish Jews, using either Arabic or Hebrew, distinguished themselves in poetry, philosophy, and history. Among the most famous Jewish writers of Spain were the poet Judah ha-Levi and the philosopher Maimonides (qq.v.). The latter contributed to law, logic, medicine, and mathematics, as well as to philosophy. His treatise *Guide of the Perplexed* (about 1190) is one of the greatest products of Jewish religious philosophy. Many renowned Talmudic scholars lived in France, particularly in Provence; others lived in Germany, particularly in the Rhineland.

The ninth period (1204–1492) also had outstanding Jewish scholars in Spain, Portugal, Provence, Italy, and Germany. The first Hebrew books ever printed were published in Italy at Reggio di Calabria (1475), Mantua (1476), and Ferrara (1477). Joshua Soncino (fl. late 15th cent.), a member of a wide-ranging family of Italian-born Jewish printers, issued the first complete Hebrew Bible (1488). Some twenty years later, the Dutch Christian printer Daniel Bomberg (d. 1549) established a Hebrew press in Venice and published the first complete editions of the Palestinian and Babylonian Talmuds.

During the tenth period (1492–1755) numerous works in Hebrew and in many European languages were written by Jewish theologians, philosophers, jurists, historians, mathematicians, poets, Biblical commentators, lexicographers, and grammarians. Among the most important were the German-born Elijah Levita (1469–1549), the Spanish Isaac Abrabanel (*see under* ABRABANEL), the Dutch Baruch Spinoza (q.v.), one of the greatest philosophers of all time, and the Italian-born Moses Hayyim Luzzatto (1707–47), a mystic and moralist.

The eleventh period (1755–1880) is noted for the work of Moses Mendelssohn (q.v.), whose publications in German, particularly his translations of parts of the Pentateuch (q.v.) in 1783 and of the Psalms about the same time, were of great importance in spreading Jewish culture among the Jews of central Europe. His friend-

Moses Mendelssohn, 18th-century German Jew whose translations from Hebrew into German contributed to a broader understanding of Jewish culture.
German Information Center

ship with eminent German writers and his writings on religious tolerance helped improve the social and political position of the Jews in Germany. One of the first of modern literary journals in Hebrew, *Meassef* ("Collector"), was published by the group of scholars of which Mendelssohn was the center. Among other Jewish writers and scholars of the early part of this period were the Talmudist Elijah Wilna (q.v.), the philosopher Salomon Maimon (1754–1800), and the philosopher of Jewish history Nachman Krochmal (1785–1840), all three of eastern Europe. Especially noteworthy was the German Leopold Zunz (q.v.), who placed the study of Judaism (q.v.) on a firm scientific basis. Among the writers and scholars of later generations were the Germans, the Talmudist Zacharias Frankel (1801–75), the medievalist Salomon Munk (1803?–67), the theologian Abraham Geiger (q.v.), and Heinrich Graetz (q.v.), author of the monumental *History of the Jews from the Earliest Times* (11 vol., 1853 et seq.).

Modern Writers. The twelfth period (1880 to the present) has seen a renascence of Hebrew literature on secular themes, in the works chiefly of the Ukrainian-born essayist Asher Ginzberg (q.v.), (called Achad Ha-am) and the

JEWISH MUSIC

Shmuel Yosef Agnon, winner of the Nobel Prize in literature in 1966. Government Press Office, State of Israel

Russian-born poets Chaim Nachman Bialik (q.v.) and Saul Tchernikhovsky (1875–1943); and by a revival of religious thoughts, mainly through the influence of the writings in German of Hermann Cohen (1842–1918), Martin Buber (q.v.), and Franz Rosenzweig (1886–1929). An upsurge of modernist Hebrew prose and poetry in Israel is represented by the publications of Shmuel Joseph Agnon (q.v.), Uri Zvi Greenberg (1894–), and Sh. Shalom (1904–), among others; and a rich literary output has been published in Yiddish, English, and most modern European languages. In the United States, particularly significant contributions to Jewish scholarship were made by the theologian Solomon Schechter (q.v.), the Talmudist Louis Ginzberg (1873–1953), the theologian Mordecai Kaplan (1881–), and the historian Salo W. Baron (1895–). Among contemporary Jewish writers are the American novelists Bernard Malamud and Saul Bellow (qq.v.), the Transylvanian-born Elie Wiesel (1928–), who writes his novels in French, the American poet Karl Shapiro (1913–), and the German poet Nelly Sachs (q.v.).

N.N.G.

JEWISH MUSIC, music of the Jews from the time of the Old Testament to the present. Ancient Jewish music seems to have been used principally in public worship, but it was utilized as well on such quasi-ritualistic occasions as coronations and victory celebrations. Indeed, as many passages in the Old Testament indicate, it would have been difficult for the Jews to imagine a joyful occasion without music: ". . . I might have sent thee away with mirth, and with song, with tabret, and with harp" (Gen. 31:27).

Instruments. The ancient Jews used a number of stringed instruments, the most characteristic of which was the *kinnor* or lyre; this was probably the instrument of King David (q.v.). Other stringed instruments were the *nevel*, or harp, and the *asor*, or zither. Such instruments as the *ugab*, or reed-pipe and the *halil*, or oboe, having orgiastic connotations in Israel as in Greece, were frowned upon by the priests. The *hasosra*, or trumpet and the *shofar*, or ram's horn were ritual instruments used in the Temple and in connection with royalty; the *shofar* still plays a role in Jewish rites. Percussion instruments included the *tof* (a tambourine-like frame drum played by women), the *pa'amon*, a bell or chime, and the *msiltayim*, or cymbals.

The melodies used in the Temple liturgy (see LITURGY) appear to have been both tetrachordal (based on a scale-series of four notes) and modal (see MODE). The liturgical texts were chanted by the priests, and an orchestra of professional musicians accompanied the priests with ornamented instrumental versions of the chanted melodies. Congregational singing was also antiphonal: the priests or a trained choral ensemble chanted one part and the congregation chanted the other. Rhythm usually followed the accents of the syllables of the words in the text.

Synagogue Music. Following the Diaspora (q.v.) and the later destruction of the Temple by the Romans in 70 A.D., the ancient institution of the synagogue assumed an ever-increasing importance in Jewish worship. The liturgical practice of cantillation (chanting of Scripture), which had originated in the 5th century B.C. and had been performed by sacerdotal musicians from about the 6th century B.C., became the duty of a single lay member of the congregation about the 1st century A.D. All accompaniment by musical instruments was henceforth forbidden, and responses, wherever they were required in the service, were sung by the entire male congregation. The practice of cantillation and the desire that it be performed correctly led to many important developments, including the beginnings of a notational system during the 5th century A.D., and the preservation of ancient chants among such extant groups as the Yemenite Jews. The investigation of Yemenite and Babylonian chant has shown that Christian chant is greatly indebted to the older Jewish model; see CHANT.

New forms did develop alongside the old, however, and these accretions to synagogal hymns and post-Biblical prayer modes, many of which were based on Arabic metrical and rhythmic systems, created a need for trained musicians. Consequently, the office of *hazan,* or cantor, was established during the early Middle Ages.

At first the cantor's principal duty was to perform the more complicated liturgy. About the 8th century, however, the cantor began the practice of improvisation in performances; over many centuries this practice, which increasingly included elements of non-Jewish songs as well as Catholic and Protestant hymn tunes, resulted in extremely elaborate cantorial melodies far removed from the original ancient prayer modes.

The ecstatic *niggunim,* or wordless hymns, of the mystics of 16th-century Cabala (q.v.) and of the 18th- and 19th-century Hasidim (q.v.) were offshoots of the ornamented cantorial style. Originally inspired by religious doctrines that stressed a spontaneous, emotionally expressive vocalization of prayer lyrics, the *niggunim* also degenerated in time as a result of frequent but inaccurate repetitions and unskilled attempts to mix native Jewish tunes with European art music.

The Hasidic material, however, is of the greatest interest. The songs and dances are ecstatic and mystical, and the music is frequently wordless. In many ways the Hasidim are like the Sufi sects of Islam in seeking enlightenment through ecstatic song and movement; *see* SUFISM.

The Reform Movement. Attempts at liturgical reform began in the 19th century. Foremost among the reformers was the Austrian Salomon Sulzer (1804–90), chief cantor of the Viennese Jewish community and a well-trained composer. Sulzer recognized the essentially Oriental character of Jewish music and strove to bring about a disciplined liturgical service that incorporated the Oriental tradition in a manner acceptable to a largely Westernized Jewry. The problem is one that still confronts many Jews, particularly Reform Jews in the United States.

In the 20th century the evolution of Jewish music, both liturgical and secular, was affected by several developments. European and American Jewish composers, among them the Swiss-American Ernest Bloch and the Frenchman Darius Milhaud (qq.v.), created modern combined orchestral and choral settings for synagogue services. Many other composers, such as the American Leonard Bernstein (q.v.) in his "Kaddish" Symphony, also incorporated Jewish home prayer tunes and secular folk melodies in their music. The training of cantors in authentic chant styles has been pursued most notably at the Cantor's Institute of the Jewish Theological Seminary (q.v.) in New York City.

In Israel, the spiritual folksongs of Oriental Jewry, so reminiscent in their musical systems of Arab music, have begun to blend with the latter and with the songs of Jews of European extraction to produce a music that many scholars believe will be a blend of Eastern and Western elements, with the former possibly predominating. Thus, the resettlement of Palestine by Jews from all parts of the world and the establishment of the state of Israel has already produced an important body of new folk music, as well as much original Israeli music that unites traditional Oriental elements with contemporary Western music. *See also* ARABIC MUSIC; FOLK MUSIC; ISRAEL; JEWS; MUSIC; PRAYER, JEWISH; RELIGIOUS MUSIC; SYNAGOGUE.   T.C.G.

JEWISH RELIGION. *See* JUDAISM.

JEWISH THEOLOGICAL SEMINARY OF AMERICA, THE, educational institution, under Conservative Jewish auspices, having the primary purpose of preparing men for the rabbinate, located in New York City. Women are admitted to certain classes and professional schools of the seminary. The seminary was founded in 1887 and chartered in 1902. Besides the rabbinical school, the seminary includes an undergraduate liberal arts program, a graduate program in Judaic studies, a teachers institute, a cantors institute, a college of Jewish music, and the University of Judaism, which is located in Los Angeles, Calif., and comprises a teachers college, a college of Judaic studies, and a graduate school. Courses of instruction offered in New York include Jewish history, religion, literature, and sacred music, and the degrees of bachelor, master, and doctor are conferred in these fields. A program of studies offered in cooperation with Columbia University (q.v.) leads to a baccalaureate degree from both institutions. In 1973 the seminary library housed more than 220,000 bound volumes and 10,000 manuscripts. In 1973 enrollment in the seminary totaled 3178 students, and the faculty numbered 163. The endowment of the seminary was about $13,000,000.

JEWISH WAR VETERANS OF THE UNITED STATES OF AMERICA, service and community relations organization for Jewish war veterans and their dependents. It acts as an intermediary between government and community agencies and veterans in such matters as medical and hospital treatment, employment aid, death benefits for dependents, and family-welfare questions. Founded in 1896 by American Civil War veterans, the J.W.V. is the oldest active U.S. veterans organization. In 1973 it had more than 300 posts. Membership was about 100,000, and Ladies Auxiliary membership about 30,000. The J.W.V. publishes a monthly magazine, *The Jewish Veteran.*

JEWS. Although, in modern usage, the terms "Hebrew", "Israelite", and "Jew" are employed synonymously, both historically and ethnically the words have different meanings. As a general historical term, Hebrew (*see* HEBREWS) has no ethnic connotation, being applied to any of numerous Semitic, nomadic tribes dwelling in the eastern Mediterranean area before 1300 B.C. In Jewish history, the term is applied specifically to those tribes which accepted Yahweh (*see* JEHOVAH) as their deity, from the time of their prehistoric origins to the time they conquered ancient Palestine, called Canaan (q.v.), and, about 1020 B.C., became a united nation ruled by a king. Israelite connotes a particular ethnic and national group, descended from the Hebrews and united culturally by their religion (*see* JUDAISM); the term is historically descriptive of this group from the conquest of Canaan to the destruction of the Kingdom of Israel by the Assyrian king Sargon II (r. 722–05 B.C.) in 721 B.C. Jew refers to a third group, the cultural descendants of the first two, from the time of their return from the so-called Babylonian Captivity (q.v.) to the present. The word itself stems from the Hebrew *yehudhi,* originally meaning a member of the Hebrew tribe of Judah, and later, as Judea (q.v.), applied to the Jewish state; the English word "Jew" is derived directly from the Latin *Judaeus,* meaning an inhabitant of Judea.

Modern Jews are members of a separate ethnic community or fellowship rather than of a race, a community that, in the face of incessant and terrible persecution, has maintained its identity for almost nineteen centuries, from the final dissolution of the Roman province of Judea in 135 A.D. to the establishment of the modern State of Israel (q.v.) in 1948. In 1970 the Israeli Knesset adopted legislation defining a Jew as one born of a Jewish mother or a convert. The remarkable preservation of Jewish group identity resulted, primarily, from strict adherence to Judaism, with which Jewish history is inextricably bound. This religion governs Jewish life in its every aspect, requires the education of the young, and includes, in its traditional doctrines, hope for and faith in the establishment of a Messianic kingdom; *see* MESSIAH. Although reform movements began to affect Judaism in the 19th century, the survival of all Jewish communities resulted from the piety with which preceding generations had adhered to the Jewish Law. A distinguishing characteristic of the Jewish people has been their respect for and devotion to education and learning, which is considered an act of worship.

THE HEBREWS IN CANAAN

The Biblical accounts of Hebrew genealogy and history are credible in most instances, as far as can be ascertained from archeological and historical research. They were written in their present form, however, centuries after the described occurrences (*see* BIBLE: *The Old Testament*), and need careful interpretation. Thus the Hebrew prophet and lawgiver Moses says to the assembled Hebrews, "An Aramaean (*see* ARAM) ready to perish was my father" (Deut. 26:5). Characterizing the ancestors of the Hebrews as Aramaean nomads ("ready to perish" signifying the nomadic state of constant economic hardship) is more or less exact. In addition to Aramaean blood, the physical ancestry of the later Israelites included a mixture of strains, such as Amorite and Hittite (*see* AMORITES; HITTITES). The physiognomy characteristic of the ancient Hebrews, as depicted in Babylonian friezes (*see* BABYLONIA; BABYLONIAN ART), was very similar to that of the Hittites. The Hebrew language was a dialect of Amorite of the western Semitic language; *see* HEBREW LANGUAGE.

The Twelve Tribes. The history of the tribes, as descendants of the patriarch Jacob, told in the Old Testament, must be viewed in the light of the national consciousness developed by the Jewish scribes who compiled and edited the historical books in the 6th and 5th centuries B.C. In their efforts to tell a continuous and detailed story establishing a common ancestry, these scribes undoubtedly recorded legends as history; nevertheless, the Biblical narrative establishes facts that are in accord with historical theory. Thus, the Scriptures tell of twelve Hebrew tribes, descended from twelve sons of the patriarch Jacob: Asher, Benjamin, Dan, Gad, Issachar, Joseph, Judah, Levi, Naphtali, Reuben, Simeon, Zebulun. Biblical scholars view the Jacob story as symbolic, with actual tribal history cloaked in the guise of personal experiences. Thus, the tribes were interrelated by blood, and some, such as Reuben, Simeon, Levi, and Judah (sons of one mother) maintained an even closer alliance. The tribes of Asher and Gad (named as descendants of servants) were subordinate tribes. Another instance of tribal history written as personal experience is the covenant (q.v.) between Jacob and Laban (Gen. 31:44–54), which is interpreted, in Biblical criticism, as an early treaty between Hebrew and Syrian tribes, delimiting the borders of their grazing lands to the north of Gilead (q.v.).

Tradition and historical theory trace the Aramaean ancestors of Israel (used collectively) to the district of Ur in Sumer, on the lower Euphrates R. About the beginning of the 2nd millennium B.C. a group of Aramaean tribes emigrated to the region around Carrhae (now Harran, Turkey), an ancient Babylonian colony. Several centuries later several family units of these tribes migrated to the west and south, settling in scattered groups around the Jordan R. The Jordan settlers became the Hebrew tribes, including the Ammonites, Moabites (qq.v.), Edomites (see EDOM), and the Yahweh-worshiping Hebrews. In the Bible this period of tribal migration is known as the age of the patriarchs; see ISAAC.

The Exodus. Some of the tribes, traditionally belonging to the Joseph group, wandered toward Egypt, probably during the period of the Hyksos kings, the predominantly Semitic conquerors of Egypt between 1694 and 1600 B.C.; see EGYPT: *History: The Middle Kingdom*. There they prospered until the Hyksos were deposed (about 1570 B.C.) and, as a result, the Hebrews were persecuted, as aliens, and forced into slavery. The exodus (see book of EXODUS), is viewed by many historians as the successful effort of the Hebrews in Egyptian bondage to be reunited with other Hebrew tribes with which they retained a sense of kinship. The fact that no archeological records of the exodus exist, even on Egyptian monuments, is probably due to the fact that the Egyptian Hebrews numbered at most a few thousand, and probably less than that. Their flight caused, evidently, no great concern in Egypt.

In Jewish history, however, the exodus assumed major proportions. It was led by Moses, the first great prophet who, on Sinai (q.v.), the sacred mountain, received the covenant with Yahweh. This early religion incorporated in itself, and bequeathed to later Judaism, nomad concepts of the position of property, the rights of human beings, sexual morality, and the essential equality of all members of the community. Personal liberty and love of freedom, characteristics of the wandering Semites, in addition to the concept of a God who is Creator, Lawgiver, and King, became part of the religion of Israel, and later its political theory. See RELIGION.

The conquest of Canaan from about 1200 to about 950 B.C. was accomplished as much by intermarriage and alliance with the Canaanites as it was by military conquest. Moreover, the invaders had an undisturbed and unique opportunity to acquire dominance: the Egyptian, Hittite, and Sumerian empires were no longer powerful, and Assyria (q.v.), the potential great power, had not yet organized its forces. Under Joshua, the successor to Moses, the Yahweh tribes crossed the Jordan R., conquered the town of Jericho (q.v.) and the surrounding plain, and established themselves in western Palestine. Although numerically they were not superior to the Canaanites already resident, the Yahweh tribes were united by their religious covenant, their tradition of common descent, and their democratic ideal. During the period of the judges (see book of JUDGES), the great military and civil leaders, the Hebrews, now known as the Israelites, secured their land. They fought off invasions by the Moabites, and Midianites, and, most powerful of all, the Philistines (q.v.) who migrated from the territory around the Aegean Sea.

THE KINGDOM

With the accession of Saul, the first Israelite king, about 1020 B.C., the Israelites became truly united as a political entity. With David, Saul's successor, the kingdom acquired greatness.

The Kingdom under David. In both Jewish history and religion, David is considered second only to Moses. He is regarded as the true founder of Israel, the instrument of the religious and political system foreshadowed on Mt. Sinai. He captured Jerusalem (q.v.), the strongest fortress in Palestine, and made it his capital. Under his direction, the Israelite army broke the power of the Philistines, and conquered Edom, Ammon, and Moab. David organized religious services and arranged the duties of the priesthood, establishing the religion of Israel as supreme in Palestine. At his death all the countries surrounding the Israelite kingdom were either subjugated or bound by treaties of friendship.

The Kingdom under Solomon. David's son and successor Solomon is known as the builder of the Temple at Jerusalem (see TEMPLE), which became a symbol of Israelite glory and splendor. Solomon was a strong and powerful ruler who brought prosperity to his people by careful use of the treasures inherited from his father, by unifying the internal administration of his kingdom, and by promotion of commerce and industry. The extent of his commercial enterprises has been verified by the recently discovered remains of the Solomonic copper refinery and naval base at Ezion-geber, on the Gulf of 'Aqaba, and of the remains of the Solomonic city at Megiddo, Israel; see BIBLE SCHOLARSHIP: *Palestinian Archeology*. Besides stimulating economic activity, Solomon tried to strengthen the political position of his kingdom by marrying influential women of many of the neighboring principalities. However, forced labor and high

JEWS

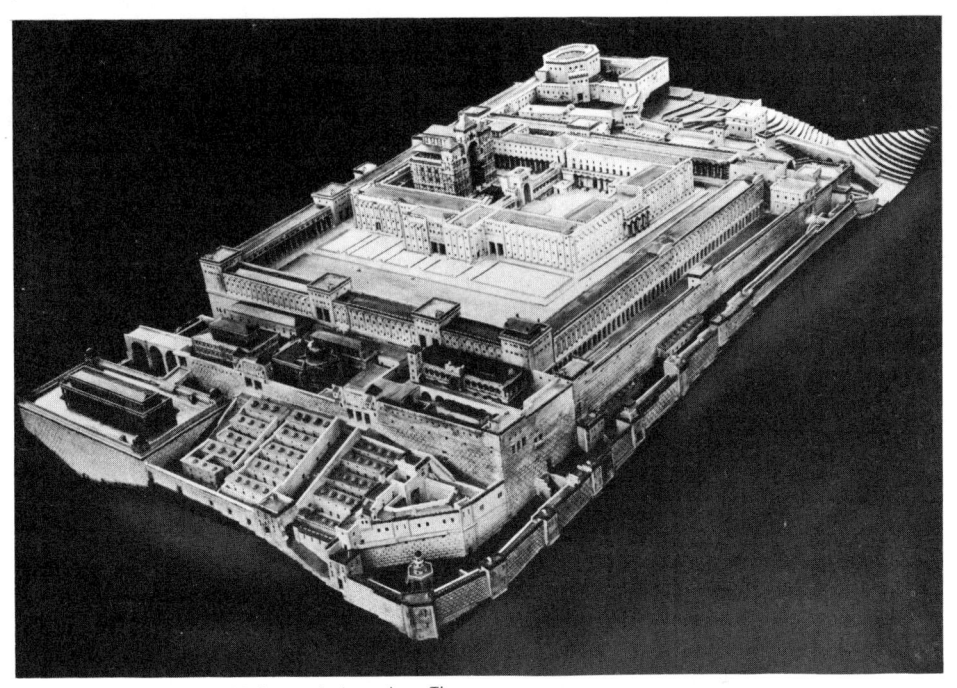

A model of the Temple of Solomon in Jerusalem. The temple was constructed about 950 B.C. of the wood of giant cedar trees from Lebanon.   Bettmann Archive

taxes provoked dissatisfaction and resentment among the population and caused political instability. Edom, in the southeast, successfully revolted, and the district of Damascus (q.v.), in the northwest, made itself independent of Israelite influence. The oppression of Solomon's rule and the king's sybaritic way of life, which was directly opposed to the stern, nomadic traditions of the Israelite religion with its democratic ideal, resulted in the division of the kingdom after Solomon's death, about 920 B.C.

The Divided Kingdom. When a delegation under Jeroboam requested guarantees of reform from Solomon's successor, Rehoboam, they were refused. In the dissension that followed, Jeroboam was supported by Sheshonk I, King of Egypt, called Shishak in the Bible (r. 940?–919 B.C.), who invaded and plundered the kingdom of Rehoboam and despoiled the Temple. The rebel leader became the first king of the autonomous northern kingdom of Palestine, known as Israel; *see* ISRAEL, KINGDOM OF. According to Biblical tradition, its inhabitants included ten of the twelve tribes, all except Judah and Benjamin. The southern kingdom, Judah, about 300 sq.mi. in area, was reduced to a secondary power. Separate religious shrines and sanctuaries were established at Dan and Bethel (qq.v.) in Israel and, although the two states retained their feeling of blood kinship, they were completely divided politically.

Jewish history for the next two centuries became a series of struggles between petty states, as Israel, Judah, Moab, Edom, and Damascus warred against each other. For a time, in the early 9th century B.C., Israel became the major Palestinian power under the great king Omri. King Omri founded Samaria (q.v.), about 870 B.C., as the capital of Israel and, under his direction, a period of peace was instituted. Under Ahab, his son and successor, however, Israel was shaken by internal strife concerning the most vital topic possible: religion. Ahab's wife, Jezebel, a princess of Tyre (q.v.), attempted to incorporate her pagan deity, the Phoenician god Melkarth (*see* BAAL), into the religion of Israel. Idolatrous influences had long been filtering into both Israelite kingdoms, but Jezebel's boldness resulted in great popular protest. Such protest was political as well as religious, for the ethical system of the Mosaic Law (*see* TORAH) concerned government as much as it did worship, and autocracy could be construed as sin. A series of lay prophets (*see* PROPHECY) waked the conscience of the Israelites. In the northern kingdom Elijah, Elisha, Amos, and Hosea called for a return to the rugged, democratic desert principles. In Judah, Isaiah and Micah inveighed against idolatry and luxury. Thus religious struggle was added to military conflict. When, in the 8th century B.C., the power of Assyria, grown to a position of dominance in the Middle East, advanced to the frontiers of the disorganized states, disaster was inevitable.

Assyria had, for over a century, attempted to conquer ancient Palestine. In 853 B.C. the first major Assyrian invasion, led by Shalmaneser III, had been turned back at the Battle of Karkar by a coalition of the little states, including Israel, under Benhadad II, King of Damascus (fl. middle 9th cent. B.C.). Assyria withdrew, but its forces continued to harry the Palestinian borders. In 734 B.C., when incessant quarreling among the weakened Palestinian states precluded another coalition, an Assyrian army under Tiglath-pileser III (r. 745–727 B.C.) invaded and conquered Israel. Only the fortress of Samaria held out until 722–721 B.C., when the Assyrians successfully assaulted and took the city. The kingdom of Israel was destroyed and many of its inhabitants were deported. Thenceforth they were known as the "Lost Tribes" (q.v.). Samaria was repopulated with immigrants from Mesopotamia who adopted the Israelite religion and became a sect known as Samaritans (q.v.). Although the kingdom of Judah became a tributary of Assyria, the southern state retained its nominal independence. Judah's survival was perhaps due to her small size, her quick submission to Assyria, and stable government.

The Fall of Jerusalem to Nebuchadnezzar. During the next century Judah maintained its identity while the balance of Near Eastern power shifted from Assyria to Egypt and, finally, to the renascent Babylonian Empire of the Chaldeans. The Judean kingdom, however, refused to submit to Chaldea as it had to Assyria. In 597 B.C. Nebuchadnezzar II, ruler of Chaldea, faced with defiance in Judah, conquered and sacked Jerusalem. The Judean nobles, warriors, and craftsmen were taken to Babylon, and Nebuchadnezzar made the Davidic prince Zedekiah king of Judah. In 588 B.C. Zedekiah led a revolt against Chaldea and, two years later, Nebuchadnezzar's army destroyed Judah and razed Jerusalem. All Judeans who were potential leaders of revolt were taken to Babylon. Another group fled to Egypt, taking with them, despite his protests, the prophet Jeremiah. Only the poorest Judean peasants were allowed to remain on their land. The Babylonian Captivity marked the end of the political independence of ancient Israel, except for a brief revival more than four centuries later.

SUBJECT JUDEA
At the time of the dissolution of Judah there were Judeans living in Egypt, in Babylon, and among the peasants in Palestine.

Life in Babylon. The most important of these communities was in Babylon. There the exiles found a thriving colony of their coreligionists, composed of the Judeans deported in 597 B.C. and others who had settled there during the destruction of the Israelite kingdom in 721 B.C. Under the direction of the priest and reformer Ezekiel, the Babylonian community retained its separate identity by replacing political Israel with spiritual Israel. The religion was ritualized and made liturgical to govern the life of the exiles. Scribes began to compile the traditions of the Israelites in the books destined to become the Bible. Prayer meetings took the place of worship in the Temple. An anonymous prophet, called Deutero-Isaiah, whose speeches form the second part of the Biblical book of Isaiah (q.v.), prepared the faithful exiles for a new life in a rebuilt Jerusalem.

Return to Jerusalem. In 539 B.C. Cyrus the Great, founder of the Persian Empire (see PERSIA), conquered Babylon. The next year he issued an edict emancipating the Jews. About 42,000 members of the Babylonian community prepared to return to Palestine, taking all their wealth, contributions from those remaining in Babylon, and, according to tradition, contributions from Cyrus himself. Led by Zerubbabel, a prince of the house of David, the expedition journeyed to Jerusalem. The country was still lying waste from the havoc of the Chaldean wars, and the emigrants despaired at the enormous task confronting them. The resulting apathy of the returned Jews was alleviated by the work of two religious leaders, the prophets Haggai and Zechariah, who held out, as Ezekiel had done before them, the rewards of spiritual life as the ultimate goal. The Jews turned their attention to rebuilding and in 516 B.C. the second Temple was completed. The latter date is regarded, in the Jewish tradition, as the true end of the exile in Babylon, which thus endured seventy years (586–516 B.C.).

The Jewish high priest was elected ruler of the province of Judah, or Judea, which thereupon became a theocracy. The task of rebuilding proceeded slowly, and about 445 B.C. Nehemiah, a Jewish favorite of Artaxerxes I, King of Persia (r. 464–424), was given permission to direct the reconstruction. Under his management Jerusalem again became a great city. During the same period, the Babylonian community, hearing reports of religious laxity, may have sent Ezra, a famous teacher and scribe, to institute religious reforms; the possibility of confusion of the identity of Artaxerxes, as mentioned in the book of Ezra (q.v.), however, makes a date of 398 or

JEWS

397 B.C. for Ezra's return also plausible. By the middle of the 4th century, Judea had become a country organized in accordance with formalized doctrines of belief and dominated by a powerful priesthood. The Torah, the books of the Law, governed every aspect of Jewish life, and the scribes and teachers of the Law gave the Scriptures final form. Judea prospered. Thus, adjusting to adverse circumstances, the Jews had, in about 150 years, transformed themselves from a political entity to a people almost entirely motivated by religion.

The Diaspora. In the late 4th century B.C., the dominant power in the ancient world became Macedonia (q.v.), under Alexander III, known as the Great. After the Macedonian subjugation of Persia, in 331 B.C., Judea became a province of Alexander's empire. According to tradition, Alexander showed special consideration to the Jews; thousands of Jews migrated to Egypt after the founding of Alexandria (q.v.); they were granted full Greek citizenship. With the growth of commercial opportunities, under the united empire, Jews migrated to colonies throughout the known world: on the shores of the Black Sea, on the Greek islands, and along the coasts of the Mediterranean Sea. These migrations assumed such large proportions that they became known collectively as the *Diaspora* (Gr., "Dispersion"). Far removed from the center of Jewish life in Judea, the emigrants had to learn and use the Greek language, rather than Hebrew, and adopt Greek customs and ideas. The Pentateuch (q.v.) was translated into Greek during the 3rd century B.C., and the Greek version, the Septuagint, which later included the other parts of the Hebrew Bible, became standard among the Jews of the Diaspora. The Greek way of life and Greek culture, known as Hellenism (*see* GREECE: *History: Ancient Greece*) became very influential among Jews of the Diaspora.

After the death of Alexander (323 B.C.), the Greeks became a political as well as a cultural danger to the Jews. Alexander's empire was divided among his generals, and Judea was first invaded by Ptolemy I, King of Egypt. Jewish territory, as the trade route to Arabia (q.v.), was strategically important, and it became the subject of intense conflict between Egypt and the Seleucidae (q.v.) of Syria. At length, in 198 B.C., in the Battle of Panion, Antiochus III, King of Syria, overwhelmed Egypt and added Judea to his domains. The Seleucid rulers began a campaign to replace Judaism with Hellenism. The campaign reached its height under Antiochus IV, King of Syria, who, in 168 B.C., proclaimed the Jewish religion illegal and replaced the altar to Yahweh in the Temple with an altar to Zeus; *see* GREEK RELIGION AND MYTHOLOGY.

The Hasmonaean Period. An inevitable Jewish rebellion began the same year under Mattathias, a Jewish priest, and his sons, called the Maccabees (q.v.). After a bitter military struggle, the Jewish forces defeated Syria. The Hasmonaean dynasty, or Maccabees, became the leaders and, finally, the kings, of an independent Jewish state. *See* books of the MACCABEES.

Under the Hasmonaeans, the Jews concentrated their efforts to keep their religion pure and free of foreign influence. The two major political parties that came into being, the Sadducees and Pharisees (qq.v.), differed as much in religious doctrine as they did in political theory. Other religious factions of the period included Jewish religious brotherhoods that maintained a monastic way of life in communal settlements; *see* ESSENES. The Hasmonaeans established the Sanhedrin (q.v.), a council of state composed of seventy-one Jewish leaders and sages that was the supreme authority for civil and religious legal decisions. The kingdom was expanded and, under John Hyrcanus, came to include Samaria and Edom, known as Idumaea, where the inhabitants were compelled to accept Judaism.

Like its predecessors, the Hasmonaean Jewish kingdom faced widespread factional conflict. During a civil conflict between the brothers Hyrcanus III (*see under* MACCABEES) and Aristobulus II (*see under* ARISTOBULUS), Antipater, an Idumaean and nominally a supporter of Hyrcanus, intrigued with the Roman general Pompey, called the Great. Rome entered Judea, and in 47 B.C. the kingdom became directly subject to Rome, with Antipater as procurator. His son Herod the Great became king in 37 B.C.

Christianity Appears. The last century of the ancient Jewish state was marked by religious and political upheaval. At the beginning of the Christian era there were about 8,000,000 Jews in the ancient world, living, outside of Judea, mainly in Alexandria, Cyrenaica (northern Africa), Babylon, Antioch (now Antâkya, Turkey), Ephesus (q.v.), and Rome. This dispersion created, in addition to the force of Hellenism, several movements that struck at Judaism. One was directed against all Jews, and took the form of anti-Jewishness based on business competition, religious differences, and the political privileges granted to many Jews who rose to high office. A second movement came from within Judaism itself, as Christianity (q.v.). The Greek Jews who came to believe in Jesus (Heb. *Yeshua,* or Joshua; *see* JESUS CHRIST) as the prom-

A relief from the Arch of Titus, in Rome, depicts Roman soldiers removing sacred utensils from the temple in Jerusalem after the Jewish rebellion against Roman authority, about 66 A.D.

ised Messiah far outnumbered the Judeans who accepted Jesus. Moreover, as the disciples of Jesus traveled through the ancient world, many pagans were converted to the new belief. Christianity was originally regarded as a Jewish sect, but as more and more pagans were accepted into Christianity, their faith revolved almost entirely about the person and preaching of Jesus. The Judeo-Christians, on the other hand, remained, essentially, Jews. The Jewish answer to these new movements was to permit no laxity in observance of the forms of traditional religion.

The Great Revolt. During the 1st century A.D. religious conflict caused bloody battles. The Roman governors of Judea were despotic and gave little respect to the Jewish religion. In 66 A.D. a violent insurrection, led by the Zealots (q.v.), a fanatic Jewish sect, began against Rome. Nero, then emperor, sent the Roman general Vespasian (later emperor) to put a final end to the conflict. By 70 A.D. the revolt was crushed, the Temple was destroyed, and Jerusalem was razed; Masada, the last fortress, fell in 73 A.D.

Nominally, Judea continued to exist. The center of Jewish learning was transferred to Jabneh (Jamnia, now Yavne, Israel) under the direction of the great sage Johanan ben Zakkai. For the next generation Judea was more or less peaceful, under strict Roman control. Then the Roman emperor Hadrian ordered Jerusalem rebuilt as a pagan city, to be called Aelia Capitolina, in honor of Jupiter (q.v.); at the same time he issued an edict banning circumcision (q.v.). This double insult caused consternation among the Jews of the Diaspora as well as those of Judea.

Bar Cocheba. A violent revolt occurred in Judea, under Simon Bar Cocheba. From 132 to 135 the Jews made a desperate stand against the Roman legions and were, for a time, successful. When the rebellion was finally put down by Rome, Judea was prostrate. By order of the emperor the very name of the province was discarded, and changed to Syria Palaestina. Jerusalem was made a pagan city, and the death penalty was decreed for any Jew who entered its gates. Persecution of Jews became common throughout the empire. Moreover, the fall of Judea created a greater rift between Jews and Christians. The Jews considered the loss a calamity, but the Christians saw it as a manifestation that God had abandoned the Jews and viewed themselves as the true bearers of divine grace (q.v.). During the first three centuries of the Christian era, Christianity became increasingly powerful. After 313, when Constantine I, Emperor of Rome, accepted the new religion for himself and his empire, Christian antagonism against, and, later, persecution of Jews became widespread.

POSTEXILIC JEWS

The destruction of the second Jewish state and the surge of anti-Jewishness did not disorganize the Jews.

Religious Development in Exile. Their answer was the development of the postexilic religion known as Judaism. Their continued unity was based upon a common language, a literary heritage that all Jews were required to know and study, a well-knit community life and organization, and their abiding Messianic hope.

JEWS

Aaron, the first Jewish high priest (19th-century French lithograph).   Jewish Museum, N.Y.

During the first six centuries of the exile, the teachers and rabbis set down the great body of oral law and religious interpretation in the Mishnah and Gemara, known collectively as the Talmud (qq.v.). The principal centers of Jewish learning became academies in Palestine, notably in Galilee (q.v.) and in Babylonia, first under the rule of the Parthians, then from 227 A.D. of the Sassanians or Neo-Persians. An important Jewish community had lived in Babylonia since the 6th century B.C., and it became the greatest influence on the exiled Jews. The Jewish colony was headed by an administrator known as an exilarch. The two Babylonian academies at Sura and Pumbeditha became renowned throughout all Jewish communities. The scholars who worked in the 1st and 2nd centuries A.D. on the codification and amplification of the oral law were the Tannaim (from Aramaic, "to teach"). They were succeeded in the 3rd century by the Amoraim (Aramaic, "speakers") and in the 5th century by editors called Saboraim (from Aramaic, "reflect"). With completion of the Gemara, the commentary on the Mishnah, the Babylonian Talmud was completed by the beginning of the 6th century. The less complete Palestinian Talmud (or Talmud of Jerusalem had received its present form about a century earlier. The later heads of the Babylonian academies were called *Geonim* (plural form of Heb. *gaon,* "excellence"); they received queries on religion from every part of the medieval world, and their answers, or "responses" came to be incorporated into standard religious practice.

Islamic Tolerance. The rise of Islam (q.v.) created no great disturbance in the Jewish communities of Babylonia. Muslim armies conquered Mesopotamia (q.v.) in 637 and the religion of Islam became the state religion. A series of nominal restrictions against Jews was decreed by the Code of Omar, promulgated by Caliph Omar I (q.v.). Jews were permitted to hold no political office and could have no Muslim servants. They could not bear arms, build or repair synagogues, or worship in loud voices. Moreover, they were required to wear yellow patches on their sleeves as a distinguishing mark. The caliphs of Baghdad (q.v.) did not consider themselves bound by the code and permitted the Jews to retain virtual autonomy; *see also* CALIPH. The historical importance of these restrictions resulted from their later importation into Europe by Christians, who imposed them on European Jews for centuries.

The period of Islamic tolerance was marked by cooperation between Muslims and Jews that resulted in a development of culture based on a combination of Greek, Muslim, and Jewish learning at a time when Europe was still in the so-called Dark Ages.

Jews in Medieval Europe. In the middle of the 10th century the center of learning, both secular and religious, shifted from Mesopotamia to Spain, then a Muslim country. Colonies of Jews had existed in Spain since before the ascendancy of the Roman Empire and had long suffered persecution, particularly after the Visigothic rulers accepted Catholicism in the 6th century; *see* GOTHS: *Visigoths.* The Muslim conquest brought peace to the Spanish Jews, who came to occupy prominent positions as statesmen, physicians, financiers, and scholars. Jewish scholars contributed to the beginning of the Renaissance in Europe by their translations of Greek classics, brought for the first time to western Europe.

The peaceful Spanish era ended in the middle of the 13th century, with the waning of Muslim domination in the Iberian peninsula. Under the Catholic monarchs, Spanish Jews were forced into the lowly position of other European Jews. During the Middle Ages persecution of Jews in Christian countries was the rule. Much of this persecution was unleashed by mobs who condemned every Jew as one who had taken part in the martyrdom of Jesus. During the Crusades (q.v.), thousands of Jews were massacred in the religious fervor of the period. In 1215 the fourth Lateran Council of the Roman Catholic Church, called by Pope Innocent III, proclaimed an official policy of restrictions, similar to the Code of Omar, and ordered all Jews to wear distinctive badges; *see also* LATERAN COUNCILS. Throughout Europe Jews were despised. In cities they were forced to live in special areas (*see* GHETTO) and not permitted freedom of movement. During the 13th and 14th centuries several European monarchs filled their treasuries by confiscating Jewish property and expelling the owners. In 1290 Edward I, King of England beggared and expelled the English Jews. Charles VI, King of France followed the English example in 1394, virtually ending Jewish history in France until modern times. During the period of the so-called black death (*see* PLAGUE), during the 14th century, massacres of Jews were common throughout Europe, on the charge that Jews had caused the plague by poisoning Christian wells. In Spain systematic persecution by the church resulted in mass conversions by Jews attempting to save their lives. In many cases, such conversions were merely outward; a class of converts called *marranos* (Sp., "swine") arose, professing Catholicism but adhering to Judaism in secret. The Spanish Inquisition, instituted in 1478, persecuted the *marranos*, and in 1492 Spain expelled the Jews. The expulsion from Portugal followed in 1497.

The exiles from western Europe found refuge in the eastern part of the continent. Thousands of Spanish Jews migrated to European Turkey, which preserved the Islamic policy of toleration, and Constantinople (now İstanbul) became the site of the largest Jewish community in Europe during the 16th century. Most of the Jews expelled from England, France, Germany, and Switzerland settled in Poland and Russia; by 1648 the Polish community included more than 500,000 Jews. The Polish Jews came to possess their own autonomous organization, within the Polish kingdom, and became the center of Jewish activity. Then came the persecutions of 1648–58, carried out by followers of Bogdan Chmielnicki (1593–1657), leader of cossacks in the Ukraine, in which countless Jewish communities of Poland were destroyed and a decline of eastern European Jewry was initiated.

Jews then being barred from the professions, from craft guilds, farming and large commercial enterprises, were forced to live by petty commerce.

JEWS IN MODERN LIFE
By the end of the 16th century only remnants of the old Jewish communities remained in western Europe.

The Reformation and the French Revolution.
With the gradual increase in political and social freedom following the Protestant Reformation (q.v.), however, tolerance for Jews was reestablished in the west. The new freedom came first to England, where the migration of Jews was encouraged, after 1650, by the Commonwealth under the military and political leader Oliver Cromwell. Jews were also encouraged to settle in the English colonies in America by such influential men as the philosopher John Locke and the colonial preacher Roger Williams. In France the Jews were enfranchised by the National Assembly in 1791, as part of the democratic concepts of the French Revolution (q.v.), and Napoleon I, Emperor of France, during his military campaigns, opened ghettos and emancipated the Jews as he marched across Europe; *see* GHETTO. A revival of repression occurred after 1815, when the states once subject to Napoleon refused to adopt his policies, including Jewish emancipation, which they regarded as a tendency to liberalism. This temporary reaction, however, lasted for only a few decades, and, in the 1860's, Jewish emancipation in western Europe was nominally secure.

Eastern European Persecution. In eastern Europe, on the other hand, the previous policy of Jewish tolerance was reversed; and Poland and Russia instituted official policies of Jewish persecution to offset any possible liberal tendencies. Such persecution equaled that of medieval Jews, particularly after the partition of Poland and the incorporation of eastern Poland into the Russian empire between 1772 and 1796; *see* POLAND: *History*. The new Russian territory contained most of the Polish Jews, for whom severe restrictions were laid down. Jews were forbidden to live outside of specific areas, and their educational and occupational opportunities were rigidly circumscribed. In addition, the imperial government encouraged and even financed periodic massacres of Jews, called pogroms (*see* POGROM), in order to divert the attention of the Russian populace from their discontent with the feudal system still prevailing in the late 19th century. The government instituted even sterner anti-Jewish measures, as it tried to isolate and render ineffective any possible political influence by Russian Jews, who were importing western European ideas and knowledge into Russia. This intense persecution endured until the Russian Revolution (q.v.), which overthrew the Czarist regime in 1917. As a result of the pogroms, about 2,000,000 Jews emigrated to the United States, between 1890 and the end of World War I, from areas under

JEWS

Anti-Semitic signs are removed from a shop window in Leeds, England, in 1960. Although anti-Semitism has declined as a political factor since World War II, many countries remain subject to periodic outbreaks of such vandalism. UPI

Russian control. Other colonies of eastern European Jews were founded in Canada, South America (notably in Argentina), the Union of South Africa, and in Palestine.

Jews in the Western Hemisphere. Jewish emigration to the Western Hemisphere began almost immediately after the founding of the first American colonies. Numerous Sephardic Jews (of Spanish or Portuguese descent) first settled in Brazil; only *marranos* were permitted, however, and persecution by the Inquisition resulted in their subsequent flight from Brazil. The first North American community of Jews was established in 1654 by some of these Brazilian *marranos*, thenceforth openly professing Judaism, in the Dutch colony of Nieuw Amsterdam (now New York City). Other groups of Jews settled in such cities as Philadelphia; Newport and Providence, in Rhode Island; and Savannah, in Georgia. At the time of the American Revolution, about 1780, the Jewish population of the colonies numbered an estimated 2000. Several of these colonial Jews became prominent during the period, notably Aaron Lopez (1731–82) of Rhode Island and Massachusetts, one of the leading merchants in the colonies, and Haym Salomon, a famous financier and one of the principal contributors to the financing of the Revolutionary army. During the early 19th century, most Jewish immigrants to the U.S. came from Germany, after 1815, as a result of anti-Jewish feeling following the downfall of Napoleon, and after 1848, following an unsuccessful German revolution. Among these German-Jewish families was that of U.S. Senator Judah P. Benjamin, who became a leading figure in the Confederate cabinet, and Isaac Mayer Wise, the organizer of American Reform Judaism. By 1880 about 250,000 Jews lived in the U.S. These early immigrants had come either as separate individuals or in family groups. During the next forty years, almost 3,000,000 Jews came to the U.S., mainly from eastern Europe. This flood of immigrants, however, constituted the population of entire communities and even provinces, which preserved their communal identity upon settling in the large cities along the Atlantic coast. Large-scale immigration ceased in 1924, when quota restrictions were enacted.

Life in Western Europe. The emancipation of the Jews had far-reaching religious and cultural, as well as political, effects. Slowly, as Jews took their place in the modern world, the wall erected around the Jewish community by strict, traditional Judaism began to crumble. Moses Mendelssohn exerted one of the greatest influences in bringing about the adjustment of Judaism, both as a religion and as a way of life, to the outside world. This great philosopher, by translating the Pentateuch into German and teaching the value of cultural affiliations between Jews and their non-Jewish environment, opened the route for the cultural contributions made by later Jews, both to the Jewish community and to the world. One of the results of his work was the Reformed Judaism initiated by German Jews. Many Jewish families discarded Judaism entirely, becoming Christian to increase their cultural and civic opportunities, and this action did not occasion the stern condemnation that it would have if taken only a century before. Among such families was that of Mendelssohn's own grandson, Felix Mendelssohn, the famous German composer. One of the greatest German poets, Heinrich Heine, was born Jewish and, though he was converted to Christianity, retained his love for Judaism. Benjamin Disraeli, one of the most notable British statesmen, was the son of a converted Jew.

In every country of western Europe, as well as in the U.S., Jews made monumental contributions, not as members of a Jewish community, but as citizens and members of national cultures. The German political theorist Karl Marx originated the modern Socialist and Communist movements. In France Henri Bergson and in Germany Hermann Cohen (1842–1918) and Martin Buber profoundly influenced modern philosophy. Sigmund Freud, a Jewish physician in Vienna, originated psychoanalysis (q.v.). In the graphic arts, such Jews as the painters Amedeo Modigliani (born in Italy), Camille Pissarro (of Portuguese and French parentage), and Marc Chagall (born in Russia), and the sculptors Jacob Epstein (born in the U.S.) and Jacques Lipchitz (born in Lithuania), became famous in international art circles. The physicist Albert Einstein (born in Germany) revolutionized theories of physics and mathematics with his concept of relativity (q.v.). In many fields of human knowledge and endeavor, Jews distinguished themselves as separate and equal members of all societies. The Jewish community itself underwent a cultural renaissance in the 19th century. Known as the *Haskalah* (Heb., "Enlightenment"), this renaissance was begun in eastern Europe. Jews once again began to write in Hebrew, to study the new science of the British biologists Charles Robert Darwin and Thomas Henry Huxley, and even to study the Bible so as to provide scholarly and scientific interpretations of the once sacrosanct Sriptures. Hebrew poetry, novels, and history were published, and Hebrew again became a living language. The Yiddish language (q.v.) of the eastern European Jews was dignified by its use as a literary language in the works of such great Jewish writers as Mendele Mocher Setorim, pen name of Shalom Jacob Abramovich (about 1836–1917), Shalom Aleichem, pen name of Solomon Rabinowitz; Judah Leb Peretz (1852–1915); and Sholem Asch; *see* YIDDISH LITERATURE. The cultural revival of the *Haskalah,* which was specifically Jewish, played an important role in the revival of Jewish hope for a homeland in Palestine by its study of the Jewish heritage.

Israeli soldiers, standing at stiff attention, take part in a parade marking the beginning of three years' active service. The army of Israel depends primarily on drafted citizens. UPI

Anti-Semitism. World events in the late 19th century indirectly aided the political hopes engendered by the *Haskalah.* In Germany and France, particularly, a movement opposing the Jews came into being. It was called anti-Semitism (q.v.) because its followers based their opposition not on the Jewish religion, but on what they considered the Jewish race: the Semites. Political parties were formed in such countries as Germany, France, Austria, and Hungary, to keep Jews from occupying positions of eminence. In France, anti-Semitism became a predominant political issue with the trial, on false evidence, of a Jewish army officer, Alfred Dreyfus (*see* DREYFUS AFFAIR). One of the spectators at the Dreyfus trial, an Austrian writer named Theodor Herzl, became convinced that the only solution to the problem of anti-Semitism was a Jewish national state. In 1896 Herzl became the founder of political Zionism (q.v.). For the next fifty years the Zionist organization fought and planned to achieve its ambition, finally realized in the State of Israel.

During the first half of the 20th century, and particularly in the period between the two

JEW'S HARP

World Wars, anti-Semitism became a dominant factor in European politics, notably in Germany. In the 1930's the growth of National Socialism (q.v.), incorporating anti-Semitic doctrines, threatened all Jews, many of whom considered themselves not Jews but assimilated members of various national groups. During the supremacy of the National Socialists in western Europe, an estimated 6,000,000 European Jews were systemically slaughtered in concentration camps, both in Germany and in German-controlled states; see CONCENTRATION CAMP.

For information on the population of the Jewish people, see JUDAISM: *Jewish Population*. See separate articles on those individuals mentioned above whose birth and death dates are not given. *See also* JEWISH ART; JEWISH LITERATURE; JEWISH MUSIC. N.N.G.

JEW'S HARP *or* **JEWS' HARP,** musical instrument consisting of a small horseshoe-shaped metal frame with a strip or tongue of metal mounted at the center. The ends of the frame are held between the teeth and the metal strip, which is free to vibrate at one end, is twanged with the thumb. The instrument produces one tone only, but various harmonics (q.v.) of this tone are made prominent by changing the size and shape of the mouth. The jew's harp was known in China as early as the 12th century, and has since been used in both Europe and America.

JEZEBEL *or* **JEZABEL** (fl. 9th cent. B.C.), Tyrian princess, daughter of Ethbaal, King of Tyre (now Sur, Lebanon) and Sidon (now Saida, Lebanon), and wife of Ahab (q.v.), King of Israel. According to the Old Testament books of Kings and Chronicles, Ahab married a princess of Tyre to cement a political alliance. Jezebel introduced the worship of Baal (q.v.) into Israel, thereby inciting a mutual enmity with the prophets of Jehovah (q.v.); *see* PROPHECY. She is portrayed as the most bitter opponent of the prophet Elijah (q.v.) and as instigating the murder of one Naboth for possession of his vineyard (1 Kings 21). Jezebel survived her husband by fourteen years and was killed by Jehu (q.v.) when he seized the thrones of Israel and Judah about 842 B.C. (2 Kings 9). The name of Jezebel was held in reproach among the Jews because she introduced tyrannical government and the worship of foreign gods. In the New Testament, in Revelation (Rev. 2:20), the name Jezebel is given to a wicked woman who is exerting a corrupting influence. In English it has come to signify a brazen or forward woman, probably from the translation of 2 Kings 9:30, "Jezebel . . . painted her face, and tired [that is, attired, as by donning a headdress] her head, and looked out at a window".

JEZREEL, PLAIN OF *or* **ESDRAELON,** large plain in northern Israel, between the Sea of Galilee (Lake Tiberias) and the Jordan R. on the E. and the Mediterranean Sea on the W. The plain, of triangular shape, is marked roughly by Mt. Tabor on the N.E., Mt. Gilboa on the S., and Mt. Carmel on the N.W. It is approximately 36 mi. long and has an average width of 15 mi. The Plain of Jezreel is watered by the Kishon, a small and intermittently dry river that ends at the Mediterranean Sea near Haifa, and by other small streams. The soil of the plain is fertile, and wheat, cotton, corn, sesame, tobacco, millet, and a variety of vegetables are grown.

The Plain of Jezreel has figured prominently in the history of Palestine. According to Josh. 19:17–23 it was assigned to the tribe of Issachar (q.v.) in the division of Canaan (q.v.) among the twelve Hebrew tribes; *see* JEWS: *The Hebrews in Canaan*; book of JOSHUA. There, in the 14th century B.C., the Israelites under the leadership of Barak defeated the Canaanites commanded by Sisera (Judg. 4). In the 13th century B.C. Jezreel was the site of a great victory by the Israelite hero Gideon (q.v.) over the Midianites (Judg. 6–7) and in the 11th century B.C. King Saul (q.v.) was finally defeated there (1 Sam. 28–31) by the Philistines (q.v.). Necho II, Pharaoh of Egypt (r. 609–593 B.C.) killed Josiah (q.v.), King of Judah, on the plain, near Megiddo, in 609 B.C. (2 Kings 23:29–30). The Hebrew prophet Elijah (q.v.) is thought to have engaged in a contest of "miracles" with the prophets of Baal (q.v.) on the western border of Jezreel (1 Kings 18:19–40); *see* PROPHECY.

The armies of ancient Assyria and Egypt (qq.v.) frequently met in battle on the Plain of Jezreel. In 1187 Saladin (q.v.), Sultan of Egypt and Syria, destroyed a fortress erected on the plain by the Knights Templars (q.v.), and in 1799 Napoléon Bonaparte, later Napoleon I (q.v.), Emperor of France, with an army of 4000 defeated a numerically superior Muslim force there.

The plain has been thought to be the battlefield referred to in Rev. 16:14–16, where "the kings of the earth and of the whole world" would gather for the battle of the "great day of God"; *see* ARMAGEDDON.

JHANSI, city of the Republic of India, in Uttar Pradesh State, and capital of Jhansi District, 130 miles S.W. of Kanpur. The city is a rail, trade, and industrial center, with railway workshops and iron and steel mills. Products manufactured in the city include brassware, rugs, rubber, and silk goods. The city developed around a fort built in 1613 and strengthened in 1742. It was the scene of a massacre of British residents in 1857 during the Indian Mutiny (q.v.). Pop. (1968) 172,987.

JIBUTI. See Djibouti.

JIDDA, or JEDDA, city and chief seaport of Saudi Arabia, in Hejaz Province, on the Red Sea, about 50 miles w. of Mecca. Railroads and roads connect Jidda with the larger cities in the country and an international airport is nearby. A commercial center, Jidda derives income from port activities. Industries in the city include iron and steel plants, oil refineries, and the manufacture of bricks, furniture, and tiles. The residential area is the site of many diplomatic missions and ministries, and through the city each year pass thousands of pilgrims on their way to Mecca (q.v.). The city is about three centuries old and was surrounded by walls until 1947. Pop. (1968 est.) 250,000.

JIG or **GIGUE**, fast dance in triple or 6/8 time. It was especially popular in England during the 16th century. In the 17th and 18th centuries, under its French name, "gigue", it was incorporated into concert music as one of the movements of the classical suite (q.v.). The jig was introduced into America in the 19th century where it became a part of the minstrel show (q.v.). Today, the jig is danced mainly in Ireland and Scotland.

JIGGER. See Chigger; Chigoe.

JIGS AND FIXTURES, devices for holding cast or forged metal parts in correct positional relationship to machine tools (q.v.). A jig, in addition to holding a piece of work, guides a machine tool accurately to predetermined locations on the work. A fixture is simply a holding device. These two devices make it possible to machine each of a number of metal parts in exactly the same manner and to such accuracy that the parts are interchangeable. For example, a jig assures that cylinder holes drilled in one automobile engine block will be in exactly the same locations and of the same size as those in all engine blocks drilled on the same jig.

The forms of jigs and fixtures are unlimited. The form used depends upon the shape and requirements of the piece of work to be machined. Accordingly, a jig or fixture is usually designed and built for a particular job.

The positioning of work in a jig is accomplished by means of locating pins and so-called rest surfaces which themselves are machined to very close tolerances. The pins and surfaces are hardened so that they may withstand wear without losing tolerance. All jigs include the same essential features: locating pins and rest surfaces, clamping devices for holding the piece of work firmly in position, and guides for directing a machine tool to desired locations on the work.

The automobile industry uses large special-purpose machines in which jigs are incorporated. These jigs automatically clamp the work and guide multiple drills or other machine tools to the work at any desired angle. The machine operator need only load and unload the parts to be machined. The simpler fixture anchors a piece of work firmly in place for machining operations, but does not act as a guide for a tool. A fixture has a part, called a set block, which includes locating pins and rest surfaces.

The use of jigs and fixtures makes possible the employment of practically unskilled labor to perform very accurate machining operations. The interchangeability of parts machined on jigs and fixtures, moreover, has made possible the assembly line procedures that are the basis of mass production.

JIMÉNEZ, Juan Ramón (1881–1958), Spanish poet, born in Moguer, Huelva Province, and educated at the College of El Puerto de Santa María and at the University of Seville. In 1901 he moved to Madrid, where he met the Nicaraguan poet Rubén Darío (1867–1916), the leader of the modernist movement in Spanish poetry, who profoundly influenced Jiménez' work. During several trips to France as a young man Jiménez became familiar with the work of the Symbolists (q.v.), who also helped shape his style. His first publication was *Almas de Violeta* ("Violet Souls"), a volume of verse. Among his other works of poetry are *Balades de Primavera* ("Ballads of Spring", 1910), *Diario de un Poeta Recién Casado* ("Diary of a Newly Married Poet", 1917), and *Sonetos Espirituales* ("Spiritual Sonnets", 1942). His Platero y Yo (1917; Eng. trans., *Platero and I,* 1956), a volume of prose poems, is a masterpiece of modern Spanish literature. The delicate fusion of fantasy and realism has endeared this poem to children as well as adults.

Shortly after the outbreak of the Spanish Civil War in 1936 Jiménez went to the United States. Subsequently he taught literature at the University of Puerto Rico and the University of Maryland. He was awarded the 1956 Nobel Prize in literature.

Jiménez' poetry is distinguished for its technical innovations, exquisite delicacy of feeling, subtle nuances of rhythm and tone, and soft lyrical quality. His poems are suffused with melancholy, a gentle brooding over solitude and suffering, and with a platonic sense of beauty.

R.J.Se.

JIMSONWEED

JIMSONWEED, or THORN APPLE or JAMESTOWN WEED, common name applied to *Datura stramonium* and related species of the Nightshade family, Solanaceae. Jimsonweed, naturalized in most parts of the world, is a large, coarse, annual herb found in pastures, roadsides, waste areas, and barnyards. Some varieties are occasionally cultivated in flower gardens.

Jimsonweed, Datura stramonium

The plants, which may grow as high as 5 ft., bear large, alternate, simple, irregularly bluntpointed leaves, and very large, conspicuous, petunialike tubular flowers with five to ten blunt points at the margin of the white or purple corolla tube. The fruit is a large, spiny, globose pod, green at first, later becoming brown, and opening at the top as it dries. The cavities within are filled with numerous large, black, flat seeds.

The name "Jimsonweed" is a corruption of "Jamestown weed" and derives from the mass poisoning of soldiers sent to Jamestown, Va., in 1676 to quell the uprising now known as Bacon's Rebellion (q.v.). Jimsonweed contains several alkaloids of the tropane configuration, which react with the nervous system to produce in man symptoms of delirium, incoherence, hallucinations, and incomprehension. The pupils of the eyes are widely dilated and vision may be disturbed. Severe cases display convulsions, coma, and not uncommonly, death. Poisoning may take place in several ways. Children have been poisoned by sucking the nectar from the base of the flowers. Some persons are poisoned when they make an infusion from the plant for the relief of asthma. One unusual case of poisoning resulted from grafting tomato tops onto jimsonweed roots, a practice intended to produce larger tomatoes. In this instance the tomato tops were grafted too high on the jimsonweed stem with the result that alkaloids produced in the jimsonweed part of the plant were transferred to the tomatoes and made them poisonous. Recently, Jimsonweed seeds and other parts of the plant have come into vogue for willfully producing hallucinations. This practice is extremely dangerous.   J.M.K.

JINJA, city of Uganda, in the Eastern Region, at the N. end of Napoleon Gulf of Lake Victoria, 45 miles N.E. of Kampala. Situated in an area of sugar plantations, the city is a lake-fishing port and the trade center of eastern Uganda. Industries include copper smelting, soybean and grain processing, cotton and sugar milling, brewing, and the manufacture of plywood and cigarettes. At Owen Falls, 1½ mi. to the N., are a dam and large hydroelectric plant. Bugembe, traditional capital of the former Busoga Kingdom, is nearby. Pop. (1965) 29,741.

JINNAH, Mohammed Ali (1876–1948), Indian Muslim statesman, first governor-general of Pakistan, born in Karachi, and educated there and in Bombay. He studied law in England, and was called to the bar in 1896. A year later he became the first Indian to appear as an advocate before the high court at Bombay, and he quickly developed a lucrative practice in criminal law. At the same time he worked fervently for the Indian National Congress, believing that Hindu-Muslim unity would strengthen India in the cause of freedom from British rule.

In 1910 Jinnah was elected to the Imperial Legislative Council, and he remained a member of the council for more than thirty years. In 1913 he joined, and three years later became president of, the All-Indian Muslim League, a political group organized to advance the interests of the Muslim minority in India. He was reelected president of the league in 1920, and after 1934 was reelected annually.

Jinnah supported the movement for noncooperation with the British, launched in the 1920's by the Indian nationalist leader Mohandas Karamchand Gandhi (q.v.), but he broke with the Indian National Congress because he felt that the promises made by the congress to the Muslim minority had not been honored. He then determined to lead the Muslims in political moves to obtain independence from the rest of India.

In 1940 Jinnah projected the separation from the rest of India of those areas with Muslim majorities, and the establishment of these Muslim areas as an independent nation. His objective was realized in 1947, when the creation of an independent Pakistan (q.v.) was approved by the British government, and Jinnah was appointed governor-general. He held that post until his death the following year. See INDIA: *History: Increasing Internal Tension*; INDIA, REPUBLIC OF: *History: Indian Independence Act*.

JIVARO, South American Indian people, numbering about 20,000, divided into four large groups and apparently constituting a distinct racial and linguistic stock. They live in E. Ecuador and the adjoining portions of N. Peru on the lower E. slopes of the Andes (q.v.) in the river basins of the Marañón, Santiago, and upper Pastaza rivers. They are a vigorous and warlike people, who remained wholly independent for centuries, successfully resisting attempts at conquest by the Incas in the pre-Spanish period and thwarting efforts at settlement and Christianization by Spanish missionaries during the 16th century. By the late 1950's, however, they had become more peaceful.

The Jivaro live in oval wooden houses called *jivarías,* each of which is the home of an extended family of some forty persons. An agricultural people, the Jivaro cultivate corn, cassava (q.v.), beans, bananas, and cotton, and weave their own cotton cloth. In warfare they are skilled soldiers, using blowguns, bows and arrows, lances, and shields. The most notable Jivaro custom was that of shrinking and preserving the heads of enemies slain in battle, in the belief that this action would prevent the return of the vengeful spirits of their victims. This custom, however, has virtually disappeared.

JOACHIM, Joseph (1831–1907), Hungarian violinist and composer, born in Kittsee, Austria. He began to study the violin at the age of five, and appeared in public in Budapest at the age of seven. From 1841 to 1843 he studied in Vienna; in the latter year he went to Leipzig, where he was warmly received by the German composer Felix Mendelssohn (*see under* MENDELSSOHN) with whom he studied for a time. Joachim was appointed (1853) concertmaster and solo violinist to George V, King of Hannover (*see under* GEORGE), retaining this post for thirteen years. In 1868 he became head of the music school in the Royal Academy of Arts in Berlin.

Joachim was one of the first virtuoso performers whose repertory included many works of other composers, past and contemporary, and not merely works of his own creation. His taste for 18th-century music helped make him a friend of such classically oriented composers as the German symphonist Johannes Brahms and the Italian opera composer Giuseppi Verdi (qq.v.). His advice about the technical capabilities of the violin was often sought by his colleagues when they wrote for the instrument. His own compositions were greatly influenced by the style of Robert Schumann (q.v.); the best known is the Hungarian Concerto for Violin, opus 11.

JOAN, Pope, legendary female occupant of the papal throne. Her "pontificate" is placed, in different accounts, variously in the 9th, 10th, and 11th centuries. According to one version, she was born in England (or in Germany of English parents) and fell in love with a Benedictine monk, with whom she fled to Athens disguised as a man. After her lover's death she entered the priesthood, became a cardinal, and, following her election to the papacy as John VIII (for the actual John VIII, *see under* JOHN) to succeed Pope Leo IV (800?–855), died in childbirth during a papal procession. The myth was first published in the 13th century, by the religious writer Stephen of Bourbon (d. 1261), and was repeated by many writers in the following three centuries. Given full credence by the church itself as well as the general public, the story was first questioned by the Bavarian historian Johannes Aventinus (1477–1534). Subsequently, other writers, including the French Calvinist theologian David Blondel (1590–1655), attacked the myth, which was completely demolished by the German Catholic theologian and historian Johann Döllinger (q.v.) in 1863.

JOAN OF ARC, Saint (Fr. *Jeanne d'Arc*), also called THE MAID OF ORLÉANS (1412–31), French national heroine, born of peasant parentage in Domrémy (now Domrémy-la-Pucelle). When she was thirteen years old, she believed she heard celestial voices. As they continued, sometimes accompanied by visions, she became convinced that they belonged to Saint Michael and to the early martyrs Saint Catherine of Alexandria (qq.v.), and Saint Margaret (255?–75). Early in 1429, during the Hundred Years' War (q.v.), when the English were about to capture Orléans, the "voices" exhorted her to help the Dauphin, later Charles VII (q.v.), King of France. Charles, because of both internal strife and the English claim to the throne of France, had not yet been crowned king. She succeeded in convincing him that she had a divine mission to save France. A board of theologians approved her claims, and she was given troops to command. Dressed in armor and

JOAN OF ARC

carrying a white banner representing God blessing the French royal emblem, the fleur-de-lis, she led the French to a decisive victory over the English. At the subsequent coronation of the Dauphin in the cathedral in Reims (q.v.), she was given the place of honor beside the king.

Although Joan had united the French behind Charles and had put an end to English dreams of hegemony over France, Charles opposed any further campaigns against the English. Therefore, it was without royal support that in 1430 Joan conducted a military operation against the English at Compiègne, near Paris. She was captured by Burgundian soldiers, who sold her to their English allies. The English then turned her over to an ecclesiastical court at Rouen to be tried for heresy and sorcery, and she subsequently underwent fourteen months of interrogation. She was accused of wrongdoing in wearing masculine dress and of heresy for believing she was directly responsible to God rather than to the Roman Catholic Church. The court condemned her to death, but she penitently confessed her errors, and the sentence was commuted to life imprisonment. Because she resumed masculine dress after returning to jail, however, she was treated as a relapsed heretic and again condemned to death. On May 30,

An equestrian statue of Joan of Arc stands in a square in Orléans, France. French Government Tourist Office

1431, Joan was burned at the stake in the Old Market Square at Rouen.

Twenty-five years after her death, the church retried her case, and she was pronounced innocent. In 1920 she was canonized by Pope Benedict XV (*see under* BENEDICT); her traditional feast day is May 30.

Joan of Arc in Literature and Art. Notable examples of the theme of Joan include the statue by the French sculptor François Rude, in the Luxembourg Museum, Paris, and that by the American sculptor Anna Hyatt Huntington, on Riverside Drive, New York City. A painting of her by the French painter Jules Bastien-Lepage (1848–84) is in the Metropolitan Museum of Art, New York City. She has been the subject of such plays as *Die Jungfrau von Orleans* (1801), by the German dramatist Johann Christoph Friedrich von Schiller; *Saint Joan* (1923), by the British playwright George Bernard Shaw; and *Joan of Lorraine* (1946), by the American playwright Maxwell Anderson. The French composer Arthur Honegger wrote of her in his oratorio *Jeanne d'Arc au Bûcher* ("Joan of Arc at the Stake"), which was first performed in 1938. Samuel Langhorne Clemens, the American humorist Mark Twain, wrote the biography *The Personal Recollections of Joan of Arc* (1896); she was the major figure in a notable chapter of the *History of England* (1754–62), by the Scottish historian

David Hume; and Voltaire, the French philosopher, commemorated her in his narrative poem *La Pucelle d'Orléans* ("The Maid of Orléans", 1756). See separate articles on each of the artists, composers and writers mentioned.

JOÃO PESSOA, formerly PARAHYBA, city in Brazil, and capital of Paraíba State, on the Paraíba do Norte R., 11 mi. inland from its port, Cabedelo, on the Atlantic Ocean, and 65 miles N. of Recife. It is a leading trade and distribution center. Industries include the manufacture of cement, footwear, and cigars. The city was founded in 1585. Pop. (1970 prelim.) 197,398.

JOASH *or* **JEHOASH,** name of two Biblical kings. In Hebrew, the name means "Jehovah gives".

Joash (844?–800 B.C.), according to 2 Kings 11–14 and 2 Chron. 22–25, King of Judah (837–800 B.C.), son of King Ahaziah (r. 842 B.C.). He was saved, as an infant, from death at the hands of his grandmother Athaliah (r. 842–837 B.C.) usurper of the throne, by his aunt Jehosheba (fl. 9th cent. B.C.), and placed on the throne at the age of seven. He reigned for "forty years" (a round number, signifying an uncertain figure), before he was assassinated by his servants.

Joash (d. 786 B.C.), according to 2 Kings 13–14 and 2 Chron. 25, King of Israel (801–786 B.C.), son and successor of Jehoahaz (r. 815–801 B.C.). His reign was supported by the prophet Elisha (q.v.). He succeeded in defeating Amaziah (q.v.), King of Judah, at Beth Shemesh (now in Israel), and reduced Judah to vassalage.

JOB, book of the Old Testament (*see* BIBLE), in the King James Version, THE BOOK OF JOB. Bible scholars have dated the book variously from Mosaic to postexilic times; *see* BABYLONIAN CAPTIVITY; MOSES. The time presently favored by most modern scholars, however, is the later postexilic period, or from 500 to 250 B.C. The author, who is unknown, is thought to have used an Israelite or Edomite (*see* EDOM) folktale or epic dating perhaps from the beginning of the Israelite monarchy (*see* JEWS: *The Kingdom*) as a framework for his poetic dialogue. Later, another writer (or editor) added the speeches of a youthful fourth friend (chapters 32–37). The book, part of the Wisdom literature of the Old Testament, includes Ecclesiastes and Proverbs (qq.v.).

The book of Job consists of five distinct sections: a prose prologue (chapters 1–2); a series of dramatic discourses between Job and three of his friends, Eliphaz, Bildad, and Zophar (chapters 3–31); a discourse between Job and Elihu, a fourth friend (chapters 32–37); the Lord's speeches from the whirlwind (38:1–42:6); and a prose epilogue (42:7–17).

The Prologue. Job is a "man . . . perfect and upright . . . one that feared God, and eschewed evil" (1:1). He is pious, rich, and the head of a large, contented family. Then on a day "when the sons of God came to present themselves before the Lord" (1:6), the Lord asks Satan (q.v.) what he thinks of Job's piety and righteousness. Satan proposes that Job would curse the Lord if he were to lose all his wealth; so God and Satan agree to test Job. Satan proceeds to take away Job's possessions, even his sons, and finally to afflict Job with extremely painful boils. Job refuses, however, to curse God. Three of his friends, having heard of his misfortunes, now arrive to comfort him, but they are dumbfounded at their first sight of Job.

Job and His Friends. The second section, after Job's first complaint (chapter 3), consists of three cycles of speeches. During each cycle each one of his three friends speaks once and Job, directly replying to each in turn, answers three times. The gist of the speeches of the three friends is that Job's misfortunes and suffering must result from some wickedness on the part of Job, and therefore he is justly served. Job, steadfastly proclaiming his innocence, soon becomes irritated, then angry, with his friends for their apparently unwarranted, superficial judgments; still he continues to seek an explanation for his suffering: "Oh that one would hear me! behold, my desire is, that the Almighty would answer me" (31:35).

The third section consists of the speeches of Elihu. His wrath is kindled against Job "because he justified himself rather than God" (32:2) and against "his three friends . . . because they had found no answer, and yet had condemned Job" (32:3). Elihu contends that Job has added "rebellion to his sin" (34:37) by questioning God's judgment. His support for this contention is the belief that "touching the Almighty, we cannot find him out: he is excellent in power, and in judgment, and in plenty of justice" (37:23).

God Speaks. In the fourth section, God speaks from out of a whirlwind. He seems to ignore completely Job's desire for an explanation or justification of his suffering: instead, He humbles Job by challenging him to explain how the universe was created and how it is ordered. Job's "error", apparently, is his presumption that God's ways and His omnipotence are humanly comprehensible. In seemingly irrelevant questions (40:8), God both rebukes Job and makes His most direct reply to Job's earlier question: "What is the Almighty, that we should serve him? and what profit should we have, if we pray unto him?" (21:15). Recognizing at last that he

JOB

has spoken out of ignorance and that he may come no closer to God than his vision of Him, Job now repents (42:1–6).

The Epilogue. In the last section, God rebukes Job's three friends (Elihu does not appear) because they "have not spoken of me the thing that is right, as my servant Job hath" (42:7). He gives to Job twice the wealth and possessions he formerly owned, seven sons and three beautiful daughters, and a contented old age. Like the prologue, the epilogue is in prose and most clearly reflects the probable folktale basis of the poetic discourses.

JOB, Hebrew folk hero whose afflictions are related in the Old Testament book that bears his name; see book of JOB.

JOCASTA, wife of Laius, King of Thebes, and mother of Oedipus (qq.v.), King of Thebes. When an oracle foretold that Jocasta's son would kill his father, Laius had the child exposed on a mountain. Believing her son dead, Jocasta did not recognize Oedipus when he reappeared in Thebes as a young man. The youth saved the city from a dread monster and, as a reward, was married to Jocasta. When she learned that she and Oedipus were mother and son, as well as husband and wife, she committed suicide in horror and despair at their incestuous relationship.

JODHPUR, city of the Republic of India, in Rajasthan State, about 175 miles S.W. of Jaipur. The city is the trade center for the surrounding region in which grains are grown. An important rail junction, Jodhpur also maintains an airport. The handicrafts industry turns out embroidered items, decorated leather goods, and ivory, lacquer, and metal ornaments. Points of interest include a wall surrounding the old part of Jodhpur and a fort, containing several old palaces, on a nearby hilltop. The city was founded in 1459 and was the capital of the former native State of Jodhpur, or Marwar, until 1949. Pop. (1971) 318,894.

JODRELL BANK OBSERVATORY *or* **NUFFIELD RADIO ASTRONOMY LABORATORIES,** department of the Victoria University of Manchester, located in Cheshire, England; it was founded shortly after World War II and placed under the direction of Sir Bernard Lovell (1913–). In 1947–48, a fixed 218-ft.-aperture radio tel-

The 2000-ton radio telescope of the Jodrell Bank Observatory, England. It is the largest and the only automatically steerable radio telescope in the world, capable of analyzing phenomena in outer space at a distance of 1,000,000,000 light-years.
British Information Services

escope was installed. It was replaced in 1957 by a steerable radio telescope 250 ft. in diameter, the largest in the world. Another steerable radio telescope, 125 ft. in diameter and controlled by a digital computer, was placed in operation in 1964. The observatory is concerned primarily with investigating the universe by studying radio emissions received from distant radio galaxies (see GALAXY), quasars, the Milky Way (qq.v.), and nearby extragalactic nebulae (see NEBULA). Radar studies of the moon and planets are also undertaken. See RADIO ASTRONOMY.

JOEL, book of the Old Testament (see BIBLE), in the King James Version, JOEL. It is one of twelve short prophetic books of the Old Testament known, primarily because they are all brief, as the Minor Prophets (see BIBLE, CANON OF THE). In Hebrew (Jewish) versions of the Old Testament the book is divided into four chapters; chapter 3 in the Hebrew versions appears as 2:28–32 in the King James Version, and chapter 4 appears as chapter 3.

The book falls into two distinct parts. In the first part (1–2:27), the prophet depicts the devastation resulting from a plague of locusts. The people are summoned to a solemn fast at "the house of the Lord" (1:14) and urged to pray there for deliverance. The prophet, interpreting the plague as a portent of the coming Day of the Lord (1:15), warns the people that only heartfelt repentance can save them on that day. If they repent, the Lord will not only remove the locusts; He will also restore to the land its former fruitfulness, and He will restore to the people their former plenty. They shall know that the Lord is "in the midst of Israel" (2:27).

In the second part (2:28–3:21), Joel prophesies an age of deliverance, in which the Lord will pour out His "spirit on all flesh" (2:28), and "shew wonders in the heavens and in the earth" (2:30), and "gather all nations" (3:2) into the "valley of decision" (3:14) for a final judgment. The enemies of Judah (q.v.) will then be laid waste for "violence against the children of Judah", but "Judah shall dwell for ever, and Jerusalem from generation to generation" (3:19-20).

Tradition attributes the book to the Hebrew prophet Joel (q.v.), about whom Bible scholars currently know nothing except his name. From references in the text, however, most scholars have concluded that the book dates from the immediate postexilic period; see BABYLONIAN CAPTIVITY. Christian theologians have always found considerable significance in the second part of Joel. Saint Peter (q.v.) believed that the passage about the Lord's Spirit was a prophecy concerning the descent of the Holy Ghost (q.v.), and he cited this passage from Joel (Acts 2:16–21) on the day of Pentecost (q.v.). Bible scholars see in the second part of Joel an early, well-realized example of the Apocalyptic style; see APOCALYPTIC WRITINGS; ESCHATOLOGY.

JOEL (Heb., "Jehovah is God"), author of the Old Testament book of Joel (q.v.). Called "the son of Pethuel" (Joel 1), he is grouped with the twelve Minor Prophets; see BIBLE. He apparently lived in or near Jerusalem about the 5th century B.C., and nothing else is known about him.

JOE-PYE WEED. See EUPATORIUM.

JOFFRE, Joseph Jacques Césaire (1852–1931), French army officer, born in Rivesaltes, and educated at the École Polytechnique, Paris. He joined the French army in 1870 at the beginning of the Franco-German War (q.v.), and remained in the army, serving in French colonies overseas. In 1911, as a major general, he became chief of staff of the French army and, at the beginning of World War I (q.v.) in August, 1914, became commander in chief of all French armies; later he was in command of all the Allied armies in France. He is known chiefly for the victorious attack the French army carried out under his direction against the German armies that had invaded France at the beginning of the war and that, by September, 1914, had almost reached Paris. Joffre's victory in the first battle of the Marne caused the Germans to abandon their march on Paris and to fall back to the Aisne R.; see MARNE, BATTLE OF THE: *First Battle of the Marne.* This success made Joffre a national hero; his subsequent failure to break the German lines, however, and the German onslaughts against the strongly fortified French city of Verdun (q.v.), which they nearly captured in 1916, caused dissatisfaction with Joffre's leadership. On Dec. 13, 1916, General Robert Georges Nivelle (1858–1924), succeeded him as actual commander of the French armies, although Joffre still retained the title of commander in chief. Subsequently Joffre was named marshal of France. In 1918 he was elected a member of the French Academy.

JOGJAKARTA. See DJOKJAKARTA.

JOGUES, Saint Isaac (1607–46), French Jesuit missionary, born in Orléans. He joined the Jesuits (q.v.) in 1624. After being ordained a priest in 1636, he was sent at his own request to Canada as a missionary to the Huron (q.v.) Indians. In the New World he undertook a mission to the Indians known as the Tobacco Nation in 1639 and to the Algonquin in 1641. He was captured, mutilated, and enslaved by the Mohawk (q.v.) in 1642; in the following year he was rescued by

A view of Johannesburg from the President Hotel.
South African Tourist Corp.

Dutch settlers. He returned to France and in 1644 was sent by the French government on a peace mission to the Iroquois. After concluding a treaty of peace with them, he went to Québec to plan the establishment of a permanent mission to the Indians. In 1646 he was captured by a hostile band of Mohawks, who charged him with sorcery and murdered him near the site of the present town of Auriesville, N.Y. His *Journal* and *Description of New Netherlands in 1642* are important sources for early American history. He was canonized in 1930 with seven other martyrs, known in the United States as the North American Martyrs and in Canada as the Canadian Martyrs. Their joint feast day is Oct. 19.

JOHANAN BEN ZAKKAI, *or* JOCHANAN BEN ZAKKAI (d. about 80 A.D.), Jewish teacher, student of the great teacher Hillel (q.v.). He preserved the laws and rituals of the Jewish religion after the destruction of the Temple at Jerusalem by Titus (q.v.), later Roman emperor, in the year 70. During the siege of Jerusalem by the Roman armies, Johanan, a prominent member of the Pharisees (q.v.), escaped from the city to the Roman encampment, according to tradition in a coffin borne by his pupils. He founded a school at Jabneh (near Gaza, in what is now the Arab Republic of Egypt) with the permission of the Roman emperor, Vespasian (q.v.), who treated him well. Jabneh became the headquarters of the Jewish council, the Sanhedrin (q.v.), of which Johanan was a member. For the next half century Johanan's school replaced Jerusalem as the spiritual center of Judaism. There, work began, in Johanan's lifetime, on the first part of the Talmud, the Mishnah (qq.v.).

JOHANNESBURG, city of the Republic of South Africa, in Transvaal Province, on the slopes of the Witwatersrand (q.v.) at an altitude of about 6000 ft. The city is about 800 miles N.E. of Cape Town and about 300 miles N.W. of Durban. It is the largest city of the Republic of South Africa and the industrial and commercial center of South Africa and the center of the country's gold-mining industry and site of the Johannesburg Stock Exchange. The city is a strategic rail, highway, and air hub, with international air traffic handled at Jan Smuts Airport. Besides mining, important industries include the manufacture of mining and railroad equipment, automobile parts, chemicals, textiles, and electrical and communications equipment. A modern city with many skyscrapers, Johannesburg is the cultural and educational center of South Africa. It has a municipal art gallery and a number of museums devoted to fields such as geology, transportation, and African history and ethnology, as well as several theaters, a symphony orchestra, and an opera company. The city is the site of a number of educational institutions, including the University of Witwatersrand (found 1922), and Witwatersrand Technical

College (1925). On the fringe of the city is the Republic Observatory.

The Johannesburg area was virtually uninhabited until 1886 when gold was discovered; by 1900 the population had grown to more than 100,000. Control of the Witwatersrand region was one of the causes of the South African War (q.v.) between the British and Dutch settlers. Johannesburg did not achieve city status until 1928. Most of the manual labor in Johannesburg, especially in the mines, is performed by the non-European population, principally the Bantu (q.v.). Within the Johannesburg metropolitan area are several Bantu townships where, in keeping with the South African policy of apartheid, the non-European population resides. Pop. (greater city; 1970 prelim.) 1,407,963.

JOHN OF DAMASCUS, Saint or **JOHN DAMASCENE, Saint** (645?–750?), theologian, writer, scholar, and Father of the Church and doctor of the Church, born in Damascus, Syria; see FATHERS OF THE CHURCH. The dates of his life are uncertain, but he is said to have lived to 104. Although a Christian, he served as a high-ranking financial officer under the Saracen caliph of Damascus; see SARACENS. Because of the caliph's hostility to Christians, John resigned his post around 700. He retired to the monastery of Mar Saba, near Jerusalem, where he was ordained a priest before the outbreak of the controversy over iconoclasm (q.v.). John opposed and fought the edicts of Leo III, Byzantine Emperor (about 680–741), against the veneration of statues and images; he was able to do so with impunity because he was not Leo's subject. He spent the rest of his life in religious study, except for a period shortly before his death, when he journeyed throughout Syria preaching against the iconoclasts.

John was considered one of the ablest philosophers of his day and was known as *Chrysorrhoas* (Gr., "Golden Stream"), because of his oratorical ability. He was the author of the standard textbook of dogmatic theology in the early Greek Church. His textbook, the *Source of Knowledge,* is divided into three parts: *Heads of Philosophy, Compendium of Heresies,* and *An Exact Exposition of Orthodox Faith.* The third and most important section contains a complete theological system based on the teachings of the early Greek Church Fathers and church synods from the 4th to the 7th century; see ORTHODOX CHURCH. John of Damascus was canonized by the Roman Catholic Church as well as the Greek Church. He is known also as John Damascenus, and his feast day in the Roman Church is March 27, in the Greek, Dec. 4.

JOHN OF NEPOMUK, Saint or **JOHN OF POMUK, Saint** (1340?–93), patron saint of Bohemia (now part of Czechoslovakia), born in Pomuk (now Nepomuk), near Pilsen (now Plzeň), Czechoslovakia. In 1380 he became pastor and later cathedral canon and vicar-general to the archbishop of Prague. According to tradition, he was later appointed confessor to Queen Joanna (d. 1386), wife of Wenceslaus IV, King of Bohemia and Germany and Holy Roman Emperor (1361–1419). The king had John tortured and put to death for his refusal to divulge the queen's confessions and for his defense of ecclesiastical rights. Pope Benedict XIII canonized him in 1729. His feast day is May 16.

JOHN OF THE CROSS, Saint. See SPANISH LITERATURE: *Renaissance and Golden Age;* THERESA, SAINT.

JOHN THE BAPTIST, Saint (between 8 and 4 B.C.–about 27 A.D.), according to all four Gospels (see GOSPEL) the precursor of Jesus Christ (q.v.), born in Judea, the son of the priest Zacharias and Elisabeth, cousin of Mary (q.v.), the mother of Jesus. John was a Nazarite (q.v.) from birth and prepared for his mission by years of self-discipline in the desert. At about the age of thirty

Saint John the Baptist beneath the Cross, detail from the Crucifixion scene on the Isenheim altar by the 16th-century German artist Matthias Grünewald.
Bettmann Archive

233

JOHN THE EVANGELIST

he went into the country around the Jordan R. preaching penance in preparation for the imminent coming of the Messiah (q.v.). He baptized penitents with water as a symbol of the baptism (q.v.) of the Holy Spirit which was to come; see HOLY GHOST. With the baptism of Jesus, his office as precursor was accomplished, and his ministry came to a close soon afterward. John incurred the anger of Herod Antipas (see under HEROD), Judean ruler, by denouncing him for marrying Herodias (14? B.C.–after 40 A.D.), the wife of his half brother Herod Philip (d. 34 A.D.), and was imprisoned (Luke 3:1–20). At the request of Salome (q.v.), daughter of Herodias and Herod Philip, John was beheaded (Matt. 14:3–11).

In art John the Baptist is represented as wearing camel's hair and often carries a staff or scroll with the words *"Ecce Agnus Dei"*, or "Behold the Lamb of God", a reference to John 1:29. The feast of his birth is celebrated (in the West) on June 24; the feast of his death, on Aug. 29.

JOHN THE EVANGELIST, Saint, *or* SAINT JOHN THE DIVINE, (d. about 101 A.D.), in the New Testament, one of the twelve Apostles (see APOSTLE), son of Zebedee and younger brother of Saint James the Great (see under JAMES). He became a disciple first of John the Baptist (q.v.) and then of Jesus, who made him an Apostle and called him and James *Boanerges* (Gr., "sons of thunder"), for their zeal (Mark 3:17). John, together with James and Peter (q.v.), made up the privileged group of disciples who witnessed Jesus' Transfiguration and were present during the Agony in Gethsemane (q.v.). Next to Peter, John was the most active of the Apostles in organizing the early Church in Palestine and, later, throughout Asia Minor. According to tradition, during a period of persecution of Christians by the Romans, John was banished to Pátmos, where he was believed to have written the Apocalypse, or book of Revelation (q.v.). Later he was believed to have gone to Ephesus, where the same tradition relates that he wrote three Epistles (see JOHN, EPISTLES OF) and the fourth Gospel (see JOHN, GOSPEL ACCORDING TO SAINT). He is venerated as the patron of Asia Minor. In art he is represented by several emblems, among them an eagle (see EVANGELISTS, SYMBOLS OF THE FOUR), relating to his office as evangelist (q.v.), and a kettle, referring to the tradition that he survived an attempt to execute him by immersion in burning oil. His feast day is Dec. 27.

JOHN, name of twenty-one popes and three antipopes. The numbering of popes named John is complicated by the omission of a John XX, whose existence modern scholars deny. According to the *Annuario Pontificio* (the official yearbook of the Vatican City), John XVI was an antipope. See also the two subentries under *John XXIII*, below. The first of these concerns the third antipope named John. The first antipope of this name was unnumbered; see *John*, below. The major figures of this name follow. For the regnal dates of prelates not listed, see POPE.

Saint John I (470–526), pope from 523 to 526, born in Tuscany. He was sent by Theodoric (q.v.) the Great, King of the Ostrogoths, who controlled Italy, to Constantinople (now Istanbul, Turkey) in 523. There, he was to obtain from Justin I (452–527), the Byzantine emperor, an abatement of Justin's repression of the Arian heretics (see ARIUS), Theodoric's coreligionists. John's orthodoxy prevented him from completely fulfilling the mission, however, and Theodoric, in anger, had John imprisoned at Ravenna, where the pontiff died. His feast day is May 18.

John II (d. 535), original name MERCURIUS, pope from 533 to 535. He was the first pope to adopt a new name upon elevation to the papacy. In his pontificate, John II secured in 533 from Athalaric, King of the Ostrogoths in Italy (516–34), confirmation of the decree against simony (the purchase or sale of church offices or preferment) issued by the Roman Senate. In the following year John obtained a profession of orthodox faith from Byzantine Emperor Justinian I (q.v.), the Great, a significant fact in the light of the current strength of the Monophysites (q.v.) in the Byzantine Empire.

John VII (d. 707), pope from 705 to 707. He apparently approved the decrees of the Quinisext Council against the See of Rome, sent to him by Byzantine Emperor Justinian II (669–711), although his predecessor had rejected them all.

John, antipope in 844. At the death of Pope Gregory IV (r. 837–44), Sergius II (r. 844–47) was lawfully chosen pope over John, a deacon, in a disputed election. The Roman populace, however, proclaimed John pope. Sergius' supporters then seized John and confined him in a monastery. His further fate is unknown.

John VIII (820?–82), pope from 872 to 882, born in Rome. He is often considered one of the ablest pontiffs of the 9th century. Among the various reforms achieved during his pontificate was a notable administrative reorganization of the papal curia. With little help from European kings, he attempted to expel the Saracens (q.v.) from Italy, after they had penetrated as far as Rome. He failed and as a result was forced to pay tribute. John defended Saint Methodius (see CYRIL AND METHODIUS) against his German enemies, who objected to his use of the Slavonic language in the liturgy. John later confirmed the permission to use Slavonic that had been originally granted by Pope Adrian II (r. 867–72), John's predecessor. In 879 he recognized the reinstatement of the learned Photius (q.v.) as the legitimate patriarch of Constantinople; Photius had been condemned in 869 by Pope Adrian II. In 878 John crowned Louis II, King of France (see under LOUIS). He also crowned two Holy Roman emperors: Charles II (q.v.), the Bald, in 875; and Charles III (see under CHARLES), in 881.

John X (860?–928), pope from 914 to 928. He was elevated to the papacy through the influence of a Roman noble family. During his pontificate he crowned Berengar I, King of Italy (d. 924), as Holy Roman emperor; in 915 he headed the allied forces that routed the Saracens (q.v.) at the Garigliano R.; and he attempted to bring the Bulgarians into communion with Rome. But John's determination to be dominated by no papal faction induced his domestic enemies, led by Marozia (fl. 10th cent.), a daughter of the family that had sponsored him for the papacy, to imprison him and effect his murder.

John XI (906–36), pope from 931 to 935 or 936. He was the son of Marozia, perhaps by Pope Sergius III (see under SERGIUS), and was chosen pope at the age of twenty-five through his mother's influence. Marozia and John's half brother Alberic (d. 954), sometimes called Alberic II to distinguish him from his father, Alberic, Marquess of Spoleto (d. 925), controlled John in all affairs except strictly spiritual matters. From the ecclesiastical view, probably John's only worthwhile deed was to confer extensive privileges upon the Cluniac Congregation, at Cluny, France, then recently organized. Alberic may eventually have seized John and kept him in prison until his death.

John XII (938–64), original name OTTAVIANO, sometimes called the BOY POPE, pope from 955 to 964. Grandson of Marozia and son of Alberic II, he was born in Rome and elected pope when he was only eighteen years old. During his pontificate, which was one of the papacy's darkest periods, he secured the aid of Otto I, King of Germany (see under OTTO), against Berengar II, King of Italy (d. 966), who had occupied the Papal States (q.v.). John crowned Otto as Holy Roman emperor in 962 but later conspired against him for assuming papal prerogatives. Otto thereupon summoned a synod that deposed John in 963. The synod elected Leo VIII (d. 965) as pope. John fled, but after Otto's departure for Germany he returned and wreaked vengeance on Leo's supporters. Leo then fled.

Before Otto could return to reinstate Leo, John died suddenly of paralysis and was succeeded by Benedict V (d. 966).

John XIII (d. 972), pope from 965 to 972. He was the nephew of Marozia and was bishop of Narni when elevated to the papacy through the influence of Otto I. Because John was the imperial papal candidate, Roman nobles opposed to imperial power imprisoned him before his pontificate was three months old. John escaped and was enabled to return to Rome when Otto invaded Italy in 966. John crowned Otto II (see under OTTO) as joint emperor with his father in 967.

John XV (d. 996), pope from 985 to 996. He became pope as the choice of Johannes Crescentius Nomentanus the Younger (d. 998), a powerful Roman aristocrat, who dominated John's pontificate. John mediated in English and French politics and was the first pope to canonize a saint, namely, Ulrich (890–973), bishop of Augsburg (canonized in 993).

John XVI (d. 1013?), original surname PHILAGATHUS, antipope in 997–98, born in Rossano, Italy. He had been a monk and had served Holy Roman emperors Otto II and Otto III (see under OTTO) as a diplomat. John was archbishop of Piacenza, Italy, when the patrician Johannes Crescentius Nomentanus the Younger (d. 998), who seized control of Rome when Otto III left the city, promoted him to the papacy in 997. Gregory V (r. 996–99) had become pope through the influence of Otto III and was expelled when Otto left. When the emperor returned to Rome, however, John fled from the city; imperial soldiers captured him and he was blinded and facially mutilated, deposed, and eventually confined to a monastery until his death.

John XIX (d. 1032 or 1033), original name ROMANO, pope from 1024 to 1032 or 1033, born in Italy. Although he was a layman, John succeeded his brother, Pope Benedict VIII (see under BENEDICT). During his pontificate, popular opinion forced John to refuse the request of Basil II, the Byzantine emperor (see under BASIL), to recognize the title of ecumenical patriarch for the patriarchs of Constantinople. In 1027 John crowned Conrad II (q.v.), Holy Roman Emperor. John is said to have been the first pope to grant indulgence (q.v.) as a reward for almsgiving.

John XXI (1215?–77), original name PEDRO, known as PETRUS JULIANUS or PETRUS HISPANUS, pope in 1276–77, born in Lisbon, Portugal, the son of a physician. John was renowned for his studies in philosophy, theology, and medicine. In 1247 he became professor of medi-

JOHN (Popes)

cine at the University of Siena; there he wrote several treatises on medicine and *Summulae Logicales* ("Logical Summaries"), a manual on logic famous for almost 300 years. Pedro became archbishop of Braga in 1273, cardinal bishop of Tusculum later in 1273, and pope in 1276. In his eight-month pontificate John improved the condition of the church in Portugal, excommunicated Alfonso III, King of Portugal (see under ALFONSO), for persistent interference in Portuguese episcopal elections, sent legates to the Great Khan of the Tatars (see KUBLAI KHAN) in an effort to form a crusade against the Saracens (q.v.), effected a temporary reunion of Eastern and Western Christendom, and prevented war between France and Castile (q.v.).

John XXII (1249–1337), original name JACQUES DUÈSE, pope from 1316 to 1334, born in Cahors, France. He taught law successively at Toulouse and Cahors, and was made bishop of Fréjus in 1300, archbishop of Avignon in 1310, and cardinal bishop of Porto in 1312. His pontificate was spent at Avignon (q.v.) under French influence. John was involved in a long dispute with Louis of Bavaria, later Louis IV (q.v.), Holy Roman Emperor, whom he finally excommunicated in 1324. Four years later Louis IV named Pietro Rainalducci, a Franciscan (see FRANCISCANS), antipope as Nicholas V (see under NICHOLAS). In 1330, however, Nicholas made humble submission to John and abdicated. Another difficulty, earlier in John's pontificate, arose from controversies among a group of radical Franciscans. Several of these friars, who were called "fraticelli" because they adhered to extremely austere views, and from whose number Nicholas V came, began to profess opinions that the pope branded as heretical. Some of the Spirituals refused to accept this papal decision on their views and, fleeing to the emperor for protection, constituted themselves an anti-Johannine party. A third conflict came from John's insistence upon his own views about the Beatific Vision, the vision of God that, according to Catholic doctrine, is granted to the faithful departed. The novelty of his opinions aroused much opposition among French theologians. Under their pressure John eventually withdrew his interpretation and returned to the traditional belief on this matter. Administratively, John applied himself to enlargement and reorganization of the papal curia and instituted several far-reaching changes in ecclesiastical finances, among whose results was a vast improvement in the previously tottering papal treasury.

John XXIII (1370?–1419), original name BALDASSARE COSSA, antipope from 1410 to 1415, born in Naples. He studied law in Bologna and in 1401 became a cardinal deacon. He was a leader in the Council of Pisa in 1409, when Pope Gregory XII (r. 1406–15) and Benedict XIII (1328–about 1423), an antipope, were deposed, and Alexander V (1340?–1410) was elected to heal the Western Schism; see SCHISM, WESTERN OR GREAT. When Alexander V died, Cossa succeeded him as John XXIII. John's principal sponsor was Louis, Duke of Anjou (see under LOUIS), whose claim to the kingdom of Naples John supported. In 1413 John convoked a council in Rome, the chief accomplishment of which was the condemnation of the writings of two religious reformers, the Englishman John Wycliffe and the Bohemian John Huss (qq.v.). At the Council of Constance held from 1414 to 1418 to heal the schism in the Western Church, John was forced, in 1415, to abdicate; see CONSTANCE, COUNCIL OF. He resumed his original name and was confined in various German cities until 1418. Reconciled with Pope Martin V (see under MARTIN), whose election in 1417 ended the schism, Cossa was made cardinal bishop of Tusculum in 1419, five months before his death.

John XXIII (1881–1963), original name ANGELO GIUSEPPE RONCALLI, pope from 1958 to 1963, born near Bergamo, Italy. He studied successively in Bergamo and Rome and was ordained a priest in 1904. Subsequently, he became secretary to the bishop of Bergamo, taught church history in the local seminary, and organized Catholic Action groups. In 1925 he was consecrated as archbishop. He served later as papal diplomat to Bulgaria (1925–35), Turkey (1935–45), and France (1945–53). In 1953 he was made a cardinal and appointed patriarch of Venice. He succeeded Pius XII (see under PIUS) as supreme pontiff.

In 1962 John convoked an ecumenical council, known as Vatican Council II (see VATICAN COUNCILS), for the purpose of effecting reform and renewal of the Roman Catholic Church (q.v.) and of taking steps to promote the unity of all Christians; see ECUMENICAL MOVEMENT. John issued eight encyclicals (see ENCYCLICAL LETTERS), the chief of them being "Christianity and Social Progress" (1961) and "Peace on Earth" (1963), which were the first papal encyclicals ever to be addressed to all men of good will. He created a new climate in interfaith relations and won the esteem and affection of the world for his personal qualities and for his work for peace and Christian unity. He received many Protestant leaders in audience. John set a precedent by journeying frequently outside Vatican City, in all about 150 times.   T.M.H.

Pope John XXIII prays during the ceremony that accompanied the opening of Vatican Council II in 1962. UPI

JOHN, name of a number of European monarchs. Brief accounts of less important rulers are included in this article under the names of the countries that they ruled. The more important monarchs are described in separate biographical articles following this entry, to which the reader is referred.

The English name *John* appears in Danish as *Hans, Jan, Johan,* or *Johann;* in French as *Jean;* in German as *Hans, Johann,* or *Johannes;* in Greek as *Ioannes;* in Hungarian as *Janos;* in Norwegian as *Hans* or *Johan;* in Polish as *Jan;* in Portuguese as *João;* in Spanish as *Juan;* and in Swedish as *Johan* or *Johannes.*

ARAGÓN

John I (1350–95), King of Aragón (1387–95), the son of Pedro IV (1319–87). He gave little attention to governmental affairs during his reign, but avoided involvement in the Hundred Years' War (q.v.).

John II (1397–1479), King of Aragón (1458–79) and King of Navarre (1425–79), the son of Ferdinand I, King of Aragón (*see under* FERDINAND) and father-in-law of Isabella I (q.v.), Queen of Spain. John represented his brother Alfonso V (q.v.), King of Aragón, Naples, and Sicily, in Aragón as lieutenant general and succeeded him to the throne of Aragón. John in 1420 had married Blanche of Navarre (1385?–1441), who inherited the throne of Navarre in 1425. For many years John struggled with his son, Charles, later Charles IV, King of Navarre (*see under* CHARLES) for control of the two kingdoms. After Charles' death in 1461, John suppressed a series of revolts led by former adherents of Charles in the province of Catalonia. During the latter part of his reign, John engaged in war against Louis XI (q.v.), King of France and was forced to cede to him the provinces of Cerdagne (in Spain and France) and Roussillon (in France).

BOHEMIA

John (1296–1346), King of Bohemia (1310–46), the son of Henry VII (q.v.), Holy Roman Emperor. He became count of Luxembourg in 1309. In the struggle between Austria and Bavaria for the crown of the Holy Roman Empire, John gained victory for Louis IV (q.v.), Holy Roman Emperor, in the battle of Mühldorf in 1322. From 1333 to 1335 John waged an unsuccessful campaign in Italy on behalf of the Guelphs; *see* GUELPHS AND GHIBELLINES. He became blind about 1340 but continued his active life. He was killed while assisting the French against the English at Crécy; *see* CRÉCY, BATTLE OF. His son became Holy Roman emperor as Charles IV (*see under* CHARLES).

BYZANTINE EMPIRE

John I Zimisces (925–76), Byzantine Emperor (969–76). In 969 he conspired with his aunt Empress Theophano (d. after 976) to murder his uncle, Emperor Nicephorus II Phocas (913?–969), and seize the throne. His reign was marked

JOHN (Rulers)

by campaigns against the Russians, whom he expelled from Bulgaria and Thrace between 970 and 973, and against the Saracens, from whom he recovered Syria during 974–76.

John II Comnenus (1088–1143), Byzantine Emperor (1118–43), the son of Alexius I Comnenus (q.v.). John was too preoccupied with military matters to reform the corrupt imperial administration. He defeated the Serbs in 1122 and the Hungarians in 1124. After 1126 he successfully fought the Seljuks (q.v.) in Asia Minor regaining much of the territory lost by earlier emperors.

John III Ducas (1193–1254), Byzantine Emperor (1222–54). After distinguishing himself as a soldier, he was chosen to succeed his father-in-law, Theodore I Lascaris (d. 1222). His reign was at first limited to the area of Nicaea, the remnant of the Byzantine Empire inherited from his predecessor, but he expanded his territories by recovering in 1241 the Latin conquests in Asia Minor. A strong administrator, John did much to improve economic conditions.

John IV Lascaris (1250?–1300?), Byzantine Emperor (1258–61), the son of Theodore II Ducas (1221–58). He reigned briefly at Nicaea until his regent deposed, blinded, and imprisoned him and assumed the throne as Michael VIII Palaeologus; see PALAEOLOGUS.

John V Palaeologus (1332–91), Byzantine Emperor (1341–76, 1379–91), the son of Andronicus III Palaeologus (1296–1341). After a civil war from 1341 to 1347, the empire was controlled by the regent John VI Cantacuzene (q.v.) as coemperor from 1347 to 1355. John V was deposed by his son Andronicus IV (d. 1379) in 1376, but regained the throne in 1379 with the aid of Turkey and Venice. Both internal dissension and extension of Ottoman Turkish control over the Balkans caused progressive decline in John's power. He sought Western aid by offering to submit to papal authority, but in 1371 was forced to acknowledge himself tributary to the Turks.

John VI Cantacuzene or **John V Cantacusene** (1292?–1383). See JOHN VI CANTACUZENE Byzantine Emperor.

John VII Palaeologus (1360–1412), Byzantine Emperor (1390, 1398–1412), the grandson of John V Palaeologus. He seized the throne for a short time in 1390 and after 1398 served as coemperor with his uncle Manuel II Palaeologus (see under MANUEL). John defended Constantinople (now Istanbul), the capital, against the Turks.

John VIII Palaeologus (1391–1448). see JOHN VIII PALAEOLOGUS, Byzantine Emperor.

CASTILE AND LEÓN

John I (1358–90), King of Castile and León (1379–90), the son of King Henry II (q.v.). John attacked Portugal to defeat the schemes of John of Gaunt (q.v.), Duke of Lancaster, who had assumed the title king of Castile, and of Ferdinand I, King of Portugal (see under FERDINAND). Ferdinand submitted in 1382 and made peace, giving his daughter to John I in marriage. On Ferdinand's death in 1383, John again made war on Portugal, but was defeated at Aljubarrota in 1385 by John I (q.v.), King of Portugal. In 1386–87 he repulsed John of Gaunt's invasion of Spain and settled their differences by a treaty and by arranging the marriage of one of John of Gaunt's daughters to his son Henry, later Henry III, King of Castile and León (see under HENRY).

John II (1405–54), King of Castile and León (1406–54), the son of Henry III. He reigned under the regencies of his mother and his uncle, Ferdinand I, King of Aragón (see under FERDINAND), until 1419. John entrusted the government to Don Álvaro de Luna (1388?–1453), his chief counselor. In 1450, after the death of John's wife, Luna arranged the king's marriage with a Portuguese princess, who promptly broke Luna's power by encouraging the king to assert his independence. In 1453 John ordered Luna's execution. John reportedly died of remorse over this treachery.

DENMARK

John I (1455–1513), King of Denmark (1481–1513), as John I, King of Norway (1483–1513), and as John II, King of Sweden (1497–1501). He was the son of Christian I (q.v.), King of Denmark. His reign was marked by his difficulties with Sweden, where Sten Sture (1440?–1503) was regent from 1470 to 1497 and from 1501 to 1503. John, aided by Swedish nobles, was able to assert his royal power in Sweden only between 1497 and 1501. In the latter year Sture regained control of Sweden and resumed the war for independence from Denmark.

ENGLAND

John (1167?–1216). See JOHN, King of England.

FRANCE

John I (1316), King of France and Navarre (1316), the son of King Louis X (see under LOUIS). John was born five and one-half months after his father's death and lived only five days. It was alleged, but never proved, that his uncle, Philip V (q.v.), who succeeded him as king, had John abducted or killed.

John II, called JOHN LE BON ("the Good") (1319–64), King of France (1350–64), the son of King Philip VI (q.v.). During his reign he debased the coinage to raise funds for prosecution of the Hundred Years' War (q.v.). John was captured in 1356 by Edward (q.v.), the Black Prince, at Poitiers (q.v.) and was imprisoned in England.

JOHN (Rulers)

His son Charles, later Charles V (q.v.), acted as regent during his captivity. John was returned to France in 1360 to raise his ransom under the terms of the Peace of Brétigny; see BRÉTIGNY, PEACE OF. Because he was unsuccessful in collecting the 3,000,000 crowns required, in 1364 John honorably resumed his captivity in England, where he soon died.

HUNGARY

John Zápolya (1487–1540), King of Hungary (1526–40). From 1511 to 1526 he was governor of Transylvania, and he also acted as regent during the minority of King Louis II (*see under* LOUIS). After Louis' death John was elected king by the Diet in 1526; his election involved him in war for twelve years with his rival for the throne, Ferdinand I (q.v.), Holy Roman Emperor. With Turkish aid he regained much of Hungary by 1529. Ferdinand recognized John as king of Hungary in 1538.

John Sigismund Zápolya (1540–71), King of Hungary (1540–71), the son of John I. He was elected king in the year of his father's death and of his own birth. His rule was supported by Suleiman I (q.v.), Sultan of Turkey, who helped him maintain his claim to the throne against the renewed aggression of Ferdinand I and of Maximilian II, Holy Roman emperors (1527–76).

NAVARRE

John (1397–1479). *See* JOHN II, under *Aragón*, above.

NORWAY

John I (1455–1513). *See* JOHN I, under *Denmark*, above.

POLAND

John I or **John Albert** (1459–1501), King of Poland (1492–1501), the son of Casimir IV (1427–92). During his reign the nobility and the gentry secured increased privileges at the expense of the burghers and the peasants. He waged unsuccessful wars against both Hungary and Moldavia over access to the Danube R.

John II Casimir (1609–72). *See* JOHN II CASIMIR, King of Poland.

John III Sobieski (1624–96). *See* JOHN III SOBIESKI, King of Poland.

PORTUGAL

John I (1357–1433). *See* JOHN I, King of Portugal.

John II (1455–95). *See* JOHN II, King of Portugal.

John III (1502–57), King of Portugal (1521–57), the son of Emanuel (q.v.), King of Portugal. At his accession Portugal was at the height of its power, but during his reign its influence began to wane. Colonial enterprise, however, continued, and Portuguese title to Brazil was confirmed by the Congress of Badajoz in 1524. John established the Inquisition (q.v.) in Portugal in 1531 and allowed the Jesuits (q.v.) to enter the country in 1540.

John IV, called JOHN THE FORTUNATE (1605–56), King of Portugal (1640–56), the first of the Braganza (q.v.) kings. He governed Portugal with energy and ability, restoring finances and promoting commerce and agriculture. He proclaimed himself king after driving out the Spanish usurpers in 1640 and finally routed them at the Battle of Montijo in 1644. In 1649 and 1654 the Portuguese won important naval victories over the Dutch off the coast of Brazil, thereby regaining their possessions in South America. By his capable administration John succeeded in restoring Portugal to a respected place in Europe.

John V (1689–1750), King of Portugal (1706–50), the son of Pedro II (1648–1706). His accession occurred during the War of the Spanish Succession, in which he allied himself with the British; *see* SPANISH SUCCESSION, WAR OF THE. He fought several unsuccessful campaigns in Spain, but obtained a favorable peace with France in 1713 and with Spain in 1715. Although his court was characterized by extravagance, John devoted much attention to ecclesiastical matters and in 1749 received for himself and his successors the title "Most Faithful King" from Pope Benedict XIV (*see under* BENEDICT).

John VI (1767–1826). *See* JOHN VI, King of Portugal.

SAXONY

John, in full JOHANN NEPOMUK MARIA JOSEPH (1801–73), King of Saxony (1854–73), the son of Prince Maximilian (1759–1838), born in Dresden. He succeeded his brother Frederick Augustus II (q.v.). John favored a liberal constitution. He assisted Austria against Prussia in the Seven Weeks' War (q.v.) in 1866; entered, under Prussian compulsion, the North German Confederation (q.v.); supported Prussia in the Franco-German War (q.v.); and helped to found the German Empire in 1871. John was a student of German and Italian literature and an amateur artist; he wrote poetry and published an annotated, metrical German translation of *The Divine Comedy* by Dante Alighieri (q.v.).

SWEDEN

John I (1201?–22), King of Sweden (1216–22). During his reign he entrusted the government to the clergy and occupied himself with several unsuccessful invasions of Estonia.

John II (1455–1513). *See* JOHN I, under *Denmark*, above.

John III (1537–92), King (1568–92), the second son of Gustavus I (q.v.). John became duke of

239

JOHN VI CANTACUZENE

Finland in 1556. His elder brother, Eric XIV (1533-77), plotted to have him condemned to death and imprisoned him from 1563 to 1567 on suspicion that John was conspiring to restore a Roman Catholic monarchy to Sweden. In 1568, with his younger brother Charles, later Charles IX (q.v.), John conspired against Eric and was elected king. Eric died of poisoning in 1577, a deed probably inspired by John. Converted to Roman Catholicism in 1578, he attempted to impose that religion upon his people, but soon abandoned the effort. Meanwhile, in alliance with the Poles, John warred against Russia, which was compelled in 1583 to cede parts of Estonia to Sweden.

JOHN VI CANTACUZENE or **JOHN V CANTACUZENE** (about 1292-1383), Byzantine Emperor (1341-55). He was the friend and first minister of Andronicus III, Byzantine Emperor (see under ANDRONICUS), after whose death he claimed the throne and went to war against the defenders of the legitimate heir, nine-year-old John V Palaeologus (q.v.). Cantacuzene triumphed largely through the aid of the Ottoman Turks, and is considered responsible for their entry into Europe. He had reigned only seven years when Palaeologus fought for the crown with Genoese help and forced him to abdicate. He became a monk and wrote his memoirs which constitute one of the major documents of Byzantine history.

JOHN VIII PALAEOLOGUS (1390-1448), Byzantine Emperor (1425-48), eldest son and successor of Emperor Manuel II (q.v.). By the time John became emperor, the empire was reduced by the Ottoman Turks to the city of Constantinople (now İstanbul, Turkey). Desperate for Western aid, John agreed to the union of the Eastern and Western churches. In 1439, the Union of Florence unified the churches, and in 1443 Pope Eugenius XI (see under EUGENIUS) authorized a crusade to rescue Constantinople. Both the Byzantine populace and the clergy bitterly opposed the union, the crusade was a complete failure, and the empire fell to the Turks under John's brother and successor, Constantine XI Palaeologus; see PALAEOLOGUS.

JOHN, often called JOHN LACKLAND (1167?-1216), King of England (1199-1216), best known for signing the Magna Charta (q.v.). John was the youngest son of King Henry II and Eleanor of Aquitaine (qq.v.); Henry provided for the eventual inheritance of his lands by his older sons before John was born. By 1186, however, only Richard I (q.v.), known as Richard the Lion-Hearted, and John were left as Henry's heirs. In 1189, as Henry neared death, John joined Richard's rebellion against their father, and when Richard was crowned he gave John many estates and titles. While Richard was off on the Third Crusade, John's efforts to usurp the crown failed; upon returning to England, Richard forgave him. When Richard died in 1199, John became king. A revolt ensued by the supporters of Arthur of Brittany (1187-1203), the rightful heir to the throne. Arthur was defeated and captured in 1202, and it is believed that John had him murdered. Philip II (q.v.), King of France continued the war until John had to surrender nearly all his French possessions in 1204. In 1207 John refused to accept the election of Stephen Langton (q.v.) as archbishop of Canterbury. Pope Innocent III (see under INNOCENT) excommunicated John and began negotiating with Philip for an invasion of England. Desperately, John surrendered England to the pope and in 1213 received it back as a fief; see FEUDALISM. John tried to regain his French possessions but he was decisively defeated by Philip in 1214. John's reign had become increasingly tyrannical; to support his wars he had extorted money, raised taxes, and confiscated properties. His barons united overwhelmingly to force him to respect their rights and privileges. John had little choice but to sign the Magna Charta presented to him by his barons at Runnymede (q.v.) in 1215, and making him subject, rather than superior, to the law. Shortly afterward John and the barons were at war. He died in the middle of the campaign, and was succeeded by his son Henry III (q.v.).

JOHN II CASIMIR, sometimes known as CASIMIR V (1609-72), King of Poland (1648-68). John was the younger son of King Sigismund III (1566-1632). He became a Roman Catholic cardinal in 1640. When his older brother Ladislaus IV, King of Poland (1595-1648) died, John was elected to succeed him. His reign was marked by the invasions by Tatars and Cossacks (qq.v.) in 1649, a disastrous thirteen-year war with Russia from 1654 to 1667, and a war with Sweden from 1655 to 1660. After abdicating in 1668, John retired to an abbey in Nevers, France.

JOHN III SOBIESKI (1642-96), King of Poland (1674-96), born in Olesko (now in the Ukrainian S.S.R.). John entered public life as a military leader in 1648. After distinguishing himself in battles against the Tatars, the Cossacks (qq.v.), the Russians, and the Swedes, he was made commander of the Polish army in 1668. He defeated the Ottoman Turks at Khotin (now in Ukrainian S.S.R.) in 1673, and was elected king of Poland in 1674. In 1683, he formed an alliance with Leopold I, King of Hungary (1640-1705).

JOHN OF GAUNT

Leading combined Hungarian and Polish forces, he lifted the Turkish siege of Vienna. By decisively defeating the Turkish army, which was three times larger than his own, John ended the threat of a Muslim conquest of Europe. During the final years of his life, after failing to secure access to the Black Sea, he suffered loss of prestige and increasing opposition among the Polish nobility. His death marked the virtual end of Polish independence.

JOHN I (1357–1433), King of Portugal (1385–1433), the illegitimate son of King Pedro I (1320–67). In 1384, after cooperating in the national revolt against Spanish influence, John became regent. In 1385 he was elected king despite the rival claim of John I, King of Castile and León (*see under* JOHN). Castilian invasions failed and John cemented his friendship with England by a treaty and by marrying a daughter of John of Gaunt (q.v.), Duke of Lancaster. John was a popular monarch; his reign featured administrative reforms, the flourishing of Portuguese culture, an emphasis on chivalry, the conquering of Ceuta in North Africa from the Moors, and the discovery of the islands of Porto Santo and Madeira. He was succeeded by his son Edward (1391–1438).

JOHN II, called JOHN THE PERFECT (1455–95), King of Portugal (1481–95), the son of King Alfonso V (q.v.), born in Lisbon. He acted as regent from 1475 to 1477 during his father's absences from the kingdom. As king, John limited the power of the aristocracy and dealt severely with the nobles who opposed him, condemning one to death and killing another by his own hand. During his reign the western coast of Africa was explored by Portuguese navigators; Diogo Cam (q.v.) discovered the mouth of the Congo R., and Bartholomeu Dias (q.v.) discovered the Cape of Good Hope. By the Treaty of Tordesillas in 1494, Portugal and Spain settled rival colonial claims by dividing the non-Christian world between themselves; *see* PORTUGAL: *History*. John was succeeded by his cousin and brother-in-law Emanuel (q.v.).

JOHN VI, (1769–1826), King of Portugal (1816–26), son of Maria I (1734–1816), Queen of Portugal, and her prince consort Peter III (1717–86). John became prince of Brazil in 1788. In 1792, after Maria became insane, John ruled in her name; in 1799 he formally became regent. During the Napoleonic Wars (q.v.), in 1801 and 1807, the French invaded Portugal. John fled to Brazil and made it the center of his government; *see* BRAZIL: *History*. Brazil was declared a separate kingdom in 1815, and when Maria died John succeeded her. While he was in Brazil, a democratic constitution was adopted in Portugal. John swore to abide by the new constitution, appointed his son Pedro later Pedro I (q.v.), Emperor of Brazil, regent of Brazil. John returned to Portugal in 1821. In 1824 John suppressed a revolt against the liberals led by his wife and his younger son, Dom Miguel (1802–66).

JOHN OF BRIENNE (1148–1237), Latin King of Jerusalem (1210–25). John, a French nobleman, became king by his marriage to Marie de Montferrat (d. 1212), Queen of Jerusalem. When Marie died, their young daughter Yolande (d. 1228) succeeded as queen under John's regency. After playing an important part in the Fifth Crusade (*see* CRUSADES), John lived and traveled in western Europe until 1229, seeking support. In 1222 he betrothed Yolande to Frederick II (q.v.), Holy Roman Emperor. Upon their marriage in 1225 Frederick quickly claimed the crown of Jerusalem. John, also claiming the crown, commanded papal troops in an attack upon Frederick's possessions. On his return to Jerusalem, 1229, he was elected regent of Constantinople (now İstanbul, Turkey) and served during the minority of Baldwin II, Emperor of Constantinople (*see under* BALDWIN).

John of Gaunt

JOHN OF GAUNT, Duke of Lancaster (1340–99), English soldier and statesman, the fourth son of Edward III, King of England and brother of Edward (qq.v.), the Black Prince, born in Ghent (ME. *Gaunt*). In 1359 John married

JOHN OF LANCASTER

Blanche (d. 1369), daughter of Henry, Duke of Lancaster (1299?–1361), and when Henry died, John became duke. John of Gaunt played an important part in the wars of the period between England and France and between England and Spain. He commanded a division of the English army, led by the Black Prince, that defeated the army of Henry, later Henry II (q.v.), King of Castile and León, at Nájera in 1367. As a result of his second marriage, to Constance (d. 1396), daughter of Pedro el Cruel (q.v.), King of Castile and León, John laid claim to the throne of Castile. During the Hundred Years' War (q.v.) he aided the Black Prince against France in 1370–71 and established English rule over most of southern France. After a severe illness forced the return of the Black Prince to England, John took command of the English armies; by 1380 he had lost much of the territory the English had previously won. In 1386 John invaded Castile, but was defeated by John I, King of Castile and León (see under JOHN). John of Gaunt gave up his claim to Castile and León in 1387 when his daughter married Henry, later Henry III, King of Castile and León (see under HENRY).

John of Gaunt was also prominent in English affairs. Together with Alice Perrers (d. 1400), his father's mistress, John dominated the English government. His rule was opposed by Parliament and by the Black Prince. In 1376 Parliament banished Alice Perrers and curtailed John's powers. The death of the Black Prince that year and the dissolution of Parliament, however, enabled John to regain his power. In 1377, on the death of Edward III and the accession of Richard II (q.v.), John's nephew and son of the Black Prince, John gave up his control of the government and thereafter played the role of peacemaker and supported the king, by whom he was made (1390) duke of Aquitaine. In 1396, after the death of his second wife, John married his mistress Catherine Swynford (1350?–1403), and Richard legitimized their children the following year. Saddened by the exile (1398) of his son, Henry of Lancaster, later Henry IV (q.v.), King of England, John died the following year.

JOHN OF LANCASTER, Duke of Bedford (1389–1435), English soldier and statesman, third son of Henry IV (q.v.) King of England. John was made lieutenant of England when his brother Henry V (q.v.), King of England, invaded France in 1415 during the Hundred Years' War (q.v.). In 1416 John commanded the English fleet that defeated the French at the mouth of the Seine R. In 1422, after his brother's death, John was designated "protector and defender of the kingdom" of the young Henry VI (q.v.), King of England. Transferring his duties in England to his brother Humphrey, Duke of Gloucester (see GLOUCESTER), John took over the conduct of English affairs in France in order to consolidate the English position against further French opposition. After reaffirming the alliance made in 1420 by Henry V with Philip the Good, Duke of Burgundy (1396–1467), John and Philip in 1424 gained a victory at Verneuil, France over the Dauphin, later Charles VII (q.v.), King of France. In 1429 John was defeated by the French heroine Joan of Arc (q.v.), at the Battle of Orléans. Two years later, when Joan, who had been captured by the Burgundians, was turned over to the English, John allowed her to be burned at the stake as a witch. Thereafter John's plans for the conquest of France were frustrated by the defection to France of Philip the Good.

JOHN OF AUSTRIA (Sp. *Juan de Austria*) (1547–78), Spanish general, an illegitimate son of Charles V (q.v.), Holy Roman Emperor born in Regensburg, Germany. Charles recognized his son, commonly called Don John, in his will, and entrusted him to the care of his legitimate son Philip II (q.v.), King of Spain. In 1568 John was given the command of a squadron that operated against the Barbary pirates (see BARBARY COAST), and in 1569–70 he suppressed a revolt of the Moors (q.v.) in Granada. Upon the formation in 1571 of the Holy League by the pope, Spain, and Venice, to put down the Ottoman Turks, John was given the supreme command of a large fleet of galleys, with which he won a great victory over the superior forces of the Turks at the naval Battle of Lepanto; see LEPANTO, BATTLE OF. He took Tunis from the Turks in 1573. In 1576 Philip II appointed him governor-general of the Netherlands, which at that time was rebelling against Spanish rule. In 1578 he defeated the Dutch in the Battle of Gembloux, but his campaign failed shortly before his death because of lack of Spanish support. See NETHERLANDS, THE: *History*.

JOHN, Augustus Edwin (1878–1961), British painter, born in Tenby, Wales, and educated at the Slade School of Fine Art in London. While traveling in France, he was influenced by the proponents of the artistic movement known as postimpressionism (q.v.). He developed a vigorous and original style, marked by fluent brush technique and striking character portrayal. His use of large areas of brilliant color, broad rhythms, and a free technique established him as one of the leaders of the modern art movement in England. His many vivid portraits include likenesses of Elizabeth II, Queen of Great Britain, the British writers George Bernard Shaw,

James Joyce, Thomas Hardy, and Dylan Thomas; the British-American sculptor Sir Jacob Epstein (qq.v.); and the American actress Tallulah Bankhead (q.v.). John also painted and etched many gypsy scenes, based on his own nomadic experiences in the British Isles. His works are found in the leading museums of London, Paris, Washington, D.C., and New York City. John was elected to the Royal Academy of Arts in 1928. His memoirs are entitled *Chiaroscuro: Fragments of Autobiography* (1952).

JOHN BIRCH SOCIETY, ultraconservative organization established to combat Communist influences in the United States. It was founded in 1958 by Robert Henry Winborne Welch (1899–   ), a Boston businessman. With a membership of between 90,000 and 100,000, the society maintains offices in Washington, D.C., and publishes a handbook, *The Blue Book,* and a monthly bulletin, *American Opinion.* John Birch, for whom the society is named, was a former Baptist missionary, killed in 1945 by Chinese Communists while on a mission for the Office of Strategic Services.

JOHN BULL, popular nickname for what is presumed to be the typical Englishman, and also for the English people, or their government. The name was in use for some time before John Arbuthnot (q.v.) wrote *The History of John Bull* (1712), a satire in which he made his now celebrated literary portrayal of John Bull as "an honest plain-dealing fellow, choleric, bold, and of a very inconstant temper." Through long usage John Bull has become a stereotype, personifying the English people. In cartoons stocky John Bull is usually depicted wearing a squat top hat, neckcloth, waistcoat, tailcoat, tight breeches, and boots.

JOHN DOE and **RICHARD ROE,** in law, originally the names of the fictitious plaintiff and fictitious defendant, respectively, in common-law actions of dispossession. Each of these names has come to be used in law to refer to a party whose identity is unknown or concealed. The more frequently used is John Doe; and criminal proceedings against an alleged offender whose identity is unknown are often called *John Doe* proceedings.

JOHN DORY or **JOHN DOREE,** common name for a marine food fish, *Zeus faber,* of the family Zeidae, found in both the Atlantic and Pacific oceans. It measures up to 22 in. long, with a maximum weight of 18 lb. It is a deep-bodied, compressed fish, with long dorsal spines and a large mouth with a protractile upper jaw. A dark spot behind each of the gills caused the legend that the spots were left by Saint Peter's finger and thumb when he took the tribute money from the fish's mouth.

JOHN, EPISTLES OF, three books of the New Testament (*see* BIBLE), in the King James Version, THE FIRST EPISTLE GENERAL OF JOHN, THE SECOND EPISTLE OF JOHN, and THE THIRD EPISTLE OF JOHN. Ecclesiastical tradition has ascribed the three Epistles to Saint John; *see* JOHN THE EVANGELIST. Today, however, considerable scholarly disagreement exists over the authorship of the five books ascribed to John: the three Epistles, the Gospel of John, and Revelation. Thus, for example, despite close similarities in language, literary style, and theological beliefs between the Three Epistles and the Gospel (*see* JOHN, GOSPEL ACCORDING TO SAINT), some modern scholars attribute the Gospel and the first letter to one person, John the Evangelist, and the second and third letters to another author, perhaps "the elder" (that is, elder or officer of a church; *see* ELDER), named in 2 John 1:1 and 3 John 1:1. Other scholars attribute all four works to the same person, possibly "the elder", instead of to John the Evangelist. And still other scholars, making no mention of

John Bull as depicted by the 19th-century American artist Thomas Nast.   Bettmann Archive

JOHN, EPISTLES OF

the Gospel, attribute 1 and 2 John to one author and 3 John to another. The view currently favored by most commentators is that one author, who may have been "the elder", wrote all three letters and the Gospel. Scholars generally agree that the letters date from about the turn of the 1st century A.D. *See also* REVELATION.

The first Epistle is in the form of a homily, rather than in that of a traditional Epistle, with its characteristic salutation (giving the name of the writer and the destination of the letter) and closing greetings. Probably, it was written for circulation among the churches of a region, perhaps Asia Minor, instead of to a specific church or congregation. The author's primary concern, never specified in the letter, appears to have been certain "false prophets" (4:1) who denied "that Jesus Christ is come in the flesh [and] is of God" (4:2). The teaching of these "antichrists" (2:18) was apparently an incipient form of Gnosticism (q.v.), a religious philosophy that so disrupted the unity of the early churches that the author approved of the withdrawal by some of these "antichrists" from the Christian community (2:19). A second major concern was to counteract the "spirit of error" (4:6) introduced by the false prophets. The author reminds the faithful of the true revelation, that "God is love", that "he loved us, and sent his Son to be the propitiation for our sins", and therefore that "if God so loved us, we ought also to love one another" for "if we love one another, God dwelleth in us, and his love is perfected in us" (4:8–12).

The second Epistle, a very brief letter, is addressed to "the elect lady and her children" (1:1). Scholars agree that "the elect lady" here referred to is not a woman but a church, possibly one of the churches in Asia Minor. The author presents the main points of 1 John in a much abridged form (1:4–9), adding, however, the warning that "If there come any unto you, and bring not this doctrine, receive him not into your house" (1:10). Such a person "is a deceiver and an antichrist" (1:7); and he that shows him hospitality "is partaker of his evil deeds" (1:11).

The third Epistle, also a very brief letter, is addressed to an individual named Gaius (1:1), apparently an exemplary church member. The occasion for writing seems to have been the behavior of another member, "Diotrephes" (1:9). Diotrephes has refused to recognize the authority of "the elder", who promises to deal personally with Diotrephes at a later time (1:10). The author praises Gaius for behaving properly (1:3–7) and urges him to continue being a fellow helper "to the truth" (1:9).

JOHN F. KENNEDY CENTER FOR THE PERFORMING ARTS. *See* SMITHSONIAN INSTITUTION.

JOHN, GOSPEL ACCORDING TO SAINT, book of the New Testament (*see* BIBLE), in the King James Version, THE GOSPEL ACCORDING TO SAINT JOHN. Ecclesiastical tradition, dating from the latter part of the 2nd century, has maintained that it was written by Saint John (*see* JOHN THE EVANGELIST) toward the end of his life and published late in the 1st century, possibly in the ancient Greek city of Ephesus (q.v.). Tradition also has held that it is the latest of the Gospels, a view shared and substantiated by modern scholars; hence its placement in the New Testament canon after the three Synoptic Gospels; *see* BIBLE, CANON OF THE; GOSPEL. The Synoptic Gospels share a common viewpoint and common subject matter.

The Author. Since the 19th century the identity of the author of the Gospel of John has generated heated controversy. Roman Catholic and conservative scholars today generally accept John the Evangelist as the author; *see* BIBLE SCHOLARSHIP. But other scholars, unable wholly to embrace the view that the author was an eyewitness to the events recorded in the book and an Apostle (q.v.), have proposed several differing hypotheses, chief among them: that the fourth canonical Gospel was written by "the elder" mentioned in the Second and Third Epistles of John (*see* JOHN, EPISTLES OF); that it was composed by a disciple of John the Evangelist (and so was based, in part, on John's recollections of the Gospel events); that it may have been written by a friend of Jesus Christ, Lazarus of Bethany (*see under* LAZARUS); or that it was written by an anonymous Christian in Alexandria (q.v.) in the first half of the 2nd century. Most non-Catholic, liberal scholars now date John from sometime in the last decade of the 1st century or early in the 2nd century.

Treatment of the Gospel. The Gospel of John falls into four distinct sections. The first (1:1–18) is a brief prologue on the nature of Jesus Christ as the incarnation of "the Word" (1:1–2, 14), or Logos, a word signifying the reason that in ancient Greek philosophy is the governing principle in the universe. Logos also designates a Christian doctrine explaining how the divine agent is manifested in the creation, ordering, and salvation of the world. The second section (1:19–11:57 or, as some scholars divide John, 1:19–12:50) presents testimony that Jesus is the true Christ, or Messiah (qq.v.); that He is, in other words, the manifestation of the incarnate Logos. This testimony is provided partly by John the Baptist and the first disciples, but chiefly by the miracles, or "signs" (20:30) done by Jesus, which "manifested forth his glory" (2:11). These miracles are: the changing of water into wine at Cana (2:1-11); the healing of an official's son (4:46-54); the healing of a man who had been lame for thirty-eight years (5:1-9); the feeding of the 5000 (6:1-15), the only miracle recorded in each of the four Gospels; the healing of a man who had been blind from birth (9:1-7); and the raising of His friend Lazarus from the dead (11:1-46). The sight of Jesus walking on the sea (6:16-21) also is classed as a miracle, or sign, by some scholars. Other scholars, uncertain as to whether this act should be regarded as a miracle, consider as additional miracles His death (19:30) and appearances as the risen Christ (20:1-29).

The third section of John is said by some scholars to begin with Christ's final trips to Bethany and Jerusalem, which marked the end of His public ministry (chapter 12); and according to them, the section comprises the Passion and Resurrection of Jesus (chapters 12-20). Others, favoring a thematic outline and following the doctrine of the Logos set forth in the prologue, see as the main theme of this section the return of the incarnate Son to the Father. According to these scholars, the third section thus begins after Christ's public ministry with chapter 13, continuing through chapter 20. Divided either way, the section includes an account of the Last Supper; Christ's last discourse and prayer, the so-called "High Priestly Prayer"; largely narrative passages treating dramatically the betrayal, arrest, trial, crucifixion, and burial of Jesus; and dramatic and inspirational personal testimony to the empty sepulchre, and the appearances of the risen Christ to Mary Magdelene, the disciples, and the doubting disciple Thomas. The fourth section of John (chapter 21) is an appendix, or postscript. In it the risen Christ, appearing a third time to His disciples, commands Saint Peter (q.v.) to "Feed my lambs" and "my sheep", foretells Peter's death, and speaks about a disciple whom He loves. This disciple is identified as the author of the Gospel (21:24).

The author of John wrote when the false beliefs of mystery cults and Gnosticism (q.v.) were circulating in the early Church beside the first doctrines of Christianity. He apparently primarily intended his Gospel to be a theological reinterpretation of Jesus' person and mission. He presented his message in terms related to the philosophical trends of his time, in a form perhaps more understandable both to Christians of the later Church and to Hellenistic Gentiles; see PHILOSOPHY: *Hellenistic and Roman Philosophy*. The author's main specific purpose apparently was to counteract a teaching of Docetic Gnosticism that Christ was a divine being who appeared in human form but was incapable of mortal feeling or of dying. The express purpose of the Gospel is revealed in 20:30-31.

John and the Synoptics. It has long been recognized that the Gospel of John differs from the earlier Synoptic Gospels. Among the more conspicuous and significant differences are: the absence in John of any records or descriptions of such biographical and historical matters as Jesus' birth, His childhood, His Temptation, the Transfiguration, the institution of the Eucharist (*see* LORD'S SUPPER), and the Agony in the garden of Gethsemane (q.v.); and the mention only in John of Christ's miraculous changing of water into wine at Cana, His miraculous raising of Lazarus, His washing of the disciples' feet at the Last Supper (13:1-20), the baptizing by Jesus and His disciples (3:22-36; 4:1-2), Nicodemus (3:1-21), the Samaritan Woman (4:7-26), and an incident originally not part of the Gospel, that of the woman caught in adultery (7:53-8:11). Important chronological differences also are revealed when John is compared with the Synoptics. In John, Christ's public ministry extends over several years, the Last Supper is eaten before the Passover (*see* PESACH), and Jesus is crucified before the first day of that holiday.

See also GOSPELS: *John.*

JOHN MUIR NATIONAL HISTORIC SITE, site in Martinez, Calif., of the John Muir House and adjacent Martinez Adobe, commemorating Muir's contribution to conservation.

JOHNS HOPKINS UNIVERSITY, THE, institution of higher learning, situated in Baltimore, Md., and founded in 1876. Funds for the establishment of the university were provided in a bequest of $3,500,000 by the American financier Johns Hopkins (1795-1873), who left an equal amount to found a hospital. The Johns Hopkins Hospital serves as a training institution for the students of the university school of medicine, which was opened in 1893 and is widely recognized as one of the best equipped and most advanced in the world. In addition to the medical school, the principal divisions of the university include the arts and sciences, hygiene and public health, health services, advanced international studies, and the evening college. There are also an applied physics laboratory and a summer school. All divisions are coeducational. The degree of bachelor is conferred in the liberal arts and sciences, business, engineering sciences, mathematical sciences, and international studies; the degree of master is conferred in the liberal arts and sciences, engineering sciences, mathematical sciences, and public health and hygiene; and the degree of doctor is conferred in engineering sciences, arts and sciences, medicine, public health and hygiene, and international studies. In 1972 the university libraries housed more than 2,000,000 bound volumes. In the same year enrollment was approximately 9500 students, the faculty numbered 1200, and the endowment of the university was about $180,400,000.

JOHNSON, name of two distinguished American explorers, writers, and motion-picture producers who were husband and wife.

Martin Elmer Johnson (1884–1937), born in Rockford, Ill. From 1910, together with his wife Osa Helen Johnson, he made many photographic expeditions to the South Pacific and Africa, taking motion pictures of the people and the animal life. Johnson is most famous for a movie record he made of the vanishing wildlife in Africa for the American Museum of Natural History (q.v.) in New York City. With his wife he also wrote many books, including *Cannibal Land* (1922), *Camera Trails in Africa* (1924), and *Lion—African Adventure with the King of Beasts* (1929).

Osa Helen Johnson (1894–1953), born in Chanute, Kans., and educated at Rollins College, Fla. After the death of her husband, she continued to write and produce motion pictures based on her adventures. Among her best-known books are *I Married Adventure* (1940) and *Bride in the Solomons* (1944).

JOHNSON, Alvin Saunders (1874–1971), American economist, educator, and editor, born near Homer, Nebr., and educated at the University of Nebraska and Columbia University. Between 1901 and 1916 he taught economics at various American colleges and universities, including Bryn Mawr, Columbia, Cornell, and Chicago, and between 1916 and 1918 he was professor of political science at Stanford University. He was director of the New School for Social Research, in New York City, from 1923 until 1945, when he became president emeritus. During that time he established a graduate faculty of political and social sciences for refugee scholars from that part of Europe controlled by the Axis Powers (q.v.). He also served in 1938–39 as professor of economics and director of general studies at the Graduate School of Yale University.

Between 1917 and 1923 Johnson edited the weekly periodical *The New Republic,* and from 1927 until 1934 he was an associate editor of the *Encyclopedia of the Social Sciences.* He became chairman of the American Association of Adult Education in 1936 and president in 1939. In 1936 he also assumed the presidency of the American Economic Association. From 1943 until 1945 he was the head of the New York State Committee on Discrimination in Employment. Among his writings are *Rent in Modern Economic Theory* (1903), *The Public Library: A People's University* (1938), *The Clock of History* (1946), *Pioneer's Progress: An Autobiography* (1952), and *A Touch of Color* (1963).

JOHNSON, Andrew (1808–75), seventeenth President of the United States, born in Raleigh, N.C. In 1826 he moved to the mountain country of eastern Tennessee and settled in Greeneville, Tenn., where he opened a tailor shop. Lacking a formal education, he was instructed in writing and arithmetic by his wife, the former Eliza McCardle (1810–76), a schoolteacher. His forensic skills and his support of the small farmers and workers of his community brought him election as alderman when he was only twenty-one. A member of the Democratic Party (q.v.), he subsequently served in the State legislature, and in the U.S. House of Representatives. After a term as governor of Tennessee, he was a U.S. Senator from 1857 to 1862.

In the Senate he continued to support the people of his region, advocating a homestead bill granting public land to settlers (*see* HOMESTEAD LAWS) and urging the popular election of Federal judges and senators. He criticized many of the abolitionists (q.v.) and believed that the question of emancipation should be decided by the States. His opposition to the interests of the large landowners in his State, however, led him to oppose their calls for secession (q.v.), and when Tennessee left the Union in June, 1861, he remained in the Senate. Denounced as a traitor by his Southern colleagues, he nonetheless supported the lenient attitude of President Abraham Lincoln (q.v.) toward the South. As military governor of Tennessee, he successfully restored civil government and, though still a Democrat, he gained the support of the Republican Party (q.v.). Elected Vice-President on the National Union ticket in 1864, he assumed the Presidency after the assassination of President Lincoln on April 14, 1865.

Johnson's plan for the Reconstruction (q.v.) of the Southern States differed in some respects from Lincoln's, but both proposals called for the restoration of normal activity under Presidential authority. When Johnson proceeded to carry out his plan without calling Congress into special session, he was violently opposed by the so-

JOHNSON, HUGH SAMUEL

Andrew Johnson, photograph by the 19th-century American photographer Mathew B. Brady.
Library of Congress

called Radical Republicans led by Representative Thaddeus Stevens of Pennsylvania and Senator Charles Sumner (qq.v.) of Massachusetts. Johnson's veto of a bill extending the power of the Freedmen's Bureau (q.v.) was overridden, and the Congressional elections of 1866 failed to bring him sufficient backing to sustain his later vetoes. His intemperate attacks on his opponents, and his rejection of a succession of acts limiting the powers of the executive, led the Radicals to enact the Tenure of Office Act in March, 1867, again over Johnson's veto. This measure made it a misdemeanor for the President to remove, without consent of the Senate, officials whose original appointment had required Senatorial confirmation. Johnson attempted to test the constitutionality of the act by dismissing one of his principal opponents, Secretary of War Edwin McMasters Stanton (q.v.). After a bitter dispute the President was subjected, for the first time in American history, to proceedings for impeachment (q.v.). During his trial in the Senate, Johnson's defenders noted that Stanton was a Lincoln appointee and that Johnson was therefore not obliged to retain him. Johnson's opponents failed by one vote to obtain the two-thirds majority needed to convict, and the President was acquitted on May 16, 1868. His supporters included seven Republicans and twelve Democrats.

The remainder of Johnson's term was marked by the increasing power of the Congressional Republicans. After the inauguration of President Ulysses Simpson Grant (q.v.), Johnson retired to Tennessee. He died five months after his return to the Senate in 1875. Severely criticized during his Presidency, Johnson has been somewhat more favorably regarded by several later historians. N.W.P.

JOHNSON, Byron Bancroft, known as BAN JOHNSON (1864–1931), American baseball promoter, born in Norwalk, Ohio, and educated at Oberlin and Marietta colleges. In 1900, after working as a sportswriter for a Cincinnati newspaper, Johnson created the American League from the disbanded Western League and presided over it until 1927. Ten years later he was elected to the National Baseball Hall of Fame; see BASEBALL HALL OF FAME AND MUSEUM, NATIONAL. Johnson formulated the plans for reorganizing professional baseball and proposed the annual contest between pennant-winning teams, the World Series. See BASEBALL.

JOHNSON, Hiram Warren (1866–1945), American political leader, born in Sacramento, Calif., and educated at the University of California. He was admitted to the California bar in 1888. His success in prosecuting San Francisco politicians on charges of bribery and corruption led to his election as governor of California in 1910, a position he held until 1917. As governor, he fought the influence of the Southern Pacific Railroad on the State government and instituted broad social and political reforms.

Johnson was associated with former President Theodore Roosevelt (q.v.) in founding the Progressive Party (q.v.), and was the unsuccessful Vice-Presidential candidate on the Progressive ticket with Roosevelt in 1912. When the Progressive Party declined, Johnson joined the Republican Party (q.v.), and became one of the most influential leaders of the progressive wing. In 1916, he was elected to the United States Senate and served until his death. Although a Republican, he supported Democratic Presidential nominee Franklin Delano Roosevelt (q.v.) in 1932. Later, however, he opposed Roosevelt's foreign policy and American membership in the United Nations.

JOHNSON, Hugh Samuel (1882–1942), American army officer and journalist, born in Fort Scott, Kans., and educated at the United States Military Academy at West Point, N.Y. He served in 1916 in Mexico against the Mexican guerrilla chief Francisco Villa (q.v.). In World War I he formulated the plan for conscription (q.v.) passed by Congress in May, 1917, as the Selective Conscription Act (see SELECTIVE SERVICE) and was in charge of the draft through 1918. In the

JOHNSON, JACK

latter year he became a brigadier general. He resigned from military service in 1919 and entered private business. In 1933 he was appointed by President Franklin Delano Roosevelt (q.v.) to direct the National Recovery Administration (N.R.A.), a Federal agency authorized by the National Industrial Recovery Act (q.v.). In 1934 Johnson began writing a column for the Scripps-Howard newspapers; see NEWSPAPER: *United States Newspapers.*

JOHNSON, Jack, professional name of JOHN ARTHUR JOHNSON (1878–1946), American boxer, born in Galveston, Texas. He began his professional boxing career in 1899 and fought his last bout in 1927. He won a disputed world's championship heavyweight title from the Canadian boxer Tommy Burns (1881–1955) in 1908 in Sydney, Australia. In 1910 in Reno, Nev., Johnson knocked out the former heavyweight champion, American boxer James J. Jeffries (q.v.), who was attempting to regain the title. With this victory Johnson was officially recognized as the first Negro heavyweight champion of the world. He lost the title to the American boxer Jess Willard (1883–1968) in Havana, Cuba, in 1915, after being knocked out in the twenty-sixth round. Johnson's life was the subject of *The Great White Hope* (1968), a Pulitzer Prize-winning drama by the American playwright Howard Sackler (1929–   ).

JOHNSON, James Weldon (1871–1938), American writer, born in Jacksonville, Fla., and educated at Atlanta and Columbia universities. He was admitted to the Florida bar in 1897 and practiced law in Jacksonville. Johnson served as United States consul in Venezuela (1906–09) and in Nicaragua (1909–12). He was secretary of the National Association for the Advancement of Colored People (q.v.) from 1916 to 1930. He became a professor of creative literature at Fisk University in 1930 and a visiting professor at New York University in 1934. His best-known book was the novel *Autobiography of an Ex-Colored Man* (1912). He also wrote *Along This Way* (1933), an autobiography; several volumes of poetry; studies of Negro American life; and the words of many popular songs, which were set to music by his brother, the American singer and composer John Rosamond Johnson (1873–1954).

JOHNSON, Lyndon Baines (1908–73), thirty-sixth President of the United States, born near Stonewall, Texas, where his father was a farmer and legislator. He graduated from Southwest Texas State Teachers College and taught high school. He married Claudia Alta ("Lady Bird") Taylor (1912–   ) in 1934. An active member of the Democratic Party (q.v.), he entered the

Lyndon B. Johnson is sworn in as the thirty-sixth President of the U.S. aboard the Presidential airplane shortly after the assassination of President John F. Kennedy in Dallas, Texas, Nov. 22, 1963. To the President's right is Mrs. Johnson; to his left, Mrs. Kennedy. UPI

Lyndon B. Johnson (right), as outgoing President of the U.S., meets with the combined Congressional leadership at the White House on Jan. 7, 1969, to discuss his final budget and State-of-the-Union message. Declining to run for reelection in 1968, President Johnson was succeeded by Richard M. Nixon. UPI

United States House of Representatives in 1937. In 1948 he was elected to the United States Senate, becoming majority leader in 1954. Regarded as one of the most effective leaders in the history of the Senate, he was instrumental in passing much important legislation during the administration of President Dwight David Eisenhower (q.v.).

After unsuccessful attempts to gain the Democratic nomination for President, Johnson was elected Vice-President under President John Fitzgerald Kennedy (q.v.) in 1960. Johnson's selection for the Vice-Presidency was important in gaining Southern votes for the Democratic Party ticket. His travels to Southeast Asia and his vigorous support of the space program (see ASTRONAUTICS) were distinguishing characteristics of his term as Vice-President. When President Kennedy was assassinated on Nov. 22, 1963, Johnson assumed office with a commitment to support the late President's tax measures and civil-rights legislation; see CIVIL RIGHTS AND CIVIL LIBERTIES. Johnson's skillful handling of this legislative program, and his pledge to avoid extensive military involvement in Asia and elsewhere, won him wide support in the election of 1964. With Senator Hubert Horatio Humphrey (q.v.) of Minnesota as his running mate, he received 43,129,484 votes, a popular majority larger than that of any previous American Presidential nominee, in defeating his Republican opponent, Senator Barry Morris Goldwater (q.v.) of Arizona, by 15,951,296 votes.

The beginning of President Johnson's full term was marked by a continuance of his legislative program. To bring about his conception of "The Great Society", in which "men are more concerned with the quality of their goals than the quantity of their goods", he supported new civil-rights legislation and called for a number of social-welfare measures. The latter, comprising the President's so-called war on poverty, were designed to encourage the economic development of depressed cities and rural areas and to improve housing for the poor; see POVERTY. The Economic Opportunity Act (1964), the National Defense Education Act (1964), and the Elementary and Secondary Education Act (1965) funded plans to improve American education at every level; see EDUCATION IN THE UNITED STATES. In 1965, Johnson encouraged amendments to the social-security laws that extended medical insurance to elderly citizens; see MEDICARE AND MEDICAID; SOCIAL LEGISLATION.

Beginning in 1965 the President became increasingly involved in controversies concerning foreign policy. His dispatch of troops to suppress a rebellion in the Dominican Republic provoked considerable criticism; see DOMINICAN REPUBLIC: *History*. Widespread opposition was aroused by his decision to increase greatly the U.S. military involvement in Vietnam and by the subsequent military and economic consequences of this involvement; see VIETNAM, WAR IN.

JOHNSON, PHILIP CORTELYOU

In March, 1968, President Johnson announced that he would not seek reelection. The last year of his term was devoted to the arrangement of a preliminary conference in Paris, France, of the major participants in the war in Vietnam. The President also appointed several commissions to study problems of domestic violence and dissension; see UNITED STATES OF AMERICA: *History: The Johnson Administration.* After the inauguration of President Richard Milhous Nixon (q.v.) in 1969, Johnson retired to his ranch near Johnson City, Texas, where he gave a number of interviews dealing with his Presidency. He published his memoirs, *The Vantage Point: Perspectives of the Presidency,* in 1971. N.H.C.

JOHNSON, Philip Cortelyou (1906–), American architect, born in Cleveland, Ohio, and educated at Harvard University. His book *International Style: Architecture Since 1922* (1932), written in collaboration with the American architectural historian Henry-Russell Hitchcock (1902–), was influential in introducing new concepts of architecture from Europe into America. Originally a commentator on and proponent of modern architecture, Johnson was chairman of the architecture department of the Museum of Modern Art, New York City, from 1932 to 1934 and from 1945 to 1954.

Johnson began designing buildings in 1942. Usually luxurious in scale and materials, with an expansive use of interior space and an elegant grace, his many important works include his own home, the famous Glass House (1949) in New Canaan, Conn.; the Seagram Building (1958), New York City, a bronze skyscraper he designed in collaboration with his mentor, the American architect Ludwig Mies van der Rohe (q.v.); and the New York State Theater (1964) at the Lincoln Center for the Performing Arts (q.v.), New York City.

See also AMERICAN ARCHITECTURE: *Modern American Architecture: Recent Trends and Achievements; The International Style.*

JOHNSON, Richard Mentor (1781–1850), ninth Vice-President of the United States, born in Bryants Station (now part of Louisville), Ky., and educated at Transylvania University (now Transylvania College). He practiced law and in 1804 entered public life as a member of the Kentucky legislature. Johnson served in the United States House of Representatives from 1807 to 1819. He was a colonel in the War of 1812 (q.v.) and, according to traditional accounts, killed the Indian chief Tecumseh (about 1768–1813) in the Battle of the Thames. Johnson was a United States Senator from 1819 to 1829, when he again became a member of the House, serving until 1837. In the Presidential election of 1836 he was the running mate of the Democratic nominee, Martin Van Buren (q.v.). Because no Vice-Presidential candidate won a majority in the electoral college (q.v.) that year, the contest was thrown into the U.S. Senate, which elected Johnson to the Vice-Presidency in March, 1837. With Van Buren he unsuccessfully sought reelection in 1840.

JOHNSON, Samuel (1696–1772), American clergyman, educator, and philosopher, born in Guilford, Conn., and educated at the Collegiate School of Connecticut (now Yale University). In 1718 he became a Congregational minister, but in 1723 he was ordained in the Church of England. Between 1724 and 1754 Johnson served as rector of an Anglican church in Stratford, Conn. He became the first president of King's College (now Columbia University), in 1754, but resigned to return to his pastoral work in 1763. Johnson was a friend and disciple of the British philosopher George Berkeley (q.v.) and was the major American exponent of Berkeleian idealism. His writings include *Ethices Elementa* (1746), later expanded and published as *Elementa Philosophica* (1752).

JOHNSON, Samuel (1709–84), known as DR. JOHNSON, British writer and lexicographer, born in Lichfield, Staffordshire, England, and educated at the local grammar school. In this school he achieved considerable proficiency in the Latin language. From 1725 to 1727 he continued his education at home, reading extensively in the large library of his father, Michael Johnson (1656–1731), a struggling bookseller, and acquiring a vast and diversified knowledge, particularly in Latin literature. From 1728 to 1731 he attended Pembroke College, University of Oxford. There his classical learning, ungainly appearance, and eccentric behavior drew much attention to him. Obliged to leave Oxford in 1731 without taking a degree because of lack of funds, he became a teacher at a small school in Leicestershire in the following year. Thereafter he went to Birmingham, where he prepared an abridged translation of an obscure Latin work, the *Historical Voyage to Abyssinia* by the Portuguese Jesuit missionary Jerônimo Lobo (d. 1678). In 1735 Johnson married Mrs. Elizabeth Jarvis Porter (1688?–1752), a widow many years his senior. With her small inheritance he opened a boarding school for boys near Lichfield, but the school soon failed. His first student was David Garrick (q.v.), who later became the most celebrated actor of his time.

Early Life and Difficulties in London. In 1737, Johnson left for London accompanied by Garrick, and by the following year had become a regular contributor to the *Gentleman's Magazine.* In that year also his *London,* an adaptation of the third satire of the Roman poet Juvenal (q.v.) was published anonymously. The work was an immediate success, and when his identity was disclosed, he received the critical acclaim of the British poet Alexander Pope (q.v.), who tried to obtain for Johnson an academic degree and the mastership of a grammar school. Pope did not succeed in these attempts, however, and Johnson was forced to spend most of the ensuing years as a bookseller's hack writer. In 1747 several booksellers commissioned him to compile a new dictionary of the English language, a work he did not complete for several years. In 1749 he published a poem, *The Vanity of Human Wishes,* based upon Juvenal's tenth satire and generally considered the finest of Johnson's verse productions. *Irene,* a tragedy that Johnson had written at Lichfield many years before, was produced by Garrick at the Drury Lane Theatre in February of the same year, but had only a moderate success. From 1750 to 1752 Johnson edited the semiweekly publication the *Rambler,* consisting of short moral essays written for the most part by himself. The wisdom of his observations and the eloquence of his diction soon attracted a wide circle of readers.

The Dictionary. His *Dictionary of the English Language* was published in 1755. Although he had little knowledge of the English language and literature of earlier periods, resulting in sometimes unreliable etymologies, his extensive reading of 17th-century prose and poetry enabled him to illustrate the correct use of words by instructive quotations. Johnson's work was the finest English dictionary published up to that time, and it was unsurpassed for almost a century; see DICTIONARY.

In 1758 Johnson began contributing to the *Universal Chronicle* a series of essays titled the *Idler,* patterned in style and tone after his *Rambler* papers. A year later he wrote the prose romance *Rasselas, Prince of Abyssinia,* a work in which are epitomized the loftiest sentiments of both the *Rambler* and the *Vanity of Human Wishes.* In 1762 Johnson was at last relieved of his oppressive penury by an annual royal pension of about $1500. In the following year the aging critic and lexicographer made the acquaintance of the British lawyer James Boswell (q.v.). Between the two men, very different in temperament and habits, a strong friendship developed, and Boswell soon began taking notes for an exhaustive biography of his distinguished friend. It is mainly to his fond and faithful recollections that posterity owes an intimately detailed knowledge of Johnson.

The Literary Club. In 1764 Johnson founded his literary Club, which included Garrick, Boswell, and other celebrities such as the poet Oliver Goldsmith, the novelist Fanny Burney, the economist Adam Smith, the historian Edward Gibbon, the statesman Edmund Burke, and the

Samuel Johnson — British Information Services

painter Sir Joshua Reynolds (qq.v.). Probably in 1765 Johnson met Henry Thrale (d. 1781), a wealthy British brewer, and his wife Hester (see PIOZZI, HESTER LYNCH), a writer who, captivated by Johnson's conversational powers, presently took him to live at their estate and to accompany them on subsequent trips to France and throughout Great Britain. In 1765 Johnson's critical edition of the works of the English dramatist William Shakespeare (q.v.) was published. It is notable for Johnson's acute comments on Shakespeare's characters as human beings. Under the title *A Journey to the Western Islands of Scotland* he next wrote an account of his trip with Boswell to Scotland and the Hebrides in 1773. His literary career closed with the *Lives of the Poets* (10 vol., 1779–81), by general consent the best of his writings in both critical content and style. He died in London and was buried in Westminster Abbey. A monument was later raised to his memory in Saint Paul's Cathedral.

Johnson exerted considerable influence on the literature of the later 18th century through his literary criticism and his conversation, an art in which he was the acknowledged master of his time. His criticism favored clarity, reasonableness, and smoothness of sound in literature, and his conversation, enriched as it was by encyclopedic knowledge and sharp wit, enforced his opinions among his contemporaries. His writings and conversation dealt also with politics, in support of the Tory Party and religion, in which he affirmed the most conservative doctrines of the Anglican Church. His religious writings included a number of prayers and meditations that expressed an intense personal religious feeling. Johnson's literary style is characterized by a Latinized vocabulary and by a complex, balanced sentence structure.

Many of his physical and mental traits were effects of an attack of scrofula and other illnesses suffered during his childhood. He had a melancholic, indolent disposition aggravated by physical handicaps. Johnson had a mottled complexion, myopia, and jerky muscular movements; he was a hypochondriac and he had a morbid fear of death; he suffered from prolonged fits of absentmindedness, and he was slovenly in personal appearance and habits. Johnson, however, was a compassionate and generous man. L.T.

JOHNSON, Thomas (1732–1819), American jurist, born in Calvert County, Md. He was a leader of the pre-Revolutionary agitation in Maryland and was a prominent member of the Continental Congress (q.v.), in which he proposed in 1775 the appointment of George Washington (q.v.) as commander in chief of the Continental Army. Early in 1777 Johnson was elected governor of Maryland and held that office through 1779. He became a supporter of the Constitution of the United States (q.v.) and was a member of the Maryland convention that ratified the Constitution in 1788. He became associate justice of the Supreme Court of the United States (q.v.) in 1791.

JOHNSON, Walter Perry (1887–1946), American professional baseball player, born in Humboldt, Kans. Johnson joined the Washington Senators of the American League as a pitcher in 1907 and remained with the club in that capacity until 1927. One of the greatest major-league pitchers, Johnson won 414 games and lost 276. He established a career strikeout record with 3497. Johnson was voted the most valuable player in the American League in 1913 and 1924. He managed the Newark Bears (1928), the Washington Senators (1929–32), and the Cleveland Indians (1933–35). In 1936 Johnson was elected to the Baseball Hall of Fame; see BASEBALL HALL OF FAME AND MUSEUM, NATIONAL.

JOHNSON, Sir William (1715–74), British soldier and colonial official in America, born in County Meath, Ireland. He emigrated to America in 1738 and settled on a tract of land in the Mohawk R. valley of New York. As a trader, he established friendly relations with the Indians, especially the Mohawk of the confederacy of the Iroquois (qq.v.). In 1746 Governor George Clinton (q.v.) appointed Johnson superintendent of Iroquois affairs, and in 1750 he was commissioned a member of the governor's council. Largely through his influence, the Iroquois were allied with the British during the French and Indian War (q.v.). Johnson was commissioned a major general in 1755 and was appointed sole superintendent of Indian affairs for the region north of the Ohio R. in 1756. For distinguished services he was created a baronet in 1755. Four years later he commanded the British force that captured Niagara from the French, and in 1760 he took part in the capture of Montréal. Johnson founded Johnstown, N.Y., in 1762.

JOHNSON CITY, city of Tennessee, in Washington Co., about 90 miles N.E. of Knoxville. The city is the trade and shipping center for the surrounding farming and lumbering area, and is an important market for Burley tobacco. Industrial establishments in Johnson City include textile mills, flour mills, iron foundries, brickworks, dairy-processing plants, and factories manufacturing furniture, hardwood flooring, foodstuffs, building supplies and materials, wearing apparel, chemicals, surgical supplies, and tools. The city is served by several railroads and airlines. Johnson City is the site of the East Tennessee State University, established in 1911, and a United States soldiers' home. The city was settled before 1800, and incorporated in 1869. Pop. (1960) 31,187; (1970) 33,770.

JOHNSON CITY, village of New York, in Broome Co., 3 miles N.W. of Binghamton, and 5 miles E. of Endicott. Johnson City is an industrial village noted especially for the manufacture of shoes. Binghamton, Endicott, and Johnson City comprise the so-called Triple Cities, in which are located mills of the Endicott Johnson Corporation, a large shoe-manufacturing concern. Other leading industries in Johnson City are the manufacture of machinery, wooden heels and lasts, felt, cameras, and candy. The village was incorporated in 1892. Pop. (1960) 19,118; (1970) 18,025.

JOHNSON GRASS, common name of *Sorghum halepense*, and belonging to the Grass family; see GRASSES. Johnson grass is a vigorous perennial forage grass which was introduced to South Carolina from Turkey about the middle of the 19th century. It has thrived throughout the moist, cotton-growing regions of s. United States. Johnson grass spreads rapidly by proliferation of rootstocks. It is valuable for pasture, and can often produce two or three hay crops per year. Johnson grass may yield as much as 15 tons of hay or 8 to 10 bushels of seed per acre each year. Fresh Johnson grass sometimes contains small quantities of hydrocyanic acid (q.v.), which is poisonous to livestock, but dried Johnson grass is usually safe for feeding purposes.

JOHNSTON, Albert Sidney (1803–62), American army officer, born in Washington, Ky., and educated at Transylvania University (now Transylvania College) and the United States Military Academy at West Point. He entered the United States Army in 1826 and later fought in the war against the Sac Indian chief Black Hawk (q.v.). In 1834 he resigned his commission, and two years later he enlisted as a private in the army of the Republic of Texas. Within a year he rose to the rank of brigadier general and was given command of the Texan army. In 1838 he was made secretary of war of the republic, a position he held for two years. After Texas had been admitted to the Union in 1845, Johnston served as colonel of a regiment of Texas volunteers during the Mexican War (q.v.). He reentered the U.S. Army in 1849, but in 1861 when the American Civil War broke out, he resigned his commission as brevet brigadier general and became a general in the Confederate army. In his first battle of the war he surprised the Union army at Shiloh, Tenn., in April, 1862; see SHILOH, BATTLE OF. Johnston's death in the battle was a severe blow to the Confederate hopes of winning the war. See CIVIL WAR, THE AMERICAN.

JOHNSTON, Joseph Eggleston (1807–91), American army officer, born in Prince Edward County, Va., and educated at the United States Military Academy at West Point. He was the grandnephew of the American colonial patriot Patrick Henry (q.v.). In 1829 Johnston was commissioned a second lieutenant in the United States Army. While fighting in the Seminole Wars (q.v.), he was wounded twice. In the Mexican War (q.v.), during which he was wounded five times, he was promoted to the rank of colonel. At the outbreak of the American Civil War, he resigned from the U.S. Army and joined the Confederate army, which commissioned him a brigadier general; see CIVIL WAR, THE AMERICAN.

At the first Battle of Bull Run in July, 1861, Johnston came to the assistance of General Pierre Beauregard (q.v.) and is given much of the credit for that first important Confederate victory; see BULL RUN, BATTLE OF. Soon after the battle, he was promoted to full general and assigned to command in northern Virginia. The following year he was severely wounded near Williamsburg (q.v.). Although disabled, he returned to duty, and in 1863 was placed in command of the Confederate forces along the Mississippi R. Johnston, however, was unable to prevent the capture of Vicksburg by General Ulysses S. Grant (q.v.); see VICKSBURG, CAMPAIGN OF. Later in the year he commanded the Army of the Tennessee opposing the advance of General William Tecumseh Sherman (q.v.) toward Atlanta. His forces were inadequate for the task, and he retreated gradually before the superior Union army, fighting a series of delaying engagements. On July 17, 1864, he was relieved of his command, but was reinstated by General Robert E. Lee (see under LEE) on Feb. 23, 1865. Johnston could not check the Union advance and on April 26, 1865, he surrendered to Sherman.

From 1879 to 1881 Johnston represented Virginia in the United States House of Representatives, and from 1887 to 1891 he was commissioner of railroads, a post to which he was appointed by President Grover Cleveland (q.v.). Johnston wrote *Narrative of Military Operations during the Civil War* (1874).

JOHNSTOWN, city in New York, and county seat of Fulton Co., about 22 miles N.W. of Schenectady. Situated in a mountain region, Johnstown is known mainly for glovemaking, but it is also a nucleus of heavy industries, including the manufacture of iron, steel, concrete, industrial equipment, machinery, leather goods, and wood and paper products. Pop. (1960) 10,390; (1970) 10,045.

JOHNSTOWN, city of Pennsylvania, in Cambria Co., on the Conemaugh R., at the confluence of Stony Creek and the Little Conemaugh R., 55 miles S.E. of Pittsburgh. It is served by railroads and maintains a municipal airport. The city is the center of an important mining area producing bituminous coal and iron ore. The surrounding region also contains clay pits, limestone quarries, and large stands of timber. Johnstown is principally an iron-processing and steelmaking center. Other industries include the manufacture of chemicals, textiles, furniture, cement blocks, glass, and rubber goods.

The site of Johnstown was settled in the 1790's by a Swiss immigrant, Joseph Johns. Originally called Conemaugh, the name of the town was later changed to honor Johns. Johnstown, situated in a deep narrow valley, has been subject to many floods. The most disastrous of these, the Johnstown flood, occurred on May

31, 1889, when the South Fork Dam on the Conemaugh R., 9 miles E. of the city, broke after unusually heavy rains, releasing about 78,000,000 tons of water in the Conemaugh River Reservoir. The swollen river swept through the valley, submerging Johnstown under 30 ft. of water and touching off fires. The loss of life in the disaster was about 2200 persons, and property losses were estimated at $10,000,000. Grandview Cemetery in Johnstown contains a large plot in which are buried 777 unidentified victims of the flood. In 1964 the flood site was memorialized as the Johnstown Flood National Memorial. The city was speedily rebuilt, and relief was sent to the inhabitants from all over the nation. Another flood in 1936 destroyed $40,000,000 worth of property and caused the loss of twenty-five lives. Since 1947 the city has been protected by a flood-control project constructed by the United States Army Corps of Engineers at a cost of more than $8,000,000. Johnstown was incorporated as a city in 1889. Pop. (1960) 53,949; (1970) 42,476.

JOHORE BAHRU, or JOHORE BHARU, city in Malaysia, and capital of Johore State, on Johore Strait, 14 miles N.W. of Singapore. It is the southernmost city of the Malay Peninsula, connected with the island of Singapore by a rail and road causeway; the road and rail systems of the peninsula begin here. The surrounding area produces rubber, palm oil, pineapples, and bauxite, and the city has fruit-canning and oil-milling plants. Within the city are a large mosque, the sultan's palace and gardens, and botanical and zoological gardens. The suburbs have resort beaches. Pop. (1970) 135,936.

JOINT CHIEFS OF STAFF. See DEFENSE, DEPARTMENT OF.

JOINTS, in anatomy, regions of union between bones or cartilages in the skeleton (q.v.). Synarthroses are rigid, immovable joints, such as the connections between the bones of the skull; symphyses are slightly movable joints, such as the junction of the bones making up the front of the pelvis; and diarthroses are movable joints, such as the meeting of the bones of the limbs with those of the trunk at the hip and shoulder.

Immovable joints are held together by actual intergrowing of bone or by strong fibrous cartilage. Slightly movable joints are held together by elastic cartilage. Typical movable joints consist of an external layer of fibrous cartilage giving rise to strong ligaments which support the separate bones. The bones of movable joints are covered with smooth cartilage and lubricated by a thick fluid, called synovial fluid, produced between the bones in membranous sacs, known as bursae. Bursitis, or inflammation of the bursae, is a common painful condition of movable joints. See also ARTHRITIS.

The human body has several types of movable joints. Ball-and-socket joints, which allow free movement in all directions, are found in the hip and shoulder. Hinge joints, allowing movement in one plane only, are found in the elbows, knees, and fingers. Pivot joints, permitting rotation only, are found between the first two vertebrae; the head rotates from side to side on a joint of this type called the axis. Gliding joints, in which the surfaces of the bones move a short distance over each other, are found between the various bones of the wrist and ankle.

JOINVILLE, Jean de (1224?–1317), French chronicler, born probably in Joinville. In 1248 he joined the Sixth Crusade (see CRUSADES), led by Louis IX (q.v.), King of France. At the age of almost eighty, under the patronage of the French queen consort Jeanne de Navarre (d. 1305), he undertook to assemble and expand notes he made on the crusade. His work, entitled *Histoire de Saint Louis* ("Story of Saint Louis", 1309), is valuable as a historical source, and is a notable example of early French prose.

JÓKAI, Maurus, or JÓKAI, MOR (1825–1904), Hungarian writer, born in Komárom, and educated at the College of Pápá. He took part in the Revolution of 1848 and, although granted amnesty, he was considered a political suspect by the Austrian authorities for many years; see HUNGARY: *History*. After the reestablishment of the Hungarian constitution in 1867, he became a member of parliament, and served until 1897, when he was appointed to a membership in the upper house. Jókai was the editor of several periodicals, both literary and political, the most important being the influential political newspaper *Hon* ("Nation"), which he founded in 1863. His novels were extremely popular; they had intricate plots and Romantic themes depicting heroism and love. He wrote more than 100 volumes of fiction, poetry, and drama.

JOLIET, city in Illinois, and county seat of Will Co., on the E. bank of the Des Plaines R., about 30 miles S.W. of Chicago. In the vicinity are limestone quarries and coal mines. Joliet is an important manufacturing and rail center. The principal industries are publishing, printing, and the manufacture of foodstuffs, apparel, pulp and paper, metals, wire, chemicals, building materials, and machinery. Joliet is the site of the College of Saint Francis for women, founded in 1930, and the Illinois State Penitentiary. The area was first settled in 1831, and was incorporated in 1837. Pop. (1960) 66,780; (1970) 80,378.

Drawing showing certain functions of human bone structures. Top and center: Ends of bones fit together in joints to permit movement of limbs, as in the ball-and-socket and hinge joints. Bottom: Spongy areas of long bones are sites of manufacture of red blood cells.

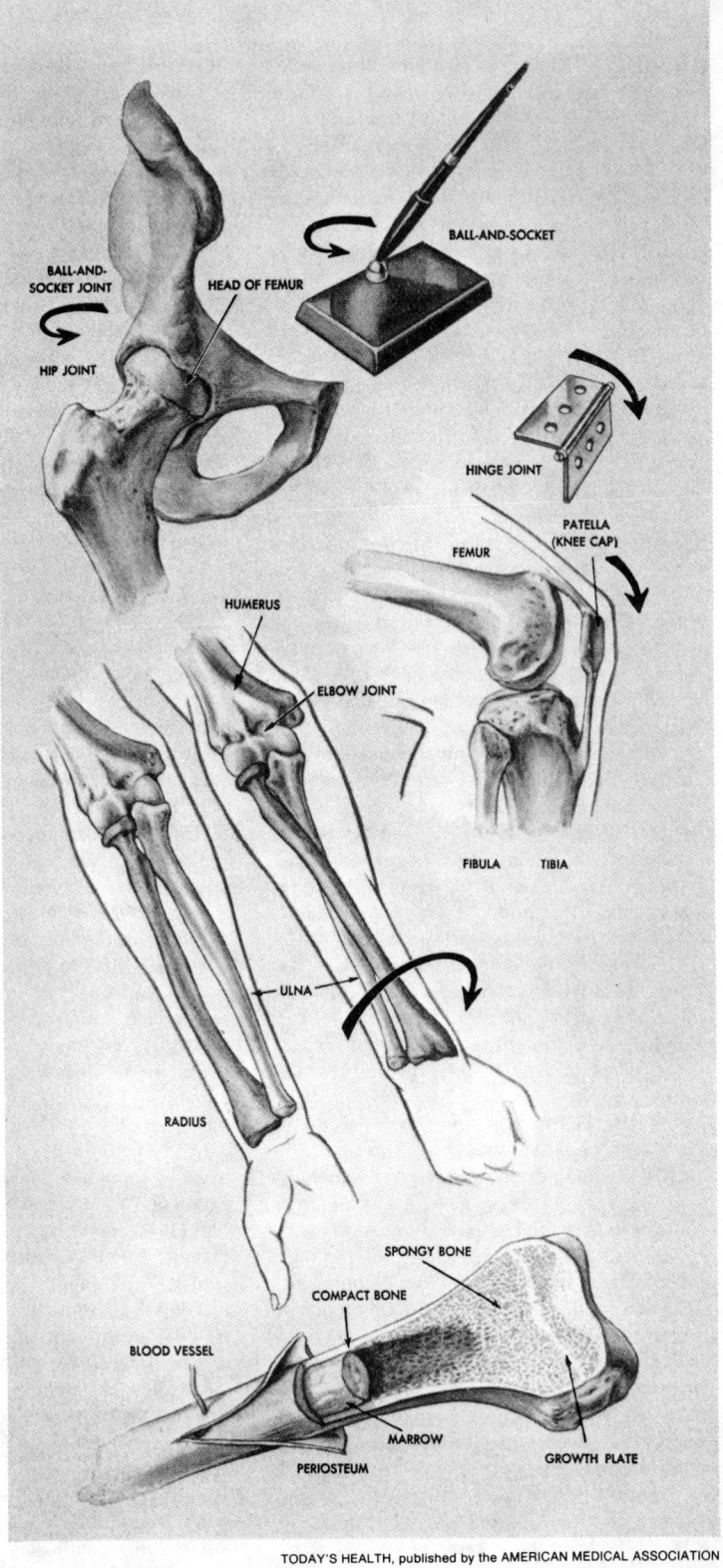

TODAY'S HEALTH, published by the AMERICAN MEDICAL ASSOCIATION

JOLIOT-CURIE

JOLIOT-CURIE, name of two French physicists who were husband and wife: **Irène Joliot-Curie** (1897–1956) and **Frédéric Joliot-Curie,** originally FRÉDÉRIC JOLIOT (1900–58).

Irène Joliot-Curie was born in Paris, the daughter of French physicists Marie and Pierre Curie (*see under* CURIE). She was educated at the University of Paris, and beginning in 1918 she assisted her mother at the Institute of Radium of the University of Paris. Frédéric Joliot-Curie, born in Paris, was educated at the School of Industrial Physics and Chemistry in Paris and at the University of Paris. While assisting also at the Institute of Radium, he met Irène, whom he married in 1926. They subsequently worked together as a scientific team and both assumed the name of Joliot-Curie. The Joliot-Curies specialized in the field of nuclear physics; *see* ATOMIC ENERGY. In 1933 they made the important discovery that radioactive elements can be artificially prepared from stable elements. In their experiments they bombarded boron with alpha particles, producing a radioactive form of nitrogen. For their contribution to nuclear research the Joliot-Curies were awarded the 1935 Nobel Prize in chemistry. See also RADIOCHEMISTRY.

In 1936 Irène served in the French cabinet as undersecretary of state for scientific research. She was a member of the French Atomic Energy Commission from 1946 to 1951 and director of the Institute of Radium after 1947. She became an officer of the Legion of Honor in 1939 and received many other honors for her contributions to nuclear science. Her death was caused by leukemia (q.v.), which she contracted in the course of her work with radioactive substances. *See also* RADIOCHEMISTRY.

Frédéric was appointed professor of physics at the Collège de France and director of the Laboratoire de Synthèse Atomique at Ivry in 1937. During the German occupation of Paris in World War II he was president of the Front National, the underground resistance movement in Paris university circles. In 1946 he was a French representative to the United Nations Atomic Energy Commission (q.v.) and was appointed high commissioner in charge of atomic-energy research in France. A member of the Communnist Party after 1946, he was dismissed in 1950 from his post as high commissioner because of his statement that no progressive scientist would contribute his scientific knowledge for the purpose of war against the Soviet Union. He retained his position, however, as a member of the French National Committee for Scientific Research. In 1956 he succeeded his wife as director of the Institute of Radium.

JOLLIET, Louis *or* **JOLIET, Louis** (1645–1700), French-Canadian explorer, born probably in Beaupré (now in Québec Province, Canada), and educated in a Jesuit seminary for the priesthood. He also studied briefly in France, but in 1668, upon his return to Canada, he abandoned the church to become a trader among the Indians. The following year he met the Jesuit missionary Jacques Marquette (q.v.). In 1672 Jolliet, already familiar with the region, was chosen to lead an expedition in search of the upper reaches of the Mississippi River (q.v.). Father Marquette was named chaplain for the party. The expedition, joined by five woodsmen, left Saint Ignace (now in Michigan) on May 17, 1673. They crossed Lake Michigan, ascended the Fox R., and descended the Wisconsin R. On June 17, 1673, the expedition entered the Mississippi R. The party then followed the Mississippi southward to a point below the mouth of the Arkansas R. before turning back. Marquette remained at Lake Michigan while Jolliet in 1674 continued on to Québec. On the return portion of the voyage Jolliet lost his records of the expedition in a canoe accident, but he replaced the records from memory. Later Jolliet explored in the region of Labrador and Hudson Bay. In 1697 he was appointed royal hydrographer of Canada.

JOLO. See SULU ARCHIPELAGO.

JOLSON, Al, assumed name of ASA YOELSON (1886–1950), American actor and singer, born probably in Saint Petersburg (now Leningrad), Russia. In 1899 he made his first appearance on the stage in *Children of the Ghetto,* at the Herald Square Theater, New York City. He subsequently was a circus performer and a café entertainer, and toured in vaudeville and with a theatrical company known as Dockstader's Minstrels. In 1911 he made his debut in musical comedy in New York City, appearing in *La Belle Paree* at the Winter Garden theater. He achieved national popularity by starring in many musical comedies, including *The Honeymoon Express* (1913), *Robinson Crusoe, Jr.* (1916), *Sinbad* (1918), *Bombo* (1921), *Big Boy* (1925), and *Wonder Bar* (1931). Jolson popularized the minstrel style of singing, appearing in "blackface" makeup that eventually became his trade mark. He entered the motion-picture field as the star of *The Jazz Singer* (1927), the first important talking film. He later played leading parts in motion pictures. Although he did not appear in *The Jolson Story* (1946) or *Jolson Sings Again* (1949), motion pictures based on events of different periods of his life, Jolson's voice was dubbed into the sound track. The success of these films resulted in an enthusiastic revival of interest in his career. Jolson was a national favorite, making numerous radio appearances and recordings. He was noted for the personal appeal of his singing and acting.

JONAH, book of the Old Testament (*see* BIBLE), in the King James Version, JONAH. It is one of twelve brief prophetic books of the Old Testament known, chiefly because of their brevity, as the Minor Prophets (*see* BIBLE, CANON OF THE). The book relates a number of incidents in the life of the Hebrew prophet Jonah (q.v.). In the first incident, Jonah is commanded by the Lord to "go to Nineveh, that great city, and cry against it; for their wickedness is come up before me" (1:2). Jonah, however, seeks to flee by ship from "the presence of the Lord" (1:3, 10). A tempest arises; the frightened, reluctant mariners cast Jonah overboard (on Jonah's request), and he is swallowed by "a great fish" (1:17). In consequent incidents, Jonah prays to the Lord from the belly of the fish (2:1–9), is subsequently "vomited out . . . upon the dry land" (2:10), and again is commanded to "go unto Nineveh . . . and preach unto it" (3:2). Jonah preaches (3:3, 4), the people repent (3:5–9), and God, seeing their works, spares them (3:10). In the final incident, God reproves Jonah for being "displeased . . . exceedingly" (4:1) after He spares "Nineveh . . . wherein are more than sixscore thousand persons that cannot discern between their right hand and their left hand" (4:11).

Many modern Bible commentators and scholars regard the book as an allegory or a parable (qq.v.), because little has been found to support it as an historical narrative. No word, for example, of any mass repentance like that described in Jonah is preserved among the known historical records of ancient Assyria (q.v.). Moreover, on the basis of internal evidence, some modern scholars now maintain that Jonah is the work of an unknown, postexilic author (not, as tradition holds it to be, the work of the historical prophet Jonah). This evidence includes the late form of Hebrew used by the writer and his apparent familiarity with certain Biblical books dating from the immediate preexilic and the postexilic periods; *see* BABYLONIAN CAPTIVITY. Other scholars still believe that it may date from some time between Jonah's age and the destruction of Nineveh (q.v.); that is, between the middle of the 8th century B.C. and 612 B.C.

Much discussion has also arisen over interpretations of the book considered as allegory or parable. The story of Jonah and the fish that swallows and later disgorges him is often taken by Christians to prefigure the entombment and resurrection of Jesus Christ. Indeed, in the Gospel of Matthew (*see* MATTHEW, GOSPEL ACCORDING TO SAINT), Jesus Himself compares His entombment with Jonah's confinement in the belly of the whale (Matt. 12:39–41). Other commentators see in the story of Jonah a parable concerning the unwillingness of the Jews to proclaim God's Word to the eager Gentiles and their consequent historical fate. Jews, on the other hand, interpret the book as an illustration of God's universal mercy.

JONAH (fl. about 8th cent. B.C.), fifth of the twelve Minor Prophets; *see* PROPHECY. Jonah (Heb., "dove") is the principal figure of the book of the Old Testament that bears his name; *see* book of JONAH. The son of Amittai, Jonah was born in Gath-hepher in the district known later as Galilee (now in Israel). Jonah's prophecy of the Israelite victory over the Syrians (8th cent. B.C.) is related in 2 Kings 14:25. The only other references to Jonah occur in the later story told in the book of Jonah, which is also referred to in the New Testament (Luke 11:29–32).

JONATHAN (fl. about 10th cent. B.C.), in the Old Testament books of Samuel (1 Sam. 13–2 Sam. 21), eldest son of Saul (q.v.), King of Israel. Jonathan was famous as a warrior and helped his father free Israel from the Philistines (q.v.). He is chiefly known, however, for his firm friendship with David (q.v.), the future king. Jonathan tried to reconcile David and Saul after the two men had quarreled and David had become an outlaw. Jonathan, together with his father and two brothers, was killed at Mt. Gilboa in a battle against the Philistines. David's famous lament for Saul and Jonathan (2 Sam. 1:19–27) is considered one of the finest examples of ancient Hebrew poetry.

JONES, Sir Harold Spencer (1890–1960), British astronomer, born in London, England, and educated at Jesus College, University of Cambridge, and the University of London. He became chief assistant at the Greenwich Observatory (q.v.) in 1913. In 1923 he was appointed astronomer at the observatory at the Cape of Good Hope, South Africa. On his return to England in 1933, Jones became astronomer royal at the Greenwich Observatory, and until his retirement in 1955, he supervised the transfer of the Greenwich Observatory from its original site to East Sussex. He was president of the British Astronomical Association from 1937 to 1939 and was knighted in 1943. Jones made many contributions to the study of astronomy, including investigations on proper motions of stars, stellar magnitudes, stellar parallaxes, orbits of double stars, the variation of latitude, the mass of the moon, and the mean distance of the earth from the sun; see EROS; STARS. Among his writings are *General Astronomy* (1922), *Worlds without End* (1935), and *Life on Other Worlds* (1940).

JONES, Henry Arthur (1851–1929), British playwright, born in Grandborough, Buckinghamshire, England. He was forced to earn his living at an early age and held a variety of jobs before he turned to writing. His first successful play, a melodrama, *The Silver King* (1882), established his literary reputation and made him financially independent. Jones was one of the first British dramatists to deal realistically with social issues in his plays. He wrote about sixty melodramas and comedies, including *Saints and Sinners* (1884) and *Mrs. Dane's Defence* (1900). See also DRAMA: *National Drama: England*.

JONES, Inigo (1573–1652), English architect, born in London. He studied in Italy, paying particular attention to the ancient ruins and the buildings designed by the Italian architect Andrea Palladio (q.v.). Jones then served as architect to the Danish court, and after his return to England he designed scenery for court theatricals written by the English playwright Ben Jonson (q.v.) and others for presentation before King James I (q.v.) and the English court. In 1615 he was appointed surveyor general of the royal buildings, and in that capacity greatly influenced contemporary English architecture. He borrowed heavily from Palladio in designing the first comprehensive examples of Renaissance architecture in England. Jones is most famous for his design of the Banqueting Hall at Whitehall, and his repairs of Saint Paul's Cathedral. His other works include the piazza of Covent Garden (q.v.), the Queen's House at Greenwich, and Ashburnham House in Westminster.

JONES, James (1921–), American author, born in Robinson, Ill. At the age of eighteen he joined the United States Army. His five-year Army experience provided the background for his first and most successful novel, the brutally realistic and powerful *From Here to Eternity* (1951), which was successfully filmed (1953). His later fiction includes *Some Came Running* (1957), *The Pistol* (1959), *The Thin Red Line* (1962), and *The Merry Month of May* (1971).

JONES, John Paul, real name JOHN PAUL (1747–92), American naval officer, born in Kirkcudbright, Scotland. At the age of twelve he went to sea for the first time, as a cabin boy, sailing to Fredericksburg, Va. By 1766 he was first mate of a slaver brigantine. In 1769–70, while in the West Indies, he flogged a crewman who later died. John Paul was subsequently arrested but proved his innocence. In 1773, as

John Paul Jones

commander of a merchant vessel in Tobago (now Trinidad and Tobago) in the West Indies, he killed the leader of a mutinous crew. Rather than wait in prison for trial he escaped from the island and later returned to Fredericksburg. The British thereafter considered him a pirate and a fugitive from justice. To hide his identity he added the surname Jones.

In 1775, on the outbreak of the American Revolution (q.v.), Jones went to Philadelphia and entered the newly established Continental Navy. He was commissioned a lieutenant and attached to the first American flagship, *Alfred*. In 1776 he was promoted to captain, and given command of the sloop *Providence*. During his first cruise on the *Providence* he destroyed the British fisheries in Nova Scotia and captured sixteen British prize ships. In 1777 he commanded the sloop *Ranger*, and after sailing to France, he cruised along the coast of Great Britain, capturing and destroying many British vessels.

Jones was next promoted to commodore and placed in command of a mixed fleet of five French and American vessels. His flagship was the *Duras*, the name of which he changed to *Bonhomme Richard* (q.v.). In this ship, on Sept. 23, 1779, off the British coast, Jones defeated the British man-of-war *Serapis* in one of the outstanding engagements of naval history. He returned to the United States in 1781 and supervised the building of the *America*, the largest vessel in the United States Navy, which he was scheduled to command, but which was presented to France. After the war he was sent to Paris to collect money from the French for the prizes he had taken and delivered to France. He last visited the U.S. in 1787 and was given a gold medal by Congress. He was the only naval officer so honored. In 1788 he accepted an offer by Catherine II (q.v.), Empress of Russia, to enter her navy, and he took a leading part in several engagements against the Ottoman Turks. Jealousy and intrigues on the part of Russian rivals hampered him and prevented him from receiving proper credit for his successes. He retired and in 1790 went to Paris. In 1792 he was appointed U.S. consul to Algiers, but he died before the commission arrived. In 1905 his remains were brought to the U.S. from their long-forgotten grave in Paris and in 1913 were buried in the United States Naval Academy chapel.

JONES, Robert Edmond (1887–1954), American stage designer, born in Milton, N.H., and educated at Harvard University. In 1911 in New York City Jones began to design stage scenery markedly different from the minutely detailed and realistic sets of his contemporaries. In his stage designs he strove to simplify sets in order to convey an abstract idea or to evoke a certain mood. Thereafter he designed the stage sets for numerous outstanding musicals, plays, and films. In *The Dramatic Imagination* (1941) he presents his ideas about stage craft.

JONES, Robert Tyre, known as BOBBY JONES (1902–71), American amateur golfer, born in Atlanta, Ga., and educated at the Georgia Institute of Technology and at Harvard University, where he majored in law. Jones won the United States national open golf championship in 1923, 1926, 1929, and 1930; he was U.S. national amateur champion in 1924, 1925, 1927, 1928, and 1930. Jones competed in Great Britain, winning the British national open championship in 1926, 1927, and 1930. He was the first player to win both the U.S. and British national open championships in the same year (1926), and the only player ever to win both national amateur and open contests in both countries in the same year (1930); see GOLF. He retired from active competition in 1930.

JONESBORO, city in Arkansas, and county seat of Craighead Co., 120 miles N.E. of Little Rock. The city is the trading and distribution center for the surrounding region in which agriculture and livestock raising are the principal occupations. Among the industrial establishments in Jonesboro are rice mills and factories manufacturing plumbing fixtures, electrical equipment, and shoes. Jonesboro was settled in 1859 and incorporated in 1883. Pop. (1960) 21,418; (1970) 27,050.

JONGKIND, Johan Barthold (1819–91), Dutch painter and etcher, born in Lattrop, the Netherlands, and trained in art at The Hague. In 1846 he went to Paris and studied with the French artist Eugène Isabey (1804–86). Jongkind's work attracted the attention of the French art critics Edmond and Jules de Goncourt (*see under* GONCOURT), who helped establish his reputation in artistic circles. Jongkind painted some excellent forest landscapes, but his main body of work dealt with seascapes. He developed a technique to illustrate the effects of light by using juxtaposed strokes of unmixed colors. This technique influenced the French painter Claude Monet (q.v.) and other impressionist artists; *see* IMPRESSIONISM. He revisited his own country often, painting the countryside around Rotterdam and Dordrecht. As an etcher he ranks high, having executed numerous fine Dutch village scenes and seascapes. He has been generally acknowledged as the finest Dutch painter of his time. His works are found in the Metropolitan Museum of Art in New York City ("Sunset on the Scheldt", 1865) and in other leading museums.

JONKOPING, city in Sweden, and capital of Jönköping County, about 180 miles s.w. of Stockholm. Throughout the county oats and rye are grown, and cattle is raised. The city is one of the leading industrial centers in Sweden, producing machinery, paper, and textiles; it is also famous for its match industry, founded in 1844. The Gota Canal links the city with the Baltic Sea. Points of interest include several 14th and 17th-century churches, and a 17th-century courthouse. The city of Jönköping was chartered in 1284. In the war between Sweden and Denmark in 1612, the city was destroyed by the inhabitants on the order of King Gustavus II (q.v.), but was rebuilt shortly afterward. Pop. (1970) 107,656.

JONQUIL. See NARCISSUS.

JONSON, Ben (1573?–1637), English dramatist and poet, born in Westminster, and educated at the Westminster School. In 1592, after serving briefly with the English army in Flanders, he returned to London and joined the theatrical company of the English theater manager Philip Henslowe (d. 1616). Johnson served Henslowe as an actor and as an apprentice playwright, revising plays already in the repertory.

Early Works. The first play written completely by Jonson that has survived is *Every Man in His Humour*. It was performed in 1598 by another company, the Lord Chamberlain's, at the Curtain Theatre; William Shakespeare was a member of the cast. His next play, *Every Man Out of His Humour* (1599), was written in the same vein. Jonson had invented a kind of topical comedy involving eccentric characters, each of whom represented a humour, or temperament, of mankind. During the next four years Jonson also wrote a number of comedies in which he satirized his fellow writers, especially the dramatists Thomas Dekker and John Marston (qq.v.). Among these are *Cynthia's Revels* (1600)

Ben Jonson — Bettmann Archive

and *The Poetaster* (1601). Dekker and Marston retaliated by attacking Jonson in their *Satiromastix* (1600).

Later Works. After 1603, when James I (q.v.) ascended the throne of England, Jonson began to write masques (*see* MASQUE). In these works, devised for the entertainment of the court, he displayed his erudition, wit, and versatility. Some of his best lyric poetry was written to be sung in these masques. His influence at court grew, until in 1636 Charles I (q.v.) appointed him poet laureate (q.v.). The masques written by Jonson, including *The Satyr* (1603), *Masque of Beauty* (1608), and *Masque of Queens* (1609), were usually performed in elaborate settings designed by the noted English architect Inigo Jones (q.v.). At the same time that he was writing for the court, Jonson continued to write for the commercial theater. During this period he produced two tragedies, *Sejanus* (1603) and *Catiline* (1611), and the four brilliant comedies upon which his reputation as a playwright primarily rests: *Volpone* (1603), *Epicene, or the Silent Woman* (1609), *The Alchemist* (1610), and *Bartholomew Fair* (1614). His many nontheatrical pieces, including epigrams, epistles, and lyrics, are collected in *The Forest* (1616) and *Underwoods* (posthumously published, 1640). The first-named includes his most famous song, "Drink to Me Only with Thine Eyes".

Influence. In spite of his literary feuds, Jonson was the acknowledged leader of the men of letters of his time, the dean and the leading wit of the group of writers who often gathered at the Mermaid Tavern in the Cheapside district of London.

Although the creative talents of Jonson were many and varied, his considerable effect on English literature of the Jacobean and Carolinian periods was probably the result of his critical theories; *see* ENGLISH LITERATURE: *The Renaissance*. He sought to advance English drama as a form of literature, attempting to make it a conscious art through adherence to classical forms and rules. He protested particularly against the mixing of tragedy and comedy, and was an effective advocate of the principles of drama established by the Greek philosopher Aristotle (q.v.), which he praised at the expense of the flexibility and improvisational qualities of dramatists such as Shakespeare. Jonson's importance today rests upon his comedies of manners and their portrayal of contemporary London life.

G.N.S.

JOPLIN, city of Missouri, in Jasper and Newton counties, 140 miles S. of Kansas City. The city is the commercial center and shipping point for the surrounding agricultural and mining region, and is served by several railroads and airlines. Among the industrial establishments in Joplin are factories manufacturing chemicals, tools, earth crushers, store fixtures, missile parts, hydraulic pumps, steel castings, explosives, insulation materials, roofing, feeds, garments, and leather goods. The city is also an important livestock market, and has several meat-packing plants. Joplin is the northern gateway to the many lake and recreational areas in the Ozark Mts. Joplin was settled about 1840, and incorporated as a city in 1873. Pop. (1970) 39,256.

JOPLIN, Scott. *See* JAZZ: *Origins of Jazz: Ragtime*.

JOPPA. *See* JAFFA.

JORDAENS, Jakob (1593–1678), Flemish painter, born in Antwerp (now in Belgium), where he studied with the Flemish artist Adam van Noort (1562–1641). About 1615 Jordaens was admitted to the Antwerp art guild. By 1621 he had his own workshop with many students and was head of the guild. His talent attracted the

JORDAN, HASHEMITE KINGDOM OF

attention of the Flemish master Peter Paul Rubens (q.v.), who employed Jordaens as an assistant. Jordaens was clearly influenced by Rubens, and although his style was not as refined as that of Rubens, he is nevertheless considered one of the leaders of Baroque (q.v.) art. Aided by his students he painted large decorative works, especially subjects of revelry, grand banquets, and vivacious genre scenes. His color is brilliant and sensuous, emphasized by luminous whites and deep reddish tones. Vigorous and prolific, Jordaens became famous, and was overwhelmed with commissions, the most important coming after the death of Rubens in 1640. Although Jordaens executed many religious paintings, today he is best known for his bourgeois scenes and lively nudes. They include "Allegory of Fecundity" (Fine Arts Museum, Brussels), "As the Old Sing, So the Young Pipe" (Alte Pinakothek, Munich), and "Feast of the Bean, the King Drinks" (Museum of Fine Arts, Vienna).

JORDAN, river in S.W. Asia, flowing 200 mi. from north to south. The river originates in several headstreams in the mountains of S. Lebanon and Syria, then flows to Lake Tiberias (q.v.) and finally into the Dead Sea (q.v.). Below Lake Tiberias the river passes through the El Ghor valley, a depression extending 65 mi. from north to south. The river, the valley, and the two seas lie within the Great Rift Valley, a depression extending from Syria to Mozambique in S.E. Africa. The Jordan descends several thousand feet from its source to the Dead Sea. The northern part of the river forms part of the boundaries between Israel and Syria and between Israel and Jordan; the southern part lies completely within Jordan. The Jordan R. is frequently referred to in the Bible; in the New Testament it is mentioned as the site of the baptism of Jesus Christ (*see* JOHN THE BAPTIST). The power created by the currents of the river makes possible the construction of hydroelectric power stations and the use of the water for irrigation, especially in the desert of the Negev (q.v.).

JORDAN, David Starr (1851–1931), American natural scientist and educator, born in Gainesville, N.Y., and educated at Cornell University and Indiana Medical College. Jordan taught natural sciences at several universities from 1871 until 1885, when he became president of Indiana University. From 1891 to 1913 he was president of Stanford University. Jordan was an expert on fishes, and he served on several international and national ichthyological commissions. He was also deeply interested in the pre-World War I peace movement, and was director of the World Peace Foundation and president of the World Peace Congress. Jordan wrote several books on politics and education, and many well-known zoological works.

JORDAN, HASHEMITE KINGDOM OF (Ar. *al Mamlaka al Urduniya al Hashemiyah*), kingdom of S.W. Asia, formerly known as Transjordan, or Transjordania. It is bounded on the N. by Syria, on the E. by Iraq and Saudi Arabia, on the S. by Saudi Arabia and the Gulf of 'Aqaba, and on the W. by Israel. The country is located between about lat. 35° N. and lat. 35°50′ N., and between long. 25°50′ E. and long. 30°40′ E. The area of Jordan, including that part W. of the Jordan R. which was occupied by Israel in 1967 (see *History*, below), is 34,820 sq.mi.

THE LAND

The principal geographical feature of Jordan is an arid plateau that thrusts abruptly upward on the E. shores of the Jordan River and the Dead

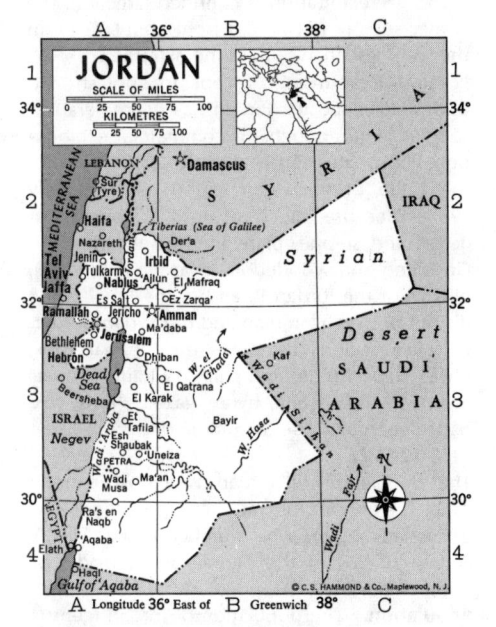

INDEX TO MAP OF JORDAN

Cities and Towns

'Ajlun	A 2
Amman (cap.)	B 3
'Aqaba	A 4
Bayir	B 3
Bethlehem	A 3
Dhiban	A 3
El Karak	A 3
El Mafraq	B 2
El Qatrana	B 3
Esh Shaubak	A 3
Et Tafila	A 3
Ez Zarqa'	B 2
Hebron	A 3
Irbid	A 2
Jenin	A 2
Jericho	A 3
Jerusalem (Old City)	A 3
Ma'an	A 3
Ma'daba	A 3
Nablus	A 2
Ramallah	A 3
Ra's en Naqb	A 4
Tulkarm	A 2
'Uneiza	A 3
Wadi Musa	A 3

Physical Features

'Aqaba (gulf)	A 4
'Araba (dry river)	A 3
Dead Sea (lake)	A 3
Ghadaf (dry river)	B 3
Hasa (dry river)	B 3
Jordan (river)	A 2
Petra (ruins)	A 3
Syrian (desert)	C 2

JORDAN, HASHEMITE KINGDOM OF

Sea (qq.v.) to a height of 2000 to 3000 ft., then slopes gently downward toward the Syrian Desert in the extreme E. of the country. The rolling hills and highlands W. of the Jordan R. are separated from the rest of the country by the Great Rift Valley, which is about 700 ft. below sea level in the area of Lake Tiberias (Sea of Galilee) and nearly 1300 ft. below sea level at the Dead Sea. Deep canyons and mountainous outcroppings with elevations of over 5000 ft. characterize the Arabian Plateau in the S. portion of the country.

Climate. The climate of Jordan is marked by sharp seasonal variations in both temperature and precipitation. Temperatures below freezing are not unknown in January, the coldest month, but the average winter temperature is above 45° F. In the Jordan valley summer temperatures may reach 120° F. in August, the hottest month, but the average summer temperature in Amman is 78° F. Precipitation is confined largely to the winter season and ranges from about 26 in. in the W. to less than 5 in. in the extreme E.

Natural Resources. Except for potash and phosphate deposits, Jordan has no mineral resources large enough for commercial exploitation. Phosphates constituted almost one third of the value of Jordanian exports in the early 1970's. Because much of Jordan consists of desert and steppe, plant life is not abundant. Grassland and wooded areas are largely in the hills W. of the Jordan R. and in the Jebel 'Ajlun district between Amman and the Syrian border. In these regions the trees include oak, ilex, olive, Aleppo pine, and palm. Wildlife consists mainly of the hyena, hyrax, gazelle, ibex, fox, partridge, mongoose, and mole rat.

THE PEOPLE

The population of Jordan is almost entirely Arab. The only sizable racial minority consists of Circassians (q.v.), who number about 12,000. Nearly 220,000 of the people are nomadic or seminomadic.

Population. The population of Jordan (census 1961) was 1,706,226; the United Nations estimated (1971) 2,383,000, including about 720,000 Palestinian Arab refugees. The overall population density is about 62 per sq.mi. (U.N. est. 1970). About half of the Jordanian population is urban.

Political Divisions. Jordan is divided into 8 administrative districts or governates, Amman, Irbid, El Balqa, El Karak, and Ma'an, on the E. side of the Jordan R., and Hebron, Jerusalem, and Nablus, on the W. side. The last three, known as the West Bank, were occupied by Israel in 1967. An extensive district farther E. is known as the desert area.

Principal Cities. Amman (q.v.), the capital and largest city of Jordan, grew in population from a census estimate of 321,000 in 1966 to an estimate of 560,000 in 1973, because of the influx of West Bank refugees in the wake of the Six-Day War with Israel in 1967. Other important cities, with populations estimated in the mid-1960's, include the "Old City" of Jerusalem (60,500), Nablus (45,800), Hebron (43,000), Bethlehem (35,700), and Jericho (10,000), all of which were occupied by Israel in 1967, and the East Bank cities of Irbid (44,700), Es Salt (16,100), Jenin (14,400), and Ez Zarqa' (1971 est., 200,000). 'Aqaba (q.v.), the only seaport, had a population of less than 10,000.

Religion and Language. The great majority of the people are Sunnite (q.v.) Muslims. Christians number about 180,000. Islam is the state religion, and Arabic the official language. English and French are commonly spoken in the towns.

Education. Jordan has made significant strides in education in recent years, despite the influx of hundreds of thousands of refugees and the very large share of the national budget assigned to the armed forces. Public education at the primary level is free and compulsory beginning at the age of six. In practice, however, about 90 percent of the male and only about half the female children go to school. The nomadic habits of much of the pastoral population make attendance difficult to enforce.

ELEMENTARY AND SECONDARY SCHOOLS. In the early 1970's some 422,000 pupils were attending elementary schools, 111,000 students were attending junior high schools, and 47,300 were enrolled in general secondary schools. More than 63 percent of students were enrolled in government schools and almost 20 percent in schools operated by the United Nations Relief and Works Agency (U.N.R.W.A.)

SPECIALIZED SCHOOLS. At the secondary level the country maintains schools devoted to commerce, industry, agriculture, and teacher training. Adult education is also stressed, and an adult literacy campaign currently has 170 training centers and some 3000 participants.

UNIVERSITIES AND COLLEGES. The University of Jordan, near Amman, established in 1962, has faculties of arts, science, economics and commerce, Islamic law, and medicine. Enrollment totals more than 3000. Other facilities for higher education include the Statistical Center, the College of Nursing, and institutes of banking studies, social work, public administration, and cooperatives. The American School of Oriental Research, the British School of Archeology, and

Cities of Jordan. Above: A busy shopping street in Amman, the capital of Jordan. Right: A street scene in Nablus, a populous city in a region of Jordan seized by Israel in the 1967 Arab-Israeli war.

JORDAN, HASHEMITE KINGDOM OF

the French School of Archeology and Biblical Studies are devoted to linguistic and historical studies and to archeological surveys and excavations. The Muslim Educational College, the Armenian Patriarchate Seminary, and the Greek Catholic Seminary of Saint Anne specialize in the preparation of clergy to oversee the holy places of Jerusalem and to conduct research on religious subjects.

Libraries and Museums. The major libraries of Jordan are the Public Library of Amman (15,000 vol.), the French Biblical School Library (40,000 vol.), the British Council Libraries (18,000 vol.), the Saint Anne Seminary Library (16,000 vol.), the Franciscan Library (7000 vol.), and the Gulbenkian Armenian Library (55,000 vol.).

Four major museums containing religious and archeological treasures are the Islamic Museum, the Jordan Archeological Museum, the Franciscan Biblical Museum, and the Palestine Archeological Museum.

Archeology. The annexation by Jordan of all that part of Palestine, including the Old City of Jerusalem, which remained in Arab hands after the armistice with Israel in April, 1949 (see *History*, below), made the country a prime attraction for tourists, historians, and archeologists. The Old City and Bethlehem (q.v.), with sites sacred to Jews, Muslims, and Christians, were of major importance to Jordan in terms of tourist revenues alone. With the occupation of the West Bank districts by Israel in 1967, however, the only prime archeological site currently in Jordan is the ancient city of Petra (q.v.).

THE ECONOMY

Underdeveloped industrially, poor in natural resources, the major part of its territory too arid for agriculture, Jordan is not economically self-supporting. Revenues from the export of goods plus services in the early 1970's provided only about 43 percent of the gross national product. A recent national budget estimate showed annual revenues of about $183,000,000 and expenditures of about $255,000,000. Grants and loans from other countries totaled approximately $15,700,000.

Agriculture. Although Jordan is predominantly an agricultural country, with about 75 percent of the population engaged in farming or livestock raising, only about 10 percent of the land area is cultivated, and only about 6 percent of the cultivated area is irrigated. With so much of its agriculture dependent on rainfall, annual production figures fluctuate widely. Wheat and barley are the major grain crops, but production is not sufficient to meet the needs of the country. Annual wheat production in the early 1970's was about 170,000 tons and barley about 26,000 tons. Some fruit crops, primarily olives, almonds, figs, grapes, and apricots, and such vegetables as tomatoes and cucumbers are grown for export. Even in the best agricultural years, food imports exceed food exports. In the same period sheep, the most important livestock animal, totaled about 665,000 head; cattle numbered about 43,000 head. It is estimated that the West Bank accounted for about 20 to 25 percent of the grain, 70 percent of the fruit, and 40 percent of the vegetable produce of Jordan before the 1967 war with Israel.

Industry. Jordan lost only about 19 percent of its industrial production as a result of the Israeli occupation of the West Bank. The soap, olive oil, and cigarette industries of the West Bank, moreover, were small and produced almost entirely for the domestic market. The major industries, including phosphates, cement, oil refining, and hydroelectric power, are concentrated east of the river. Industrialization, starting from a very small base only a few years ago, has proceeded rapidly, even since the 1967 war. Both local and foreign-owned firms are encouraged through fiscal concessions from the government and high protective tariffs. The Jordan Development Board, in accordance with the 1964–70 economic plan and one scheduled for 1973–75, is setting up textile, pharmaceutical, drug, food-processing, sugar, paper, housewares, and glass industries on the East Bank. Plans for doubling the oil-refining capacity, agreements with a Yugoslav company for oil exploration and with India for increased phosphates purchases (Jordan was producing about 918,000 tons of phosphates annually in the early 1970's), and the discovery in 1967 of additional potash deposits augur well for continued industrial development.

Currency and Banking. Jordan since 1950 has issued its own currency, the Jordan dinar (1 dinar equals U.S.$2.8500; 1973), which is divided into 1000 fils. Although Jordan is a member of the sterling area, the dinar was not devalued following the drop of the British pound from $2.80 to $2.40 in November, 1967. In fact, the dinar increased in value, in terms of gold and foreign currency reserves, throughout the mid-1960's, even while the gap between import costs and export earnings widened. The health of the dinar is directly linked to large-scale foreign aid and cash grants. The United States, in the decade 1957–67, contributed loans, food shipments, and cash totaling $500,000,000; in 1968 it ceased its direct budgetary support because Jordan was receiving large subsidies from Arab countries.

Workmen load potassium salts for transfer to plants in northern Jordan, where it is processed into potash. **United Nations**

Beginning in 1967, oil-rich Saudi Arabia, Libya, and Kuwait provided Jordan with cash grants of $112,000,000 annually; in 1971, however, Libya and Kuwait began to withhold the grants because of Jordanian activities against the Palestinian guerrillas; in 1972 the U.S. resumed certain forms of aid. The Central Bank of Jordan administers all funds, including sterling assets and currency commitments.

Commerce and Trade. The principal exports of Jordan, apart from agricultural produce which is shipped to neighboring countries, are phosphates and potash. Tourism, which was a larger source of income in prewar Jordan than all of its export commodities combined, has fallen off sharply since 1967. The principal imports are food, chemicals, textiles, machinery, rubber, and electrical equipment, with Great Britain, the U.S., West Germany, Lebanon, Japan, Syria, and Saudi Arabia the chief suppliers. In 1971 the total value of Jordanian imports was about $215,000,000, about the same as in 1966. The total value of exports was $32,000,000, compared to $24,500,000 in 1966.

Transportation and Communications. All major cities are linked by asphalted roads, and small towns by oiled or dirt roads. In the early 1970's passenger automobiles numbered about 15,200 and commercial vehicles about 5500. The only railroad runs from the Syrian border through Amman as far south as Ma'an, a total of 227 mi. West Germany has provided a loan of $12,000,000 for the extension of the line to the port of 'Aqaba. From the 110-mi. section of the Trans-Arabian Pipeline that crosses Jordan the government receives $5,000,000 yearly in transit fees. The air terminal in Amman is served by the Royal Jordanian Airlines and some ten other international lines.

In the early 1970's Jordan had in use about 33,000 telephones, 410,000 radios, and 61,000 television sets. Publications include two daily newspapers and four weeklies.

GOVERNMENT

Under the 1951 constitution, Jordan is a limited monarchy. King Hussein I (q.v.), chief executive and head of state, shares executive power with a premier and sixteen other cabinet members who are responsible to parliament.

Central Government. Legislative power rests in a house of representatives of sixty members elected by male suffrage to four-year terms and a senate of thirty members appointed by the king subject to house approval. As chief executive, Hussein may declare war, conclude peace, and convene, adjourn, and prorogue the house. He is also commander in chief of the armed forces. The Jordan Arab Army, formerly called the Arab Legion, of about 53,000 men, strongly loyal, represents a major buttress to royal authority.

Political Parties. Although political parties were banned in 1963, King Hussein since the 1967 war has endeavored to promote national unity by bringing opposition leaders into the government. The government-created El Nahda (Revival) Party is opposed by seven groups: the Arab Constitutional Bloc (conservative); the Muslim Brotherhood, the Arab Palestine Bloc, and the Liberation Bloc (rightist); and the Ba'ath, the National Front, and the National Socialist Party (leftist and influenced by Egyptian and Syrian policies).

Local Government. Each of the eight administrative districts of Jordan is headed by a governor appointed by the king. The nomadic population, divided into East and West Bank jursidictions, is administered separately.

Judiciary. Jordan, like many Arab countries, has a civil and a religious court system. Magis-

JORDAN, HASHEMITE KINGDOM OF

trate courts, the lowest in the civil system, hear minor criminal and civil cases; the more important go to courts of first instance. Decisions of these courts are subject to review by courts of appeal. The supreme court, the High Court of Justice, presides over cases against the state, hears appeals, and interprets the law.

Shari'a courts rule on marriage, divorce, interdiction, wills, and guardianship cases for Muslim citizens desiring traditional Islamic interpretation rather than civil decisions. Non-Muslim minorities may resort to religious courts of their own traditions in personal status cases. The nomadic tribes may bring cases to tribal courts.

HISTORY

The territory comprising modern Jordan was the site of some of the earliest settlements and political entities known to historians. The Ammonites (q.v.) and the kingdoms of Edom, Gilead, and Moab (qq.v.), situated east of the Jordan R., are referred to repeatedly in the Bible. These kingdoms were successively conquered by, or made tributary to, the Egyptians, Assyrians, Babylonians, Persians, and Romans. Jordan was wrested from the Byzantine Empire (q.v.) by the Arabs between 633 and 636, and has remained an Arab and Islamic country ever since. During the Crusades (q.v.) parts of Jordan were briefly governed by Christians. From 1517 until 1918 Jordan was ruled by the Ottoman Turks (see OTTOMAN EMPIRE).

The Trappist monastery at Latrun is famous for its vineyards, which are worked by the monks. UPI

Transjordan Independence. The liberation of Jordan from Turkish sovereignty was achieved in September, 1918, during World War I, by joint action of British and Arab troops. After the war Jordan, along with the territory comprising present-day Israel (q.v.), was awarded to Great Britain as a mandate by the League of Nations (q.v.). The British in 1922 divided the mandate into two parts, designating all lands west of the Jordan R. Palestine, and those east of the river Transjordan. Transjordan was placed under the nominal rule of Abdullah ibn-Husein (q.v.) in 1921. In February, 1928, Transjordan obtained qualified independence in a treaty concluded with Great Britain.

The government of Transjordan cooperated with Great Britain during World War II, making its territory available as a base of British operations against pro-Axis forces, which had gained control of the government of Iraq. In 1945 Transjordan became a member of the Arab League, an organization created for the purpose of coordinating Arab policy in international affairs and of curbing Jewish national aspirations in Palestine. The British government relinquished its mandate over Transjordan on March 22, 1946. By the terms of a treaty concluded by the two nations on that date, Transjordan received recognition as a sovereign independent state. The treaty also established an Anglo-Transjordanian military and mutual-assistance alliance, with the British securing military bases and other installations in the country in exchange for an agreement to train and equip the Transjordanian army. Abdullah ibn-Husein was proclaimed king the following May.

The Arab League and Jordan. The Jordanian army, known at that time as the Arab Legion, joined, with the armed forces of the other nations of the Arab League, in a concerted attack in May, 1948, on the newly formed State of Israel. During the war the Legion occupied sections of central Palestine, including the Old City of Jerusalem. Transjordan signed an armistice with Israel on April 3, 1949.

On April 24, 1950, despite strong opposition from other Arab League members, King Abdullah formally merged all of Arab-held Palestine with Transjordan. From that point on the prefix trans (across) became inaccurate, and the kingdom has been called Jordan. The word Hashimite (q.v.) refers to Hashim, the grandfather of Muhammed, from whom the Jordanian royal house claims direct descent.

King Abdullah was assassinated by a sup-

JORDAN, HASHEMITE KINGDOM OF

porter of a rival Arab claimant to the West Bank on July 20, 1951, and was succeeded by his son Talal I (1911?–72) the following September. The Jordanian parliament on Aug. 11, 1952, deposed Talal, who suffered from a mental disorder, and elevated his son, as Hussein I, the same day. A regency council acted for the new king until he reached the age of eighteen on May 2, 1953.

Armed Jordanian and Israeli detachments were involved in frequent frontier clashes during the early 1950's. A major source of friction were Israeli irrigation and hydroelectric schemes that would have reduced the volume of the Jordan R. waters, which were considered vital to Jordanian development.

Arab Problems and Disunity. Jordan became a member of the United Nations (q.v.) on Dec. 14, 1955, and during the latter half of the following year Jordanian and Israeli U.N. delegates registered bitter and increasingly frequent charges of border violations and armed raids.

By the provisions of a ten-year pact signed on Jan. 19, 1957, Egypt, Syria, and Saudi Arabia agreed to furnish Jordan with an annual subsidy of $36,000,000. The pact was designed to free Jordan from dependence on Western nations, especially Great Britain, the policies of which were considered anti-Arab and pro-Israel. The Jordanian premier and other leftists in the government were dismissed by the king in April, however, and the following June, Syria and Egypt revoked the aid pact.

On Feb. 14, 1958, two weeks after Egypt and Syria merged to form the United Arab Republic, the more conservative governments of Jordan and Iraq announced the formation of the Arab Federation. When the Iraqi government was overthrown in July, however, largely as a result of U.A.R. propaganda and intrigue, the federation was dissolved and Jordan severed diplomatic relations with the U.A.R. Although ties were restored in August, 1959, relations between Hussein and President Gamal Abdel Nasser (q.v.) of the U.A.R. remained strained. When the Jordanian premier, Hazza Majuli, was assassinated in August, 1960, the king charged Nasser with direct responsibility.

Tranquillity in the Early 1960's. During 1961 and 1962 Jordan was relatively free of domestic political strife and of anti-government agitation by the volatile refugee population. One sign of growing strength on the part of the throne was the general acceptance and even popularity of the king's marriage, in May, 1961, to Antoinette Avril Gardiner (1941–), of Great Britain, who was granted the title Princess Muna. After the elections of December, 1962, political parties, which had been banned during the height of Jordanian-U.A.R. tensions, were reactivated. Foreign relations were less relaxed, however. In September, 1961, Jordan recognized the new regime in Syria, which had just seceded from the U.A.R., and Nasser retaliated by breaking diplomatic relations with Jordan; see SYRIA: *History*.

After the fall of one premier and the resignation of another in the spring of 1963, political parties were again banned. Elections in July installed a new cabinet and inaugurated another two-year period of relative domestic tranquillity. Diplomatic relations with the U.A.R. were restored in 1964 as a result of mounting pressure for Arab League unity against Israel. Renewed clashes with Israel over Jordan R. water rights led to an Arab summit conference in Cairo in September, 1964, which Hussein attended.

Growing Tensions and War with Israel. Relations with the revolutionary and left-leaning Ba'athist regime in Damascus (see SYRIA: *History*) deteriorated in the mid-1960's. Despite calls for unity, Arab nations tended to polarize into an extremist camp including Syria, the U.A.R., and Iraq, and a moderate group including Jordan, Saudi Arabia, and Tunisia. For a time the Jordanian frontier with Syria was as troubled as that with Israel. Arab guerrilla fighters of the Palestine Liberation Organization (P.L.O.), infiltrating Jordan from Syria, launched terrorist attacks against Israel for which Jordan suffered Israeli reprisals. In July, 1966, Jordan withdrew support from the P.L.O., but a massive Israeli raid in November created intense pressure on Hussein to back the terrorists. When he refused, the P.L.O. called for his overthrow, and clashes on the Syrian border increased.

Arab-Israeli tensions were meanwhile mounting steadily. When war seemed imminent, Hussein, in an unprecedented gesture of Arab solidarity, flew to Cairo and signed a defense treaty with Nasser on May 30, 1967. This action greatly enhanced his position with the refugees, but it also committed Jordan to active involvement when the Six-Day War broke out on June 5. On June 7, its air force destroyed and the West Bank occupied, Jordan accepted a U.N. cease-fire.

Jordanian postwar diplomacy aimed at reinforcing ties with the West and achieving an Israeli withdrawal from the occupied area. Hussein took no unilateral initiatives toward a peace settlement, however, and the U.A.R. (which in 1971 changed its name to Arab Republic of Egypt; q.v.), Algeria, and Syria meanwhile hardened their anti-Israel position with calls for a sustained guerrilla offensive against Israel, which was staged from bases in Jordan.

Early in 1973, King Hussein of Jordan and his new queen, Alia, are escorted to a formal dinner at the White House by President Richard M. Nixon. UPI

The situation in Jordan reached the point of civil war in September, 1970, when Palestinian guerrillas supported by Syria fought Jordanian troops in Amman and other areas of northern Jordan. After heavy casualties, a cease-fire agreement was reached requiring a number of concessions from Hussein. In 1971, however, Hussein ordered Premier Wasfi Tal (1920–71) to take military action against the guerrillas, and the movement was completely crushed. Arab reaction against Jordan was strongly hostile. On Nov. 28, while attending an Arab League meeting in Cairo, Premier Tal was assassinated by members of the Black September guerrillas.

In 1972 Hussein proposed creation of a federated Arab state comprising Jordan and the Israeli-occupied west bank of the Jordan R. Arab opinion was unanimously opposed, and the Palestinian guerrilla group Al Fatah called for the overthrow of Hussein.

In February, 1973, King Hussein visited the U.S. and received promises of continued U.S. economic and military aid. On Sept. 18 Hussein granted amnesty to 1500 political prisoners, including some 750 Palestinian commandos; the move was viewed as a peace gesture following meetings with leaders of Egypt and Syria that had brought about reconciliation among the three countries.

When, on Oct. 6, full-scale war again broke out between Israel and Egypt and Syria, Jordan at first remained neutral. Under pressure from Arab leaders, however, and, it was believed, because of the early success of the Arab drive, King Hussein sent units of the Jordanian army to join Syrian forces on the Golan Heights. Kuwait, which had cut off economic assistance to Jordan in 1971, resumed its aid after Jordan joined in the attack on Israel.

JORULLO, volcano in S.W. Mexico, in Michoacán State, 33 miles S.E. of Uruapan. Jorullo was formed in 1759 with a violent upheaval, destroying a fertile agricultural area. The volcano has been inactive for over a century. In the course of volcanic activity six cones have been formed; the highest is 4331 ft. above sea level.

JOSEPH, Saint (fl. beginning of the 1st cent. A.D.), according to all four Gospels (see GOSPEL) in the New Testament, a carpenter of Nazareth (now in Israel) in the province of Galilee, the husband of the Virgin Mary (see MARY, SAINT). The earliest genealogy (Matt. 1:1–17) of Jesus (see JESUS CHRIST) makes Joseph a descendant of David (q.v.), King of Israel and Judah. He plays an important role in the infancy narratives (Matt. 1, 2; Luke 1, 2) but later in the Gospels is mentioned infrequently, for the last time in Luke 2:43. Mentioned only incidentally elsewhere in the New Testament, Joseph is often referred to in later traditions, and in modern times he has become a popular saint, revered especially by Roman Catholics; his feast day is March 19. According to some accounts Joseph was Mary's nominal husband, eighty years old and the father of a grown-up family of sons by a former wife (an explanation of the Biblical reference to the "brethren of the Lord") at the time of his formal espousal of Mary. This version first occurs in the Apocryphal gospels, earliest of which is apparently the *Protevangelium of James,* a 2nd-century work quoted by the Christian teacher, writer, and theologian Origen and mentioned by the theologian and church father Clement of Alexandria and the Christian apologist Saint Justin (qq.v.). The controversy as to the "brethren of the Lord" has been waged from Saint Jerome (q.v.) downward. Two opinions previously prevailed: (1) that they were sons of

JOSEPH OF ARIMATHEA

Joseph by a former wife, as held by most orthodox Christians and by fathers such as Clement of Alexandria, Origen, and Eusebius of Caesarea (q.v.) and the later Greek writers; or (2) that they were sons of both Joseph and Mary, as maintained by the ecclesiastical writer Tertullian (q.v.), the Roman heretic Helvidius (fl. 4th cent.), and heretical Arabian sects.

JOSEPH, name of two rulers of the Holy Roman Empire.

Joseph I (1678–1711), King of Hungary (1687–1711), King of Germany (1690–1711), Holy Roman Emperor (1705–11), born in Vienna, Austria, the eldest son and successor of Leopold I, Holy Roman Emperor (*see under* LEOPOLD). Holding liberal opinions, he granted privileges to the Protestants of his dominions, especially in Silesia. In alliance with Britain, he prosecuted the War of the Spanish Succession against France; he supported the claim of his brother, who succeeded him as Charles VI (q.v.), to the throne of Spain. Joseph died before the war ended. *See* SPANISH SUCCESSION, WAR OF THE.

Joseph II (1741–90), King of Germany (1764–90), and Holy Roman Emperor (1765–90), born in Vienna, Austria, the son of Francis I, Holy Roman Emperor, and Maria Theresa (qq.v.), and the first emperor of the royal German family known as the House of Hapsburg-Lorraine; *see* HAPSBURG. Joseph was a zealous reformer who abolished serfdom and feudal dues, gave peasants great freedom, made the penal code more humane, and allowed for a great measure of freedom of worship. At the same time he suppressed Roman Catholic religious orders and reduced the number of the clergy. Joseph was unable to make many of his reforms permanent because of resistance from the clergy and nobility and because his methods sometimes caused unrest among his subjects.

JOSEPH (Heb., "he shall add"), in the Old Testament, the eleventh son of the patriarch Jacob (q.v.), or Israel, by his favorite wife, Rachel. According to the account in Genesis (30–50), Joseph was the favorite son of Jacob because he was the firstborn of Rachel. Joseph was envied by his brothers, particularly after Jacob expressed his partiality toward him by giving him a "coat of many colors", and they sold him into slavery. Taken to Egypt (now the Arab Republic of Egypt) by his master, Joseph later won the favor of the pharaoh by interpreting his dream and prophesying from it seven years of prosperity to be followed by seven years of famine. The pharaoh made Joseph his highest official and charged him with collecting food to be used during the years of famine. When the famine came, the Egyptians were able to survive as a result of Joseph's foresight. Joseph's brothers came to Egypt for supplies, and Joseph revealed himself to them. In the reconciliation that followed, Jacob moved his entire family to Egypt and settled in Goshen (q.v.), where his descendants remained and multiplied until the Hebrew prophet and lawgiver Moses (q.v.) led them out of Egypt.

Biblical scholars believe Joseph represents one of the northern tribes of the Hebrew confederacy; *see* JEWS: *The Hebrews in Canaan*. The story of the enmity of his brothers toward him is thought to represent a coalition of other tribes of the confederacy against the tribe of Joseph after the latter had grown strong; this view is believed to have been combined by later Hebrew writers with accounts of a sojourn in Egypt by some of the Hebrew tribes and with the story of a Hebrew who rose to a high position there. The first Biblical enumeration of the Hebrew tribes, in Exodus (q.v.), makes no mention of the tribe of Joseph; some authorities suggest that when the other tribes allied against it, the tribe of Joseph split into the tribes of Ephraim and Manasseh (qq.v.), who are identified in the Bible as the sons of Joseph.

JOSEPH, Chief. *See* INDIAN WARS; NEZ PERCÉ.

JOSEPH, Father, real name FRANÇOIS LE CLERC DU TREMBLAY (1577–1638), French monk and statesman, born in Paris. He joined the Order of Capuchins (q.v.) in 1599. About 1612 he became associated with the French statesman and cardinal Duc de Richelieu (q.v.). Father Joseph became Richelieu's confidant and adviser and in subsequent years was entrusted with many important secret diplomatic missions in France and elsewhere in Europe. In contrast to Richelieu, who was called the *Éminence Rouge* ("Red Eminence") from the color of his clerical robes, Father Joseph became known as *Éminence Grise* ("Gray Eminence"). The activities of Father Joseph were motivated by religious zeal. He hoped to restore Roman Catholicism throughout Europe, and therefore aided Richelieu in efforts to convert the French Protestants (*see* HUGUENOTS), and proposed a crusade against the Ottoman Turks who then controlled much of Europe.

JOSEPH OF ARIMATHEA, according to all four Gospels (*see* GOSPEL) of the New Testament, a rich Jew of Arimathea who, after the crucifixion of Jesus Christ (q.v.) requested the body from the Roman procurator Pontius Pilate (q.v.) and placed it in his own tomb. According to some ancient writers he was, later, the founder of Christianity in Britain and of a mon-

JOSÉPHINE

astery at Glastonbury (q.v.); scholars, however, reject these claims. In the Arthurian Cycle (q.v.) of romances and in late medieval legend he brings the Holy Grail into Britain; see GRAIL, THE HOLY.

JOSÉPHINE, Empress of France. See under BEAUHARNAIS.

JOSEPHUS, Flavius, original name JOSEPH BEN MATTHIAS (37 or 38–about 101), Jewish historian, born in Jerusalem of both royal and priestly lineage (see PRIEST). A man both learned and worldly, he was a member of the Pharisees (q.v.) and also a public figure who, before the Jewish revolt against Rome (66), had made friends at the court of Emperor Nero (q.v.).

The parts played in the revolt by the Zealots (q.v.), and their opponents the Pharisees, who considered it impracticable, led to ambiguity in the historical record of the role of Josephus, a Pharisee, in the conflict. His own writings present two conflicting accounts of his mission in the province of Galilee (in what is now Israel). According to one account, he took command of the Jewish forces there to lead the Galilean phase of the revolt, but the other, later, account contends that he sought to subdue the revolt rather than lead it. Whichever story may be true, apparently he prepared Galilee for the coming onslaught and in 67 valorously repulsed the advance of Vespasian (q.v.), the Roman general who was soon to become emperor, defending the fortress of Jotapata for forty-seven days before surrendering. Josephus would have been sent as a prisoner to Nero had he not had the wit to prophesy that his captor, Vespasian, would himself one day be emperor. This prophecy accorded with Vespasian's ambitions and the general kept Josephus with him, thus probably saving his life. While Vespasian's prisoner, Josephus saw the subjugation of Galilee and Judea. Subsequently freed, he adopted Vespasian's family name, Flavius, and in the entourage, now, of another future emperor, Vespasian's son Titus (q.v.), he witnessed Titus' siege of Jerusalem. Thereafter, enjoying imperial patronage under Vespasian, Titus, and the latter's brother and successor, Domitian (q.v.), Josephus lived in Rome and devoted himself to his writing.

His works include *The Jewish War* (in seven books), which he wrote to dissuade his people and other nations from courting annihilation by further revolt against an all-powerful Rome; *Jewish Antiquities* (in twenty books), a history of the Jews from the Creation (q.v.) to 66 A.D. that constitutes an eloquent, sympathetic narrative of his people, showing how they had flourished under the law of God; an autobiography, *Life*; and *Against Apion*, a refutation of charges against the Jews made by the anti-semitic Greek grammarian Apion (fl. 1st cent.) and other anti-Semitic writers. The last-named is invaluable because Josephus recapitulates writings on Jewish history that are no longer extant.

JOSH BILLINGS. See BILLINGS, JOSH.

JOSHUA, book of the Old Testament (see BIBLE), in the King James Version, THE BOOK OF JOSHUA; in other versions, the title is sometimes rendered as Iosue (in the Vulgate, q.v.) or Josue (Douay). According to the traditional view, its author was the ancient Israelite leader Joshua (q.v.). Most modern Bible scholars, however, reject this view; their studies have shown that the book contains material drawn from a number of different sources. Attempts to date the various strands have largely been inconclusive. The only conclusion widely accepted today is that the oldest passages of the book, which some scholars date from the middle of the 10th century B.C., were completely rewritten and much elaborated upon in the 7th century B.C. by a member (or members) of the so-called "Deuteronomic" school (see DEUTERONOMY; PENTATEUCH). Later, probably after 500 B.C., editors concerned primarily with priestly matters added to or rewrote much of the latter half of the book.

Joshua concludes the accounts begun in the books of Genesis, Exodus (qq.v.), and Deuteronomy of the origin and early history of the Jews (q.v.). It begins (chapters 1–6) with an account of the entry by the Hebrews into the Promised Land, Canaan (q.v.), and the sack of the ancient Palestinian walled city of Jericho (q.v.). It then relates (chapters 7–12) how the Hebrews established themselves throughout Canaan by their conquest of another ancient city, Ai, by "a league" (9:15) with the fearful Gibeonites (see GIBEON), by their bloody rout of an army led by the kings of five other southern Canaanite cities, and by the slaughter of an army gathered by yet other Canaanite kings "at the waters of Merom" (11:5) in the north. Much of the latter half (chapters 13–24), of the book describes how Joshua distributed the conquered land among the twelve tribes of Israel (q.v.). Joshua's final exhortation (chapter 23) to Israel to honor the covenant entered into with God on Mount Sinai (qq.v.) and an account of the last gathering of the tribes under Joshua (chapter 24), at which time the people and Joshua enter into another covenant to serve and obey God, conclude the book.

The central theme of Joshua is that God will lead His people if they observe His law; but if they deny Him, He will turn from them, giving them over to marauding nations and to foreign rule. *See also* HEXATEUCH.

JOSHUA (Heb., "Jehovah is salvation"), in the Old Testament, leader of the Hebrews in the invasion and occupation of Canaan (q.v.) and the principal figure of the story told in the book that bears his name; *see* book of JOSHUA. He was the son of Nun (Exod. 33:11), of the tribe of Ephraim (q.v.), and was born probably in Goshen, a district of ancient Egypt, where his parents were slaves. Joshua is first mentioned in Exod. 17:9 as the one chosen by the Hebrew prophet and lawgiver Moses (q.v.) to command the Israelites (*see* JEWS) in the battle against the Amalekites (q.v.) at Rephidim, a place of uncertain location in Sinai (now a disputed territory between Israel and the Arab Republic of Egypt). Shortly afterward he was one of the twelve spies sent (Num. 13) to explore the land of Canaan and was one of the two who favored an advance. Upon the death of Moses, Joshua succeeded him and led the conquest of western Palestine. He was much revered as the successor of Moses, but scholars generally reject the historical accuracy of the book of Joshua, in which he is idealized. *See* PALESTINE: *History.*

JOSHUA TREE NATIONAL MONUMENT, region of natural interest in S. California; *see* NATIONAL PARK SERVICE.

JOSIAH (Heb., "may Jehovah give"), in the Old Testament, king of Judah (640–609 B.C.), son and successor of Amon (r. 642 B.C.). During his reign (recounted in 1 Kings 22, 23; 2 Chron.), a book of law, probably Deuteronomy (q.v.), was discovered by workers who were repairing the Temple (*see* TEMPLE: *Temple at Jerusalem*). Largely influenced by precepts contained in its text, Josiah reestablished the worship of Jehovah (q.v.), removed foreign influences, and instituted the rites prescribed. When the Egyptian pharaoh, Necho II (r. about 609–593 B.C.), sought to revive the Assyrian empire (*see* ASSYRIA), which had been weakened by the death some twenty years before of King Ashurbanipal (q.v.), Josiah opposed him. The armies of Judah and Egypt met in 609 at Megiddo, in Mesopotamia (q.v.), and Josiah was slain by Egyptian archers.

JOUHAUX, Léon (1879–1954), French labor leader, born in Paris. When Jouhaux was about twelve years old he left school and went to work to supplement the family income. Later while working in a government match factory he became active in the labor movement. In 1909 he became secretary-general of the trade union, the Confédération Générale du Travail ("General Confederation of Labor"), commonly called the C.G.T. During World War I Jouhaux moderated his radical-extremist views and supported the policies of the Socialist Party. He espoused the cause of state socialism after the war, and was instrumental in forming the International Labor Organization (q.v.). Before the outbreak of World War II, he brought the C.G.T. into the center-left French coalition government, the Popular Front. The C.G.T. was disbanded when the Germans occupied France. Jouhaux was subsequently arrested and sent to Buchenwald, a German concentration camp (q.v.). Returning to France in May, 1945, he served as a secretary-general of the C.G.T. until December, 1947, when he resigned to organize an anti-Communist labor organization. He was a founder in 1949 of the International Confederation of Free Trade Unions; *see* TRADE UNION: *International Organization.* He was awarded the 1951 Nobel Peace Prize.

JOULE, James Prescott (1818–89), British physicist, born in Salford, Lancashire, England. An invalid throughout life, he suffered from a spinal disorder and did not attend school. Although the chemist John Dalton (q.v.) was one of his instructors at home, for the most part he gained his scientific knowledge through private study. One of the outstanding physicists of his day, Joule is best known for his researches in electricity and thermodynamics (qq.v.). In the course of his investigations of the heat emitted in an electrical circuit he formulated the law, now known as Joule's Law of electric heating, which states that the amount of heat produced each second in a conductor by a current of electricity is proportional to the resistance of the conductor and to the square of the current. Joule gave experimental verification to the law of conservation of energy in his study of the transfer of mechanical energy into heat energy; *see* ENERGY. Using many independent methods he determined the numerical relation between heat and mechanical energy, or the mechanical equivalent of heat, often called Joule's equivalent; *see* HEAT: *Heat Units.* He received many honors from universities and scientific societies throughout the world. His *Scientific Papers* in two volumes were published in 1885 and 1887.

JOURNALISM, gathering (by reporters), evaluating (by editors), and disseminating (through various media) of facts of current interest. Originally journalism encompassed only such printed matter as newspapers and periodicals. In the 20th century, however, it is construed as including other media used in disseminating news, such as radio, television, and documentary or newsreel films.

JOURNALISM

Historical Survey. The earliest known journalistic effort was the *Acta Diurna* ("Journal of the Day") of ancient Rome; in the 1st century B.C. the Roman statesman Gaius Julius Caesar (q.v.) ordered these handwritten news bulletins posted each day in the Forum (q.v.). The first printed newspaper, produced from wood blocks, appeared in Peking, China, in the 7th or 8th century A.D. In the middle of the 15th century, wider and faster dissemination of news was made possible by the invention in Europe of movable type. At first newspapers consisted of one sheet and dealt with a single event. Gradually a more complex product evolved.

Germany, the Netherlands, and England produced newsletters of varying sizes in the 16th and 17th centuries. French influence rose with the development of the magazine or literary journal late in the 17th century. By the early 18th century politicians had begun to realize the enormous potential of newspapers in shaping public opinion. Consequently the journalism of the period was largely political in nature; journalism was regarded as an adjunct of politics, and each political faction had its newspaper. It was during this period that the great English journalists flourished, among them writers like Daniel Defoe, Jonathan Swift, Joseph Addison, and Sir Richard Steele (qq.v.). Also at this time began the long and continuous struggle for freedom of the press.

In the English colonies of America, the first newspaper was *Publick Occurrences, Both Foreign and Domestick,* published in Boston in 1690; it was suppressed and its editor, Benjamin Harris (fl. 1673–1716), was imprisoned after having produced four issues. The precedental case involving freedom of the press in America was the trial of the publisher John Peter Zenger (q.v.) in 1735, which resulted in the acquittal of Zenger on charges of criminal libel based on articles critical of the colonial authorities in New York. The Alien and Sedition Acts (q.v.), passed in 1798, included provisions for censorship of the press. After provoking a great deal of opposition, these acts were allowed to expire.

Journalism in the 19th century was affected by the Industrial Revolution (q.v.). Newly invented machines made widespread, cheap production and distribution of newspapers possible. As education became available to the general public, the demand for reading matter increased. As a result, hundreds of newspapers and specialized periodicals began publication throughout the world. Competition among them, both for circulation and to obtain the news as fast as possible, was intense. Great pub-

President Lyndon B. Johnson, during his years in office, 1963–69, preferred to meet journalists at informal news conferences in his office at the White House. UPI

Journalistic photography is especially difficult and hazardous when covering a war. To get the good shot, the photographer must always take the lead. Nguyen Thanh Tai – UPI

lishing empires, consolidating many newspapers and periodicals, were founded. Gradually a few important daily newspapers emerged, eventually reaching millions of readers; these included the *Daily Express* and *Daily Mirror* of London, the New York *Times* and the *Daily News* of New York City, and the Chicago *Daily Tribune*. Wire services, such as Reuter's (*see* REUTER, BARON PAUL JULIUS VON) and the Associated Press, were organized to facilitate the gathering of news.

The Growth of Editorialization. At the same time, journalism began its permanent double life, split into opposing camps as editors found that, freed from the political affiliations of the previous century, they could indulge their own interests in promoting either responsible factual journalism or sensationalism. The profession of newspaper editing therefore became a powerful and often respected one.

Synonymous with sensationalism in newspaper publishing is the phrase "yellow journalism". The term probably derives from a competition in the 1890's between rival American newspapers both of which were publishing versions of a popular comic strip (q.v.) featuring a character known as the Yellow Kid; the comics were printed in yellow. In order to attract readers away from the rival newspaper, these competing papers began to use lurid headlines and emphasize sensational items, usually crimes of passion or alleged atrocities of the Spanish-American War (q.v.), rather than serious news. Largely a result of the work of two American publishers, Joseph Pulitzer and William Randolph Hearst (qq.v.), the era of yellow journalism is generally regarded as having ended with the outbreak of World War I. Some of its aspects, however, such as eye-catching headlines, comics in color, and heavy use of illustration (q.v.), have continued.

Editors and publishers have also found that journalism can be a potent force for progress. Early in the 20th century, President Theodore Roosevelt (q.v.) accused some crusading journalists, especially writers for such weekly magazines as *McClure's* and *Everybody's*, of being muckrakers. While sympathizing with their goals, he characterized them as unable to lift their gaze above the corruption in business and government they alleged to be basic in American life. Their work in calling this corruption to public attention was effective, however, in accomplishing social, economic, and political reforms, for example, important antitrust legislation (*see* TRUST). Most American newspapers and newsmagazines are now identified with a continuing editorial policy of support for causes deemed worthy by their publishers. Ideally such editorializing is presented on the so-called editorial page or in a special section. It may also take the form of a series of articles, clearly separated from the bulk of factual news.

The ability of journalists to report all the news they feel should be reported has often been curtailed. Forces outside the publishing industry, including governmental, military, religious, and corporate authorities, have at various times throughout the history of journalism determined what could or could not be printed. This has been particularly true for the press in a totalitarian regime. Occasionally, even in the U.S. political and military authorities are charged with news manipulation.

JOURNALISM

Audio-Visual Journalism. In the second decade of the 20th century a new era in journalism began. Radio made it easier for the public to obtain the news; one had only to turn on the set and listen to simplified, excerpted bulletins. The reader became the listener. During the same period, a third journalistic medium rose in importance, as newsreels were shown in motion-picture theaters throughout the world. These brief filmed reports had the added advantages of visual excitement and immediacy.

The increasing popularity of television in the 1950's and 1960's marked the end of the theatrical newsreel. Television could bring an even greater sense of immediacy, directly to the viewer in his home. Often the viewer was able to witness an important news event at the moment it occurred. For example, live telecasts showed American astronauts orbiting in their spacecraft and walking on the moon, and millions of viewers watched the coronation of Elizabeth II, Queen of Great Britain and Northern Ireland, and the funerals of President John Fitzgerald Kennedy, civil-rights leader Martin Luther King, Senator Robert Francis Kennedy, and British Prime Minister Sir Winston Churchill (qq.v.). More controversial has been the coverage of such events as the U.S. military involvement in Southeast Asia and riots by minority groups in various American cities.

Editorial opinion has been less emphasized in television than in the other news media. A few radio commentators such as H. V. Kaltenborn (1878–1965), Edward R. Murrow (q.v.) and Eric Sevareid (1912–), who had been immensely influential in the 1930's and 1940's remained at work in the 1960's. A regulation of the Federal Communications Commission (q.v.), however, requires that opponents of a stated opinion be allowed equal broadcast time in which to state their rebuttal case.

Current Trends. As television became more popular, newspapers became fewer in number. Newspapers are now relied upon for more extensive coverage, including the background and significance, of those events which television newscasts can present only superficially. At the same time, the number of other, more specialized periodicals, such as newsmagazines and special interest publications, increased. In the period from 1940 to 1969, the number of newspapers in the United States decreased from approximately 13,000 to 11,000, while the number of periodicals increased from 6000 to 9000.

A phenomenon of the late 1960's was the growth of the so-called underground press, produced largely by and for young people. The publishers of these periodicals claimed to reach some 9,000,000 readers a week by 1971. About 200 of the publishers formed a loosely structured press association dedicated to spreading their views on political and social matters not discussed by other journalistic media or presented there in terms found objectionable by underground journalists. The periodicals, sometimes tending toward anarchism, were written with little attention to literary forms.

Schools of Journalism. An important development in the early 20th century was the founding of the first schools of journalism at various educational institutions. The first of these was established at the University of Missouri in 1908. A school of journalism was founded at Columbia University in New York City in 1912. Today schools of journalism exist throughout the world and courses in journalism are taught even at the secondary level. Many journalists receive their early training on school newspapers.

The concept of what is included in journalism and what a journalist does is still in the process of extension. In addition to training in reporting, interviewing, writing, editing, proofreading, and page makeup, present-day schools of journalism may also include courses in public relations, photography, and radio and television newscasting and programming, and courses in modern technological methods of printing and transmitting information.

See CENSORSHIP; FREEDOM OF THE PRESS; NEWSPAPERS; PERIODICALS; PHOTOGRAPHY: *Photography As Art: Beginnings of Photojournalism;* PRINTING; RADIO AND TELEVISION BROADCASTING; TELEVISION.

JOURNEYMAN. See GUILD.

JOUST. See TOURNAMENT.

JOVE. See JUPITER.

JOWETT, Benjamin (1817–93), British educator and Greek scholar, born in Camberwell, England, and educated at the University of Oxford. In 1842 he was ordained a clergyman in the Church of England, and in the same year became tutor at Balliol College, Oxford. In 1855 he was appointed professor of Greek at Oxford. His translation of the *Epistles of Saint Paul* (1855) aroused controversy among theologians because the work was a liberal interpretation of the writings of the Apostle. Several years later, *Essays and Reviews* (1860), of which he was a coauthor, brought this controversy to a head. Charges of heresy were brought against him, but he was acquitted by a chancellor's court at Oxford.

Jowett was elected Master of Balliol College in 1870, a position he held until his death; he was also vice-chancellor of Oxford from 1882 to

1886. His fame as one of the most important English educators rests on the numerous reforms he instituted for the benefit of undergraduates.

As a scholar Jowett's fame rests on his English translation (4 vol., 1871) of the *Dialogues* of the Greek philosopher Plato (q.v.). He also translated other ancient Greek works, notably the *History of the Peloponnesian War* (2 vol., 1881) by Thucydides (q.v.), *Politics* (2 vol., 1885) by Aristotle (q.v.), and the *Republic* (3 vol., 1894) by Plato (q.v.).

JOYCE, James (Augustine Aloysius) (1882–1941), Irish novelist and poet, born in Dublin, and educated at Jesuit schools, including University College, Dublin. Raised in the Roman Catholic faith, he broke with the Church while he was in college. During his undergraduate days he also began his literary career; his first publication is "Ibsen's New Drama" (1900), an essay. Joyce left Dublin in 1904 with Nora Barnacle (1886–1951), whom he later married, and settled eventually in Trieste. There he was employed mainly as a language instructor. In 1907 he suffered an attack of iritis, the first of the severe eye troubles that led finally to near blindness.

Major Works. Joyce's first book, *Chamber Music* (1907), consists of thirty-six highly finished love poems, which reflect the Elizabethan lyricists and the Victorian lyric poets of the 1890's. In his second work, *Dubliners* (1914), a collection of fifteen short stories, Joyce deals with crucial episodes of childhood and adolescence and of family and public life in Dublin. In 1919 he settled in Zürich, Switzerland, where he remained until 1919. His first long work of fiction, *A Portrait of the Artist as a Young Man* (1916), is largely an autobiographical novel recreating his youth and home life in the story of its protagonist Stephen Dedalus. In this work Joyce made considerable use of stream of consciousness (q.v.) or so-called interior-monologue, technique, a literary device that renders all the thoughts, feelings, and sensations of a character with scrupulous psychological realism.

Moving to Paris in 1920, Joyce and his family lived there for twenty years. He attained international fame with the publication (1922) of *Ulysses*, a novel based upon the Greek poet Homer's *Odyssey* (q.v.). Primarily concerned with a twenty-four-hour period in the life of an Irish Jew, Leopold Bloom, *Ulysses* describes also the same day in the life of Stephen Dedalus, and the story reaches its climax in the meeting of the two characters. The main themes are Bloom's symbolical search for a son and Dedalus' growing sense of dedication as a writer. Joyce developed the stream of consciousness in this work as a remarkable means of character portrayal, combining it with the use of mimicry of speech and the parody of literary styles as an overall literary method.

Finnegans Wake (1939), Joyce's last work, is an attempt to embody in fiction a cyclical theory of history. The novel is written in the

James Joyce, a portrait by the French artist Jacques Emil Blanche (1861–1942), hangs in the National Portrait Gallery, London. Bettmann Archive

form of an interrupted series of dreams during one night in the life of the character Humphrey Chimpden Earwicker. Symbolizing all mankind, Earwicker, his family, and his acquaintances blend, as characters do in dreams, with each other and with various historical and mythical figures. Joyce carried his linguistic experimentation to its furthest point in *Finnegans Wake* by writing English as a composite language based upon combinations of parts of words from various languages.

In 1940, during World War II, when the German armies invaded France, Joyce went to Zürich, where he died. His other works include a play, *Exiles* (1918), two collections of verse, *Pomes Penyeach* (1927) and *Collected Poems* (1936), and the posthumously published *Stephen Hero* (1944), an early version of *A Portrait*.

JUAN DE FUCA STRAIT

Literary Position. Joyce was one of the most influential novelists of the 20th century. In his prose he employs symbols to create what he called an "epiphany", the revelation of certain inner qualities. Thus, the earlier writings reveal individual moods and characters and the plight of Ireland and the Irish artist in the early 1900's. The two later works reveal man in all his complexity as an artist and lover and in the various aspects of his family relationships. Using experimental techniques to convey the essential nature of realistic situations, Joyce merged in his greatest works the literary traditions of realism, naturalism, and symbolism (qq.v.). His various achievements influenced many of the foremost British and American writers of the 20th century.

JUAN DE FUCA STRAIT, water passage of the Pacific Ocean, between the State of Washington and Vancouver Island, British Columbia, Canada. The strait leads into Puget Sound on the s. and the Strait of Georgia on the N. Juan de Fuca Strait is 100 mi. long, and varies in width from 15 to 20 mi.

JUAN FERNÁNDEZ ISLANDS, sparsely inhabited island group in the South Pacific Ocean, belonging to Chile, 400 miles w. of Valparaíso, Chile. The main island is Marino Alejandro Selkirk. The islands are rocky, and volcanic in origin. The main occupation is lobster fishing. The island group was discovered probably in 1563 by the Spanish explorer Juan Fernández (1536?–1602), for whom the islands were named. An English sailor, Alexander Selkirk (q.v.), was marooned on the main island, between 1704 and 1709, and his experiences are supposed to have suggested the plot and central character for the novel *The Life and Adventures of Robinson Crusoe* by the British writer Daniel Defoe (q.v.). Area about 70 sq.mi.

JUÁREZ, Benito Pablo (1806–72), Mexican statesman, born near the town of Oaxaca of Indian parents, and educated in the law. Juárez became governor of the State of Oaxaca in 1847 and was imprisoned when the Mexican general, Antonio López de Santa Anna (q.v.), seized the national government in 1853. Juárez escaped to New Orleans, La., but returned to Mexico in 1855 to take part in the revolution that overthrew Santa Anna. Juárez became minister of justice in the new government and instituted a series of liberal reforms that were embodied in the constitution of 1857. The following year Juárez became provisional president after the outbreak of a revolt led by conservative elements. Soon afterward he was forced to flee the national capital, Mexico City, and established a new seat of government at Veracruz. He initiated a number of sweeping reforms, including the reduction of the civil power of the Roman Catholic Church by confiscating ecclesiastical property. He defeated the conservative forces in 1860 and 1861, when he established his government in Mexico City and was constitutionally elected president.

Benito Pablo Juárez

Facing financial chaos caused by five years of civil war, Juárez suspended payments to foreign creditors in 1861. France, Spain, and Great Britain intervened, however, and landed troops at Veracruz. Juárez reached a settlement with Great Britain and Spain; those countries withdrew from Mexico, but the French remained and captured Mexico City. Maximilian, Archduke of Austria, the puppet of emperor Napoleon III (qq.v.), Emperor of France, was crowned emperor of Mexico in 1864. Juárez moved his capital to the north and continued military resistance. When Maximilian's government fell in 1867, Juárez returned to Mexico City and was reelected president. In 1871 the statesman Porfirio Díaz (q.v.), an unsuccessful political candidate against Juárez, began a revolt which eventually was quelled, but Juárez died of apoplexy during the uprising. Juárez is regarded as one of the greatest national heroes in Mexican history.

See MEXICO: *History.*

JUBBULPORE *or* **JABALPUR,** city of the Republic of India, in Madhya Pradesh State, near the Narmada R., about 150 miles N.E. of Nagpur. In the surrounding agricultural district wheat, rice, millet, and mangoes are grown. Jubbulpore is an important trading and industrial center. The chief manufactures are textiles, telephone parts, furniture, building materials, ammunitions, and glassware. The city is the seat of Jabalpur University, founded in 1957. Pop. (1971) 425,122.

JUBILEES, book of the Pseudepigrapha (*see* BIBLE: *The Apocrypha*). It is called variously the Book of Jubilees, the Lesser Genesis, the Apocalypse of Moses, and the Testament of Moses. Modern Bible scholars generally agree that Jubilees was written by a single unknown author, who probably was a Levite priest or a Pharisee; *see* LEVITES; PHARISEES. Because the work apparently reflects the period of the early Hasmonaean monarchy (*see* JEWS: *Subject Judea*; MACCABEES), it is commonly held to date from the latter half of the 2nd century B.C. Hebrew most likely was the language of the original; substantial portions of the book written in Hebrew have been discovered recently at Qumran; *see* DEAD SEA SCROLLS.

Jubilees is now regarded as a Midrashic (*see* MIDRASH) commentary on the book of Genesis (q.v.), and scholars find it valuable mainly as a source for the understanding of early Haggadah and Halakah (qq.v.). The purpose of the work seems to have been to encourage greater devotion to the Torah (q.v.), or Law, at a time when Judaism (q.v.) was undergoing strong alien influences. The book itself consists of a history of the world, purportedly revealed by an angel to the Hebrew lawgiver and prophet Moses (q.v.) on Mt. Sinai (*see* SINAI). The historical account is divided into Jubilees, cycles of fifty years consisting of seven Sabbatical years, as described in Lev. 25:8–12. Much material, mostly of a legendary nature, is added to the Biblical account in Genesis and Exodus (q.v.) in order to demonstrate the supremacy of the Torah, and all objectionable acts and practices of the Hebrews and the Hebrew patriarchs recounted in the Bible are omitted.

Jubilees is itself of little theological importance, but close study of its eschatological passages have added to the understanding and appreciation of Old and New Testament books employing apocalyptic and eschatological methods and themes; *see* APOCALYPTIC WRITINGS; ESCHATOLOGY.

JUBILEE, YEAR OF, among the ancient Jews, extraordinary Sabbatical year, following the seventh Sabbatical year since the last year of Jubilee, that is, celebrated every fiftieth year. In the year of Jubilee the land was completely left to rest, as in the ordinary Sabbatical year; all debts were remitted; land that had been alienated was restored to its original owners; and all Jews who, through poverty, had been obliged to hire themselves out as servants were released from bondage (Lev. 25).

The Christian Church adopted the concept of a year of remission and the term Jubilee from the Jews; the Jubilee Year, or Holy Year, as it is officially designated, in two forms, the "ordinary" and "extraordinary", is still an institution in the Roman Catholic Church. During such years a solemn plenary indulgence (q.v.) is granted to Roman Catholics, under conditions depending upon the papal document that proclaims the Holy Year. The ordinary Holy Year is that which is celebrated at stated intervals. It was instituted by Pope Boniface VIII (*see under* BONIFACE) in 1300, and the interval between Holy Years was fixed at twenty-five years by Pope Paul II (r. 1464–71) in 1470. Observance of the Holy Year requires a pilgrimage to Rome or equivalent works specified in the papal proclamation. Extraordinary Holy Years, or Jubilees, which involve similar observances, are proclaimed on special occasions, as, for example, the fiftieth anniversary of the ordination of the pope to the priesthood. The most recent Holy Year, an ordinary Jubilee, was 1950.

JUDAEA. See PALESTINE.

JUDAH, in the Old Testament, name of the fourth son of Jacob (q.v.) and of one of the twelve tribes of Israel (*see* JEWS: *The Hebrews in Canaan*); the early history of the tribe may be represented in the story of Jacob's son (Gen. 29, 35, 38). According to Exodus (q.v.) the tribe formed the vanguard in the march through the wilderness out of Egypt (now the Arab Republic of Egypt), and the succeeding Biblical books recording the later history of Israel portray Judah as predominant. After the reign of Solomon (q.v.), King of Israel and Judah, the tribes of Judah and Benjamin (q.v.) formed a separate, southern kingdom (1 Kings 12–2 Kings 25); *see* JEWS: *The Kingdom*.

JUDAH HA-LEVI, or JUDAH BEN SAMUEL HALEVI (1080?–1140?), Jewish poet, philosopher, and physician, born in Toledo, Spain, and a resident of Cordoba during most of his life. Ha-Levi, who lived during the time when Christian power and culture were superseding Moorish power and Arabic culture in Spain, was schooled in the Hebrew Bible, rabbinic literature, Arab poetry, and Greek philosophy and medicine. While earning a prosperous living as a physician, he wrote what is generally acclaimed as the greatest Jewish poetry of the Middle Ages and a noteworthy work of Hebrew philosophy, *Ha-Kuzari* ("The Khazar"). Late in his life he took leave of his family and friends in Spain to realize a long-cherished dream of visit-

JUDAISM

ing Palestine. En route, he spent time in the Egyptian cities of Alexandria and Cairo. No record of the remainder of his journey exists, but, according to legend, he was ridden down by an Arab horseman before the gates of Jerusalem. Ha-Levi wrote liturgical poems for the Jewish sabbath and holy days, and secular poems celebrating friendship, love, his yearning for Zion, his feeling about the suffering of his people, and his hope for their messianic redemption. Ha-Kuzari, a dialogue originally written in Arabic, explains the Jewish faith to a new convert.

JUDAISM, religious system, doctrine, rites, and customs of the Jews (q.v.). Although the term Judaism specifically refers to the religion of the ancient Hebrew tribe of Judah (q.v.), it has come to connote the entire culture of the Jewish people.

Primitive Judaism. Judaism arose among the Hebrews (q.v.), a northern Semitic group of tribes. At first a polytheistic religion similar to that of other Semitic tribes, Judaism was characterized by animism (q.v.) and by worship of the sun and nature deities. The religion of the Hebrews became monotheistic, however, by the acceptance of Yahweh, the god of the patriarchs Abraham, Isaac, and Jacob (qq.v.), as the one true God; see JEHOVAH; MONOTHEISM. The monotheistic aspect of Judaism was symbolized by a covenant (q.v.), or contract, in which Yahweh promised the Hebrew people His protection in return for their worship of Him as the one and only God. The original covenant between Yahweh and Abraham (Gen. 17), confirmed by the rite of circumcision (q.v.), was reiterated to Moses (q.v.) on Mt. Sinai (q.v.) and confirmed there by the receiving of the divine law, known as the Decalogue (q.v.) or Ten Commandments (Exod. 20–23).

When the Hebrew tribes (subsequently known as Israelites) conquered Canaan (q.v.) they had, in common with all other agricultural peoples, sacrificial customs and seasonal festivities intended to placate their deity. Belief in evil spirits, adherence to dietary regulations, the practice of death rites and the rite of circumcision, the myths of the creation (q.v.) and the flood (see DELUGE), and the legends of Cain, Esau (qq.v.), and the patriarchs were incorporated into other ancient religions of the Middle East. What set Judaism apart, therefore, was the covenant with Yahweh and its ethical considerations, principally the rights of human beings, the sacredness of the family unit, and unswerving loyalty to God.

The Prophets. The original tribes of Canaan were not monotheistic; they worshiped local deities as representatives of natural phenomena. In direct contravention of the covenant with Yahweh, the Israelites increasingly assimilated the idolatry and paganism of the Canaanites. In the 8th century B.C., a group of Israelite laymen, called prophets, arose to denounce the corruption of Judaism. These men, among them Amos and Isaiah (qq.v.), and such later figures as Jeremiah (q.v.), claimed to derive their authority from Yahweh and foretold the ruin of the Israelites should they persist in their iniquities. They called for a return to the precepts and implications of the Mosaic Law, and several of them preached the coming of a Messiah (q.v.), who would establish a perfect kingdom upon earth. See PROPHECY.

The Law. During the Babylonian Captivity (q.v.) of the 6th century B.C., the Israelites kept their identity as a religious and national group only through prayer meetings and by reestablishing the Mosaic Law as a rigid code of behavior. When the Israelites were permitted to return to Canaan, the practice of Judaism was revived, largely under the efforts of the reformer Ezra (q.v.). The Temple at Jerusalem which had been destroyed when the Israelite kingdom fell to the Babylonians, was rebuilt (see TEMPLE), the Old Testament was written down, and the Mosaic Law was formally reaffirmed. In its final form the Law embodied the code set forth in the Biblical book of Leviticus (q.v.). The prayer meetings held in Babylon during the exile led to the establishment of the synagogue (q.v.) as a place in which religious ceremonies could be carried on outside the Temple at Jerusalem. A new order of teachers, called scribes, assumed the religious leadership of the Jews and the responsibility for transmitting the Mosaic Law to succeeding generations.

During the following centuries a great body of oral law was built up that embodied both religious and ethical precepts as well as historical tradition. Both civil and religious matters were governed by this body of law. The Hebrew text of the Old Testament underwent constant editing, principally by a group of scholars called the Masoretes (see MASORA), and became fixed in its present form about 100 A.D. When the Sadducees (q.v.), a party formed of the elements of the priestly, aristocratic class, arose in the 2nd century B.C. the tradition of the scribes was carried on by another group, the Pharisees (q.v.). The Sadducees regarded the first five books of the Bible, the Pentateuch or written Torah (qq.v.), as the only binding law; the Pharisees supported traditional law, or the oral Torah, as well as the Pentateuch, differing as well in matters of doctrine, such as the Pharisaic belief in the immortality of the soul, divine providence, and future retribution, none of which is contained in the Pentateuch. During the 1st century A.D. the rabbis, or teachers, of the Pharisees became the accepted religious leaders of the Jewish people, under great sages such as Akiba ben Joseph, Johanan ben Zakkai, and Hillel (qq.v.). Under the pressure of the Roman Empire and a new sect, the Christians, who were originally regarded as heretical Jews, the rabbis laid down the foundations of a religion devoted to the preservation of a Jewish community. One of the outstanding characteristics of Judaism, however, as opposed to the earlier authoritarian religion of the Israelites (see SANHEDRIN), is that no rabbinical decision regarding laws, religious ceremonies, or customs was or is represented as mandatory. Judaism became the religious expression of all Jewish people, as well as of the priests, prophets, scholars, and teachers. Each point of doctrine or tradition was presented together with statements of the discussions and controversies that preceded their formulation. See also RABBI.

The Talmud. The aggregation of decisions and opinions of the rabbis concerning both the civil and religious law came to be called the Talmud (q.v.). From the time the Talmud was first committed to writing, during the first six centuries of the Christian era, until the development of Reform Judaism in the 19th Century (see *Modern Judaism*, below) its authority was recognized by all Jews with the exception of a small 8th-century sect, called Karaites (q.v.). Rabbinical Judaism, as governed by the Torah and delineated in the Talmud, although legalistic in form, became the basis of a cultural life shared throughout succeeding centuries by Jews in all countries. No separation was made between the secular aspects of living; the tradition governed problems of ethics, business, hygiene, and family life as firmly as it governed religious ritual. The synagogues (q.v.), each synagogue completely autonomous, replaced the Temple, and worship through prayer and study of the Torah replaced the sacrificial rites of the Temple.

Centers of religious study were first established in Babylon and about the 10th century removed to Spain. About this period arose a class of logicians and scholars who codified and organized the scriptural commentaries in a reasoned, didactic fashion that was strongly influenced by Aristotelian logic; see ARISTOTLE: *Philosophy*. The most prominent of these scholars was an 11th-century French rabbi, called Rashi, and a 12th-century Spanish rabbi and

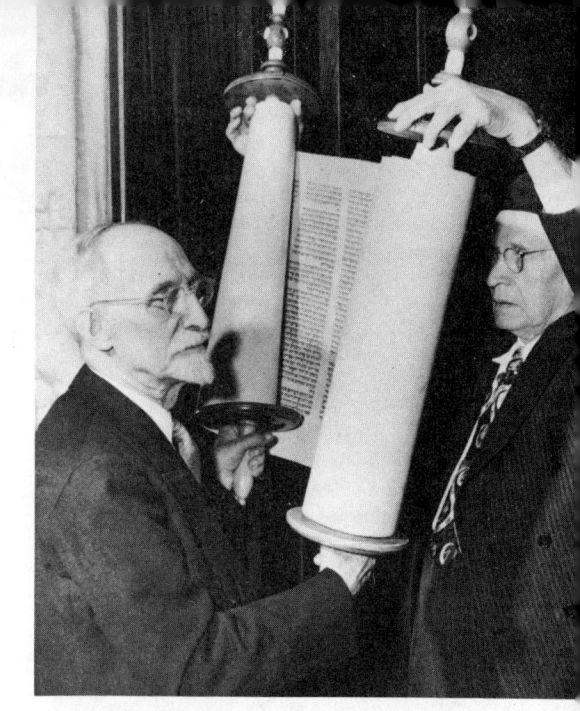

A Torah scroll, containing the Pentateuch, or Law of Moses, contained in the first five books of the Old Testament, is carefully unrolled. The Torah is among the most sacred possessions of a Jewish congregation. UPI

scholar, Maimonides (qq.v.). At about the same time another tradition was developing, that of the Cabala (q.v.), a mystical system combining demonology, astrology, and angelology with traditional Judaism and concerned with the divine element in man, rather than with the reasoned veneration of God. One Cabalistic offshoot, Hasidism, became a compound of lofty ethical tenets and popular superstition concerning demons and evil spirits; see HASIDIM.

Religious Theory and Practice. The main currents of Judaism, although varying in detail during the stages of its developments, remained relatively stable from the beginnings of rabbinical scholarship in about the 1st century A.D. until the 19th-century reform movement. In essence, Judaism is contained in a phrase repeated at the commencement of all Jewish services: *Sh'ma Yisroël, Adonai Elohenu, Adonai Echod* ("Hear, O Israel, the Lord our God is one Lord", Deut. 6:4). He is the God not only of Jews but of all creation, and the Talmud states in support of this concept that, when God spoke to Moses, He spoke in seventy languages, all those known at the time. The second Judaic concept is the election and mission of the Jewish people; God has chosen them to bring to the world the knowledge and acceptance of His existence so that all men can be delivered through the acceptance of His law. To that end, God has made a covenant with the Jews that is contained in

JUDAISM

the Torah and emphasizes the principles of justice, human rights, and ethics. In sum, therefore, Judaism is the consciousness of God as expressed in the Torah and embodied in the life of the Jewish people.

Once having accepted the existence, holiness, eternity, and universality of God, the Jew can appeal to and praise Him directly. In Judaism, unlike the religion of the Israelites, no priestly class exists and no Jew needs an intermediary between himself and God. Judaism thus accepts the possibility of prophecy, regards the prophets of the Scriptures as divinely inspired, and views Moses as the supreme prophet, although the Mosaic Law is by no means regarded as supreme revelation. Judaism involves no public declaration of principles, as do Christian creeds, and no fixed formulas of belief, though the prayer services, called the Order of the Day, are regulated by the Talmud. In traditional Judaism, moreover, the Jew accepts an expected personal Messiah as the political redeemer of the Jewish people, and bodily resurrection (q.v.) during the temporality of the existence of the Messiah on earth. To all Jews who have believed and faithfully practiced the Law the coming of a Messiah is regarded in the nature of a reward for their faith and a victory for Judaism.

In practice, the Law is primarily concerned with ethics, and its primary goal is the welfare of society. Freedom of the will is a basic concept, and each Jew bears the responsibility for his religious and moral actions; see FREE WILL. When he contravenes the Law, which is the standard for conduct, divine retribution is inevitable, although the sinner cannot know in what form or how it will occur. Divine retribution, in the form of both reward and punishment, is an essential part of Judaism. These retributive aspects of Judaism, including the coming of the Messiah, are all based on the degree of faithfulness with which the Jew has believed and practiced the Law, particularly in its ethical aspects. The cardinal principle of Judaic ethics is: Love thy neighbor as thyself (Lev. 19:18). Education, charity, care of the sick, respect for the rights of others, and honor of family are all exacted by Law.

Synagogues are centers not only of worship and education, but of social service as well. In the synagogue all Jews are equal before God, and any Jew is eligible to lead the assembly in worship. In Orthodox synagogues it is customary to separate male and female worshipers. Even during the life of the ancient theocratic state of Israel, however, women were accorded all legal rights, although they were disqualified as witnesses for civil and criminal cases because they were regarded as more emotional than men. During the postexilic period women were venerated; they were regarded as guardians of the home, and the sanctity of the home was the cornerstone of the Jewish community.

The mission of the Jews does not make Judaism a proselytizing religion. Judaism accepts but does not seek converts, nor does it condemn those who are not Jews. During the time of the ancient national state, several periods of active missionary work did occur, and during the development of rabbinical Judaism conversion was fairly common. In the 7th century A.D., for example, the bulk of the population of the Khazar nation, in what is now the south central portion of the Soviet Union, near the Caspian Sea, was converted to Judaism; see KHAZARS. Since the late 18th century when the Jews began to be released from their ghetto (q.v.) existence, conversion has been permitted only for those who can convince a congregation that they are truly desirous of accepting the Law.

The dietary and Sabbath (q.v.) regulations of Judaism are restrictive in nature. Following the tenets of the Mosaic Law, dietary regulations permit Jews to eat only the meat of animals that have cloven hooves and chew a cud, and of fish that have both gills and scales. The eating or drinking of milk products and meat or meat products at the same meal is prohibited, and separate utensils must be used for meat and milk foods; see KOSHER. The observance of the Sabbath as a day of rest and a weekly feast is cardinal. No work, travel, or business transactions are permitted on the Sabbath, which is reserved for prayer and study at the synagogue and in the home. Among the traditions of Judaism are included the observance of many holy days and feast days, such as Yom Kippur, Sukkoth, Pesach, Hanukkah, Purim, Shabuoth, and Rosh Hashanah (qq.v.), all commemorating events in Jewish history or observing solemn occasions of the Jewish year; see also FESTIVALS AND FEASTS: *Jewish Festivals*. The tradition governs the entire life of a Jew in detail, from the circumcision of a male infant, to the rending of garments in token of mourning for the dead, and the lighting of a memorial candle on the anniversary of a death.

The followers of Judaism living in non-Jewish states formerly depended for deliverance from their subordinate political positions for the most part on the coming of the Messiah. No laws in Judaism, however, prevent Jews from recognizing the civil law of the state in which

Pesach, or Passover, commemorates the liberation of the Jews from slavery in Egypt. UPI

they live. Economic, social, and political relationships with Gentiles are not forbidden; only intermarriage with non-Jews is explicitly prohibited.

Modern Judaism. The present-day division of Judaism into several groups occurred in the 19th and 20th centuries as a result of social, intellectual, and political pressures on its followers. The 18th-century rationalists of Judaic thought were led by Moses Mendelssohn (*see under* MENDELSSOHN), a German philosopher who became one of the greatest scholars of modern Judaism. To prepare the Jew, who for many centuries had been confined to the ghetto, for life in the modern world, Mendelssohn began to organize Judaic thought on the basis of 18th-century Rationalism (q.v.) and to translate parts of the Bible into German. With the expansion of mercantilism, many Jews found that the observance of strict dietary laws and the complete cessation of week-day activity on the Sabbath were exceedingly difficult. On an intellectual level the strict legal precepts of Judaism were resented by many Jews as being too rigid to meet the problems of a constantly changing world. Traditional Judaism, moreover, emphasized prayers for the restoration of a Jewish national state and the Temple at Jerusalem, and the Messianic concept. Thus, the nationalistic elements of Judaism became the target of pressure from many sides. Under the influence of such pressures, both from Jews and non-Jews, the Reform movement began in Germany. Some Reform congregations introduced several changes in worship; they changed the observance of the Sabbath to Sunday, rather than the traditional observance from sundown on Friday to sundown on Saturday, and eliminated many dietary restrictions. The reformers, led by a German rabbi named Abraham Geiger (q.v.), placed their emphasis on the ethical considerations of Judaism rather than the strict law of the Torah and the Talmud. They rejected the concept of a personal Messiah who would reconstitute the Jewish national state and instead conceived of their Messiah as the leader who would institute the brotherhood of man and bring about an era of justice and peace for all nations. Thus, Reform Judaism accepted the spirit of the Law but not its letter. Reform Judaism spread throughout Western Europe and became particularly prominent in Germany and in the United States. To counter the Reform movement, those Jews who continued to believe in the tradition as well as the Torah reiterated their faith in orthodox practices. Calling their movement Conservative Judaism, these Jews proposed to modernize Judaism on the basis of rational understanding, without relinquishing any of its basic traditional characteristics. They differed from the older generation of pious traditionalists, such as the Hasidim, in that they endeavored to comprehend the basic meaning of the Law, rather than to practice it by rote.

Religious and political motivations combined in the late 19th and 20th centuries in Zionism (q.v.), a movement that anticipated the restoration of Israel (q.v.) as a state. Spurred by anti-semitism (q.v.), particularly the planned extermination of European Jews during World War II under the system of National Socialism (q.v.), the United Nations set up the modern post-war nation of Israel. Israel is not a religious state by definition, but its existence has had effects on Judaism.

The shofar, a ram's horn, is blown to signify the close of Yom Kippur, the day of atonement. This holiest day of the year is devoted to fasting, meditation, and prayer. UPI

With the establishment of the State of Israel in 1948 the city of Jerusalem (q.v.) was divided between Israel and Jordan. Reunification of the ancient metropolis under Israeli rule after the Six-Day War in June, 1967, reemphasized the importance of the city to Judaism. After a prohibition lasting for centuries, Jews were able to pray at the Wailing Wall, the only remains of the Temple. Resumption of Jewish activities in the Old City of Jerusalem had an electrifying impact on world Judaism and brought widespread support to Israel in its struggle with the surrounding Arab nations.

Influence. Judaism has been one of the most important factors in the development of modern civilization, not only through its direct influence on its followers but also through its role in the development of Christianity and Islam (qq.v.). From Judaism Christianity inherited the concept of monotheism, the Old Testament, the prayer service, many liturgies, the concept of the Sabbath, and, most important of all, the basis for the Christian ethics. Muslims, who received Judaic doctrine both directly and through Christianity, base their theology on Judaic monotheism, their dietary laws on those of the Torah, and their ethics on the Mosaic Law. The Muslim mosque (q.v.) is similar to the synagogue and continues the Judaic custom of prayer services.

Jewish Population. In the late 1960's the Jewish population of the world was estimated to be 13,875,000. Of this total, about 5,870,000 live in the U.S., the present center of world Jewry; more than 2,521,000 are concentrated in New York State and 1,836,000 in the area of New York City. In the same period about 2,620,000 Jews were living in the U.S.S.R., some 2,497,000 in Israel, and about 194,000 in Africa. South and Central America have about 720,000 Jewish inhabitants. In addition, Jewish communities of various sizes exist in almost every country.

Jews in the U.S. enjoy political and religious equality and are generally well integrated into the life of the country. They worship in 5700 synagogues. American Judaism has Orthodox, Conservative, and Reform branches. Each branch has a national organizational unit, and all are represented in the Synagogue Council of America by lay and clerical members.

Soviet Jews are also granted a measure of legal equality as citizens, but the observance of Judaism is curtailed in accord with Communist antireligious tenets; see JEWISH AUTONOMOUS OBLAST.

See BIBLE; BIBLE, CANON OF THE; RELIGION: *The Religious.*

JUDAS, Saint. See THADDAEUS.

JUDAS ISCARIOT (d. about 28 A.D.), in the New Testament, Apostle (q.v.) who betrayed Jesus Christ (q.v.) to the Sanhedrin (q.v.). Said to be a native of Kerioth, possibly a town in Judea (q.v.), he served as steward to Jesus and His other disciples. In the Gospel of John (see JOHN, GOSPEL ACCORDING TO SAINT), Judas is portrayed as covetous and dishonest from the beginning (12:6). It was the temptation of money, according to the Gospels of Matthew and Mark, that made him betray Jesus to the chief priests for thirty pieces of silver; see MARK, GOSPEL ACCORDING TO SAINT; MATTHEW, GOSPEL ACCORDING TO SAINT. The Synoptic Gospels (Matthew, Mark, and Luke) represent Jesus as conscious of the meditated treachery, which He plainly foretells. When Judas sees the consequences of his guilt, he is filled with despair and kills himself. The two accounts of his death in the New Testament differ in their details (Matt. 27:3–5, Acts 1:16–20).

JUDAS MACCABAEUS. See MACCABEES.

JUDAS TREE, common name applied to trees and shrubs of the genus *Cercis,* belonging to the Pea family, Leguminoseae. The genus is widely distributed in temperate regions of the Northern Hemisphere. Flowers of the genus, which are usually pink or red, are borne in umbel-like clusters, and have a five-toothed calyx, five-lobed, irregular corolla, ten stamens, and a single pistil. The fruit is a flat, winged, many-seeded pod. The rounded, heart-shaped leaves appear in early spring following flowering. The

Eurasian Judas tree, *C. siliquastrum,* derived its name from the tradition that Judas Iscariot (q.v.) hanged himself on a tree of the species; it attains a height of 30 ft. The redbud, or American Judas tree, *C. canadensis,* is smaller, 15 to 20 ft., although some individuals are taller, and is native to the eastern and central United States, and cultivated throughout the U.S. and s. Canada. Flowering of the Judas tree is one of the traditional harbingers of spring in many parts of the U.S.

JUDE, book of the New Testament (*see* BIBLE), in the King James Version, THE GENERAL EPISTLE OF JUDE. This Epistle of only twenty-five verses proclaims itself in its first verse as having been written by "Jude, the servant of Jesus Christ, and brother of James". Early ecclesiastical tradition variously attributed it to several persons mentioned in the New Testament: among them Judas (or Judah), a "brother" of Jesus Christ (Matt. 13:55, Mark 6:3); and Judas "the brother of James" (Acts 1:13). Modern Bible scholars, aware that the problem of identification in this case is quite complicated, either leave it unresolved or suggest as the author an unknown person who called himself, or was named, Jude. Suggested dates of composition range from about 70 A.D. to the beginning of the 2nd century. *See also* THADDAEUS.

The Epistle of Jude is addressed to Christians in general. It exhorts them to "contend for the faith" (1:3) against "certain men crept in unawares" (1:4) who, "mockers in the last time, . . . walk after their own ungodly lusts" (1:18). These persons, "sensual, having not the Spirit" (1:19), will be judged by the Lord and given over to "darkness for ever" (1:13). The author draws examples from the Old Testament, and also cites passages from two noncanonical works, the book of Enoch (q.v.) and the Assumption of Moses, to remind his readers of the doom that awaits all unbelievers, malcontents, and boasters.

JUDE, Saint. *See* THADDAEUS.

JUDEA. *See* PALESTINE.

JUDGES, book of the Old Testament (*see* BIBLE), in the King James Version, THE BOOK OF JUDGES. It recounts the history of Israel (q.v.) from the death of the Hebrew leader and prophet Joshua to the time just prior to the birth of the Hebrew prophet Samuel (qq.v.); that is, roughly from the end of the Israelite conquest of Canaan (q.v.) to the beginning of the monarchy; *see* ISRAEL, KINGDOM OF; JEWS. Tradition has ascribed the book to Samuel, but most present-day Bible commentators and scholars consider it to be a composite work. Parts of it, for example,

Flowers of the redbud or American Judas tree, Cercis canadensis
Jack Dermid — National Audubon Society

the Song of Deborah (chapter 5), are believed to be very ancient, perhaps the oldest preserved Old Testament writings, whereas other portions (chapters 17–21) are thought to be additions made by priestly editors during the period following the Babylonian Captivity (q.v.). The bulk of the book (2:6–16:31) is generally regarded as the work of Deuteronomic editors of the 7th and 6th centuries B.C.; *see* DEUTERONOMY; PENTATEUCH.

Judges falls into three distinct sections. The first section (1:1–2:5) briefly summarizes the Israelite conquest of Canaan, beginning with Joshua's death. This account differs, however, from the account of the conquest in the book of Joshua (q.v.). In the latter, for instance, the Israelite tribes unite under Joshua and conquer or kill all the Canaanites; in Judges they fight separately for territories that they occupy only partially. This failure of the Israelites to kill or drive out all the former inhabitants of Canaan portends evil for them (Judg. 2:1–5).

The second section (2:6–16:31) tells of how the children of Israel a number of times were delivered over to various alien nations, "which the Lord left, to prove Israel by them" (3:1), and how each time a hero (or heroine) appeared to defend the Israelites. These heroes are not titled "judges" in the text, but most of them are described as having "judged" Israel for a certain amount of years. The deliverers, or judges, featured in this part of the book are Othniel (3:8–11), Ehud (3:12–30), Deborah (chapters 4, 5), Gideon (chapters 6–8), Jephthah (10:17–12:7), and Samson (chapters 13–16). Also included in this section are brief references to the exploits of six minor heroes and a chapter (chapter 9) devoted wholly to Abimelech, Gideon's son, who "reigned three years over Israel" (9:22) and then was killed for "the wickedness . . . he did unto his father, in slaying his seventy brethren" (9:56).

The third section of Judges (chapters 17–21)

JUDGMENT

recounts two stories. The first tells of the migration of the tribe of Dan (q.v.) "unto Laish" (19: 27). The second is an account of an intertribal war against the tribe of Benjamin (q.v.); it starts after some Benjaminites abuse a concubine belonging to a Levite (see LEVITES).

Judges has considerable historical value as a source, the only Biblical one, for determining both the events and the social conditions of the period between the Israelite conquest of Canaan and the time of Samuel. It is also valuable because of the much older fragments of Hebrew literature preserved in it. See also DEBORAH; GIDEON; JEPHTHAH; SAMSON.

JUDGMENT, in law in England and the United States, judicial determination of the rights and obligations of the parties to a civil action; see CIVIL LAW. Judgments are generally classified as final judgments and interlocutory judgments. In a final judgment, a court or referee makes a complete and definitive disposal of all issues in the action; final judgments made in cases in which the defendant interposes no defense to the complaint made by the plaintiff are called default judgments. In an interlocutory judgment, the court determines some of the rights of the parties, but reserves for future determination the unsettled issues in the action and the extent of the relief to be given the plaintiff. The party to whom relief is given in the form of a judgment for money damages (q.v.) is called a judgment creditor and the adverse party is called a judgment debtor. By statute in most jurisdictions in the U.S., a final judgment constitutes a lien (q.v.) on the real property of a judgment debtor; see PROPERTY. By law in most States, unpaid judgments are presumed to have been paid or satisfied after twenty years.

The judgments in equity actions usually are called decrees; see LAW: Equity. Decrees are enforced by proceedings, to punish for contempt of court, known as contempt proceedings; see CONTEMPT. In actions for divorce or separation (qq.v.), a judgment directing a husband to pay alimony (q.v.) is enforceable by contempt proceedings. Judgments for money are enforced by a process called execution, which may be against property or against earnings. Executions against property are directions to a sheriff or marshall to levy upon the property of the judgment debtor, to sell the same, and to apply so much of the proceeds as are necessary to pay the judgment. Executions against earnings, sometimes called income executions or garnishment (q.v.), direct the employer to pay a portion of earnings to the sheriff or marshall, to be applied to pay the judgment.

An examination of the property or earnings of the judgment debtor may be made, under codes of civil procedure, for the judgment creditor. In some States application must be made to the court for such an order; in other States, the attorney for the judgment creditor may issue a subpeona (q.v.) for the examination. The order or subpoena usually contains a provision restraining the judgment debtor from transferring any of his property without further order of the court.

See also VERDICT.

JUDITH, book of the Old Testament Apocrypha (see BIBLE: The Apocrypha), in the King James Version, JUDITH. Judith is included in the Roman Catholic canon; see BIBLE, CANON OF THE; DEUTEROCANONICAL BOOKS. The book falls into two roughly equal parts. In the first part (chapters 1–7), the Babylonian king Nebuchadnezzar II (see under NEBUCHADNEZZAR) sends his general, Holofernes, to punish the western nations because they have refused to join him in a war against Media (q.v.). Holofernes marches against them, and all except the Israelites submit. At this point in the narrative an adviser warns Holofernes that God will defend the Israelites so long as they remain faithful to Him. But Holofernes, disregarding the warning, surrounds the Israelites in the ancient Palestinian town of Bethulia, near Jerusalem.

In the second part of the book (chapters 8–16) the pious and beautiful widow Judith (Heb., "Jewess"), after rebuking the Israelites for losing faith in God when under siege, volunteers to deliver them. She goes to the Assyrian camp, pretending to be an informer against her people, and charms Holofernes, who invites her to a banquet in his tent. At the banquet, Holofernes becomes drunk and falls asleep. Judith, seizing a sword, beheads him, wraps the severed head in a bag, and returns with it to her people. The jubilant Israelites now attack the Assyrians, and the latter, leaderless, flee in panic. Judith leads the people in a song of celebration and praise; then all go to Jerusalem to offer thanksgiving.

Most modern scholars recognize that Judith does not reflect history. It contains too many errors: Nebuchadnezzar, for instance, who actually was the king of Babylon before the Babylonian Captivity (qq.v.) is depicted as the king of Assyria, and the tale is set in a time after the destruction of the Assyrian capital Nineveh (q.v.) in 612 B.C. and after the fall of Jerusalem in 587 B.C. Judith is thought, therefore, to be a symbolic narrative, written probably some time during or just after the Maccabean period (see MACCABEES). Most likely the author wrote it to encourage the Jewish people in their efforts at that time to maintain their religious and political freedom.

JUDITH, Jewish folk heroine whose exploits, probably fictional, are recounted in the Apocryphal Old Testament book that bears her name; see book of JUDITH.

JUDO. See JUJITSU.

JUGGERNAUT *or* **JAGANNATH** (Skr. *Jagannatha,* "lord of the world"), form of Krishna, one of the avatars (incarnations) of the Hindu god Vishnu (q.v.). The town of Puri, in Orissa State, India, is the center of Jagannath worship. There, during the annual (June and July) festival of Rathayatra, an idol representing the god and supposedly containing the bones or ashes of Krishna is taken from its temple and drawn on an enormous wooden car to a summer garden house about a mile away. Occasionally, in the past a small number of the multitude of Hindu pilgrims annually gathered at Puri have, in a frenzy, thrown themselves under the huge wheels of the car, which crushed them to death. This practice, stopped by the British during their occupation of India, gave rise to the term "juggernaut", now often used to characterize an invincible crushing force, as in the expression "military juggernaut". The worship of Jagannath at Puri is believed to date from the 4th century A.D. The present temple, begun in the 6th century, was completed in the 12th century.

JUGOSLAVIA. See YUGOSLAVIA.

JUGURTHA (d. 104 B.C.), King of Numidia (113–104 B.C.), grandson of King Masinissa (238?–149 B.C.). After the death of his uncle, Micipsa (d. 118 B.C.), who succeeded Masinissa on the throne, Jugurtha invaded the dominions of Micipsa's son, Adherbal (d. 117 B.C.?), and usurped the throne. He was defeated in a war with the Romans, the so-called Jugurthine War, which took place from 111 B.C. to 106 B.C. He was taken to Rome as a prisoner and was exhibited in the triumph of the Roman general Lucius Cornelius Sulla (q.v.) in 104 B.C. He died in prison. See NUMIDIA.

JUILLIARD SCHOOL, THE, institution of higher learning, located in New York City. The school was named the Juilliard School of Music in 1946, when it was formed by the amalgamation of the Institute of Musical Art and the Juilliard Graduate School. The Institute of Musical Art had been founded by the American conductor Frank Heino Damrosch (1859–1937) and the American philanthropist James Loeb (1867–1933), in 1905, and the Juilliard Graduate School had been established in 1924 through a legacy of the American music patron Augustus D. Juilliard (1836–1919). In 1968 a drama division was added, and in 1969 the school's name was changed to The Juilliard School. The degree of either bachelor of music or fine arts is awarded upon completion of both a musical curriculum and a course of studies in the humanities or liberal arts. The master of music and the doctor of musical arts degrees are also conferred. Professional training is given in all the performing arts. In 1973 the library housed 30,000 music scores, 5000 records and tapes, and 12,000 books on music, dance, and drama. In the same year the enrollment was about 700 full-time students, and the faculty numbered 186. The Juilliard School moved into Lincoln Center for the Performing Arts (q.v.) in October, 1969.

JUIZ DE FORA, city of Brazil, in Minas Gerais State, on the Paraíbuna R. in the mountainous Serra da Mantiqueira region, 80 miles N. of Rio de Janeiro. Sometimes called the "Manchester of Brazil", the city is a major textile center; other manufactures include knitted goods, metal products, tires, food and dairy products, sugar, and rubber. Hydroelectric power is available nearby, and the surrounding area grows coffee, sugarcane, grains, timber, cotton, and tobacco. The city has schools of law, pharmacy, dentistry,

The Juilliard School, completed in 1969, is a unit of the Lincoln Center for the Performing Arts.
Ezra Stoller

and engineering, as well as a noted museum. Founded in the 1800's, Juiz de Fora was formerly called Parahybuna, an old spelling of the river name. Pop. (1970 prelim.) 218,832.

JUJITSU *or* **JIUJITSU,** *or* JUJUTSU (Japanese *ju,* "yielding"; *jutsu,* "art"), Japanese method of personal combat without weapons in which opposing force or movement is utilized to one's own advantage. In practicing jujitsu, a studied knowledge of leverage and of the weak points in the human anatomy are essential. In its milder forms, jujitsu is known popularly as judo.

In essence, the jujitsu expert, by yielding or moving with the attacking force of an opponent, seeks to throw the opponent off balance, and to use that same force to disable his adversary. A person skilled in jujitsu can disable his opponent by striking a nerve, by cutting off the circulation of blood, or by dislocating a joint or breaking a bone. Using similar methods, he can disable an opponent permanently or even kill him. The closed fist is not used in jujitsu; disabling blows are delivered by slashing with the margin of the open palm. The three chief elements of jujitsu are *nagewasa,* tricks to throw or down an opponent; *katamewaza,* pinning or locking holds; and *atewaza,* striking and kicking blows.

Especially important to a practitioner of jujitsu is knowing how to fall without incurring injury; this maneuver is accomplished by twisting the body so as to fall upon pads of muscle, rather than upon the base of the spine or upon a joint. Body weight and muscular development are unimportant in jujitsu, the most important requisites are agility, speed, and presence of mind.

Jujitsu has been in use in Japan since the early 7th century B.C. Until the fall of the feudal system, the art was practiced only by the Japanese nobility, especially the samurai (q.v.), who kept its methods secret. In the 19th century the Japanese began to teach the milder techniques of jujitsu in their public schools, and private jujitsu academies were opened. The art was taught to members of the military and police forces. Students of jujitsu were kept on strict diets, and the study of the art became a method of physical culture that is still widely used in Japan. Control of temper, necessary for effective practice of jujitsu, was stressed; students who became angry when provoked were not allowed to continue their jujitsu studies. Techniques of killing an opponent by means of jujitsu were still kept secret, and were known to only a few experts in the country.

Judo. Near the end of the 19th century, Professor Jigoro Kano, a nobleman of Tokyo, collected many of the simple techniques of jujitsu into a new system that he called judo. The system was introduced into Europe and the United States, and several schools were established. During World War II, the soldiers of many countries, including the U.S., were taught modified jujitsu holds in hand-to-hand fighting. Forces, such as commandos and rangers, were taught techniques in more detail; *see* COMMANDO; SPECIAL FORCES. Since then, police forces of many cities in the United States and Europe have been trained in the art. Numerous private schools and academies continue to teach jujitsu, especially in conjunction with the Japanese-Korean form of combat known as karate (q.v.). Like karate, judo is practiced as a competitive sport around the world using rules established by Kodokan College in Tokyo. In the U.S. it was recognized as a sport in 1953 by the Amateur Athletic Union.

JUJUBE, common name of evergreen and deciduous shrubs and trees of the genus *Zizyphus,* in the Buckthorn family. Jujubes are native to tropical and subtropical regions all over the world. Plants of the genus have small, regular flowers which produce drupaceous fruits. The common jujube, *Z. jujuba,* native to warm regions of Eurasia, and the Indian jujube, *Z. mauritiana,* native to India, produce fruits that are dried as sweetmeats. The common jujube is widely cultivated in China for its fruit and is grown as an ornamental plant in warm areas of the United States. The lotus tree, *Z. lotus,* is a North African species which produces a mealy fruit used by the Africans to make cakes.

JUKES, fictitious name for a family investigated in 1874 by the Prison Association of New York. The report of the association was prepared by the American sociologist Richard Louis Dugdale (1841–83), and published in 1875 under the title of *The Jukes: A Study in Crime, Pauperism, Disease, and Heredity.* Hundreds of Jukes were traced, representing several generations, and the majority proved to be mentally, socially, and economically inadequate. The cost of the family to the State of New York over a seventy-five year period was estimated at more than $1,250,000. A later study, *The Jukes in 1915,* showed that the condition of the family had greatly improved since Dugdale's study. *The Kallikak Family* (1912) by the American psychologist Henry Herbert Goddard (1866–1957) is the study of a similar kinship group, likewise known under a fictitious name and often compared with the Jukes. Today, the original hereditary interpretations of crime and degeneracy are believed to be less significant than environmental factors.

JULIA (39 B.C.–14 A.D.), only child of the Roman emperor Augustus (q.v.). She was married at the age of fourteen to her cousin Marcus Claudius Marcellus (d. 23 B.C.). After her husband's death, two years later, she was married to the Roman general Marcus Vipsanius Agrippa (q.v.), to whom she bore three sons and two daughters. He died in 12 B.C., whereupon Julia was given in marriage to Tiberius (q.v.), stepson of Augustus and later emperor. Julia became notorious for profligacy and vice, and was banished from Rome by her father.

JULIAN (Lat. *Flavius Claudius Julianus*) (331–63), Roman Emperor (361–63), born in Constantinople (now İstanbul, Turkey). In 355 he was appointed as caesar to govern Gaul, Britain, and Spain. He became popular with his troops, who proclaimed him emperor in 361, and following the death of his cousin Constantius II (*see under* CONSTANTIUS), he succeeded to the throne. In March, 363, he set out on an expedition against the Persians, and was fatally wounded in a battle in the desert near Ctesiphon (q.v.). Julian became known as Julian the Apostate because he openly embraced paganism and renounced Christianity.

JULIANA (1909–   ), in full JULIANA LOUISE EMMA MARIE WILHELMINA, Queen of the Netherlands (1948–   ), only daughter of Wilhelmina (q.v.) and Duke Henry of Mecklenburg-Schwerin (1876–1934), born at The Hague. In 1937 she married Prince Bernhard of Lippe-Biesterfeld (1911–   ), to whom she subsequently bore four daughters; the heiress presumptive is Princess Beatrix (1938–   ). In World War II when Germany occupied the Netherlands in 1940 Juliana moved to Canada with her family, going from there to England in 1944, and returning to the Netherlands in 1945. On Oct. 14, 1947, because of the illness of her mother, Juliana temporarily assumed royal power in the Netherlands, ruling as princess regent until Dec. 1, 1947, when Wilhelmina resumed her rule. She became regent for the second time on May 14, 1948, and on Sept. 4 of that year Queen Wilhelmina, after fifty years as ruler of the Netherlands, abdicated in favor of Juliana. On Sept. 6, 1948, Juliana was crowned queen of the Netherlands in Amsterdam.

JULIAN CALENDAR. See CALENDAR: *The Roman Calendar*.

JULIUS CAESAR. See CAESAR, GAIUS JULIUS.

JULIUS II, original name GIULIANO DELLA ROVERE (1443–1513), pope from 1503 to 1513, born in Albisola Superiore, Italy. During his

Queen Juliana of the Netherlands and her husband, Prince Bernhard, pose for an official portrait in 1961.
UPI

reign the territory of the papacy was greatly expanded. By joining the League of Cambrai (1508) against the Republic of Venice and by forming (1511) the Holy League against France, Julius secured his hold on the Papal States (q.v.) and extended papal rule over parts of northern Italy. Julius was the patron of many Italian Renaissance artists, notably the architect Bramante and the painters Raphael and Michelangelo (qq.v.).

JULLUNDUR, city of the Republic of India, in Punjab State, 260 miles N.W. of Delhi. Sugar refining, flour milling, and textile manufacturing are the chief industries of the city. Until the city of Chandigarh (q.v.) was built in the 1950's, Jullundur was the capital of Punjab State. Pop. (1971) 296,103.

JULY, seventh month of the year in the modern calendar, consisting of thirty-one days. It was the fifth month of the year in the early Roman calendar and thus was called *Quintilis*, or fifth month, by the Romans. It was the month in which the Roman general and statesman Gaius Julius Caesar (q.v.) was born, and in 44

JULY REVOLUTION

B.C., the year of his assassination, the month was named *Julius*, in his honor. See CALENDAR.

JULY REVOLUTION, French revolution of July, 1830, in Paris, which overthrew the Bourbon dynasty, in possession of the throne of France since the restoration of King Louis XVIII (q.v.) in 1815; see FRANCE: *History*. The main cause of the July Revolution was the reactionary policy followed by Louis and his brother, Charles X (*see under* CHARLES), who became king in 1824. Two classes, the nobility and the clergy, foes of democratic progress, were shown special favor. A partial indemnity was granted by Charles to the nobles for the lands the state had confiscated during the French Revolution (q.v.); the Jesuits, who had been driven out of the country during that war, were readmitted and education was placed under clerical control. In addition, Charles also took severe measures against the liberty of the press. In March, 1830, the Chamber of Deputies, the lower legislative house, demanded the dismissal of several of the ministers of the king. In response the king dissolved the legislature. The returns from the elections ordered by the king to select a new parliament indicated that the new legislature would be even more strongly opposed to the policies of Charles than its predecessor.

On July 26, a few days before the new legislature was to meet, the minister of domestic affairs issued ordinances completely suspending the liberty of the press and declaring the new elections null and void. Led in part by the noted general, the Marquis de Lafayette (q.v.) and by the statesman Jacques Laffitte (1767–1844), the middle and working classes of Paris rose in revolt and took possession of the municipal government in the Hôtel de Ville. By July 29, the entire city was in the hands of the insurrectionists, and Charles withdrew his minister's ordinances. It was too late, however, to save his throne. The opposition demanded that he abdicate in favor of Louis Philippe (q.v.) of the house of Bourbon-Orléans. On July 30, Louis Philippe arrived in Paris. Although he was opposed by the workers, the liberal forces supporting him were strong enough to cause Charles to abdicate and flee the country, and to have the legislature elect Louis Philippe as king.

The July Revolution acted as a signal for democratic uprisings on the European continent, particularly in Belgium, Germany, Italy, and Poland. See the *History* sections of the various countries mentioned. See also EUROPE: *History*.

JUMNA (anc. *Jomanes*), river in N. India, principal tributary of the Ganges (q.v.), rising in the w. Himalaya near Mt. Kamet. After a southerly course of about 95 mi. it enters the plains N. of Saharanpur, and follows a winding route past Delhi and Agra to Allahabad (qq.v.), where it joins the Ganges, after a total course of about 860 mi. The confluence of the Jumna and Ganges is a place of pilgrimage for Hindus. The river is navigable by barge and is used for irrigation purposes.

JUMPING. See TRACK AND FIELD.

JUMPING BEAN, seeds of tropical and subtropical New World shrubs of the genera *Sebastiania* and *Sapium*, belonging to the Spurge family. The seeds are usually infested with larvae of a small moth, *Carpocapsa saltitans*, related to the codling moth. The larva occupies about one fifth of the interior of the seed, and, when the seed is placed on a flat surface, its movements disturb the balance of the seed, causing the seed to roll from side to side, turn over endwise, or actually jump. Warmth, as from the palm of a hand, results in livelier movement. The seeds are commonly called Mexican jumping beans in the United States.

JUNAGADH *or* **JUNAGARH,** city of the Republic of India, in Gujarat State, about 220 miles N.W. of New Delhi. Nearby is the forest of Gir, the only place in India where lions are still found. The city contains a college, a library, and a museum. Manufactured products include copper and brass ware and gold and silver embroidered work. Cotton, rice, millet, sesame, and sugarcane are raised in the surrounding area. Pop. (1971) 193,709.

JUNCO *or* **SNOWBIRD,** common name for any American bird in the genus *Junco* of the Finch family, Fringillidae. Juncos are slate-colored birds with white abdomens, white outer tail feathers, and pink bills. They are about 5¼ to 6 in. long. The birds breed in cold regions such as the arctic regions of Canada and Alaska or the tops of high mountains. In wintertime they are found farther south. The common junco of N.E. United States is *J. hyemalis*, the slate-colored junco, which winters from S. Canada to central America. *J. oreganus*, the Oregon junco, is found in N.W. U.S.; it winters in the South and S.W. U.S. The Mexican junco, *J. phaeonotus*, is found in the mountains of S.W. U.S.

JUNCTION CITY, city in Kansas, and county seat of Geary Co., about 60 miles W. of Topeka. The city is a trading and shipping center for the surrounding area, which raises livestock and produces dairy and farm products. Limestone quarries are nearby. Pop. (1970) 19,018.

JUNDIAÍ, city of Brazil, in São Paulo State, about 30 miles N.W. of São Paulo, with which it is connected by rail. Grapes, coffee, timber, and grains are produced in the area, and an annual grape festival is held here. The city manufactures steel, textiles, wine, hardboard, cement, and pottery. Tungsten is mined nearby. Goods are shipped by rail 75 miles S.E. to the port of Santos on the Atlantic Ocean. The city was founded in 1655; the name was formerly spelled Jundiahy. Pop. (1970 prelim.) 145,785.

JUNE, sixth month of the year in the Gregorian calendar, consisting of thirty days. The etymology of the name is uncertain. Different authorities derive the name from the Roman goddess Juno (q.v.) or from the name of a Roman *gens,* Junius. Another theory traces the origin of the name to the Latin *iuniores* as opposed to *maiores* for May, the two months being dedicated to youth and old age, respectively. June was the fourth month in the old Roman calendar. At the time that the Roman general and statesman Gaius Julius Caesar (q.v.) instituted reform of the calendar, June had 29 days, to which Caesar added a thirtieth. In the Northern Hemisphere it signals summer. See CALENDAR.

JUNEAU, city, capital, and port of entry of Alaska, in the Southeastern Senatorial District, on Gastineau Channel, opposite Douglas Island, about 525 miles S.E. of Anchorage. A scenic backdrop to the city is provided by Mt. Juneau and Mt. Roberts. Juneau is served by steamships and airlines. It is the fourth-largest city in Alaska and the center of all government administrative activities of the State. Sources of revenue in the city and vicinity are fishing and fish processing, lumber mills, and dairy and fur farming. The Alaska-Juneau Mine on Mt. Roberts, operative until 1944, was one of the largest gold mines in the world. Glacier Bay National Monument (q.v.) is about 60 miles N.W. of Juneau. The site of Juneau was first settled in 1880 as a gold-mining center. It was made the capital of Alaska in 1900, and in 1906 the governmental offices were moved to Juneau from Sitka. Pop. (1960) 6797; (1970) 6050.

JUNE BEETLE or **JUNE BUG,** common name for any of several beetles in the Scarab family, so called because the adults are most common in June. In the northern United States the name is applied to the numerous species in the genus *Phyllophaga,* known as "May bugs" in the South, where they emerge earlier. The brown, stout-bodied adults are about one inch long and feed on leaves. The larvae, known to horticulturists as "white grubs", burrow in soil, feed on the roots of plants, and often do damage to grass lawns. The larval stage persists for two to three years.

In the southern U.S. the name "June beetle" is applied to the figeater, *Cotinus nitida,* a green and brown insect that, in the adult stages, feeds on ripe figs and other fruit. The larvae, like those of the northern June beetle, live in the ground and eat plant roots, but do little damage to important plants. The name "June beetle" is applied in Europe to beetles of the genus *Rhizotrogus,* closely related and similar in habits to the June beetles of the northern U.S. See SCARAB.

JUNEBERRY. See SHADBUSH.

JUNG, Carl Gustav (1875–1961), Swiss psychiatrist and founder of analytic psychology, born in Kesswil, and educated at the universities of Basel and Zürich, where he received a medical degree in 1902. Jung collaborated with the Austrian psychoanalyst Sigmund Freud (q.v.) from 1907 to 1913, and founded the International Psychoanalytic Association in 1910. His revolutionary book *Wandlungen und Symbole der Libido* (1912; Eng. trans., *Psychology of the Unconscious,* 1916) interpreted unconscious symbols historically and mythologically. His *Psychologische Typen* (1921; Eng. trans., *Psychological Types,* 1923) introduced his concepts of extroversion and introversion. Jung traveled widely from 1920 to 1937, studying various cultural groups. He founded the Swiss Society for Practical Psychology in 1935, and the Carl Gustav Jung Institute, in Zürich, for training analysts, in 1948.

Jung was one of the earliest converts to the psychoanalytic doctrines of Freud, and he remained a disciple until 1911, when he founded an independent neo-Freudian school under the name of analytic psychology, with a center at

Carl Gustav Jung (right) at his home near Zürich, Switzerland, talks with Dr. Carleton Sprague Smith (1905–), American art authority, during a visit in 1955.

Swiss National Tourist Office

JUNGFRAU

Zürich. Analytic psychology rejects the Freudian concepts of the libido (q.v.) as sexual in nature and of psychoneurosis as sexual in origin, placing emphasis on the libido as a creative force or will to live, and on the conflicts of patients in psychotherapy as products of immediate problems. The unconscious is considered to contain a collective or racial factor, as well as an individual content. Jung also introduced the concept of the complex as a psychological fixation that dominates the personality. His collected works, translated into English, and edited by the British writer Herbert Read (1893–   ) and others, include *Two Essays on Analytical Psychology* (1953), *Psychology and Alchemy* (1953), *Psychology and Religion: West and East* (1958), *The Structure and Dynamics of the Psyche* (1960), *Alchemical Studies* (1968), and *Analytical Psychology: Its Theory and Practice* (1969). See PSYCHOANALYSIS: *Psychoanalytic Schools: Carl Jung.*

JUNGFRAU, mountain of the Bernese Oberland, Switzerland, located on the border between the cantons of Bern and Valais and rising to a height of 13,642 ft. above sea level. The Jungfrau was ascended for the first time in 1811. A railroad, the highest in Europe, ascends the mountain to Jungfraujoch, a point about 11,340 ft. above sea level.

JUNGLE FOWL, common name for any of the wild, galliform forest birds of the genus *Gallus* common in the Orient. The red jungle fowl, *G. gallus,* of India is believed to be the ancestor of the common fowl (q.v.); a well-known subspecies is the bankiva, found in Java. Three other species are known: *G. sonnerati,* the gray jungle fowl, of India; *G. varius* of Malaysia; and *G. lafayetti* of Ceylon. These birds are hunted as game.

JUNGLE SHEEP. See MUNTJAC.

JUNIPER, common name of evergreen trees and shrubs of the genus *Juniperus,* belonging to

Branch of Rocky Mountain juniper, Juniperus scopulorum. U.S. Forest Service

the Pine family. The genus includes about sixty species, native to cold and temperate regions of the Northern Hemisphere. Junipers produce two types of leaves: needlelike, sharply pointed, articulated leaves without oil glands, arranged in twos or whorls of three; and small scalelike leaves with oil glands on the lower surfaces. Some juniper plants produce the different types of leaves on separate plants, others produce needlelike leaves on younger plants, and scalelike leaves on older plants, and some plants bear both kinds simultaneously. In most species, male and female cones are borne on separate plants. Male cones are dry, and bear pollen-producing chambers on shield-shaped scales. Female cones, which are fleshy when mature, have fused scales, giving a solid, berrylike appearance. The "berry", which varies from $\frac{1}{4}$ to $\frac{1}{2}$ in. in diameter, is red or purple, and contains one to eight bony seeds.

Common juniper, *J. communis,* is a shrub or small tree, 6 to 13 ft. in height, which grows on dry soil throughout the temperate and cold regions of Eurasia and North America. Unripe fruits of common juniper yield oil of juniper, which is used in the manufacture of varnish, and in medicine, as a diuretic. Ripe fruits are used for flavoring gin (q.v.). Creeping juniper or savin, *J. horizontalis,* is a prostrate shrub, bearing scalelike leaves, which grows on rocky or sandy banks in northeastern United States and eastern Canada. The red cedar or red savin, *J. virginiana,* native to temperate North America, may grow as a shrub or tree. The trees may grow as tall as 100 ft. and the trunk may be as much as 5 ft. in diameter. Red cedar produces cedar oil, used as a clearing agent in histology, and as immersion oil. The tree has ragged bark and red, durable, aromatic heartwood, used extensively for manufacture of pencils, woodwork, clothing chests, fence posts, and telegraph poles. Cedar chests are especially desirable as clothing chests because the wood contains a pungent oil which repels insects, such as moths. Wood of a related species, the Bermuda cedar, *J. bermudiana,* native to Bermuda, is used for the same purposes.

Other species native to North America include: California juniper, *J. californica,* native to southwestern U.S.; Rocky Mountain juniper, *J. scopulorum,* native to the northern Rocky Mts.; Mexican or rock juniper, *J. mexicana,* native to Mexico and Texas; western juniper, *J. occidentalis,* native to Washington, Oregon, and California; and alligator juniper, *J. deppeana,* native to the southern Rocky Mts. After the common juniper, the most abundant juniper of Europe is the savin, *J. sabina,* which grows throughout the mountains of central Europe. It has scalelike, glandular leaves, and the inflorescences yield oil of savin, formerly used in medicine as a stimulant, diaphoretic, anthelmintic, and emmenagogue. The Chinese juniper, *J. chinensis*, a species native to western Asia, grows as tall as 60 ft., and bears bright-green leaves.

Many species of juniper, particularly Chinese juniper, red cedar, common juniper, and savin, are cultivated in the U.S. as ornamental trees and shrubs. Prostrate varieties are commonly used in borders, and columnar trees are popular adjuncts of lawns and informal gardens.

JUNÍPERO, Serra. See SERRA, JUNÍPERO.

JUNIUS, pen name of the unknown author of a series of sixty-nine polemical letters published between Jan. 21, 1769, and Jan. 21, 1772, in a London newspaper, the *Public Advertiser*. The principal intent of the writer was to discredit the administration of Prime Minister Augustus Henry Fitzroy, 3rd Duke of Grafton (1735–1811). Junius charged Grafton and other members of the government with personal immorality, and vented his wrath on George III (q.v.), King of Great Britain. Grafton was eventually compelled to resign from office as a result of these attacks. The letters, written in a vigorous prose style, were widely read; before 1772 at least twelve unauthorized editions had been published. In 1772 the collection was revised by the author, who added a dedication to the people of Great Britain and a preface. Speculation about the identity of the author persisted for many years following the appearance of the first letters; more than forty persons, at various times, were held to be the author. The probable author, in the view of many scholars, is the British government official and writer Sir Philip Francis (1740–1818).

JUNK, wooden, high-pooped sailing vessel of the Far East, used for fishing and river transportation and by some families for living quarters. The prow, or bluff-bow, is broad and flat rather than pointed, and the bottom is either flat or small-keeled with a low rudder. Junks have a deck and high masts, most commonly three, with four-cornered, coarse cotton sails, called lugsails, braced flat by bamboo strips or battens; see SAIL. Long oars may also be used on the boats. Larger, more seaworthy junks, reaching a length of 70 ft. and a displacement of up to 100 tons, are used in coastal waters. The vessels are used chiefly by the Chinese, Japanese, and Javanese. See also FISHING VESSELS: *Asiatic Types*. Compare SAMPAN.

JUNO, one of the planetoids (q.v.), the third to be discovered, first observed by the German astronomer Karl Ludwig Harding (1765–1834) in 1804. It revolves about the sun in 1592 days.

JUNO, in Roman mythology, queen of the gods, the wife and sister of the god Jupiter (q.v.). She was the protectress of women and was worshiped under several names. As Juno Pronuba she presided over marriage; as Juno Lucina she aided women in childbirth; and as Juno Regina she was the special counselor and protectress of the Roman state. Her special festival, the Matronalia, was celebrated on March 1. Juno is the Latin counterpart of the Greek queen of the gods Hera (q.v.). The month of June was named after her.

JUPITER, largest planet in the solar system and, after Venus, the brightest planet. The mean distance of Jupiter from the sun is 483,300,000 mi., about 5.2 times that of the earth. Jupiter takes 11.87 years to make a complete revolution about the sun. Jupiter is markedly flattened at the poles, the polar diameter being 82,900 mi. and the equatorial diameter 88,800 mi. The volume of Jupiter is approximately 1300 times that of the earth; because its mass is nearly 317 times that of the earth, its mean density is one fourth that of the earth, or 1.4 times that of water. The rotation period of the planet is approximately 9 hr. 50 min.; the period of rotation of areas close to the equator is apparently slightly less than that of areas at higher latitudes.

The Surface. The planet, as seen through a telescope, is marked by a number of parallel bands or belts of different widths. The belts themselves and the spots and other markings observed in these belts undergo considerable variation. The most notable marking on Jupiter is a large, oval spot, the so-called great Red Spot, which is about 8700 mi. wide and 25,000 mi. long. The spot is definitely known to have been observed in 1878, but was probably seen at an earlier date. This mark has diminished in color with the passing of the years, and except for a period of time in 1937 when its color was very pronounced, it has faded considerably; only its outline has remained partially visible.

The variable nature of the surface features, the difference in rotation period in different latitudes, the high reflecting power, the existence of the great Red Spot over a long period of time, and the low density of the planet indicate that the planet is probably composed of a relatively small solid core surrounded by a very thick layer of atmosphere. Spectroscopic studies show that the atmosphere of Jupiter contains mostly hydrogen, methane, and ammonia. Temperature measurements indicate that the temperature of the visible surface is about −135° C. (−211° F.).

JUPITER

Scientists believe that the semipermanent markings may be clouds of droplets of ammonia because ammonia is close to its boiling point at the temperature and pressure of the atmosphere of Jupiter. In 1955 radio waves from the planet were detected for the first time by means of radio telescopes; see RADIO ASTRONOMY. Studies of the signals suggest that the radio waves result from large-scale disturbances in the atmosphere of Jupiter. They also indicate that the planet possesses a radiation belt similar to, but considerably more intense than, the Van Allen belt of the earth; see RADIATION BELTS.

Jupiter's Satellites. Four of the twelve known satellites, were seen by the Italian astronomer Galileo Galilei (q.v.) in 1610, and were the first celestial bodies to be discovered by means of the telescope. They are easily visible with a pair of binoculars. These so-called Galilean satellites are named Io, Europa, Ganymede, and Gallista, but are generally designated by the Roman numerals I, II, III, IV, in order of their distance from the planet; they are all comparable in size and mass with the earth's satellite, the moon. The other eight satellites are too small and faint to be seen except with very powerful telescopes.

Jupiter is also associated with a family of comets (see COMET), the orbits of which bear a definite relationship to the orbit of Jupiter. According to one theory of the origin of comets, the comet family associated with Jupiter resulted from eruptions thrown out from the planet. Because of its great size Jupiter causes serious perturbations (q.v.) in the orbits of other planets, of all planetoids (q.v.), and of comets, and its influence on the motion of other heavenly bodies makes it extremely important in the science of celestial mechanics.

JUPITER, or JOVE, in Roman mythology the ruler of the gods, the son of the god Saturn (q.v.), whom he overthrew. Originally the god of the sky and king of heaven, Jupiter was worshiped as god of rain, thunder, and lightning. As the protector of Rome he was called Jupiter Optimus Maximus ("the best and most high") and was worshiped in a temple on the Capitoline hill. As Jupiter Fidius he was guardian of law, defender of truth, and protector of justice and virtue. The Romans identified Jupiter with Zeus (q.v.), the supreme god of the Greeks, and assigned to the Roman god the attributes and myths of the Greek divinity; the Jupiter of Latin literature, therefore, has many Greek characteristics, but the Jupiter of Roman religious worship remained substantially untouched by the Greek influence. With the goddesses Juno and Minerva (qq.v.) Jupiter formed the triad whose worship was the central cult of the Roman state.

JURA, mountain range of Europe, on the border between France and Switzerland. Beginning in E. France on the N. bank of the Rhone R. in Ain Department, the range extends northward, forming the W. bank of the river until it reaches the Swiss frontier near Geneva. From that point

A view of the Doubs River in the forests of the Jura Mts. in western Switzerland.
Swiss National Tourist Office

Skeleton of Ceratosaurus, *a dinosaur of the late Jurassic Period.*   Smithsonian Institution

it passes through the Jura and Doubs departments, following the boundary line between France and Switzerland in a long curve toward the northeast. The range finally passes wholly into Switzerland, and terminates on the S. bank of the Rhine R. west of its confluence with the Aare R. The range thus defined is the Jura proper, but many geographers apply the name also to the mountains N. of the Rhine and S. of the Rhône, considering that these rivers merely make two breaks in an otherwise continuous chain. South of the Rhône the chain is known as the Jura Alps and merges with branches of the western Alps. North of the Rhine an irregular chain extends E. of the Black Forest (q.v.) in the State of Baden-Württemberg, Germany, and through the State of Bavaria as far as the Main R. This chain, called the German or Swabian Jura, is similar to the Jura proper in the character of rock formations, but different in structure, being formed entirely by faulting; see FAULT.

The Jura proper consists of a series of parallel folds in the strata, forming together a plateau nearly 200 mi. long and 20 to 35 mi. wide. These folded ridges have in many places suffered transverse fractures, which, in the form of steep gorges known as cluses, add greatly to the picturesque character of the landscape. The general height of the range is from 3000 to 5000 ft. It is highest near the S. end, W. of Lake Geneva, where the Crêt de la Neige has an altitude of 5652 ft. The Jura are formed of limestone rich in fossils; for this reason the geological period called the Jurassic Period (q.v.) of the Mesozoic Era (q.v.) was named after the range. *See also* GEOLOGY: *Historical.*

JURASSIC PERIOD, in geology, time unit of the Mesozoic Era, after the Triassic Period and before the Cretaceous Period (qq.v.). The period began roughly 180,000,000 years ago and lasted for approximately 45,000,000 years. It was named for the Jura (q.v.) mountain range of Europe, where extensive geological deposits belonging to the time unit occur. In Europe the rock system of the period is divided into eighteen series, but in the United States geologists recognize only three series: the Lower, Middle, and Upper Jurassic.

During the Jurassic Period the Atlantic shoreline of the United States was located farther east than at the present time. As a result, no Jurassic deposits of marine origin occur in the eastern U.S. In the western U.S., however, a large trough, known as the Rocky Mountain geosyncline, extended from northwestern Canada to Mexico, following approximately the present line of the Rocky Mts. This great trough was invaded by the ocean from the north, covering portions of Montana, Wyoming, Idaho, North Dakota, South Dakota, Nebraska, Colorado, and Utah. Toward the end of the period the sea receded, leaving extensive marine deposits, among them the Morrison formation, which has yielded more fossils of large dinosaurs than any other group of rocks. In some portions of the mountain States thick beds of windblown sand were laid down at this period, the so-called red beds. At the very end of the Jurassic Period, a tremendous upheaval in the Southwest, the Sierra Nevada or Nevadan revolution, produced the Sierra Nevada and Cascade ranges.

In other parts of the world, marine Jurassic deposits are found in Australia, England, the Himalaya Mts. and Japan. Some of these Jurassic formations contain coal and other minerals of economic importance, such as lithographic limestone. The gold deposits of the Sierra Nevada are of Jurassic origin.

293

JURISPRUDENCE

Flora. The vegetation of the Jurassic Period was abundant and consisted in great part of evergreens, palms, and tree ferns. Smaller plants such as herbaceous ferns and scouring rushes formed the undergrowth in the forests. The flora of the period was very widely distributed, and many of the same species were found in Siberia, the arctic, North America, and England. Geologists deduce from this cosmopolitan distribution that the climate of the period was mild, even in the regions of the subarctic and subantarctic.

Fauna. The most conspicuous animals belonging to the period were the dinosaurs, among them the *Brontosaurus* and *Tyrannosaurus*. Other reptiles included the flying pterodactyls and the marine ichthyosaurs. A group of marine reptiles that has survived to the present day, the turtles, also made their first appearance in Jurassic times. *Archaeopteryx*, the first known bird, which represents the link between the reptiles and modern birds, belongs to the Jurassic Period. The mammals of the period were small and apparently lived on all of the continents except Australia. See GEOLOGY, HISTORICAL; PALEONTOLOGY.

JURISPRUDENCE (Lat. *jurisprudentia*, from *jus*, "law", and *prudentia*, "knowledge"), knowledge of the law and its interpretation, or the science and philosophy of law. In ancient Rome the term was used in the former sense. Those who were so skilled in the law, whether they were of unofficial position or judges, that they could declare what the rule would be in a novel or otherwise doubtful case were called *juris prudentes;* the body of law built up by their concurrent interpretation was called *juris prudentia*. This development of law by interpretation is akin to what among English-speaking peoples is called "case" law, law arising from a body of decided cases, and in France and Spain the term "jurisprudence" is still used in that sense.

Science of the Law. Commonly, in modern times, English-speaking peoples use the word "jurisprudence" to describe what was often called at an earlier period the philosophy of law, and what Continental writers now call the theory or the science of the law. An English or American treatise on jurisprudence, or on the science or principles of law, undertakes to determine what law is by defining the essential elements in our conception of law; the relation that law bears to the cognate social sciences, politics, ethics, and economics; the way in which law originates, in popular customs, judicial usage, and legislation, and the way in which it ceases to exist by desuetude, change of usage, abrogation, or repeal; its application with reference to persons, time, and place, and the way in which it is enforced. Jurisprudence formulates and classifies the conceptions with which law operates, that is, legal relations, rights, and duties. It may undertake to classify law and to construct a system or framework in which every rule of modern law, or perhaps of all law, past and present may find an appropriate place. It may, although it more rarely does, attempt to classify all the relations which the law recognizes or creates and which it regulates or orders, that is, the relations of state and government to other forms of association and to individuals, and the relations of private associations and of individuals to each other. It may, although it still more rarely does, analyze the fundamental conceptions of the family, of property, and of succession.

Schools of Jurisprudence. The principal modern schools of jurisprudence are the natural-law school, the analytical school, the historical school, the comparative school, and the sociological school. The first three differ mainly in their views of the nature and origin of law and its relation to ethics (q.v.).

To the natural-law jurist, law is antecedent to the state; to the analytical jurist, it is the creation of the state; and to the historical jurist, state and law are social products, developing side by side, each influencing the other. To the natural-law jurist, law is cognizable by pure reason; to the analytical jurist, it is the command of the sovereign power; to the historical jurist, it is the formulated wisdom of man. To the natural-law jurist, law is applied ethics, and, in the extreme form of the theory, that which is not right is not law. To the analytical jurist, a law that commands what is ethically wrong or forbids what is ethically right is not the less a law if it proceeds from the political sovereign. The historical jurist accepts in this respect the position taken by the analytical school, but points out that it is difficult for a lawmaker to act otherwise than in accord with the contemporary sense of right, and that laws which run counter to that sense are not likely to be enforced. Historical jurisprudence differs from analytical jurisprudence chiefly in emphasizing the great part played by social custom in developing and establishing law. To the analytical jurist customary law, including judicial custom, is an anomaly; he would abolish it by covering the whole field of social relations with written codes.

The natural-law school has its roots in the Stoic philosophy (*see* STOICISM) and the Roman jurisprudence; it was increasingly dominant in Europe from the Reformation (q.v.) to the close of the eighteenth century; see NATURAL LAW. The theory of the analytical school was first sharply formulated by the English philosopher Thomas Hobbes (q.v.) in his *Leviathan* (1651). The views of this school, however, did not originate in England. The tendency to exalt the function of the legislator appeared on the Continent at the close of the Middle Ages and was associated with the efforts of the national states to rid themselves of the chaos of varying provincial and local customs that had taken form during the Middle Ages. This end could be attained only by national legislation, and has been fully attained only by the adoption of national codes. See CODE.

The historical school dates from the nineteenth century, as a reaction against natural-law ideas. The German jurist Friedrich Karl von Savigny (1779–1861), first clearly defined the principles of historical jurisprudence in 1814. No great antagonism exists between the historical and the comparative school. This latest school, or tendency, of which the leading early exponents were the German legal scholar Rudolf von Jhering (1818–92), and Albert Hermann Post (1839–95), represents a widening of the field of investigation. Not only is each national law studied historically but the various national systems are compared at similar stages of development. As a result of this process, not only may the normal course of legal development be discovered, but that which is universal and human may be separated from that which is particular to a single nation or to a special stage of development; and then, as Jhering hoped, it may eventually become possible to write a history of the law of the world. Among the leading British and American writers on comparative law were James Barr Ames (1846–1910), Oliver Wendell Holmes (*see under* HOLMES), Henry Sumner Maine (1822–88), Frederick William Maitland (q.v.), and Sir Frederick Pollock (1845–1937).

The sociological school of jurisprudence is largely a product of the 20th century. Its approach to the analysis of law differs from that of the other schools in that it is concerned less with the nature and origin of law than with its actual functions and end results. The proponents of sociological jurisprudence seek to view law within a broad social context rather than as an isolated phenomenon distinct from and independent of other means of social control. They are concerned with practical improvement of the legal system and feel that this can be achieved only if legislation and court adjudications take into account the findings of other branches of learning, particularly the social sciences. The American jurist Roscoe Pound (q.v.) was a prominent figure in the school of sociological jurisprudence.

A loose application of the term "jurisprudence" makes it practically equivalent to the word "law" itself, as in the phrase "medical jurisprudence", meaning the law connected with the field of medicine. W.O.D.

JURY (Lat. *juratus*, "sworn", from *jus*, "right", "law"), in law, sworn body of laymen who are constituted the judges of the truth of factual evidence (q.v.) on trial (q.v.) of an action or proceeding, and, on instruction of the court, apply the law to the facts. Such a jury is a petit jury or trial jury. *See also* CORONER; GRAND JURY.

History. The exact origin of the jury system is not known; various writers have attributed it to different European peoples who at an early period developed methods of trial not unlike the early jury trials in England. It seems probable that the jury in England was derived directly from the Norman institution of recognition by sworn inquest, which was substituted by the Norman conquerors for the method of trial by battle. The *Curia Regis*, or King's Court, might direct the sheriff to select four knights of the county, who then chose twelve knights to serve as *recognitors*. The duty of the latter, after being duly sworn, was to inquire as to various matters of interest to the new rulers of England that might be the subject of public inquiry. Such matters might include the taxation of a subject. As early as the 12th century, it had become customary for suitors in certain cases affecting the title to real estate to apply to the King's Court for the summoning of recognitors to ascertain either from their own knowledge or upon inquiry from others, the truth of the matter in issue; the verdict of the court, if unanimous, was accepted as conclusive. It was natural that other questions of fact arising in the King's Court should be disposed of in a similar manner, and the gradual transformation of the recognitors into the jury in common law (q.v.) followed as a matter of course. Originally the jurymen were not only judges of fact, but they were witnesses often selected because of their knowledge of the customs and the people of the locality, and possibly of the suitors themselves. In the early 15th century, however, the judges of the courts of common law restricted the jury to the performance of its function as a judge of fact upon the evidence submitted to it, which is the single function of the jury in modern practice.

JURY

Selection of a Jury. The first step toward summoning a jury is the issuing of a writ or precept of a court to the trial of any case, whether civil or criminal, having jurisdiction over jury trials, directed to the sheriff and called at common law a *venire facias* ("cause to come"), commanding him to summon citizens residing in the county to attend at a term of court for the purpose of serving as jurors. In the United States each State has its own qualifications for those who must serve as jurymen. In general, all jurors must be U.S. citizens, of twenty-one years of age or over, and of approved integrity. The group of jurors called at any one time is known as a panel. Both the State courts and the Federal courts have independent lists of jurors that are made up under the direction of officials known as commissioners of jurors. Jurors are paid, as provided by statute, for time spent serving on juries. At the trial the selection of the jury is made subject to the direction of the presiding judge. The names of the jurymen are drawn by lot by the clerk of the court, and as their names are called the jurymen take their seats in the jury box until twelve are thus chosen. The parties to the action or their attorneys may then exercise their right to eliminate undesirable members from the jury by means of challenge. Both the defense and the prosecution may examine the jurors for the purpose of ascertaining whether cause for challenge in any particular case exists.

Function of a Jury. After a satisfactory jury has been drawn, the jury is sworn, and the trial proceeds. In general, during the progress of a trial, all questions of law are determined by the court and questions of fact by the jury. The limits of the inquiry as to facts are determined by the pleadings and the rules of evidence. Whether evidence is properly admissible or not is a question for the court, but the weight and credibility of the evidence admitted are determined by the jury. The court, however, may decide a question of fact without sending the question to the jury if no conflict of evidence exists on the point. The court may also interpret written instruments received in evidence without the aid of the jury.

After all the evidence has been presented, the counsel, first for the defendant and later for the plaintiff or prosecution, "sum up", that is, each addresses the jury, reviewing the evidence in the case and commenting upon it in a manner favorable to his side of the case. The judge then makes his charge to the jury. The charge is a statement of the rules of law applicable to the evidence in the case, and it is given for the purpose of aiding the jury to render a correct verdict. The jury then retires from the courtroom and is locked into a room until an agreement as to the verdict is reached, or until the presiding judge deems the jury is hung, or cannot reach an agreement. In the event no agreement is reached, a new trial may be called. All the twelve members of a jury must agree upon a verdict, which in a civil trial may be "for the plaintiff" or "for the defendant", and in a criminal trial "guilty" or "not guilty". The verdict of a jury is decisive and cannot be disturbed unless rendered contrary to law or against the weight of evidence, in which case it may either be set aside by the presiding judge, or the judgment rendered thereon may later be set aside on appeal. *See* VERDICT.

Special juries, such as those specially selected in order to secure jurymen of more than common intelligence, were known at common law and were expressly authorized by statutes. Statutes in many States of the U.S. now provide for the selection of special juries for the trial of cases of great importance or difficulty.

JUSSERAND, Jean Jules (1855–1932), French historian and diplomat, born in Lyon. He studied law and in 1876 entered the diplomatic service. After serving in the French diplomatic corps in Great Britain, Turkey, and Denmark, he was appointed ambassador to the United States. Between 1902 and 1925 Jusserand did much in this capacity to promote U.S.-French relations, partly through his friendship with President Theodore Roosevelt (q.v.). Also a historian, Jusserand received the 1917 Pulitzer Prize in history for *With Americans of Past and Present Days* (1916).

JUSTICE, DEPARTMENT OF, an executive department of the Federal government of the United States, created by Congress in 1870 to assume the functions performed until then by the Office of the Attorney General, established in 1789. The Department is headed by the attorney general (q.v.), who is appointed by the President with the approval of the Senate.

Functions. The functions of the department include providing means for the enforcement of Federal laws and investigating violations thereof; supervising the Federal penal institutions; furnishing legal counsel in cases involving the Federal government and conducting all suits brought before the Supreme Court of the United States in which the Federal government is concerned; interpreting laws relating to the activities of the other Federal departments; and rendering legal advice, upon request, to the President and members of the cabinet.

The attorney general is assisted by the deputy attorney general. The third-ranking official of

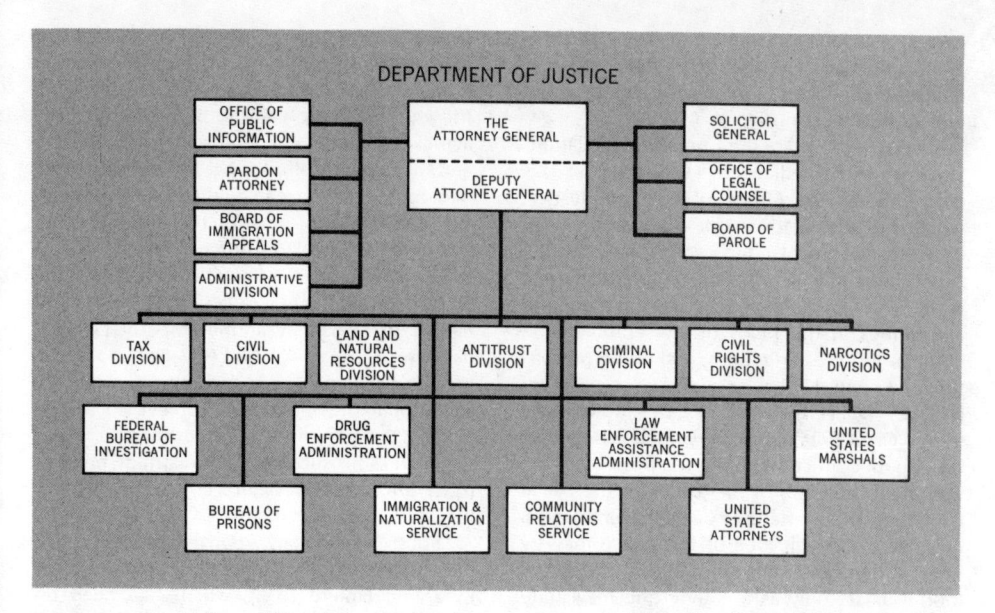

JUSTICE, DEPARTMENT OF

DEPARTMENT OF JUSTICE

```
                          THE ATTORNEY GENERAL
    OFFICE OF PUBLIC INFORMATION            SOLICITOR GENERAL
    PARDON ATTORNEY                         OFFICE OF LEGAL COUNSEL
                          DEPUTY ATTORNEY GENERAL
    BOARD OF IMMIGRATION APPEALS            BOARD OF PAROLE
    ADMINISTRATIVE DIVISION

    TAX DIVISION | CIVIL DIVISION | LAND AND NATURAL RESOURCES DIVISION | ANTITRUST DIVISION | CRIMINAL DIVISION | CIVIL RIGHTS DIVISION | NARCOTICS DIVISION

    FEDERAL BUREAU OF INVESTIGATION | DRUG ENFORCEMENT ADMINISTRATION | LAW ENFORCEMENT ASSISTANCE ADMINISTRATION | UNITED STATES MARSHALS

    BUREAU OF PRISONS | IMMIGRATION & NATURALIZATION SERVICE | COMMUNITY RELATIONS SERVICE | UNITED STATES ATTORNEYS
```

the department is the solicitor general, who directs all U.S. government litigation in the Supreme Court and who is concerned generally with the conduct of the appellate litigation of the government. Nine assistant attorneys general head the divisions of the Justice Department. The functions of the department are carried out regionally by U.S. attorneys and U.S. marshals; one of each is appointed to the ninety-four Federal judicial districts by the President, with the consent of the Senate.

Structure. The department includes the antitrust, civil, civil rights, criminal, land and natural resources, narcotics, tax, and administrative divisions and the Office of Legal Counsel. The Antitrust Division is charged with the enforcement of the Federal antitrust laws and related enactments against industrial and commercial monopolies; the most important of these laws are the Sherman Antitrust Act (q.v.) of 1890 and the Clayton Act (q.v.) of 1914 and 1950; *see also* TRUST. The Civil Division supervises all matters relating to civil suits and claims involving the U.S. and its departments, agencies, and officers. Its jurisdiction includes cases involving patents, fraud, tort claims, customs, and veterans' affairs. The Civil Rights Division is responsible for enforcing the Civil Rights Acts of 1957, 1960, and 1964, and the Voting Rights Act of 1965. It is also charged with enforcing the criminal statutes against terrorist conspiracies and police brutality.

The Criminal Division is entrusted with enforcing Federal criminal statutes relating to such matters as organized crime, kidnapping, bank robbery, fraud against the government, racketeering, and certain civil matters such as extradition proceedings and seizure actions under the Federal Food, Drug and Cosmetics Act. The Criminal Division also is charged with the prosecution of all cases involving subversives and with the enforcement of all statutes relating to subversive activities. The Land and Natural Resources Division protects Federal government ownership, conservation, or use of land and natural resources; acquires land for Federal purposes; and protects certain rights and properties of American Indians.

The Narcotics Division, created in 1973, has responsibility for Federal prosecution of narcotics law violators and for providing other legal support to the Drug Enforcement Administration (q.v.).

The Tax Division is responsible for the conduct of all civil suits arising out of the internal-revenue laws. The Administrative Division supervises the business management of the Justice Department. The Office of Legal Counsel advises and assists the attorney general in the performance of his duties.

Associated Agencies. Other agencies include the Federal Bureau of Investigation (q.v.), which investigates violations of Federal laws and collects evidence in cases in which the U.S. may be involved; the Bureau of Prisons, which supervises the Federal Prison System; the United States Board of Parole, which has the authority to release Federal prisoners before the end of their sentences; the Pardon Attorney, who receives and investigates applications to the President for pardon or clemency; the Drug Enforcement Administration; the Immigration and Naturalization Service (q.v.); and the Board of Immigration Appeals.

Special sections are the Community Relations Service, which mediates racial disputes in U.S. communities; the Office of Criminal Justice, which provides a forum for discussion of the difficult issues involved in criminal law; and the Law Enforcement Assistance Administration, which, through grants, works to strengthen local capabilities in the fields of law enforcement, criminal justice, corrections, and crime prevention and control.

JUSTICE OF THE PEACE, in the judicial system of Great Britain and the United States, a judicial public officer with limited powers. In the U.S. the jurisdiction of the justice of the peace is defined by the statutes of the several States. In some States a justice of the peace may try only misdemeanors; in other States he has authority to act only as a committing magistrate and has no trial jurisdiction in criminal cases; in still other States, he has authority to try civil disputes in matters involving up to $300, as well as limited criminal jurisdiction.

The office of justice of the peace, established as early as 1630, was one of the first instrumentalities of government created by the American colonists. The principal function of the official was the maintenance of order; his jurisdiction was primarily over criminal matters. He had limited civil jurisdiction and performed certain administrative duties, such as the performance of marriage ceremonies. With the development of the legal system, most of his criminal jurisdiction was withdrawn.

JUSTIN, Saint, or JUSTIN THE MARTYR (100?–165 A.D.), one of the earliest apologists of the Christian Church, born in Flavia Neapolis (now Nablus, Jordan), a Roman city built on the site of the ancient Shechem, in Samaria. His parents were pagans. As a young man Justin devoted himself to the study of Greek philosophy, notably the writings of Plato (q.v.) and the Stoic philosophers; see STOICISM. His study of the Old and New Testaments caused him to convert to Christianity, and thereafter, he strove by his teachings and writings to bring others to the truths he had discovered. Justin was beheaded during the reign of the Roman emperor Marcus Aurelius (q.v.) because he refused to offer sacrifice to the pagan gods. Justin was included in the martyrology of the Roman Catholic Church (q.v.) in the 9th century; his feast day is April 14. The books that are ascribed to him with certainty are the two *Apologies for the Christians* (actually one work in two parts, the first addressed "to Antoninus Pius", the second "to the Roman Senate"), and the *Dialogue with Trypho the Jew,* which professes to be the record of an actual discussion at Ephesus. As a philosopher and theologian Justin sought to reconcile Christian doctrine and pagan culture. His writings are valuable for the information they give about the 2nd century Christian Church. G.E.D.

JUSTINIAN I, in full FLAVIUS PETRUS SABBATIUS JUSTINIANUS, called JUSTINIAN THE GREAT (483–565), Byzantine Emperor (527–65), nephew of Emperor Justin I (452–527), born in Illyricum, in Illyria (q.v.), and educated in Constantinople (now Istanbul, Turkey). In 518 he became the administrator for Justin, who named Justinian as his successor. He married Theodora (q.v.), a former actress, in 523. On the death of his uncle in 527 Justinian was elected emperor.

Almost immediately upon his accession Justinian inaugurated a policy of restoration of the Byzantine Empire (q.v.), which had been reduced by the barbarian invasions of the 5th century; see ROME, HISTORY OF: *The Empire: Decline and Fall.* The eastern front of the empire was secured by an "eternal peace" signed with Persia in 532. Internal unrest was crushed by the great general Belisarius (q.v.). In 533 an imperial army set out against the Vandal kingdom (see VANDALS) in northern Africa, which was reincorporated into the empire in 534. Almost simultaneously another imperial army attacked the Ostrogoths (see GOTHS: *Ostrogoths*) in Italy; however, the Ostrogoths resisted annihilation for another twenty years. A third campaign, undertaken against the Visigoths (see GOTHS: *Visigoths*), reconquered southeastern Spain. By the emperor's death most of the former Roman territory around the Mediterranean Sea, except for Gaul and northern Spain, was again part of the empire in spite of a resumption of the Persian war in 540 and gradual Slavic infiltration (see SLAVS) in the Balkans.

The centralized empire envisaged by Justinian required a uniform legal system. Therefore an imperial commission headed by the renowned jurist Trebonianus (fl. 6th cent.) worked for ten years to collect and systematize existing Roman law (q.v.). Their work was incorporated into the enormous *Corpus Juris Civilis* (Lat., "Body of Civil Law"), also called the Justinian Code, promulgated in 534 and kept up to date by the addition of new decrees, or *Novellae.* This formidable legislative codification still remains the basis for the law of most European countries. Simultaneously with this legal reform, attempts were made to rectify administrative abuses.

Emperor Justinian I and his retinue, a mosaic from the 6th-century Church of San Vitale, in Ravenna, Italy.
Bettmann Archive

The final goal of Justinian was the reconciliation of all Christian groups after the quarrels of the preceding two centuries. Originally strictly orthodox in his recognition of the 5th-century Council of Chalcedon, Justinian had thereby affected the reunion of Rome and Constantinople; see CHALCEDON; COUNCIL. In 553, seeking to find a formula satisfactory to the Monophysites (q.v.) in the East and perhaps under the influence of Theodora, who favored their views, the emperor called the second council of Constantinople (Council of the Three Chapters), which condemned as Nestorian certain views accepted at Chalcedon; see CONSTANTINOPLE, COUNCILS OF; NESTORIANS. This attempt at compromise, imposed by force where necessary, achieved only superficial pacification, and it proved altogether satisfactory to none of the parties.

To insure the safety of the frontier territories Justinian restored the entire system of border fortifications and had it extended. At the same time he sponsored an extensive building program of churches and public buildings. Most beautiful among his churches still standing in western Europe are San Vitale and Sant' Apollinare in Classe, both in Ravenna. The main concern of the emperor was for his capital, Constantinople, where the magnificent Church of the Holy Wisdom (Hagia Sophia), adorned with multicolored marble and gold mosaics, became the marvel of all Christendom; see SAINT SOPHIA.

The ambitious program of Justinian proved ruinously costly; it required oppressive taxes, which contributed to the constant internal unrest. His failure to repress governmental abuses or to achieve religious reconciliation also intensified the unrest. The constant wars exhausted the state and jeopardized its stand against the new dangers that were to manifest themselves after the emperor's death. Nevertheless, at the close of his life Justinian could justifiably claim that as emperor he had fulfilled his mission of reviving the military might and the intellectual and artistic splendor of the Roman Empire.

JUSTINIAN CODE. See CODE; JUSTINIAN I; ROMAN LAW.

JUTE, fiber of either of two species of woody herbs belonging to the Linden family, *Corchorus capsularis* and *C. olidorius*. The plants are cultivated in tropical countries throughout the world. They are annuals with sparsely branching stems, often growing as tall as 14 ft. The small yellow flowers, which grow singly or in pairs, give rise to capsular fruits. The fibers of the inner bark, called bast fibers or phloem fibers, are glossy and tenacious, but are brittle and easily injured by moisture.

Most cultivated jute is grown in alluvial soils of the river valleys of India. The herb is planted, cultivated, and harvested by hand, the harvesting following planting by four to five months. At harvest, roots and foliage are removed from the plants, and the stems, tied in bunches, are

JUTES

soaked in water, retted on for two to three weeks. At the end of the retting process, the fibers are easily separable from most of the remaining stem tissue. While still in water, the stems are pounded with wooden mallets. They

Jute, Corchorus capsularis

are then rinsed, wrung thoroughly to remove any remaining nonfibrous material, and hung up to dry. The dried fibers are yellowish-white, soft, and lustrous. Jute is used in the manufacture of low-grade twine, burlap, and cheaper varieties of paper. See CORCHORUS.

JUTES, early Germanic tribe of Denmark or northern or Rhenish Germany which, between 400 and 500 A.D., conquered southeastern Britain. Little is known of the tribe prior to their settling in Kent, parts of Hampshire, and the Isle of Wight. The people are believed to be related to the inhabitants of Jutland (q.v.). Their territory bordered that of the Saxons who, with the Angles, also settled Britain and drove the Britons (qq.v.) westward into present-day Wales. Through assimilation the Jutes gradually lost their identity as a people, and by the 8th century the term Jute had almost completely disappeared from the English language. See ENGLAND: *History.*

JUTLAND (Dan. *Jylland*), in physical geography, peninsula of N.W. Europe, extending northward from the Eider R. and bounded on the N. by the Skagerrak strait, E. by the Kattegat strait, and the Lille Baelt channel, and on the W. by the North Sea. In political geography, Jutland comprises part of Schleswig-Holstein (q.v.), West Germany, and all of the Danish mainland; see DENMARK. The name is applied, in common usage, only to the Danish portion of the peninsula.

Danish Jutland extends about 210 mi. in a N. and S. direction and has a maximum width of about 110 mi. The terrain is generally low, except for a range of hills on the east-central portion of the peninsula. Within the hills is the country's highest point, Yding Skovhøj, 568 ft. above sea level. Jutland is traversed by numerous small streams of which Gudenaa R., 98 mi. in length, is the longest. The W. coast of the peninsula, which consists of a continuous sandy beach, has only one good harbor, that of Esbjerg (q.v.). The E. coast is indented by numerous bays and fjords. Bordering the E. coast are fertile, undulating fields and meadows. Agricultural activity, confined largely to this region, includes cattle raising, dairy farming, and general farming. Fishing is also an important industry. Aarhus (q.v.) is the largest city of Danish Jutland. Besides Esbjerg, other leading towns include Aalborg (q.v.), Horsens, and Randers.

The ancient Romans called the peninsula Chersonesus Cimbrica, a reference to the native Cimbri (q.v.). In the 5th century the peninsula was occupied by the Jutes (q.v.), a Germanic tribe that participated, along with the Angles and Saxons (qq.v.), in the invasion of Britain. The Jutes were succeeded on the peninsula by the Norsemen (q.v.), the ancestors of the modern Danes. Area of Danish Jutland, 11,441 sq.mi.; pop. (1971) 2,197,970.

JUTLAND, BATTLE OF, major naval engagement fought between the British and German fleets during World War I. The British Grand Fleet was under the command of Admiral John Rushworth Jellicoe (q.v.), and the German High Seas Fleet was commanded by Vice-Admiral Reinhard Scheer (q.v.). The action took place about 75 mi. off the Danish coast of Jutland on May 31 and June 1, 1916. The first phase of the battle began when, at 3:48 P.M., May 31, the battle cruisers and destroyers of Vice-Admiral David Beatty (q.v.) made contact with a squadron of German battle cruisers. Both sides opened fire simultaneously and the action lasted for 55 min. At 4:43 P.M., the German squadron was joined by the remainder of the High Seas Fleet. Beatty, who was still waiting for Jellicoe to bring up the rest of the Grand Fleet, fought a delaying action until the British supporting force could reach the scene. With the arrival of the Grand Fleet, a contest of high naval strategy began between Jellicoe and

Scheer. Jellicoe maneuvered the German fleet into a "V" formed by British ships. Elements of the two fleets engaged each other intermittently throughout the late evening and early morning. Due to a series of British blunders, including confusion of orders and poor intelligence reports, and a brilliant retreat maneuver by Scheer, the German fleet escaped under cover of darkness, thus ending the battle. Out of a total of 110 German vessels engaged in the battle, Scheer lost 11. German casualties totaled 2545 officers and men. The British lost 14 of 149 ships and 6274 officers and men. Although the material and human losses of the British were the greater, the German fleet made no further attempts to break the Allied blockade of the coast of Germany. Allied supremacy on the North Sea remained unchallenged for the duration of the war. See WORLD WAR I: *The War at Sea (1914–18)*.

JUVENAL, in full DECIMUS JUNIUS JUVENALIS, Roman poet, born in Aquinum, in southern Italy, about 65 A.D. His known literary activity extended from 98 to 128. The sixteen extant satires of Juvenal are brilliant but exaggerated attacks upon the follies and vices of Roman life, composed with bitterness and irony. Many of his satires reveal a deep sympathy with the poor and dislike of the wealthy. His poems were admired by the 17th- and 18th-century British satirists, including John Dryden, Alexander Pope, and Samuel Johnson (qq.v.). Many of these authors translated works of Juvenal and modeled their satires after his.

JUVENILE COURT, authority charged with the disposition of cases of juvenile delinquency (q.v.). Juvenile courts are sometimes referred to as children's courts or family courts, but they are always responsible for the adjudication of charges against children. Juvenile courts also have jurisdiction in some States of the United States in cases of dependency and neglect. Jurisdiction extends to age 16, 17, or 18, the usual age limit, and in a few States to age 21, depending on the law of the State. The Federal Juvenile Delinquency Act of 1938 considers any person a juvenile who has not attained his eighteenth birthday. Some courts have power to try adults for contributing to the delinquency of a child.

Prior to 1899, when the first juvenile courts were established in the U.S., all children were tried in regular criminal courts along with adults. Special institutions, usually called reformatories (q.v.), began to be established in the 1820's for children in order to separate them from adult prisoners. Advocates of special juvenile courts argued that children's cases should not be tried in public but in semiprivacy. Indictment by grand jury, trial by jury, confrontation of accuser, and representation of counsel were denied children in juvenile courts on the theory that the court hearing was civil in nature rather than criminal. The power of the State to deal with children in this manner was based on the doctrine of *parens patriae,* which considered the child as a ward of the State. The State was concerned with the child's best interests.

In the Gault case of 1967 the Supreme Court of the United States (q.v.) extended to juvenile offenders some of the legal guarantees granted to adults. This decision requires juvenile courts to accord children the following basic rights: notice of charges; right to counsel; right to confrontation and cross-examination; and privilege against self-incrimination. Indictment by grand jury and trial by jury are not required, and children need not be advised at the time of arrest of right to counsel and the right to remain silent with respect to charges.

In Great Britain, the courts of chancery had jurisdiction over property rights of minors before the establishment of children's courts in 1908 to deal with delinquency.

An important adjunct of juvenile courts is probation (q.v.). Probation officers conduct social studies or investigations prior to sentencing; if the offender is placed on probation they supervise the child during the period of probation. It is generally agreed that a knowledge of behavioral sciences and training in social service work should be a requirement for probation officers. The juvenile court itself should have properly staffed detention facilities, medical and psychological evaluation clinics, and other essential social services. R.A.C.

JUVENILE DELINQUENCY, term employed variously to denote (1) most narrowly, a violation of law committed by a child or youth; (2) more broadly, the official adjudication by a juvenile court (q.v.) that a child within a stipulated age range (minimum usually seven, maximums variously sixteen, seventeen, or eighteen) has committed certain acts in violation of laws or ordinances, or is following a course of conduct or living in a situation justifying court intervention in his interests and in those of society; and (3) most broadly, the conduct of children or youths whose aggressive misbehavior, lack of respect for authority, or deviant patterns of social adjustment, although perhaps not strictly in violation of any law, is nevertheless disturbing to the community.

Causes of Delinquency. Determination of the causes of juvenile delinquency is extremely dif-

JUVENILE DELINQUENCY

ficult, one of the reasons being the variety of meanings delinquency can have in the lives of the delinquents themselves. Delinquency may consist of a single superficial or incidental act arising out of some temporary situation or stress not likely to recur. It may reflect a stage in a youth's development, to be followed by maturation into socially acceptable adulthood. It may be a fairly normal adjustment to an abnormal environment in which certain family, neighborhood, or juvenile-group standards may differ from and conflict with those of the community as a whole. Some delinquents may be mentally or emotionally maladjusted. Finally, delinquency may be chronic, that is, deeply rooted in the personality of the child and a stage in his development toward more serious antisocial or criminal behavior.

Another source of difficulty in determining the causes of delinquency is the methods employed by students of the subject. For example, researchers have often erred in assuming that certain conditions were causes of delinquency simply because statistical studies showed them to be present in high incidence in the groups of delinquents studied. Yet the same apparent causes may affect one child quite differently than another, and frequently the same causes may be shown statistically to exist among nondelinquents. Statistical studies of large groups of delinquents cannot give the same kind of insight as comparison studies of carefully selected pairs of individuals. The delinquency or nondelinquency of a child can never be predicted on the basis of a group statistical tendency.

In the past many unsuccessful efforts were made to find a single cause of delinquency. The Italian criminologist Cesare Lombroso (q.v.) and his followers developed in the 19th century the concept of an innate so-called criminal type marked from birth by certain physical stigmata. During the late-19th and early-20th century, social conditions such as poor housing, inadequate schooling, and child labor were stressed as causes. In the 1920's and 1930's considerable attention was given to the supposedly determining effect of mental retardation, and such concepts as "moral imbecile" and "sex moron" were widely accepted. Studies of hereditary degeneracy among certain notorious families had considerable impact during this period. Endocrine glands were also for a period considered as determining agents. During the 1930's and the early 1940's so-called delinquent areas and problem neighborhoods received much attention. In recent years the psychiatric explanation of delinquency holds that tensions may not spur antisocial behavior unless the vulnerable personality favors it.

Present-day students of delinquency generally reject any single explanation of its cause. Instead, they look for a combination of causes to be found in the home, the school, the neighborhood or community, and in the personality of the child himself.

The home situation has long been recognized as of special importance in the development of delinquency and in attempts to prevent or control it. Children deprived of one or both parents are, as a group, more prone to delinquency than those living in homes where both parents are present. Lack of positive discipline within the home, conflict between the parents or other disturbing interfamilial relationships, and expressions of antisocial or criminal attitudes are frequently cited as contributing to delinquency. Other conditions of stress in the family situation, such as serious poverty, deprivation, or illness, may also have harmful effects.

Children spend thousands of hours of the most significant years of their lives in school. Studies have indicated some close relationships between maladjustment in school on the one hand and the development of delinquency on the other. A significantly high percentage of delinquents are found to have been chronic truants. Similarly, the majority of delinquents are one or more years educationally retarded. They show also a rather high incidence of specific learning disabilities, such as difficulty in learning to read. The dull-normal slow learners, those with intelligence quotients ranging approximately from 75 to 90, are represented disproportionately among delinquents. Some studies have shown a significantly higher degree of conflict with the school or teacher among delinquents than among nondelinquents.

Some studies have emphasized the importance of the neighborhood or community in the development of delinquency. Certain neighborhoods have abnormally high rates of delinquency and crime. Generally of low socioeconomic status, such neighborhoods additionally have developed, for various reasons, social, cultural, or behavioral standards different from those of the community as a whole. Frequently people living in such neighborhoods feel apart from and oppressed by the larger community. Often within such a setting a juvenile society characterized by gang groups with aggressive or otherwise antisocial standards and patterns of behavior will develop. In such cases the primary loyalty of the child or youth is often

Efforts to curb juvenile delinquency begin in the home. A counselor talks with the family of a disturbed youth.
Family Service Assn. of America

to his friends rather than to the alien standards of the school or community.

Many studies of the causes of delinquency have turned to a deeper exploration of the personality and inner dynamics of the child himself. These studies have been concerned with the child's feelings of anxiety, frustration, inferiority, deprivation, or rejection as causes of such neurotic manifestations as unusual aggressiveness, hostility, instability, or egocentricity. Although emphasizing the individual, studies of this kind recognize that faults in the home, school, or community environments may provoke antisocial behavior in already disturbed children. See CHILD PSYCHOLOGY.

In recent years students of delinquency have attempted to discover what special causes underlie the apparent marked increase in juvenile delinquency since World War II. Long-term statistics on delinquency reveal a fairly even picture over twenty- or thirty-year periods, with cycles of increase or decrease within those periods. Statistical evidence of an increase in delinquency must be carefully interpreted, however. Statistics may reflect changes in the methods of research and analysis. They may reflect enactment of new laws relating to children or periods of severity or relaxation in the enforcement of laws. They may reflect, in part, actual changes in the culture that open up new possibilities for delinquent conduct, for example, the development and widespread use of the automobile. In 1967 the task force on juvenile delinquency of the President's Commission on Law Enforcement and Administration of Justice, established by President Lyndon Baines Johnson (q.v.), focused attention on such problems as urban slums, educationally handicapped children, and unemployed parents.

It is probable that drastic changes in social patterns have caused an increase in delinquency. The changes caused or accelerated by World War II and its aftermath have undoubtedly been profoundly disturbing to many young people. Peacetime military service in many cases has delayed their assumption of adult responsibilities. The war and the continued threatening world situation may also have contributed to the vogue of violence reflected in comic books, motion pictures, and television plays which, in the view of some researchers, is capable of precipitating delinquent behavior in especially susceptible children. Educational and

An innovation in the rehabilitation of juvenile delinquents is the prerelease center, in which inmates live for a period before their discharge. Under partial supervision, the youths find employment and contribute to their support.   U.S. Bureau of Prisons

psychological doctrines of extreme permissiveness are indicated by other authorities. Others hold that the gap between the "good life" emphasized in America and the limited access to it causes frustration and alienation among underprivileged youths who desire economic advancement. Without doubt, however, the most important changes in social patterns affecting delinquency have been those in American family life. An increasing disorganization of the family, a loss of the feeling of family integration and cohesiveness, is apparent in the growing number of divorces and desertions. Of great significance too has been the diminution of the father's status in the family, the loss of his role as the standard-setting and behavior-controlling authority.

Prevention and Control of Delinquency. Just as the causes of delinquency are to be found in a combination of conditions in the home, the school, the community, and the personality of the child, so efforts to prevent or control delinquency must, to be effective, deal with all four of these areas.

The home situation, which probably has the greatest influence in the determination of delinquency, is also the most difficult to remedy. Case work by social-service agencies with the family as a whole, with the parents, or with the children alone often has proved of some supporting or ameliorating benefit. The assistance of the church to which the family belongs is sometimes very helpful, as are the contributions of public agencies if poverty, unemployment, or illness is present. When the home situation cannot be much improved by outside assistance, efforts by the school, child-guidance clinics, or other agencies working directly with the child may help to increase his resistance to the harmful effects of the home environment.

The schools can do much to prevent or control delinquency not only by cooperating with other interested agencies but by correcting those defects in the school itself that may be helping to create delinquency. Among the contributions that a school can provide directly to the child are an efficient attendance service, designed to search out and deal with the causes of nonattendance, and a well-rounded student-service program, including health examinations, psychological counseling, vocational guidance, and special work with the physically or mentally handicapped. The school can do much also by analyzing and correcting the causes of unnecessary failure and retardation, thereby reducing the harmful effects of such experiences on young people. More adequate curriculum provisions for slow learners can somewhat reduce educational and other maladjustments among this group. Anything that contributes to the improvement of teachers' attitudes, understanding, and effectiveness with children and to making the school a happier and more satisfying experience for the child contributes signally to the prevention of delinquency.

The cooperation of many agencies is necessary to treat effectively those causes of delinquency that can be traced to the neighborhood or community environment. Public-health, housing, sanitation, and park departments may eliminate some of the physical conditions conducive to delinquency. Public and private social-service agencies, child-guidance centers, vocational-counseling and employment services, religious institutions, and cultural and recreational groups may deal with different aspects of the human problem. Experience has proved the desirability of coordinating the activities of all these varied agencies in dealing with a neighborhood or community, particularly one of the serious problem neighborhoods that in some cities provide an inordinate amount of the total delinquency. Probably the most important need is for better public understanding of the fact that the word "delinquency" denotes a wide variety of social maladjustment, not a single type of misbehavior.

Once a child has been officially adjudged a delinquent, his rehabilitation and retrainings are generally in the hands of legally constituted authorities. For this aspect of the delinquency-control program, extension of positive juvenile-court practices is necessary. To function adequately, a juvenile court requires a professionally trained staff both for preliminary study of the child and for probationary and follow-up supervision, close coordination with other community agencies, and the availability of a variety of resources for delinquents who have to be taken out of their homes and neighborhoods for brief or longer periods of time. Such resources include detention homes, study and diagnostic centers, residential treatment centers, specialized private institutions, foster homes, the services of volunteer workers, and adequately planned and staffed public institutions.

History. Since ancient times enlightened legal systems have distinguished between the juvenile delinquent and the adult criminal. The immature were not considered free agents and so were not morally responsible for their behavior. Hebraic law exempts the male child from sin until the age of thirteen. Under Roman law children under seven were not held responsible for their acts under any circumstances; those from seven to the age of puberty were not responsible if it were officially ruled that they lacked understanding of the nature of their actions; those from puberty to twenty-five years of age were to have their youthfulness taken into consideration in the prescription of punishment. Under the Napoleonic Code in France limited responsibility was ascribed to children under sixteen. In England from the time of Edward III (q.v.), King of England, in the 14th century, it has been understood that a child under seven is in all circumstances incapable of guilt for crime. A child from eight to fourteen years of age is presumed to be incapable of guilt unless evidence is given of the ability to "discern between good and evil".

Despite the apparent humanity of some of these statutes, the punishment of juvenile offenders until the 19th century was often incredibly severe, harsh punishments having been regarded as an effective deterrent to others. Less than two hundred years ago, under British law and the laws of the British colonies in North America, very young children could be put to death or deported for relatively minor offenses. Lashing, flogging, and other extreme corporal punishments were in vogue. The first institution expressly for juveniles, the House of Refuge, was established in New York City in 1824 so that institutionalized delinquents could be kept apart from adult criminals. Other children's reformatories were established in Pennsylvania in 1828 and in Massachusetts in 1847. The movement spread rapidly throughout the United States and abroad. These early institutions, however, frequently known as "industrial schools", were often very rigid and punitive.

In the second half of the 19th century increased attention was given to the need for special legal procedures that would protect and guide the juvenile offender rather than subject him to the full force of criminal law. Massachusetts in 1870 and 1880 and New York in 1892 provided for special hearings for children in the courts. In 1899 a committee of the Chicago Bar Association made studies leading to the preparation of the first juvenile-court law. The founders of the Chicago juvenile court believed that the child should not be dealt with as a criminal but as one in need of the type of care, custody, or discipline that "shall approximate as nearly as may be that which should be given by its parents". Most civilized countries throughout the world have established juvenile courts. In Norway, Denmark, and Finland special boards of child welfare deal with children's cases, and the Soviet Union entrusts the matter to the education authorities.

Besides the juvenile court, a number of other innovations in working with juvenile delinquents have appeared in the 20th century, among them child-guidance clinics, juvenile-aid bureaus attached to police departments or other official agencies, and special programs in schools. During the 1930's widespread enthusiasm was shown for local coordinating councils that brought together all those community agencies whose work related to child welfare. Youth-correction authorities have been established in various States, notably California, Massachusetts, and Minnesota, to coordinate the courts and other official agencies dealing with delinquency in a single comprehensive approach to the delinquency problem. The Office of Juvenile Delinquency and Youth Development of the Department of Health, Education, and Welfare (q.v.) provides information and coordination at the Federal level.

Understanding of the many problems related to juvenile delinquency and effectiveness in dealing with these problems have not increased steadily. From time to time apparent crises of various kinds have evoked demands for a return to such age-old and thoroughly discredited methods of coping with delinquency as harsh punitive measures against the offenders. Actually the problems of delinquency prevention and control are only part of the broader responsibility of society to help each child reach his highest level of personal and social achievement.

R.A.C.

K, eleventh letter and eighth consonant in the English alphabet. The letter appeared in its modern form in the Roman alphabet, in which it corresponded to the Greek letter *kappa,* which was written either as a somewhat simplified form of an earlier Phoenician letter or as a reversal of this form. The Phoenician letter, which was equivalent to the Hebrew *caph* or *kaph,* was in turn derived from an Egyptian hieratic character based on the hieroglyph for a bowl. The distinctive forms taken by the letter during its history may be summarized as follows:

K	𐤊 or K	𐤊	𓂝	🥣
Roman	Early Greek	Phoenician	Egyptian Hieratic	Hieroglyphic Bowl

The *k* sound was indicated usually in Latin and the Romance languages by the letter c, and in the scripts of these languages the k form survived only in certain abbreviations and words of foreign origin. Even in Anglo-Saxon, c was used for the *k* sound, but in the Middle English period c acquired an *s* or *sh* sound before certain vowels in many words of Latin origin (as in cinder and ocean), so that the letter c became phonetically ambiguous. Accordingly, k was substituted for c in words of Anglo-Saxon origin that kept the *k* sound before the vowels e, i, and y (such as keen, kin, and king, from AS. *cene, cyn,* and *cyning,* respectively). More recently k has been used in the spelling of a number of loan words from a great variety of sources.

In all the languages in which k has been a part of the alphabet, it has indicated substantially the same sound, that of a voiceless guttural stop or mute with the point of closure farther forward or back in the mouth according to the preceding or following vowel. This sound is also frequently expressed by c, ck, ch, and q. The ck spelling represents a form of consonant doubling frequent in Anglo-Saxon after a short vowel; when the sound is a final stop, as in back, buck, and stick, the doubling is, strictly speaking, unnecessary, and in modern English the spelling is accordingly often simplified by omitting the k, as in music(k), traffic(k), and public(k). The letter k is still found as a silent letter in initial positions before n in such words as knight and know.

As an abbreviation, the capital K is used for titles such as Knight or King, and for the king in chess. The capital or lowercase K is used for kilo or kilogram. In chemistry K is the symbol for potassium (originally kalium); in assaying and jewelry work, k stands for carat (or karat), and in physics for cathode (Gr. *kathodos*); in the phrase vitamin K, it stands for coagulation (Dan. *koagulation*). As a symbol the capital or lowercase K is used to indicate the tenth or, when J is used for the tenth, the eleventh in a class, order, group, or series. K was used in medieval Roman numerals for the number 250, or, in the form K̄, for 250,000. In mathematics and physics K is a common symbol for a constant, particularly as a coefficient; in spectroscopy it stands for a Fraunhofer spectral line (*see* FRAUNHOFER LINES) caused by calcium; and in physics it indicates temperature on the Kelvin scale (*see* HEAT: *Temperature Scales*). As a qualifying noun, K is used in compound words to describe something having the form of the capital K. M.P.

K2, mountain peak in Asia. *See* KARAKORAM.

KAABA. *See* MECCA.

KABALEVSKY, Dmitri (Borisovich) (1904–), Soviet composer, born in Saint Petersburg (now Leningrad), and educated at the Scriabin Music School and the Moscow Conservatory. His music, which often makes use of Russian folk melodies, is heavily nationalistic and politically oriented. Symphony No. 3 is subtitled *Requiem* for Lenin; and his opera *Before Moscow*, written for the 25th anniversary of the Russian Revolution in 1942, celebrates the defense of the capital in World War II. Kabalevsky also wrote a chorale, *Our Great Fatherland*, in 1942. He wrote the musical score for a number of Soviet films.

KABUKI. See JAPANESE DRAMA; JAPANESE MUSIC: *Dramatic Music*.

KABUL, city and capital of Afghanistan, and capital of Kabul Province, on the Kabul R., about 75 miles W. of Jalalabad. Kabul is the political, economic, and cultural center of the country. The city commands the important trade routes into India and West Pakistan Province, notably the Khyber Pass (q.v.). Kabul has fruit canneries, textile plants, and munitions plants. Places of interest include a royal palace, Kabul University, and a fortress called the Bala Hissar. Invasions of India were made through the city by Alexander III, King of Macedonia, called the Great, and the Mongol conquerors Baber and Genghis Khan (qq.v.). In 1504 Kabul was made the capital of Baber's conquests; between 1526 and 1738 it belonged to the Empire of Delhi; it became the capital of Afghanistan in the 18th century. The city was occupied by British forces in 1839, 1842, and 1879; see AFGHANISTAN: *History*. Pop. (1971 est.) 318,094.

KABUL, chief river of Afghanistan, rising at the base of the Unai pass in the Paghman range. After flowing generally E. across Afghanistan and entering W. Pakistan through the Mohmand Hills, the river joins the Indus R. at Attock. It passes through the Afghan cities of Kabul and Jalalabad. The Kabul is used chiefly for irrigation; a dam has been constructed for this purpose at Jalalabad. The river is about 360 mi. long and is navigable below Jalalabad.

KABYLES, Berbers (q.v.) of coastal Algeria, Tunisia, and of some oases in the Sahara, organized in a confederation of tribes. The Kabyles of

On a street in Kabul, a primitive Ferris wheel draws a crowd of youngsters. The ride is driven by man power. **UPI**

KÁDÁR

the mountainous coastal region of Algeria inhabit a region known as Kabylia. The region is divided by the Sahel-Soummam valley into Greater Kabylia on the west, with mountains rising 7500 ft. above sea level, and Little or Lesser Kabylia on the east, with an average height of about 3000 ft.

The vernacular of the Kabyles is Hamitic; see HAMITIC LANGUAGES. The people have relatively long heads and fair skin, resembling Europeans. The so-called Libyan type, comprising both brown-eyed brunettes and blue-eyed blondes, is the oldest pure strain of the Kabyle people, and the blond type may be descended from the blond Libyans represented on ancient Egyptian monuments. Intermixture of Libyan Kabyles with Arab and Negroid peoples has taken place.

The Kabyles are monogamous and patriarchal. They generally follow an agricultural economy and include almost 1,000,000 sedentary cultivators. During the French occupation of Algeria they were introduced to such occupations as trading, field labor, industrial work, and soldiering. The family group lives together in a compound composed of rectangular houses. Their pottery, which is made by the women without the use of a potter's wheel, is decorated in geometric patterns; it has been closely studied by archeologists because it resembles the pottery of ancient Greece; see GREEK ART AND ARCHITECTURE: *Geometric Period*. The Kabyles are Muslims of the Sunnite sect; see SUNNITES.

KÁDÁR, János, original name JÁNOS CSERMANCK (1912–   ), Hungarian Communist Party leader, born in a Hungarian village (then in Austria-Hungary) and educated in the village school. In 1931 he joined the outlawed Hungarian Communist Party and was arrested several times during the 1930's for illegal political activities. In 1946 he was elected a deputy secretary-general of the Hungarian Communist Party and in 1949 he became minister of the interior and head of the secret police. He was arrested in 1951 by Mátyás Rákosi (q.v.), Hungarian premier, and charged with treason. After his release in 1953 he quickly rose to influence again and was instrumental in forcing Rákosi to resign in 1956. Later that year he became first secretary of the Socialist Workers' Party (a coalition of parties including the Communist Party) and deputy premier in the government formed by the moderate Communist Imre Nagy (1898–1956). After the downfall of Nagy, following the suppression of the Hungarian revolution by the Soviet army in November, 1956, Kádár immediately formed a new government and was its premier until 1958. He held the premiership again from 1961 to 1965. See HUNGARY: *History*.

KADDISH. See PRAYER, JEWISH.

KADIKÖY, city of Turkey, on the Sea of Marmara, about 4 miles S.E. of İstanbul, of which it is a residential suburb. It is the Asian rail terminus and is connected to the Galata Bridge steamer port by ferry. Few traces remain of more than 2500 years of history. Kadiköy was possibly a Phoenician site; the first known settlement was the colony of Chalcedon, established by Greeks from Megaris in 685 B.C. Later Kadiköy was under Persian, Greek, Bithynian, Roman, and Byzantine rule; the 4th General Ecumenical Council was held here in 451 A.D. Ravaged in the 6th century, Kadiköy fell to the Ottoman Turks in 1350; it was first named Kaleca Dünya. Pop. (1970) 237,519.

KADUNA, city of Nigeria, in Kano State, on the Kaduna R., 130 miles S.W. of Kano. A major rail junction, the city trades in cotton, livestock, durra sorghum, and ginger. Manufactures include textiles, machinery, steel, aluminum and petroleum products, and bearings. Kaduna is the site of a teachers' college, a technical institute, a museum, and a library. Pop. (1963) 149,910.

KAESŎNG, independent city of North Korea, coextensive with Kaesŏng District, 30 miles N.W. of Seoul. An industrial and trade center, the city is famous for its porcelain. Grain and ginseng are grown in the area. Nearby to the S.E. is Panmunjŏm, site of the armistice negotiations ending the Korean War in 1953; in 1965 a freedom pavilion was built on the South Korean side of the border. Tombs of ancient kings are found in Kaesŏng, which was an ancient cultural center and the Korean capital from the 10th to the 14th century. It served as capital of the Koryu dynasty until 1392 and was sacked by the Mongols in 1231. Sometimes called Songdo, the city was called Kaijo under Japanese rule from 1910 to 1945. Pop. (1970 est.) 175,000.

KAFKA, Franz (1883–1924), Austrian novelist and short-story writer, born in Prague (now in Czechoslovakia), and educated in law at the University of Prague. A civil servant who wrote in his spare time, he suffered from poor health, depression, and feelings of inferiority.

Kafka is considered one of the most significant 20th-century writers. The themes of his work are the frustration, anxiety, and loneliness of modern man. Kafka's heroes, oppressed by an inherent sense of guilt, find themselves in constant conflict with incomprehensible forces of good and evil. Their efforts to understand the authorities by whom they are pursued and the laws by which they are judged are doomed to failure. Kafka's stories blend reality and fantasy, and include passages of religious serenity. His style is remarkably lucid even when his subject matter is bizarre. In his most famous short story, "Die Verwandlung" (1915; Eng. trans., "The Metamorphosis", 1937), the hero awakens to find that he has turned into an enormous cockroach; rejected by his family, he is left to die alone. Kafka's philosophy is akin to that of the Danish philosopher Sören Aabye Kierkegaard (q.v.) and to the 20th-century philosophical and literary movement known as existentialism (q.v.). In literary technique his work has the qualities of both expressionism and surrealism (qq.v.).

Most of Kafka's works were published posthumously, although before he died he asked that his manuscripts be destroyed. Kafka is best known for three unfinished novels edited by his friend, the Austrian writer Max Brod (q.v.): *Der Prozess* (1925; Eng. trans, *The Trial*, 1937); *Das Schloss* (1926; Eng. trans., *The Castle*, 1930); and *Amerika* (1927; Eng. trans., 1938). Kafka's few short stories include "Das Urteil" (1913; Eng. trans., "The Judgment", 1945); "Ein Landarzt" (1919; Eng. trans., "A Country Doctor", 1945); "In der Strafkolonie" (1920; Eng. trans., "In the Penal Colony", 1941); and "Ein Hungerkünstler" (1922; Eng. trans., "A Hunger Artist", 1938). Letters written (1912–17) by Kafka to a German girl named Felice Bauer (to whom he proposed marriage) were published as *Letters to Felice* (1973). Several of Kafka's works were the sources of plays and motion pictures, notably in the film *The Trial* (1962) by Orson Welles (q.v.).

KAGAWA, Toyohiko (1888–1960), Japanese social reformer and evangelist, born in Kobe, and educated at the Kobe Presbyterian Theological College and Princeton University. Originally a Buddhist, he became a Christian while in his teens and not long afterward began a long and ultimately successful struggle for social reform in the slums of Tokyo. On his return in 1918 to Japan following study in the United States he achieved prominence as an organizer of labor unions and rural cooperatives. During World War II he advocated pacificist views, and after the war, he led in the fight for the democratization of Japan. His writings include *Christ and Japan* (1934) and *Behold the Man* (1941).

KAGOSHIMA, city and seaport in Japan, and capital of Kagoshima Prefecture, on S. Kyushu Island, on the N.W. shore of Kagoshima Bay, about 90 miles S.E. of Nagasaki. Kagoshima is the commercial and cultural center of S. Kyushu. The leading manufactures of the city include a famous type of earthenware known as Satsuma ware, silk and cotton goods, arms, and cigars. The city was formerly the seat of the Satsuma princes, and was the center of the Satsuma Rebellion in 1877. Severe damage was wrought in the city in 1914, when a volcanic island in Kagoshima Bay erupted. Pop. (1970 est) 403,000.

KAGUAN. See COLUGO.

KAIFENG, city of the People's Republic of China, in Honan Province, just S. of the Hwang Ho (Yellow R.), about 325 miles N.W. of Nanking. Kaifeng is a busy commercial center located in a rich agricultural region. Livestock, wheat, sorghum, millet, and cotton, the leading products of the surrounding area, are traded extensively in the city. Cotton weaving is the leading manufacturing industry. Among the noteworthy points of interest in Kaifeng is a pagoda constructed of glazed tiles. The city is also the site of the Kaifeng College of Chemical Technology. Founded in the 3rd century B.C., throughout the reign of the Five Dynasties (907–60 A.D.) and the Sung dynasty (960–1127), the city, then known as Pienliang, served as the capital of China. Kaifeng has been devastated by floods, earthquakes, and fires on various occasions. Late in the 12th century a colony of Jews settled in the city. The colonists maintained their racial purity and religious faith for many centuries, but were gradually assimilated, through intermarriage, by the Chinese. In 1948 Kaifeng was occupied by Communist forces. In 1954 the city was replaced as provincial capital by Chengchow. Pop. (1970 est.) 330,000.

KAILUA-LANIKAI, unincorporated community of Hawaii, in Honolulu Co., on Kailua Bay, on the eastern coast of Oahu, 13 miles N.E. of Honolulu. The community is industrial as well as residential, manufacturing metal and machine products and engineering equipment. At Kailua is a beach park, and nearby to the N. is the Kaneohe Marine Corps Air Station. Lanikai, a residential village and road terminus to the S., also has beaches. Pop. (1970) 33,783.

KAIROUAN, city in Tunisia, and capital of Kairouan Governorate, 80 miles S. of Tunis. The city, a trade center for cereals, olives, sheep, wool, and skins, produces leather goods, handicrafts, copperware, and ceramics. It was formerly known for its carpets and rose oil. Called the "City of 100 Mosques", Kairouan is one of the holiest of Muslim cities. The buildings, with Moorish and Saracenic inscriptions, date from the 9th century, and older Cufic inscriptions and Roman ruins are also found. Turreted walls and gates give the city the aspect of a medieval Arab fortress. Founded by an Arab emir in 671, the city became capital of the Ifrika

KAISER

Province of the caliphate in the 8th century and of the Aghlabite dynasty in the 9th century. In the 11th century Kairouan was capital of the Zirid dynasty, and in the 15th century it was an administrative center under the Almoravids. It was occupied by the French in 1881. The name is also spelled Kairwan and Quairwan. Pop. (1966) 82,299.

KAISER, Georg. See GERMAN LITERATURE: *Expressionism.*

KAISER, Henry J. (1882–1967), American industrialist, born in Canajoharie, N.Y. From 1914 to 1929 he headed his own company, which engaged in highway construction in British Columbia, Cuba, and Washington and California. In 1931, as chairman of the executive committee of Six Companies, Inc., Kaiser supervised the construction of Boulder Dam in Colorado. He subsequently was a director of the companies that built the Bonneville Dam in Oregon and the Grand Coulee Dam in Washington; see DAM. In World War II he managed Pacific-coast shipyards that handled a great deal of the wartime shipbuilding for the United States government. At this time he developed prefabrication and assembly methods that revolutionized the shipbuilding industry by dramatically increasing the speed of ship construction. In 1945, in association with the automobile manufacturer Joseph W. Frazer (1892–1971), Kaiser organized the Kaiser-Frazer Corporation, which was for a period one of the largest automobile-manufacturing concerns in the U.S.; the manufacture of automobiles was subsequently discontinued, however. He was also the founder of the Kaiser Steel and Kaiser Aluminum and Chemical Corporations. His son, Edgar Fosburgh Kaiser (1908–), is active in many enterprises formerly of concern to his father.

KAISERSLAUTERN, city of West Germany, in Rhineland-Palatinate State, about 35 miles w. of Mannheim. Among the important industries of the city are iron founding and the manufacture of cottons and woolens, machinery, structural steel, and bicycles. The city existed as early as 882 and was probably a royal residence during the Carolingian (q.v.) period. An imperial city until 1357, it has been the scene of many military engagements; the castle built by Frederick I (q.v.), Holy Roman Emperor, in 1152 was destroyed by the French in 1713. Following World War II, the city was incorporated within the French Zone of Occupation. Pop. (1970) 100,700.

KAKINADA or **COCANADA,** city and seaport of the Republic of India, in Andhra Pradesh State, on the Bay of Bengal and on the Godavari R. delta, about 315 miles N.E. of Madras. Navigable channels connect Kakinada with the Godavari delta canal system. In the city are rice and cottonseed-oil mills, salt works, and tobacco factories. The principal exports are cotton, rice, and oilseeds. Pop. (1971) 164,172.

KALAHARI DESERT, arid and semiarid plateau region of s. Africa, in s.w. Botswana and N. South Africa, between the Orange R. and the Okovanggo R. valley to the N. The surface is generally covered with red soil, except in the E., where large patches of sand are found. When a heavy rain occurs, pans of water form in the extensive mud flats. The Kalahari was crossed in 1849 by the British explorer David Livingstone (q.v.). Many of the Boers (q.v.) who attempted to trek across the Kalahari on their way from the Transvaal to Angola in 1878–79 died of thirst in the Kalahari. The desert is inhabited by Hottentots and Bushmen (qq.v.). Area, about 275,000 sq.mi.

KALAMAZOO, city in Michigan, and county seat of Kalamazoo Co., on the Kalamazoo R., about 130 miles w. of Detroit. The city is a manufacturing center and also an important trading and shipping center for an agricultural area noted for the production of peppermint, celery, orchard fruits, and grapes. The principal industries in the city are the manufacture of paper, drugs, fishing tackle, furnaces, heaters, truck transmissions, and air-conditioning machinery. Educational and cultural facilities in Kalamazoo include Kalamazoo College (Baptist, 1833), Nazareth College (Roman Catholic, for women, 1897), and Western Michigan University (1903), an institute of arts, a natural history museum, and a number of different musical organizations.

Kalamazoo was founded in 1829 as a trading post by Titus Bronson and was known as Bronson until 1836, when it was renamed Kalamazoo. The city was incorporated as a village in 1838 and chartered as a city in 1883. Pop. (1960) 82,089; (1970) 85,555.

KALB, Johann, known as BARON DE KALB (1721–80), German-born soldier who fought in the American Revolution, born in Hüttendorf, near Bayreuth. At the age of twenty-two he became a lieutenant in a German regiment of the French army, and fought with distinction in the War of the Austrian Succession and the Seven Years' War, rising to the rank of brigadier general by 1761. In 1768 Kalb was sent to America as an agent of the French government to determine the attitude of the colonies toward Great Britain. He returned to America in 1777, and joined the Revolutionary army with the rank of major general. He served briefly under General George Washington (q.v.) before the winter encampment at Valley Forge, and later was second in command to General Horatio Gates (q.v.) at the disastrous Battle of Camden, S.C., in August, 1780. Kalb's troops were finally forced to retreat before the army of Lord Charles Cornwallis (q.v.), but Kalb himself was wounded and captured by the British. He died of his wounds three days after his capture. See AMERICAN REVOLUTION.

KALE, or BORECOLE, common name given to a hardy biennial variety of cabbage, *Brassica oleracea* var. *acephala,* the leaves of which are similar in shape to those of the wild plant from which cabbage was bred. Colewort, *B. oleracea,* the wild ancestor, still grows along the coasts of western Europe. The leaves are usually curly and often finely divided. They ascend directly from the rootstock and do not form a head. The essential structure and method of culture are identical with those of cabbage. Kale is grown in the southern United States in fall and early winter for winter and spring harvest. The foliage is used in cooking as greens.

The collard is a vegetable plant in the same cabbage family as kale, but can be grown in warmer climates. Rich in vitamin A, the leaves, or collards, can be cooked and eaten in the same manner as kale. See CABBAGE.

KALEVALA, national epic poem of Finland (*see* FINNISH LITERATURE), written in eight-syllable trochaic verse. The anonymous poem tells of the adventures of three legendary Finnish heroes, Väinämöinen, Ilmarinen, and Lemminkäinen. The most important series of episodes deals with Väinämöinen's attempts to marry the daughter of Louhi, a hero of the northern land Pohjola. Another prominent story tells of the adventures of the heroes in their attempts to win possession of the Sampo, a magic mill that endlessly grinds out salt, meal, and gold for its possessor. The poem also gives an allegorical account of the creation of the world and of the defeat of paganism by Christianity in Finland. The songs on which the *Kalevala* is based were transmitted orally from one generation to another, and were not written down or published until the 19th century. A number of fragments were compiled and edited in 1822 by the Swedish-Finnish writer Zachris Topelius (1818–98). About twelve thousand lines, collected and edited by the Finnish scholar Elias Lönnrot (1802–84), were published in 1835; and an edition containing nearly twenty-three thousand lines was published in 1849. The *Kalevala* has been translated into English, German, French, Swedish, and other languages. Musical works based on the *Kalevala* include the symphonic poems *Lemminkäinen's Return* (1895) and *Pohjola's Daughter* (1906) by the Finnish composer Jean Sibelius (q.v.). A.G.

KALGAN *or* **CHANGKIAKOW,** city of the People's Republic of China, in Hopei Province, at the edge of the Mongolian plateau, near the Nankow Pass of the Great Wall (q.v.) of China, about 75 miles N.W. of Peking. Because of its location, Kalgan is sometimes referred to as "The Gate to Mongolia". An important commercial center, the city is linked by rail with Peking; a modern highway connects Kalgan with Ulan Bator, Mongolia, to which it exports considerable quantities of tea. Among the leading imports from Mongolia are wool, hides, and furs. Fur processing is the chief manufacturing industry. Late in 1948, during the civil war between the Chinese Nationalists and Communists, Kalgan was occupied by Communist forces. From 1928 until 1956 Kalgan was capital of the former Chahar Province. Pop. (1970 est.) 1,000,000.

KALI (feminine form of Skr. *kala,* "time"), consort of the Hindu god Siva (q.v.) in her manifestation of the power of time. She represents an aspect of the terror of Shakti, or the dynamic energy of a Hindu god, personified as his female consort. Kali is frequently depicted as being black, naked, wearing a garland of human skulls, having a frightening visage, laughing, and with blood-stained teeth and protruding tongue. She usually has four arms, symbolizing absolute dominion over all finite things. One hand holds a sword, the second holds a severed human head, the third is believed by her devotees to be removing fear, and the fourth is often interpreted as granting bliss. Kali, omnipotent, absolute, and all-pervasive, is beyond fear and finite existence and is therefore believed able to protect her devotees against fear and to give them limitless peace. Finally, as absolute night, devouring all that exists, she is sometimes depicted as standing on the corpse of Siva, which, like the garland of skulls, symbolizes the remains of finite existence. Kali's worshipers reportedly appeased her in the past with human sacrifices. She is propitiated today with the blood of animals, particularly goats, and birds. Under the title Bhavani, she was invoked by the secret brotherhood of murderers called Thugs (q.v.). The city of Calcutta (q.v.) received its name from Kali; Calcutta is the anglicized form of Kalighata, the name of a large temple, dedicated to her. See HINDUISM; INDIAN MYTHOLOGY.

KĀLIDĀSA *or* **KALIDASA** (fl. 5th century A.D.), Hindu poet and dramatist. He belonged to the second period of Sanskrit literature (q.v.), when the writing of the anonymous Vedic hymns gave way to the writings of secular drama and poetry by known authors. Kālidāsa is an outstanding figure in Oriental literature. He is particularly noted for his dramas, the most famous of which is *Sakuntala*. Kālidāsa also wrote two epic poems and many lyric poems, characterized by their fine descriptions of nature and of poignant emotions. His principal works have been translated into many languages including English. So many poems of different types are attributed to Kālidāsa that some critics believe them to be the work of three poets, all named Kālidāsa. See also DRAMA: *Drama of India*.

KALININ, formerly TVER, city of the Soviet Union, in the Russian S.F.S.R., and capital of the Kalinin Oblast, at the confluence of the Volga and Tvertsa rivers, 100 miles N.W. of Moscow. Kalinin is a major industrial and transportation center, producing textiles, heavy machinery, and railroad equipment. Known as Tver until 1933, the city was renamed for the Soviet leader Mikhail Ivanovich Kalinin (q.v.). Pop. (1970) 345,112.

KALININ, Mikhail Ivanovich (1875–1946), Russian statesman, born in Tver Province (now Kalinin Oblast). In 1898 he joined the Russian Social Democratic Labor Party, and the following year was imprisoned for political activities. With his release ten months later, Kalinin again engaged in revolutionary activities as a supporter of Bolshevism (q.v.) until 1904, when he was exiled to Siberia. He returned to Saint Petersburg (now Leningrad) the next year and participated in the 1905 revolution. In 1913 he was again exiled to Siberia, but he escaped and remained in St. Petersburg until the Bolshevik Revolution of 1917, in which he took an active part. After the establishment of the Soviet republic he was elected a member of the central committee of the Supreme Soviet. He became the first chairman of the Presidium of the Supreme Council in 1923 and as such was president of the U.S.S.R. He held the position until his death.

KALININGRAD, formerly KÖNIGSBERG, city of the Soviet Union, in the Russian S.F.S.R., and capital of Kaliningrad Oblast, on the Pregel R., about 200 miles S.W. of Riga. It is a major industrial and commercial center and is connected by a channel with Baltiysk, its outer port on the Baltic Sea. Among the principal industries of the city are shipbuilding and the manufacture of machinery, railroad equipment, chemicals, paper, lumber, and tobacco products. Kaliningrad is the site of many historic landmarks, notably the Schloss, or Castle, built in 1255, and the cathedral, begun in 1333. Adjoining the cathedral is a tower containing the tomb of the German philosopher Immanuel Kant (q.v.). Kaliningrad State University (formerly the University of Königsberg), founded in 1544, has a notable observatory.

Founded in the 13th century, the city was originally a fortress built around the Schloss erected by the Teutonic Knights (q.v.); it was named Königsberg (Ger. "King's Town") to honor Ottokar II, King of Bohemia (1230?–78). From 1457 to 1525 it was the official residence of the grand master of the Teutonic Knights, and from 1525, when the grand master proclaimed himself duke of Prussia, to 1618, the city was the residence of the dukes of Prussia. Frederick I (q.v.) was crowned the first king of Prussia in the castle chapel in 1701. During World War I the city was the scene of heavy fighting between the Germans and Russians. Following the war, Königsberg was made the capital of the former province of East Prussia (q.v.). The city was heavily bombed during World War II, and in 1945 was occupied by Soviet troops. By the terms of the Potsdam Conference (q.v.), the Soviet Union annexed the city and surrounding territory in 1945. A year later it was renamed Kaliningrad, in honor of Mikhail Ivanovich Kalinin (q.v.), president of the U.S.S.R. Pop. (1970) 218,000.

KALMAR, city of Sweden, and capital of Kalmar County, opposite Öland Island on Kalmarsund, a sound on the Baltic Sea, about 150 miles S.W. of Stockholm. Dairying, sheep raising, and stone quarrying are the important occupations of the county. In the town are shipyards and match factories. Parts of the fortress of Kalmarnahus, built on an island in the harbor, date from the 12th century. In 1397 the Union of Kalmar agreement, uniting Sweden, Norway, and Denmark under the Danish crown, was signed in the town; see SWEDEN: *History*. Pop. (1970) 52,774.

KALMIA, genus of evergreen shrubs, native to North America, belonging to the Heath family. The genus is named after the Swedish botanist Peter Kalm (1715–79), who traveled in North America. The regular, almost perfectly pentagonal flowers, borne in terminal corymbs, have a five-parted calyx, a five-lobed corolla, ten stamens, and a solitary, five-celled pistil. The fruit is a globular, many-seeded capsule. Mountain laurel, calico bush, or spoonwood, *K. latifolia*, is common on rocky slopes and sandy soils of the northeastern United States and eastern Canada. The shrub grows 3 to 6 ft. tall in the north, and as tall as 35 ft. in the southern part of its range. The bowl-shaped flowers are waxy-white or pink. Mountain laurel is the State flower of Pennsylvania and Connecticut. Sheep laurel lambkill, or wicky, *K. angustifolia*, is a smaller shrub, seldom more than 3 ft. high, native to bogs, pastures, and swamps of eastern Canada and the eastern U.S. It has crimson or pale-crimson flowers with pink-tinted stamens. Pale laurel, *K. polifolia*, is a straggly shrub, usually about 12 in. high, native to cool bogs and mountains of the U.S. and Canada. It produces small, rose-purple flowers. All three genera flower from late May to early July. Kalmias are cultivated in cool, shady gardens of the U.S. Leaves of kalmias contain a poisonous crystalline substance, $C_{31}H_{50}O_{10}$, harmful to livestock.

KALMUCKS, *or* KALMYKS, name of one of the major tribal divisions of the Mongols (q.v.), who lived originally in Chinese Turkestan (now Sinkiang-Uighur Autonomous Region). From the 15th to the 17th centuries A.D. the Kalmucks were nomadic herdsmen who competed with China for control of Peking (q.v.). In the 18th century they migrated to the lower Volga R. region in E. Europe. About 1771 a group of about 300,000 Kalmucks decided to return to China to escape the domination of Russia. They took part in one of the largest and most difficult mass migrations in recorded history. Attacked en route by Russians and Turkic tribes, only one third of the group reached Chinese Turkestan. There they were protected by the Chinese and eventually settled in the fertile basin of the Ili R. Some Kalmucks stayed on the steppes of the Volga region, and their descendants still live there. Kalmucks are also found throughout central Asia.

The czarist government of Russia attempted to settle the Kalmuck nomads on a reservation near Astrakhan', and the Soviet government established a republic for them in 1935. During World War II the Kalmucks collaborated with the invading Germans against the Soviet government. As punishment the Soviet government abolished the Kalmuck republic and exiled thousands of the people to Siberia. Many Kalmucks escaped, however, to Europe and the United States. In 1958 the Kalmuck Autonomous Soviet Socialist Republic was reconstituted, and many of the people were returned to the Volga R. region. Today they constitute more than half of the total population of about 248,000 in the republic. The people engage chiefly in farming.

The Kalmucks are unique among Mongols in practicing the Buddhist religion; *see* BUDDHISM. They are followers of the Dalai Lama of Tibet. The Kalmuck language, one of the Ural-Altaic languages (q.v.), contains a recorded literature consisting of myths, poems, legal codes, and historical narratives.

KALUGA, city of the Soviet Union, in the Russian S.F.S.R., and capital of the Kaluga Oblast, on the Oka R., about 100 miles S.W. of Moscow. The city is an important river port and manufacturing center, served by river vessels and several railway lines. Among the leading industries are smelting, brickmaking, brewing, and the manufacture of lumber, machinery, leather products, and foodstuffs. The first historical record of Kaluga dates from 1389. The city was incorporated into the grand duchy of Moscow in 1518. Under the Soviet government Kaluga became the capital of a separate oblast in 1944. Pop. (1970) 211,000.

KAMA, river of the Soviet Union, the largest tributary of the Volga R., situated mainly in the extreme W. of the Asian portion of the country. The river rises in the central Ural Mts. and flows in a circuitous course, successively N.W., N.E., S.E., S., and S.W. before emptying into the Volga about 40 miles S. of the city of Kazan. The river, about 1260 mi. long, is an important component of the national inland-waterway system.

KAMARHATI, city of India, in West Bengal State, on the Hooghly R., 7 miles N. of Calcutta. It is a part of the greater Calcutta area and chiefly an industrial city, with jute and cotton mills, tanneries, and plants manufacturing cement, paint, metal and rubber products, and pottery. Kamarhati is the site of Brahmmananda Kesabchandra College. Pop. (1970 est.) 198,523.

Mountain laurel, Kalmia latifolia — State of North Carolina

KAMCHATKA

KAMCHATKA, oblast of the Soviet Union, in the Russian S.F.S.R., in N.E. Siberia. The oblast includes the entire Kamchatka Peninsula and a small part of the mainland. The peninsula extends S.W. from the mainland for a distance of about 750 mi., separating the Sea of Okhotsk from the Bering Sea and the Pacific Ocean. The capital and chief city is the port of Petropavlovsk-Kamchatskiy (pop. in 1970, 154,000). The Koryak National Area, occupying the N. section of the peninsula, and the Komandorskiye Islands (q.v.), situated in the Bering Sea, are attached to the Kamchatka Oblast for administrative purposes.

The peninsula is traversed by two active volcanic mountain ranges extending from N.W. to S.E. and set apart by a wide, level, central area. The highest peak is Klyuchevskaya Sopka volcano in the E. range, which rises to a height of 15,584 ft. A tundra (q.v.) region, averaging about 2150 ft. above sea level, forms the W. coast of the peninsula, and the E. coast is bordered by cliffs. The principal river, the Kamchatka, empties into the Bering Sea near Ust'-Kamchatsk. Fishing is the chief industry in this area, the Caspian Sea being the only larger source of fish in the Soviet Union. Hunting is also important; the region has an abundance of polar bears, deer, seals, sables, otters, and mountain sheep. Natural resources include oil, gold, iron, copper, coal, and sulfur. Potatoes, vegetables, and grain are grown. The inhabitants of Kamchatka are composed of Koryaks, Kamchadals, Chinese, Koreans, Russians and Tungus (q.v.). Area, about 200,000 sq.mi.; pop. (1970) 287,000.

KAMEHAMEHA. See HAWAII: *History.*

KAMENSK-URAL'SKIY, city of the Soviet Union, in the Russian S.F.S.R., in the foothills of the Central Ural Mts., on the Iset R., 55 miles S.E. of Sverdlovsk. It is a rail junction and a major bauxite-mining and aluminum-refining center. Pig iron, pipe, tools, building materials and wood and food products are also manufactured. A power station is located here. The city was founded in 1682 as Kamenskiy Zavod, the first iron-smelting works in the Ural Mts. The name was changed first to Kamensk and then, about 1930, to its present form. Most of the industry has developed since the city was chartered in 1935. The name is sometimes spelled Kamensk-Uralski. Pop. (1970) 169,000.

KAMERLINGH ONNES, Heike (1853–1926), Dutch physicist, born in Groningen, and educated at the University of Groningen. He was professor of physics at the University of Leiden from 1882 until his death. Best known for his work in cryogenics (q.v.), or the study of the production and effects of extremely low temperatures, he succeeded in liquefying helium (q.v.) for the first time in 1908. He studied the effects of extreme cold on a number of gases and metals, and made significant discoveries relating to increased electrical conductivity at temperatures approaching absolute zero. He was awarded the 1913 Nobel Prize in physics.

KAMIKAZE. See WORLD WAR II: *Invasion of the Philippines; Battles for Iwo Jima and Okinawa.*

KAMPALA, city and capital of Uganda, in Buganda Region, near Lake Victoria, about 75 miles N.E. of Entebbe, and about 300 miles N.W. of Nairobi, Kenya. The city trades in livestock, hides, coffee, cotton, and sugarcane; industries include flour and sugar milling, cotton ginning, tanning, coffee processing, and manufacturing of textiles, cigarettes, and cement. Port Bell, a lake port 6 miles to the S.E., is connected with Kampala by road and rail. Kampala is the site of government buildings, of the National Theater, and of the Uganda Museum, which was government headquarters from 1900 to 1905. On Old Kampala Hill a tablet marks the site of a fort established by the British in 1890, and on Kasaubi Hill are tombs of the kabakas (kings) of Buganda. Nearby to the N.W. is Makerere, with the University College of East Africa, founded in 1938. Mengo, to the S.W., was the traditional capital of the kingdom of Buganda, formally dissolved in 1967. Kampala was capital of the British protectorate from 1900 to 1905 and succeeded Entebbe when the country became independent in 1962. Pop. (greater city; 1969) 330,700.

KANARESE, name of a group of Dravidian (q.v.) peoples of India, who speak a Dravidian language called Kannada, or Kanarese. Located principally in Mysore and Andhra Pradesh states, they number about 14,500,000. Their language, which closely resembles Tamil and Telugu, two other important members of the Dravidian family, is transcribed in an alphabet derived from ancient Hindi. A large body of literature, some of which dates from as early as the 12th century A.D., is written in Kannada.

KANAWHA *or* **GREAT KANAWHA,** river of west-central West Virginia, formed by the confluence of two headstreams, the New and Gauley rivers at Gauley Bridge in Fayette Co. The Kanawha is navigable and flows about 97 miles N.W. across the State until it meets the Ohio R. at Point Pleasant. The largest city on the course of the river is Charleston. The Little Kanawha R. is a parallel tributary of the Ohio R.

KANAZAWA, city and seaport in Japan, on Honshu Island, 290 miles N.W. of Tokyo. Kanazawa is an industrial center producing machinery, textiles, porcelain and lacquer ware. The 22-acre Kenroku Park contains the largest landscaped gardens in Japan. Pop. (1970) 361,379.

KANCHENJUNGA, peak of the Himalaya and the third-highest mountain in the world, on the frontier between Nepal and Sikkim. The mountain has five peaks; the highest is 28,208 ft. above sea level. In 1929 a Bavarian expedition attempted to climb the mountain, but failed. In 1931 a German party set out to make the ascent. Two members of the party were killed in a fall, and the group was forced to abandon the climb. The summit was finally reached in 1955 by a British expedition led by Welsh educator and mountaineer Dr. Charles Evans (1918–), who led the expedition that conquered Mt. Everest (q.v.). But in deference to local superstition they did not scale the crest.

KANCHIPURAM, *or* CONJEEVERAM, city of the Republic of India, in Tamil Nadu State about 45 miles s.w. of Madras. The only important industry is the weaving of cotton and silk fabrics. It was important before the Christian era, and is one of the most sacred cities of southern India, and is known as the Benares of the South. The city contains a number of imposing temples and shrines, some of which are many centuries old. Pop. (1971) 110,505.

KANDAHAR *or* **QANDAHAR,** city of Afghanistan, in Kandahar Province, about 250 miles s.w. of Kabul. Kandahar, the second-largest city and chief commercial center of the country, lies on a fertile, irrigated plain about 3400 ft. above sea level. The leading products of the province are fruit, grain, tobacco, silk, cotton, and wool. The city itself has fruit processing and canning plants and textile mills. A thick wall of mud construction encloses the city. Points of interest include bazaars and mosques, the tomb of the first Amir of Afghanistan, Ahmad Shah (q.v.), and the nearby ruins of the original city, which was destroyed by the Persian king Nadir Shah (1688–1747) in 1738. According to legend, ancient Kandahar was founded by Alexander III (q.v.), King of Macedonia, known as Alexander the Great. Pop. (1971 est.) 133,799.

KANDINSKY, Vasily (1866–1944), Soviet painter and author, born in Moscow. He left a legal career to study art in Munich at the Azbe School and with the German painter Franz von Stuck (1863–1928). With the German painter Franz Marc (1880–1916), in 1912 he founded in Munich the Blaue Reiter (Blue Rider) school of expressionist painting. Returning to the Soviet Union in 1918, he taught art and was director of the Museum of Pictorial Culture in Moscow in 1919. Two years later he helped found the Soviet Academy of Arts and Sciences. In 1922 he returned to Germany as a teacher at the Bauhaus (q.v.). He taught there until 1933, when he left Germany to live in Paris.

An excellent colorist and a highly skilled technician, Kandinsky's earlier works were marked by an interplay of rhythmic lines and exotic color, an intermediate stage between expressionism (q.v.) and abstract art; *see* ABSTRACT AND NONOBJECTIVE ART: *Kandinsky and Mondriaan.* His later work was more precisely geometric in form and completely abstract or nonobjective in content. Kandinsky was also a writer and theorist on art, and was regarded as an important

"La Flèche" (1943), by Vasily Kandinsky.
Kunstmuseum, Basel

KANDY

spokesman for abstract painting. His best-known book is *The Art of Spiritual Harmony* (1912; Eng. trans., 1914). Many of his works are at the Solomon R. Guggenheim Museum in New York City.

KANDY, or CANDY, city in Ceylon (Sri Lanka), about 80 miles N.E. of Colombo. Tea, cacao, and coffee are cultivated in the area, which is also a noted commercial center. Kandy was the ancient capital of the kings of Ceylon. The city is also famous as the site of perhaps the most sacred of Buddhist temples, Dalada Maligawa. Pop. (1971 prelim.) 94,000.

KANE, Elisha Kent (1820-57), American explorer, physician, and scientist, born in Philadelphia, Pa., and educated at the universities of Virginia and Pennsylvania. In 1842 he became an assistant surgeon in the United States Navy. He served in 1850 with the United States Coast Survey as surgeon and naturalist in the first expedition sent to search for the party of the British explorer Sir John Franklin (q.v.), who had been lost in the Arctic Region in 1845. In 1853 Kane was appointed head of an arctic exploration party, in command of the *Advance*. He sailed through Baffin Bay and Smith Sound into the basin now bearing his name and there his expedition remained for twenty-one months. The expedition explored as far as 80° 35' N., farther than man had previously gone. When provisions ran low, Kane and his group abandoned the *Advance* and set out for the Danish settlements in Greenland, reaching Upernivik in August, 1855, after a hazardous overland journey of three months. For his book entitled *Arctic Explorations: The Second Grinnell Expedition* (2 vol., 1856), Kane was awarded medals by Congress and the Royal Geographical Society. Other writings include *The U.S. Grinnell Expedition in Search of Sir John Franklin* (1853).

KANGAROO, common name for any of fifty-two species of diprotodont marsupial animals constituting the family Macropodidae, found in Australia and neighboring islands. Typical kangaroos have sheeplike heads, large, movable ears, slender chests, and heavy hind parts. They have short forelegs, with five unequal digits, and long powerful hind legs, with which they make their characteristic leaps. A large-sized kangaroo can cover a distance of 25 ft. in a single leap. The hind feet typically have four toes; the toe adjacent to the outside digit bears a long sharp claw, used in defense. The long powerful tail is used to balance the animal when sitting upright or leaping. The hide is tough, often covered with soft woolly fur; the animal is

Giant kangaroo, Macropus giganteus, *with a joey in her pouch.* Australian News & Information Bureau

hunted for its hide and for its flesh. Kangaroo hunting is a popular sport in Australia, and a special breed of greyhound is trained for the hunt. The kangaroo, although ordinarily a timid animal, is dangerous when at bay, pummeling its attacker with its forepaws and slashing with its claws. The kangaroo can be trained, and occasionally boxing matches are arranged between the animals and human beings.

Typical kangaroos are terrestrial, grazing animals that subsist chiefly on vegetation and occasionally do much damage to pasture crops. Female kangaroos, like the females of other marsupials, have special abdominal pouches. The newly born young finds its way into the pouch by following a path of fur that the mother's tongue has moistened. These pouches, in which the young are kept until about six months old, contain four mammary glands of which two are functional. Female kangaroos when pursued lift their young out of the pouches and cast them aside.

The best-known and largest species of kangaroo are the giant, or great gray, kangaroo, *Macropus giganteus*, and the red, or woolly, kangaroo, *M. rufus*. Both species reach a body length of slightly more than 5 ft. exclusive of the tail, which is 4 to 4½ ft. long. The filander, *M. brunii*, of the Aru Islands, observed in 1682 by the Dutch explorer Kornelis Philander de Bruyn (1652–1726), was the first kangaroo known to Europeans. *M. robustus*, a somewhat stouter species, is known as the wallaroo or euro.

Kangaroos of smaller size are commonly called wallabies, and are usually brighter in color than the large species. Many of these species are about the size of a rabbit; those of the genus *Lagorchestes*, particularly, so resemble rabbits that they are called hare wallabies or hare kangaroos. Similar species in the genus *Onychogalea* are called nail-tailed wallabies because their tails are tipped with a horny claw or nail. The red-necked wallaby, or brush kangaroo, *Wallabia rufogrisea*, inhabits thickets, while the rock wallabies of the genus *Petrogale* live in crevices in rocks. Unlike most other kangaroos the rock wallabies are chiefly nocturnal. The only arboreal kangaroos are the small tree kangaroos or tree wallabies of the genus *Dendrolagus*, whose forelimbs are almost as long as their hind limbs. These marsupials are inefficient in making their way either on the ground or in trees, but prefer an arboreal habitat.

The potoroos, or "rat" kangaroos, are small members of the Kangaroo family that form a subfamily by themselves. These animals resemble jumping mice, or jerboas (q.v.). Many of the species, although terrestrial, have a prehensile tail. The best-known genera are *Potorous*, containing the typical "rat" kangaroos, and *Bettongia*, containing the short-nosed "rat" kangaroos.

The musk kangaroo, *Hypsiprymnodon moschatus*, is a ratlike wallaby living in the rain-forest of N. coastal Queensland; it differs from all other kangaroos in having five toes on each hind foot and in having the tail almost completely naked and scaly. Scientists believe that this animal may be a connecting link between the kangaroo and the closely related phalanger (q.v.). See MARSUPIALS.

KANGAROO RAT, common name for two completely unrelated animals: a small ratlike kangaroo (q.v.) of Australia; and a kangaroolike rodent of western United States, treated in this article.

The American kangaroo rat, also called the pocket rat, is a member of the Pocket-Mouse family, Heteromyidae and like other members of the family has storage pouches on the outside of its cheeks. The animal is given its popular name because it hops about on its extremely long hind legs like a kangaroo. Typical kangaroo rats are about 1 ft. long; one species, the pygmy kangaroo rat, *Microdipodops megacephalus*, is only 6 in. long. The animals have soft silky fur and robust bodies. They live in colonies and burrow into the ground in desert regions, from which they emerge at night to seek the seeds and vegetation on which they subsist. Kangaroo rats are capable of surviving for long periods without water. A typical species is *Dipodomys agilis*, found in California. This animal is tan above and white below, and has a black tail. A black half-moon across its nose and a white stripe on each side extends over its haunches backward to the tip of the tail.

KANKAKEE, city in Illinois, and county seat of Kankakee Co., on the Kankakee R., 55 miles S.W. of Chicago. The city is the trade center and shipping point for a rich agricultural area producing grain. In the vicinity are large limestone quarries and coal mines. The principal industries include the manufacture of food products, furniture, farm implements, foundry products, hosiery, and chemicals. The city is the site of Olivet Nazarene College, established in 1907. Kankakee was first settled in 1832, and chartered as a city in 1855. Pop. (1960) 27,666; (1970) 30,944.

KANKAKEE, river of N.W. Indiana and N.E. Illinois. Rising near South Bend, Ind., the Kankakee flows S.W. and W. into N. Illinois until it meets the Iroquois R. From there it flows N.W. to its confluence with the Des Plaines R., about 12 miles

KANKAN

s.w. of Joliet. At their junction the Des Plaines and the Kankakee form the Illinois River (q.v.). The Kankakee is about 225 mi. long.

KANKAN, city in Guinea, and capital of Kankan Region, on the Milo R., about 175 miles s.w. of Bamako, and about 300 miles N.E. of Conakry. It is the inland terminus of the railroad to Conakry and at the head of navigation in high-water season on the Milo, a tributary of the Niger R. Rice is grown and livestock is raised in the area, and gold is mined nearby. The city, a trade center for cattle, sheep, rice, rubber, corn, potatoes, and yams, also manufactures bricks and soap. Normal and technical colleges are located here. Kankan was occupied by the French in 1891. Pop. (1964 est.) 29,100.

KANNAPOLIS, unincorporated community of North Carolina, in Cabarrus and Rowan counties, 22 miles N.E. of Charlotte. A company-owned mill town, Kannapolis was built in 1906 around textile mills founded in 1877. Sheets, towels, blankets, and other household goods are manufactured here. Pop. (1960) 34,647; (1970) 36,293.

KANO, city in Nigeria, and capital of Kano State, about 550 miles N.E. of Lagos. The city is walled and the houses are built of clay. The principal industries include the production of peanuts and the manufacture of morocco leather goods, metal wares, and cotton. In addition, there is a large trade in the farm produce and livestock of the surrounding area. The Kano area was one of the original Hausa (q.v.) states, dating from 900 A.D. Islam was adopted probably between the 12th and 14th centuries. The area was conquered by the Fula (q.v.) in the 19th century and held by them until 1903, when it was seized by the British. Pop. (1963) 295,432.

KANPUR, or CAWNPORE, city of the Republic of India, in Uttar Pradesh State, on the Ganges R., about 40 miles s.w. of Lucknow. The largest city in the State, Kanpur is an important rail and trade center and is noted for the manufacture of woolen fabrics. Its industrial establishments include textile mills, engineering works, tanneries, and factories for the manufacture of leather products. In 1857, during the Indian Mutiny (q.v.) against British rule, the British garrison and population, while fleeing from Kanpur, were massacred on the banks of the Ganges less than a mile from the city; see INDIA: *History.* Pop. (1971 prelim.) 1,151,975.

KANSA, or KAW, American Indian tribe of the Siouan stock (*see* SIOUX), speaking a dialect of the Osage language, and originally occupying several villages on the lower Kansas R. when Father Jacques Marquette (q.v.), the French explorer and cartographer, visited them in 1673. In the early 19th century their numbers were estimated at about 1300, but the population has steadily decreased since that time to about 200. Before 1840 their lands, along with those of the neighboring Osage Indians, were acquired by the United States government through treaty purchase and incorporated in the so-called Indian Territory to which many of the principal Indian tribes were being removed. In 1846 the Kansa themselves were removed to a reservation west of the Osage R. within the present borders of Oklahoma, where they have since remained. The culture of the Kansa was typical of that of the Plains Indians of the central U.S., since it was based in the main upon buffalo hunting and a nomadic or seminomadic life. The Kansa obtained social prestige and honor only in combat. Their villages consisted of large, semipermanent earth lodges. A celebrated tribal member was Charles Curtis, born in Topeka, Kans., Vice-President of the U.S. under President Herbert Hoover (qq.v.).

See PLAINS INDIANS.

KANSAS, one of the West North Central States of the United States, bounded on the N. by Nebraska, on the E. by Missouri, on the s. by Oklahoma, and on the w. by Colorado. The State is situated in the geographical center of the continental U.S. Kansas is rectangular in shape, the only irregularity occurring in the N.E. portion where the boundary is delineated by the Missouri River (q.v.). Kansas measures about 410 mi. from E. to w. and about 208 mi. from N. to s.

Area (13th State in rank)	82,264 sq.mi.
Land	81,787 sq.mi.
Inland water	477 sq.mi.
Population	(1970, 28th in rank) 2,249,071
	(1960, 28th in rank) 2,178,611
	(1950) 1,905,299
Altitude	680 ft. to 4039 ft.
Capital	Topeka (1970) 125,011
Largest city	Wichita (1970) 276,554
Entered Union (34th State)	Jan. 29, 1861
Nickname	The Sunflower State
Motto	Ad Astra per Aspera (To the Stars Through Difficulties)
Song	"Home on the Range"
Flower	native sunflower
Bird	western meadowlark

THE LAND

The terrain of Kansas falls into two great regional divisions. The smaller of these, comprising about a third of the area of the State, lies within the central prairies of the U.S. The larger division, extending westward from the prairie region, lies within the Great Plains; it rises from an elevation of about 2000 ft. in the E. to a maximum of 4039 ft. at Mt. Sunflower on the west-central boundary. A gently undulating plain broken by occasional hills and valleys, the Kansas prairies slope upward from an elevation of

KANSAS

INDEX TO MAP OF KANSAS

Cities and Towns

Abbyville	D 4
Abilene ⊙	E 3
Ada	E 2
Admire	F 3
Agenda	E 2
Agra	C 2
Albert	C 3
Alden	D 3
Alexander	C 3
Allen	F 3
Alma ⊙	F 2
Almena	C 2
Altamont	G 4
Alta Vista	F 3
Alton	D 2
Altoona	G 4
Americus	F 3
Andale	E 4
Andover	E 4
Anthony ⊙	D 4
Arcadia	H 4
Argonia	E 4
Arkansas City	E 4
Arlington	D 4
Arma	H 4
Ashland ⊙	C 4
Assaria	E 3
Atchison ⊙	G 2
Athol	D 2
Atlanta	F 4
Attica	D 4
Atwood ⊙	B 2
Auburn	G 3
Augusta	F 4
Aurora	E 2
Axtell	F 2
Baileyville	F 2
Baldwin City	G 3
Barnard	D 2
Barnes	F 2
Bartlett	G 4
Basehor	G 2
Baxter Springs	H 4
Bazine	C 3
Beattie	F 2
Beaumont	F 4
Belle Plaine	E 4
Belleville ⊙	E 2
Beloit ⊙	D 2
Belpre	C 4
Belvue	F 2
Benedict	G 4
Bennington	E 2
Bentley	E 4
Benton	E 4
Bern	F 2
Beverly	E 2
Big Bow	A 4
Bird City	A 2
Bison	C 3
Blue Mound	H 3
Blue Rapids	F 2
Bluff City	E 4
Bogue	C 2
Bonner Springs	H 2
Brewster	A 2
Bronson	H 4
Brookville	E 3
Brownell	C 3
Bucklin	C 4
Bucyrus	H 3
Buffalo	G 4
Buhler	E 3
Bunker Hill	D 3
Burden	F 4
Burdett	C 3
Burdick	F 3
Burlingame	G 3
Burlington ⊙	G 3
Burns	F 3
Burr Oak	D 2
Burrton	E 3
Bushton	D 3
Caldwell	E 4
Cambridge	F 4
Caney	G 4
Canton	E 3
Carbondale	G 3

⊙ County seat

Carneiro	D 3
Cassoday	F 3
Catharine	C 3
Cawker City	D 2
Cedar Vale	F 4
Centerville	H 3
Centralia	F 2
Chanute	G 4
Chapman	E 3
Chase	D 3
Chautauqua	F 4
Cheney	E 4
Cherokee	H 4
Cherryvale	G 4
Chetopa	G 4
Chicopee	H 4
Cimarron	B 4
Circleville	G 2
Claflin	D 3
Clay Center ⊙	E 2
Clayton	B 2
Clearwater	E 4
Clifton	E 2
Clyde	E 2
Coats	D 4
Codell	C 2
Coffeyville	G 4
Colby ⊙	A 2
Coldwater ⊙	C 4
Collyer	B 2
Colony	G 3
Columbus ⊙	H 4
Colwich	E 4
Concordia ⊙	E 2
Conway Springs	E 4
Coolidge	A 3
Copeland	B 4
Corning	F 2
Cottonwood Falls ⊙	F 3
Council Grove ⊙	F 3
Courtland	E 2
Coyville	G 4
Crestline	H 4
Cuba	E 2
Cullison	D 4
Culver	E 3
Cunningham	D 4
Damar	C 2
Danville	E 4
Dearing	G 4
Deerfield	A 4
DeSoto	H 3
Delia	G 2
Delphos	E 2
Denison	G 2
Dennis	G 4
Denton	G 2
Derby	E 4
Dexter	F 4
Dighton ⊙	B 3
Dodge City ⊙	B 4
Dorrance	D 3
Douglass	F 4
Dover	G 3
Downs	D 2
Dresden	B 2
Dunlap	F 3
Durham	E 3
Dwight	F 3
Eastborough	E 4
Easton	G 2
Edgerton	H 3
Edna	G 4
Edwardsville	H 2
Effingham	G 2
El Dorado ⊙	F 4
Elgin	F 4
Elk City	G 4
Elk Falls	F 4
Elkhart ⊙	A 4
Ellinwood	D 3
Ellis	C 3
Ellsworth ⊙	D 3
Elmdale	F 3
Elsmore	G 4
Elwood	H 2
Emmett	F 2
Emporia ⊙	F 3
Englewood	C 4
Ensign	B 4
Enterprise	E 3
Erie ⊙	G 4

Esbon	D 2
Eskridge	F 3
Eudora	G 3
Eureka ⊙	F 4
Everest	F 2
Fairview	G 2
Fall River	G 4
Florence	E 3
Fontana	H 3
Ford	C 4
Formoso	D 2
Fort Dodge	C 4
Fort Scott ⊙	H 4
Fowler	B 4
Frankfort	F 2
Franklin	H 4
Fredonia ⊙	G 4
Frontenac	H 4
Fulton	H 4
Galena	H 4
Galesburg	G 4
Galva	E 3
Garden City ⊙	B 4
Garden Plain	E 4
Gardner	H 3
Garfield	C 3
Garnett ⊙	G 3
Gas	G 4
Gaylord	D 2
Gem	B 2
Geneseo	D 3
Geuda Springs	E 4
Girard ⊙	H 4
Glade	C 2
Glasco	E 2
Glen Elder	D 2
Goddard	E 4
Goessel	E 3
Goff	G 2
Goodland ⊙	A 2
Gorham	D 3
Gove ⊙	B 3
Grainfield	B 2
Grandview Plaza	F 2
Grantville	G 2
Great Bend ⊙	D 3
Greeley	G 3
Green	E 2
Greenleaf	E 2
Greensburg ⊙	C 4
Grenola	F 4
Gridley	G 3
Grinnell	B 2
Gypsum	E 3
Haddam	E 2
Hallowell	H 4
Halstead	E 4
Hamilton	F 4
Hanover	F 2
Hanston	C 3
Hardtner	D 4
Harper	D 4
Hartford	F 3
Harveyville	F 3
Havana	G 4
Haven	E 4
Havensville	F 2
Haviland	C 4
Hays ⊙	C 3
Haysville	E 4
Hazelton	D 4
Healy	B 3
Hepler	H 4
Herington	E 3
Herndon	B 2
Hesston	E 3
Hiattville	H 4
Hiawatha ⊙	G 2
Highland	G 2
Hill City ⊙	C 2
Hillsboro	E 3
Hillsdale	H 3
Hoisington	D 3
Holcomb	B 3
Holton ⊙	G 2
Holyrood	D 3
Home	F 2
Hope	E 3
Horace	A 3
Horton	G 2
Howard ⊙	F 4
Hoxie ⊙	B 2

Hoyt	G 2
Hudson	D 3
Hugoton ⊙	A 4
Humboldt	G 4
Hunter	D 2
Huron	G 2
Hutchinson ⊙	D 3
Independence ⊙	G 4
Ingalls	B 4
Inman	E 3
Iola ⊙	G 4
Isabel	D 4
Iuka	D 4
Jamestown	E 2
Jennings	B 2
Jetmore ⊙	B 3
Jewell	D 2
Johnson ⊙	A 4
Junction City ⊙	E 2
Kanopolis	D 3
Kanorado	A 2
Kansas City ⊙	H 2
Keats	F 2
Kechi	E 4
Kendall	A 4
Kensington	C 2
Kincaid	G 3
Kingman ⊙	D 4
Kinsley ⊙	C 4
Kiowa	D 4
Kirwin	C 2
Kismet	B 4
Labette	G 4
La Crosse ⊙	C 3
La Cygne	G 3
Lafontaine	G 4
La Harpe	G 4
Lake City	D 4
Lakin ⊙	A 4
Lamont	F 3
Lancaster	G 2
Lane	G 3
Lansing	H 2
Larned ⊙	C 3
Latham	F 4
Lawrence ⊙	G 3
Leavenworth ⊙	H 2
Leawood	H 3
Lebanon	D 2
Lebo	G 3
Lecompton	G 2
Lehigh	E 3
Lenora	C 2
Leon	F 4
Leonardville	F 2
Leoti ⊙	A 3
Le Roy	G 3
Lewis	C 4
Liberal ⊙	B 4
Liberty	G 4
Liebenthal	C 3
Lincoln ⊙	D 2
Lincolnville	F 3
Lindsborg	E 3
Linn	E 2
Linwood	G 2
Little River	E 3
Logan	C 2
Longford	E 2
Long Island	C 2
Longton	F 4
Lorraine	D 3
Lost Springs	E 3
Louisburg	H 3
Louisville	F 2
Lucas	D 2
Luray	D 2
Lyndon ⊙	G 3
Lyons ⊙	D 3
Macksville	D 4
Madison	F 3
Mahaska	E 2
Maize	E 4
Manchester	E 2
Manhattan ⊙	F 2
Mankato ⊙	D 2
Manter	A 4
Maple Hill	F 2
Mapleton	H 3
Marienthal	A 3
Marion ⊙	F 3
Marquette	E 3

Continued on page 322

KANSAS

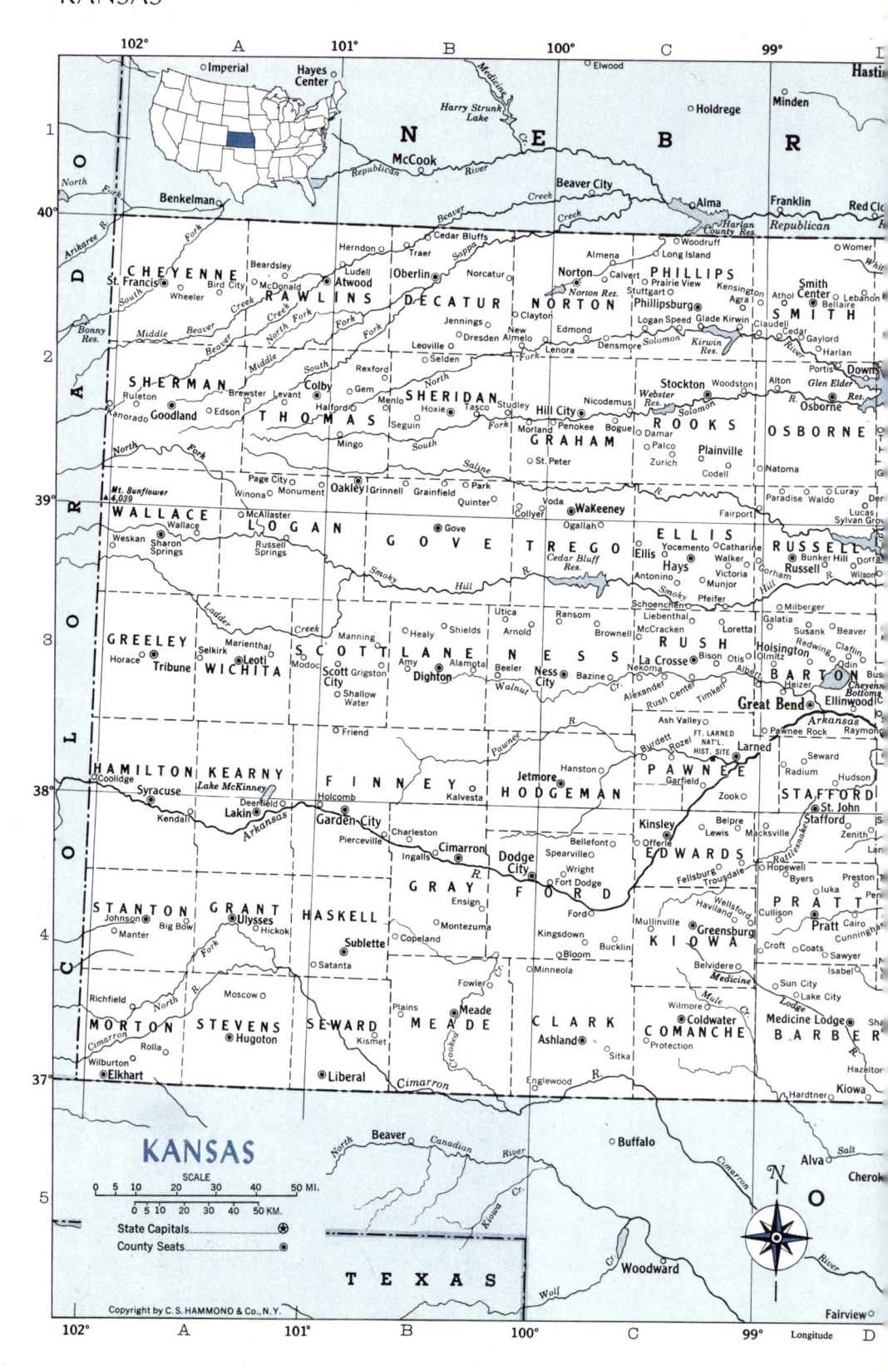

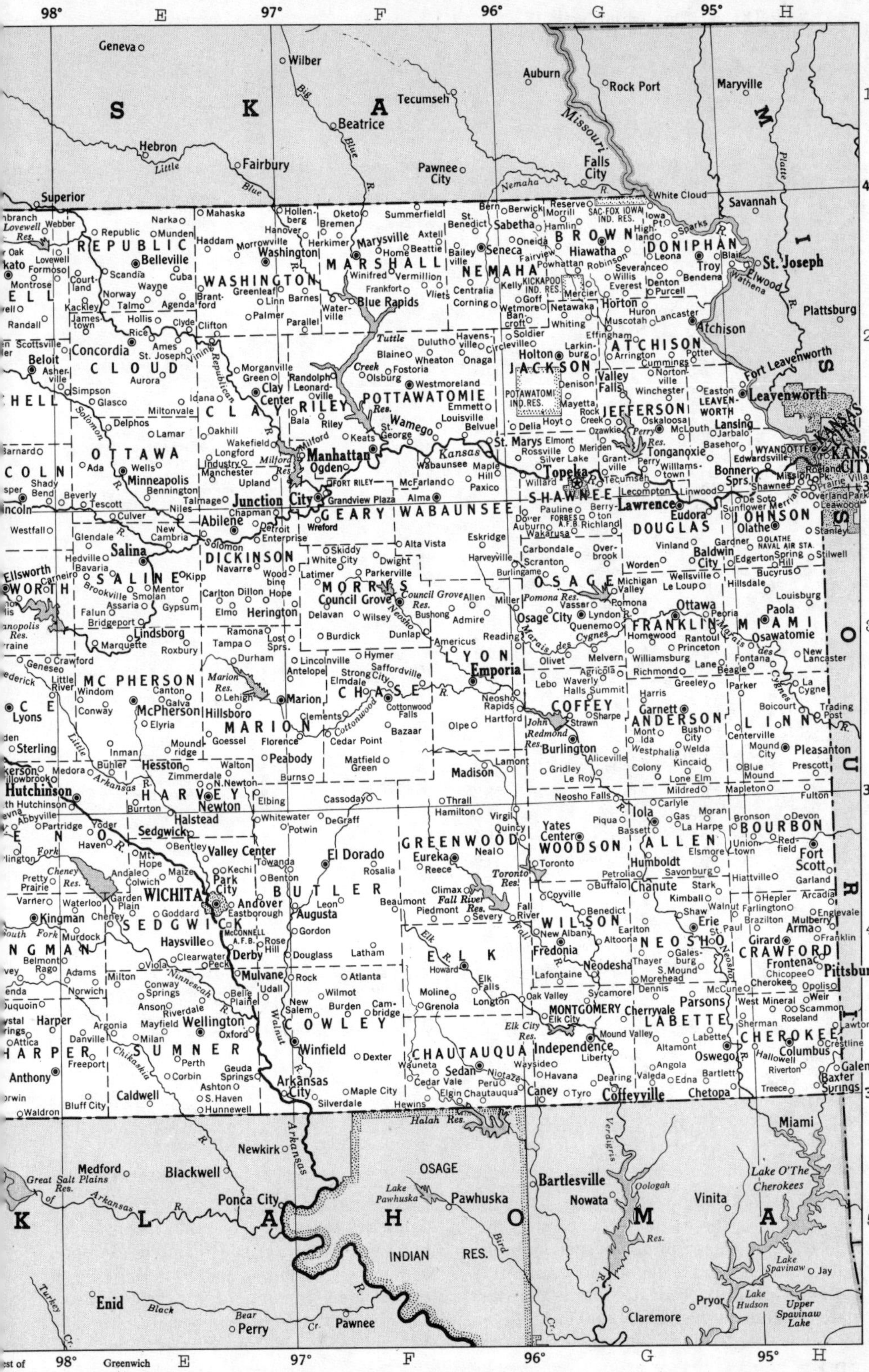
98°
E
97°
F
96°
G
95°
H
1
2
3
4
5
40°
39°
38°
37°
N E B R A S K A
M I S S O U R I
O K L A H O M A
REPUBLIC
WASHINGTON
MARSHALL
NEMAHA
BROWN
DONIPHAN
CLOUD
CLAY
RILEY
POTTAWATOMIE
JACKSON
ATCHISON
JEFFERSON
LEAVENWORTH
WYANDOTTE
OTTAWA
DICKINSON
GEARY
WABAUNSEE
SHAWNEE
DOUGLAS
JOHNSON
SALINE
MORRIS
OSAGE
FRANKLIN
MIAMI
MC PHERSON
MARION
CHASE
LYON
COFFEY
ANDERSON
LINN
HARVEY
RENO
BUTLER
GREENWOOD
WOODSON
ALLEN
BOURBON
SEDGWICK
KINGMAN
ELK
WILSON
NEOSHO
CRAWFORD
HARPER
SUMNER
COWLEY
CHAUTAUQUA
MONTGOMERY
LABETTE
CHEROKEE
Geneva
Wilber
Auburn
Rock Port
Maryville
Tecumseh
Beatrice
Hebron
Fairbury
Pawnee City
Falls City
Superior
White Cloud
Savannah
St. Joseph
Plattsburg
Belleville
Washington
Marysville
Seneca
Sabetha
Hiawatha
Troy
Atchison
Concordia
Clay Center
Manhattan
Wamego
Holton
Leavenworth
Beloit
Minneapolis
Junction City
Abilene
Topeka
Lawrence
Olathe
Kansas City
Salina
Ellsworth
Council Grove
Lyndon
Ottawa
Paola
Osawatomie
Lindsborg
McPherson
Marion
Emporia
Burlington
Garnett
Pleasanton
Hutchinson
Newton
Halstead
Iola
Fort Scott
El Dorado
Eureka
Yates Center
Humboldt
Chanute
WICHITA
Augusta
Kingman
Fredonia
Erie
Girard
Pittsburg
Derby
Mulvane
Wellington
Winfield
Independence
Parsons
Oswego
Columbus
Galena
Anthony
Caldwell
Arkansas City
Sedan
Coffeyville
Chetopa
Baxter Springs
Miami
Newkirk
Medford
Blackwell
Ponca City
Pawhuska
Bartlesville
Nowata
Vinita
Enid
Perry
Pawnee
Claremore
Pryor
Jay
OSAGE
INDIAN RES.
Lake O' The Cherokees
Missouri R.
Kansas R.
Arkansas R.
Neosho R.
Verdigris R.
Greenwich

KANSAS

Index to Map of Kansas — Continued from page 319

Marysville ⊙	F 2	Palmer	E 2
Mayetta	G 2	Paola ⊙	H 3
Mayfield	E 4	Paradise	D 2
McCracken	C 3	Park	B 2
McCune	G 4	Park City	E 4
McDonald	A 2	Parker	H 3
McFarland	F 2	Parsons	G 4
McLouth	G 2	Partridge	D 4
McPherson ⊙	E 3	Pauline	G 3
Meade ⊙	B 4	Pawnee Rock	D 3
Medicine Lodge ⊙	D 4	Paxico	F 2
Medora	E 3	Peabody	E 3
Melvern	G 3	Peck	E 4
Meriden	G 2	Perry	G 2
Merriam	H 3	Peru	F 4
Milan	E 4	Petrolia	G 4
Milford	F 2	Pfeifer	C 3
Miltonvale	E 2	Phillipsburg ⊙	C 2
Minneapolis ⊙	E 2	Piedmont	F 4
Minneola	C 4	Pierceville	B 4
Mission	H 2	Pittsburg	H 4
Moline	F 4	Plains	B 4
Montezuma	B 4	Plainville	C 2
Monument	A 2	Pleasanton	H 3
Moran	G 4	Plevna	D 4
Morganville	E 2	Pomona	G 3
Morland	B 2	Portis	D 2
Morrill	G 2	Potwin	F 4
Morrowville	E 2	Powhattan	G 2
Moscow	A 4	Prairie View	C 2
Mound City ⊙	H 3	Prairie Village	H 2
Moundridge	E 3	Pratt ⊙	D 4
Mound Valley	G 4	Prescott	H 3
Mount Hope	E 4	Preston	D 4
Mulberry	H 4	Pretty Prairie	D 4
Mullinville	C 4	Princeton	G 3
Mulvane	E 4	Protection	C 4
Munden	E 2	Quenemo	G 3
Munjor	C 3	Quinter	B 2
Murdock	E 4	Ramona	E 3
Muscotah	G 2	Randall	D 2
Narka	E 2	Ransom	C 3
Nashville	D 4	Rantoul	G 3
Natoma	D 2	Raymond	D 3
Neodesha	G 4	Reading	F 3
Neosho Falls	G 3	Redfield	H 4
Neosho Rapids	F 3	Reece	F 4
Ness City ⊙	C 3	Republic	E 2
Netawaka	G 2	Reserve	G 2
New Cambria	E 3	Rexford	B 2
Newton ⊙	E 3	Richfield	A 4
Nickerson	D 3	Richland	G 3
Niotaze	F 4	Richmond	G 3
Norcatur	B 2	Riley	F 2
North Newton	E 3	Riverton	H 4
Norton ⊙	C 2	Robinson	G 2
Nortonville	G 2	Rock	F 4
Norwich	E 4	Rock Creek	G 2
Oakley ⊙	B 2	Roeland Park	H 2
Oberlin ⊙	B 2	Rolla	A 4
Offerle	C 4	Rose Hill	E 4
Ogden	F 2	Roseland	H 4
Oketo	F 2	Rossville	G 2
Olathe ⊙	H 3	Roxbury	E 3
Olivet	G 3	Rozel	C 3
Olmitz	D 3	Rush Center	C 3
Olpe	F 3	Russell ⊙	D 3
Olsburg	F 2	Sabetha	G 2
Onaga	F 2	Saint Francis ⊙	A 2
Oneida	G 2	Saint George	F 2
Opolis	H 4	Saint John ⊙	D 3
Osage City	G 3	Saint Marys	G 2
Osawatomie	H 3	Saint Paul	G 4
Osborne ⊙	D 2	Salina ⊙	E 3
Oskaloosa	G 2	Satanta	B 4
Oswego ⊙	G 4	Savonburg	G 4
Otis	C 3	Sawyer	D 4
Ottawa ⊙	G 3	Scammon	H 4
Overbrook	G 3	Scandia	E 2
Overland Park	H 3	Schoenchen	C 3
Oxford	E 4	Scott City ⊙	B 3
Ozawkie	G 2	Scranton	G 3
Palco	C 2	Sedan ⊙	F 4

Sedgwick	E 4	Whitewater	E 4
Selden	B 2	Whiting	G 2
Seneca ⊙	F 2	Wichita ⊙	E 4
Severance	G 2	Williamsburg	G 3
Severy	F 4	Wilsey	F 3
Sharon	D 4	Wilson	D 3
Sharon Springs ⊙	A 3	Winchester	G 2
Shawnee	H 2	Windom	E 3
Silver Lake	G 2	Winfield ⊙	F 4
Simpson	E 2	Winona	A 2
Smith Center ⊙	D 2	Woodbine	E 3
Smolan	E 3	Woodston	C 2
Soldier	G 2	Yates Center ⊙	G 4
Solomon	E 3	Yoder	E 4
South Haven	E 4	Zenda	D 4
South Hutchinson	D 3	Zurich	C 2
Spearville	C 4		
Spring Hill	H 3	**Physical Features**	
Stafford	D 4		
Stanley	H 3	Arkansas (river)	D 3
Sterling	D 3	Beaver (creek)	A 2
Stilwell	H 3	Big Blue (river)	F 1
Stockton ⊙	C 2	Cedar Bluff (res.)	C 3
Strong City	F 3	Cheney (res.)	E 4
Sublette ⊙	B 4	Cheyenne Bottoms	
Summerfield	F 2	(lake)	D 3
Sun City	D 4	Chikaskia (river)	E 4
Sunflower	H 3	Cimarron (river)	B 4
Sycamore	G 4	Cottonwood (river)	F 3
Sylvan Grove	D 2	Elk River	F 4
Sylvia	D 4	Fall (river)	G 4
Syracuse ⊙	A 3	Fall River (res.)	F 4
Tampa	E 3	Forbes A.F.B.	G 3
Tecumseh	G 2	Fort Larned Nat'l	
Tescott	E 2	Hist. Site	C 3
Thayer	G 4	Fort Leavenworth	H 2
Timken	C 3	Fort Riley	F 2
Tipton	D 2	Glen Elder (res.)	D 2
Tonganoxie	G 2	Hulah (res.)	F 5
Topeka (cap.) ⊙	G 2	John Redmond (res.)	G 3
Toronto	G 4	Kanapolis (res.)	D 3
Towanda	E 4	Kansas (river)	F 2
Treece	H 4	Kickapoo Ind. Res.	G 2
Tribune ⊙	A 3	Kirwin (res.)	C 2
Troy ⊙	G 2	Ladder (creek)	A 3
Turon	D 4	Leavenworth, Fort	H 2
Tyro	G 4	Little Arkansas (river)	E 3
Udall	E 4	Little Blue (river)	E 1
Ulysses ⊙	A 4	Marais des Cygnes	
Uniontown	G 4	(river)	H 3
Utica	B 3	McConnell A.F.B.	E 4
Valeda	G 4	McKinney (lake)	A 3
Valley Center	E 4	Medicine Lodge	
Valley Falls	G 2	(river)	D 4
Vermillion	F 2	Middle Beaver	
Victoria	C 3	(creek)	A 2
Vining	E 2	Milford (res.)	E 2
Viola	E 4	Missouri (river)	G 1
Virgil	F 4	Nemaha (river)	G 1
Wakarusa	G 3	Neosho (river)	G 4
WaKeeney ⊙	C 3	Ninnescah (river)	E 4
Wakefield	E 2	Olathe Naval Air Sta.	H 3
Waldo	D 2	Pawnee (river)	B 3
Walnut	G 4	Perry (res.)	G 2
Walton	E 3	Potawatomi Ind. Res.	G 2
Wamego	F 2	Rattlesnake (creek)	D 4
Washington ⊙	E 2	Republican (river)	E 2
Waterville	F 2	Riley, Fort	F 2
Wathena	H 2	Sac-Fox-Iowa Ind. Res.	G 2
Waverly	G 3	Saline (river)	D 3
Weir	H 4	Sappa (creek)	B 2
Welda	G 3	Smoky Hill (river)	C 3
Wellington ⊙	E 4	Solomon (river)	E 2
Wellsville	G 3	Sunflower (mt.)	A 2
Weskan	A 3	Toronto (res.)	F 4
West Mineral	H 4	Tuttle Creek (res.)	F 2
Westmoreland ⊙	F 2	Verdigris (river)	G 5
Westphalia	G 3	Walnut (creek)	B 3
West Plains (Plains)	B 4	Walnut (river)	E 4
Wetmore	G 2	Webster (res.)	C 2
Wheaton	F 2	White Rock (creek)	D 2
White City	F 3	Wilson (res.)	D 3
White Cloud	G 2		

about 750 ft. in the E. The lowest point in the State, 680 ft. above sea level, is situated in the S.E. In this region is also situated the only mountainous area, a projection of the Ozark Mts. The mean elevation of the State is 2000 ft.

Rivers and Lakes. The two principal rivers are the Kansas River (q.v.), which joins the Missouri R. on the N.W. boundary, and the Arkansas River (q.v.) in the S. The important tributaries of the Kansas R. are the Republican River (q.v.) and the

Smoky Hill R., which, with its two principal affluents, the Solomon and the Saline, drains the N.W. quarter of the State. The S.E. region is drained by the Neosho and Verdigris rivers, which flow S. and enter the Arkansas R. in Oklahoma. Natural lakes are few in Kansas. The eighteen major reservoirs in the State include Milford Reservoir on the Republican R., Kanapolis Reservoir, on the Smoky Hill R., Cheney Reservoir on the North Fork of the Ninnescah R., Kirwin Reservoir on the Solomon R., Tuttle Creek Reservoir on the Big Blue R., Toronto Reservoir on the Verdigris R., and the Fall River Reservoir.

Climate. Kansas has a continental climate, with characteristically changeable temperature and precipitation. The annual mean temperature ranges from about 58° F. on the south-central and S.E. border to 52° F. in the N.W. The highest temperature recorded in the State was 121° F. (at Fredonia); the lowest, −40° F. (at Alton). Precipitation ranges from an average of 40 in. in the S.E. to 30 to 35 in. in the N.E., decreasing gradually westward to the Colorado border, where the average is 16 to 18 in. Snowfall averages about 10 in. annually in the south-central counties and increases gradually to 24 in. in the N.W.

The average annual number of days with measurable precipitation is 76 in Goodland, 83 in Wichita, 90 in Concordia, and 95 in Topeka. Storms and tornadoes are of limited extent and duration, although in dry periods dust storms occur occasionally in the W., and blizzards or severe snowstorms sometimes last as long as 48 hours.

Climate	Goodland	Topeka	Wichita
Normal temperatures (in ° F.)			
January maximum	41.5	38.3	41.4
January minimum	13.7	17.7	21.2
July maximum	90.5	89.2	91.7
July minimum	61.0	67.2	69.6
Annual	50.6	54.3	56.6
Normal precipitation (in inches)			
Wettest month	2.92	5.80	4.49
Driest month	.37	.97	.85
Annual	16.65	34.66	30.58
Latest frost	May 5	April 19	April 5
Earliest frost	Oct. 9	Oct. 26	Nov. 11
Mean number of days between latest and earliest frost	157	200	210

Plants and Animals. The E. area of Kansas has many native species of deciduous trees, including oaks, maples, and hickories. Kansas is the only State without native pines; the only evergreen plants are the Eastern red cedar and the yucca. The wild flowers of the E. region include asters, gentians, and many species of orchids.

The Kansas State capitol, in Topeka.   Kansas Industrial Development Commission

Some forest-dwelling animals such as the fox squirrel, previously restricted to E. Kansas, now occur in the W. along with such western species as the black-tailed prairie dog and the spotted ground squirrel. Under protection, the white-tailed deer has rebuilt substantial populations after virtual extinction in many areas; it is now the only big-game animal in Kansas. Of their once vast herds, only a few bison and pronghorns remain, and they are protected. Although considered to be a rather dry State, Kansas has at least 130 species of fish in streams and reservoirs.

Parks and Other Places of Interest. Fort Larned National Historic Site (q.v.), in Pawnee County, is a pioneer fortification on the Santa Fe Trail. Fort Scott Historic Area and other Kansas Historic Areas commemorate events in Kansas before and during the Civil War. The State maintains almost forty parks, including Clark State Park, in the S.; Atchison State Park, in the N.E.; Kingman State Park, near Kingman, with a fish and game nursery and quail farm; Lake Meade State Park, in the S.W., with buffalo and elk herds; Crawford State Park, in the center of the State; and Lake Scott State Park, in the W., containing El Quartelejo, the ruins of 17th-cen-

KANSAS

tury Pueblo Indian dwellings. Cheyenne Bottoms, near Great Bend, is a recreational area and waterfowl refuge. Historic points of interest include the Old Shawnee Methodist Mission, at Fairway; Hollenberg Station of the Pony Express, near Hanover; the Beecher Bible and Rifle Church, at Wabaunsee; and a replica of the main street of the cowboy town Dodge City.

Sports. Most of the sport fishing in Kansas is in stocked artificial lakes owned by the Federal, State, and county governments. Fish species found are black bass, catfish, walleye and northern pike, sauger, and crappie. Small-game animals and game birds are hunted, including cottontail rabbit, jackrabbit, gray and fox squirrels, bobwhite and scaled quail, ring-necked pheasant, and waterfowl.

THE PEOPLE

According to the 1970 decennial census, the population of Kansas was 2,249,071, an increase of 3.2 percent over the 1960 population. As calculated by the Census Bureau, the urban segment comprised 1,484,234 persons, 66.1 percent of the total, compared with 61.0 percent in 1960. The rural segment comprised 762,344 persons, 33.9 percent of the total, compared with 39.0 percent in 1960. Ethnically, the 1970 population was distributed as follows: white persons, 2,122,068; nonwhites, 124,510, including 106,977 Negroes, 8672 Indians, 1584 Japanese, 1233 Chinese, and 6044 others. The percentage of native-born residents was 98.8; of foreign-born, 1.2. The major countries of origin of the foreign-born, in order of rank, were Germany, Great Britain, and Yugoslavia. The 1970 population density averaged 27.5 per sq.mi., compared with 26.6 in 1960.

The chief cities are Topeka, the capital and third-largest city, a manufacturing center and the site of the Menninger (psychiatric) Clinic; Wichita, the largest city, a grain and livestock market, and a major industrial center; and Kansas City, the second-largest, a meat-packing and grain-storage center.

Kansas has four Indian reservations, occupied by the Iowa, Kickapoo, Potawatomi, and (jointly) Sac and Fox tribes.

Education. The public-school system of Kansas was established in 1855. Education is free and compulsory for all children between the ages of seven and sixteen.

ELEMENTARY AND SECONDARY SCHOOLS. In 1970 public elementary schools numbered about 1450 and public secondary schools, about 580. Enrollment in 1971 was about 346,000 in elementary schools and about 157,000 in secondary schools. Teachers in the public-school system in 1972 numbered about 13,000 in elementary schools and about 12,800 in secondary schools. In 1970 private institutions included about 200 elementary schools and 45 secondary schools; enrollment in 1971 was about 33,000 elementary and 10,000 secondary students. Teachers in private schools numbered about 2120 in the late 1960's.

UNIVERSITIES AND COLLEGES. In 1970 Kansas had fifty-three institutions of higher education, twenty-seven of which were public. University and college enrollment was about 101,000. State institutions include the University of Kansas (q.v.), Kansas State University, Fort Hays State College, Kansas State Teachers College, Kansas State College of Pittsburg, and Wichita State University. Washburn University of Topeka is a municipal institution. Private institutions include Baker University, Kansas Wesleyan University, Ottawa University, College of Emporia, McPherson College, and Benedictine College.

Libraries and Museums. The outstanding library in the State is the Kansas State Historical Society Library, in Topeka, with about 250,000 volumes. Museums include the Chanute African Museum, with exhibits of trophies from the expeditions of Osa and Martin Johnson; the Sod Town Prairie Historical Museum in Colby, with reproductions of the sod dwellings invented by the settlers of this treeless area; the Menninger Foundation Museum and Archives, in Topeka, with a psychiatric library including manuscripts of Sigmund Freud (q.v.), Benjamin Rush (see under RUSH), and others; and the Wichita Art Museum. Of special interest in Abilene are the Eisenhower Museum and Home, boyhood home of Dwight D. Eisenhower (q.v.), thirty-fourth President of the United States, and the Eisenhower Library, containing material pertaining to his Presidency.

THE ECONOMY

Kansas has a diversified economy. The per capita income in 1972 was $4455, or 99 percent of the average in the U.S. About 69 percent of all personal income is derived from private nonfarm sources, about 22 percent from governmental sources (including social security and military benefits), and more than 6 percent from agriculture. Most nonagricultural wage earners are employed, in descending order of numbers, in wholesale and retail trade, national and local governments, manufacturing, and services. Kansas has about 1130 hotels, motels, and other travelers' accommodations, with an aggregate annual income of about $46,000,000.

Manufacturing. According to a recent survey of manufactures (1971), production workers in Kansas totaled 89,600. The largest groups were

KANSAS

employed in the manufacture of transportation equipment; another significant segment was employed in the manufacture of food and kindred products. Almost 25 percent were employed in the Standard Metropolitan Statistical Area (q.v.) of Wichita, and a third of these worked in the city of Wichita. The Kansas area of the Standard Metropolitan Statistical Area of Kansas City employed another 22 percent. The value added by manufacture (see VALUE) in the largest industries totaled $553,300,000 for transportation equipment and $345,500,000 for food and kindred products. The production of chemicals and allied products, although ranking sixth in employment, ranked third in value added, at $328,200,000. According to the most recent published figures, the value added by all manufacturing in 1971 was $2,560,600,000.

Agriculture. Kansas has diversified agriculture, with a concentration on the production of livestock and livestock products. Principal commodities include cattle, wheat, hogs, and sorghum grain. In the early 1970's, according to latest available statistics, Kansas ranked first among the States in production of wheat and fourth in cattle and calves. Other major crops included corn and hay. Farms in Kansas numbered about 85,000 in 1972, totaling some 49,900,000 acres, and averaging 587 acres each. Cash income from crops, livestock, and government payments in 1971 was $2,194,200,000.

Mining. The mineral resources of Kansas include petroleum, natural gas, helium, cement, and natural-gas liquids. In 1971, according to the latest available statistics, mineral production was valued at $589,400,000 annually, representing almost 2 percent of the U.S. total. In quantity of production Kansas ranked first in helium.

In value and volume of petroleum, Kansas ranked seventh among the States. The leading counties in mineral production in 1971 were Grant, Ellsworth, Ellis, Seward, Barton, Butler, and Russell counties. Petroleum was produced in eighty-two counties, primarily Ellis, Barton, Butler, and Russell counties. Natural gas was produced in fifty-six counties, including Grant, Stevens, Kearny, and Morton; and natural-gas

Modern equipment harvests the rich wheat crop of Kansas. Kansas Industrial Development Commission

liquids in fourteen, including Ellsworth, Grant, and Seward. Cement was produced in Allen, Montgomery, Neosho, Wilson, and Wyandotte counties. The proved reserves of crude oil in 1971 were 539,305,000 bbl, and indicated additional reserves in the State were 20,500,000 bbl.

Forestry. The forest land of Kansas consists almost entirely of hardwoods. Entirely under private ownership, the commercial forest land comprises some 1,200,000 acres. It produces a net annual cut of sawtimber of some 36,000,000 bd.ft.

Transportation. The first railroad in Kansas was the Maryville, Palmetto & Roseport R.R., inaugurated on April 23, 1860, and now a part of the Union Pacific R.R. In addition to the Union Pacific, the State is served by ten Class 1 railroads, including the Atchison, Topeka & Santa Fe System, the Missouri Pacific R.R., with a total of about 8000 mi. of track. Rural and municipal roads totaled 133,987 mi. in 1970. Highways of the Federally aided Interstate Highway System totaled 822 mi. in 1970; Federally aided primary and secondary roads totaled 32,311 mi. There were 119 public and 176 private airports in 1971. Two international and several smaller airlines serve the major cities.

The refinery of the Skelly Oil Company at El Dorado is a typical installation of one of the major industries of Kansas. Kansas Industrial Development Commission

Communications. The first newspaper in Kansas was the *Shawnee Sun,* an Indian-language publication founded in 1835. The first English-language paper was the *Kansas Weekly Herald,* founded in Leavenworth in 1854. The State in 1971 had 50 daily newspapers with a total circulation of 651,000 and 15 Sunday papers. Among the leading papers were the Wichita *Eagle* and *Beacon,* the Topeka *Capital-Journal,* and the Hutchison *News.* Of some 58 AM and 25 FM radio stations operating in 1971, one of the earliest was KFH (1922), in Wichita. Television stations numbered twelve.

GOVERNMENT

Kansas is governed under the constitution of 1859, as amended. Executive authority is vested in a governor, a lieutenant governor, an attorney general, and a secretary of state, all elected for two-year terms, and other elected and appointed officials. Legislative authority is exercised by the Senate with 40 members and the House of Representatives with 125 members, elected for four-year and two-year terms, respectively. The legislature meets annually. The judicial system includes a seven-member supreme court, district courts, and various local and special courts. The State is divided into 105 counties.

Two Senators and five Representatives represent Kansas in the United States Congress.

Voting Qualifications. Suffrage is extended generally to U.S. citizens eighteen years of age who meet the residence requirements (six months in the State and thirty days in the town and election district).

HISTORY

The earliest known inhabitants of present-day Kansas included the Pawnee, the Osage, and the Kansa Indians (qq.v.). In 1541 the Spanish explorer Francisco Vásquez de Coronado (q.v.) and a force of men crossed the region from southwest to northeast in search of the land of "Quivira", which proved to be only a village of Wichita tepees. Little was known about the area until after 1803, when the greater portion passed into the possession of the United States as part of the Louisiana Purchase (q.v.). Between 1804 and 1819 the Lewis and Clark Expedition (q.v.), Lieutenant Zebulon Montgomery Pike (q.v.), and Lieutenant Stephen Harriman Long (1784–1864) successively explored parts of present-day Kansas. The region formed part of Missouri Territory until 1821, and it remained unorganized from that time until 1854. In 1854 the Illinois Senator Stephen Arnold Douglas (q.v.) introduced a proposal in the United States Senate for the organization of the territories of Kansas and Nebraska; *see* KANSAS-NEBRASKA ACT. The proslavery faction in Congress incorporated in the act a declaration repealing the Missouri Compromise (q.v.) of 1820, and leaving the question of slavery to be decided by the inhabitants of the territory. Passed in May, 1854, the act removed the final legislative barrier to the extension of slavery into the West. As soon as the bill received Congressional approval, proslavery immigrants from Missouri and Arkansas and abolitionists from the Northern States entered Kansas. The region became an arena of struggle between the contending groups, and factional violence was not to end until 1858.

On June 10, 1854, a meeting of proslavery adherents declared slavery existent in the territory. Settlers from Missouri founded Leavenworth in June and Atchison in July. Before the end of the year New England colonists, sent out by the Massachusetts Emigrant Aid Society, settled Lawrence, Topeka, Osawatomie, and other towns. On Nov. 29, 1854, during an election for a territorial delegate to Congress, armed bodies of men from Missouri took possession of the polls and cast 1700 votes out of a total of 2843. Elections were held in the following March for a territorial legislature. The Missourians again took over the polls and elected proslavery delegates from every district. Out of a total of 6218 votes, delegates in favor of slavery received more than 5400; however, the number of lawful voters in the territory was less than 3000. The

KANSAS

territorial governor set aside the returns from six of the districts and ordered new elections. Free-Soil candidates were victorious, but the proslavery party had a majority in the territorial legislature. Using Missouri statutes as models, the legislature passed stringent laws aimed at the antislavery movement. It became a capital offense to assist slaves in escaping to or from the territory, and a felony to circulate antislavery publications. Among other and similar legislation was a law requiring all voters to swear to support the Fugitive Slave Law. In July, 1855, Andrew H. Reeder (1807–64), the territorial governor, broke off relations with the legislature and became an active partisan of the Free-Soil Party (q.v.). He was replaced on July 31. The Free-Soil faction, refusing to acknowledge the legality of the territorial government, organized a rump convention, which met at Topeka on Oct. 23, 1855. The delegates adopted a State constitution prohibiting slavery after July 4, 1857, and excluding Negroes from the State. Following approval of the constitution in a referendum, an election for State officers and a legislature was held, on Jan. 15, 1856, and Charles Robinson (1818–94) was elected governor.

Statehood. Although the Free-Soil government sought to avoid hostilities with the territorial authorities, mutual antagonisms and provocations by proslavery followers deepened the crisis. The leaders of the Free-Soil Party were indicted for treason and imprisoned, following an incident at Lawrence. Shortly thereafter, on May 21, 1856, a proslavery mob sacked Lawrence. The retaliatory massacre of five men at Pottawatomie Creek by John Brown (q.v.) and his sons on May 23, 1856, marked the beginning of guerrilla warfare, which mounted in fury until broken up by U.S. troops toward the end of June. On July 4, 1856, the Free-Soil legislature met at Topeka but was dispersed by the Federal forces. A second attempt (Jan. 6, 1857) of the legislature to convene led to the arrest of its members. Governor Robert J. Walker (1801–69), who had become head of the territorial government in March, 1857, succeeded in reaching an agreement with Free-Soil leaders. The latter abandoned the Topeka constitution and agreed to take part in an election for a territorial legislature to be held in October, 1857. The Free-Soil Party triumphed at the polls. Meanwhile the proslavery party had summoned a convention. On Nov. 7, 1857, this body adopted the so-called Lecompton Constitution, guaranteeing the possession of all slave property already in Kansas. Only one constitutional clause, an article that legalized slavery for all time, was submitted to the electorate, and the Free-Soil partisans boycotted the referendum. Immigration from the North had meanwhile given the antislavery forces a majority in Kansas, and when the Lecompton Constitution as a whole was submitted to the people, in the following January, it was decisively rejected. The Free-Soil Party captured control of the territorial government on this occasion. The so-called English Bill, a compromise measure, was defeated at an election (August, 1858) ordered by Congress. On July 5, 1859, a constitutional convention met at Wyandotte (now a part of Kansas City, Kansas) and adopted (July 27) a constitution prohibiting slavery. This constitution was ratified in the following October. Delegates to Congress and members of the territorial legislature were chosen in November of that year, and on Jan. 29, 1861, Kansas was admitted to the Union.

In the Civil War Kansas sent to the field a larger number of Union soldiers, in proportion to its population, than any other State. The Kansas-Missouri border region was the scene of bitter guerrilla warfare throughout the conflict. Antislavery raiders before the Civil War and Unionist guerrilla bands that operated during the

Madonna of the Trail, a monument at Council Grove, commemorates the women pioneers of the western frontier.
KIDC (Kansas) Photo

KANSAS

war were popularly known as jayhawkers; see JAYHAWKER. On Aug. 21, 1863, the Confederate guerrilla commander William Clarke Quantrill (q.v.) and his men burned the town of Lawrence and massacred about 150 of the inhabitants.

For nearly fourteen years after the Union victory, which was followed by a great influx of immigrants into Kansas, the State was involved in recurrent wars with the Indians. Railway-building projects were instituted, and by 1872 more than 2000 mi. of track were in operation. Between 1878 and 1880 more than 40,000 Negroes migrated to Kansas. Prohibition became an important question in State politics after 1880. The movement encountered considerable opposition at first, but in 1890 an amendment to the State constitution was adopted outlawing the sale and manufacture of intoxicating beverages. Kansas remained a "dry" state until 1948, when the amendment was repealed; a liquor-control act was passed by the legislature in 1949.

The Republican Party has been predominant in Kansas. Of the twenty-eight Presidential elections held in Kansas, the Republican Party has been victorious in twenty-one. In 1968 the Democratic candidate, Lyndon B. Johnson, defeated his Republican opponent, Barry M. Goldwater (qq.v.). In 1972 Kansas gave the Republican candidate, President Richard Milhous Nixon (q.v.), 619,812 votes and the Democratic candidate, Senator George S. McGovern (1922–   ) of South Dakota, 270,287 votes.

KANSAS, river of N.E. Kansas, formed by the confluence of the Smoky Hill and Republican rivers at Junction City. It flows in a generally easterly direction for about 170 mi. to the adjoining cities of Kansas City, Kans., and Kansas City, Mo., where it joins the Missouri R. Other cities along the river are Lawrence and Topeka. In Kansas the river is known as the Kaw.

KANSAS CITY, city in Kansas, and county seat of Wyandotte Co., at the junction of the Kansas and Missouri rivers, opposite Kansas City, Mo. With Kansas City, Mo., it forms one of the major trade, industrial, and cultural centers in the Midwest. Livestock trading and meat packing are the chief industries in Kansas City, Kans., and the stockyards and packing plants of the city rank second only to those of Chicago. Kansas City is also noted as a flour-milling and grain-storage center. Other important industrial establishments include soap works, iron foundries, lumber mills, and oil refineries.

The city lies on both banks of the Kansas R. and on the s. bank of the Missouri R. Overlooking the industrial districts are many residential areas on nearby hills. Three hundred acres of land are devoted to public parks. The Soldiers' and Sailors' Memorial Building, with a large auditorium, and the Old Shawnee Mission are among the noteworthy public buildings. Educational and cultural institutions in the city include the school of medicine of the University of Kansas (q.v.), Kansas City Kansas Community Junior College (1923), Central Baptist Theological Seminary (1901), and Kansas City Conservatory of Music.

The site on which the city developed was settled in 1843 by a tribe of Ohio Indians, the Wyandot (q.v.). They sold their land to the Federal government in 1855 with the understanding that their burial ground, still preserved, should be maintained by the government. The lands of the Wyandot were settled in 1857, and the following year the settlement was incorporated as Wyandotte. Kansas City developed as a settlement near Wyandotte; in 1886 Kansas City, Wyandotte, and other surrounding communities were consolidated to form the present city. A commission form of government was instituted in 1909. Pop (1970) 168,213.

KANSAS CITY, second-largest city and port of entry of Missouri, in Jackson and Clay counties, at the confluence of the Kansas and Missouri rivers, adjoining Kansas City, Kans., with which it forms Greater Kansas City, one of the leading commercial communities in the United States. Transportation includes railroads and airlines.

Kansas City is the site of an important livestock exhibition, the annual American Royal Livestock Show; the livestock-exchange building is the largest of its kind in the U.S. The city is frequently the site of national conventions, and is the site of the Federal Reserve Bank of the 10th District. It is the home of the Chiefs, a professional football team of the American Conference of the National Football League, and of the Royals, a professional baseball team of the American League; and it is the part-time home (with Omaha, Nebr.) of the Kings, a professional basketball team of the National Basketball Association.

Among the educational institutions in Kansas City are the University of Missouri, Kansas City, established in 1929 as the University of Kansas City; Rockhurst College (1910), the College of Saint Teresa (1867), a college of osteopathy and surgery, a college of pharmacy, a conservatory of music, and four schools of theology. Cultural facilities include the Kansas City Art Institute, the Nelson-Atkins Art Galleries, and the Mary Atkins Museum of Fine Arts. Municipal parks cover more than 7030 acres. The city is governed under the council–city manager system.

Commerce and Industry. Because of its location near the geographic center of the U.S. and the excellence of its transportation, grain-elevator, and warehousing facilities, Kansas City is one of the most important markets and distribution centers in the country. It ranks high among U.S. cities as a market for livestock and hard wheat and as a distributing point for agricultural machinery. Major industries are wheat-flour production, oil refining, motor car and truck assembly, engineering, banking, and the manufacture of vending machines, iron and steel products, chemicals, and paints. Retail sales and Federal, State, and local government are important sources of employment.

History. The site of the present city was first permanently settled by French fur traders in 1821. The settlement was incorporated as the Town of Kansas in 1850 and received its first charter as Kansas City in 1853. In its early days the town was an important river terminal for trade with the southwest and one of the principal stations for wagon trains going westward. The coming of the first railroad in 1866 marked the beginning of the city's commercial importance.

Population. Between 1910 and 1950 the population of Kansas City increased from 248,381 to 456,622. In 1960 it was 475,539; in 1970 it was 507,087.

KANSAS-NEBRASKA ACT, popular name of a law enacted by the United States Congress on May 30, 1854, establishing the territories of Kansas and Nebraska in the former territory of the Louisiana Purchase (q.v.) and repealing the Missouri Compromise (q.v.).

Behind the bill lay Midwestern determination to compete with the South in building a transcontinental railroad, an ambition which required that Nebraska formally become a territory. Because the new territory lay north of the Missouri Compromise line, the South protested and slaveholding became an issue in the controversy. The bill, with repeal of the Missouri Compromise, was strongly supported by the administration of President Franklin Pierce (q.v.) and by the South. The chief sponsor of the act was Senator Stephen Arnold Douglas (q.v.), Chairman of the Senate Committee on Territories, who was accused by many abolitionist leaders of having Presidential ambitions. The act provided, in essence, that the question of slavery (q.v.) within the territories was to be decided by the inhabitants of the areas concerned before statehood was achieved. Although it was intended as a compromise measure, suitable to both the pro- and antislavery forces, the act precipitated so many armed conflicts, particulary in Kansas, that the territory became known as "bleeding Kansas". The most famous leaders in these conflicts were the abolitionist John Brown and the American desparadoes and Southern sympathizers Jesse James and William Quantrill (qq.v.). The members of the Whig Party, acused their leaders of catering to Southern interests. This dissension weakened the Whig Party, indirectly contributed to the rise of the Republican Party under the leadership of Abraham Lincoln (q.v.), and led ultimately to the American Civil War; see CIVIL WAR, THE AMERICAN.

KANSAS, UNIVERSITY OF, coeducational State university, founded in 1866 and situated in Lawrence, Kans., except for the school of medicine, which is in Kansas City, Kans. The university offers courses in the liberal and fine arts, engineering, architecture, journalism, law, pharmacy, medicine, education, nursing, and business. The degree of bachelor is conferred in all of these fields; the degree of master is conferred in some of the professional curricula and in the liberal arts; and doctorates are conferred in medicine, philosophy, and education. Founded in 1927, the Museum of Natural History contains about 300,000 specimens, including important collections in ornithology, vertebrate paleontology, and entomology. In 1968 the university library housed more than 1,250,000 bound volumes. Student enrollment in 1968 totaled 17,790, the faculty numbered 1211, and the endowment of the university was about $24,000,000.

KANT, Immanuel (1724–1804), German philosopher, born in Königsberg (now Kaliningrad, U.S.S.R.). He received his education in the Collegium Fredericianum and the university of his native city. At the college he studied chiefly the classics, and at the university he studied physics and mathematics. After his father died, he was compelled to halt his university career and earn his living as a private tutor. In 1755, aided by a friend, he resumed his studies and obtained his doctorate. Thereafter for fifteen years he taught at the university, lecturing first upon science and mathematics, but gradually enlarging his field to cover almost all branches of philosophy. Although his lectures and works written during this period established his reputation as an original philosopher, he did not receive a chair at the university until 1770, when he was made professor of logic and metaphysics. For the next twenty-seven years he continued to teach at the university and attracted a large number of pupils to Königsberg. Kant's unorthodox religious teachings, which were based on rationalism

KANT

rather than revelation, brought him into conflict with the government of Prussia, and in 1792 he was forbidden by Frederick William II (q.v.), King of Prussia, to teach or write on religious subjects. Kant obeyed this order for five years until the death of the king, and then felt released from his obligation. In 1798, the year following his retirement from the university, he published a summary of his religious views.

Kant's Philosophy. The keystone of Kant's philosophy, sometimes called critical philosophy, is contained in his *Critique of Pure Reason* (1781), in which he examines the bases of human knowledge and creates an individual epistemology (q.v.). Like earlier philosophers, Kant differentiates modes of thinking into analytic and synthetic propositions. An analytic proposition is one in which the predicate is contained in the subject, as in the statement, "Black houses are houses." The truth of this type of proposition is evident, because to state the reverse would be to make the proposition self-contradictory. Such propositions are called analytic because truth is discovered by the analysis of the concept itself. Synthetic propositions, on the other hand, are those that cannot be arrived at by pure analysis, as in the statement, "The house is black". All the common propositions that result from experience of the world are synthetic.

Propositions, according to Kant, can also be divided into two other types: empirical and a priori. Empirical propositions depend entirely on sense perception, but a priori propositions have a fundamental validity and are not based on such perception. The difference between these two types of proposition may be illustrated by the empirical, "The house is black", and the a priori, "Two plus two makes four". Kant's thesis in the *Critique* was that it is possible to make synthetic a priori judgments. This philosophical position is usually known as transcendentalism. In describing how this type of judgment is possible Kant regards the objects of the material world as fundamentally unknowable; from the point of view of reason, they serve merely as the raw material from which sensations are formed. Objects of themselves have no existence, and space and time exist only as part of the mind, as "intuitions" by which perceptions are measured and judged. In addition to these intuitions Kant states that a number of a priori concepts, which he calls categories, also exist. He divides the categories into four groups: those dealing with quantity, which are unity, plurality, and totality; those dealing with quality, which are reality, negation, and limitation; those dealing with relation, which are substance-and-accident, cause-and-effect, and reciprocity; and those dealing with modality, which are possibility, existence, and necessity. The intuitions and the categories can be applied to make judgments about experi-

Immanuel Kant — Bettmann Archive

ences and perceptions, but cannot, according to Kant, be applied to abstract ideas such as freedom and existence without leading to inconsistencies in the form of pairs of contradictory propositions or "antinomies", in which both members of each pair can be proved true.

In the *Metaphysics of Ethics* (1797) Kant describes his ethical system, which is based on a belief that the reason is the final authority for morality. Actions of any sort, he believed, must be undertaken from a sense of duty dictated by reason; and no action performed for expediency or solely in obedience to law or custom can be regarded as moral. Kant describes two types of commands given by reason: the hypothetical imperative, which dicates a given course of action to reach a specific end, and the categorical imperative, which dictates a course of action that must be followed because of its rightness and necessity. The categorical imperative is the basis of morality and was stated by Kant in these words: "Act as if the maxim of your action were to become through your will a general natural law"

Kant's ethical ideas are a logical outcome of his belief in the fundamental freedom of the individual as stated in his *Critique of Practical*

Reason (1788). This freedom he did not regard as the lawless freedom of anarchy but rather as the freedom of self-government, the freedom to obey consciously the laws of the universe as revealed by reason. He believed that the welfare of each individual should properly be regarded as an end in itself and that the world was progressing toward an ideal society in which reason would "bind every law giver to make his laws in such a way that they could have sprung from the united will of an entire people, and to regard every subject, in so far as he wishes to be a citizen, on the basis of whether he has conformed to that will". In his treatise *Perpetual Peace* (1795) Kant advocated the establishment of a world federation of republican states.

Kant had a greater influence than any other philosopher of modern times. Kantian philosophy, particularly as developed by the German philosopher Georg Wilhelm Friedrich Hegel (q.v.), was the basis on which the structure of Marxism was built; the dialectical method, used by both Hegel and Karl Marx (q.v.) was an outgrowth of the method of reasoning by "antinomies" that Kant used. Kant's pupil the German philosopher Johann Gottlieb Fichte (q.v.) rejected his teacher's division of the world into objective and subjective parts, and developed an idealistic philosophy that also had great influence on 19th-century socialists. One of Kant's successors at the University of Königsberg, Johann Friedrich Herbart (q.v.), incorporated some of Kant's ideas in his system of pedagogy.

Other Works. In addition to works on philosophy, Kant wrote a number of treatises on various scientific subjects, many in the field of physical geography; see GEOGRAPHY. His most important scientific work was his *General Natural History and Theory of the Heavens* (1755), in which he advanced the hypothesis of the formation of the universe from a spinning nebula, a hypothesis that later was developed independently by Pierre Simon de Laplace (q.v.); see COSMOGONY. See also AESTHETICS; LOGIC.

Among Kant's other writings are *Prolegomena to Every Future Metaphysic of Ethic* (1783), *Metaphysical Rudiments of Natural Philosophy* (1786), *Critique of Judgment* (1790), and *Religion within the Boundaries of Pure Reason* (1793).

KANTOR, MacKinlay (1904–), American writer, born in Webster City, Iowa. While still in high school, he joined the local newspaper as a reporter and columnist, professions he was to follow for several years in Chicago, Ill., and in both Cedar Rapids and Des Moines, Iowa. Following the publication of his first novel, *Diversey* (1928), Kantor wrote an average of one book each year. These include such popular novels as *The Voice of Bugle Ann* (1935), *Midnight Lace* (1948), *Spirit Lake* (1961), and *The Children Sing* (1973); they deal with such diverse subjects as foxhound breeding and Americans in the Orient. His autobiography, *But Look, the Morn*, was published in 1947. For *Andersonville* (1955), one of his authoritative and absorbing works on the American Civil War, Kantor was awarded the 1956 Pulitzer Prize in fiction.

KANYE, town in Botswana, and capital of Ngwaketse District, 45 miles S.W. of Gaberones and about 180 miles N.W. of Johannesburg, South Africa. It is chiefly a trade center in an irrigated farming and stock-raising region, with asbestos mines nearby. The town, one of the largest native settlements in southern Africa, is headquarters of the Bangwaketse tribal reserve. Pop. (1964) 34,045.

KAOHSIUNG, independent city in Taiwan, and capital of Kaohsiung Co., on Taiwan Strait, about 175 miles S.W. of Taipei. It is a fishing center and the second port of Taiwan. Fish, rice, sugar, pineapples, and bananas are exported. The chief industries are oil refining, shipbuilding, fish and fruit processing and canning, rice and sugar milling, and iron casting. The port, which was once under Dutch occupation, developed after 1858; the industrial center developed under Japanese rule from 1895 to 1945. The city was known as Takow (Japanese Taku) until 1920 and as Takao by the Japanese from 1920 to 1945. The name is also spelled Kaosiung or Kaohiung. Pop. (1970 est.) 735,000.

KAOLIN (Chin. *kaoling*, "high ridge"), or CHINA CLAY, a pure, soft, white clay, of variable but usually low plasticity, retaining its white color when fired. The material was first obtained from a hill called kauling, and was sent to Europe in the early eighteenth century. Pure kaolin is used in the manufacture of fine porcelain and china; impure varieties are used in making pottery, stoneware, and bricks, and as filler for pigments and in the manufacture of paper. The chief constituent of kaolin is the mineral kaolinite, a hydrous aluminum silicate, $Al_2Si_2O_5(OH)_4$, formed by the decomposition of aluminum silicates, particularly feldspar. Kaolin is now mined chiefly in South Carolina, North Carolina, Georgia, Pennsylvania, and Alabama. The term kaolin is often extended to include other porcelain clays which are not discolored by firing.

KAPITZA, Peter Leonidovich (1894–), Soviet physicist, born in Kronshtadt, and educated at the Petrograd Polytechnic Institute. For two years he taught electrical engineering at the institute. In 1921 he went to England to study at the University of Cambridge, and soon after he became an assistant to Sir Ernest Rutherford (q.v.), the director of magnetic research at the Cavendish Laboratory in Cambridge. Kapitza returned to the Soviet Union in 1934 to attend a scientific conference and remained there to become director of the Institute for Physical Problems of the U.S.S.R. Academy of Sciences. He is best known for his achievements in the liquefaction of gases and especially for originating simple methods for producing liquid helium and hydrogen. He also investigated the effects of low temperatures and strong magnetic fields on metals; *see* CRYOGENICS; MAGNETISM. In 1955 he was appointed director of the Soviet earth-satellite program; *see* ASTRONAUTICS; SATELLITE, ARTIFICIAL.

KAPODISTRIAS, Count Ioannes Antonios *or* **CAPO D'ISTRIA, Count Giovanni Antonio.** See GREECE: *History: The War of Independence.*

KAPOK. See CEIBA; FIBER: *Vegetable Fibers.*

KARACHI, largest city and principal port of Pakistan, on the Arabian Sea, N.W. of the Indus R. delta, about 650 miles S.W. of Lahore, and 550 miles N.W. of Bombay, India. The city is the distributing hub and shipping outlet for the produce of the Indus valley; a maritime and rail terminus; and a major air link with Europe and the East, as well as with domestic points. The port of Karachi has the capacity to ship about 4,000,000 tons of cargo annually. Produced in the surrounding countryside are wheat, in abundance, and cotton. Exports from Karachi include wheat, cotton, leather skins, and raw wool. Industries include cotton and wool textiles, chemicals, oil refining, iron and steel, and shipbuilding. New towns with the purpose of housing Muslim refugees from India have been incorporated into Karachi; one of these is Korangi, constructed to provide housing for about 500,000 persons. The University of Karachi is located in the city. Karachi was founded about 1725. When it was ceded in 1843 to the British, it was a small fishing village with a natural harbor. Karachi was the capital of Pakistan from 1947, when the country was established, until 1961. Pop. (greater city, 1972 prelim.) 3,469,000.

KARAGANDA, city of the Soviet Union, in the Kazakh S.S.R., and capital of the Karaganda Oblast, about 350 miles S.W. of Novosibirsk. The oblast is one of the principal coal-producing areas of the Soviet Union. Tungsten copper, and iron are also mined, and farming and livestock production are important. The city is the industrial center of the oblast and focal point for transport from western Siberia and the Urals. The industries of the city include the production of steel and flour. Pop. (1970) 523,000.

KARAITES, *or* CARAITES (from Heb. *qārā,* "to read"), Jewish sect, considered heretical by Orthodox Jews, which believes in the strict interpretation of the Jewish Scriptures and rejects the Talmud (q.v.) and the rabbinical traditions incorporated into Judaism (q.v.) during the first six centuries A.D. The sect was founded in Baghdad (now in Iraq) about 765 by Anan ben David (q.v.), a Jewish religious leader. The doctrine of Karaism is also called Ananism. The sect survives today in several Middle East countries, where it claims more than 10,000 adherents.

KARAJAN, Herbert von (1908–   ), Austrian conductor, born in Salzburg, and educated in music there and in Vienna. Although he began his career as a pianist, by the time he was twenty-one he was serving as musical director of the opera house in Ulm, Germany. After seven years at Ulm he moved to Aachen and then to Berlin, where he conducted from 1938 to 1945.

Following his appointment as conductor for life of the Gesellschaft der Musikfreunde of Vienna in 1951, Karajan's reputation grew to international proportions. He toured the world, both as guest conductor and leading such groups as the Philharmonia Orchestra of London and the Berlin Philharmonic Orchestra. He

At an annual tribal fair near Karachi, a trained camel is directed in the steps of the drum dance. UPI

made his American debut with the last-named organization in Washington, D.C., in 1955. From 1956 to 1964 he was director of the Vienna State Opera. Artistic director of the Salzburg (q.v.) Music Festival from 1957 to 1959, he was appointed to its board of directors in 1965.

A meticulous conductor, Karajan also achieved a reputation as a highly original stage director and designer of operatic productions, particularly of the works of the Austrian composer Wolfgang Amadeus Mozart and the German composer Ludwig van Beethoven (qq.v.).

KARAKORAM, mountain range on the northern border of Jammu and Kashmir (q.v.) containing K^2 or Mt. Godwin Austen (28,250 ft.), the second highest peak in the world. *See also* GODWIN-AUSTEN, HENRY HAVERSHAM.

KARAKUL. *See* SHEEP.

KARA-KUM DESERT, region of the Soviet Union, occupying most of the Turkmen S.S.R. and the S.W. portion of the Kazakh S.S.R. The desert extends from the Ust'-Urt plateau on the N., to the Amu-Dar'ya R. on the E., to the Kopet-Dagh mountains on the S., and nearly to the Caspian Sea on the W. Consisting chiefly of large expanses of hard-packed clay and rolling sand dunes, the terrain is generally devoid of vegetation. Certain species of steppe bushes and a few varieties of flowering plants occur in limited areas, mainly in the S.E. the area of Kara-Kum Desert is about 110,000 sq.mi.

KARA SEA, southern arm of the Arctic Ocean along the N. coast of the U.S.S.R., situated between the islands of Novaya Zemlya and the N.W. coast of Siberia (qq.v.), Russian S.F.S.R. It has an area of more than 300,000 sq.mi. and an average depth of about 650 ft. Ice-locked for most of the year, the sea is usually a navigable fishing grounds during August and September, and is an outlet for the Yenisey, Pyasina, Taymyr, and Ob' rivers. Chief ports, all in the Russian S.F.S.R., are Dikson, Tambey, and, in the Gulf of Ob' extending inland, to Novy Port. The Matochkin Strait, dividing Novaya Zemlya, connects the Kara Sea with the Barents Sea (q.v.).

KARATE (Jap. "empty hand"), martial art of unarmed self-defense in which directed or focused blows of the hands and feet, dealt with special breathing and shouts, are used from poised positions. More than a method of combat, karate emphasizes self-discipline, positive attitude, and high moral purpose. It is taught professionally at different levels, and under different Oriental names, for basic self-defense, competitive sport, and free-style exercise.

History. The art of karate is more than 1000 years old and originated in the ancient Orient, first as monastic training and later as a defense by Chinese peasants against armed bandits. During the 17th century it became highly developed as an art on the island of Okinawa, Japan. In 1922 karate was introduced to the Japanese public by the Okinawan professor Funakoshi Gichin (1867–1955), and the art is today chiefly associated with Japan. It was introduced into the United States after the military occupation of Japan following World War II. Many schools of karate, including Korean and Chinese styles, are presently taught in the U.S.

Technique and Training. Karate is related to judo but stresses striking techniques, through lethal kicks and punches, rather than wrestling or throwing of an opponent. The three elements of speed, strength, and technique are vital to karate expertise. Constant alertness and a keen sense of timing and surprise are also requisites. On the other hand, resistance to pain must be developed. In competition, vital attack zones are limited to areas above the waist.

Great attention is given to knowing the most vulnerable points of the human body, which may be attacked by the hands, elbows, knees, or feet. These areas include the face, neck, solar plexus, spinal column, groin, and kidneys. In ordinary karate competitions or exhibitions, only the area of the body above the waist is allowed as a target and all blows are to be pulled. The most common blows used are chops or knife hands, knuckle punches, hammerblows, finger jabs, and front, side, back, round, jump, and stamping kicks. In actual fighting, any of these blows can be fatal. The ability of a karate master to break boards or bricks with a chop of his bare hand is proverbial.

The karate trainee toughens his hands and feet by striking sandbags and special punching boards and by driving them into containers of sand, rice, or gravel. Constant exercises are also important for limbering up and strengthening the muscles of the body. Deep-breathing exercises are also useful because exhalation and sudden shouts accompany the directed blows, particularly the final or so-called killing blows. Such breathing and cries help the rhythm of attack, focus more force in each blow or block, and psychologically invigorate a person while disconcerting his opponent. *See* YOGA.

Instruction and Achievement. The language of karate is chiefly Japanese. A karate training hall or gym is called a dōjō, and the white, pajamalike garment worn in all training is called the gi. More than 200 specific Japanese terms are used for the various blows and moves that are employed in the kata, or form patterns.

KARATE

Degrees of achievement are formally recognized in karate training, each represented by a cloth belt of a particular color worn around the gi, the usual colors being, in ascending order, white, green, purple, brown, and black. Qualifications for belts differ from school to school, depending upon the style and standard of karate taught. The black belt, or dan, signifies the highest proficiency in karate and, like the other belts, is itself qualified by degrees of honor or skill, the highest dan being the ninth or tenth degree.

Competition. The Japan Karate Association, established by Funakoshi in 1955, held the first all-Japan karate championships in 1957. Since then the association has grown to an international membership of more than 100,000, with more than 130 affiliated karate clubs around the world. Countless other karate schools have also come into being, particularly in the U.S., where it has become highly popular as a sport and a method for self-protection for women and children as well as men. Karate has also been incorporated in training programs for policemen, soldiers, and college athletes.

An international karate organization has not yet come into being, largely because of the difficulties presented in standardizing the many different schools and styles of karate. In the U.S., although no single organization exists to conduct official national competitions, hundreds of tournaments are held each year throughout the country. In some of these, hundreds of competitors participate. Among the best-known competitions are the annual American championships of the Japan Karate Association, held usually on the West Coast or in Hawaii, and the All-American Open Karate Championships, annually contested at Madison Square Garden in New York City.

See also JUJITSU.

KARBALA', city in Iraq, and capital of Karbala' Province, 60 miles s.w. of Baghdad, on the edge of the Syrian desert. It is connected to the Hindiya branch of the Euphrates R. by canal. Karbala', one of the holiest Islamic cities, is the center of pilgrimage for the Shi'ites, one of the Muslim sects (q.v.). In the center of the city is the shrine of Hasan (629?–680), a Muslim martyr. The chief industries are the manufacture of religious goods, textiles, shoes, and cement and food processing. Pop. (1966) 83,301.

A karate expert demonstrates the dropkick, leaping high to attack his opponent with his right foot. UPI

KARELIAN AUTONOMOUS SOVIET SOCIALIST REPUBLIC, or KARELIA, autonomous republic of the Soviet Union, in the Russian S.F.S.R. It is in the N.W. Soviet Union and is bounded on the N. by the Murmansk Oblast, on the E. by the White Sea and the Arkhangelsk Oblast, on the S. by the Volga and Leningrad oblasts, and on the W. by Finland. The chief cities are the capital, Petrozavodsk, and Vyborg (qq.v.). The terrain, a low plateau, is rugged and similar to that of Finland (q.v.). Karelia abounds in mineral resources, and is the leading producer of mica in the Soviet Union. Zinc, iron ore, and magnetite are also mined, and building stone is quarried. Forests of pine and fir cover about 70 percent of the area. Throughout the republic are many rivers and thousands of lakes, the most notable being lakes Ladoga and Onega (qq.v.), the two largest lakes in Europe. The climate is so severe that inland waters are frozen for more than six months a year. Less than 1 percent of the land is used for agricultural purposes. The principal industries are fishing, hunting, lumbering, and processing timber and wood products. Karelia was annexed to the Russian Empire in 1721 by Emperor Peter I (q.v.). It was made an autonomous republic of the Russian S.F.S.R. in 1923, and in 1940, with 16,170 sq.mi. of territory acquired from Finland after the Russo-Finnish War (q.v.), it was established as the Karelo-Finnish Soviet Socialist Republic. In 1956 Karelia reverted to the status of an autonomous republic in the Russian S.F.S.R. Area, 66,540 sq.mi., pop. (1970) 714,000.

KARENS, tribal people of Burma, numbering about 3,000,000 and living principally in Kayah State in Burma. In physical characteristics they resemble the Burmese; see BURMA, UNION OF: *People.* The Karens are monogamous and practice a form of nature worship, although about 10 percent of them practice Christianity and Buddhism (qq.v.). The Karen language, a member of the Tai branch of the Sino-Tibetan languages (q.v.), is one of the pre-Chinese languages spoken in Lower Burma and on the borders of Thailand. The relationship of this language with other primitive Indochinese languages has not yet been completely determined.

KARLFELDT, Erik Axel (1864–1931), Swedish poet, born in Folkärna, Dalarna County, and educated at Uppsala University. He served as a teacher and librarian of the Swedish Academy from 1904 to 1912 and then as its secretary until his death. Karlfeldt declined the 1912 Nobel Prize in literature, feeling that his work was unknown outside of Sweden. The prize, however, was awarded to him posthumously in 1931. Karlfeldt drew his themes from peasant life and from nature. His poetry is often touched with humor, with underlying spiritual depths. He wrote in many verse forms, and was especially noted for his skillful use of meter and archaic expressions. His collections of poetry include *Vildmarks och Kärleksvisor* ("Ballads of the Wilderness and Love", 1895), *Fridolins Visor* ("Ballads of Fridolin", 1898), *Fridolins Lustgård* ("Fridolin's Garden", 1901), and *Hösthorn* ("Cornucopia", 1927). Some of his poems are available in English translation in the volumes *Some Swedish Poems* (1909) and *Arcadia Borealis* (1938).

KARL-MARX-STADT, formerly CHEMNITZ, city in East Germany, and capital of Karl-Marx-Stadt District, at the foot of the Erzgebirge Range, on the Chemnitz R., about 40 miles S.W. of Dresden. The district was created in 1952 from the former Saxony (q.v.) State in the Soviet Occupation Zone. It is a leading textile manufacturing center and also produces locomotives, textile and mining machinery, and chemicals. Chemnitz was founded in the 12th century, and during the 14th century it developed as a textile center. The trade and industry of Chemnitz was almost completely ruined in the 17th century, during the Thirty Years' War (q.v.), but later, with the introduction of cotton manufacture, it began to recover. Industrial growth in the 19th century and early years of the 20th century was rapid. The city received its name, Karl-Marx-Stadt, in 1953. Pop. (1970 est.) 298,472.

KARLOVY VARY (Ger. *Karlsbad* or *Carlsbad,* "Charles' bath"), city and resort of Czechoslovakia, on the Ohře R., about 70 miles N.W. of Prague. The city has long been noted for healthful mineral springs, which were believed to have been discovered in 1347 by Charles IV (*see under* CHARLES: *Holy Roman Empire*). The town was chartered as Vary in 1370, and later to honor the emperor the name Karlovy was added to the name. Among the important occupations in the city are the processing of mineral salts and the bottling of mineral waters for export, and the manufacture of ceramic and porcelain ware and leather goods.

The repressive Karlsbad Decrees, designed to curb liberalism in Austria-Hungary and the German states, were drawn up here in 1819, after the assassination of the German dramatist and antiliberal pamphleteer August von Kotzebue (1761–1819) by Karl Ludwig Sand (1795–1820), a student leader. Pop. (1970 est.) 45,000.

KARLSBAD DECREES. See KARLOVY VARY.

KARLSKRONA, city and naval port in Sweden, and capital of Blekinge County, on the Baltic

Sea, and about 240 miles S.W. of Stockholm. The city occupies five islands and part of the adjoining mainland, which are connected by bridges. Among the industries of the city are shipbuilding, brewing, granite quarrying, and the manufacture of clothing, naval equipment, metal products, and porcelain. Since 1680 Karlskrona has been the headquarters of the Swedish navy. Harbor installations include forts, dry docks, and an arsenal. Pop. (1970) 36,405.

KARLSRUHE, or CARLSRUHE (Ger., "Charles' Rest"), city of West Germany, in Baden-Württemberg State, about 40 miles N.W. of Stuttgart and 30 miles S.W. of Heidelberg. Karlsruhe is a major railway junction, is connected by canal to the nearby Rhine R. The city is the site of the Schloss, or palace, of the former margraves of Baden, which was badly damaged in World War II. It houses several research institutions, institutes of the arts and music, and the Federal Court on constitutional questions. The principal manufactures include locomotives, metal goods, chemicals, machinery, and perfumes. The city was founded in 1715 by the Margrave Charles William of Baden (1709–38) who constructed a hunting lodge on the site. Pop. (1970) 259,100.

KARLSTAD, city and inland port in Sweden, and capital of Värmland County, partly on Tingvalla Island, on the N. shore of Lake Vänern. Karlstad is near the estuary of the Karälv R. and about 160 miles W. of Stockholm. During the Middle Ages (q.v.) it was known as Thingvalla. The city was chartered and the present name was adopted in 1584. Karlstad is an episcopal see and has a cathedral. Machines, matches, lumber, iron goods, and textiles are the chief industrial products. Pop. (1970) 72,467.

KARLSTADT or **CARLSTADT** or **KAROLSTADT,** real name ANDREAS RUDOLF BODENSTEIN (about 1480–1541), German religious reformer, born in Karlstadt, and educated at the universities of Cologne, Erfurt, and Wittenberg. He adopted doctrines later espoused by Martin Luther (q.v.), the German inaugurator of the Reformation (q.v.). Becoming associated with Luther in 1517, Karlstadt joined him in theological disputation with the German Roman Catholic theologian Johann Eck (q.v.) at Leipzig, Germany, in 1519. He was the leader of the Protestant cause during Luther's absence at the castle of Wartburg in 1521–22, but he later championed radical reforms that brought him into conflict with Luther and the latter's protector, Frederick III, Elector of Saxony (1463–1525). Karlstadt was banished from Saxony in 1524 and during his exile was accused of participation in the Peasants' War (q.v.). Upon retracting statements, made earlier, of disbelief in the Lutheran doctrine of the Lord's Supper (q.v.), he was allowed to return to Wittenberg on Luther's request. Once again, though, he engaged in disputation on the Lord's Supper and in 1529 had to flee to Switzerland, where he was warmly received by the Swiss religious reformer Huldreich Zwingli (q.v.) and became professor of theology at the University of Basel.

KARMA. See HINDUISM.

KÁRMÁN, Theodor von (1881–1963), Hungarian-American aeronautical engineer, born in Budapest, and educated at the Technical University of Budapest and at the University of Göttingen. He taught at the latter university, and in 1912 he was appointed director of the Aeronautical Institute at the University of Aachen. In 1930 he went to the United States and became professor and director of the Guggenheim Aeronautics Laboratory at the California Institute of Technology. Von Kármán rejected a request by the German government to return to Germany and in 1936 became an American citizen. He did extensive research in rocketry, and during World War II he was chairman of an advisory board to the United States Air Force. He made theoretical contributions to aerodynamics (q.v.), hydrodynamics, and mathematical analysis in thermodynamics. Von Kármán also developed (1935) the first theory of supersonic drag, designed supersonic wind tunnels, and initiated research that led to the first breaking of the sound barrier by an aircraft; see SUPERSONICS.

Kármán produced many scientific works including *Aerodynamics* (1954), and received many honors, including the Wright Brothers Memorial Trophy (1954), the Robert H. Goddard Memorial Award (1960), and the first United States National Science Medal (1963).

KARNAK. See EL KARNAK.

KARO, Joseph ben Ephraim. See CARO, JOSEPH BEN EPHRAIM.

KÁROLYI, Count Mihály (1875–1955), Hungarian statesman, born in Budapest, and educated at the university in Budapest. He served in the short-lived parliament of 1905–06 and was again in parliament from 1910 to 1918. He led the radical section of the Independence Party in the period before World War I (q.v.), heading the opposition to the militaristic policies of Prime Minister István Tisza (q.v.). During the war Károlyi actively supported the cause of pacifism. The defeat of the Hungarian armies late in 1918 was followed by the near collapse of the Austro-Hungarian monarchy. In October, 1918, with the acquiescence of Emperor Charles I (q.v.), Károlyi formed an independent government. On Nov. 16, 1918, the Hungarian People's Republic was established, and in January, 1919, Károlyi was elected provisional president. He was unable to stem the political and social unrest that followed the war, however, and in March, 1919, he resigned from the presidency and handed over the governmental powers to his prime minister, the Communist leader Béla Kun (q.v.). Károlyi went into exile soon afterward, residing chiefly in Paris. During World War II he supported the Allies, and after the war he returned to Hungary. From 1947 to 1949 he was Hungarian minister to France.

KAROO (Hottentot *Karusa*, "barren", "dry"), semidesert plateau regions of the Republic of South Africa, in Cape of Good Hope Province. The Southern Karoo, or Little Karoo, is located E. of Cape Town between the coastal range of mountains on the S. and the Swartberg range about 15 mi. to the N. The Southern Karoo is bounded on the N.E. by the Great Karoo, or Central Karoo, a vast plateau extending about 350 miles E. and W. and bounded by mountain ranges. Some authorities classify a third plateau, which extends N. from the Great Karoo to the Orange R. as the Northern Karoo. During most of the year the Karoos are parched. Some parts are irrigated, however, and are very fertile. The general elevation of the plateau is between 1000 and 4000 ft. above sea level. Area, more than 100,000 sq.mi.

KARRER, Paul (1889–1971), Swiss chemist, born in Moscow, Russia (now the U.S.S.R.), and educated at the University of Zürich. In 1911–12 he was an assistant at the Chemical Institute of the University of Zürich, and he served there as professor of chemistry (1918–59) and director (1919–59). In 1935 he synthesized the vitamin riboflavin (q.v.), and as a result of this work and other work on carotinoids and flavins, he received the 1937 Nobel Prize in chemistry. His writings include *Lehrbuch der Organischen Chemie* ("Manual of Organic Chemistry", 1930), which has appeared in editions in several languages, and *Carotinoide* ("Carotinoids", 1948).

KARS, city in Turkey, and capital of Kars Province, about 175 miles S.E. of Trabzon, and about 40 miles S.W. of Leninakan, U.S.S.R. The city is on a rail line and a roadway joining Turkey and the Soviet Union. It is a commercial hub as well as an administrative center; manufactures include woolens, rugs, leather goods, and processed milk. In the 9th and 10th centuries Kars was the center of an independent Armenian principality. Turks besieged the city in the 11th century, Mongols in the 13th and 14th centuries, and Persians in the 18th century. Following the Russo-Turkish War, 1877–78, Kars was ceded to Russia. The city reverted to the Turks in 1921 by a treaty between the U.S.S.R. and Turkey. Pop. (1965) 32,141.

KARUN, only navigable river of Iran, rising in the central section of the Zard Kuh Mts. After following a circuitous route for about half its length, the river turns S.W., is joined by the Ab-i-Diz R. about 24 miles S. of Shushtar, and flows S.W. past Ahwaz to its confluence with the Shatt-al-'Arab R. at Khorramshahr. The total course of the river is about 450 mi., and it is navigable from its mouth to Shushtar.

KASAI, river of south-central Africa, chief southern tributary of the Congo River (q.v.). The Kasai rises in the central highlands of Angola and flows for over 1000 miles N. to the Congo. The river forms part of the boundary between Angola and the Republic of Zaire (formerly the Democratic Republic of the Congo). Most of the rivers and streams of the Kasai R. system flow from S. to N. The chief tributaries of the system are the Fimi, Sankuru, Lulua, and the Kwenge (the largest) rivers. The system is navigable by steamboat for more than 1500 mi.

KASAVUBU, Joseph. See ZAIRE, REPUBLIC OF: *History*.

KASHAN, city of Iran, in Tehran Province, about 150 miles S. of the city of Tehran. It is noted for its fine carpets. Woolen and silk goods, brass and copper work, and jewelry are also produced in Kashan. The city dates from ancient times and was formerly important as a site along the caravan route from Kerman to Isfahan. Pop. (1966) 81,651.

KASHGAR or SHUFU, city of the People's Republic of China, in the Sinkiang-Uigur Autonomous Region, on the Kashgar R., at the junction of several important trade routes, about 700 miles S.W. of Urumchi, and about 300 miles S. of Alma-Ata, U.S.S.R. Principal products of the nearby irrigated oasis are grains, cotton, and fruits. Oil wells and copper mines are worked in the vicinity. Textiles woven of gold and silver thread, carpets, gold and silver goods, leather work, woolens, sheepskins, dressed furs, and cotton cloth are the chief products of the city. Kashgar was wrested from the Huns by the Chinese in the 1st century B.C. In the 10th and 11th centuries it was a part of the Turkish Uigur Kingdom. The region was in succeeding centuries taken by invading armies, including those of the Mongol conquerors Genghis Khan and Tamerlane (qq.v.), being finally recaptured by the Chinese in 1759. Pop. (1970 est.) 175,000.

KASHMIR

KASHMIR. See JAMMU AND KASHMIR.

KASKASKIA, village of Illinois, in Randolph Co., on the Mississippi R., near the mouth of the Kaskaskia R., about 40 miles S.E. of East Saint Louis. It is the oldest permanent settlement in the Mississippi Valley, and the first capital of Illinois. In 1675 the French missionary Jacques Marquette (q.v.) established a mission at the Indian village of Kaskaskia, on the Illinois R. in what is now La Salle County. About 1700 the mission and village were moved to the present site of Kaskaskia, and the settlement became an important trading center as well as one of the leading French communities in the West. In 1763 the region was ceded to England by the Treaty of Paris and Kaskaskia became a headquarters for the British in the area. George Rogers Clark (see under CLARK), the American revolutionary soldier, captured the town on July 4, 1778. From 1809 to 1817 it was the capital of Illinois Territory, and in 1818 it became the capital of the newly created State of Illinois. After the removal of the seat of government to Vandalia in 1819 the town declined rapidly. Near the end of the 19th century, a change in the course of the Mississippi R. obliterated most of the old section of the town. The site of the French Fort Kaskaskia, built in 1736 and destroyed about 1767, is in nearby Fort Kaskaskia State Park. Pop. (1960) 97; (1970) 79.

KASKASKIA, river of Illinois, rising in Champaign Co., W. of Urbana. It flows generally S.W. about 300 mi. until it joins the Mississippi R. a few miles N.W. of Chester. It is navigable from its mouth to Vandalia, a distance of about 150 mi.

KASSALA, city in Sudan, and capital of Kassala Province, at the foot of the Jebel Kassala, on the Gash R., 15 mi. from the Ethiopian border and 260 miles E. of Khartoum. It is the center of a major cotton-growing region and of the Gash irrigation project, which covers 75,000 acres. Irrigated gardens in the area produce vegetables, fruits, corn, and millet. Kassala is a trade center, marketing hides, wheat, palm products, and gum arabic. Agricultural equipment is imported and maintained here, and industries include tanning, flour milling, and vegetable processing. The city is the headquarters of the Khatmiya Islamic religious sect. Founded by the Egyptians in 1834 as a military camp, Kassala was held by the rebelling Mahdists (see MAHDI) from 1885 to 1894 and by Italy from 1894 to 1897 and for a short period during World War II. Pop. (1964 est.) 49,000.

KASSEL or **CASSEL,** city of West Germany, in Hesse State, on the Fulda R., about 80 miles S.W. of Hannover. The city is notable as a center of heavy industry. Railway equipment, machines, porcelain ware, textiles, and scientific instruments are the chief manufactures. Kassel was originally a Roman colony. In the 12th century it was incorporated within Thuringia (q.v.), and in the 13th century it was acquired by the landgraves of Hesse (q.v.). During the 17th century Kassel was settled by many French Huguenots (q.v.), who founded a new town above the old one. The city became capital of the Prussian province of Hesse-Nassau in 1866. Many of the gabled houses date from the 17th century. Among the notable buildings are a 14th-century church, the former residence of the electors of Hesse-Kassel, several museums, an art gallery, and an industrial-art school. Pop. (1970) 214,800.

KASSITES (Akkadian *Kashshū* or *Kushshū*; Gr. *Cossaioi* or *Cissii*), people of ancient southwestern Asia. Early in the 17th century B.C. they descended from their habitat in the Zagros Mts. between Iraq and Iran and settled in much of northern Babylonia (q.v.). About 1550 B.C. the Hittites (q.v.) attacked Babylonia, weakening its military power. Subsequently the Kassites captured Babylon, deposed the dynasty of Hammurabi (q.v.), and established a new dynasty which ruled southern and eastern Mesopotamia for four centuries. The Kassites adopted the Babylonian language and culture during that period and were virtually absorbed by the native population. About 1230 B.C. the Assyrian king Tukulti-Ninurta I (r. 1256–1233 B.C.) captured Babylon and greatly weakened the political power of the Kassite dynasty. The Kassites, however, remained on the throne of Babylonia until about 1160 B.C., when they were conquered by Shutruk-Nahhunte I (q.v.), King of Elam.

Except for names of numerous persons, places, and deities, little is known of the Kassite language. Scholars believe that it was neither an Indo-European nor a Semitic language and that it resembled the language of the Elamites.

E.I.G. & S.N.K.

KASTLER, Alfred (1902–), French physicist, born in Guebwiller, Alsace, Germany (now in France), and educated at the École Normale Supérieure, Paris. He taught in several high schools and at the universities of Bordeaux and Clermont-Ferrand before 1941, when he returned to the École Normale Supérieure as a professor of physics. Kastler was awarded the 1966 Nobel Prize in physics for his discovery and development of methods of atomic research. He had developed the technique of optical pumping in 1951, a method of bombarding gas atoms with light waves and radio waves which laid the groundwork for development of the laser (q.v.).

KATANGA. See Lubumbashi.

KATHIAWAR, peninsula of the Republic of India, in Gujarat State. The peninsula extends s.w. into the Arabian Sea and is bounded on the n.w. by the Gulf of Kutch and on the s.e. by the Gulf of Cambay. Area, about 23,000 sq.mi.

KATHMANDU, city and capital of Nepal, on the n. bank of the Baghmati R., in the Valley of Nepal, about 75 miles n. of the Indian frontier. The city, which was founded in 723, is the economic, political, and cultural center of Nepal. Rice, wheat, maize, and truck produce grown in the countryside are marketed in Kathmandu. Notable sites include many Hindu and Buddhist temples and the royal palace. Pop. (1966 est.) 195,260.

KATMAI NATIONAL MONUMENT, region of natural interest in Alaska, on the n.e. coast of the Alaska Peninsula, on Shelikof Strait, 100 miles n.w. of Kodiak Island. The monument includes Katmai Volcano (6715 ft. above sea level) and the Valley of Ten Thousand Smokes. The volcano was considered extinct until an eruption in 1912 blew off the top of the mountain and showered volcanic ash over much of the Alaskan mainland and Kodiak Island. Several minor eruptions occurred in 1914. The main volcanic crater, 3 mi. wide and about 3700 ft. deep, is lined with glaciers, some of which flow into the blue-green lake on its floor. In 1916 the valley was discovered by an expedition sent out by the National Geographical Society. Steam and gases issue from the thousands of openings in the earth that mark the valley. The monument is administered by the National Park Service (q.v.).

KATOWICE (Ger. *Kattowitz*), city in Poland, and capital of Katowice Province, on the Rawa R., about 40 miles n.w. of Cracow. The province is rich in coal and zinc, and the city is one of the principal mining and industrial centers of the country, producing iron castings, machinery, and ironware. In 1867 Katowice was chartered as a town by Prussia, of which it was then a part. When Silesia (q.v.) was partitioned between Poland and Germany in 1921, Katowice was incorporated within Poland. It was occupied by German troops from the beginning of World War II until 1945. Pop. (1970) 303,264.

KATRINE, LOCH, lake in s.w. Perth County, Scotland, 5 miles e. of Loch Lomand and 10 miles w. of Callander. It is 8 mi. long, 1 mi. wide, and less than 500 ft. deep, and was enlarged in 1859 to become the chief water supply for the city of Glasgow. Situated at the foot of Ben Venue, a mountain 2393 ft. high, and w. of the wooded valley known as The Trossachs (q.v.), the loch is noted for its beauty. It is celebrated in literature in *The Lady of the Lake,* the romantic poem by the Scottish poet and novelist Sir Walter Scott (q.v.). The village of Glengyle, at the s.e. head of the lake, was the birthplace of the Scottish freebooter known as Rob Roy (q.v.).

KATSURA, Prince Taro (1847–1913), Japanese statesman and soldier, born in Choshu Province, now part of the Yamaguchi Prefecture. He actively supported the restoration of the Japanese emperor to political power in 1867, and was later sent twice to Europe, in 1870 and 1884, to study German military tactics. On his return to Japan, Katsura became one of the *Genro,* or "elder statesmen", who were thereafter one of the greatest influences on Japanese policies. During the Sino-Japanese War in 1894 (*see* China: *History;* Japan: *History*), he commanded a division and from 1898 to 1900 served in the cabinet as minister of war. After he became prime minister in 1901, he negotiated one of the most significant pacts in modern Japanese history, the Anglo-Japanese Alliance, and directed the government until the end of the Russo-Japanese War (q.v.) in 1905. Katsura was one of the most conservative leaders of Japan and adhered entirely to the principle that government officials should be responsible only to the emperor, not to the people. He served as prime minister again from 1908 to 1911 and in 1912–13, when his appropriations for warships helped create the modern Japanese navy. For his services, Katsura was successively created viscount (1895), count (1902), marquess (1906), and prince (1911).

KATTEGAT, strait between the s.w. coast of Sweden and the e. coast of the Jutland peninsula, Denmark. It is connected to the North Sea on the n.w. by the Skagerrak strait and to the Baltic Sea on the s. by the Øresund sound and the Store Baelt and Lille Baelt channels. The Kattegat varies from 37 to 100 mi. in width and is about 140 mi. long.

KATYDID, common name for any of several American, long-horned grasshoppers characterized by the sound resembling "katydid" that the male of the species makes. Katydids are arboreal insects and are most commonly heard at night during summer and early fall. The best-known is *Pterophylla camellifolia,* found throughout the United States east of the Rocky Mts. The insect is usually green in color, has broad, leaf-shaped wings, and is about 2½ in. long. Other species of katydids found in eastern U.S. belong to the genus *Amblycorypha; A. oblongifolia* differs from the common katydid in having long, narrow wings and a more slender body. The katydids of southern and western U.S. belong to the

Angular-winged katydid, Microcentrum laurifolium
New York Zoological Society

genus *Microcentrum,* and closely resemble *A. oblongifolia.*

KATZ, Sir Bernard (1911–), British biophysicist, born in Leipzig, Germany. In 1934, immediately upon receiving an M.D. degree from the University of Leipzig, he emigrated to England. For four years he performed biological research at University College, University of London. Then, in 1939, he accepted a research fellowship at the University of Sydney, Sydney, Australia. During World War II he served in the Royal Australian Air Force. After the war, in 1946, he returned to University College as a British citizen and member of the biophysics research unit; in 1952 he was named head of the biophysics department of the college. Katz, who was knighted in 1969, shared the 1970 Nobel Prize in medicine and physiology with the American biochemist Julius Axelrod and the Swedish physiologist Ulf Svante von Euler (qq.v.). He was cited for his research on the function of a chemical substance, acetylcholine, released from nerve endings in the transmission of impulses.

KAUAI, island and county of Hawaii, fourth-largest island of the State, 74 miles N.W. of Oahu, from which it is separated by Kauai Channel, and 18 miles E. of Niihau, from which it is separated by the Kaulakahi Channel. The island, formed by volcanic action, is covered with mountains, the highest being Kawaikini Peak, at 5170 ft. above sea level. Much of the soil, especially in the north, is fertile, and sugarcane and tropical fruits are raised. Kauai is seamed with canyons, the deepest of which, Waimea, is almost 10 mi. long and more than ½ mi. deep. The island and the county are coextensive. The chief towns are Lihue, and the county seat Kapaa. Area, 555 sq.mi.; pop. (1960) 28,176; (1970) 29,761.

KAUFMAN, George S(imon) (1889–1961), American playwright, director, and producer, born in Pittsburgh, Pa. After having worked for some years as a newspaperman in Washington, D.C., and New York City, he devoted himself exclusively to the writing of plays. His fame rests principally on works that he wrote in collaboration with several other noted American playwrights, among which are several of the most successful comedies and musical comedies of his time. Kaufman's chief contribution to these collaborations was acidly satirical and often hilarious dialogue. With Marc Connelly (q.v.), he wrote *Dulcy* (1921), *Merton of the Movies* (1922), and *Beggar on Horseback* (1924); with Morris Ryskind (1895–), *Animal Crackers* (1928), *Of Thee I Sing* (1931), which won a Pulitzer Prize, and *Bring on the Girls* (1934); with Ring Lardner (q.v.), *June Moon* (1928); with Moss Hart (q.v.), *Once in a Lifetime* (1930), *You Can't Take it With You* (1936), which won a Pulitzer Prize, *I'd Rather Be Right* (1937), *The Man Who Came to Dinner* (1939), and *George Washington Slept Here* (1940); with John P. Marquand (q.v.), *The Late George Apley* (1944); with Edna Ferber (q.v.), *Minick* (1924), *Dinner at Eight* (1932), *Stage Door* (1936), and *The Land Is Bright* (1941); with his wife, Leueen MacGrath (1914–), *The Small Hours* (1951); and with Abe Burrows (1910–), *Silk Stockings* (1955). Kaufman is sole author of such hits as *The Butter and Egg Man* (1925) and *Strike Up the Band* (1927). He directed and produced many of these plays.

KAUNAS (Russ. *Kovno*), city of the Soviet Union, in the Lithuanian S.S.R., at the confluence of the Niemen and Viliya rivers, about 130 miles s. of Riga. The city is the trading center for the surrounding region that produces lumber and grain. The leading industries of Kaunas are the manufacture of textiles and metal goods. A notable building in the city is the 15th-century Lithuanian-Gothic Church. Also in Kaunas are an agricultural school, a polytechnical institute, an art museum, and a historical museum. The city was founded about the 11th century, and later during the Middle Ages it was fortified against the Teutonic Knights (q.v.). In the 15th century the city passed to the Kingdom of Poland and in 1795, after the third partition of Poland, Kaunas was acquired by the Russians. Kaunas was occupied by the German army during

World War I. It served as the capital of the newly independent republic of Lithuania from 1918 to 1940. Kaunas was heavily damaged and was occupied by Soviet troops during World War II. Pop. (1970) 305,116.

KAUNITZ, Count Wenzel Anton von, Prince von Kaunitz-Rietberg (1711–94), Austrian statesman, born in Vienna, and educated in the law. In 1735 he became councilor to Charles VI (q.v.), Holy Roman Emperor. In 1748 he was the delegate of Austria in negotiations with other European powers, which brought to a close the War of the Austrian Succession (see AIX-LA-CHAPELLE, TREATIES OF) and established the right of Maria Theresa (q.v.) to succeed her father, Charles VI, to the Hapsburg dominions. As ambassador to France from 1750 to 1753, Kaunitz negotiated an alliance between Austria and France. In 1753, when he became state chancellor and director of foreign policy, he transformed the alliance with France into a coalition against Frederick II (q.v.), King of Prussia; this development was a contributing factor to the outbreak of the Seven Years' War (q.v.). He represented Austria at conferences that arranged the first partition of Poland in 1772 (see POLAND: History), and in 1775 he acquired for Austria the province of Bukovina, formerly held by the Ottoman Turks. He retired in 1792.

KAURI, or KAURI PINE, common name of a coniferous tree, Agathis australis, belonging to the Pine family. The kauri is native to New Zealand, where it grows in extensive forest tracts. The tree, which sometimes grows as tall as 150 ft., produces dense, dark, evergreen foliage. The yellowish lumber of the tree, which is used in building construction and shipbuilding, is closegrained, flexible, and durable. The resin produced by the kauri, called dammar, is either collected fresh from the trees or found in large pieces, some weighing as much as 100 lb., buried in forests where kauris grow.

KAUTSKY, Karl Johann (1854–1938), German socialist, born in Prague, and educated at the University of Vienna. He was a friend and disciple of the communist leaders Karl Marx and Friedrich Engels (qq.v.). In 1883 he founded the newspaper Die Neue Zeit, which, under his editorship, became one of the leading socialist periodicals of Europe. After joining the German Social Democratic Party, he won recognition as one of the foremost Marxist theoreticians of his time, esteemed for his defense of revolutionary doctrines against the more liberal theories of the social democratic leader Eduard Bernstein (q.v.), (1850–1932). Later, Kautsky himself adopted more liberal views.

During World War I, which he denounced as an imperialist venture, Kautsky was a pacifist. In 1917 he was one of the leaders of a left-wing faction that split from the Social Democratic Party and formed the Independent Social Democratic Party; see SOCIALISM. Kautsky regarded the Russian Bolshevik revolution of November, 1917 (see BOLSHEVISM), and declined to follow a large section of his party into the newly formed United German Communist Party, which supported the Soviet regime. He wrote a number of polemics against the Bolshevik leaders, of which one of the best known is "Dictatorship of the Proletariat" (1918). After World War I he resided chiefly in Vienna, directing the activities of the Austrian socialists. After the annexation of Austria by Germany in 1938, he went to Amsterdam, the Netherlands where he died shortly afterward.

Kautsky's greatest contribution to Marxist theory is Theories of Surplus Value (4 vol., 1905–10), a work based on manuscripts and notes left by Marx and originally intended as the basis for a fourth volume of Marx's Capital. Theories of Surplus Value has been published in several European languages. Several of Kautsky's other writings are also regarded as Marxist classics; among these are Ethics and the Materialist Conception of History (1907) and Foundations of Christianity (1908).

KAVERI, or CAUVERY, river of S. India, about 475 mi. long, rising in the Western Ghats mountains and flowing S.E. across Mysore and Tamil Nadu, entering the Bay of Bengal through two principal mouths. Although of no value for commercial navigation, the Kaveri is highly important for irrigation purposes, chiefly in its Tanjore delta region, where there are extensive irrigation works, ancient and modern. In Mysore the falls of the river are utilized for the generation of electric power. The entire course of the Kaveri is holy ground to the Hindus, who call the river Dakshini Ganga, the "Ganges of the south".

KAW. See KANSA.

KAWABATA, Yasunari (1899–1972), Japanese author, born in Osaka. He graduated from Tokyo Imperial University in 1924, already well known as a writer of short stories. For a few years after his graduation Kawabata belonged to a group of young writers who favored lyricism over social realism and were known as neo-sensationists. He gradually evolved his own painstaking, episodic style, frequently concerning himself with the exploration of loneliness, resulting in a remarkable probing of the feminine mind and of the outer fringes of human sexual-

KAWAGUCHI

ity. Kawabata won the 1968 Nobel Prize in literature, the first Japanese to be so honored; he was cited for his "narrative mastership, which with great sensibility expresses the Japanese mind". Two of Kawabata's novels, *Snow Country* (1956) and *Thousand Cranes* (1959), were reissued (1969) in a one-volume edition. *The Master of Go* (posthumously published, 1972) is his fictional memoirs. See JAPANESE LITERATURE: Modern Period.

KAWAGUCHI, city of Japan, in Saitama Prefecture, on the Arakawa (Ara) R., on the island of Honshu, adjoining Tokyo on the N., and 8 mi. from the city center. Kawaguchi, linked to the capital by the Kohoku bridge, manufactures textiles, glass, and iron products. Pop. (1970) 305,886.

KAWASAKI, city of Japan, on the island of Honshu, in Kanagawa Prefecture, about 15 miles s. of Tokyo. Kawasaki, part of the metropolitan area fronting Tokyo Bay, is a major industrial center; industries include shipbuilding and repair, textiles, steel, chemicals, and machinery. Largely destroyed in World War II, Kawasaki was later restored. Pop. (1970) 973,486.

KAYAK. See CANOE.

KAYE, Danny, professional name of DAVID DANIEL KOMINSKI (1913–), American actor, born in New York City. He left high school in his senior year to become a professional entertainer, performing from 1929 to 1933 as singer, dancer, and comedian in the summer resorts of the Catskill Mts. of New York State. From 1933 to 1939 he toured the United States, England, and the Orient in a vaudeville troupe, perfecting his art as a pantomimist. Several months after making his New York City theatrical debut in *Straw Hat Revue* (1939), he married Sylvia Fine, the writer-composer who had provided him with his most successful material. He appeared to great critical acclaim in two musicals, *Lady in the Dark* (1940) and *Let's Face It* (1941), before making his motion-picture debut in *Up in Arms* (1944). His later films include *The Secret Life of Walter Mitty* (1947), *Hans Christian Andersen* (1952), and *The Madwoman of Chaillot* (1969). Meanwhile he toured throughout the world, raising funds as ambassador at large for the United Nations Children's Fund (UNICEF), entertained American troops stationed abroad, and played a season as star of "The Danny Kaye Show" (1963–64), on television. In 1970 he returned to the musical-comedy theater in New York City in *Two by Two*.

KAYSERI, city in Turkey, and capital of Kayseri Province, 165 miles S.E. of Ankara. It is the trading center for the agricultural products of the province and is important for the manufacture of textiles and carpets. Pop. (1970) 167,696.

KAZAKH SOVIET SOCIALIST REPUBLIC, constituent republic of the U.S.S.R., in w. central Asia, bounded on the N. by the Russian S.F.S.R., on the E. by China, on the s. by the Kirghiz S.S.R., the Uzbek S.S.R., and the Turkmen S.S.R., and on the w. by the Caspian Sea and the Kalmuck A.S.S.R. The Kazakh S.S.R. is composed largely of arid plains, notable among which is the Kyzyl-Kum desert. The Ural, Emba, Ishim, Sary Su, and Irtish are the principal rivers. Within the republic are the Aral Sea and several large lakes, including lakes Balkhash and Zaysan. On the E. border of Kazakh are located the Tien Shan Mts. Alma-Ata (q.v.) is the capital. Other important towns are Semipalatinsk, Karaganda, Uralsk, Petropavlosk, and Chimkent (qq.v.). Native Kazakhs comprise about half of the population; the remainder of the inhabitants are mainly Russian colonists and Uzbeks. Before 1917 the people of Kazakh lived as nomads, and their principal occupation was the breeding of livestock. Today, with the aid of irrigation canals and hydroelectric power, crops are raised. The chief agricultural products include grain, cotton, sugar beets, potatoes, vegetables, fruit, cattle, and sheep. About half of the total U.S.S.R. deposits of copper, lead, and zinc are in Kazakh. Coal, oil, tungsten, Iceland spar, nickel, chromium, bauxite, iron manganese, molybdenum, and other minerals are mined, in addition to copper, lead, and zinc. The production of iron and steel, nonferrous metals, chemicals, and textiles are among the leading industries.

Danny Kaye and Gwen Verdon (1925–) in a dance created for "The Danny Kaye Show" on C.B.S. television.

KAZAN'

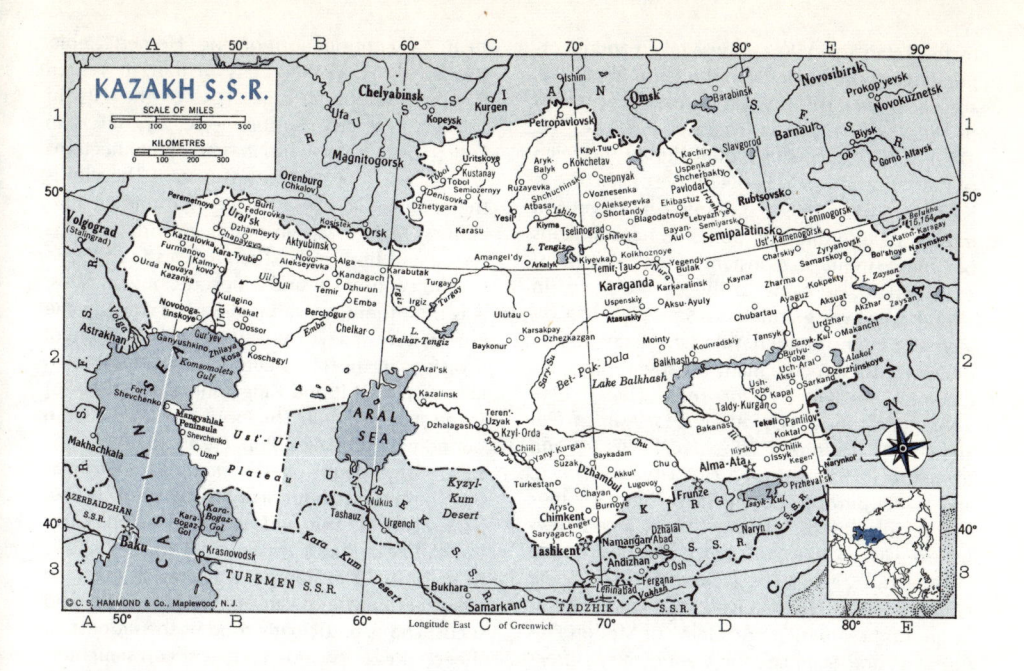

INDEX TO MAP OF KAZAKH S.S.R.

Cities and Towns

Akkul'	D 2	Dzhezkazgan	C 2	Makanchi	E 2	Ush-Tobe	D 2
Aktyubinsk	B 1	Ekibastuz	D 1	Makat	B 2	Uspenska	D 1
Alekseyevka	D 1	Emba	B 2	Mointy	D 2	Uspenskiy	D 2
Alga	B 1	Fort Shevchenko	A 2	Narynkol'	E 2	Ust'-Kamenogorsk	E 1
Alma-Ata (cap.)	D 2	Ganyushkino	B 2	Novaya Kazanka	A 2	Uzen'	B 2
Amangel'dy	C 1	Gur'yev	B 2	Novobogatinskoye	B 2	Zaysan	E 2
Aral'sk	C 2	Iliysk	D 2	Panfilov	D 2	Zharma	D 2
Aryk-Balyk	C 1	Kachiry	D 1	Pavlodar	D 1	Zhilaya Kosa	B 2
Arys'	C 2	Kalmykovo	B 2	Petropavlovsk	C 1	Zyryanovsk	E 2
Atasuskiy	D 2	Kandagach	B 2	Ruzayevka	C 1		
Atbasar	C 1	Kara-Tyube	B 2	Semipalatinsk	D 1	**Physical Features**	
Ayaguz	E 2	Karaganda	D 2	Semiyarsk	D 1		
Balkhash	D 2	Karkaralinsk	D 2	Shchuchinsk	C 1	Alakol' (lake)	E 2
Baykonur	C 2	Karsakpay	C 2	Shevchenko	B 2	Aral (sea)	B 2
Berchogur	B 2	Katon-Karagay	E 2	Stepnyak	D 1	Balkhash (lake)	D 2
Bol'shoye Narymskoye	E 2	Kazalinsk	C 2	Taldy-Kurgan	D 2	Bet-Pak-Dala (desert)	C 2
Chapayevo	B 1	Kiyma	C 1	Temir	B 2	Caspian (sea)	B 2
Charskiy	E 2	Kiyevka	D 1	Temir-Tau	D 2	Chu (river)	D 2
Chelkar	B 2	Kokchetav	D 1	Teren'-Uzyak	C 2	Emba (river)	B 2
Chiili	C 2	Koschagyl	B 2	Tobol	C 1	Ili (river)	D 2
Chimkent	C 2	Koundradskiy	D 2	Tselinograd	C 1	Irtysh (river)	D 1
Chu	D 2	Kustanay	C 1	Turgay	C 2	Komsomolets (gulf)	B 2
Dossor	B 2	Kzyl-Orda	C 2	Turkestan	C 2	Mangyshlak (pen.)	B 2
Dzerzhinskoye	E 2	Kzyl-Tuu	D 1	Uch-Aral	D 2	Syr-Dar'ya (river)	C 2
Dzhambul	D 2	Lebyazh'ye	D 1	Uil	B 2	Tengiz (lake)	C 1
Dzhetygara	C 1	Lenger	C 2	Ural'sk	B 1	Ural (river)	B 2
		Leninogorsk	E 1	Urda	A 2	Ust'-Urt (plateau)	B 2
		Lugovoy	D 2	Uritskoye	C 1	Zaysan (lake)	E 2

The area now covered by the Kazakh S.S.R. was once a part of the empire of the Mongol conqueror Genghis Khan (q.v.). Between 1730 and 1819 it was incorporated within Russia. Kazakh was admitted to the U.S.S.R. as a constituent republic in 1936. The launching of the Vostok and Voskhod manned space vehicles took place at Baykonur in the central part of the republic. Area, 1,048,030 sq.mi. Pop. (1970) 12,-850,000.

KAZAN', city and river port in the Soviet Union, and capital of the Tatar A.S.S.R., on the Kazanka R., 3 mi. above the confluence of the Kazanka and Volga rivers, about 200 miles S.E. of Gor'kiy. It is an important industrial, commercial, and cultural center of the middle Volga region. In the city aircraft, machinery, chemicals, and textiles are produced, and furs and animal hides are processed. Kazan' was formerly a leading center of Muslim culture and is presently a center of Tatar culture. Books, bulletins, and periodicals are published in the Tatar language, and several Tatar schools, including a university, a teachers college, and an agricultural school, are in the city. The city was founded in the 15th century as the capital of the Khanate established

343

by the Tatars (q.v.). Kazan' was taken and incorporated into Russia by Ivan the Terrible in 1552; see under IVAN. The city was destroyed by troops of the Cossack soldier Emelyan Pugachev (d. 1775) in 1774 and later rebuilt during the reign of Catherine II (q.v.). Pop. (1972 est.) 904,000.

KAZAN, Elia (1909–), American stage and motion-picture director, born Elia Kazanjoglous of Greek parents, in Constantinople (now İstanbul), Turkey. He came to the United States in 1913. Kazan was graduated from Williams College and later attended Yale University School of Drama. He directed many Broadway plays, including *The Skin of Our Teeth* (1942), *One Touch of Venus* (1943), *A Streetcar Named Desire* (1947), *Death of a Salesman* (1949), *Tea and Sympathy* (1953), *Cat on a Hot Tin Roof* (1955), and *Sweet Bird of Youth* (1959). The many motion pictures he directed include *A Tree Grows in Brooklyn* (1945), *A Streetcar Named Desire* (1951), *Viva Zapata* (1952), and *A Face in The Crowd* (1957). He received the best-director award of the American Academy of Motion Picture Arts and Sciences for *Gentleman's Agreement* (1947) and for *On the Waterfront* (1954). A portion of his early experiences is recounted in his novel *America, America* (1962), which was made into a motion picture in 1963. Kazan wrote and directed the film adaptation. A second novel, *The Arrangement* (1966), was made into a motion picture by Kazan in 1968. His third novel, *The Assassins*, was published in 1972.

KAZANTZAKIS, Nikos (1885–1957), Greek author, born in Candia, Crete, and educated at the University of Athens. After receiving his law degree, he went to France, where he studied philosophy under Henri Bergson. During the 1930's he traveled extensively in Europe, Asia, and Africa, and he wrote a number of books combining travel description and personal and philosophic commentary. His best-known novels in English are *Zorba the Greek* (1943; Eng. trans., 1952), the story of an aging Greek miner possessed with an unconquerable zest for life, and *The Greek Passion* (1948; Eng. trans., 1954), concerning the reenactment of a passion play in a Greek village. Successful motion pictures were made from both these novels.

He published several books on religious-philosophical themes, including *The Last Temptation of Christ* (1960) and *Saint Francis* (1962). Kazantzakis translated Dante, Goethe, and several ancient Greek classics into the modern Greek language, of which he was one of the great masters. He also wrote philosophical essays, tragedies, and lyric and epic poetry, including *The Odyssey: A Modern Sequel* (1938; Eng. trans., 1958), a continuation of the Homeric epic.

KAZVIN or **QAZVIN,** city of Iran, in Tehran Province, about 90 miles N.W. of the city of Tehran. The city is connected by rail with Tehran and Tabriz and has road connections with other important cities in Iran. The city is the commercial center of the surrounding agricultural region. Kazvin produces wine and has textile and flour mills. The city was founded in the 3rd century A.D. and a mosque, now in ruins, was built there by Harun al-Rashid (q.v.) in the 8th century. Kazvin was damaged by Mongol invasions in the 13th century. Later, the Persian kings repaired it and King Tahmasp I (1524–76) made it his capital. The city has suffered from periodic earthquakes. Pop. (1966) 103,791.

KEA, large parrot, *Nestor notabilis,* that inhabits the mountainous sections of South Island, New Zealand. The bird, which is named after the call *keaa* that it usually delivers in flight, is from 18 to 19 in. long and is grayish green in color. It feeds on carrion, insects, fruit, and seeds, and is particularly fond of the kidneys of sheep. Keas swarm about sheep-slaughterhouses, where they pick up the refuse; they occasionally attack a live sheep, burying their beaks in the back to get at the kidneys. Bounties are paid for dead keas.

KEAN, the name of a family of noted English actors.

Edmund Kean (1787–1833), born in London, the son of an actress. He made his first stage appearance at the age of four in a ballet. He had little schooling, but studied the art of acting with his uncle. From 1801 to 1814 he played leading roles in a number of theatrical companies, including that of the famous actress Mrs. Sarah Siddons (q.v.), but it was not until the latter year, when he appeared at the Drury Lane Theatre (q.v.), London, as Shylock, that he established his reputation as a Shakespearean tragedian. The principal roles he played in his subsequent career were those of Richard III, Hamlet, Othello, Iago, Macbeth, and Shylock; he was also celebrated for his performance as Sir Giles Overreach in *A New Way to Pay Old Debts,* by the English playwright Philip Massinger (q.v.). Kean first appeared in New York City in 1820 as Richard III; he made a number of American tours. His last performance was at Covent Garden Theatre (q.v.), London, in the part of Othello, in 1833. Though he suffered the handicap of small stature, his expressive eyes, command of facial expression, powerful and musical voice, and deep understanding of the characters he played, made him the foremost English tragedian, after David Garrick (q.v.).

KEARNY

Charles John Kean (1811–68), son of Edmund, born in Waterford, Ireland, and educated at Eton College. He made his first stage appearance at the Drury Lane Theatre in *Douglas* by the British clergyman and playwright John Home (1722–1808). Charles Kean acted in many plays with his father and made a successful appearance as Hamlet in London in 1838. He made several successful tours of the United States and after 1850 produced a series of notable revivals of the plays of Shakespeare at the Princess Theatre, London. Charles Kean was most successful in melodramatic rather than tragic roles. Among his best performances were those he gave in the plays *Louis XI* and *The Corsican Brothers*, both adapted by Dion Boucicault (q.v.) from the French.

KEARNEY, city in Nebraska, and county seat of Buffalo Co., in the valley of the Platte R., 125 miles w. of Lincoln. It has an airport and is served by railroad. Kearney is the shipping and distributing point of a fertile agricultural area producing grain and livestock. The industries of the city include the manufacture of irrigation pumps and other farm equipment, cement, valves, and truck generators. The city was named for Fort Kearney, an army outpost used from 1848 to 1871 to protect travelers on the Oregon and Overland trails. The remains of the fort nearby are in Fort Kearney State Park. The city is the site of Kearney State College. The name "Kearney", although misspelled, was to honor the American general Stephen Watts Kearny (see under KEARNY). The city was incorporated in 1873. Pop. (1960) 14,210; (1970) 19,181.

KEARNEY, Denis (1847–1907), American labor leader, born in Oakmount, County Cork, Ireland. About 1868 he settled in San Francisco, Calif., where he became a foreman of stevedores; later he went into the draying business. Kearney became an American citizen in 1876. When California experienced an economic depression in 1877, Kearney began to hold meetings of workers in sand lots near San Francisco to protest against the increasing influx of Chinese laborers. He held that their extremely low wages represented unfair competition with American workers for jobs. He condemned unemployment, dishonest banking, and unfair taxes. Several newspapers supported him, and he organized the Workingman's Party of California. In 1878 the Workingman's Party, which had affiliated with the Granger movement (q.v.), sent a large number of delegates to a State convention to draft a new constitution for California. In 1878 Kearney also toured the eastern States, making speeches in the larger cities, but was unsuccessful in his attempts to extend his party outside of California. The party gradually sank into obscurity and Kearney retired from political life in 1884.

KEARNY, town of New Jersey, in Hudson Co., at the head of Newark Bay, between the Passaic and Hackensack rivers. It is served by railroad and has an extensive water frontage with docking facilities for oceangoing ships. Kearny is a suburb of Newark and New York City and also an important manufacturing center. The principal industries are food processing and the manufacture of chemicals, plastics, linoleum, machinery, and radio and electrical equipment. The site of the present town and the surrounding region was settled about 1668. In 1867 the present community was separated from the adjoining town of Harrison. Kearny was named for the American general Philip Kearny (see under KEARNY). It was incorporated as a town and given its present name about 1895. Pop. (1960) 37,472; (1970) 37,585.

KEARNY, name of a family of American military leaders; best known are the following.

Stephen Watts Kearny (1794–1848), army officer, born in Newark, N.J., and educated at Kings College (now Columbia University). He joined the army in 1812, serving with distinction at the Battle of Queenston Heights; see WAR OF 1812, THE. As brigadier general during the Mexican War (q.v.) he was placed in command of the Army of the West and conquered New Mexico. Kearny, with the aid of the American naval officer Robert Field Stockton (1795–1866), occupied Los Angeles, Calif., early in 1847. A dispute arose between Kearny and Stockton as to who was chief in command, and John Charles Frémont (q.v.), whom Stockton had appointed civil governor of California, refused to obey Kearny's orders. Kearny was sustained as military governor by orders from Washington, and he had Frémont court-martialed. In June, 1847, Kearny was ordered to Mexico, where he served a few months as civil governor of Veracruz and then of Mexico City.

Philip Kearny (1814–62), army officer, born in New York City, and educated at Columbia College (now Columbia University). The nephew of Stephen Watts Kearny, he served under his uncle along the frontier. He also fought with the French army in Algeria (1840) and in Italy (1859). He lost his left arm in 1847 during the Mexican War. As a major general of Union army volunteers, he was killed on a reconnoitering expedition at Chantilly, Va., during the American Civil War; see CIVIL WAR, THE AMERICAN.

KEATON, Joseph Francis, popularly known as "BUSTER" KEATON (1895-1966), American motion-picture actor, born in Piqua, Kans. The son of vaudeville performers, Keaton received his training early as a member of "The Three Keatons". In his early films he played a stooge with Roscoe "Fatty" Arbuckle, an already established silent-film comic. Keaton's first featured roles were in *The General* (1926), *Steamboat Bill, Jr.* (1927), and *The Cameraman* (1928). His deadpan expressions, floppy bow tie, and remarkable sense of timing made him one of the most popular comics in silent pictures. After sound became a permanent part of motion pictures, Keaton appeared in fewer films. His later film roles included appearances in *Sidewalks of New York* (1931), *Sunset Boulevard* (1950), and *It's A Mad, Mad, Mad, Mad World* (1963).

KEATS, John (1795-1821), British poet, born in London, England, the son of a livery-stable owner. He was educated at the Clarke School, Enfield, and at the age of fifteen was apprenticed to a surgeon. Subsequently, from 1814 to 1816, Keats studied medicine in London at Guy's and Saint Thomas' hospitals; in 1816 he became a licensed apothecary but never practiced his profession, deciding instead to follow a career as a poet.

Early Works. Keats had already written a translation of Vergil's *Aeneid* and some verse; his first published poems (1816) were the sonnets "Oh, Solitude if I with Thee Must Dwell", and "On First Looking into Chapman's Homer". Both poems appeared in the *Examiner,* a literary periodical edited by the British essayist and poet Leigh Hunt (q.v.), one of the principal champions of the Romantic movement in English literature; *see* ENGLISH LITERATURE: *The Romantic Age.* Hunt introduced Keats to a circle of literary men, including the British poet Percy Bysshe Shelley (q.v.); the group's influence enabled Keats to see his first volume published, *Poems by John Keats* (1817). The principal poems in the volume were the sonnet on Chapman's Homer, the sonnet "To One Who Has Been Long in City Pent", and "I Stood Tip-Toe upon a Little Hill" and "Sleep and Poetry", which defended the principles of Romanticism as promulgated by Hunt and attacked the practice of Romanticism as represented by the British poet George Gordon Byron (q.v.).

Keats' second volume, *Endymion,* was published in 1818. It is based upon the myth of Endymion (q.v.) and the moon goddess, and was violently attacked by two of the most influential critical magazines of the time, the *Quarterly Review* and *Blackwood's Magazine.* The latter called the Romantic verse of Hunt's literary circle "the Cockney school of poetry", declared *Endymion* to be nonsense, and recommended that Keats give up poetry.

Last Works. In 1820 Keats became ill with tuberculosis. The illness may have been aggravated by the emotional strain of his devoted attachment to Fanny Brawne (1801?-65), a young girl with whom he had fallen passionately in

John Keats

love. Nevertheless, the period 1818-20 was one of great creativity for Keats. In July, 1820, the third and best of his volumes of poetry, *Lamia, Isabella, The Eve of St. Agnes, and Other Poems,* was published. The three-title poems, dealing with mythical and legendary themes of ancient, Renaissance, and medieval times, are rich in imagery and phrasing. The volume also contains the unfinished poem "Hyperion", containing some of Keats' finest work, and three poems considered among the finest in the English language, "Ode on a Grecian Urn", "Ode on Melancholy", and "Ode to a Nightingale".

In the fall of 1820, under his doctor's orders to seek a warm climate for the winter, Keats went to Rome. He died there in February, 1821, and was buried in the Protestant cemetery. Some of his best-known poems were posthumously published; among them are "Eve of St. Mark" (1848) and "La Belle Dame sans Merci" ("The Beautiful Woman without Mercy", first version published

1888). Keats' letters, praised by many critics as among the finest literary letters written in English, were published in their most complete form in 1931; a later edition appeared in 1960.

Although Keats' career was short and his output small, critics agree that he was one of the leading poets of the Romantic period and has a lasting place in the history of British and world literature. Characterized by exact and closely knit construction and by force of imagination, his poetry gives transcendental value to the physical beauty of the world. His verbal music is well suited to the unique combination of romantic sentiment and classical clarity his work expresses. L.T.

KEBLE, John (1792–1866), British poet and clergyman, born in Fairford, Gloucestershire, and educated at the University of Oxford. In 1816 he was ordained a priest in the Church of England, and in 1827 his poetic work *The Christian Year* was published anonymously. This popular work, based on the *Book of Common Prayer* (q.v.), includes hymns for each Sunday, each festival, and each saint's day of the church. From 1831 to 1841 Keble was professor of poetry at Oxford and after 1835 was vicar of Hursley, Hampshire. His sermon *National Apostasy*, which he preached at Oxford in July, 1833, advocated a return to the dogmas of the church as laid down by its earliest theologians; see FATHERS OF THE CHURCH. This sermon occasioned a long controversy between advocates of orthodox, or High Church, principles and believers in church liberalism. Keble's sermon marked the beginning of the Oxford movement (q.v.), also known as Tractarianism, which supported the High Church position. He contributed four pamphlets to the series of ninety, known as *Tracts of the Times*, written by leaders of the movement and issued at Oxford (1833–41). In addition to the writings mentioned above, Keble edited (1836) the definitive edition of *Laws of Ecclesiastical Polity*, written by the English theologian Richard Hooker (q.v.) in the 16th century, and was the author of *Lyra Innocentium: Thoughts in Verse on Christian Children, Their Ways, and Their Privileges* (1846), *On Eucharistical Adoration* (1857) and *The Life of Thomas Wilson* (1863).

KECSKEMÉT, city of Hungary, 50 miles S.E. of Budapest. It is the trade center for the fruit, grain, and cattle raised in the surrounding agricultural region. Industries in the city are tanning, wine making, fruit processing, and flour milling. Pop. (1970 est.) 77,000.

KEDIRI, city of Indonesia, in East Java Province, on the Brantas R., 65 miles S.W. of Surabaja. It is the trade center of an important sugar-producing area that also grows rice, rubber, coffee, and tobacco. Industries in the municipality include sugar, rice, and textile milling, tobacco processing, sawmilling, and metalworking. The ruins of Hindu temples are nearby. Kediri was the capital of a Hindu kingdom from the 11th to the 13th century and was capital of Kediri Residency under Dutch rule. Pop. (1971) 178,865.

KEDUSHAH. See PRAYER, JEWISH.

KEELER, William Henry (1872–1923), American professional baseball player, born in Brooklyn, N.Y. Because he was five feet four and one half inches in height, he was nicknamed "Wee Willie". He was an outfielder with the Baltimore team of the National League from 1894 to 1899, with the Brooklyn Dodgers of the National League from 1899 to 1903, with the New York Yankees of the American League from 1903 to 1910, and with the New York team of the National League in 1910. Keeler was a noted "place hitter", that is, one who dexterously bats the ball to unguarded portions of the field, in contrast to the "power hitter", who drives the ball long distances. During his career he played in 2124 games and had a lifetime batting average of .345. He led the National League in batting in 1897 and 1898. Keeler was elected to the Baseball Hall of Fame in 1939. See BASEBALL HALL OF FAME AND MUSEUM, NATIONAL.

KEELING ISLANDS. See COCOS ISLANDS, TERRITORY OF.

KEELUNG, or CHILUNG, city and chief seaport of Taiwan, on the N. coast of the island, at the head of a deep, well-sheltered bay, immediately N.E. of Taipei. The principal export is coal. Gold and sulfur are mined near the town. Pop. (1970 est.) 330,000.

KEENE, city in New Hampshire, and county seat of Cheshire Co., on the Ashuelot R., about 40 miles S.W. of Concord. The city is the shipping point, and retail and wholesale trading center of S.W. New Hampshire. The principal industries are the manufacture of machinery, metal goods, paper goods, leather products, and furniture. It is the site of Keene State College and is in the center of a popular ski area. Annual events in Keene are a winter carnival and a spring music festival. The first permanent settlement was established on the site in 1750, and Keene was chartered as a town in 1753 and incorporated as a city in 1874. Pop. (1960) 17,562; (1970) 20,467.

KEENE, Laura, real name MARY MOSS (about 1826–73), Anglo-American actress, born in London. Her first stage appearance was in the role of Pauline in *The Lady of Lyons* by the British writer Edward Bulwer-Lytton (*see under* LYTTON). She played in Australia from 1852 to 1855.

From 1856 to 1863 she managed Laura Keene's Theater in New York City, where she appeared in comedies and melodramas that she herself produced. Her most successful production was *Our American Cousin* by the British playwright Tom Taylor (1817–80) in 1858. Her company was acting this play at Ford's Theatre, Washington, D.C., on April 14, 1865, when President Abraham Lincoln (q.v.) was assassinated there.

KEFALLINÍA or **CEPHALONIA** (anc. *Cephallenia*), Greek island in the Ionian Sea, which together with nearby small islands forms Kefallinía Department. Kefallinía is the largest of the Ionian Islands, with an area of about 290 sq.mi. It has an irregular coastline 30 mi. long and from 3 to 20 mi. wide. It is mountainous; the highest point, Mt. Ainos, is 5315 ft. above sea level. The chief towns are Argóstolian, which is the capital of the department, and Lixoúrion. The principal crops are currants, olives, grapes, citrus fruits, and cotton. The principal industry is handicrafts.

Kefallinía, like the other Ionian Islands, was seized and ruled by a succession of foreign powers from the time of its fall to the Romans in 189 B.C. until its annexation by Greece in 1864. It was occupied by Italy in World War II. Pop. of department (1961) 46,314. *See* IONIAN ISLANDS.

KEFAUVER, (Carey) Estes (1903–63), American lawyer and legislator, born in Madisonville, Tenn., and educated at the University of Tennessee and at Yale Law School. In 1927 he began to practice law in Chattanooga, Tenn. In May, 1939, he was elected on the Democratic ticket to serve out the unexpired term of United States Representative from the Third Congressional District of Tennessee. He retained his seat in the succeeding four Congresses. Kefauver was elected to the United States Senate in November, 1948. In 1950 he became chairman of the newly created Special Committee to Investigate Organized Crime in Interstate Commerce. Popularly known as the Kefauver Committee, it accumulated substantial evidence of close ties between crime syndicates and local political officials. Kefauver resigned as committee chairman on May 1, 1951. He was a leading contender for the Democratic Presidential nomination in 1952 and the unsuccessful candidate for Vice-President in 1956. Kefauver was reelected to the Senate in 1954 and 1960.

KEITEL, Wilhelm (1882–1946), German field marshal, born in Helmscheroda, near Brunswick. He entered the army in 1901 and served as a captain in World War I. Following the war he remained in the Reichswehr, rising to the rank of colonel in 1931, and major general three years later. A staunch supporter of the German dictator Adolf Hitler (q.v.), he was made chief of the administrative department in the ministry of war in 1935, and in 1938 was put in supreme command of the combined armed forces of Germany. He was made a field marshal in 1940, and in 1941, during World War II (q.v.), he commanded the German forces on the Soviet front. Four years later, in May, 1945, he signed the terms of military surrender of the German Reich to the Allies. He was arrested that same year to face charges at the war crimes trial in Nuremberg, and was found guilty of conspiracy to wage aggressive warfare and of crimes against humanity. He was hanged in 1946. *see* WAR-CRIMES TRIALS: *Nuremberg Trials.*

KEITH, Sir Arthur (1866–1955), British anthropologist, born in Aberdeen, Scotland, and educated at the universities of Aberdeen, London, and Leipzig. He was appointed professor and conservator of the museum at the Royal College of Surgeons in 1908, and was professor of comparative anatomy at the Royal Institution from 1917 to 1923. Keith was an expert in the reconstruction of prehistoric man from fragments of fossil remains. He was elected a fellow of the Royal Society in 1913 and knighted in 1921. He wrote *Ancient Types of Man* (1911), *The Human Body* (1912), *Nationality and Race* (1919), *Concerning Man's Origin* (1927), *Darwinism and Its Critics* (1935), *New Theory of Human Evolution* (1949), and *Autobiography* (1950).

KEKULÉ VON STRADONITZ, Friedrich August (1829–96), German chemist, born in Darmstadt. He studied architecture at the University of Giessen, but turned to chemistry after he heard the lectures of the German chemist Justus von Liebig (q.v.). In 1856 he became assistant professor of chemistry at the University of Heidelberg and in 1858 was appointed to a similar position at the University of Ghent. From 1865 until his death Kekulé was professor of chemistry at the University of Bonn.

The results of his investigations into the linking of carbon atoms in organic compounds were of inestimable importance in the development of organic chemistry. He introduced the concept of tetravalent carbon atoms joined to each other and to other atoms in the molecules of organic compounds, and in 1865 formulated the theory of the ring structure of benzene; *see* AROMATIC COMPOUNDS; CHEMISTRY: *Valency;* CHEMISTRY, ORGANIC.

KELLER, Gottfried (1819–90), Swiss novelist and poet, born in Zürich. In his youth he studied art; a stipend granted him by the Swiss government after the publication of his first volume, *Gedichte* ("Poems", 1846), enabled him to study philosophy at the University of Heidelberg. He lived in Berlin from 1850 to 1855, and from 1861 to 1867 held a government post in Switzerland. Keller is regarded as one of the major German novelists and poets of the second half of the 19th century. His novels and short stories are realistic, with touches of Romantic imagination; Keller is a master of intense tragedy and lively humor. He is best known for his autobiographical novel *Der grüne Heinrich* ("Green Heinrich", 4 vol., 1854–55), considered one of the masterpieces of modern German literature, and for his short stories about Swiss provincial life *Die Leute von Seldwyla* ("People of Seldwyla", first series, 1856, second, 1874). The latter includes the humorous tale *Die Drei Gerechten Kammacher* ("The Three Kammacher Lawyers"), and the tragic story *Romeo und Julia auf dem Dorfe,* which served as the basis for the libretto of the opera *A Village Romeo and Juliet* (1900–01) by the British composer Frederick Delius (q.v.). Among others of Keller's works are the books of short stories *Sieben Legenden* ("Seven Legends", 1872) and *Züricher Novellen* ("Zürich Stories", 1878); the book of poems *Gesammelte Gedichte* ("Collected Poems", 1883); and the novel *Martin Salander* (1886).

KELLER, Helen Adams (1880–1968), American author and lecturer, born in Tuscumbia, Ala. When nineteen months old, she was stricken with an acute illness that left her deaf and blind. No way could be found to educate her until her seventh year, when she began her special education in reading and writing with Anne Mansfield Sullivan, later Macy (1866–1936), of the Perkins Institute for the Blind. She quickly learned to read by the Braille system (q.v.) and to write by means of a specially constructed typewriter. In 1890 she learned to speak after only one month of study. Ten years later she was able to enter Radcliffe College, from which she was graduated with honors in 1904. She then served on the Massachusetts Commission for the Blind, and shortly thereafter lectured throughout the world, using her life as an inspiration for other afflicted persons. After World War II she visited wounded veterans in hospitals all over the United States, and in 1946 spoke in England, France, Italy, and Greece on behalf of the physically handicapped. She received the Presidential Medal of Freedom in 1964. Her writings include *The Story of My Life* (1903), *The World I Live In* (1908), *Out of the Dark* (1913), *Midstream—My Later Life* (1930), *Let Us Have Faith* (1940), *Teacher: Anne Sullivan Macy* (1955), and *The Open Door* (1957). Her life is the subject of a film, *The Unconquered* (1954), and a play, "The Miracle Worker" (1960) by the American author William Gibson (1914–   ).

KELLEY, Edgar Stillman (1857–1944), American composer and writer on music, born in Sparta, Wis., and educated in Chicago and in Stuttgart, Germany. From 1893 to 1895 he was music critic for the San Francisco *Examiner,* and from 1898 to 1902 he taught at the Yale University School of Music. During the next eight years Kelley taught privately in Berlin, Germany, returning to the United States in 1910 to teach at the Cincinnati Conservatory of Music. His best-known works are the incidental music to the play, *Ben Hur,* op. 17; and the symphony, *New England,* op. 33. Among his writings is *Chopin, the Composer* (1913).

KELLOGG, Frank Billings. See under KELLOGG-BRIAND PACT.

KELLOGG, John Harvey (1852–1943), American surgeon and hygienist, born in Tyrone,

Helen Keller, left, demonstrates how she was able to "hear" her teacher, Anne Sullivan, by feeling the vibration of her lips. UPI

Mich., and educated at Bellevue Hospital Medical College. He set up practice in Battle Creek, Mich., where he became superintendent of the Battle Creek Sanitarium in 1876. He was the founder, and from 1923 to 1926 the president, of Battle Creek College, and the founder and medical director of the Miami-Battle Creek Sanitarium in Miami Springs, Fla. Kellogg was interested in public health and nutrition and developed processes for improving cereal foods. Among his writings are *The Art of Massage* (1895), *The Home Book of Modern Medicine* (1906), *Life, Its Mysteries and Miracles* (1910), and *Neurasthenia* (1914).

KELLOGG-BRIAND PACT. multilateral treaty, more formally known as the Pact of Paris, renouncing war as an instrument of national policy and signed by fifteen nations in Paris on August 27, 1928. The pact was sponsored and drafted by the American jurist and statesman Frank Billings Kellogg (1856–1937), then secretary of state of the United States, and Aristide Briand (q.v.), then foreign minister of France. For his role in promoting the pact, Kellogg was awarded the 1929 Nobel Peace Prize. The 1920's, following the peace conferences closing World War I, were a period in which several antiwar and disarmament conferences were held; see DISARMAMENT; LOCARNO. These conferences were the genesis of the Kellogg-Briand Pact. On April 6, 1927, the tenth anniversary of the entry of the U.S. into World War I, Briand suggested, in a statement to American press correspondents in Paris, that the U.S. and France abolish the possibility of war between them. In the exchange of notes between Kellogg and Briand that followed, the U.S. expressed its desire to include the proposal in a general treaty among all the world powers. As a result of these negotiations, the Pact of Paris bound its signatories to renounce aggressive warfare and settle disputes by peaceful means. Defensive war was not outlawed; moreover, the preamble to the treaty declared that the breaking of the agreement by any signatory automatically released the others from their obligations. The Pact of Paris was signed by Germany, Belgium, Great Britain, Canada, Australia, New Zealand, the Union of South Africa, the Irish Free State, India, Italy, Japan, Poland, Czechoslovakia, France, and the U.S.; it was ratified by the United States Senate on Jan. 15, 1929. In 1932 the pact was invoked through the League of Nations in a futile attempt to halt the Japanese invasion of China. It was again invoked, by more than sixty governments, but to no avail, against the Italian invasion of Ethiopia in 1936.

KELLY, Emmett Leo (1898–), American circus performer, born in Sedan, Kans. Before joining the circus in 1921, Kelly was a cartoonist. His cartoon character, called "Wearie Willie", later was the model on which Kelly created his famous clown "Willie", the woebegone, sorrowful tramp. Kelly appeared on television and in such motion pictures as *The Greatest Show on Earth* (1952), in which he appeared as "Willie", and *Wind Across the Everglades* (1952). His autobiography *Clown: My Life in Tatters and Smiles* was published in 1954.

KELLY, Grace (Patricia) (1929–), former American motion-picture actress, now Princess Grace of Monaco, born in Philadelphia, Pa. After attending the American Academy of Dramatic Arts (q.v.) in New York City, she made her stage debut in 1949 in the Broadway production of *The Father* by August Strindberg (q.v.). Her first motion picture was *Fourteen Hours* in 1951. The following year she starred with the American actor Gary Cooper (q.v.) in *High Noon*. In 1954, she won the best-actress award of the Academy of Motion Picture Arts and Sciences for her role in *The Country Girl*. That year she also appeared in *Rear Window*, and *Dial M for Murder*. *High Society* and *The Swan* were released in 1956, the same year she married Prince Rainier III (q.v.) of Monaco.

KELP, common name applied to large, foliose, marine, brown algae, a type of seaweed, belonging to the class Phaeophyceae, and to ashes of these algae, used as a source of iodine and soda. The principal genera of kelp are *Laminaria*, the true kelps, *Macrocystis*, the giant kelps, and *Nereocystis*, the bladder kelps, belonging to the families Laminariaceae and Lessoniaceae. The ashes of *Fucus*, the rockweeds, belonging to the family Fucaceae, are also referred to as kelp. True kelps and rockweeds are distributed throughout the temperate and boreal areas of the oceans of the world, but giant kelps and bladder kelps are restricted to the northern Pacific Ocean. True kelps, giant kelps, and bladder kelps have independent gametophyte and sporophyte generations. The sporophyte plant consists of a basal holdfast, a long slender stalk, and a long, leaflike blade. Clusters of unicellular spore-producing organs, called sporangia, bear microscopic spores. The gametophyte plant, which develops from a spore, is a minute filament composed of about twenty to fifty cells. Male filaments produce many sperms, and female filaments produce a few eggs; both sperms and eggs are produced in specialized gametangia; uniting, they give rise to new sporophyte plants.

Because kelp contains considerable potash, it is used as a fertilizer, especially in agricultural areas situated near the coast. In the Orient it is used extensively as a food because of its high mineral and vitamin content. Ashes obtained by burning the plants were formerly a major commercial source of iodine and soda.

Rockweed, a kelp of the genus Fucus.

KELT. See CELTIC PEOPLES AND LANGUAGES.

KELVIN, 1st Baron, William Thomson (1824–1907), also known as LORD KELVIN, British mathematician and physicist, born in Belfast, Ireland, and educated at the universities of Glasgow and Cambridge. He accepted a professorship at the University of Glasgow in 1846 and held it until 1899, during which time he became recognized as one of the leading physical scientists and greatest teachers of his time.

In the field of thermodynamics (q.v.) Thomson developed the work done by the British physicist James Prescott Joule (q.v.) on the interrelation of heat and mechanical energy and in 1852, they collaborated to investigate the so-called Joule-Thomson cooling effect. In 1848 he proposed the absolute scale of temperature, that still bears his name; see HEAT: *Temperature Scales*. His work in the field of electricity (q.v.) was of practical importance in telegraphy; see TELEGRAPH. He studied the mathematical theory of cable signaling and devised improvements in the manufacture of cables and in the construction of the mirror galvanometer and the siphon recorder. He was employed as scientific advisor in the laying of the Atlantic telegraph cables in 1857–58 and 1865–66. Thomson also investigated the oscillatory nature of electrical discharge, the electrodynamic properties of metals, and the mathematical treatment of magnetism (q.v.), and contributed to the theory of elasticity. With the German physiologist and physicist Hermann Ludwig Ferdinand von Helmholtz (q.v.), Thomson estimated the age of the sun and later calculated the energy radiated from the surface of the sun. Among the many devices he devised or improved were a tide predictor, a harmonic analyzer, and an apparatus for taking soundings in shallow and deep waters (see SOUNDING). In addition he reconstructed and improved the mariner's compass (see COMPASS: *Magnetic Compass*).

Thomson was knighted in 1866 and was raised to the peerage with the title of Baron Kelvin of Largs in 1892. He was president of the Royal Society in 1890, and in 1902 received the Order of Merit. Many of his scientific papers were collected in his *Reprint of Papers on Electricity and Magnetism* (1872), *Mathematical and Physical Papers* (1882, 1883, 1890), and *Popular Lectures and Addresses* (1889–94).

KEMAL ATATÜRK

KEMAL ATATÜRK, previously KEMAL PASHA, and earlier MUSTAFA KEMEL or MUSTAPHA KEMAL (1881–1938), Turkish soldier, national leader, and first president of the Republic of Turkey, born in Salonika, and educated at the military college in Constantinople (now İstanbul). In accordance with an ancient Turkish practice, he began life without a surname, but was called Kemal, meaning "perfection", because of his excellence in mathematics.

Military Leadership. He worked against the sultanate, but in 1908, finding the reforms instituted by the Young Turks too moderate, he left politics and devoted himself to his military career. In 1911 and 1912 he served in the Turko-Italian War. He became chief of staff of an army in 1913, during the second Balkan War, and from 1913 to 1914 he was military attaché at Sofia, Bulgaria. He opposed Turkish participation on the German side in World War I because he regarded defeat as inevitable; nevertheless he served with distinction as a commander during the Gallipoli and Dardanelles Campaign (q.v.) in 1915, in the Caucasus from 1916 to 1917, and in Palestine in 1918. In recognition of his military services, he was given the title of pasha.

After World War I, Mustafa Kemel rallied national resistance to the execution of the harsh

351

KEMBLE

peace terms imposed upon Turkey. He was exiled by the sultan to Anatolia, where he set up a rival government in 1920, and was elected president. In military actions, he suppressed the newly-created Armenian Republic (see ARMENIA: History) and defeated the Greek army of occupation. For his victory against the Greeks at the battle of the Sakarya River in 1921, he received the official designation of Ghazi, meaning "victorious". See TURKEY: History.

President of the Republic. His victories secured milder peace terms at a conference with representatives of the allied powers at Lausanne in 1922. The same year the sultan was deposed, and a year later the Ghazi was unanimously elected president of the republic. Reelected in 1927, 1931, and 1935, he ruled as a dictator, tolerating no opposition. In the ten years from 1924 to 1934 he completely transformed traditional Turkey. His reforms included the separation of the Moslem church from the state, the abolition of the caliphate (see CALIPH) and the monasteries; the suppression of ancient modes of dress and of the practice of polygamy; the introduction of the Roman alphabet, the Gregorian calendar, and new civil and penal codes; and the adoption of family names to simplify the compilation of civil and military listings of the population. In 1934 the National Assembly conferred upon him the surname of Atatürk, or "chief Turk".

His national policy was directed toward making Turkey a European rather than an Oriental country, and to this end he promoted extensive industrialization. Fearing the foreign political domination which often accompanies foreign capital investments, he sought to finance commerce and industry through the use of Turkish national funds, secured by heavy taxation. Thus industry and trade were largely state-controlled. In foreign policy, Kemal Atatürk maintained friendly relations with the Soviet Union, and concluded treaties of friendship with the Balkan countries, Hungary and Greece. In 1936, by agreement with the great powers, Turkey was allowed to fortify the straits of the Bosporus and the Dardanelles.

KEMBLE, name of a famous British family of actors. Among its most important members are the following.

Roger Kemble (1721–1802), born in Herefordshire. He formed a traveling theatrical company soon after his marriage to British actress Sarah Ward (1735–1807) in 1753, and subsequently she and their children toured with the company. The oldest of their twelve children, Sarah Kemble Siddons (q.v.), became one of the great actresses of her time. Roger Kemble never became famous, although he scored a success at the Haymarket Theatre, London, in 1788 as Falstaff in William Shakespeare's *King Henry IV.*

John Philip Kemble (1757–1823), eldest son of Roger, born in Prescot, Lancashire, and educated at the English College in Douai, France. As a child he had acted in his father's company, and he returned to the stage after studying for the priesthood, bringing to his roles an austerity and quality of spirituality that contributed to his success. He was most noted for his acting of the great tragic parts. A star at the Drury Lane Theatre (q.v.) in London from 1783, he often palyed there together with his famous sister, Sarah Kemble Siddons, and managed the theater from 1788 to 1802. He later managed Covent Garden Theatre (q.v.), where in 1817 he made his farewell appearance in the title role of Shakespeare's *Coriolanus,* his best part. Among the many other parts in which he was celebrated are the title roles in Shakespeare's *Hamlet, Macbeth,* and *King Lear.*

Fannie Kemble, in full FRANCES ANNE KEMBLE (1809–93), older daughter of Charles, born in London. She became immediately popular after her London debut in 1829 at Covent Garden Theatre as Juliet in Shakespeare's *Romeo and Juliet.* She was suited for both comedy and tragedy, and her success continued in other Shakespearean plays and in Restoration comedies until she retired in 1834 upon her marriage to an American plantation owner. After her return to the stage in 1847, she was most successful giving readings, in England and America, from the plays of Shakespeare. She wrote a number of plays and several books of memoirs about her acting career and her life in America.

KEMEROVO, city of the Soviet Union, in the Russian S.F.S.R., and capital of Kemerovo Oblast, on the Tom R., about 125 miles E. of Novosibirsk. Served by a branch of the Trans-Siberian Railroad, Kemerovo is one of the principal coal-mining centers for the Kuznetsk Basin of southern Siberia. The city has a large chemical industry, as well as glassworks, sawmills, and a power plant. Founded in 1916 as Shcheglovsk, the city was named in 1935. Pop. (1970) 385,000.

KEMPIS, Thomas A. See THOMAS A KEMPIS.

KENDALL, Edward Calvin (1886–1972), American biochemist, born in South Norwalk, Conn., and educated at Columbia University. After he began his career in 1910 as a research chemist in the pharmaceutical industry, he subsequently joined the staff of Saint Luke's Hospital in New York City. In 1914 he became head of the biochemistry section of the Mayo Clinic in

Rochester, Minn., and in 1921 was appointed professor of physiological chemistry in the Mayo Foundation for Medical Education and Research, University of Minnesota. After 1952 he served as professor of chemistry at the James Forrestal Research Center of Princeton University. His extensive research in endocrinology led to the isolation of thyroxine, glutathione, and several adrenal cortex hormones; see ENDOCRINE SYSTEM. Kendall's outstanding achievement was the isolation of cortisone (q.v.). He shared the 1950 Nobel Prize in medicine and physiology with the American physician Philip Showalter Hench and the Polish-Swiss chemist Tadeus Reichstein (qq.v.).

KENDREW, John Cowdery (1917–), British biophysicist, born in Oxford, England, and educated at the universities of Oxford and Cambridge. He worked with the World War II ministry of aircraft production from 1940 to 1945. He then returned to Cambridge; in 1953 he became deputy director of the Medical Research Council Laboratory of Molecular Biology, a government agency. Kendrew shared the 1962 Nobel Prize in chemistry with his Cambridge associate, the Austrian-British biochemist Max Ferdinand Perutz (q.v.). Kendrew was responsible for determining the structure of a protein pigment called myoglobin, which is similar to hemoglobin. Through crystallography, the bombardment of a molecule with X rays, he determined the spatial arrangement of the myoglobin atoms.

KENILWORTH, Great Britain, urban district of Warwickshire, England, on a tributary of the Avon R., about 80 miles N.W. of London. During the 12th century the town was granted to the English royal treasurer, Geoffrey de Clinton (fl. 1130), who built a castle there. The castle was given to the English noble, Simon de Montfort (q.v.) in the 13th century. In 1562 Queen Elizabeth I (q.v.) gave the castle to her favorite Robert Dudley, 1st Earl of Leicester (see under DUDLEY). The castle was later celebrated in the romance *Kenilworth* by the Scottish novelist Sir Walter Scott (q.v.). In addition to ruins of the castle, remains of a 12th-century priory are in Kenilworth. Pop. (1971 est.) 19,980.

KÉNITRA, city of Morocco, in Rabat Province, on the Sebou R., 10 mi. inland from the Atlantic Ocean, 22 miles N.E. of Rabat. The city is on the coastal railroad and is a major port and naval base served by the outport at Mehdia. Exports include grains, wine, citrus fruits, and vegetables from the Gharb plain to the E., zinc from the Midelt mines, and cork from the nearby Mamora forests to the S. Petroleum and natural gas are found to the E. Industries in the city include textile milling, fish and tobacco processing, and fertilizer manufacturing. Founded by Marshal Louis Herbert Gonzalve Lyautey (q.v.) in 1912, when the French protectorate was established, Kénitra was called Port-Lyautey from 1932 to 1956. The port was opened in 1913, and the city was the site of a United States naval air station until 1963. Pop. (1971) 139,206.

KENMORE, village of New York, in Erie Co., adjoining Buffalo, and 5 miles N. of the downtown area. Manufactures include machinery, chemicals, wood and metal products, and electric appliances. The surrounding area has many farms. The village was incorporated in 1899. Pop. (1960) 21,261; (1970) 20,980.

KENNAN, George Frost (1904–), American diplomat, born in Milwaukee, Wis., and educated at Princeton University. He began his diplomatic career in 1925 in Hamburg, Germany. His four tours of duty in the Soviet Union included service as the United States ambassador in 1952 and, until his retirement, 1953. As a result of his experience, Kennan was regarded as an authority on the U.S.S.R. In 1961, recalled to the diplomatic service by President John F. Kennedy, he began two years of duty as ambassador to Yugoslavia. Also an educator, he joined the Institute for Advanced Studies in Princeton, N.J., in 1953. And as an author, he twice won both the Pulitzer Prize in history and the National Book Award: for Vol. I of his two-volume work *Soviet-American Relations,* entitled *Russia Leaves the War* (1957); and for *Memoirs: 1925–1950* (1967). Volume II of the first-named work is *Decision to Intervene* (1958); his autobiography is continued in *Memoirs: Vol. II, 1950–1963* (1972).

KENNEBEC, river of W. Maine, rising in Moosehead Lake and flowing generally S. about 150 mi. before joining Androscoggin R. to form Merrymeeting Bay, an arm of the Atlantic Ocean. The river is dammed at Bingham, Skowhegan, Waterville, and Augusta to provide hydroelectric power. The river is navigable to Augusta.

KENNEDY, name of an American family, prominent in public affairs. The most notable members of the family are the following.

Joseph Patrick Kennedy (1888–1969), businessman and diplomat, born in Boston, Mass., and educated at Harvard University. He amassed a fortune through various business enterprises, including motion pictures and real estate. He served as first chairman of the Securities and Exchange Commission (q.v.), an independent agency of the United States government, in 1934 and 1935; as chairman of the Federal Maritime Commission in 1937; and as

As President-elect, John F. Kennedy poses with members of his family at his father's home in Hyannis Port, Mass. Seated, left to right, are his sister, Mrs. R. Sargent Shriver, Jr.; his parents, Mr. and Mrs. Joseph P. Kennedy; his wife, Jacqueline; his brother, Edward M. Kennedy. Standing, left to right, his sister-in-law, Mrs. Robert F. Kennedy; his brother-in-law, Steven Smith; Mrs. Smith; Kennedy; his brother, Robert F. Kennedy; his sister, Mrs. Peter Lawford; R. Sargent Shriver, Jr.; Mrs. Edward M. Kennedy; and Peter Lawford. UPI

ambassador from the United States to Great Britain from 1938 to 1940. His wife, Rose Fitzgerald Kennedy (1890–), was the daughter of the political leader John Francis Fitzgerald (1863–1950), mayor of Boston from 1906 to 1907 and from 1910 to 1914. The oldest son of Joseph Patrick and Rose Fitzgerald Kennedy, naval officer Joseph Patrick Kennedy, Jr. (1915–44), was killed in combat in World War II.

John Fitzgerald Kennedy (1917–63), 35th President of the United States, the son of Joseph Patrick. See separate article.

Robert Francis Kennedy (1925–68), political leader and legislator, the son of Joseph Patrick, born in Brookline, Mass. Kennedy interrupted his undergraduate studies at Harvard University to serve in the United States Navy during World War II. After the war he returned to Harvard and in 1948 received a B.A. degree. He was awarded an LL.B. degree from the University of Virginia in 1951. Later that year he became an attorney in the United States Department of Justice, leaving that post the following year to manage the senatorial campaign of his older brother, John F. Kennedy (q.v.). Following the campaign Robert Kennedy returned to government service as counsel to several Senate subcommittees. He first gained national prominence as chief counsel (1955–57) of the Senate permanent investigations subcommittee in its investigation of Teamster Union executives David Beck (1894–) and James Hoffa (1913–). In 1960, following the election of his brother to the Presidency, Robert Kennedy was appointed U.S. attorney general. His tenure in that office was marked by active enforcement of civil-rights laws. He resigned his cabinet post in 1964, and in the same year was elected U.S. Senator from New York. As Senator, Kennedy showed himself to be particularly concerned with the problems of urban ghettos and of the poor and disadvantaged.

In the spring of 1968 Kennedy, who sharply differed with some of the policies of President Lyndon B. Johnson (q.v.), campaigned for the Democratic Party nomination. By June, 1968, he had won major preference primaries in Indiana, Nebraska, and California. Upon leaving a celebration in Los Angeles, after his victory in the California primary was assured, Kennedy was shot by the Jerusalem-born Jordanian Sirhan Bishara Sirhan (1944–). Kennedy died the following day, June 6, 1968. His gravesite in Arlington National Cemetery (q.v.) is near that of President Kennedy.

354

Edward Moore Kennedy (1932–), political leader and legislator, the son of Joseph Patrick, born in Brookline, Mass. He attended Harvard University from 1951 to 1952, served in the United States Army as an enlisted man from 1952 to 1954, then returned to Harvard and was awarded a B.A. degree in 1956. He attended the International Law Institute, The Hague, the Netherlands, in 1956 and 1957, and received an LL.B. degree from the University of Virginia Law School in 1959. He served as assistant to the district attorney of Suffolk County, Mass., from 1960 until 1962, when he resigned and was elected to the United States Senate, to fill the unexpired term of his brother John. He was reelected U.S. Senator from Massachusetts in 1964 and 1970. During the organization of the Ninety-first Congress in January, 1969, members of his party elected Kennedy party whip. As party whip, a position he retained for two years, Kennedy took his place among the leaders of the Democratic Party, serving as liaison between them and party members in the Senate.

KENNEDY, John Fitzgerald (1917–63), thirty-fifth President of the United States, born in Brookline, Mass. He was the second son of the financier Joseph Patrick Kennedy (*see under* KENNEDY), who served as chairman of the Securities and Exchange Commission (q.v.) and as ambassador to Great Britain during the administration of President Franklin Delano Roosevelt (q.v.). John Kennedy studied at the London

Hans Knopf — Pix, Inc.

Above: John Fitzgerald Kennedy and his wife, Jacqueline, on the campaign trail in New York City during his successful race for the Presidency in 1960. Below: John F. Kennedy takes the oath of office to become President of the United States. Administering the oath is Chief Justice Earl Warren. At right is Vice-President Lyndon B. Johnson.

UPI

A fixture of President Kennedy's office was his rocking chair, in which he sits here to converse with aides, including Assistant Secretary of State for African Affairs G. Mennen Williams (facing camera). Camera Press — Pix, Inc.

Governor Adlai Ewing Stevenson (*see under* STEVENSON) of Illinois in 1956, Kennedy received the Democratic nomination for President in 1960. His campaign included a series of televised debates with his Republican opponent, Vice-President Richard Milhous Nixon (q.v.). Kennedy and his running mate, Senator Lyndon Baines Johnson (q.v.) of Texas, were elected by a small popular majority.

Policies as President. In his inaugural address, Kennedy, noting that "the torch has been passed to a new generation", called for a commitment to the national welfare and to the defense of freedom. His first major crisis in foreign policy occurred in April, 1961, when he approved an invasion of Cuba by refugees operating with the help of U.S. agencies, which had been planned by the preceding Administration; *see* CUBA: *History*. The swift failure of the invasion at the Bay of Pigs resulted in personal humiliation for the President. In October, 1962, however, his blockade and threatened military invasion of Cuba forced the Soviet Union to remove its long-range missiles from the island. His popularity in Europe was heightened by a visit

The funeral procession for President John F. Kennedy moves along Connecticut Avenue in Washington, D.C., on Nov. 25, 1963. Behind the caisson walk Mrs. Kennedy and other members of the family and President and Mrs. Lyndon B. Johnson. UPI

School of Economics in 1935–36, was graduated from Harvard University in 1940, and served in the United States Navy during World War II, notably as the commander of the patrol torpedo boat PT-109. While on duty in the Pacific Ocean in August, 1943, he saved the lives of several of his crewmen, earning a citation for valor. A member of the Democratic Party (q.v.), he was elected to the United States House of Representatives in 1946 and to the United States Senate in 1952. In 1953 he married the daughter of a New York City financier, Jacqueline Lee Bouvier (1929–   ); they were the parents of two children who survived infancy, Caroline Kennedy (1957–   ) and John Fitzgerald Kennedy, Jr. (1960–   ). Mrs. Kennedy married the Greek shipping magnate and business executive Aristotle Socrates Onassis (1906–   ) in 1968. During recovery from a series of spinal operations, Kennedy completed his biographical study of several U.S. Senators who had resisted political pressures in their adherence to personal ideals. This book, *Profiles in Courage* (1956), received a Pulitzer Prize in 1957.

After an unsuccessful attempt to gain the nomination for Vice-President on a ticket with to West Berlin, where he pledged continued U.S. support for West Germany. Maintaining the commitment of previous administrations, he intensified U.S. involvement in South Vietnam; see VIETNAM: *History;* VIETNAM, WAR IN. One of his most notable achievements in foreign policy was the establishment of the Peace Corps (q.v.).

The President's program of domestic legislation was intended to stimulate economic growth and to broaden public welfare. An extensive civil-rights bill became part of his program in 1963. Lacking Congressional support, however, he was able to enact relatively little legislation. More successful were his efforts in support of racial integration at the University of Mississippi and elsewhere. His program of space exploration called for a landing of men on the moon before the end of the 1960's; see ASTRONAUTICS.

President Kennedy was assassinated on Nov. 22, 1963, during a political trip to Dallas, Texas. The fourth President to be assassinated, he died shortly after being fired upon in an open car. A commission headed by Chief Justice Earl Warren (q.v.) later confirmed that the assassin had been Lee Harvey Oswald (1939–63), a former U.S. Marine who had returned to the U.S. after being refused Soviet citizenship; see WARREN REPORT. On Nov. 25, the President was given a state funeral and buried in Arlington National Cemetery (q.v.). The period of national mourning was followed, during the Johnson administration, by enactment of much of the legislation first proposed by Kennedy.

Kennedy, the youngest man and the first Roman Catholic to be elected to the Presidency, achieved considerable popularity during his brief term. For 1000 days the world watched as the vigorous young President, with the members of his large and glamorous family surrounding and assisting him, placed his individual stamp on both domestic and foreign affairs. Kennedy was noted for the high literary standard of his speeches.

See *also* UNITED STATES OF AMERICA, THE: *History: The Kennedy Administration.* N.H.C.

KENNEDY, CAPE. See CAPE KENNEDY.

KENNEDY, MOUNT. See YUKON TERRITORY.

KENNESAW MOUNTAIN, BATTLE OF, Civil War action fought on June 27, 1864, at Kennesaw Mt. in Cobb County, Ga., about 20 miles N.W. of Atlanta. Confederate general Joseph Johnston (q.v.), who had been steadily retreating before Union general William Tecumseh Sherman (*see under* SHERMAN), ordered his 18,000 troops to throw up breastworks near the mountain on June 18, 1864, and there he made a stand. On the morning of June 27 Sherman ordered his 16,000 troops to attack the fortified lines of the enemy. The battle was waged over a 10-mi. front and lasted for 2½ hr. The assault failed, and the Union troops withdrew. Total Confederate losses were about 800; total Union losses, 2500. The defeat was the most severe suffered by Union forces during the Georgia campaign. Kennesaw Mountain National Battlefield Park is on the site at which the battle was fought. See CIVIL WAR, THE AMERICAN.

KENNETH, name of two kings of Scotland.

Kenneth I, called MACALPINE (d. about 858 A.D.), traditionally, the founder and first king of Scotland. About 834 he succeeded his father, Alpine, as king of the Gaelic Scots in Galloway. In a series of battles from 841 to 846 he conquered the Pictish kingdom (*see* PICTS) and, uniting it with his own, called his increased domains Scotland. The kingdom is sometimes called Scone, after Kenneth's capital. In later years the king led six invasions of Lothian, southern Scotland, then part of Saxon Northumbria.

Kenneth II, (d. 995), king from 971 to 995, the son of Malcolm I MacDonald (d. 954). From the beginning of his reign Kenneth waged war against the Saxons, particularly the earls of Northumbria who occupied southern Scotland, and against the Norwegians, who controlled Scotland north of the Spey R. Although his wars were not successful, Kenneth consolidated central Scotland into a strong kingdom. See *also* SCOTLAND: *History.*

KENNEWICK, city of Washington, in Benton Co., on the Columbia R., about 73 miles S.E. of Yakima. The city has some manufacturing. The Atomic Energy Commission has a plant nearby. Pop. (1960) 14,244; (1970) 15,212.

KENNY, Elizabeth (1886–1952), Australian nurse, commonly known as Sister Kenny, born in Warrialda, New South Wales, and educated at Saint Ursula's College in Armidale. During successive periods of service from 1911 to 1918 as a nurse in the Australian bush country and with the Australian army, she developed the so-called Sister Kenny method for the treatment of infantile paralysis; see POLIOMYELITIS. Subsequently she improved this treatment, and in 1933 established a clinic at Townsville, Queensland. In 1940 she came to the United States and began further research on the symptoms and treatment of infantile paralysis. In 1943 the Elizabeth Kenny Institute was established in Minneapolis. Her method, consisting essentially of the stimulation and reeducation of the muscles affected by infantile paralysis, provoked strong controversy within the medical profession, but

KENO

she persisted in her claims and continued to arouse interest by her lectures before medical and lay audiences. Among her writings are *Kenny Concept of Infantile Paralysis and Its Treatment* (1942), and an autobiography, *And They Shall Walk* (1943).

KENO, game of chance, played with numbered cards and counters by any number of people. Keno is a variant of bingo (q.v.), which it closely resembles. In both games the players are issued cards divided into rows of numbered squares, no two cards having exactly the same numbers. In keno the possible numbers in each of twenty-five squares extend from 1 to 90, while in bingo the possible numbers extend only from 1 to 75. There is no free number in the center square in keno as there is in bingo. When keno is played, the operator of the game draws or releases numbered balls, one at a time, from a container known as the "keno goose". There are no duplicate numbers in the "goose". Each number is marked off by the operator on a large board that usually is illuminated. Winners are those who first cover on their cards all five numbers in a vertical, horizontal, or diagonal row.

KENOSHA, city and port in Wisconsin, and county seat of Kenosha Co., on Lake Michigan, about 30 miles S. of Milwaukee. The city is a major manufacturing center that produces automobiles, fire-fighting equipment, brass and copper products, textiles, plumbing fixtures, fertilizers, industrial tools, wire rope and cable, and dairy machinery. Kenosha has railroad service and harbor facilities for lake and deepwater vessels. The site of the city was settled about 1835 and the settlement was known as Southport from 1837 until 1850, when it was chartered as a city and renamed Kenosha. Pop. (1960) 67,899; (1970) 78,805.

KENSINGTON AND CHELSEA, ROYAL BOROUGH OF, Great Britain, borough of Greater London, England, on the N. bank of the Thames R. Before 1965 the two districts of Kensington and Chelsea were separate boroughs. Kensington, which is chiefly a residential district, was a manor as early as the 11th century. About the end of the 17th century, William III (q.v.), King of England, bought Nottingham House in Kensington and established his court there. Later remodeled by the British architect Sir Christopher Wren (q.v.), it became known as Kensington Palace. Kensington Gardens, adjoining Hyde Park, was laid out as part of the palace grounds during the reign of Queen Anne (q.v.) and in 1851 was the site of the Great Exhibition. The British Museum of Natural History; the Geological Museum; the Victoria and Albert Museum; the Imperial Institute; the Royal Colleges of Science, of Art, and of Music; and the Royal Albert Hall are all located in Kensington.

The Chelsea district, located s. of Kensington, is also mainly residential. It is noted for the manufacture, in the 18th century, of Chelsea china, and for its literary and artistic associations. At various times in the 18th, 19th, and 20th centuries, Chelsea was the home of satirist Jonathan Swift; essayist, playwright, and statesman Sir Richard Steele; novelist Tobias Smollett; statesman Sir Robert Walpole; landscape painter and illustrator Joseph Turner; poet and painter Dante Gabriel Rossetti; American painter James McNeill Whistler; essayist and poet Leigh Hunt; Scottish essayist and historian Thomas Carlyle; Anglo-American novelist Henry James; and American artist John Singer Sargent (qq.v.). Among the landmarks of the district are the Royal Hospital (for disabled soldiers), completed under the supervision of Sir Christopher Wren in 1692; the Sloane Botanic Gardens; and the Chelsea Embankment on the Thames, a tree-lined promenade laid out from 1871 to 1874 and flanked by fine houses. Pop. (1971 est.) 186,570.

KENSINGTON RUNE STONE, supposed relic of an expedition of thirty Norsemen (q.v.) to North America in 1362. Found on a farm near Kensington, Minn., in 1898, the stone is inscribed with runes (q.v.) that were deciphered by the American author Hjalmar Rued Holand (1872–1963) in 1907. Although Holand later wrote several books about the stone, many scholars doubt the stone's authenticity.

KENT, Great Britain, maritime county of S.E. England, on the Strait of Dover. It is drained by the Darent, the Medway, and the Stour rivers and by the Thames estuary, which bounds the county on the N. The North Downs, a range of chalk hills, extend from E. to W., and terminate on the strait in the famous White Cliffs. The estuary of the Medway contains several islands, including the fertile Isle of Sheppey. The Isle of Thanet (see THANET, ISLE OF) is separated from the mainland by the branches of the Stour R.

The chief towns include Canterbury, a county borough, Chatham, Dover, Gravesend, and the county town, Maidstone (qq.v.). Fishing, the grazing of cattle and sheep, and the raising of hops and fruits are important occupations. The principal industrial establishments are paper mills, engineering shops, breweries, and cement works.

The Roman conquerors invaded England through Kent in the 1st century B.C. and established a series of ports along the coast. Through the ancient site of Canterbury ran the Roman

KENTUCKY

road now called Watling Street. During the Anglo-Saxon period the area now included in the county formed the Kingdom of Kent. From the time of the Norman Conquest in 1066 until the 14th century Kent was an earldom; see ENGLAND: *History*.

Area, 1525 sq.mi.; pop. (1971) 1,396,030.

KENT, James (1763–1847), American jurist, born in Fredericksburgh, N.Y., and educated at Yale College (now Yale University). He was admitted to the bar in 1785 and practiced law at Poughkeepsie from 1785 to 1793. During this period he was twice elected to represent Dutchess County in the State Assembly. In 1793 Kent was appointed one of two masters in Chancery in New York City, and in the same year he became the first professor of law at King's College (later Columbia College). In 1796 Kent was again elected to the State Assembly, and in 1798 he was appointed judge of the New York Supreme Court. He became chief justice in 1804 and held that position until 1814, when he was appointed chancellor of the New York Court of Chancery. As chancellor he handed down decisions that influenced the subsequent development of American equity jurisprudence. He resigned as chancellor in 1823 to devote himself to the teaching of law at Columbia College. His lectures there constituted the basis for his four-volume work, *Commentaries on American Law* (1826–30).

KENT, Rockwell (1882-1971), American painter and illustrator, born in Tarrytown, N.Y. He studied with several American artists, including William Merritt Chase (1849–1916) in 1898 and Abbott Handerson Thayer (q.v.) in 1903, while attending the Columbia University School of Architecture. Thayer's influence was most lasting. After 1905 Kent spent most of his time traveling and painting in Maine, New Hampshire, Newfoundland, Greenland, and South America.

Kent preferred painting the stark, bleak aspects of nature. Simple but strong, his landscapes feature formally balanced, decorative areas; "Winter" (1907, Metropolitan Museum of Art, New York City) is a typical example of his work. Kent is regarded as one of America's foremost illustrators; his drawings for *Moby Dick*, *The Canterbury Tales*, and the plays of the English playwright William Shakespeare are his finest achievements in this field.

Often the center of controversy because of his espousal of left-wing political causes and feelings of friendship for the Soviet Union, Kent gave 80 of his paintings and 800 drawings to the Soviet Union in 1960. In 1967 he was awarded the Lenin Peace Prize.

Kent wrote about his travels and his involvement in political controversies in a number of books, including *Wilderness* (1920), *Voyaging Southward from the Strait of Magellan* (1924), *N by E* (1930), *Greenland Journal* (1962), and *It's Me O Lord* (autobiography, 1955). He also illustrated all his works.

KENT'S CAVERN, *or* KENT'S HOLE, limestone cave near Torquay, Devonshire, England, one of the earliest sites to yield evidence of the contemporaneous existence of man and now extinct or no longer indigenous animals. Excavations were begun in 1825, and later investigations were carried on in 1840, from 1865 to 1880, and in 1926. Six levels of deposits were discovered. The upper layers contain relics of the Roman period and the early Iron and Bronze ages. These include polished stone and metal artifacts, pottery, and human bones, which indicate cannibalistic customs. On deeper levels below layers of limestone and black mold are deposits of red cave earth and black earth containing human and animal bones and Paleolithic implements. The animal remains include those of the mammoth, woolly rhinoceros, reindeer, and giant deer.

KENTUCKY, one of the East South Central States and one of the four Commonwealths of the United States, bounded on the N. by Indiana and Ohio, on the E. by West Virginia and Virginia, on the S. by Tennessee, and on the W. by Missouri and Illinois. Kentucky is approximately triangular in shape; it measures about 425 mi. from E. to W. and about 180 mi. from N. to S.

Area (37th State in rank)	40,395 sq.mi.
Land	39,650 sq.mi.
Inland water	745 sq.mi.
Population	(1970, 23rd in rank) 3,219,311
	(1960, 22nd in rank) 3,038,156
	(1950) 2,944,806
Altitude	257 ft. to 4145 ft.
Capital	Frankfort (1970) 21,902
Largest city	Louisville (1970) 361,958
Entered Union (15th State)	June 1, 1792
Nickname	The Bluegrass State
Motto	United We Stand, Divided We Fall
Song	"My Old Kentucky Home"
Flower	goldenrod
Bird	cardinal

THE LAND

Kentucky may be divided into three main regions. The S.E. third of the State is a mountainous region, the northward continuation of the Cumberland Plateau. The Kentucky portion of this plateau has been carved by streams into a maze of narrow, steep-sided valleys separated by equally narrow ridges with an average elevation of 2000 ft.

The second topographic division, a continuation of the highland rim of Tennessee, extends from the mountain region westward across the

359

The State capitol of Kentucky, at Frankfort.   UPI

s. half of the State to the Mississippi R. Parts of this region are level, other parts are rolling and hilly, and still other parts are composed of sinkhole basins. The region contains the Mississippi Pennyrile, an uneven area of about 8000 sq.mi., which is underlaid by many caves. One of the caves, Mammoth Cave (*see* MAMMOTH CAVE NATIONAL PARK), is the largest in the world. A major area of the cavern, under exploration in 1969, has disclosed artifacts showing that previous civilizations were familiar with it. North of the Pennyrile lie the w. coalfields, which contain about half of the considerable coal reserves of the State. In the s.w. corner of the region is the Jackson Purchase, a great tract bought from the Chickasaw Indians in 1818 by Andrew Jackson (q.v.), later the seventh President of the U.S.

The third division of Kentucky is the Lexington plain, known as the bluegrass region; a circular, gently rolling area with a diameter of 90 to 110 mi., it is situated in the north-central part of the State. Bordering the bluegrass region on three sides is the Knobs, a crescent-shaped plain dotted with hilly formations. The highest point in Kentucky is Black Mt. (4145 ft.), in Harlan County; the lowest, 257 ft., is a point on the Mississippi R. in Fulton County.

Rivers and Lakes. The State has a fine drainage system consisting of a number of navigable rivers and hundreds of smaller streams. The Mississippi R. flows for 80 mi. along the w. border and receives the entire drainage of the State, over 95 percent of which enters it by way of the Ohio R. The latter, the principal river of the State, flows along the entire N. boundary in a winding course of nearly 600 mi. and, with its larger tributaries, forms an important system of inland navigation. Other major streams are the Kentucky, Big Sandy, Licking, Cumberland, Green, Barren, and Tennessee rivers. Man-made lakes formed by large power and flood-control dams include Kentucky Lake on the Tennessee R.; Lake Cumberland, formed by Wolf Creek Dam on the Cumberland R.; Herrington Lake, formed by the Dix Dam on the Dix R.; and Rough River Reservoir on the Rough R. Lake Barkley was formed by Barkley Dam on the Cumberland R., which was completed in the late 1960's.

Climate. Kentucky has a continental climate, with wide extremes of temperature and precipitation. It lies in the belt of storm-bearing westerly winds, which bring occasional cold spells in winter and hot spells in summer. In general, summers are warm and humid and winters mild. The highest temperature recorded in the State was 114° F. (at Greensburg); the lowest, −34° F. (at Bonnieville and Cynthiana). Precipitation is abundant, averaging from 36 in. in the N. to 50 in. in the s. Thunderstorms are frequent during spring and summer. Snowfall varies from year to

KENTUCKY

INDEX TO MAP OF KENTUCKY

Cities and Towns

Adairville … D 7	Cains Store … H 6	Faubush … H 6	Hopkinsville ʘ … B 7
Adams … M 4	Calhoun ʘ … C 5	Ferguson … H 6	Horse Cave … F 6
Adolphus … E 7	Calvert City … D 3	Firebrick … L 3	Huddy … N 5
Aflex … N 5	Calvin … K 7	Fishtrap … N 6	Hustonville … H 6
Albany ʘ … G 7	Campbellsburg … G 3	Flat Fork … L 5	Hyden ʘ … L 6
Alexandria ʘ … J 3	Campbellsville ʘ … G 6	Flatgap … M 5	Ilsley … B 6
Allen … M 5	Campton ʘ … K 5	Flat Lick … K 7	Independence ʘ … H 3
Allensville … C 7	Canada … N 5	Flatwoods … M 4	Inez ʘ … N 5
Allock … L 6	Caneyville … E 6	Fleming … M 6	Irvine ʘ … K 5
Alton … H 4	Cannel City … L 5	Flemingsburg ʘ … K 4	Irvington … E 5
Anchorage … G 4	Carlisle ʘ … J 4	Florence … J 2	Island … C 6
Anco … L 6	Carpenter … K 7	Fonde … K 7	Ivel … M 5
Anna … E 6	Carrollton ʘ … G 3	Fordsville … D 5	Jackson ʘ … L 5
Anneta … E 6	Catlettsburg ʘ … M 4	Forks of Elkhorn … H 4	Jamestown ʘ … G 7
Annville … K 6	Cave City … F 6	Fort Knox … F 5	Jeff … L 6
Arjay … K 7	Cawood … L 7	Fort Mitchell … K 2	Jeffersontown … G 4
Arlington … C 3	Cecilia … F 5	Fort Thomas … L 1	Jeffersonville … K 5
Artemus … K 7	Centertown … C 6	Fort Wright-Lookout	Jenkins … M 6
Ashland … M 4	Central City ʘ … C 6	Heights … K 1	Junction City … H 5
Auburn … D 7	Chaplin … G 5	Fountain Run … F 7	Kayjay … K 7
Audubon Park … F 4	Chavies … L 6	Frankfort (cap.) ʘ … H 4	Keaton … L 5
Augusta … J 3	Clarkson … E 6	Franklin ʘ … D 7	Keavy … J 6
Austin … F 7	Clay … B 6	Fredonia … B 6	Keene … H 5
Auxier … M 5	Clay City … K 5	Freeburn … N 5	Kehoe … L 4
Bagdad … G 4	Clearfield … K 4	Frenchburg ʘ … K 5	Kenton … J 3
Balkan … K 7	Clinton ʘ … C 3	Fullerton … L 3	Kenvir … L 7
Bandana … C 2	Closplint … L 7	Fulton … C 4	Kings Mountain … H 6
Banner … M 5	Clover Bottom … L 7	Gamaliel … F 7	Kingswood … E 5
Barbourville ʘ … K 7	Cloverport … D 5	Gapcreek … H 7	Kirksville … J 5
Bardstown ʘ … G 5	Cold Spring … L 2	Garrett … M 6	Kite … M 6
Bardwell ʘ … C 3	Collista … M 5	Garrison … L 3	Knottsville … D 5
Barlow … C 3	Columbia ʘ … G 6	Gatliff … K 7	Kona … M 6
Baskett … B 5	Columbus … C 3	Georgetown ʘ … H 4	Kuttawa … E 3
Beattyville ʘ … K 5	Combs … L 6	Germantown … K 3	La Center … C 3
Beauty … N 5	Coopersville … H 7	Ghent … G 3	La Grange ʘ … G 4
Beaver Dam … D 6	Corbin … J 7	Girdler … K 7	Lakeside Park … K 2
Bedford ʘ … G 3	Corydon … B 5	Glasgow ʘ … E 7	Lancaster ʘ … H 5
Beechwood … F 4	Cottle … L 5	Glencoe … H 3	Lawrenceburg ʘ … H 4
Bee Spring … E 6	Cottonburg … J 5	Glendale … F 5	Lawton … L 4
Bellevue … L 1	Covington ʘ … K 1	Glens Fork … G 6	Leatherwood … L 6
Belmont … F 5	Coxton … L 7	Glomawr … L 6	Lebanon ʘ … G 5
Belton … D 6	Crab Orchard … H 6	Gooserock … K 6	Lebanon Jct. … F 5
Benham … M 7	Crayne … E 2	Goshen … F 4	Leeco … K 5
Benton ʘ … D 3	Crescent Springs … K 1	Gracey … B 7	Leitchfield ʘ … E 6
Berea … J 5	Crestview … L 1	Graham … C 6	Lejunior … L 7
Bernstadt … J 6	Crestwood … G 4	Grand Rivers … D 3	Levee … K 5
Berry … J 3	Crittenden … H 3	Gray … K 7	Level Green … J 6
Betsy Layne … M 5	Crofton … C 6	Gray Hawk … J 6	Lewisburg … C 6
Beverly … L 7	Cromwell … D 6	Graysbranch … M 3	Lewisport … D 5
Big Clifty … E 5	Cumberland … M 6	Grayson ʘ … M 4	Lexington ʘ … J 4
Big Creek … K 6	Cunningham … C 3	Greensburg ʘ … F 6	Liberty ʘ … H 6
Bloomfield … G 5	Cynthiana ʘ … J 4	Greenup ʘ … M 3	Liggett … L 7
Blue Diamond … L 6	Danville ʘ … H 5	Greenville ʘ … C 6	Ligon … M 6
Boldman … M 5	David … M 5	Greenwood … J 7	Lily … J 6
Bond … J 6	Dawson Springs … B 6	Guthrie … C 7	Littcarr … M 6
Bonnieville … F 6	Daysville … C 7	Haddix … L 6	Livermore … C 5
Bonnyman … L 6	Dayton … L 1	Hadley … D 6	Livingston … J 6
Boonesboro … J 5	Delphia … L 6	Haldeman … L 4	Lloyd … M 3
Booneville ʘ … K 6	Depoy … C 6	Hall … M 6	London ʘ … J 6
Boston … F 5	Dewitt … K 7	Hanson … C 6	Lone Oak … C 3
Bowling Green ʘ … D 7	Dexter … D 3	Happy … L 6	Lookout … N 6
Bradfordsville … G 6	Dixon ʘ … B 5	Hardburly … L 6	Loretto … G 5
Brandenburg ʘ … E 4	Dorton … M 6	Hardin … D 3	Lost Creek … L 6
Bremen … C 6	Dover … K 3	Hardinsburg ʘ … D 5	Lothair … L 6
Brightshade … K 7	Drakesboro … D 6	Hardy … N 5	Louellen … L 7
Brodhead … J 6	Dry Ridge … H 3	Harlan ʘ … L 7	Louisa ʘ … M 4
Bromley … K 1	Earlington … B 6	Harned … E 5	Louisville ʘ … F 4
Bronston … H 7	East Bernstadt … J 6	Harold … M 5	Lovelaceville … C 3
Brooks … F 4	East Point … M 5	Harrodsburg ʘ … H 5	Lovely … N 5
Brookside … L 7	Echols … D 6	Hartford ʘ … D 6	Lowmansville … M 5
Brooksville ʘ … J 3	Eddyville ʘ … E 3	Hatfield … N 5	Loyall … L 7
Browder … D 6	Edgewood … K 2	Hawesville ʘ … D 5	Ludlow … K 1
Brownsville ʘ … E 6	Edmonton ʘ … F 7	Hazard ʘ … L 6	Lynch … M 7
Bruin … L 4	Elizabethtown ʘ … E 5	Hazel … D 4	Lynnview … F 4
Brushart … L 3	Elkhorn City … N 6	Hazel Green … K 5	Maceo … D 5
Buckner … G 4	Elkton ʘ … C 7	Hebron … J 1	Madisonville ʘ … B 6
Buechel … F 4	Elsmere … K 2	Heidrick … K 7	Majestic … N 5
Bulan … L 6	Eminence … G 4	Henderson ʘ … B 5	Manchester ʘ … K 6
Burgin … H 5	Emlyn … J 7	Hendricks … L 5	Mannington … C 6
Burkesville ʘ … G 7	Ennis … D 6	Hickman ʘ … C 4	Marion ʘ … E 2
Burlington ʘ … J 2	Eolia … M 6	High Bridge … H 5	Marrowbone … F 7
Burna … D 2	Erlanger … K 2	Highland Heights … L 1	Marshes Siding … H 7
Burning Springs … K 6	Essie … L 6	Hillsboro … K 4	Martin … M 5
Burnside … H 6	Eubank … H 6	Hima … L 6	Mary … K 5
Burton (Bypro) … M 6	Evarts … L 7	Himlerville (Beauty) … N 5	Mayfield ʘ … D 3
Bush … K 6	Ewing … K 4	Hindman ʘ … M 6	Mays Lick … K 3
Butler … J 3	Ezel … L 5	Hiram … L 7	Maysville ʘ … K 3
Cadiz ʘ … B 7	Fairdale … F 4	Hiseville … F 6	McAndrews … N 5
	Fairfield … G 5	Hitchins … M 4	McCarr … N 5
	Fairview … C 7	Hodgenville ʘ … F 5	McDowell … M 6
	Falcon … L 5	Hope … K 4	McHenry … D 6
ʘ County seat	Falmouth ʘ … J 3	Hopeful Heights … J 2	McKee ʘ … K 6

Continued on page 364

361

KENTUCKY

KENTUCKY
SCALE
0 5 10 20 30 40MI.
0 5 10 20 30 40KM.
State Capitals
County Seats
H 30′ J 84° K 30′ L 83° M 30′ N 82°
O H I O
CINCINNATI
Covington
Newport
Ft.Thomas
BOONE
KENTON
CAMPBELL
Florence
Erlanger
Hamilton
Batavia
Hillsboro
Georgetown
West Union
Peebles
Waverly
Portsmouth
McArthur
Huntington
Ashland
Ironton
Maysville
Vanceburg
Flemingsburg
Carlisle
Paris
Cynthiana
Georgetown
Lexington
Versailles
Winchester
Mount Sterling
Owingsville
Morehead
Grayson
Louisa
Paintsville
Prestonsburg
Pikeville
Richmond
Berea
Danville
Lancaster
Stanford
Somerset
London
Manchester
Hazard
Whitesburg
Harlan
Pineville
Middlesboro
Barbourville
Corbin
Williamsburg
Williamson
Jenkins
Norton
Wise
Kingsport
Bristol
Elizabethton
Rogersville
La Follette
Oneida
Jellico
W E S T
V A.
V I R G I N I A
T E N N E S S E E
Ohio River
Cumberland Gap
Norris Lake
South Holston Lake
West of Greenwich

KENTUCKY

Index to Map of Kentucky — Continued from page 361

McKinney ....H 6	Pleasant View ....J 7	South Williamson ....N 5	Williamstown ⊙ ....H 3
McRoberts ....M 6	Pleasure Ridge Park ...F 4	Spottsville ....C 5	Willisburg ....G 5
Meally ....M 5	Pleasureville ....G 4	Springfield ⊙ ....G 5	Wilmore ....H 5
Means ....K 5	Poole ....B 5	Stab ....J 6	Winchester ⊙ ....J 5
Melbourne ....L 2	Powderly ....C 6	Staffordsville ....M 5	Wingo ....C 4
Mentor ....J 3	Premium ....M 6	Stamping Ground .....H 4	Winston Park ....L 2
Middlesboro ....K 7	Preston ....K 4	Stanford ⊙ ....H 5	Woodbine ....J 7
Middletown ....G 4	Prestonsburg ⊙ ......M 5	Stanley ....C 5	Woodburn ....E 7
Midway ....H 4	Princeton ⊙ ....B 6	Stanton ⊙ ....K 5	Woodlawn ....L 1
Millersburg ....J 4	Providence ....B 6	Stearns ....J 7	Woodlawn ....D 3
Mills ....K 7	Pryorsburg ....D 3	Stillwater ....K 5	Wooton ....L 6
Millstone ....M 6	Quicksand ....L 5	Stone ....N 5	Worthington ....M 3
Milltown ....G 6	Raceland ....M 3	Strunk ....J 7	Wrigley ....L 4
Milton ....G 3	Radcliff ....E 5	Sturgis ....B 5	Wurtland ....M 3
Minerva ....K 3	Ravenna ....K 5	Sullivan ....A 6	Yancey ....L 7
Mitchellsburg ....H 5	Relief ....L 5	Sulphur ....G 4	Yeaddiss ....L 6
Monticello ⊙ ....H 7	Revelo ....J 7	Sulphur Well ....F 6	Yosemite ....H 6
Moores Creek ....K 6	Richmond ⊙ ....J 5	Summer Shade ....F 7	Zebulon ....M 5
Moorman ....C 6	Rineyville ....F 5	Summersville ....F 6	
Morehead ⊙ ....L 4	Robards ....B 5	Susie ....H 7	**Physical Features**
Moreland ....H 6	Robinson ....J 4	Tateville ....H 7	
Morganfield ⊙ ......E 1	Rochester ....D 6	Taylor Mill ....K 2	Abraham Lincoln
Morgantown ⊙ .....D 6	Rockholds ....J 7	Taylorsville ⊙ ....G 4	Birthplace Nat'l
Morris Fork ....K 6	Rockport ....D 6	Thealka ....M 5	Hist. Site ....F 5
Mortons Gap ....B 6	Rose Hill ....H 5	Tinsley ....K 7	Barkley (lake) ....B 7, E 3
Mountain Ash ....J 7	Rosine ....D 6	Tollesboro ....K 3	Barren (river) ....D 6
Mount Eden ....G 4	Rowletts ....F 6	Tompkinsville ⊙ .....F 7	Barren River (res.) ....E 7
Mount Olivet ⊙ .....J 3	Royalton ....M 5	Travellers Rest ....K 6	Beech Fork (river) ....G 5
Mount Sterling ⊙ ....J 4	Rumsey ....C 5	Trenton ....C 7	Big Sandy (river) .....M 4
Mount Vernon ⊙ ....J 6	Russell ....M 3	Twila ....L 7	Black (mt.) ....M 7
Mount Washington ...F 4	Russell Springs ....G 6	Tyner ....K 6	Buckhorn (res.) ....K 6
Mouthcard ....N 6	Russellville ⊙ ....D 7	Ulysses ....M 5	Campbell, Fort ....C 7
Muldraugh ....E 5	Sacramento ....C 6	Union ....H 3	Chaplin (river) ....G 5
Munfordville ⊙ .....E 6	Sadieville ....H 4	Uniontown ....B 5	Clarks, East Fk. (river) .D 3
Murray ⊙ ....D 4	Saint Charles ....B 6	Upton ....F 6	Cumberland (lake) ...H 7
Nancy ....H 6	Saint Francis ....G 5	Utica ....C 5	Cumberland (mt.) ....L 7
Nebo ....B 6	Saint Mary ....G 5	Vada ....K 5	Cumberland (river) ...D 2
Neon ....M 6	Saint Matthews ......F 4	Valley Station ....F 4	Cumberland Gap Nat'l
New Castle ⊙ ......G 4	Saldee ....L 6	Vanceburg ⊙ ....L 3	Hist. Park ....K 7
New Concord ....J 4	Salem ....D 2	Van Lear ....M 5	Dale Hollow (lake) ...G 8
Newfoundland ....L 4	Salt Lick ....K 4	Verona ....H 3	Dewey (lake) ....M 5
New Haven ....F 5	Salvisa ....H 5	Versailles ⊙ ....H 4	Dix (river) ....H 5
New Liberty ....H 3	Salyersville ⊙ ....L 5	Vicco ....L 6	Drakes (creek) ....E 7
Newman ....C 5	Samuels ....G 5	Villa Hills ....K 1	Dry (creek) ....K 2
Newport ....L 1	Sandgap ....J 6	Vine Grove ....F 5	Eagle (creek) ....H 4
Nicholasville ⊙ ......J 5	Sandy Hook ⊙ ......L 4	Virgie ....M 6	Fishtrap (res.) ....N 6
North Middletown ...J 4	Savoy ....J 7	Visalia ....J 3	Fort Campbell ....C 7
Nortonville ....C 6	Sawyer ....J 7	Waco ....J 5	Grayson (res.) ....L 4
Oak Grove ....C 7	Saxton ....J 7	Waddy ....G 4	Green (river) ....C 5
Ogle ....K 6	Science Hill ....H 6	Walker ....K 7	Herrington (lake) .....H 5
Oil Springs ....L 5	Scottsville ⊙ ....E 7	Wallins Creek ....K 7	Hinkston (creek) .....J 4
Okolona ....F 4	Scranton ....K 5	Waltersville ....J 5	Kentucky (lake) ......E 3
Old Landing ....K 5	Sebree ....B 5	Walton ....H 3	Kentucky (river) ......H 3
Olive Hill ....L 4	Seco ....M 6	Warfield ....N 5	Land Between the
Olmstead ....D 7	Sedalia ....D 4	Warsaw ⊙ ....H 3	Lakes Nat'l Rec.
Olympia ....K 4	Sextons Creek ....K 6	Washington ....K 3	Area ....E 3
Oneida ....K 6	Sharpsburg ....K 4	Watergap ....M 5	Laurel River (res.) ....J 6
Owensboro ⊙ ....C 5	Shelbiana ....M 6	Water Valley ....C 4	Licking (river) ....J 3
Owenton ⊙ ....H 3	Shelbyville ⊙ ....G 4	Waverly ....B 5	Little (river) ....B 7
Owingsville ⊙ ......K 4	Shepherdsville ⊙ .....F 4	Wayland ....M 6	Mammoth Cave Nat'l
Paducah ⊙ ....D 3	Shively ....F 4	Waynesburg ....H 6	Park ....F 6
Paint Lick ....J 5	Sibert ....K 6	Webbs Cross Roads ...G 6	Mayfield (creek) .....C 3
Paintsville ⊙ ....M 5	Siloam ....M 3	Webbville ....M 4	Mud (river) ....D 7
Paris ⊙ ....J 4	Silver Grove ....L 2	Weeksbury ....M 6	Nolin (river) ....E 6
Park City ....E 6	Sizerock ....L 6	Wellington ....K 5	Obion (creek) ....C 3
Park Hills ....K 1	Slaughters ....B 6	West Liberty ⊙ ......L 5	Ohio (river) ....C 2
Parksville ....H 5	Slemp ....L 6	West Point ....E 4	Paint Lick (river) .....J 5
Peabody ....K 6	Slickford ....H 7	Westport ....F 4	Panther (creek) ......C 5
Pembroke ....C 7	Smilax ....L 5	West Somerset ......H 6	Pine (mt.) ....L 7
Perryville ....H 5	Smithland ⊙ ....D 3	West Van Lear ......M 5	Pond (river) ....C 6
Petersburg ....H 2	Smith Mills ....B 5	Westwood ....M 4	Red (river) ....K 5
Pewee Valley ....G 4	Smiths Grove ....E 6	Wheatcroft ....B 5	Red (river) ....C 7
Phelps ....N 6	Smith Town ....H 7	Wheelwright ....M 6	Rockcastle (river) ....J 6
Philpot ....D 5	Soft Shell ....L 6	Whitehouse ....M 5	Rolling Fork (river) ...F 5
Pierce ....F 6	Somerset ⊙ ....H 6	White Plains ....C 6	Rough (river) ....D 5
Pigeonroost ....K 6	Sonora ....F 5	Whitesburg ⊙ ....M 6	Rough River (res.) ....E 5
Pikeville ⊙ ....N 6	Southgate ....L 1	Whitesville ....D 5	Saline (river) ....D 1
Pine Hill ....J 6	South Irvine ....J 5	Whitley City ⊙ .....J 7	Salt (river) ....F 5
Pine Knot ....H 7	South Park View .....F 4	Wickliffe ⊙ ....C 3	Tennessee (river) ....D 3
Pineville ⊙ ....K 7	South Portsmouth ....L 3	Williamsburg ⊙ .....J 7	Tradewater (river) ...B 6
Pittsburg ....J 6	South Shore ....M 3	Williamsport ....M 5	Tug Fork (river) .....N 5

year but averages from 6 to 10 in. in the s.w. to 15 to 20 in. in the s.e. The average annual number of days with measurable precipitation is 121 at Louisville and 128 at Lexington. Tornadoes occur occasionally, about once a year.

Plants and Animals. The most distinctive and characteristic plant found in Kentucky is the goldenrod, which flowers in profusion in the autumn. The pennyroyal, or "pennyrile", grows in the w. areas. The north-central region is famous for its bluegrass, so called because its pollen-carrying stamens, which develop in May, have a bluish-gray hue. Other wild plants growing in various regions include the azalea, dog-

Climate	Lexington	Louisville
Normal temperatures (in °F.)		
January maximum	41.3	42.0
January minimum	24.5	24.5
July maximum	86.4	87.3
July minimum	65.9	66.4
Annual	55.2	55.6
Normal precipitation (in inches)		
Wettest month	4.83	5.05
Driest month	2.12	2.35
Annual	44.49	43.11
Latest frost	April 13	April 1
Earliest frost	Oct. 28	Nov. 7
Mean number of days between latest and earliest frosts	198	220

wood, bluebell, and rhododendron; the hazelnut, walnut, and beechnut; and the wisteria, poison ivy, and Virginia creeper. Kentucky has extensive forests containing a wide variety of trees. Among these are the black and white walnut, black cherry, poplar, sycamore, maple, black and white oaks, honey locust, black locust, cedar, beech, ash, pine, linden, basswood, hemlock, gum, hickory, elm, and ten species of willows.

Kentucky was formerly the habitat of a wide variety of animal life. Bison, white-tailed deer, and wapiti (elk) roamed the region south of the Ohio R. Small game and songbirds also were plentiful. Much of the wildlife of the region was slaughtered by early settlers. Efforts are presently being made to restore and maintain deer, bear, game birds, and waterfowl. Among the small mammals that currently abound are the gray squirrel, opossum, raccoon, woodchuck, eastern cottontail rabbit, muskrat, and mink. Birds include the mockingbird, Carolina chickadee, cardinal, golden-crowned kinglet, yellow-bellied sapsucker, bronzed grackle, catbird, grasshopper sparrow, great blue heron, and American egret. One of the major bird migration routes passes over the w. part of the State.

Parks, Forest, and Other Places of Interest. Kentucky has two national parks, Mammoth Cave National Park, near Cave City, a series of underground passages, 150 mi. of which have been explored; and Cumberland Gap National Historical Park (*see* CUMBERLAND GAP), near Middlesboro (the remainder in Tennessee and Virginia), a mountain pass of the Wilderness Road. The Abraham Lincoln Birthplace National Historic Site (q.v.), near Hodgenville, is the traditional birthplace cabin of Lincoln. Daniel Boone National Forest, with headquarters at Winchester, comprises more than 460,000 acres and encompasses the w. rim of the Cumberland Plateau; Cumberland Falls State Park and Natural Bridge State Park are within the forest. Kentucky is one of the most extensive State park systems in the U.S. Breaks Interstate Park, on the

A granite monument honoring Kentuckians who lost their lives in one of the last battles of the American Revolution stands in Blue Licks Battlefield State Park, near Paris, Ky. Kentucky Dept. of Public Information

Virginia border at Elkhorn City, Ky., is jointly operated by the two States. My Old Kentucky Home State Park, at Bardstown, contains the house in which the American composer Stephen Foster (q.v.) is said to have written the famous song.

Other points of interest in Kentucky include Churchill Downs, scene of the Kentucky Derby (q.v.); many horse farms noted for producing championship thoroughbred horses are situated near Lexington. Shakertown is the site of a Shaker community founded in 1805. At Fairview, birthplace of Jefferson Davis (q.v.), is a monument to the Confederate president.

Sports. The many rivers and lakes in Kentucky provide abundant sport fishing. Species to be had all year include rainbow trout, several varieties of bass, walleye and northern pike, sauger, muskellunge, chain pickerel, rockfish, and crappie. Small-game animals and game birds hunted include white-tailed deer, cottontail rabbit, gray squirrel, wild turkey, ruffed grouse, and bobwhite quail.

THE PEOPLE

According to the 1970 decennial census, the population of Kentucky was 3,219,311, an increase of 6 percent over the 1960 population. As calculated by the Census Bureau, the urban segment comprised 1,684,053 persons, 52.3 percent

KENTUCKY

of the total, compared with 44.5 percent in 1960. The rural segment comprised 1,534,653 persons, 47.7 percent of the total, compared with 55.5 percent in 1960. Ethnically, the 1970 population was distributed as follows: white persons, 2,981,766; nonwhites, 236,940, including 230,793 Negroes, 1531 Indians, 1095 Japanese, and others. The percentage of native-born residents was 99.5; of foreign-born, 0.5. The 1970 population density averaged 81.2 per sq.mi., compared with 76.2 in 1960.

The chief cities are Frankfort, the capital, a distilling and trade center; and, in order of population, Louisville, a port on the Ohio R. and an industrial and rail center; Lexington, a tobacco and agricultural market and horse-breeding center, site of the University of Kentucky; and Covington, a port on the Ohio R. and a center for agricultural marketing and manufacturing.

Education. The public-school system of Kentucky was established in 1849. Education is compulsory for all children between the ages of seven and sixteen.

ELEMENTARY AND SECONDARY SCHOOLS. In the early 1970's public elementary schools numbered about 1255 and public secondary schools, about 355. Annual enrollment was about 509,000 in elementary and about 211,000 in secondary schools. Teachers in the public-school system numbered 18,170 in elementary and about 11,725 in secondary schools. In the early 1970's private institutions included about 255 elementary schools with some 55,000 students, and about 75 secondary schools with about 21,000 students. Teachers in private schools numbered about 3600 in the late 1960's.

UNIVERSITIES AND COLLEGES. In the early 1970's Kentucky had 35 institutions of higher learning, 28 of which were privately supported. University and college enrollment was about 87,000. Public colleges include the University of Kentucky (q.v.), Murray State University, Eastern Kentucky University, Western Kentucky University, Morehead State University, and the University of Louisville. The private institutions include Berea College (q.v.), Bellarmine College, Cumberland College, Kentucky Wesleyan College, and Asbury College.

Libraries and Museums. The Louisville Free Public Library has some 700,000 volumes and an audio-visual department comprising 2500 films, 15,000 phonograph records, and 75,000 electronically taped programs. The library also operates a museum of natural science and history. The Kentucky Department of Libraries, in Frankfort, has about 700,000 volumes. Cultural institutions include the Behringer Museum of Natural History, in Covington; the Kentucky Historical Society in Frankfort, housed in the Old State House; and the Audubon Memorial Museum, in Henderson, devoted to memorabilia of the American naturalist and painter John J. Audubon (q.v.).

THE ECONOMY

Kentucky has a diversified economy. The per capita personal income in 1972 was $3609, or 80 percent of the average in the U.S. More than 70 percent of all personal income is derived from private nonfarm sources, about 25 percent from governmental sources (including social security and military benefits), and more than 4 percent from agriculture. Most nonagricultural wage earners are employed, in descending order of numbers, in manufacturing, wholesale and retail trade, national and local governments, and services. Mineral industries employ a sizable group of workers. Kentucky has about 965 hotels, motels, and other travelers' accommodations, with aggregate annual income of about $65,000,000.

At the disposal of electric utilities and industrial plants in the State, according to the latest available statistics (1968) were some 671,000 kw of developed waterpower; an estimated 1,485,000 kw remained for future development. Steam is the prime generator of 91.8 percent of power.

Manufacturing. According to a recent survey of manufactures (1971), production workers in Kentucky totaled 187,100. The largest groups were engaged in the manufacture of electrical machinery, apparel, and nonelectrical machinery, and in food processing. More than 40 percent were employed in the Standard Metropolitan Statistical Area (q.v.) of Louisville. Another manufacturing center was Lexington. The value added by manufacture (see VALUE) in the largest industries totaled $844,300,000 for the electrical-machinery industry, $724,300,000 for nonelectrical machinery, and $673,800,000 for food processing. The clothing industry, which ranked second in employment, ranked eighth in value added, at $234,900,000. Tobacco manufactures, ranking fourth, contributed $438,000,000 toward value added by manufacture. According to the most recent published figures, the value added by all manufacturing in Kentucky in 1971 was $5,168,200,000.

Agriculture. Kentucky has a diversified agriculture; its principal commodities are tobacco, cattle, dairy products, and hogs. Among major crops besides tobacco are corn, hay, and soybeans. In 1971 according to latest available statistics, Kentucky ranked second among the States in production of tobacco. In 1972 farms numbered about 121,000, totaling about 16,-

700,000 acres and averaging 138 acres each. Cash income from crops, livestock, and government payments in 1971 was $954,200,000.

Mining. The mineral resources of Kentucky include coal, stone, petroleum, and natural gas. In 1971, according to the latest available statistics, mineral production was valued at $925,900,000 annually, representing slightly more than 3 percent of the U.S. total. In quantity of production Kentucky ranked first among the States in bituminous coal, with 22 percent of the total; it ranked third in fluorspar. The leading counties in total production were Breathitt, Muhlenberg, Hopkins, Harlan, Floyd, and Union. Deposits of coal are in forty-two counties, the leading producers being Muhlenberg, Pike, Hopkins, and Harlan. Union County led the fifty-nine petroleum-producing counties; and Livingston, Jefferson, and Christian led in stone production. The proved reserves of crude oil in 1971 were 73,103,000 bbl, and indicated additional reserves were 786,000 bbl.

Forestry. The forest land of Kentucky consists predominantly of hardwoods. Primarily under private ownership, the commercial forest land comprises some 11,800,000 acres. It produces a net annual cut of sawtimber of approximately 728,000,000 bd.ft.

Transportation. The first railroad in Kentucky was the Lexington & Ohio R.R., inaugurated on Jan. 30, 1834, and now a part of the Louisville & Nashville R.R. In addition to the latter line, the State is served by ten Class 1 railroads, including the Chesapeake & Ohio Ry. and the Illinois Central R.R., with a total of some 3600 mi. of track. Rural and municipal roads totaled 69,071 mi. in 1970. Highways of the Federally aided Interstate Highway System totaled 738 mi. in 1970; Federally aided primary and secondary roads totaled 19,787 mi. There were 47 public and 26 private airports in 1971. Major cities were served by 3 international and 7 smaller airlines in 1973. The commercial navigable rivers are part of the Mississippi R. system. They are the Ohio R. and its links, the Kentucky, Barren, and Green rivers, Bear Creek, and Rough R.; and the Tennessee, Cumberland, and Big Sandy rivers.

Communications. The first newspaper in Kentucky was the *Kentucky Gazette*, founded in 1787 in Lexington. The State in 1971 had 27 daily newspapers with a total circulation of 769,000 and 13 Sunday papers. Of some 100 AM and 60 FM radio stations operating in 1971, among the earliest were WLAP in Lexington and WHAS in Louisville, both established in 1922. Television stations numbered 10. In 1969, Kentucky was among the national leaders in Educational Television Network systems, the State system comprising 12 broadcast transmitters in addition to producing studios in several regions at colleges and universities.

The Kentucky Derby, run annually at Churchill Downs in Louisville, has been a colorful tradition since 1875.
Louisville Chamber of Commerce

GOVERNMENT

Kentucky is governed under the constitution of 1890–91, as amended. Executive authority is vested in a governor, a lieutenant governor, an attorney general, and a secretary of state, all elected for four-year terms, and other elected and appointed officials. Legislative authority is exercised by the General Assembly, consisting of the Senate with 38 members and the House of Representatives with 100 members, elected for four-year and two-year terms, respectively. The legislature meets biennially in even-numbered years. The judicial system includes a seven-member court of appeals, circuit courts, and various local and special courts.

Kentucky is represented in the United States Congress by two Senators and seven Representatives.

Local Government. Kentucky is divided into 120 counties, the chief units of local government. Each county is presided over by a county judge. Major elected county officials include sheriffs, county clerks, and county judges. Each county is subdivided into magisterial districts for purposes of actual government. The municipalities enjoy limited self-government. The three main forms of municipal government are

KENTUCKY

the council-manager, mayor-council, and commission plans.

Voting Qualifications. Suffrage is extended generally to U.S. citizens eighteen years of age who meet the residence requirements (one year in the State, six months in the county, and sixty days in the election precinct).

HISTORY

The region known presently as Kentucky was inhabited in prehistoric times by primitive tribes whose extant remains include a wealth of artifacts. In more recent centuries the rich meadow lands and hunting grounds of Kentucky attracted such Indian tribes as the Shawnee, Wyandot, Delaware, and Cherokee. The French explorer Robert Cavelier, Sieur de La Salle (q.v.), visited the area during his descent (completed 1682) of the Mississippi R.; it is believed that he may also have visited the region in 1669. Notable among subsequent penetrations of the area were those made by the American physician and explorer Thomas Walker (1715–94) in 1750 and the American frontiersman Christopher Gist (1706?–59) in 1751. In 1767 the American pioneer Daniel Boone (q.v.) and five companions visited eastern Kentucky, but it was not until 1774 that the American pioneer and soldier James Harrod (1742–93), and forty associates from the Monongahela country established the first permanent settlement in Kentucky, which was given the name Harrodsburg. In 1775 Daniel Boone established a settlement, which he named Boonesboro. The land policy of Virginia encouraged immigration to the new country, but hostile Indians made the region dangerous. In 1774 a Virginian force decisively defeated the Northwestern Indians at Point Pleasant (now in W. Va.), and forced them to retire beyond the Ohio R. In the same year Boone concluded a treaty with the Cherokee by which they sold for 10,000 pounds sterling their flimsy claim to the lands between the Ohio and Cumberland rivers and west and south of the Kentucky R. (amounting to 17,000,000 acres, or about half of the present State of Kentucky) to Richard Henderson (q.v.) and his associates who styled themselves the Transylvania Company. Virginia claimed the territory in question and refused to recognize the validity of the sale, but the Virginia legislature consented in 1778 to give the company a title to 200,000 acres and to confirm the sales already made.

Statehood. Attempts to make the region into a State began in May, 1775. Colonel Henderson convoked at Boonesboro a convention that adopted a code of nine laws for the government of the self-constituted commonwealth; this action was, however, disallowed by the legislature of Virginia. The following year, by act of the legislature, the new county was organized under the name of Kentucky County, with Harrodsburg as the county seat and with separate representatives in the Virginia legislature. Kentucky was admitted to the Union on June 1, 1792. In July, 1799, the second constitution of Kentucky was passed, making the governor and other State officers elective by the people instead of by the electors. In the War of 1812 Kentucky sent 7000 men into action; about one fourth of the army of General Andrew Jackson (q.v.) at the Battle of New Orleans consisted of Kentucky riflemen.

Upon the outbreak of the Civil War Kentucky attempted to maintain a position of neutrality,

A towboat moves a nineteen-barge shipment of more than 35,000 tons of coal along the Ohio River. Bituminous coal is a chief source of mineral wealth in Kentucky.

West Kentucky Coal Co.

but the geographical position of the State made the plan impossible. The governor rejected the appeal of President Abraham Lincoln (q.v.) for troops, and when the Confederate and Union armies began to pour into the State from opposite directions, formal demands were made for their withdrawal. The Union armies soon took possession, and by 1862 the Confederate forces had evacuated the State. Important military operations in Kentucky were the battles of Mill Springs, Richmond, and Perryville, the invasion of General Braxton Bragg (q.v.), the five successive cavalry raids of the Confederate General John Hunt Morgan (1825–64), and the Confederate raid on Paducah under the direction of General Nathan Bedford Forrest (q.v.). Including the so-called Home Guards and those who enlisted but were never mustered in, Kentucky furnished more than 90,000 troops to the Union army and 40,000 to the Confederacy. Throughout the war Kentucky remained a slave State; its slaves were freed only after the adoption in 1865 of the Thirteenth Amendment to the Constitution of the United States (q.v.).

In the controversy during the 1960's surrounding the decision by the United States Supreme Court to end racial segregation in public schools, Kentucky took a generally pro-integration stand. In 1966 the State passed a law broader than the 1964 Federal Civil Rights Act, barring racial discrimination in employment and public accommodations. Open-housing demonstrations were held in Louisville in 1967 and, as a result, the city Board of Aldermen adopted an ordinance banning discrimination in the sale or rental of housing.

Since the Civil War Kentucky has voted Democratic in all Presidential elections except those of 1896, 1924, 1928, 1948, 1956, 1960, and 1968. In 1972 Kentucky gave the Republican candidate, President Richard M. Nixon (q.v.), 670,937 votes and the Democratic candidate, Senator George S. McGovern (1922–) of South Dakota, 369,082 votes.

KENTUCKY, river of central Kentucky, rising in Lee Co. in the Cumberland Plateau, and flowing 259 mi. first w. and then N. to join the Ohio R. near Madison, Ind. The Kentucky R. is formed by the junction of the North Fork and the Middle Fork. A series of locks make the river navigable from the Ohio to Frankfort.

KENTUCKY AND VIRGINIA RESOLUTIONS, resolutions adopted in 1798 by the legislatures of Kentucky and Virginia to protest the enactment by the Federal government of the Alien and Sedition Acts (q.v.).

The Kentucky Resolutions, drafted by then Vice-President Thomas Jefferson (q.v.), argued that the government was formed by a compact among the States and that the Federal powers were limited to those delegated to it in the Constitution. In addition, the validity of laws passed by the government under supposedly unauthorized powers should be determined by the members of the compact, the States. A second resolution, passed by the Kentucky legislature in 1799, called for the States to formally nullify any law deemed objectionable.

The Virginia Resolutions were drawn up by the American statesman James Madison (q.v.), later the fourth President of the United States. The resolutions argued similarly that the States had the right to interfere with any alleged unconstitutional exercise of power by the Federal government. Madison wrote, "that, in a case of a deliberate, palpable, and dangerous exercise of other powers not granted by the said compact, the states, who are parties thereto, have the right and are in duty bound to interpose for arresting the progress of the evil".

The Kentucky and Virginia Resolutions, when presented for approval to the legislatures of the other States, were largely ignored or rejected. The principles stated in the resolutions later formed the basis of the doctrines of States' rights, nullification, and secession (qq.v.).

KENTUCKY DERBY, famous American annual horse race. The Kentucky Derby has been run continuously at Churchill Downs racetrack, in Louisville, Ky., on the first Saturday of May since 1875, when the track was built. The race is limited to horses three years of age. The distance for the race was 1½ mi. from 1875 to 1895, and since 1896 the distance has been 1¼ mi. The record speed for the 1½-mi. distance, 2 min. 34½ sec., was run by a horse named Spokane in 1889. The record for the 1¼-mi. distance, 2 min., was set by Northern Dancer in 1964. Wagering at the Kentucky Derby has been governed by pari-mutuel rules since 1908.

The Kentucky Derby is one of three races for three-year-olds of the so-called Triple Crown. The other two races are the Preakness at Pimlico in Baltimore, Md., and the Belmont Stakes, run at Belmont Park, Elmont, N.Y. Eight horses have won the Triple Crown: Sir Barton in 1919; Gallant Fox in 1930; Omaha in 1935; War Admiral in 1937; Whirlaway in 1941; Count Fleet in 1943; Assault in 1946; and Citation in 1948. Two jockeys, Eddie Arcaro (q.v.) and Bill Hartack (1933–), have each ridden five Kentucky Derby winners. Eight of the winners have been bred by Calumet Farms. For a list of the winners of the Kentucky Derbies, see next page.

KENTUCKY, UNIVERSITY OF

KENTUCKY DERBY WINNERS

Year	Winner	Year	Winner
1875	Aristides	1925	Flying Ebony
1876	Vagrant	1926	Bubbling Over
1877	Baden Baden	1927	Whiskery
1878	Day Star	1928	Reigh Count
1879	Lord Murphy	1929	Clyde Van Dusen
1880	Fonso	1930	Gallant Fox
1881	Hindoo	1931	Twenty Grand
1882	Apollo	1932	Burgoo King
1883	Leonatus	1933	Broker's Tip
1884	Buchanan	1934	Cavalcade
1885	Joe Cotton	1935	Omaha
1886	Ben Ali	1936	Bold Venture
1887	Montrose	1937	War Admiral
1888	Macbeth II	1938	Lawrin
1889	Spokane	1939	Johnstown
1890	Riley	1940	Gallahadion
1891	Kingman	1941	Whirlaway
1892	Azra	1942	Shutout
1893	Lookout	1943	Count Fleet
1894	Chant	1944	Pensive
1895	Halma	1945	Hoop, Jr.
1896	Ben Brush	1946	Assault
1897	Typhoon II	1947	Jet Pilot
1898	Plaudit	1948	Citation
1899	Manuel	1949	Ponder
1900	Lieutenant Gibson	1950	Middleground
1901	His Eminence	1951	Count Turf
1902	Alan-a-Dale	1952	Hill Gail
1903	Judge Himes	1953	Dark Star
1904	Elwood	1954	Determine
1905	Agile	1955	Swaps
1906	Sir Huon	1956	Needles
1907	Pink Star	1957	Iron Liege
1908	Stone Street	1958	Tim Tam
1909	Wintergreen	1959	Tomy Lee
1910	Donau	1960	Venetian Way
1911	Meridian	1961	Carry Back
1912	Worth	1962	Decidedly
1913	Donerail	1963	Chateaugay
1914	Old Rosebud	1964	Northern Dancer
1915	Regret	1965	Lucky Debonair
1916	George Smith	1966	Kauai King
1917	Omar Khayyam	1967	Proud Clarion
1918	Exterminator	1968	*Dancer's Image
1919	Sir Barton	1969	Majestic Prince
1920	Paul Jones	1970	Dust Commander
1921	Behave Yourself	1971	Canonero II
1922	Morvich	1972	Riva Ridge
1923	Zev	1973	Secretariat
1924	Black Gold		

* In subsequent litigation, the second-place horse, Forward Pass, was awarded (1972) the first-place purse because post-race examination showed traces of a banned drug in Dancer's Image, which however retained the winning title.

KENTUCKY, UNIVERSITY OF, coeducational State-supported institution of higher learning, situated in Lexington, Ky. Thirteen community colleges affiliated with the university are located throughout Kentucky. The university was established in 1865 as a land-grant college (*see* LAND-GRANT COLLEGES) forming part of Kentucky University (now Transylvania College). By successive acts of the State legislature of Kentucky the college became the State College of Agriculture and Mechanic Arts in 1878, the State University of Kentucky in 1908, and the University of Kentucky in 1916. The University of Kentucky comprises colleges of arts and sciences, agriculture, allied health, architecture, engineering, education, law, home economics, business and economics, library science, social professions, medicine, nursing, dentistry, and pharmacy; it also includes a graduate school. The degrees of bachelor, master, and doctor are awarded. In 1973 the university library housed more than 1,000,000 bound volumes. Enrollment totaled 33,612 students, the faculty numbered 2200, and the endowment was $1,281,185.

KENYA, republic in E. Africa, a member of the Commonwealth of Nations. It is bounded on the N. by the Sudan and Ethiopia, on the N.E. by Somalia, on the E. by the Indian Ocean, on the S. by Tanzania, and on the W. by Lake Victoria and Uganda. Kenya lies between about lat. 4°40′ N. and 4°40′ S. and long. 34° E. and 42° E. The area is 224,960 sq.mi.

THE LAND

Physiographically, Kenya falls into several well-defined zones extending from the coast upward to lofty mountain ranges that reach elevations in excess of 10,000 ft. above sea level. From a low coastal strip the terrain rises gradually to a broad, arid plateau known as the Nyika (steppe). The succeeding region contains great volcanic mountain chains, of which the principal peak is Mt. Kenya (17,058 ft.). The S. and S.E. portions of the country are heavily forested; on the W. the immense depression of the Great Rift Valley is demarcated by a succession of steep cliffs. The chief river of Kenya is the Tana.

Climate. Kenya is traversed by the equator, the region to the N. being hot and dry with comparatively little rain. The region to the S. falls into three meteorological zones, the coast, the highlands, and the lake country. The coast is humid, the mean annual temperature ranging from 76° F. in June and July to 82° F. in February, March, and April. In the highlands the climate is relatively temperate, and in the lake region it is tropical. The rainy seasons occur from October to December and April to June.

Natural Resources. The main resource of Kenya is its land, of which about 10 percent is suitable for agriculture. About one third of this is arable, with the remainder suitable for grazing. The N. two thirds of the country are desert, suitable for limited grazing.

Plants and Animals. The plant life of Kenya is luxuriant and diversified. Along the coast are forests containing palm, mangrove, teak, copal, and sandalwood trees. Forests of baobab, euphorbia, and acacia trees cover the lowlands to an elevation of approximately 3000 ft. The rubber vine grows both on the coast and in the lowlands. Extensive tracts of savanna (grassland), interspersed with groves of acacia and papyrus tree, characterize the terrain from 3000 to 9000 ft. The principal species in the dense rain forest of the E. and S.E. mountain slopes are the camphor and bamboo. The alpine zone (above 11,000 ft.) contains large, leafy plants of the *Senecio* and *Lobelia* genera.

KENYA

INDEX TO MAP OF KENYA

Regions

Central	B 3
Coast	B 3
Eastern	B 3
Nairobi (district)	B 3
North Eastern	B 2
Nyanza	A 3
Rift Valley	A 2
Western	A 2

Cities and Towns

Baragoi	B 2
Buna	C 3
Bura	B 3
Eldoret	A 2
El Wak	C 2
Embu	B 3
Fort Hall	B 3
Garba Tula	B 2
Garissa	B 3
Gazi	B 4
Gilgil	B 3
Isiolo	B 2
Kajiado	B 3
Kakamega	A 2
Karungu	A 3
Kericho	A 3
Kiambu	B 3
Kilifi	B 3
Kipini	C 3
Kisii	A 3
Kisumu	A 2
Kitale	A 2
Kitui	B 3
Kolbio	C 3
Kwale	B 4
Laisamis	B 2
Lamu	C 3
Lodwar	A 2
Lokitaung	A 1
Lolgorien	A 3
Machakos	B 3
Magadi	A 3
Malindi	C 3
Mambrui	C 3
Mandera	C 2
Maralal	B 2
Marsabit	B 2
Meru	B 3
Mombasa	B 3
Moyale	B 2
Muddo Gashi	B 2
Nairobi	B 3
Naivasha	B 3
Nakuru	A 3
Nanyuki	B 2
Narok	A 3
North Horr	B 2
Nyeri	B 3
Port Victoria	A 3
Rumuruti	B 2
South Horr	B 2
Taveta	B 3
Thika	B 3
Thomson's Falls	B 2
Tsavo	B 3
Vanga	B 4
Voi	B 3
Wajir	C 2
Witu	C 3

Physical Features

Dawa (river)	C 1
Elgon (mt.)	A 2
Formosa (bay)	C 3
Galana (river)	B 3
Gedi (ruins)	B 3
Kenya (mt.)	B 3
Lorian (swamp)	B 2
Natron (lake)	A 3
Nyiru (mt.)	B 2
Patta (isl.)	C 3
Royal Tsavo Nat'l Park	B 3
Rudolf (lake)	B 2
Tana (river)	B 3
Victoria (lake)	A 3

Kenya is renowned for the great variety of its wildlife, especially the big game animals associated with the African savanna. The major species are elephant, rhinoceros, zebra, giraffe, and lion and other large cats. Many of these are protected in national parks and game preserves. The country also abounds in reptiles and birds.

Waterpower. Since World War II hydroelectric power projects have been developed to meet the increasing demand for electric power. Notable among these is the $95,000,000 hydroelectric project on the Tana R. In the early 1970's Kenya produced about 555,000,000 kw hours of electricity, of which about 319,000,000 kw hours were produced by hydroelectric plants. More power will soon be provided by these plants.

THE PEOPLE

Most of the population is African, but Kenya has considerable Asian and European minorities, with a smaller Arab community living mainly on the coast. The African population is ethnically very diverse. It is composed of over forty tribes belonging to four main linguistic groups: Bantu, Nilo-Hamitic, Nilotic, and Hamitic peoples; see AFRICA: *Ethnology.* Most numerous are the Bantu tribes, which include the Kikuyu, the largest and most influential tribe in Kenya.

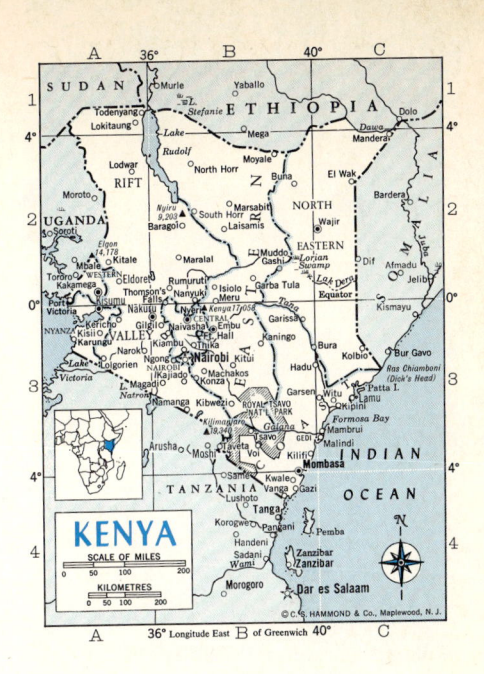

Population. The population of Kenya (census 1969) was 10,942,705; the United Nations estimated (1971) 11,694,000. The overall population density is about 49 per sq.mi. (U.N. est. 1970). More than 90 percent of the people live in rural villages.

Political Divisions and Principal Cities. Kenya is divided into seven administrative provinces: Coast, Eastern, Central, Rift Valley, Nyanza, North Eastern, and Western, as well as the Nairobi district. Local government matters are handled by provincial advisory councils, whose members are appointed by the president.

Nairobi (q.v.) is the capital and largest city. The major seaport is Mombasa (q.v.), built on an offshore island of the same name. Other cities are Nakuru, the capital of Rift Valley Province,

Jomo Kenyatta, architect of Kenyan independence. UPI

Kenyan girls perform a traditional dance. Africapix

Kisumu, a port city on Lake Victoria, and Eldoret, a rail center N.E. of Kisumu.

Religion. Accurate figures on religious affiliations are not available. The most recent sampling (1962 census) gives the following estimates: 37 percent Protestant, 22 percent Roman Catholic, and about 3 percent Muslim. The remaining 38 percent are largely followers of traditional tribal religions.

Language. Nearly all the African tribes have their own distinct languages, although there are linguistic groups of very similar dialects. Since the early 20th century Swahili (q.v.) has become the dominant African tongue, and is now the official language of Kenya. Gujerati and Punjabi are spoken in the Asian community. See AFRICAN LANGUAGES.

Education. Education is not compulsory for African children, but between 35 and 40 percent of all African children of school age attend school; of these an estimated 90 percent are now enrolled at the elementary level (first seven years). A nonracial educational system at all levels has been instituted recently. African children now attend elementary and secondary schools formerly limited to European and Asian students. The literacy rate, however, was estimated at only 20 percent in the late 1960's.

ELEMENTARY AND SECONDARY SCHOOLS. In the early 1970's, about 1,400,000 children attended elementary schools, and almost 126,000 were enrolled in secondary school courses (generally for a duration of four years). The majority of the schools are maintained by the government, and the rest receive government support.

SPECIALIZED SCHOOLS. Kenya Polytechnic Institute at Nairobi provides advanced training in technical subjects. Teacher-training institutes and trade schools had a total annual enrollment of more than 8000.

UNIVERSITIES AND COLLEGES. The University of East Africa, which had colleges in Nairobi, Kampala in Uganda, and Dar es Salaam in Tanzania, was disbanded in 1970. The University of Nairobi, opened in 1970, provides courses in arts, science, education, agriculture, medicine, art, architecture, engineering, veterinary medicine, law, and domestic science. Initial student enrollment was about 1200.

Culture. European influence is still strong, particularly in the cities, but a growing appreciation of traditional African themes has begun to influence art, social life, and politics. Outside the cities, the Bantu have traditionally been skilled farmers. Pastoral Nilo-Hamitic peoples, such as the Masai and Turkana, attach great socioeconomic importance to their cattle, as do the Hamitic nomads of northern Kenya to their camels. The number of animals owned is an index of tribal status.

THE ECONOMY

Agriculture is the chief source of economic wealth, accounting for about 40 percent of the gross domestic product. Mining activity is on a relatively small scale, but the growing manufacturing industry is more important in Kenya than in most black African nations. After World War II Kenya experienced one of the highest rates of economic growth in the world because of large-scale foreign investments and the influx of European management and technical personnel. The government adopted the policy that the growth of the economy should be left to private enterprise and that government aid should be restricted to emergencies. Kenya joined with Tanzania and Uganda, in 1967, to form the East African Community, an economic association to further the development of a common market in goods and services among the member states. By 1970 four autonomous corporations had been organized to operate harbor, railroad, airways, and communications services of the three countries. In a recent year the budget showed about $262,000,000 in revenue and slightly lower expenditures.

Agriculture. The Kenyan agricultural system is highly diversified, producing almost every basic foodstuff. Sugarcane, corn, coconuts, sisal, cot-

A scientist examines the nest of a Sudan dioch, a subspecies of weaverbird that is a serious pest to Kenyan farmers.
United Nations

ton, and cashew nuts are grown on the coast and in the lowlands; coffee, tea, cotton, cereal grains, beans, potatoes, peanuts, and tobacco are grown in the highlands, the main producing area. Stockbreeding and dairy farming are important; in the early 1970's Kenya had about 8,500,000 head of cattle, some 3,700,000 sheep, 75,000 pigs, and about 500,000 poultry. Dairy production included butter, 4000 tons; cheese, 1000 tons; and milk, 840,000 tons.

Forest and Fishing Industries. Kenya produces hard woods (musheragi, muiri, mukeo, camphor, musaise) and soft woods (pids, cedar, cypress). Wattle bark, used in tanning, is an important export item. Commercial fishing on the coast and on Lake Victoria is sufficient to satisfy the local market. Small quantities of fish are exported.

Mining. The overall importance of mining has steadily declined in the last three decades, with the output of soda ash dropping by nearly 50 percent in the 1955–65 decade to about 117,000 tons per year. Gold, silver, salt, lime, limestone, and other minerals are being produced in increasing quantities, however.

Manufacturing. Although expanding, most industry is still on a small scale, and consists mainly of food and raw material processing for local consumption. Flour milling, brewing, and cement manufacturing are among the leading industries.

Currency, Commerce, and Trade. The currency unit is the Kenya shilling consisting of 100 cents (1 shilling equals U.S.$.14; 1972). Domestic commerce, hitherto dominated by Asians, is now being progressively taken over by Africans. Exports go principally to Great Britain and the sterling area (which form over 20 percent of the export market), West Germany, and the United States. They include coffee (the largest cash crop), tea, wattle-bark extract, sisal, soda ash, hides and skins, pyrethrum extract (used in insecticides), and lumber. Imports come mainly from Great Britain and the sterling area (about one third of the total), Japan, the United States, West Germany, and Iran. They consist chiefly of clothes, heavy equipment, and a small range of fuels. Uganda and Tanzania currently purchase about 25 percent of Kenyan manufactured goods. In 1971 Kenyan imports were valued at about $515,000,000 and exports totaled about $219,000,000.

Transportation. Kenya is served by the East African Railways Corporation, which operates about 4000 mi. of railroad, linking Kenya with Uganda and Tanzania. Roads in Kenya total about 25,400 mi., of which about 1850 mi. are surfaced. The chief port is Mombasa; steamer services are maintained on Lake Victoria, with connections to Albert and Kioga lakes. River transportation, however, is not extensive. Nairobi International Airport is a major terminus for East African Airways and other international airlines; regular local air services are also maintained.

Communications. Kenya has two English-language daily newspapers and one Swahili-language daily. The Voice of Kenya operates radio and television stations with English-, Asian-, and African-language programs.

Labor. In the late 1960's some 600,000 persons were gainfully employed, of whom about 10 percent were Europeans and Asians. The bulk of the population are not wage earners but engage in farming and herding at a subsistence level. Over 35 percent of the African labor force in

KENYA

Kenya was employed in agriculture and forestry. Nearly 30 percent of Kenyan workers are employed in such public works as highway maintenance. An industrial relations charter signed by labor representatives and employers in 1962 set out the responsibilities of management and unions.

GOVERNMENT

According to the constitution that came into effect on Dec. 12, 1964, Kenya is an independent republic with a parliamentary form of government.

Central Government. Executive authority is exercised by a president, elected for a four-year term by popular vote. A cabinet, appointed by the president, is collectively responsible to the legislature, the Kenyan National Assembly. The assembly consists of 158 directly elected members and 12 members elected by the assembly. HEALTH AND WELFARE. Hospitals are maintained by the government in urban areas and district capitals; they are augmented by mission and private hospitals throughout the country. Health centers, dispensaries, and mobile units provide health services in rural areas and among the nomadic tribes. Hospitals are free for children and outpatients. The European, Asian, and Arab communities finance their own hospital services.

Workers enjoy a statutory monthly minimum wage that varies from city to city and includes a housing allowance. Employers must provide medical care and benefits for injuries sustained at work, but workers are not obliged to participate in a compensation fund.

Local Government. The higher local authorities are divided into two categories: municipalities and county councils; and four types of lower authority: urban councils, township authorities, area councils, and local councils. Although all of these are responsible to the central government, considerable local autonomy is encouraged. Many of the councils raise their own revenues to finance public health measures, road and construction projects, and social welfare schemes. They also contribute to local education costs.

Judiciary. The judicial system consists of a high or supreme court and subordinate courts. The chief justice and eleven puisne judges of the high court are appointed by the president.

Defense. The army consists of four infantry battalions and a paratroop brigade with a total strength of about 4700 officers and men. A small air force is being developed with British assistance. The navy operates coastal patrol boats on Lake Victoria and the Indian Ocean.

HISTORY

Little is known about the early history of the area that comprises Kenya today. Arab traders arrived on the coast in the 7th century and gradually penetrated the interior in search of slaves, ivory, gold, and iron. They set up a series of city-states along the coast of modern Kenya, Tanzania, and Mozambique. Here the Swahili language evolved and later spread throughout eastern Africa.

Modern Colonialism. Soon after 1500 Portugal captured the Arab trade and destroyed most of their cities. With the aid of their countrymen from Oman, the Arabs ousted the Portuguese in the 17th century, and Oman controlled the Kenya coast until the late 19th century.

In July, 1895, after conventions signed between Great Britain and Germany defining the respective spheres of influence of the two countries in East Africa, the territory assigned to Great Britain, which had originally been settled in 1888 by a chartered private company, was taken over by the British crown and named the East African Protectorate. The territory included a coastal strip extending 10 mi. inland, comprising the mainland dominions of the sultan of Zanzibar, held by the British on lease. The first railroad (Mombasa to Lake Victoria), begun in 1896 and completed five years later, afforded a considerable impetus to large-scale European colonization of the temperate highlands.

BRITISH ANNEXATION. In 1920 the British East Africa Protectorate, excluding the coastal dominions of the sultan of Zanzibar, was annexed by the British government, proclaimed a crown colony, and renamed Kenya. The sultan's possessions were officially designated Kenya Protectorate.

During World War II a British and Kenyan force launched a successful offensive against Italian positions in Ethiopia and Italian Somaliland. At the end of the war a vigorous movement for the advancement of African political rights began to agitate the country.

MAU MAU TERRORISM. Following pressure from the nationalist Kenya African National Union (KANU), founded in 1944 and led from 1947 by the Kikuyu leader Jomo Kenyatta (q.v.), the first African was appointed to the colonial executive council in 1952. Early in 1952 the Mau Mau (variously interpreted to mean "hidden ones" or "those things"), a secret society sworn to expel all whites from Kenya, launched a campaign of terror against Europeans and natives friendly to Europeans. The Mau Mau was composed mainly of Kikuyu tribesmen, who are most numerous in the region north of Nairobi. In October the government proclaimed a state of emergency

Mount Kenya, an extinct volcano and the principal peak of the Aberdare range. At 17,058 ft., it is the second-highest mountain in Africa.
Bruno Barbey – Magnum

Kenya. Plate 1.

View of downtown Nairobi, the capital and largest city of Kenya and a major business center of eastern Africa.
Swissair

Kenya. Plate 2. *Above: Conical huts made of mud and wattle are typical dwellings of Kenyan tribal families. Below: Moloi children, members of a Kenyan tribe.*

Bruno Barbey – Magnum

throughout the colony. Detachments of British marines and soldiers were assigned to duty in Kenya the same month. Despite severe reprisals, the campaign of terror continued over the next three years. According to a government announcement, Mau Mau casualties to January, 1956, totaled 10,173 killed and 2274 captured. Mau Mau activity dwindled after February, 1956, following the capture of several leaders of the movement. The government announced on Nov. 13 that military operations against the Mau Mau had been suspended. At that time their forces were estimated at less than 300. The Mau Mau had killed an estimated 2800 people, most of them African.

AFRICAN ELECTORAL RIGHTS. On the recommendation of a government commission, Africans who had completed an intermediate school course or met other specified qualifications were made eligible to vote in the elections for the legislative council. Of the 400,000 Africans who were eligible, 126,508 registered and voted in the March, 1957, elections. Eight Africans were elected, but they refused to serve; instead, they pressed demands for an extended native franchise and free universal primary-school education. On Nov. 4, 1958, African elected members of the legislative council began a boycott of its sessions and were joined later by the Asian elected members. The boycott ended on April 29, 1959. On Jan. 12, 1960, the state of emergency declared to suppress the Mau Mau movement was ended.

CONSTITUTIONAL REFORM. A new constitution, providing for increased African control of the government and adopted during conferences in London early in 1960, came into effect on Dec. 8. In the elections held from Jan. 18 through March 16, 1961, the KANU, headed by the African labor leader Tom Mboya (1930–69), won 16 of the 53 seats on the common electoral roll, more than any other party. On Aug. 21 Kenyatta, who, despite his denials of involvement, had been imprisoned as an instigator of the Mau Mau, was given full liberty and assumed the leadership of Mboya's party.

In anticipation of independence Kenyan political leaders of various factions met in London between Feb. 14 and April 6, 1962, to negotiate the provisions of a new national constitution. The constitution, as approved, divided Kenya into eight administrative regions.

Kenyan Independence. When countrywide elections were held in May, 1963, KANU won 75 house seats and 19 senate seats, and the Kenya African Democratic Union (KADU) won 33 house seats and 16 senate seats. Kenyatta became prime minister when the colony became internally self-governing on June 1, 1963, and an all-African cabinet assumed office. On Dec. 12, 1963, Kenya gained full independence.

One year later Kenya became a republic, with Kenyatta as president. In 1964, Kenya launched a development plan projected to 1970. In 1966, following a split in KANU, a new party was founded, the Kenya People's Union (K.P.U.), and the constitution was amended to amalgamate the two houses of parliament into a national assembly. In 1968 legislation was enacted to provide that candidates for public office be nominated only by the ruling party, KANU, or the opposition party, K.P.U. In 1969, however, the government proscribed the K.P.U.

The political and social stability of Kenya was threatened at the end of the 1960's by tensions resulting from the assassination of Tom Mboya, a member of the Luo tribe and a leading figure in the government. A Kikuyu was tried, found guilty of the murder, and sentenced to death in September, 1969. The assassination sparked an outbreak of tribal violence that led to the banning of the K.P.U. on the grounds that it was subversive. In December, in the first general elections since independence, more than two thirds of the incumbent KANU candidates were defeated. Kenyatta, the only candidate for the office, was reelected as president.

As the new decade began, Kenya continued to show a satisfactory rate of economic growth, led by a thriving tourist business. In general, the nation maintained good relations with its neighbors and with Western nations, at the same time adhering to the principle of nonalignment. In 1972 and 1973, however, Kenya ousted a large number of noncitizen Asians, most of whom held British passports.

KENYA, MOUNT, extinct volcano, 17,058 ft. high, second highest mountain in Africa after Kilimanjaro (q.v.). *See* KENYA: *The Land.*

KENYATTA, Jomo (1893–   ), African nationalist leader, born near Nairobi, Kenya (then part of British East Africa), and educated at a mission school. He became active in African nationalist movements in 1921. He traveled widely in the 1930's, during which time he studied two years at Moscow University and later attended the University of London. He wrote *Facing Mount Kenya* (1938), an anthropological study of the Kikuyu tribe, of which he was a member. During World War II, the British colonial government of Kenya began removing all Africans to reservations. In response to this action Kenyatta, in 1948, helped form the Mau Mau, a terroristic secret society. In 1952 Kenyatta and five other persons were arrested and convicted of leading the outlawed movement; he was released in 1959. Four years later Kenya was granted independence, and Kenyatta, the leader of the dominant native political party, became prime minister. See KENYA: *History*.

KEOKUK, city in Iowa, and county seat of Lee Co., near the junction of the Illinois and Missouri State lines, on the Mississippi R., about 150 miles S.E. of Des Moines. Manufactures include metal and wood products, clothing, and rubber products. It is the site of Keokuk Community College, founded in 1953. Keokuk Dam (1913) extends across the Mississippi R. to Hamilton, Ill. Keokuk is the site of a national cemetery, established in 1862. Named for the Sac Indian chief Keokuk (1780–1848), the city was incorporated in 1847. Pop. (1960) 16,316; (1970) 14,631.

KEPLER, Johannes (1571–1630), German astronomer, born in Weil, Württemberg. He studied theology and the classics at the University of Tübingen; there he became acquainted with the teachings of the Polish astronomer Nicolaus Copernicus (q.v.), which greatly influenced his later career. He held the chair of astronomy and mathematics at the University of Graz from 1594 until 1600, when he became assistant to the Danish astronomer Tycho Brahe (q.v.) in the latter's observatory near Prague. Upon the death of Brahe in 1601 Kepler assumed his position as imperial mathematician and court astronomer to Rudolf II (q.v.), Holy Roman Emperor. In 1612 Kepler became mathematician to the states of Upper Austria. He moved to Ulm in 1626, where he completed and published the *Rudolphine Tables,* astronomical tables started by Tycho Brahe, which served as an indispensable aid to 17th-century astronomers.

In his official capacities Kepler edited astrological almanacs, but his serious occupation was the study of mathematics and planetary motion. He was attracted to the Copernican system (q.v.) because of the mathematical simplicity afforded by the Copernican concept of the solar system and because he regarded the sun, in a mystic as well as naturalistic sense, as the center of the universe. In his search for elucidation of his conviction that God had created the world according to an underlying mathematical harmony he formulated and verified the three laws of planetary motion for which he is best known; see KEPLER'S LAWS. These laws summarized and systematized the vast amount of empirical data on planetary motion amassed by the astronomers of his time and served as the foundation for the principles subsequently set forth by the English mathematician, physicist, and astronomer Sir Isaac Newton (q.v.). *See also* CELESTIAL MECHANICS.

Kepler also made contributions in the field of optics and developed a system of infinitesimals in mathematics, which was a forerunner of calculus (q.v.). A few of his more important writings are *Astronomia Nova de Motibus Stellae Martis* ("Commentaries on the Motions of Mars", 1609), *Harmonice Mundi* ("World Harmony", 1619), and *Epitomes Astronomiae Copernicanae* ("Epitome of Copernican Astronomy", 1618–21).

KEPLER'S LAWS, three laws concerning the motions of planets enunciated by the German astronomer Johannes Kepler (q.v.) early in the 17th century; see PLANET; SOLAR SYSTEM.

Kepler based his laws on planetary data collected by the Danish astronomer Tycho Brahe (q.v.), to whom he was an assistant. The proposals broke with a centuries-old belief based upon the Ptolemaic system (q.v.) advanced by the Alexandrian astronomer Ptolemy (q.v.), in the 2nd century A.D., and the Copernican system (q.v.) put forward by the Polish astronomer Nicolaus Copernicus (q.v.) in the 16th century, that the planets moved in circular orbits. According to Kepler's first law, the planets orbit the sun in elliptical paths, with the sun at one focus of the ellipse (q.v.). The second law states that the areas described in a planetary orbit by the straight line joining the center of the planet and the center of the sun are equal for equal time intervals, that is, the closer a planet comes to the sun, the more rapidly it moves. Kepler's third law states that the squares of the periods required for different planets to describe a complete orbit are proportional to the cubes of their mean distances from the sun.

These laws played an important part in the work of the 17th-century English astronomer, mathematician, and physicist Isaac Newton (q.v.), and are important for the understanding of the orbital paths of the moon, the natural satellite of the earth, and the paths of the artificial satellites launched from the earth; see SATELLITE, ARTIFICIAL. *See also* NEWTON'S LAWS OF MOTION.

KERALA, State of the Republic of India, bordered on the N. by Mysore State, on the E. by Tamil Nadu State, and on the S. and W. by the Arabian Sea. A belt of lowlands lies along the coast, extending from 10 to 20 mi. in width. Inland are alluvial plains, about 30 to 40 mi. in width. In the eastern section of the State rise the Western Ghats, a highland area with elevations of some 7000 ft. The principal agricultural products of the State are rice, tapioca, coconut, areca nuts, oilseeds, pepper, sugarcane, rubber, tea, coffee, and cardamom; almost all Indian black pepper and Indian rubber products come from Kerala. Among the livestock raised are buffalo and other cattle, sheep, and goats. Most of the industrial concerns in the State are owned or sponsored by the government. Privately owned industries include cashew processing and the manufacture of coir. Other manufactures are tiles, textiles, ceramics, fertilizers and chemicals, and glass. In addition, there are numerous factories processing the agricultural and mineral products of the State. Fishing is also a flourishing activity. The capital of Kerala is Trivandrum.

Kerala State was formed in 1956 from portions of the former Travancore-Cochin State and the former Madras State, including much of the Malabar Coast. Area, 15,002 sq.mi.; pop. (1971 prelim.) 21,280,397.

KERCH', city and seaport of the Soviet Union, in the Ukrainian S.S.R., on the E. shore of the Crimea Peninsula, about 110 miles N.E. of Yalta. The city is on the Kerch' Strait between the Sea of Azov and the Black Sea. Kerch' is an important industrial center in a region producing iron ore and natural gas. The city has iron and steel mills, shipyards, fisheries, canneries, and chemical plants. Kerch' was founded during the 6th century B.C. as the Greek colony of Panticapaem. For several centuries before the Christian Era, the port and the environs composed the independent kingdom of the Bosporus. Later, the city was ruled by Byzantium, held briefly by the Tatars, and then ruled by the Italian city-state of Genoa. After a subsequent period of Turkish rule, Kerch' was captured in 1771 by Russia during one of the Russo-Turkish Wars (q.v.). The city was severely damaged during the Crimean War and again during World War II. Pop. (1970) 127,608.

KERENSKI, Aleksandr Feodorovich (1880–1970), Russian revolutionary leader, born in Simbirsk (now Ul'yanovsk), and educated at the University of Saint Petersburg (now Leningrad University). In his youth he secretly joined the Socialist Revolutionary Party, which was at that time officially banned as a subversive organization. Publicly, however, he declared himself a member of the Group of Toil, a moderate legal political party; and in 1912, as a representative of that group, he was elected a deputy to the Duma (q.v.). In March, 1917, during the Russian Revolution (q.v.), after the overthrow of the emperor and the establishment of a provisional republican government, Kerenski was appointed minister of justice, and two months later he became minister of war. In June he attempted to rally the troops for an offensive against the Germans, but large numbers of soldiers refused to obey their officers, left their posts, and returned to their homes. In the reorganization of the government that followed, Kerenski succeeded Prince Georgi Evgenievich Lvov (q.v.) as provisional prime minister of Russia.

One of Kerenski's first acts as prime minister was the suppression of the Bolshevik Party (see BOLSHEVISM), led by Vladimir Ilich Lenin (q.v.). Lenin went into hiding in Finland; other Bolshevik leaders, including Leon Trotsky (q.v.), were arrested. Kerenski's failure to counteract the steady deterioration in the economic and military situation of the country, however, enabled the Bolsheviks to undermine his government and to concentrate the power of government in the soviets, or councils, of workers, soldiers, and peasants, which constituted a dual governmental structure parallel to the provisional government.

On the political right, Kerenski was beset by the agitation conducted by monarchists and other counterrevolutionaries, who sought to overthrow the provisional government and crush the revolution. Kerenski vacillated between the Bolsheviks and counterrevolutionists. In September, when the commander in chief of the Russian armies, General Lavr Georgievich Kornilov (q.v.), attempted to march on the capital, Petrograd (now Leningrad), and establish himself as a military dictator, Kerenski failed to take decisive measures; the attempted coup was aborted by the action of the Bolsheviks, who utilized the advantages accruing to them as a result of their initiative to seize power on Nov. 7, 1917. Kerenski, who, in the meantime had gone to the front in an effort to win support among the troops, organized a military force and attempted to capture Petrograd, but the troops refused to fight. He fled to Paris where he led several anti-Bolshevik organizations and for some years edited the newspaper *Dni*. He eventually settled in the United States, where he lectured on political and social science. His writings include *Prelude to Bolshevism* (1919), *The Catastrophe* (1927), *The Crucifixion of Liberty* (1934), and *Russia and History's Turning Point* (1965), a memoir updating some of his earlier work.

KERGUÉLEN ARCHIPELAGO, group of about 300 islands and islets of volcanic origin, in the S. Indian Ocean, about 1200 miles N. of Antarctica, and about 2000 miles S.E. of Madagascar. The only island of importance in the group is Kerguélen. The island is rocky and mountainous; the highest peak is Mt. Ross, 6120 ft. above sea

KÉRKIRA

level. The island is so deeply indented by fiords that, although it is 100 mi. long and 79 mi. wide, no point on the island is more than 12 mi. from the sea. Penguins and other sea birds frequent it, but no fauna is indigenous to Kerguélen. The native flora is of great antiquity and is thought possibly to have reached the island from distant South America rather than from comparatively nearby Africa. Especially notable is the Kerguélen cabbage, a vegetable long valued by explorers of those waters for its antiscorbutic qualities. The island was discovered in 1772 by the French navigator Yves Joseph de Kerguélen-Trémarec (1734?–97). The British explorer Captain James Cook (q.v.) visited it in 1776 and named it Desolation Island. France annexed Kerguélen in 1893 and has established permanent scientific research stations there. The only inhabitants are the personnel at the stations. Area, about 2700 sq.mi.

KÉRKIRA, known in English as CORFU, island and town in Greece, part of the Ionian Islands, of which the island of Kérkira is the most northerly. The island is separated from the N.W. coast of the Greek mainland and the S.W. coast of Albania by a strait 2 to 15 mi. wide. With the small islands of Paxói and Antipaxos, it forms the department (or nome) of Kérkira (pop. 1971, 92,261), the capital and largest town of which is the port of Kérkira (pop. 1971, 26,658) on the E. coast of Kérkira Island. Practically all the commerce of the island passes through the town of Kérkira. Except for its twin-peaked citadel, a palace of white Maltese stone, and some other noteworthy buildings, the town is architecturally unimpressive.

The island (area, 229 sq.mi.) is about 38 mi. in length and varies from 3 to 20 mi. in breadth. The N. part of the island is mountainous, the central part hilly, and the southern part low and fairly level. The entire island is well watered and highly fertile. Olive trees are grown, and olive oil is the principal product. Other products are oranges, figs, and wine, the last of which is used chiefly for home consumption.

History. Kérkira is the ancient Corcyra. Its early history, though identified as the Homeric island of Scheria (Phaeacia), is mythical. In early Greek times, about 734 B.C., it was colonized by the Corinthians; soon it attained wealth and maritime power and asserted its independence. After the Persian Wars, in which Corcyra took no part, a further dispute with Corinth led the Corcyreans to ally themselves with Athens (435 B.C.), and the intervention of the latter city was a factor contributing to the outbreak of the Peloponnesian War; see GREECE: *History: Ancient Greece.*

Constant internal dissensions and varying foreign control characterized the history of the island until it was taken under Roman protection in 229 B.C. During the greater part of the

The sun-drenched streets of Kérkira, or Corfu, bear little witness to the island's long history.
Greek National Tourist Office

Middle Ages it belonged to the Byzantine Empire (q.v.); later it passed into the possession of the Venetians, who called it Corfu and held it until 1797, in spite of several attacks by the Ottoman Turks. Since that time Kérkira has shared the fortunes of the other Ionian Islands, becoming a part of Greece in 1864. The French during World War I took temporary military possession of Kérkira on Jan. 11, 1916, to provide a refuge for the exhausted Serbian army, driven through Albania and faced with starvation. The Greek government protested against this breach of its neutrality but offered no active opposition. The Serbian parliament met there for the first time on Sept. 10, 1916; and on Kérkira, July 20, 1917, the Declaration of Corfu, proclaiming the union of the Yugoslavs, was signed by the exiled government of Serbia and the Yugoslav Committee. In 1923 an Italian general, a delegate on a commission for the delimitation of the boundaries between Greece and Albania, was assassinated on Greek soil by persons unknown. The Italian dictator, Benito Mussolini (q.v.), holding the Greek government responsible, sent Italian naval forces to bombard the town of Kérkira and to occupy the island. The matter was brought before the League of Nations (q.v.) by Greece, and was settled by Italian evacuation of Kérkira in September, 1923, and the payment of a large indemnity to Italy by Greece. In World War II the island was seized by Italian forces.

KERMADEC ISLANDS, group of islands in the Pacific Ocean, annexed by New Zealand in 1887, 600 miles N.E. of New Zealand. The largest of the islands is Raoul, or Sunday Island, which has an area of 11 sq.mi., and is the site of a meteorological station and airfield. Total area, 13 sq.mi.; pop. (1971) 9.

KERMAN, city in Iran, and capital of Kerman Province, 500 miles S.E. of Tehran. Kerman carpets are the principal manufactured product; goat wool shawls are also produced. Notable historic buildings include an 11th-century mosque, and a restored citadel and fort. Pop. (1966) 118,344.

KERMANSHAH, city in Iran, and capital of Kermanshah Province, in the Karkheh R. valley, about 90 miles S.W. of Hamadan. The city is the commercial center for grain and other produce of the countryside. Flour, textiles, refined oil, beet sugar, and carpets are produced there. Founded in the 4th century, Kermanshah has long been an important market center by virtue of its position on the caravan route from Hamadan to Baghdad. East of the city lies the Behistun inscription (q.v.) of Darius the Great (*see under* DARIUS), which became the key to the decipherment of several ancient Middle Eastern writings. Pop. (1966) 187,930.

KERN, Jerome David (1885–1945), American composer, born in New York City, and educated at the New York College of Music and in England and Germany. After completing his studies he returned to New York City, where his score for *The Red Petticoat,* an operetta produced in 1911, won critical praise. During the next twenty years Kern achieved numerous successes composing for the Broadway stage. Especially noteworthy are his scores for *Very Good Eddie* (1915), *Oh Lady, Oh Lady* (1918), *Sally* (1920), *Stepping Stones* (1923), *Sunny* (1925), and *Show Boat* (1927). The last-named production, based on the novel by Edna Ferber (q.v.) and with lyrics by Oscar Hammerstein 2nd (*see under* HAMMERSTEIN), is generally considered his greatest work (*see* MUSICAL COMEDY). Beginning in 1930 Kern, besides writing for the stage, composed the music for many popular motion pictures, including *Men of the Sky* (1930), *Swing Time* (1936), *High, Wide, and Handsome* (1937), *You Were Never Lovelier* (1942) and *Can't Help Singing* (1945). Some of his works for the stage during this period are *The Cat and the Fiddle* (1931), *Music in the Air* (1932), *Roberta* (1933), and *Very Warm for May* (1939).

Kern was remarkably adept at infusing his music with the flavor of the dramatic situations and the lyrics for which he composed. Among the finest of his songs are "Ol' Man River", "Look for the Silver Lining", "They Didn't Believe Me", "Why Do I Love You?", "Smoke Gets in Your Eyes", and "The Last Time I Saw Paris".

KERNITE. *See* BORAX.

KEROSINE. *See* PETROLEUM.

KERR, Walter Francis (1913–), American drama critic and author, born in Evanston, Ill., and educated at Northwestern University. Kerr taught drama at Catholic University of America, Washington, D.C., from 1938 to 1949. In New York City he directed theatrical productions of *Sing Out, Sweet Land* (1944), for which he wrote the libretto, and *Touch and Go* (1949), a review with sketches and lyrics by Kerr and his wife Jean Collins Kerr (1923–). He also directed Mrs. Kerr's play *King of Hearts* (1954). Kerr was drama critic for *Commonweal* magazine (1950–52), The New York *Herald Tribune* (1951–66), and The New York *Times* (1966–67). In September, 1967, he became a weekly contributor to the *Times.* His books include *How Not to Write a Play* (1955), *The Decline of Pleasure* (1962), and *Tragedy and Comedy* (1967).

KERRVILLE, city in Texas, and county seat of Kerr Co., on the Guadalupe R., 65 miles N.W. of

KERRY

San Antonio. Sheep, goat, and cattle herding are prevalent in the area, and the city is a market for wool and mohair. Kerrville's high altitude and warm climate make it a popular health and tourist resort. The city was incorporated in 1856. Pop. (1960) 8901; (1970) 12,672.

KERRY, maritime county of the Republic of Ireland, in s.w. Munster Province, on the Atlantic Ocean. The county has an irregular coastline indented by many bays and inlets. The region is largely mountainous with several peaks more than 3000 ft. above sea level. Carrantuohill, at 3414 ft., is the highest point in Ireland. In the center of the county are the picturesque Lakes of Killarney; see KILLARNEY, LAKES OF. The principal rivers are the Feale, the Maine, the Inny, and the Kenmare. Many islands lie off the coast. The capital, Tralee, is the most important town. Dairying, the raising of sheep and goats, fishing, the quarrying of slate and limestone, the manufacture of coarse woolens and linens, and tourism are the chief sources of income. Area, 1815 sq.mi.; pop. (1971) 112,941.

KERRY BLUE TERRIER, breed of terrier (q.v.) that originated in County Kerry, Ireland, before the beginning of the 19th century. The Kerry blue retrieves well from either land or water, and is used in Ireland and England for hunting birds and small game. It is also employed as a sheep and cattle herder and as a watchdog. The breed first became well known in the United States in the third decade of the 20th century. A typical Kerry blue has a long head and a flat skull, small or medium-sized eyes that are usually hazel in color; a deep chest, a moderately long neck, and a soft curly coat that may be any of several shades of blue. The male dog is about 18 in. high at the shoulder and weighs from 33 to 38 lb.; the bitch is slightly under 18 in. in height and weighs from 32 to 36 lb. The Kerry blue is an extremely alert and intelligent dog, with unusual powers of endurance. Because of its loyalty and its unusual gentleness toward children it is an admirable pet.

KESTREL. See FALCON.

KETCH, class of fore-and-aft-rigged, two-masted sailing vessel, having the mizzen or jigger mast to the fore of the rudder post. Until the 19th century, square-rigged ketches were used both as warships and for off-shore fishing, but today they are popular for yachting (q.v.). See also SAIL.

KETCHIKAN, city and seaport of Alaska, in the Southeastern Senatorial District, on Revillagigedo Island, about 250 miles S.E. of Juneau, and about 600 miles N.W. of Seattle, Wash. The city is the commercial center of a fishing, mining, and lumbering area. Industrial establishments in the town and vicinity include salmon canneries, cold-storage plants, and lumber mills. Ketchikan is headquarters for a huge commercial fishing fleet and is one of the largest salmon-fishing ports in the world. Pop. (1960) 6483; (1970) 6994.

KETONES, class of organic compounds that contain the structure C—C—C in which the lines represent covalent bonds. The simplest ketone is acetone, CH_3—CO—CH_3, and it corresponds to the general ketone formula with three hydrogen atoms attached to each of the end carbon atoms. Acetone is a product of the metabolism (qq.v.) of fats, but under ordinary conditions it oxidizes quickly to water and carbon dioxide; see CHEMICAL ANALYSIS: *Organic Analysis.* In diabetes mellitus (q.v.), however, acetone accumulates in the body and may be detected in the urine. Other ketones are camphor, many of the steroids, some fragrances, and some sugars. Ketones are relatively reactive organic compounds, and thus are invaluable in the synthesis of other compounds; they are also important intermediates in cell metabolism. See CHEMISTRY: *Organic Chemistry.*

KETTERING, city of Ohio, in Montgomery Co., adjoining Dayton on the s. Important industries include the manufacture of auto and aircraft parts, electronic equipment, tools, and machine products. Settled in the 18th century, Kettering was incorporated as a village in 1952 and as a city in 1955, absorbing all of unincorporated Van Buren Township. Pop. (1960) 54,462; (1970) 69,599.

Kerry blue terrier — Walter Chandoha

KETTERING, Charles Franklin (1876–1958), American engineer, inventor, and manufacturer, born in Ashland County, Ohio, and educated at Wooster College and Ohio State University. He was an electrical designer for the National Cash Register Company in Dayton, Ohio, in 1904, and in 1908 organized the Dayton Engineering Laboratories, for which he developed and manufactured lighting and ignition systems for automobiles and a self-starting system. He is best known for the latter invention. His inventions were marketed under the proprietary name "Delco"; a lighting and power system, based on a generator driven by an internal-combustion engine, and developed in 1914 for use in isolated communities, was called the Delco Farm Light System. Kettering's studies of antiknock fuels resulted in the use of tetraethyl lead in gasoline. From 1917 until 1947 he was vice-president and general manager of the General Motors Research Corporation, also serving as vice-president of the General Motors Corporation from 1920 until 1947. He was cosponsor of the Sloan-Kettering Institute for Cancer Research founded in 1948.

KETTLEDRUM, or TIMPANO, musical instrument consisting of a copper or brass hemispherical shell with a sheepskin head tuned by stretchers and sounded by soft-headed drumsticks. Large orchestras include three or more in different sizes, each of which can be varied in pitch by means of a foot pedal that changes the tension on the drum head. See DRUM.

KEY, in mechanics, small part fitting a prepared recess cut in two joined parts or components, and thus employed to lock these parts together. Keys are most commonly used to lock wheels or gears firmly in their axles; see GEARING; WHEEL AND AXLE. Such a key is often composed of a thin strip of metal that fits tightly into a transverse groove cut in the axle shaft and into a parallel groove in the inner diameter of the wheel hub. Some keys are designed to prevent any play between wheel and axle, and others are so arranged as to allow the wheel to slide along the axle but not to turn relative to it. When sliding motion is necessary, engineers, rather than using a key, usually prefer to use a splined shaft. Instead of separate keys, such shafts have several ridges or splines machined on the shaft; these splines fit into corresponding grooves cut in the hub.

The term "key" is also applied to the inserted locking device, a small, shaped cut of metal, used to move or release a bolt or catch in a complementary mechanism. See LOCK. Key also refers to levers of musical instruments.

KEY, Francis Scott (1779–1843), American lawyer and poet, born in Frederick County (now Carroll County), Md. He practiced law in Maryland and in the District of Columbia. During the War of 1812 Key witnessed the British bombardment of Fort McHenry, the most important of

Francis Scott Key

the ring of fortifications about Baltimore. The sight of the American flag still flying over the fort at daybreak inspired him to write the poem "The Star Spangled Banner" (q.v.). The poem and the music to which it was set became the national anthem of the United States, first by popular usage, and in 1931 by Act of Congress. Key was also the author of the essay *The Power of Literature and Its Connection with Religion* (1834) and *Poems* (posthumously published, 1857).

KEYNES, John Maynard, 1st Baron of Tilton (1883–1946), British economist, born in Cambridge, England, and educated at Eton College and the University of Cambridge. He began his career in the India Office of the British government, and wrote a highly regarded book, *Indian Currency and Finance* (1913). During World War I he worked in the treasury, which he represented at the Paris Peace Conference (1919). Opposed to the economic terms of the Treaty of Versailles (see VERSAILLES, TREATY OF) he resigned his position, and wrote *The Economic Consequences of the Peace* (1919), in which he correctly predicted that the staggering reparations levied against Germany would goad that country into economic nationalism and a resurgence of militarism. During the next decade he made a fortune speculating in international currencies, taught at Cambridge, and wrote *Treatise on Probability* (1921), a mathematical work, and *A Treatise on Money* (1930). In the latter, he sought to explain why an economy operates so unevenly, with frequent cycles of booms and depressions. Like other treatments of the subject, his work failed to explain the problem of prolonged depression, a phenomenon which did not conform to the then generally accepted notion that recessions were self-correcting. It was then felt that during recessions savings would accumulate, causing interest rates to fall and would thereby encourage business to invest and the economy to expand. Keynes closely examined the problem of prolonged depression in his major work, *The General Theory of Employment, Interest, and Money* (1936). This book, which provided a theoretical defense for programs that were already being tried in Great Britain and by President Franklin Delano Roosevelt (q.v.) in the United States (see NEW DEAL), proposed that no self-correcting mechanism to lift an economy out of a depression existed. It stated that unused savings prolonged economic stagnation and that business investment was spurred by new inventions, new markets, and other factors not related to the interest rate on savings. Because business investment necessarily fluctuated, it could not be depended upon to maintain a high level of employment and a steady flow of income through the economy. Considering this, Keynes proposed that government spending must compensate for insufficient business investment in times of recession. Keynes' ideas have profoundly influenced the economic policies of many governments since World War II, and his book is considered by many to be one of the most significant theoretical works of the 20th century.

Shortly after Great Britain entered World War II, Keynes published *How to Pay for the War* (1940), in which he urged that a portion of every wage earner's pay should automatically be invested in government bonds. In 1942 he was made a baron, and two years later he headed the British delegation to the United Nations Monetary and Financial Conference, the Bretton Woods Conference (q.v.). At the conference he promoted establishment of the International Bank for Reconstruction and Development and the International Monetary Fund (qq.v.).

See ECONOMICS: *History: 20th-Century Theory.*
KEYSERLING, Count Hermann Alexander (1880–1946), German philosopher, born in Estonia (now the Estonian S.S.R.), and educated at the universities of Heidelberg and Vienna. He lived in France and England from 1903 to 1905, in Berlin from 1906 to 1907, and on his estates in Estonia from 1908 to 1918. During the Russian Revolution he was deprived of his estates and fortune, and settled in Darmstadt, Germany. Keyserling's interest in Oriental philosophy, which strongly influenced his own works, led him to establish a "School of Wisdom" in 1920. Thereafter he traveled and lectured in many countries, including the United States. His translated works include *The Travel Diary of a Philosopher* (1925), *The World in the Making* (1927), *Europe* (1928), *The Recovery of Truth* (1929), and *South American Meditations* (1932).

KEY WEST, city and port of entry in Florida, and county seat of Monroe Co., on Key West Island, near the w. end of the Florida Keys (q.v.), about 130 miles S.W. of Miami. Key West is connected with the mainland by the Overseas Highway, a 123-mi. long highway completed in 1938. Key West is the southernmost city in the United States, and a popular winter vacation resort. Coconut and date palms, banana, almond, avocado, and many other tropical trees and shrubs grow in abundance in Key West. Tourism is the chief source of income; other industries include commercial shrimp-fishing and the manufacture of cigars. The city is particularly noted for turtle canneries, and canned turtle meat and turtles are exported to northern markets. Key West is also a military post, naval air station, and submarine base. Fort Taylor, built in 1846 and later improved, is now a U.S. Coast Guard base. Key West was settled about 1822, prior to which it is believed to have been a pirate refuge. The city was of military importance in several wars in the 19th century because of its strategic location. Pop. (1960) 33,956; (1970) 27,563.

KHABAROVSK, city of the Soviet Union, in the Russian S.F.S.R., and capital of the Khabarovsk Territory, on the Amur R., just E. of the border of Manchuria. The Khabarovsk Territory includes the Jewish Autonomous Oblast (q.v.). Khabarovsk is the most important industrial center in the Soviet Far East. Major industries are iron and steel manufacturing, petroleum refining, flour milling, meat packing, and brewing and distilling. The Trans-Siberian Railroad traverses Khabarovsk, making the city an important railway center. Khabarovsk was founded in 1858 as an imperial fortress. Pop. (1970) 437,000.

KHACHATURIAN, Aram (1903–), Soviet composer, born in Tbilisi, Russia (now Georgian S.S.R.), and educated at the Moscow Conservatory. His early work, such as Trio for Clarinet, Violin and Piano (1932) and First Symphony (1934), demonstrated lyrical power, the skillful use of dissonance, traditional techniques, and the influence, apparent in his subsequent work, of Armenian folk music. Some of Khachaturian's later compositions are Piano Concerto (1935); *Poem for Stalin* (1938), a choral-orchestral piece; Violin Concerto in D minor (1940); *Gayane* (1942), a ballet that includes the well-known *Sabre Dance;* Second Symphony (1943); Cello Concerto (1946); and Rhapsody for Violin and Orchestra (1960). He also composed scores for stage productions and motion pictures. In 1959 he received the Lenin Prize.

KHAFRE or KHAFRA (Gr. *Khephren* or *Chephren*) (fl. 2565 B.C.), king of IV Dynasty of Egypt and builder of the second pyramid at Giza (q.v.). See EGYPT; ARAB REPUBLIC OF: *History: The Old Kingdom;* PYRAMIDS.

KHALKÍS, or CHALKIS or CHALCIS, city in Greece, and capital of the Aegean island department of Euboea, on the Strait of Evripos, about 40 miles N.W. of Athens, with which it is connected by rail. The ancient city, inhabited by Ionians, was an important commercial and industrial center. In the 7th and 8th centuries A.D. it was a base for the establishment of colonies in Macedonia (there giving name to the peninsula of Chalcidice) and in Sicily. It was successively, thereafter, an Athenian, a Macedonian, and a Roman possession. During the Middle Ages it was a prosperous community under the Venetians, who held it from 1209 until its conquest by the Ottoman Turks in 1470. Pop. (1971) 36,381.

KHAN (Turk. *khān*, "lord"), title for the ruler of China and leader of the Mongol, Tatar, and Turkish tribes. After the Mongol conqueror Temujin overran northern China and was proclaimed Genghis Khan (q.v.) in 1206, a succession of khans reigned over the Mongols throughout the Middle Ages; *see* MONGOL DYNASTIES. Local chieftains and high-ranking men in India and Pakistan and central Asia have also been called khans.

KHANH HUNG, city in South Vietnam, and capital of Ba Xuyen Province, in the Mekong Delta area near the mouth of the Bassac R. (Song Hau Giang), 95 miles S.W. of Saigon. It is the center of an intensive rice-growing region and is also a communications hub for highway and canal traffic. The city was formerly called Soc Trang. Pop. (1962 est.) 34,610.

KHANIÁ or CANEA (anc. *Cydonia*), city and seaport in Greece, and capital of the island of Crete, 170 miles S. of Athens. Although the harbor cannot accommodate large ships the town is an important export center, principally for soap, oil, leather, and agricultural products. One of the oldest cities of Crete, Khaniá was conquered (69 B.C.) by the Romans, and in 826 A.D. fell under Arab rule. Reconquered (961) by the Byzantines, it became a Venetian colony. Despite the enormous wall with which the Venetians surrounded Khaniá, it fell to the Ottoman Turks in 1646. In 1913, when the Turks ceded Crete to Greece, Khaniá became a Greek possession. During World War II the town suffered heavy damage in 1941, during the German airborne invasion of Crete. Among the notable buildings of Khaniá are Turkish mosques and Greek churches. Pop. (1971) 40,452.

KHARAGPUR, city of India, in West Bengal State, S. of the Cossye R., 8 miles W. of Midnapore and 70 miles S.W. of Calcutta. In an area producing rice, grains, and vegetables, Kharagpur is a road and rail junction and has repair shops, engineering works, rice mills, and plants manufacturing textiles, chemicals, and leather products. The city is the site of Kharagpur College, an institute of technology, a city museum, and the shrine of a local saint venerated by both Hindus and Muslims. The name of the city was sometimes spelled Kharakpur. Pop. (1971) 161,911.

KHARIJITES. *See* MUSLIM SECTS: *Kharijites.*

KHAR'KOV, city of the Soviet Union, in the Ukrainian S.S.R., and capital of the Khar'kov Oblast, at the junction of the Khar'kov and Lopan rivers, 235 miles E. of Kiev. It is the second largest city (after Kiev) of the Ukrainian S.S.R. and one of the largest cities in the U.S.S.R. Located near the rich coal mines in the basin of the Donets R. and linked by railroad to the iron-ore deposits of Krivoy Rog (q.v.) in south-central Ukraine, the city has become one of the greatest industrial centers of the Soviet Union. It produces chiefly farm machinery, electric generators, chemicals, paper, and machine tools. Neither the Lopan nor the Khar'kov river is navigable, and a network of railroads radiates from the city. Khar'kov is the seat of the State University of Khar'kov, founded in 1804. The city is also the site of the Palace of Industry, which acts as the coordinating center for all Ukrainian industries.

Khar'kov was founded as a fortress town about 1654. In 1765 it became the administrative center of the Ukraine. With the development of the vast mineral wealth of the territory in the late 19th century, the city rapidly became an industrial center. During World War I (q.v.) Khar'kov was the scene of violent fighting, first between German and Russian troops, and later between opposing forces in the Russian Revolution (q.v.) that began in 1917. The city was made

Firewood is unloaded from dhows, Arab riverboats of shallow draft, on the bank of the Nile River near Khartoum for use in the city. United Nations

the capital of the newly organized Ukrainian S.S.R. in 1920, but was replaced as the capital by Kiev in 1934. Khar'kov was occupied by German troops during World War II from 1941 to 1943. Pop. (1972 est.) 1,280,000.

KHARTOUM *or* **KHARTUM**, city and capital of the Republic of the Sudan, and capital of Khartoum Province, on the Blue Nile R., near the junction with the White Nile R., about 1000 miles s. of Cairo, Egypt. Khartoum is the governmental, educational, and commercial center of the country. The city has an international airport and is served by river steamboats and by railroad. Khartoum is the site of the University of Khartoum, founded in 1903 by the British as Gordon Memorial College; two museums; zoological gardens; and many mosques and churches. The city was founded as a military camp by the Egyptians about 1820. The town developed as the center of the Sudanese slave trade, a practice that was ended by the British general Charles George Gordon (q.v.) in 1875. Gordon later returned to the Sudan, and in 1884–85, during the revolt led by the Muslim leader Mohammed Ahmed (see Mahdi), he was killed defending Khartoum. The city was destroyed by the Mahdists and abandoned for Omdurman, now a suburb on the opposite side of the Blue Nile. Khartoum was recaptured by an Anglo-Egyptian army in 1898. See Sudan, Republic of the: *History.* Pop. (1971 est.) 261,840.

KHARTOUM NORTH, city of Sudan, in Khartoum Province, on the Blue Nile R. just above its confluence with the White Nile, opposite Khartoum on the N. Served by a railroad, the city has dockyards, workshops, and meat-packing, textile-weaving, and brewing industries. Goods manufactured in the city include rubber products, concrete, and canvas shoes. Livestock, cotton, wheat, barley, and fruit are traded. Pop. (1971 est.) 127,672.

KHAYYÁM, Omar. See Omar Khayyám.

KHAZARS *or* **CHAZARS,** extinct people who flourished from about 200 A.D. to about 950, living at first in the region of the Caucasus Mts. and the Caspian Sea and later on the steppes of southeastern Russia. At the height of their power, in the 9th century, the Khazars controlled Russia west to the Dnieper R. and north to the middle course of the Volga R. They carried on an extensive commerce, centered in their capital at Itil (now Astrakhan'). The ethnology of the Khazars was complicated by racial mixture and dispersion; most authorities classify them as a Turkish or, less probably, a Georgian people; see Georgian Soviet Socialist Republic. In the 7th century their Khakan, or sovereign, embraced Judaism (q.v.), and a large part of the population was converted thereafter. Khazar power came to an end when, after a series of wars, they were overcome and assimilated by the Russians. The Khazars were a significant factor in preventing Arab expansion to the Caucasus; see Russia: *Origins of the Russian People.*

KHEDIVE, hereditary title granted to the viceroy of Egypt, Ismail Pasha (q.v.), by the sultan of Turkey in 1867 when Egypt was under the rule of the Ottoman Empire. It was abolished in 1914 when Egypt became a British protectorate.

KHERSON, city of the Soviet Union, in the Ukrainian S.S.R., and capital of the Kherson Oblast, on the Dnieper R., about 15 mi. from its mouth on the Black Sea, and about 100 miles N.E. of Odessa. The city is an important port where agricultural products and manganese ore are exported and oil is imported. The chief industries are flour milling, textile processing, and the manufacture of machinery. Kherson was founded in 1778 by the Russian prince Grigori Potëmkin (q.v.) as a naval port. Pop. (1970) 261,000.

KHINGAN, name of two mountain ranges, the Great Khingan and the Lesser Khingan, in N.E. China. The Great Khingan, reaching to a height of about 8000 ft., runs in a N.-S. direction in upper Inner Mongolia. The Lesser Khingan lies mainly in the Heilungkiang Province on the border between Siberia and Manchuria, China.

KHÍOS, or CHIOS, island and department of Greece, in the Aegean Sea, about 8 mi. off the W. coast of Asian Turkey. The island is about 30 mi. long, and 8 to 15 mi. wide. The capital and chief town is Khíos (pop. 1971, 24,074), a seaport on the E. coast. In the N. the island is mountainous, but the land in the S. is open and fertile. Gum mastic, from which a liqueur is made, and wine are the principal products of the island. Other products include olives, figs, and oranges. Coastal trade is important economically; industry includes the mining of antimony and calamite, marble quarrying, and tanning.

The island contains relics of ancient times, when it was an important Greek state, the home of noted poets and sculptors, and a participant in the wars that marked the history of ancient Greece and Rome. Khíos was occupied by the Seljuk Turks in the 11th century A.D., and later became a possession, successively, of the Venetians, Genoese, and Ottoman Turks. During the Balkan War of 1912, it again became a Greek possession; see BALKAN WARS.

KHIVA (anc. *Chorasmia;* later *Khwarizm* and *Khorezm*), formerly a large khanate of west-central Asia, S. of the Aral Sea, now part of the Uzbek S.S.R. and the Turkmen S.S.R. Khiva is also the name of a town in the Khorezm Oblast of the Uzbek S.S.R.; the town is noted for its many historic buildings, such as the Islam-Khodzha Minaret and the mausoleum of the khans. In ancient times the Oxus R. (now Amu-Dar'ya R.), which passes through the khanate, emptied into the Caspian Sea and thus provided the ancient kingdom with a waterway to Europe. When the course of the river shifted to the Aral Sea, ancient Khiva declined in importance. Khiva was taken by the Arabs in 680 A.D. and later by the Mongol leaders Genghis Khan and Tamerlane (qq.v.). Russia annexed part of the khanate in 1873, and in 1919 the U.S.S.R. deposed the khan of Khiva, dissolving the khanate. Khiva became the Khorezm Soviet People's Republic in 1920, and in 1924 it was absorbed into the two Soviet republics, Uzbek S.S.R. and Turkmen S.S.R.

KHORANA, Har Gobind (1922–), American geneticist, born in Raipur, India. He received a B.S. degree in 1943 and an M.Sc. degree in 1945, both from the University of Punjab. He received a doctorate in chemistry from the University of Liverpool in 1948. During the next twelve years he held posts at the Federal Institute of Technology in Zürich, Switzerland; the University of Cambridge, England; the University of British Columbia in Vancouver, and the Rockefeller Institute (now Rockefeller University) in New York City. In 1960 Khorana joined the Enzyme Institute at the University of Wisconsin, eventually becoming its co-director. He shared the 1968 Nobel Prize in medicine and physiology with Robert W. Holley and Marshall W. Nirenberg (qq.v.) for independent studies of how genes within a cell determine the function of that cell. See NUCLEIC ACIDS.

KHORAT. See NAKHOM RATCHASIMA.

KHORSABAD. See ASSYRIA.

KHOSRAU or **KHUSRAU** or **KHOSRU,** name of two kings of the Sassanid dynasty (226–641 A.D.) of Persia.

Khosrau I, known as KHOSRAU ANUSHIRVAN ("having an immortal soul") (d. 579), King (531–79), the son of Kavadh I (r. 485–531). Khosrau I is considered one of the greatest kings of the ancient Persian Empire; see PERSIA. In a series of wars with the Eastern Roman Empire (531–32, 540–45, 571–76) he extended his domain to the Black Sea. Other military conquests extended the frontier of Persia to the Indus R. in the east, and from the Arabian Sea far into central Asia. He was successful in all his Byzantine wars until 576, when the forces of Emperor Justin II (d. 578) defeated the Persians at Melitene (now Malatya).

Khosrau's military prowess was equalled by his administrative ability. His reformation of the provincial administration and tax system, advancement of industrial and commercial development, and encouragement of learning and literature caused his reign to be known as the golden age of ancient Persian literature; see PERSIAN LANGUAGE AND LITERATURE. Khosrau became the central figure of many Persian legends.

Khosrau II, known as KHOSRAU PARVEZ ("The Victorious") (d. 628), King (590–628), the grandson of Khosrau I. He was assisted in gaining the throne by Mauricius, Emperor of Byzantium (539?–602), and, in gratitude, restored to the Eastern Roman Empire many of the Byzantine territories conquered by his grandfather. When Mauricius was deposed and murdered in 602, Khosrau turned against Byzantium and for the remainder of his reign waged war against that empire. He reconquered the territories restored in 592 and invaded most of southwest Asia, including Syria and Palestine. The Persian armies captured Egypt in 616 and a year later conquered Chalcedon, opposite Constantinople (now İstanbul, Turkey). Intrigues and insurrections against Khosrau began to arise in Persia, and Heraclius, Byzantine Emperor (575?–641), took advantage of this domestic weakness to defeat the Persian monarch in a campaign from 623 to 628. After this defeat Khosrau was deposed and murdered by his son, later Kavadh II (r. 628).

Nikita S. Khrushchev, in his position as premier of the Soviet Union, visited the United Nations headquarters in New York City in 1959. At left is the late U.N. Secretary-General Dag Hammarskjöld. United Nations

KHRUSHCHEV, Nikita S(ergeyevich) (1894–1971), Soviet Communist leader, born in Kalinovka, in what is now the Russian S.F.S.R. The son of a miner, he worked in his early years as a shepherd and locksmith. After serving in the czarist army in World War I (q.v.) and participating in the Bolshevik Revolution (see BOLSHEVISM), he joined the Communist Party and Red Army in 1918 and fought in the civil war. He attended a Communist Party high school in 1921 and was active as a party organizer until 1929. For the next two years he attended the Industrial Academy in Moscow. Khrushchev advanced rapidly in the party, becoming a member of the Central Committee in 1934. From 1935 to 1937, as first secretary of the Moscow Regional Committee, he directed the industrialization program of the second Five-Year Plan (q.v.). In 1938 he was transferred to the Ukraine as first secretary of the Ukrainian party organization and made a provisional member of the All-Union Political Bureau of the party; he became a full member in 1939 and was also appointed to the presidium of the U.S.S.R. Supreme Soviet.

During World War II (q.v.) Khrushchev headed the guerrilla forces in the Ukraine and the political department of the Red Army on the southern front. In 1944, after the Germans were driven from the Ukraine, he was entrusted with restoring agricultural production, establishing order, and punishing traitors. Returning to Moscow in 1949, he was appointed a member of the Secretariat of the party's All-Union Central Committee. Subsequently he emerged as the foremost Soviet agricultural expert. In 1953 he became first secretary of the Central Committee, in effect, the head of the Communist Party of the U.S.S.R. and the chief architect of Soviet policy. Khrushchev denounced the late dictator Joseph Stalin (q.v.) in 1956 and in 1957 he demoted many of Stalin's former close associates. He became premier of the Soviet Union upon the resignation of Nikolai Bulganin (q.v.) in 1958. Khrushchev boasted of Soviet destructive might but advocated peaceful methods to overcome capitalism. Khrushchev was deposed as premier and party head on Oct. 14–15, 1964. He was then accused of political "errors", including fomenting the 1962 Cuban missile crisis, establishing a "cult of personality", and disorganizing the economy. By the end of the year he held no government office. In 1966 he was dropped from the party Central Committee. In 1970 *Khrushchev Remembers* was published in English; Khrushchev denied, however, he had authorized the book. See COMMUNISM; UNION OF S.S.R.: History; Foreign Affairs in the 1950's and 1960's.

KHUFU, *or* (Gr.) **CHEOPS,** Pharaoh of Egypt (2680–2657 B.C.). Khufu was the first king of the IV Dynasty, also known as the Memphite Dynasty. The outstanding event of his reign was the construction of the Great Pyramid at Giza, near Cairo; see EGYPTIAN ARCHITECTURE AND ART; PYRAMIDS. This colossal monument became famous as one of the seven wonders of the world (q.v.), and remains one of the most notable structures in the history of architecture. Khufu virtually impoverished his country to effect its completion, enlisting the services of almost the entire adult male population. In 1954 the 125-ft. solar funeral ship of Khufu was discovered near the Great Pyramid; see EGYPTIAN ARCHEOLOGY. In the ritual of the funerary cult as practiced by Khufu and his contemporaries, such vessels were constructed for the purpose of transporting the souls of the departed through the heavens in the path of the sun god.

KHULNA, city of Pakistan, in former East Pakistan (now Bangladesh) on the Kazi Bacha R. in the Ganges Delta, 80 miles S.W. of Dacca, and about 70 miles N.E. of Calcutta, India. An industrial city and trade center, it is a rail terminus and junction for river traffic; oceangoing vessels are serviced at the port of Chalna, 18 miles to the S. The surrounding swampy area contains forests and peat deposits and grows rice, sugar-cane, dates, coconuts, jute, and tobacco. Among industries in the city are rice, oilseed, and jute milling; cotton-textile weaving; shipbuilding; fishing; sawmilling; and the manufacture of newsprint, matches, and salt. The power station is the center of an irrigation project for the area. Pop. (1971 est.) 403,000.

KHUSRAU. See KHOSRAU.

KHYBER PASS, most important pass connecting Afghanistan and West Pakistan. It winds N.W. through the Safed Koh Range (q.v.) near Peshawar, West Pakistan, for 30 mi. to Kabul, Afghanistan, varying in width from 5 to 150 yd. The mountains on either side can be climbed only in a few places and the precipitous walls vary in height from 1404 to about 3500 ft. For centuries the Khyber Pass was used by invaders to enter India. During the Afghan Wars (see AFGHANISTAN: *History*), the pass was the scene of numerous skirmishes between Anglo-Indian soldiers and native Afghans. Particularly well known is the battle of January, 1842, in which about 16,000 British and Indian troops were killed. The British constructed a road through the pass in 1879 and converted it into a highway during the 1920's.

KIAMUSZE (Jap. *Chia-mu-ssu*), city of the People's Republic of China, in Heilungkiang Province, on the lower Sungari R., 195 miles N.E. of Harbin. A major river port and supply base for surrounding Manchurian coalfields, it forms, with its northern suburb of Lienkiangkow, an important rail junction, with spurs to the coal regions. Industries include sawmilling, flour and soybean milling, tanning, beet-sugar refining, and the manufacture of paper, wood pulp, and brick and tile. A power plant is situated here. Developed while under Japanese control, Kiamusze served as capital of Sankiang Province in Manchukuo from 1934 to 1946, and of the former Hokiang Province until 1949 after its return to China. The city was created in 1934. Pop. (1970 est.) 275,000.

KIANG. See Ass.

KIBBUTZ, cooperative village, or communal farm, in Israel (q.v.), where all property is collectively owned and work is organized on a collective basis. Each member contributes by working according to his capacity and in return receives food, clothing, housing, and other domestic services according to his needs. Dining rooms, kitchens, and stores are central, and schools and children's dormitories are communal. Each village is governed by an elected assembly. Although most kibbutzim are entirely agricultural, some have established manufacturing industries. In 1968 there were 230 kibbutzim, with a total of 80,000 members. The first kibbutz, called Degania, was founded in 1909. *See also* CHILD PSYCHOLOGY; COMMUNE; FAMILY.

KICKAPOO, Algonquian tribe of North American Indians that lived originally in central and

Indian of the Kickapoo tribe.   Bureau of American Ethnology

KIDD

southern Wisconsin. The name Kickapoo is derived from the Algonquian *Kiwigapawa*, "he moves about". These Indians spoke the Algonquian language (*see* AMERICAN INDIAN LANGUAGES) and were extremely successful warriors; they served as mercenaries for the French, Spanish, British, and Mexicans. In the period before the American Revolution, the Kickapoo moved southward into the Wabash region now included in the States of Illinois and Indiana, and during the revolution and the War of 1812 they joined the other tribes of the Ohio Valley in siding with the British against the Americans. In subsequent years they made treaties with the United States government under the terms of which they settled in Missouri and later in Kansas. About 1852 a large portion of the tribe made another migration southward through Texas into Mexico, where they became known as the Mexican Kickapoo. At the present time Kickapoo communities are found in northern Coahuila State, Mexico, as well as in northeastern Kansas and Oklahoma.

See PLAINS INDIANS.

KIDD, William (1645?–1701), known as "Captain Kidd", English pirate and privateer, born in Greenock, Scotland. He went to sea as a young man, and by 1690 was established in New York City as a shipowner. In that same year, as captain of one of his own vessels, he served the English against the French privateers in the West Indies. He was awarded £150 in 1691 for loyal service in the insurrection instigated by the German-born fur trader in New York Jacob Leisler (1640?–1691).

During a visit to London in 1695 Kidd received from King William III (q.v.), sometimes called William of Orange, a commission as a privateer, with orders to act against pirates in the Indian Ocean. His expedition financed by private citizens, Kidd sailed from England in April, 1696, but after a year at sea, during which time they captured no prizes, and his crew mutinied at Madagascar, Kidd and his crew turned to piracy. During the next two years they seized many merchant ships, the richest of which was the *Quedagh Merchant,* an Armenian vessel.

Upon arriving in the West Indies in 1699 and learning that he was wanted for piracy, Kidd immediately set sail for New England. He landed at Oyster Bay, L.I., and from there wrote Richard Coote, 1st Earl of Bellamont (1636–1701), the governor of New England, that he could justify his piracy, and sent Bellamont some plunder. Confident of pardon, he proceeded to Boston, where he and several of his crew were arrested. They were sent to London and imprisoned at Newgate. On May 23, 1701, Kidd was hanged, after being tried, convicted on three piracy indictments, and judged guilty of fatally wounding a crew member during the Madagascar mutiny. The small amount of treasure recovered from his ship and from Gardiners Island (q.v.), off the east coast of Long Island, led to the belief that the rest of Kidd's treasure is buried somewhere near New York City, on the Atlantic coast.

KIDDERMINSTER, Great Britain, municipal borough of Worcestershire, England, on the Stour R. and the Staffordshire and Worcester Canal, about 15 miles N. of Worcester. The borough is noted for its carpet manufactures, which were established in 1735. The Kidderminster carpet was one of the earliest ingrain carpets to be made in England. From the 9th to the 12th centuries Kidderminster was a royal manor; in 1636 it was incorporated. Pop. (1971 est.) 47,640.

KIDDUSH. *See* PRAYER, JEWISH.

KIDNAPPING, in criminal law, offense of wrongfully taking and conveying away a person against his will, either by force, fraud, or intimidation. The word was originally applied only to the abduction of children, but very early in English law it was employed to designate the same offense with regard to adults. The early common law also confined the offense to the taking of a person from his own to another country, but such a restriction does not exist in the common law today.

In nearly all the States of the United States the crime of kidnapping is defined by statute. Merely enticing a competent adult person away is not sufficient to constitute the crime. The crime can only exist when an abduction is carried out against the will of the person, either actually or constructively. For example, inducing a laborer to go to a distant place to work, by holding out extravagant promises that the employer does not intend to fulfill, does not come within the scope of this crime; but getting a sailor intoxicated and taking him aboard a strange ship, with design to detain him until the vessel is under way, and then to persuade or coerce him to serve as a seaman, has been held to constitute kidnapping. The crime is also committed if the consent to such removal is induced by fraud, or if the victim is legally incompetent to give a valid consent, as in the case of a young child or of a feeble-minded person. The essential elements of kidnapping and of false imprisonment are about the same, except that the former includes, in addition to a detention, the act of carrying away the victim to another place, usually for the purpose of avoiding discovery.

The penalty for kidnapping is generally severe in the U.S.; and most States also make it a crime to attempt or conspire to commit a kidnapping. A Federal law, popularly known as the Lindbergh Act, which was enacted in 1932 after the kidnapping of the child of the American aviator Charles Augustus Lindbergh (q.v.), makes it a Federal crime, punishable by life imprisonment, to kidnap a person and transport him to another State; this law was amended in 1934 to make a conspiracy to commit a kidnapping also a Federal crime. In 1968 the Supreme Court of the United States (q.v.) invalidated that section of the Lindbergh Act that gave the jury the power to recommend the death penalty for the crime of kidnapping.

A person legally entrusted with the custody of another may not, of course, be guilty of kidnapping him. A parent, however, may be guilty of kidnapping his own child if the custody of such child has been given to another by court order or decree. When the parents have separated without legal decree, one may take his child from the other even by trick or deception, without committing the offense of kidnapping. See also ABDUCTION.

KIDNEY, one of a pair of glands whose function is the elaboration and excretion of the urine.

Structure. In humans, kidneys are situated in the region of the loins, one on each side of the spine, and are embedded in fatty tissue. They are bean-shaped, possessing a convex outer border and a concave inner border. A small ductless gland, the adrenal gland (q.v.), is on the upper end of each kidney, the average length of which is slightly more than 4 in. and the usual weight of which is from 4 oz. to 6 oz. The left kidney is often slightly longer and narrower than the right. The concave inner border presents an indentation, the hilum, at which the blood vessels enter and leave. In front is the renal vein carrying blood from the kidney; behind it lies the renal artery carrying blood to the kidney. Most posterior is the ureter, a tube that conveys urine to the bladder (q.v.; see URINE AND URINARY SYSTEM). The hilum arises from a deeper indentation, the sinus of the kidney, in which the ureter dilates to form a small sac, the pelvis. The kidney also embodies glomeruli, tuftlike aggregations or loops of capillaries enclosed within thin envelopes of endothelial lining called Bowman's capsules, located at the blind beginning ends of the renal tubules.

Function. Urine, produced in the glomeruli and renal tubules, is carried to the pelvis by collecting tubules. The glomeruli act as simple filters, through which water, salts, and waste products from the blood pass into the spaces of Bowman's capsules and from there down into the renal tubules. Most of the water and salt is reabsorbed from these tubules; the remainder is excreted as urine. The renal tubules also secrete other salts and waste products from the blood into the urine. The average amount of urine secreted in 24 hr. is about 50 oz., but the quantity varies considerably, depending on intake of fluid and loss from such sources as the skin in perspiration or from vomiting; see EXCRETION. Losses in the stool may be large in diarrhea (q.v.).

The kidneys are also important in maintaining a balance of fluid and salt and a normal degree of acidity. When disorders upset these delicate equilibria, the kidneys act to restore balance by

STRUCTURE OF THE KIDNEY

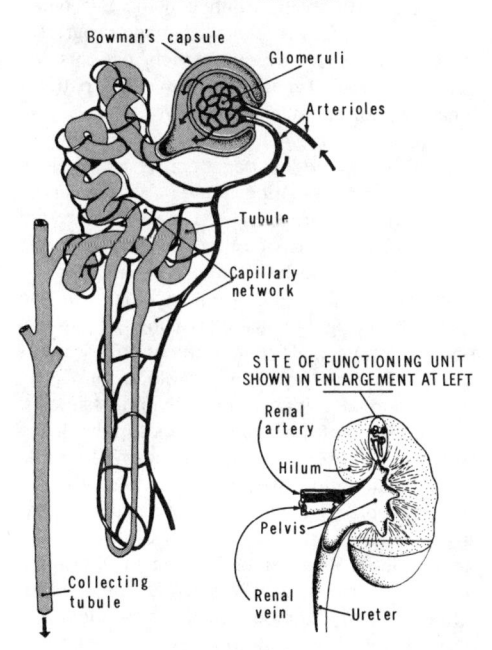

SITE OF FUNCTIONING UNIT SHOWN IN ENLARGEMENT AT LEFT

excreting more or less water, salt, and hydrogen ions. The kidneys are also involved in the maintenance of normal blood pressure (q.v.) and in the elaboration of a hormone that stimulates the production of red blood cells; see BLOOD: *Blood Cells—Erythrocytes.*

Diseases of the Kidney. Nephritis (q.v.), or inflammation of the kidney, is one of the commonest kidney diseases. Many different types of nephritis are attributable to a variety of causes, only some of which are known. Symptoms vary; in many cases there may be none. Its chief characteristics are the appearance in the urine of such elements as albumin, a condition known as albuminuria; red and white blood cells; and hyaline or granular casts, all revealed by microscopic examination of the urine. It is much more common in childhood and adolescence than in middle age.

The commonest form of nephritis is called glomerulonephritis; it often occurs within three to six weeks following a streptococcal infection. The patient often complains of chills, fever, headache, backache, puffiness or edema of the face, especially around the eyes, nausea, and vomiting. Urine may become scanty and smoky in appearance. Prognosis is generally good, and most cases recover completely. A small percentage of cases fail to recover, however, and develop chronic nephritis.

Chronic nephritis can be distinguished from the acute form only arbitrarily because of the very gradual transition between the two types. In chronic nephritis, kidney damage progresses over many years, during which patients are symptom-free. Eventually, however, patients may develop uremia and kidney failure.

The nephroses include a variety of types of nephritis marked by degenerative changes in the tubules of the kidney. Pure nephrosis is rare; more common are those types associated with glomerulonephritis or other diseases affecting the kidney. Nevertheless, the term nephrosis is still used for a syndrome characterized by the presence of generalized swelling or edema, large amounts of albumin in the urine, considerable cholesterol (q.v.) in the blood, and relatively normal urinary output. Nephrosclerosis, or hardening of the small arteries supplying the kidney, is a disorder characterized by the presence of albumin, casts, and occasionally white or red blood cells in the urine; it usually accompanies hypertensive vascular disease. Its fundamental lesion is a sclerosis of the small arteries of the kidney, with secondary atrophy of the glomeruli and pathological changes in the interstitial tissue. The condition may develop at any age, but its onset is most common between forty and fifty years.

Renal calculi, nephrolithiasis, or stones in the kidney, may form in the kidney or renal pelvis from crystals deposited from the urine. Infection or obstruction may play a part in their formation. Sometimes they occur when the level of blood calcium is abnormally high, as may be the case when there is overproduction of hormone (see HORMONES) by the parathyroid glands (q.v.). Occasionally, stones may develop when the blood level of uric acid is too high, as may be the case in gout (q.v.). Certain other diseases may also be associated with the tendency to deposit crystalline substances in the kidney to form stones. In most cases, however, the cause for their formation is not known. Stones are more frequent in males than in females and may cause bleeding, secondary infection, or obstruction. Many stones, particularly large ones, may cause no symptoms for years. They tend to be stationary, but can produce soreness in the back on the affected side. The soreness may vary from a dull ache to severe pain. Small kidney stones tend to travel from the pelvis down the ureter toward the bladder, where their movement is usually accompanied by severe pain. Colic caused by stones usually requires one or more injections of narcotics for relief. The pain may develop suddenly after muscular exercise. Once a stone drops into the bladder, it may be passed with the urine unnoticed, and the pain ceases. If the stone is too large to pass, surgery is necessary. X ray (q.v.) examination of the kidney region is indispensable in diagnosis.

Uremia is a poisoning caused by accumulations in the blood of waste products normally excreted by the kidney, but retained because of insufficient renal function. It occurs most often as the end stage of any chronic kidney disease and is characterized by drowsiness, headache, nausea, inability to sleep, spasms, seizures, and coma. Prognosis is poor. Recently, however, such techniques as repeated periodic dialysis, treatment with an artificial kidney to clear the blood of accumulated waste products and toxins, and kidney-transplant operations offer new hope to patients heretofore doomed.

Pyelonephritis is an infection of the kidney with bacteria. Acute pyelonephritis is often accompanied by fever, chills, pain on the affected side, and urinary frequency and burning on urination. Chronic pyelonephritis, like chronic glomerulonephritis, is a slowly progressive, usually symptom-free disease that may eventually lead to destruction of the kidney and to uremia. Pyelonephritis is more common in women than men, and more usual in diabetics.

Of the tumors of the kidney, Wilms' tumor, a highly malignant form, is most frequent in young children. In adults, the majority of malignant kidney tumors are carcinomas; fortunately, they are uncommon. Benign tumors of the kidney, including cysts and benign solid tumors, are more frequent; they generally cause no symptoms. See TUMOR.

Tuberculosis (q.v.) of the kidney is caused by tubercle bacilli, which are carried to the kidney by the bloodstream from some other infected organ, such as the lung, where it most usually originates. Because treatment with antituberculosis drugs is usually effective, the disease is rare today.

A host of other less common diseases, such as lupus erythematosus (a morbid skin condition) and amyloid disease (starchlike accumulations in the tissues), may also involve the kidney. It may be affected by carbon tetrachloride and other poisons, by shock, and by injury. It may also be the site of a variety of congenital malformations.   L.J.V.

KIEL, city and port of West Germany, in Schleswig-Holstein State, on the Baltic Sea at the E. entrance of the Nord-Ostsee Canal (q.v.), about 50 miles N. of Hamburg. The city has been noted as a port since the 10th century because of its excellent harbor, which is a tideless fjord about 11 mi. long, averaging 40 ft. in depth. The chief industries of the city, aside from shipbuilding and naval maintenance, are the manufacture of soap, food products, machinery, and woolen goods; the city also contains breweries, printing plants, sawmills, foundries, and fish-curing plants. Kiel has been for centuries a great trading center; the chief items of commerce are coal, oil, fish, timber, machinery, and cereal grains. In 1284 the city became a member of the Hanseatic League (q.v.). In 1773 it came under Danish rule; in 1866, as part of Schleswig-Holstein, it became part of Prussia. In World War I the city was the headquarters of the German Imperial Fleet, and in World War II its important naval base was heavily bombed by the British and Americans. Following World War II the city was included in the British Zone of Occupation. Pop. (1970) 271,000.

KIEL CANAL. See NORD-OSTSEE CANAL.

KIELCE, city of Poland and capital of Kielce Province, in the Holy Cross Mts., about 90 miles S. of Warsaw. The city is a rail junction and a processing and market center for the agricultural and mineral resources of the surrounding area. Local minerals include iron, marble, and limestone. Iron goods and processed foodstuffs are produced. Founded in 1173, the city has a medieval cathedral and a castle dating from 1638. A regional museum has displays on provincial life and resources. Pop. (1970) 125,952.

KIERKEGAARD, Søren Aabye (1813–55), Danish philosopher and theologian, born in Copenhagen, and educated at the University of Copenhagen. He studied theology but was never ordained, and after two years of travel in Germany he settled in Copenhagen in 1842 and remained there until his death. His ill health and morbid, retiring temperament, coupled with his custom of issuing his writings under various pen names, prevented Kierkegaard's reputation from spreading far beyond his immediate circle. The originality of his thought, however, and the force and brilliance of his aphoristic, often obscure style eventually exerted a strong influence upon the literature and theology of his country.

Kierkegaard opposed the speculative philosophers of Denmark and the objective, rationalistic thought of such figures as the German philosopher Georg Hegel (q.v.). Kierkegaard based his philosophy on the dichotomy between faith and knowledge and between thought and reality. In his theology he carried to an extreme the Protestant doctrine that religion is a matter for the individual soul; he analyzed the fundamental principles of Christianity, employing the systematic method of inquiry developed by the ancient Greek philosopher Socrates (q.v.).

In his later work Kierkegaard opposed the theology and practices of the established church and treated suffering as a basic element in the relations of God and man. In recent years Kierkegaard has been intensively studied in Europe and America as one of the pioneers of modern Protestantism, and more specifically as a major influence upon the philosophical school of existentialism (q.v.), and upon the writings of the Austrian novelist Franz Kafka (q.v.). Kierkegaard's most important books are *Either/Or* (1843), *Fear and Trembling* (1843), *Philosophical Fragments* (1844), *Stages on Life's Way* (1845), *Concluding Unscientific Postscript* (1846), *The Sickness unto Death* (1849), and *The Attack upon Christendom* (1854–55).

KIESELGUHR. See DIATOMACEOUS EARTH.

KIESINGER, Kurt Georg. See GERMANY: *History: Recent Developments.*

KIEV, city in the Soviet Union, and capital of the Ukrainian S.S.R. and the Kiev Oblast, on the Dnieper R., about 585 miles S.W. of Moscow. Kiev is the third largest city of the U.S.S.R. and a leading cultural and industrial city. The city is a center for trading in grain, fruits, livestock, sugar beets, and other agricultural products. The many factories manufacture chemical apparatus, hardware, machinery, clothing, sugar, and paper. In 1947 the first silk-weaving mill in the Ukraine was established at Kiev.

Kiev is built principally on hills overlooking the right bank of the Dnieper and has three main sections: the old section, with hills surmounted by ancient castles and fortifications dating back to the 11th century; the Pechersk hill, site of a famous monastery; and the Podol, the commercial section on lower ground adjoining the river. Kiev was one of the foremost religious centers of the former Russian empire, and contains many church buildings, including the Cathedral of Saint Sophia (now a museum) which was built in the 11th century and is the most ancient cathedral in the Soviet Union. The Pechersk, or Cave, monastery, founded in the 11th century, is one of the most sacred edifices of the Russian Orthodox Church, famous for its catacombs. Other noted structures include the former imperial palace, the city hall, the All-Ukrainian Historical Museum, the public library, and an art museum. Kiev is the seat of a state university and the Ukrainian Academy of Sciences.

History. Kiev was settled in the 4th century A.D. The position of the city, on the Dnieper R. and in the center of a rich agricultural region, made Kiev one of the wealthiest and most important of Russian cities. In the 9th century Kiev became the capital of the earliest major Russian state, the Varangian-Russian principality. During the reign of Vladimir I (956?–1015), the first Christian ruler of Russia, the inhabitants of Kiev adopted the Greek Orthodox faith, and the city became the earliest center of that church in Russia. Its wealth and exposed position near the Russian frontier made Kiev a constant prey to attack. The armies of the Mongol leader Batu Khan (q.v.) sacked and destroyed the city in 1240. Kiev remained under Mongol domination until 1320, when it came under the rule of Lithuania, and in 1483 was again destroyed by a Crimean army. Under Polish rule from 1559 to 1654, the city was annexed by Russia in 1668. In the 18th century Peter I (q.v.), Emperor of Russia, made the city one of the most heavily fortified cities in his empire. Kiev was occupied by German troops during World War I and was the scene of violent fighting from 1917 to 1920 during the Russian Revolution (q.v.). In 1934 Kiev replaced Khar'kov (q.v.) as the Ukrainian capital. German forces occupied the city in 1941, during World War II, but were driven out during the Soviet reconquest of the Ukraine in 1943. Pop. (1972 est.) 1,764,000.

KIGALI, city and capital of the Republic of Rwanda, about 60 miles S.E. of Kisenyi. Kigali, which is served by an international airport, is the commercial and administrative center of the country. There are tin mines in the vicinity, and the city has markets for coffee, cattle, hides, and local food produce. A town of German East Africa from 1899 to 1916, Kigali was the capital of Ruanda, part of the territory of Ruanda-Urundi, which was a League of Nations mandate administered by Belgium from 1923 and a United Nations trust territory from 1946. The city became the capital of the independent Republic of Rwanda in 1961. Pop. (1967 est.) 25,000.

KIKUYU, tribe of African people in Kenya. See AFRICA: *The People: Ethnology;* KENYA: *The People; History;* KENYATA, JOMO.

KILAUEA, active volcanic crater in the south-central part of the island of Hawaii, located on the southeastern slope of the great volcanic mountain Mauna Loa, at an elevation of 3646 ft. above sea level, almost 10,000 ft. below the summit of the mountain. The crater forms a great cavity in the side of the mountain and has an area of about 4 sq.mi.; the walls of the crater are from 200 to 700 ft. high. Except for occasional lava flows across the floor of the crater, volcanic activity in recent times has been restricted to a subsidiary inner crater called Halemaumau, which measures about 3000 ft. across and has a depth of about 1300 ft.

Normally, lava streams constantly flow into the floor of the crater from subterranean sources and either cool and harden or accumulate until they drain off into other subterranean passages, but the lava is subject to sudden changes of level during great volcanic activity, when it may escape from vents on the lower slope toward the sea. The most famous overflows occurred in 1790, 1823, 1840, 1868, 1920–21, 1950, 1955, 1959, 1965, and 1969. In 1924, the eruption was preceded by an overflow that created a lake of boiling lava covering 50 acres. Since 1911 an observatory has been maintained on the brink of the crater. Kilauea is included in Hawaii Volcanoes National Park (q.v.).

KILDARE, inland county of the Republic of Ireland, in Leinster Province, bordered on the N.W. by Westmeath, on the N. by Meath, on the E. by Dublin and Wicklow, on the S. by Carlow, and on the W. by Laoighis. The county town is Naas, about 18 miles S.W. of Dublin. The terrain of Kildare is flat and the soil is fertile. Agriculture is the chief industry; sugar beets, grains, and livestock are raised. The N. section contains many marshes, including the Bog of Allen (*see* BOG). The central portion of the county contains the Curragh, a 5000-acre plain that has pastures and courses for race horses. The principal rivers are the Boyne, the Barrow, and the Liffey. Area, 654 sq.mi.; pop. (1971) 71,977.

KILIMANJARO, highest known mountain in Africa, in N.E. Tanzania near the border with Kenya. The two volcanic peaks of Kilimanjaro stand about 7 mi. apart, and are connected by a broad saddle; Kibo, the higher peak, rises to 19,340 ft. above sea level and the summit of Mawensi is 16,892 ft. above sea level. The crater of

The towering mass of Mt. Kilimanjaro looms above a herd of grazing wildebeest. UPI

Kibo is covered with an ice-cap which is pierced by several small craters. The entire mass is isolated, rising to more than 16,000 ft.

KILKENNY, inland county of the Republic of Ireland, in Leinster Province, bordered by Laoighis on the N., by Carlow and Wexford on the E., by Waterford on the S., and by Tipperary on the W. The terrain is mainly flat with a few isolated hills. The chief river is the Nore; the Barrow and Suir rivers flow along the E. and the S. boundaries respectively. Few bogs are found in Kilkenny. The chief crops are oats, barley, turnips, and potatoes. Coal, iron, and manganese are mined, and limestone and slate are quarried. The principal manufactures are ale, whiskey, shoes, and flour. The county town is Kilkenny. Area, 796 sq.mi.; pop. (1971) 61,811.

KILLARNEY, LAKES OF, three lakes in the S.W. of the Republic of Ireland, in the vicinity of the resort town of Killarney in County Kerry. The lakes contain numerous islands and are part of a national park. The wooded slopes of the mountains of Kerry rise abruptly from the lake shores. On the island of Ross in Lough Leane, the largest lake (about 8 sq.mi.), stands an ancient ruined castle. Between Lough Leane and Muckross Lake is the ruin of a Franciscan abbey founded in 1440. The outlet of the lakes is the Laune R. which flows N.W. into Dingle Bay, an arm of the Atlantic Ocean.

KILLDEER, or **KILLDEE** or **KILDEER,** common name of a bird, *Charadrius vociferus,* in the Plover family, Charadriidae, so named from the sound of its shrill, two-syllabled note. The bird, which is found throughout North America, repeats this note frequently from morning until well into the night. The killdeer is about 8 in. long, grayish brown above, and white below with two black bands traversing its breast. The killdeer is a powerful flier and rapid runner. Breeding occurs usually on farmlands near streams. In a shallow depression in the ground the female lays four acutely pointed eggs which, because of their shape, rotate in a small circle when the wind blows them and thus remain in the ground.

KILLEEN, city of Texas, in Bell Co., 45 miles S.W. of Waco and bordering Fort Hood. Wood products and machine parts are manufactured, and the surrounding area grows livestock, cotton, and corn. The city is the site of the Fort Hood Center of Mary Hardin–Baylor College (1845; Baptist; women). Settled in 1882, Killeen was incorporated in 1908. Pop. (1960) 23,377; (1970) 35,507.

KILLER WHALE. See WHALE.

KILLIFISH, common name for any of more than 300 species of very small, esociform fishes

KILMARNOCK

constituting the family Cyprinodontidae. The killifish are all less than 1 ft. in length and are brightly colored, occasionally striped with black. The species are found in salt water and fresh water in all warm regions of the world. Killifish are sometimes used as bait, and are often kept in home aquariums, where they thrive on either prepared fish foods or on shrimps, worms, insect larvae, or, occasionally, algae. The fish are oviparous, or egg-laying. The striped topminnow, *Fundulus notatus*, is a common killifish off the eastern and southern coasts of the United States, and so is the mayfish, *F. majalis*. The rainwater fishes of the genus *Lucania*, found in swamps and stagnant streams in southeastern U.S., and the topminnows of the genus *Zygonectes*, of central U.S., are useful because they eat mosquito larvae.

KILMARNOCK, Great Britain, burgh in Scotland, and county town of Ayr County, about 20 miles s.w. of Glasgow. Kilmarnock is in a coal-mining district, and the principal industries include the production of pig iron, hydraulic machinery, carpets, leather, and whiskey. The poems of the Scottish poet Robert Burns (q.v.) were first published here in 1786, and the town has a museum honoring the poet. Pop. (1971 est.) 48,992.

KILMER, family name of two American poets. **(Alfred) Joyce Kilmer** (1886–1918), born in New Brunswick, N.J., and educated at Rutgers College and Columbia University. From 1909 to 1917 he was on the staff of the *New Standard Dictionary* as well as various periodicals. He volunteered for service in the United States Army in 1917, and was killed in action in France, in July, 1918, during the second Battle of the Marne. His lyric poem "Trees", included in the collection *Trees and Other Poems* (1914), won him international fame. His other works are *Summer and Love* (1911), and *Main Street and Other Poems* (1915).

Aline Murray Kilmer (1888–1941), wife of Joyce Kilmer, born in Norfolk, Va. Her volumes of verse include *Candles That Burn* (1919) and *A Buttonwood Summer* (1929).

KILN, any of several kinds of furnace, heated by the combustion of fuel, used for the firing of pottery or other ceramic products, the roasting of ores, or the production of cement. In modern engineering usage, little distinction is made between a furnace (q.v.) and a kiln, although the term "kiln" is always applied to the heating units used in ceramic and cement manufacture.

Kilns in general are divided into two types: intermittent kilns in which the fire must be extinguished while the kiln is being unloaded and recharged with another batch of material to be fired; and continuous kilns in which loading and unloading is accomplished while the kiln is lit. Modern kilns are of both types, although the various forms of continuous kilns are particularly suited to mass production methods of manufacture. The two most important types of continuous kiln are the tunnel kiln, in which the material heated is moved through a long combustion chamber or heating zone on carts or conveyors, and the rotary kiln, in which the material is moved through a long, inclined, rotating combustion chamber by the force of gravity. For description of the operation of specific kilns see CEMENT, PORTLAND; POTTERY.

KILOWATT. See ELECTRICAL UNITS: *Practical Units.*

KILPATRICK, William Heard (1871–1965), American educator, born in White Plains, Ga., and educated at Mercer, Johns Hopkins, and Columbia universities. From 1909 until 1938, when he was named professor emeritus of educational philosophy, Kilpatrick taught at Teachers College of Columbia University. A disciple and the principal popularizer of the educational theories of his colleague the American philosopher John Dewey (q.v.), he emphasized project-oriented rather than subject-oriented education, strongly centered on the individual child himself. Among his many books are *Education and the Social Crisis* (1932) and *The Educational Frontier* (1933).

KIMBERLEY, city of the Republic of South Africa, in the Cape of Good Hope Province, about 250 miles s.w. of Johannesburg. Kimberley is the center of the South African diamond-mining region. The principal industries include diamond cutting, the processing of lime and wolfram, and the manufacture of cement and bricks. The city was founded in 1870 as a result of the discovery of diamond fields around its site. In 1887 the De Beers Consolidated Mines, Ltd., assumed control of all Kimberley mines. Pop. (1970 prelim.) 103,789.

See DIAMOND: *Formation and Occurrence.*

KIMCHI, David or **KIMHI, David** (1160–1235), Jewish lexicographer and Biblical scholar, born in Narbonne, France. He was the prominent member of a southern European family of Jewish scholars. Kimchi is the author of *Sefer ha-Shorashim* ("Book of Roots"), a dictionary of the Hebrew language; the work is noted for its etymological derivations. He also wrote *Et Sofer* ("Pen of the Scribe"), a guide to the proper copying of Biblical manuscripts; and commentaries on a number of books of the Old Testament, including Genesis, Chronicles, and Psalms

The modern kindergarten is designed to provide a pleasant environment for the child's first educational experience away from home.
Musée Pédagogique

(qq.v.). His Biblical commentaries were so valuable and popular that the earliest printed Hebrew Bibles included them.

KIMMEL, Husband Edward. *See* PEARL HARBOR.

KINCARDINE, *or* THE MEARNS, Great Britain, maritime county of Scotland, bounded on the N. by Aberdeen County, on the E. by the North Sea, and on the S. and W. by Angus County. The Grampian Mts. occupy the N. and N.W. portions of Kincardine; Mt. Battock (2555 ft.) is the highest summit. The chief rivers of the county are the Dee and North Esk, which form respectively part of the N. and S. boundaries of the county. Farming, livestock raising, and fishing are the principal industries. The chief crops are oats, barley, turnips, wheat, and potatoes. Stonehaven, about 15 miles S. of Aberdeen, is the county town. Area, about 379 sq.mi.; pop. (1969 est.) 25,694.

KINDERGARTEN (Ger. "Children's Garden"), a school or section within an elementary school where a program is offered that is designed to establish the growth and development patterns of young children. It always precedes the first grade level. Space and equipment are provided to encourage constructive play. The play stimulates informal experiences in the language arts, arithmetic, science, health, and creative arts, thereby establishing educational concepts and work habits that are necessary for successful future schooling. Experts agree that the physical, social, and emotional growth that is stimulated by these activities is invaluable.

The kindergarten curriculum includes such activities as listening to the reading of poetry and stories, singing, rhythmic movement, dramatic play, blockbuilding, vigorous outdoor play involving climbing, crawling, pulling, pushing, painting, modeling clay, puzzles and other games that require the manipulation of materials of various sizes and shapes.

The first kindergarten came into existence in 1837 when the German educator Friedrich Froebel (q.v.) opened a school for children between the ages of three and seven in Blankenburg, Thuringia, putting into effect educational ideas he had been advocating for twenty years. His program for preschool-age children was slow to be accepted, but eventually kindergartens became common throughout the world.

In the United States most kindergartens are operated for five year olds. Some provisions are made for a two-year experience beginning at age four. In Europe, many kindergartens provide a two-year experience. In the Soviet Union, for example, the experience is four years, from ages three to seven. Generally, kindergarten groups are privately operated or part of a public-school system. A kindergarten may have full-day sessions, as in the Soviet Union, or offer morning and afternoon sessions, as in much of the U.S.

Some research studies indicate that kindergarten experiences have a direct measurable effect on the future academic achievement of the children. It has been difficult, however, to measure accurately the later academic attainments of children who attended kindergarten because current studies have so far not been comprehensive enough. *See also* NURSERY SCHOOL AND DAY NURSERY; PRESCHOOL EDUCATION.

L.L.

KINDI, AL-, in Arabic ABU-YŪSUF YA'QŪB IBN-ISHĀQ AL-KINDI (d. after 870), first important Islamic philosopher, born in Al Kufa, Iraq, and educated at Basra and Baghdad. Al-Kindi was one of the earliest Arab students of the Greek philosophers and one of the first translators of the ancient Greek philosopher Aristotle (q.v.) into Arabic. Called "the philosopher of the Arabs" because he was descended from Arab nobility, he is known to be the author of more than 270 works, most of them short tracts covering a wide range of topics including philosophy, medicine, mathematics, optics, and astrology. Some of his works were translated into Latin during the Middle Ages and had a wide influence on European scholars.

The philosophy of al-Kindi was strongly influenced by Neoplatonic Aristotelianism; (see NEOPLATONISM). He attempted to provide a philosophical basis for the speculative theology of the Mu'tazilites (see ISLAM: *Theology and Philosophy*). Although he claimed that the conclusions of philosophy and religion are essentially harmonious, he nevertheless placed revelation above philosophy, and prophetic insights above reason. Al-Kindi's influence on Muslim thinkers continued for about a century after his death.

KINESCOPE. See TELEVISION: *Television Receivers: Kinescopes.*

KINETIC ENERGY. See ENERGY; KINETIC THEORY.

KINETIC THEORY, physical theory which accounts for the behavior of matter, particularly matter in the gaseous state, by the motions of atoms and molecules. According to the kinetic theory, the molecules of all matter can be regarded as tiny elastic spheres which are in constant motion, moving rapidly at high temperatures and slowly at low temperatures, and reaching a state of rest only at absolute zero, about $-273°$ C. ($-459°$ F.).

Effects of Heat upon Atoms. According to the kinetic concept, the atoms in a solid substance are not fixed rigidly but are in a stable equilibrium with respect to the forces between them. Heat causes the atoms to oscillate about the positions of equilibrium, but not to oscillate so far that the equilibrium is lost. The motions of each atom under the influence of heat cause motions of the surrounding atoms, and these motions are in turn transmitted to atoms still farther away. This is one of the ways that heat is conducted through solid substances. A similar transference accounts for the phenomenon of friction. When two solid objects are rubbed together, the atoms on the surfaces of the objects are set into motion, thus heating first the surfaces and then, by conduction, the entire objects.

If a solid substance is heated sufficiently, its atoms will eventually acquire enough energy so that they will move so far from their positions of equilibrium that they can no longer return. When this point is reached, and the atoms are constantly wandering from one position to another, the substance is in a liquid rather than in a solid state. After this change has taken place, the term "molecule" is properly applicable to groups of atoms which remain closely attached. The range of motion of molecules in a liquid is much greater than that of atoms in a solid. Molecules at and near the surface of a liquid sometimes have so much energy that they move completely out of the liquid and do not return to it. In this case the molecule is free of the effects of the other molecules in the liquid and can be regarded as a molecule of gas. This is the mechanism of evaporation; evaporation is always accompanied by the converse process of condensation, the return of gas molecules to the liquid. With increasing temperature the number of molecules escaping from the liquid increases until all the molecules are free. When this condition occurs, the substance is in the gaseous or vapor state. The density of a substance in the gaseous state is often less than one thousandth of the density of the same substance in the solid or liquid state under normal conditions.

When a gas is in a normal state (see THERMODYNAMICS) its molecules are moving in all possible directions and at a variety of speeds, and are colliding with each other and with the walls of the container in which they are held. No energy is lost by collisions between molecules because the molecules are perfectly elastic; moreover, the net change of momentum as a result of intermolecular collisions is zero. The momentum produced by collision with the container walls causes the gas to exert pressure on the walls; moreover, such collisions may be inelastic, so that energy is transferred between gas and walls. If the gas is heated, the molecules move at greater velocities and hence expend more momentum in collisions, and as a result the pressure of the gas increases. Mathematical analysis shows that the pressure of a gas is equal to $\frac{1}{3}nmV^2$ when n is the number of molecules in a given volume of the gas (the same for all gases), m is the mass of the individual molecules, and V is the statistical average veolocity of the molecules (the root-mean-square of the individual velocities). In gas mixtures the pressure is the sum of the pressures of the component gases.

Behavior of Gases. From this mathematical expression, laws concerning the behavior of gases can be demonstrated. When temperature is constant (and the value of V, the velocity, therefore does not change) the pressure of the gas is proportional to nm, which is the density of the gas. This statement of proportions is equivalent to Boyle's Law (q.v.). Similarly, from the equation it can be seen that if the temperature varies, resulting in a change in the value of V, the pressure will vary also. This law or principle, which had been demonstrated experimentally prior to the development of kinetic theory, is equivalent to Charles' Law. The equation also shows that if the pressures and temperatures of two gases are equal, the numbers of molecules per unit volume are also equal. This law, Avogadro's, had also been discovered before the kinetic theory was developed. See articles on most of the laws named.

Two other important facts may be learned from the equation $p = \frac{1}{3}nmV^2$. Given the density and pressure of a gas, it is possible to calculate the average velocity of the molecules in the gas (the quantity V) and also the number of individual molecules in a given quantity of the gas. In the case of hydrogen the speed of the molecules is 1839 meters per second at atmospheric pressure (760 mm. of mercury) and 0° C. (32° F.). The velocity of oxygen molecules under the same conditions is 461 meters per second. The number of molecules in a cubic centimeter of any gas under the same standard temperature and pressure is 27,000,000,000,000,000,000 (2.7 × 10^{19}). Similarly the kinetic theory permits the calculation of the radii of individual molecules. Typical values are 0.0000000136 cm. for hydrogen and 0.0000000181 cm. for oxygen.

The kinetic theory is a satisfactory explanation of most of the physical phenomena which are the result of the motions of atoms or molecules as a whole. The theory does not, however, give a satisfactory explanation of phenomena resulting from dynamic changes within the atom; see ATOM AND ATOMIC THEORY; QUANTUM MECHANICS.

KING, title of a male ruler vested with authority over a single state, nation, or tribe, usually for life and by hereditary succession. Originally the title of king indicated a higher rank than that of emperor (q.v.), but the ancient Roman emperors assumed the names imperator and caesar (q.v.) to indicate authority over subjugated kings. The early Teutonic kings were usually elected; this practice ended, however, with the institution of primogeniture (q.v.). Under the influence of Christianity kings came to be crowned and anointed by ecclesiastical authority, a practice justified theoretically by the doctrine of the divine right (q.v.) of kings. Kingship by divine right was not successfully challenged until the English revolution of 1688, or Glorious Revolution, when the power of kings was limited by constitution or custom. Among the civil powers enjoyed by such constitutional monarchs in modern times have been appointments to office, the approval or rejection of legislative measures, the negotiation of treaties, and the granting of clemency and pardon.

KING, Ernest Joseph (1878–1956), American naval officer, born in Lorain, Ohio, and educated at the United States Naval Academy at Annapolis, and at the Naval War College. From 1901 until the outbreak of World War I, King served successively with the West Indies fleet, as an instructor in the ordnance and gunnery department of the Naval Academy, and on the staff of the commander in chief of the Atlantic fleet. Between 1914 and 1919 he commanded a destroyer division, and for further service with the Atlantic fleet was awarded the Navy Cross and promoted to the rank of captain. From 1926 to 1928 he commanded the submarine base at New London, Conn., and directed the raising of the sunken submarines U.S.S. *S-51* and *S-4*. He then turned to aviation, qualifying as a naval aviator, and served from 1938 to 1939 as vice-admiral in command of aircraft of the battle force of the U.S. fleet. With the entry of the U.S. into World War II (q.v.), King was appointed commander in chief of the U.S. fleet, and from March, 1942, until Nov., 1945, King concurrently served as chief of naval operations, the highest position in the United States Navy. He was promoted to the rank of fleet admiral in 1944.

KING, Martin Luther, Jr. (1929–68), American clergyman and Negro civil-rights leader, born in Atlanta, Ga. In 1935, both King and his father, Martin Luther King, Sr. (1899–   ), changed their first given name from Michael to Martin. He received a B.A. degree from Morehouse College in 1948, a B.D. degree from Crozer Theological Seminary in 1951, and a Ph.D. degree from Boston University in 1955. Ordained a minister in his father's church (Ebenezer Baptist Church, Atlanta) in 1947, King became pastor of the Dexter Avenue Baptist Church, Montgomery, Ala., in 1954. In 1955, after a Negro woman was arrested for refusing to give up her seat on a Montgomery bus to a white person, King began his active leadership of the civil-rights movement by taking charge of a successful 382-day boycott of the Montgomery bus system. In this, as in all his later civil-rights campaigns, King emphasized the need to act in nonviolent ways, in accordance with the teachings of the Indian nationalist leader Mohandas K. Gandhi and the American naturalist Henry David Thoreau (qq.v.).

In 1957 he was instrumental in founding the Southern Christian Leadership Conference (S.C.L.C.), a group of southern Negro ministers and other professional persons that became one

Martin Luther King, Jr., center, receives congratulations from Crown Prince Harald, left, and King Olav V, of Norway, after receiving the Nobel Peace Prize in 1964. Mrs. King is at his left. UPI

of the leading civil-rights organizations. In 1960 he was named co-pastor of his father's church in Atlanta. In 1963 King led a second massive civil-rights campaign in Birmingham, Ala.; this was followed by major campaigns for Negro voter registration in the South, for desegregation, and for better education and housing. These campaigns were later extended to the northern States. During the course of these non-violent campaigns, he was arrested several times.

On April 4, 1968, King was in Memphis, Tenn., preparing to lead a march of striking sanitation workers when he was assassinated by James Earl Ray (1928–   ). In 1969, Ray was convicted of the murder of King and sentenced to ninety-nine years in prison. After the assassination, rioting broke out in 125 American cities, including Chicago, Ill., and Washington, D.C. King's colleague, the Rev. Ralph David Abernathy (q.v.), took over leadership of the S.C.L.C. King's widow, Coretta Scott King (1927–   ) and the Rev. Andrew J. Young, Jr. (1932–   ), have assisted Abernathy in directing the organization.

King, who received the 1964 Nobel Peace Prize, was the author of several books, including *Stride Toward Freedom* (1958), *Strength to Love* (1963), *Why We Can't Wait* (1964), and *The Trumpet of Conscience* (1968). See also CIVIL RIGHTS AND CIVIL LIBERTIES; NEGROES IN THE UNITED STATES: *The Civil-Rights Movement*. B.E.M.

KING, Rufus (1755–1827), American political leader, born in Scarboro, Maine, and educated at Harvard College (now Harvard University). After studying law he was admitted to the bar in 1780, and in 1783 he became a judge in the Massachusetts General Court, to which he was re-elected several times. From 1784 to 1787 he was a delegate to the Continental Congress (q.v.), and introduced, in 1785, a resolution prohibiting slavery in the Northwest Territory (q.v.), which had been ceded to the United States by Great Britain three years before. The substance of King's resolution was subsequently incorporated into the Ordinance of 1787, which made slavery illegal in the Northwest Territory.

King was prominent in the proceedings of the Federal Constitutional Convention in 1787, and the following year helped procure the ratification of the Constitution by Massachusetts. In 1788 he moved to New York City, and a year later was elected to the New York State Assembly. Later in 1789 he was elected to the United States Senate, and became known as an outstanding leader in the Federalist Party (q.v.). From 1796 to 1803 he was U.S. minister to Great Britain. He was subsequently twice nominated, in 1804 and 1808, by the Federalists as Vice-Presidential candidate, but was defeated both times. He was a U.S. Senator from 1813 to 1825; in 1816 he was the unsuccessful Federalist candidate for the Presidency. He was again minister to Great Britain in 1825–26.

KING, William Lyon Mackenzie (1874–1950), Canadian statesman, born in Berlin (now Kitchener), Ontario, and educated at Toronto

University. He was a reporter on the *Toronto Globe* from 1895 to 1896 and a fellow in political science at Harvard University from 1897 to 1900. As an expert on labor questions, he was called upon by the Canadian government for help in organizing the Department of Labor in 1900, and was deputy minister of labor from 1900 to 1908, serving as chairman of royal commissions on industry and immigration, and as conciliator for the government in various strikes. In 1906 he represented Canada in negotiations with the British government on immigration problems, and in 1908 he was elected to the Dominion Parliament as a Liberal, representing North Waterloo, Ont. A year later, he was appointed minister of labor in the cabinet of Sir Wilfrid Laurier (q.v.). During World War I King went to the United States under the auspices of the Rockefeller Foundation, serving as adjustor and investigator of industrial relations and production to various large corporations.

In 1919 he was chosen leader of the Liberal Party of Canada at the National Liberal Convention at Ottawa, succeeding Sir Wilfrid Laurier, and was elected to Parliament as representative for Prince County, Prince Edward Island. He was leader of the opposition in the Dominion House of Commons from 1919 to 1921 while the Conservative Party held the majority. In 1921 the Liberals were returned to power, and King became prime minister and secretary of state for external affairs, serving until 1926. During this period he represented Canada at the imperial conferences in London in 1923 and 1926. In 1926 King was reelected to Parliament as representative from Prince Albert, Saskatchewan, and in 1928 he served again as prime minister of Canada. He signed the Kellogg-Briand Pact (q.v.) on behalf of Canada that same year.

His government fell in 1930, but in 1935 King, as head of the victorious Liberal Party, became prime minister of his country for the third time. He was chairman of the Canadian delegation to the United Nations Conference in San Francisco in 1945 and to the Paris Peace Conference a year later. He resigned as minister of external affairs in 1945 and as premier in 1948. After 1945 he represented Glengarry, Ontario, in the Canadian Parliament. His works include *Industry and Humanity, A Study in the Principles Underlying Industrial Reconstruction* (1918), *Canada at Britain's Side* (1941), and *Canada and the Fight for Freedom* (1944).

KING, William Rufus De Vane (1786–1853), American politician, born in Sampson County, N.C., and educated at the University of North Carolina. He studied law, and was admitted to the bar in 1806. In the same year he was elected to the State legislature, serving until his election to the United States House of Representatives in 1810. In 1816 he was appointed secretary to the U.S. legation at Saint Petersburg (now Leningrad), Russia. On his return in 1818 he settled at Cahaba, Ala., as a cotton planter. In 1819 he became a member of the United States Senate, and remained in the Senate until 1844, serving after 1833 as president pro tempore. He resigned in 1844 to assume the post of minister to France. Two years later he was recalled, and from 1848 until his death again served in the U.S. Senate. In 1852 King was elected Vice-President of the U.S. on the Democratic Party ticket. He was sworn into office but died before undertaking his duties.

KINGBIRD, common name for any of several American flycatchers (q.v.) in the genus *Tyrannus* of the family Tyrannidae. The birds, which average about 6¾ to 7½ in. in length, are courageous and pugnacious, attacking birds as large as hawks when such birds threaten their nests. Kingbirds feed on flying insects, selecting only the stingless drones for their meals. Kingbirds nest in trees and build their nests of twigs lined with feathers. The female lays three or four eggs in a clutch.

The eastern kingbird, *Tyrannus tyrannus,* is found throughout the United States, except in the southwest. It is dark slate above and white below. The head is black with a crest of feathers that conceals a crimson patch on the top. The tail of the bird bears a white transverse stripe at its tip. The gray kingbird, *T. dominicensis,* found from the southeastern U.S. to Central America and N. South America is a somewhat similar bird without a white tail stripe. The western kingbird, *T. verticalis,* is found in the western U.S.; Cassin's kingbird, *T. vociferans,* is found from central California and S. Montana to Guerrero, Mexico.

KING CRAB *or* HORSESHOE CRAB, or HELMET CRAB, common name for any of five species of crablike marine arthropods constituting the class Merostomata. One species, *Limulus polyphemus,* is found along the E. coast of North America from Nova Scotia, Canada, to Yucatán, Mexico; the other species are found on the E. coast of Asia. The animals are intermediate in structure between crustaceans (see CRUSTACEA) and arachnids, and were formerly classified as an order of the class Arachnida (q.v.).

The king crab is dark brown, and reaches a length of about 2 ft. The head and thorax are fused into a cephalothorax, which is covered above with a hard, thick, horseshoe-shaped

King crab, of the genus Limulus. Gordon S. Smith – National Audubon Society

shell. The abdomen is small, covered with a narrow shell hinged in front to the main shell, and terminating in a long sharp spine, which makes up half the total length. The king crab has a large compound eye on each side of its cephalothorax and two pairs of smaller, simple eyes set between the compound eyes. The mouth is located in the middle of the underside of the cephalothorax; on each side of the mouth is a row of five legs bearing pincers. The bases of the legs are specially adapted for crushing food. The abdomen bears six additional pairs of appendages modified as gills. The king crab digs its way into the sand and mud of the ocean bottom near the shores where it leads a sedentary life, feeding on small invertebrates. In late spring the female lays its eggs in the intertidal zone along the shores of bays and estuaries. King crabs are used to feed poultry and swine, and for fertilizer.

KINGFISHER, *or* HALCYON, common name for any bird in the subfamily Cerylinae of the family Alcedinidae. Kingfishers have large heads, usually crested, with long thick bills, and short stout bodies with short tails. Their legs and feet are small. The birds frequent sandbanks near freshwater streams throughout the world, and are especially abundant in the islands of the Pacific Ocean. In the side of a sandbank the females dig tunnels about 2 to 3 ft. long at the ends of which they deposit from 5 to 8 white eggs. The birds subsist on fish.

The belted kingfisher, *Megaceryle alcyon*, is found throughout North America. It is about 12 in. long, and has a large tufted crest of feathers on its crown. The male is bluish above and white below, with a thick blue stripe across its upper breast. The sides of its neck are white. The female has an additional reddish brown stripe across its breast. The green kingfisher, *Chloroceryle americana,* is found from s. Texas to South America. This bird, which is about 8 in. long, has no crest on its crown. It is greenish above and white below. The male has a reddish brown band across its breast with a row of green spots below the band; the female is not striped below, and has two rows of green spots across its breast. The ringed kingfisher, *M. torquata,* of tropical America, is a large, crested species which averages 16 in. in length.

KING GEORGE'S WAR, third of four North American wars, waged by the British and French from 1744 to 1748, and corresponding to the European War of the Austrian Succession; see Succession Wars. During the period of peace after Queen Anne's War (q.v.), irreconcilable conflicts arose between the French and British for control of North America. In 1744 the French captured and destroyed a British fort at Canso, Nova Scotia, and carried the prisoners to the French fortress of Louisbourg on Cape Breton Island. Governor William Shirley (q.v.) of Massachusetts, fearing French invasion, appealed for aid to the other colonies. A force of about 4000 militiamen was raised and placed under the command of Sir William Pepperell (q.v.), a Maine merchant. In April, 1745, the colonial troops sailed in British ships from Boston against Louisbourg. On June 15, after seven weeks of attack, the colonials captured the supposedly impregnable fortress. The next year France sent a fleet to retake Louisbourg and attack Boston, but the fleet was scattered by a storm. In 1747 a second fleet sent for the same purpose was intercepted and defeated by a British squadron. At the end of the war in 1748, Louisbourg was returned to the French by the Treaty of Aix-la-Chapelle, in return for British control of Madras, India; see Aix-la-Chapelle, Treaties of. The settlement disgruntled the colonists, and the British only partly placated the colonists by bearing the entire expenses of the Louisbourg expedition. The question of colonial control was later resolved in the French and Indian War (q.v.).

KING JAMES VERSION *or* **AUTHORIZED VERSION.** See Bible, English Translations of the.

KING LEAR, tragedy in five acts written by the English playwright William Shakespeare (q.v.). Its first recorded performance was in 1606. Printed in 1608, it was also included in the edition of Shakespeare's plays that was published in 1623 and is known as the First Folio.

The tragedy tells the story of Lear, a legendary king of ancient Britain, who is driven mad after dividing his kingdom among his three daughters. Although the author piles one incident of melodramatic horror upon another, the play is a remarkably penetrating study of sanity and madness, temporal power, and primary familial relationships. The principal plot concerning Lear and his daughters is interwoven with a subordinate plot involving the duke of Gloucester and his sons, each story reinforcing and illuminating the other.

Because of its enormous scope and complexity, *King Lear* is often regarded as the most difficult of all the Shakespearean tragedies to produce. It is, nevertheless, frequently performed, the title role having served as a vehicle for many of the world's leading actors in their maturity.

Sources used by Shakespeare in writing this work include *Historia Regum Britanniae* (1135?) by the English chronicler Geoffrey of Monmouth (q.v.); *Chronicles of England, Scotland, and Ireland* (1577) by the English chronicler Raphael Holinshed (q.v.); the second book of *The Faerie Queene* (1590) by the English poet Edmund Spenser (qq.v.); the pastoral romance *Arcadia* (1590) by the English writer Sir Philip Sidney (q.v.); and an anonymous play, *The True Chronicle History of King Leir and His Three Daughters* (published 1605).

KINGLET, common name for any of the small American and European birds in the genus *Regulus* in the same family as the Old World warblers, Sylviidae. Kinglets are usually greenish gray birds with brightly colored patches on the tops of their heads. The birds measure from 3½ to 4 in. in length. They move about in a quick, eccentric fashion and, when moving around in trees, continuously flick their wings nervously. Most species utter thin, weak notes. Kinglets feed on insects injurious to cultivated crops and trees, especially grasshoppers, scale insects, and aphids.

The firecrest, *Regulus ignicapillus,* and the goldcrest, *R. regulus,* are some common European species, with bright red and yellow-orange crown patches respectively. The small golden-crowned kinglet, or golden-crested wren, *R. satrapa,* is widely distributed in the United States. This bird is about 3½ in. long. The adult male has an orange crown patch, bordered with a circle of yellow, around which is another circle of black. The female has a yellow patch surrounded by black. The bird is found in small groups in trees, especially in orchards. The ruby-crowned kinglet *Regulus calendula,* with a similar range, is about 3¾ in. long. The male has a bright red crown patch; the female has no crown patch.

KING PHILIP'S WAR. See PHILIP, sachem of Wampanoag tribe.

KINGS, two books of the Old Testament (*see* BIBLE), in the King James Version, THE FIRST BOOK OF THE KINGS, COMMONLY CALLED THE THIRD BOOK OF THE KINGS, and THE SECOND BOOK OF THE KINGS, COMMONLY CALLED THE FOURTH BOOK OF THE KINGS. In the King James Version, 1 Kings and 2 Kings immediately follow the two books of Samuel (q.v.). Originally, these four books existed as two books; the present 1 Samuel and 2 Samuel formed one, the present 1 Kings and 2 Kings the second. Their division into four books was begun by the translators of the Septuagint (q.v.). The titles of the two books of the Kings in the King James Version, and in a number of other English versions of the Bible used by Roman Catholics, reflect the numbering of the Septuagint and a preference by Saint Jerome (q.v.) for the title *Regum* (Lat., "Kings"). The Hebrew title is *sepher melakhim,* "Book of Kings".

Content. The books of the Kings recount the history of the kingdoms of Israel and Judah (qq.v.) from the death of the Hebrew king David and the enthronement of his son Solomon (qq.v.) to the Babylonian Captivity (q.v.), or roughly the period of time extending from the early part of the 10th century B.C. to the latter half of the 6th century B.C. Specifically, the contents of the two books concern: the enthronement and reign of Solomon, and the building of

Ruby-crowned kinglet, Regulus calendula
Karl H. Maslowski — National Audubon Society

KINGS

the first Temple (1 Kings 1–11); the division and history of the two kingdoms through the reigns of the Israelite king Ahab and the Judean king Jehoshaphat (qq.v.; 1 Kings 12–22); the history of the divided kingdoms continued until the fall of Samaria (q.v.) and the dispersion of Israel in 721 B.C. (2 Kings 1–17); the history of Judah from the end of the kingdom of Israel to the fall of Judah in 586 B.C., and the subsequent release from prison of the Judean king Jehoiachin (r. 598–597 B.C.) in the thirty-seventh year of his exile (2 Kings 18–25). *See also* JEWS; TEMPLE: *Temple at Jerusalem.*

Authorship. The two books were ascribed by Talmudic scholars (*see* TALMUD) to the Hebrew prophet Jeremiah (q.v.). Modern Bible scholars, however, currently attribute their authorship to two or more anonymous authors or editors of the Deuteronomic school; *see* DEUTERONOMY; PENTATEUCH. These writers, either in composing or in compiling the present texts of the books, are thought to have drawn their material from a number of earlier sources, several of which are actually mentioned in the texts. These acknowledged sources are: The Book of the Acts of Solomon (mentioned in 1 Kings 11:41); The Book of The Chronicles of the Kings of Israel (as in 1 Kings 14:19); and The Book of The Chronicles of the Kings of Judah (as in 1 Kings 14:29). All three "books" probably belonged to official archive collections and were annals or historical records (The Book of the Acts of Solomon also contained legendary information). The Old Testament books now called the Chronicles (q.v.), however, were compiled at a later time. Other earlier sources employed but not referred to in the present texts have been identified and variously designated by scholars. They include: the so-called Davidic court narrative, or "Early Source of Samuel" (found in 2 Sam. 9–20 and 1 Kings 1–2); two independent story cycles concerning respectively the Hebrew prophets Elijah and Elisha (qq.v.), and including both historical and legendary material (1 Kings 17–19, 21, 2 Kings 1–13); and the so-called "Isaiah source", a body of legends about the Hebrew prophet Isaiah (q.v.) which was incorporated first in 2 Kings (2 Kings 18:13–20:19) and later largely duplicated in chapters 36–39 of the book of Isaiah (q.v.).

The first anonymous writer's work is believed by most scholars to date from just before the death of the Judean king and religious reformer Josiah (q.v.) in 609 B.C. The second writer's work is thought to date from about 550 B.C., mainly because the last historical event recorded occurred in 561 B.C. and no mention is made of the fall of Babylon in 539 B.C. As members of the Deuteronomic school, neither author was dispassionate. Both authors evaluated, interpreted, and commented on the reigns, acts, and events each reported guided by a firm belief that the national existence depended above all on obedience to the God of Israel and Judah.

KINGS CANYON NATIONAL PARK, conservation and recreation area on the W. slope of the Sierra Nevada Mts., in S.E. Fresno and N.E. Tulare counties, Calif., about 60 miles E. of the city of Fresno. The park contains giant sequoia trees, mountain wilderness, and deep canyons. It is bordered on the S. by Sequoia National Park (q.v.), and includes the former General Grant National Park, which is separated from the main body of the park. The park, covering 460,330.90 acres, was established in 1940. It is administered by the National Park Service (q.v.).

KINGSLEY, Charles (1819–75), British novelist and clergyman, born in Dartmoor, Devonshire, England, and educated at King's College (later part of the University of London) and the University of Cambridge. In 1842 he became a priest in the Church of England. He was appointed chaplain to Victoria (q.v.), Queen of Great Britain, in 1859 and in 1873 became a canon of Westminster Abbey (q.v.). From 1860 to 1869 he was professor of modern history at Cambridge. Kingsley held liberal economic, political, and theological views. He was a leader in the two important English economic and political reform movements of the time, Christian socialism and Chartism (q.v.), and opposed the strict orthodoxy of the Oxford movement (q.v.) in the Anglican Church. Kingsley's personal and theological attacks on the British prelate John Henry Newman (q.v.), later Cardinal Newman, evoked in 1864 the latter's famous *Apologia pro Vita Sua* (Lat., "Apology for His Life").

Kingsley's novels *Alton Locke* (1849) and *Yeast* (1849) display his sympathy with the economically and politically oppressed classes of the England of his day. He is most widely known, however, for his novels laid in foreign lands or in former times, such as *Hypatia* (1853), *Westward Ho!* (1855), *Two Years Ago* (1857), and *Hereward the Wake* (1866). His tales for children include *The Heroes* (1856), a book of Greek fairy tales, and *The Water-Babies* (1863).

KINGSLEY, Sidney (1906–), American playwright, born in New York City, and educated at Cornell University. He began writing plays while at Cornell, and in 1933 his first professionally staged play, *Men in White,* was produced. The play, which was awarded the 1934 Pulitzer Prize for drama, revealed with penetrating realism secrets of the medical profession. His second play, *Dead End* (1935), a bitter story of the lives of New York City slum children, was also very successful. He was given the Drama Critics Circle Award for *The Patriots* (1942), a historical drama, and for *Darkness at Noon* (1952), an adaptation of the book by the Hungarian-born British novelist Arthur Koestler (q.v.). One of his most popular plays was *Lunatics and Lovers* (1954), a broad farce. His most recent work was *Night Life* (1962), a melodrama of big-city life.

KINGS MOUNTAIN, BATTLE OF, military engagement of the American Revolution (q.v.) fought on Oct. 7, 1780, in York Co., S.C., near the border with North Carolina. The battle took place on a low, narrow, isolated ridge called Kings Mt. The American troops, some 900 frontiersmen under a divided command, trapped a force of about 1000 Loyalist militia at the top of the ridge. After an hour of heavy fighting, the British commander, Major Patrick Ferguson (1744–80) was killed, and the British surrendered. The American casualties were twenty-eight killed and sixty-two wounded, while the entire British force was either killed, wounded, or captured. The site of the battle is in the 3950-acre Kings Mountain National Military Park.

KING SNAKE, common name for American constricting snakes in the genus *Lampropeltis*, common examples of which are the chain snake and milk snake (qq.v.). King snakes like all snakes are carnivorous reptiles. They feed on other snakes (including poisonous snakes) and on birds and rodents, enmeshing these animals in their coils and squeezing them to death. King snakes are not susceptible to the venom of snakes of the Viper or Pit-Viper families. They are gentle when kept in captivity.

KINGS POINT, village of New York, in Nassau Co., on W. Long Island, near New York City. In 1941 the United States government purchased a 65-acre estate overlooking Long Island Sound in Kings Point, and established the United States Merchant Marine Academy (q.v.), there. The academy trains officers for both the merchant marine and the naval reserve. Kings Point was incorporated in 1924. Pop. (1960) 5410; (1970) 5525.

KINGSPORT, city of Tennessee, in Sullivan Co., on the Holston R., in the Appalachian Mts. near the Virginia border, about 85 miles N.E. of Knoxville. In an agricultural area, the city is an industrial center; its enterprises include printing and publishing, distilling, and the manufacture of film, paper and pulp, plastic products, hosiery, synthetic yarn, bookbinding cloth, glass, chemicals, bricks, leather goods, and cement. It is the site of the Kingsport Center of East Tennessee State University (1911). On the site of a fort built on the Wilderness Road (Boone Trail) in 1761, the community bore many names until shortly before the city was incorporated in 1917. Pop. (1960) 26,314; (1970) 31,938.

KINGSTON, city in New York, and county seat of Ulster Co., on the W. shore of the Hudson R., at the mouth of Rondout Creek, about 50 miles S. of Albany. Kingston is the manufacturing and shipping center of a dairying and agricultural region. The principal industries of the city include the production of boats, bricks, clothing, and electronic and refrigeration equipment.

The Dutch built a fort on the site of the present city in 1614, and the first permanent settlement, known as Esopus, was established by the Dutch in 1652. Nine years later the settlement was chartered as Wiltwyck, and in 1669 it was renamed Kingston. The first State constitution of New York was adopted at Kingston on April 20, 1777. During the American Revolution, the British sacked and burned the town. Kingston was chartered as a village in 1805 and chartered as a city in 1872. Pop. (1960) 29,260; (1970) 25,544.

KINGSTON, borough of Pennsylvania, in Luzerne Co., on the Susquehanna R., opposite Wilkes-Barre. The borough is in an important anthracite coal area. In addition to coal mining, the principal industries are the manufacture of nylon, rayon, and cigars. Kingston was settled in 1769. In 1778 many of the settlers of the region were killed in the Wyoming Massacre; see WYOMING VALLEY. Kingston was incorporated as a borough in 1857. Pop. (1960) 20,261; (1970) 18,325.

KINGSTON, city of Canada, in Ontario Province, and capital and chief city of Frontenac Co., on Lake Ontario, about 95 miles S.W. of Ottawa. The city, an important transshipping port, with outlets to the Saint Lawrence R., has shipyards, dry docks, and other harbor facilities. The principal industrial products include locomotives, aluminum goods, textiles, and chemicals. Kingston is the site of the Royal Military College, Queen's University, and Fort Henry, a fortress built during the War of 1812. Founded in 1673 as a French trading post, Kingston was settled by the British about 1783; it was the capital of Canada from 1841 to 1844. Kingston was incorporated as a city in 1846. Pop. (1971) 59,047.

KINGSTON, city, capital, and chief seaport of Jamaica, on a deep harbor on the S.E. coast of the island. The harbor admits the largest vessels, and an active import and export trade is carried

405

KINGSTON

on. The railways of the island are centered here, and an international airport is nearby. The city is most important as a tourist resort. Kingston is the site of the University of the West Indies and the College of Arts, Sciences, and Technology. Near the city are the ruins of the former chief settlement, Port Royal, which was destroyed by an earthquake in 1692. Kingston, founded soon afterward, became the capital in 1872. The city has been subject to severe hurricanes, and on Jan. 15, 1907, an earthquake caused many deaths and severe damage. Pop. (1970 prelim.) 117,400.

KINGSTON. See Dun Laoghaire.

KINGSTON-UPON-HULL. See Hull.

KINGSTOWN. See Saint Vincent.

KINGSVILLE, city in Texas, and county seat of Kleberg Co., on Tranquitas Creek, 35 miles s.w. of Corpus Christi. It serves as headquarters for the huge King Ranch of almost 1,000,000 acres, which adjoins on the s. and e. The city is a trade and shipping center for an area of livestock, oil and gas, and grain production. Manufactures include chemicals, concrete, metal, and wood and leather products, and the city has rail shops and cotton-processing plants. It is the site of Texas College of Arts and Industries (1925). Settled in 1902, the town was incorporated in 1911 and the city in 1916. Pop. (1960) 25,297; (1970) 28,711.

KINGTEHCHEN, or FOWLIANG, city of the People's Republic of China, in Kiangsi Province, on the Chang R., about 30 miles s.w. of Shanghai. The city has long been noted for the manufacture of porcelain. Pop. (1970 est.) 300,000.

KING WILLIAM'S WAR, first of four North American wars, waged by the English and French from 1689 to 1697, and part of a larger European war fought by the Grand Alliance (q.v.) against France over the succession to the throne of England. The French and English colonists, aided by Indians, raided each other's settlements. Following a series of English raids in Canada, in 1690 the French governor of Canada, Comte de Frontenac (q.v.), planned counterattacks on New York City and Boston. As initial steps in his campaign, the French and their Indian allies burned Schenectady, N.Y., laid waste Salmon Falls, N.H., and destroyed Fort Loyal, Maine, while French privateers based in Nova Scotia harried New England shipping. The New England colonists raised an expeditionary force and placed it under the command of the new governor of Massachusetts, Sir William Phips (1651–95). This force captured Port Royal in Nova Scotia, and unsuccessfully attacked Québec. For the rest of the war the French and their Indian allies ravaged the northern frontiers of the English colonies. The Peace of Ryswick (see Ryswick, Peace of) in 1697 restored Port Royal to the French, but left the colonial problem unresolved. Warfare resumed in 1702 in Queen Anne's War (q.v.).

KINKAJOU, common name for a small carnivorous mammal, *Potos flavus,* in the Raccoon family, found in the trees of tropical America. The kinkajou, which attains a body length of about 3 ft., has a round, catlike head and a slender body covered with soft, yellowish brown, woolly fur. It has a long, prehensile tail. The animal is gentle in disposition and can be readily tamed as a pet. It feeds on insects, small birds and mammals, birds' eggs, fruit, and honey.

KINO, Eusebio Francisco, surname also spelled CHINI, CHINO, or QUINO (1645–1711), Italian explorer and missionary in southwestern North America, born in Segno. Educated in mathematics and astronomy at Jesuit schools in Italy and Germany, he became a member of the Society of Jesus in 1669. In 1681 he arrived in New Spain and in 1682 he published a pamphlet in Mexico City concerning his observations of a comet in Cádiz, Spain, in 1680.

Later in 1682, as mapmaker and Jesuit superior of an exploring and colonizing mission to Baja California (q.v.), he began the work that was to occupy him for the rest of his life. In the region known as Pimería Alta, comprising what is now the southern part of Arizona and most of the Mexican State of Sonora, Kino spent nearly thirty years preparing maps, founding missions that eventually became towns and cities, and introducing agriculture and stock raising to the Indians. His maps, one of which first showed Baja California to be a peninsula rather than an island, remained standard for more than a century. His historical and autobiographical work, *Favores Celestiales,* published in English as *Kino's Historical Memoir of Pimería Alta* (2 vol., 1919; reissued 1948), is of great value to historians of the Southwest.

KINSEY, Alfred Charles (1894–1956), American biologist, born in Hoboken, N.J., and educated at Bowdoin College and at Harvard University. He began teaching at Indiana University in 1922 and became professor of zoology in 1929. His early research included studies in insect taxonomy, notably of gall wasps. In 1942 he founded the Institute for Sex Research, Inc., to investigate human sexual behavior. With financial support from the National Research Council, the Rockefeller Foundation, and Indiana University, he conducted an extensive survey based on interviews with thousands of men and women. Kinsey and his assistants reported their initial findings in *Sexual Behavior in the Human*

Male (1948) and *Sexual Behavior in the Human Female* (1953). Though highly technical and designed primarily for professionals in medical and sociological fields, the works achieved wide popular attention and caused much controversy. They were denounced by some people who feared the moral consequences of broadly disseminating such information. The works were also criticized by scientists who challenged the methodology of the survey. Kinsey's other writings included several biological studies.

KINSHASA, formerly LÉOPOLDVILLE, city and capital of the Republic of Zaire (formerly the Democratic Republic of the Congo), coextensive with Kinshasa Province, on the s.w. side of Stanley Pool, about 750 miles s.w. of Kisangani, and opposite Brazzaville, Republic of the Congo. The chief commercial center of the country, the city has an international airport and is served by railroad, and by steamers operating on the Congo R. system. Industrial establishments include shipyards, textile mills, and plants processing food. In Kinshasa are two universities, a tropical-medicine research institute, and a museum of African life. The British-American explorer Sir Henry Morton Stanley (q.v.) founded the city in 1881, and named it Léopoldville in honor of King Leopold II of Belgium; *see under* LEOPOLD. It became the capital of Belgian Congo in 1926, and capital of the newly independent Democratic Republic of the Congo (now Zaire) in 1960. The city was renamed Kinshasa in 1966. Pop. (1970) 1,323,039.

KINSTON, city in North Carolina, and county seat of Lenoir Co., on the Neuse R., about 65 miles s.e. of **Raleigh**. It is an important market for bright-leaf tobacco, and the center and shipping point of an agricultural area producing tobacco, cotton, corn, and livestock. The major industrial establishments in the city produce chemicals, cured tobacco, and textiles. The site of Kinston was settled about 1740; it was incorporated as a city in 1849. Pop. (1960) 24,819; (1970) 22,309.

KIOTO. *See* KYOTO.

KIOWA, tribe of North American Indians, speaking a language constituting an independent linguistic stock, and originally living along the Arkansas and Canadian rivers in a region now included in the States of Colorado, New Mexico, and Oklahoma. The Kiowa were among the most predatory and warlike Indians of this region. After constant warfare with whites, they were subdued by United States Army troops under George Armstrong Custer (q.v.) in 1868 and were settled with considerable difficulty on a reservation in Oklahoma. In 1874 they broke out of the reservation and resumed active warfare with white settlers in the vicinity; they were subdued, however, in the following year, with the loss of all their horses and arms and the deportation of a number of their chiefs and warriors to Florida. Since that time they have remained in Oklahoma. In 1901 they were granted U.S. citizenship, and their number in a recent year was about 2600.

In their primitive state the Kiowa displayed a typical Plains Indian culture, with an especially elaborate and effective military organization. The Kiowa made a closer approach to a written language than the great majority of Indian peoples, having a system of pictographic signs which were painted on deer, antelope, and buffalo hides and were used both as primitive calendars and as chronological records of events. *See* PLAINS INDIANS.

KIPCHAK. *See* GOLDEN HORDE.

KIPLING, Rudyard (1865–1936), British writer, born in Bombay, India, and educated in England. From 1882 to 1889 he was on the editorial staff of the *Civil and Military Gazette* of Lahore, India, to which he also contributed short stories. His first works published in book form were the volume of satirical verse *Departmental Ditties* (1886), dealing with civil and military cantonment life in British colonial India, and a collec-

Rudyard Kipling — Elliott & Fry, Ltd., London

tion of his magazine stories called *Plain Tales from the Hills* (1887). Kipling's literary reputation was established by six stories of English life in India, published in India between 1888 and 1889 in paper-covered volumes containing one story each, and which revealed Kipling's profound identification with, and appreciation for, the land and people of India. Thereafter he traveled extensively in Asia and America, married (1892) an American girl, lived (1892–97) in Vermont, and finally settled (1903) in England. He was a prolific writer of short stories, poems, and novels, most of which attained wide popularity. He received the 1907 Nobel Prize in literature.

Kipling is regarded as one of the greatest of English short-story writers. As a poet he is remarkable for rhymed verse written in the slang used by the ordinary British soldier. His writings constantly projected three ideas: intense patriotism, the duty of Englishmen to lead lives of strenuous activity, and England's destiny to become a great empire. In the later works of his long career Kipling's insistent imperialism was an echo of the Victorian past of England.

Among Kipling's important short fictional works are *Many Inventions* (1893), *The Jungle Book* (1894), and *The Second Jungle Book* (1895), which are collections of animal stories considered by many critics to be his finest writing; *Just So Stories for Little Children* (1902), and *Puck of Pook's Hill* (1906). The highly popular novels or long narratives include *The Light that Failed* (1891), about a blind artist; *Captains Courageous* (1897), a sea story; *Stalky & Co.* (1899), based on Kipling's boyhood experiences at the United Services College; and *Kim* (1901), a picaresque tale of Indian life that is generally regarded as his best long narrative. Among his collections of verse are *Barrack-Room Ballads* (1892), which contains the popular poems "Danny Deever", "Mandalay", and "Gunga Din"; *The Seven Seas* (1896); and *The Five Nations* (1903), which contains the well-known poem "Recessional". Kipling was also the author of the autobiography *Something of Myself* (posthumously published, 1937).

KIRBY-SMITH, Edmund (1824–93), American army officer and educator, born in Saint Augustine, Fla., and educated at the United States Military Academy. He resigned from the U.S. Army April 6, 1861, at the beginning of the American Civil War (*see* CIVIL WAR, THE AMERICAN), and was appointed lieutenant colonel of cavalry in the army of the Confederate States of America (q.v.). He became brigadier general in June, 1861, and major general in October of that year. From 1863 to 1865, after the Trans-Mississippi Department was cut off from the rest of the Confederacy, he acted as civil and military administrator of the department. He was made a general in 1864. On June 2, 1865, Kirby-Smith became the last of the Confederate commanders to surrender. From 1870 to 1875 he was chancellor of the University of Nashville, and from 1875 to his death he was professor of mathematics at the University of the South in Sewanee, Tenn.

KIRCHHOFF, Gustav Robert (1824–87), German physicist, born in Königsberg (now Kalingrad, U.S.S.R.), and educated at the University of Königsberg. He was professor of physics at the University of Breslau from 1850 until 1854, when he accepted a similar position at the University of Heidelberg. From 1875 until his death he was professor of physics at the University of Berlin. With the German chemist Robert Wilhelm Bunsen (q.v.), Kirchhoff developed the modern spectroscope for chemical analysis. In 1860 the two scientists discovered the elements cesium and rubidium (qq.v.) by means of spectrum (q.v.) analysis. He conducted important investigations of radiation heat transfer, and also postulated two rules, now known as Kirchhoff's laws of networks, concerning the distribution of current in electrical circuits; *see* ELECTRIC CIRCUIT; HEAT TRANSFER.

KIRGHIZ SOVIET SOCIALIST REPUBLIC, or KIRGHIZIA, constituent republic of the Soviet Union, bounded on the N. by the Kazakh S.S.R., on the E. by China, on the S. by the Tadzhik S.S.R., and on the W. by the Uzbek S.S.R. The chief city and capital is Frunze. Kirghizia is within the great mountain area of central Asia. Notable uplifts are the Tien Shan and Kungey Ala Tau ranges and the Pamir region. The highest elevation is on the border with China, at Pobeda Peak, 24,406 ft. above sea level. Lakes are numerous; the largest, Issyk-Kul', is almost a mile above sea level. The country contains vast mineral resources, including coal, oil, mercury, antimony, and lead. The leading industrial plants are sugar refineries, tanneries, textile and lumber mills, and engineering and metallurgical enterprises. The principal occupation is the raising of sheep, cattle, pigs, and goats. Most of the Kirghizians lead a nomadic existence, wandering through the river valleys and mountain slopes with their herds. Although less than 10 percent of the land is sown to crops, the republic is a major producer of cotton and grains. Kirghizia is also one of the leading silk-producing regions in the Soviet Union. Kirghizia became an autonomous soviet socialist republic of the Russian S.F.S.R. in 1926, and ten years later was

KIROV

INDEX TO MAP OF KIRGHIZ S.S.R.

Cities and Towns

Atbashi	C 2
Dzhalal-Abad	B 2
Frunze (cap.)	B 2
Kant	B 2
Kyzyl-Kiya	B 2
Naryn	C 2
Osh	B 2
Przheval'sk	C 2
Sulyukta	A 3
Talass	B 2
Tashkumyr	A 2
Tomak	B 2
Tyup	C 2
Uzgen	B 2

Physical Features

Chu (river)	B 2
Issyk-Kul' (lake)	C 2
Kokshaal (river)	C 2
Naryn (river)	B 2
Pobeda (peak)	D 2
Sonkol' (lake)	B 2
Talass (river)	A 2

formed as a constituent republic. Area, 76,460 sq.mi.; pop. (1970) 2,933,000.

KIRIN, city and port of the People's Republic of China, in Kirin Province, at the head of navigation on the upper Sungari R., 135 miles S. of Harbin. The Fengman Dam and the large Sungari R. Reservoir lie 15 miles S.E., where a hydroelectric station is located. A rail junction and trade center of a grain- and tobacco-growing area, the city has flour and soybean mills and sawmills and manufactures chemicals, paper, and matches. Founded in 1673 as a military fortress and administrative center, Kirin formerly traded in ginseng and timber and had a junk-building industry. Pop. (1970 est.) 1,200,000.

KIRKCALDY, Great Britain, seaport and burgh in Fife County, Scotland, on the N. shore of the Firth of Forth, 10 miles N. of Edinburgh. Kirkcaldy is the largest British producer of oilcloth and linoleum. Other manufactures include textiles and farm machinery. It has an important coasting trade and export trade with the United States. Kirkcaldy was the birthplace of the famed economist Adam Smith (q.v.), and the city has several fine churches. Pop. (1971 est.) 50,091.

KIRKCUDBRIGHT, Great Britain, county of S.W. Scotland on Solway Firth and Wigtown Bay, in the Galloway district. The county is a hilly region drained by the Cree and Dee rivers. The chief occupation is raising dairy cattle. Sheep-raising is also important, and oats and other grains are grown. Kirkcudbright, the county town, is the principal community. Area, 899 sq.mi.; pop. (1971 est.) 27,448.

KIRKLAND, Samuel (1741–1808), American Congregationalist missionary, born in Norwich, Conn., and educated at the College of New Jersey (now Princeton University). He was ordained in 1766, and in the same year he went to what is now Madison County, N.Y., to work with the Oneida (q.v.) Indians. Shortly before the American Revolution, he secured a declaration of neutrality from the Six Nations, the powerful confederation of Iroquois (q.v.) tribes. He served during the war as a military chaplain. In 1793 he founded Hamilton-Oneida Academy (now Hamilton College, in Clinton, N.Y.), for the education of Indian boys. His letters and journals furnish a unique picture of life among the Iroquois.

KIRKSVILLE, city in Missouri, and county seat of Adair Co., about 87 miles N. of Columbia. The city has varied manufacturing. It is the site of Northeast Missouri State College, founded in 1867, and of the Kirksville College of Osteopathy and Surgery, founded in 1892. See OSTEOPATHY. Pop. (1960) 13,123; (1970) 15,560.

KIRKUK, city of Iraq, and capital of Kirkuk Province, about 150 miles N. of Baghdad. The city is in one of the richest oil fields of Iraq and is the origin of pipelines of the Iraq Petroleum Company extending to the Mediterranean coast. In addition, the city is the marketing center of an area in which sheep are raised and grains and fruit are grown. Ruins dating back about 3000 years have been found on the site of the city. Pop. (1965) 462,027.

KIRKWOOD, city of Missouri, in Saint Louis Co., on the Meramec R., 12 miles S.W. of downtown Saint Louis. Although the city is chiefly residential, machine parts, nursery products, cement, and wood products are manufactured. It is the site of Meramec Community College. Laid out in 1852, Kirkwood was incorporated in 1865. Pop. (1960) 29,421; (1970) 31,890.

KIROV, formerly VYATKA, city of the Soviet Union, in the Russian S.F.S.R., and capital of Kirov Oblast, on the Vyatka R., about 250 miles N.W. of Perm'. It is an important industrial and transportation center, with lumber mills, breweries, metalworking plants, and facilities for processing hides, furs, flour, meat, and dairy products. Votyaks, a people of Finnish stock, settled at Kirov in the 12th century. In the 14th century Russian traders established themselves there. The settlement had various names until

409

KIROVABAD

1780, when it became known as Vyatka. The present name was adopted in 1934 in honor of the Soviet Communist leader Sergei Mironovich Kirov (1888–1934). Pop. (1970) 332,000.

KIROVABAD, formerly GANDZHA, city of the Soviet Union, in Azerbaidzhan S.S.R., about 200 miles w. of Baku. It is on the railway line from Baku to Batumi and is an important marketing and industrial center for locally grown cotton. Textiles, cottonseed oil, agricultural machinery, canned fruits, and wine are produced in Kirovabad. An ancient city, it was the home of the 12th century Persian poet Nizami (q.v.). The city was taken by Russia in 1804. It was renamed in honor of the Soviet Communist leader Sergei Mironovich Kirov (1888–1934) in 1935. Pop. (1970) 190,000.

KIROVOGRAD, city of the Soviet Union, in the Ukrainian S.S.R., and capital of Kirovograd Oblast, on the Ingul R., about 200 miles s.w. of Kharkov. It is the center for a grain-producing area. The most important manufactures of Kirovograd are agricultural machinery and implements. The city was founded in the 18th century as the fortress Elisabethgrad. During the Russian Revolution it was the scene of bitter fighting. In 1936 the city was renamed Kirovograd in honor of the Soviet Communist leader Sergei Mironovich Kirov (1888–1934). Pop. (1970) 189,000.

KISANGANI, formerly STANLEYVILLE, city of the Republic of Zaire, and capital of Orientale Province, on the Congo R., below the Stanley Falls, about 760 miles N.E. of Kinshasa. The city is served by several railroads, maintains an airport, and is a terminus for steamers from Kinshasa. In the surrounding region farming and livestock raising are the chief occupations. Kisangani is a transshipment and small-scale manufacturing center, and is the site of an agricultural institute and the Free University of the Congo. A post was established near the site of the present-day city by the British-American explorer Sir Henry Morton Stanley (q.v.) in 1882. Sixteen years later Stanleyville was made a city; the name was changed to Kisangani in 1966. Pop. (1969 est.) 229,596.

KISFALUDY, name of two Hungarian brothers, who as poets and dramatists were influential in the rise of nationalistic literature in Hungary in the early 19th century.

Sándor Kisfaludy (1772–1844), poet, born in Sümeg, and educated in Györ and Bratislava. His best-known volume of sonnets, *The Loves of Himfy,* was inspired by the works of the 14th-century Italian poet Francesco Petrarch (q.v.). The poems were published in two parts, the first part in 1801 and the second in 1807. Sándor also wrote a popular volume of prose tales, *Legends of the Olden Time in Hungary* (1807), and several historical dramas.

Károly Kisfaludy (1788–1830), dramatist, born in Téte. After serving in the Napoleonic Wars from 1804 to 1811, he later turned to painting and writing. His play, *The Tatars in Hungary* (1819), was the first successful Hungarian national historical drama. Károly wrote other historical dramas and tragedies and comedies based on Hungarian life.

See also HUNGARIAN LITERATURE.

KISH. See SUMER: *Archeology.*

KISI, city of the People's Republic of China, in Heilungkiang Province, on the Maling R., near the Soviet border, about 200 miles s.e. of Harbin and about 150 miles N.W. of Vladivostok, U.S.S.R. A rail junction and coal-mining center of the Mishan Basin, Kisi produces mining equipment and metal products. The city grew after Japanese rail development while it was a part of Manchukuo in the 1930's. The city was established in 1956. The name is also spelled Chi-hsi. Pop. (1970 est.) 350,000.

KISKADDEN, Maude. See ADAMS, MAUDE.

KISMET (Turk., from Ar. *qismah,* "lot, portion"), Turkish word for destiny, often expressing the notion that human intervention cannot change a fated course of events.

KISSING BUG, common name for any of several large species of true bugs that suck the blood of man, so called because their favorite site of attack is on the face about the lips. These bugs belong to the carnivorous Assassin-Bug family, Reduviidae, distributed throughout the world. The common kissing bug of the United States is the masked bedbug hunter, *Reduvius personatus,* an insect about ¾ in. long. Although the bug lives in human habitations, it only rarely attacks man; it usually feeds on insects, especially bedbugs. The masked bedbug hunter is so called because the numerous sticky hairs on its face collect dust, giving it a masked appearance. The so-called "big bedbug" or conenose of the southern and southwestern U.S. is *Triatoma sanguisuga,* a black insect, margined on its sides with red. This inch-long species commonly bites humans, but also lives outdoors, feeding on grasshoppers and potato beetles. The South American barbeiro, or conenose, *T. megistus,* is the principal vector of the parasite causing Chagas' disease, a Brazilian form of sleeping sickness (q.v.).

KISSINGER, Henry Alfred (1923–), American educator and public official, born in Fürth, Germany, and educated at Harvard University. He was brought to the United States by his parents in 1938 and became a citizen five years later. From 1943 to 1946 Kissinger served as an enlisted man in the United States Army.

Kissinger's first book, *Nuclear Weapons and Foreign Policy* (1957), grew out of studies undertaken by the Council on Foreign Relations, a nonprofit study group. In this book Kissinger advocated flexibility in U.S. foreign military activities; it is regarded as a primary source book in American foreign policy. He began to teach in the department of government at Harvard in 1954, the year in which he was awarded a PH.D. degree. In the 1950's and 1960's he served as an occasional foreign-policy adviser to Presidents Dwight David Eisenhower, John Fitzgerald Kennedy, and Lyndon Baines Johnson (qq.v.); he conducted studies for a number of government agencies, as well as for the Rockefeller Brothers Fund, a foundation that supports philanthropic activities, and for Brookings Institution (q.v.).

In 1968 Kissinger took a leave of absence from Harvard to become the assistant to President Richard Milhous Nixon (q.v.) for national security affairs. In this post he became influential in establishing and effecting U.S. foreign policy. He accompanied President Nixon to China and the U.S.S.R. in 1972. He also represented the U.S. in negotiations toward settlement of the war in Indochina. In January, 1973, Kissinger's efforts finally resulted in an agreement establishing a cease-fire in Vietnam. For this achievement he shared the 1973 Nobel Peace Prize with the North Vietnamese diplomat Le Duc Tho (q.v.). In August, 1973, President Nixon appointed Kissinger secretary of state; he was the first foreign-born citizen to hold this post. Kissinger retained his national security affairs post.

KISTNA (Hindi *Krishna*), river of S. India, rising in the Western Ghats mountains in Mysore State and flowing generally E. for about 800 mi. before emptying into the Bay of Bengal near False Divi Point. The mouth of the river forms the N. limit of the Coromandel Coast (q.v.). The river is not navigable, but its waters are used for irrigation. The source of the Kistna is sacred to Hindus.

KITAKYUSHU, city of Japan, in Fukuoka Prefecture, at the N. end of Kyushu Island on the Hibiki Sea and Shimonoseki Strait, 35 miles N.E. of Fukuoka. The city was formed in 1963 when the five cities of Kokura, Moji, Tobata, Wakamatsu, and Yawata were combined.

The combined city of Kitakyushu features a great iron and steel industry, supplied by the large Chukuko coalfields, lying to the S. and W. It is also an important transportation center, home of light industries, and a major export center.

Of the five previously autonomous cities, Kokura is a port at the mouth of the Murasaki R. Industries include cotton-textile weaving, rice milling, and the manufacture of chemicals and porcelain. Moji, connected with Shimonoseki Strait by road and rail, is a steamer terminus for the Inland Sea. It exports lumber, cement, cotton products, glass, sugar, flour, and beer. After completion of the railroads in 1887 and opening of the port to foreign trade in 1899, Moji (known in feudal times as Mojigaseki) developed rapidly. Tobata and Wakamatsu are joined by the Wakato bridge over an inlet of the Hibiki Sea. Fishing is important in Tobata, and plants produce sugar, glass, cotton thread, and alcohol. Wakamatsu exports sugar and imports raw materials for the industries of the city. Yawata, or Yahata, is the chief iron- and steel-milling center; the Yahata ironworks were established in 1897. The population of the combined city (1970) was 1,042,000.

KITAZATO, Shibasaburo (1852–1931), Japanese bacteriologist, born in Kumamoto, and educated at the University of Tokyo. From 1885 to 1891 he was in Berlin, studying under the German bacteriologist Robert Koch (q.v.). After his return to Japan he served in various academic, research, and administrative capacities at the University of Tokyo, Keio University, the Imperial Japanese Institute, and his own research laboratory, which he founded in 1915. Kitazato isolated three important bacilli, those that cause tetanus (1889), anthrax (1889), and dysentery (1898), and prepared (1890) a diphtheria antitoxin. In Tokyo, in 1894, he discovered the infectious agent of bubonic plague; at the same time the Swiss bacteriologist Alexandre Yersin (1863–1943) made the same discovery in Hong Kong.

KITCHEN CABINET, in American political history, name given to a small, unofficial group of intimate advisers of President Andrew Jackson (q.v.). Shortly after his first inauguration in 1829, Jackson, instead of consulting his official cabinet on important matters of state, went to his personal associates for advice. The original group included Isaac Hill (1789–1851), editor of the New Hampshire *Patriot*; Francis Preston Blair (q.v.), editor of the Washington *Globe*; and Amos Kendall (1789–1869), a minor government official and the reputed leader of the group. After the cabinet was reorganized in 1831, the kitchen cabinet declined in influence.

KITCHENER, city of Canada, in Ontario Province, and county seat of Waterloo Co., in the Grand R. valley, 35 miles N.W. of Hamilton and 55 miles S.W. of Toronto. Industries include meat packing, tanning, and the manufacture of

KITCHENER

foundry and steel products, electrical and electronic equipment, food products, plastic and rubber products, furniture, chemicals, and textiles. The city is the site of the Kitchener Conservatory of Music and a vocational school; Waterloo Lutheran University (1911) and the University of Waterloo (1959) are in Waterloo, 2 mi. to the N.W. Founded in 1806 by Pennsylvania Germans, Kitchener was called Sand Hills, Mount Pleasant, and, after a second wave of German immigrants arrived about 1830, Berlin. In 1916 the city was renamed for the British field marshal Horatio Herbert Kitchener (q.v.). Pop. (1971) 109,954; metropolitan area, 224,390.

KITCHENER, Horatio Herbert, 1st Earl Kitchener of Khartoum and of Broome (1850–1916), British military officer and statesman, born in Ballylongford, County Derry, Ireland, and educated at the Royal Military Academy at Woolwich. He was commissioned second lieutenant in the Royal Engineers in 1871 and was promoted to captain in 1883 for distinguished service in Palestine, Cyprus, and Egypt. In 1884 Kitchener accompanied Viscount Garnet Joseph Wolseley (1833–1913) in an unsuccessful attempt to relieve the British general Charles George Gordon (q.v.) at Khartoum (q.v.). Kitchener served as governor general of the Eastern Sudan in northeast Africa from 1886 to 1888. He was appointed British sirdar or commander in chief of the Egyptian army in 1892. A ruthless but capable military leader, in 1895 he started the successful invasion of the Sudan. His forces annihilated the army of the Arab leader Abdullah et Taaisha (1846?–99), known as The Khalifa, at Omdurman in 1898 and became firmly established at Khartoum, capital of the Sudan. See SUDAN, REPUBLIC OF THE: *History.*

Kitchener was promoted to the rank of major general in 1896 and raised to the peerage as Baron Kitchener of Khartoum in 1898. After serving in the South African War (q.v.) between Great Britain and the Boer republics, in 1902 he was made a viscount and received the Order of Merit. He served as commander in chief of the British forces in India from 1902 to 1909, when he was promoted to field marshal. Although he greatly strengthened Britain's power, he was refused the viceroyship of India. Instead, in 1911 he was appointed consul general in Egypt, and for his services in Egypt he was made Earl of Broome in 1914.

At the outbreak of World War I Kitchener was appointed secretary of state for war; in that capacity from 1914 until 1916 he was responsible for recruiting the volunteer British army. He was lost at sea when the cruiser *Hampshire*, on which he was traveling, struck a mine and sank.

KITCHEN MIDDEN, in archeology, refuse heap left at the site of a primitive camp or village. Such heaps, often containing buried relics of industry and art, have been found in all parts of the world. They are of particular importance in investigations of cultures that left no written records or permanent architectural remains, such as the communities of the North American Indians, and of Stone, Bronze, and early Iron Age Europeans; see ARCHEOLOGY: *History.* The earliest kitchen middens studied by archeologists are in Denmark, where *kjökkenmöddings* ("kitchen leavings"), so large and ancient that they were originally thought to be natural formations, were excavated in the 19th century. The primitive custom of locating camps on the abandoned refuse piles of former habitations created some middens more than 1000 ft. long and 10 ft. deep along the Danish beaches (in other parts of the world middens as deep as one hundred feet have been found), and archeologists have unearthed from them not only animal debris such as shells and bones but artifacts such as piercers, knives, scrapers, hammers, slingstones, and pottery. Middens found near ocean shores or around inland waters where mollusks abound are often called shell heaps; they have been particularly valuable as records of nomadic or seminomadic peoples who regularly settled in temporary homes on the seashore. In North America, for example, vast shell heaps have been studied along the east coast and on the coasts of British Columbia, Oregon, and southern California; such heaps have served as an important source of information about the primitive life of these regions, particularly in the south where centuries of Spanish acculturation have greatly modified the native Indian cultures. See also ARCHEOLOGY: *Methods;* MAN, ANCIENT.

KITE, or FORKTAIL, common name for any of the graceful, medium-sized birds comprising several subfamilies of the Hawk family, *Accipitridae.* Kites are found in the warmer portions of all continents. They have long, slender wings, and long tails, deeply forked in some species. Their legs and feet are smaller and weaker than those of most other hawks, and consequently their diet, which varies among different species, is made up of very small animals or of carrion. Most species of kites build their nests of twigs on high trees, but some species nest in trees only a few feet above water. The female in most species lays three or four white eggs, blotched brown and purple.

Four species of kite are found in North America. The swallow-tailed or fork-tailed kite, *Elanoïdes forficatus,* is found in the Gulf States. This bird is about 21 in. long, and is black above and white below. Its head, neck, and hind parts are white, and the wing tips, rear of wing, and tail are black below. The bird feeds on snakes, frogs, and insects. The white-tailed kite, *Elanus leucurus,* is found in California, Texas, and Florida in the United States, and throughout Central America and most of South America. It is about 14½ in. long and is light gray above and white below, with a white head and tail, and with black-streaked wings. The everglade kite, *Rostrhamus sociabilis,* is found from Florida to South America, and feeds only on one species of freshwater snail *(Pomacea).* The Mississippi kite, *Ictinia misisippiensis,* formerly abundant in the southern and central U.S., is occasionally found in the Gulf States, but is now uncommon. It feeds on insects, small amphibians, and small reptiles.

The common European kite, or glede, *Milvus milvus,* is a large species, about 26 in. long. It is chestnut, streaked with black, and has a grayish head. The bird feeds on small mammals, birds, frogs, insects, and carrion, and so does the pariah or black kite of India, *M. migrans,* which is often tamed and trained as a scavenger.

KITE, wind-supported flying device, consisting of a wooden or similar framework covered with paper, cloth, or synthetic material, used as a rudimentary airfoil for pleasure or study. Attached to a long string, it can be sent aloft through the action of the wind on its surfaces; its distance or height is controlled from the ground by playing out the string. Kites are of ancient origin, kite flying having been practiced by various Asian peoples and the ancient Egyptians. Today kite flying is a popular pastime and a competitive sport. In eastern Asia special competitions are held in which the flown kites are elaborately decorated in the form of birds, fishes, or dragons, and they are often equipped with whistles or pipes that emit musical noises as the wind blows through them.

Kites have been employed for practical purposes as well as for pleasure. The kite-flying experiments of the American statesman and scientist Benjamin Franklin (q.v.) for the investigation of atmospheric electricity are well known, and kite studies were also made by the American physicist and inventor Alexander Graham Bell (q.v.). Beginning in the 1890's and continuing for about forty years, box kites, consisting of two or more open-ended, connected boxes were used for sending aloft meteorological instruments to measure wind velocity, temperature, barometric pressure, and humidity; *see* METEOROLOGY. In the late 19th and early 20th century, kites were used for lifting military observers to heights from which they could observe the disposition of enemy forces. During World War II, kites were also used as gunnery targets. Present-day applications include the use of kites as signals in air-sea-rescue operations.

See also BALLOON.

An early English illustration of a kite, published in 1634 in The Mysteries of Nature and Art *by John Bates.*
Hallmark Gallery

KITHAIRŌN (anc. *Cithaeron*), mountain of E. central Greece on the border between the departments of Attikí and Voiotía; 4623 ft. high. At the foot of the N. slope are the ruins of the ancient city of Plataea (q.v.); to the N. stood the ancient fortress city of Thebes (q.v.). The mountain is mentioned in Greek mythology as the scene of Dionysian rites (*see* DIONYSUS; MYSTERIES, CLASSIC) and as the place where King Laius of Thebes abandoned his son Oedipus (q.v.).

KITIMAT, city of Canada, in British Columbia, at the head of the Douglas Channel, about 425 miles N.W. of Victoria. Kitimat is a planned community built by the Aluminium Co. of Canada in 1951 to house the workers for a smelter it constructed concurrently 5 mi. from the center of the city. The area was chosen because of its deepwater harbor and abundant supply of hydroelectric power nearby. The aluminum smelter, one of the largest in the world, went into operation in 1954. Pop. (1971) 11,824.

KITTIWAKE

KITTIWAKE, common name for any of several gulls constituting the genus *Rissa,* so called from the sound of their cry. The kittiwake is characterized by an extremely short hind toe. The bird is chiefly pure white in color, except for its back and wings, which are grayish with black wing tips. The bird averages about 14½ in. in length. It is rarely seen near shore except during the breeding season, when it is found in large colonies on cliffs. The kittiwake prefers to search for food in the open sea. The Atlantic or black-legged kittiwake, *Rissa tridactyla,* is found in arctic and cold temperate regions on both sides of the North Atlantic Ocean; it has a greenish-yellow bill and black legs and feet. A subspecies is common in the North Pacific Ocean. The red-legged kittiwake, *R. brevirostris,* is found in the Bering Sea; it has red legs.

KITTREDGE, George Lyman (1860–1941), American educator and scholar, born in Boston, Mass., and educated at Harvard University. He began teaching at Harvard in 1888 and was professor of English there from 1894 until 1936. He was a famous Shakespearean scholar, and his one-volume edition, the *Complete Works of Shakespeare* (1936), is generally considered authoritative. Among his many studies still in print are *Study of Gawain and the Green Knight* (1916) and *Witchcraft in Old and New England* (1929). He was also an editor of *Webster's New International Dictionary, Second Edition* (1934) and an editor of several series on English grammar, Scottish and English ballads, and Anglo-Saxon literature.

Brown kiwi, Apteryx australis   New Zealand Information Service

KITTY HAWK, peninsula of North Carolina, in the Atlantic Ocean, site of the Wright Brothers National Memorial. The memorial commemorates the first successful flight of an aircraft, made by the American inventors Orville and Wilbur Wright (*see under* WRIGHT) on Dec. 17, 1903; see NATIONAL PARK SERVICE. See also AVIATION: *Kitty Hawk and After.*

KIUSHU. See KYUSHU.

KIWANIS INTERNATIONAL, organization of men's service clubs, composed of businessmen and professional men, founded to render service to the community and to promote better business and professional standards. The motto of the Kiwanis clubs is "We build". Local clubs are active in their communities, supporting law-enforcement and public-service agencies and promoting good citizenship. Many local Kiwanis clubs regularly send underprivileged children to summer camps. The first Kiwanis club was organized in Detroit, Mich., in 1915. The name was derived from an Indian word *Keewanis* "to make oneself known". In 1917 Kiwanis clubs were chartered in Canada, and the name Kiwanis International was adopted at the national convention in 1924. The Kiwanis International is now composed of about 5700 local clubs located in 33 countries. In 1970 the membership of Kiwanis International totaled approximately 275,000. The *Kiwanis Magazine,* a monthly, is published from the national headquarters in Chicago, Ill.

KIWI, common name applied to flightless birds belonging to the family Apterygidae, and related to the extinct moa (q.v.). The bird, known also as the apteryx, is named for its characteristic cry. The three species are restricted to New Zealand.

The kiwi is usually about the size of a large hen, but the brown kiwi (*Apteryx australis*) has a total length of 22 in. Although incapable of flight, the kiwi has rudimentary wings, hidden by the downy, gray-brown feathers that thickly cover the body. The legs are short, stout, and covered with scales, and the beak is long and slender, with nostrils near the tip. The three anterior toes are armed with strong claws, used in scratching and as weapons, and the posterior fourth toe is short and raised from the ground. The kiwi hides during the day in holes in the ground and comes out in the twilight to forage for worms or insects. The female lays one or two very large white or greenish eggs, which hatch after an incubation period of seventy-five to eighty days. Incubation is by the male. Game laws protect the kiwi because it is threatened with extinction.

KIZILIRMAK (anc. *Halys*), longest river in Turkey, rising in N. central Turkey, near Kızıl Dağ mountain, E. of Sivas. From the source, the river flows in a broad arc s.w. to the vicinity of Nevşehir, N.W. to Kalecik, and then generally N.E. to Cape Bafra on the Black Sea. The total length of the Kizilirmak is more than 700 mi.

KJÖLEN MOUNTAINS, mountain range and plateau of the Scandinavian peninsula, mostly in Norway, where it extends from North Cape to the s.w. end of the country. North of 63° N. latitude the range coincides with the border between Sweden and Norway. Kebnekaise in N.W. Sweden, at 6946 ft. above sea level, is the highest peak in the range.

KLAGENFURT, city in Austria, and capital of Carinthia Province, on the Glan R., about 60 miles s.w. of Graz. The city is a noted winter sports resort in a scenic mountain area. It is also the marketing center of a rich mining and agricultural region. Manufactures in the city include textiles and leather goods. Klagenfurt is a Roman Catholic bishopric and has a cathedral built in the 16th century. Klagenfurt became a city in the late 13th century. Pop. (1971) 74,618.

KLAIPĖDA, formerly MEMEL, city and port of the Soviet Union, in the Lithuanian S.S.R., on the Baltic Sea, 75 miles N.E. of Kaliningrad. It is an important industrial center and has shipyards and factories engaged in the manufacture of lumber and paper products, textiles, soap, bricks, and processed food. The city was settled in 1252 by the Teutonic Knights. It belonged to Prussia and briefly to Sweden (1629–35). It remained in Prussia until 1919, when the Treaty of Versailles placed it under French administration. In 1920 the city became the capital of the Memel Territory (q.v.). Pop. (1970) 140,000.

KLAMATH, river of s.w. Oregon and N.W. California, rising in Upper Klamath Lake, Ore., and flowing s.w. and then sharply N.W. before emptying into the Pacific Ocean near Regua, Calif. The river is about 275 mi. long. In N. California the river is dammed to form Copco Lake.

KLAMATH FALLS, city in Oregon, and county seat of Klamath Co., at the s. end of Upper Klamath Lake, about 235 miles s.e. of Portland, and about 15 miles N. of the California boundary. It is served by three railroads and maintains a municipal airport. The city is the distribution center of an extensive lumbering and agricultural area. The principal industries in the city are lumber mills and lumber-processing plants. Kingsley Air Force Base is nearby. The city is the site of the Oregon Technical Institute, founded in 1947.

Klamath Falls is also the center of a resort and recreational area. In the vicinity are many lakes, as well as numerous streams, which afford facilities for fishing. Founded about 1867, the city was known as Linkville until 1893, when it was renamed Klamath Falls. In 1906 Klamath Falls was incorporated as a city. Pop. (1960) 16,949; (1970) 15,775.

KLANG, city of Malaysia, in Selangor State, on the Klang R., 20 miles s.w. of Kuala Lumpur. A road hub, it lies on the Kuala Lumpur-Port Swettenham branch railroad, 5 miles N.E. of the latter town, which is the second port of Malaya. The surrounding area grows fruits, oil palms, and coconuts and has rubber plantations. Rubber products are manufactured and pineapples are canned in the city. At Connaught Bridge, 2 mi. to the E., is a steam-power station. Klang is the second-largest city of the country and site of the palace of the sultan. Pop. (1970) 113,269.

KLAPROTH, Martin Heinrich (1743–1817), German chemist, born in Wernigerode. He learned chemistry as an apothecary's assistant and worked as an apothecary in Hannover, Berlin, and Danzig. He set up his own chemistry laboratory in 1780 and was appointed chemistry lecturer at the Artillery School in Berlin in 1792. When the University of Berlin was founded in 1810, he was appointed the first professor of chemistry, and served in this position until his death. An outstanding chemist and mineralogist, sometimes referred to as the father of analytical chemistry, Klaproth is famous for his discovery of the new elements uranium (1789), zirconium (1789), chromium (1798), and cerium (1803). His researches included devising new, quantitative methods of mineral analysis, and he also pioneered the application of chemical analysis to archeology (q.v.); *see* CHEMISTRY: *Major Divisions of Chemistry: Analytical Chemistry.*

KLEE, Paul (1879–1940), Swiss painter, born near Bern. In 1898 he went to Munich, where he studied with the German painter Franz von Stuck (1863–1928). His first work was a series of bizarre etchings. Between 1908 and 1911 he became acquainted, through exhibitions in Munich, with the work of the French painters Paul Cézanne and Henri Matisse and the Dutch painter Vincent van Gogh (qq.v.). Klee's work at this period began to reflect the influence of cubism (q.v.); his use of delicate colors and a curious sense of fantasy set his paintings apart. In 1912 he joined the movement called *Blaue Reiter* ("Blue Rider") with the Russian painter Vasily Kandinsky (q.v.) and the German painter Franz Marc (1880–1916). Through their exhibitions, this group spread the doctrine of ex-

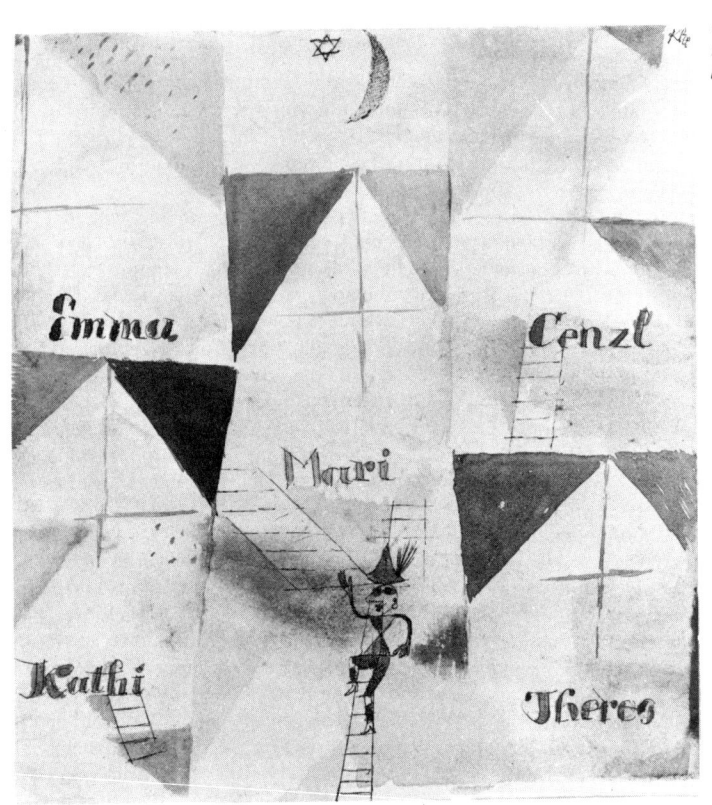

"The Bavarian Don Giovanni", watercolor by Paul Klee, painted in 1919.
Solomon R. Guggenheim Museum

pressionism (q.v.) throughout Europe. In 1920 Klee became a teacher at the Bauhaus (q.v.) in Weimar, the most advanced art school in Germany. In 1925 he moved with the Bauhaus to Dessau, and from 1930 until 1933 he taught at Düsseldorf.

Klee's most important and influential paintings represent a combination of abstract linear patterns, naïve and fantastic subject matter, exotic color harmonies, and an eerie humor. Many of his works are reminiscent of Egyptian hieroglyphics, children's drawings, or the painting and ornaments of primitive peoples. He experimented continually in painting on such original surfaces as cloth, blotting paper, newsprint, and cement. Representative examples of his art include "They're Biting" (1920, The Tate Gallery, London) and "Arab Song" (1932, Phillips Gallery, Washington, D.C.). Much of his writing on art, including *Pädagogisches Skizzenbuch* (1925; Eng. trans., *Pedagogical Sketch Book*, 1944), has been published. See ABSTRACT AND NONOBJECTIVE ART: *Other Experimenters;* BAUHAUS.

See ABSTRACT AND NONOBJECTIVE ART: *Other Experimenters;* BAUHAUS.

KLEIST, Ewald Christian von (1715–59), soldier and poet, born in Zeblin, near Köslin (now Koszalin, Poland), and educated at the University of Königsberg. He served in the Danish army and from 1740 until his death he was an officer in the Prussian army. During the Seven Years' War (q.v.), he was mortally wounded at Kunersdorf (now Kunowice, Poland). His principal literary works were the lyric poem *Der Frühling* ("The Spring", 1749), modeled on *The Seasons* by the Scottish poet James Thomson (q.v.), *Ode an die Preussische Armee* ("Ode to the Prussian Army", 1757), and the brief epic of two ancient Greek soldiers, *Cissides und Paches* (1759).

KLEIST, Heinrich von (1777–1811), dramatist, grandnephew of Ewald, born in Frankfurt-an-der-Oder. He served in the Prussian army from 1792 to 1799. During the next eleven years, he studied law and philosophy in Frankfurt, was a government official in Berlin and Königsberg (now Kaliningrad, Russian S.F.S.R.), and journeyed through Europe. In 1808 Kleist and the German economist Adam Heinrich Müller (1779–1829) founded *Phöbus,* a literary and philosophical periodical. In *Phöbus* Kleist published several of his poems, including the tragedy *Penthesilea* (1808), and the novelette *Michael Kohlhass* (1808). By 1803 he had written his first important play, the tragedy *Die Familie Schroffenstein* ("The Schroffenstein Family"). His other important works included the romantic drama of courtly love *Das Käthchen von Heilbronn* ("Kathy of Heilbron", 1810), the comedy *Der Zerbrochene Krug* ("The Broken Jug", 1811), and the historical play *Der Prinz von Homburg* (1811). In 1810 he became editor of the newspaper *Berliner Abendblätter* (*Berlin Evening News*), which was suppressed in 1811 for attacks on the policies of the Prussian chancellor Prince Karl August von Hardenberg (q.v.). This misfortune and the failure of Kleist to find a publisher or a producer for his plays left him despondent. In 1811 he killed both himself and his mistress. Despite his short career, he is considered one of the outstanding German dramatists. *See* DRAMA: *National Drama: Germany.*

KLEMPERER, Otto (1885–1973), German conductor, born in Breslau (now Wrocław, Poland), and educated at the Hoch Conservatory in Frankfurt and at the Klindworth Scharwenka and Stern conservatories in Berlin. In 1907 he was appointed conductor at the German Theater in Prague, and during the next twenty years he directed many German opera houses and conducted orchestras in Great Britain, the United States, and South America. In 1927 he was named director of the Berlin State Opera. But in 1933 Klemperer left Germany (then under the dictator Adolf Hitler) to settle in the U.S. Until 1939 he was conductor of the Los Angeles Philharmonic orchestra. Partially paralyzed following an operation for a brain tumor in 1939, Klemperer often had to conduct in a sitting position. Nevertheless he continued to appear with many of the great orchestras of the world, specializing in the works of two Austrian composers, Wolfgang Amadeus Mozart and Klemperer's own benefactor, Gustav Mahler (qq.v.). In 1959 he was named principal conductor of the Philharmonia Orchestra of London and remained in that capacity with its successor, the New Philharmonia, until 1972.

KLEPTOMANIA, impulse to steal that is obsessive and unrelated to rational motives. Persons afflicted with the obsession are usually aware of the immorality of stealing and of the social consequences of theft. Nevertheless, the desire to steal is so irresistible that thefts are frequently committed with little or no attempt at concealment. Because kleptomaniacs obtain gratification from the act of stealing rather than from possession of the stolen articles, they often steal objects of little value that they could easily buy. Although psychiatrists regard kleptomania as a neurosis (*see* MENTAL DISORDERS), the obsession is not recognized as a legal defense for theft in American or British courts. The kleptomaniac is not legally responsible for his thefts, however, if he cannot distinguish right from wrong.

KLEVE *or* **CLEVE** (Fr. *Clèves*), town of West Germany, in North Rhine-Westphalia State, about 2 mi. from the Rhine R., to which it is connected by canal, and 12 mi. by rail S.E. of the Dutch town of Nijmegen. It is built in Dutch architectural style on three hills. Leather, shoes, and machinery are manufactured in the town, and industries include tobacco and cotton. With mineral springs in the vicinity, Kleve is frequented as a summer resort. In the center of the town is the famous Schwanenburg, or Swan's Castle, said to have been founded by the Roman statesman and general Gaius Julius Caesar, and associated with the "Knights of the Swan" legend, immortalized in Richard Wagner's opera *Lohengrin.* Among other notable buildings is a 14th-century Roman Catholic church built in Gothic style and containing the tombs of the counts and dukes of Kleve. The town became the seat of the counts of Kleve in the 11th century, and later was the capital of the Duchy of Kleve, which was created in 1417. In 1614 the duchy, which embraced land on both sides of the Rhine, came into the possession of Brandenburg (q.v.) and was later incorporated with the electorate. The part of the duchy east of the Rhine was ceded to France in 1795; the remaining portion was seized by France from Prussia during the Napoleonic Wars. Both portions were restored in 1815 except for some small sections which were made part of the Netherlands. Following the conclusion of World War II Kleve was included in the British zone of occupation in Germany. Pop. (1970) 43,600.

KLINE, Franz Josef (1910–62), American painter, born in Wilkes-Barre, Pa., and educated at the School of Fine and Applied Art of Boston University and Heatherly School of Fine Arts in London. Kline settled in New York City in 1938, soon becoming associated with the abstract expressionist school of painting as it evolved during and immediately after World War II. With his first one-man exhibition in 1950, Kline attracted a great deal of attention because of his use of bold black areas against a plain white background. In later years Kline sometimes added touches of strong color to his basically black-and-white canvases. During the 1950's Kline taught art at Black Mountain College in North Carolina, Pratt Institute in Brooklyn, N.Y., the Philadelphia Museum School of Art, and Cooper Union in New York City. *See also* ABSTRACT AND NONOBJECTIVE ART.

KLINGER

KLINGER, Max (1857–1920), German painter, etcher, and sculptor, born in Leipzig, and trained in art in Karlsruhe, Berlin, and Paris. He chose chiefly mythological and allegorical subjects, often achieving striking and unorthodox designs. His paintings, such as "Christ on Olympus" (Museum of the 20th Century, Vienna), and his etchings reveal a restless, tortured imagination as well as powerful technical accomplishments. Sculpture became his chief medium after 1894. He created a large statue of the German composer Ludwig van Beethoven and a bust of the German philosopher Friedrich Nietzsche (qq.v.).

KLIPSPRINGER. See ANTELOPE.

KLONDIKE, region of Canada, covering about 800 sq.mi. in Yukon Territory near the E. border with Alaska. The vaguely defined region, which is drained by the Klondike R., is not far from the Arctic Circle and is subject to harsh, long winters. The region became famous after gold was discovered on Aug. 17, 1896, in Bonanza Creek, a tributary of the Klondike R. After the news reached the United States a year later, thousands of gold prospectors went to the Klondike, many of them temporarily settling in Dawson.

A prospector extracts gold on a street in Nome, Alaska, during the Klondike gold rush.   Bettmann Archive

In 1900, the greatest production year, the gold produced in the Klondike was valued at $22,000,000. Continually decreasing amounts of gold were found after that year, and this, together with the extreme hardships of Klondike winters, resulted in the decline of the gold fields. See ALASKA: *History.*

KLOPSTOCK, Friedrich Gottlieb (1724–1803), German poet and dramatist, born in Quedlinburg, and educated at the classical school at Schulpforte and the universities in Jena and Leipzig. Klopstock was one of the earliest important writers of the German classical period; see GERMAN LITERATURE: *The Classical and Romantic Period.* He played an important part in freeing German literature from French and other foreign influences. His principal poetic work was *Der Messias* ("The Messiah"), a religious epic. He began it while studying at Schulpforte and completed it in four volumes between 1751 and 1773. *Der Messias* has been widely translated and imitated. Klopstock's reputation as a lyric poet, however, has endured better than his fame as an epic or dramatic poet. His best lyrics are contained in the volume *Oden* ("Odes", 1747–80), a collection of poems on religion, friendship, and nature. Klopstock also wrote religious dramas in verse with themes taken from the Old Testament. He was an ardent nationalist; in a trilogy of prose dramas, *Hermanns Schlacht* ("Hermann's Battle", 1769), *Hermann und die Fürsten* ("Hermann and the Princess", 1784), and *Hermanns Tod* ("Hermann's Death", 1787), he glorified Arminius, or Hermann, a German national hero of the early part of the 1st century A.D.

KLYSTRON. See ELECTRONICS: *Microwave Electron Tubes.*

KNELLER, Sir Godfrey, real name GOTTFRIED KNILLER (1646–1723), British painter, born in Lübeck, Germany, and educated as a painter in Amsterdam. He emigrated to England in 1675 with an established reputation as a portrait painter. His patrons included the English monarchs Charles II, James II, William III, Queen Mary II, Queen Anne, and George I (qq.v.). Kneller also painted other European reigning monarchs and innumerable portraits of celebrities. His work is marked by forceful characterization and careful technical finish. Many of his paintings are in Hampton Court Palace, London, including one of his best-known works, "Ten Beauties of the Court of William III".

KNICKERBOCKER, Diedrich, pen name used by the American writer Washington Irving (q.v.) for his satire *A History of New York* (1809).

KNIFE. See CUTLERY.

KNIGHT, mounted man-at-arms of medieval Europe, who served a king or other feudal superior, usually in return for the tenure of a tract of land; see FEUDALISM. The knight was generally a man of noble birth, who had served in the subordinate ranks as page and squire before being ceremoniously inducted into knighthood by his superior. At his induction the knight usually swore to be brave, loyal, and courteous and to protect the defenseless, especially women. After the 15th century, knighthood came to be conferred on civilians as a reward for public services.

In modern Great Britain, knighthood is an honor conferred by the monarch on both men and women in recognition of outstanding personal merit. The knight is usually created through appointment to an order of knighthood. The title sir is prefixed to his first name, and initials standing for his order of knighthood follow his name. For example, John Smith, on receiving the title of Knight Commander of the Order of the Garter, is afterward known as Sir John Smith, K.G. Other titles of British knightly orders include Knight Commander of the Order of the British Empire (K.B.E.), Knight Commander of the Bath (K.C.B.), Knight Commander of the Order of Saint Michael and Saint George (K.C.M.G.), Knight Commander of the Royal Victorian Order (K.C.V.O.), Commander of the Indian Empire (K.C.I.E.), and Knight Commander of the Star of India (K.C.S.I.). Knighthood is also occasionally conferred without membership in a particular order. A knight so created is known as a Knight Bachelor, and his name is followed by the abbreviation Kt., standing for knight. See CHIVALRY.

KNIGHTHOOD, ORDERS OF, in modern usage, honorary societies, membership in which is generally conferred by a nation or a head of state on noblemen or persons who have performed some unusually meritorious service. Three categories of orders may be distinguished: royal orders, generally limited to noblemen of royal blood or of the highest grade; noble or family orders, open to noblemen generally; and orders of merit, bestowed on persons of all classes as a reward for distinguished service. Persons admitted to membership in an order generally receive a badge or medal and a formal title, such as "Knight Commander" or "Knight of the Grand Cross". The orders are believed to have originated during the age of feudalism (q.v.), when many noblemen, impoverished by their heavy expenditures during the Crusades (q.v.) or virtually disinherited through the operation of the law of primogeniture (q.v.), became professional soldiers in the service of various kings or other nobles. These knights formed organizations known as orders, which had special uniforms and insignia and were given distinctive names. Modern orders use the symbols and nomenclature of the feudal orders, but serve a purely honorary function.

In modern times, orders of knighthood have been created and conferred most often by monarchies, a few empires, and the Holy See of the Roman Catholic Church. Orders were abolished, in some instances by law, in such countries as Austria, Germany, and the U.S.S.R. But in the mid-20th century, with the emergence of many independent republics in Africa and Asia, there has been a proliferation of orders created by the authorities of those nations. This situation is reminiscent of the late Middle Ages (q.v.), when many local rulers established orders of knighthood in order to increase their prestige; frequently these orders lasted only through the lifetime of the ruler who established them. Of the profusion of orders born in the Middle Ages, several remain extant in modern times. These include the Order of the Garter (Great Britain), the Order of the Elephant (Denmark), and the Order of the Golden Fleece (Spain, formerly shared with Austria).

KNIGHTS HOSPITALERS

ORDERS OF KNIGHTHOOD

Country	Order	Founded	Founder	Description of Badge and Motto
Belgium	Leopold	1832	Leopold II	8-pointed white cross edged with gold on a wreath of oak and laurel, suspended from a royal crown; a medallion center bearing a golden lion on a black field, surrounded by a fillet bearing the motto L'Union Fait la Force ("In Union There Is Strength").
Denmark	Elephant	1462	Christian I; renewed by Christian V in 1693	Silver star bearing a purple medallion on which is mounted a silver or diamond cross surrounded by a silver laurel wreath.
France	Legion of Honor	1802	Napoleon I	5-rayed white enamel and gold star; a female head on the obverse representing the republic, two crossed flags on the reverse.
Great Britain	Bath	1725	George I	Military: gold Maltese cross botonée, enamelled white; in each of the four angles a lion of England and in the center a rose, thistle, and shamrock; Civil: gold filigree oval, the external filled, containing a motto, and encircling the same device as the military. Tria Juncta in Uno ("Three In One") is the motto.
Great Britain	British Empire	1917	George V	Motto: For God and the Empire
Great Britain	Garter	1350	Edward III	Motto: Honi Soit Qui Mal Y Pense ("Evil to Him Who Evil Thinks").
Great Britain	Merit	1902	Edward VII	Red and blue enamelled cross, central blue medallion bearing the motto For Merit in gold, encircled by laurel wreath; the addition of two crossed swords indicates naval and military members.
Great Britain	Thistle	1687	James II	For royalty and 16 Scottish nobles; 8-pointed star with figure of Saint Andrew and cross, and thistles on collar, motto Nemo Me Impune ("No One Harms Me With Impunity").
Italy	Annunziata	1362	Amadeus VI, Count of Savoy	Gold medal, representing the Annunciation, entwined with chain of knots and roses.
Netherlands	Netherlands Lion	1815	William I	8-pointed cross with gold W between the arms and a lion in the center.
Norway	Saint Olaf	1847	Oscar I	8-pointed white cross botonée, national arms on red ground.
Rome, See of	Christ	1318	Diniz of Portugal	Gold-edged Latin cross of red and white enamel, surmounted by 8-pointed star.
Rome, See of	Holy Sepulcher	1496?	Alexander VI	Red enamel cross potent with small crosses between the arms.
Spain	Alcantara	1215	Salamanca noblemen of Estremadura	Brown, leafless pear tree on gold field.
Spain	Calatrava	1158	Sancho III	Red fleur-de-lis cross.
Spain	Golden Fleece	1429	Philip the Good, Duke of Burgundy	Golden fleece suspended from flaming flintstone in enamel; motto Pretium Laborum non Vile ("Not Cheap Is the Reward of Labor").
Spain	Saint James of the Sword	1170?	Ramiro II, King of Leon?	Gold shield, with lily-hilted sword in cruciform.
Sweden	Seraphim	1285	Magnus I	8-pointed white cross, seraph's heads in angles; blue medallion with I.H.S.

Although certain religious orders such as the Knights of Saint John of Jerusalem (q.v.), fraternal or service orders such as the Knights of Pythias (q.v.), and various labor organizations and secret societies employ the word "knight" in their names, they are in no way related to the orders of knighthood.

The accompanying chart lists eighteen significant orders of knighthood.

KNIGHTS HOSPITALERS. See KNIGHTS OF SAINT JOHN OF JERUSALEM.

KNIGHTS OF COLUMBUS, chief organization of Roman Catholic laymen in the world, founded in Connecticut in 1882 as an American fraternal society for Roman Catholic men. The society was organized to promote benevolence and fraternity among its members, to encourage religious and racial tolerance and patriotism, and to further the interests of the Roman Catholic Church (q.v.). The Knights of Columbus has branches throughout the United States and its possessions, and also in Mexico, Cuba, the Philippines, Canada, Guatemala, Guam, and the Virgin Islands. It maintains an insurance plan for members; noninsured members are called associates. In 1973 membership totaled 1,165,681. An associated organization, the Circles of Columbian Squires, founded in 1928, is open to Roman Catholic boys between the ages of fourteen and eighteen and stresses leadership training.

KNIGHTS OF LABOR, THE NOBLE ORDER OF THE, American labor union, originally established as a secret fraternal order (q.v.). It is notable in United States labor history as the first organization of workers to advocate the inclusion in one union of all workers in the country. As its ideal, the Knights of Labor projected a society based on cooperative industrial and agricultural enterprises owned and operated by the workers, farmers, clerks, and technicians comprising them.

The Noble Order of the Knights of Labor was founded in Philadelphia, Pa., in 1869 by the American garment worker Uriah Smith Stephens (1821–82) and a number of his fellow workers. Workers in all trades were eligible for membership; physicians (prior to 1881), lawyers, bankers, professional gamblers or stockholders, and liquor dealers were excluded. For the first few years of its existence, the Knights of Labor functioned as a secret society using an elaborate, mystic ritual. It grew slowly until the economic depression of the 1870's, when large numbers of workingmen joined the organization. The secret and fraternal nature of the order was eliminated in 1881, and it began to function as a trade union. It adopted a policy of militant action against employers and played an important part in the strikes by coal miners and railroad workers in 1877.

The first general assembly of representatives of local organizations of the Knights of Labor met in Reading, Pa., in 1878. The assembly projected a number of sweeping reforms, including institution of the eight-hour workday, abolition of convict labor, prohibition of the employment of children under fourteen years of age, institution of equal opportunities and wages for women in industry, and establishment of a Bureau of Labor Statistics in the Federal government. The assembly also adopted the policy of inclusive unionism, whereby all workers, regardless of race, creed, craft, trade, or degree of skill, and all other individuals and groups expressing sympathy for labor were eligible for membership in the Knights of Labor.

For about five years after the convocation of the general assembly of 1878, the Knights of Labor employed the strike (q.v.) weapon on numerous occasions. During this period, however, the national leadership of the organization began to advocate the use of less radical measures. In 1883 Terence Vincent Powderly (1849–1924), an American machinist who was the order's leading exponent of moderate policies, was elected to head the organization.

In 1886 the membership began to decline rapidly, partly because of opposition by Powderly and other organization leaders to a one-day general strike as a means of winning the eight-hour day; see HOURS OF LABOR. Members were alienated also by their leaders' denunciation of the eight anarchists whose conviction for complicity in the Haymarket Square Riot (q.v.) in Chicago was widely believed to be unjust. Another factor contributing to membership decline was the defeat that the organization sustained in a strike against the railroads in the southwestern part of the U.S. Also in 1886 factional strife broke out between the members who continued to support the original policy of inclusive unionism and those who favored craft unionism; see TRADE UNIONS IN THE UNITED STATES.

Terence Vincent Powderly, General Master Workman of the Knights of Labor, is introduced to the 1886 convention of the organization in Richmond, Va. (contemporary engraving). Library of Congress

This dissension led to the secession of a number of large craft unions, which, in December of that year, participated in the organization of the American Federation of Labor (q.v.). The last important struggle in which the Knights of Labor participated was the 1894 strike by workers against many of the principal railroads of the U.S. The total defeat of this strike, due partly to the opposition of the American Federation of Labor, resulted in the virtual collapse of the Knights of Labor. The organization was formally dissolved in 1917.

KNIGHTS OF MALTA, name given to the Knights of Saint John of Jerusalem (q.v.), as a result of their long residence (1530–1798) on the island of Malta (q.v.).

KNIGHTS OF PYTHIAS, American benevolent society, founded in Washington, D.C. in 1864, to promote fraternity and universal brotherhood. The name Pythias is derived from the ancient Greek legend about Damon and Pythias (q.v.), and represents undying friendship. The Knights of Pythias support a wide variety of humanitarian causes: they maintain a home for the aged, indigent, and ill, a summer camp for poor boys, a broad scholarship fund, and provide financial and voluntary hospital aid.

Social activities are arranged by an auxiliary society, The Dramatic Order, Knights of Khorassan. Two other auxiliary societies are a junior order, for fourteen to eighteen year old boys, and the order of the Pythian Sisters, for women. An unaffiliated group, the Knights of Pythias of

KNIGHTS OF RHODES

North and South America, Europe, Asia, and Africa, has exclusively Negro membership.

The organization is governed by the Supreme Lodge, Knights of Pythias of the World. Subordinate to it are the grand lodges in various States, Canada, the Panama Canal Zone, the Philippine Islands, Alaska, and Israel. Members may attain to three ranks: page, esquire, and knight. Membership is about 250,000; headquarters are in New York City.

KNIGHTS OF RHODES, name given to the Knights of Saint John of Jerusalem (q.v.) from 1309 to 1523.

KNIGHTS OF SAINT JOHN OF JERUSALEM, known as HOSPITALERS or KNIGHTS HOSPITALERS, shorter forms of their full name, The Sovereign Military Order of the Hospital of Saint John of Jerusalem, of Rhodes, and of Malta. Historically the Knights Hospitalers were the protectors of a hospital built in Jerusalem before the first Crusade by the Blessed Gerard (d. 1120). The order was founded after the formation of the Latin Kingdom of Jerusalem, approved by Pope Paschal II (see under PASCHAL) in 1113, and again approved by Pope Eugene III (see under EUGENIUS) in 1153. The brothers were sworn to poverty, obedience, and chastity and to assistance in the defense of Jerusalem. Gerard, their first leader, was called rector; later heads of the order were called grand masters. Of necessity, the order became a military one, and the armed knights were of noble birth. They formed a community under the Rule of Saint Augustine (q.v.). At first devoted to the care of pilgrims and crusaders, the order left the Holy Land with the failure of the Crusades (q.v.).

Knights of Rhodes. After 1309 the order had its headquarters on the island of Rhodes. It formed a territorial state and its navy kept the eastern Mediterranean Sea free of Muslims. The properties of the Knights Templars (q.v.) were given to the order in 1312. The Knights of Rhodes, as they came to be called, formed national units of the order elsewhere; they were called Tongues (Fr. *Langues*). Forced to leave Rhodes when it was seized by Suleiman II (q.v.), ruler of the Ottoman Turks, in 1522, they had no home until 1530, when they were ceded the island of Malta (q.v.).

Knights of Malta. The order figured in European history until well into the 19th century. As the Knights of Malta, it lost its English and German properties during the Reformation (q.v.) and its French holdings during the French Revolution (q.v.). The Russians granted the order protection, but the French under Emperor Napoleon I (q.v.) seized Malta. The convent was moved to Trieste in 1798 and to Rome in 1834. By this time the Russians had confiscated all properties held by them in Russian territories.

The Knights of Malta, as recognized by Pope John XXIII (see under JOHN) in 1961, form a religious community and an order of chivalry; see also CHIVALRY. Organized in five grand priories and a number of national associations, they carry on diplomatic relations with the Vatican and with individual countries. As a religious community, they maintain hospitals, first-aid centers, and facilities to care for war casualties and refugees. They wear a black cloak on which is applied an eight-pointed Maltese cross. The grand master is titled prince and holds a church rank equal to that of a cardinal. The membership of the order was about 8000 in the late 1960's.

KNIGHTS OF THE GOLDEN CIRCLE, American secret society organized in the South in 1855 to promote slavery and to extend the institution, particularly into northern Mexico. Later, during the American Civil War, the society spread to Ohio, Illinois, and Indiana, and also functioned in the border states of Kentucky and Missouri. During the war, the Northern members militated for peace and for reducing the increasing powers of the Federal government. Public charges were made that the Northern groups were engaged in treasonable activities such as spying and planning armed insurrections against the Union. In 1863 the organization was renamed the Order of American Knights, and early in 1864 the group was reorganized as the Sons of Liberty under the leadership of the American politician Clement Laird Vallandigham (q.v.). In 1864 the membership reached a maximum, estimated to be between 200,000 and 300,000. Some of the members interfered with the Union war effort chiefly by hindering enlistments in the Union army and encouraging desertions from it. The society dissolved before the end of the war for several reasons, including an abortive attempt to free Confederate prisoners in Illinois and Ohio in the summer of 1864, the imminent Union victory, and strong opposition by some Northern governors. See CIVIL WAR, THE AMERICAN.

KNIGHTS TEMPLARS, members of a medieval religious and military order officially named the Order of the Poor Knights of Christ, and popularly known as the Knights of the Temple of Solomon or Knights Templars because their first quarters in Jerusalem adjoined a building known at the time as Solomon's Temple. The order developed from a small military band formed in Jerusalem in 1119 by two French knights, Hugh des Payens and Godfrey of Saint-Omer; its aim was to protect pilgrims visiting Palestine after the First Crusade (see CRUSADES). Military in purpose from its beginning, the order thus differed from the other two great 12th-century religious societies, the Knights of Saint John of Jerusalem (q.v.) and the Teutonic Knights (q.v.), which began as charitable institutions.

The Knights Templars obtained papal sanction for their order, and in 1128 at the ecclesiastical Council of Troyes they were given an austere rule closely patterned on that of the monastic order of Cistercians (q.v.). The Knights Templars were headed by a grand master, under whom were three ranks: knights, chaplains, and sergeants. The knights were the dominant members, and they alone were allowed to wear the distinctive dress of the order, a white mantle with a large red Latin cross on the back. The headquarters of the Knights Templars remained at Jerusalem until the fall of the city to the Muslims in 1187; it was later located successively at Antioch, Acre, Caesarea (qq.v.), and in Cyprus.

Banking Activities. Because the Knights Templars regularly transmitted money and supplies from Europe to Palestine, they developed an efficient banking system, upon which the rulers and nobility of Europe came to rely. The knights gradually became bankers for a large part of Europe and amassed great wealth. After the last Crusades had failed and interest had waned in an aggressive policy against the Muslims, the Knights Templars were no longer needed to police Palestine. Their immense riches and power had aroused the envy of secular as well as ecclesiastical powers, and in 1307 the impoverished Philip IV (q.v.), King of France, with the aid of Pope Clement V (see under CLEMENT), arranged for the arrest of the French Grand Master Jacques de Molay (1243?–1314) on charges of sacrilege and Satanism. Molay and the leading officers of the order confessed under torture and were eventually burned at the stake. The order was suppressed in 1312 by Clement V and its property assigned to the rival Knights Hospitalers, although most of it was in fact seized by Philip and by Edward II (q.v.), King of England, who disbanded the order in that country.

Knights Templars now are members of the York Rite of the Masonic system; see FREEMASONRY.

KNITTING, art of forming a fabric through the use of a needle or needles, by the interlocking of a yarn or yarns in a series of connected loops by means of hand or mechanized needles. Originally connected with the knotting of fishnets and snares by peoples of ancient times, the art of knitting did not develop in Europe until the 15th century. The Scots have claimed both its invention and its introduction to France.

All knitting was done by hand until 1598, when an English clergyman named William Lee (d. 1610) invented a machine that could knit stockings. Elizabeth I (q.v.), Queen of England, refused Lee a patent for his machine, considering the new invention a threat to many of the hand knitters in the country. The machine, however, was used in other countries, and paved the way for further improvements. The first addition came in 1758, when a British cotton spinner, Jedediah Strutt (1726–97), invented an attachment to the stocking frame that could produce ribbed goods. In 1816, the British engineer Marc Isambard Brunel (1769–1849), father of the more famous engineer Isambard Kingdom Brunel (q.v.), invented a circular knitting frame, to which he gave the name of *tricoteur*. The knitting of heavier yarns became possible when another British inventor, Matthew Townsend, introduced the latch needle, a needle having a latch-closed hook at one end, which was patented by him in 1858. In 1864, William Cotton, also in Great Britain, introduced an improvement in power machines known as Cotton's system. The improved machine was capable of shaping the heels and toes of hosiery, and laid the basis for the modern full-fashioned machines. Automatic knitting machines were first introduced in 1889.

See also LOOM; SEWING MACHINE; TEXTILES.

KNOSSOS or CNOSSUS, ancient city of Crete, on the N. side of the island, about 3 mi. from the coast, near the modern city of Iráklion. About 2000 B.C., Knossos was a center of the highly developed Aegean civilization (q.v.) of the Bronze Age. The city is frequently mentioned in Greek mythology; the Dictaean cave, legendary home of the infant Greek god Zeus (q.v.), is nearby, and the labyrinth, home of the monster known as the Minotaur (q.v.), is within the palace of Minos. The prehistoric culture of Crete is known as Minoan (q.v.), from Minos (q.v.), the name of several legendary kings of Knossos.

The city was founded before 3000 B.C. After about 1000 B.C. it was dominated by the Dorians (q.v.), and about the 3rd century B.C. it became a Roman colony. In modern times the city has been the site of extensive archeological investigations. The first excavations were made about 1900 by the British archeologist Sir Arthur John Evans (q.v.). Evans excavated the royal palace, the greatest of a series of magnificent buildings. Knossos' decline dates from the destruction of the palace by fire in 1400 B.C. See ARCHEOLOGY.

KNOTS AND ROPEWORK

KNOTS AND ROPEWORK, art of joining together pieces of such flexible objects as rope, and of forming loops or designs in ropes, string, or fibers. It is one of the oldest human skills, and may have a utilitarian or a decorative purpose; in some instances it has magical or religious significance.

The art of knotting and working with rope predates recorded history. It is a vital part of many trades and crafts and is particularly connected with the sailor's trade. The sailors who worked the large square-rigged cargo ships in the 19th century knew and used hundreds of knots and probably were the most accomplished practitioners of the craft. The total number of knots, bends, and hitches known amount to several thousand, many of them exceedingly complicated and each designed for a single specific purpose.

Although most rope joinings are commonly known as knots, the term should properly be limited to arrangements in which the rope is led through a loop formed by itself. Knots used to attach one rope to another or to attach a rope to an object are known as bends and hitches. Another division of ropework is splicing, in which a rope is joined to another or to itself by separating the strands and braiding them together. Ropes are frequently tied by various forms of seizings, which are secure windings of smaller string or rope. String is also used for whipping the end of a rope to prevent the strands from separating. Fancy ropework is the making of complicated decorative knots and the weaving and braiding of rope and string to produce ornamental objects or coverings. Sections of rope are sometimes protected against moisture and wear by worming, parceling, and serving. Worming consists of winding small cords or strings around the rope in the grooves between the individual strands, for an even surface. After worming, the rope is parceled by winding it with narrow strips of canvas, often tarred, to make a waterproof covering. Over the parceling (and wound in the opposite direction to the lay of the rope, the worming, and the parceling) is placed the serving, a protective layer of closely wound string.

Common Knots. The simplest of all knots is the overhand knot, formed by passing one end of a rope over and around the other end. The overhand knot is the basis for a wide variety of more complicated knots. The figure-of-eight knot, made by doubling the end of a rope to form a loop and passing the free end around and under the standing part and then through the loop, is the most decorative of all simple knots. Its practical use is confined to stopper knots on the ends of lines, but it is frequently incorporated into decorative rope designs.

The square knot, also known as the reef knot because of its use in tying reefs in ships' sails, is believed to be the oldest of all practical knots and is one of the most useful. The square knot is formed by tying two overhand knots, one on top of the other, in opposite directions, which brings the rope ends out of the knot at either end on the same side of the loop. If two overhand knots are tied in the same direction, the result is a granny knot, in which the rope ends come out of the knot on different sides of the loops. The granny is less secure than the square knot, and is more likely to jam if tension is applied to one end. Another variant on this simple knot is the fool's knot or thief knot, which is similar to the square knot except that the loose ends emerge diagonally from opposite corners of the knot. This kind of knot will slip if the slightest tension is placed on it.

The simplest form of sliding knot or slip knot is the running eye knot, made by tying a simple overhand knot around the body of the rope. The loop formed by the running eye knot can be made smaller by pulling on the standing part of the rope. The bowline is used for a fixed loop that will not slip. It is made by forming a loop in the rope some distance from the end and then passing the end of the rope through the loop, around the standing part, and back through the loop. The bowline has been called the king of knots; it will hold under tension, will never jam and can always be easily untied.

The bow knot in its simplest form is a modification of the square knot. The first overhand knot is tied with the ends of the rope as in the square knot, but in tying the second overhand knot the ends are doubled into loops and the knot is tied with the loops rather than the ends. The bow knot is simpler to untie than the square knot, because it can be loosened by pulling on the ends. It is also more decorative, and is frequently used for tying neckties, shoelaces, and packages. The bow knot can be tied either in square or granny form. The loops of the square bow knot are parallel to the standing part of the knot, whereas the loops of the granny bow knot are perpendicular to the standing part. The square bow knot is less likely to slip or to jam than the granny bow knot.

The sheepshank is used to shorten a rope temporarily. It is made by doubling a portion of the central part of the rope over on itself one or more times. At each end of the doubled-over portion a half-hitch is taken over the looped

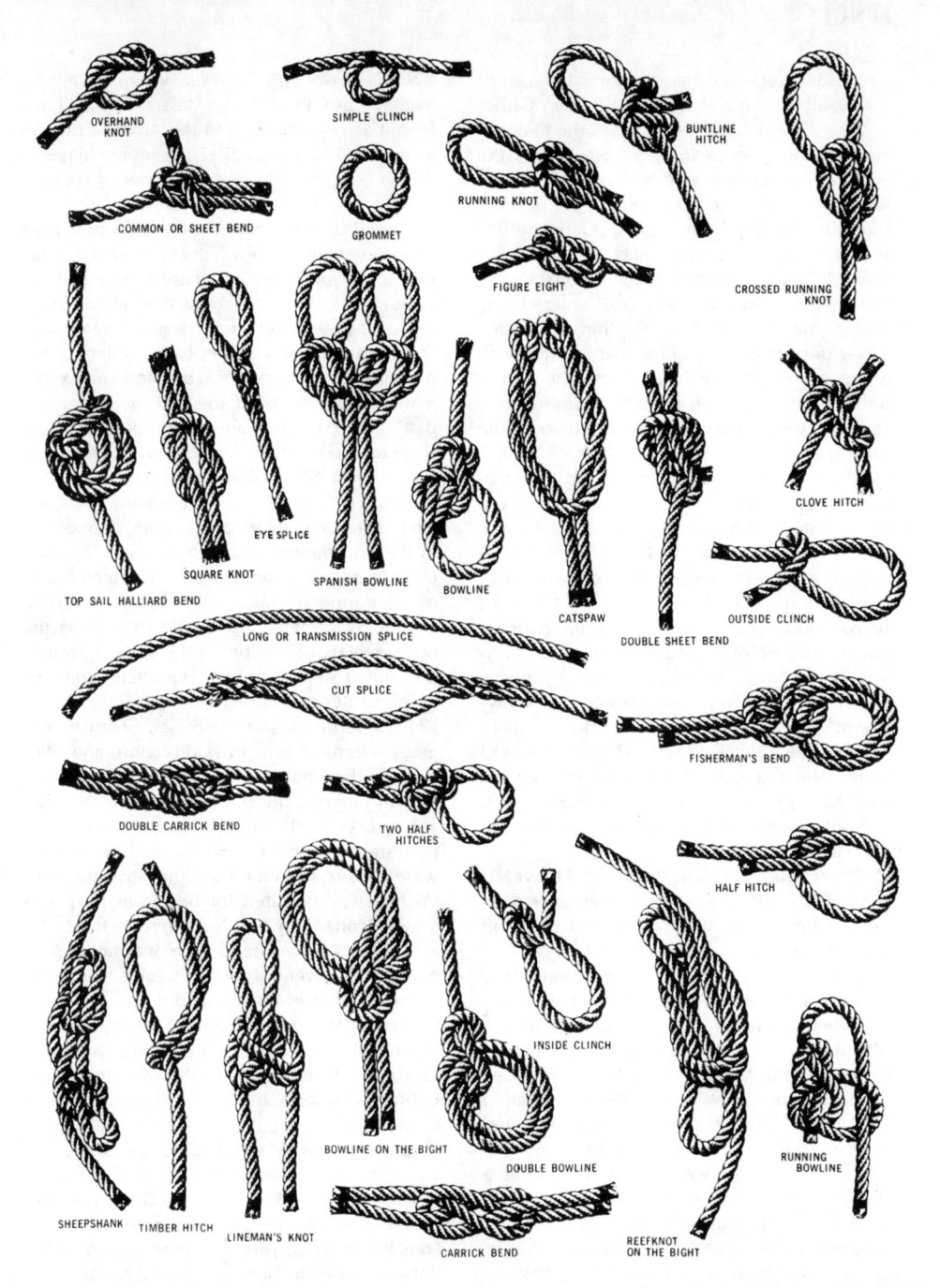

Common knots used by sailors and in various trades and crafts. — Whitlock

ends with the standing part of the rope. The half-hitches, which are formed by making a loop in the rope with the end portion under the standing part, hold the doubled-over part of the rope in place. Two half-hitches placed one on top of the other are frequently used to fasten a rope to a spar or other object.

KNOWLEDGE, THEORY OF. See EPISTEMOLOGY.

KNOW-NOTHINGS, in American history, popular name of a secret political party that existed from 1849 to about 1860. The party organized in

425

KNOX

clandestine societies that discriminated against immigrants and members of the Roman Catholic Church. Such societies included the Order of the Sons of America in Pennsylvania and the Order of the Star Spangled Banner in New York. The chief aims of the party were to prevent foreign-born citizens from holding political office and to check foreign influences and ideas. Between 1825 and 1855 more than 5,000,000 foreigners, mostly Roman Catholics, entered the United States. The Know-Nothings became powerful because of popular fear of a growing strength among these immigrants. The Know-Nothing Party acquired its name from its practice of secrecy; a member questioned about the party always answered "I don't know". In 1854 the group officially adopted the name American Party, and that same year its candidates won the governorships in Massachusetts and Delaware. The party was also quite successful in several State gubernatorial elections the following year. In the Presidential election of 1856, however, the party attempted to straddle the slavery issue and in so doing lost a great majority of its partisans in the North and West to the aggressive Republican Party (q.v.). As a result, the Know-Nothing candidate, former President Millard Fillmore (q.v.), received only 871,731 votes and carried only the State of Maryland. By 1861 the party had no representation in Congress, and soon afterward it totally disappeared from the political scene.

KNOX, Frank, in full WILLIAM FRANKLIN KNOX (1874–1944), American newspaper publisher and politician, born in Boston, Mass., and educated at Alma College. Knox began his newspaper career in 1898, and until 1900 worked successively as reporter, city editor, and circulation manager of the Grand Rapids (Mich.) *Herald*. In 1901, he became the owner of the Sault Sainte Marie (Mich.) *News*, and later, of newspapers in New Hampshire. From 1928 to 1931 he was manager of the chain of newspapers owned by the American publisher William Randolph Hearst (q.v.). After 1931 he acquired a controlling interest in the Chicago *Daily News*. Consistently active as a Republican in politics, Knox was active in Republican Party politics in Michigan and New Hampshire, and in 1936 he was nominated to run for the Vice-Presidency of the United States on a ticket headed by the American political leader Alfred M(ossman) Landon (q.v.). They were defeated by the Democratic Party ticket headed by President Franklin Delano Roosevelt (q.v.). In 1940 the President appointed Knox secretary of the navy, a post he held until his death.

KNOX, Henry (1750–1806), American military leader, born in Boston, Mass. In 1775 Knox fought as a volunteer with the American forces at Bunker Hill and at the subsequent siege of British-occupied Boston. Dorchester Heights, overlooking Boston, was fortified largely by means of artillery that Knox transported from Fort Ticonderoga, New York. The British were eventually forced to evacuate Boston in 1776. Commander in chief George Washington (q.v.) made Knox a brigadier general the same year and placed him in charge of the artillery of the American army. Knox took part in many of the major engagements of the war, including the battles of Princeton and Monmouth and the siege of Yorktown. He became major general in 1781; from 1782 to 1784 he was in command of the fortress of West Point, New York. Knox was United States secretary of war from 1785 to 1789 in the government established under the Articles of Confederation (q.v.); he remained in this office during the administration of President George Washington from 1789 to 1794 as the first secretary of war under the Constitution of the United States. See separate articles on many of the battles mentioned.

KNOX, John (about 1505–72), Scottish religious reformer, born in Haddington, and educated at the University of Glasgow. Originally a Roman Catholic priest, Knox became attracted about 1543 to the preachings of the Scottish Protestant reformer George Wishart (q.v.). Knox was called to the Protestant ministry and, after Wishart was executed for heresy in Saint Andrews, Scotland in 1546, preached in the castle and parish church there. Knox was taken prisoner in 1547 when a French fleet captured St. Andrews; he spent a year and a half in French galleys and was released only at the intercession of Edward VI (q.v.), King of England. On his return to England he joined the ministry of the Church of England, and in 1551 was appointed a royal chaplain.

Opposition to Mary Tudor. When Mary Tudor, a Catholic, became Mary I (q.v.), Queen of England, in 1553 Knox fled to Geneva, Switzerland, where he became acquainted with the French Protestant reformer John Calvin (q.v.). Knox remained in Geneva until 1559, except for a period in 1555 when he visited Scotland. After his return to Geneva from this visit, he carried on a correspondence with the Protestant nobles of Scotland, the Lords of the Congregation, and also wrote his treatise *The First Blast of the Trumpet against the Monstrous Regiment of Women* (1558), a polemic against government by women. This work was directed chiefly against the Catholic regent of Scotland, Mary of Guise (1515–60), ruling for her daughter Mary, Queen of Scots (q.v.).

When he returned to Scotland in 1559, Knox aided a Protestant revolt against the regency. His preaching at Perth and St. Andrews won those towns to his cause, and his labors in Edinburgh stimulated the development of a strong antigovernment party. The Protestant reformers, however, could not hope to succeed alone against the regent, who was supported by French troops. Knox therefore induced the

John Knox

queen of England, Elizabeth I (q.v.), to intervene. With English aid, and furthered by the death of Mary of Guise and the consequent withdrawal of French troops, the Protestant party came into control of the Scottish government. On Aug. 17, 1560, the Protestant reformers' Confession of Faith, written chiefly by Knox, was adopted by the Scottish parliament; it remained the authorized Scottish creed for two centuries. See CALVINISM; PRESBYTERIANISM; SCOTLAND, CHURCH OF.

The return to Scotland of the Roman Catholic Mary, Queen of Scots, in the following year revived all the old dissensions as well as created new ones. As minister of Saint Giles Cathedral in Edinburgh, Knox publicly condemned Mary's governmental policies and personal conduct. A sermon in St. Giles led to the first of a series of personal interviews between Mary and Knox, the record of which forms a remarkable portion of Knox's *History of the Reformation in Scotland* (published posthumously, 1586 and 1664).

Knox's violent opposition to Mary alienated one of his chief supporters, James Stewart, Earl of Moray (1531?–70), half brother to Mary and one of her principal advisers; the marriage (1565) of Mary and Henry Stewart, Lord Darnley (q.v.), a Catholic, reunited them, however, for both regarded it as a menace to the new Protestantism.

Final Years. The events of the next two years, including the murder of Darnley, Mary's marriage to James Hepburn, 4th Earl of Bothwell (q.v.), and her flight into England, gave control of national affairs to the Protestant party. Moray became regent, and the acts of 1560 in favor of the reformed religion were ratified by the Scottish parliament. Knox's influence remained a formidable force, and his sermons at the 1567 coronation of James VI of Scotland, later James I (q.v.), King of England, and at the opening of the Scottish parliament had the importance of public manifestos.

In 1572 Knox retired to St. Andrews after a paralytic stroke. There he completed his last book, *An Answer to a Scottish Jesuit* (1572).

See also SCOTLAND: *History.*

KNOX, Philander Chase (1853–1921), American lawyer and politician, born in Brownsville, Pa., and educated at Mount Union College. Knox was admitted to the Ohio bar in 1875. In the course of his law practice in Pittsburgh, Pa., he became known as one of the most successful corporation lawyers in the country. In 1892, during the steel strike in Homestead (q.v.), Pa., he was counsel for the Carnegie Steel Corporation, and in 1901 was appointed United States attorney general by President Theodore Roosevelt (q.v.). During his tenure of office he toured Latin America; his attempts to protect American financial interests abroad came to be known as "dollar diplomacy" and were often criticized.

KNOXVILLE, city in Tennessee, and county seat of Knox Co., on the Tennessee R., 110 miles N.E. of Chattanooga. It is served by railroad and a municipal airport. Knoxville is the largest city in E. Tennessee and is an important commercial and manufacturing center. The surrounding agricultural area produces tobacco, fruits, corn, small grains, livestock, poultry, and dairy products. In the vicinity of the city are large marble quarries and coal, iron, zinc, and copper mines. Industrial establishments in Knoxville include railroad shops, tobacco warehouses, and plants manufacturing wearing apparel, finished marble, cement, furniture, plastics, aluminum, and steel products. The city is the site of the University of Tennessee (see TENNESSEE, UNIVERSITY OF), Knoxville College, which was established in

Koala, Phascolarctos cinereus — Air France

1875, and the Tennessee School for the Deaf. Among the places of interest in Knoxville is the home, built in 1792, of William Blount (q.v.), governor of Tennessee before it became a State. The site of Knoxville was first settled in 1786. In 1791 a town was laid out and named in honor of Henry Knox (q.v.), then secretary of war of the United States. Knoxville was capital of the territory from 1792 to 1796 and capital of the State from 1796 to 1812 and from 1817 to 1819. During the American Civil War the city fell to Federal troops, who successfully withstood a Confederate siege from Nov. 16 to Dec. 4, 1863. Pop. (1960) 111,827; (1970) 174,587.

KOALA, or AUSTRALIAN NATIVE BEAR or AUSTRALIAN NATIVE SLOTH, common name for an arboreal marsupial animal, *Phascolarctos cinereus,* belonging to the Phalanger family. In appearance the animal somewhat resembles the toy Teddy Bear, which was modeled after it; in habits it somewhat resembles a sloth. The koala reaches a maximum length of about 2½ ft. and has a maximum life-span of about twenty years. It has a large, round head with large, round, furry ears, and a stout body covered with thick ashy gray fur. The animal has a vestigial tail. Its legs are short; its "hands" and "feet" are large, and each has five toes, two of which are opposable to the other three. Each toe bears a strong claw. The female gives birth to one young at a time. The young koala is kept in the marsupial pouch for about six months after birth, at the end of which time the female carries it upon her back until it is about half grown. Koalas are found only in eucalyptus forests of eastern Australia. The animals frequent high eucalyptus trees, feeding only on the leaves and flowers of certain species of eucalyptus. The animal is lethargic, and often remains in the same tree for days. The males are more active than the females and feed during the day; the females sleep all day and feed at night. Koalas sleep curled up on the limbs of trees, firmly grasping the limbs with their specially adapted "hands" and "feet". The animal does not relax its hold even when it is mortally wounded by gunfire. Koalas were formerly killed for their soft, thick fur, sold in the United States as "wombat" fur; they are now protected by laws in Australia. A wounded koala whimpers like a hurt child. In captivity koalas are gentle animals which make excellent pets. They are so sedentary that they will not run off, even when kept in unfenced eucalyptus regions, as they are in several Australian parks.

KOBE, city and chief commercial port in Japan, and capital of Hyogo Prefecture, on Osaka Bay on Honshu Island, at the western end of the 30-mile metropolitan industrial area that includes Osaka. Since the 1890's several adjoining cities, including Hyogo, have been absorbed by Kobe. Agricultural produce of the locality includes rice and other grains, fruits and vegetables, and tea. Shipbuilding and rubber goods are primary among the manufactures of the city. Chemicals, machinery, electrical equipment, textiles, refined sugar, flour, and sake are also produced.

Behind the narrow coastal site of the city are mountains on which suburban residences and hotels have been built. Many Christian churches, Shinto and Buddhist temples and shrines, two famous statues of Buddha, a fine arts museum, and a municipal museum with a collection on Western cultural contact are in Kobe. The city did not become important until the 1860's when Japan was opened to foreign trade. Before that time Hyogo, now a part of Kobe, had for centuries been a major Japanese port. Pop. (1970) 1,289,000.

KØBENHAVN. See COPENHAGEN.

KOBLENZ or **COBLENZ,** city of West Germany, in Rhineland-Palatinate State, at the junction of the Mosel and Rhine rivers, about 35 miles N.W. of Frankfurt-am-Main. Koblenz is an important center of tourism and of trade, particularly in German wines. The principal industries include the manufacture of machinery, pianos, paper, textiles, and chemicals. Among the principals buildings are the Church of Saint Castor, completed in 1208; the house where the Austrian statesman Prince Klemens von Metternich (q.v.) was born in 1773; and a palace, completed in 1786.

History. Originally a Roman military outpost, constructed about 9 B.C., the town that subsequently developed on the site was a residence of Carolingian (q.v.) kings. In the 13th century the city was a prosperous member of the league formed by the Rhenish cities to promote their common commercial and political interests.

After the French Revolution, Koblenz became a French possession and was later made the chief town of the department of Rhine and Moselle. Following the defeat of Napoleon I (q.v.), Emperor of France, the Congress of Vienna awarded Koblenz to Prussia; see VIENNA, CONGRESS OF. In 1822 it was made the capital of the Rhine Province of Prussia. After World War I Koblenz was the headquarters of the Allied Rhineland High Commission and was occupied for a time by American and French troops. Because of its importance as a rail and manufacturing center, the city was heavily damaged during World War II. After the defeat of Germany in 1945, the city of Koblenz was included in the French zone of occupation.

Pop. (1970) 120,100.

KOCH, Robert (1843–1910), German physician and bacteriologist, born in Clausthal-Zellenfeld, and educated at the University of Göttingen. He practiced medicine at Wollstein between 1872 and 1880, when he became a professor at the School of Medicine at Berlin. In 1885 he was appointed professor at the University of Berlin and director of the Institute of Health, and in 1891 he was appointed director of the Institute for Infectious Diseases in Berlin. While he was still in medical practice at Wollstein, Koch began bacteriological research. In 1876 he isolated the bacillus that causes the disease known as anthrax (q.v.); seven years later he discovered a method of preventive inoculation against the disease. In 1882 he succeeded in isolating the tuberculosis (q.v.) bacillus, and in 1883, while on an official mission to Egypt and India to study cholera, he identified the comma bacillus as the cause of Asiatic cholera (see CHOLERA, ASIATIC). In 1890 Koch produced a substance called tuberculin, which he at first considered to be a cure for tuberculosis, but which proved to be useful only in the diagnosis of the disease. He also investigated the cattle plague or rinderpest in South Africa and in 1896 developed a means of vaccination against the disease. He investigated bubonic plague (see PLAGUE) in Bombay and malaria (q.v.) and sleeping sickness in Africa. Koch's improved methods of bacteriological investigation and his many valuable discoveries gave great impetus to the development of the science of bacteriology (q.v.). He was awarded the 1905 Nobel Prize in medicine and physiology. Koch was a prolific writer; his works were collected and published posthumously in 1912.

KOCHER, Emil Theodor (1841–1917), Swiss surgeon, born in Bern, and educated at the universities of Bern, Berlin, Paris, and London. He taught at the University of Bern from 1866 until his death, becoming professor and director of the university surgical clinic in 1872. Kocher was the first surgeon to treat goiter (q.v.) by removing the thyroid gland. His later work included pathological studies of the thyroid and stomach, research on hernia and osteomyelitis (qq.v.) and the development of techniques for numerous surgical operations. He received the 1909 Nobel Prize in medicine and physiology. Among his writings are several texts on surgical procedure.

KOCHI, city in Japan, and capital of Kochi Prefecture, on Shikoku Island, at the mouth of the Kagami R. on Urado Bay, an inlet of Tosa Bay, about 90 miles S.E. of Hiroshima. Urado, its port, ships dried bonito, paper, lumber, and cement. Kochi processes fish, brews sake, and produces raw silk and ornamental coral. The city is the site of a medieval castle; nearby are beaches, boating facilities, and the Ryugado Cave. Pop. (1970) 240,481.

KODÁLY, Zoltán (1882–1967), Hungarian composer, folkmusic collector, and music educator, born in Kecskemét, and educated at the University of Budapest and the Budapest Academy of Music. Beginning about 1905 he and the Hungarian composer Béla Bartók (q.v.) collected and popularized Hungarian folkmusic, which had been forgotten for centuries by the educated classes. In his compositions Kodály quoted or imitated the forms, harmonies, rhythms, and melodic shapes of Hungarian folkmusic. His finest works include the *Psalmus Hungaricus* ("Hungarian Psalm", 1923) for tenor, chorus, and orchestra, the opera Háry János (1926), *Galántai táncok* ("Dances of Galánta", 1933) for orchestra, and the *Missa brevis* ("Short Mass", 1945). After 1945 he developed a system of music education for the public schools of Hungary. His method, which emphasizes the singing of songs either borrowed from or based on folkmusic, has been adopted by many schools in the United States and elsewhere.

KODIAK, largest island of the Kodiak archipelago in the Gulf of Alaska, about 40 miles S.E. of the Alaska Peninsula, from which it is separated by Shelikof Strait. The island is 100 mi.

long and from 10 to 16 mi. wide, with a greatly indented coastline. The archipelago was discovered about 1762 by a Russian fur trader, Stepan Gottov. The first Russian colony in North America was founded in 1784 at Three Saints Bay, on S.E. Kodiak Island, and until 1804 the colony was the center of Russian activity in Alaska. In 1867, when the United States purchased Alaska from the Russian Empire, Kodiak became an American possession. Grass is abundant, and the land is used extensively for cattle grazing. Salmon fishing is the chief industry. The island is noted as the habitat of the large, brown Kodiak bear. The principal city is Kodiak City, (pop., 1970, 3798). Population of the island, 1970, 6357. Area, 3465 sq.mi.

KOESTLER, Arthur (1905–), British novelist, journalist, and essayist, born in Budapest, Hungary, and educated at the University of Vienna. During the 1920's and 1930's he was a foreign correspondent for a number of European newspapers. He joined the Communist Party in 1931, but left it in disillusionment in 1937. During World War II he served in the British army and afterwards became a British subject.

His first novel, *The Gladiators* (1939), uses the theme of a revolution that failed. During the 1930's he was twice imprisoned, in Spain and France, and during the Spanish Civil War was condemned to death in Spain but later released. His period under sentence of death inspired *Reflections on Hanging* (1957). His best-known work is *Darkness at Noon* (1941), a novel based on the Moscow purges and political trials in the 1930's. The book was translated into thirty languages and in 1951 became a successful play. *Arrow in the Blue* (1952) and *The Invisible Writing* (1954) are autobiographical works. In *The Ghost in the Machine* (1968) Koestler hypothesized that mankind's apparent urge for self-destruction may be explained on a physiological basis, especially in the pathology of the brain. *The Call Girls* (1973) is a tragicomic novel about the survival of mankind.

KOFFKA, Kurt. See Gestalt Psychology.

KOFORIDUA, city in Ghana, and capital of the Eastern Province, near the Densu R., 37 miles N. of Accra. The city is on the Accra-Kumasi rail line and is a road and trade center. It ships cocoa, processes palm products, and manufactures furniture. The surrounding area produces cacao, palm products, kola nuts, corn, and cassava. Pop. (1970) 69,804.

KOFU, city in Japan, and capital of Yamanashi Prefecture, on Honshu Island, about 75 miles w. of Tokyo. Industries include the growing of silkworm cocoons and the manufacture of raw silk and crystal ware. Grapes are grown in the rich agricultural plain on which Kofu lies. Recent development of the hot springs and of the natural surroundings have resulted in a growth of tourism. Fuji (q.v.) lies about 30 miles s. of Kofu. Pop. (1970) 182,669.

KOH-I-NOOR. See Diamond: *Famous Diamonds.*

KOHLER, Kaufmann (1843–1926), American rabbi and educator, born in Fürth, Germany, and educated at the universities of Munich, Leipzig, Berlin, and Erlangen. In 1869 Kohler emigrated to the United States and was chosen rabbi of the Beth El Congregation in Detroit, Mich. Two years later he went to Chicago, and he was rabbi of Temple Sinai there until 1879, when he succeeded as rabbi of the congregation of Temple Beth-El in New York City. In 1885 he was instrumental in calling a rabbinical conference held in Pittsburgh, Pa., which formulated a platform that first embodied the principles of American Reform Judaism. From 1903 until 1922 he served as president of Hebrew Union College in Cincinnati, Ohio. A well-known Jewish scholar, Kohler was one of the editors of the *Jewish Encyclopedia* and wrote several textbooks on Reform Judaism, including *Backwards or Forwards — Lectures on Reform Judaism* (1885).

KÖHLER, Wolfgang. See Gestalt Psychology.

KOHLRABI, common name of *Brassica oleracea,* var. *caulorapa,* a variety of cabbage (q.v.).

Kohlrabi, Brassica oleracea

The edible portion of kohlrabi is the swollen, turniplike, green or purple stem. The plant is harvested while the stems are small and tender; if allowed to mature, the stems become woody and develop a strong flavor. Kohlrabi is grown from seed and is usually planted for early spring or fall harvesting.

KOKIU, city of the People's Republic of China, in Yünnan Province, in the Red R. valley, about 125 miles S.E. of Kunming. The leading tin-mining center of China, the city is linked by rail to Hanoi and to the port of Haiphong, both in North Vietnam. The products of the tin-smelting and -processing plants of Kokiu are also exported by rail through Kunming. The name of the city is sometimes spelled Kochiu. Pop. (1970 est.) 250,000.

KOKOMO, city in Indiana, and county seat of Howard Co., on Wildcat Creek, 50 miles N. of Indianapolis. Kokomo is a manufacturing center, producing automobile parts and accessories, machinery, and aluminum die castings. The city is the site of a regional campus of Indiana University. The American inventor Elwood Haynes (q.v.) built one of the first American automobiles at Kokomo in 1893, and the first trial run of the automobile took place there in 1894. In addition, the city was among the first to manufacture pneumatic rubber tires, aluminum castings, and stainless steel. Kokomo was settled in 1842 and named after a chief of the Miami (q.v.) Indians, who inhabited the region at the time. It became the county seat in 1844 and was incorporated as a city in 1865. Pop. (1960) 47,197; (1970) 44,042.

KOKOSCHKA, Oskar (1886–   ), Austrian-British painter, born in Pöchlarn (then part of Austria-Hungary). He studied art in Vienna in 1906 and 1907, and was a professor at the Dresden Academy from 1918 to 1924. One of the early exponents of the style of expressionism (q.v.) in German painting, Kokoschka began by painting psychologically penetrating portraits of Viennese physicians, architects, and artists. Among the works he did then is his "Self-Portrait" (1913, Museum of Modern Art, New York City). This phase of his work gradually gave way to a period of robust, brilliantly colored landscapes and figure pieces, painted with great freedom and exuberance. Many of them are views of harbors, mountains, and cities. Examples from this period include "Harbor of Marseilles" (1925, City Art Museum of Saint Louis, Mo.) and "View of Cologne" (1956, Wallraf-Richartz-Museum, Cologne, Germany).

Kokoschka, one of the artists denounced by the National Socialist government of Germany

Oskar Kokoschka, self-portrait, 1966.
Marlborough-Gerson Gallery

as degenerate, moved to England in 1938 and became a British subject in 1947. Best known as a painter, Kokoschka is also a writer. His literary works include poetry and plays not translated into English and the collection of short stories *Spur im Treibsand* (1956; Eng. trans., *A Sea Ringed with Visions*, 1962).

KOKURA. See KITAKYUSHU.

KOLA NUT. See COLA NUT.

KOLAR GOLD FIELDS, city of India, in Mysore State, 45 miles E. of Bangalore. The city is a rail-spur terminus and the center of the gold-mining region of India, which began operations in 1882. The city comprises several mining and industrial areas and the residential section of Robertsonpet. Industries include gold and silver processing, tanning, tobacco curing, meat processing, and brick and tile manufacturing. A commercial college is located here. Pop. (1971) 185,136.

KOLCHAK, Aleksandr Vasilievich (1874–1920), Russian admiral and counterrevolutionist, born in Saint Petersburg (now Leningrad), and educated at the Russian naval academy. Kolchak entered the Russian navy in 1888, served with distinction in the Russo-Japanese War of 1904–05, and was appointed rear admiral in command of the Baltic fleet during World War I. In 1917 he was promoted to the rank of vice-admiral and

431

placed in command of the Black Sea fleet. After the Bolshevik Revolution of November, 1917 (see BOLSHEVISM), he organized a counterrevolutionary army in Siberia and assumed the title of Supreme Ruler of Russia, establishing his capital at Omsk. During 1918 and early 1919 he scored a number of successes against the Soviet armies, but in November, 1919, he lost Omsk to the Soviets. Kolchak transferred his government farther east to Irkutsk, but the citizens of that city refused to accept his rule and set up a socialist government instead. Kolchak was compelled to resign, and he transferred the command of his armies to the anti-Bolshevik general Anton Ivanovich Denikin (1872–1947). Shortly afterward Kolchak was captured and executed by the Soviet forces.

KOLHAPUR, city of India, in Maharashtra State, about 200 miles S.E. of Bombay. Pottery, paper, and textiles are manufactured in the city. In about the 3rd century B.C., Kolhapur was an important Buddhist religious center. The city was the capital of the former princely State of Kolhapur, which became part of the Republic of India in August, 1947. The former State, which extended from the Western Ghats mountains E. to the Deccan plain, was a stronghold of the Hindu people known as Marathas (q.v.). Pop. (1971) 259,068.

KOLLÁR, Jan (1793–1852), Slovak poet and scholar, born in Mošovce, Slovakia (now in Czechoslovakia). Kollár was instrumental in developing Slovak as a literary language; his principal work was a cycle of patriotic sonnets, *Daughter of Slava* (1824). He also compiled a collection of Slovakian folk songs (2 vol., 1823–27) and wrote a philological work in German on root forms and dialects of the Slovak language (1837). See CZECH LANGUAGE; CZECH LITERATURE: *Fourth Period.*

KOLLWITZ, Käthe Schmidt (1867–1945), German artist, born in Königsberg (now Kaliningrad, U.S.S.R.), and educated in Berlin and Königsberg. In 1898 her illustrations for *Die Weber* ("The Weavers"), a play by the German playwright Gerhart Hauptmann (q.v.), first presented the figures of a mother, a child, and death, dominant motives in all her work. Almost exclusively a graphic artist, Käthe Kollwitz produced in her etchings, woodcuts, and lithographs sensitive and compassionate portrayals of the toil of the working classes. Her work, based upon bitter and tragic subjects and drawn with monumental simplicity, was denounced by the National Socialist regime in Germany, and she lived in virtual seclusion from 1933 until her death.

KOLMAR. See COLMAR.
KÖLN. See COLOGNE.
KOL NIDRE. See PRAYER, JEWISH.
KOLOZSVÁR. See CLUJ.
KOLWEZI, town of the Republic of Zaire (formerly the Democratic Republic of the Congo), in Katanga Province, 150 miles N.W. of Lubumbashi. The town is on the Benguela Railway and is the center of a major copper- and cobalt-mining area; uranium, radium, oxide ores, and lime deposits also occur. In the town are concentrating plants for copper and cobalt ores, which are then shipped by rail to Likasi, 85 mi. to the E., for processing. Kolwezi is also the trade center for the surrounding agricultural area. Pop. (1970 est.) 25,000.

KOMANDORSKIYE ISLANDS, or COMMANDER ISLANDS, group of four islands of the Soviet Union, lying E. of the peninsula of Kamchatka in the Bering Sea. They are administered as part of the Kamchatka Oblast, in the Russian S.F.S.R. Beringa (607 sq.mi.) is the largest island; the others are Mednyy (180 sq.mi.) and two small uninhabited islands (63 sq.mi. together). These islands and the American Pribilof Islands (q.v.) are the sole remaining Bering Sea breeding grounds of the fur seal. Although the climate of the islands is comparatively mild, only a few Russians and Aleuts inhabit them.

KOMI AUTONOMOUS SOVIET SOCIALIST REPUBLIC, subdivision of the Soviet Union, in the Russian S.F.S.R., located in the N.E. portion of European Russia. Part of Komi lies N. of the Arc-

"Death Tears a Child From Its Mother", lithograph by Käthe Kollwitz. Collection the Museum of Modern Art— Mrs. John D. Rockefeller, Jr. Purchase Fund

tic Circle in the tundra, a region in which reindeer breeding is the chief occupation. South of the tundra are vast forests, which comprise two thirds of the area of the republic. The principal products from Komi are lumber, coal, asphalt, and building materials. Hunting, fishing, and livestock raising are other sources of income. The inhabitants, known as Komi or Zyrians, speak the Finno-Ugric languages (q.v.). Syktyvkar is the administrative center of the republic, which was constituted as such in 1936. Area, 160,540 sq.mi.; pop. (1970) 965,000.

KOMODO DRAGON or KOMODO LIZARD. See Monitor.

KOMSOMOL. See Union of Soviet Socialist Republics: *Government: The Communist Party.*

KOMSOMOL'SK, city of the Soviet Union, in the Russian S.F.S.R., on the Amur R., about 600 miles N.E. of Vladivostok, and about 150 miles N. of the border between the U.S.S.R. and China. Principal industries are shipbuilding, tanning, woodcutting, and the manufacture of steel, tin, and machinery. Komsomol'sk was built, beginning in 1932, by members of the Communist youth organization known as the Komsomol. The city expanded greatly after World War II. Pop. (1970) 218,000.

KÖNIGSBERG. See Kaliningrad.

KONOYE, Prince Fumimaro (1891–1945), Japanese prime minister and diplomat, a descendant of the noble Fujiwara clan, born in Tokyo, and educated at Kyoto Imperial University. Prince Konoye was a member of the Japanese delegation to the Paris Peace Conference in 1919 after World War I. He returned to Japan and entered the House of Peers, becoming president of that body in 1933. Prince Konoye abstained from party politics, tacitly supporting the military leaders who acquired control of the government. In 1937, shortly before the beginning of the Sino-Japanese War, he became prime minister. Although he resigned in 1938 as a protest against Japanese militarists, he was again chosen prime minister in 1940. In the same year he aligned Japan with the Axis powers (q.v.). Before the United States entered World War II he offered to negotiate with United States diplomats, but was forced out of office and replaced by General Hideki Tojo (q.v.) in late 1941. After the war Prince Konoye was arrested as a war criminal by the Allied powers. In December, 1945, he committed suicide.

See Japan: *History: War with China.*

KONRAD VON WÜRZBURG (about 1220–87), Middle High German poet, born probably in Würzburg. He lived and worked chiefly in Strasbourg. Konrad von Würzburg was the author of short literary or art epics (see Epic Poetry), and of legends, poetic narratives, and romances. Many of his writings were derived from older Latin and French sources. Konrad von Würzburg's work marked the transition in German literature from the period of the Minnesingers to that of the Meistersinger (qq.v.). Among his writings were *Der Schwanritter* ("The Knight of the Swan"), a tale later adapted by the German composer Richard Wagner (q.v.) for the libretto of his opera *Lohengrin; Die Goldene Schmiede* ("The Golden Smithy"); *Der Welt Lohn* ("The Reward of the World"); and the unfinished *Trojanerkrieg* ("The Trojan War").

KONSTANZ or CONSTANCE, city of West Germany, in Baden-Württemberg, on the Rhine R. at its exit from the Lake of Constance, and contiguous to the Swiss commune of Kreuzlingen. Two old city gates mark the remains of its ancient fortifications. The cathedral, founded in the 11th century and rebuilt in the 15th, has fine hand-carved oak portals and choir stalls. It was there that the religious reformer John Huss (q.v.) was sentenced to be burned at the stake. Notable secular buildings include the Kaufhaus, containing the hall in which the conclave of cardinals met to elect a pope at the time of the Council of Constance (see Constance, Council of) in 1417; the Rosgarten, the former guildhall of the butchers, containing an interesting museum; the town hall, with the ancient city archives; and the Barbarossa Inn, where Frederick I (q.v.), Holy Roman Emperor, known as Frederick Barbarossa, signed a treaty with the cities of the Lombard League in 1183. The principal industries in Konstanz are the manufacture of linen and cotton goods, carpets, and chemicals.

History. The Roman *Constantia* was known as early as the 3rd century. In 570 it was made the seat of a bishopric, which existed as one of the most powerful in Germany until its suppression in 1821. In 780 Konstanz was given municipal rights and in 1192 was made a free imperial city. Because it had joined the Schmalkaldic League (q.v.), the city was deprived of its imperial privileges in 1548 and presented to Ferdinand, Archduke of Austria, later Ferdinand I (q.v.), Holy Roman Emperor. In 1805 Konstanz was given to Baden. In 1945, during World War II, the city was taken by the French first army, and was subsequently included in the French Zone of Occupation. Pop. (1970) 61,600.

KONYA, or KONIA, city in Turkey, and capital of Konya Province, on the Plain of Konya, about 150 miles S. of Ankara. The city produces carpets and leather and carries on trade in minerals. The surrounding area is noted for the breeding of horses and camels. Konya has irrigated gardens, several fine mosques, and a monastery of the Maulawiyah, or dancing dervishes, with the tomb of Jalal-ud-din Rumi (1207–73), the founder of that group; see DERVISH.

Under the Persian Empire, Konya, then called Iconium, was the frontier city of Phrygia. The Romans joined it to Lycaonian district and made it the capital. Saint Paul and Barnabas (qq.v.) preached there. At that time it probably had a considerable Jewish population and became the center from which Christianity spread in south Galatia. In Byzantine times it was the seat of an archbishop. Konya was the scene of a defeat of the Ottoman Turks by the Egyptians in 1832. Pop. (1970) 200,760.

KOO, Vi Kyuin Wellington, original name KU WEI-CHUN (1888–   ), Chinese diplomat and statesman, born in Shanghai, and educated at Columbia University. From 1915 to 1922 he was successively Chinese minister to Mexico, the United States, and Great Britain. He served as Chinese minister plenipotentiary to the Paris Peace Conference in 1919, after World War I. From 1922 to 1924 he was minister for foreign affairs and acting prime minister and from 1926 to 1927 minister of finance. In 1931 he once more became minister for foreign affairs. From 1932 to 1934 he represented China at the League of Nations (q.v.). Koo was Chinese minister, then ambassador, to France (1932–41), and ambassador to Great Britain (1941–46) and to the U.S. (1946–56). In 1946 Koo headed the Chinese delegation to the first General Assembly meeting of the United Nations (q.v.). He was senior adviser to Nationalist Chinese president Chiang Kai-shek (q.v.) from 1956 until he was elected judge of the International Court of Justice in 1957. He retired from the court in 1966.

KOODOO. See KUDU.

KOOKABURRA, common name for several species of birds in the kingfisher family, Alcedinidae, living in Australia and New Guinea. The kookaburra, a stocky grayish bird about 12 in. in length, is the largest member of the family. It rarely catches fish, living mainly on large insects, mice, small birds, and small snakes. It is sometimes nicknamed "laughing jackass" because its call sounds like loud laughter. The most common species in Australia is *Dacelo novaeguineae*, however, in northern Australia the blue-winged kookaburra, *D. leachii,* predominates. Two other species of kookaburra live in New Guinea. The bird is heard at dawn, noon and dusk; hence its name of "bushman's clock".

KOOTENAI *or* **KOOTENAY. 1.** River of Canada and the United States, rising in the Rocky Mts. of S.E. British Columbia. The Kootenai (spelled Kootenay in Canada) flows in an arc S. into Lincoln County, Mont., then N.W. through Idaho, and across the Canadian border again through Kootenay Lake to its confluence with the Columbia River (q.v.). Among important towns on the river, which is 400 mi. long, are Libby, Mont.; Bonners Ferry, Idaho; Creston, B.C.; and Nelson, B.C. **2.** Long narrow lake in S.E. British Columbia. It is about 60 mi. long and from 1 to 4 mi. wide and covers an area of about 220 sq.mi. The surrounding region is noted for its scenic beauty. **3.** Canadian national park, in the Rocky Mts. of British Columbia near the Alberta boundary, S.W. of Banff. The park contains the sources of the Kootenay R. Area, 587 sq.mi.

KOPEYSK, city of the Soviet Union, in the Russian S.F.S.R., 8 miles S.E. of Chelyabinsk. The major lignite-mining center in the vicinity includes the Gornyak suburb of Kopeysk. Mining excavators and agricultural machinery are manufactured. A mining settlement called Ugolnye Kopi was established here before 1917; the name was changed to Goskopi and then to Kopi between 1928 and 1933. The city was chartered in the latter year. The name is sometimes spelled Kopeisk. Pop. (1970) 156,000.

KORAN (Ar. *Qur'ān,* from *qara'a,* "to read"), *or* ALCORAN, sacred Scripture of Islam (q.v.). The name was applied by Muhammad (q.v.) to each individual portion of the revelations which, according to the beliefs of the religion, he received from Allah (q.v.), or God, but the name was later used for the book containing all the divine revelations given to Muhammad. Whenever Muhammad told of his revelations, secretaries wrote them down and his followers memorized them. The whole collection as it is now was compiled by his followers a few years after his death in 632. An authorized version was produced in the early 650's by a group of Arabic scholars under Othman; see CALIPH: *The Immediate Successors.* They destroyed variant copies, some of which are now accepted.

The Koran is the earliest known work in Arabic prose; it is divided into 114 *suras* (chapters) of various lengths, and contains the Islamic religious, social, civil, commercial, military, and legal codes. The chief doctrines laid down in the Koran are: only one God and one true religion exists; all men will undergo a final judgment, and the just will be rewarded with eternal bliss and the sinners punished; when mankind turned from truth, God sent prophets to lead the way back, and the greatest of the prophets were Moses, Jesus Christ, and Muhammad. Punishments and rewards are depicted with vivid imagery and are exemplified by stories, many of which also are found in the Jewish and Christian Scriptures and Apocrypha. Laws and directions and admonitions to virtue also parallel those of the Jewish writings.

Accepted by Muslims as the miraculous utterance of the Almighty, the Koran is regarded as above criticism and a work not to be proved but itself the standard of merit. The tone of the book is authoritative and dogmatic throughout; the second chapter opens, "This is the book in which there is no doubt. . . ." Copies of the Koran are treated by Muslims with great reverence; they are never held below the girdle and are not touched without prior purification of the person. Texts from the Koran are characteristic decorations for banners, buildings, weapons, and other objects; see ISLAMIC ART AND ARCHITECTURE. Commentaries on the Koran have been extremely numerous; one library alone, that of Tripoli in Syria, reportedly contains twenty thousand commentaries.

KORÇË (Slavonic *Koritza*), city in Albania, and capital of Korçë District, about 70 miles S.E. of Tiranë, and about 30 miles N.W. of Kastoría, Greece. The city is a commercial center producing knitwear, leather, carpets, and flour; brewing and sugar refining are also important. Places of interest in the city include a 15th-century mosque. Pop. (1967) 45,860.

KORČULA, island in the Adriatic Sea, belonging to Yugoslavia, and administered as part Croatia. The island is about 30 mi. long, and averages about 5 mi. in width. Farming, notably the cultivation of olives and grain, and fishing are the principal industries. Korčula and Blato are the most important towns. Area, 107 sq.mi.; pop. (1961) 19,758.

KOREA (Korean *Choson* or *Tai Han*; Jap. *Chosen*), peninsula of the E. Asian mainland, divided into two political entities, the Democratic People's Republic of Korea (North Korea) and the Republic of Korea (South Korea). The peninsula is bounded on the N. by mainland China and the Soviet Union; on the E. by the Sea of Japan; on the S.E. and S. by the Korea Strait, which separates it from Japan; and on the W. by the Yellow Sea. The peninsula lies between about lat. 33°1′ N. and lat. 43°1′ N. and long. 124°11′ E. and long. 131°52′ E. It has a length, in a north-to-south direction, of about 500 mi.; its average width is about 135 mi. On the southeast, south, and west, the peninsular coast, which has an aggregate length of about 5300 mi., is deeply in-

KOREA

dented; the E. coast is relatively regular and has few natural harbors. Numerous off-lying islands are in the S. and W. Cheju (area, about 700 sq.mi.), due S. of the mainland, is the largest island.

The area of South Korea is about 36,152 sq.mi.; of North Korea, about 48,814 sq.mi.

THE LAND
Except in the S.W., a region of low hills and valleys, Korea is extremely mountainous. The main uplift extends generally N. to S. along the entire E. coast of the peninsula, and many spurs and parallel ranges mark the central and N. sections. Mount Paektu (9003 ft.), on the Chinese border, is the highest peak. Most of the peninsular rivers are short, swiftly flowing mountain streams. The Yalu River (q.v.), which forms most of the boundary with mainland China, is navigable by small craft for the greater part of its length; the Tumen R., which demarcates the Soviet–North Korean frontier and the remainder of the Chinese frontier, is navigable by small craft for about 50 mi. Among the larger rivers entirely within Korea are the Naktong, Taedong, and Han. The country has no large lakes.

Climate. The climate of Korea is characterized by sharp regional and seasonal variations. In the N. and N.W. regions, long, cold winters prevail and the mean annual temperature is about 38° F. January temperatures in these regions frequently fall below 8° F. Freezing temperatures are common during the winter in central and southern Korea, but the cold season is relatively brief. Mean annual temperatures in the central and S. regions are about 50° F. and 57° F. respectively. Summers are generally warm and equable. Annual precipitation varies between 35 and 53 in.; the season of maximum precipitation extends from April to November. Droughts and floods occur occasionally.

Natural Resources. Korea is rich in mineral resources. Substantial deposits of coal and iron ore exist. Among other basic resources are gold, silver, copper, lead, zinc, tungsten, limestone, and graphite. The division of the country after the Korean War (q.v.), however, left most of these deposits in North Korea. The land is suitable for agriculture, and the surrounding seas afford an abundance of fish.

Plants and Animals. The flora and fauna of Korea are rich and varied. In the higher regions of the N. the predominant trees are pine, fir, spruce, birch, and larch. In the central part maple, elm, poplar, and ash are the major species. Laurel, bamboo, and evergreen oak flourish in the mild S. coastal areas. Among the large indigenous mammals are tigers, leopards, bears,

435

The throne room of the Changduk royal palace, near Seoul, typifies ancient Korean architecture. United Nations

boars, deer, wolves, and foxes. Birds include eagles, hawks, herons, storks, cranes, swans, pheasants, quail, and snipe. Venomous serpents are rare.

Waterpower. Most of the development of waterpower resources took place during the Japanese occupation, and in North Korea where the industrialization was the heaviest. Electric power in North Korea is almost completely derived from hydroelectric stations. In the mid-1970's total electric power production approached 17,000,000,000 kw hours. Although hydroelectric power represents a small proportion of the electricity supply of South Korea, installed capacity had increased to more than 340,000 kw by 1971. The Ch'unch'ŏn hydroelectric power plant in South Korea, completed in the mid-1960's, provides irrigation for farming areas as well as power.

THE PEOPLE

Little is known of the origin of the Korean people. Because of the mixed racial character of the present-day Korean population, which contains representatives of northeastern Asian Mongoloid, Oceanic Mongoloid (Malaysian), and Ainu physical types, it is believed that the ancestors of the Koreans probably included immigrants from the islands of the Malay Archipelago (q.v.), as well as from the northeastern Asiatic mainland. Koreans have characteristically Mongoloid features, but are frequently taller than the average Mongol, with somewhat lighter skin coloring.

Population. The mountains and hill country of South Korea are sparsely populated. The population is concentrated in the Seoul-Inch'ŏn area and in the fertile plains in the s. The total population of South Korea (census 1970) was 31,469,132; the United Nations estimated (1971) 31,917,000. The overall population density was about 840 per sq.mi. (1970 est.). North Korea, except in the N.W. where the large cities are located, is sparsely populated, with only 299 persons per sq.mi. in 1970. According to a U.N. estimate, the population of North Korea was 14,281,000 in 1971.

Political Divisions. South Korea is divided into nine provinces and two cities which rank as provinces: Kyŏnggi, North Ch'ungch'ŏng, South Ch'ungch'ŏng, North Chŏlla, South Chŏlla, North Kyŏngsang, South Kyŏngsang, Kangwŏn, and Cheju provinces and Seoul City and Pusan City. North Korea is divided into six administrative districts and four cities which rank as administrative units equal to the districts: North P'yŏngan, South P'yŏngan, North Hwanghae, South Hwanghae, North Hamgyŏng, South Hamgyŏng, Chagang, Kangwŏn, and Yanggang districts and P'yŏngyang City, Kaesŏng City, Hamheung City, and Ch'ŏngjin City.

Principal Cities. The capital and largest city of South Korea is Seoul, with a population (1970) of 5,536,377. Other important South Korean cities are the port of Pusan (1,880,710); Taegu (1,082,750), noted for its silk-spinning and cotton-ginning mills; the seaport of Inch'ŏn (646,013), trading center for soya beans and rice; and Kwangju (502,753), a commercial center. P'yŏngyang is the capital of North Korea and its largest city, with an estimated population of 1,500,000. Other leading North Korean cities are the ports of Hŭngnam-Hamhŭng (200,000) and Ch'ŏngjin (250,000).

Religion. Buddhism and Confucianism were introduced from China at an early date, the latter becoming predominant in the late 14th century. Christianity was introduced into Korea about 1785 by Catholic converts from China, but

KOREA

INDEX TO MAP OF KOREA

NORTH KOREA

Cities and Towns

Anak	A3
Anju	A3
Aoji-dong	D1
Changyŏn	A3
Chasŏng	B2
Ch'ŏngjin	D2
Chŏngju	A3
Ch'osan	B2
Haeju	A3
Hamhŭng	B3
Hoeryŏng	C1
Hongwŏn	B2
Huch'ang	B2
Hŭich'ŏn	B2
Hŭngnam	B3
Hyesan	C2
Kaesŏng	B3
Kanggye	B2
Kilchu	C2
Kimchaek	C2
Koksan	B3
Musan	C1
Najin	C1
Namp'o	A3
Nanam	C2
Ongjin	A4
Paekam	C2
P'anmunjŏm	B3
Pukch'ŏng	B2
P'yŏngyang (cap.)	B3
P'yŏngsan	B3
Sariwŏn	A3
Sinch'on	A3
Sinŭiju	A2
Sohung	B3
Sŏnch'ŏn	A3
Sŏngrim	A3
Sunch'ŏn	A3
Tanch'ŏn	C2
Uiju	A2
Unggi	D1
Unsan	B3
Wŏnsan	B3
Yangdŏk	B3
Yongamp'o	A3
Yŏnghŭng	B3

Physical Features

Changjin (res.)	B2
Paektu (mt.)	B2
Puksubaek (mt.)	B2
Taedong (river)	B3
Tumen (river)	C1
Yalu (river)	B2

SOUTH KOREA

Cities and Towns

Andong	C4
Changhŭng	B5
Changsŏng	B5
Chech'ŏn	C4
Cheju	B6
Chinhae	C5
Chinju	C5
Ch'ŏnan	B4
Ch'ŏngju	B4
Chŏngŭp	B5
Chŏnju	B5
Ch'unch'ŏn	C4
Ch'ungju	B4
Inch'ŏn	B4
Iri	B5
Kanggyŏng	B4
Kangnŭng	C4
Kimch'ŏn	C4
Koch'ang	B5
Kongju	B4
Kunsan	B5
Kwangju	B5
Kyŏngju	C5
Masan	C5
Miryang	C5
Mokp'o	B5
Namwŏn	B5
P'anmunjŏm	B4

P'ohang	C4
Pusan	C5
Samch'ŏk	C4
Samnangjin	C5
Sangju	C4
Seoul (cap.)	B4
Sŏsan	B4
Sunch'ŏn	B5
Suwŏn	B4
Taegu	C5
Taejŏn	B4

Ŭisŏng	C4
Ulchin	C4
Ulsan	C5
Wŏnju	C4
Yŏngch'ŏn	C5
Yŏngdŏk	C4
Yŏngju	C4
Yŏsu	B5

Physical Features

Cheju (isl.)	B6
Cheju (strait)	B6
Halla (mt.)	B6
Han (river)	B4
Kŏje (isl.)	C5
Korea (strait)	C5
Kŭm (river)	B4
Naktong (river)	C5
Quelpart (Cheju) (isl.)	B6
So (isl.)	B5
Ullŭng (isl.)	D4

A street scene in modern Seoul.   United Nations

because of persecution of Christians, European missionaries did not arrive until about 1882. The faith of the majority of the people is Buddhism. Christians comprise the third-largest religious community in South Korea.

Language. The language of Korea, Korean, is a member of the Ural-Altaic family of languages. It is similar to Japanese in its grammar, although not in its vocabulary, and it has its own alphabet. Chinese characters, however, are widely used for literary purposes.

Education. Primary education in South Korea is free and compulsory for all children between the ages of six and twelve. In North Korea, education is free and compulsory through the middle-school, or ninth-year, level. In addition, the government provides scholarships for study at institutions of higher education.

ELEMENTARY AND SECONDARY SCHOOLS. South Korea in the early 1970's had about 5500 elementary schools, with an annual enrollment of about 5,800,000 pupils, and almost 2000 middle schools and vocational and academic high schools, with an aggregate annual enrollment of 1,921,000.

In North Korea in the early 1970's, some 9260 schools—including primary and secondary schools and institutes of higher education (excluding universities)—were attended by 3,200,000 students. Of this total, about 214,000 were students in some 570 institutes, and two thirds of these were studying technical and engineering subjects.

UNIVERSITIES AND COLLEGES. In the early 1970's South Korean institutions of higher education included about 70 universities and colleges, which were annually attended by about 180,000 students, and some 50 graduate schools with an enrollment of about 5000. More than 40 junior colleges and technical colleges are also maintained by South Korea.

The principal universities of South Korea include Korea University, Pusan National University, Seoul National University, Yonsei University, and Ewha Women's University.

North Korea in the early 1970's had three universities, chief among which is Kim Il Sung University, at P'yŏngyang, with a total enrollment of about 10,000.

Culture. The Korean people respect their cultural heritage, and efforts have been made to preserve traditions. Korean dynasties, which ruled the country from 669 A.D. to 1910, encouraged the arts. Musicians and dancers were attached to the court, and during the Yi dynasty from 1392 to 1910, particularly, all the arts flourished. During this dynasty the capital was established at Seoul, the phonetic alphabet was invented, books were printed from movable type, and universities were founded. Chinese and Buddhist influences on the Korean culture have been strong. During the thirty-five years that Japan controlled the country before the end of World War II, however, the growth of national cultural aspirations was discouraged.

LIBRARIES AND MUSEUMS. The National Central Library is the most important library in South Korea. Other significant collections are found in eight university libraries and several other libraries. The United States also maintains an information center library in South Korea. The National Museum is located in Seoul, as is the Museum of Fine Arts. South Korea also has an art gallery at Kyongbok Palace in Seoul. North Korea has a Central Library, and several libraries are located in provinces and cities. In addition to the Korean Revolutionary Museum, North Korea has five national museums.

LITERATURE. Earliest Korean literature was based on oral tradition and reflects the influences of China. Korea has a long tradition of written works. As early as 600 A.D. a 100-volume history was compiled, and the first Korean encyclopedia was completed in the 15th century. Korean thinkers later published discourses on such varied topics as medicine, agriculture, geology, astronomy, music, and military science.

ART. Nature permeates all artistic expression in Korea. Painting is a major art form, and although Korean painting shows strong Chinese influences, it has distinct qualities which developed during the Yi dynasty. Since the end of World War II Western influence and trends have become increasingly apparent in all art forms.

MUSIC. Korea has a rich heritage of ancient music. The earliest songs were associated with festivals in honor of the harvest, and through the years songs about common labors have

A farm woman in a village near Pusan washes clothes in a stream.   United Nations

Korean elders attend a citizens' meeting in Pusan.   United Nations

A Korean mother with her baby.   United Nations

been passed down. The Yi Palace Orchestra, founded some 500 years ago, still performs court music in the old tradition. Korean music compares with European music in its richness and emotional complexity. It is founded on a three- or six-beat system and in sound resembles spirited waltzes. The dances of Korea tell historic stories in the manner of ballets.

THE ECONOMY

The Korean economy is dependent primarily on agriculture. The Korean conflict greatly disrupted the economic development of the country. The division of the country at the 38th parallel has left most of the heavy industry in the north, although the south has some mineral and hydroelectric potential for development.

Much rehabilitation in South Korea has been achieved by the United Nations Commission for the Unification and Rehabilitation of Korea (UNCURK). Two five-year economic development plans (1962–66 and 1967–71) achieved annual average growth rates of 8.3 percent and 11.4 percent, respectively. The gross national product rose from about $742,000,000 in 1961 to almost $8,000,000,000 in 1971. The country is currently operating under a third five-year plan (1972–76), emphasizing development of the rural economy, increased exports, and establishment of heavy and chemical industries. In 1971 budget figures showed revenues of $1,700,000,000 and expenditures of $1,820,000,000.

In North Korea all industry was nationalized with the establishment of the Democratic People's Republic. Agriculture is collectivized. Successive economic plans have given emphasis to development of heavy industry and to mechanization of agriculture. For 1971 the government reported increases of 180 percent in output of machine tools and of 50 percent in tractors over the preceding year. Output of steel was reported at about 2,500,000 tons in 1972, and production for the first half of that year was estimated to be up by 20 percent over the same period of 1971. Coal production in 1972 was placed at about 21,000,000 tons. Recent annual budget figures were balanced at about $6,000,000,000 in revenue and expenditures.

Agriculture. South Korea contains a large proportion of the farms and cultivable lands. About 45 percent of the labor force is engaged in agriculture; in North Korea the proportion is about 40 percent. For the country as a whole the area under cultivation normally totals about 11,300,000 acres, but as a result of wartime neglect of irrigation facilities and of the land, an estimated one third of the arable acreage is nonproductive. Land-distribution programs were carried out in both sections of the country in the post-World War II period.

In North Korea, large-scale mechanization has greatly increased the grain yield. In the early 1970's unusually large harvests were reported, especially in rice, which accounts for more than half of the total agricultural output. Other crops reported to be yielding unusually rich harvests were wheat, barley, corn, potatoes, and oil-bearing crops. Livestock in North Korea number about 1,370,000 pigs, 740,000 cattle, and 190,000 sheep.

In South Korea agrarian reform was instituted in 1948. A marked migration from farming and fishing villages to the cities occurred during the 1960's. The trend began to show a reversal in the early 1970's, however, as a result of the government movement to develop rural areas. Agricultural methods are being revolutionized by programs of irrigation and mechanization.

The chief crops of South Korea, with the approximate number of tons produced in 1971, are rice (3,998,000), barley and wheat (2,197,000), pulse (263,000), and corn (64,000). An important development in the early 1970's was the expansion in fruit production, which more than doubled within a decade.

Forest and Fishing Industries. The Korean fisheries and forests are major sources of wealth. Practically all of the timber resources are in the mountainous regions of North Korea. In the mid-1960's timber production annually totaled more than 127,000,000 cu.ft. The principal catch of the fishing industry in terms of value consists of sardines, the source of a commer-

KOREA

cially important oil and fertilizer. The catch also includes mackerel, pollock, herring, and a variety of shellfish, mainly oysters, clams, abalone, and shrimp, and seaweeds, mother-of-pearl, and sponges. In the early 1970's the annual South Korean catch totaled about 1,000,000 tons, and fish exports were valued at about $104,000,000. Whaling is also carried on. In the early 1970's the North Korean fish catch was about 1,000,000 tons.

Mining. More than 100 varieties of minerals are found in the peninsula. With few exceptions the most valuable mineral deposits are in North Korea, which has substantial deposits of iron ore, coal, graphite, tungsten, magnesite, lead, zinc, and copper. In the early 1970's production of coal was about 24,000,000 tons. Iron ore and graphite also were mined.

South Korea has one of the largest deposits of tungsten in the world. In the early 1970's annual production was about 4000 tons, and a tungsten-processing plant was under construction. Production of anthracite coal totaled some 24,000,000 tons. Other minerals exploited include iron ore, amorphous graphite and lead ore.

Manufacturing. South Korean manufacturing industries, traditionally consumer goods–oriented, are shifting significantly to capital goods. Among the industries showing marked increases in production are textiles and apparel, iron and steel, shipbuilding, oil refining, petrochemicals, rubber, cement, and fertilizers. In the early 1970's new plants were either in operation or under construction in most of these industrial areas. Other manufactured products include plywood, glass, and ceramics.

The basic manufacturing industries of the peninsula are in North Korea. Among these industries, which were established in the main by the Japanese, are iron and steel making and the manufacture of cement, chemicals, textiles, and pig iron. In the early 1970's annual production of steel and pig iron was about 2,500,000 tons each; of cement, about 4,500,000 tons; and of chemical fertilizer, about 1,700,000 tons. North Korea has in addition the bulk of the hydroelectric facilities of the nation, but the output of these plants and industrial productivity generally were greatly reduced as a result of United Nations air attacks during the Korean War.

Currency and Banking. The unit of currency in South Korea is the won, introduced in 1962 (395 won equal U.S.$1; 1973). The unit of currency of North Korea is the won, which is divided into 100 jun (2.57 won equal U.S.$1; 1972).

The Bank of Korea is the South Korean bank of issue. South Korea also has six commercial banks. North Korea has three banks, of which the Korean Central Bank is the issuing bank.

Commerce and Trade. Following the disruption of South Korean foreign trade during the war years, the decade 1961–71 showed an average annual increase of exports of 41 percent. In 1972 major exports included manufactured goods (86 percent of the total), machinery and transportation equipment, plywood, and food products. Imports included fertilizers, textile fibers, and petroleum. Imports totaled $2,522,000,000; and exports, $1,633,000,000. The princi-

A cement plant goes into operation in Korea. It is one of two built with United Nations assistance, to meet the domestic need for cement.
United Nations

KOREA

pal trading partners were the U.S. and Japan. The bulk of North Korean foreign commerce is with the Soviet Union, China, and other Communist nations. Minerals and metals constitute the majority of exports, and fuels, chemicals, and machinery represent major imports.

Transportation and Communications. The highway and railroad network of the peninsula was almost completely destroyed during the Korean War. The South Korean railroad system, consisting of some 3300 mi. of track, is government-operated. It carries annually about 120,000 passengers and 48,000,000 tons of freight. South Korea has more than 20,000 mi. of road. The North Korean railroad network, with more than 6500 mi., is connected with those of the U.S.S.R. and China. South Korea has some 45 daily newspapers, about 570 weekly and monthly periodicals, and about 200 other publications. North Korea has about 30 principal newspapers, periodicals, and foreign-language publications.

Radio service in South Korea is provided by a governmental network of seventeen stations and by three commercial stations, two church-affiliated stations, and stations of the United Nations Command and the American Armed Forces Korea Network. In North Korea the Central Broadcasting Committee broadcasts nationally, while local programming is supplied by local committees. Loudspeakers are placed in factories and in open areas of the towns.

Labor. In South Korea sixteen unions are affiliated with the Federation of Korean Trade Unions, which had a total membership in the late 1960's of about 415,000. The major industrial, technical, and agricultural unions in North Korea are affiliated with the General Federation of Trade Unions with a total membership of about 2,000,000. Professional workers, including artists, writers, musicians, lawyers, and scientists, have their own trade organizations.

GOVERNMENT

South Korea is a republic governed under the terms of a constitution that became effective on Dec. 27, 1972. The promulgation ended a period of martial law dating from October, 1972.

North Korea is governed according to the provisions of the constitution of Sept. 8, 1948. This document closely resembles the organic law of other countries within the Soviet sphere of influence.

Central Government. In South Korea the president, popularly elected for a four-year term, is the head of state. As chief executive, he formulates national policy and appoints the premier and cabinet.

In North Korea executive authority is exercised by the council of ministers. The members of this body, which is headed by a premier, are elected by the Supreme People's Assembly (see *Legislature,* below) and are responsible to it. In practice, however, all power is in the hands of the political committee of the Workers' (Communist) Party and its general secretary, Marshal Kim Il Sung (1912–   ).

HEALTH AND WELFARE. The South Korean government provides welfare services for the aged, handicapped, wounded veterans, and war widows. In North Korea the government provides rest homes, sanatoria, and free medical services.

Legislature. The legislature of South Korea is the unicameral National Assembly, comprising 146 elected members and 73 members chosen by the National Conference for Unification from a list recommended by the president. In North Korea legislative power is vested in the Supreme People's Assembly, a body consisting of one member for every 30,000 persons, elected by direct vote for four-year terms. The assembly is convened in regular session twice annually and, when it is not in session, the Presidium of the assembly is the highest responsible organ of government.

Political Parties. Political parties were suspended in South Korea in 1961 but were reinstated in 1963. The two major parties are the Democratic Republican Party (the government party), and the New Democratic Party, an opposition coalition formed in 1967.

The dominant party in North Korea is the Workers' Party of Korea. Two other small parties are formally recognized: the North Korean Democratic Party and the Religious Chungwoo Party, but they do not oppose basic policies of the government.

Local Government. The nine provinces and two special cities of South Korea are headed by appointed governors who are responsible to the executive branch of the national government. The constitution stipulates that provinces and lower territorial subdivisions shall have elected councils with limited legislative powers. Each local administrative unit of North Korea (district, city, county, and township) has its own elected people's assembly.

Judiciary. Judicial power in South Korea is vested in three types of courts. The supreme court, the highest court, has the power to change laws which it finds unconstitutional and to decide the manner in which the law is to be interpreted and when it is applicable. It is also authorized to dissolve political parties. The supreme court consists of up to sixteen judges, appointed by the president upon the recommen-

A farmer ploughs his rice paddy. Rice, barley, and wheat are important Korean agricultural products.
United Nations

dation of the chief justice. The other courts are the courts of appeal and district courts.

In North Korea the judicial system consists of the supreme court, provincial courts, people's courts of cities and counties, and special courts. Members of the courts are elected by the people's assemblies. The supreme court supervises the work of all lower courts.

Defense. A U.N. force has the responsibility of protecting the frontier between South and North Korea (see *History*, below). Military service in South Korea lasts for 2 years in the army, and 3 years in the navy and air force. In the early 1970's the armed forces of South Korea totaled about 600,000 men. In North Korea military service is compulsory at eighteen years of age. North Korean armed forces were estimated at about 500,000.

HISTORY

Chinese colonies, established during the Han (q.v.) dynasty flourished in northern and central Korea in the first three centuries of the Christian era. The last of these, Naknang (Lo-lang), with its capital at modern P'yŏngyang, was overwhelmed by the Koreans early in the 4th century.

Early Korean Kingdoms. The first purely native state to emerge in the peninsula was Koguryo, established by a branch of the Tungus, a people of northern Manchuria (q.v.) who moved down into the mountainous area of the upper Yalu R. about the 2nd century B.C. Another branch of the same stock, the Han, had established a number of small tribal territories in southeastern Korea by the 3rd century A.D. By about 400 A.D. the Korean peoples had been consolidated into three kingdoms: Koguryo in the north, Silla in the southeast, and Pakche in the southwest. A fourth, smaller territory, Kaya, on the extreme south coast, was conquered about 562 by Silla and Pakche. The so-called Three Kingdoms Period lasted until 660 when first Pakche and then Koguryo were conquered by the combined armies of China and Silla. The kingdom of Silla proved strong enough to drive out the Chinese and to form the first unified Korean state.

Silla was supplanted as the dominant power in Korea in 918 by Koryo, a northern state occupying the former territory of Koguryo. The Koryo dynasty lasted until 1392, although in the last century of its rule it was under the domination of the Mongol overlords of China; *see* MONGOL DYNASTIES.

Japanese Invasion. In 1392 a Koryo general, Yi Song-gye, usurped the throne and established a dynasty that remained in existence until 1910, the longest-lived dynasty in history. Weakened by factionalism within the government, Korea was invaded by Japanese armies in the late 16th century, and Seoul was captured in 1592. In the following year, however, the invaders were driven back with aid from China. The Japanese attempted another invasion in 1597 but were repelled, and the Japanese fleet was destroyed by

KOREA

a Korean naval force in a brilliant sea engagement. After 1627 Korea was a tributary state of the Manchu rulers of China; see CHINA, PEOPLE'S REPUBLIC OF: *History: Imperial Power: The Manchu, or Ch'ing, Dynasty.*

In the late 19th century Korea became the center of a struggle for power between China, Russia, and Japan, which led first to the Sino-Japanese War (see JAPAN: *History: Restoration of Imperial Rule*) and later to the Russo-Japanese War (q.v.). In 1895 the Japanese engineered a revolt in Seoul that led to the murder of the queen and the flight of the king. In 1906, a Japanese resident-general was appointed, and in the following year the Korean army was disbanded. In 1910 Korea was formally annexed to Japan and named Chosen; it remained under Japanese control until 1945; see JAPAN: *History: The 20th Century.*

Post-World War II Period. In 1945 following the defeat of Japan in World War II, Korea was occupied by U.S. and Soviet forces. Complete independence was guaranteed to Korea after a maximum five-year period of Allied trusteeship.

The U.S. and Soviet military commanders were subsequently unable to agree on terms for the formation of an all-Korean provisional government. In September, 1947, the U.S. referred the matter to the United Nations (q.v.). The U.N. General Assembly established in November a commission to arrange all-Korean elections, but the North Korean authorities, with the support of the Soviet Union, refused to cooperate with the commission.

NORTH KOREA AND SOUTH KOREA. In February, 1948, the U.N. approved a resolution providing for elections in the U.S. zone of Korea. In the same month the draft of a Soviet-style constitution for a "Democratic People's Republic of Korea" was promulgated.

United Nations-supervised elections for a constituent assembly were held in South Korea on May 10, 1948. On July 12, when it completed its labors, the assembly adopted a constitution proclaiming the Republic of Korea. The constituent assembly, which then assumed the functions of the national legislature, elected the right-wing nationalist leader Syngman Rhee (q.v.) president of the republic on July 20. On Aug. 15 U.S. military authorities formally relinquished power to the South Korean government. Meanwhile, on July 10, the North Korean People's Council had approved the draft constitution. Single-slate elections for the Supreme People's Assembly took place on Aug. 25. On Sept. 9 the people's assembly, meeting in P'yŏngyang, formally proclaimed establishment of the North Korean republic and elected the Moscow-trained Communist Kim Il Sung to the premiership.

During the fall and early winter months of 1948 abortive uprisings occurred in various parts of South Korea. Approximately 15,000 insurgents were killed in the most serious revolt, which centered on Cheju Island. In November the South Korean National Assembly formally asked the U.S. government to retain its military forces on South Korean soil pending the organization of an adequate South Korean defense force. The U.N. General Assembly, in a resolution adopted on Dec. 12, implicitly approved this request and recognized the South Korean government as the only legitimate state authority on the peninsula.

The cleavage between the rival republics deepened during 1949. Occasional frontier clashes along the 38th parallel posed the threat of full-scale civil war, and the authorities of both regimes inflicted harsh reprisals on opposition groups. In March the North Korean government signed a ten-year economic and cultural agreement with the Soviet Union.

DEPARTURE OF UNITED STATES FORCES. Withdrawal of all U.S. forces in South Korea, except a 500-man military advisory group, was completed on June 30, 1949. In July the National Assembly enacted a military conscription bill authorizing the creation of a standing army of 200,000 men. In October the U.S. Congress granted South Korea $60,000,000 for economic assistance.

Communist guerrilla activity in South Korea increased during the first half of 1950. Popular disapproval of brutal police measures against dissidents, rampant inflation, and a prolonged cabinet crisis added to the general unrest.

Korean War. The North Korean government proposed to the U.N. on June 10 that elections for an all-Korean legislature be held in August. But on June 25 the armed forces of the Communist regime invaded South Korea, precipitating the struggle generally known as the Korean War (q.v.). Overrunning South Korean frontier positions, the invaders seized Seoul on June 28 and began a sustained drive southward. Meanwhile, on June 25, the U.N. Security Council, able to function in the crisis only because of the prevailing boycott of its sessions by the Soviet delegate, had passed a cease-fire resolution and ordered the North Koreans to withdraw. On June 27 President Harry S. Truman (q.v.), basing his action on the cease-fire resolution, ordered American naval and air forces to the defense of the beleaguered South Koreans and the Security Council invoked military sanctions against North Korea, transforming the civil war into an

KOREA

international conflict. American ground forces were committed to the defense of South Korea on June 30 (for details of the fighting, see KOREAN WAR). On Dec. 1, 1950, the U.N. General Assembly created the United Nations Korean Reconstruction Agency (UNKRA), an organization charged with speeding the rehabilitation of war-torn South Korea.

TRUCE AT PANMUNJOM. On July 10, 1951, despite the strenuous opposition of the South Korean government, the U.N. and Communist commands began discussions on terms of a truce. The truce agreement was signed at Panmunjom on July 27, three years and thirty-two days after the start of hostilities.

FOREIGN AID AND TREATIES. Rehabilitation programs were instituted in both parts of the country following cessation of hostilities. In August the U.S. Congress appropriated $200,000,000 for relief and reconstruction in South Korea and the Soviet government allocated $1,110,000,000 for "restoration of the destroyed national economy of Korea". The U.S. government revealed plans later in August for a long-range rehabilitation program costing $1,000,000,000.

By the terms of the Korean armistice document the U.N. and the Communists agreed to convene a top-level political conference within three months "in order to insure the peaceful settlement of the Korean question". Direct negotiations regarding the composition, agenda, and opening date of the conference began at Panmunjom on Oct. 28. On Dec. 12 the U.N. delegate withdrew from the negotiations because the Communists had accused the U.S. of "perfidy". As a consequence of their refusal to retract the charge, the talks were not resumed.

South Korea and the U.S. ratified a mutual-defense treaty in January, 1954. The treaty granted the U.S. the right to maintain land, sea, and air forces in South Korea and stipulated that U.S. military assistance would be forthcoming only in the event of external attack on South Korea.

President Rhee won his third term as chief executive in a national election held on May 15, 1956. On June 9 the U.N. Command ordered all its members to leave South Korea. On Nov. 28, the U.S. and South Korea signed a treaty of friendship, commerce, and navigation.

ELECTIONS AND REPATRIATION. In elections for the South Korean National Assembly in May, 1958, President Rhee's Liberal Party won 125 of the 233 seats. In December a proposed revision of the national-security law provoked strong opposition from the Democratic Party, whose members in the assembly went on a sit-down strike. All opposition members were evicted on Dec. 24, and legislation was passed providing penalties for criticizing the president. In April, 1959, operation of the opposition paper, *Kyung Hyang Shinmun*, was suspended by the government, and in July Cho Bong Am (1899–1959), losing candidate for the presidency in 1952 and 1956, was hanged as a Communist agent. Rhee was reelected president on March 15, 1960, after a campaign during which an opposition-party official was beaten to death. Violent antigovernment demonstrations and riots in April forced Rhee to resign on April 27 and to go into exile in Honolulu, Hawaii, late in May. In July freedom of publication and assembly was proclaimed, and many of Rhee's former officials were tried in Seoul. On July 29 general elections for the National Assembly were held, giving the Democratic Party more than two thirds of the seats in both houses. A new president, Posun Yun (1892–   ), took office on Aug. 13, and on Aug. 19 John Myun Chang (1899–1966) assumed the premiership.

North Koreans held in Japan during World War II began to be repatriated in December, 1959. On Feb. 28, 1961, the South Korean legislature approved an economic- and technical-aid agreement with the U.S. expected to add about $43,000,000 to the $207,000,000 in American aid already budgeted for the fiscal year. Following a prolonged period of disorderly demonstrations, led particularly by student groups, the government of Premier Chang was overturned on May 16 by a military coup led by Major General Chung Hee Park. With an avowed purpose of preventing Communist inroads in South Korea, the new ruling junta dissolved the legislature and assumed the right to govern by decree. As head of the junta, Park initiated an austerity program and arrested many businessmen and officals. Elections to end the military rule were promised for 1963.

Korea in the 1960's and 1970's. The South Korean president Posun Yun resigned on March 21, 1962, in protest against Park's decision to exclude all members of previous regimes from the government. Park assumed the presidency on March 24. A new constitution, approved by a national referendum held on Dec. 17, was to go into effect with the scheduled 1963 elections. In early 1963 Park considered postponing the elections for several years but was pressured into adhering to his promise of a 1963 vote by public protests and American refusal to extend further aid if elections were not held. Park, running against Posun Yun, won the election on Oct. 15 by a slim margin. The legislative elections, held Oct. 26, gave his newly formed Democratic Re-

445

public Party a majority in the new unicameral parliament. Park was reelected to a second term in 1967. A referendum in October, 1969, approved a constitutional amendment permitting Park to seek a third term in 1971.

An international crisis was precipitated at the beginning of 1968 with the capture of the U.S. intelligence ship *Pueblo* and its eighty-three-man crew, by North Korean naval units on Jan. 23. Following months of negotiations, the eighty-two surviving crewmen and the body of one, who died as a result of wounds received during the action, were released on Dec. 23.

In October, 1972, Park declared a state of martial law, dissolving the legislature, banning all political activity, and closing the universities. In November a referendum approved a new constitution, extensively strengthening the powers of the president. President Park asserted that the document had as its goal the unification of the two Koreas.

In December, 1972, martial law was ended, and an election was held for members of the National Unification Conference. The main function of this body is selection of the president, thus eliminating popular election for that office. The conference met on Dec. 23, and Park was reelected for a six-year term.

Moves toward unification began in 1971 with a meeting of representatives of North and South Korea, under the auspices of the Red Cross. Further such meetings were held frequently in 1972 and 1973, but the two sides still remained far apart on basic political principles.

KOREAN WAR, military struggle fought on the Korean Peninsula from June, 1950, to July, 1953; see KOREA: *History: Post-World War II Period: Korean War.* Begun as a war between South Korea (Republic of Korea) and North Korea (Democratic People's Republic of Korea), the conflict swiftly developed into a limited, international war involving the United States and nineteen other nations. From a general viewpoint, the Korean War was one of the by-products of the cold war (q.v.), the global political and diplomatic struggle between the Communist and non-Communist systems, following World War II (q.v.). Specifically, the Korean War, excluding its early, solely national stage, resulted from a so-called police action undertaken by the United Nations (q.v.) against Communist aggression. No formal declaration of war was made, however. The U.N. action was unique because, despite numerous, earlier provocations, neither the U.N. nor its predecessor, the League of Nations (q.v.), had employed collective, military measures to repel an aggressor.

Fighting began when, on June 25, 1950, the North Korean army, substantially equipped by the Soviet Union, invaded South Korea. South Korean positions along the 38th parallel, which marked the frontier between the two republics, were swiftly overrun, and the Communist forces drove southward. North Korea was aided during the war by personnel and equipment from both Communist China and the Soviet Union. The U.N. Security Council (q.v.), with the Soviet delegate voluntarily absent, invoked military sanctions against North Korea on June 27 and called upon member states to aid the Republic of Korea. Almost simultaneously U.S. President Harry S. Truman (q.v.) ordered American military forces into action against the invaders. American forces, those of South Korea, and, ultimately, combat contingents from Australia, Belgium, Luxembourg, Canada, Colombia, Ethiopia, France, Great Britain, Greece, Netherlands, New Zealand, Philippines, South Africa, Thailand, and Turkey, with medical units from Denmark, India, and Sweden, were placed under a unified U.N. command headed by the U.S. commander in chief in the Far East, General of the Army Douglas MacArthur (q.v.). The participating ground forces of these nations, the U.S., and South Korea, were eventually grouped in the United States Eighth Army.

Seoul, the South Korean capital, fell to the invaders on June 28, three days after the war began. During July the U.N. forces retired to a perimeter-defense line about 50 mi. from Pusan, a leading seaport on the southeastern coast. Fierce North Korean attacks failed to dislodge them. On Sept. 15, 1950, the U.N. command launched a powerful offensive. The U.N. army made an amphibious landing at Inch'ŏn, on the west coast 200 mi. above Pusan, cutting the lines of communication of the North Koreans, and the Pusan defenders, breaking out of the perimeter, drove toward Seoul. The South Korean capital was recaptured on Sept. 26. The U.N. forces then pressed across the 38th parallel, captured the North Korean capital, P'yongyang, on Oct. 19, and in some sectors advanced to the Yalu R., the boundary between China and Korea. The enemy had ceased to be effective, and the way seemed open to a speedy end of hostilities.

Later in October, however, Communist Chinese divisions crossed the Yalu and engaged advanced elements of the U.N. army. Undeterred, General MacArthur ordered, on Nov. 24, a so-called end-the-war offensive. This offensive was almost immediately frustrated by a massive Chinese counteroffensive. The U.N. troops, overextended, outnumbered, and ill-equipped to fight a fresh enemy in the bitter North Korean winter, were soon in general retreat. On November 26 the Communists cut the escape route of some 40,000 U.S. soldiers and marines in northeast Korea, who fought their way out and were later evacuated from the port of Hungnam. They reoccupied P'yongyang on December 5, and, sweeping into South Korea, recaptured Seoul on Jan. 4, 1951. The Communist offensive was halted by January 15 along a front substantially south of Seoul. The U.S. Eighth Army took the offensive on January 25, and the entire U.N. command mounted the powerful attack known as Operation Killer on February 21. Under pressure of superior firepower, the Chinese slowly withdrew from South Korea. Seoul fell to the U.N. again on March 14. By April 22 U.N. forces had occupied positions slightly north of the 38th parallel along a line that, with minor variations, remained stationary for the rest of the war.

Air power, in particular, played a key role in the war, which proved to be the first battlefield in history for supersonic jet aircraft. U.N. aircraft were instrumental in support of ground forces, in destroying Chinese supply lines, and in crippling North Korean airfields. At the start of the war the U.S. Fifth Air Force was still equipped chiefly with conventional, or World War II, aircraft, namely the F-51 Mustang and B-26 Invader. The first jet-against-jet engagement in history occurred Nov. 9, 1950, when an American F-80 destroyed a Communist jet fighter. The Soviet MiG-15 employed by the powerful Chinese Communist air force quickly proved superior to the American jets, however, and the U.S. responded with a crash program that produced the formidable F-86 Sabre. The ensuing MiG-Sabre confrontations increased greatly from late 1951 on, and large-scale air battles, mostly over so-called MiG Alley in northwest Korea, resulted ultimately in the loss of some 58 Sabres and 800 MiG's. By the end of the war, U.N. planes had been responsible for about 75 percent of the enemy tanks destroyed and for an estimated 39,000 enemy fatalities; see AIRPLANE: *Airplane Types and Uses: Military Airplanes;* UNITED STATES AIR FORCES: *History;* JET PROPULSION.

The war had assumed a new dimension, meanwhile, as U.N. bombers, hitherto virtually unopposed in strikes against Communist rear positions, were challenged by increasing numbers of Soviet-built jet aircraft operating from bases in Manchuria (q.v.). On the basis of this development and the Chinese intervention, General MacArthur concluded that victory

A column of soldiers moves toward the front as Korean civilians flee from the war. UPI

could be achieved only by attacking Communist bases in Manchuria, blockading the Communist Chinese coast, and reinforcing the U.N. command with Nationalist Chinese ground forces brought from Taiwan. MacArthur's public advocacy of this strategy, which entailed the risk of a general war with China and the Soviet Union, conflicted with policies established by his civilian and military superiors. As a result, he was relieved of his command by President Truman on April 11, 1951. His successor, U.S. Lieutenant General Matthew Ridgway (1895–   ), pursued the limited objective of inflicting maximum personnel loss upon the enemy along the fixed battle front and from the air. This strategy, while severely punishing the Chinese and the rehabilitated North Korean army, could not drive them from the field. In the ensuing stalemate, the Communists were unable to force the U.N. from North Korea, and the U.N. was unwilling to pay the price necessary to drive the enemy into Manchuria.

Some of the most desperate battles of the war took place in the area popularly known as the Iron Triangle, and on the hills called Old Baldy, Capital, Pork Chop, T-Bone, and Heartbreak Ridge. The U.N. air force, retaining command of the skies despite opposition from enemy interceptors, devastated North Korean supply bases, railroads, bridges, hydroelectric plants, and industrial centers. North Korean coastal points were systematically pounded by U.N. naval units. The war was marked also by violent riots and demonstrations in the U.N. prisoner-of-war compounds; by Communist charges, never substantiated, that the U.S. had waged germ warfare against North Korea and China; by the exchange of sick and wounded prisoners of war; and by disclosures that the Communists had been guilty of atrocities against captured U.N. personnel.

In June, 1951, as the positional-warfare pattern began to crystallize, the Soviet delegate to the U.N. formally proposed that the belligerents in Korea open discussions for a cease-fire. On July 10, 1951, following preparatory talks, representatives of the U.N. and Communist commands began truce negotiations at Kaesŏng, North Korea. These negotiations were to be carried on intermittently for more than two years.

Though conducted in an atmosphere of mutual suspicion and recrimination, negotiations finally resulted in settlement of all except one of the major issues. The chief obstacle to agreement was Communist refusal to accept the principle, adhered to by the U.N., that a prisoner of war should not be returned against his will to his respective army. Negotiations broke down in October, 1952, and were not resumed until April, 1953. In late spring of that year, the two sides agreed that prisoners unwilling to return to their own countries would be placed in the custody of a neutral commission for a period of ninety days following the signing of the truce. It was also established that during this period each side could attempt to persuade its nationals to return home. The two sides agreed to hold a top-level peace conference within three months of the effective date of the armistice, but this date was later postponed until April, 1954.

On July 27, 1953, the truce agreement was signed at P'anmunjŏm. Thus, pending ultimate settlement at the projected peace conference, the Korean War was terminated after more than three years of conflict. The U.S. suffered 157,530 casualties; deaths from all causes totalled 33,629, of which 23,300 occurred in combat. South Korea sustained 1,312,836 military casualties, including 415,004 dead; casualties among other U.N. allies totaled 16,532, including 3094 dead. Estimated Communist casualties were 2,000,000. The economic and social damage to the Korean nation was incalculable.

See UNITED NATIONS, THE: *The Korean War*.

M.B.R.

KORNBERG, Arthur (1918–), American biochemist, born in Brooklyn, N.Y. He received a B.S. degree from the College of the City of New York in 1937 and a medical degree from the University of Rochester in 1941. From 1942 to 1953 Kornberg held a position with the United States Public Health Service, working on enzymes at the National Institute of Health in Bethesda, Md. Academic appointments followed, at Washington University in Saint Louis, the University of California at Berkeley, New York University, and Stanford University, Calif.,

A scene in Seoul after the expulsion of Communist armies during the Korean War. UPI

at the last of which he became head of the department of biochemistry. At Washington University in 1956 Kornberg and his associates artificially produced a chemically exact but inert molecule of deoxyribonucleic acid (DNA), a basic substance of genes. For this achievement he shared the 1959 Nobel Prize in medicine and physiology with Severo Ochoa (q.v.), a Spanish-American biochemist. At Stanford in 1967 Kornberg headed a team which carried his previous achievement a step farther by synthesizing DNA, this time in a biologically active state. See NUCLEIC ACIDS.

KORNGOLD, Erich Wolfgang (1897–1957), Austrian-American composer, born in Braunau, Austria. When only eleven years old he wrote a pantomime, *Der Schneemann* ("The Snowman"), which was produced at the Royal Opera of Vienna in 1910. Soon afterward the youthful composer gave a concert in Berlin, where he was acclaimed by many musical celebrities. His works, including songs, chamber music, orchestral pieces, and operas (*The Dead City*, 1920), show skill in thematic development and orchestration. Coming to the United States in 1934, he worked as conductor and composer of motion-picture scores. He became a naturalized U.S. citizen in 1943.

KORNILOV, Lavr Georgievich (1870–1918), Russian general of Cossack descent, born in Ust'-Kamenogorsk, and educated at the Artillery College in Saint Petersburg (now Leningrad). He received his commission in the army in 1892 and later served with distinction in the Russo-Japanese War in 1904 and 1905. During World War I he was captured by the Austrians in 1915, escaped in 1916, and returned to Russia. After the Russian Revolution (q.v.) of March, 1917, he was appointed commander in chief of the Russian Army by the revolutionary leader Aleksandr Feodorovich Kerenski (q.v.). Kornilov immediately submitted plans to the government to reestablish the fighting morale of the army, but his plans were rejected when he subsequently demanded concurrent powers that Kerenski feared would lead to a military dictatorship. In September, 1917, Kornilov led a counterrevolutionary attack against Kerenski, which ended a few days later with Kornilov's arrest and imprisonment. With the help of units of the Cossacks (q.v.), he escaped after the November revolution, organized an anti-Bolshevik force of Cossacks, and was killed in action against the Communist forces.

KOROLENKO, Vladimir Galaktionovich (1853–1921), Russian writer, born in Zhitomir, and educated at the University of Saint Petersburg (now Leningrad) and the Moscow School of Agriculture. From 1879 to 1885 he was in forced exile in Siberia for advocating social reforms for Russia. In 1895 he became editor of the review *Russian Wealth*, for which he wrote articles condemning injustices. Korolenko is best known for his well-written and sympathetic stories of Russian peasant life. Among his writings are the novel *The Blind Musician* (1886), the volume of short stories *Siberian Tales* (1901), and an autobiography.

KOROSEAL. See RUBBER, SYNTHETIC: *Types of Synthetic Rubber: Other Specialty Rubbers.*

KOS, or COS, island of Greece, in the Aegean Sea, off the s.w. coast of Turkey, second-largest of the Dodecanese Islands, see DODECANESE. It is about 25 mi. long and 5 mi. wide and consists mostly of fertile and well-tilled plains, and partially of hilly country. Farming and stock raising are the principal occupations of the island, and grapes, figs, olives, lettuce, tomatoes, almonds, wheat, barley, and corn are the most important crops. Kos contains many architectural remains of ancient Greek civilization. It is thought to be the birthplace of the physician Hippocrates (q.v.).

The principal town and port of the island, also named Kos, contains a 14th-century fortress erected by the Knights of Rhodes. During the reign of the Egyptian king Ptolemy II (*see under* PTOLEMY) the town was an important center for learning. Area of island, 111 sq.mi.; pop. (1961) 18,187.

KOSCIUSKO, Thaddeus, original name TADEUSZ ANDRZEJ BONAWENTURA KOŚCIUSZKO (1746–1817), Polish national hero and military leader, born near Brest (now in the U.S.S.R.), and educated in military engineering in Warsaw and in Germany, Italy, and France. Imbued with contemporary French liberal philosophy, he went to America in 1776 to serve with the colonial forces in the American Revolution (q.v.). He fought under General Horatio Gates (q.v.), directed the construction of fortifications at West Point, N.Y., served under General Nathanael Greene, and became an aide to General George Washington (qq.v.). In 1783, in recognition of his services, Kosciusko was granted American citizenship, a pension and estates, and the rank of brigadier general.

In 1784 he returned to Poland, attaining the rank of major general in the Polish army. Following the second partition (1793) of Poland, among Russia, Prussia, and Austria, he led a successful rebellion for Polish independence. After some initial military successes in fighting the Russian and Prussian invading forces, however,

KOSHER

Thaddeus Kosciusko — Bettmann Archive

he was defeated and wounded at Maciejowice. He was then held prisoner in Russia until 1796, when he was released and exiled. In exile he visited America, where he was awarded $15,000 and a grant of Ohio land. From 1798 until his death he lived in France and Switzerland, unsuccessfully seeking independence for Poland. See POLAND: *History*.

Kosciusko not only fought for national independence, but also supported the principle of political equality among men. He emancipated the serfs on his estates in Poland shortly before his death and he ordered in his will that his Ohio property be sold to provide education for Negro Americans.

KOSHER (from Heb. *kāshēr*, "fit, proper"), term meaning ritually proper for use according to Jewish law. It is especially applied to the food that Jews are permitted to eat. Only animals that have cloven hooves and that are ruminant, that is, chew the cud, are considered to be kosher. These animals must be killed according to the traditional rabbinical ritual, and must be soaked, salted, and washed to remove any traces of blood. Milk or milk products must not be eaten with meat, and shellfish is to be avoided. During the festival of Pesach (q.v.) no leavened bread is to be eaten. Although originally these dietary regulations were designed to preserve health standards, they are today for the most part observed only by Orthodox Jews.

KOŠICE (Hung. *Kassa*; Ger. *Kaschau*), city of Czechoslovakia, and capital of the Východoslovenský Region, on the Hornád R., about 130 mi. N.W. of Budapest, Hungary. Košice is an important industrial center with a petroleum refinery and various light industries; an iron and steel center is close to the city. Among the many historic places of interest in the city is the Gothic Cathedral of Saint Elizabeth, built in the 14th and 15th centuries. Košice was created a town in 1241 by the Hungarian King Bela IV (1206–70). Since then it has been held at various times by the Austrians, Turks, Hungarians, and Russians. By the terms of the Treaty of Trianon in 1920 the city was ceded by Hungary to Czechoslovakia. It reverted to Hungary in 1939, at the beginning of World War II, but was recovered by Czechoslovakia at the close of the war. Pop. (1970 est.) 142,000.

KOSSEL, Albrecht (1853–1927), German physiological chemist, born in Rostock, and educated at the University of Strasbourg. He served as a lecturer at Strasbourg from 1881 to 1883, when he became director of the chemical division of the Physiological Institute at Berlin. He was appointed professor of physiology at the University of Marburg in 1895 and at the University of Heidelberg in 1910. Kossel's studies were devoted to the chemical composition of cells, of cell nuclei, and of protein (q.v.); he discovered the bases adenine and thymine of animal nucleic acid (q.v.). For these researches in biochemistry he received the 1910 Nobel Prize in medicine and physiology.

KOSSUTH, Lajos (1802–94), Hungarian patriot and statesman, born in Monor, Hungary (then part of Austria), and educated at Sárospatak and Budapest. After briefly practicing law he began his political career in 1825 in the Hungarian national diet, or parliament. Kossuth reported his observations of political activities in the form of a parliamentary gazette, which attracted the attention of the Austrian imperial police, who arrested Kossuth and imprisoned him for high treason in 1837. He was freed by popular demand in 1840 and the following year he became editor of the *Pesti Hirlap* ("Pest Journal"), a magazine advocating political reform and an independent legislature for Hungary.

In 1847 Kossuth was returned to the diet. He continued to advance his liberal views in a series of brilliant speeches demanding a constitution not only for Hungary, but for Austria as well. His campaign was successful in winning a separate constitution for Hungary within the

Austrian Empire, and when the new government was formed in March, 1848, Kossuth was named minister of finance.

Kossuth's extreme Hungarian nationalism antagonized the Slavic peoples of Austria-Hungary, who joined the German-speaking Austrians in opposing him, and in July, 1848, Kossuth called the Hungarian nation to arms to defend their independence. In April, 1849, he was named governor and virtual dictator of the newly declared Hungarian Republic. The Hungarian forces won victories early in the uprising but were crushed after the Russian army intervened on the Austrian imperial side.

Kossuth resigned in August and fled to Turkey. He subsequently visited England and the United States, where he was received with enthusiasm and delivered speeches on behalf of Hungarian independence. He spent the last forty-five years of his life in exile in England and in Italy, constantly attempting to promote his ideal of Hungarian independence. *See* HUNGARY: *History: The 18th and 19th Centuries.*

KOSTROMA, city of the Soviet Union, in the Russian S.F.S.R., and capital of Kostroma Oblast, at the confluence of the Volga and Kostroma rivers, about 200 miles N.W. of Moscow. Kostroma is an industrial city noted for the manufacture of linen; other industries include the processing of flour, lumber, and tobacco. Among the places of interest in the city are a 14th-century monastery and the Uspenski Cathedral, built in the 13th century. Kostroma, founded 1152, is one of the oldest commercial centers in the U.S.S.R. Pop. (1970) 223,000.

KOSYGIN, Aleksei Nikolayevich (1904–), Soviet Communist leader, born in Saint Petersburg (now Leningrad). Kosygin attended the Leningrad Cooperative Technical School Technicum (1921–24) and the Leningrad Kirov Textile Institute (1929–35), and was graduated from the latter as a textile engineer. After working in several textile plants, he became director of a spinning mill in 1937. He was an active member of the Leningrad Communist Party and in 1938 was elected chairman of its executive committee, a position equivalent to mayor. During World War II, Kosygin helped evacuate 500,000 people from Leningrad when it was under German siege. He was appointed an alternate member of the Politburo in 1946 and a full member in 1948. In 1959 he was appointed chairman of the State Planning Commission, and in 1960, he became a member of the Presidium and first deputy chairman of the Council of Ministers, a position he shared with Anastas I. Mikoyan (q.v.). In October, 1964, following the ouster of Nikita S. Khrushchev (q.v.), Kosygin was elected Chairman of the Council of Ministers, a post in the Soviet Union equivalent to prime minister. At the same time, Leonid Ilyich Brezhnev (q.v.) became First Secretary of the Communist Party and co-leader with Kosygin of the U.S.S.R. At the close of the 1960's, however, Kosygin was relegated to a lesser leadership position as Brezhnev's power increased.

KOTA, *or* KOTAH, city of the Republic of India, in Rajasthan State, on the Chambal R., 120 miles s. of Jaipur. The city is a trade center for an area growing cotton, millet, wheat, and oilseeds; industries include cotton and oilseed milling, textile weaving, distilling, dairying, and the manufacture of metal handicrafts. The rail junction, a road hub, lies 3 miles to the N. The

Premier Aleksei N. Kosygin, left, is welcomed by President Lyndon B. Johnson as the two leaders began a meeting at Glassboro, N.J., in 1967. At center is Viktor Sukhodrev, an interpreter. UPI

Crosthwaite Institute is located in Kota, as are old and new palaces of the maharao (the maharajah). The city was formerly capital of the princely State of Kota, formed in 1572 from Bundi State. Pop. (1971) 213,005.

KOUFAX, Sandy, in full SANFORD KOUFAX (1935–), American baseball player, born in New York City. He earned a scholarship to the University of Cincinnati. In a career that was prematurely ended because of an arthritic condition in his left elbow, Koufax became the dominant left-handed pitcher in the major leagues. During his major-league years, 1955 to 1966, he pitched for the Brooklyn (N.Y.) Dodgers, which later became the Los Angeles (Calif.) Dodgers, and won 165 games, lost 87, compiled an earned-run average of 2.76, and struck out 2396 batters in 2325 innings. During his last five seasons he posted won-lost records of 14–7, 25–5, 19–5, 26–8, and 27–9. He set major-league records by pitching four no-hit games and striking out 382 batters in one year. He twice tied the then record of strikeouts (18) in a nine-inning game. Koufax won the Cy Young Memorial Award as the best pitcher in the major leagues in 1963, 1965, and 1966. In 1972, he was elected to the Baseball Hall of Fame; see BASEBALL HALL OF FAME AND MUSEUM, NATIONAL.

KOUSSEVITZKY, Serge (Alexandrovitch) (1874–1951), Russian-American conductor and virtuoso on the double bass, born in Vishny-Volotchok, and educated in music in Moscow. In 1920 he settled in Paris, where he established a series of concerts of modern works. He appeared as guest conductor in Europe and the United States. From 1924 to 1949 he was conductor of the Boston Symphony Orchestra (q.v.). After 1936 he directed the orchestral concerts of the Berkshire Festival (q.v.) each year. In 1940 he established the Berkshire Music Center. Koussevitzky became a U.S. citizen in 1941.

KOVNO. See KAUNAS.

KOWLOON, peninsula on the mainland of China, opposite the island of Hong Kong (q.v.). Kowloon, about 3 sq.mi. in area, was ceded to the British crown colony of Hong Kong by China in 1860. The city of Greater Kowloon is the principal industrial and transportation center of the colony and is connected by rail to Canton, China.

KOZHIKODE, formerly CALICUT, city and seaport of the Republic of India, in Kerala State, on the Arabian Sea, about 350 miles S.W. of Madras. It is a railroad junction and the shipping center of a rich agricultural region. Coffee, coconuts, tea, ginger, pepper, and other spices are the chief exports. Industrial establishments include sawmills, textile mills, coffee-processing plants, and factories producing soap and tile. Kozhikode was visited in 1487 by the Portuguese explorer Pedro de Covilhão (1450?–1545?). In May, 1498, the Portuguese navigator Vasco da Gama (q.v.) arrived there after completing the first voyage from Europe to Asia around the Cape of Good Hope. Portuguese attempts to establish a trading post at Kozhikode, then a prosperous cotton-weaving center, succeeded in 1513. The Portuguese withdrew in 1525. Trading stations were founded in the city by the English East India Company in 1664 and by the French in 1698. The British seized Kozhikode in 1790 in retaliation against attempts by the local rulers to expel European merchants. In 1792 the British annexed the city, with much of the surrounding region. Pop. (1971) 333,980.

KRAFFT-EBING, Baron Richard von (1840–1902), German neuropsychologist, born in Mannheim, and educated at the University of Heidelberg. He served as professor of psychology at the universities of Strasbourg, Graz, and Vienna between 1872 and 1902. In his most important and influential work, *Psychopathia Sexualis* (1886; Eng. trans. 1892), Krafft-Ebing presented the largest collection of case histories of sexual deviation ever made up to that time. He was interested in the psychological aspect of criminal behavior and in the legal aspects of sexually deviant behavior. Krafft-Ebing was often consulted by the courts in criminal cases. He also studied genetic roots in insanity and experimented with hypnosis (q.v.) as a form of treatment for mental disorders (q.v.).

KRAFT, Adam or **KRAFFT, Adam** (1460?–1508?), German stone sculptor, born probably in Nuremberg. Kraft worked in the naturalistic, elaborately ornamented, so-called late Gothic style of sculpture. Among his chief works are a family tomb in the Church of Saint Sebald, Nuremberg; the tabernacle for the Church of Saint Lawrence, Nuremberg; and several bas-reliefs of the Stations of the Cross (q.v.), of which most are in the Germanic Museum in Nuremberg.

KRAGUJEVAC, city of Yugoslavia, in the Republic of Serbia, on the Lepenica R., 60 miles S.E. of Belgrade. The city is a center for the making of munitions and also produces canned vegetables, foundry products, and flour. First mentioned in the 17th century, the city has a cathedral of Byzantine architecture. Kragujevac was the capital of the Serbian prince Miloš Obrenovich I (1780–1860) from 1818 to 1839, during the revolts against Turkey. The Serbian national assembly met here from 1868 to 1880. Pop. (1971) 71,180.

KRAKATAU, or KRAKATOA, small volcanic island of Indonesia, in the Sunda Strait between Java and Sumatra, about 100 miles w. of Djakarta. Until the night of Aug. 26–27, 1883, Krakatau had an area of about 18 sq.mi.; at that time a volcanic eruption and its consequent explosions destroyed most of the island, so that the present area is only 6 sq.mi. The waves produced by the submarine earthquake that accompanied the eruption attained a height of 50 ft. and traveled some 8000 mi.; they killed thousands of people along the coasts of Java and Sumatra and destroyed incalculable amounts of property. One of the explosions produced the loudest noise ever heard by man, which was heard at a distance of 3000 mi. The rock ejected was in the form of fine dust, which was diffused by aerial currents throughout the upper atmosphere; for three years thereafter observers all over the world reported brilliant colorations of sunrise and sunset, caused by the refraction of the rays of the sun by these tiny particles. The island displayed volcanic activity again in 1927, and the inhabitants were evacuated; the island is now uninhabited.

KRAKÓW. See CRACOW.

KRAMER, Jack, in full JOHN (ALBERT) KRAMER (1921–), American tennis player and promoter, born in Las Vegas, Nev. In 1936 he was the national boys' singles champion and two years later won the national interscholastic championship. In 1939 he was named to the first of many U.S. Davis Cup squads. He led the Davis Cup team in 1946 and 1947 in victories over the Australian team. In those same two years Kramer won the prestigious United States singles championship. His sole British (Wimbledon) championship was won in 1947. He retired in 1954 to become a full-time tennis promoter. Kramer, a master of the serve-and-volley "big game", is often ranked with William Tilden and Donald Budge (qq.v.) as one of the U.S. best tennis players of all time.

KRANACH, Lucas. See CRANACH, LUCAS.

KRASNODAR, formerly EKATERINODAR, city of the Soviet Union, in the Russian S.F.S.R., and capital of the Krasnodar Territory, N. of the Caucasus Mts., on the Kuban R. and the Sea of Azov, about 160 miles s. of Rostov. A railroad hub and river port, the city is a processing and distribution center for the rich Kuban agricultural region. In addition to food processing, important industries include petroleum refining and the manufacture of machinery, machine parts, and chemicals. The city has several theaters, museums, and teaching institutes. It was founded as a Cossack fort in 1794 during the reign of Empress Catherine II (q.v.), for whom it was originally named. It was a center for White Russian activities during the Russian civil war (1917–20). The city was renamed Krasnodar in 1920. In World War II it was occupied by German Forces for six months in 1942 and 1943. Pop. (1970) 465,000.

KRASNOYARSK, city and port of the Soviet Union, in the Russian S.F.S.R., and capital of Krasnoyarsk Territory, in central Siberia, on the Yenisey R., about 2100 miles S.E. of Moscow. The territory has an extensive lumbering industry; farming, trapping, and livestock raising are also carried on; and such minerals as aluminum, gold, nickel, and uranium are found. A major river port and rail center, the city has large railroad repair shops, and facilities for building and repairing ships. Krasnoyarsk is also an important manufacturing center with plants producing building and mining equipment, cement, farming and shipbuilding equipment, and textiles. Founded as a fortress in 1628, Krasnoyarsk grew rapidly after the construction of the trans-Siberian railway in the 1890's. Pop. (1970) 648,000.

KREBS, Hans Adolf (1900–), German-born, British biochemist, born in Hildesheim, and educated at the universities of Göttingen, Freiburg, Munich, Berlin, and Hamburg. He served as a research assistant (1926–30) at the Kaiser Wilhelm Institute of Biology. After working briefly at the University of Freiburg, he left Germany in 1933 and settled in England. There he became a Rockefeller research student at the University of Cambridge. Associated with the University of Sheffield after 1935, he was professor of biochemistry and director of research in cell metabolism from 1945 to 1954; in 1954 he was appointed to similar posts at the University of Oxford. Krebs made fundamental contributions to the chemistry of body processes. He developed the so-called Krebs cycle or citric acid cycle, which explains how the various chemical factors in food are turned into physical energy in the human body.

Krebs shared the 1953 Nobel Prize in medicine with the American biochemist Fritz Albert Lipmann (q.v.).

KREFELD, formerly CREFELD or KREFELD-UERDINGEN, city of West Germany, in North Rhine-Westphalia State, about 15 miles N.W. of Düsseldorf and approximately 10 miles w. of the Rhine R. Krefeld is noted for the manufacture of fine silks and velvets; other products include chemicals, dyes, foodstuffs, machinery, and steel. Chartered in 1373, the city was incorporated into Prussia in 1702 and was part of the Prussian Rhine Province until shortly before World War II. Pop. (1970) 222,700.

KREISLER, Fritz (1875–1962), Austrian-American composer and violinist, born in Vienna, and educated at the Vienna and Paris conservatories. At the age of fourteen, Kreisler toured the United States with the Polish pianist Moriz Rosenthal (1862–1946). Following his return to Vienna in 1889, he withdrew from the concert stage for varying periods during the next decade to study medicine and art and to serve briefly as an officer in the Austrian army. Kreisler resumed his musical career in 1899 but suffered a brief hiatus early in World War I when he was wounded while serving in the Austrian army. After 1915 he lived mainly in the U.S., becoming a naturalized citizen in 1943.

Kreisler attained recognition as the most accomplished concert violinist of his time. He composed numerous pieces for the violin, such as *La Précieuse*, *Praeludium and Allegro*, and *Variations on a Theme by Corelli*, which he attributed originally to 17th- and 18th-century masters. Among his other compositions are *Caprice Viennois*, *Liebesfreud*, *Liebesleid*, and *Tambourin Chinois*, all for violin; a string quartet; and the operettas *Apple Blossoms* (1920), *Sissy* (1933), and *Rhapsody* (1944).

KREMLIN. See MOSCOW.

KRENEK, Ernst (1900–   ), Austrian-American composer and writer on music, born in Vienna. He studied with the Austrian composer Franz Schreker (1878–1934) in Vienna and Berlin, and achieved recognition soon after World War I through performances of several of his chamber-music and orchestral compositions. Between 1925 and 1927 he was conductor and stage director at several small theaters in Germany. His *Jonny Spielt Auf* ("Johnny Strikes up the Band", 1925–26; first performed in Leipzig, 1927; in New York City, 1929), a comic opera composed in a style based on American jazz, brought Krenek worldwide recognition and was subsequently translated into eighteen languages. Between 1928 and 1938, when he settled permanently in the United States, Krenek made his home in Vienna and often appeared throughout Europe as a pianist. During these years he began using the twelve-tone system (q.v.) developed by the Viennese composer Arnold Schönberg (q.v.); see MUSIC: *The 20th Century*. Krenek was professor of music at Vassar College from 1939 to 1942 and from 1942 to 1947 headed the music department at Hamline University, Saint Paul, Minn. He became an American citizen in 1945.

Among Krenek's other compositions are the operas *Orpheus and Eurydice* (1923, text by the Austrian painter and poet Oskar Kokoschka; q.v.) and *Karl V* (1931–33; first performed in Prague, 1938), five symphonies, many orchestral works, songs, chamber music, and piano pieces. He wrote *Music Here and Now* (1939); *Studies in Counterpoint* (1940), a work on the twelve-tone method; and *Modal Counterpoint* (1959).

KREUGER, Ivar (1880–1932), Swedish industrialist and financier, born in Kalmar. In 1908 he organized the construction firm of Kreuger & Toll. The firm acquired interests in the Swedish match industry, and expanded them steadily; in 1917 Kreuger organized the Swedish Match Co. as a holding company for the numerous match factories and allied enterprises under his control. He proceeded to establish an international match monopoly, gaining the monopoly of the manufacture and sale of matches in various countries, including Estonia, Latvia, Greece, Germany, and Ecuador, by making large loans to the governments. Kreuger was considered a financial genius and people all over the world and from all walks of life invested in his enterprises. The world economic depression that began in 1929 caused financial stress upon the huge economic empire established by Kreuger & Toll. Kreuger resorted to speculation and fraudulent practices to remain solvent, but by 1932 bankruptcy was imminent and he committed suicide.

KRISHNA, in Hinduism and Indian mythology (qq.v.), the eighth avatar, or incarnation, of the god Vishnu (q.v.). Tradition says that Vishnu appeared as Krishna to rid the world of a tyrannical king named Kamsa, the son of a demon. Kamsa's half-sister Devaki was Krishna's mother; Krishna was her eighth child, her first six children having been slain by Kamsa because he had been told that one of her children would kill him. Devaki's seventh child, Krishna's brother Bala-Rama, was miraculously saved by Vishnu. Krishna, also saved, was secretly exchanged for the child of the cowherd Nanda. Nanda and his wife Yasoda became Krishna's foster parents; and thus Krishna grew up among cowherds, playing boyish pranks and seducing the *gopis* (cow girls) and other rustic maidens, all of whom found his flute playing irresistible. He is said to have had more than 16,000 wives in his lifetime, of whom his favorite was Radha, the daughter of his foster father.

Numerous legends describe Krishna's miracles and heroic exploits. He slew or defeated scores of evil demons and monsters, eventually killing, as predicted, the tyrannical Kamsa. He appears prominently, and as a diety, in the epic poem *Mahabharata* (q.v.), in which he sides with the Pandavas, one of two contending fami-

KRISHNA

Krishna holding Mount Govardhan over the people of Braj, a 16th-century illustration from a Persian translation of the Sanskrit Mahabharata, the Razm-nama.
Metropolitan Museum of Art — Edward C. Moore, Jr., Gift Fund

lies, and acts as the charioteer of the hero Arjuna. It is to Arjuna, troubled on the eve of the decisive battle, that Krishna delivers the celebrated discourse on duty and life known as the *Bhagavad-Gita* (q.v.). Later additions to the *Mahabharata* also portray Krishna as divine; the *Puranas* (q.v.), Sanskrit accounts of legendary, ancient times written between the 6th and 16th centuries A.D., subsequently elaborated on and expanded his divine character. Today, Krishna is probably the most celebrated god of the Hindu pantheon.

For his part in the struggle between the Pandavas and their enemies, the Kauravas, legend says that Krishna and all his race were cursed by Gandhari, the mother of the slaughtered Kaurava brothers. Thereafter, Krishna's people quarreled among themselves, ultimately exterminating one another in a single day by fighting with uprooted reeds grown from a magical iron powder. Krishna and his brother Bala-Rama alone survived. They retired into a nearby forest, where a serpent crawled out of Bala-Rama's mouth, leaving him dead. The solitary Krishna was then killed by a hunter who mistook him for a deer and shot him with an arrow tipped with the same magical iron that had destroyed his people.

Krishna is represented in art as dark, usually blue-skinned. Modern scholars believe that both Krishna and Bala-Rama represent ancient heroes of the non-Aryan tradition who were

455

adopted into the Hindu pantheon at a fairly late date.

KRISTIANIA. *See* OSLO.

KRISTIANSAND, city and seaport in Norway, and capital of Vest-Agder County, on Skagerrak Strait, about 170 miles s.w. of Oslo. The city ships fish products, paper, pulp, and timber. Kristiansand was founded in 1641 by Christian IV (q.v.), King of Denmark and Norway. The city became an Episcopal see in 1682. Pop. (1971 est.) 56,975.

KRIVOY ROG, city of the Soviet Union, in the Ukrainian S.S.R., on the Ingulets R., about 225 miles s.e. of Kiev. Situated within a rich iron-mining region, the city supplies ores for the coal centers of the Donets Basin and is, itself, a major engineering, mining, and steel center of the Soviet Union. Krivoy Rog also produces chemicals, processed foods, and wood products. Founded in the 17th century, the city became industrially important in the early 1880's, when mining was begun in the region. Most of its industry and mines, destroyed when the city was occupied by the Germans in World War II, have since been rebuilt and modernized. Pop. (1970) 573,000.

KROEBER, Alfred L(ouis) (1876–1960), American anthropologist, born in Hoboken, N.J., and educated at Columbia University. He taught at the University of California from 1901 to 1946, becoming professor of anthropology in 1916. He was also successively curator and director of the Anthropological Museum of the university between the years 1908 and 1946. Kroeber led a number of expeditions investigating the North American Indians, particularly in the southwestern United States, and participated in expeditions outside the U.S. to Mexico in 1924 and 1930 and to Peru in 1925, 1926, and 1942. He was recognized as one of the foremost authorities on the languages, religion, and culture of these regions. He was influential in the planning and execution of anthropological field work in the West, and, largely through his textbook, *Anthropology* (1923, rev. 1948), in the teaching of the subject in American colleges. In 1917 he founded the American Anthropological Society. Among Kroeber's other works are *Handbook of Indians of California* (1925), *Peruvian Archaeology* (1944), and *Style and Civilization* (1957).

KROGH, (Schack) August (Steenberg) (1874-1949), Danish physiologist, born in Grenaa, and educated at the University of Copenhagen. He served successively as an assistant in physiology and a lecturer in zoophysiology at the University of Copenhagen from 1899 until 1916, when he was promoted to a professorship in animal physiology. His early experiments were in the field of respiration, and many of his important discoveries in the field were described in his *Mechanism of Gas Exchange in Lungs* (1906). Subsequently he discovered the mechanism whereby blood is brought to and withdrawn from the muscles by the action of capillaries; this discovery earned him the 1920 Nobel Prize in medicine and physiology. He was also a Fellow of the Royal Society of London and a member of the National Academy of Sciences in Washington, D.C.

KROL, John Joseph, Cardinal (1910–), Roman Catholic ecclesiastic, born in Cleveland, Ohio. He studied at Saint Mary's Seminary, Cleveland, and was ordained a priest in 1937. He continued his studies at the Gregorian University in Rome and at the Catholic University in Washington, D.C.; he returned to Cleveland in 1942. He was chancellor of the diocese of Cleveland from 1951 to 1953 and auxiliary bishop and vicar-general of the diocese from 1953 to 1961. Consecrated a bishop in 1953 and appointed archbishop of Philadelphia in 1961, Krol was elevated to the cardinalate by Pope Paul VI in 1967. Cardinal Krol became president of the National Conference of Catholic Bishops in 1971, succeeding John Francis, Cardinal Dearden (q.v.).

KRONSHTADT *or* **KRONSTADT,** city of the Soviet Union, in the Russian S.F.S.R., on Kotlin Island in the Gulf of Finland, about 35 miles w. of Leningrad (q.v.). Peter I (q.v.), called the Great, recognized the value of the island for the defense of Saint Petersburg (now Leningrad), and in the first decade of the 18th century seized it from Sweden and erected fortifications. For almost two centuries it was the port for St. Petersburg, but in 1885 a canal was completed permitting large vessels to discharge at St. Petersburg, and since then Kronshtadt has been exclusively a naval port. The history of the naval station is a violent one; the personnel, sailors, and special troops, have frequently rebelled against government authority. They participated in revolutionary uprisings in 1825, 1882, and 1905–06. In the revolution of March, 1917, they fought successfully against czarist forces, and then in July of the same year mutinied against the provisional government of the liberal leader Aleksandr Kerenski (q.v.). Kronshtadt sailors allied themselves with the Bolsheviks in the November, 1917, revolution, but in March, 1921, they mutinied against the Soviet government and were crushed by Soviet troops.

KROPOTKIN, Prince Pëtr Alekseevich (1842–1921), Russian geographer and anarchist, born in

Moscow. He was in the army from 1862 to 1867, and during this time conducted two successive exploratory expeditions in Siberia and Manchuria, which resulted in valuable geographic discoveries. In 1867 he went to Saint Petersburg (now Leningrad), where he was appointed an official of the Russian Geographic Society. On behalf of the society he conducted a series of explorations of the glaciers of Finland and Sweden between 1871 and 1873. While engaged in these activities, Kropotkin also studied the writings of the leading political theorists, and eventually adopted the socialist revolutionary views of the International Workingmen's Association (q.v.). He later abandoned that body and became an exponent of the still more radical doctrine of anarchism (q.v.).

Returning to Russia, he began to disseminate anarchist propaganda, and in 1874 was arrested and imprisoned. He escaped two years later and went to Switzerland, where he joined an international anarchist society, the Jurassic Federation. He subsequently settled in France, and in 1883 was arrested and sentenced to five years' imprisonment for anarchistic activities. He won his release after only three years, and thereafter lived and worked in England for a number of years. After the Bolshevik Revolution of 1917 he returned to the Soviet Union, settling near Moscow; although he was openly opposed to the Bolshevik government, as he was to all governments, he took no active part in Soviet political life.

The central theme of Kropotkin's numerous writings is the abolition of all forms of government in favor of a communistic society operating solely on the principle of mutual aid and cooperation, rather than through governmental institutions. Kropotkin wrote in both French and English; his writings include *Paroles d'un Révolté* (1885; Eng. trans. *Memoirs of a Revolutionist,* 1899); *Fields, Factories, and Workshops* (1899); *Terror in Russia* (1909); and *Ethics, Origin and Development* (1924).

KRUGER, Stephanus Johannes Paulus, known as OOM PAUL (1825–1904), South African statesman, born in Colesburg, Cape Colony (now the Cape of Good Hope). He went with his parents on the Great Trek, a migration (1835–40) of Boer settlers from the Cape to the territory north of the Orange R. His family was among the founding families of the Transvaal State, the independence of which Great Britain recognized in 1852. Kruger's early experiences as a fighter against the Zulus and other African natives who opposed the Boer settlers contributed to his election as commandant general of the Transvaal forces in 1864. After the British annexed the Transvaal in 1877, Kruger continued in office under the British government, but he was dismissed the following year because of his agitation for the independence of the Transvaal. When the Boer rebellion broke out in 1880, Kruger was one of the military leaders of his people, and, in 1881, became one of the negotiators of the peace agreement with Great Britain. In 1883 Kruger was elected president of the Transvaal, and he was reelected to this office until 1902 when the Boers accepted British supremacy. During the South African War (q.v.), which broke out in 1899, Kruger, who was too old to take the field with his countrymen, went to Europe, where he attempted to gain the aid of various Continental powers for the Transvaal. After the defeat of the Boers in South Africa, Kruger lived in exile, principally in Utrecht, Netherlands, where he dictated *The Memoirs of Paul Kruger* (1902).

KRUGERSDORP, city of South Africa, in Transvaal Province, in the Witwatersrand region, 20 miles N.W. of Johannesburg. The chief city of the West Rand district, it is a center for the mining of gold, uranium, and manganese, has metalworking and tanning industries, and manufactures chemicals and paint. A technical college and a large sports ground are in the city. The Paardekraal monument commemorates the victory of the Boers over the Zulus in 1838 and was the site of the meeting of Boer leaders in 1880 that led to the restoration of the republic. Nearby to the N.W. are the Sterkfontein caves, where the remains of protohumans have been found. Founded in 1887, Krugersdorp was named for Stephanus Johannes Paulus Kruger (qq.v.), the last Boer president of the South African Republic. Pop. (1968 est.) 100,525.

KRUPP, name of a family of German industrialists who became world famous as owners of Fried. Krupp of Essen, a vast steel and munitions concern, founded by Friedrich Krupp (1727–1826) with the intention of manufacturing a high-quality steel to equal or surpass that of English origin. The following were among its most important members.

Alfred Krupp (1812–87), known as the Cannon King, son of Friedrich, born in Essen. He developed the process, begun by his father, of making cast steel. In 1847 he introduced a muzzle-loading cannon (q.v.) of cast steel. In 1851 at the Great Exhibition in London, he showed a flawless block of cast steel weighing more than 2 tons, an accomplishment that brought him international recognition. Another of his achievements was the development of the seamless

KRUPP

Alfred Krupp — Library of Congress

railway wheel, which was afterward widely adopted. Krupp artillery and breech-loading rifles, first used by the Prussian army in 1861, proved their superiority to conventional weapons in the siege of Paris during the Franco-German War (q.v.) in 1871. During the 1860's Alfred acquired coal and iron mines, creating an integrated industrial empire, which was one of the earliest in Germany.

Friedrich Alfred Krupp (1854–1902), son of Alfred, born in Essen. He devoted himself to the financial side of the munitions business and greatly expanded the Krupp interests. He acquired other steel plants and more coal and iron mines, purchased shipyards, and operated a steamer fleet.

Bertha Krupp (1886–1957), daughter of Friedrich Alfred, born in Essen. She inherited the Krupp holdings from her father and headed the firm until shortly after her marriage in 1906 to Gustav von Bohlen und Halbach. Afterward she concentrated mainly on developing extensive social-welfare programs for employees of the firm. The famous "Big Bertha" cannon, which was used by Germany in World War I, was named for her.

Gustav von Bohlen und Halbach (1870–1950), husband of Bertha Krupp, born in The Hague, the Netherlands. To prevent the Krupp name from dying out, he took the name Krupp von Bohlen und Halbach and became head of the firm. During the years before World War I, the Krupp works supplied armor plate and guns for new ships in the rapidly expanding German navy. At this time, also, the firm became internationally famous for the manufacture of heavy-siege mortars and long-range cannon. After World War I, the firm was forced by the Allies to reduce steel capacity and was forbidden to manufacture firearms. Krupp concentrated on peacetime goods and rebuilt the enterprise. He was, however, a supporter of National Socialism (q.v.) and of the rearmament program instituted by the German dictator Adolf Hitler (q.v.) in the early 1930's. Thus the Krupps produced arms once again. After the defeat of Germany in World War II Krupp was indicted as a war criminal, but because of his poor health, he was not tried by the International Military Tribunal; *see* WAR-CRIMES TRIALS: *Nuremberg Trials.*

Alfried Alwyn Felix Krupp von Bohlen und Halbach (1907–67), son of Gustav, last of the family to control the Krupp firm, born in Essen. He succeeded his father as head of the Krupp industry in 1942 and thereafter coordinated the National Socialist war industries. In 1948 a United States tribunal convicted Alfried of plundering industries in occupied countries and using slave labor during World War II. He was

The last member of the Krupp family, Alfried Krupp von Bohlen und Halbach (right), who held sole control of the company, seen here chatting shortly before his death, with apprentices in the Krupp engineering works at Essen, West Germany.
German Information Center

sentenced to twelve years in prison, and his properties were confiscated. In 1951 he was released and his properties restored. By the terms of a direct agreement made in March, 1953, with the Allied High Commission, Krupp was to divest himself of his iron, steel, and coal interests. This arrangement was never put into effect, however, because no buyers appeared. In the 1960's the Krupp empire went heavily into debt, and in 1967 Alfried was forced to relinquish family ownership of the firm in order to obtain necessary financing. His only son and heir, Arndt Krupp von Bohlen und Halbach (1939–), in return for renouncing his right to the business, was given an annual stipend of about $500,000.

KRUTCH, Joseph Wood (1893–1970), American critic, educator, and naturalist, born in Knoxville, Tenn., and educated at the University of Tennessee and Columbia University in New York City. From 1924 to 1951 he was the drama critic of the liberal weekly The Nation and taught dramatic literature at Columbia University and several other institutions. In these years he also published books at the rate of one each year, including biographies and essays on drama, science, and nature. In the early 1950's Krutch moved to the Arizona desert, seeking better health and an escape from urban life.

His work thereafter, including The Measure of Man (1954), for which he won the 1955 National Book Award in nonfiction, reflects his increasing concern with ecology and his expertise as a naturalist. In the early 1960's Krutch appeared on network television as star and co-producer of two documentary films, tours of the Sonoran Desert near Tucson, Ariz. (1963), and of the Grand Canyon of the Colorado (1965). Critics list among his important books Edgar Allan Poe: A Study in Genius (1926), The Modern Temper (1929), The American Drama since 1918 (1939; revised, 1957), the autobiographical More Lives than One (1962), and The Best Nature Writing of Joseph Wood Krutch (1970), an anthology.

KRYPTON, element, member of the group of inert gases (q.v.), with at.no. 36, at.wt. 83.80, b.p. $-152.3°$ C. ($-242.1°$ F.), m.p. $-157.21°$ C.^{549mm} ($-250.978°$ F.^{549mm}), sp.gr. 3.74, and symbol Kr. It was first isolated in 1898 by the British chemists Sir William Ramsay (q.v.) and Morris William Travers (1872–1961) by fractional distillation (q.v.) of a mixture of the inert gases. Krypton is present in the atmosphere to the extent of 1 part in 20,000,000 by volume or 1 part in 7,000,000 by weight. It is a colorless, odorless gas. Several compounds of krypton were discovered in 1962 and 1963. Krypton is used alone or with argon and neon (qq.v.) in incandescent bulbs. It emits a characteristic bright orange-red color in an electric discharge tube; such tubes filled with krypton are used in lighting airfields because the red light is visible at a distance and penetrates fog and haze to a greater extent than ordinary light. In 1960 the International Commission on Weights and Measures meeting in Paris adopted as the length of the standard meter 1,650,763.73 wavelengths of light (q.v.) emitted by the isotope krypton-86. See also C.G.S. SYSTEM; WEIGHTS AND MEASURES.

KUALA LUMPUR, city and capital of Malaysia, in Selangor State, about 200 miles N.W. of Singapore. The city is the transportation center of a region noted for tin mines and rubber plantations. It has an international airport and is connected by rail and road with Port Swettenham on the Strait of Malacca. The seat of administration for the Malay states after 1895, Kuala Lumpur became capital of the Federation of Malaya in 1948. In 1963 the city became capital of the newly formed Federation of Malaysia. Pop. (1970) 451,728.

KUBELIK, name of two Czech musicians, father and son.

Jan Kubelik (1880–1940), violinist, born near Prague, Czechoslovakia (then Austria-Hungary), and naturalized (1903) as a Hungarian citizen under the surname Polgar. He was trained at the Prague Conservatory and made his debut as a violinist in Vienna in 1898. Thereafter he made concert tours throughout the world. He visited the United States for the first time in 1901 and often performed in the U.S. until 1935. Kubelik attracted large audiences because of his technical skill and superb interpretation of violin music by many different composers.

(Jeronym) Rafael Kubelik (1914–), conductor, son of Jan, born near Kolin (then in Austria-Hungary), and trained as a composer, conductor, and violinist at the Prague Conservatory. He made his conducting debut with the Czech Philharmonic Society orchestra, which he led from 1936 to 1939. He later served as conductor of the National Theater, Brno, Czechoslovakia (1939–41); the Czech Philharmonic orchestra, Prague (1941–48); the Chicago Symphony Orchestra (1951–53); and the Royal Opera House, Covent Garden, London (1955–58). In 1961 he was appointed chief conductor of the Bavarian Radio Symphony Orchestra, Munich, and in 1973 became music director of the Metropolitan Opera Company (q.v.), New York City. He also wrote operas, symphonies, and string quartets.

KUBITSCHEK, Juscelino (1902–), Brazilian surgeon and twentieth president of Brazil, born in Diamantina, Minas Gerais State, and educated at Minas Gerais University. After postgraduate work at hospitals in Paris, Vienna, and Berlin, he practiced surgery in Brazil until 1933, when he was appointed secretary to the federal administrator of Minas Gerais. Later that year Kubitschek was elected to the Brazilian chamber of deputies; he served until it was dissolved in the coup d'état of 1937. In 1939, after two years in private practice, he was elected mayor of Belo Horizonte, capital of Minas Gerais. From 1946 to 1950, he was again a member of the chamber of deputies. From 1950 to 1955 he was governor of Minas Gerais. Elected president of Brazil as a labor-center coalition candidate, he served from 1956 to 1960. In June, 1964, Kubitschek was barred from voting or holding political office for ten years because of alleged corruption during his presidency.

KUBLAI KHAN or **KHUBILAI KHAN** or **KUBLA KHAN** (1215–94), Mongol military leader, founder and first Emperor of the Mongol Yüan dynasty (see MONGOL DYNASTIES) in China, grandson of the Mongol conqueror Genghis Khan (q.v.) and his best-known successor. Kublai Khan completed the conquest of China

Kublai Khan, from an ancient Chinese painting.

which was begun by his grandfather; see CHINA: History. From 1252 to 1259 he aided his brother Mangu Khan (1207?–59) in the conquest of southern China, penetrating successfully as far as Tibet and Tonkin. Upon the death of Mangu in 1259 he became the khan or ruler. Between 1260 and 1279 he succeeded in driving the Kin Tatars out of northern China, and in subduing rebellious factions among the Mongols. In 1264 he founded his capital on the site now occupied by Peking; it was called Khanbalik, which is romanized as Cambaluc or Cambalu. He relinquished all claims to the parts of the Mongol Empire outside of China, consolidated his hold on China, and in 1280 established the Yüan dynasty as the successor to the Southern Sung dynasty. He undertook foreign wars in attempts to enforce tribute claims on neighboring states, conquering Burma and Korea. However, his military expeditions to Java and Japan met with disaster.

His name was known all over Asia and also in Europe. The court at Cambaluc attracted an international group of adventurous men, including the famous Venetian traveler Marco Polo (q.v.). Kublai Khan did much to encourage the advancement of literature and the arts. He was a devout Buddhist and made Buddhism the state religion, but during his reign other religions were also tolerated.

KUCHING, city in Malaysia, and capital of Sarawak State, on the Sarawak R., 18 miles above its mouth on the South China Sea, about 450 miles E. of Singapore. A road center and chief port for the W. coast of Borneo, the city exports timber, bauxite from nearby mines, pepper, sago, and jelutong, or jungle rubber, and trades in rice, fish, and livestock. It manufactures lumber and furniture, food products, alcohol, matches, cigarettes, and soap and has vegetable-oil and boat-building industries. The large Chinese section of the city has several temples. Outstanding buildings are the Sarawak Museum and Library and, across the river, the Astana, residence of the white rajas of the Brooke family from 1841 to 1946 (see BROOKE, SIR JAMES), and now the governor's residence. Also in Kuching are Anglican and Roman Catholic cathedrals, a mosque, and a teacher-training center. The city became the state capital in 1963. It was also formerly called Sarawak. Pop. (1969 est.) 70,000.

KUDU, or KOODOO, common name for either of two African antelope namely, the species *Tragelaphus strepsiceros,* the greater kudu, and *Strepsiceros imberbis,* the lesser kudu. The greater kudu is one of the largest antelope, measuring about 5 ft. high at the shoulder. The animal is grayish brown, with a longitudinal white stripe along the middle of its back, and with several transverse white stripes on each side. The male has long, spiraling horns, sometimes more than 4 ft. in length; the female is hornless. Greater kudus, found in the forests and dense brush of Tanzania, and less commonly in Kenya and Uganda, are timid, gentle animals and feed on leaves, fruit, and grass. The lesser kudu is similar in color to the greater, but measures only about 40 in. at the shoulder. This animal is also found in thick forests in eastern Africa.

KUDZU, common name of a leguminous vine, *Pueraria thunbergiana,* belonging to the Pea family. The plant, which is native to China and Japan, is a coarse-growing perennial with large trifoliate leaves having coarsely lobed leaflets.

Kudzu, Pueraria thunbergiana

The flowers, borne on long racemes, are large and purple. The fruit is a flat, papery pod covered with a tawny down. Kudzu plants often fail to bloom or, after blooming, fail to produce normal seed. Most kudzu plants are grown from root cuttings; kudzus produce long, lateral runners that generate roots at intervals.

Kudzu produces edible roots, and the stems yield a fiber, called ko-hemp. Since the introduction of kudzu into the United States in 1876, it has become important as a source of hay and forage and for its use in controlling soil erosion. Kudzu is well adapted to the southern U.S.; in northern regions, growth is exceeded by that of other legumes, such as clover and alfalfa. As a hay plant, the viny nature of kudzu makes it difficult to harvest, but as pasturage kudzu is valuable for its high protein and vitamin A and D content. The value of kudzu in reducing soil erosion arises from the binding capacity of the long runners which it produces.

KUHN, Richard (1900–67), Austrian chemist, born in Vienna, and educated at the universities of Vienna and Munich. He was *Privatdocent* at the University of Munich from 1925 until 1926, when he was appointed professor of chemistry at the University of Zürich. In 1935 he became professor and director of the chemistry department at the Kaiser Wilhelm Institute for Medical Research (now the Max Planck Institute in Berlin). Kuhn is best known for his researches on carotinoids and vitamins, for which he was awarded the 1938 Nobel Prize in chemistry. He was forced by the National Socialist government of Germany to decline the award, receiving it finally in 1949. In addition to writings on carotenes, he wrote *Chemistry of the Present and Biology of the Future* (1927).

KUHN, Walt (1880–1949), American painter, born in New York City. After studying in many European countries, he helped organize the famous Armory Show (International Exhibition of Modern Art, New York City, 1913). He is noted chiefly for his vigorous studies of circus performers, chorus girls, and trapeze athletes. His "The Blue Clown" (1931) in the Whitney Museum of American Art, New York City, is the most popular example of his work. He also did a number of brilliant studies of still lifes. Kuhn contributed substantially to the introduction of the techniques and theories of modern art to the American public and to many American artists.

KUIBYSHEV. See KUYBYSHEV.

KU KLUX KLAN, name of a secret terrorist organization active in the Southern States during the period of Reconstruction (q.v.) that followed the American Civil War (*see* CIVIL WAR, THE AMERICAN), and which was reactivated on a wider geographic basis in the 20th century. The original Klan was organized in Pulaski, Tenn., on Dec. 24, 1865, by six former Confederate army officers who gave their society a name adapted from the Greek work *kuklos* ("circle"). Although the Ku Klux Klan began as a prankish social organization, its activities soon were directed against the Republican Reconstruction governments and their leaders, both Negro and white, which came into power in the Southern States in 1867. *See also* CARPETBAGGERS.

Original Targets and Tactics. The Klansmen regarded the Reconstruction governments as hostile and oppressive. They also generally believed in the innate inferiority of Negroes and therefore mistrusted and resented the rise of former slaves to a status of civil equality and often to positions of political power. Thus the Klan became an illegal underground committed to destroying the Reconstruction governments from the Carolinas to Arkansas. Attired in robes or sheets and wearing masks topped with

Ku Klux Klan members parading in Binghamton, N.Y., in the 1920's, when the Klan became active in the North. UPI

pointed hoods, the Klansmen terrorized public officials in efforts to drive them from office and Negroes in general to prevent them from voting, holding office, and otherwise exercising their newly acquired political rights. It was customary for the Klansmen to burn crosses on hillsides and near the homes of those they wished to frighten. When such tactics failed to produce the desired effect, their victims might be flogged, mutilated, or murdered; *see* LYNCHING. These activities were justified by the Klan as necessary measures in defense of white supremacy and the inviolability of white womanhood.

A secret convention of Klansmen, held in Nashville, Tenn., in 1867, adopted a declaration of principles expressing loyalty to the Constitution of the United States and its government and declaring the determination of the Klan to "protect the weak, the innocent and the defenseless . . . ; to relieve the injured and oppressed; [and] to succor the suffering. . . ." The convention designated the Klan as an Invisible Empire and provided for a supreme official, called Grand Wizard of the Empire, who wielded virtually autocratic power and who was assisted by ten Genii. Other principal officials of the Klan were the Grand Dragon of the Realm, who was assisted by eight Hydras; the Grand Titan of the Dominion, assisted by six Furies; and the Grand Cyclops of the Den, assisted by two Nighthawks.

From 1868 to 1870, while Federal occupation troops were being withdrawn from the Southern States and Radical regimes replaced with Democratic administrations, the Klan was increasingly dominated by the rougher elements in the population. The local organizations, called klaverns, became so uncontrollable and violent that the Grand Wizard, former Confederate General Nathan Bedford Forrest (q.v.), officially disbanded the Klan in 1869. Klaverns, however, continued to operate on their own. In 1871, Congress passed the Force Bill to implement the Fourteenth Amendment to the Constitution of the U.S. guaranteeing the rights of all citizens; *see* CONSTITUTION OF THE UNITED STATES: *Amendments to the Constitution.* In the same year President Ulysses S. Grant (q.v.) issued a proclamation calling on members of illegal organizations to disarm and disband; thereafter hundreds of Klansmen were arrested. The remaining klaverns gradually faded as the political and social subordination of Negroes was reestablished.

Invisible Empire, Knights of the Ku Klux Klan. The name, rituals, and some of the attitudes of the original Klan were adopted by a new fraternal organization incorporated in Georgia in 1915. The official name of the new society, which was organized by a former preacher, Colonel William Joseph Simmons (d. 1945), was Invisible Empire, Knights of the Ku Klux Klan. Membership was open to native-born, white, Protestant males, sixteen years of age or older; Negroes, Catholics, and Jews were excluded and were increasingly made targets of defamation and persecution by the Klan. Until 1920 the society exercised little influence. Then, in the period of economic dislocation and political and social unrest which followed World War I, the Klan expanded rapidly and became active in almost all States, notably Oregon, Colorado, Kansas, Oklahoma, Texas, Alabama, Georgia, Illinois, Indiana, Ohio, Pennsylvania, and New Jersey. Although the Klan everywhere fiercely preached white supremacy, it focused its attack on what it considered to be alien-outsiders, particularly the Roman Catholic Church, which it believed was threatening traditional American ways and values. All non-Protestants, aliens, liberals, trade unionists, and striking workers were denounced as subversives.

Like its prototype, the Klan burned fiery crosses to frighten its victims. Masked Klansmen also marched through the streets of many communities, carrying placards threatening various persons with summary punishment and warning others to leave town. Many persons were kidnapped, flogged, and mutilated by the Klan; a number were killed. Few prosecutions of Klansmen resulted, and in some communities they were abetted by local officials.

Journalistic disclosures of crimes committed by the Klan and of corruption and immorality in its leadership led to a Congressional investigation in 1921, and for a time the Klan changed its tactics. After 1921 it experienced a rapid growth of membership and became politically influential throughout the nation. One estimate of its membership, made in 1924, when the Klan was at the peak of its strength, was as high as 3,000,000. In that year a resolution denouncing the Klan, introduced at the national convention of the Democratic Party (q.v.), precipitated a bitter controversy and was defeated.

In the middle 1920's, inept and exploitive leadership, internal conflict, and alleged Klan immorality and violence badly damaged the Klan's reputation, and political opposition increased. By 1929 it had been reduced to several thousand members. During the economic depression of the 1930's the Ku Klux Klan remained active on a small scale, particularly against trade-union organizers in the South. It also openly threatened Negroes with dire punishment if they exercised their right to vote. In 1940 the Klan joined with the German-American Bund, an organization financed in part by the National Socialist government in Germany, in holding a large rally at Camp Nordland, N.J.

After the entry of the U.S. into World War II, the Klan curtailed its activities. In 1944 it disbanded formally when it was unable to pay back taxes owed to the Federal government. Revival of Klan activities after the war led to widespread public sentiment for the suppression of the organization. It suffered a setback in its national stronghold, Georgia, when that State revoked the Klan charter in 1947. With the death of its strongest postwar leader, the obstetrician Dr. Samuel Green, (1890–1949), of Atlanta, Ga., Klan unity broke down into numerous, independent, competing units, which often did not last long enough to be placed on the list of subversive organizations issued by the U.S. attorney general.

Recent Activity. The Supreme Court ruling, on May 17, 1954, that racial segregation in public schools was unconstitutional, stirred the Klan into new attempts at recruitment and violence but did not bring internal unity or greatly increased membership, power, or respectability in the South. Most opponents of desegregation chose other leaders, such as the White Citizens Councils, while the Klans chiefly attracted the fringe elements of society and remained more of a status than a resistance movement.

As the civil-rights movement gained force in the late 1950's and as massive resistance to integration began to diminish throughout the South, the Klan continued to offer hard-core opposition to civil-rights programs and was believed to be involved in many incidents of racial violence, intimidation, and reprisal, particularly bombings. After the U.S. Civil Rights Act of 1964 it experienced a marked increase in membership to an estimated 40,000 in 1965. Most of its members were drawn from urban and small-town working classes. Currently the major organizations are the United Klans, with headquarters in Tuscaloosa, Ala., and the National Knights, operating out of Tucker, Ga. The most violence-prone groups were believed to be the closely allied National States Rights Party and the White Knights of the Ku Klux Klan of Mississippi.   D.M.C.

KULTURKAMPF (Ger., "culture" and "struggle"), name applied to the conflict between the Roman Catholic Church (q.v.) and the German Empire between 1871 and 1883. In 1870 the Vati-

KUMAMOTO

can Council promulgated the dogma of papal infallibility (*see* INFALLIBILITY). The German chancellor Prince Otto von Bismarck (q.v.) felt that the subsequent increase of the authority of the Roman Catholic Church in Germany, as well as its support by the Center Party, composed of Catholic groups, threatened the power of the empire. In 1872 Bismarck passed a law suppressing the order of the Society of Jesus, and all Jesuits (q.v.) were expelled from the empire; the following year the May Laws, or Falk Laws, making the Roman Catholic clergy in Germany subject to the authority of the state, were promulgated. During the next two years, in spite of bitter opposition from the Catholic elements in Germany, civil marriage was made obligatory; all religious orders, except nursing orders, were dissolved; and various other laws repressing the power of the Roman Catholic clergy were passed. Under the new laws hundreds of priests were imprisoned, and half the Roman Catholic bishops in Germany were displaced, many of them being forced to flee abroad. After the accession of Pope Leo XIII (*see under* LEO) in 1878, negotiations between the Vatican and the German Empire were reopened, and the various repressive laws were gradually abandoned. A compromise was reached in 1883, and the only repressive laws remaining in effect were the proscription of the Jesuits and the law making civil marriages compulsory. *See* GERMANY: *History.*

KUMAMOTO, city in Japan, and capital of Kumamoto Prefecture, on the w. coast of the island of Kyushu, about 50 miles E. of Nagasaki. The city is the marketing and processing center for the surrounding region in which tobacco and vegetables are grown. Local industries include the manufacture of bamboo ware and pottery. Kumamoto is also the seat of two universities and a junior college. Founded in the 16th century, the city was a stronghold of feudal Japan and one of the centers of the Satsuma Rebellion in 1877. Pop. (1970) 440,020.

KUMASI, formerly COOMASSIE, city in Ghana, and capital of the Ashanti region, in a dense forest belt about 125 miles N.W. of Accra. It is the commercial and transportation center for a rich cacao-producing area. The principal industry is food processing. The city is the site of the University of Science and Technology and four research institutes of the Ghana Academy of Sciences. Kumasi was founded about 1700 as capital of a confederacy of Ashanti (q.v.) tribes. During the 19th century, it was the site of several battles between the Ashanti and the British. The city was the scene of a native uprising in 1900, after which the region was annexed to the British Gold Coast Colony; *see* GOLD COAST. Pop. (1970) 342,986.

KUMQUAT, common name of small evergreen shrubs of the genus *Fortunella,* closely related to the citrus genus, and of the edible orange-colored fruits produced by these trees. Native to China and Indochina, the shrubs are extensively cultivated in Japan and in the

Kumquat, Fortunella margarita

United States in Florida and California. The two principal species are *F. japonica,* which bears a globular fruit, and *F. margarita,* which bears an elliptical fruit. Fruits of both species are sweet and palatable, and grow about as large as a small plum. Both species of kumquat are fairly hardy and are grown as ornamental tub plants in northern U.S. and as outdoor plants in southern U.S. Commercial kumquats are usually hybrids between *Fortunella* and *Citrus* (q.v.). They are frequently preserved in syrup and eaten as dessert.

KUN, Béla (1886–1937), Hungarian communist leader, born in Szilágy-Cseh, Transylvania. He became an exponent of Marxian socialism in his youth, and later joined the Hungarian Social-Democratic Party. Upon the outbreak of World War I he was drafted into the Austro-Hungarian army; he was captured by Russian troops in 1915 and sent to a prison camp in Siberia. Kun spent the ensuing two years disseminating revolutionary socialist propaganda among his fellow-prisoners. Subsequent to the Bolshevik Revolution of November, 1917, Kun was allowed to go to

Moscow, where he became the leader of a group of Hungarian communists. One year later he led this group to Budapest and launched a movement to overthrow the recently established Hungarian People's Republic; see HUNGARY: *History*. In February, 1919, he was arrested by the government and imprisoned, but in the following month the head of the government, Count Mihály Károlyi (q.v.), realizing his regime was faced with imminent collapse, handed the governmental power over to Kun and the communists, who immediately proclaimed the establishment of the Hungarian Soviet Republic. Kun launched a military offensive against the Czech armies then poised threateningly on the Hungarian border, and after winning a series of victories set up a soviet republic in Slovakia in June, 1919. He was persuaded to withdraw his troops, however, by the promise made by the Rumanian government, which had sent an invading army into Hungary, to recall its forces, and the pledge of the French government to accord formal recognition to Kun's regime.

Meanwhile the domestic situation in Hungary had deteriorated as a result of some of the policies initiated by Kun, especially the hastily executed nationalization of the large landed estates and of the factories, which alienated large sections of the population. In August, 1919, when the Rumanian army advanced to the outskirts of Budapest, the Hungarian Soviet collapsed and Kun fled to Vienna and then to the Soviet Union in 1920. Welcomed by the leaders of the Soviet government, Kun was given an important official position in the administration. Little is known of his subsequent activites; reputedly, he was charged with participation in a widespread conspiracy against the Soviet regime in 1937, and was executed.

KUNIYOSHI, Yasuo (1893–1953), American painter, born in Okayama, Japan. He came to the United States in 1906 and studied in Los Angeles and at the Art Students League in New York City. Kuniyoshi's early paintings were marked by somber black and gray hues, severely stylized forms, and traces of Oriental tonalities. He subsequently established himself as one of the foremost artists of the U.S. with a series of still-life paintings of early American objects such as weathervanes and old crockery. In his arrangement of these motifs Kuniyoshi imparted an exotic flavor to his commonplace subject matter. He was also known for large studies of nudes and of female circus performers. He received the Temple Gold Medal at the Pennsylvania Academy of Fine Arts in 1934, and in 1935 a Guggenheim fellowship.

KUNLUN MOUNTAINS, mountain chain of central Asia. It forms the N. wall of the Tibetan plateau, as the Himalayas do the S. The peaks measure from 18,000 to more than 25,000 ft. in altitude, and the passes from 13,000 to 18,000 ft.

KUNMING, formerly YÜNNAN or YÜNNANFU, city in the People's Republic of China, and capital of Yünnan Province, on the fertile Yünnan Plateau, about 6300 ft. above sea level, on the N. shore of Tien Chih Lake and about 380 miles S. of Chengtu. Kunming consists of a walled inner city that is almost completely surrounded by a modern section. The city is an important transportation center. The major industries manufacture chemicals, textiles, and machinery, and smelt tin and copper. The city is the site of Yünnan University. Kunming dates from the Shang dynasty (about 1766 B.C.–about 1122 B.C.). During World War II, it served as the E. terminus of the famed Burma Road (q.v.) and as an Allied military base. Pop. (1970 est.) 1,700,000.

KUNSAN, city of South Korea, in North Cholla Province, on the Yellow Sea, at the mouth of the Kum R., 27 miles N.W. of Chonju, and 115 miles S.W. of Seoul. A port, rail terminus, and industrial city, it exports rice, leather, paper, soybeans, and gold. Industries include rice and paper milling, sake brewing, fishing, and the manufacture of machine tools and plywood. The Kunsan Fisheries Junior College is in the city. Under Japanese rule from 1910 to 1945 the city was called Gunzan. Pop. (1970 est.) 105,000.

KUNZITE. See SPODUMENE.

KUOMINTANG (Chin., "Nationalist People's Party"), political party of China organized during the Revolution of 1911, by which the Manchu dynasty was overthrown and a republican government in China established; see CHINA: *The Republican Period*. The Kuomintang was founded by the Nationalist revolutionary leader Sun Yat-sen (q.v.), whose election in 1911 as provisional president of the republic established the Kuomintang as the leading party in the new government. In the following year, however, Sun was succeeded as president by the military leader Yüan Shih-k'ai (q.v.) who, finding his autocratic policies opposed by the Kuomintang governmental representatives, expelled the party from the government.

After World War I the Kuomintang set up a separate government in southern China and attempted to secure the recognition of the major foreign powers, but succeeded in gaining only that of the Soviet Union. The party held its first national congress in 1924; included among the delegates were numerous non-Kuomintang groups, notably the representatives of the Chinese Communist Party, who exercised great influence on the decisions of the congress. Between 1924 and 1927 the power of the Communists within the Kuomintang increased sharply, but in the latter year Chiang Kai-shek (q.v.), then a military officer and leader of a right-wing faction of the party, expelled the Communists and began a military campaign aimed both against them and at the conquest and unification of all China under the Kuomintang banner. By late 1928 this campaign had largely succeeded, and the Kuomintang then inaugurated a period of "political tutelage", during which the party was to conduct the government while educating the people in the use of their political rights. This period, originally scheduled to end in 1935, was extended, because of the war against Japan, until the end of 1947, when a new constitution was promulgated and the end of Kuomintang one-party government was proclaimed.

Meanwhile, following the conclusion of World War II, the Communists, operating from bases in northern China and Manchuria, had resumed hostilities against the Kuomintang-led Nationalist government. Attempts in 1946 by the United States government to mediate the strife ended in failure. In the bloody fighting that ensued the Nationalist armies suffered a succession of grave defeats, and by the middle of 1949 the Communists controlled most of the Chinese mainland. The Kuomintang and remnants of its armies withdrew in the summer of 1949 to the island of Taiwan (q.v.). With U.S. economic help and under the leadership of Chiang Kai-shek, the Kuomintang gradually transformed Taiwan into one of the chief anti-Communist strongholds in the Far East.

KUOPIO, city in Finland, and capital of Kuopio Province, on the N.W. shore of Lake Kallavesi at the head of the Saimaa lake system, about 210 miles N.E. of Helsinki. A transportation center, with water, rail, and road facilities, Kuopio is the commercial, industrial, and educational center of the province. Principal industries in the city include food processing and the manufacture of machinery and textiles. Pop. (1970 est.) 65,000.

KURA, river in the S. European Soviet Union, the longest river of the Transcaucasia region (see CAUCASIA), approximately 950 mi. in length, of which only the last 300 mi. are navigable. The river rises as the Kuruçay in the mountains of N.E. Turkey. It flows N.E. into the Georgian S.S.R. to a point near Gori where it arcs and turns S.E. At Zemo-Avchala, a village 8 miles N. of Tbilisi, is a hydroelectric station. Continuing S.E. past Rustavi, the river enters the Azerbaidzhan S.S.R. A dam and hydroelectric plant have been built at Mingechaur; the dam forms the 40-mi.-long Mingechaur Reservoir. At Sabirabad, the Kura receives the Araks (q.v.), the most important tributary. The Kura enters the Caspian Sea (q.v.) about 75 miles S. of Baku (q.v.).

KURCHATOVIUM, name assigned in 1964 by Soviet scientists to claimed discovery of chemical element number 104. The priority of discovery of this element is in dispute, and the name has not yet been accepted internationally. See ELEMENTS, CHEMICAL.

KURDISTAN, extensive region of Asia in E. Turkey, S.W. Armenian S.S.R., N.W. Iran, N.W. Iraq, and a small part of N.E. Syria. The area is extremely mountainous and includes two large lakes, Lake Van in Turkey and Lake Urmia in Iran. Among the largest cities in the area are Mosul and Kirkuk in Iraq, Kermanshah in Iran, and Diyarbakir and Erzurum in Turkey. Area, about 74,000 sq.mi. See KURDS.

KURDS (anc. *Carduchi*), seminomadic tribes inhabiting Kurdistan (q.v.). The Kurds are Sunnites (q.v.) or orthodox Muslims many of whom live in small villages and are engaged in agriculture and sheep raising. Their chief manufacture is finely-woven rugs. They speak Kurdish, a language of the western Iranian branch of the Indo-European languages (q.v.). The Kurds resisted invasions by many warring peoples, but were subjugated by the Seljuks (q.v.) in the 11th century and brought into the Ottoman Empire (q.v.) in the 14th century. According to the Treaty of Sèvres, concluded by the Allies with Turkey in 1920, the Kurds were promised an independent state, but this promise was not kept; see SÈVRES, TREATY OF. After 1925 Kurdish revolts have occurred sporadically in Turkey, Iraq, and Iran. In 1970, after more than eight years of almost continuous war, the Iraqi government granted the Kurds autonomy over a region in northwestern Iraq. Kurds were given cabinet status in the central government to deal with problems of the region. Kurdish also became one of the official languages of Iraq.

KURE, city and seaport of Japan, in Hiroshima Prefecture, on the W. coast of Honshu Island, about 125 miles S.W. of Kobe. Kure has extensive shipbuilding facilities and dockyards and, before the occupation of Japan by Allied forces in 1945, was one of the largest naval bases of the Japanese Empire. Pop. (1970) 235,193.

KURGAN, city of the Soviet Union in Asia, in the Russian S.F.S.R., capital of Kurgan Oblast, on the Tobol R., 180 miles E. of Chelyabinsk. Kurgan is served by the Trans-Siberian Railroad; see SI-

BERIA: *Production and Industry*. It is also the industrial center for a rich agricultural region. Industries include the manufacture of agricultural and other machinery and the processing of agricultural products. The city's name means tumulus, or burial ground, and refers to the ancient burial grounds in the area. Pop. (1970) 244,000.

KURIA MURIA ISLANDS, group of five barren islands, belonging to Oman, in Kuria and Muria Bay, off the S.E. coast of Arabia. They were ceded to Great Britain in 1854 by the Sultan of Oman for a station of the Red Sea telegraph cable. The islands were returned to Oman in 1967. Area, 30 sq.mi.

KURIL ISLANDS *or* **KURILE ISLANDS** (Russ. *kurit*, "to smoke"), chain of about thirty large and twenty small volcanic islands in the N. Pacific Ocean, belonging to the Soviet Union, and extending N.E. about 700 mi. from the N.E. tip of Hokkaido to the S. end of Kamchatka Peninsula. The Kurils are heavily forested and contain many active volcanoes. Hunting, fishing, and sulphur mining are the chief occupations of the inhabitants, the most interesting of whom are the Ainu (q.v.). The Kurils were settled by both the Russians and Japanese in the 18th century. In 1875 Japan ceded to Russia the nearby island of Sakhalin (q.v.) in exchange for full Japanese possession of the Kurils. The islands were returned to the U.S.S.R. by an agreement reached at the Yalta Conference (q.v.) during World War II. The islands are administered as part of Sakhalin Oblast. Area, about 6020 sq.mi.

KURISCHES HAFF, or COURLAND LAGOON, inlet of the Baltic Sea, extending about 60 mi. along the coast of the Lithuanian S.S.R. and the Kaliningrad Oblast, of the Soviet Union.

KURLAND. See LATVIA: *History*.

KURLAND, Bob, in full ROBERT ALBERT KURLAND (1924–), American basketball player, born in Jennings, Mo. Kurland, 7 ft. ¾ in. tall, played on the basketball team of the Oklahoma State University of Agriculture and Applied Science (known as Oklahoma A. & M.), at Stillwater, Okla. With Kurland at center, the team won National Collegiate Athletic Association (N.C.A.A.) titles in 1945 and 1946. After he was graduated he played for the Phillips Oilers of Bartlesville, Okla., the national Amateur Athletic Union (A.A.U.) champions of 1947, 1948, and 1950. Kurland also played on championship United States teams in the Olympic Games of 1948 and 1952.

KUROPATKIN, Aleksei Nikolaevich (1848–1926), Russian military leader, possibly born at Pskov. He entered the army at the age of sixteen, and after fighting in Turkestan and Algeria he distinguished himself in the Russo-Turkish War of 1877–78. He was lieutenant general and governor of the Transcaspian territories (now part of Soviet Central Asia) from 1890 to 1898 and was minister of war for the six years that followed. Although he was opposed to the Russo-Japanese War because of Russia's unpreparedness, he fought in Manchuria as supreme commander of Russian forces in the Far East. His troops were defeated at Mukden in 1905, and he was relieved of command. In World War I he fought on the Western front. He was governor of Turkestan in 1916–17. He wrote *The Russian Army and the Japanese War* (1909).

KUROSAWA, Akira (1910–), Japanese motion-picture director, born in Tokyo. Intending to become a painter, he briefly attended the Tokyo Academy of Fine Arts. In 1937 he became an assistant director and screenwriter at the Toho film studios in Tokyo. The first film he directed, *Sugata Sanshiro* (two parts, 1943–44), was one of three minor works he produced during World War II. His first international success was *Rashomon* (1950; United States release, 1952), one of the many films in which Kurosawa directed the Japanese actor Toshiro Mifune (1920–). Critics have characterized his productions of *Ikiru* (1952; U.S. release, *To Live!*, 1960) and *Schichinin o Samurai* (1954; U.S. release, *The Seven Samurai*, 1956) as masterpieces. While Kurosawa's adaptation of traditional Oriental techniques gives his films a peculiarly Japanese sensibility, their visual beauty and dramatic strength appeal to Western audiences as well. Among his later films shown in the U.S. are *High and Low* (1963) and *Red Beard* (1964).

KUROSHIO CURRENT, or JAPAN CURRENT, fast moving ocean current (max. speed, about 3½ knots). It flows northeastward from Taiwan to the Ryukyu Islands, passing close to the coast of Japan, and into the North Pacific Ocean. To the east of northern Japan the Kuroshio is met by the Oyashio Current, a southwest-flowing current that supports rich plankton life. The Oyashio originates in the Bering Sea and flows along the coast of the Kamchatka Peninsula before turning east to join the Kuroshio.

The Kuroshio Current springs from the Pacific North Equatorial Current, which divides when it reaches the Philippines, one part heading south, the other to the north. Like the Gulf Stream (q.v.), the Kuroshio is a warm current. It is believed to reach a depth of about 2300 ft. See OCEAN AND OCEANOGRAPHY: *Ocean Currents*.

KURSK, city of the Soviet Union, in the Russian S.F.S.R., and capital of Kursk Oblast, near the confluence of the Seym and Tuskor rivers, about 125 miles N. of Khar'kov. Kursk is the railroad and industrial center of an area important for agriculture and iron ore. Industries in the city include the processing of agricultural products and the manufacture of pig iron, machinery, and chemicals. Kursk is one of the oldest cities in the Soviet Union, dating from the 11th century. During World War II (q.v.), the city was occupied by the Germans from 1941 to 1943. Pop. (1970) 284,000.

KURUME, city of Japan, in Fukuoka Prefecture, on the island of Kyushu, on the Chikugo R., 20 miles S.E. of Fukuoka. A road and rail junction, it is an industrial city and trade center for the Chikugo Plain rice and agricultural region. It manufactures cotton textiles, rubber products, machinery, chemicals, and lacquerware. Kurume was formerly a castle town of a princely family. Pop. (1970) 194,178.

KUSCH, Polykarp (1911–), German-American physicist, born in Blankenburg, Germany, and educated at the Case Institute of Technology, Cleveland, Ohio, and the University of Illinois. He taught successively at the universities of Illinois and Minnesota and at Columbia University from 1931 to 1941. During World War II he was engaged in vacuum-tube research for the war effort. He returned to Columbia in 1946 and became professor of physics in 1949. He was chairman of the physics department from 1949 to 1952 and from 1960 to 1963. He was executive director of the Columbia Radiation Laboratory from 1952 to 1960. In 1969 Kusch was appointed vice-president and dean of faculties at Columbia University. Kusch is noted for his investigations of atomic structure. His best-known contribution was the precise evaluation of the magnetic moment of the electron. For his research into new and more accurate methods of atomic calculations, he was awarded the 1955 Nobel Prize in physics, jointly with the American physicist Willis Eugene Lamb, Jr. (q.v.).

KUSHIRO, city of Japan, in Hokkaido Prefecture, on the Pacific Ocean, at the mouth of the Kushiro R., 145 miles E. of Sapporo. A road and rail junction, it is a port and center of an extensive fishing industry. Timber, coal, and processed fish are exported, and the city cans fish, processes fish oil and agricultural and marine products, and manufactures paper, pulp, and wood products. Dairying is carried on in the vicinity, and nearby to the W. is the Kushiro coalfield. Akan National Park, with volcanic formations and health resorts, lies to the N. Pop. (1970) 191,948.

KUSKOKWIM, second largest river in Alaska, rising in the Alaska Range, and flowing about 600 miles S.W. to Kuskokwim Bay, an inlet of the Bering Sea. It is navigable for about 500 mi.

KÜSTENJA. See CONSTANŢA.

KUTAISI or **KUTAIS,** city of the Soviet Union, in the Georgian S.S.R., on the Rion R., about 60 miles N.E. of Batumi. An industrial center, within the Caucasia (q.v.) region, the city receives much of its power from a hydroelectric station on the river. The chief manufactures are chemicals, foodstuffs, mining and transportation equipment, textiles, and trucks. During the 8th century B.C. Kutaisi was capital of the ancient country of Colchis (q.v.). After a long history of wars, the city was occupied by Russians in the 18th century. Pop. (1970) 161,000.

KUTCH, GULF OF, inlet of the Arabian Sea on the W. coast of India. It is about 30 mi. wide and extends for about 100 mi. between the Kutch and Kathiawar peninsulas. The head of the gulf adjoins the vast salt marsh known as the Little Rann of Kutch.

KUWAIT, independent sheikhdom of Asia, on the N.W. coast of the Persian Gulf. It is bounded

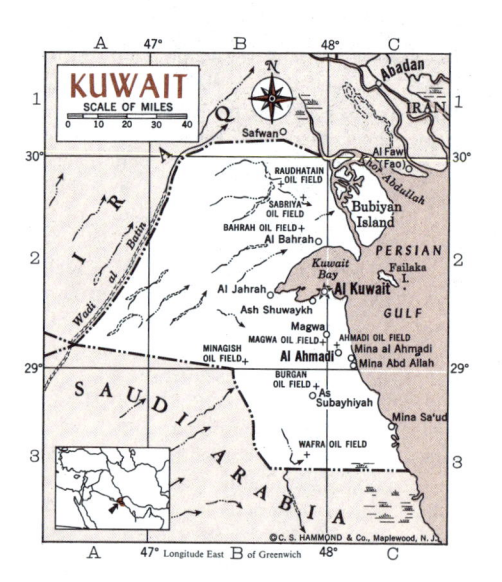

INDEX TO MAP OF KUWAIT

Cities and Towns

Al Ahmadi	B 2
Al Bahrah	B 2
Al Jahrah	B 2
Al Kuwait (cap.)	C 2
As Subayhiyah	C 3
Ash Shuwaykh	B 2
Magwa	B 2
Mina Abd Allah	C 2
Mina al Ahmadi	C 2
Mina Sa'ud	C 3

Physical Features

Abdullah, Khor (bay)	C 2
Ahmadi (oil field)	C 2
Bahrah (oil field)	B 2
Batin (dry river)	A 2
Bubiyan (isl.)	C 2
Burgan (oil field)	B 3
Failaka (isl.)	C 2
Kuwait (bay)	B 2
Magwa (oil field)	B 2
Minagish (oil field)	B 2
Raudhatain (oil field)	B 2
Sabriya (oil field)	B 2
Wafra (oil field)	B 3

468

Seif Palace, seat of the sheik of Kuwait.

on the N. and N.W. by Iraq, on the E. by the Persian Gulf, and on the S. by Saudi Arabia. It lies between about lat. 28°30′ N. and lat. 30°5′ N. and long. 46°30′ E. and long. 48°20′ E. Total area, including the islands of Bubiyan and Failaka, is about 9375 sq.mi.

Physical Characteristics. The terrain is mostly barren desert with an intensely hot and dry climate and an annual rainfall of less than 4 in. Oil is the prime natural resource.

Population. The people are of Arabic stock. The population of Kuwait (official census 1970) was 737,909; the United Nations estimated (1971) 831,000. The overall population density is about 122 persons per sq.mi. (U.N. est. 1970). Al Kuwait (1970 pop., 80,405) is the capital and chief port. Islam is the predominant religion. The national language is Arabic, but English is widely spoken.

Education is free and is divided into pre-primary, primary, intermediate, and secondary levels. School enrollment annually totaled about 140,000 pupils in 190 schools of all levels in the late 1960's, according to the latest available statistics. Kuwait University, opened in 1966, has an annual enrollment of about 1320 students. About 1300 Kuwaitis were studying abroad.

The Economy. Kuwait is entirely dependent upon oil production for its domestic development and foreign exchange. Manufacturing is slight, and farming is on a subsistence level.

Crude-oil production totaled about 146,800,000 tons annually in the early 1970's, of which about 90 percent was exported. Principal customers are the United States, Japan, Italy, and Great Britain. Revenue from the oil trade annually averages close to $1,500,000,000 and accounts for the largest share of the national budget. Major imports are automobiles and trucks, textiles, cigarettes and tobacco, and machinery. Total value of imports was about $650,000,000 in the early 1970's. Leading suppliers were the U.S., Great Britain, Japan, and West Germany. In a recent year annual budget figures were balanced at about $1,000,000,000 in revenue and expenditures.

The currency unit is the Kuwait dinar, composed of 1000 fils (1 dinar equals U.S.$3.52; 1973).

Transportation and Communications. Kuwait has no railroads, but a highway system is rapidly being developed. An international airport began operations in 1962. Telephone and telegraph systems are maintained by the state; about 25,000 telephones, 100,000 radios, and 75,000 television sets are in use.

Government. The state is headed by a hereditary sheikh. His power is exercised through a prime minister and council of ministers appointed by the sheikh. A fifty-member national

KUWAIT

assembly is elected every four years by adult males, except policemen and servicemen. The state provides an extensive social welfare program, including free medical service for all citizens. Kuwait has a small British-trained army.

History. The sheikhdom developed around Al Kuwait, which was settled early in the 18th century. Kuwait was nominally under Ottoman Turkish rule until 1899, when the reigning sheikh asked for, and obtained, British protection. In 1914 Great Britain reaffirmed its protective role and formally recognized the independence of the sheikhdom. Subsequently Wahhabis (q.v.) from the Saudi Arabian province of Nejd attacked Kuwait. The British aided the principality, and peace was restored in 1921 by a treaty establishing the Kuwait-Nejd boundary; a neutral zone was created in 1922. Petroleum was discovered in Kuwait in 1938. Operating under a concession, the Kuwait Oil Company, owned jointly by the Gulf Oil Corporation of the U.S. and the British Petroleum Company, began full-scale exploitation of the reserves in 1946. Under the provisions of a 1951 agreement the sheikh shared equally in the profits of the company. Japanese, Dutch, and other American companies also share interests in oil fields in Kuwait and the former neutral zone.

British protection of the sheikhdom ended on June 19, 1961. Kuwait is a member of the Arab League (q.v.) and became the 111th member of the United Nations in 1963. The first constitution of the country was proclaimed in January, 1963, and the first national assembly was elected on Jan. 23. The present ruler, Sheikh Sabah al-Salem al-Sabah (1913–), succeeded his brother in November, 1965. In February, 1966, Kuwait and Saudi Arabia reached agreement on a mutual border, eliminating the neutral zone and providing for sharing of the oil resources of that area.

In the aftermath of the Arab-Israeli war of 1967, Kuwait joined Lebanon and Saudi Arabia in providing substantial financial aid to the government of Jordan. In 1971, however, Kuwait began withholding its aid because of Jordanian actions against the Palestinian guerrilla movement.

In 1973 Kuwait signed a participation agreement with British and U.S. oil firms, under which Kuwait would immediately receive a 25 percent interest in existing concessions; the interest was to rise to 51 percent in ten years.

KUWAIT, capital of Kuwait. See AL KUWAIT.
KUYBYSHEV, formerly SAMARA, city of the Soviet Union, in the Russian S.F.S.R., and capital of Kuybyshev Oblast, on the great bend of the Volga R. and at the mouth of the Samara R., about 560 miles S.E. of Moscow. The city is the processing and shipping center for farm products and petroleum from the surrounding region. Kuybyshev is an important river port and rail and industrial center. The principal manufactures include aircraft, automobiles, ball bearings, chemicals, locomotives, machinery, synthetic rubber, and textiles. Founded in the 16th century, the city was an important grain center; its industrial expansion began in the early 20th century. In 1941, during World War II, when Moscow was threatened by invading German armies, Kuybyshev was chosen as the alternative administrative center of the Soviet Union. Pop. (1972 est.) 1,094,000.

KUZNETS, Simon (Smith) (1901–), American economist and statistician, born in Kharkov, Russia (now Ukrainian S.S.R.). He emigrated to the United States in 1922 and was educated at Columbia University. He joined the staff of the National Bureau of Economic Research, New York City, in 1927, and became professor of economics and statistics at the University of Pennsylvania in 1936. He was professor of political economy at Johns Hopkins University from 1954 until 1960 when he became professor of economics at Harvard University. Kuznets was named professor emeritus of economics at Harvard when he retired in 1971. The 1971 Alfred Nobel Memorial Prize in economics was awarded to Kuznets, and his interpretation of economic growth was cited as having led to new insights into the world economic and social structure. Kuznets is regarded by economic theorists as an empiricist; he developed the concept of the gross national product (q.v.), the sum of the goods and services of a nation, which is used to determine the rate of the economic growth of the nation. He is the author of several important works on economics, including *National Income and Its Composition* (2 vol., 1941), *Modern Economic Growth* (1966), and *Toward a Theory of Economic Growth* (1968).

KUZNETSK BASIN, rich iron and coal mining area of the Soviet Union, in the Russian S.F.S.R., in W. Siberia, in the basin of the Tom R., between the Alay Range and the Salair Ridge. Excellent coking coal, fairly close to the surface, is mined there. An estimated 450,000,000,000 tons lie in the basin. During the early 1930's, the region was an integral part of the Ural-Kuznetsk Industrial Combine. Iron ore from the Ural Mts. was exchanged for the coal of the Kuznetsk Basin. After World War II, with the exploitation of coal deposits in the Urals and of iron ore in the basin, the combine declined in importance. Area, about 10,000 sq.mi.

KWAJALEIN. See MARSHALL ISLANDS.

KWAKIUTL, confederacy of North American Indian tribes, living in Canada on Queen Charlotte and N. Vancouver Island, and along the shores of British Columbia. They form one of the divisions of the Wakashan linguistic stock; see AMERICAN INDIAN LANGUAGES. Like most of the tribes of the Pacific Northwest, the Kwakiutl hunt and fish. Government is by secret societies. The population is stratified for political and religious purposes into three hereditary classes: a nobility of chiefs, a middle class, and a class of slaves. The Kwakiutl life is one of fierce and unremitting rivalry. The Kwakiutl are often regarded as an aggressive people. Private property, reckoned in blankets and copper plates, is the main index of personal social status, which is often independent of hereditary class. Conspicuous displays of wealth play a prominent part in social life. During competitive ceremonies, such as the potlatch (q.v.), a ceremonial exchange of gifts is accompanied by ritualistic boasting and denunciation. The wealthiest Kwakiutl use the potlatch as an occasion for the public destruction of their property, an act accepted as the most valid proof of individual status and wealth. The Kwakiutl were extensively studied in the late 19th century by the German-American anthropologist Franz Boas (q.v.).

KWEILIN, city of the People's Republic of China, in Kwangsi Chuang Autonomous Region, on the Kwei R., about 250 miles N.W. of Canton. Situated where the railroad meets the river, the city is at the head of navigation on the Kwei. It also lies on the historic Kweilin Route, one of the three major links between north and south. Kweilin has two sections, an old walled city and a modern industrial area, linked by a bridge. It is the trade center of a region that grows rice, grains, cotton, vegetables, and timber; industries include sugar, paper, and tung-oil milling and cotton processing. The city is a cultural center and the site of a university and a medical college. The traditional capital of Kwangsi except for the period 1913–36, it was superseded by Nanning in the 1950's, under Communist rule. It became a municipality in 1930. During World War II an American air base was located here. The name is also spelled Kuei-lin. Pop. (1970 est.) 225,000.

KWEIYANG, city in the People's Republic of China, and capital of Kweichow Province, 200 miles S. of Chungking. A rail hub and center of roads leading W., the city, located at a height of about 3500 ft., lies in an area growing cotton, grains, tobacco, fruits, and livestock. Industries include cotton, silk, and tobacco processing, paper milling, and the manufacture of glass, chemicals, pharmaceuticals, ink, wine, and matches. Coal mines are in the vicinity. Kweiyang is the site of a university and a medical college. The city was created in 1930. Pop. (1970 est.) 1,500,000.

KYANITE. See CYANITE.

KYD, Thomas or **KID, Thomas** (about 1557–95), English dramatist, born in London and educated at the Merchant Taylors' School, London. Kyd was one of the most important dramatists of the Elizabethan period before the time of William Shakespeare (q.v.). The one play that is definitely ascribed to him, *The Spanish Tragedy* (published 1594), was one of the most successful English plays of its time. His use of shocking and horrifying melodramatic situations was imitated by subsequent English dramatists; Shakespeare's *Titus Andronicus,* for example, shows evidences of Kyd's influence. Many literary experts believe that Shakespeare used a play (now lost) attributed to Kyd as a source for his tragedy *Hamlet*; other plays attributed to Kyd are *The Tragedy of Solyman and Perseda* (written about 1588) and *The First Part of Ieronimo* (published 1605), a prologue to *The Spanish Tragedy.*

KYOTO or **KIOTO,** city in Japan, and capital of Kyoto Prefecture, on Honshu Island, about 30 miles N.E. of Osaka. The city is famed for such fine handicrafts as silk brocades, bronzes, cloisonné and damascene work, porcelain, and lacquer ware; the few industries of Kyoto include the manufacture of aircraft parts, chemicals, and electrical equipment. Long a leading religious and cultural center, the city is the site of more than 2000 ancient temples and shrines. Noteworthy landmarks include the imperial palace, several old tombs, Kyoto and Doshisha universities, and the municipal museum. Kyoto served as the capital of Japan almost continuously from 794 to 1868, when the seat of administration was removed to Tokyo. Because of its cultural importance, the city was not bombed during World War II. Pop. (1970) 1,419,165.

KYUSHU, or KIUSHU, island of Japan, the most southerly of the four main Japanese islands. It is separated from the island of Honshu by Shimonoseki Strait, and from Shikoku by Bungo Strait. Kyushu is an irregularly shaped, mountainous island. The coalfields in the N. yield about half of the coal mined in Japan. The principal agricultural crop is rice. Kitakyushu is the largest city and the major industrial center of the island. Area, 16,196 sq.mi.; pop. (1970) 12,996,000.

L l

L, twelfth letter and ninth consonant in the English alphabet. The form of the capital letter and the name by which it is known in English first appeared in Latin, in which it was adapted from the early Greek letter *lambda*. This in turn was derived from a Phoenician letter corresponding to the Hebrew *lamedh*. The letter appeared first in ancient Egyptian, which had both a hieratic character and the hieroglyph (representing a lioness) upon which the hieroglyph is based. The stages through which the form of the capital L evolved may be summarized as follows:

L	Λ	V or ᒐ	⌇ξ	𓃭
Roman or Late Latin	Greek	Phoenician	Egyptian Hieratic	Egyptian Lioness Hieroglyph

The sound of *l* is technically a voiced lateral consonant or semivowel, sometimes loosely known as a liquid; it is normally produced in English words by bringing the tip of the tongue into contact with the upper teeth or (more often) the adjacent palatal ridge and allowing air to flow past the edges of the tongue, with the lips held well apart. Because the vocal cords are vibrating and the current of air does not stop, l is known as an open consonant, in distinction to shut consonants such as p, t, and k; and because the air current is not so forced as to produce a rubbing or hissing effect, l is called a sonorous consonant, in distinction to fricative consonants such as f or s. The normal *l* sound varies in different languages as the point of contact of the tip of the tongue is higher or lower in the mouth and as the surface of the tongue is more or less concave. The most extreme variations from the English *l* sound are in such languages as Tamil, in which is heard a so-called cerebral l, a consonant pronounced with the tongue curled far back to touch the roof of the mouth at a point somewhere on the hard palate, and in Chinese, in which contact is made with the sides of the concave tongue, and the air is sent through the trough at the tip. In Chinese the *l* is in effect substituted for the ordinary English lingual *r*, resulting in the distinctive confusions of *l* and *r* in the pronunciation of English by native Chinese speakers. In Welsh, *ll* is prounced without vibration of the vocal cords (voiceless).

Because of its sonority and stability, l, along with the other sonorous consonants (m, n, and r), is often given a preceding neutral vowel sound and the value of an unaccented syllable, as in battle and able; this syllabic l usually comes down to modern English through the reduction of unaccented but fully spelled syllables, such as -al, -el, and -ul, in which the vowel letter has been lost. An opposite process, in which a formerly sounded l is no longer pronounced but is retained in spelling, is found in the silent l in some modern English words, especially after a or o and before k, m, and f, as in walk, folk, palm, and half.

As an abbreviation the capital L is used for Latin, left, and lake, and for titles such as Lord and Lady. In botanical names L stands for Linnaeus, and in photometry it stands for the lambert, the unit of brightness. It also stands for heliocentric longitude in astronomy and terrestrial longitude in geodesy. The capital or lowercase L, and also the form £, are abbreviations for a pound or pounds of currency (from Lat. *libra*). The lowercase l stands for liter, length, and lira; the form *l-* is used in chemistry as an abbreviation for levo- (or levorotatory).

As a symbol, the capital or lowercase L is used to indicate the eleventh or, when J is the tenth, the twelfth in a class, order, group, or series. In Roman numerals the capital L represents the number 50, or in the form L̄, 50,000. The capital or lowercase L indicates inductance in electrical computations. The capital letter is used either with or without a qualifying noun to indicate anything having the shape of the capital L, such as a short, right-angled pipe fitting that connects two pipes at right angles, or an L-shaped object. In architecture it denotes a wing or extension attached at right angles to a main building, giving the ground plan of the entire structure the form of an L; the term is sometimes less properly extended to denote a narrower or lower extension or wing built in the same direction as the main length of the building.   M.P.

LABIATAE. See Mint.

LABICHE, Eugène Marin (1815–88), French playwright, born in Paris. *L'Avocat Loubet,* the first of his nearly 100 farces and comedies, was produced in 1838. Many of his plays were written in collaboration with other writers, but it was Labiche's gifts for writing farces, vaudeville, and pure comedy that made the collaborations successful. His early plays were typical French farces, gay, fast moving, and broadly humorous, but he soon developed his farcical comedies into satires on middle-class life in France which raised them to the level of the comedy of manners and character. Among his most successful plays were *Le Chapeau de Paille d'Italie* (1851; Eng. trans., *The Italian Straw Hat,* 1967), *Le Voyage de Monsieur Perrichon* (1860; Eng. trans., *The Journey of Mr. Perrichon,* 1924), and *La Cagnotte* (1864; Eng. trans., *Pots of Money,* 1961). *Le Chapeau de Paille d'Italie* was made into a motion picture by the French producer-director René Clair (q.v.), and produced in the United States for the Federal Theatre Project in 1936 under the title *Horse Eats Hat* by Orson Welles (q.v.) and John Houseman (1902–   )

LABOR, in economics, effort necessary to satisfy human needs. It is one of the three leading factors in production, the other two being land (natural objects) and capital (q.v.); *see* Wealth.

In industry labor has a great variety of functions, which may be classified as follows: production of raw materials, as in mining and agriculture; manufacturing in the widest sense of the word, or transformation of raw materials into objects serviceable to man; distribution, or transference of useful objects from one place to another, as determined by human needs; operations involved in the management of production, such as accounting and secretarial work; and personal services such as those rendered by physicians and teachers.

Many economists distinguish between productive and unproductive labor. The former consists of those kinds of exertion that produce utility embodied in natural objects. Unproductive labor, like that of the musician, is both useful and honorable, but does not add to the material wealth of the community.

As a result of the industrial revolution (q.v.) at the end of the 18th century, most workers were employed in large factories and similar undertakings. These workers were not protected from economic exploitation nor from the consequences of illness, disability, or unemployment. In the early decades of the 19th century, however, increasingly prevalent ideas of freedom caused great changes in the conditions of labor. Workers began to form trade unions and cooperative societies that enabled them to participate in many types of political activities and to protect themselves by political and economic means. Laws for the regulation of labor are now intended not to fix wages as formerly, but to protect the workers. *See* Factories and the Factory System; Labor Relations; Trade Union; Trade Unions in the United States.

LABOR DAY, legal holiday celebrated on the first Monday in September in all of the States of the United States and also in the District of Columbia, Puerto Rico, the Canal Zone, and the Virgin Islands. The celebration of Labor Day, in honor of the working class, was initiated in 1882 by the Knights of Labor (q.v.), who held a large parade in New York City. In 1884 the Knights of Labor held a parade on the first Monday of September, and passed a resolution to hold all future parades on that day and to designate the day as Labor Day. Subsequently workers of other organizations throughout the country began to agitate for action by State legislatures in declaring the day a legal holiday. In March, 1887, the first law to that effect was passed in Colorado, followed by New York, Massachusetts, and New Jersey. In 1894 the Congress of the United States made the day a legal holiday. Labor Day is celebrated by parades and meetings at which addresses are made by prominent labor leaders and political figures.

LABOR, DEPARTMENT OF, an executive department of the Federal government of the United States, administered by a secretary, who is appointed by the President with the approval of the Senate. The department was created by an act of Congress in 1913 as a cabinet-level agency "to foster, promote, and develop the welfare of the wage earners of the United States, to improve their working conditions, and to advance their opportunities for profitable employment". Predecessor agencies were the Bureau of Labor in the Department of the Interior (1884) and the Department of Commerce and Labor (1903).

The secretary of labor is a member of the

LABOR, DEPARTMENT OF

President's cabinet and is his chief adviser on labor matters. He is assisted by an under secretary, six assistant secretaries (for manpower; employment standards; occupational safety and health; labor-management relations; policy, evaluation, and research; and administration and management), the solicitor of labor, and the commissioner of labor statistics.

There are seven principal operating units:

The Manpower Administration oversees programs to furnish job training and placement services; supervises payment of unemployment compensation under Federal and State laws; conducts experimental and demonstration programs to improve manpower procedures; and includes the U.S. Employment Service, Unemployment Insurance Service, Office of Manpower Development Programs, and Bureau of Apprenticeship and Training.

The Employment Standards Administration enforces laws regulating wages and hours and child labor and prohibiting sex and age discrimination in employment; administers workmen's compensation (q.v.) for work-connected disabilities of Federal and certain other employees; supervises equal opportunity requirements for Federal contractors; promotes opportunities for women workers; and includes the Wage and Hour Division, Office of Workmen's Compensation Programs, Office of Federal Employees Compensation, Office of Federal Contract Compliance, and Women's Bureau.

The Occupational Safety and Health Administration enforces the Occupational Safety and Health Act and issues regulations, conducts inspections, issues citations, operates safety-education programs, and authorizes State enforcement under Federal standards.

The Labor-Management Services Administration administers laws that regulate certain activities of unions and private pension plans and protect the reemployment rights of veterans, administers Federal labor-management relations, and helps strengthen free collective bargaining procedures.

The Office of Policy, Evaluation, and Research assists in developing department policies and legislative initiatives and stimulates and coordinates evaluation and research activities.

The Bureau of Labor Statistics serves as the government's principal fact-gathering agency in the field of labor economics, and publishing statistics on such subjects as employment wages, hours of work, work stoppages, prices, and occupational safety and health.

The solicitor of labor is responsible for the legal activities of the department.

LABOR PARTY, in United States history, name given to various political parties formed at different periods by workingmen; see POLITICAL PARTIES IN THE UNITED STATES. Generally included in this definition are those political parties based on a coalition of workers and farmers organized for the advancement of their joint interests; generally excluded are those parties, many of which were largely composed of workers, which sought to attain their ends by the application of the principles of revolutionary socialism (q.v.). The general motivation for the formation of labor parties was the conviction that the existing parties were either unwilling or unable to serve the interests of labor.

The earliest of the labor parties was the Workingmen's Party, organized by the Mechanics' Union of Trade Associations of Philadelphia in 1828; this party, which sought to achieve such reforms as the establishment of a public-school system and the abolition of imprisonment for debt, served as the model for similar parties formed soon afterward in New York, New Jersey, and several other States. The activities of these parties were severely curtailed by the economic crisis of 1837. Organization of labor parties on a national scale did not occur until after the American Civil War, when a rapid growth of large-scale industrial enterprises was followed by the development of a large wage-earning class. The labor forces of this period recognized that they alone could not marshal sufficient strength to attain their ends, and therefore formed coalitions with reformist agrarian groups, which consisted chiefly of small-scale farmers. Such was the origin of the Greenback-Labor Party (q.v.), formed in 1878, which put forth demands including the establishment of a labor bureau in the Federal government and a reduction of working hours. This party was supplanted in 1891 by the Populist Party (see POPULISM), which drew much of its membership from the recently organized American Federation of Labor (q.v.) and demanded the eight-hour workday, a graduated income tax, government ownership of the railroads, and direct popular election of United States Senators. In 1896, when the Populists succeeded in gaining control of the Democratic Party (q.v.), their own independent organization disappeared. It was not replaced until 1919, a year of widespread labor unrest; in that year, after labor groups in several States had made preparations for the organization of State labor parties, the National Labor Party was established, with a membership drawn almost exclusively from the trade unions; see TRADE UNIONS IN THE UNITED

LABOR RELATIONS

STATES. The indispensability of agrarian support led to the supercession of this party in 1920 by the Farmer-Labor Party (q.v.), the platform of which included demands for a larger share for labor in industrial management and the elimination of the practice of discrimination against Negroes; see NEGROES IN THE UNITED STATES. The Farmer-Labor Party won 265,411 votes in the 1920 Presidential election campaign, and in the campaign of 1924 supported the candidate of the Progressive Party (q.v.), Robert Marion La Follette (see under LA FOLLETTE). In 1925 the Farmer-Labor Party was dissolved; its only surviving branch was the Minnesota Farmer-Labor Party, which subsequently exercised a large measure of control over the State government and over the election of Congressional representatives to the Congress from Minnesota.

A new attempt to organize a nationwide labor party occurred in 1936, when a group of labor leaders in New York State founded the American Labor Party (q.v.). Although this party did not thereafter attain any influence outside New York State, thus defeating the original purpose of the founders, it became a power in State politics, electing or helping to elect many municipal, State, and Federal representatives and officers. In 1936, 1940, and 1944, the American Labor Party supported the Presidential candidacy of Franklin Delano Roosevelt (q.v.). In May, 1944, a right-wing group within the party charged that the party had come under Communist domination, and withdrew to form a separate organization, the Liberal Party (q.v.) of New York State. In the 1948 and 1952 Presidentail elections the American Labor Party supported the candidates of the Progressive Party. Polling an insufficient number of votes, in 1954 the party lost the right to appear on future ballots.

LABOR RELATIONS, broadly, all dealings, transactions, and activities affecting the determination and enforcement of the terms and conditions of employment.

The relations between employers and employees developed differently in various parts of the world. In particular, the goals and activities of European trade unions differ considerably from those of trade unions in the United States. In Europe customs and laws bearing on labor relations are often basically dissimilar even in neighboring countries. European trade unions are primarily national organizations allied closely with political movements and parties. By contrast, the trade-union movement in the U.S. developed with a marked degree of uniformity. The typical U.S. trade union is primarily a local organization devoted to the advancement and protection of the economic interests of its members. It usually has national and State-wide affiliations but no loyalty to a particular political ideology. This article is concerned mainly with labor-relations developments in the U.S.; see AMERICAN FEDERATION OF LABOR AND CONGRESS OF INDUSTRIAL ORGANIZATIONS; TRADE UNION; TRADE UNIONS IN THE UNITED STATES.

History. In the early-19th century, before the growth of the factory system (see FACTORIES AND THE FACTORY SYSTEM), wages and hours of work were usually arranged in direct dealings between employers and individual employees. The prevailing legal and social opinions and the economic situation did not favor the development of workers' organizations. Because the disparity in bargaining power between employers and employees caused many abuses, however, the workers in various industries organized trade unions, which demanded better terms of employment and enforced their demands by means of the strike (q.v.). In addition, three types of regulation, namely, protective legislation, labor-relations legislation, and collective agreements between unions and employers, were developed successively to remedy abuses and preserve industrial peace.

Protective legislation, the earliest type of regulation, was enacted by States, and to a lesser extent, by the Federal government, principally during the early-20th century. Such legislation regulated the maximum hours of work, and minimum wages of women and minors and hazardous practices affecting them as employees. Some of these protections were extended later to adult male employees; see CHILD LABOR; FAIR LABOR STANDARDS ACT OF 1938; HOURS OF LABOR; MINIMUM WAGE; WOMEN, EMPLOYMENT OF. Another type of protective legislation is that under which industrial employees become entitled to benefits. Such legislation includes laws guaranteeing workmen's compensation (q.v.) for industrial accidents and social-security (q.v.) legislation, such as unemployment insurance (q.v.), old-age insurance, survivors' insurance, and disability insurance; see OLD-AGE PENSIONS; SOCIAL LEGISLATION. Since 1945 numerous statutes have forbidden discrimination (q.v.) in employment and, increasingly, in union membership, removing restrictions based on such factors as age, race, and sex; see CIVIL RIGHTS AND CIVIL LIBERTIES.

Federal and State labor-relations laws guarantee to workers the right of free association in unions, establish procedures for determining appropriate bargaining units and selecting unions as exclusive bargaining agents, and outlaw certain unfair practices of employers. The prin-

A young spinner in a cotton mill, 1909. Lewis W. Hine – George Eastman House

cipal statutes of this type are the National Labor Relations Act (q.v.) of 1935 and the Labor-Management Relations Act of 1947, which amends the N.L.R.A. by requiring employers and unions to bargain in good faith and enumerating practices prohibited to each group; see NATIONAL LABOR RELATIONS BOARD. The Labor Management Reporting and Disclosure Act of 1959 includes a series of measures protecting employees from unfair practices on the part of either the employee or the union and extending the rights of union members to participate in the decision-making processes of the union. The act also prohibits the closed-shop agreement (q.v.), in which union membership is required as a condition of employment. Pension benefit plans are regulated by the Welfare and Pension Plan Disclosure Act of 1959.

Labor-relations legislation requires that employers and unions deal and bargain with each other, but does not itself fix terms and conditions of employment as did the earlier protective legislation. The bargaining of employers and unions results in collective agreements setting forth the principal terms and conditions of work. Thus the most important determinant of these matters in the more highly industrialized States is no longer protective legislation but the collective-bargaining agreement. During the 1960's the right to collective bargaining, but without the right to strike, was extended to employees in the public service.

Modern Practices. The larger employers of labor now have labor-relations, or industrial-relations, departments dealing with problems in the negotiation and administration of agreements. Such departments are usually divided into two branches, one responsible for day-to-day administration of agreements relating to wages and salaries, the other responsible for such matters as assignments to work, schedules of work, lay-offs, promotions, discipline, grievances, and arbitration (q.v.). Many of the international unions adapted their organizational structures to those of the principal companies with which they deal. These unions have specialists trained and assigned to deal with management specialists in matters relating to negotiations, grievances, arbitrations, legal services, social-security and welfare services, industrial engineering, economics, and public relations.

When the employees in a plant are not represented by a union, the terms and conditions of employment are usually determined by direct arrangements between management and employee. A union seeking to deal with an em-

LABOR RELATIONS

ployer as the exclusive bargaining representative of its employees may try to persuade the employer to recognize it on the basis of authorization cards signed by a majority of employees in an appropriate bargaining unit and signifying the desire of these employees to be so represented. Failing such recognition, the union may file a representation petition with the appropriate Federal or State agency. The agency will then proceed to determine the unit appropriate for collective bargaining and, if warranted, conduct a secret ballot election among the employees in that unit.

The management is obliged to bargain in good faith with the union selected by the employees. The Labor-Management Relations Act requires that a notice of contract negotiations be given to the Federal Mediation and Conciliation Service (q.v.) and to the State mediation agency, where one exists. These agencies make available the services of their staff mediators to assist the parties in achieving agreement if their unassisted negotiations are not fruitful. Such services are optional; neither party to a negotiation is required to accept them. If agreement on contract terms cannot be reached through bargaining the union is allowed to strike, except in certain industries, such as the railroads, in which strike action is delayed because a strike would be against the public interest. Most agreements provide for the filing of grievances by employees and by the union with respect to alleged violations of the agreement and required consideration of a grievance in a prescribed time sequence by union and management officials with progressively greater authority and responsibility. The agreements provide also that a grievance not so resolved may be appealed to arbitration for a final, binding decision. A party to such an agreement has the right to call upon Federal courts and many State courts to compel the other party to arbitrate.

Arbitrators of labor-management disputes are impartial, disinterested professionals chosen directly by the parties involved or selected from lists of nominees as submitted, for example, by the American Arbitration Association (q.v.). In some instances arbitration is conducted by a board of arbitrators of which all members except a neutral chairman with the deciding vote are interested individuals. Arbitration is conducted either by an arbitrator selected especially for a case or by an umpire, referee, or chairman designated for the duration of the collective agreement. Arbitrators' awards are enforceable, when filed, as judgments of a court of law, and may be set aside only for specific causes, such as lack of authority, fraud, interest, or misconduct on the part of the arbitrator.

With some notable exceptions, the dealings between most present-day representatives of managements and unions are characterized by

A goal of labor relations is the avoidance of strikes through negotiation or mediation. Here, Arthur J. Goldberg, secretary of labor in the Kennedy administration, presides at signing of a strike-averting agreement in 1962 between company and union officials. UPI

The labor movement in action is typified by this march of workers from the Brooklyn Navy Yard, to protest the shutting down of the facility in 1964. UPI

mutual respect, the product of years of negotiation and joint administration of agreements. The mutual confidence thus engendered fosters more pacific and cooperative labor relations than prevailed formerly. Labor-management arbitration contributes greatly to industrial peace because it substitutes the binding award of a respected neutral for the exertion of economic force during the term of a collective agreement. Although labor and management continue to differ on various economic problems that produce conflicts, both groups recognize that they have a number of common objectives. They generally realize also that neither group can reach its own goals without the assistance of the other.

See also INDUSTRIAL MANAGEMENT; INDUSTRIAL PSYCHOLOGY. P.S. & S.G.K.

LABOUR PARTY, political party in Great Britain organized as in its present form in 1906. The party originated in 1900 with the adoption by the Trades Union Congress at Plymouth of a resolution calling a conference of trade unions, as well as socialistic, cooperative, and other labor bodies, to consider the problem of securing adequate parliamentary representation for labor. The conference, held in 1906, created a committee, known as the Labour Representation Committee, under the secretaryship of the British statesman James Ramsay MacDonald (q.v.). Its objective was to secure the election of candidates identified with labor interests, or to support candidates sympathetic to labor. The committee was composed chiefly of representatives of the trade unions, but the Fabian Society (q.v.) and the Independent Labour Party were

Clement R. Attlee, left of microphone, after the Labour Party victory of 1945 that made him prime minister of Great Britain. Acme – UPI

Harold Wilson, leader of the British Labour Party, photographed after the 1964 election victory that made him prime minister of Great Britain, a post he held for six years.
London DAILY EXPRESS

each given one representative on the executive committee. From Jan. 24 to Nov. 4, 1924, the party was in control as the first Labour government in British history.

The Labourites regained power in June, 1929, but in August, 1931, a coalition cabinet was formed.

After a series of governments formed by the Conservative Party, the Labour Party returned to power after World War II with an overwhelming majority in August, 1945, under the leadership of Clement Attlee (q.v.). It immediately launched a broad program of socialization. The Bank of England (q.v.), the railroads, the coal mines, the iron and steel industry, and other industries were nationalized; legislation providing for a comprehensive, cradle-to-the-grave social-security program was enacted. The Labour Party remained in power following elections in February, 1950, winning a majority of ten seats. Emergence of a left-wing faction within the party weakened the government's tenuous control of Parliament, and Prime Minister Attlee proclaimed a general election for Oct. 25, 1951. The Conservatives were returned to power by a small majority. In the elections of October, 1964, the Labour Party gained a majority of four seats, forming a government under Harold Wilson (q.v.). The Labour Party increased its majority to ninety-seven seats after the elections of 1966. Four years later, Labour lost 59 seats, and a new government was formed under Conservative Party leader Edward Richard George Heath (q.v.). See GREAT BRITAIN: *History.*

LABRADOR, triangular-shaped peninsula, forming the eastern tip of Canada, and comprising the mainland section of the province of Newfoundland (q.v.).

LABRADORITE. See FELDSPAR.

LABRADOR CURRENT *or* **ARCTIC CURRENT,** cold ocean current that passes S. from the Arctic Ocean through Davis Strait into the North Atlantic Ocean, and along the E. coast of North America S. of Labrador and Newfoundland. The Labrador Current meets the warm Gulf Stream (q.v.) off the Grand Banks (q.v.). The meeting of the two currents produces whirlpools and fog. See OCEAN AND OCEANOGRAPHY: *Ocean Currents.*

LABRADOR RETRIEVER. See RETRIEVER.

LA BRUYÈRE, Jean de (1645–96), French essayist and moralist, born in Paris, and educated principally at the University of Orléans. From 1684 he was associated with the French noble house of Condé (q.v.), first as tutor in history and then as secretary to Louis de Bourbon, grandson of Louis II de Bourbon, Prince de Condé (q.v.), known as the Great Condé. La Bruyère is famous for a single literary work, *Les "Caractères" de Théophraste, Traduits du Grec, avec les Caractères ou les Moeurs de ce Siècle* ("The 'Characters' of Theophrastus, Translated from the Greek, with Characters or Customs of This Century", 1688). This work is a translation of character sketches written by the Greek philosopher Theophrastus (q.v.) in the late 3rd century B.C.; in addition, it contains frank and often satirical literary portraits by La Bruyère of eminent contemporaries, maxims by La Bruyère of a philosophic and moralistic nature, and critical comments by him on the French social life of the time. The book, written in brief and incisive style in contrast to the usual elaborate manner

479

of the period, won immediate popularity. Nine editions were published between 1688 and 1696, for each of which the author supplied new literary portraits of contemporaries and other material. *Les Caractères* brought La Bruyère the enmity of those he had ridiculed; their influence in the French Academy was strong enough to prevent his election to that body for a time, but he was finally elected in 1693; *see* INSTITUTE OF FRANCE.

LABURNUM, genus of trees and shrubs belonging to the Pea family, native to temperate and subtropical Eurasia. Laburnums bear yellow flowers, similar in structure to those of the pea, in late spring. Common laburnum or golden chain, *L. anagyroides,* is a small tree which grows as high as 40 ft. It produces hard, heavy, fine-grained, dark-brown or dark-green wood, which is used in cabinetmaking. The leaves, bark, and seeds contain cytisine, $C_{11}H_{14}NO_2$, a bitter, very poisonous, crystalline alkaloid used in medicine as a cathartic or diuretic. Several varieties are widely cultivated in warm regions of the United States, including: var. *aureum,* which produces yellow leaves; var. *autumnale,* which produces flowers in both late spring and late summer; var. *bullatum,* which produces curled leaves; var. *pendulum,* which has drooping branches; and var. *quercifolium,* which produces lobed leaves. Scotch laburnum, *L. alpinum,* is a related species with larger leaves and darker yellow flowers. It is hardier and blooms about two weeks later than the common laburnum. Both species are grown from layers or seeds, and the choicer varieties are often grown by grafting or budding.

LABYRINTH, name given to a number of ancient buildings, consisting of intricate mazelike chambers or passages. The buildings were so designed that a person, having entered one would find it difficult to make his way out. Of these structures the most celebrated were the Egyptian, which contained three thousand chambers, and the Cretan, which perhaps existed in myth only, and the idea of which was possibly derived from the elaborate plan of the Minoan palace at Knossos (q.v.). In Greek mythology, the Cretan labyrinth was constructed by the Athenian craftsman Daedalus as the prison of the Minotaur (qq.v.), a monster part bull and part man. The true purpose of the ancient labyrinths is uncertain. In England labyrinths consisting of a maze of paths walled by yew or holly hedges have been constructed in gardens for the mystification of those unfamiliar with the pattern of the maze and the consequent amusement of those who, knowing the key turnings, can readily find their way out. One of the finest of the English labyrinths still in existence was built at Hampton Court Palace, London, in the 17th century.

LAC, resinous substance secreted by the lac insect upon the twigs and young branches of certain trees, the chief of which are species of the genus *Ficus.* Lac is a product of southern Asia, particularly northern India. The term is the same as the numerical "lac" or "lakh", meaning one hundred thousand, and denotes the myriads of insects that swarm upon the trees. The lac insect, *Coccus lacca,* belongs to the family Coccidae; the female insects insert their long proboscides into the bark of the twigs or branches, drawing their foodstuff from the sap. They exude a secretion which accrues and coalesces, forming hard, resinous layers which completely cover their bodies. The ovaries of the females contain a crimson fluid, called lac dye, and resembling cochineal (q.v.), once used as a dye.

Crude lac, known as stick-lac, consists of the resin, the incrusted insects, lac dye, and twigs. When crushed, and washed free of the dye, twigs, and insects, it becomes granular and is known as seed-lac or grained lac. After melting and further purification the resulting lac resin is solidified into thin layers or flakes which constitute commercial shellac.

Shellac varies in color from yellow to deep orange. When bleached it is known as white shellac. It is used in making phonograph records, as stiffening in the manufacture of felt hats, in sealing wax, and in lacquer (q.v.). The term "shellac" is often applied to a solution of the resin in alcohol, used as a varnish (q.v.).

The demand for lac has greatly lessened as synthetic plastic materials have replaced it in many uses.

LACCADIVE, MINICOY, AND AMINDIVI ISLANDS, group of twenty-four coral islands in the Arabian Sea, about 150 miles w. of the Malabar Coast of India. Only ten of the islands are inhabited. The inhabitants, who are Muslim, fish and cultivate coconuts for copra. The group is administered as a Union Territory of the Republic of India. Area, 11 sq.mi.; pop. (1961) 24,108.